PROCEEDINGS OF THE IFIP TC 11 23rd INTERNATIONAL INFORMATION SECURITY CONFERENCE

IFIP – The International Federation for Information Processing

IFIP was founded in 1960 under the auspices of UNESCO, following the First World Computer Congress held in Paris the previous year. An umbrella organization for societies working in information processing, IFIP's aim is two-fold: to support information processing within its member countries and to encourage technology transfer to developing nations. As its mission statement clearly states,

> *IFIP's mission is to be the leading, truly international, apolitical organization which encourages and assists in the development, exploitation and application of information technology for the benefit of all people.*

IFIP is a non-profitmaking organization, run almost solely by 2500 volunteers. It operates through a number of technical committees, which organize events and publications. IFIP's events range from an international congress to local seminars, but the most important are:

- The IFIP World Computer Congress, held every second year;
- Open conferences;
- Working conferences.

The flagship event is the IFIP World Computer Congress, at which both invited and contributed papers are presented. Contributed papers are rigorously refereed and the rejection rate is high.

As with the Congress, participation in the open conferences is open to all and papers may be invited or submitted. Again, submitted papers are stringently refereed.

The working conferences are structured differently. They are usually run by a working group and attendance is small and by invitation only. Their purpose is to create an atmosphere conducive to innovation and development. Refereeing is less rigorous and papers are subjected to extensive group discussion.

Publications arising from IFIP events vary. The papers presented at the IFIP World Computer Congress and at open conferences are published as conference proceedings, while the results of the working conferences are often published as collections of selected and edited papers.

Any national society whose primary activity is in information may apply to become a full member of IFIP, although full membership is restricted to one society per country. Full members are entitled to vote at the annual General Assembly, National societies preferring a less committed involvement may apply for associate or corresponding membership. Associate members enjoy the same benefits as full members, but without voting rights. Corresponding members are not represented in IFIP bodies. Affiliated membership is open to non-national societies, and individual and honorary membership schemes are also offered.

PROCEEDINGS OF THE IFIP TC 11 23rd INTERNATIONAL INFORMATION SECURITY CONFERENCE

IFIP 20th World Computer Congress, IFIP SEC'08,
September 7-10, 2008, Milano, Italy

Edited by

Sushil Jajodia
George Mason University
USA

Pierangela Samarati
University of Milano-Bicocca
Italy

Stelvio Cimato
University of Salerno
Italy

Springer

Editors
Sushil Jajodia
George Mason University
USA

Pierangela Samarati
University of Milano-Bicocca
Italy

Stelvio Cimato
University of Salerno
Italy

p. cm. (IFIP International Federation for Information Processing, a Springer Series in Computer Science)

ISSN: 1571-5736 / 1861-2288 (Internet)
ISBN: 978-1-4419-3520-5 e-ISBN: 978-0-387-09699-5

Printed on acid-free paper

springer.com

IFIP 2008 World Computer Congress (WCC'08)

Message from the Chairs

Every two years, the International Federation for Information Processing hosts a major event which showcases the scientific endeavours of its over one hundred Technical Committees and Working Groups. 2008 sees the 20th World Computer Congress (WCC 2008) take place for the first time in Italy, in Milan from 7-10 September 2008, at the MIC - Milano Convention Centre. The Congress is hosted by the Italian Computer Society, AICA, under the chairmanship of Giulio Occhini.

The Congress runs as a federation of co-located conferences offered by the different IFIP bodies, under the chairmanship of the scientific chair, Judith Bishop. For this Congress, we have a larger than usual number of thirteen conferences, ranging from Theoretical Computer Science, to Open Source Systems, to Entertainment Computing. Some of these are established conferences that run each year and some represent new, breaking areas of computing. Each conference had a call for papers, an International Programme Committee of experts and a thorough peer reviewed process. The Congress received 661 papers for the thirteen conferences, and selected 375 from those representing an acceptance rate of 56% (averaged over all conferences).

An innovative feature of WCC 2008 is the setting aside of two hours each day for cross-sessions relating to the integration of business and research, featuring the use of IT in Italian industry, sport, fashion and so on. This part is organized by Ivo De Lotto. The Congress will be opened by representatives from government bodies and Societies associated with IT in Italy.

This volume is one of fourteen volumes associated with the scientific conferences and the industry sessions. Each covers a specific topic and separately or together they form a valuable record of the state of computing research in the world in 2008. Each volume was prepared for publication in the Springer IFIP Series by the conference's volume editors. The overall Chair for all the volumes published for the Congress is John Impagliazzo.

For full details on the Congress, refer to the webpage http://www.wcc2008.org.

Judith Bishop, South Africa, Co-Chair, International Program Committee
Ivo De Lotto, Italy, Co-Chair, International Program Committee
Giulio Occhini, Italy, Chair, Organizing Committee
John Impagliazzo, United States, Publications Chair

WCC 2008 Scientific Conferences

TC12	**AI**	Artificial Intelligence 2008
TC10	**BICC**	Biologically Inspired Cooperative Computing
WG 5.4	**CAI**	Computer-Aided Innovation (Topical Session)
WG 10.2	**DIPES**	Distributed and Parallel Embedded Systems
TC14	**ECS**	Entertainment Computing Symposium
TC3	**ED_L2L**	Learning to Live in the Knowledge Society
WG 9.7 **TC3**	**HCE3**	History of Computing and Education 3
TC13	**HCI**	Human Computer Interaction
TC8	**ISREP**	Information Systems Research, Education and Practice
WG 12.6	**KMIA**	Knowledge Management in Action
TC2 **WG 2.13**	**OSS**	Open Source Systems
TC11	**IFIP SEC**	Information Security Conference
TC1	**TCS**	Theoretical Computer Science

IFIP

- is the leading multinational, apolitical organization in Information and Communications Technologies and Sciences
- is recognized by United Nations and other world bodies
- represents IT Societies from 56 countries or regions, covering all 5 continents with a total membership of over half a million
- links more than 3500 scientists from Academia and Industry, organized in more than 101 Working Groups reporting to 13 Technical Committees
- sponsors 100 conferences yearly providing unparalleled coverage from theoretical informatics to the relationship between informatics and society including hardware and software technologies, and networked information systems

Details of the IFIP Technical Committees and Working Groups can be found on the website at http://www.ifip.org.

Foreword

These proceedings contain the papers selected for presentation at the 23rd International Information Security Conference (SEC 2008), co-located with IFIP World Computer Congress (WCC 2008), September 8–10, 2008 in Milan, Italy. In response to the call for papers, 143 papers were submitted to the conference. All papers were evaluated on the basis of their significance, novelty, and technical quality, and reviewed by at least three members of the program committee. Reviewing was blind meaning that the authors were not told which committee members reviewed which papers. The program committee meeting was held electronically, holding intensive discussion over a period of three weeks. Of the papers submitted, 42 full papers and 11 short papers were selected for presentation at the conference.

A conference like this just does not happen; it depends on the volunteer efforts of a host of individuals. There is a long list of people who volunteered their time and energy to put together the conference and who deserve acknowledgment. We thank all members of the program committee and the external reviewers for their hard work in the paper evaluation. Due to the large number of submissions, program committee members were required to complete their reviews in a short time frame. We are especially thankful to them for the commitment they showed with their active participation in the electronic discussion. We are also very grateful to the following individuals who gave their assistance and ensured a smooth organization process: Sabrina De Capitani di Vimercati and Giulio Occhini, who served as General Chairs for the conference; Judith Bishop and Ivo De Lotto, who chaired WCC'08 within which this conference is organized; Stelvio Cimato, who served as Publication Chair and collated these proceedings; and Eros Pedrini, who served as Publicity Chair, maintained the Web pages, and helped in organizing the material for the proceedings.

Last, but certainly not least, our thanks go to all the authors who submitted papers and all the attendees. We hope you find the program stimulating.

Sushil Jajodia and Pieragela Samarati
Program Chairs

Contents

PRIVACY PROTECTION

Hiding in Groups: On the Expressiveness of Privacy Distributions 1
Karsten Nohl and David Evans

Practical Privacy-Preserving Benchmarking 17
Florian Kerschbaum

Enhancing Privacy in Remote Data Classification 33
A. Piva, C. Orlandi, M. Caini, T. Bianchi, and M. Barni

WEB APPLICATIONS SECURITY AND MALWARE

Minimizing SSO Effort in Verifying SSL Anti-phishing Indicators 47
Yongdong Wu, Haixia Yao and Feng Bao

Robbing Banks with Their Own Software—an Exploit Against Norwegian Online Banks 63
Yngve Espelid, Lars–Helge Netland, André N. Klingsheim, and Kjell J. Hole

Collaborative architecture for malware detection and analysis 79
Michele Colajanni, Daniele Gozzi, and Mirco Marchetti

SENSOR AND WIRELESS SECURITY

Realizing Stateful Public Key Encryption in Wireless Sensor Network ... 95
Joonsang Baek, Han Chiang Tan, Jianying Zhou and Jun Wen Wong

Establishing secure links in low-rate wireless personal area networks 109
Maurizio Adriano Strangio

An Asynchronous Node Replication Attack in Wireless Sensor Networks . 125
Jianying Zhou, Tanmoy Kanti Das, and Javier Lopez

SECURITY POLICIES

A B Formal Framework for Security Developments in the Domain of Smart Card Applications 141
Frédéric Dadeau, Marie-Laure Potet, Régis Tissot

An Implementation of a Privacy Enforcement Scheme based on the Java Security Framework using XACML Policies 157
Thomas Scheffler, Stefan Geiß, Bettina Schnor

Negotiation of Prohibition: An Approach Based on Policy Rewriting 173
Nora Cuppens-Boulahia, Frédéric Cuppens, Diala Abi Haidar, Hervé Debar

ACCESS CONTROL IN DISTRIBUTED SYSTEMS

An Integrity Lock Architecture for Supporting Distributed Authorizations in Database Federations 189
Wei Li, Lingyu Wang, Bo Zhu, and Lei Zhang

Role Signatures for Access Control in Open Distributed Systems 205
Jason Crampton and Hoon Wei Lim

Policies and Security Aspects For Distributed Scientific Laboratories ... 221
Nicoletta Dessí, Maria Grazia Fugini, R. A. Balachandar

INTRUSION DETECTION

A Fuzzy Model for the Composition of Intrusion Detectors 237
Inez Raguenet and Carlos Maziero

Investigating the problem of IDS false alarms: An experimental study using Snort 253
G.C.Tjhai, M.Papadaki, S.M.Furnell, N.L.Clarke

User Session Modeling for Effective Application Intrusion Detection 269
Kapil Kumar Gupta, Baikunth Nath (Sr. MIEEE) and Kotagiri Ramamohanarao

ANOMALY DETECTION

A Product Machine Model for Anomaly Detection of Interposition Attacks on Cyber-Physical Systems 285
Carlo Bellettini and Julian L. Rrushi

Anomaly Detection with Diagnosis in Diversified Systems using Information Flow Graphs 301
Frédéric Majorczyk, Eric Totel, Ludovic Mé, Ayda Saïdane

Behavioral Intrusion Detection Indicators ... 317
Jacques Saraydaryan, Luc Paffumi, Veronique Legrand and Stephane Ubeda

ROLE MINING AND CONTENT PROTECTION

Leveraging Lattices to Improve Role Mining ... 333
Alessandro Colantonio, Roberto Di Pietro, Alberto Ocello

A Parallelization Framework for Exact Knowledge Hiding in Transactional Databases ... 349
Aris Gkoulalas-Divanis and Vassilios S. Verykios

Efficient Coalition Detection in Traitor Tracing ... 365
Hongxia Jin, Jeffery Lotspiech and Nimrod Megiddo

VOIP AND NETWORK SECURITY

SPIT Identification Criteria Implementation: Effectiveness and Lessons Learned ... 381
S. Dritsas, Y. Soupionis, M. Theoharidou, Y. Mallios, D. Gritzalis

Detecting More SIP Attacks on VoIP Services by Combining Rule Matching and State Transition Models ... 397
Dongwon Seo, Heejo Lee, and Ejovi Nuwere

A Decentralized Bayesian Attack Detection Algorithm for Network Security ... 413
Kien C. Nguyen, Tansu Alpcan, and Tamer Başar

NETWORK DEVICES SECURITY AND CYBER WARFARE

An Operation-Based Metric for CPA Resistance ... 429
J. Pan, J.I. den Hartog, and E.P. de Vink

YASIR: A Low-Latency, High-Integrity Security Retrofit for Legacy SCADA Systems ... 445
Patrick P. Tsang and Sean W. Smith

Adversary Modeling and Simulation in Cyber Warfare ... 461
Samuel N. Hamilton and Wendy L. Hamilton

SECURITY COMPLIANCE

Interactive Selection of ISO 27001 Controls under Multiple Objectives ... 477
Thomas Neubauer, Andreas Ekelhart, and Stefan Fenz

Feasibility of Automated Information Security Compliance Auditing ... 493
Longley D., Branagan M., Caelli W.J. and Kwok LF

Software Licence Protection and Management for Organisations 509
Muntaha Alawneh and Imad M. Abbadi

RISK AND SECURITY ANALYSIS

A Vulnerability Prioritization System Using A Fuzzy Risk Analysis Approach 525
Maxwell G. Dondo

ASTRA : A Security Analysis Method Based on Asset Tracking 541
Daniel Le Métayer and Claire Loiseaux

A Knowledge-Based Bayesian Model for Analyzing a System after an Insider Attack 557
Qutaibah Althebyan, Brajendra Panda

IDENTITY AND TRUST MANAGEMENT

Portable User-Centric Identity Management 573
Gail-Joon Ahn, Moo Nam Ko and Mohamed Shehab

Ubiquitous Privacy-Preserving Identity Managment 589
Kristof Verslype and Bart De Decker

Facilitating Privacy Related Decisions in Different Privacy Contexts on the Internet by Evaluating Trust in Recipients of Private Data 605
Indrajit Ray and Sudip Chakraborty

VIRTUALIZATION AND DIGITAL FORENSICS

Using Virtualization to Create and Deploy Computer Security Lab Exercises 621
Brian Hay, Ronald Dodge, and Kara Nance

DigForNet: Digital Forensic in Networking 637
Slim Rekhis, Jihene Krichene, and Noureddine Boudriga

A Live Digital Forensic system for Windows networks 653
Roberto Battistoni, Alessandro Di Biagio, Roberto Di Pietro, Matteo Formica, and Luigi V. Mancini

SHORT PAPERS

HoneyID : Unveiling Hidden Spywares by Generating Bogus Events 669
Jeheon Han, Jonghoon Kwon, Heejo Lee

A Security Protocol for Self-Organizing Data Storage 675
Nouha Oualha, Melek Önen and Yves Roudier

Protecting Financial Institutions from Brute-Force Attacks 681
Cormac Herley and Dinei Florêncio

Agency Theory: Can it be Used to Strengthen IT Governance? 687
Shaun Posthumus and Rossouw von Solms

A new Accounting Mechanism for Modern and Future AAA Services.... 693
Alexandros Tsakountakis, Georgios Kambourakis, and Stefanos Gritzalis

A user survey on the sense of security, Anshin........................ 699
Yasuhiro Fujihara, Yuko Murayama and Kentarou Yamaguchi

Multi-Layer Encryption for Multi-Level Access Control in Wireless Sensor Networks 705
Po-Yuan Teng, Shih-I Huang, and Adrian Perrig

A Comparative Study of Anomaly Detection Techniques in Web Site Defacement Detection 711
Giorgio Davanzo, Eric Medvet and Alberto Bartoli

Managing the lifecycle of XACML delegation policies in federated environments 717
Manuel Sánchez, Óscar Cánovas, Gabriel López, Antonio F. Gómez-Skarmeta

Assessing the Likelihood of Privacy Policy Compliance 723
George O.M. Yee, Larry Korba, and Ronggong Song

Classification features for detecting Server-side and Client-side Web attacks 729
Benferhat Salem and Tabia Karim

Index 735

Organization

General Chairs

Sabrina De Capitani di Vimercati, *Università degli Studi di Milano Italy*
Giulio Occhini, *AICA, Italy*

Program Chairs

Sushil Jajodia, *George Mason University, USA*
Pierangela Samarati, *Università degli Studi di Milano, Italy*

Publication Chair

Stelvio Cimato, *Università degli Studi di Milano, Italy*

Publicity Chair

Eros Pedrini, *Università degli Studi di Milano, Italy*

Program Committee

Claudio Ardagna, *Università degli Studi di Milano, Italy*
Vijay Atluri, *Rutgers University, USA*
Tuomas Aura, *Microsoft Research, UK*
Aditya Bagchi, *Indian Statistical Institute, India*
Jan Camenisch, *IBM Zurich Research Laboratory, Switzerland*
Marco Casassa Mont, *HP Laboratories, UK*
Yves Deswarte, *LAAS-CNRS, France*
Bart DeDecker, *K.U.Leuven, Belgium*
Kevin Du, *Syracuse University, USA*
Jan Eloff, *University of Pretoria, South Africa*
Simone Fischer-Huebner, *Karlstad University, Sweden*
Steven Furnell, *University of Plymouth, UK*
Sara Foresti, *Università degli Studi di Milano, Italy*
Michael Gertz, *University of California at Davis, USA*

Dimitris Gritzalis, *Athens University of Economics and Business, Greece*
Dieter Gollmann, *Technische Universitt Hamburg, Germany*
Le Gruenwald, *University of Oklahoma, USA*
Yong Guan, *Iowa State University, USA*
Jaap-Henk Hoepman, *Radboud University Nijmegen, Netherlands*
Angelos Keromytis, *Columbia University, USA*
Yongdae Kim, *University of Minnesota, USA*
Peng Liu, *Pennsylvania State University, USA*
Javier Lopez, *University of Malaga, Spain*
Refik Molva, *Institut Eurcom, France*
Yuko Murayama, *Iwate Prefectural University, Japan*
Peng Ning, *North Carolina State University, USA*
Stefano Paraboschi, *Università di Bergamo, Italy*
Philippos Peleties, *Universal Bank Public Ltd, Cyprus*
Gnther Pernul, *University of Regensburg, Germany*
Sihan Qing, *Chinese Academy of Sciences, China*
Kai Rannenberg, *Goethe University Frankfurt, Germany*
Indrajit Ray, *Colorado State University, USA*
Kent Seamons, *Brigham Young University, USA*
Cristina Serban, *AT&T, USA*
Stephanie Teufel, *University of Fribourg, Switzerland*
Jozef Vyskoc, *VaF, Slovak Republic*
LingYu Wang, *Concordia University, Canada*
Sean Wang, *University of Vermont, USA*
Tatjana Welzer, *University of Maribor, Slovenia*
Louise Yngstrom, *SU/KTH, Sweden*

Additional Reviewers

Emmanuel Adigun
Andreas Albers
Mohammad Ashiqur Rahaman
Kun Bai
Richard Brinkman
Jiayong Cai
Zhen Cao
Ebrima Cessay
Lukasz Chmielewski
Nathan Clarke
Marijke Coetzee
Bart De Win
Andre Deuker
Moses Dlamini
Stelios Dritsas
Stefan Dürbeck
Anas Abou El Kalam
Conny Franke
Lothar Fritsch
Ludwig Fuchs
Mohammed Gad El Rab
David Galindo
Flavio Garcia
Anna Granova
Marko Hlbl
Karin Hone
Yuan Hong
Karthick Jayaraman
Yoon-Chan Jhi
Qingguang Ji
Xiaoqi Jia
Jianchun Jiang
Michael Kohn
Jan Kolter
Thomas Leiber
Corrado Leita
Dequan Li
Fengjun Li
Gaicheng Li
Lunquan Li
An Liu
Wenming Liu
Ling Long
Leonardo Martucci
Patrick Merten
Noman Mohammed
Djedjiga Mouheb
Vincent Nicomette
Eiji Okamoto
Melek Önen
Nouha Oualha
Keshnee Padayachee
Maria Papadaki
Van-Hau Pham
Mike Radmacher
Kamil Reddy
Denis Royer
Tobias Scherner
Rolf Schillinger
Christian Schlger

Jan Schlueter
Anirban Sengupta
Qingni Shen
Abdullatif Shikfa
Yannis Soupionis
Martin Steinert
Thorsten Strufe
Zhouxuan Teng
Marianthi Theoharidou
Bill Tsoumas
Hein Venter
Kristof Verslype
Vesa Virta
Falk Wagner
Guan Wang
Yiming Wang
Stefan Weiss
Xi Xiong
Zhen Yu
Dayong Zhang
Shengzhi Zhang
Wentao Zhang
Xinyu Zhang
Zutao Zhu

Hiding in Groups: On the Expressiveness of Privacy Distributions

Karsten Nohl and David Evans

Abstract Many applications inherently disclose information because perfect privacy protection is prohibitively expensive. RFID tags, for example, cannot be equipped with the cryptographic primitives needed to completely shield their information from unauthorized reads. All known privacy protocols that scale to the anticipated sizes of RFID systems achieve at most modest levels of protection. Previous analyses found the protocols to have weak privacy, but relied on simplifying attacker models and did not provide insights into how to improve privacy. We introduce a new general way to model privacy through probability distributions, that capture how much information is leaked by different users of a system. We use this metric to examine information leakage for an RFID tag from the a scalable privacy protocol and from a timing side channel that is observable through the tag's random number generator. To increase the privacy of the protocol, we combine our results with a new model for rational attackers to derive the overall value of an attack. This attacker model is also based on distributions and integrates seamlessly into our framework for information leakage. Our analysis points to a new parameterization for the privacy protocol that significantly improves privacy by decreasing the expected attack value while maintaining reasonable scalability at acceptable cost.

1 Introduction

RFID labels in consumer products promise a world of new, convenient applications such as smart homes and automated checkout, but also raise serious privacy concerns. Among the many privacy intruding uses of RFID technology are corporate spying and customer profiling. The profiles encode information similar to Internet traces and, hence, have a certain monetary value.

Karsten Nohl and David Evans
University of Virginia, Computer Science Department, e-mail: {nohl,evans}@cs.virginia.edu

Please use the following format when citing this chapter:

Nohl, K. and Evans, D., 2008, in IFIP International Federation for Information Processing, Volume 278; *Proceedings of the IFIP TC 11 23rd International Information Security Conference*; Sushil Jajodia, Pierangela Samarati, Stelvio Cimato; (Boston: Springer), pp. 1–15.

Privacy protocols can protect a tag's identity from an attacker, but incur extra cost that grows with the degree of privacy; the cost becomes prohibitive for perfect privacy. Thus, practical protocols must trade some privacy for lower cost and higher scalability. Previous analyses of scalable protocols concluded that the privacy loss is high [5, 9]. In these analyses, the attacker is not assumed to be rational. Furthermore, although these analyses reveal a lack of privacy, they do not provide practical insights into how to improve the protocols.

We present a new way of measuring privacy that not only captures the privacy of the whole system but also the variance in privacy experienced by different users. Unlike previous approaches that represent privacy in a single value (e.g., the average group size), our analysis measures privacy loss as a distribution of how much information is leaked by different tags. We use our new privacy metric to derive distributions of information leakage for two example cases: an RFID random number generator that encodes a timing side channel and the tree protocol. Our metric works equally well in modeling these two very different sources of information and can further be used to model almost any source of deterministic or probabilistic information [10].

To derive a better understanding about the economics of privacy attacks and how to improve protection against them, we model a realistic attacker who attempts to collect traces because of their potential financial value. Our attacker is modeled as a function that maps traces to their value. We derive an upper bound on the shape of this function that allows us to model the most capable, yet rational attacker. Analyzing the privacy distribution of the tree-based hash protocol in light of this rational attacker leads to an adjustment of the tree parameters that provides substantially more privacy while incurring no extra tag cost and reasonable additional reader cost. Restructuring the tree improves privacy significantly while preserving scalability.

Our main contribution is a new way of representing privacy in form of a probability distributions which we demonstrate on a timing side channel in Section 3 and on a privacy protocol in Section 4. We then use this metric to analyze the value that an attack has to a rational attacker (Section 5), and propose a simple way for adjusting the tree protocol to better trade-off attack value and protection cost (Section 6).

2 Background

This section provides background information and describes previous work on defining privacy and measuring the privacy properties of RFID systems.

RFID Systems. The RFID tags we consider are small, cheap, passive radio-readable labels. The tags have unique identification numbers that a reader can read from the tag. The reader uses this ID to look up information from a back-end database. Adding privacy protection to RFID tags leads to higher per-tag costs and lower reading ranges (due to the increased power consumption), as well as increased computational cost in the backend system. To support RFID systems with billions of tags, this backend cost must grow sub-linearly with the size of the system.

Privacy Protocols. Several RFID privacy protocols have been proposed, all of which sacrifice at least one of scalability, availability, or strong privacy. The basic hash protocol, in which a tag hashes a random nonce with a secret key, provides strong privacy but does not scale well [16]. The database must try the keys of all tags to find the one that matches. This computational overhead is prohibitive for large systems.

A more scalable protocol assigns several secrets to each tag [9]. The secrets are structured in a tree with the tags as the tree leaves. A tag t_i is assigned the secrets $s_{i,1}, s_{i,2}, ...s_{i,d}$ where d is the depth of the tree (all secrets but the last are shared with some of the other tags). When queried, tag t_i responds with $H(s_{i,1}, r_1), r_1, H(s_{i,2}, r_2), r_2, \cdots, H(s_{i,d}, r_d), r_d$ where $H(\cdot,\cdot)$ is a strong one-way function and the r_j values are random nonces. The database executes the basic hash protocol for each tree level to finds the secret used on each level. Once a leaf is reached, the path from the root to the leaf uniquely identifies the tag. In the standard tree protocol, a tree with a constant branching factor at each level is used. This tree-based hash protocol scales well beyond billions of tags. The drawback of the protocol, however, is that secrets are shared among several tags and extracting the secrets from some tags potentially allows tracking others. An attacker can uniquely identify a tag with higher probability when more secrets of that tag are known. We show in Section 6 that increasing the branching factor at the lowest tree level improves privacy and that optimal trees for many scenarios have only two levels. In previous proposals, a binary tree was discussed [9], which according to our analysis has the least privacy of all possible trees.

Buttyan et al. also propose an algorithm for finding the optimal tree of secrets [4]. Their algorithm optimizes for a metric based on the average group size and generally increases the depth of trees. In follow-up work, the same authors and Avoine propose a new protocol that is equivalent to the two-level tree we propose [1]. They show that even in the metric they optimize for, the two-level tree is always superior to the trees their optimization algorithm finds. Our work provides the missing link between measuring privacy and improving privacy within the same framework and explains why trees with fewer levels provide more privacy.

Privacy Definition. The highest level of privacy possible in an identity system is *strong privacy* as defined in [7]. Strong privacy requires that an attacker cannot distinguish between a pair of uncompromised tags after interacting with all the tags in the system and extracting secrets from some tags. The only known way to efficiently achieve strong privacy for large-scale systems is by using asymmetric cryptography. Implementing the required public key ciphers on cheap RFIDs, however, is not possible [8].

The basic hash protocol can achieve strong privacy without asymmetric cryptography, but it requires the reader to perform as many cryptographic hashing operations as there are tags in the system. Strong privacy cannot be achieved while also matching the cost and scalability requirements of RFID systems [9, 11].

We define privacy as the state in which no *rational* attacker will attempt to compromise the system. Our definition of privacy acknowledges the fact that some amount of information is always leaked in the real world and that any definition which is too strong cannot be fulfilled. A rational attacker will only attack a system when the expected monetary (or other) return value exceeds the expected cost. Our definition allows for some tags to have relatively weak privacy protection as long as a large majority of tags experience strong protection and the attacker is very unlikely to see many weakly protected tags. In our definition, privacy can be deduced from information leakage, but the exact conversion between the two varies for different attackers and systems. We present a general approach to estimating the value of an attack from a distribution of information leakage in Section 5. Our model is abstract in that we do not assume any specific value of readings, but rather show ways to measure and improve privacy against any rational attacker.

Measuring Privacy. The privacy of the tree-based hash protocol has been estimated in several research papers. A first analysis calculated the probability that two readings from the same tag can be linked [2]. The paper concluded that the tree-based protocol provides insufficient privacy. We believe that this is too strong a privacy definition, which cannot be achieved, and advocate that the ability of an attacker to build whole traces should instead be considered. An alternative way of calculating the privacy of a system is by measuring the average anonymity of all tags. One such metric measures the average number of tags from which each tag cannot be distinguished [4]. A more precise metric measures the entropy of these groups [11]. Both approaches measure privacy as a single value, which is limiting in two ways. First, condensing privacy into a singular value presumes how the attacker will use the leaked information. Different attackers, however, use the information in diverse ways and hence the privacy of a system depends on the attacker's incentives and capabilities. Secondly, when averaging the information leakage over all tags in a system, information is lost about which parts of the system are mostly responsible for privacy deficits. Understanding the distribution of the information leakage is crucial for reducing the amount of information leaked. In this paper, we use a metric based on Shannon entropy from our previous work that measures the amount of information disclosed by the tags [11]. We extend this metric to consider the distribution of information leaked by tag groups. The tags fall in different groups that can be distinguished while tags within each group cannot. In a group of size g in a system with N tags, $\log_2(N/g)$ bits of information can be learned from each tag.

3 Side Channel Information Leakage

Privacy is potentially compromised at many layers including side channels. Side Channels are often caused by physical variance across different tags and can be observed as different timing, power consumption, or antenna characteristics. We are analyzing the varying lag between the moment a tag is supplied with power and when it starts operating. Because this latter time cannot be observed directly, we measure it indirectly through the tag's choice of random number that is used during anti-collision. These random numbers are required to match certain statistical randomness properties but do not guarantee randomness in a cryptographic sense

[6]. In particular, an attacker can often bias the distribution of values, which, besides breaking anti-collision, potentially compromises privacy.

Random number generators found on current tags (including cryptographic tags) generate random numbers using a linear feedback shift register (LFSR) with constant initial condition [12]. Each random value, therefore, only depends on the number of clock cycles elapsed between the time the tag is powered up (and the register starts shifting) and the time the random number is extracted. The variation in the choice of random number is hence a timing side channel that allows different groups of tags to be distinguished. Since the random numbers on current tags are generated deterministically, they are only unpredictable to attackers who cannot measure the timing with accuracy smaller than the wrap-around time of the generator (which for 16-bit random number is 0.6 seconds at 106 kHz [12]). Realistic attackers will more likely measure with micro- or nano-second accuracy. An attacker can even make a tag generate the same "random" number repeatedly by querying the tag at exactly the right time. In theory, the numbers generated for a given timing should be the same for all tags, because the circuitry that generates the numbers is the same and no physical randomness is used. Therefore, no information about the tag should be learned from the choice of number. In practice, however, we observe that due to manufacturing differences, groups of tags can be distinguished based on how quickly they start operating after the reader field is switched on. The distribution of process variance follows a typical normal (Gaussian) distribution and so does the average expected value generated by different tags. Most tags have too little variance to be distinguishable while few tags power up sufficiently slower or faster than the average so that the expected random value is slightly before or after the average value in the LFSR sequence. Figure 1a shows a typical distribution of expected average values for different tags that we estimated from our experiment. In this experiment we queried several different cards for a random number after exactly the same time. The average of each tag is slightly biased from the average of all tags.

The number and size of the groups that can are distinguishable due to their random numbers depends on the amount of process variation and the measuring accuracy of the attacker. The more variation exists among the tags and the better the attacker can control the timing of the tag, the more groups can be distinguished. For simplicity of our example, we assume the expected values to follow a normal distribution with standard deviation σ and an attacker with a timing resolution of 2σ. Virtually all tags can be placed in one of four groups as shown in Figure 1: Those having expected values slightly smaller or larger than the average, or significantly smaller or larger than the average.

An attacker learns more information from tags in smaller groups. A group of z tags corresponds to $\log_2(N/z)$ bits of leaked information where N is the total number of tags that an attacker potentially encounters (and is the total number of tags in the system unless the attacker has extra knowledge to exclude some tags). For the convenience of the following calculations, we calculate information in *nats* rather than *bits*. Nats are similar to bits but computed with base e; 1 nat equals $1/\ln(2)$ bits (approx. 1.33 bits). A group size z therefore corresponds to $\ln(N/z)$

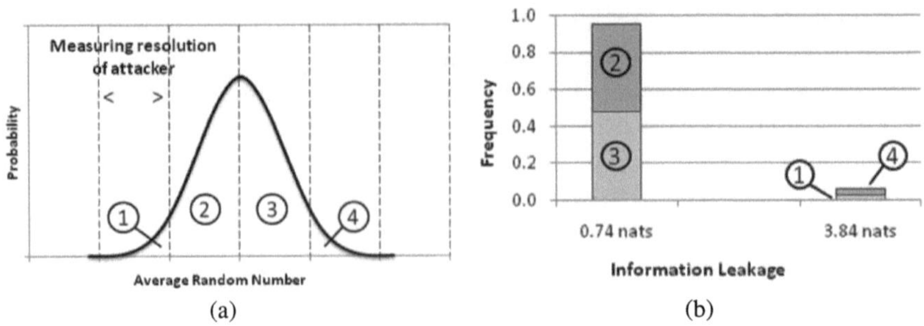

Fig. 1 Information disclosure of weak random number generator (a) distribution of varying expected value due to process variation; (b) distribution of information leakage.

nats of information. The distribution of information leakage for tags equipped with the weak random number generator is shown in Figure 1b.

In our example, each of the two groups around the average value holds 47.7% of the tags. The information leakage from tags in these two large groups is $\ln(1/0.477) = 0.74\text{nats} = 0.98\text{bits}$. The leakage from tags in the two smaller groups that divert more from the average value is consequently much higher at 3.84 nats (5.10 bits).

The privacy of a system is directly related to the distribution of information leakage. For the analyzed random number generator, privacy is therefore also directly related to the amount of process variation. Privacy can be significantly increased by lowering the process variation or by excluding a small number of outliers from the system. A better lesson still to be learned from this analysis is that any RNG design that gives control over the generated numbers to the attacker is clearly flawed, especially when also used for purposes other than anti-collision.

4 Tree Protocol Information Leakage

In the same way that we found the distribution of information leakage for the number generator, we can find similar distributions for most other sources. To analyze the privacy of the tree protocol, we need to know the distribution of group sizes and the likelihood that a randomly chosen tag falls into a group of a certain size. Tags are indistinguishable to the attacker if they use the same subset of the secrets known to the attacker. The larger the group of indistinguishable tags is, the more privacy is provided for the tags in the group. The distribution of group sizes depends on the tree parameterization and the set of secrets known to the attacker.

The tree protocol provides strong privacy if none of the secrets are known to the attacker: all N tags in circulation are in one large group of size N. As the attacker learns secrets from the tree, however, smaller groups of tags can be distinguished and strong privacy is lost. For example, in a tree of size $N = 256$ with spreading factor $k = 4$ with one compromised tag, an attacker can group the tags into groups of sizes 3, 12, 48, and 192 tags [11].

For $z = 3, 12, 48, 192$ there are z tags in a group of size z and z/k tags in smaller groups. In our example, there are 48 tags in a group of size 48 and 12+3+1 tags in smaller groups. For all other values of z there are less than $z + z/k$ tags in groups smaller or equal to z. Therefore, the probability that a randomly chosen tag falls into a group of size z or smaller after the secrets on a single tag have been captured is upper-bounded by

$$\Pr(Z \leq z) \leq \frac{k}{k-1} \cdot \frac{z}{N}. \tag{1}$$

The one broken tag is no longer considered part of the system and Equation 1 is defined over the range of group sizes actually found in the tree; that is, $k-1 \leq z \leq N \cdot \frac{k-1}{k}$.

To simplify the following calculations, we consider only the upper bound of Equation 1. This bound corresponds to the case where one group for each possible size $(1, 2, 3, ...)$ exists. These groups each hold $k/(k-1)$ tags. While this case is impossible to achieve in reality because a group of size z should have z members, it provides a close enough upper bound on the real distributions of groups.

This upper bound on the cumulative distribution is shown in Figure 2a along with the values of the real distribution. Note that the upper bound diverges most from the real distribution for those groups that leak the least information, and least for the more important groups that leak the most information. In our example tree of 256 tags with one broken tag, there are 4/(4-1) = 1.33 tags in a group of size one, another 1.33 tags in a group of size 2, and so forth. This configuration never appears in reality but provides a close upper bound on the real distribution; and unlike the real values, this bound can be expressed in a closed-form probability distribution.

The probability that x or more nats are leaked (as defined in Section 3) by a randomly chosen tag is upper bounded by:

$$\Pr(X \geq x) \leq \frac{k}{k-1} \cdot \frac{1}{e^x}.$$

This is defined over the range of inputs that correspond to group sizes actually found in the tree; that is, $\ln\left(\frac{k}{k-1}\right) \leq x \leq \ln\left(\frac{N}{k-1}\right)$.

So far, we only considered the case of a single broken tag. Assuming tags are evenly distributed, each additional broken tag adds the same number of members to each group (with the exception of the largest group which shrinks in size). For b broken tags[1], the probability that at least x nats of information for a given tag are disclosed becomes

$$\Pr(X \geq x) \leq b \cdot \frac{k}{k-1} \cdot \frac{1}{e^x} \tag{2}$$

for the range $\ln\left(\frac{k}{k-b}\right) \leq x \leq \ln\left(\frac{N}{k-1}\right)$.

The probability that the system defeats an attacker who requires at least x nats of information to be successful is: $\Pr(X < x) = 1 - \Pr(X \geq x)$. Figure 2b shows

[1] Our approximation is closest if b<k, but still valid otherwise.

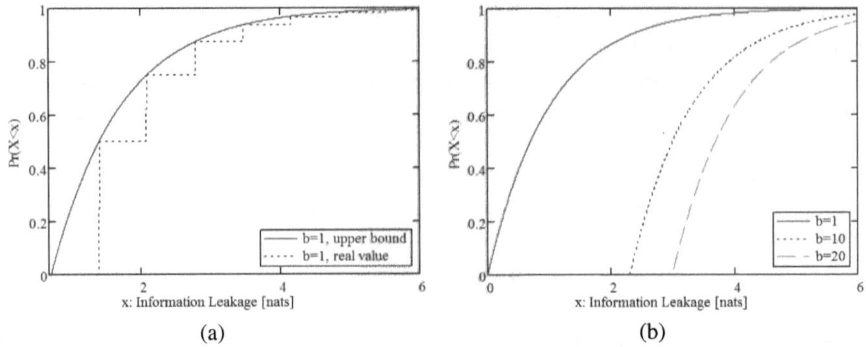

Fig. 2 Probability that for a tree with b broken tags less than x nats of information are leaked by a randomly selected tag, k is large. (a) real value vs. upper bound, one broken tag; (b) upper bound for different numbers of broken tags.

this probability for different numbers of broken tags. Note that the distribution is independent of the number of tags in the system and for large trees it is essentially independent of the spreading factor, k. A realistic attacker will certainly behave more complex than this simple threshold. We address this concern in the Section 5 with an extended model that acknowledges the rational and adaptive behavior of realistic attackers.

Multi-Tag Attack. A sophisticated attacker will use all available information to distinguish individuals. In particular, all tags that a person carries will be used to track that person. Suppose each individual carries m tags that are randomly selected from the tree. To create an identifier for a person, the attacker simply concatenates the information learned from the various tags the person carries. The different identifier that can be build this way separate all individuals into separate groups, which can again be reflected by a distribution of information leakage. The information learned from each of the tags follows the exponential distribution described by Equation 2. Summing several exponential distributions leads to a gamma distribution. Hence, the probability that a total of x nats of information are leaked from a person that carries m tags is:

$$\Pr(X = x) = \frac{x^{m-1}}{(m-1)\,!} \cdot b \cdot \frac{k}{k-1} \cdot \frac{1}{e^x}.$$

This distribution is shown in Figure 3a for different m. The probability that not more than c nats of information are leaked from a randomly chosen tag can be calculated as the integral of this function up to c, which is shown in Figure 3b. Note that the graph shows the probability that the system is *not* compromised, so lower values indicate a higher probability of privacy compromise.

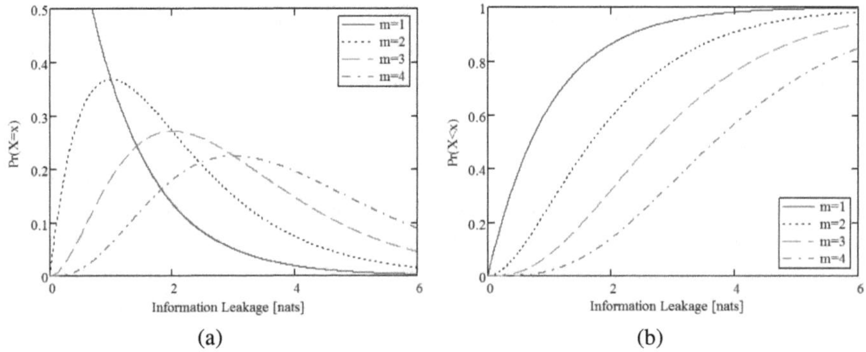

Fig. 3 (a) Distribution of information leaked by collection of m tags. (b) Probability that information leaked by m tags is smaller than x nats.

5 Distinguishing Traces

Privacy-intruding uses of RFIDs include surveillance of individuals, corporate espionage, and profiling of consumers. Rogue customer profiling is the most frequently discussed scenario in the context of RFID privacy. Traces collected by a rogue reader could be used in ways similar to Internet traces to build customer profiles and enable price discrimination [13], and therefore constitute a certain value. In many scenarios, RFIDs primary purpose is to build such profiles and customers are often provided with price incentives to participate in loyalty schemes. But while legitimate collecting of consumer data is transparent and provides incentives to the customer, rogue readers will try to read the same information from the tags without owner consent. Another rational attack scenario is corporate espionage where information is collected from RFID labels on products to learn their internal business information of competitors. Lastly, tracking attackers keep individuals under surveillance through RFID readings. Our analysis of the expected attack value in this section and the proposed modification of the tree protocol in Section 6 apply equally to all three types of attacker. In this analysis, we avoid making restrictive assumptions about the actual use of collected traces or attempt to quantify their value. Instead, we assume that in any attack, the attackers' objective is to distinguish tags in order to build traces, which is more likely when the attacker has more information about the tags. Our privacy metric, therefore, measures the amount of information the attacker learns about different tags. Privacy is achieved when the expected cost of any attack exceeds the expected return.

Other Information Sources. Attackers are not limited to information from the tree protocol or random number generator. Our approach of modeling information leakage as a probability distribution applies just as well to all other information sources such as physical side channels. Sources that might be used in an attack include the physical characteristics of the tag (e.g., radio fingerprint), meta-information (e.g., location and time of read), and information from other detection systems, such as biometric identification systems like face and voice recognition. The exact distribution of many of these sources is as of yet unknown. In the next section we show how all these additional sources can be modeled as attacker strategy.

Threat Model. We are considering an attacker that mines RFID data sets for profitable traces, where a *trace* is a set of readings from the same tag. In order to build traces, an attacker wants to link the different RFID readings collected from the same individual. Each reading consists of time, place, the randomized tag identifier, and potentially further metadata. The attacker's goal is to extract individual traces form a collection of many intermingled traces. The likelihood that the attacker will be successful grows with the amount of information leaked by the tags the individual carries. Readings have higher value to the attacker when they carry more information.

The data set the attacker collects is composed of many intermingled traces from different tags. We assume that each individual trace becomes valuable only when it can be separated from all other traces thus identifying a set of readings from a single tag (or a conjoined group of tags). Whether a trace can be separated using data from the protocol level depends on the secrets known to the attacker. The previous section derives the expected sizes of tag groups distinguishable on the protocol level for an attacker with a given number of compromised tags. To separate those traces that are indistinguishable at the protocol level, the attacker will further employ data mining techniques, use additional information sources such as the weak random numbers from Section 3, other side channel information, or contextual information such as place and time of read to distinguish traces. To capture the success of the attacker in doing so, we introduce two functions: the *attacker strategy function*, which describes the sophistication of the attack, and the *binning function*, which captures the clustering of traces.

The attacker strategy function encodes the probability with which an attacker can distinguish traces that are indistinguishable at the protocol level. The function captures the side channel information and data mining techniques that are available to the attacker, and varies widely for different attackers. Even though the function is generally unknown—even to the attacker—we can derive an upper bound on it.

First, we define P as the average probability that a set containing two traces can be distinguished. This average probability is closely related to the success of our attacker who is interested in collecting a large number of traces with high probability. Previous analyses measure the least privacy experienced by any of the tags [3]. In contrast, privacy in our model is achieved if the average protection is high enough to discourage all rational attackers from attacking a system while the actual protection experienced by different users depends on the set of secrets an attacker possesses.

Given a set of any number of readings known to come from two different tags, the attacker can separate the readings into two groups based on the tag from which they were generated with probability P. It follows that traces cannot be separated from groups of three intermingled traces with average probability better than P^2. If the chances of extracting a trace from a set of three traces were higher, an attacker could distinguish two traces with a probability higher than P by intermingling an additional trace. We can generalize to any number of intermingled traces:

Trace Extraction Theorem: *Let the average probability over all traces that two traces can be distinguished be P. Then a trace cannot be extracted from a set with* $g > 1$ *traces with an average probability better than* $P^{(g-1)}$.

To prove this theorem we show that when a trace is added to a set of traces, extracting that trace from the set is at least as difficult as distinguishing the trace from every member of the set. We further show that this probability is always maximized when, given the average probability of distinguishing two traces, P, all pairs of traces can be distinguished with the same probability. The strategy function is, hence, upper-bounded by: $S(g) = P^{(g-1)}$. The proof is given in the full version of this paper.

Second, the binning function describes the distribution of traces into the different groups that can be distinguished in the tree using protocol information leakage. Given a distribution of groups as derived in Section 4, a system with size N, and a data set with $t+1$ intermingled traces, the probability that at most g traces from a group of size z are included in the data set is:

$$B(z,g) \leq \binom{t}{g} \cdot \left(1 - \frac{z}{N}\right)^{t-g}.$$

Expressed in terms of encoded information, the probability that g indistinguishable traces with x nats of entropy (that is, traces from a group with size $z = N/e^x$) are found in the set is:

$$B(x,g) = \binom{t}{g} \cdot \left(1 - \frac{1}{e^x}\right)^{t-g} \cdot \left(\frac{1}{e^x}\right)^{g}.$$

The binning function is shown in Figure 4a for traces with different entropies.

Last, the *success function* encodes the probability that a trace with given entropy can be extracted. This is the likelihood that the trace is intermingled with $(g-1)$ other traces, $B(x,g)$, multiplied by the probability that the attacker can extract a trace from a set of g traces, $S(g)$, and summed over all possible mixes ($g = 0, 1, ..., t$; where $g = 0$ is a single, not intermingled trace):

$$Su(x) = \sum_{g=0}^{t} \left(B(x,g) \cdot S(g)\right).$$

The success function is shown in Figure 4b. To determine whether an attack is successful, the success function needs to be interpreted in light of the attacker's requirements. The value of an attack to the attacker depends on the likelihood that traces can be extracted from the collected data, which is encoded in the success function. Multiplying the success function with the likelihood that a trace with given entropy occurs (from Section 4), and integrating over all possible entropies (that is, the entropies from that largest to the smallest group) gives us the expected value of the attack:

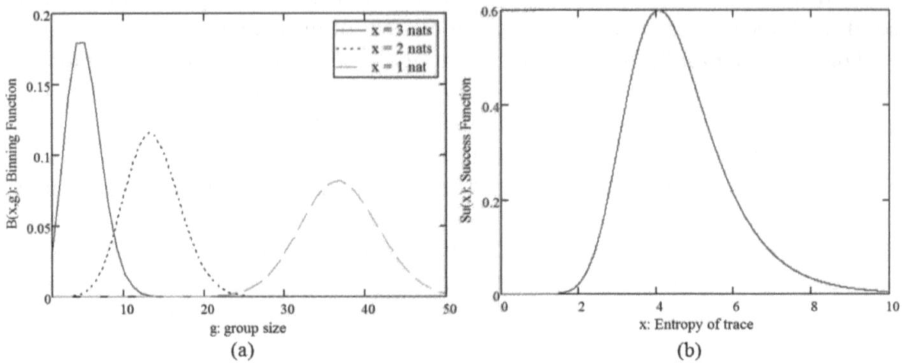

Fig. 4 Binning Function: probability that a trace with x nats of entropy is intermingled with g other traces; data set with $t = 100$ traces. (b)Success Function: probability that a trace with x nats of entropy can be extracted; $t = 100$.

$$Value = \int_{ent(lrg)}^{ent(sm)} (Su(x) \cdot \Pr(X = x))\, dx \tag{3}$$

where $ent(lrg)$ and $ent(sm)$ are the entropies of the largest and smallest groups in the system. As shown in Figure 3b, only certain group sizes have a high likelihood to contain useable information. In both the random number generator and the tree protocol, this is due to the fact that a large majority of the tags hides in few large groups, but only the few tags in small groups can easily be distinguished. Hence, the majority of the attack value is generated by these groups of the smaller sizes while the majority of tags contributes only very little. In the next section, we use this insight to design a protocol modification that decreases the attack value and defeats a rational attacker.

6 Minimizing Attack Value

We assume rational attackers have financial goals. Such an attacker will only attack a system if the expected value of the traces acquired exceeds the cost of the attack. The value of an attack is given by Equation 3. The insight that the bulk of the attack value is generated by the tags in smaller groups points to a simple but very effective improvement of the tree protocol: restructure the tree so that no tags fall in groups smaller than some threshold. Moving tags from these smallest groups to larger groups decreases the attack value significantly.The most scalable tree for a given tree depth, d is a balanced, fixed-k tree that has a constant spreading factor of $k = N^{1/d}$. We assume that d is fixed because it is limited by the tag memory and by the maximum reading time. Varying the spreading factor for the whole tree does not provide an effective trade-off. Varying the spreading factor only at the last level of the tree, however, preserves most of the scalability, while significantly improving privacy.

The privacy-improved tree is constructed by dividing the tags into groups of some threshold size c and constructing a balanced, fixed-k tree with these groups as the leaves. The threshold is chosen to be larger than the largest group size that still carries a high value to the attacker. The computational time required to find a tag is the time to find the correct leaf plus the time to identify the correct tag within that leaf:

$$Cost = \left(\frac{N}{c}\right)^{\frac{1}{d-1}} \cdot (d-1) + c.$$

In comparison, the balanced tree has a maximal cost of $N^{1/d}d$. Increasing c increases privacy and computational cost. The attack value of the modified tree is computed using Equation 3 but with a larger minimum group size. The attack value is:

$$V_{all}(c) = \int_{\ln\left(\frac{k}{k-b}\right)}^{\ln\left(\frac{N}{c-1}\right)} V_{gen}.$$

For each choice of the minimum group size, c, we get a different point on the trade-off curve between privacy and cost that is depicted in Figure 5 for an example scenario. A fixed-k tree for the example setup requires a spreading factor of 56. Increasing the size of the groups on the last level beyond 56 decreases the attack value. It falls to 40% of the maximum value at a group size of 1100 tags while increasing the reader cost 9 times. Limiting the attack value to 20% leads to a 30-fold cost increase. These correspond to 1139 and 3729 hashing operations, which is still orders of magnitude below the 107 operations required to reduce the attack value to zero using the basic hashing scheme with no shared keys.

For a large group of attackers and for virtually all RFID systems, minimal group sizes of $\sqrt{N}$ will provide sufficient privacy. The resulting tree has only two levels,

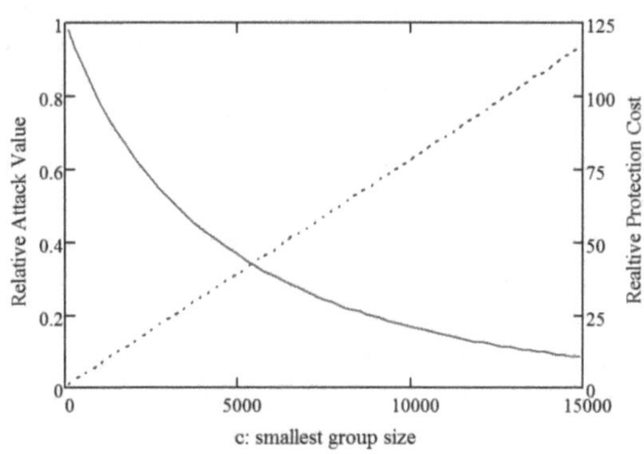

Fig. 5 Trade-off between attacker value and protection cost. Scenario of a large system with many broken tags and many tags per person, specifically $N = 10^7$, $d = 4$, $b = 50$, $m = 10$, $P = \frac{1}{2}$, and $t = 100$.

which requires smaller memories on the tag and leads to quicker reading times when compared to a deeper tree. The computational cost is still not prohibitive even for very large systems. In a system with one billion tags, each read requires about 6000 hashing operations, which takes only a fraction of a second on a general-purpose processor.

The attacker value can be further reduced by decreasing k on the first level and increasing it on the second level. A hashing computer build from FPGAs can execute on the order of a billion hashing operations per second at reasonable cost [14]. For a system with a billion tags, this would support authenticating more than 100,000 tags per second on a single such server. The appropriate tree for many RFID privacy scenarios therefore has only two levels and is hence the opposite configuration from the initially proposed binary tree [9].

7 Conclusions

Modeling information disclosure as a probability distribution of leaked information exposes the parts of a system responsible for most of the privacy lost. Analyzing secret-trees and side channels using such distributions helps to identify a small subset of tags as the source of most of the privacy loss and provides new insights into the trade-off between cost and privacy. The privacy distribution of secret trees and many other sources can be approximated by an exponential distribution. When information from several tags or other sources is combined by an attacker, the overall information leakage can be modeled using a single gamma distribution. Our approach of expressing all privacy leaks in the form of probability distributions enables designers of privacy protection to identify the weakest link and thereby estimate the privacy of the overall system, which has not previously been possible.

When combined with a rational attacker model, identifying the weakest part of the tree protocol enabled us to find new parameters for the tree with much improved privacy. Our attacker model takes into account the value of different traces and assumes that an attack is successful only if the overall value exceeds the attack cost. Attackers can be modeled by a function that assigns values to different amounts of information leakage. Without making restrictive assumptions on the actual incentives of the attacker we can prove an upper bound on the value function that corresponds to the most capable attacker. This overall value is mostly generated by the tags in the smallest groups at the last level of the tree. Varying the size of these groups trades increased computational cost for decreased attack value. Although our parameterization might seem obvious in retrospect, it was not stated prior to our analysis. In fact, the previously proposed binary tree appears to provide the least privacy of all possible setups. This underlines that good models for information leakage and a good understanding of the attacker's incentives are needed when designing new privacy protocols.

Acknowledgment. This work has been partly supported by the National Science Foundation through Award 0541123.

References

1. Avoine, G., Buttyan, L., Holczer, T. and Vajda, I. Group-Based Private Authentication International. *Workshop on Trust, Security, and Privacy for Ubiquitous Computing*, 2007.
2. Avoine, G., Dysli, E. and Oechslin, P. Reducing Time Complexity in RFID Systems. *Selected Areas in Cryptography*, 2005.
3. Avoine, G. and Oechslin, P. RFID Traceability: A Multilayer Problem. *Financial Cryptography*, 2005.
4. Buttyan, L., Holczer, T. and Vajda, I. Optimal Key-Trees for Tree-Based Private Authentication. *Workshop on Privacy Enhancing Technologies*, 2006.
5. Damgard, I. and Ostergaard, M. RFID Security: Tradeoffs between Security and Efficiency. *Cryptology ePrint Archive*, 2006.
6. EPCGlobal Inc. Class 1 Generation 2 UHF Air Interface Protocol Standard v1.0.9, 2005.
7. Juels, A. and Weis, S. Defining Strong Privacy for RFID. *Cryptology ePrint Archive*, 2006.
8. Kumar, S. and Paar, C. Are standards compliant elliptic curve cryptosystems feasible on RFID? *Workshop on RFID Security*, 2006.
9. Molnar, D. and Wagner, D. Privacy and Security in Library RFID: Issues, Practices, and Architectures. *ACM CCS*, 2004.
10. Nohl, K. and Evans, D. Quantifying Information Leakage in Tree-Based Hash Protocols. *University of Virginia, CS Dept., Technical Report UVA-CS-2006-20*, 2006.
11. Nohl, K. and Evans, D. Quantifying Information Leakage in Tree-Based Hash Protocols. *Conference on Information and Communications Security*, 2006.
12. Nohl, K., Evans, D., Starbug and Ploetz, H. Reverse-Engineering a Cryptographic RFID Tag. *USENIX Security*, 2008.
13. Odlyzko, A. Privacy, Economics, and Price Discrimination on the Internet. *International Conference on Electronic Commerce*, 2003.
14. Satoh, A. and Inoue, T. ASIC-Hardware-Focused Comparison for Hash Functions MD5, RIPEMD-160, and SHS. *International Symposium on Information Technology*, 2005.
15. Tsudik, G. YA-TRAP: Yet Another Trivial RFID Authentication Protocol. *International Conference on Pervasive Computing and Communications*, 2006.
16. Weis, S., Sarma, S., Rivest, R. and Engels, D. Security and Privacy Aspects of Low-Cost Radio Frequency Identification Systems. *International Conference on Security in Pervasive Computing*, 2003.

Practical Privacy-Preserving Benchmarking

Florian Kerschbaum

Abstract Benchmarking is an important process for companies to stay competitive in today's markets. The basis for benchmarking are statistics of performance measures of a group of companies. The companies need to collaborate in order to compute these statistics.

Protocols for privately computing statistics have been proposed in the literature. This paper designs, implements and evaluates a privacy-preserving benchmarking platform which is a central entity that offers a database of benchmark statistics to its customers. This is the first attempt at building a practical privacy-preserving benchmarking system and the first attempt at addressing all necessary trade-offs.

The paper starts by designing a protocol that efficiently computes the statistics with constant cost per participant. The protocol uses central communication where customers only communicate with the central platform which facilitates a simple practical orchestration of the protocol. The protocols scale to realistic problem sizes due to the constant communication (and computation) cost per participant of the protocol.

1 Introduction

Benchmarking is the comparison of one company's key performance indicators (KPI) to the statistics of the same KPIs of its peer group. A key performance indicator (KPI) is a statistical quantity measuring the performance of a business process. Examples from different company operations are make cycle time (manufacturing), cash flow (financial) and employee fluctuation rate (human resources). A peer group is a group of (usually competing) companies that are interested in comparing their KPIs based on some similarity of the companies. Examples formed along different

Florian Kerschbaum
SAP Research, Karlsruhe, Germany, e-mail: florian.kerschbaum@sap.com

Please use the following format when citing this chapter:

Kerschbaum, F., 2008, in IFIP International Federation for Information Processing, Volume 278; *Proceedings of the IFIP TC 11 23rd International Information Security Conference*; Sushil Jajodia, Pierangela Samarati, Stelvio Cimato; (Boston: Springer), pp. 17–31.

characteristics include car manufacturers (industry sector), Fortune 500 companies in the United States (revenue and location), or airline vs. railway vs. haulage (sales market).

Privacy is of the utmost importance in benchmarking. Companies are reluctant to share their business performance data due to the risk of losing a competitive advantage or being embarrassed. Several privacy-preserving protocols that can be used for benchmarking that keep the KPIs confidential within one company have been proposed in the literature [2, 5, 9, 10, 13, 20]. None of those matches the requirements of a large service provider offering a benchmarking service entirely. Instead this paper proposes a new practical, constant cost, centralized privacy-preserving benchmarking protocol and evaluates it.

A benchmarking platform is a central service provider that offers a database of statistics of peer groups and KPIs to its customers. Customers, i.e. companies, would first subscribe with the service provider and then would be able to retrieve relevant statistics. On the service provider's request the subscribed companies would engage in a protocol to recompute the statistics.

The benchmarking platform is not supposed to acquire the plain text KPIs from the companies acting as a trusted third party, but rather the KPIs are to be kept entirely private to the companies. In the privacy-preserving protocol the benchmarking platform is a regular participant without any input. While the privacy protects the confidentiality of the KPIs for the companies, it alleviates the benchmarking platform from the burden of storing and handling them and protects it from the potential embarrassment due to accidental revealation.

Another important aspect of the service provider model is that the subscribed companies only communicate with the service provider, but never amongst each other. Anonymity among the subscribed companies is a required feature and can only be achieved, if they do not need to address messages to others. The precise requirement for anonymity is that subscribers do not know or refer to any static identifier of other customers (e.g. IP addresses, public keys, etc.). Any static identifier will reveal changes in the composition of the peer group to the subscribers in subsequent executions of the protocol which is undesirable and may break the privacy of the entire system. In many cases, the service provider wants to know the identity of the subscribers for billing purposes, which simplifies communication.

In order to keep the proposed protocols practical, they need to be optimized in computation and communication cost. One measure is the number of rounds that are needed to complete the protocol. A round in the service provider model is a step in the protocol that all subscribers need to complete before any subscriber can initiate the next step. The proposed protocols have a constant number of rounds. Another measure is the communication complexity of the protocol. Our protocol has a constant (i.e. linear in the length of the security parameter) communication complexity for each subscriber independent of the number of subscribed companies.

This paper presents from our view the first practical implementation of privacy-preserving benchmarking. It addresses a number of trade-offs in its distributed systems (single central platform) and security (key distribution and security assumptions) architecture that are tuned for practical performance and economic benefit.

E.g. one central platform is crucial for economic acceptance. Alternatives using multiple mutually distrustful server are economically inacceptable due to the necessarily different business model. Nevertheless for the central communication model no linear cost protocols are known, so we had to sacrifice some security in the key distribution model. Furthermore, not only linear performance is required, but also low constant factors. We know from [20] that a two-party variation of a sub-protocol has superb practical performance. Therefore we are willing to accept the multiplicative hiding assumption (Section 5.1.2) resulting in a significantly improved performance. Our performance evaluation results show that such a solution is at the borderline of what is currently practically feasible.

In summary this paper contributes and evaluates the first privacy-preserving benchmarking platform that combines the following three features:

- *practical*: It addresses all trade-offs from a distributed systems and security point of view for practical performance and economic benefit.
- *centralized*: Each participant communicates only with a central server (or set of servers).
- *constant-cost*: Cost per participant is constant:
  - constant number of rounds
  - constant communication cost

The remainder of the paper is structured as follows: After a short description of the economic motivation for using privacy in Section 2, we introduce some building blocks used and notation in Section 3. Then we describe the registration of companies with the service provider in Section 4. The protocols to recompute the statistics are described and analyzed in Section 5. The practical evaluation using a prototype is presented in Section 6. Related work is discussed in Section 7 before the conclusions are presented in Section 8.

2 Economic Motivation

The privacy requirement of the benchmarking platform is designed for the economic advantage of the service provider. Two advantages can be separated: customer acceptance and competitive advantage.

Privacy is anticipated to increase customer acceptance. The intuition is that customers are reluctant to share business critical data and private benchmarking can alleviate the risk. This in turn leads to more potential customers, a larger market size and in last consequence to larger revenue.

Privacy can also provide a competitive advantage. The risk and cost of sharing KPIs to engage in benchmarking can be lowered by privacy. Thereby offering a higher benefit to customers, justifying a higher price or increasing the market share.

Also given the realistic possibility of privacy-preserving benchmarking with similar results to and the same price as non-privacy-preserving benchmarking, there is no reason to engage in non-privacy-preserving benchmarking. As mentioned above, the privacy feature also alleviates the service provider from handling and storing the individual KPIs and the embarrassment in case of an accidental disclosure, which reduces the operating costs of the service provider.

3 Preliminaries

3.1 Homomorphic Encryption

Our protocols are built using homomorphic encryption. In homomorphic encryption one operation on the cipher texts produces an encryption of the result of a homomorphic operation on the plain texts. In particular, we require the homomorphic operation to be addition (modulo a constant). Several such encryption systems exist [3, 8, 24, 27, 28]. We suggest Paillier's encryption system [28] which has been generalized in [8]. Let $E_X(x)$ denote the encryption of x with public key $\overline{K}_X$, then Paillier's encryption system has the following property:

$$E_X(x) \cdot E_X(y) = E_X(x+y)$$

From which the next property can be easily derived:

$$E_X(x)^y = E_X(x \cdot y)$$

3.2 Oblivious Transfer

Oblivious Transfer (OT) was introduced in [30] and generalized to 1-out-of-2 OT in [12]. In 1-out-of-2 OT the sender has two secrets x_0 and x_1 and the receiver has one bit b. After the execution of the OT protocol, the receiver has obtained x_b, but has learnt nothing about $x_{\neg b}$. The fastest known implementation of OT is described in [25]. It was proven secure under the (computational and decisional) Diffie-Hellman assumptions in the random oracle model. An OT protocol between a sender S and a receiver R (where the parameters are clear from the context) is denoted by

$$S \xrightarrow{\text{OT}} R$$

3.3 Message Authentication Codes

A message authentication code (MAC) is a function parameterized by a secret key k that is easy to compute and compresses an input x of finite arbitrary length to an output $MAC(x,k)$ of fixed finite length [29]. More importantly, MACs provide computation-resistance, i.e. given any number of authenticated texts $\langle x_i, MAC(x_i,k)\rangle$ it is computationally infeasible to compute another authenticated text $\langle x, MAC(x,k)\rangle$ $(x \neq x_i)$ without knowing the key k. A successful attempt of producing an authenticated text is called MAC forgery.

3.4 Secret Sharing

A secret sharing scheme divides a secret s into n shares $S = \{s_1, \ldots, s_n\}$ such that any subset of S of size t can be used to recover s. Modular addition can be used for secret sharing where $t = n$, if $s = \sum_i^n s_i \bmod m$ [19]. It can be replaced by exclusive-OR $s = s_1 \oplus \ldots \oplus s_n$ (where $\oplus$ denotes exclusive-OR). Both secret sharing schemes are perfect, i.e. less than t shares yield absolutely no information, in the information-theoretic sense, about s.

4 Registration

When companies subscribe to the benchmarking platform, a trusted third party is involved. This trusted third party only needs to be involved once during registration, but we assume that it does not maliciously collaborate with the service provider. A practical candidate for such a third party would be PKI certification authority. The issued certificates will be used to establish secure and authenticated channels between the subscribers and the service provider.

Furthermore, we extend the third party's functionality to a dealer. The trusted third party will distribute secrets to the subscribers. In particular, the trusted third party distributes to all subscribers:

- K_{common}: A private key in the homomorphic encryption system of Section 3.1. This private key is shared among the subscribers, but unknown to the service provider. The corresponding public key $\overline{K}_{common}$ is known to the service provider.
- s_{common}: A key for the MAC algorithm, also shared among the subscribers and unknown to the service provider.

5 Protocols

This section will present protocols for computing the following statistics:

- mean
- variance
- maximum

These protocols will be executed for each peer group and each KPI. Let x_i denote the input (KPI) of the i-th subscriber X_i. For reason explained later the subscribers know the size n of the peer group and therefore computation of the mean ($\mu = \frac{1}{n}\sum_i^n x_i$) is equivalent to summation. Furthermore, for practical reasons, we compute mean and variance in different rounds, such that the mean has been revealed before the variance is being computed. In this case computation of the variance is also equivalent to summation (of $(x_i - \mu)^2$). Note that, the summation of the variance should be done using a different shared key pair $\langle K_{common'}, \overline{K}_{common'} \rangle$, if the cost of distributing it to all subscribers is affordable.

Summation using homomorphic encryption is quite natural: Each subscriber submits $E_{common}(x_i)$ to the service provider which, after receiving all inputs, computes the encrypted sum as $\prod_i^n E_{common}(x_i) = E_{common}(\sum_i^n x_i)$.

Maximum computation for two parties was first presented and evaluated in [20] and the following protocol builds upon the successful experiences. The subscriber sends $E_{common}(x_i)$ to the service provider who maintains an encrypted (intermediate) maximum $E_{common}(max)$. The service provider chooses two large random numbers r and r' (e.g. size $O(m^2)$ where m is the maximum KPI possible), such that $r' < r$. He sends to the subscriber $E_{common}(c) = E_{common}(r \cdot (x_i - max) + r')$. It holds that $c < 0 \Leftrightarrow x_i < max$ where "< 0" is interpreted in a mapping of integers $[-d, d-1]$ to $[0, 2d-1]$ according to congruence in modular arithmetic.

Furthermore, the service provider flips a coin $r'' \in \{0,1\}$ and if r'' is 1, then he negates c resulting in c'. The subscriber and the service provider share c as $c = c' \oplus r''$. They then engage in an OT where the service provider sends one of $\langle E_{common}(x_i + r'''), E_{common}(max + r''') \rangle$ where r''' is a random number chosen by the service provider to hide the encrypted value. The service provider switches the values, if he negated c. Then the subscriber chooses according to c', rerandomizes the value (by homomorphically adding $E_{common}(0)$) and returns it to the service provider which can then obtain a new $E_{common}(max)$ by subtracting r'''.

After executing the protocols the service provider has the encrypted values $E_{common}(sum)$ for the mean and variance and $E_{common}(max)$ for the maximum.

The intention of the protocol is that the service provider obtains the result to store it in the database for all subscribers and future subscribers until the statistics are recomputed. For software engineering reason the subscribers are not supposed to keep a record of the protocols, but rather obtain the results via a database query. The service provider submits therefore the encrypted results $E_{common}(result)$ to all subscribers and they respond with the decrypted $result$. We chose to submit to all subscribers, such that no single subscriber may obtain the correct result, but return an incorrect result to the service provider (and the other subscribers). The service provider can compare all *result* values and detect the presence of malicious subscribers if there is at least one honest subscriber. He can identify the malicious subscribers, if there is a majority of honest subscribers.

Round 1:

$$
\begin{array}{llll}
X_i & \longrightarrow & SP & E_{common}(x_i) \\
SP & \longrightarrow & X_i & E_{common}(c) = E_{common}(-1^{r_3} \cdot (r_1 \cdot (x_i - max) + r_2)) \\
SP & \xrightarrow{\text{OT}} & X_i & E^c = \begin{cases} E_{common}(x_i + r_4) & \text{if } c \geq 0 \oplus (r_3 = 0) \\ E_{common}(max + r_4) & \text{if } c < 0 \oplus (r_3 = 0) \end{cases} \\
X_i & \longrightarrow & SP & E_{common}(max') = E^c \cdot E_{common}(0) \\
SP & & & E_{common}(max) = E_{common}(max' - r_4)
\end{array}
$$

Round 2:

$$
\begin{array}{llll}
SP & \longrightarrow & X_i & E_{common}(sum) = E_{common}(\sum_{i=1}^{n} x_i) \\
 & & & E_{common}(max) \\
X_i & \longrightarrow & SP & sum \\
 & & & MAC(sum|i, s_{common}) \\
 & & & max \\
 & & & MAC(max|i, s_{common}) \\
 & & & E_{common'}((x_i - \frac{sum}{n})^2)
\end{array}
$$

Round 3:

$$
\begin{array}{llll}
SP & \longrightarrow & X_i & E_{common'}(sum') = E_{common'}(\sum_{i=1}^{n}(x_i - \frac{sum}{n})^2) \\
 & & & H(MAC(sum|1, s_{common}), \ldots, MAC(sum|n, s_{common})) \\
 & & & H(MAC(max|1, s_{common}), \ldots, MAC(max|n, s_{common})) \\
X_i & \longrightarrow & SP & sum' \\
 & & & MAC(sum'|i, s_{common})
\end{array}
$$

Round 4:

$$
SP \longrightarrow X_i \; H(MAC(sum'|1, s_{common}), \ldots, MAC(sum'|n, s_{common}))
$$

Fig. 1 Benchmarking Protocol

5.1 Security Assumptions

5.1.1 Semantic Security

Semantic security means it must be infeasible for a probabilistic polynomial-time adversary to derive information about a plaintext when given its cipher text and the public key. A more formal definition can be found in [15]. The property of semantic security has been proven equivalent to cipher text indistinguishability. If an encryption scheme possesses the property of indistinguishability, then an adversary will be unable to distinguish pairs of ciphertexts based on the message they encrypt. Paillier's encryption system has been proven semantically secure against chosen plain-text attacks under the Decisional Composite Residuosity Assumption [28].

5.1.2 Multiplicative Hiding

We assume that a number x is effectively hidden by multiplying it with a random number r in a large domain (e.g. $O(x^2)$) and adding another random number $r' < r$. Let $\mathbb{D}$ denote the domain of numbers hidden in this form. Then we assume that $d \in \mathbb{D}$ reveals no relevant information about the hidden x.

5.2 Security in the Semi-Honest Model

Following Goldreich's definitions [14] we define the view $VIEW_i$ of the i-th party as

Definition 1 *The view of the i-th party during an execution of our protocols on* $(x_1,\ldots,x_m)$, *denoted* $VIEW_i(x_i, \ldots, x_m)$ *is* $\{x_i, r_i, m_1, \ldots, m_\phi\}$, *where* r_i *represents the outcome of the i-th party's internal coin tosses, and* m_i *represents the i-th message it has received.*

The result is implicit in the view. Further following Goldreich's definitions of semi-honest security (for deterministic functions), we define security against a semi-honest attacker:

Definition 2 *Let* $f : (\{0,1\}^*)^m \mapsto (\{0,1\}^*)^m$ *be an m-ary functionality, where* $f_i(x_1,\ldots,x_m)$ *denotes the i-th element of* $f(x_1,\ldots,x_m)$. *For* $I = \{i_1,\ldots,i_t\} \in \{1,\ldots, m\}$, *we let* $f_I(x_1,\ldots,x_m)$ *denote the (sub-)sequence* $f_{i_1}(x_1,\ldots,x_m), \ldots, f_{i_t}(x_1,\ldots,x_m)$ *and let* $VIEW_I(x_1,\ldots,x_m) = (I, VIEW_{i_1}(x),\ldots,VIEW_{i_t}(x))$. *We say that our protocols privately compute* f *if there exists a polynomial-time simulator, denoted S, such that for every I of size t, such that* $S(I, (x_{i_1},\ldots,x_{i_t}), f_I(x_1,\ldots,x_m))$ *is computationally indistinguishable from* $VIEW_I(x_1,\ldots,x_m)$.

We also use the composition theorem from [14]. It states that if a function g is privately reducible to f and there exists a protocol to privately compute f, then there exist a protocol for privately computing g. A protocol privately reduces g to f, if it privately computes g when f is replaced by an oracle (according to the ideal model). We use this to replace the use of OT in our protocols.

We show security against a semi-honest subscriber by giving a simulator of his view. In the first round, he receives a random value $d \in \mathbb{D}$ and an encrypted random share $E_{common}(r)$. In the second round he receives encryptions of $E_{common}(sum)$ and $E_{common}(max)$. The third round repeats $E_{common}(sum')$ for the variance.

We show security against a semi-honest service provider by giving a simulator of his view. In the first round he receives $E_{common}(x_i)$, $E_{common}(max)_i$ from each participant. Due to the semantic security these encryptions appear as random numbers. In the second round he receives the results *sum* (mean) and *max*, as well as another encryption $E_{common}((x_i - \mu)^2)$ and in the third round he receives sum' (variance) (again from each participant).

5.3 Security in the Constrained Malicious Model

Security against a malicious attacker provides security against any deviations from the protocol, such that secrecy of the computation can be reduced to the semi-honest security. Security against a malicious attacker provides no security against protocol abortion (from the platform provider) or providing false inputs. In particular, a malicious subscriber can submit the maximum possible KPI value and thereby falsify the result of the maximum computation. Differently from an auction, where the maximum value or at least its submitter (Vickrey auctions) are revealed, this is not case for benchmarking. We therefore abandon security against a malicious attacker and its cost in favor of a lesser security definition.

We are particularly concerned with secrecy of the KPIs. We therefore assume a constrained malicious attacker that can deviate from the protocol in order to obtain additional information (except what can be inferred by the result and the local input). The constraint is that the attacker is to deliver the correct result to the other parties. Such behavior can be enforced for a service provider by contract obligations. It is also economically motivated, since we can assume that all subscribers and the service provider have a vested interest in obtaining the correct result.

Consider the following attacker impersonating a service provider: When obtaining the result, he simply resends an encrypted, originally submitted, KPI $E_{common}(x_i)$. Then he can compute the mean, variance and maximum locally and store the correct results in the database where the subscribers will retrieve them. He deviated from the protocols, obtained all individual KPIs and still delivered the correct result to all subscribers.

The following protocol should prevent any constrained malicious attacker. When obtaining the result the subscribers not only return the decrypted result *result*, but also send a MAC for the value received $MAC(result|i, s_{common})$ (where $|$ denotes concatenation). In a further round the service provider proves to all subscribers that he submitted the same value for decryption to all of them by sending them $\theta = H(MAC(result.1, s_{common}) \mid \ldots \mid MAC(result.n,\ s_{common}))$ (where $H()$ denotes a cryptographic hash function).

Formally, we define an attacker in the constrained malicious model:

Definition 3 *Let* $f : (\{0,1\}^*)^m \mapsto (\{0,1\}^*)^m$ *be an m-ary functionality,* $I = \{i_1, \ldots, i_t\} \subset \{1, \ldots, m\}$, $\neg I = \{1, \ldots, m\} \setminus I$ *and* $(x_1, \ldots, x_m)_I = (x_{i_1}, \ldots, x_{i_t})$. *A pair* (I, C), *where* C *is a polynomial-size circuit family, represents an adversary* A *in the real model. The joint execution of our protocols under* C *and* $\neg C$ *where* $\neg C$ *coincides with the strategies defined by our protocols, denoted as* $REAL(x)$, *is defined as the output resulting from the interaction between* $C(x_I)$ *and* $\neg C(x_I)$. *An adversary* A *is admissible (for the constrained malicious model) if* $REAL_{\neg C(x)} = f_{\neg C(x)}$.

Then we extend the output of subscriber X_i in the ideal model with a verification bit b_i. In the ideal model b_i is always true, in the real protocol it is computed by verifying $\theta \stackrel{?}{=} H(MAC(result.1, s_{common})| \ldots |MAC(result.n,\ s_{common}))$. Recall, that due to software engineering reasons of decoupling retrieval from computation the subscribers are not to keep a record of the recomputation, but rather obtain the results via database query.

Finally we state the following theorem:

Theorem 1 *Our benchmarking protocols privately compute average, variance and maximum in the presence of a constrained malicious service provider.*

Proof Sketch: The view of the service provider offers no information (i.e. all received messages appear as random numbers) until he receives the first decrypted result. This implies that all deviations from the protocol until the first decrypted result reveal no information to him. After the first decrypted result he will obtain further decrypted result which provide information. All decryptions solely depend on the encryption sent by the service provider. Our verification bit protocol ensures that if every subscribers outputs "true" as his verification bit, the service provider has submitted the same encryption to all subscribers and obtains the exact same information from all of them (or he has successfully forged a MAC). By definition of the constrained malicious attacker, this is the correct result, i.e. the service provider only obtains the correct result and nothing else.

The final protocols with security against a constrained malicious service provider are depicted in Figure 1. The protocol uses a constant number of rounds (4) and constant message size in each round (i.e. linear in a fixed security parameter K of the homomorphic encryption scheme). It is independent of the number of participants, the number of KPIs or peer groups and the subscribers never need to exchange message even indirectly and therefore remain entirely anonymous amongst each other.

6 Performance Evaluation

The goal of the benchmarking protocols is to act as the basis of a real-world benchmarking platform. Therefore the protocols need to be evaluated under realistic conditions. We implemented a prototype version of the protocols (with partial anonymity among the subscribers only) based on web services. The web service stack consists of a Tomcat 5.5 [1] web application server using the Axis2 1.1 [2] web service engine. All our implementation was done in Java 1.5. The implementation includes our own implementation of Paillier's [28] encryption system.

The test bed includes a central server with a 3.2GHz 32-bit Intel processor with 2GB of RAM of which 256MB were available to the Tomcat Java Virtual Machine. The clients were emulated using VMware [3] as a virtual machine monitor each having 256MB of RAM of which 64MB were available to each Tomcat Java Virtual Machine. Each emulated client ran five Tomcat web application servers acting as

[1] http://tomcat.apache.org/

[2] http://ws.apache.org/axis2/

[3] http://www.vmware.com/

five subscribers in the protocol. Up to fifteen such clients were emulated on two servers. We expect realistic peer group sizes to be between 10 and 25 subscribers, such that 75 subscribers as the maximum peer group size should underpin the protocol's scalability.

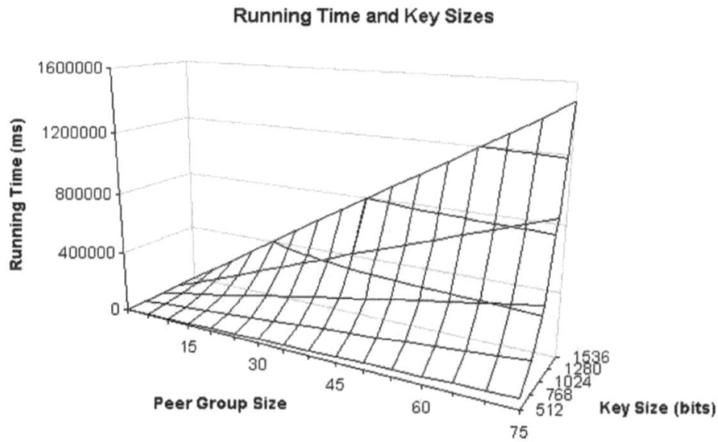

Fig. 2 Computation performance over key size and peer group size

The first experiment was to measure the computational cost by increasing both the peer group size and the key size of Paillier's encryption system, but independently of each other. We computed one KPI repeatedly for varying peer group sizes and key lengths. The entire system including server and clients was emulated on one machine disabling network cost. In the results depicted in Figure 2 one can see the expected linear increase of running time with peer group size as expected from the constant cost per participant, but running time increases quickly with key size. While the computational cost for one participant is below 1 second for 512 bit key length, it is almost 20 seconds for 1536 key length. Paillier's encryption system uses RSA-type keys [31], such that 768 or 1024 bit key lengths can be expected to be the most common ones. The conclusion from this experiment is to be conservative when choosing the key length for large peer groups, but realistic key sizes, such 768 or 1024 bits are feasible even for large peer groups.

The second experiment was to measure network cost by increasing the delay of the network. We computed one KPI first over the shared local area network (LAN), then with dummynet [32] as a wide-area network (WAN) emulator. We increased the round trip time to 200 milliseconds which corresponds roughly to the round trip time in the Internet from Germany to Japan or Australia. From the results in Figure 3 we can see that the performance on LAN is dominated by the computation cost and that the performance on WAN is dominated by communication cost. As expected leads the constant communication cost to a linear increase in running time. The conclusion

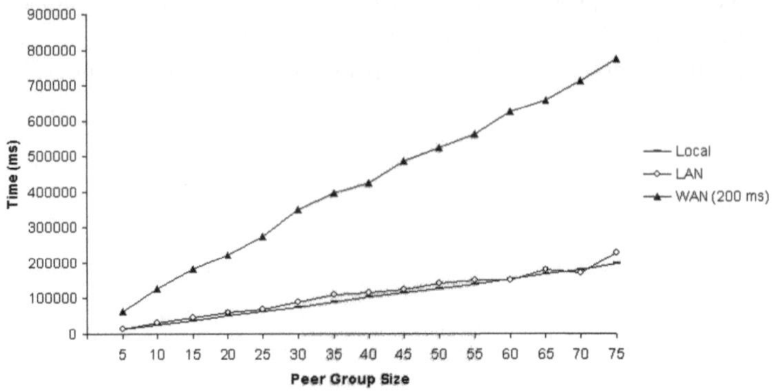

Fig. 3 Performance under different network conditions

	Centralized	No. Central Servers	Cost per Participant	Anonymizable	Implemented
[2]	n	n/a	$O(n^2)^1$	n	n
[20]	n	n/a	$O(\log^2 n)^1$	y	n
[9, 10]	y	1	$O(n)$	n	n
[13]	y	2	$O(1)$	y	y
[5]	y	3, 5, 7	$O(1)$	y	y
this paper	y	1	$O(1)$	y	y

Table 1 Overview of Related Work

from this experiment is that for a protocol to be practically realizable over current network conditions the focus should be on communication cost. A peer group of 75 subscribers computes one KPI in approximately 12 minutes. We expect up to 200 KPIs, but computations can be performed concurrently, such that an estimate of the combined running time is difficult.

7 Related Work

The application of private collaborative benchmarking has been first described in [2]. The authors present important applications of a secure division protocol, where one party performs the blinded division after the others have agreed on the blinding. Filtering outlying values before benchmarking has been considered in [20], where also the initial idea for the comparison (maximum) protocol was presented, but all communication was done in a peer-to-peer model. Although both papers are concerned with benchmarking as an application, they consider different computations than our statistics.

Other examples of privacy-preserving statistical computations include the computation of the mean [11, 21]. Here two party each have a mean as a fraction and want to compute the combined mean. In [1] the median is being computed as a two or peer-to-peer multi-party protocol.

All these and many more protocols are special protocols of general secure (multiparty) computation (SMC) protocols. SMC was introduced in [34] and generalized to multi-party computations in [4, 16] with computational security [16] and information-theoretic security [4]. The draft by Goldreich [14] gives a general construction and very extensive background on the security models. The protocols by Yao were implemented in [23].

The motivation to build special protocols for important problems was realized soon [17]. Besides benchmarking a related application are auctions. For auctions similar models to our service provider model have been introduced. A model applicable to general multi-party computations is introduced in [26] which has been extended in [18, 22]: Two mutually distrusting servers execute a binary circuit with the input of multiple external parties. The separation of input clients and computation servers has been picked-up in [6] and extended in [7]. The protocols in [6] and the recent result by [7] for constant-round SMC for any function requires at least three servers. All implementations of SMC [5, 13] except ours use this model.

In [13] the model has been applied to online surveys which computes the same statistics as our protocols. Their implementation is based on [23] and uses the two server model of [26]. They do not report absolute performance figures, but indicate that the computation is practical. They even present an idea on how to verify the entries which unfortunately does not apply in our case.

In [5] the model is applied to secure auctions which can be extended to benchmarking. Their implementation is based on variations of [6] and they report performance for three, five and seven servers. They do not report figures for the entire application, but again indicate that the computation is practical.

The problem with both implementations and the model in general is that it requires multiple computation servers. These servers need to be mutually distrustful in order for the protocol to be secure which implies separate business entities in a practical realization. This is a major obstacle for a single service provider business model, since one has to organize and finance several collaborating, but mutually distrustful partners. Therefore we argue that different protocols are needed.

The single server model has been used in theory for maximum [9] and mean [10] computations. Both protocols have linear communication cost in the number of participants as opposed to our constant. Furthermore our protocols achieve full anonymity (no static identifier), even for the provider of the maximum (auction winner), which is not the case in [9, 10] where companies refer to each other by public keys. Static identifiers reveal changes in peer group composition to subscribers in subsequent executions of the protocol which is undesirable. We also strengthen the security against the central platform provider to the constrained malicious model, since this is our main economic motivator.

Table 1 provides an overview over the related papers for protocols and implementation. Although none of the previous work considers anonymity as a feature, we anticipate that anonymous versions can be built from the work as indicated in the table. Our protocols are not only the first constant-cost, anonymous, centralized benchmarking protocols, but also the first implementation not based on the multiple server model.

One can view our problem also as a database privacy problem. We compute a non-sensitive database from sensitive distributed entries. A simple approach for secure query evaluation on a sensitive database, based on homomorphic encryption, is evaluated for performance in [33] and found lacking the necessary performance.

8 Conclusions

In this paper we have presented and evaluated a constant-cost, anonymous, centralized privacy-preserving benchmarking protocol. The secrecy of individual KPIs is maintained against the service provider in any case, if he delivers the correct result. It can be used to realize a (central) privacy-preserving benchmarking platform that computes the statistics of the key performance indicators of the subscribers.

Full anonymity, i.e. everybody except the central service provder remains anoynmous, can be achieved using an anonymous communication channel. Then participation in multiple peer groups is possible.

The practical evaluation shows that the effort for building a constant-cost (independent of the number of participants) protocol is fruitful and yields computation times on the order of minutes even over WAN network conditions. The protocols are among the first practically evaluated secure multi-party computation systems.

Based on our positive economic evaluation of privacy we intend to continue to build practical systems on top of the protocols.

References

1. G. Aggarwal, N. Mishra, and B. Pinkas. Secure computation of the kth-ranked element. *Proceedings of EUROCRYPT*, 2004.
2. M. Atallah, M. Bykova, J. Li, K. Frikken, and M. Topkara. Private collaborative forecasting and benchmarking. *Proceedings of the ACM workshop on Privacy in the electronic society*, 2004.
3. J. Benaloh. Verifiable Secret-Ballot Elections. *PhD thesis, Yale University*, 1987.
4. M. Ben-Or, and A. Wigderson. Completeness theorems for non-cryptographic fault-tolerant distributed computation. *Proceedings of the 20th ACM symposium on theory of computing*, 1988.
5. P. Bogetoft, I. Damgard, T. Jakobsen, K. Nielsen, J. Pagter, and T. Toft. A Practical Implementation of Secure Auctions Based on Multiparty Integer Computation. *Proceedings of Financial Cryptography*, 2006.
6. I. Damgard, R. Cramer, and J. Nielsen. Multiparty Computation from Threshold Homomorphic Encryption. *Proceedings of EUROCRYPT*, 2001.
7. I. Damgard, and Y. Ishai Constant-Round Multiparty Computation Using a Black-Box Pseudorandom Generator. *Proceedings of CRYPTO*, 2005.

[1] Different computations than statistics

8. I. Damgard, and M. Jurik. A Generalisation, a Simplification and some Applications of Pailliers Probabilistic Public-Key System. *Proceedings of International Conference on Theory and Practice of Public-Key Cryptography*, 2001.
9. G. Di Crescenzo. Private Selective Payment Protocols. *Proceedings of Financial Cryptography*, 2000.
10. G. Di Crescenzo. Privacy for the Stock Market. *Proceedings of Financial Cryptography*, 2001.
11. W. Du, and M. Atallah. Privacy-preserving Cooperative Statistical Analysis. *Proceedings of the 17th Annual Computer Security Applications Conference*, 2001.
12. S. Even, O. Goldreich, and A. Lempel. A randomized protocol for signing contracts. *Communications of the ACM 28(6)*, 1985.
13. J. Feigenbaum, B. Pinkas, R. Ryger, and F. Saint-Jean. Secure Computation of Surveys. *Proceedings of the EU Workshop on Secure Multiparty Protocols*, 2004.
14. O. Goldreich. Secure Multi-party Computation. Available at *www.wisdom.weizmann.ac.il/~oded/pp.html*, 2002.
15. O. Goldreich. The Foundations of Cryptography Vol. 2. *Cambridge University Press*, 2004.
16. O. Goldreich, S. Micali, and A. Wigderson. How to play any mental game. *Proceedings of the 19th ACM conference on theory of computing*, 1987.
17. S. Goldwasser. Multi party computations: past and present. *Proceedings of the 16th ACM symposium on principles of distributed computing*, 1997.
18. A. Juels, and M. Szydlo. A two-server, sealed-bid auction protocol. *Proceedings of the 6th Conference on Financial Cryptography*, 2002.
19. E. Karnin, J. Green and M. Hellman. On Secret Sharing Systems. *IEEE Tranactions on Information Theory 29(1)*, 1983.
20. F. Kerschbaum, and O. Terzidis. Filtering for Private Collaborative Benchmarking. *Proceedings of the International Conference on Emerging Trends in Information and Communication Security*, 2006.
21. E. Kiltz, G. Leander, and J. Malone-Lee. Secure Computation of the Mean and Related Statistics. *Proceedings of Theory of Cryptography Conference*, 2005.
22. H. Lipmaa, N. Asokan, and V. Niemi. Secure Vickrey auctions without threshold trust. *Proceedings of the 6th Conference on Financial Cryptography*, 2002.
23. D. Malkhi, N. Nisan, B. Pinkas, and Y. Sella. Fairplay - A Secure Two-party Computation System. *Proceedings of the USENIX security symposium*, 2004.
24. D. Naccache, and J. Stern. A New Public-Key Cryptosystem Based on Higher Residues. *Proceedings of the ACM Conference on Computer and Communications Security*, 1998.
25. M. Naor, and B. Pinkas. Efficient Oblivious Transfer Protocols. *Proceedings of the symposium on data structures and algorithms*, 2001.
26. M. Naor, B. Pinkas and R. Sumner. Privacy Preserving Auctions and Mechanism Design. *Proceedings of the 1st ACM Conference on Electronic Commerce*, 1999.
27. T. Okamoto, and S. Uchiyama. A new public-key cryptosystem as secure as factoring. *Proceedings of EUROCRYPT*, 1998.
28. P. Paillier. Public-Key Cryptosystems Based on Composite Degree Residuosity Classes. *Proceedings of EUROCRYPT*, 1999.
29. B. Preneel. Cryptographic hash functions. *European Transactions on Telecommunications 5(4)*, 1994.
30. M. Rabin. How to exchange secrets by oblivious transfer. *Technical Memo TR–81, Aiken Computation Laboratory*, 1981.
31. R. Rivest, A. Shamir, and L. Adleman. A Method for Obtaining Digital Signatures and Public-Key Cryptosystems. *Communications of the ACM 21(2)*, 1978.
32. L. Rizzo. Dummynet: a simple approach to the evaluation of network protocols. *ACM Computer Communication Review 27(1)*, 1997.
33. H. Subramaniam, R. Wright, and Z. Yang. Experimental Analysis of Privacy-Preserving Statistics Computation. *Proceedings of the Workshop on Secure Data Management*, 2004.
34. A. Yao. Protocols for Secure Computations. *Proceedings of the IEEE Symposium on foundations of computer science* 23, 1982.

I. Damgård and M. Jurik. A Generalisation, a Simplification and some Applications of Paillier's Probabilistic Public-Key System. In Proceedings of International Conference on Theory and Practice of Public-Key Cryptography, 2001.

Enhancing Privacy in Remote Data Classification

A. Piva, C. Orlandi *, M. Caini, T. Bianchi, and M. Barni

Abstract Neural networks are a fundamental tool in data classification. A protocol whereby a user may ask a service provider to run a neural network on an input provided in encrypted format is proposed here, in such a way that the neural network owner does not get any knowledge about the processed data. At the same time, the knowledge embedded within the network itself is protected. With respect to previous works in this field, the interaction between the user and the neural network owner is kept to a minimum without resorting to general secure multi-party computation protocols.

1 Introduction

Recent advances in signal and information processing together with the possibility of exchanging and transmitting data through flexible and ubiquitous transmission media such as internet and wireless networks, have opened the way towards a new kind of services whereby a provider sells its ability to process and interpret data remotely, e.g. through an internet web service. Examples in this sense include access to remote databases, processing of personal data, processing of multimedia documents, interpretation of medical data for remote diagnosis. In this last scenario, a patient may need a diagnosis from a remote medical institute that has the knowledge needed to perform the diagnosis. Health-related data are of course sensitive, and the patient may do not want to let the institute to know the data he owns; on the other hand, the medical institute is interested in protecting his expertise.

In 2000 two papers [19, 1] proposed the notion of privacy preserving data mining, meaning the possibility to perform data analysis on a distributed database, under some privacy constraints. After the publication of these papers, security constraints were added to several machine learning techniques: decision trees [19], neural networks [6], support vector machines [18], naive bayes classifiers [16], belief networks [24], clustering [14]. In all these works, we can identify two major scenarios: in the first one Alice and Bob share a dataset and want to extract knowledge from it without revealing their own data (we define this scenario as privacy preserving data mining). In the other scenario, which is the one considered in this paper, Alice owns her private data x, while Bob owns an evaluation function C, where in most cases C is a classifier (we define it a remote data classification). Alice is interested in having her data processed by Bob, but she does not want that Bob learns either her input or the output of the computation. At the

Alessandro Piva, Michele Caini, Tiziano Bianchi
Department of Electronics and Telecommunications, University of Florence e-mail: {piva, caini, bianchi}@lci.det.unifi.it

Claudio Orlandi
Department of Computer Science, University of Aarhus, e-mail: orlandi@daimi.au.dk

Mauro Barni
Department of Information Engineering, University of Siena e-mail: barni@dii.unisi.it

* Work done while working at University of Florence.

Please use the following format when citing this chapter:

Piva, A., et al., 2008, in IFIP International Federation for Information Processing, Volume 278; *Proceedings of the IFIP TC 11 23rd International Information Security Conference*; Sushil Jajodia, Pierangela Samarati, Stelvio Cimato; (Boston: Springer), pp. 33–46.

same time, Bob does not want to reveal the exact form of C, representing his knowledge, since, for instance, he sells a classification service through the web (as in the remote medical diagnosis example).

A fundamental tool in data classification is represented by neural networks (NNs), because of their approximation and generalization capabilities. For this reason, it can be of interest to design a protocol whereby a user may ask a service provider to run a neural network on an input provided in encrypted format. Previous works on privacy preserving NN computing are limited to the systems presented in [3, 6]. However, such studies resort extensively to highly inefficient general secure multi-party computation (SMC) [25] for the computation of the non-linear activation functions implemented in the neurons.

This is not the case with our new protocol which does not resort to general SMC for the evaluation of the activation functions. In a nutshell, the protocol has been designed to ensure that the data provided by the user (say Alice), representing the input of the neural network, are completely protected and, at the same time, to not disclose Bob's classifier (the NN). The proposed protocol relies on homomorphic encryption that allows to perform directly in the encrypted domain all the linear computations. For the non linear functions that can not be handled by means of homomorphic encryption, a limited amount of interaction between the NN owner and the user is introduced to delegate the user (say Alice) to perform some of the computations. Comparing our work with previous ones, another advantage can be highlighted: the proposed protocol can handle every kind of feedforward NN (not only simple layered networks), without disclosing neither the number of neurons nor the way they are connected.

This protocol can be seen as an improvement of the one proposed in [3] from both privacy and efficiency side. In particular, in [3] the authors resorted to a general technique to protect the output value of the neurons, while here we introduce ad-hoc techniques (Section 4.3) for the same purpose. Another difference is in the protection of the network topology, that has been improved and now can cope with more general kind of networks. Finally, in this paper we describe also a practical implementation of our system, proving the feasibility of our technique, for a real set-up. As the best of our knowledge, this is the first practical implementation of a protocol for the private evaluation of a neural network based classifier.

The rest of this paper is organized as follows. In Section 2, a brief overview on Neural Networks that can be used with our protocol is given. In Section 3 our scenario will be described, focusing on the privacy constraints and reviewing the properties to be achieved by our protocol. The way the protocol works is described in Section 4. Section 5 is devoted to the experimental results obtained developing a distributed application that runs the protocol. Some concluding remarks are given in Section 6, while in Appendix how to deal with non integer computation will be discussed.

2 Neural Networks

Neural networks have a great ability to model any given function [17, 13]. Moreover neural networks are provided with good learning algorithms, are robust against noise and generalize well on unseen examples. In this section we will introduce several types of network that can be used with our protocol. The notation is consistent with the one in [5], where a detailed treatment of neural networks is given.

2.0.1 Perceptron

The simplest neural network is the *perceptron* (Figure 1 (a)). It can discriminate between two different classes of instance, and its classification function consists of a linear combination of the input variables, the coefficients of which are the parameters of the model. The discriminant function is of the form $a(\mathbf{x}) = \mathbf{w}^T\mathbf{x} + w_0$ where $\mathbf{x}$ is the input vector, $\mathbf{w}$ is the vector of weights and w_0 is a threshold[2]. The instance $\mathbf{x}$ is assigned to class c_1 if $a(\mathbf{x}) \geq 0$ and to class c_2 if $a(\mathbf{x}) < 0$. This method can easily be extended to the multiclass case using one discriminant function $a_k(x)$ for each class C_k such that $a_k(\mathbf{x}) = \mathbf{w}_k^T\mathbf{x}$.

[2] From now on we can forget about w_0 simply appending it at the end of the vector and obtaining $a(\mathbf{x}) = [\mathbf{w}\ w_0]^T[\mathbf{x}\ 1]$

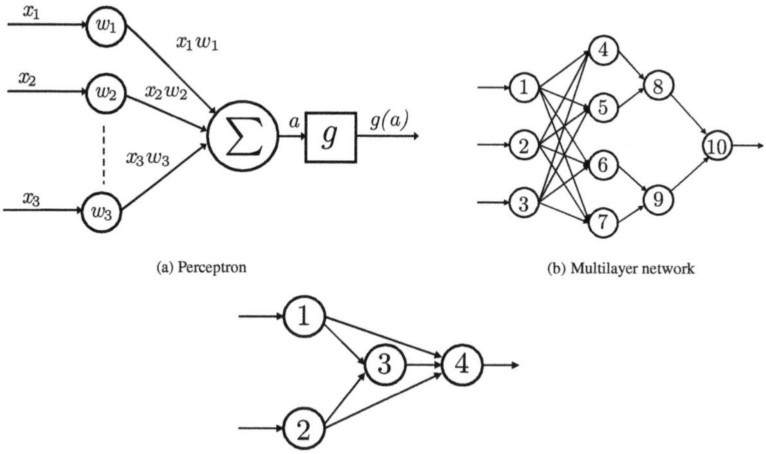

(a) Perceptron

(b) Multilayer network

(c) General feedforward network

Fig. 1: Three kinds of different networks that can be used with the proposed protocol. Figure (a) shows a single layer network, known as *perceptron*; Figure (b) shows a *multi-layer feedforward network* , while Figure (c) shows a *general feedforward network*. Note that in feed-forward networks it is possible to number neurons such that every neuron gets inputs only from neurons with smaller index.

2.0.2 Feed-Forward Networks

To allow for more general classifications it is possible to consider a network of interconnetted neurons. Networks consisting of successive layers of adaptive weights are called *layered networks*: in such a network every unit in one layer is connected to every unit in the next layer, but no other connections are permitted, as shown in Figure 1 (b). The units that are not treated as output units are called *hidden* units.

The output of the j-th hidden unit in the i-th layer is obtained by first forming a weighted linear combination of its l input values to give:

$$a_j^{(i)} = \sum_{k=1}^{l} w_{jk}^{(i)} x_k$$

Here $w_{jk}^{(i)}$ denotes the weight associated to an edge going from the k-th neuron of the previous layer to the neuron j of i-th layer. The activation of the hidden unit is obtained by transforming the linear sum using an activation function $g(\cdot)$ to obtain $z_j^{(i)} = g\left(a_j^{(i)}\right)$.

This procedure is iterated until the output layer is reached, obtaining the final output $y_k = g(a_k)$. We will refer to a L-layer network as a network having L layers of adaptive weights, regardless of the input units.

Since there is a direct correspondence between a network diagram and its mathematical function, we can develop more general network mappings by considering more complex network diagrams. To be able to run the computation, however, we shall restrict our attention to the case of *feed-forward* networks, in which there are no feed-back loops, as shown in Figure 1 (c).

The activation function of the hidden neurons are usually sigmoidal functions, i.e. $g(a) = \frac{1}{1+e^{-a}}$. The differentiability of this kind of functions leads to a powerful and computationally efficient learning method, called *error backpropagation* [22].

The proposed protocol can deal with sigmoid activation functions and also with linear activation functions. The latter is sometimes desirable because the use of sigmoid units at the outputs would limit the range of possible outputs to the range attainable by the sigmoid.

3 Remote Data Classification

As we already disclosed in the introduction, by remote data classification we mean a scenario where two users, Alice and Bob, remotely cooperate to allow Alice to perform an evaluation or classification applied to her private data set x, by exploiting Bob's knowledge (represented by the classifier own by Bob).

There are two trivial solutions for this problem: Alice can send her data and Bob performs the classification, or Bob sends his classifier and Alice performs the classification. Both these solutions have a clear drawback. Alice doesn't want to disclose to Bob her data nor the output of the classification (in the case of the previous medical example, Alice doesn't want to reveal if she is actually healthy or not). On the other hand, Bob might not be happy to disclose the classifier, since he probably invested time and money in training his network.

Again we can find a trivial solution to these security requirements by resorting to a trusted third party (TTP) that takes inputs from Alice and Bob, and gives back to Alice the output of the computation. Of course this scenario is not the ordinary one: if Alice and Bob distrust each other, it could be hard to agree on a common TTP.

The goal of this work is to propose a protocol for remote data classification that respects the above privacy constraints without resorting to a TTP, and where cryptography and some randomization will play the role of the TTP. As many other protocols in literature, we will make the assumption that both Alice and Bob are semi-honest. This means that they will follow the protocol properly, but they can later analyze the protocol transcripts trying to discover information about other party inputs. We will also assume that Alice and Bob can communicate over a secure (private and authenticated) channel, that can be implemented in practice as a standard SSL connection.

To grant protection against malicious adversary (i.e. adversary that can behave differently from what they are supposed to do), there are standard constructions to produce a protocol secure in the malicious scenario from a semi-honest one [11]. Moreover in our protocol, there is no evidence that a cheating player can discover significant information about other party inputs, and therefore we can assume that semi-honest behavior is forced by external factors i.e. Bob being a service provider that doesn't want to lose his reputation, and Alice is interested in having her data correctly classified.

3.1 Protocol Requirements

In the following, a discussion of the requirements satisfied by the designed protocol to deal with the above scenario is given.

3.1.1 Correctness.

It means that Alice wants to have a correct classification of her data. As Bob gets no output, only Alice has interest in this property. We are not concerned here with the accuracy of Bob's NN, nor we could be. What we mean here is that Bob could maliciously give an incorrect answer to Alice, i.e. in the medical example, a corrupted Bob could be instructed to reply "ill" to a given list of people. We could avoid this kind of cheating by running our protocol over an anonymized network as is [9]. In general as our protocol is only secure against semi-honest adversaries, we can't ensure correctness: to do so, we should transform our protocol into a protocol secure against malicious adversary using standard compiler techniques [11].

3.1.2 Alice's Privacy.

Alice's data are completely protected. In fact, Alice gives her input in an encrypted format and receives the output in an encrypted format. So Alice's privacy relies on the security of the underlying cryptosystem that is, in our case, semantic security.

3.1.3 Bob's Privacy.

While it's clear what we mean with Alice's privacy, it's not the same with Bob's privacy. We need again to refer to the TTP ideal scenario: as long as Alice gets her data classified, she's learning something about Bob classifier. She learns in fact how Bob classifies a vector data. Suppose that she is allowed to run the protocol an arbitrarily number of times: she could submit every (or a very large database of) instances to be classified by Bob, so that she could easily build a table with the classification of every vector, obtaining in that way a classifier that works the same of Bob's one for the classified vector, and that will classify also new vectors.

This result does not depend on the protocol security (we are talking about the TTP ideal scenario) but simply on the fact that from the input and the output of a computation it is always possible to learn something about the computed function (and this is exactly the goal of machine learning). A question is therefore: is it possible to model this kind of attack, where a user interacts many times with the classifier to understand his structure? How many interactions does the attacker need? This question is partially answered in watermarking literature under the name *sensitivity attack*. For a linear classifier (perceptron) the number of iterations to completely disclose it is very low [15]. For a more complex function, like a multi-layer network, it's harder to say, but there are still solutions allowing to extract a local boundary even without knowing anything about the nature of the classifier [7].

The proposed protocol is able to protect the structure and the hidden neurons output of the Bob's NN.

Concerning the structure of the Network, the protocol is designed to completely protect the way the neurons are connected, and to partially protect the number of neurons actually present in the network, so that Alice will get an upper bound B for the number of neurons. Bob can adjust this bound B in a way to achieve a good level of privacy and at the same time an efficient protocol.

Concerning the hidden neurons output, we have to protect them, since they represent an unneeded leakage of information. Given a hidden neuron with sigmoid activation function, it is possible to split its output in two parts, one that we can perfectly protect, while the other will be partially disclosed.

- *State of the Neuron:* this is the most important part of the output. Depending on the sign of the weighted sum of the inputs, every neuron can be *on* (i.e. output > 0.5) or *off* (i.e. output < 0.5). We will perfectly protect this information, flipping it with probability one half, achieving a one-time pad kind of security.
- *Associated Magnitude:* the activation of every neuron has also a magnitude, that gives information about "how much" the neuron is *on* or *off*. We will hide those values in a large set of random values, in such a way that Alice will not learn which values are actually part of the computation and which ones are just random junk. Of course the bigger the set is, the more privacy it comes, and more computational resources are needed.
- *Neuron's Position:* the last trick to achieve security is to completely randomize the position of the hidden neurons in such a way that Alice will not discover which outputs correspond to which neurons. Therefore Alice may learn a bit of information at every execution (meaning something about the magnitudes of them), but she'll not be able to correlate those information in order to gain advantage from repeated executions of the protocol.

3.1.4 Round Complexity.

We would like to run the computation with no interaction (except the minimum needed to input the vector and get the output). Unluckily, there are only few kinds of algorithms that can be computed in such a way, that is NC^1 circuits [23], and *NLOGSPACE* problem [4]. Round complexity, i.e. the number of messages between the players, is an important measure for the complexity of a cryptographic protocol. The round complexity of our protocol is given by the number of layers of the network. Given that a network with three layers can approximate any function, we can consider our protocol to have a constant round complexity.

4 Privacy-Preserving Protocol for Remote Data Classification

We will continue to use the notation introduced before, together with some new symbols to refer to the encrypted version of the data. The input of the neuron is $\mathbf{x}$ and its encrypted version is $\mathbf{c}$, while the encrypted version of the activation a of every neuron will be referred as d.

4.1 Building blocks

We describe first of all the building blocks that are required for the correct behavior of the proposed protocol.

4.1.1 Homomorphic Encryption.

The chosen public-key cryptosystem to instantiate our protocol is the Damgård-Jurik modification [8] of the Paillier encryption scheme [20].

This cryptosystem is based on the hardness to decide the n-th residuosity of elements modulo n^{s+1}, where n is an RSA modulo. At the end, the encryption and the decryption procedures are the following:

Set-up: select p,q big primes. Let $n = pq$ be the public key, while the secret key, called λ, is the least common divisor between $(p-1)$ and $(q-1)$.

Encryption: let $m \in \mathbb{Z}$ be the plaintext, and s such that $n^s > m$. Select a random value $r \in \mathbb{Z}^*_{n^s}$; the encryption c of m is:

$$c = E_{pk}(m,r) = (1+n)^m r^{n^s} \mod n^{s+1}$$

Decryption: the decryption function D_{sk} depends only on the ciphertext, and there is no need to know the random r in the decryption phase. We refer to the original paper for the complete description.

The main advantage of this cryptosystem is that the only parameter to be fixed is n, while s can be adjusted according to the plaintext. In other words, unlike other cryptosystems, where one has to choose the plaintext m to be less than n, here one can choose an m of arbitrary size, and then adjust s to have $n^s > m$ and the only requirement for n is that it must be unfeasible to find its factorization.

The trade-off between security and arithmetic precision is a crucial issue in secure signal processing applications. As we will describe in more detail in the Appendix, the possibility to quantize the input samples and to work with an arbitrary precision allows us to neglect that we are dealing with integer modular numbers, so that we can consider to have an arbitrarily accurate non-integer homomorphic encryption scheme.

For the sake of simplicity from now on we will indicate the encryption just as $c = E(m)$, as the keys are chosen once and are the same for all the protocol length, and the random parameter r is just to be chosen at random. If $x_1 = x_2$ we will write $E(x_1) \sim E(x_2)$. The encryption of a vector $\mathbf{c} = E(\mathbf{x})$ will be simply the vector composed of the encryption of every component of the plaintext vector.

As said, this cryptosystem satisfies the homomorphic property so, given two plaintexts m_1 and m_2, the following equalities are satisfied:

$$D(E(m_1) \cdot E(m_2)) = m_1 + m_2 \tag{1}$$

and

$$D(E(m)^a) = am. \tag{2}$$

Concerning the security of this cryptosystem, it provides semantic security against chosen-plaintext attacks; more details can be found in the original paper [20].

4.1.2 Privacy Preserving Scalar Product (PPSP).

A secure protocol for the scalar product allows Bob to compute an encrypted version of the scalar product between an encrypted vector given by Alice $\mathbf{c} = E(\mathbf{x})$, and one vector $\mathbf{w}$ owned by Bob. The protocol guarantees that Bob gets nothing, while Alice gets an encrypted version of the scalar product that she can decrypt with her private key. Such a protocol is easily achievable exploiting the two homomorphic properties shown in the Equations 1 and 2:

Input: $\mathbf{c} = E(\mathbf{x})$; Bob: $\mathbf{w}$
Output: Alice: $d = E(\mathbf{x}^T\mathbf{w})$
PSPP(**c**;**w**)
(1) Bob computes $d = \prod_{i=1}^{N} c_i^{w_i}$
(2) Bob sends d to Alice

After receiving d, Alice can decrypt this value with her private key to obtain the weighted sum a.

It is worth observing that though the above protocol is a secure one in a cryptographic sense, some knowledge about Bob's secrets is implicitly leaked through the output of the protocol itself. If, for instance, Alice can interact N times with Bob (where $N = |\mathbf{x}| = |\mathbf{w}|$ is the size of the input vectors), she can completely find out Bob's vector, by simply setting the input of the i-th iteration as the vector with all 0's and a 1 in the i-th position, for $i = 1,\ldots,N$. If we use the scalar product protocol described above to build more sophisticated protocols, we must be aware of this leakage of information. This is again a *sensitivity attack*, as introduced before. Note that the problems stemming from sensitivity attacks are often neglected in the privacy preserving computing literature.

4.1.3 Evaluation of the Activation Function

If the function g is known and it's invertible, like in the case of the sigmoid function, the information given by a or $y = g(a)$ is the same. So Bob can simply give a to Alice that can compute y by herself.

4.2 Perceptron Protocol

The blocks described above allow to run a privacy preserving remote data classification protocol for a single layer network. Let us suppose that the network has I inputs and 1 output. The protocol is the following:

Input: $\mathbf{c} = E(\mathbf{x})$; Bob: $\mathbf{w}$
Output: Alice: classification of $\mathbf{x}$
PERCEPTRON(**c**;**w**)
(1) Alice and Bob run the PPSP protocol.
(2) Alice decrypts the output $a = D(d)$
(3) Alice computes $g(a)$

If the network has more than one output neuron, say O, just run in parallel O instances of the previous protocol.

4.3 Handling with Hidden Neurons

We consider now the more interesting case of a feedforward network. As already defined, a feedforward network is composed by N neurons that can be ordered in a way that neuron j gets in input the output of a finite set I_j of neurons having index lower than j, like the ones in Figure 1. We use this ordering to label every neuron. The weight of the connection from neuron i to neuron j is indicated by w_{ij}. The input vector of neuron j is $\mathbf{x}_j$ while the associated weights vector $\mathbf{w}_j$. The aim is now to protect the output of hidden neurons and the network topology.

4.3.1 Hidden Neurons Output Protection.

In the perceptron protocol, Bob gives to Alice the linear sum a of the output neurons, and then Alice computes by herself the activation function output. The simple iteration of the perceptron protocol for every neuron in the network will disclose the activation value of every hidden neuron, but Alice is not supposed to get this information.

The linear sum a can be viewed as $a = sign(a) \cdot |a|$. Depending on $sign(a)$ the output of the sigmoid function will be "almost 1" (i.e. $0.5 \leq y < 1$) or "almost 0" (i.e. $0 < y \leq 0.5$). We can perfectly protect the value $sign(a)$ by exploiting the fact that the sigmoid function is actually antisymmetric as shown in Figure 2, i.e. $g(-a) = 1 - g(a)$.

Bob can randomly change the sign of a just before sending it to Alice thanks to the homomorphic property, since $E(a)^{-1} = E(-a)$. Then Alice can decrypt as usual the value received, compute the activation function on the received input $g(-a)$ and send $E(g(-a))$ back to Bob. Bob can recover the value he needs simply performing the subtraction (only for the scrambled values), that is $E(g(a)) = E(1 - g(-a)) = E(1)E(g(a))^{-1}$.

In this way Alice will not discover which (nor how many) neurons are actually activated or not. We will deal with the protection of the value $|a|$ later.

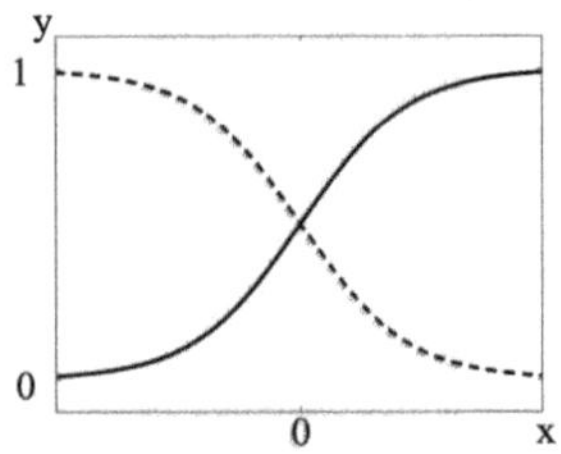

Fig. 2: The Sigmoid is antisymmetric with respect to $(0, 1/2)$, i.e. $g(-a) = 1 - g(a)$.

4.3.2 Network Embedding.

To protect the network topology, i.e. the number of hidden neurons N_H and the way they are connected, we will embed the network in a multilayer network, composed of L layers of M neurons each. Of course $LM \geq N_H$. The added $LM - N_H$ neurons will be called *fake neurons*. They have to look the same as the real neurons and so they will be initialized with some incoming connections from other neurons, with random weights. They will not influence the computation as no real neurons will take their outputs as input.

A good embedding is one where every neuron only gets inputs from neurons that are in previous layers. An example of a legal embedding of the network in Figure 1 (b) is given in Figure 3.

In this way Alice will only learn an upper bound LM for the actual number of hidden neurons N_H, while she will not learn the way they are connected or the connection weights, as Bob can perform the PPSP for every neuron by himself just picking up the necessary inputs and make the weighted sum with his private weights. The number L also gives a bound about the longest path between input and output neurons. Instead M is not the upper bound of the incoming connection for a neuron, given that we can split one original layer into two or more layers in the embedded network. Every neuron in layer l can take inputs from any neuron belonging to any previous layer.

The more we increase L, the more we protect the network topology. At the same time L will be the number of interaction round of the protocol, so we have to find a tradeoff between round complexity and network topology protection.

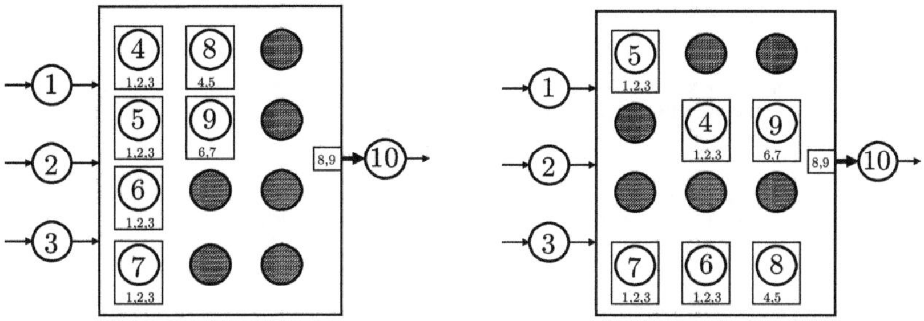

(a) Network Embedding (b) Network Scrambling

Fig. 3: Figure (a) is a natural embedding of the network in Figure 1 (b) into a 3×4 network. The big box refers to the protected zone. The numbers under the neurons indicate which inputs are given to that neuron. Filled neurons refer to fake neurons, that are meaningless for the actual computation. In the setup phase we need to assign some inbound connection for these neurons, to be sure that their output will be undistinguishable from that of real hidden neurons. Figure (b) shows a legal scrambling of the network.

4.3.3 Network Randomization.

At this point we have to deal with the protection of the value $|a|$. We are concerned with the disclosing of $|a|$ because if Alice is allowed to run the protocol several times, she can use this additional information to actually understand the network weights. The solution we propose is to scramble all the network at every different execution. A legal scrambling is one that preserves the property of the embedding, i.e. every neuron only gets input from neurons belonging to previous layers, as the one shown in Figure 3 (b). We note that there are at least $L \cdot M!$ legal scramblings, the ones that permute only neurons between the same layer. Increasing the number of neurons per layer M we can get a higher number of different permutations and so a better protection for the network, at the cost of a higher computational burden.

We define the *embedding ratio* as the ratio between the number of hidden neurons of the embedded network and the number of hidden neurons in the original network LM/N_H. As this ratio increases, Alice will see more meaningless values, and therefore she won't be able to understand which values refers to real hidden neurons and which ones don't. Together with the network scrambling, this is a countermeasure to Alice's attempt to run a sensitivity attack against the protocol.

4.4 Multi-Layer Network Protocol

The final protocol is the following:

System Setup: Bob chooses L, M and finds a legal embedding of his network in the $L \times M$ one.

Execution Setup: Alice and Bob agree on a parameter s required by the used cryptosystem, and on a quantization factor Q, that will be used to obtain integer values from the input samples. Alice generates a pair of public and private keys and gives the public one to Bob. Bob will randomly scramble the neuron positions in the network to reach another legal configuration.

Execution: we will consider real neurons and fake ones as the same, as there's no difference, but the fake one's output will never be used again.

```
Input: Alice: $\mathbf{c}$; Bob: $\mathbf{w}_j^{(i)}$ with $i = 1,\ldots,L$, $j = 1,\ldots,M$
Output: Alice: classification of $x$
PPDC($\mathbf{c}$; $\{\mathbf{w}_j^{(i)}\}_{i=1,\ldots,L;j=1,\ldots,M}$)
    for $i = 1$ to $L$
        for $j = 1$ to $M$
            Bob runs PPSP($\mathbf{c}_j^{(i)}$; $\mathbf{w}_j^{(i)}$) and gets $d = E(a)$
            Bob picks $t_j \in \{+1, -1\}$ at random
            if $t_j = -1$
                Bob sets $d = d^{-1}$
            Bob sends $d$ to Alice
            Alice decrypts $d$, evaluates $g(a)$, and sends $z = E(g(a))$ back to Bob
            if $t_j = -1$
                Bob sets $z = E(1)z^{-1}$
    for $j = 1$ to $O$ //out-degree of the network
        Bob runs PPSP($\mathbf{c}_j$; $\mathbf{w}_j$) and gets $d = E(a)$
        Bob sends $d$ to Alice
        Alice decrypts $d$ and evaluates her output $g(a)$
```

The security of this protocol follows from the previous considerations.

5 Implementation of the Protocol

In this section a practical implementation of the proposed protocol is described, and a case study execution that will give us some numerical results in terms of computational and bandwidth resources needed is analyzed.

5.0.1 Client-Server Application.

We developed a Java application based on Remote Method Invocation technology[3]. The software, which makes use of a modified implementation of the Damgård-Jurik cryptosystem available on Jurik's homepage[4], is composed of two parts: the client and the server. The former sets the environment creating a couple of public/private keys and choosing the number of bits of the modulus, and it chooses a server to connect to. The latter can load several neural networks into the system and choose an appropriate quantization factor and embedding ratio.

5.0.2 Experimental Data.

Two datasets were selected from the UCI Machine Learning Repository [21], and two kinds of neural networks were trained starting from those data sets:

- *Sonar:* this dataset refers to the classification of sonar signals by means of a neural network; the dataset contains patterns corresponding to sonar signals bounced off a metal cylinder (bombs) and signals bounced off a roughly cylindrical rock; we have trained a NN with the standard backpropagation algorithm, containing 60 input neurons, 12 hidden neurons, and 1 output neuron.

---

[3] `http://java.sun.com/javase/technologies/core/basic/rmi/`

[4] `http://www.daimi.au.dk/~jurik/research.html`

- *Nursery:* this dataset was derived from a hierarchical decision model originally developed to rank applications for nursery schools [12]; we have trained a NN with 8 input neurons, 20 hidden neurons, and 5 output neurons.

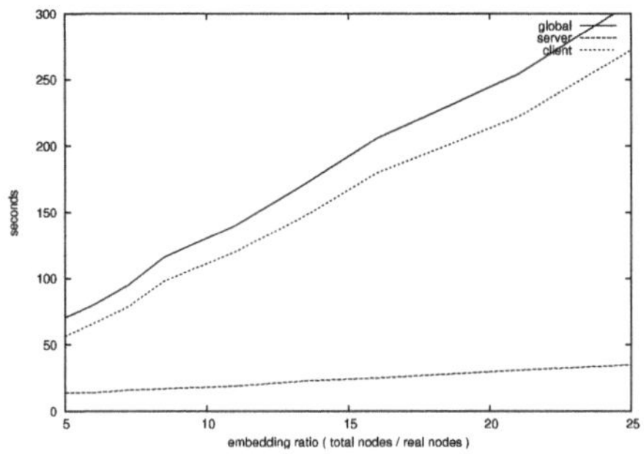

(a) *Nursery* neural network

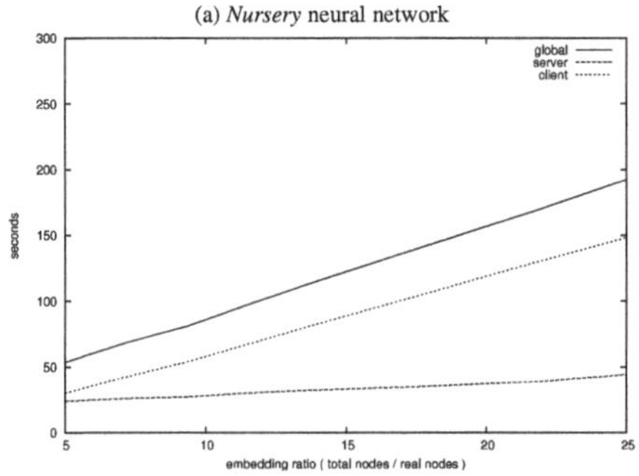

(b) *Sonar* neural network

Fig. 4: Protocol execution time, according to different values of the embedding ratio.

5.0.3 Experimental Setup.

We loaded these NNs into the server changing the embedding ratio at every execution. The quantization factor has been set to $Q = 10^9$, obtaining a reasonable accuracy in the computation to prevent quantization error. In the key generation algorithm the key length has been set to $n = 1024$ to obtain a reasonable level of security [2].

Then we deployed the application on two mid-level notebooks, connected on a LAN. The execution time increases linearly with respect to the embedding ratio, as also the communication overhead does. Choosing carefully the embedding ratio, we can find the desired trade off between execution time and achieved security. Experiments showed that an embedding ratio value of 10 offers a reasonable execution time. Of course the level of security we need is mostly application-based. Results are pictorially represented in Figure 4, where we can distinguish between the running time on the client, on the server, and the total time. Given that the application was executed on a LAN, the communication time is negligible. The amount of exchanged bytes is reported in Table 1 for some values of the embedding ratio. It is worthy to note that even if the *Sonar* NN has 73 neurons (60 input + 12 hidden + 1 output) while the *Nursery* NN has only 33 neurons (8 input + 20 hidden + 5 output), the former is computed in shorter time. This is due to the fact that the only piece of the network that has to be embedded are the hidden neurons[5]. Therefore the *Nursery* NN, having more hidden neurons than the *Sonar* NN, needs more time and bandwidth for the computation.

Neural Network	embedding ratio				
	5	10	15	20	25
sonar	153kB	256kB	359kB	470kB	579kB
nursery	232kB	368kB	544kB	722kB	894kB

Table 1: bandwidth occupation

5.0.4 Workload.

Looking at client and server side workload we can notice that something (apparently) strange happens: the client side workload is greater than the server side one, despite the server seems to do more work than anyone else.
Actually, taking into consideration the protocol, during the evaluation of every hidden layer the client performs encryptions and decryptions once for every neuron while the server has to do a lot of multiplications and exponentiations at every step (that is, for every neuron) to compute the activation value. This is why we are allowed to think that the server side workload has to be greater than the client side one.
Nevertheless, this is not true. We should consider also the nature of things, not only the amount of them. In fact, the client performs heavier operations than the server (encryptions and decryptions are more expensive than multiplications and exponentiations, of course) and so the client side workload is greater than the other one. So, as shown in Fig. 4, with a little amount of nodes the global workload seems to be fairly shared among the parts, and increasing the number of hidden nodes the client side workload grows faster and the performance gets worse.
That behavior allows the protocol to work fine with NNs that are composed by a relatively small set of hidden neurons (that is, between 100 and 300 hidden neurons) because of the nature of the operation involved, no matter which kind of computer the server offers. In any case, we can notice in Fig. 4 that also with an embedding ratio equal to 25 it is possible to achieve a satisfactory computation time, so that it is possible to handle without problems a NN with more than 500 hidden neurons, as we did with sonar and nursery neural networks during the experimental tests.
As far as we know this is the first protocol of this kind that was implemented, as no experimental results are mentioned in [6]. Therefore we can't compare our approaches.

6 Conclusions

Several modern artificial intelligence applications require the protection of the privacy of the data owner, unwilling to reveal his/her input data to the owner of the classifier. In this framework, the availability of tools to process data and signals directly in the encrypted domain allows to build secure and privacy preserving protocols solving the mentioned problem. Given the central role that neural network computing plays in artificial intelligence field, a protocol for NN-based privacy-preserving computation has been designed, where the knowledge embedded in the NN as well as the data the NN operates on are protected. The proposed protocol relies on homomorphic encryption for the linear computations, and on a limited amount of interaction between the NN owner and the user for non linear operations. However, the interaction is kept to a minimum, without resorting to general multiparty computation protocols. Any

[5] The input and output layers represent the input and the output of the function: adding fake inputs or outputs, or scrambling their position will result in a meaningless computation.

unnecessary disclosure of information has been avoided, protecting all the internal computations, so that at the end the user will only learn the final output of the NN computation.

Acknowledgements The work described in this paper has been supported in part by the European Commission through the IST Programme under Contract no 034238 - SPEED. The information in this document reflects only the authors views, is provided as is and no guarantee or warranty is given that the information is fit for any particular purpose. The user thereof uses the information at its sole risk and liability.

References

1. Agrawal, R., Srikant, R.: Privacy-preserving data mining. In: SIGMOD '00: Proceedings of the 2000 ACM SIGMOD International Conference on Management of Data, pp. 439–450 (2000)
2. Barker, E., Barker, W., Burr, W., Polk, W., Smid, M.: Recommendation for Key Management–Part 1: General. NIST Special Publication pp. 800–57 (2005)
3. Barni, M., Orlandi, C., Piva, A.: A privacy-preserving protocol for neural-network-based computation. In: MM&Sec '06: Proceeding of the 8th Workshop on Multimedia and Security, pp. 146–151 (2006)
4. Beaver, D.: Minimal-latency secure function evaluation. Proc. of EUROCRYPT00, LNCS pp. 335–350 (2000)
5. Bishop, C.: Neural Networks for Pattern Recognition. Oxford University Press (1995)
6. Chang, Y., Lu, C.: Oblivious polynomial evaluation and oblivious neural learning. Theoretical Computer Science **341**(1), 39–54 (2005)
7. Comesana, P., Perez-Freire, L., Perez-Gonzalez, F.: Blind newton sensitivity attack. Information Security, IEE Proceedings **153**(3), 115–125 (2006)
8. Damgård, I., Jurik, M.: A generalisation, a simplification and some applications of Paillier's probabilistic public-key system. In: Public Key Cryptography, pp. 119–136 (2001)
9. Dingledine, R., Mathewson, N., Syverson, P.: Tor: The second-generation onion router. In: Proceedings of the 13th USENIX Security Symposium (2004)
10. Fouque, P., Stern, J., Wackers, G.: CryptoComputing with rationals. Financial-Cryptography.-6th-International-Conference, Lecture-Notesin-Computer-Science **2357**, 136–46 (2003)
11. Goldreich, O., Micali, S., Wigderson, A.: How to play any mental game or a completeness theorem for protocols with honest majority. In: STOC '87: Proceedings of the twentieth annual ACM symposium on Theory of computing, pp. 218–229 (1987)
12. Gorman, P., et al.: UCI machine learning repository (1988). URL `http://archive.ics.uci.edu/ml/`
13. Hornik, K., Stinchcombe, M., White, H.: Multilayer feedforward networks are universal approximators. Neural Netw. **2**(5), 359–366 (1989)
14. Jha, S., Kruger, L., McDaniel, P.: Privacy Preserving Clustering. 10th ESORICS (2005)
15. Kalker, T., Linnartz, J.P.M.G., van Dijk, M.: Watermark estimation through detector analysis. In: ICIP98, vol. I, pp. 425–429. Chicago, IL, USA (1998)
16. Kantarcioglu, M., Vaidya, J.: Privacy preserving naive bayes classifier for horizontally partitioned data. In: In IEEE Workshop on Privacy Preserving Data Mining (2003)
17. Lapedes, A., Farber, R.: How neural nets work. Neural information processing systems pp. 442–456 (1988)
18. Laur, S., Lipmaa, H., Mielikäinen, T.: Cryptographically private support vector machines. In: KDD '06: Proceedings of the 12th ACM SIGKDD International Conference on Knowledge discovery and data mining, pp. 618–624 (2006)
19. Lindell, Y., Pinkas, B.: Privacy preserving data mining. In Advances in Cryptology - CRYPTO '00, volume 1880 of Lecture Notes in Computer Science **1880**, 36–54 (2000)
20. Pailler, P.: Public-key cryptosystems based on composite degree residuosity classes. In: Proceedings of Eurocrypt'99, Lecture Notes is Computer Science vol. 1592, pp. 223–238. Springer-Verlag (1999)
21. Rajkovic, V., et al.: UCI machine learning repository (1997). URL `http://archive.ics.uci.edu/ml/`
22. Rumelhart, D., Hinton, G., Williams, R.: Learning internal representations by error propogation. Parallel distributed processing: Explorations in the microstructure of cognition **1**, 318–362 (1986)
23. Sander, T., Young, A., Yung, M.: Non-Interactive CryptoComputing For NC 1. IEEE Symposium on Foundations of Computer Science pp. 554–567 (1999)
24. Yang, Z., Wright, R.N.: Improved privacy-preserving bayesian network parameter learning on vertically partitioned data. In: ICDEW '05: Proceedings of the 21st International Conference on Data Engineering Workshops, p. 1196 (2005)
25. Yao, A.: How to generate and exchange secrets. In: IEEE FOCS'86 - Foundations of Computer Science, pp. 162–167 (1986)

Appendix: Handling Non-integer Value

In this appendix we will describe how we can obtain an arbitrarily accurate real number Damgård-Jurik cryptosystem. First of all we map, as usual, the positive numbers in $\{0,\ldots,\frac{n^s-1}{2}\}$, and the negative ones in $\{\frac{n^s-1}{2}+1,\ldots,n^s-1\}$, with $-1 = n^s - 1$. Then, given a real value $x \in \mathbb{R}$, we quantize it with a quantization factor Q, and approximate it as $\bar{x} = \left\lfloor \frac{x}{Q} \right\rfloor \simeq \frac{x}{Q}$ for a sufficiently thin quantization factor. Clearly the first homomorphic property still stands i.e.

$$D(E(\bar{x}_1) \cdot E(\bar{x}_2)) = \bar{x}_1 + \bar{x}_2 \simeq \frac{x_1 + x_2}{Q}.$$

This allows Bob to perform an arbitrarily number of sums among ciphertexts. Also the second property holds, but with a drawback. In fact:

$$D(E(\bar{x})^{\bar{a}}) = \bar{a} \cdot \bar{x} \simeq \frac{a \cdot x}{Q^2}$$

The presence of the Q^2 factor has two important consequences: (i) the size of the encrypted numbers grows exponentially with the number of multiplications; (ii) Bob must disclose to Alice the number of multiplications, so that Alice can compensate for the presence of the Q^2 factor. The first drawback is addressed with the property of Damgård-Jurik cryptosystem that allows us, by increasing s, to cipher bigger numbers. The second one imposes a limit on the kind of secure computation that we can perform using the techniques proposed here. Luckily in our application we perform only one multiplication for each ciphertext in the scalar product protocol.

An estimation of the s parameter to be chosen in a way that the value inside the ciphertext after the computation will fit into n^s is the following: let X be the upper bound for the norm of Alice's input vector, and W an upper bound for the weight vectors norm. Every scalar product computed in the protocol is then bounded by $|\mathbf{x}||\mathbf{w}|\cos(\widehat{\mathbf{x}\mathbf{w}}) \leq XW$. Given a modulo n sufficiently large for security purposes, it is possible to select the parameter s such that:

$$s \geq \left\lceil \log_n \frac{2XW}{Q^2} \right\rceil$$

(the factor 2 is due to the presence of both positive and negative values). Other solutions for working with non integer values can be found in [6] where a protocol to evaluate a polynomial on floating-point numbers is defined (but the exponent must be chosen in advance), and [10], where a cryptosystem based on lattice properties allowing computation with rational values is presented (even in this case, however, a bound exists on the number of multiplications that can be carried out to allow a correct decryption).

Minimizing SSO Effort in Verifying SSL Anti-phishing Indicators

Yongdong Wu, Haixia Yao and Feng Bao

Abstract In an on-line transaction, a user sends her personal sensitive data (e.g., password) to a server for authentication. This process is known as Single Sign-On (SSO). Subject to phishing and pharming attacks, the sensitive data may be disclosed to an adversary when the user is allured to visit a bogus server. There has been much research in anti-phishing methods and most of them are based on enhancing the security of browser indicator. In this paper, we present a completely different approach of defeating phishing and pharming attacks. Our method is based on encrypted cookie. It tags the sensitive data with the server's public key and stores it as a cookie on the user's machine. When the user visits the server so as to perform an on-line transaction, the sensitive data in the cookie will be encrypted with the stored public key of the server. The ciphertext can only be decrypted by the genuine server. Our encrypted cookie scheme (ECS) has the advantage that the user can ignore SSL indicator in the transaction process. The security is guaranteed even if the user accepts a malicious self-signed certificate. This advantage greatly releases user's burden of checking SSL indicator, which could be very difficult even for an experienced user when the phishing attacks have sophisticated vision design.

1 Introduction

With the rapid development of Internet and web technologies, most of the online applications such as e-banking and e-government are built on or assisted by WWW. For example, after China Government endorsed the "Digital Signature Law" in 2005, more and more China citizens open e-banking accounts (over 60 million in 2007) such that the transaction amount is in-

Cryptography and Security Department, Institute for Infocomm Research, Singapore
e-mail: \{wydong,hxyao,baofeng\}@i2r.a-star.edu.sg

Please use the following format when citing this chapter:

Wu, Y., Yao, H. and Bao, F., 2008, in IFIP International Federation for Information Processing, Volume 278; *Proceedings of the IFIP TC 11 23rd International Information Security Conference*; Sushil Jajodia, Pierangela Samarati, Stelvio Cimato; (Boston: Springer), pp. 47–61.

creased at a rate of 30% annually [1]. Usually, an on-line transaction is built based on client/server model. When a user initiates a transaction with a web browser (*e.g.*, Internet Explorer or Firefox), she will send a request to the web server with its URL (Universal Resource Locator). On a request, the server sends back a form to request the user's personal information. Once the server authenticates the browser with the user's input, the web server sends the confidential page within the browser window which will be shown to the user.

Most web sites currently authenticate users with a simple password submitted via an HTML form similar to Fig.1. Because the personal data are involved, information submitted via HTML forms has proven to be highly susceptible to phishing [2, 3] which exploits the visual mistake to lure victims. Evidence suggests somewhere 3-5% of phishing targets disclose sensitive information and passwords to spoofed web sites [4, 5]; about two million users gave information to spoofed websites resulting in direct losses of $1.2 billion for US banks and card issuers in 2003 [6]. Presently, phishing attacks are becoming more and more sophisticated [7]. As a result, good phishing techniques can fool even the most vigilant users [8, 9], and the countermeasures such as trusted paths [10, 11] and multi-factor authentication schemes [12] are susceptible to phishing.

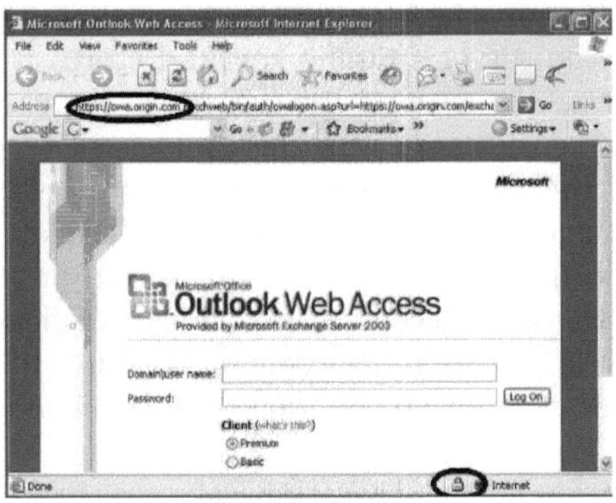

Fig. 1 HTTPS GUI of Microsoft Internet Explorer (IE) for self-signed certificate. Firefox will highlight the background of URL status besides those in IE.

To understand the workflow of phishing, let's recall that an on-line transaction has three links which know the personal data: server, transmission channel and user/browser. Hence, to provide secure transaction, the security of each link should be ensured. Nowadays, the server usually installs heterogeneous firewalls, IDS (Intrusion Detection System) *etc* so as to guarantee the safety of the server; meanwhile, the transmission channel is managed with SSL (Secure Socket Layer [13]) protocol which is secure enough for message transmission in an on-line transaction from the viewpoint of a cryptographer. To provide a trustworthy browser/user interface, the browser renders some security indicators so as to provide the user information about the authenticity of the website. Concretely, a browser provides user interface which includes at least three indicators: a HTTPS other than HTTP is shown in the URL bar, besides the target domain name; (2) A closed lock is shown in the status bar if the SSL protocol is performed successfully and the URL bar matches the certificate of server, both (1) and (2) are highlighted with circles in Fig.1; (3) If the user clicks on the closed lock, the visited server certificate will be shown in a pop-up window. If and only if all of the above items are checked carefully, all the links are protected and thus the target server is authentic in principle.

Nonetheless, the transaction scheme may still be vulnerable in practical since the client/browser interface can be easily reproduced with "Web spoofing" technique [14, 15, 16]. Friedman *et al.* [17] summarized that it is difficult for average users to determine whether a browser connection is secure due to the follows:

- It is trivial to insert a spoofed image with any security indicator where one does not exist [14].
- Many users do not understand the meaning of the SSL security indicator. Hence, they ignore the security indicator such that a non-SSL malicious website is mis-regarded as a trusted server.
- Many users do not notice the absence of SSL lock icon.
- The lock icon only indicates that the current page was delivered to the user securely with SSL protocol. However, the page content including the user input can be sent to other website insecurely, or is accessible to other frame shown in the same browser instance in a multi-frame page [18].
- Regardless certificate is critical in verifying the authenticity of the server, few common users understand SSL certificates, and rare users go through the effort of checking SSL certificates and certificate authorities (CAs). Indeed, there are too many cryptology jargons in the definition of digital certificate.
- Some browsers provide warnings to inform the user when data is submitted insecurely, or server certificate is problematic such as expiry or self-signed, but many users ignore these warnings or turn them off.

In summary, the major reason that an attacker can start phishing or pharming attack is that users do not reliably notice the absence of a security indicator, and do not know how to use. Hence, the browser must provide ease of use interface, and minimize the effort in checking the security indicators. In contrast, if an anti-pharming solution is too complicated, it will likely be misused by average users.

This paper presents an anti-phishing scheme called as ECS which enhance the security of the user/browser link. ECS upgrades the browser with handling cookies so as to minimize the user effort in on-line transaction. To this end, the cookie including the password as well as the public key of the target server is generated in the user registration process. To perform an on-line transaction, the browser builds an SSL channel with the server, then the browser merges the password with SSL session key, and encrypts them with the stored public key. The ciphertext is sent to the target server as an encrypted cookie. After the SSL server decrypts the ciphertext, it will recover the password since it knows the session key. This improvement enables that a user is free from checking SSL indicators at any time except the registration period. As a result, the present protection scheme provides to the user the following advantages:

- free from identifying closed lock;
- free from identifying HTTPS and URL in the status bar;
- free from identifying the certification;
- free from identifying self-signing certificate.
- free from dictionary attack.

The organization of the paper is as follows. Section 2 introduces the preliminaries. Sections 3 describes the present scheme. Section 4 addresses our implementation. Section 5 analyzes relevant work. Section 6 concludes the paper.

2 Preliminaries

2.1 Phishing and Pharming

In a phishing attack, an adversary duplicates a known site of business (*e.g.*, `www.paypai.com` mimics `www.paypal.com`) and then sends spams to encourage users to visit the malicious site. When users click on the link within the spam email, they are taken to the fake site to divulge critical information.

Pharming accomplishes the same thing as phishing, but with more stealth and without spam email. In this case, the adversary plants false code on the domain name server (DNS) itself, so that anyone who enters the correct website address will be directed by the DNS to the fake site.

2.2 HTTPS-enabled Browser

Of all security techniques against Internet attacks, SSL3.0 [13] is the *de facto* standard for end-to-end security and widely applied to do secure transactions such as Internet banking. When the client's web browser makes a connection to an SSL-enabled web server over HTTPS, the browser must verify the server's certificate, all the CA's certificates, name of the server certificate against URL status, and expiry. If any of these checks fails, the browser warns the user and asks the user if it is safe to continue. If the user chooses positively, she may permit the SSL connection to continue even though any or all of these checks have failed [19], expiry or self-signed certificates. In reality, researchers have shown that users routinely ignore such security warnings [20, 21, 22]. Unfortunately, this kind of ignorance enables the phishing attack. In other words, SSL merely guarantees that the received message is authentic and confidential in the transmission, but it does not care about the message before or after transmission.

2.3 HTTP Cookie

HTTP cookies (see `http://en.wikipedia.org/wiki/HTTP_cookie`) are parcels of text sent by a server to a web browser and then sent back unchanged by the browser each time it accesses that server. Since cookies may contain sensitive information (user name, a token used for authentication, etc.), their values should not be accessible to other computer applications.

A cookie contains the name/value pair, an expiration date, optional secure flag and version number, a path/domain name. The name/value pair is the content of the cookie; the expiration date tells the browser when to delete the cookie; if the secure flag is set, the cookie is intended only for encrypted connections; the path/domain tells the browser where the cookie has to be sent back. For security reasons, the cookie is accepted only if the server is a member of the domain specified by the domain string. Therefore, a cookie is actually identified by the triple name/domain/path, not only the name. In other words, same name but different domains or paths identify different cookies with possibly different values. Generally, the browser objects including cookie are under control of same origin policy.

2.4 Same Origin Policy

The same-origin policy is an important security measure in modern web browsers for client-side scripting (mostly JavaScript)[1]. It governs access control among different web objects and prevents a document or script loaded from one "origin" from getting or setting properties of a document from a different "origin", where an "origin" is defined using a tuple <domain name, protocol, port>.

[1] Internet Explorer uses an alternative approach of security zones in addition to the same-origin (or "same-site") policy.

3 The Encrypted Cookie Scheme

3.1 Attack Model

Fig.2 illustrates the participants involved in on-line transaction model: user, SSL server, client/browser and attacker. The user will authenticate herself with SSO (Single-Sign-On) to the SSL server, while the SSL server authenticates itself with a certificate issued by a certificate authority. The browser is an application such as Firefox^{TM} or Microsoft Internet Explorer^{TM} which helps the user to make transactions. When a user requests a secure page, the browser will verify the server's certificate with HTTPS/SSL protocol. If the server is authentic, both sides will negotiate a session key for the secure communication, and the user's browser status line shows a security lock. Additionally, if the user clicks the security lock, a popup window will show the security information on server certificate. The attacker aims to impersonate an innocent user by forging an SSL site and luring an innocent user to disclose sensitive data.

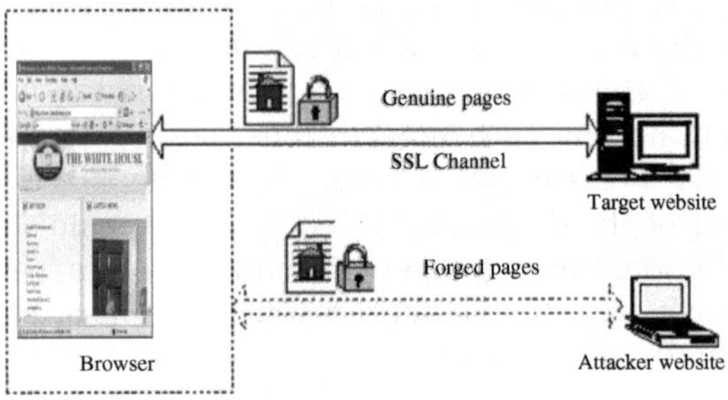

Fig. 2 Attack model

In this paper, suppose that an adversary can create an arbitrary self-sign certificate, but the user ignores the security warning and accepts the certificate in any transaction period. Thus, the attacker can insert, delete and tamper the communication data at will. This phishing attack is powerful such that many countermeasures are invalid. For example, SecurID [23] provides One-Time Password for two-factor authentication and has been deployed in a lot of financial institutions, but it is still vulnerable to the phishing attack.

3.2 ECS Modules

Suppose a server generates a public/private key pair PK/SK, and obtains a certificate C_A from a CA (*e.g.*, `www.verisign.com`) whose public key is hard-coded in the user's browser. To improve the browser's security against phishing attack, ECS encrypts the user's sensitive data with server's public key PK and transmits the encrypted cookie to the server. To this end, ECS has 3 modules: Registering cookie, reading cookie, and verifying cookie.

3.2.1 Registering cookie

After the browser builds an SSL channel with the registration server, it displays a form as Fig.1 for registration. Before filling in the form, a user should carefully verify all the security indicators, *i.e.*, closed lock, HTTPS URL status and attributes of server certificate (subject, issuer, expiry, etc). If all the SSL indicators are in place, the user will input her personal data <**`username`**, **`password`**>, and send the complete form to the server. Then the server will return a cookie whose content as

$$C = PK \parallel m \parallel Aux, \tag{1}$$

where m =<**`username`**, **`password`**>, Aux is the auxiliary information such as certificate version of the server in case of certificate upgrading. Moreover, the server saves **`username`** and the hash of **`password`** into a database $\mathbb{B}$.

3.2.2 Reading Cookie

As we mentioned in the Section 2.4, same origin policy makes sure that a cookie is read only when the requested source is the same as the stored one. If a user visits a HTTPS website whose domain matches the cookie domain, the browser will read the cookie after setting up an SSL channel with the transaction server. Then the browser will encrypt the **`username/password`** pair to generate a cookie whose content is

$$c = \mathcal{E}(PK, m \oplus k \oplus C_A, r), \tag{2}$$

where r is a random number, k is the the SSL session key, and $\mathcal{E}(PK, \cdot)$ is a CCA2 encryption algorithm (*e.g.*, ElGamal cryptosystem). Afterwards, the browser generates cookie $\mathbf{C}$, further sends to the server the cookie as an SSL traffic, *i.e.*, cookie's encryption $\mathcal{F}(k, \mathbf{C})$, where $\mathcal{F}(\cdot)$ is a symmetric cipher such as AES such that no adversary can eavesdrop the traffic.

Remark: a client can not distinguish an adversary from a genuine server by comparing the received public key with the stored public key PK in the transaction since a genuine server may update its public key (ref. Subsection 4.3) from time to time.

3.2.3 Verifying cookie

After receiving the encrypted cookie $\mathcal{F}(k, \mathbf{C})$, the server decrypts it to obtain cookie content c. Then it calculates $m = \mathcal{D}(SK, c) \oplus k \oplus C_A$ with the decryption algorithm $\mathcal{D}(\cdot)$ and its private key SK. Based on the user database $\mathbb{B}$, the server can verify the identity of the user.

3.3 Security Analysis

Based on same origin policy, a cookie will not be read from the user's machine unless the transaction URL domain is identical to the registration URL domain. Hence, to launch a phishing attack, the following diagram should be employed.

- an attacker $\mathcal{A}$ forges a website with the same URL as the genuine site;
- $\mathcal{A}$ selects a public/private key pair, and self-signs his public key to create a certificate $\tilde{C}_A$. Please note that public key of $\mathcal{A}$ must be different from that of a genuine server, otherwise, $\mathcal{A}$ can not setup SSL channel with the user;
- $\mathcal{A}$ lures a user to visit the bogus site. For example, by sending spam email;
- The user visits the bogus site and ignores the certificate warning.

To obtain the sensitive data of a user so as to impersonate her with the above diagram, an adversary $\mathcal{A}$ will start man-in-the-middle attack as follows,

- attacker $\mathcal{A}$ produces a bogus certificate $\tilde{C}_A$, and sends a polynomial number n_1 of queries to the client so as to obtain the ciphertext

  $$c_i = \mathcal{E}(PK, m \oplus k_i \oplus \tilde{C}_A, r_i), i = 1, 2, \ldots, n_1,$$

  where k_i is the SSL session key, and r_i is random.
- attacker $\mathcal{A}$ tries to impersonate the user by connecting to the genuine server. Both $\mathcal{A}$ and server negotiate an SSL session key k with the server. Clearly, $k \oplus C_A \neq k_i \oplus \tilde{C}_A$ for any $i \in [1, n_1]$
- attacker $\mathcal{A}$ continues to send a polynomial number n_2 of queries to the user so as to obtain the ciphertext

  $$c_j = \mathcal{E}(PK, m \oplus k_j \oplus \tilde{C}_A, r_j), j = n_1 + 1, \ldots, n_1 + n_2,$$

  where k_j is the SSL session key, r_j is random, and $k \oplus C_A \neq k_j \oplus \tilde{C}_A$ for any $j \in [n_1 + 1, n_1 + n_2]$.

Since $\mathcal{E}(\cdot,\cdot)$ is CCA2, it is semantically secure such that the distribution of $\mathcal{E}(\cdot,\cdot)$ is uniform for any m. Thus,

$$\mathcal{H}(m) = \mathcal{H}(m \mid c_i, k_i \oplus C_A), i = 1, 2, \ldots, n_1 + n_2, \quad (3)$$

where $\mathcal{H}(X)$ represents the entropy of variable X. Informally, m is independent from c_i due to the random number r_i, thus the query results provide negligible information to adversary $\mathcal{A}$ in generating an encryption $c = \mathcal{E}(PK, m \oplus k \oplus C_A)$. Therefore, to impersonate a user, $\mathcal{A}$ has to generate a well-formed ciphertext $c = \mathcal{E}(PK, m \oplus k \oplus C_A, r)$ from (PK, k, C_A) and some r but without knowing m.

If $\mathcal{A}$ succeeds in generating c at non-negligible probability, $\mathcal{A}$ queries the server with c so as to obtain $m \oplus k \oplus C_A$. Thus $\mathcal{E}(PK, \cdot)$ is not secure against chosen ciphertext attack, *i.e.*, $\mathcal{E}(PK, \cdot)$ is not CCA2. It contradicts with our assumption on $\mathcal{E}(PK, \cdot)$.

On the other hand, Eq.(2) demonstrates that the present scheme is secure against dictionary attack.

4 ECS Implementation

In our implementation, Firefox browser (`http://developer.mozilla.org/en/docs/Download_Mozilla_Source_Code`) and Apache server are used as testbed for demonstrating ECS. A module in Firefox is used to encrypt `<username, password>` to generate an encrypted cookie in the reading stage, and a PHP program is used to generate cookie and verify the encrypted cookie.

4.1 Registration Process

The registration is performed for the first time when a user visits an SSL server without a cookie. In order to make use of on-line transaction, users usually obtain sensitive data such as password via out-of-band channel (*e.g.*, face-to-face delivery, mail) in advance. To register a user on line, the server will send a form Fig.1.

After a user checks all the security indicators (*i.e.*, lock, URL,certificate), she fills in the form and submits the complete form to the SSL-server. Afterwards, the client will receive an HTTPS page generated with code segment in Fig.3 from the SSL-server. When the browser cookie is enabled, the new cookie will be stored in the user site.

```
<?php
$value = C;
$expiry=3600× 24× 365;
setcookie("ECS_USER", $value, time()+$expiry, "/", "192.168.137.211", 1);
?>
```

Fig. 3 Setting up an example cookie. The cookie name is ECS_USER, its value is the string C which is generated in Eq.(1), its expiry is of 365 days. The path/domain `/192.168.137.211` tells the browser to send the cookie when requesting a page of the domain `192.168.137.211`.

4.2 Transaction Process

After registration, a cookie which including the `username/password` and server public key is stored in user's machine. If a user likes to make a transaction, it is unnecessary to input her password any more, *i.e.*, Fig.2 will not be shown in the transaction period. With regard to Fig.4, the cookie will be read when the user visits the authentic server based on the same origin policy, and processed according to the proposed scheme in Section 3. Afterwards, the encrypted cookie is sent to the server for verification. Concretely,

- In the member function *nsCookieService::GetCookieInternal*() of the source file *mozilla\netwerk\cookie\src\nsCookieService.cpp*, we add ECS code for searching the cookie with name "ECS_USER", reading the cookie value, parsing the value according to Eq.(1), and generating c with Eq.(2). Moreover, since either IETF RFC2109 or cookie processing module uses semi-colon (`0x3B`), addition (`0x2B`), comma (`0x2C`), LF (`0x0A`) and NUL (`0x00`) as separators, and the ciphertext c may have the separators, ECS encodes c such that these separators do not occur in cookie. Technically, As shown in the following table, ECS scans ciphertext c byte by byte, and replaces byte "\" (or ";" ,"+", ",", LF, NUL) with two bytes "\\" (or "\A", "\B","\C","\D", "\E" respectively).

Original symbol(ASCII code)		Coded symbols
backslash (`0x5C`)	↔	"\\" (`0x5C5C`)
semi-colon (`0x3B`)	↔	"\A" (`0x5C41`)
addition (`0x2B`)	↔	"\B" (`0x5C42`)
comma (`0x2C`)	↔	"\C" (`0x5C43`)
LF (`0x0A`)	↔	"\D" (`0x5C44`)
NUL (`0x00`)	↔	"\E" (`0x5C45`)

- At the server side, after receiving the cookie, the server decodes the value to ciphertext c by replacing two bytes "\\" (or "\A", "\B","\C","\D", "\E") with one byte "\" (or ";" , "+", ",", LF, NUL resp.) sequentially, then decrypts c with its private key. If the decrypted password matches the stored one, the user is authentic.

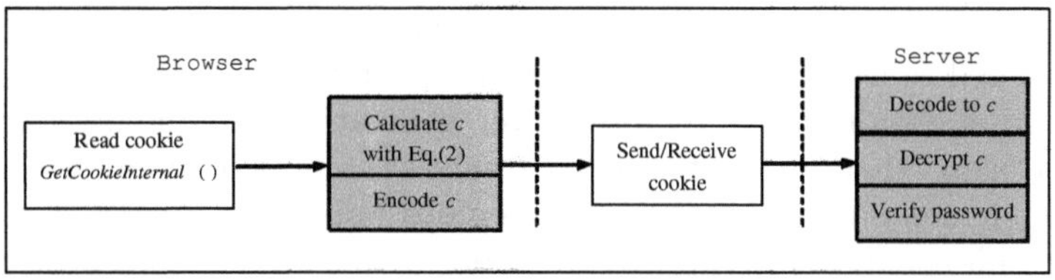

Fig. 4 User authentication process. The shadow units are developed for ECS.

4.3 Refreshment Process

When the server receives the cookies from the client, it will check the version, and select the private key based on the version. The private key enables the server to decrypt the ciphertext correctly. If the `username/password` matches a registration record of database $\mathbb{B}$, the user is authenticated to perform on-line transaction. Furthermore, if the version is not latest, the server will send a new cookie $\tilde{c}$ with Eq.(1) including the old password, new public key and new version. If the new cookie $\tilde{c}$ has the same password as that of the old cookie c, the client/browser will replace the old cookie with the new one.

5 Related work

Since phishing attack is a realistic risk in on-line transaction, there are many countermeasures on phishing attacks based on different security models.

5.1 Manual-checking Mechanism

Synchronized Random Dynamic (SRD) scheme [27, 28] defines an internal reference window whose color is randomly changed, and sets up the boundary of the browser window with different colors according to certain rules. If the boundary of a pop-up window de-synchronizes with that of the reference window, the user concludes that a web-spoof attack is under way. However, it is impractical for the device of small screen (such as hand-held device) because it is inconvenient to open two windows and switch between the windows. Moreover, the attacker can create a bogus reference window to overlap the original reference window.

RFC2617 [29] proposes a Digest Access Authentication scheme which employs password digest to authenticate a user. PwdHash [11] authenticates a user with a one way hash of the tuple <password, domain name> instead of password only so as to defeat the visual mistake on URL. Moreover, Dynamic

Security Skins (DSS) [30] creates a dedicated window for inputting username and password so as to defeat bogus window. After both server and client will negotiated a session key, a remote server generates a unique abstract image called as "skin" that automatically customizes the browser window or the user interface elements in the content of a remote web page. Similarly, the client browser independently computes the same image. To authenticate content from an authenticated server, the user needs to perform one visual matching operation to compare two images. In addition, since `username` should be disclosed to the server before authentication, `username` will be known to the phishing attacker.

Adelsbach *et al.* [31] combines all concepts in an adaptive web browser toolbar, which summarizes all relevant information and allows the user to get this crucial information at a glance. As this toolbar is a local component of the user's system, a remote attacker cannot access it by means of active web languages. The advantage of this implementation is that a user has a permanent and reliable overview about the status of his web connection. Once a user has personalized the browser's GUI, users achieve sufficient security against visual attacks. Users only have to verify the web browser's personalization and the certificate information, which is always displayed. A disadvantage of the toolbar described above is that the user must recognize his personal image at each login.

5.2 Auto-checking mechanism

As an improvement on [31], ADSI (Automatic Detecting Security Indicator) [32] generates a random picture and embeds it into the current web browser. It can be triggered by any security relevant event occurred on the browser, and then performs automatic checking on current active security status. When a mismatch of embedded images is detected, an alarm goes off to alert the users. Since an adversary is hard to replace or mimic the randomly generated picture, the web-spoofing attack can not be mounted. However, ADSI can not prevent man-in-the-middle phishing attack with self-sign certificate.

Adida [33] presents a FragToken scheme which employs the URL fragment as an authenticator, and change-response for authentication. FragToken is only useful in low-security environment (*e.g.*, Blog) since it is vulnerable to man-in-the-middle attack.

By examining the domain name, images and links, SpoofGuard [34] examines web pages and warns users when a certain page has a high probability based on the blacklist in the server site.

Cache Cookie [35] utilizes the browser cache files to identify the browser. It does not install any software into the client side and hence is easy of deployment. Another cookie based scheme is called Active cookie scheme [36] which stores both the user's identification and a fixed server IP address.

When a client visits the server, the server will redirect the client to the fixed IP address. In short, Active cookie scheme acts as replacing URL domain name with IP address so as to defeat pharming attack.

Karlof *et al.* [18] proposed the locked same-origin policy (LSOP) enforces access control for SSL web objects based on servers' public keys. LSOP grants access only if the stored public key is identical to the public key sent with a new connection. Applying the locked same-origin policy to SSL-only cookies yields locked cookies, an extension to SSL-only cookies which binds them to the public key of the originating server. However, as pointed out in [18], LSOP does not consider the input problem such as SSO. For example, LSOP is vulnerable to the most popular phishing attack which asks an innocent user to fill in a password/account page as Fig.1.

For comparison, Table 1 lists the security performance of related countermeasure and ECS. It demonstrates that the user effort for transaction security is minimal. The weakness is that ECS asks the client to install a patch in the client browser once. Nonetheless, this one-time installation is worthy for the minimal effort in the transaction in comparison with the tedious certificate management work in client-side SSL scheme.

Table 1 Comparison in terms of client effort in on-line transaction.

	Free from checking URL	Free from checking SSL lock	Free from checking Cert warn	Free from checking GUI	Free from MiMA	Free from installing patch
Pwdhash[11]	✓	✓	×	✓	×	×
Client SSL [13]	✓	✓	×	✓	✓	✓+
LSOP[18]	×	✓	×	×	×	×
SRD[28]	✓	✓	×	×	×	×
DigestAccess[29]	×	×	×	✓	×	✓
DSS[30]	×	✓	×	×	×	×
FragToekn[33]	×	×	×	✓	×	✓
SpoofGuard[34]	×	×	×	✓	×	×
ActiveCookie[36]	✓	×	×	×	×	✓
Present ECS	✓	✓	✓	✓	✓	×

URL: https://domain;
SSL lock: the closed SSL lock on the status bar;
Cert warn: a pop-up window for self-signed/non-signed certificate;
GUI: the browser window against a reference window;
MiMA: man-in-the-middle attack; It has minor difference from general MiMA.
Patch: (source/exectutable) code inserted in browser;
+: Client-side SSL does not install any software patch, but it has to manage certificates with much effort.

6 Conclusions

Users' psychological acceptance of an authentication mechanism is vital to its success [37]. However, users' interpretations of "secure" web connections vary significantly, and many users have trouble accurately interpreting browser security indicators and cues, such as URL bar, locked icon, certificate dialogs, and security warnings [21].

The encrypted cookie scheme ECS minimizes the user effort and guarantees that only the target server can obtain the cookie. It does not modify the access role and protocol but the cookie reading module, hence it is easy for deployment.

References

1. Zhensheng Guan, Invited talk in International ICT Security Exhibition & Conference, Guangzhou, China, Nov. 28, 2007.
2. Edward W. Felten, Dirk Balfanz, Drew Dean, and Dan S. Wallach, "Web spoofing: An Internet Con Game," 20th National Information Systems Security Conference,1997. http://www.cs.princeton.edu/sip/pub/spoofing.html
3. Serge Lefranc, and David Naccache, "Cut and Paste Attacks with Java," http://eprint.iacr.org/2002/010.ps
4. Evgeniy Gabrilovich, and Alex Gontmakher, "The homograph attack," *Communications of ACM*, 45(2):128, 2002.
5. Martin Johns, "Using Java in anti DNS-pinning attacks," `http://shampoo.antville.org/stories/1566124/,February2007.`
6. Avivah Litan, "Phishing Attack Victims Likely Targets for Identity Theft," in Gartner First Take FT-22-8873. 2004, Gartner Research
7. Microsoft. Microsoft security bulletin MS01-017: Erroneous VeriSign-issued digital certificates pose spoofing hazard,March 2001. `http://www.microsoft.com/technet/security/Bulletin/MS01-017.mspx`
8. Tyler Close, "Waterken YURL," `http://www.waterken.com/dev/YURL/httpsy/`
9. Russell Housley, Warwick Ford, Tim Polk, and David Solo, "Internet X.509 public key infrastructure certificate and Certificate Revocation List (CRL) profile," 2002. `http://tools.ietf.org/html/rfc3280`
10. V. Benjamin Livshits, and Monica S. Lam, "Finding security vulnerabilities in Java applications using static analysis," USENIX Security Sym., pp.271-286, 2005.
11. Blake Ross, Collin Jackson, Nick Miyake, Dan Boneh, and John C. Mitchell, "A Browser Plug-in Solution to the Unique Password Problem," Usenix Security Symposium, 2005.
12. mozilla.dev.security, "VeriSign Class 3 Secure Server CA?," `http://groups.google.com/group/mozilla.dev.security/browse_thread/threa%d/6830a8566de24547/0be9dea1c274d0c5`, March 2007.
13. A. Freier, P. Kariton, and P. Kocher, "The SSL Protocol: Version 3.0," Netscape communications, Inc., 1996.
14. Tieyan Li, and Yongdong Wu, "Trust on Web Browser: Attack vs. Defense," First MiAn International Conference on Applied Cryptography and Network Security, LNCS 2846, pp.241-253, 2003.
15. Jeffrey Horton, and Jennifer Seberry, "Covert Distributed Computing Using Java Through Web Spoofing," ACISP, pp.48-57, 1998. http://www.uow.edu.au/ jennie/WEB/JavaDistComp.ps.

16. F. De Paoli, A.L. DosSantos, and R.A. Kemmerer, "Vulnerability of Secure Web Browsers," National Information Systems Security Conference, 1997.
17. Batya Friedman, David Hurley, Daniel Howe, Edward Felten, and Helen Nissenbaum, "Users' Conceptions of Web Security: A Comparative Study," Conference on Human Factors in Computing Systems, pp.746-747, 2002.
18. Chris Karlof, Umesh Shankar, J.D. Tygar, and David Wagner, "Dynamic pharming attacks and the locked same-origin policies for web browsers," CCS 2007.
19. Security Space and E-Soft, "Secure Server Survey," `http://www.securityspace.com/s_survey/sdata/200704/certca.html`, May 2007.
20. Stephen Bell, "Invalid banking cert spooks only one user in 300," ComputerWorld New Zealand, `http://www.computerworld.co.nz/news.nsf/NL/-FCC8B`
21. Rachna Dhamija, J. D. Tygar, and Marti Hearst, "Why phishing works," SIGCHI Conference on Human Factors in Computing Systems, pp.581-590, 2006.
22. Min Wu, Robert C. Miller, and Simson Garfinkel, "Do security toolbars actually prevent phishing attacks?" the SIGCHI Conference on Human Factors in Computing Systems, pp.601-610, 2006.
23. RSA Security Inc, "SecurID product description," `http://rsasecurity.com/node.asp?id=1156`.
24. Sudhir Aggarwal, Jasbinder Bali, Zhenhai Duan, Leo Kermes, Wayne Liu, Shahank Sahai, and Zhenghui Zhu,"The Design and Development of an Undercover Multipurpose Anti-Spoofing Kit (UnMask)," 23rd Annual Computer Security Applications Conference, 2007.
25. M. Burnside, Blaise Gassend, Thomas Kotwal, Matt Burnside, Marten van Dijk, Srinivas Devadas, and Ronald Rivest, "The untrusted computer problem and camera-based authentication," International Conference on Pervasive Computing, LNCS 2414, pp.114-124, 2002.
26. Pim Tuyls, Tom Kevenaar, Geert-Jan Schrijen, Toine Staring, and Marten van Dijk, "Visual Crypto Displays enabling Secure Communications," Proceeding of First International Conference on Security in Pervasive Computing, pp.12-14, 2003.
27. Yougu Yuan, Eileen Zishuang Ye, and Sean Smith, "Web Spoofing," 2001. `http://www.cs.dartmouth.edu/reports/abstracts/TR2001-409/`
28. Eileen Zishuang Ye, and Sean Smith, "Trusted Paths for Browsers," ACM Transactions on Information and System Security,8(2):153-186, 2005.
29. J. Franks, P. Hallam-Baker, J. Hostetler, S. Lawrence, P. Leach, A. Luotonen, and L. Stewart. HTTP Authentication: Basic and Digest Access Authentication, June 1999. `http://www.ietf.org/rfc/rfc2617.txt`.
30. Rachna Dhamija, and J.D. Tygar, "The Battle Against Phishing: Dynamic Security Skins," Symposium On Usable Privacy and Security (SOUPS) 2005.
31. Andre Adelsbach, Sebastian Gajek, and Jorg Schwenk, "Visual Spoofing of SSL Protected Web Sites and Effective Countermeasures," Information Security Practice and Experience(ISPEC), LNCS 3469, pp.204-216, 2005.
32. Fang Qi, Tieyan Li, Feng Bao, and Yongdong Wu, "Preventing Web-Spoofing with Automatic Detecting Security Indicator," ISPEC, LNCS 3903, pp. 112-122, 2006.
33. Ben Adida,"BeamAuth: Two-Factor Web Authentication with a Bookmark," CCS 2007.
34. Neil Chou, Robert Ledesma, Yuka Teraguchi, Dan Boneh, and John C. Mitchell, "Client Side Defense Against Web-based Identity Theft," `http://crypto.stanford.edu/SpoofGuard/#publications`
35. Ari Juels, Markus Jakobsson, and Tom N. Jagatic, "Cache Cookies for Browser Authentication," IEEE Symp. on Security and Privacy, pp.301-305, 2006.
36. Ari Juels, Markus Jakobsson, and Sid Stamm,"Active Cookies for Browser Authentication," `http://www.ravenwhite.com/files/activecookies--28_Apr_06.pdf`.
37. J. H. Saltzer, and M. D. Schroeder, "The protection of information in computer systems," *Proceedings of the IEEE*, 63(9):1278-308, Sept. 1975.

Robbing Banks with Their Own Software—an Exploit Against Norwegian Online Banks*

Yngve Espelid, Lars–Helge Netland, André N. Klingsheim, and Kjell J. Hole

Abstract The banking industry in Norway has developed a new security infrastructure for conducting commerce on the Internet. The initiative, called BankID, aims to become a national ID infrastructure supporting services such as authentication and digital signatures for the entire Norwegian population. This paper describes a man-in-the-middle vulnerability in online banking applications using BankID. An exploit has been implemented and successfully run against two randomly chosen online banking systems to demonstrate the seriousness of the attack.

Key words: Public-key infrastructure, man-in-the-middle attack, online banking

1 Introduction

The Norwegian banking community has created a new infrastructure for secure e-commerce, called BankID.[1] As of October 2007, BankID had more than 700,000 users. This number is expected to approach 2.5 million come 2009. At the time of writing, the infrastructure is mainly used for authentication of Internet banking customers, but BankID is extending into other markets, such as the government sector and e-commerce in general. It has also been used in conjunction with e-voting in some companies. BankID won a European prize, namely the *eema Award for Ex-*

Y. Espelid, L-H. Netland, A. N. Klingsheim, and K. J. Hole
NoWires Research Group
Department of Informatics
University of Bergen, Norway
e-mail: {yngvee, larshn, klings, kjellh}@ii.uib.no

* A short version of our work was presented at the conference Financial Cryptography and Data Security 2008 (FC '08) [10].

[1] Not to be confused with the Swedish BankID initiative.

Please use the following format when citing this chapter:

Espelid, Y., et al., 2008, in IFIP International Federation for Information Processing, Volume 278; *Proceedings of the IFIP TC 11 23rd International Information Security Conference*; Sushil Jajodia, Pierangela Samarati, Stelvio Cimato; (Boston: Springer), pp. 63–77.

cellence in Secure Electronic Business in 2006. Within a few years, the Norwegian banking industry wants BankID to become a nationwide identity system.

No detailed technical information about BankID has been released to the general public. Our request to see in-depth descriptions of the architecture and design was met with a non-disclosure signature prerequisite. Moreover, no publicly available independent third party evaluation of the system confirms that BankID meets a minimum of security and privacy requirements. This is worrisome due to a number of reasons: Firstly, a report by the US National Research Council [20] states that public review is essential when developing a nationwide identity system. The social costs of a poorly thought-out system are simply too high to justify.

Secondly, unlike in the US, liability has historically been assigned to the customer in disputes with Norwegian banks. In a previously analyzed court case [16], two expert witnesses turned the ruling in favor of a bank by claiming that the banking systems were very secure. No technical documentation was provided to support this claim.

Thirdly, the banking industry both owns the BankID infrastructure and provides financial services on top of the framework. It is not clear how potential conflicts of interest, involving the bank as a service provider and operator, will be resolved. Uncontested, the combination of no trusted third party and a security-through-secrecy policy could undermine the legal protection of Norwegian bank customers.

Finally, BankID relies on two-factor authentication with One-Time Passwords (OTPs), similar to earlier online banking systems. In 2005, Schneier warned that this form of authentication failed to address recent security challenges, such as phishing, identity theft, and fradulent transactions [23].

A previous paper [18] describes a risk analysis of the BankID infrastructure. In that study, the authors give an overview of the architecture and design of BankID, and pinpoint several weaknesses. Our work was done in parallel with the mentioned evaluation, and examines the therein suggested Man-in-the-Middle (MitM) attack in detail. A short paper on our work was presented at Financial Cryptography and Data Security 2008 [10].

The remainder of this paper is organized as follows: Section 2 provides a short overview of BankID; Section 3 looks at BankID from an adversary's point of view; Section 4 describes a MitM vulnerability in BankID that has been turned into an exploit; Section 5 explains how to make the attack more effective by capitalizing on a bank customer's trust in BankID; Section 6 describes our disclosure process; Section 7 suggests improvements to BankID; Section 8 presents related work; while Sect. 9 concludes the paper.

1.1 Definitions

Individual authentication, referred to as *authentication* for simplicity, is the process of establishing an understood level of confidence that an individual is who he or she claims to be [21]. If the level of confidence is high, the authentication is said to be strong. *Authorization* is the process of deciding what an individual ought to be allowed to do. A *vulnerability* is a weakness that violates the security goals of an information system. An *exploit* is a practical attack—in the form of detailed instructions or program code—utilizing a vulnerability. The attack must have been implemented and successfully run to constitute an exploit.

2 BankID Overview

BankID is modeled after an X.509 Public-Key Infrastructure (PKI), where the banks themselves own and operate the central infrastructure. PKIs have been studied extensively by the computer security community. In addition, many vendors provide PKI solutions in the commercial marketplace. Hence, there is a strong theoretical foundation for important PKI principles as well as extensive practical experience gained from implementing and running PKIs. A good introduction to PKIs can be found in [1].

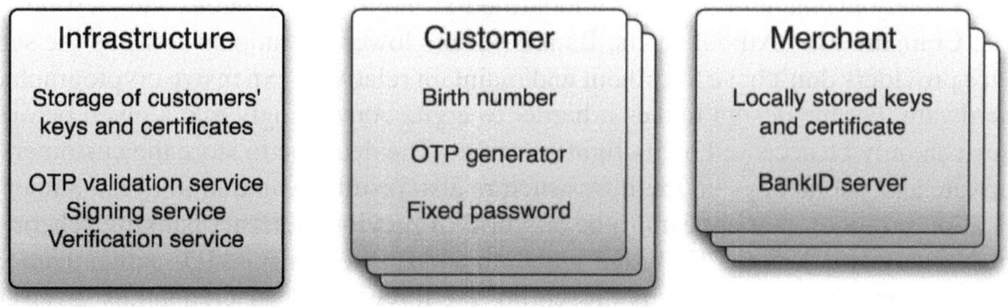

Fig. 1 Entities in BankID

Useful insights into BankID can be obtained from a white paper released by the BankID project [25], and by enrolling as a customer of the PKI. The system is built around three general entities: a central *infrastructure*, *customers*, and online *merchants*. The individual parties, their credentials, and duties are summarized in Fig. 1. An Internet bank is one example of a BankID merchant. In one of the participating banks, new customers sign up for BankID on the Web. Shortly after becoming a member, the customer receives an OTP generator and a fixed password by unregistered mail. When logging into the bank with BankID, customers use their Norwegian birth number[2] for identification, and an OTP in combination with the fixed password for authentication. People who sign up with more than one bank can choose freely among their OTP tools when using BankID. The PKI functionality provided by BankID is transparent to customers, as their private-public key pairs

[2] Norwegian birth numbers uniquely identify Norwegian citizens. These are similar to the US Social Security numbers.

are stored and controlled by the infrastructure. PKI services, such as creating and verifying digital signatures, are performed centrally on behalf of the users. Merchants store and control their own cryptographic keys and rely on server software distributed by the BankID project.

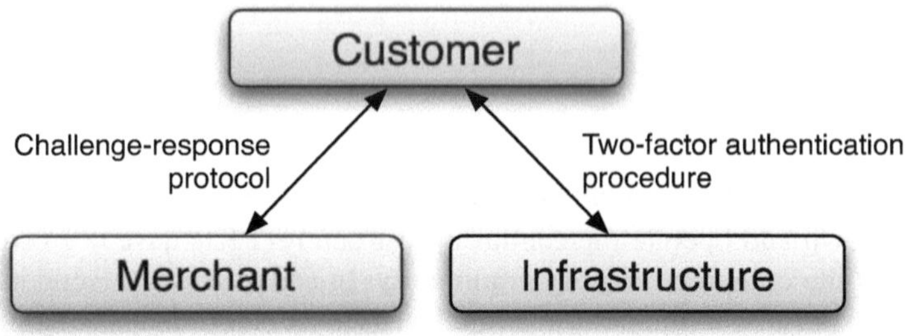

Fig. 2 BankID authentication procedure from the customer's point of view

The BankID design differs from a typical X.509 PKI, which requires private keys to be solely available to the entity identified in the matching public-key certificate [1]. Compared to textbook PKIs, BankID offers lower operational costs as the service providers don't have to roll out and maintain relatively expensive cryptographic hardware, but the design makes it harder to argue convincingly that a given private key can only be accessed by its rightful owner. The decision to store the customers' private and public keys on the infrastructure also results in an untraditional authentication protocol, that appears to be a hybrid of previous Internet banking schemes in Norway and X.509 PKI based authentication. Prior to BankID, authentication typically involved bank clients presenting the three customer credentials given in Fig. 1 to the banking system. The new design, depicted in Fig. 2, involves a longer protocol:

- The customer presents her birth number, OTP, and fixed password to the central infrastructure. This action unlocks PKI functionality on the infrastructure.
- The customer engages in a challenge-response protocol with the merchant. The infrastructure handles all PKI operations on behalf of the user.

A closer look at BankID's architecture and design can be found in [18].

2.1 The BankID Applet

A Java applet [24] is central in the authentication procedure depicted in Fig. 2. The applet is readily available from the central infrastructure.

The following scenario describes a typical BankID session involving bill payment for Internet banking customers. First, the client visits her bank's log-in page, which instructs her browser to download the applet from the central infrastructure.

The applet initiates the previously described authentication procedure. Upon successful authentication, an HTTPS session loads in the customer's browser. Now, the client can fill out payment details. Upon submitting the bill, the applet is reinitialized in the customer's browser, prompting her for credentials to sign the transaction. After submitting a fresh OTP and the private-key password, the transaction is processed. Next, the customer can continue the HTTPS session or terminate the bank session by logging out.

3 An Adverserial View into BankID

Attackers use a variety of tactics to break the security of software systems. A common strategy is to start by gathering information about the target. A detailed profile on an application allows attackers to apply their resources in the potentially most rewarding places. Upon mapping out the target, adversaries are wise to consider common vulnerabilities, as studies show that systems often fail for the same reasons. Common techniques used by attackers have been documented at length by the software security community, e.g. [4, 15, 19].

In terms of BankID, an interesting observation is the centralized key storage that contradicts advice given in the security literature. The resulting authentication protocol should draw the attention of attackers, because the development of new secure cryptographic protocols is a difficult undertaking. So much so that security experts strongly discourage the practice of "rolling your own" cryptography [26].

3.1 Reverse Engineering the Authentication Protocol

An inspection of merchant web pages reveals that the BankID applet is initialized by HTML parameters. One parameter specifies the address to the infrastructure server running the two-factor authentication procedure. Another parameter controls the location of the merchant server carrying out the challenge-response protocol. Consequently, all merchants can use the same applet by configuring these initialization parameters.

The applet initialization parameters can be altered so that the applet communicates with BankID software through a proxy controlled by an attacker. This allows adversaries to produce a blueprint of the BankID authentication procedure.

A walk-through of the customer authentication is provided by Fig. 3. The broken vertical lines represent the three main entities' lifelines. When entities interact, activation bars overlay their lifelines. The customer's activation bar represents the browser running on her computer. The grey and partially overlapping activation bar symbolizes the applet running in her browser.

Steps 1 through 4 in the figure show how merchants bootstrap the authentication process. The customer downloads an HTML page from the merchant, which

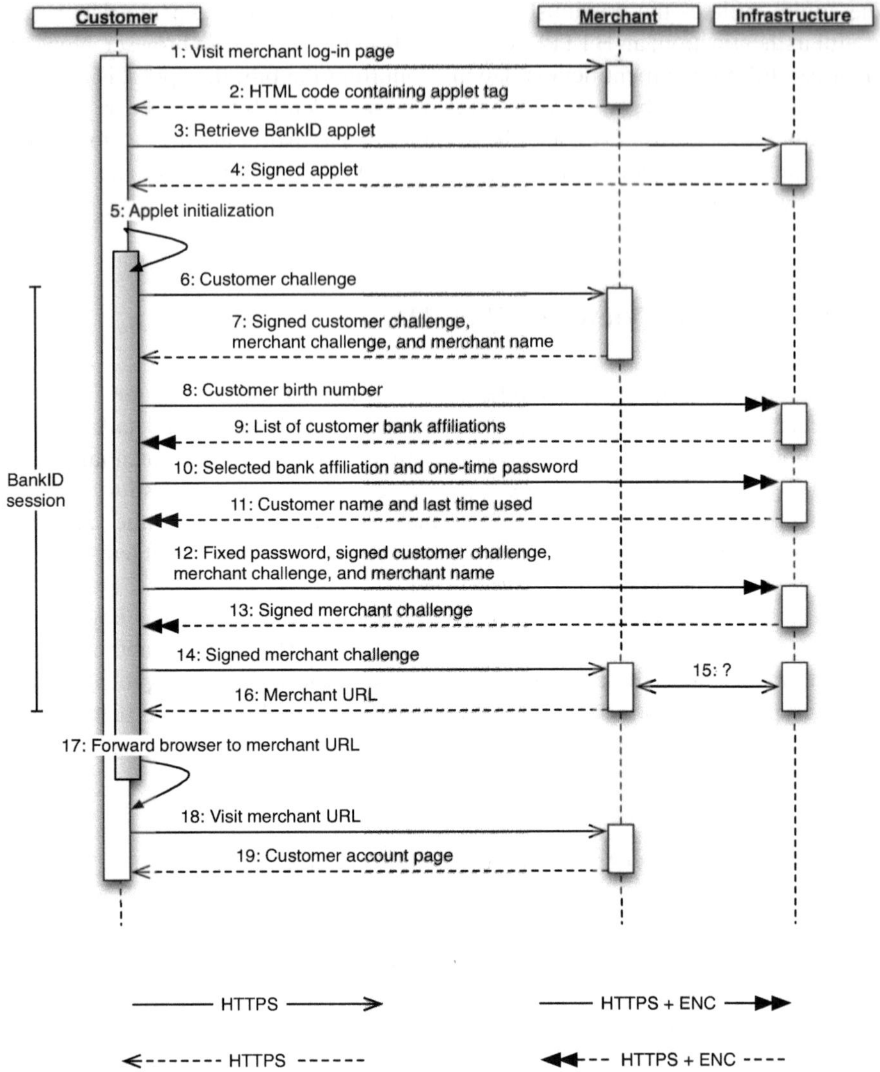

Fig. 3 Authentication process

instructs the customer's browser to retrieve the signed applet from the central infrastructure. These interactions run over HTTPS. The browser automatically verifies the applet signature, and prompts the user to trust the applet.

On customer acceptance, the applet is initialized in step 5. The applet is the catalyst for the authentication protocol and manages the BankID session, depicted as steps 6 through 16. Two stages, numbered in accordance with Fig. 3, initiate the challenge-response protocol:

6. The applet generates and sends a challenge to the merchant.
7. The merchant signs the customer challenge and generates a challenge to the customer. These challenges, along with the merchant name, are sent to the customer.

Steps 8 through 13 make up the two-factor authentication procedure necessary to unlock the customer's PKI credentials on the central infrastructure and sign the challenge. This communication has an additional layer of encryption, denoted ENC in Fig. 3, which denies the proxy the possibility to determine the content of that part of the protocol. Hence, the following dialogue is partially guesswork based on observations of network activity and the applet's response to customer input:

8. The customer inputs her birth number for identification.
9. The infrastructure returns a list of her BankID affiliations.
10. The customer chooses a bank and enters an OTP.
11. On valid OTP, the infrastructure returns the customer's name and the time when BankID was last used.
12. The signed customer challenge, the merchant challenge to sign, the name of the merchant, and the fixed customer password, are sent to the infrastructure.
13. The infrastructure verifies the merchant signature and uses the customer's private key to sign the merchant challenge, which it returns to the customer.

This concludes our guesswork. The applet now completes the challenge-response protocol with the merchant:

14. The signed merchant challenge is returned to the merchant.
15. We assume that the merchant and the infrastructure communicate to determine the customer's identity and verify the signature.
16. If the challenge-response protocol is successful, the merchant sends a URL to the customer.

Step 16 completes the authentication protocol, and the customer continues an HTTPS session with the merchant as illustrated by steps 17 through 19.

3.2 Reverse Code Engineering

Java byte code is easily reverse engineered and can reveal a program's inner workings to an attacker. When reverse engineering the BankID applet, we found the additional layer of encryption in steps 8–13 in Fig. 3 intriguing and made some interesting observations. As it turns out, three public keys belonging to the infrastructure are hardcoded in the applet. These are linked to different infrastructure services, namely OTP validation, signing, and verification.

In a customer request to the infrastructure, the applet generates a symmetric key used to encrypt the query. This key is encrypted with the service's public key and appended to the request. Using its private key, the service can decrypt the symmetric

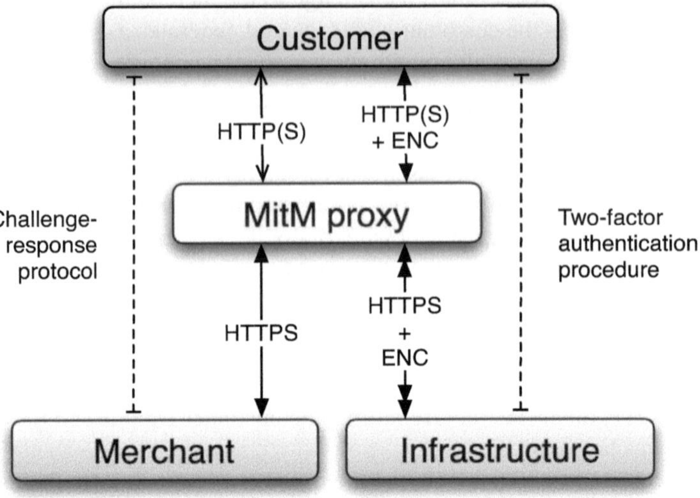

Fig. 4 The MitM proxy in the authentication protocol

key, and in turn decrypt the query. The same symmetric key is used to encrypt the response to the customer. A new key is created for each request.

Another observation from the code study is the use of the core Java class `SecureRandom`. This class provides a pseudo-random number generator. A study of the code segment generating symmetric encryption keys revealed a possible vulnerability. The running Java version affects whether the `SecureRandom` instance seeds itself or by an algorithm in the applet. Given Java version prior to 1.4, current time, amount of free memory, and loop counters are used to compute the seed. A cryptanalysis can determine the strength of both the seeding technique and the encryption algorithm. However, we chose to focus on session management issues in BankID.

4 An Exploit Against BankID

As mentioned in Sect. 3, by changing two initialization parameters, the applet willingly communicates—over either HTTP or HTTPS—with the MitM proxy depicted in Fig. 4. The proxy learns the communication between the applet and the merchant, which is sufficient to obtain an authorized session to the merchant. The attack is carried out through the following steps:

1. Trick the user into initializing the applet with malicious parameters.
2. Start the HTTPS session between the MitM proxy and the merchant to obtain a session ID (this identifier is not shown in Fig. 3.)

3. Relay the BankID session until the authentication completes.
4. Seize the HTTPS session to the merchant after the authentication is completed (step 16, Fig. 3.)

The attack can be explained in terms of session management. Conceptually, two sessions exist; a regular HTTPS session between the customer and the merchant, and the BankID session involving the infrastructure, the merchant, and the customer, as shown in Fig. 3. A discrepancy between these sessions enables the MitM attack. First, only the merchant server is authenticated in the HTTPS session, enabling the MitM proxy to initiate a session on behalf of the customer. Then the customer and the merchant are mutually authenticated through the BankID session, which is simply relayed by the MitM proxy. Finally, the authorization granted to the customer in the BankID session is transferred to the HTTPS session controlled by the MitM proxy, and the attack is successful (step 16, Fig. 3).

Note that the attack uses the signed applet from the infrastructure, turning it into an attack tool against BankID.

4.1 Proof of Concept

The previously described vulnerability was turned into an exploit against two randomly chosen Norwegian online banking systems in March 2007. Both attempts gave access to a customer account in these banks. The BankID community claimed to have fixed the problem in November 2007. A slightly modified version of the first exploit was successfully launched against BankID again in December 2007, using a version rollback attack. In short, an old version of the BankID applet was used to sidestep the countermeasures implemented in November 2007. The BankID community then introduced additional security measures in January 2008, thereby stopping our rollback attack.

5 Attack Considerations

The MitM attack can be bootstrapped in multiple ways, using well known attack strategies. Phishing attacks are already plaguing the banking industry, and can be used to trick some users into opening a webpage from the MitM proxy.

Nordic banks have been pestered over the last year by man-in-the-browser attacks [13]—trojan horses installed in web browsers. A trojan could change the parameters to the applet when the customer visits her online bank. This would be extremely difficult to detect for the average user.

5.1 Trust Management Capitalization

Trust can be defined as a positive expectation regarding the behavior of someone or something in a situation that entails risk to the trusting party [9, p. 77]. Risk is simply the possibility of suffering harm or loss. It is important to note that, unlike in the X.509 PKI specification [1], trust in this context is not a binary concept but involves many levels of trust. For any given user, there is a certain amount of trust that is needed to be willing to transact. Let this level be denoted the *cooperation threshold* [22]. In order to get the most out of the attack against BankID, an adversary wants as many customers as possible to reach the cooperation threshold. The BankID design helps achieve this goal.

Assume that an attacker decides to bootstrap the BankID attack with an e-mail phishing scheme. A press release from Gartner indicates that approximately 19% of phishing targets click on a link in a malicious e-mail, and that 3% give financial or personal information to phishers [11]. The numbers illustrate that the success rate relies firstly on the cleverness of the phishing e-mail, and secondly on the trustworthiness of the phishing site. We discuss our attack in conjunction with the latter.

Recall that the signed BankID applet is loaded unmodified from the BankID infrastructure. Hence, the user carries out a seemingly regular authentication procedure. The browser successfully validates the applet signature and displays a certificate belonging to the BankID infrastructure. This is ideal in winning the trust of customers, as they are carefully instructed to look for this when using BankID [5]. Furthermore, the user is presented with this information before the webpage is rendered. The user's attention is drawn to the applet—not to the webpage or the MitM proxy's URL in the address bar. Hence, the important first step towards the cooperation threshold is taken before the malicious webpage is shown to the user.

The next step is to present a webpage visually indistinguishable from the merchant's authentic webpage. The only indication of an attack will then be in the address bar of the victim's browser. Phishers use a variety of tactics to manipulate this bar. If a merchant website has a cross-site scripting vulnerability [19], the success rate of the attack could rise further by capitalizing on the customer's trust in the merchant's own website. Upon completing the authentication, the attacker assumes control of the real BankID session. The information sent to the customer after this point can be crafted so that the he still believes that the attack was a legitimate log-in attempt.

Norwegian banks currently use OTPs and fixed passwords to authorize transactions. Therefore, the attacker must collect at least one OTP and the password to transfer money out of the account. This can be achieved by alerting the user at the end of the log-in procedure that the previously entered fixed password and OTP were incorrect, after which the attacker asks for them again. Upon receiving the credentials, the attacker sends the customer one of the bank's standard error messages. This last step is a standard phishing technique. However, the customer has already reached the cooperation threshold and should take the bait.

6 The Disclosure Process

The discovery of the BankID MitM vulnerability and the subsequent exploit urgently called for countermeasures from the BankID community. Building on insights from the BankID risk analysis [18], our team needed less than a month to break into Norwegian Internet banks using BankID. Taking into account that the attack relies on techniques well-known to malicious hackers, it was reasonable to conclude that our attack posed a significant risk for BankID customers.

According to a survey [7], the world's largest software companies encourage some variant of *responsible disclosure* [8] when independent researchers find vulnerabilities in their products. Inspired by responsible disclosure, we informed major stakeholders in the BankID community, namely Bankenes Standardiseringskontor (BSK) and The Norwegian Banks Payment and Clearing Centre (BBS), about the MitM vulnerability in March '07. The Financial Supervisory Authority of Norway (FSAN) was also informed about the problem at this point. On request, BSK also received a technical description of how the BankID vulnerability could be turned into an exploit. They later responded that the vulnerability had been removed in January, i.e. before we developed the proof of concept code.

Unable to convince the system owners about the dangers posed by the exploit, we released the interim report "Next Generation Internet Banking in Norway" on May 16th [18]. This work points out weaknesses in BankID, and explicitly states that we had developed a proof of concept attack against BankID. Our discovery was reported by several media outlets, but did not spark a broad discussion around BankID as a nationwide identity system candidate.

In September and October '07 we demonstrated the MitM exploit for FSAN and a group of security experts with influence on the Norwegian banking industry, hoping that this would get the attention of the BankID community. A month later we distributed an early version of this paper to BSK, BBS, and the BankID coordinator. In November '07 we again told of the exploit in a large Norwegian newspaper [12]. In the subsequent debate, the banks claimed to have addressed our attack in a November patch, and questioned the lawfulness of our security testing. In early December '07 our attack caught the attention of members of the Norwegian Parliament, and was scheduled for a Question Time session.

By using a version rollback attack, the exploit was again successfully run against the previously vulnerable Internet banks on December 18th. Hence, the BankID community had spent eight months coming up with a fix that did not work. During this time period the banks neither seeked our counsel nor asked for another test. Having failed to establish a productive dialogue with the system owners, we decided to look at other alternatives for improving the situation.

Full disclosure of an exploit on a live banking system with close to one million users seemed drastic. Still, banking customers had for at least nine months believed BankID to be secure, while our exploit showed that the user community had been and continued to be exposed to an unnecessary high risk. In the end, we chose to revisit responsible disclosure, but this time with FSAN as a coordinator. In January

'08 we were informed that new countermeasures had been introduced in BankID to prevent our rollback attack. We have not analyzed these security measures in detail.

7 Possible BankID Improvements

Due to lack of complete information on the BankID system we can only give some general recommendations on how to improve the security through changes to the applet itself. In future versions of the BankID applet, the session discrepancy discussed in Sect. 4 should be corrected to mitigate the risk posed by our exploit. The applet needs to properly authenticate its communication peers, enabling it to detect a MitM proxy. Also, the applet must require end-to-end encryption when communicating with both the infrastructure and the merchant. To achieve these goals the applet can require HTTPS when connecting to the infrastructure and the merchant, and explicitly check that the authenticated server is the correct one. Input validation [19], such as a whitelisting approach, can be useful to avoid hostile communication points. We leave it to the BankID community to evaluate the feasibility of this approach.

In the long-term, the BankID community should evaluate the implications of moving to a traditional PKI where the clients possess their own private-public key pairs. The move would improve the strength of the authentication, and yield a simpler design. Also, several of the problems identified in [18] could be reduced or solved. Such a change comes with a cost. However, a national security infrastructure must fulfill minimum security requirements, including resistance to MitM attacks, and offer strong authentication. Many countries around the world have already put to use, or are contemplating national identity systems based on PKI and cryptographic smartcards. Hence, there are many experiences around the world that should be taken into consideration if the BankID community decides to offer a traditional PKI.

8 Related Work

A series of three articles analyze Norwegian banking systems [17, 16, 18]. The first paper shows that some Norwegian banks were vulnerable to a combined brute-force and distributed denial-of-service attack in 2003 and 2004. The authors go on to discuss the effects of the banks' security-through-secrecy policy, concluding that it prohibits learning and causes the same mistakes to be repeated. The second paper elaborates on the problems with a bank's non-disclosure policy in a Norwegian court case. The third paper contains a risk analysis of BankID from the customer's point of view. It concludes that users of BankID are exposed to a number of significant risks that should be mitigated. Our attack builds on the above-mentioned article series and zooms in on weaknesses touched upon in the risk analysis of BankID [18]. In particular, our work further testify to the inefficacy of the banks' security-through-secrecy policy.

According to an IBM white paper [14], the two-factor authentication schemes widely adopted by online banks are insufficient in protecting against combined phishing and MitM attacks. An adversary first sends a phishing e-mail to the banking customer with a link to a proxy controlled by the attacker. If the victim takes the bait, the adversary plays an active role in the log-in process by relaying user input to the bank and the bank's responses back to the user. Upon completing authentication, the attacker can seize the session or mix fraudulent transactions with the users legitimate transactions.

Our attack uses elements of a combined phishing and MitM attack, but goes further by using the bank's own software, the BankID applet, to gain the victim's trust. The BankID attack starts as a phishing attack with a phishing e-mail to the bank customer, but continues with loading the unmodified and digitally signed BankID applet instead of a fake applet. By doing so, an adversary abuses a crucial point of trust in BankID. The unmodifiable applet, formerly a disadvantage to an attacker, becomes an advantage in terms of gaining the trust of banking customers. After finishing the applet log-in procedure, the attack procedes as in the combined phishing and MitM attack, where the attacker must trick the victim into supplying his OTP and fixed password.

In [2], Anderson argues that a false threat model was accepted, due to the lack of feedback on why British retail banking systems failed. In doing so, the financial industry developed increasingly complex systems to protect against cryptanalysis and technical attacks, when it would have been wiser to focus on implementation and managerial failures. Analyses of banking systems published after Anderson's initial paper underscore the observation that systems fail not because of inadequate cryptographic primitives, but rather design flaws and implementation errors [6, 3].

9 Conclusion

The security of the Norwegian banking industry's new PKI solution, BankID, was repeatedly broken in '07. A MitM attack enabled attackers to access customer accounts in two online banks. Our attack used techniques well-known to cyber criminals and was based solely on public information. An exploit was demonstrated for FSAN and a group of security professionals to highlight the severity of the problem.

BankID's untraditional design hinders the system from providing a high level of security. The decision to store customers' private-public key pairs in a central location has resulted in a weak authentication protocol. A redesign of BankID is called for if the system is to offer the intended degree of security.

Our exploit underscores the importance of independent evaluation of national systems. BankID's design flaw contradicts advice given by security experts, and should have been detected and resolved long before the system was put into production. An unbiased scrutinization of the infrastructure and its documentation by leading security analysts would most likely have identified the problem.

The BankID community needs to improve their risk management processes. Today, the system owners fail to identify and quickly resolve problems. This was demonstrated to us by the nine months it took the banks to address our initial exploit. The subsequent version rollback attack further testifies to the inefficacy of BankID's current risk management processes.

As BankID is now gaining serious momentum in Norway—and is pushed by the BankID community to become the main identity system in Norway—both government and citizens need a better perception of the true level of security. In light of our attacks and the findings in [18], a thorough analysis of BankID is called for. This could increase the trustworthiness of BankID in the long run. At the time of writing the gap is too big between the actual level of security, and how the BankID community describes their system (see `www.bankid.no`.)

9.1 Final Remark

We would like to emphasize that only BankID accounts belonging to members of the NoWires Research Group were used to develop and demonstrate the MitM attack. No accounts belonging to others were involved in any way during our work with this paper.

References

1. Adams, C., Lloyd, S.: Understanding PKI—Concepts, Standards, and Deployment Considerations, 2nd edn. Addison-Wesley (2003)
2. Anderson, R.: Why cryptosystems fail. In: ACM 1st Conference on Computer and Communication Security. Fairfax, VA, USA (1993)
3. Anderson, R., Bond, M., Clulow, J., Skorobogatov, S.: Cryptographic processors—a survey. Technical Report 641, University of Cambridge (2005). URL http://www.cl.cam.ac.uk/~mkb23/research/Survey.pdf
4. Andrews, M., Whittaker, J.A.: How to Break Web Software—Functional and Security Testing of Web Applications and Web Services. Addison-Wesley (2006)
5. BankID: Hva gjør kunden ved mistanke om at noe er galt? (2007). URL http://www.bankid.no/index.db2?id=4066. Last checked March 2008 (in Norwegian)
6. Berkman, O., Ostrovsky, O.M.: The unbearable lightness of pin cracking. In: Financial Cryptography and Data Security (FC). Lowlands, Scarborough, Trinidad/Tobago (2007). URL http://www.arx.com/documents/The_Unbearable_Lightness_of_PIN_Cracking.pdf
7. Biancuzzi, F.: Disclosure Survey (2006). URL http://www.securityfocus.com/columnists/415. Last checked March 2008
8. Christey, S., Wysopal, C.: Responsible vulnerability disclosure process (2002). URL http://www.whitehats.ca/main/about_us/policies/draft-christey-wysopal-vuln-disclosure-00.txt. Last checked March 2008

9. Cranor, L.F., Garfinkel, S. (eds.): Security and Usability—Designing Secure Systems That People Can Use. O'Reilly (2005)
10. Espelid, Y., Netland, L.H., Klingsheim, A.N., Hole, K.J.: A proof of concept attack against norwegian internet banking systems. In: Proc. Financial Cryptography and Data Security (2008)
11. Gartner: Gartner study finds significant increase in e-mail phishing attacks (2004). URL `http://www.gartner.com/press_releases/asset_71087_11.html`. Last checked March 2008
12. Gjøsteen, K., Hole, K.J.: Nei, ennå ikke trygg. Aftenposten (29. Nov, 2007). URL `http://www.aftenposten.no/meninger/debatt/article2126133.ece`. Last checked March 2008 (in Norwegian)
13. Gühring, P.: Concepts against man-in-the-browser attacks (2006). URL `http://www2.futureware.at/svn/sourcerer/CAcert/SecureClient.pdf`. Last checked March 2008
14. Gundel, T.: Phishing and internet banking security (2005). URL `ftp://ftp.software.ibm.com/software/tivoli/whitepapers/Phishing_and_Internet_Banking_Security.pdf`
15. Hoglund, G., McGraw, G.: Exploiting Software—How to Break Code. Addison-Wesley (2004)
16. Hole, K.J., Moen, V., Klingsheim, A.N., Tande, K.M.: Lessons from the Norwegian ATM system. IEEE Security & Privacy **5**(6), 25–31 (2007)
17. Hole, K.J., Moen, V., Tjøstheim, T.: Case study: Online banking security. IEEE Security & Privacy **4**(2), 14–20 (2006)
18. Hole, K.J., Tjøstheim, T., Moen, V., Netland, L., Espelid, Y., Klingsheim, A.N.: Next generation internet banking in Norway. Tech. Rep. 371, Institute of Informatics, University of Bergen (2008). Available at: `http://www.ii.uib.no/publikasjoner/texrap/pdf/2008-371.pdf`
19. Huseby, S.H.: Innocent Code. Wiley (2004)
20. Kent, S.T., Millett, L.I. (eds.): IDs—Not That Easy: Questions About Nationwide Identity Systems. The National Academies Press (2002)
21. Kent, S.T., Millett, L.I. (eds.): Who Goes There? Authentication Through the Lens of Privacy. The National Academies Press (2003)
22. Marsh, S., Dibben, M.R.: Trust, untrust, distrust and mistrust—an exploration of the dark(er) side. In: iTrust 2005, *LNCS*, vol. 3477, pp. 17–33. Springer (2005)
23. Schneier, B.: Two-factor authentication: too little, too late. Communications of the ACM **48**(4), 136 (2005)
24. Sun Microsystems, Inc.: Applets. URL `http://java.sun.com/applets/`. Last checked March 2008
25. The Norwegian Banks' Payment and Clearing Centre: BankID FOI white paper (Release 2.0.0) (2006). (in Norwegian)
26. Viega, J., McGraw, G.: Building Secure Software—How to Avoid Security Problems the Right Way. Addison-Wesley (2002)

Collaborative architecture for malware detection and analysis

Michele Colajanni, Daniele Gozzi, and Mirco Marchetti

Abstract The constant increase of malware threats clearly shows that the present countermeasures are not sufficient especially because most actions are put in place only when infections have already spread. In this paper, we present an innovative collaborative architecture for malware analysis that aims to early detection and timely deployment of countermeasures. The proposed system is a multi-tier architecture where the sensor nodes are geographically distributed over multiple organizations. These nodes send alerts to intermediate managers that, in their turn, communicate with one logical collector and analyzer. Relevant information, that is determined by the automatic analysis of the malware behavior in a sandbox, and countermeasures are sent to all the cooperating networks. There are many other novel features in the proposal. The architecture is extremely scalable and flexible because multiple levels of intermediate managers can be utilized depending on the complexity of the network of the participating organization. Cyphered communications among components help preventing the leakage of sensitive information and allow the pairwise authentication of the nodes involved in the information sharing. The feasibility of the proposed architecture is demonstrated through an operative prototype realized using open source software.

1 Introduction

It is pointless to repeat once again that the global network is growing steadily and fast, and that the attached hosts are becoming more and more tightly connected (for example with the shift from dial-up PSTN connections to broadband xDSL and cable-TV connections). The increasing phenomenon of botnet infections is a real threat to organizations which rely heavily on their web presence. Some evidences

Department of Computer Engineering, University of Modena and Reggio Emilia, e-mail: michele.colajanni@unimore.it, e-mail: daniele.gozzi@unimore.it, e-mail: mirco.marchetti@unimore.it

Please use the following format when citing this chapter:

Colajanni, M., Gozzi, D. and Marchetti, M., 2008, in IFIP International Federation for Information Processing, Volume 278; *Proceedings of the IFIP TC 11 23rd International Information Security Conference*; Sushil Jajodia, Pierangela Samarati, Stelvio Cimato; (Boston: Springer), pp. 79–93.

have been found that connect large botnets with organized crime, so voiding the influence of this type of worms is not any more just a matter of computer security.

The present defense mechanisms against the most virulent forms of malware and botnets are clearly inadequate. Some estimates [1] show that the Storm worm reached two million machines, thus giving its owner a computing power theoretically higher than the world's top supercomputers. Other recent data concerning worm spread can be obtained from the ShadowServer site [2]. Any domestic personal computer is heavily targeted by self-replicating malware when it is connected to an ADSL line. (We recorded through the honeypot Nepenthes [3] 10464 infection attempts over a 178 hour period, which is about one attempt per minute on average.)

The usual defense mechanisms aim to apply patches on demand well past the first attack attempt and the discovery of a new vulnerability. For a safer diffusion of the Internet-based services, we think it is important to move from independent and late defenses to coordinated, timely and possibly preventive countermeasures.

We present an innovative collaborative architecture that aims to anticipate malware detection, analysis and related countermeasures. The cooperation between heterogeneous and geographically distributed networks can be especially useful to fight autonomously spreading malware (i.e., worms) that represents the main focus of this paper. For example, most negative effects of malware and botnet spreading can be mitigated by simple packet filtering policies that must be activated as soon as possible. Unfortunately, each network implements this type of countermeasures in an individual fashion, without any knowledge of what is happening in other networks. In our proposal that allows different networks to cooperate, all information about a new malware type (threats, how is spreading, which kind of vulnerabilities it exploits, which software application or operating system can be affected, countermeasures) gathered by one sensor is propagated in a fast, reliable and trusted way with the goal of preventing the infection in other not yet touched networks.

The proposed architecture has several innovative features. Unlike the few existing collaborative systems that are mainly oriented to spam fighting, the proposed system is oriented to malware detection, analysis and communication of security threats. Its flexibility and scalability is intrinsic in the architecture design that is based on a decentralized communication scheme and a multi-tiered hierarchy of geographically distributed components. The proposed solution is general and takes advantage of the knowledge of each participant on its network part while requiring a very unobtrusive trust scheme. Cross-organization security initiatives are rarely seen even if some interesting solutions for partial information disclosure have been presented [4].

Current initiatives which require the cooperation of many users to collect malware represent an appreciable start, but most of the analysis work is still manual and there is a strict separation between anti-malware research and deployment of countermeasures. On the other hand, the proposed architecture needs a limited or null human intervention that differentiates it from analogous solutions in similar fields. Finally, it is worth to observe that we take advantage of honeypot properties to share information without raising privacy concerns between different organizations.

The remainder of this paper is structured as follows. In Section 2, we evidence the contribution of this paper with respect to the literature. In Section 3, we give an overall description of the cooperation architecture and the details of the main components. In Section (4) we describe the implementation of a prototype version of the proposed architecture. In Section 5, we present the results of some experimental tests. Finally, in section 6 we state our conclusions and outline future research work opened by this paper.

2 Related work

A cooperative multi-tiered hierarchy of geographically distributed components for fighting malware represents an original proposal. However, other interesting cross-organization security initiatives exist. We can cite the DNS black lists (DNSBL) [5], Botnet investigation [6, 2], IDS alert correlation frameworks [7, 8], partial information disclosure [4].

DNS black lists (DNSBL) are one of the existing automated facilities for limiting the activities of suspicious hosts, but they are still highly focused on a single service (email). Our approach is general and avoids blacklists, since many home Internet connections have dynamic IP addresses and the inclusion of such addresses would be detrimental to the efficacy of the blacklist and to the user experience.

Investigation of botnets is still highly manual. The existing efforts are more oriented to help law enforcement agencies, but not so much to limit malware spread. Instead, we aim mainly to counter worm infections and botnet activities from a technical point of view. The absence of just one common countermeasure deployment approach is an intentional goal of the designed architecture that intends to avoid overreactions and prevent denials of service induced by attackers with specially crafted malware.

Current NIDS alert correlation frameworks are rarely (if at all) seen in a cross-organization deployment. We insist once again on the benefits of intrusion information sharing and we propose a cooperative architecture where each participant has to trust only two other parties (its Manager and the Collector, as evidenced in section 3) and communication is authenticated and encrypted. The pairwise trust scheme and cyphered communications among the components represent other interesting novel features of the proposal, although similar solutions have been suggested in other contexts [9, 10, 11]. The benefits of cooperation are not indirect: each participant is notified timely of security threats collected from any cooperating organization. The shared data does not need any modification for increased anonymity, since the involved hosts are an attacker and a honeypot.

Malware collection organizations, such as the *mwcollect Alliance* [12], focus on grasping the dynamics of infection spreading and detecting new malware types and variants. This operation is carried out mainly through manual analysis of binary code and extraction of call graphs. We seek to obtain a substantial reduction of the human interaction required for identifying new malware.

The system design guarantees an intrinsic flexibility and scalability that, to the best of our knowledge, cannot be found in any existing proposal as a priority architecture requirement.

3 Architecture design

The growing proliferation of Internet worms is mainly due to their non-stopping evolution of the spreading and replication mechanisms, which have traversed several stages:

1. automated infection of vulnerable network services on servers (e.g. [13]);
2. automated infection of vulnerable collateral network services on desktop computers (e.g., [14]);
3. email spreading, where the attack code is activated by unaware users (e.g., [15]);
4. email spreading, where infection is based on a mail user agent vulnerability (e.g., [16]);
5. infection of vulnerable Web applications, often carried out through XSS techniques; the search for vulnerable targets is made through web search engines (e.g., [17]);
6. infection of the client side execution environment (JavaScript or Flash) in rich Web applications, such as the lOrdOfthenOOse and EricAndrew worms [18].

The main types of malware that the present version of our architecture is targeting are those of types 1 and 2. The scheme in Figure 1 describes the main components of the proposed multi-tier system: sensors, managers, collector. In this section we describe each component and show how this solution can be scaled to become a massive geographically distributed network of cooperating honeypots.

3.1 Sensors

We define a cooperating network as a honeypot sensor installation in a remote location. The sensor is able to collect infection attempts from its location and collect the payloads of the offending worms. Ideally, each machine connected to the Internet has the same chance of being targeted by a worm, however the presence of firewalls in some organizations internal networks has the effect of slowing the infection because some protocols are blocked for inbound connections. The capillary distribution of honeypot sensors grants a thorough monitoring of malware spread, but the locally stored malware payloads have to be transferred to a collection point where they are further analyzed through some behavior and safe supervision. Malware collection should abstract from the topology of the underlying networks, and a single point of connection between the cooperating networks is aimed at preventing the disclosure of the the internal network structures.

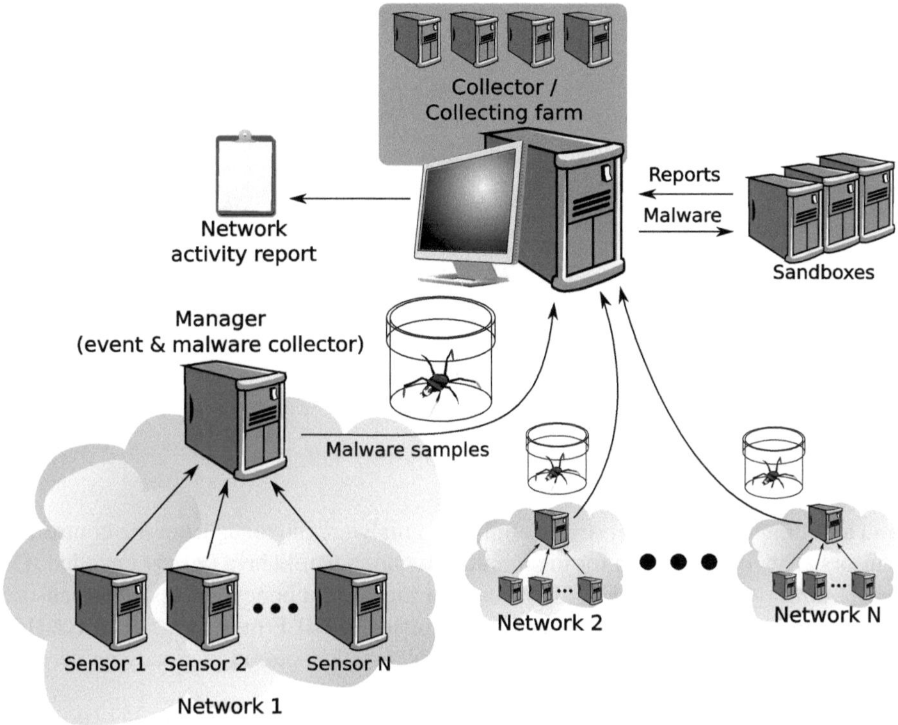

Fig. 1 Cooperative architecture for malware detection and analysis

The edge level of the proposed architecture is composed of *sensors*, which could be every type of IDMEF [19] event generator. However, low interaction honeypots, such as Nepenthes [3], are the best suited sensor type for our purpose, as they are able to collect copies of the malware payload while guaranteeing a continuous operation.

Upon collection, the malware payload samples are sorted on the basis of their MD5 hash. This solution prevents the collection of duplicate binaries, although the chance of hash collisions is not null. Novel malware is marked as different from known malware because its MD5 hash is unknown. Polymorphic malware spans over many hashes while having actually the same behavior and the operation needed for correlating the different hashes of the same malware as the mwcollect Alliance does is currently manual. We will describe in section 3.3 how to address this issue.

3.2 Managers

Managers are the architecture nodes which collect alerts and payloads from the set of sensors. A manager installation is composed by a Manager process (e.g., Prelude)

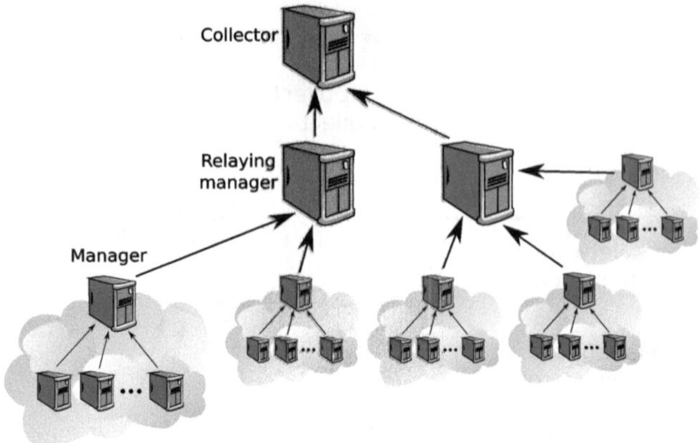

Fig. 2 Hierarchical organization of managers

and a polling agent which retrieves unknown malware payloads from the controlled sensors. The ideal location for the malware payload would be a *base64* encoded IDMEF *AdditionalData* element [19], however the current honeypots tested as sensors do not provide a payload transfer facility inside IDMEF messages. To solve this problem, we utilize a script which periodically lists captured payloads on sensors and retrieves those with an unknown MD5 hash.

The managers can be configured in a relaying way. As Figure 2 shows, the alert and payload collection nodes are connected as a hierarchy. This topology maximizes the collection capability while keeping low the number of transferred payloads, because the payloads are transferred to a higher level manager only if they are not already present there. This solution guarantees the transmission of each new malware variant to the collector .

The flexibility of the architecture is guaranteed by the possibility of having any number of manager levels. In such a way, small organizations can connect its sensor(s) directly to a remote manager; complex organizations can have multiple levels of managers that are controlled locally and connected to one or multiple remote managers.

3.3 Collector

The *Collector* is the top element of the hierarchical architecture. Each cooperating network contributes to the collection of malware hosted by the Collector. For each incoming malware sample, the collector runs an automated thorough analysis by means of local and external tools. The result of the analysis is stored and utilized to classify the malware. In our test case, the collector forwards the malware to some remote sandbox services and sends an email to the administrators of all cooperating networks with the analysis results that evidence also the ports and the protocols involved in the malware remote controlling. It is important to observe that, to avoid system bottleneck and single points of failure, the collector is one logical component that actually runs on a cluster of machines.

Cyphering and polymorphism mechanisms may be applied to the worm code both if the worm is spread in a binary form or as a script: binaries can be altered by polymorphisms, while scripts may be obfuscated. These attacker strategies makes extremely difficult the worm classification as a single phenomenon, and this problem affects mostly the reverse engineering of the worm code. Worm detection is usually done through signature checking which becomes harder because of an increased number of signatures in the case of polymorphic malware. However, the *perfect* polymorphic engine (one that can change all the malware code at each attack) has yet to come. After a first classification through the MD5 hash, the mwcollect Alliance currently employs custom hash functions to classify the variants of the same worm with polymorphic transformations. This approach is indeed effective, but a special hash function has to be designed for each different polymorphic worm and the internals of this function have to remain undisclosed, otherwise the worm author could easily prepare an immune variant.

In order to solve the problems of payload cyphering and polymorphism, our malware classification is done in two steps. During the first step, the malware is analyzed by many different antivirus engines. If the payload cannot be identified just by a signature detection, the analysis proceeds to the second step. Here, the malware is executed in a protected environment and its effects are monitored (this technique is known as *sandboxing*).

While the behavioral analysis is not as precise as signature analysis since two different worms may have similar behaviors, it is the only way to collect any data for identifying the structure of botnets. This sandbox-backed analysis, although not exact, is the way of classifying the polymorphous variants of the same malware which fits best the purpose of fighting malware spread. This method has the benefit of being completely automatic, while not as exact as signature detection. All connections to honeypots are by default intrusion attempts, so assuming that the analyzed binary is harmful, it is perfectly legitimate. The knowledge of the real activities carried out by the malware if preferable to an exact classification.

3.4 Activity report

When using multiple remote sandboxes for analysis, the corresponding results will be dis-homogeneous, often unstructured and not directly comparable. In order to allow the cooperating networks to take advantage of the report information, all the results are adapted by the collector. In particular, the endpoints of the observed network connections which are related to the malware activity are highlighted. After the adaptation phase, the reports are sent to all the cooperating networks, even to those not yet reached by the malware. In this way, all the components receive the information needed for deploying defensive countermeasures, such as blocking certain network connections, closing ports or patching some software applications. The exchange of information between the cooperating networks is the most effective measure against the spread of malware. By knowing timely how a worm is being transmitted, the administrators can deploy adequate countermeasures or at least plan some attack mitigation actions. Furthermore, the knowledge about the infection vector may be shared very early with the vendor of the targeted software, which can start correcting the problem when very few machines have been attacked. The increased bandwidth and availability of Internet connections facilitate the patch deliver in a short time.

One of the countermeasures that can be adopted against malware is the interruption of connections towards the malware distribution servers and the *Command & Control* (C&C) servers, if the payload is downloaded from a remote location or the malware has a control infrastructure. Usually these countermeasures are activated after the malware has begun spreading, not on a preventive basis. Each network implements this type of countermeasures in an individual way. On the other hand, if different networks cooperated, the information describing the way a new malware is spreading could be used to prevent the infection in networks not yet touched. It may even be feasible to deploy preventive measures before the working hours. For example, if the C&C servers are identified, it is possible to put into place new firewalling rules which prevent any infected host behind the firewall to connect and download further instructions from the malware controller; it also becomes possible to write blacklists of known C&C servers (although some recent worms such as Storm use decentralized communication systems).

3.5 Communication security

Is is essential to prevent a single node from polluting the set of collected data when we are aggregating information from many sources. The data may be misleading due to a malfunctioning or because a malicious user joined the network of cooperating sensors. In both instances, we need a way to trace back every alert to its origin. We use a public key cryptographic scheme to address this issue. The collector and the managers are provided with a public and private key pair, which are used for authenticating all the information exchanged among the architecture components. Each component knows in advance the keys of its communicating components. This choice guarantees the traceability of communications, together with the certainty that only registered managers can communicate with higher level managers and with the collector. Public key cryptography also provides confidentiality to the communication. The proposed communication scheme takes advantage of cooperation without the need of exchanging data directly between peers, since all the communications occur vertically. The only necessary trust relationship is pairwise between a sensor and a manager, or different lines of managers or between a top manager and the collector.

3.6 Malware collection

A capillary distributed network of sensors allows us to collect a set of data statistically relevant, that can be used for practical and research purposes. Most security products vendors have a similar infrastructure, but the proposed decentralized network has the advantage of being **vendor-agnostic** and possibly larger.

4 Prototype implementation

The feasibility of the proposed architecture is demonstrated through the realization of a prototype based on open source software and custom integration scripts. The prototype has been validated experimentally in controlled conditions as a whole and in its individual components through known malware. Furthermore, the prototype has been deployed in live operation, and it has been able to collect previously unknown malware. In this section we describe the technical details of the most important and novel components.

4.1 Malware collection

Malware collection is carried out by Nepenthes [3] instances. This software is a modular daemon which mainly has the following functions:

- socket binding and listening for incoming connections
- identification of targeted vulnerability
- analysis of the exploit code for the extraction of information necessary for downloading the worm payload
- payload retrieval
- logging and issuing alerts, potentially to a remote server through the IDMEF protocol

Each of these functions is implemented in a separate module, which in the Nepenthes source code is prefixed by a descriptive prefix, such as *dnsresolve-*, *download-*, *module-*, *log-*, *shellcode-*, *shellemu-*, *sqlhandler-*, *submit-*, *vuln-*. For example, modules whose name starts with "vuln" contain the vulnerability simulation logic which is needed to reply correctly to attacks so as to retrieve the payload location.

Malware distribution can occur in many ways, and the honeypot software has to support as may method as possible. Sometimes the shellcode opens a remote connection with a TCP or UDP stream from which it transfers subsequent commands; otherwise a TFTP, FTP or HTTP download is used to transfer the worm payload. Nepenthes computes a SHA512 or MD5 hash of the malware and it stores a copy of the harmful binary. Such binaries can be moved to remote servers with different methods or be submitted[1] to organizations that search for new malware, like the mwcollect Alliance [12], or Norman [20]. Nepenthes also provides a *libprelude* output module which can be used for issuing alerts to a Prelude Manager. In the prototype which we prepared, sensors use the Prelude output module to inform their respective manager of new infection attempts, while managers periodically call a script which looks in the archived payload directory of each controlled sensor. Since it would be preferable to collect malware samples as soon as possible, we plan to integrate alert issuing and payload uploading in the future.

4.2 Communication infrastructure

The critical component of the proposed distributed architecture is the communication infrastructure. Its requirements are:

- forwarding of alerts and malware binaries from sensors to managers and between managers
- transfer of unknown malware samples to the collector
- authentication of all exchanged messages
- confidentiality

In addition to these functional requirements, it is essential for the format of the exchanged messages to be a recognized standard and allow the maximum interoperability between heterogeneous threat detection systems. These considerations brought ourselves to choosing Prelude [21] as the alert management framework.

4.2.1 Prelude: a hybrid IDS

Prelude is an Open Source software which allows the deployment of a hybrid intrusion detection system - an aggregate of sensors employing different technologies and approaches to detect attacks. A typical use case is the integration of Host and Network IDSs in large networks. The format of the exchanged messages is IDMEF [19]. Prelude offers a library (*libprelude*) that security-related software can use to issue alerts and communicate with Prelude managers. Communications are encrypted using public key cryptography and relaying of messages is supported by managers, so it becomes possible to build a hierarchical network of malware-collecting nodes.

4.2.2 Transferring captured malware

A key requirement or the proposed architecture which is not natively supported by the hybrid IDS Prelude is the submission of the binaries downloaded by Nepenthes

[1] submission is done though the GOTEK protocol or with custom solutions which are different for each collection service

to a collection node. The sole propagation of IDMEF alerts is not sufficient for this. The Nepenthes developers are currently working on the integration of their work with the malware submission services of some sandboxes (CWSandbox and Norman) and online antivirus engines (VirusTotal), and they have developed the GOTEK malware distribution protocol which is actively employed by the mwcollect Alliance.

Our implementation is based on a script which is executed periodically on the collector and manager nodes. The script spawns a remote shell to each machine that is managed on the immediately lower level of the architecture, lists the collected binaries and retrieves the unknown ones. For example, the collector examines the caches of the highest level managers, which in turn collect the malware binaries from their respective subordinate managers. The lowest level managers collect binaries from their pool of honeypots.

4.2.3 Malware analysis

One of the advantages of the proposed architecture is the independency from a single malware analysis tool. It is possible to employ locally installed antivirus engines or sandboxes as well as remote public malware analysis services.

Our prototype is able to submit malware to three different remote services:

- Virustotal [22], via SMTP submission
- Norman Sandbox [23], using a custom HTTP POST request
- CW Sandbox [24], also using HTTP POST

The process of submitting the malware samples is handled by a custom modular software which is easily extendable to support other analysis services. By combining traditional signature detection and behavioral analysis (both from different vendors) we can identify clearly the actions performed by malware. Exact classification of the malware is only marginally useful since we know that the analyzed binary comes indeed from a worm, having collected it with a honeypot.

4.2.4 Report generation and sending

The results of different analysis services have heterogeneous formats and are typically semi-structured texts. Before sending the results to the administrators of the cooperating networks, the reports are tagged semantically so that an automated response may be prepared from each network accordingly to the local policies. The most important data are the location of the malware payload and the retrieval method, the address of command & control servers, the IP addresses of known infected hosts and the protocol being exploited for the infection to occur.

We remark that those reports can be easily used to generate and deploy automatic countermeasures without human intervention, thus greatly reducing the time required to react a network attack

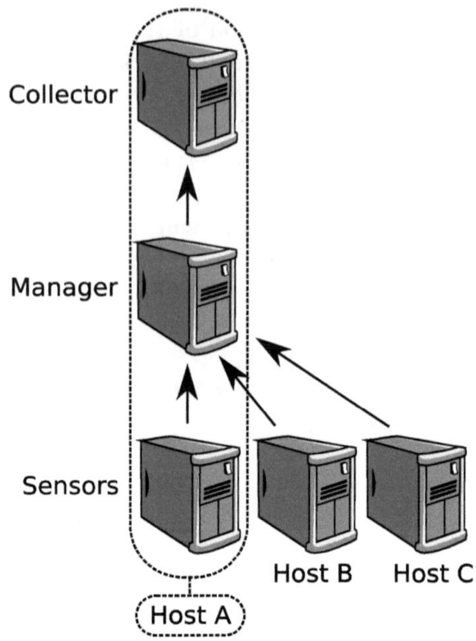

Fig. 3 Test setup

5 Experimental results

The described prototype has been validated experimentally in controlled conditions with the deployment scheme shown in Figure 3.

A single host is being used as a sensor, manager and collector, and two sensors have been installed in other machines. The manager is collecting alerts and malware samples from three sensors, and the collector is doing the same on a single manager. With this setup we can simulate:

1. the collection of binaries performed by the manager
2. the forwarding of alerts from the sensors up to the collector
3. the analysis of binaries performed by the collector
4. the collector generating a report and sending it to all the cooperating network administrators

A first test has been performed by sending known malware to the sensors. Nepenthes managed to collect the binaries and correctly issued alerts that were forwarded by the manager to the collector. Accordingly, the binary payload of the malware was transferred from the sensor to the manager and then to the collector, which proceeded with the analysis, since the hash of the binary is unknown. The payload was sent to the Norman sandbox analysis tool and the analysis outcome was interpreted and emailed to the administrators of the three simulated networks. The report included all the information gathered from the online analysis tool and was delivered timely to all the interested parties.

In order to verify the behavior of the system in a real setup, some Nepenthes sensors have been installed on home ADSL connections. This experiment led to the issuing of 3866 alerts and to the collection of 52 distinct binaries over a span of about eight hours. Seven of the collected binaries were previously unknown to our collector, and they were submitted to the available online scanning services. In many cases the behavioral analysis performed in CWSandbox has lead to the classification of malware as a worm-bot, and to the identification of several C&C hosts.

The following is a sample of the the report produced by the sandbox service:

```
0995104827bee951abc4fcc93cdf85ee :
INFECTED with W32/Malware
(Signature: W32/Malware.LNH)
    * Connects to "j4m41z.B3D3RPIERO.INFO"
      on port 6137 (TCP).
    * Connects to IRC Server.
    * Possible backdoor functionality
      [Authenticate] port 113.
Network Activity:
  Opened listening TCP connection on port: 113
    * C&C Server: 69.64.36.188:6137
    * Server Password:
```

The worm bot tries to connect to a C&C server and opens a backdoor on port 113.

```
13ff667bebcc58253faba2313dce7b89 :
INFECTED with W32/Kut.gen1
(Signature: W32/Poebot.ADT)
  * C&C Server: 140.116.199.57:8998
Network activity
  * Server Password: PING
```

In this case it has been possible to intercept the password use by the malware for *authenticating* to its C&C servers.

```
03fb1ecf2cbcfb74ab5c29dcd247e132 :
INFECTED with W32/Endom.A (Signature: Allaple.gen1)
    * Sends data stream (76 bytes) to remote
        address "124.86.6.4",
      port 139.
    * Connects to "124.86.6.4" on port 445 (TCP).
    * Sends data stream (76 bytes) to remote
        address "124.86.8.6",
      port 139.
    * Connects to "124.86.8.6" on port 445 (TCP).
      * Sends data stream (76 bytes) to remote
        address "124.86.10.8", port 139.
    * Connects to "124.86.10.8" on port 445 (TCP).
    * Connects to "124.86.6.4" on port 9988 (TCP).
       * Sends data stream (255 bytes) to remote
         address "124.86.6.4", port 9988.
```

This result demonstrates that the proposed solution allows us to detect and block malware communications even if they rely on a complex, multi-tier control network, as this bot does. Such solutions make it difficult to block the malware communications by only inspecting network traffic anomalies, because of the multiple servers and the different TCP ports. However, by examining the malware behavior we know at least the entrance points of the C&C network, and by blocking them we can prevent newly infected machines from joining the botnet.

6 Conclusions

This paper describes an innovative architecture to automate malware collection and classification with the purpose of implementing just in time countermeasures. It aims to benefit from the cooperation of multiple sensors spread over geographically distributed networks. The architecture is highly scalable and flexible because the number of component tiers can be adapted to the network characteristics of each participating organization.

We envision this proposal as a possible evolution of the existing malware collecting infrastructures, whose benefits are still dependent on a predominantly manual analysis of the collected samples.

The automatic analysis carried out on the collected malware allow the architecture to defeat most concealing techniques used by virus writers, since it includes the execution of the malware payload in a sandbox. This behavioral analysis avoids most hiding techniques found in modern malware. The related computational cost is reduced thanks to the collection of malware from multiple networks and to the rapid classification of duplicate binaries based on their MD5 hash.

Much attention has been paid to the security of the architecture that utilizes pairwise trust between the close components and ciphered communications. However, the necessary theoretical and practical validation of the security level of the architecture and consequent possible adjustments are left to future work.

We should also observe that we have implemented a prototype for the validation of the main ideas that are behind the proposed architecture. All experiments have obtained the expected results. On the other hand, a large scale deployment of the proposed architecture over the networks of different organizations lacks because of practical obstacles. Nevertheless, preliminary contacts with other academic

7 Acknowledgements

The authors would like to thank Saverio Verrascina [2] for his valuable help with the prototype implementation.

---

[2] saverio@weblab.ing.unimo.it

References

1. Sharon Gaudin (2007), Storm Worm botnet more powerful than top supercomputers, Information Week, available at http://www.informationweek.com/software/showArticle.jhtml?articleID=201804528
2. ShadowServer Foundation homepage, available at http://www.shadowserver.org
3. Nepenthes, available at http://nepenthes.mwcollect.org/
4. Xu D and Ning P (2005), Privacy-Preserving Alert Correlation: A Concept Hierarchy Based Approach, 21st Comp. Sec. App. Conf.
5. Jaeyeon Jung J and Sit E (2004) An empirical study of spam traffic and the use of DNS black lists, IMC '04: Proceedings of the 4th ACM SIGCOMM conference on Internet measurement
6. Freiling FC, Holz T, and Wicherski G (2005) Botnet Tracking: Exploring a Root-Cause Methodology to Prevent Distributed Denial-of-Service Attacks, ESORICS 2005: Proceedings of the 10th European Symposium on Research in Computer Security
7. Valeur F, Vigna G, Kruegel C, and Kemmerer RA (2004) A Comprehensive Approach to Intrusion Detection Alert Correlation, IEEE Transactions on dependable and secure computing, Jul-Sept 2004, Vol. 1 pp.146-169
8. When-Yi Hsin, Shian-Shiong Tseng, Shun-Chieh Lin (2005) A study of alert based collaborative defense, Proceedings of the 8th International Symposium on Parallel Architectures, Algorithms and Networks (ISPAN05)
9. Zhu S, Setia S, Jajodia S (2003) LEAP: efficient security mechanisms for large-scale distributed sensor networks, CCS '03: Proceedings of the 10th ACM conference on Computer and communications security
10. Perrig A, Canetti R, Tygar JD, Song D (2000) Efficient Authentication and Signing of Multicast Streams over Lossy Channels, Proc. of the 2000 IEEE Symposium on Security and Privacy
11. Przydatek B, Song D, Perrig A (2003) SIA: secure information aggregation in sensor networks, SenSys '03: Proceedings of the 1st international conference on Embedded networked sensor systems
12. mwcollect Alliance, homepage available at http://alliance.mwcollect.org/
13. Robert Tappan Morris (1988), The Morris Worm, homepage available at http://www.morrisworm.com/. Cited 17 Jan 2008.
14. Internet Storm Center (2004), Sasser Worm, LSASS exploit analysis, available at http://isc.sans.org/diary.html?date=2004-04-30
15. Computer emergency Response Team (2000), CERT®Advisory CA-2000-04 Love Letter Worm, available at http://www.cert.org/advisories/CA-2000-04.html
16. Symantec™(2004), W32.Wallon.A@mm worm description, available at http://www.symantec.com/security_response/writeup.jsp?docid=2004-051112-0815-99
17. US-CERT (2004), Technical Cyber Security Alert TA04-356A (Santy worm), available at http://www.us-cert.gov/cas/techalerts/TA04-356A.html
18. Wikipedia (2007), Timeline of notable computer viruses and worms, available at http://en.wikipedia.org/wiki/Timeline_of_notable_computer_viruses_and_worms#2006
19. IETF Intrusion Detection Working Group (2007) The Intrusion Detection Message Exchange Format (IDMEF), available at http://tools.ietf.org/html/rfc4765
20. Norman ASA, homepage available at http:/www.norman.com/
21. Prelude Hybrid IDS project, homepage available at http://www.prelude-ids.org/
22. Virustotal, a malware analysis service offered by Hispasec Sistemas, available at http://www.virustotal.com/
23. Norman SandBox Information Center, available at http://sandbox.norman.com
24. CWSandbox, Behavior-based Malware Analysis remote sandbox service, homepage available at http://www.cwsandbox.org/

Realizing Stateful Public Key Encryption in Wireless Sensor Network

Joonsang Baek, Han Chiang Tan, Jianying Zhou and Jun Wen Wong

Abstract In this paper, we present our implementation of a stateful public key encryption (stateful PKE) scheme in the wireless sensor network (WSN) environment. In order to reduce the communication overhead of the stateful PKE scheme we implement, which is of prime importance in WSN, we introduce a technique called "indexing". The performance analysis of our implementation shows that there are significant advantages of using stateful PKE in WSN in terms of computation and communication costs, compared with normal public key encryption.

1 Introduction

1.1 Motivation

Wireless sensor networks (WSNs) are useful in a variety of domains, including monitoring the integrity of buildings and building automation, early discovery of catastrophes (like forest fires and earthquakes), medical surveillance and remote diagnosis, pollution control and the battlefield and perimeter defense.

In the typical setting, a WSN consists of numerous tiny nodes communicating with a few base stations. Among those tiny nodes, there can be some nodes which have more computation and/or communication capacity. The base stations are often

---

Joonsang Baek
Institute for Infocomm Research, Singapore, e-mail: jsbaek@i2r.a-star.edu.sg

Han Chiang Tan
Institute for Infocomm Research, Singapore, e-mail: hctan@i2r.a-star.edu.sg

Jianying Zhou
Institute for Infocomm Research, Singapore, e-mail: jyzhou@i2r.a-star.edu.sg

Jun Wen Wong
Institute for Infocomm Research, Singapore, e-mail: jwwong@i2r.a-star.edu.sg

---

Please use the following format when citing this chapter:

Baek, J., et al., 2008, in IFIP International Federation for Information Processing, Volume 278; *Proceedings of the IFIP TC 11 23rd International Information Security Conference*; Sushil Jajodia, Pierangela Samarati, Stelvio Cimato; (Boston: Springer), pp. 95–107.

assumed to be powerful enough to perform computationally intensive tasks such as cryptographic computations. The sensor nodes, on the other hand, have constrained resources in terms of computation, memory and battery power.

Although WSN brings us a great variety of applications as mentioned above, it is fairly vulnerable to attacks such as eavesdropping and impersonation as sensor nodes are often deployed in physically accessible areas and often interact with environments and people. As a result it has become of prime importance to provide security services for WSNs including data encryption and node authentication.

Not long ago public key cryptography (PKC) was believed to be unsuitable for providing security services in WSN as PKC usually requires computationally-intensive cryptographic operations while sensor nodes are severely resource constrained [16]. Contrary to this common belief, it has recently been reported that PKC is in fact feasible to be realized in WSNs [9][20][21].

In this paper, we focus on the realization of PKC in WSN, specifically, efficient implementation of public key encryption for the *confidentiality* service in WSN. Before presenting our contribution, we review the previous work in this line of research.

1.2 Related Work

Although its realization on WSN is challenging, PKC will bring great simplicity and efficiency in providing a number of essential security services [10]. In this section we briefly survey the related work on implementation of PKC in WSNs.

Watro et al. [21] designed and implemented public key based protocols that allow authentication and key agreement between a sensor network and a third party as well as between two sensor networks. The specific public key algorithm they used is RSA [15] whose key size varies (512, 768 and 1024 bits). Their protocols were implemented on UC Berkeley Mica2 motes using the TinyOS [19] environment.

Wander et al. [20] presented implementation of authentication and key exchange protocols based on public-key cryptography on Atmel ATmega128L low-power 8-bit microcontroller platform. Two base algorithms for their work are RSA-1024 (RSA with 1024-bit key size) and ECC-160 (Elliptic Curve Cryptography with 160-bit key size). It was reported in their paper that ECC has a significant advantage over RSA as it reduces computation time and also the amount of data transmitted and stored.

Bellare et al. [4] discussed how to significantly speed-up the public key encryption (PKE) by simply allowing a sender to maintain "state" that is re-used across different encryptions. This new type of PKE is called *stateful PKE*. As an efficient construction, Bellare et al. presented a stateful PKE scheme based on the Diffie-Hellman assumption (Given g^a, g^b, it is computationally infeasible to compute g^{ab}).

1.3 Our Contributions

From the literature review in the previous subsection, one can notice that due to the efficiency that it could provide, ECC can be a good candidate for the algorithm that realizes PKE in WSN, which consists of sensor nodes with limited resources for computation/communication. One can also notice that stateful PKE could bring further improvement on the realization of PKE in WSN.

Having these in mind, we make the following contributions in this paper:

- In order to enhance *communication* efficiency of Bellare et al.'s [4] Diffie-Hellman (DH) based stateful PKE scheme, we modify it using a simple but useful "indexing" technique whereby the repeated part of ciphertext, which is usually long, is replaced by a short string.
- We implement the modified version of the DH based stateful PKE scheme on the MicaZ [8] platform and analyze its security and performance. To our knowledge, this is the first implementation of stateful PKE in WSN.

2 Our Modified DH-Based Stateful PKE for WSN

2.1 Basic Setting

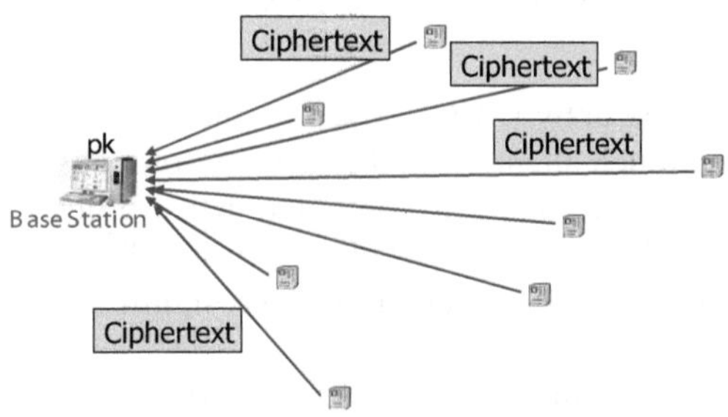

Fig. 1 Overview of Basic Setting

Security services for WSNs can vary depending on the specific requirements of each application. For our implementation, we consider a simple (single-hop) but widely applicable security service architecture in which each sensor node can encrypt data using a base station's public key *pk* as depicted in Figure 1. We assume that the public key of the base stations are embedded in each sensor node when they are deployed. On receiving each ciphertext from each sensor node, the base station uses the corresponding private key *sk* to decrypt it.

Like the case for general WSNs, we assume that the base station is powerful enough to perform computationally intensive cryptographic operations, and the sensor nodes, on the other hand, have constrained resources in terms of computation, memory and battery power. We also assume that the private key of the base station is safely stored, e.g., using smart card.

One of the advantages of employing public key encryption in this setting, where the sensor nodes do not have to perform decryption, is that a long-term private key does not need be stored inside each sensor node. In contrast, if one wants to run some key exchange protocol to share symmetric key between the base station and the sensor node and encrypts subsequent messages using the shared key, the shared key of the sensor node ought to be protected securely. (Otherwise, an attacher that has obtained the *long-term* shared key from the sensor node can freely decrypt the subsequent ciphertexts as well as the ciphertexts obtained before.)

Of course other more complex settings such as multi-hop exist and the security services for these settings should be difficult to realize. However, the focus of this paper is mainly realizing stateful PKE in the basic WSN setting we have described above, which itself is challenging due to resource constraints of sensors, rather than advocating that our scheme can solve every security (confidentiality) problem in WSN.

2.2 Some Preliminaries

Not surprisingly, there are few *public key* cryptographic tools that we can easily employ to realize the security services in WSN due to the high level of resource-constraints in WSN. Nonetheless, the following cryptographic primitives can be useful:

- Elliptic curve cryptography (ECC): Since its introduction in late 80's [13][14], ECC has attracted much attention as the security solutions for wireless networks due to the small key size and low computational overhead. It is an established fact that ECC-160 offers a similar level of security of RSA-1024. As mentioned earlier, Wander et al. [20] showed that ECC has significant advantages over RSA in the WSN setting.
- Hybrid encryption: Recall that in our basic setting presented previously, each sensor node has to send encrypted data to the base station. It is a well-known fact that normal PKE schemes solely constructed from number-theoretic primitive are too slow to encrypt a large amount of data. Hence hybrid encryption is used in practice. In a hybrid encryption scheme, a session key is generated by a public key algorithm called "Key Encapsulation Mechanism (KEM)" [12] and actual data is encrypted by a symmetric encryption algorithm specifically called "Data Encapsulation Mechanism (DEM)" [12] under the generated session key. It is shown [7] that this hybrid encryption scheme is secure against chosen ciphertext attack (CCA-secure) if both KEM and DEM are CCA-secure.

One of the PKE schemes that are based on the above primitives is Abdalla et al.'s [1] DHIES (Diffie-Hellman Integrated Encryption Scheme). But Bellare et al. has shown that DHIES can further be improved using the "stateful encryption" concept, which will be explained shortly.

2.3 Diffie-Hellman Based Stateful PKE with Indexing

Stateful PKE [4] could be understood as a special type of hybrid encryption which significantly speeds up the KEM-part of hybrid encryption by allowing a sender to maintain state which is reused across different encryptions. For example, Bellare et al's [4] DH based stateful PKE scheme, which is a stateful version of DHIES, works as follows. To encrypt a message M, the encryption algorithm computes $(rP, \mathsf{E}_K(M))$, where r is chosen at random from $\mathbb{Z}_q$ (q, a prime), $K = \mathsf{H}(rP, Y, rY)$ (P, a generator of the ECC-group of order q; H, a hash function; E, a CCA-secure symmetric encryption function) and $Y = xP$ (x, a private key; Y, a public key). Now, the value r is kept as state and rP and K do not need to be computed every time a new message is encrypted. In this way, stateful PKE brings computational efficiency gains.

But we argue that this scheme can further be improved to save energy for communication. As the sensor nodes lack sufficient amount of energy, reducing communication overhead is also of prime importance. (According to [20], power to transmit *one* bit is equivalent to approx. 2,090 clock cycle of execution on the microcontroller.) Hence, the repeated transmission of the same value $U = rP$ for a number of different sessions would be a waste of the communication resource.

Our approach to resolve this problem is to employ a natural but useful "indexing" technique whereby the value U is replaced by a much shorter string. – In our implementation, for example, the length of U is 21 bytes and the index for this which we denote by id_U is only 3 bytes. To uniquely identify U using id_U, we use an identity of a sensor node and a sequence number. (This will be explained in detail in Section 3.1.) Also, to protect id_U from modification by attackers, we hash it with a KEM-key. More precisely we describe our modified DH based stateful PKE scheme as follows. - Along with this description, readers are refered to Figure 2.

- **Setup**: The base station does the following:
  Pick a group $\mathbb{G}$ of prime order q;
  Pick a generator P of $\mathbb{G}$;
  Pick a hash function H;
  Pick a symmetric encryption scheme $\mathsf{SYM} = (\mathsf{E}, \mathsf{D})$;
  Pick x at random from $\mathbb{Z}_q^*$ and compute $Y = xP$;
  Return $pk = (q, P, Y, \mathsf{H}, \mathsf{SYM})$ and $sk = (pk, x)$ // pk and sk denote public key and private key resp.
- **I-Phase** (Indexing Phase): Using pk, a sensor node performs the following to encrypt a plaintext M:
  Pick $r \in \mathbb{Z}_q^*$ at random and compute $U = rP$;
  Pick an index $id_U \in \{0,1\}^*$ for U in such a way that id_U uniquely identifies U;

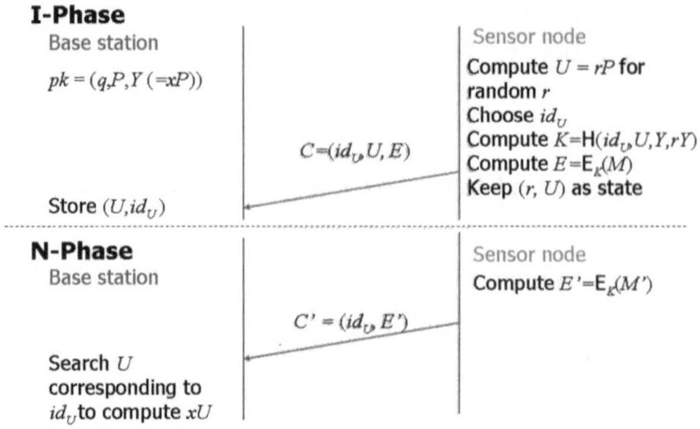

Fig. 2 Overview of DH-Based Stateful PKE with Indexing

Compute $K = \mathsf{H}(id_U, U, Y, rY)$;
Compute $E = \mathsf{E}_K(M)$; // $\mathsf{E}_K(\cdot)$ denotes symmetric encryption function under key K
Keep (r, U) as state;
Return $C = (id_U, U, E)$ as ciphertext

Note that the size of id_U is much smaller than that of U. Note also that the node can cache K to save computation further.

Upon receiving $C = (id_U, U, E)$ from the sensor node, the base station performs the following to decrypt it:

Compute $xU = xrP$ and $K = \mathsf{H}(id_U, U, Y, xU)$;
Compute $M = \mathsf{D}_K(E)$; // $\mathsf{D}_K(\cdot)$ denotes the symmetric decryption function under key K
Return M

Note in the above algorithm that M can be $\perp$ (meaning "reject").

- **N-Phase** (Normal Phase): In this phase, the sensor node performs the following to encrypt a plaintext M':

  Compute $E' = \mathsf{E}_K(M')$;
  Return $C' = (id_U, E')$ as ciphertext

  Upon receiving $C' = (id_U, E')$, the base station conducts the following to decrypt C':

  Search its database for U that corresponds to id_U;
  If the corresponding U does not exists, return $\perp$
  Else compute $xU = xrP$, $K = \mathsf{H}(id_U, U, Y, xU)$ and return $M' = \mathsf{D}_K(E')$

We remark that the choice of id_U is very important. For instance, if it were chosen at random, it would collide with $id_{U'}$ that other sensor node has chosen for other "U'" value. In this case, the base station cannot decrypt a given ciphertext as there is an ambiguity as to which one is correct. For this reason, id_U ought to uniquely identify the value U. In Section 3, we will describe how to select id_U in details.

2.4 Security Analysis

The security against chosen ciphertext attack (CCA) for stateful PKE is defined in [4], which extends the usual IND-CCA (Indistinguishability under CCA [5]) notion of normal PKE. The essence of this security definition is that an adversary does not get any significant advantage in breaking the confidentiality of ciphertext even though he uses the same state to encrypt messages for multiple receivers.

We now prove that our modified DH based stateful PKE scheme is also secure under this security definition. A basic idea of the proof[1] is that even though an attacker can replace the index of a challenge ciphertext (a ciphertext that the attacker wants to break the confidentiality) with its own, it cannot break the confidentiality (indistinguishability of encryption) since, intuitively, the hash function H prevents id_U from alteration. Formally we prove the following thorem.

Theorem 1. *Assume that the underlying symmetric encryption scheme* E *is IND-CCA secure and the hash function* H *is random oracle [6]. Then our stateful PKE scheme proposed above is secure against CCA in the sense defined in [4] under the assumption that the Gap Diffie-Hellman (GDH) problem is computationally intractable. (The GDH problem refers to a computational problem where an adversary, given* (P, aP, bP) *for random* $a, b \in \mathbb{Z}_q$*, tries to compute a DH-key* abP *with the help of DH-oracle, which, given tuple* (P, aP, bP, cP)*, can decide whether* $c = ab$ *or not.)*

Proof. (Sketch) Let A and B be a CCA adversary and an adversary for GDH respectively. Assume that B is given (P, aP, bP) as instance. B sets $U^* = aP$ and $Y_1 = bP$, where Y_1 denotes the receiver 1's public key. B picks K^* at random from the appropriate key space and sets $K^* = \mathsf{H}(id_{U^*}, U^*, Y_1, ?)$, where ? denotes "indeterminate". When A queries receiver i's public key Y_i, where $2 \leq i \leq n$, as public key registration query, B picks K_i at random from the appropriate key space and defines $K_i = \mathsf{H}(id_{U^*}, U^*, Y_i, ?)$.

Now, when A queries (id_U, U, Y, D) to H, B answers as follows:

- Pick K at random
  If $id_U = id_{U^*}$, $U = U^*$ and D is a DH-key of (U, Y) then
    - If $Y \neq Y_1$ then
      - If $Y = Y_i$ for some $i \in [2, n]$ then return K_i (which was selected by B in the beginning) as answer
      - Else pick K_i at random, set $K_i = \mathsf{H}(id_{U^*}, U^*, Y_i, D)$. and return K_i as answer
    - Else abort the game and return D as DH-key of $U^*(= aP)$ and $Y_1(= bP)$

Note that in the above simulation of H, B keeps a query-answer list, which we denote by H-List. B deals with the rest of the queries from A as follows.

When A asks for encryption of (i, M), B searches appropriate K_i, computes $E = \mathsf{E}_{K_i}(M)$ and returns (id_{U^*}, U^*, E) to A as answer. When A queries (M_0, M_1)

[1] Note that the "proof" here means the "reductionist proof" [2] widely used to provide security arguments for various schemes and protocols.

as a challenge, B picks $b \in \{0,1\}$ at random, computes $E^* = \mathsf{E}_{K^*}(M_b)$ and returns (id_{U^*}, U^*, E^*) to A as a challenge ciphertext.

There are two types of decryption queries. When A queries (id_U, U, E) for decryption, B first checks whether U is an element of group $\mathbb{G}$. If it is not, B sends off $\perp$ to A, otherwise it conducts the following:

If $id_U = id_{U^*}$ and $U = U^*$ then return $\mathsf{D}_{K^*}(E)$
Else search $K = \mathsf{H}(id_U, U, Y_1, ?)$ from the H-List

If it exists return $\mathsf{D}_K(E)$
Else pick K at random and return $\mathsf{D}_K(E)$ and update the query-answer list for H with K

When A queries (id_U, E) for decryption, B searches the H-List for U. If such U does not exist, B returns $\perp$ to A, otherwise, it conducts the same procedure as described above.

3 Our Implementation

3.1 Implementations of Symmetric Encryption and Index id_U

As shown in the preceding section, for the modified DH based stateful PKE scheme to be secure, we need to use an IND-CCA secure symmetric encryption scheme. We select the IND-CCA secure symmetric encryption scheme (DEM 3) recommended by ISO standard [12], which can be described as follows.

- Encryption: First, this algorithm splits the key $K(= \mathsf{H}(id_U, U, Y, rY))$ into K_1 and K_2 such that $K = K_1 || K_2$, where the length of K_1 is the same as the length of a plaintext M and the length of K_2 is appropriate for the key length of Message Authentication Code function MAC. Next, this algorithm computes $S = K_1 \oplus M$ and $\sigma = \mathsf{MAC}_{K_2}(S)$. Finally, it outputs a ciphertext $E = (S, \sigma)$. (Note that the particular MAC scheme used in our implementation is HMAC [3].)
- Decryption: On input $E = (S, \sigma)$ and the key K, this algorithm computes $K = K_1 || K_2$ and checks whether $\sigma = \mathsf{MAC}_{K_2}(S)$. If it is, this algorithm returns $M = S \oplus K_1$ otherwise, returns $\perp$.

As remarked at the end of Section 2.3, selecting id_U so that it uniquely identifies the value U is important. In our implementation, we construct id_U as follows:

$$id_U = ID_{\text{node}} || N,$$

where ID_{node} denotes a unique identity of a sensor node and N denotes a sequence number for the current value U. The size of ID_{node} and N is 2 bytes and 1 byte respectively. In our implementation, the base station is set to replace id_U (in its database) with new one whenever N changes. - Consequently, only *one* id_U exists for *each* sensor node.

Note that since each sensor node has a different identity ID_{node}, it is not possible to find a collision if less than $2^{16} (= 65536)$ sensor nodes exist. Hence, if constructed in the way described above, id_U uniquely identifies U depending on how many sensor nodes should be deployed. (One can of course enlarge the size of ID_{node} to increase the number of sensor nodes that can be deployed. Even if one byte is stretched, the number of deployable senor nodes increases dramatically.)

Item	Value
Transmission Frequency	2450 MHz
Transmission Power	0 dBm (=1 mW)
Data Rate	250 kbps
Energy to Transmit (Measured)	**1.56 μJ/byte**

Table 1 Characteristic Data for MicaZ

3.2 Performance Analysis

The WSN platform on which our implementation is based is MicaZ, developed by Crossbow Technology [8]. The RF transceiver for this MicaZ complies with IEEE 802.15.4/ZigBee, and the 8-bit microcontroller is Atmel ATmega128L, which is the major energy consumer. We use a laptop PC (Lenovo T60 1.83GHz (Intel Core 2) CPU, 512MB RAM) as a base station.

In Table 1, we summarize some characteristic data for the MicaZ platform, which include the energy to transmit one byte, which we measured.

Source Address (2 bytes)	Destination Address (2 bytes)	Message Type (1 byte)	Data (45 bytes)

Fig. 3 Data Format

The programming languages we used for our implementation are nesC, C and Java (mainly used for interface design on base station). The base operating system for the MicaZ platform is TinyOS [19]. The ECC component of our stateful PKE is based on TinyECC [18], which we modify for our implementation. The size of key for ECC is 160 bits.

Figure 3 illustrates the data format of a packet in our implementation. We assume that the size of each packet be 50 bytes, 5 bytes for the header and 45 bytes for the payload.

We now analyze the computational overhead of our implementation. In Table 2, we summarize and compare the energy consumptions of our implementation when a plaintext message of 20 bytes is encrypted in I-Phase and N-Phase respectively. – It would not be surprising that I-Phase needs much more energy than N-Phase since I-Phase includes two point-multiplications in order to compute $U(= rP)$ and rY, which are *not* needed in N-Phase where U and rY are reused.

	Energy cost
Encryption in I-Phase	46.76 mJ
Encryption in N-Phase	0.89 mJ

Table 2 Comparison between the energy consumptions for encryption of a 20-byte plaintext in I-Phase and N-Phase

Another interpretation of this result is that the modified DH based stateful PKE scheme we implement actually saves significant amount of energy compared with its non-stateful version in which U and rY should be computed according to the randomness of r every time a new message is encrypted. In other words, in the non-stateful version, I-Phase is repeated whenever a new plaintext message is inputted to the encryption function. – In fact, I-Phase of our modified DH based stateful PKE scheme is almost the same[2] as Bellare et al.'s DHIES [1], a normal PKE scheme based on the GDH problem, from which the DH based stateful PKE scheme in [4] is derived.

Based on this observation, we can compare the encryption cost of our modified DH based stateful PKE scheme with that of the non-stateful version. Using the measured energy costs for encryption presented in Table 2 and assuming encryption is conducted 10 times, we demonstrate the comparison between the energy cost of encryption in our modified DH based stateful PKE scheme (simply termed "stateful PKE") and that of its non-stateful version (simply termed "non-stateful PKE") in Figure 4. Notice that the non-stateful version consumes roughly 8.5 times more energy than stateful one.

Before analyzing the communication overhead, we remark that the performance of our implementation is comparable to those of the ECDSA implementation on MicaZ presented in [18] and the DH-key exchange implementation on Mica2dot presented in [20]. According to [18], the measured energy costs of signature generation and verification of the ECDSA implementation are 46.2 mJ and 58.4 mJ respectively when using 160-bit key. Also, it is reported in [20] that the energy cost for the DH-key generation is 22.3 mJ. (Note that the DH-key generation involves one point multiplication while our implementation of the DH based stateful PKE scheme needs two point multiplications in encryption.)

We now analyze the communication overhead. Recall that we use a packet size of 50 bytes. However, 50 bytes are not enough to send all the required data in I-Phase

[2] The only difference is that id_U should be chosen and hashed together with the Diffie-Hellman key.

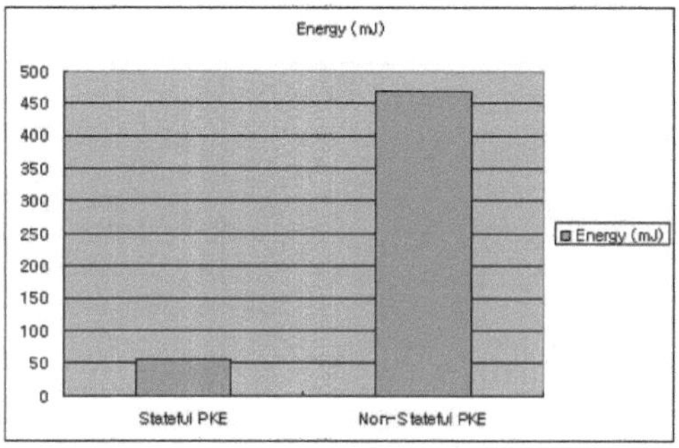

Fig. 4 Comparison between the energy costs of encryption in our modified DH based stateful PKE and its non-stateful version assuming that encryption is conducted 10 times

as the value U, which takes up 21 bytes, needs to be transmitted in this phase. So, in the actual implementation, we make a sensor node send actually two packets in I-Phase. Since U is replaced by id_U which is 3 bytes in length in N-Phase, we do not need to send two packets. On the other hand, if this "indexing" method is not used, U should be transmitted every time a new message is encrypted and hence, two packets should be transmitted every time. More precisely, we can obtain the energy consumption for transmitting two packets 1 time and one packet $n_t - 1$ times by computing

$$\begin{aligned} 1.56\mu\text{J/byte} \times \big((50+50)+50(n_t-1)\big) \text{ bytes} \\ = 78(n_t+1)\mu\text{J} \end{aligned}$$

and the energy for transmitting two packets n_t times by computing

$$1.56\mu\text{J/byte} \times (2\cdot 50n_t) \text{ bytes} = 156n_t\ \mu\text{J},$$

where n_t denotes the total number of transmissions.

The implication of this result is that our indexing method can save at least 45% of transmission energy when using stateful PKE as illustrated in Figure 5.

4 Concluding Remarks

In this paper, we presented another positive result regarding the feasibility of public key cryptography (PKC) in WSNs: We successfully implemented a statful PKE scheme on MicaZ node [8].

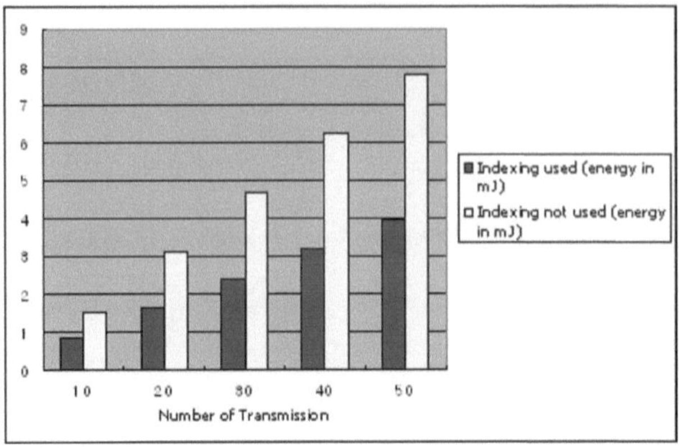

Fig. 5 Comparison between the energy costs of communication when the indexing method is used and when it is not

To enhance the communication efficiency of the stateful PKE, which is very important in WSN, we introduced a technique called "indexing". The performance analysis of our implementation showed that our indexing technique reduced the communication overhead significantly. An interesting direction of research on the indexing technique would be to provide different designs of index (id_U) for different purposes.

Finally, we note that this work focused only on how to provide confidentiality service for WSNs using PKC. How to provide authentication service for WSN using PKC is interesting future work.

Acknowledgements The authors are grateful to the anonymous referees of IFIP SEC '08 for their helpful comments. This work is partially funded by the EU project SMEPP-033563.

References

1. M. Abdalla, M. Bellare and P. Rogaway, *The Oracle Diffie-Hellman Assumptions and an Analysis of DHIES*, In CT-RSA '01, LNCS 2020, pp. 143–158, Springer-Verlag, 2001.
2. M. Bellare, *Practice-Oriented Provable-Security*, Lectures on Data Security – Modern Cryptology in Theory and Practice, LNCS 1561, pp. 1–15, Springer-Verlag 1999.
3. M. Bellare, R. Canetti and H. Krawczyk, *Keying Hash Functions for Message Authentication*, In Crypto '96, LNCS 1109, pp. 1–15, Springer-Verlag, 1996.
4. M. Bellare, T. Kohno and V. Shoup, *Stateful Public-Key Cryptosystems: How to Encrypt with One 160-bit Exponentiation*, In ACM-CCS 2006, pp. 380–389, 2006.
5. M. Bellare, A. Desai, D. Pointcheval and P. Rogaway, *Relations Among Notions of Security for Public-Key Encryption Schemes*, In Crypto '98, LNCS 1462, pp. 26–45, Springer-Verlag, 1998.
6. M. Bellare and P. Rogaway, *Random Oracles are Practical: A Paradigm for Designing Efficient Protocols*, In ACM-CCS '93, pp. 62–73, ACM, 1993.

7. R. Cramer and V. Shoup, *Design and Analysis of Practical Public-key Encryption Schemes Secure against Adaptive Chosen Ciphertext Attack*, SIAM Journal of Computing 33, pp. 167–226, 2003.
8. MicaZ Wireless Sensor Network Platform, Crossbow Technology, http://www.xbow.com/
9. G. Gaubatz, J.-P. Kaps and B. Sunar, *Public Key Cryptography in Sensor Networks Revisited*, In European Workshop on Security in Ad-Hoc and Sensor Networks 2004 (ESAS '04), LNCS 3313, pp. 2–18, Springer-Verlag, 2005.
10. G. Gaubatz, J.-P. Kaps, E. Oztruk and B. Sunar, *State of the Art in Ultra-Low Power Public Key Cryptography for Wireless Sensor Networks*, In IEEE International Workshop on Pervasive Computing and Communication Security 2005 (PerSec '05), 2005.
11. J. Hoffstein, J. Pipher, J. Silverman, *NTRU: A Ring-Based Public Key Cryptosystem.* In Algorithmic Number Theory (ANTS III), LNCS 1423, pp. 267–288, Springer-Verlag, 1998.
12. ISO 18033-2, *An Emerging Standard for Public-Key Encryption*, Working Group 2 of ISO/IEC JTC 1/SC27, 2004.
13. N. Koblitz, *Elliptic Curve Cryptosystems*, Mathematics of Computation 48, pp. 203–209, 1987.
14. V. Miller, *Use of Elliptic Curves in Cryptography*, In Crypto '85, LNCS 218, pp. 417–426, Springer-Verlag, 1986.
15. R. Rivest, A. Shamir, and L. Adleman, *A Method for Obtaining Digital Signatures and Public-Key Cryptosystems*, Communications of the ACM 21 (2), pp. 120–126, 1978.
16. A. Perrig, R. Szewczyk, J.D. Tygar, V. Wen, D.E. Culler, *SPINS: Security Protocols for Sensor Networks*. Wireless Networks 8 (2002), pp. 521–534, 2002.
17. M.O. Rabin, *Digitalized signatures and Public Key Functions as Intractable as Factorization*. Mit/lcs/tr-212, Massachusetts Institute of Technology, 1979.
18. TinyECC, http://discovery.csc.ncsu.edu/software/TinyECC/
19. TinyOS, http://www.tinyos.net/
20. A. Wander, N. Gura, H. Eberle, V. Gupta and S Shantz, *Energy Analysis of Public-Key Cryptography for Wireless Sensor Networks*, In IEEE International Conference on Pervasive Computing and Communication 2005 (PerCom '05), pp. 324–328, IEEE Computer Society, 2005.
21. R. Watro, D. Kong, S. fen Cuti, C. Gardiner, C. Lynn and P. Kruus, *TinyPK: securing sensor networks with public key technology*, In ACM workshop on Security of ad hoc and sensor networks 2004 (SASN '04), pp. 59–64. ACM Press, 2004.

7. R. Cramer and V. Shoup, Design and Analysis [illegible] Secure against Adaptive Chosen Ciphertext Attack, SIAM Journal of Computing, [illegible] 226, 2003.
8. [illegible] Wireless Sensor Network Platform, Crossbow Technology, Inc. [illegible]
[illegible]

Establishing secure links in low-rate wireless personal area networks

Maurizio Adriano Strangio

Abstract This paper presents a provably secure and efficient key agreement protocol (SNKE) using private key authentication. The distinguishing features of protocol SNKE are: (a) ease of implementation in the 802.15.4 stack (it makes use of the cryptographic services provided by the media access layer); (b) availability of two operation modes (hash-chain and key-renewal modes) with forward secrecy achieved (in key-renewal mode) with a modest computational effort.

In addition, the key distribution scheme, which may be either based on group keys or pairwise keys, combined with both operation modes offers effective levels of protection against long-term key compromise.

The protocol was designed to meet the strict power and energy constraints of low-rate wireless personal area networks (802.15.4 WPANs). Indeed, the foreseeable applications include the deployment of standard-compliant secure wireless sensor networks (WSNs).

1.1 Introduction

The latest version of the IEEE 802.15.4 standard [16] provides a comprehensive specification for the physical and media access control layers of low-rate wireless personal area networks (LR-WPAN). LR-WPANs are essentially aimed at supporting low cost, low power and reliable applications such as industrial monitoring and control, home automation, sensor networks and medical solutions. The standard specifies two different device types: (a) full-function devices (FFDs) and (b) reduced-function devices (RFDs). A FFD may operate in PAN coordinator, coordinator or device modes and interacts with both RFDs and FFDs. On the other hand, an RFD is intended for lightweight applications and can communicate only with FFDs. Three networking topologies are generally supported, i.e. star, peer-to-peer

---

Department of Mathematics, University of Rome "Roma Tre", Italy
e-mail: strangio@mat.uniroma3.it

Please use the following format when citing this chapter:

Strangio, M.A., 2008, in IFIP International Federation for Information Processing, Volume 278; *Proceedings of the IFIP TC 11 23rd International Information Security Conference*; Sushil Jajodia, Pierangela Samarati, Stelvio Cimato; (Boston: Springer), pp. 109–123.

or cluster-tree. RFDs can associate with a single FFD at a time thus forming only star network topologies. A network shall include at least one PAN coordinator which may have greater c! omputational resources than any other node in the PAN.

Over-the-air networks are inherently less secure than wired networks since attackers with the technology can intercept protocol transcripts with little effort (e.g. by making use of a portable computer with a 802.15.4 compliant radio interface or a scanner). Therefore, many applications need to ensure the confidentiality and integrity of the data flowing among the communicating nodes in the LR-WPAN. Furthermore, in hostile environments the opponent may succeed in obtaining the long-term keying material stored on a node. As a result, the attacker not only may learn confidential data exchanged in past communications (secured with previously established sessions keys) but, even worse, could modify and inject messages to influence the events for her own advantage (e.g. sensor networks deployed on a battlefield).

In this paper we present protocol SNKE, a secure and efficient key agreement scheme for establishing secure links in a LR-WPAN. The protocol makes use of private key cryptographic primitives to account for the energy constraints of devices forming the network and uses long-term shared keys to authenticate the communicating principals. In terms of energy consumption it is well known that private key algorithms are superior to public key cryptography.

Recently, many schemes based on pre-distributed keys have been proposed to avoid the computational overhead required by key agreement protocols; the general approach is to use either a unique network-wide shared key or a set of keys randomly chosen from a key pool so that two nodes share at least one key with high probability. However, the main drawbacks of these schemes is the lack of scalability and a higher vulnerability to node exposure.

To avoid the above shortcomings, protocol SNKE incorporates a key renewal mechanism; the long term private key shared by any two principals is replaced by a new value at the completion of the protocol execution. As a result, the protocol enjoys forward secrecy while requiring only a modest computational load on low resource devices (RFD nodes). As an additional benefit, protocol SKNE can be effectively implemented on top of the security services offered by the 802.15.4 media access control layer (WPAN-MAC).

1.2 Related work

There is a relatively small number of key agreement protocols based on symmetric key techniques. This is so mainly because key management is considered troublesome with symmetric key cryptosystems although the resulting algorithms are much more efficient. On the other hand, public-key cryptosystems can simplify the key management process but it turns out that ensuring the authenticity of the public keys is not less trivial than distributing symmetric keys.

Table 1.1 considers the most significant properties of key agreement protocols and compares several well known schemes found in the literature with protocol SNKE. As shown in column one, protocol SNKE competes with the others in terms of the required message flows. Column two enumerates the cryptographic primitives used as the basic building blocks, with ENC standing for "symmetric encryption" and MAC for "message authentication code" (the number in the parenthesis counts the invocations of the primitive for each side in a run of the protocol). Column three reveals whether the protocols provide key confirmation while column four clearly indicates that protocol SNKE is the only one providing forward secrecy (FS). Finally, column five indicates whether there are successful attacks against the protocols published in the literature.

Note that we do not consider key agreement protocols that are not strictly based on private key cryptography (even if they are more recent) or that require a trusted on-line third party (e.g. Kerberos key distribution); for example, SEKEN [18] albeit being an interesting proposal makes use of public keys (it is a key transport protocol) and also requires a base station to maintain an updated map of the network topology.

Table 1.1 Comparison of symmetric-cryptography key agreement protocols

↓*Protocol/Property*→	*Flows*	*Primitives*	*Key. Conf.*	*FS*	*Attacks*
Andrew RPC[28]	4	ENC(4)	-	No	Yes
2PKDP[19]	3	ENC(2)	A,B	No	No
ISO/IEC Mech. 5[17]	2	ENC(2)	A	No	No
ISO/IEC Mech. 6[17]	3	ENC(2)	A	No	No
AKEP1 [5]	3	ENC(1),MAC(2)	A,B	No	Yes
SNKE	3	ENC(1),MAC(1)	A,B	Yes	No

1.3 Protocol Specification

1.3.1 Preliminaries

If X is a finite set then $x \stackrel{R}{\leftarrow} X$ denotes the sampling of an element uniformly at random from X. If α is neither an algorithm nor a set $x \leftarrow \alpha$ represents a simple assignment statement. The symbol $\oplus$ denotes bitwise *exclusive or* on strings of equal length. Let $\mathtt{H} : \{0,1\}^* \rightarrow \{0,1\}^\ell$ denote a cryptographic hash function. We assume that hash functions behave like random functions (random oracles [6]).

A *keyed message authentication code* (MAC) is a 3-tuple of polynomial time algorithms $\langle \mathtt{key}(\cdot), \mathtt{tag}_\kappa(\cdot), \mathtt{ver}_\kappa(\cdot) \rangle$ where (a) $\mathtt{key}(\cdot)$ is a randomized key generation algorithm that returns a cryptographic key κ when the input is 1^ℓ (ℓ is the security parameter); (b) $\mathtt{tag}_\kappa(m)$ is a (randomized) algorithm that accepts message $m \in \{0,1\}^*$, key κ in input and returns a tag τ; (c) $\mathtt{ver}_\kappa(\tau)$ is a (deterministic) tag verification algorithm that accepts $(m,\ \tau)$ in input and returns 1 iff $tag_\kappa(m) = \tau$

otherwise it returns 0. We also require a correctness condition where for all m in the message space if $\texttt{tag}_{\kappa}(m) = \tau$ then $\texttt{ver}_{\kappa}(m, \tau)$ should output 1. The standard security notion for MACs requires resistance to strong unforgeability against chosen-message ! attacks (SUF-CMA, [4]).

A *private key encryption scheme* (ENC) is a 3-tuple of polynomial time algorithms $\langle \texttt{key}(\cdot), \texttt{enc}_{\kappa}(\cdot), \texttt{dec}_{\kappa}(\cdot) \rangle$ where (a) $\texttt{key}(1^{\ell})$ is a randomized key generation algorithm that returns a cryptographic key κ on input the security parameter ℓ; (b) $\texttt{enc}_{\kappa}(m)$ is a (randomized or stateful) algorithm that accepts a message $m \in \Sigma^*$ and key κ in input and returns a ciphertext c; (c) $\texttt{dec}_{\kappa}(c)$ is a (deterministic and stateless) algorithm that on input c, κ returns m (iff $\texttt{dec}_{\kappa}(\texttt{enc}_{\kappa}(m)) = m$). For a private key encryption scheme the standard security notions include *indistinguishability* of encryptions [15] and *non-malleability* [13] under chosen plaintext attacks (CPA) and chosen ciphertext attacks (CCA).

1.3.2 Protocol SNKE

Protocol SNKE (Figure 1.1) is an efficient key agreement protocol requiring only three messages to be exchanged. A symmetric authentication setting is assumed, i.e. a principal believes that its communication peer holds the shared key (securely) distributed prior to the actual communication and trusts that its partner is honest (private keys are not deliberately revealed to malicious third parties). The protocol provides key confirmation, implying that only the two principals involved in the communication should be able to establish the session key (since computation of the session key by each party requires knowledge of the shared secret), provided they were not corrupted before the protocol run. This appealing property, which makes the protocol resistant to *adaptive corruptions* [29, 9] and allows universal composability [10], is achieved by making use of a MAC to (explicitly) authenticate the transcripts with a (confirmation) key derived f! rom the actual session key. The protocol is endowed with two modes of operation:

hash-chain mode: principals A, B running the protocol establish a pair of session keys (respectively sk_A, sk_B) that are used to seed a hash chain of encryption keys. In other words, the ith message sent from A to B is encrypted under the key $sk_{A,i} = \texttt{H}(sk_{A,i-1})$ and key $sk_{A,i-1}$ is discarded (vice versa, the jth message from B to A is encrypted with $sk_{B,j}$). With this option enabled, protocol SNKE may be run once to seed the scheme of Mauw *et al.* [23] thus allowing bidirectional communication (the protocol in [23] supports only unidirectional communications);

key-renewal mode: principals A, B running the protocol receive in their local output a session key sk for subsequent encryption and a new shared long-term key $\texttt{K}'$. As a consequence, communications secured with previously established session keys are inaccessible if the parties are eventually corrupted (thus offering forward secrecy).

We point out two distinguishing features of protocol SNKE: (a) it is easily implemented in the 802.15.4 stack by making use of the cryptographic services provided by the media access layer; (b) with key-renewal mode forward security is achieved at the expense of a small resource expenditure (since it makes use of symmetric key cryptography). Observe that if the pre-shared key $\mathtt{K}$ is discarded by A, B in hash-chain mode the protocol also maintains forward secrecy. The main actions of the protocol are outlined below (refer to figure 1.1 for further details):

1. Principal A selects r_A (challenge nonce) at random from $\{0,1\}^\ell$ where $\ell \geq 64$, computes the ciphertext c_A under the symmetric key $\mathtt{K}$ and sends it to B;
2. Principal B decrypts message c_A, checks whether the resulting cleartext is correct (i.e if it contains the identity of its intended peer A), carries on by selecting r_B at random from $\{0,1\}^\ell$ and computes the 3-tuple of keys κ_B, χ_B, η_B. Thereafter, B computes the ciphertext c_B, the tag t_B authenticating message c_B, sends c_B, t_B to A and erases r_B, κ_B from its memory;
3. On receipt of c_B, t_B principal A decrypts message c_B and checks whether the resulting cleartext is correct (i.e if it contains the identity of its intended partner B). Subsequently she computes the 3-tuple of keys κ_A, χ_A, η_A verifies the tag t_B (rejecting the connection request in case of failure), sends the tag t_A to B and discards r_A, κ_A from its memory;
4. On receipt of t_A, provided the tag verification procedure is successful, principal B returns either $\mathtt{K}, \eta_B$ or χ_B, η_B depending on the operation mode (otherwise it returns null). Analogously for principal A;

Observe that in key-renewal mode when protocol SNKE returns, the calling application erases key $\mathtt{K}$ and replaces it with the new value $\mathtt{K}'$. For additional security, long-term keys may be stored in tamper-proof modules (when available); in this case all operations involving such keys would be performed inside the module (e.g. to compute χ_A, χ_B). On-line computations for both principals (regardless of the operation mode) involve one encryption and one decryption, computing and verifying a MAC tag and a hash value calculation.

1.4 Remarks on the Key Management Model

In this section we briefly comment on the key management models that may be applied with protocol SNKE. In general, adopting the appropriate scheme requires the designer to seek for an acceptable trade-off between security (resilience versus the adversarial model) and the required resource expenditure (e.g. memory usage).

The most common types of keying models are those wherein either: (1) a *network shared key* is distributed to the entire network; (2) *pairwise keys* are established among the nodes or (3) the network is partitioned into sets of nodes which are assigned *group keys*.

The network shared key model is the simplest scheme since it allows full connectivity with only one key to manage and small memory usage. However, the all

$A: \mathtt{K} = \mathtt{K}_{AB} = \mathtt{K}_{BA}$
$B: \mathtt{K} = \mathtt{K}_{AB} = \mathtt{K}_{BA}$
$\mathtt{OpMode}: 0 = \mathtt{key\text{-}renewal}, 1 = \mathtt{hash\text{-}chain}$

$A: r_A \xleftarrow{R} \{0,1\}^{\ell}$
$\quad c_A \leftarrow \mathtt{enc}_{\mathtt{K}}(r_A, A)$
$A \to B:\ c_A$
$B: r_A, B \leftarrow \mathtt{dec}_{\mathtt{K}}(c_A)$
$\quad r_B \xleftarrow{R} \{0,1\}^{\ell}$
$\quad c_B \leftarrow \mathtt{enc}_{\mathtt{K}}(r_B, B)$
$\quad \kappa_B, \chi_B, \eta_B \leftarrow \mathtt{H}(r_B, r_A, A, B, \mathtt{K})$
$\quad t_B \leftarrow \mathtt{tag}_{\kappa_B}(c_B, r_A, A)$
$B \to A:\ c_B, t_B$
$A: r_B, A \leftarrow \mathtt{dec}_{\mathtt{K}}(c_B)$
$\quad \kappa_A, \chi_A, \eta_A \leftarrow \mathtt{H}(r_B, r_A, A, B, \mathtt{K})$
$\quad$ if $\mathtt{ver}_{\kappa_A}(t_B) \neq 1$ then $\mathtt{reject}$ endif
$\quad t_A \leftarrow \mathtt{tag}_{\kappa_A}(c_A, r_B, B)$
$A \to B:\ t_A$
$B:$ if $\mathtt{ver}_{\kappa_B}(t_A) \neq 1$ then $\mathtt{reject}$ endif
$\quad$ if $\mathtt{OpMode}$=0 then return $\mathtt{K}' \leftarrow \mathtt{K} \oplus \chi_B, sk_B \leftarrow \eta_B$
$\quad$ elseif $\mathtt{OpMode}$=1 then return $sk_A \leftarrow \chi_A, sk_B \leftarrow \eta_B$
$\quad$ endif
$A:$ if $\mathtt{OpMode}$=0 then return $\mathtt{K}' \leftarrow \mathtt{K} \oplus \chi_A, sk_A \leftarrow \eta_A$
$\quad$ elseif $\mathtt{OpMode}$=1 then return $sk_A \leftarrow \chi_A, sk_B \leftarrow \eta_B$
$\quad$ endif

Fig. 1.1 Protocol SNKE

powerful adversary can gain complete control of the entire network by compromising any one of the nodes. Therefore, this scheme is detrimental if there is reason to believe that nodes may be compromised with non negligible probability (e.g. in an extremely hostile environment).

Many applications are aimed at monitoring the interactions between objects and the surrounding premises; the resulting network topology is often hierarchical with data paths optimized for the computation of aggregate data from subsets of nodes (in other words a node needs no interaction with all other nodes in the network). To this end, it may be advantageous to employ a key distribution scheme to establish pairwise links among communicating nodes. Networks established with pairwise keys are more resilient to attacks since the adversary that is able to compromise a node only learns the set of keys used by that node to communicate with neighboring devices. However, the degree of network connectivity determines the number of keys to be stored in each node (a fully connected 1-hop network having n nodes requires storing $n-1$ pairwise keys per node).

In the group key model a shared key is used by a set of nodes to establish secure links between any two nodes in the group. With this scheme one achieves a reasonable trade off between the worst case resilience to attacks displayed by the network shared key model and the large resource expenditure required by the pairwise key model.

Protocol SNKE may be profitably used either with pre-distributed group keys or pairwise keys. We assume that all nodes sharing a pre-defined key are within communication range (either because they were statically deployed over the target area or an additional self-organising mechanism is employed to bring key-coupled nodes in each others neighborhood).

A group key may be assigned to a set of RFD nodes and to one or more coordinator nodes[1] For example, the group of RFD nodes N020, N021, N022 and the FFD coordinator N02 in Figure 1.2 may have in common a group key; the nodes N0, N01, N02, N03, N012 also constitute a group based on a different key (unique in the whole network with N0 acting as the PAN coordinator).

When protocol SKNE is run in key-renewal mode, resilience to node compromise (within a group) increases with time; optimum resilience is achieved after each node has run the protocol with the coordinator node at least once (thereafter the protocol is invoked when the nodes need to communicate again with the coordinator). In hash-chain mode, the group key does not change and it suffices that each device runs the protocol only once with the coordinator since both will use the established keys for subsequent communications. Note that in this case the network (group) is not resilient to node compromise (unless as discussed before the base key is discarded; however, devices will no longer be able to communicate with other nodes in the group). Now assume that pairwise keys are pre-distributed to nodes in the WPAN. If protocol SNKE is run in key-renewal mode, compromise resilience of network nodes remains constant through out the lifetime of the WPAN (there is no need to wait until! all RFDs have run the protocol at least once with the coordinator as with group keys); i.e., forward secrecy is ensured for all sessions. Analogously, in hash-chain mode the main difference with respect to group keys is the stronger resilience to node compromise. We conclude this section by mentioning some noteworthy schemes for the key distribution problem (there is a large body of recent work in the literature concerning this problem). In [1] the authors introduce the concept of *pebbles* which are large ad-hoc networks of small resource-constrained devices that are assigned a secret group key. Communication among the devices of the same pebble is encrypted using the Traffic Encryption Key (TEK) which is derived from the group key. However, the proposed mechanism lacks a detailed analysis of the resources needed in the computation and the overhead for the subsequent distribution of the keys. Another open issue concerns the effectiveness of the probabilistic algorithm used to select the manager at each round of the key updating process. The probabilistic key distribution scheme of [14] is based on the assumption that every node in the network needs to communicate with all other nodes; this is a somewhat unp! ractical scenario for real world networks. Their scheme was later extended by [11] to allow more sophisticated probabilistic algorithms for establishing pairwise keys among sensor devices. Moreover, the authors in [22] developed a general framework called pool-based key pre-distribution wherein the schemes of [14, 11] can be considered as particular instances. These papers are all inspired by the work of [8] which describes a protocol for group key distribution based on the evaluation

[1] RFDs must store a shared key for each potential coordinator FFD they need to associate with.

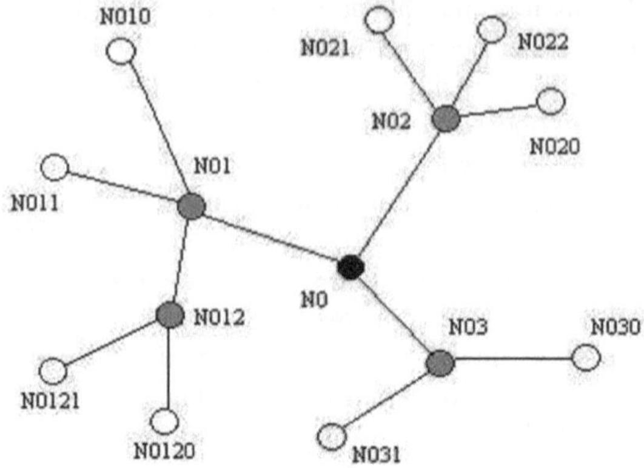

Fig. 1.2 A simple cluster tree WPAN. The black circle designates the PAN-coordinator, the gray circles indicate FFD nodes and the white circles RFD nodes. The lines between two nodes indicate that a parent-child relationship has been established due to a previous communication.

of shared polynomials. A disadvantage with all the preceding schemes is that they imply heavy computational loads on devices. The work of [26] mandates the use of a base station to distribute keys. This is not always convenient since it introduces a single point of failure into the network.

1.5 Security of Protocol SNKE

Rather than informally arguing about the desirable security properties (e.g. key independence (KI), forward secrecy (FS), etc) we adopt a more rigorous approach by proving the security of protocol SNKE in the formal model of distributed computing of Canetti-Krawczyk [9]. This model is currently considered the most comprehensive complexity-theoretic framework for protocol security analysis.

1.5.1 The Canetti-Krawczyk model

In this section we recall the main concepts of the Canetti-Krawczyk model (the presentation is mostly adapted from [9]). A `key-exchange` (`KE`) protocol is run in an interconnected network of machines (principals) executing instances of the protocol called `KE-sessions`. The set of principals are usually denoted by the letters P_i with $i = 1,\ldots,n$ (P_i's unique id corresponds to the subscript i). The input to the kth running instance of a protocol (KE session) within principal P_i is of the form $(i, j, s_{ik}, role)$ where j is the identity of the partner, s_{ik} is the session identifier and $role$ is either `initiator` or `responder` (the tuple $i, j, s_{ik}, role$ identifies the session within P_i). A session within P_i and a session within P_j are `matching` if their inputs are respectively of the form $(i, j, s_{ik},$`initiator`$)$ and $(j, i, s_{jl},$`responder`$)$ with $s_{ik} = s_{jl}$.! Matching sessions play an important role in the definition of security.

The adversary is an active "man-in-the-middle" malicious party that can intercept and modify messages, delay or prevent their delivery, inject messages of her own choice, interleave messages from different sessions, etc (i.e., the adversary is the network). To account for the potential disclosure of secret information, the adversary is allowed to perform the following types of operations on a session:

1. (`session-key query`,i, s_{ik}): the adversary learns the session key sk_{ik} corresponding to the complete session s_{ik};
2. (`party corruption`,i): the adversary learns *all* the information stored in the memory of P_i (including long-term private keys, session specific data and session keys). The result of this query depends on the current state of the protocols running within the principal; if P_i has not invoked any sessions then it returns the long-term private key otherwise it returns long-term private keys, session-specific data and session keys of completed and unexpired sessions (which have not been explicitly erased). From thereon all the actions of a corrupted principal are controlled by the attacker;
3. (`session-state reveal`,i, s_{ik}): this query is asked of a non-complete session s_{ik}. The adversary learns the (internal) session state for that particular session (which may include, for example, the secret ephemeral nonces but not the long-term private key used across all session at the party). The need for this query, in addition to party-corruption and session-key queries, stems from the possibility that private keys are given better protection than ephemeral session-specific data (e.g by using tamper-proof security modules);
4. (`session expiration`,i, s_{ik}): this action can be scheduled by the adversary for any session s_{ik} which is complete. As a result, the session key s_{ik} is erased from P_i's memory. The adversary is not allowed to perform a `session-key query` query of an expired session;

A `KE-session` $(i, j, s_{ik}, role)$ is *exposed* if the adversary has scheduled any one of the following actions on the session: (a) a `session-state reveal` query; (b) `session-key query`; (c) `party corruption` (of P_i) before the session has expired. Also, the session is exposed if its matching session $(j, i, s_{jl}, role')$ has been exposed (since matching sessions output the same session key).

The above model refers to the *unauthenticated-links* (UM) model and the corresponding adversary $\mathscr{U}$ is called the UM-adversary. There is also the *authenticated-links* (AM) model, wherein the AM-adversary [3], denoted $\mathscr{A}$, cannot inject or modify messages or neither deliver a specified message more than once. The rationale for having two models is explained by the notion of protocol *emulation*. Informally, a protocol Σ' *emulates* protocol Σ in the UM if for any adversary that interacts with Σ' in the UM there exists an adversary that interacts with the Σ in the AM such that the two interactions are computationally indistinguishable. Specific protocols, called *authenticators* (or compilers), on input the description of a protocol Σ, output a description of a protocol Σ' such that Σ' emulates Σ in the UM. Examples of authenticators are given in [3].

Formalisation of the security of a `KE` protocol follows the definitional approach of [5]. The resultant notion of an `SK-secure` protocol captures the requirement that the adversary is unable to obtain the session key of an unexposed session. An SK-game is defined wherein the goal of an UM-adversary $\mathscr{U}$ (the definition is analogous for the AM-adversary) is to distinguish the session key of a `KE-session` $(i, j, s_{ik}, role)$ with an additional `test-session` query. This query may be scheduled by the adversary only of a complete session. The adversary is provided with a value sk_{ik} as follows: an unbiased coin is tossed, if the result b equals 0 then sk_{ik} is the real value of the session key, otherwise it is a random value chosen from the same distribution of the session keys produced by the protocol but independent of the value of the real session key. After receiving sk_{ik} the adversary may continue with oth! er queries against the protocol; at the end of its game $\mathscr{U}$ outputs its guess b' of b. The adversary `succeeds` in its distinguishing attack if (1) the test session is not exposed; (2) the probability that $b' = b$ is significantly larger than $1/2$. More formally:

Definition 1 ([9]) *A* `KE` *protocol is* `SK-secure in the UM` *(resp. AM) if for any PPT* UM-*adversary* $\mathscr{U}$ *(resp.* AM-*adversary* $\mathscr{A}$*) the following conditions hold:*

a. *if two uncorrupted parties complete matching sessions in a protocol run then, except for a negligible probability, they output the same session key;*
b. $\mathscr{U}$ *succeeds (in its test-session distinguishing attack) with probability no more than 1/2 plus a negligible function in the security parameter.*

An important property of `KE` protocols not captured by the above definition is `forward secrecy` (`FS`), i.e., the assurance that once a session key is erased from the memory of the principals that have established the key, it cannot be learned by the adversary even if the principals are subsequently corrupted and (a polynomial number of) the protocol transcripts were observed (note that a passive adversary is subsumed here). Formally, this is captured via the notion of `session expiration`. A key-exchange protocol is said to be `FS-secure` if the above definition holds even when the adversary is allowed to corrupt a peer to the test session *after the test-session key expired* at that peer.

1.5.2 Security analysis of protocol SNKE

To prove that protocol SNKE (in both operational modes) is SK-secure in the UM we first show that the protocol of Figure 1.3 which we denote by SNKE-ENC[2]

[2] The values s_A, s_B represent session identifiers which are omitted from the specification of protocol SNKE for simplicity.

(since it is essentially equivalent to protocol SNKE without MACs) is secure in the AM. We then apply well known techniques and results to prove our thesis using the following MAC-authenticator ([9]): principal P_i sends a challenge nonce $N_i \stackrel{R}{\leftarrow} \{0,1\}^\ell$ to P_j and P_i responds by sending message m along with the authentication tag $\mathrm{MAC}_{k_{ij}}(j, N_i, m)$. This authenticator can be proven secure analogously to the signature-based authenticator from [3].

Theorem 1 *Assuming the encryption scheme* ENC *is* (t,ε)-IND-CPA-secure *and* H *is a random oracle then protocol* SNKE-ENC *is* SK-secure in the UM.

The proof of this theorem is in the appendix. We stress that the theorem is valid for both operation modes of protocol SNKE. By using the above MAC-authenticator to compile protocol SNKE-ENC, by virtue of Theorem 6 [9], we obtain that protocol SNKE is secure in the UM.

$$
\begin{array}{rl}
A: & \mathrm{K} = \mathrm{K}_{AB} = \mathrm{K}_{BA} \\
B: & \mathrm{K} = \mathrm{K}_{AB} = \mathrm{K}_{BA} \\
\hline
A: & r_A \stackrel{R}{\leftarrow} \{0,1\}^\ell \\
 & c_A \leftarrow \mathtt{enc}_{\mathrm{K}}(r_A, A) \\
A \rightarrow B: & s_A, c_A \\
B: & r_A, A \leftarrow \mathtt{dec}_{\mathrm{K}}(c_A) \\
 & r_B \stackrel{R}{\leftarrow} \{0,1\}^\ell \\
 & c_B \leftarrow \mathtt{enc}_{\mathrm{K}}(r_B, B) \\
 & \chi_B, sk_B \leftarrow \mathrm{H}(s_A, s_B, r_A, r_B, A, B, \mathrm{K}) \\
 & \mathrm{K}' \leftarrow \mathrm{K} \oplus \chi_B \\
B \rightarrow A: & s_B, c_B \\
A: & r_B, B \leftarrow \mathtt{dec}_{\mathrm{K}}(c_B) \\
 & \chi_A, sk_A \leftarrow \mathrm{H}(s_A, s_B, r_A, r_B, A, B, \mathrm{K}) \\
 & \mathrm{K}' \leftarrow \mathrm{K} \oplus \chi_A
\end{array}
$$

Fig. 1.3 Protocol SNKE-ENC

1.6 Implementation Issues

The 802.15.4 media access control layer offers three basic security services: (a) *message integrity*, (b) *data confidentiality* and (c) *replay protection*. The standard recommends the secure implementation of cryptographic operations and also that mechanisms should be employed to guaranteee the authenticity of stored keying material (which may be shared on a pairwise or group basis).

There are also eight different security suites in the standard which can be applied to the single frame that offer increasing grades of cryptographic protection: (a) no protection; (b) message (frame) integrity with tags of length 32, 64 and 128 bits; (c) encryption only (d) authenticated encryption with tags of length 32, 64 and 128 bits.

The upper protocol layers are responsible for setting up the keys and determining the security level to use.

We estimate the power consumption of a node in the key establishment process; of course, there are minimum energy requirements necessary to preserve an adequate level of security. By inspection of Table 1.1 (column two - *Primitives*) it is clear that protocol SNKE performs better than all the others in terms of the energy requirements involved in the execution of the cryptographic primitives and radio communications.

The practical security of any hash function lies in the appropriate choice of the output size m in order to prevent collisions (which are easier to find than pre-images and 2nd pre-images). A number of computations of size $O(2^{m/2})$ are required to find a collision for an m-bit hash function according to the "birthday attack"; whereas it requires a $O(2^m)$ effort to find either pre-images or 2nd pre-images by the brute-force attack [24]. For this reason we consider the SHA-1 construction a suitable choice for the hash function H. According to [27] the energy cost of computing SHA-1 ($m = 160$) is approximately 0.76 μJ per byte.

The 802.15.4 standard indicates the AES block cipher [12] with 128-bit keys as the designated encryption scheme (consider also the construction of [25]). In recent work it was reported that the energy cost of performing 128-bit AES encryption/decryption operations on a Rockwell WINS node (equipped with a 133 MHz StrongARM processor) is less than 0.1 mJ [21]. For greater efficiency one-time pads may be used (significant energy savings can be achieved on RFD devices); in this case the shared key should be twice the standard length (i.e. 256 bits) with each principal using a different half (128 bits) to encrypt the exchanged nonces r_A, r_B (this method can be applied when the protocol is run in key-renewal mode).

The HMAC-SHA1 [2] construction is the recommended choice for the MAC since it enjoys the SUF-CMA security property and requires a modest computational load (the underlying hash function (SHA) is applied twice with some additional padding); furthermore, it allows efficient reuse of the chip area dedicated to the hash function. Alternatively, the UMAC construction [7] which is based on a universal hash function family may offer greater efficiency. Recently, Kaps *et al.* [20] have improved the universal hash function family used in UMAC (NH) and have obtained a new construction (WH) with significant energy savings (it is shown that WH outperforms NH with respect to dynamic and leakage power, circuit area and delay at 100 MHz).

References

1. S. Basagni, K. Herrin, E. Rosti, and D. Bruschi. Secure Pebblenets. *Proceedings of the ACM International Symposium on Mobile Ad Hoc Networking and Computing*, pages 156–163, 2001.
2. M. Bellare, R. Canetti, and H. Krawczyk. Keying hash functions for message authentication. *Advances in Cryptology - CRYPTO 1996*, LNCS 1109:1–15, 1996.

3. M. Bellare, R. Canetti, and H. Krawczyk. A modular approach to the design and analysis of authentication and key exchange protocols. *In 30th Symposium on Theory of Computing*, pages 419–428, 1998.
4. M. Bellare and C. Nampempre. Authenticated encryption: Relations among notions and analysis of the generic composition paradigm. *Advances in Cryptology - Asiacrypt 2000*, LNCS 1976, 2000.
5. M. Bellare and P. Rogaway. Entity authentication and key distribution. *In Proceedings of CRYPTO 1993*, LNCS 773:232–249, 1993.
6. M. Bellare and P. Rogaway. Random oracles are practical: A paradigm for designing efficient protocols. *In 1st Conference on Computer and Communications Security*, pages 62–73, 1993.
7. J. Black, S. Halevi, H. Krawczyk, T. Krovetz, and P. Rogaway. UMAC: Fast and secure message authentication. *Advances in Cryptology - CRYPTO '99*, LNCS 1666:216–233, 1999.
8. C. Blundo, A. D. Santis, A. Herzberg, S. Kutten, S. Vaccaro, and M. Yung. Perfectly-secure key distribution for dynamic conferences. *Advances in Cryptology - CRYPTO 1992*, LNCS 740:471–486, 1993.
9. R. Canetti and H. Krawczyk. Analysis of key exchange protocols and their use for building secure channels. *Advances in Cryptology-EUROCRYPT 2001*, LNCS 2045:453–474, 2001.
10. R. Canetti and H. Krawczyk. Universally composable notions of key exchange and secure channels. *Advances in Cryptology-EUROCRYPT 2002*, LNCS 2332:337–351, 2002.
11. H. Chan, A. Perrig, and D. Song. Random key predistribution schemes for sensor networks. *Proceedings of the IEEE Symposium on Research in Security and Privacy*, pages 197–213, 2003.
12. J. Daemen and V. Rijmen. *The Design of Rijndael*. Springer-Verlag, 2002.
13. D. Dolev, C. Dwork, and M. Naor. Non-malleable cryptography. *Proceedings of the 23rd Annual Symposium on the Theory of Computing*, 1991.
14. L. Eschenauer and V. Gligor. A key management scheme for distributed sensor networks. *Proceedings of the 9th ACM Conference on Computer and Communications Security*, pages 41–47, 2002.
15. S. Goldwasser and S. Micali. Probabilistic encryption. *Journal of Computing and System Sciences*, 28:270–299, 1984.
16. IEEE-802.15.4-2006. Standard for information technology-telecommunications and inofrmation exchange between systems-local and metropoolitan area networks-specific requirements-part 15.4: Wireless medium access control (mac) and physical layer (phy) specifications for low rate wireless personal area networks (wpann). Institute of Electrical and Electronics Engineers, 2006.
17. ISO/IEC-11770-2. Information technology-security techniques-key management-part 2: Mechanisms using symmetric techniques. International Standards Organization, 1996.
18. K. Jamshaid and L. Schwiebert. SEKEN (Secure and Efficient Key Exchange for Sensor Networks. *Proceedings of IEEE Int.l Conference on Performance, Computing and Communications*, pages 415–422, 2004.
19. P. Janson and G. Tsudik. Secure and Minimal Protocols for Authenticated Key Distribution. *Computer communications*, 18(9):645–653, 1995.
20. J. Kaps, K. Yuksel, and B. Sunar. Energy Scalable Universal Hashing. *IEEE Transactions on Computers*, pages 1484–1495, 2005.
21. H. Krawczyk. The energy cost of cryptographic key establishment in wireless sensor networks. *http://eprint.iacr.org/2007/003*, 2007.
22. D. Liu, P. Ning, and R. Li. Establishing pairwise keys in distributed sensor networks. *Proceedings of the 10th ACM conference on Computer and communications security*, pages 52–61, 2003.
23. S. Mauw, I. Van Vessen, and B. Bos. Forward Secure Communication in Wireless Sensor Networks. *3rd International Conference on Security in Pervasive Computing*, 2006.
24. A. Menezes, P. V. Oorschot, and S. Vanstone. *Handbook of Applied Cryptography*. CRC Press, 1997.
25. M. Ohkubo, K. Suzuki, and S. Kinoshita. Cryptographic Approach to "Privacy-Friendly" Tags. *In RFID Privacy Workshop*, 2003.

26. A. Perrig, R. Szewczyk, V. Wen, D. E. Culler, and J. Tygar. SPINS: Security protocols for sensor networks. *In Mobile Computing and Networking*, 2001.
27. N. Potlapally, S. Ravi, A. Raghunathan, and N. Jha. Analyzing the energy consumption of security protocols. *Proceedings of Int.l Symposium on Low power electronics and Design*, pages 30–35, 2003.
28. M. Satyanarayanan. Integrating Security in a Large Distributed System. *ACM Transactions on Computer Systems*, 7(3):247–280, 1989.
29. V. Shoup. On Formal Models for Secure Key Exchange. Technical Report RZ 3120, IBM Research, 1999.

1.7 Appendix - Proof of theorem 1

The first condition of Definition 1 is easily verified in the AM (recall that AM-adversaries cannot modify or inject messages unless the sender is corrupted or the messages belong to an exposed session).

We now prove condition two of Definition 1. Recall that an encryption scheme is (t,ε)-IND-CPA-secure if the advantage of the adversary (running in time at most t) at the end of the IND-CPA-game (which captures the indistinguishability of encryptions under chosen plaintext attacks) is less than ε. The IND-CPA-game played by $\mathscr{B} = (\mathscr{B}_1, \mathscr{B}_2)$ (against challenger algorithm $\mathscr{C}$) is outlined below:

1. (Setup): $\mathscr{C}$ generates a shared key $\mathtt{K} \xleftarrow{R} \mathtt{key}(1^\ell)$ and gives 1^ℓ to $\mathscr{B}_1$;
2. (Non-adaptive queries): $\mathscr{B}_1$ asks the encryption oracle queries of its own choice;
3. (Challenge ciphertext): $\mathscr{B}_1$ chooses plaintexts m_0, m_1 (with $|m_0| = |m_1|$) and gives them to the challenger, who selects a bit b and returns the encryption of m_b under $\mathtt{K}$ (i.e. ciphertext c). $\mathscr{B}_1$ hands over c and state information to $\mathscr{B}_2$;
4. (Adaptive queries): $\mathscr{B}_2$ may issue additional queries to the encryption oracle;
5. (Output): $\mathscr{B}_2$ stops and outputs a bit b_{CPA} as its guess for b: $\mathscr{B}$ wins if $b_{CPA} = b$.

The advantage of the adversary is calculated as the difference between the probability that $\mathscr{B}$ outputs the correct value of bit b and a random guess (with probability $1/2$). Consider adversary $\mathscr{A}$ attacking the protocol in the AM. Observe that under the hypothesis that $\mathtt{H}$ is a random oracle the only one way $\mathscr{A}$ can obtain significant information (and therefore win the SK-game) about a particular session key $sk_{ij}^s = \mathtt{H}(s_i, s_j, r_i, r_j, i, j, \mathtt{K}_{ij})$ is by querying the oracle at the point $(s_i, s_j, r_i, r_j, i, j, \mathtt{K}_{ij})$. Suppose that the challenger $\mathscr{C}$ starts (the setup phase) by generating key $\mathtt{K}^* \xleftarrow{R} \mathtt{key}(1^\ell)$. Algorithm $\mathscr{B}_1$ is given in input 1^ℓ and access to the encryption oracle under key $\mathtt{K}^*$. At some stage of its game $\mathscr{B}_1$ chooses at random two principals P_{i^*}, P_{j^*} among all the n principals, selects $! \xleftarrow{R} r_i^{(0)}, r_i^{(1)} \{0,1\}^{\ell_1}$ and outputs $m_0 = (r_i^{(0)}, j^*), m_1 = (r_i^{(1)}, j^*)$. The challenger $\mathscr{C}$ chooses a random bit b and computes $c = \mathtt{enc}_{\mathtt{K}^*}(m_b)$. Algorithm $\mathscr{B}_2$ is given in input $c, 1^\ell$ and state information (which contains the values $r_i^{(0)}, r_i^{(1)}, i^*, j^*$). $\mathscr{B}_2$ generates the keying material (pairwise keys) $\mathtt{K}_{ij} \leftarrow \mathtt{key}(1^\ell)$ for any two parties i, j except for P_{i^*}, P_{j^*}; their shared key $\mathtt{K}_{i^* j^*}$ is assumed to be equal to $\mathtt{K}^*$ (of course, $\mathscr{B}_2$ does not know the value of $\mathtt{K}^*$). Note that

P_{i^*} and P_{j^*} will eventually share pairwise keys with other principals $P_k, k \neq i^*, j^*$. $\mathscr{B}_2$ also chooses at random a session id s_i^* among those where P_{i^*} is the initiator and P_{j^*} the responder (i.e. the chosen session is (i^*, j^*, s_i^*)—we omit the indi! cation of the role and the subscript counting the number of se! ssions f or simplicity). Algorithm $\mathscr{B}_2$ tries to guess b in its IND-CPA-game while running $\mathscr{A}$ as a subroutine. In particular, $\mathscr{B}_2$ must simulate a virtual SK-game played by $\mathscr{A}$ in such a way that $\mathscr{A}$'s view is indistinguishable from a real SK-game. All sessions scheduled by $\mathscr{A}$ are simulated by $\mathscr{B}_2$ according to the specification of the protocol. In particular, for sessions $s_i \neq s_i^*$ involving two principals P_i, P_j with $i \neq i^*$ or $j \neq j^*$ it outputs the transcript $\mathtt{enc}_{\mathtt{K}_{ij}}(r_i, j) \| \mathtt{enc}_{\mathtt{K}_{ji}}(r_j, i)$[3] for random r_i, r_j and sets $sk_{ji}^s = sk_{ij}^s \stackrel{R}{\leftarrow} \{0,1\}^{|\mathtt{H}(\cdot)|}$. When (eventually) session s_i^* is invoked, $\mathscr{B}_2$ submits to $\mathscr{A}$ the challenge c! iphertext $y = \mathtt{enc}_{\mathtt{K}}(m_b, j^*)$ as the message sent by the initiator P_{i^*}. In addition, $\mathscr{B}_2$ chooses $r_j^* \stackrel{R}{\leftarrow} \{0,1\}^{\ell_1}$, obtains the value $z = \mathtt{enc}_{\mathtt{K}^*}(r_j^*, i^*)$ from its encryption oracle, submits z to $\mathscr{A}$ as P_{j^*}'s response and sets $sk_{j^* i^*}^{s^*} = sk_{i^* j^*}^{s^*} \stackrel{R}{\leftarrow} \{0,1\}^{|\mathtt{H}(\cdot)|}$. For queries of the random oracle $\mathtt{H}$ at the point $(s_i, s_j, r_i, r_j, i, j, \mathtt{K}_{ij})$ submitted by $\mathscr{A}$ the answer is $v \stackrel{R}{\leftarrow} \{0,1\}^{|\mathtt{H}(\cdot)|}$. If $i = i^*$ and $j = j^*$ the record $\langle \widehat{s_i}, (s_i, s_j, r_i, r_j, i, j, \mathtt{K}_{ij}) \rangle$ is stored in the list L. When $\mathscr{A}$ invokes `session-state reveal` or `party corruption` queries that do not involve both P_{i^*}, P_{j^*} these are easily answered by $\mathscr{B}_2$ since it knows the required information (see above). If at any point $\mathscr{A}$ issues a `session-state reveal` of session s^*, a `party corruption` query of either P_{i^*} or P_{j^*} or chooses a test-session different than s^* then $\mathscr{B}_2$ aborts. At the end of its game (and when $\mathscr{A}$ has stopped) $\mathscr{B}_2$ outputs the element from the list L having $\widehat{s_i} = s_i^*$ (if it exists).

We analyze the success probability of $\mathscr{B}_2$. If there exists an entry in the list L having $\widehat{s_i} = s_i^*$ we say that event $\mathtt{qry}^*$ has occurred. We have

$$|\mathrm{Pr}_{\mathscr{B}_2}[b_{CPA}{=}b] - \frac{1}{2}| = |\mathrm{Pr}_{\mathscr{A}}[b_{SK}{=}b] - \frac{1}{2}| \leq \mathrm{Pr}_{\mathscr{A}}[\mathtt{qry}^*] + \frac{1}{2}\mathrm{Pr}_{\mathscr{A}}[\overline{\mathtt{qry}^*}] \leq \frac{1}{2}\mathrm{Pr}_{\mathscr{A}}[\mathtt{qry}^*]$$

where we used the fact that $\mathrm{Pr}_{\mathscr{A}}[b_{SK} = b | \overline{\mathtt{qry}^*}] = \frac{1}{2}$ The probability that $\mathscr{B}_2$ outputs the correct answer is (at least) $\mathrm{Pr}_{\mathscr{A}}[\mathtt{qry}^*]/q_s$ where q_s is the polynomial bound on the number of sessions run in the SK-game. Therefore, since the running time of $\mathscr{B}_2$ is essentially equal to the running time of $\mathscr{A}$ we have

$$|\mathrm{Pr}_{\mathscr{B}_2}[b_{CPA}{=}b] - \frac{1}{2}| \leq q_s \varepsilon$$

and this proves the theorem.

[3] The actual order of the messages in the transcript depends on the role (initiator or responder) played by each principal in the run of the protocol.

An Asynchronous Node Replication Attack in Wireless Sensor Networks

Jianying Zhou, Tanmoy Kanti Das, and Javier Lopez

Abstract Applications of wireless sensor network (WSN) are growing significantly, and many security protocols meant for WSN have been proposed. One of the unique problems of WSN is that the sensor nodes are not tamper resistant as the main attraction of deploying WSN is its low cost. *Node replication attack* exploits this weakness to launch an attack, in which cryptographic secrets from the compromised sensor nodes are used to create duplicate sensor nodes in large number. Then these sensor nodes are placed in critical locations of the WSN to mount attacks. Several protocols were proposed to defend WSN against the replication attack, and one of the promising among them is *distributed detection protocol* presented by Parno et al. at IEEE S&P 2005. However, we show in this paper that their distributed detection protocol is vulnerable to an *asynchronous* node replication attack. Further, we modify the protocol to make it secure for *dynamic* WSN supporting node mobility.

Keywords: Wireless Sensor Network Security, Node Replication Attack, Distributed Detection Protocol.

1 Introduction

Wireless sensor networks are quickly gaining popularity due to the fact that they are potentially low cost solutions to a variety of real-world challenges [1] and they provide a means to deploy large sensor arrays in a variety of con-

Jianying Zhou
Institute for Infocomm Research, Singapore, e-mail: jyzhou@i2r.a-star.edu.sg

Tanmoy Kanti Das
e-mail: dastanmoy@gmail.com

Javier Lopez
Computer Science Department, University of Malaga, Spain, e-mail: jlm@lcc.uma.es

Please use the following format when citing this chapter:

Zhou, J., Das, T.K. and Lopez, J., 2008, in IFIP International Federation for Information Processing, Volume 278; *Proceedings of the IFIP TC 11 23rd International Information Security Conference*; Sushil Jajodia, Pierangela Samarati, Stelvio Cimato; (Boston: Springer), pp. 125–139.

ditions capable of performing both military and civilian tasks. However, due to inherent constraints of resources (computing, communication, and storage), security in WSN poses different challenges than traditional network/computer security [9, 15].

The security threats to WSN and the countermeasures have been studied intensively in the recent years [2]. Many of the identified attacks are generic in nature and may not work under every operational considerations. Similarly, the proposed defenses against these attacks are also generic in nature. Thus there is a need to analyze those countermeasures in different operational scenarios to verify their effectiveness. In this paper, we study the defenses against the node replication attack under certain operational conditions. We show that under these operational conditions the proposed defenses are inadequate to thwart our *asynchronous* node replication attack as defined in this paper.

The rest of this paper is organized as follows. In the next section, we survey the related work on WSN security. In section 3, we review the existing techniques for detection of node replication. In section 4, we present a new node replication attack which defeats the detection mechanism. In section 5, we suggest several modifications to make the existing distributed detection protocol secure. Section 6 concludes the paper.

2 Related Work

Most of WSNs consist of off-the-shelf low cost hardware without any tamper-proof capabilities. Thus sensor nodes are vulnerable to abuse and compromise. In fact, it is pointed out in [7] that MICA2 sensor nodes can be compromised within a minute. Thus compromising a node for mounting different kinds of attack is a practical threat to any WSN. Particularly the threat is really serious where sensor nodes are deployed in adversarial conditions. The attacker can capture nodes, replicate at will and place the duplicate nodes in critical network locations to cause maximum disruption in the network operation. It should be noted that a single captured node is enough to mount these sort of attacks. Use of tamper-proof hardware is the most easy and effective solution of the problem. However, tamper-proof hardware is costly and it is simply not economical to deploy such sensor networks. So we have to look for other avenues to resist this kind of attack.

Researchers are looking into security of WSN from different perspective. Lots of attacks and countermeasures are proposed in the existing literature [3, 4, 16, 18, 19]. McCune et al. [10] highlighted the *Denial-of-Message* (DoM) attack in which a set of nodes act maliciously and prevent broadcast messages to reach certain section(s) of the WSN. They also proposed Secure Implicit Sampling algorithm to detect such attacks. Newsome et al. [13] proposed the defenses against *Sybil attack* in which a single node takes on multiple identities to deceive other nodes. Hu et al. [8] presented an algorithm, known as packet leashes, to defeat the *wormhole attack* in which the attacker captures message bits at one location and replays them in another location. Karlof et al. [11] discussed several attacks and countermeasures against routing protocols in WSNs.

To effectively resist any attack, we have to understand the goals and motivation of the attacker first. Let us consider a WSN deployed in hazardous and adversarial conditions like in a battle field. In this situation, any adversary's goal may include any/all of the following.

- Find out the network topology.
- Learn about the data collected by the sensor nodes.
- Inject false data to mislead the enemy.
- Bring down the network if possible.

It is assumed that it is not possible for the attacker to physically remove all sensor nodes. However, the attacker can capture a few of them. Thus to achieve his goals, the attacker may look for other options. One of the options available to him is to capture as many nodes as possible and turn them into malicious nodes. One technique that can be used is to quickly replicate the captured nodes and insert the duplicate nodes in strategic locations within the WSN to achieve any/all of the above goals.

In this paper, we consider a competitive scenario where two rival WSNs are deployed. The primary goal of both networks is the same: to observe some physical phenomenon. The secondary goal is to mount attacks on the rival network. Example of this type of competitive environment exists in battle field monitoring systems. Here nodes of a WSN collaborate to mount attacks on the other WSN. Attacks may be as simple as to read the secret data from the other network or more severe ones which incapacitate the attacked network to function. Under this operational scenario, we investigate the effectiveness of available defense mechanisms. We assume that the adversary can only capture a few nodes and the number of captured nodes are insignificant compared to the total number of deployed nodes. We show that the existing protocols are insufficient to prevent a new node replication attack effectively in *dynamic* WSN supporting node mobility. Our attack is different from the existing node replication attacks as at no point of time the number of malicious nodes directly involved in mounting the attack is greater than the number of captured nodes. Thus, one may argue this attack cannot be termed as node replication attack. However, the number of nodes directly involved in the attack over a period of time is much much higher than the number of captured nodes. Thus we consider this attack as a *variant* of the classical node replication attack.

3 Detection of Node Replication Attack

There are several techniques available in the existing literature to resist the *node replication attack* described above. They can be broadly categorized into three different categories: *localized* approach, *centralized* approach, and *distributed* approach [14].

In localized detection technique, neighbours of a node vouch for this node's location by voting [13]. However, this approach cannot detect the distributed node replication where the replicated nodes are more than two hops away. Other method that can reliably detect the node replication is based on centralized approach. Here each node sends its neighbours' claimed location information to the base station for verification. This method can effectively detect the node replication attack but nodes near the base station bear the burnt of excessive communication. Also nodes near the base station are subject to subversion by the attacker as failure of these nodes cripples the WSN. Thus distributed approach where all nodes in the WSN share the burden of detection, is the most preferred solution.

Parno et al. [14] presented a distributed detection and prevention mechanism for node replication attack. The *randomized multicast protocol* described in [14] is based on birthday paradox. In this protocol, each node sends its location claim having format $< ID_\alpha, l_\alpha, \{H(ID_\alpha, l_\alpha)\}_{K_\alpha^{-1}} >$ to its immediate neighbours. Here ID_α, l_α are id and location of node α, respectively; K_α, K_α^{-1} are public and private keys of the node α, respectively; $H(M)$ is the hash of message M, and $\{M\}_{K_\alpha^{-1}}$ indicates α's signature on M. Upon receiving a location claim from its neighbour α, a node verifies signature of α on it and with probability p, it selects g random locations within the network. Then it forwards the location claim to the witness nodes near the selected locations using *geographic routing* [12, 17]. Similarly, neighbours of the replica α' also forward the location claim to the witness nodes. Based on the birthday paradox, it can be assumed two nodes with the same id but different location will have at least one common witness who will flood the network about the conflicting location claims. This will in turn exclude all the malicious nodes having id ID_α from the network. It was found that if a network consists of $n = 10000$ nodes and if g=100, average degree of each node $d = 20$ and $p = 0.05$ is the probability that a neighbour will forward a location information, then the probability of detecting a single node replication is 63%. If the node is replicated twice the probability of detection is greater than 95%. The communication cost of the protocol is of the order of $O(n^2)$.

A more efficient version of the randomized multicast protocol is *line selected multicast protocol* [14]. As we know, to send a piece of information from node α to β, the information should travel through several intermediate nodes as nodes in a WSN not only act as a data collection unit but also act as a router. When a location claim travels from node α to β, all the intermediate nodes in the path are aware about that particular location claim. Thus ever a conflicting location claim crosses the path, these intermediate nodes can detect the conflict and inform others about it. This is the basic idea behind the line selected multicast protocol. It was found that the expected number of intersections c, between x randomly drawn lines (i.e. paths) within the unit circle is given by [14]

$$E(c) = x(x-1)\left(\frac{1}{6} + \frac{245}{144\pi^2}\right)$$

The exact protocol is as follows [14].

1. Let $r = p \cdot d \cdot g$, where p is the probability that a neighbour will forward a location information and d is the average degree of each node.
2. Each location claim from a node α is forwarded to r nodes by α's neighbours.
3. All the intermediate sensor nodes through which these claims travel to reach their intended recipient also store these claims in their buffer. And these intermediate nodes thus act as additional witnesses.
4. After receiving a location claim from node α', the witness node checks for the existence of similar claims among the claims already in its buffer. Here, by similar we mean that the two claims have the same id. If a similar claim α with a different location already exists, the witness node informs all other nodes about them. Consequently, α and all α's are excluded from the network.

The advantage of line selected multicast over randomized multicast comes from the fact that nodes along the path through which the claims travel also act as witnesses. It was found during Monte-Carlo simulations that if we have two paths for α originating from α's neighbour and two for α', then the probability of intersection is 56%. This probability increases to 95% if we have five such paths instead of two. Communication overhead for the entire network is $O(n\sqrt{n})$, assuming that the length of each path is $O(\sqrt{n})$. Under the similar assumption, each node requires to store $O(\sqrt{n})$ location claims.

Both the protocols described above require a loose notion of synchronization for proper detection of node replication attack. The frequency of execution of detection protocol depends on several conflicting requirements like detection efficiency, storage and communication costs etc.. In one variant of the protocol, detection algorithm runs after fixed interval T and it takes t unit of time for detection algorithm to complete. Note that $T >> t$. After the execution of the detection algorithm, all the nodes only remember the identities of revoked nodes. However, there is a lacuna in this approach. Node replication can be mounted between the two detection passes. To overcome this, all nodes also remember the list of its valid neighbours detected during previous run of detection protocol and all nodes refuse to communicate with a node unless it participates in a detection pass. In another approach, time is divided into T epochs consisting of k time slots. During each time slot, a fixed number of nodes announce their location and the standard protocols are followed thereafter. All the protocols presented here assume that each node got at least one legitimate neighbour. Otherwise, masked replication attack can be mounted, though one can easily defeat the masked replication attack with the use of pseudo-neighbour(s) [14].

4 Asynchronous Node Replication Attack

As described earlier that we are considering a competitive environment where more than one WSN is deployed. This type of situation may be available in military applications like battle field or border monitoring system. Each of the WSN has a specific set of goals and one important goal is to mount attacks on the enemy network to prevent it from functioning normally or read data from the enemy network. Cryptographic information retrieved from the captured node(s) most of the time is used for mounting such an attack. One of the widely used techniques to mount an attack based on information retrieved from the captured nodes is node replication, and here we study the protocols used to detect such an attack.

In the classical node replication attack, it is assumed that the adversary will replicate a captured node and will insert large number of duplicate nodes for malicious purpose. All the duplicate nodes are present simultaneously in the network. Distributed detection mechanism succeeds because of the presence of nodes with the same id in different locations. Classical node replication attack is very straightforward and the defense mechanism is also simple. We like to investigate the effectiveness of such defense mechanisms against an *asynchronous node replication attack* where the number of nodes actively mounting the attack at any specific point of time is not greater than the number of captured nodes, but over a period of time the total number of nodes actively participating in mounting the attack is far greater than the total number of captured nodes.

Let us denote the original WSN as "blue" network and the WSN deployed by the adversary as "gray" network. Besides the nodes actively participating in mounting an attack, all other nodes in gray network passively participate in mounting an attack, i.e., they only help active nodes by providing network resources from gray network.

4.1 Basic Strategy

Here we consider that the attacker only possesses a single captured node and blue network is running *distributed node replication detection* protocol. Let us discuss how we can mount a node replication without being detected. We will generalize this strategy later to consider that multiple captured nodes are available to the attacker. The main idea behind our attack is to use the captured cryptographic secrets by different nodes of the gray network during each detection pass. At any point of time the number of nodes mounting the attack is equal to the number of captured nodes. However, over a period of time, the total number of nodes directly used to mount the attack is much higher than the number of captured nodes. Let us present the attack in a stepwise manner (see Figure 1).

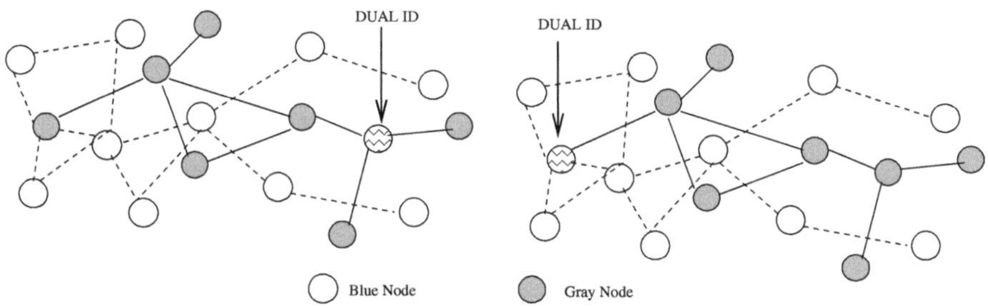

Fig. 1 Dual ID node moves in blue network

1. Deploy the gray sensor network over the same area as that of the blue network. One of the sensor node δ in the gray network holds dual id consisting of the captured id from the blue network and its own id in the gray network.
2. We assume that the nodes in the gray network can securely communicate among themselves, which means authenticity, integrity and confidentiality of message exchanged among gray nodes are guaranteed.
3. The node δ with dual id acts as the gateway between the gray and blue networks. However, the blue network is unaware of it.
4. In each detection pass of the blue network, different nodes from the gray network act as the gateway. At the beginning of the detection phase in the blue network, the nodes in the gray network decide upon a node γ, which will take over the role of the gateway δ. This node then gets all the cryptographic information from the previous gateway and participates in the detection phase as a legitimate node in the blue network. Also the previous gateway δ_p forgets the id used to communicate with the blue network. However, δ_p continues to be a part of the gray network. This way δ evades detection, as well as learns about the blue network topology and other sensitive information about the blue network. To an outside observer monitoring the blue network, it would appear that δ is changing location each time a detection pass runs. However, it would not be possible under a distributed detection environment to detect such a malicious behavior by δ.

Let us now analyze the situation from the blue network's point of view. It seems that everything runs normally. In each detection pass a node with valid id ID_δ is moving to different part of the network. Due to the distributed nature of the detection mechanism it cannot even detect this type of random disappearance/appearance of node δ from different part of the blue network each time the detection phase runs, thus unsuspecting the blue network falls pray to the attack. However, one question remains, what the attacker achieves by mounting the attack. His gain is as follows.

- Though the attacker is able to compromise only one node, he can discover the entire topology of the blue network.
- The attacker can learn about the traffic pattern of the blue network.
- The attacker can identify the nodes which are critical for network-wise communication and whose failure may partition the network.

The attack becomes more critical if the number of captured nodes becomes more than one. Then several δs can collaborate to mount more severe attacks.

4.2 Collaborative Strategy

Now we consider a more realistic scenario where an adversary captures more than one sensor node. Let the number of captured nodes be m and the nodes using the captured identity is denoted by $\delta_0, \delta_1, \ldots, \delta_{m-1}$. Note that, the number of captured nodes are insignificant compared to the total number of deployed nodes. Otherwise, if the adversary controls most of the nodes, he can control the network with ease. In the previous subsection, we have assumed that the adversary is in possession of only one captured node, thus can mount the attack through only one node. Here, we consider more than one captured node is available and they can collaborate to mount the attack. Though the basic strategy remains the same, in the present case, $\delta_0, \delta_1, \ldots, \delta_{m-1}$ can mount coordinated attack. Also, δ_i, δ_j may not be within the radio range of each other but they can communicate with each other using both blue and gray networks. Thus when δ_i, δ_j communicate through the gray network, the communication remains secret from the blue network. Let us present the attack in a stepwise manner (see Figure 2).

1. Let the total number of captured nodes be m. At the beginning of each detection pass, the gray network selects m number of nodes. Selected nodes hold dual id, one for the blue network and the other for the gray network.
2. Let us denote the nodes having dual id as $\delta_0, \delta_1, \ldots, \delta_{m-1}$. Different set of nodes from the gray network may perform the role of dual id nodes during each detection pass. Newly captured ids can also be added to increase the number of captured ids. In reality the attack can be mounted with a single captured id and one can add new captured ids as when available. Thus the attack is dynamic in nature.

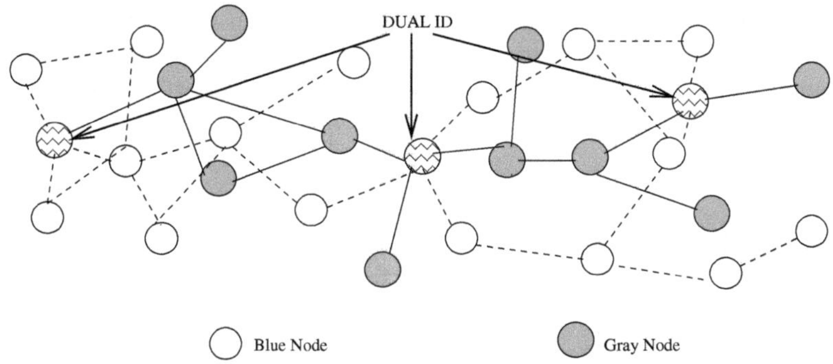

Fig. 2 Attack using several nodes

3. As part of two networks these nodes with dual id can communicate between them through both networks. Say, δ_i needs to communicate something to δ_j without giving any hint to the blue network, it routes that message through the gray network. On the contrary, when they want to communicate something which all nodes in the blue network should be aware, they route the message through the blue network.
4. Consider that a message is received by the node δ_i. According to the routing algorithm it faithfully forwards the message to node β. However, δ_i also sends the message to all other dual id nodes through the gray network. All those dual id nodes upon receiving the message, replay it there. Consequently they mount a *wormhole attack* on the blue network.
5. The gray network can inject bogus data through all δ_i in a coordinated manner to defeat the data aggregation algorithm. We will discuss this in detail afterward.

We assume that the central base station is not responsible for monitoring and supervising operations of the blue sensor network, collective efforts of the sensor nodes are responsible for smooth operation of the network. In fact this is the basis of the distributed node replication detection algorithm of [14]. A very potent attack that can be mounted on the blue network is *coordinated false data injection*. Consider that in the area A_i, certain important event is observed by both blue and gray networks, and the gray network wants to mislead the blue network about the event. All that gray network will do is to turn all the gray nodes in that area (assuming that the number of gray nodes in the area is less than the total number of captured nodes) into dual id nodes. And all the dual id nodes will send false report about the event to the blue network. This may mislead the data aggregation algorithm in the blue network if the ratio of dual id nodes and good nodes in the region A_i is close to 1. If the ratio is greater than 1, then the possibility of misleading the blue network is very high. Afterward the gray network will redeploy the dual id nodes as when required. Note that no physical movement of actual sensor nodes is required, only the captured ids are distributed properly by the gray network to mount the attack. Similarly, we can place dual id nodes in any critical location of the network without any physical movement of nodes. Thus mounting *denial of service* or *denial of message* attack becomes very easy.

5 Prevention

Before we discuss the prevention mechanism, let us first highlight the weaknesses of the distributed detection approach which was exploited to mount a successful attack. The underlying protocol over which the distributed detection is used to prevent the node replication attack, allows nodes to move from one place to other. In addition to this, distributed detection does not take into account the possible movements of nodes. We exploit this lacuna to mount the attack. Thus to prevent the node replication attack presented in the previous section, either the sensor nodes should not be allowed to move or the protocol to prevent the node replication attack should take into account the mobility of the sensor nodes.

Let us now consider that the sensor nodes remain stationary throughout the entire life of the network, i.e., movements of sensor nodes are not permitted. So the topology of sensor network remains static. Due to the restriction on sensor node movement, the attack presented in the previous section can be resisted as explained below.

- During the attack, cryptographic secrets of captured nodes are sent from one gray node to another. This is done to relocate dual id nodes from one place to another without any physical movement of gray nodes. It appeared to the blue network that certain nodes are moving from one place to another. As the movement of nodes is no longer allowed, the blue network will not allow a node to re-join the network after it changes its location. This effectively thwarts the attack as the attacker cannot insert dual id nodes anywhere in the network. Dual id node can only be inserted at the fixed location, i.e., at the original location of the captured node. Also this cannot be termed as node replication attack either.
- Consequently it is no longer possible to learn about the entire network topology using a small number of captured nodes which reduces the effectiveness of the attack.
- Another important aspect of the proposed attack was to mislead the data aggregation algorithm by injecting coordinated false data. This is done by increasing the concentration of dual id nodes in a particular region. However this is not possible if nodes are to remain stationary, so the attack cannot work. Thus, the restriction on node movement will be able to thwart the attack successfully.

However question remains how practical it is to stop mobility altogether. Some applications may require movement of sensor nodes for operational purpose and restricting the movement of nodes may prove undesirable. After all, the ad-hoc nature of the network is one of the main attractions of deploying such a WSN. Thus a stationary network may be able to prevent the attack, it may not be practical always. On the other hand, if we are to allow the movement of sensor nodes, then it is very difficult to differentiate between the malicious node movements and legitimate node movements and the problem is somewhat equivalent to intrusion detection problem. Also sensor nodes do not have much processing power to make such a complicated decision and it may require the involvement of base station at some point of time.

Another possibility is use of base station to monitor the network. When a sensor network receives a location claim from a new sensor node it forwards the location claim with probability p to the base station. This "new" sensor node may be recent addition to the network or it may be a node moved in from a different neighbourhood. Thus the base station always remains aware about the movement or addition of sensor nodes in the network. Also the base station can take appropriate action if it suspects any foul play by any malicious sensor node. However as pointed in [14], the centralized approach also has its drawbacks. Thus we need to have hybrid approach where we combine the distributed detection approach with centralized monitoring to have a secure protocol. The basic philosophy behind the hybrid approach is to allow the base station take decision regarding the nature of sensor node's movement, i.e., the base station makes the distinction between the normal and malicious node movements. However, the base station never participates in the detection process. Let us first present the extended protocol for distributed detection of node replication and movement in detail.

5.1 Distributed Detection of Node Movement

Here we present the possible modifications required to make the protocol for distributed detection of node replication secure. In the modified protocol, before the end of a detection phase, each sensor node checks whether it received location claims from all of its neighbours. If it was found that location claim from a particular neighbour α was missing, it follows a similar protocol after it receives a location claim. Only difference is that it now indicates a missing sensor node and its previously known location. The modified protocol is as follows.

Just before the end of execution of distributed detection protocol [14], each node β checks whether it heard from all the nodes it heard during the previous detection phase. If it finds that any node α is missing, then with probability p, it selects nodes present in g random locations in the network to forward α's previous location claim. This missing node alert has the format

$< M, \{ID_\alpha, l_\alpha, \{H(ID_\alpha, l_\alpha)\}_{K_\alpha^{-1}}\}, \{H(ID_\alpha, l_\alpha, \{H(ID_\alpha, l_\alpha)\}_{K_\alpha^{-1}})\}_{K_\beta^{-1}} >$. Here M indicates that it is the notification for a missing node. ID_α is the ID of α and l_α is the previous location of α. Nodes are loosely time synchronized, so one can include a time-stamp in the location claim and in the "missing node alert" to prevent any kind of replay attack.

After receiving this missing node notification by a witness node, it verifies all the required signatures to satisfy himself that it is not a forged notification. Then it checks existence of any location claim from α. If there exists a location claim from α in its buffer and it indicates a change of location, the witness node takes "appropriate" action. However, if there is no change in location of α, the witness node simply deletes the missing node notification. A missing node alert may be triggered by the loss of location claim sent by α to β due to communication error. In such a situation witness nodes find that there is no change in location and delete the alert. This eliminates the probability of false positives. Here we have described the required modifications over the randomized multicast protocol. One can also easily modify the line selected multicast protocol in a similar fashion.

After detecting a node movement, it is required to differentiate between a legitimate movement and a malicious movement to decide upon the course of remedial actions. There is no easy solution to this problem as sensor nodes themselves are resource constraint and lack processing power to analyze and decide upon whether present movement is malicious or normal. Another option is to allow limited movement, i.e., every node must stay within a predefined region and if nodes stray beyond the region, they are simply removed from the network. By removal, we mean that no node will communicate with them. However the best possible solution to node movements would be to inform the base station and let the base station analyze the movement to determine whether it is a normal or malicious movement. Thus the protocol no longer remains distributed as it requires the involvement of base station and we call it hybrid protocol.

Security Analysis

It was pointed out earlier that d is the average degree of each sensor node. Thus when a sensor node α changes its location and if all of α's neighbours detect it properly, then $p \cdot d \cdot g$ nodes receive those missing node alerts. Similarly for the current location of α, the number of witness nodes will be $p \cdot d \cdot g$. If there is a common witness between these two different sets of witnesses, then we can detect the movement of the node α. Thus according to the birthday paradox if there is a collision, we can detect the movement. The probability of collision is given by [14, 5]

$$P_c \geq 1 - e^{\frac{-p^2 \cdot d^2 \cdot g^2}{n}}$$

Using the similar setup of [14], i.e., if $n = 10000$, $g = 100$, $d = 20$, and $p = 0.05$, one can detect the movement of sensor node with the probability 63%. And if $p = 0.1$, then one can detect the sensor node movement with probability 98%. Thus the probability of successful detection of node movement is quite high.

5.2 Hybrid Protocol

One drawback of distributed detection of node movement is that it cannot detect the node movement if a node α (i) first refuses to send its location claim in a detection round, (ii) then it moves to a different location and (iii) joins a new neighbourhood in the next detection round. This way α avoids the conflict between the current location claim and the previous location claim (i.e., missing node alert). Hybrid protocol avoids this drawback by involving the base station in the detection process. Hybrid protocol consists of distributed detection of node replication/movement and centralized decision making. Involvement of base station is required to differentiate between the normal and malicious node movements. It is assumed that the base station always maintains a list of all nodes present (including those who had left the network) in the network with their claimed location.

Let us now point out the required modifications over the distributed detection protocol. After receiving the claim from a neighbour α, with probability p it forwards the location claim to g witness nodes. Now, if it is the first time that the neighbour heard from α, the list of witness nodes must include the base station. Thus even without presence of any conflict the base station can also detect both node movement and replication on its own. In the distributed detection of node movements, nodes take appropriate action once they detect movement of sensor nodes. In the hybrid protocol this "appropriate" action is forwarding the two claims, which proves the change of location, to the base station for further action. Upon receiving the claims the base station has to decide whether the present movement is malicious or not. This is somewhat equivalent to behavior-based intrusion detection [6]. Information retrieved from past behaviors constitutes the normal behavior and any major deviation causes an intrusion alert. Thus any unexpected action (i.e., movement not seen before) of the sensor node may cause the base station to revoke it. Note that, addition of base station in the witness list thwarts the attack discussed before.

One drawback of the hybrid system is that the revocation part is deterministic. It is known that after the detection of node movement by any witness node, the claims will be forwarded to the base station for remedial action. At this point a powerful attacker may try to block those messages from reaching the base station. Under these circumstances the protocol looks vulnerable. To overcome this vulnerability, we modify the protocol in the following manner.

After detecting the movement of node α, the witness node broadcasts the location claim and missing node alert to all the nodes in the network including the base station with the request of revocation of node α. Now the base station also receives those messages and analyzes the movements of α. If the movement is in the expected line then it broadcasts a message to reinstate the node α. This protocol is suitable for those networks where node moves occasionally. Otherwise, communication overhead will be too high.

6 Conclusion

In this paper, we presented a detailed analysis of the distributed node replication detection protocol [14]. One of the main motivations behind the development of distributed node replication detection protocol is that it is more secure and robust compared to centralized approach. However, we showed that the protocol is vulnerable against an *asynchronous node replication attack*. Also the communication overhead of the entire network which is of the order of $O(n\sqrt{n})$ for line selected multicast is quite high. We modified their protocol and proposed a *hybrid approach* consisting of distributed detection and centralized monitoring to make it secure even in *dynamic* WSN supporting node mobility.

Acknowledgements The authors are grateful to the anonymous referees of IFIP SEC'08 for their helpful comments. This work is partially funded by the EU project SMEPP-033563.

References

1. I. F. Akyildiz, W. Su, Y. Sankarasubramaniam, and E. Cayirci. "A Survey on Sensor Networks". *IEEE Communications Magazine*, 40(8):102-114, 2002.
2. J. Baek, E. Foo, H. C. Tan, and J. Zhou. "Securing Wireless Sensor Networks - Threats and Countermeasures". Book Chapter in *Security and Privacy in Wireless and Mobile Computing*, Troubador Publishing, 2008.
3. M. Cagalj, S. Capkun, and J. P. Hubaux. "Wormhole-Based Antijamming Techniques in Sensor Networks". *IEEE Transactions on Mobile Computing*, 6(1):100-114, 2007.
4. H. Chan, A. Perrig, and D. Song. "Secure Hierarchical In-Network Aggregation in Sensor Networks". *2006 ACM Conference on Computer and Communications Security (CCS'06)*, pp. 278-287, 2006.
5. T. Cormen, C. Leiserson, R. Rivest, and C. Stein. "Introduction to Algorithms". MIT Press, 2001.
6. D. Denning. "An Intrusion Detection Model". *IEEE Transactions on Software*, Vol. SE-13, No. 2, pp. 222-232, 1987.
7. C. Hartung, J. Balasalle, and R. Han. "Node Compromise in Sensor Networks: The Need for Secure System". *Technical Report CU-CS-988-04*, Department of Computer Science, University of Colorado at Boulder, 2004.

8. Y. C. Hu, A. Perrig, and D. B. Johnson. "Packet Leashes: A Defense against Wormhole Attacks in Wireless Networks". *2003 IEEE INFOCOMM.*
9. J. Lopez and J. Zhou (editors). "Wireless Sensor Network Security". *Cryptology & Information Security Series*, Vol. 1, IOS Press, 2008.
10. J. M. McCune, E. Shi, A. Perrig, and M. K. Reiter. "Detection of Denial-of-Message Attacks on Sensor Network Broadcasts". *2005 IEEE Symposium on Security and Privacy (S&P'05)*, pp. 64-78, May 2005.
11. C. Karlof and D. Wagner. "Secure Routing in Wireless Sensor Networks: Attacks and Countermeasure". *AdHoc Networks*, Vol. 1, Issues 2-3, pp. 293-315, Elsevier, September 2003.
12. B. Karp and H. T. Kung. "GPSR: Greedy Perimeter Stateless Routing for Wireless Networks". *2000 ACM Annual International Conference on Mobile Computing and Networking (MobiCom'00)*, pp. 243-254, 2000.
13. J. Newsome, E. Shi, D. Song, and A. Perrig. "The Sybil Attack in Sensor Networks: Analysis & Defenses". *2004 ACM International Symposium on Information Processing in Sensor Networks (IPSN'04)*, pp. 259-268, April 2004.
14. B. Parno, A. Perrig, and V. Gligor. "Distributed Detection of Node Replication Attacks in Sensor Networks". *2005 IEEE Symposium on Security and Privacy (S&P'05)*, pp. 49-63, May 2005.
15. A. Perrig, J. Stankovic, and D. Wagner. "Security in Wireless Sensor Networks". *Communications of the ACM*, 47(6):53-57, Special Issue on Wireless Sensor Networks, 2004.
16. A. Perrig, R. Szewczyk, J. D. Tygar, V. Wen, and D. E. Culler. "SPINS: Security Protocols for Sensor Networks". *Wireless Networks*, Vol. 8, pp. 521-534, 2002.
17. S. Ratnasamy, B. Karp, L. Yin, F. Yu, D. Estrin, R. Govindan, and S. Shenkar. "GHT: A Geographic Hash Table for Data-Centric Storage". *2002 ACM International Workshop on Wireless Sensor Networks and Applications (WSNA'02)*, September 2002.
18. D. Wood and J. A. Stankovic. "Denial of Service in Sensor Networks". *IEEE Computer*, Vol.35, No. 10, 2002.
19. F. Ye, H. Luo, S. Lu, and L. Zhang. "Statistical En-route Filtering of Injected False Data in Sensor Networks". *IEEE Journal on Selected Areas in Communications*, 23(4):839-850, April 2005.

8. Y. C. Hu, A. Perrig, and D. B. Johnson, "Packet Leashes: A Defense against [illegible] Attacks in Wireless Networks", [illegible]

A B Formal Framework for Security Developments in the Domain of Smart Card Applications

Frédéric Dadeau, Marie-Laure Potet, Régis Tissot

Abstract We propose in this paper a formal framework based on the B method, that supports the development of secured smart card applications. Accordingly to the Common Criteria methodology, we focus on the formal definition and modelling of access control policies by means of dedicated B models expressing, on one hand, the access control rules, and, on the other hand, the dynamics of the system. These models are then weaved to produce a security kernel. From there, we propose a conformance relationship that aims at establishing whether a concrete representation of the system complies, at the security level, with the security kernel. This embraces both a well-defined notion of security conformance as well as traceability allowing to relate basic events appearing at the level of applications with abstract security policies. This approach is put in practice on an industrial case study in the context of the POSÉ project, involving both academic and industrial partners.

Key words: Access Control, B Method, Security Model, Traceability, Common Criteria, Conformance Relation

1 Introduction

Security requirements, as functional aspects, must be taken into account along the global development process of applications. For instance, in the Common Criteria (CC) approach, security is specified as a set of security

Frédéric Dadeau, Régis Tissot
Laboratoire d'Informatique de Franche-Comté, 16 route de Gray, F-25030 Besançon cedex, e-mail: `{dadeau,tissot}@lifc.univ-fcomte.fr`

Marie-Laure Potet
Laboratoire d'Informatique de Grenoble, BP. 72 – F-38402 Saint-Martin d'Hères cedex, e-mail: `Marie-Laure.Potet@imag.fr`

Please use the following format when citing this chapter:

Dadeau, F., Potet, M.-L. and Tissot, R., 2008, in IFIP International Federation for Information Processing, Volume 278; *Proceedings of the IFIP TC 11 23rd International Information Security Conference*; Sushil Jajodia, Pierangela Samarati, Stelvio Cimato; (Boston: Springer), pp. 141–155.

functional components [7] and the development process must then supply some assurances relatively to these security requirements [8]. The main assurance classes are relative to the design of the application to be evaluated (ADV), how functional testing have to be conducted (ATE) and to the vulnerability analysis (AVA). The result is a level of confidence, based on the measures taken during the development process. Furthermore, based on the functional and assurance components which are selected, CC evaluations rely on the principle of presentations of evidences, which explain how security functionalities are really guaranteed. For instance, testing assurance must establish how security requirements are covered. On the other hand, functional specifications must be established complete and consistent with the security functionalities requirements. The CC norm is then strongly based on the notion of specifications (models) and traceability (presentations of evidences).

On the other hand, smart cards play an important role in the information systems security. They supply a medium for authentication, confidentiality and integrity. Security in smart cards is based on hardware mechanisms and operating system protections and, at the level of applications, on some security properties that can be established. Because smart cards become a central piece of every day citizen security, as high-security identification cards, public transport, payment or healthcare cards, it is crucial to produce some evidences in term of security. Due to the increasing number of such applications, methodologies must be elaborated, in order to dispose of validation processes which can be reproduced and automated.

This paper presents a formal framework dedicated to the development of secure smart cart applications, based on the B method [2]. This work has been developed in the national french ANR project named POSÉ that aims at proposing an effective approach, adapted to security and development engineer practices. Section 2 describes the context of the POSÉ project and the proposed approach. Section 3 describes the security model level and Section 4 shows how conformance between an application and a security model can be characterized. Then, Section 5 illustrates our approach on a real smart card case study and its use in a model-based testing process. Finally, conclusion and perspectives are presented in Sect. 6.

2 The Context

The POSÉ project[1] is dedicated to the validation of smart card applications, using a model-based testing approach [22]. Model-based testing consists in using the formal model to support the computation of test cases and the associated test oracle, namely, the result expected after the execution of the test case. Then, abstract test cases have to be concretized to be run on the system under test. In this process, the major difficulty is to relate the abstract data

[1] http://www.rntl-pose.info

(operations signatures and abstract values) to the concrete data of the implementation (method signatures and concrete values). The partners[2] implied in this project are Gemalto, the world leader in smart cards technology suppliers, LEIRIOS Technologies and its model-based test generation LTG tool, SILICOMP-AQL an accredited organization in security certification and two academic partners, the LIG (Grenoble) and LIFC (Besançon).

2.1 The POSÉ Approach

A model-based testing approach is deployed at Gemalto, using the Leirios Test Generator tool [14] based on B. The POSÉ project addresses the extension of this approach to take specific security properties into account. More precisely, addressed topics are how security requirements can be formalized and linked to a functional model, in order to be exploited for security model-based testing. One of the major challenge was to re-use the concretization platform, which links the abstract specifications with the APDU communication level [13]. Furthermore, also for industrial reasons, a compatibility with the Common Criteria norm was expected, in order to re-use the methodology for validation testing, to satisfy evaluations levels EAL 4, 4+ or 5 [9].

The POSÉ project focuses on access control policies for several reasons. First, as pointed out previously, data protection is a central piece of security in smart card applications. Furthermore, this aspect becomes more important when smart card standardized platforms are considered. For instance, the POSÉ case study is based on the notion of objects (data, file and directory files) which carry their own access control rules. Thus, the correctness of the access control implementation is very crucial, as well as the personalization phase which instantiates the platform for a given set of controlled objects. Access control which is considered here is the control of subjects executing some operations on some of the protected objects. These rules depend on security attributes, such as the files life cycle. Second, we are interested in the dynamic aspects of access control policy, i.e., how permissions evolve during the system execution. Thus, a security model will describe both the access control entities (subject, object, conditional rules) and the dynamic part of the controlled operations. In this way, access control can be specified as a set of admissible traces. A similar approach is adopted by F. Schneider [19] who characterizes access control by security automata.

When security is dedicated to the control of operation execution, traceability and conformance consist in establishing a correspondence between behaviors admitted by the security model and behaviors admitted by the application. Contrary to functional conformance, where a specification and an implementation are compared, there is here no direct correspondence between secured operations and the interface of applications. Thus, a mapping

[2] `http://www.gemalto.com`, `http://www.leirios.com`, `http://www.aql.fr`

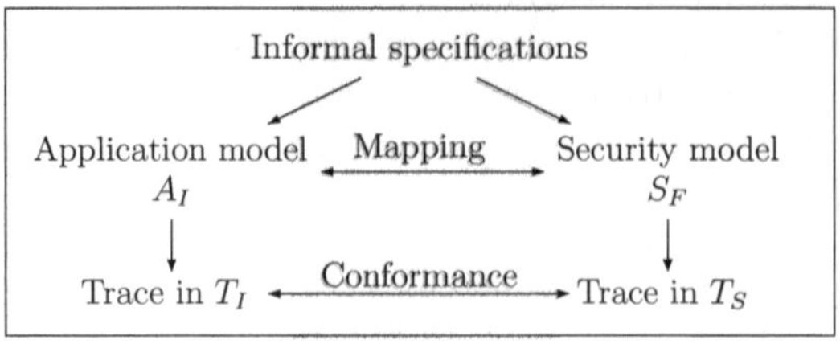

Fig. 1 Principle of the approach

relation must be given, in order to decompose application interfaces in terms of secured operations. The proposed approach is depicted in Fig. 1.

Intuitively, traces accepted by the application can also be accepted by the security model, through the mapping relation. Thus, the conformance reduces to the inclusion, apart from the mapping. In sections 3 and 4, we describe the formal framework capturing both modelling and conformance. This framework is based on the B method because B was already used in the existing model-based testing approach [6] and it is also well-suited to the definition of conformance.

2.2 A Brief Introduction to the B Method

The B method [2] is dedicated to the formal development, from high level specification to implementable code. Specifications are based on three formalisms: *data* are specified using a set theory, *properties* are first-order predicates and the *behaviors* are specified by *Generalized Substitutions*. A formal development process is supported through a refinement relation. The B method has been applied in industrial applications, such as the railway domain [3] and in the context of JavaCard application or environment [17, 5].

Generalized Substitutions can be defined by the Weakest Precondition (*WP*) semantics, introduced by E.W. Dijkstra [10], and denoted here by $[S]R$. $[x := e]\, R$ is the substitution of free occurrences of x in R by e. Table 1 presents other useful *WP* definition examples (in which z is a fresh variable).

From generalized substitutions, the following predicates can be computed (x being the state variables attached to the substitution S and x' the values of x after the substitution):

$\mathsf{trm}(S)$	$\hat{=}$	$[S]true$	termination
$\mathsf{prd}_x(S)$	$\hat{=}$	$\neg[S]\neg(x' = x)$	before-after predicate
$\mathsf{fis}(S)$	$\hat{=}$	$\exists x\ \mathsf{prd}_x(S)$	feasibility

Operation definitions are of the form $o \leftarrow op(i) \hat{=}$ PRE P THEN S END. An operation is characterized by its termination and its before-after predicate. The Event B extension [1], dedicated to dynamic aspects, is based on another execution model. Events are of the form SELECT P THEN S END.

$[x, y := e, f]\, R$	$\Leftrightarrow$ [z:=f][x:=e][y:=z]	multiple substitution
$[\mathsf{skip}]\, R$	$\Leftrightarrow R$	null substitution
$[\text{PRE } P \text{ THEN } S \text{ END}]\, R$	$\Leftrightarrow P \wedge [S]\, R$	preconditioned substitution
$[\text{SELECT } P \text{ THEN } S \text{ END}]\, R$	$\Leftrightarrow P \Rightarrow [S]\, R$	guarded substitution
$[S_1 \,;\, S_2]\, R$	$\Leftrightarrow [S_1]\,[S_2]\, R$	sequential substitution
$[\text{CHOICE } S_1 \text{ OR } S_2 \text{ END}]\, R$	$\Leftrightarrow ([S_1]R) \wedge ([S_2]R)$	bounded choice substitution
$[\text{VAR } x \text{ IN } S \text{ END}]\, R$	$\Leftrightarrow \forall$ x $[S]\, R$	substitution with local variable

Table 1 Some Weakest Precondition calculus definitions

An event is characterized by its before-after predicate and as soon as the event is feasible, it can be enabled. Feasibility is considered here as a guard.

Abstract models can be proved and refined (see Fig. 3 and 5 for examples). First, invariants can be stated: the proofs consist in showing that invariants are established by the initialization part and preserved by each operation definitions. Then, the refinement process consists in building a more concrete model and establishing the refinement relation. The refinement is based on a gluing invariant linking abstract and concrete variables. Refinement proof obligations consists in showing that the concrete initialization refines the abstract one, and that each concrete operation refines its abstract definition. A substitution S is refined by a substitution T, with respect to the gluing invariant L ($S \sqsubseteq_L T$) if and only if:

$$\boxed{L \wedge \mathsf{trm}(S) \;\Rightarrow\; [T]\neg[S]\neg L}$$

3 Formal Security Models

As stated in Sect. 2.1 we are interested by both access control rules and the dynamic evolution of security attributes. In order to be compatible with the Common Criteria security functional requirements, a security model will be constituted by two parts: a *rule-based model*, describing classical aspects of access control and a *dynamic model*, describing how security attributes evolve. The rule-based model corresponds to components of families FDP_ACC and FDP_ACF (access control policy and access control functions) of the Common Criteria, and the dynamic model corresponds to components of family FMT_MSA (Management of Security Attributes) [7]. These two models will be stated by means of B specifications. In this way, security properties can be proved as invariants relative to object, subject and security attributes.

3.1 B *Security Model*

The rule-based model describes which subjects are authorized to execute which operations on a controlled object, depending on some conditions relative to security attribute values. Permissions (the only kind considered here)

```
MACHINE e_purse_rules
SETS
   SUBJECTS={admin, bank, pda}; OPERATIONS={checkPin, credit, ...};
   MODE={perso, use, invalid}
CONSTANTS
   permission,
     /*  Security attributes:  */
   mode, isHoldAuth
PROPERTIES
   mode ∈ MODE ∧ isHoldAuth ∈ BOOL ∧
   permission ∈ (SUBJECTS ↔ OPERATIONS) ∧
     /*  Access control rules:  */
   (mode=use ⇒ (bank ↦ checkPin) ∈ permission) ∧
   ((mode=use ∧ isHoldAuth=TRUE) ⇒ (bank  ↦ credit) ∈ permission) ∧
   ...
END
```

Fig. 2 Formal model expressing the e-purse security rules

are defined as triplets belonging to a relation of the form SUBJECTS $\leftrightarrow$ OPERATIONS $\leftrightarrow$ OBJECTS, where $A \leftrightarrow B$ stands for a binary relation between A and B, and $a \mapsto b$ is the representation associated to pairs. Security attributes are specified as abstract constants and conditions are predicates on these constants. An example is given in Fig. 2.

In smart card applications, subjects generally correspond to the type of authentication and access control depends on the life cycle of the card or the applet. We illustrate this with an example of an electronic purse (e-purse), in which some operations may only be executed from specific terminals that represent the subjects. We distinguish three kinds of terminals: administrative terminals dedicated to personalization, bank and pda terminals. An access rule of the security policy states, for example, that the `checkPin` operation, that compares the holder PIN code for its authentication can only be executed from a bank terminal. In the same way, the holder authentication is also a security attribute. Another rule states that a `credit` command can be executed only if the holder has been authenticated.

The dynamic model describes how objects, subjects and security attributes evolve through a set of basic operations, including controlled operations. The dynamic model should fulfill several properties relative to the rule-based model: all controlled operations must be defined in the dynamic model; moreover, this latter must contain two special entities, named *subject* and *object*, denoting respectively the current subject and object values. The dynamic description of the `checkPin` operation is given in Fig. 3. Because, in this example, the access control does not imply any object, their related definitions are omitted.

```
MACHINE e_purse_dynamic
SETS
   SUBJECTS={admin, bank, pda}; MODE={perso, use, invalid}
VARIABLES
   subject, mode, isHoldAuth
INVARIANT
   subject ∈ SUBJECTS ∧ mode ∈ MODE ∧ isHoldAuth ∈ BOOL
INITIALISATION
   subject :∈ SUBJECTS || mode := perso || isHoldAuth := FALSE
OPERATIONS
   res ← checkPin(p) ≙
      PRE p ∈ 0..9999 THEN
         CHOICE isHoldAuth := TRUE || res := success
         OR isHoldAuth := FALSE || mode := invalid || res := blocked
         OR isHoldAuth := FALSE || res := failure
         END
      END
   ...
END
```

Fig. 3 Formal model expressing the e-purse dynamics

3.2 Security Kernel and Admissible Traces

From a rule-based model and a dynamic model, a security kernel, enforcing the rules of the first model on the second one, can be automatically generated by the Meca tool [12]. Let $out \leftarrow op(i) \mathrel{\hat{=}}$ PRE P THEN S END be the definition of operation *op* in the dynamic model. Let $C \Rightarrow (s \mapsto op \mapsto o) \in permission$ be the unique rule associated to operation *op* (to simplify). The generated kernel contains the operation given in Fig. 4, describing how the execution of the operation *op* is controlled.

The security kernel specifies behaviors that are secure. Traces can be syntactically represented as sequences of occurrences of execution calls, stated as triplets (op, v, r) where *op* is an operation name, v a valuation of input parameters and r a valuation of output parameters. Then, a trace associated to a model M is written $< init\ ;\ (c_1, v_1, r_1)\ ;\ \ldots\ ;\ (c_n, v_n, r_n) >$ with $c_i \in Oper(M)$. In order to define admissible traces, the event corresponding to the execution of an operation call has to be defined. Let $out \leftarrow op(i)$

```
out, rs ← exec_op (i) ≙
   PRE pre_typ  THEN  /* typing of parameters */
      IF  subject=s ∧ object=o ∧ C ∧ P
      THEN  S || rs := OK ELSE rs := KO
      END
   END
```

Fig. 4 General format of an operation in the security kernel

be an operation defined by the substitution PRE P THEN S END. The event $exec(op, v, r)$, corresponding to the execution of the call $op(v)$ returning the value r, can be defined by the substitution:

SELECT $[i := v]P$ THEN
  VAR out IN $[i := v]S$; SELECT $(r = out)$ THEN skip END END
END

Substitution into substitution, as $[i := v]S$, is defined as in [2]. As described in Sect. 2.2, a substitution can be characterized by its prd predicate. Here, we have $\mathsf{prd}(exec(op, v, r)) \equiv \exists\, out' \;/\; [i := v](P \wedge \mathsf{prd}(S) \wedge out' = r)$, that exactly describes the effect of an operation call for input v producing the value r as result. Now, let t be a trace of the form $< init \;;\; (c_1, v_1, r_1) \;;\; \ldots \;;\; (c_n, v_n, r_n) >$. This trace is *admissible* for the model M $(t \in T_M)$ if and only if the condition $\mathsf{fis}(init \;;\; exec(c_1, v_1, r_1) \;;\; \ldots ; exec(c_n, v_n, r_n))$ holds.

For instance, $< init; S; (\mathbf{checkpin}, < 1234 >, < success, OK >) >$ is an admissible trace if the predicate $mode = use \wedge subject = bank$ can be established after the sequence $< init \;;\; S >$. We now present a conformance relation, based on this formal framework that aims at establishing whether or not an application conforms to a security model.

4 Conformance Relationship

Smart card applications are generally built as a set of commands, in the APDU format [13]. *APDU commands* supply the card with instructions to be executed and their parameters. *APDU responses* return results and a status word that contains the result of the command execution. Values of the status word are standardized; for instance, SW=9000 indicates that the commands terminated in the right way. Conformance is then based on some relations between APDU commands and abstract controlled operations.

Relatively to the security properties which are considered, ie., the control of commands execution, the granularity between operations which are controlled and the operations of the application is the same. Nevertheless, operations at the level of application and commands designed in the access control differ. In the first case, operations are defensive and can be invoked in any case (authorized case, security error or functional restriction) whereas operations of the security model are not executed if access control conditions do not hold, since they are considered as preconditions. Moreover, although status words are standardized, APDU responses are not always predictable. In case of multiple errors (for instance two security defaults or a functional restriction and a security error) application specifications do not impose any choice. This indeterminism is very important in the sense that implementations are free to favour one cause over another. A too precise specification could introduce a cause of channel side, making the implementation behavior too predictable. As a consequence the mapping correspondence must support a form of underterminism to deal with multiple errors.

4.1 Mapping Security and Functional Models

We propose, hereafter, a definition of a mapping which is suitable for our application domain. A mapping is a set of rules stating how application calls can be related to controlled operations of the security kernel. In a more general case, a rule takes one of the two following forms:

1. $(op_{\mathrm{A}pp}, < v_{\mathrm{A}pp} >, < r_{\mathrm{A}pp} >) \rightarrow (op_{\mathrm{S}ec}, < v_{\mathrm{S}ec} >, < r_{\mathrm{S}ec}, \mathrm{OK} >)$
2. $(op_{\mathrm{A}pp}, < v_{\mathrm{A}pp} >, < r_{\mathrm{A}pp} >) \rightarrow (\mathsf{skip}, < \mathrm{KO} >)$

The first case maps an authorized behavior with a security behavior that describes a set of possible security attributes change. The second case corresponds to non authorized calls, in particular security attributes and the current subject and object must not be modified, in any way. $< v_{\mathrm{A}pp} >, < r_{\mathrm{A}pp} >, < v_{\mathrm{S}ec} >, < r_{\mathrm{S}ec} >$ denotes sequences of values or free variables. In the following, $(c_{\mathrm{A}pp}, c_{\mathrm{S}ec}) \in R$ means that there exists a rule $l \mapsto r$ and a substitution σ such that $\sigma(l) = c_{\mathrm{A}pp}$ and $\sigma(r) = c_{\mathrm{S}ec}$.

Here, we consider a restrictive case where the name of operations are identical and the input parameter values are equal. In this case, a mapping consists in establishing, for each application level command, a correspondence between results which are returned at the application level and associated result in the security model. Thus, a mapping takes the form:

$$\{< r^1_{\mathrm{A}pp} >, \ldots, < r^n_{\mathrm{A}pp} >\} \mapsto \{< r^1_{\mathrm{S}ec} >, \ldots, < r^k_{\mathrm{S}ec} >\}$$

Figure 5 describes a functional specification of our e-purse. The mapping R_1 hereafter is based on the fact that a thin observation of authorized behaviors is possible (`success`, `failure`, `blocked`):

$$\{< \mathsf{9000} >\} \rightarrow \{< success, OK >\} \quad \{< \mathsf{9202} >\} \rightarrow \{< blocked, OK >\}$$
$$\{< \mathsf{9201} >\} \rightarrow \{< failure, OK >\} \quad \{< \mathsf{9401} >, < \mathsf{9402} >\} \rightarrow \{< KO >\}$$

A mapping can be non-deterministic, meaning that some results of the application level can belong to two sets. In this case, one result at the application level can correspond to different abstract results. Non-determinism is a way to deal with multiple errors. Suppose now that the dynamic part of our example (see Fig. 3) introduces a precondition of the form $p \in \mathbb{N}$ and a condition of the form IF $p \notin 0..9999$ THEN res := data_error ELSE ... END. The mapping R_1 is changed to R_2 in which $\{< \mathsf{9401} >\} \rightarrow \{< KO >\}$ is replaced by $\{< \mathsf{9401} >\} \rightarrow \{< data\_error, OK >\}$. Nevertheless a problem arises when the two conditions $p \in 0..9999$ and $mode = use$ do not hold. Depending on the order in which the verifications are performed in the ap-

```
sw ⟵ checkPin(p) ≙
  PRE p ∈ ℕ
  THEN
     IF p ∈ 0..9999
     THEN IF mode = use ∧ terminal = bank
         THEN
              IF p = pin
              THEN isHoldAuth := TRUE || hptry := 3 || sw := 9000
              ELSE isHoldAuth := FALSE || hptry := hptry - 1 ||
                    IF hptry - 1 = 0
                    THEN mode := invalid || sw := 9202
                    ELSE sw := 9201
                    END
              END
         ELSE sw := 9402     /* mode ≠ use ∨ terminal ≠ bank */
         END
     ELSE sw := 9401     /* p ∉ 0..9999 */
     END
  END
```

Fig. 5 A functional model of the `checkPin` command

plication level, the result may differ. To overcome this problem, R_2 has to be extended, introducing a non-deterministic mapping, by adding the rule $\{< 9401 >\} \rightarrow \{< KO >\}$ (cf. Sect. 4.2).

4.2 Conformance Definition

Intuitively, an application conforms to a security model if and only if its traces are accepted by the security model, through the mapping relation. Due to the considered security policies, it means that: (*i*) all sequences of positive calls (associated to an effective execution of operations) can also be played by the security model, and, (*ii*) the application level can refuse more executions than the security level, in particular for functional reasons.

More formally, let $t_A = < init_A \ ; \ c_A^1 \ ; \ldots \ ; c_A^n >$ be a trace relative to the application and let $t_S = < init_S \ ; \ c_S^1 \ ; \ldots \ ; c_S^n >$ be a trace relative to the security model. A mapping relation R can be extended to traces in the following way:

$$(t_A, t_S) \in \ R \ \text{ iff } \ (c_A^1, c_S^1) \in \ R \ \wedge \ldots \wedge (c_A^n, c_S^n) \in \ R.$$

In this way, the set of traces associated to an application trace t_A can be computed. Now, operation calls that return KO can be assimilated to stuttering steps [16], because they do not modify security attributes. The operation *Stut* hereafter erases such calls.

$$\begin{array}{ll}
Stut(< (\mathsf{skip}, < \mathrm{KO} >) \ ; \ s >) & \hat{=} \ Stut(< s >) \\
Stut(< (c, < v >, < r, \mathrm{OK} >) \ ; \ s >) & \hat{=} < (c, < v >, < r, \mathrm{OK} >) \ ; \ Stut(< s >) > \\
Stut(<>) & \hat{=} <>
\end{array}$$

Finally, the conformance between an application A and a security model S, through a mapping relation R, is defined by:

$$\forall\ ta\ (ta \in T_A \Rightarrow \exists\ ts\ ((ta, ts) \in R \wedge Stut(ts) \in T_S))$$

With this definition, it is possible to implement some part of the access control in a wrong way, for instance in making a mistake during the update of a security attribute. The conformity relation that we propose (only) verifies that a wrong implementation can not be used to obtain rights that are not authorized. Nevertheless, it is the main expected characteristics in security: a security failure which can not be exploited in any way is not really a problem.

The relevance of the proposed approach is based on the correctness of R. For a left part $(c_{\mathrm{A}pp}, v_{\mathrm{A}pp}, r_{\mathrm{A}pp})$ of a mapping rule, let $\{(c^i_{\mathrm{S}ec}, v^i_{\mathrm{S}ec}, r^i_{\mathrm{S}ec}) \mid i \in 1..n\}$ be the set of right parts associated to it. Correctness must ensure that modification of security attributes evolve in the same way, at the application and security levels. Then correctness must be stated by:

$$\text{CHOICE } exec(c^1_{\mathrm{S}ec}, v^1_{\mathrm{S}ec}, r^1_{\mathrm{S}ec}) \text{ OR } \ldots \text{OR } exec(c^n_{\mathrm{S}ec}, v^n_{\mathrm{S}ec}, r^n_{\mathrm{S}ec}) \text{ END} \\ \sqsubseteq_L exec(c_{\mathrm{A}pp}, v_{\mathrm{A}pp}, r_{\mathrm{A}pp})$$

with L the relation linking security attributes, subjects and objects with their representation at the application level (see Sect. 2.2). For instance if the correspondence $\{< \texttt{9401} >\} \rightarrow \{< KO >\}$ is omitted in R_2 then the correctness of R_2 (cf. Sec. 4.1) does not hold, because we can not establish that $subject = terminal \wedge p \notin 0..9999 \Rightarrow mode = use \wedge terminal = bank \wedge p \notin 0..9999$, where $subject = terminal$ is the gluing invariant linking variables of the security level with variables of the application level (other variables do not differ).

5 Applications in the POSÉ Context

In order to support interoperability and security, standards have been proposed by the main manufacturers. These norms define open platforms upon which standardized consumer and business applications can be built. It is thus very interesting to propose a methodology associated to the development and validation of applications based on such platforms. The IAS application [11], chosen as the case study of the POSÉ project, offers a notion of security data objects –SDO– that carry their own access control rules –SDO security header. An application developed on IAS consists in a personalization phase, giving a set of SDOs with their instantiated security headers. The IAS platform has been chosen in the French Administration project Adèle (`https://www.ateliers.modernisation.gouv.fr/ministeres/projets_adele/a125-ter-developpement/public`).

5.1 Description of the Models

Initially, only a functional model of the application was available. This model had previously been used to validate an implementation that has been established as conform to the functional model. Since this latter is very large (60 operations for about 15000 lines of B code), it was necessary to ensure its conformance w.r.t. the security requirements. We started by designing a model of the dynamics of the system, and, separately, we considered the access control rules. The resulting model was much simpler and more abstract than the original model (13 operations for about 1000 lines of B code). This model focuses on the file life cycle and access conditions based on pin authentication. Because of the limitation of the animator tool we use, these two models are deterministic. Let us consider an example, extracted from the case study.

We consider the *VERIFY* command which works as the *checkPin* operation of the e-purse example (Fig. 3) but it is parametrized by any PIN object. VERIFY permits either to get the authentication of a PIN object, if a PIN value is given, or to check its authentication state, if no PIN value is given. In the security model, the success of the VERIFY command depends on the existence of the PIN object and the validation of the access conditions which protect the PIN. The security model also deals checks the expected PIN value and the value of its tries counter.

In the security model, the status words of the command VERIFY are abstracted to *success, blocked, failure*, whose meanings are similar to those of the `checkPin` command. We define a mapping $M1$ (given hereafter) between the status word of the implementation and the abstracted ones –in 63Cx, x represents the number of remaining tries.

Status word on functional model	Meaning	Mapping with security model
9000	Success	$\{< success, OK >\}$
6983	SDO PIN unverified and no more tries	$\{< blocked, OK >\}$
6984	SDO PIN tries counter reached 0	$\{< failure, OK >\}$
63Cx	User authentication failed or not done	$\{< failure, OK >\}$
6A88	SDO PIN not found	$\{< KO >\}$
6982	Secure messaging erroneous or invalid access conditions	$\{< KO >\}$
6700	PIN value length is out of bounds	$\{< KO >\}$

Due to the complexity of the models, the mapping relation correction was not established by proof. It has been established by a review process based on the analysis of each branch of the code. Such form of validation seems to be at the level of smart card application developers because developers must understand both the security model and the application description, stating which status word corresponds to which internal behaviors.

5.2 Testing Methodology

The conformance relation that we have proposed is able to establish whether, or not, a trace is correct w.r.t. security requirements, in our case, the access control policy. In the POSÉ project, the model based validation approach is based on the Leirios Test Generator (LTG) tool [14] that offers an animator for B specifications and technics for generating tests from B specification. Animation will be both used to verify that a sequence can be played by a model and to compute parameter values or preambles to build a correct sequence. Moreover, a script has been developed in order to apply a mapping relation to any traces relative to the functional model.

In a first (ascending) approach, tests are produced at the application level and confronted to the security model kernel. In this way, the confidence of the functional model w.r.t the security one is improved. For instance, let us consider a functional model in which we have omitted to cancel the authentication on a PIN when an subsequent authentication fails –due to an erroneous PIN value. This error is observable in the example of Fig. 5. Then, the test sequence:

< (VERIFY,<pin1,1234>) ; (VERIFY,<pin1,4321>) ; (VERIFY,<pin1,_>) >

produces the output sequence <<9000> ; <63C1> ; <9000>>. But the animation of the sequence *s* for the mapped output sequence <<success, OK> ; <failure, OK> ; <success, OK>> fails to be established on the security kernel model. In order to experiment the defined conformance relation, we have performed mutations on model and checked that tests sequences generated from this model did not conform to the security model.
As pointed out before, only deterministic models can be taken into account by LTG. As a consequence, an abstract sequence computed from an application sequence can be easily animated by this tool, provide a very effective procedure for a test oracle. If unbounded non-deterministic models are considered, the feasability of the abstract sequences can be computed through a proof process. Finally, if the mapping relation is non-deterministic, at least one sequence must be accepted by the security model.

A second (descending) approach has been experimented in the POSÉ project. It consists in exploiting the security model to generate abstract test cases, which are completed with the help of the functional model. This approach is well-suited to the industrial process, since tests are built at the security level. Let *s* be an input sequence constituted by a sequence of command invocation and their input values. *s* can be played at the security level in order to obtain a result sequence *r*. Now, sequence *s* is played by LTG at the functional level. Notice that operations at the security level may have abstracted –and removed– parameters w.r.t. the functional level; these parameters are added when replaying the sequence *s* at the functional level. Thus, the animator looks for an instantiation of input parameters that makes it possible to successively execute each operation so that this latter results in one of the expected outputs in r (modulo the mapping relation). If the instantiation is possible, we have the guarantee that the test conforms to the security requirements, and thus it can be played on the implementation. Otherwise, if the sequence is not be executable at the functional level, we not conclude on the conformance of the functional level w.r.t. the security level; indeed it is possible that the functional level is more restrictive than the security level, and requires additional operations of the functional level to be inserted along the sequence.

6 Conclusion and Future Work

As stated in the introduction, the approach proposed here has been developed in the framework of the RNTL POSÉ project, dedicated to verification and development of certifiable smart card applications. The B method has already been proved to be well-suited for smart card industries [6] and also, here, for modelling main entities of access control. Based on this method, Security Policy Model required from Common Criteria EAL5, can be easily specified, including dynamic aspects as preconized by some data protection class components. Due to the expressiveness of the B method, dynamic aspects can be captured in a more or less precise way. Moreover, notions of observability and refinement attached to the B models has been easily exploited in order to define a conformance relation including data refinement. This relation can be used both for testing or formal development approaches, as preconized by the ADV and ATE classes, particularly for high EALs.

The B method has already been used as a support for access control policies [4, 20]. In [4], the authors propose a form of modeling attached to Or-BAC access control and characterize behaviors which are conform to a given access control. The approach proposed here, can be seen as an extension of [4] and [20], in which dynamic conditions are taken into account as well as the observation of inputs, outputs and data refinement. In this way we have relate models which are stated at different levels of abstraction, as it is imposed by the Common Criteria approach. In [18], the authors use Labeled Transition Systems (LTS) to describe test purposes from Or-BAC rules specifying access control. They act as an oracle for the test execution, using based on the ioco conformity relation [21]. Our approach is similar, since they both rely on trace inclusions, and our notion of stuttering is close to the notion of quiescence. Nevertheless, our relation is not exclusively destined to be used as a test oracle. Indeed, by establishing preservation properties on our relation, it would be possible to prove properties on the implementation through the abstract security model.

We are currently leading experiments on using a combinatorial testing approach in order to generate test cases that exercise the security of the system. In this context, we plan to use the conformance relation as a test oracle, as illustrated previously.

Acknowledgements This work was supported by the RNTL POSE project (ANR-05-RNTL-01001), and partially funded by the Région Franche-Comté.

References

1. J-R. Abrial and L. Mussat. Introducing Dynamic Constrains in B. In D. Bert, editor, *Proceedings of the 2nd Int. B Conference*, volume 1393 of *LNCS*. Springer, 1998.
2. J.R. Abrial. *The B-Book*. Cambridge University Press, 1996.
3. P. Behm and all. Météor: A Successful Application of B in a Large Project. In *FM'99 - Formal Methods*, volume 1708 of *LNCS*, pages 348–387. Springer, September 1999.
4. N. Benaissa, D. Cansell, and D. Mery. Integration of Security Policy into System Modeling. In Julliand and Kouchnarenko [15].
5. D. Bert, S. Boulmé, M-L. Potet, A. Requet, and L. Voisin. Adaptable Translator of B Specifications to Embedded C programs. In *FME 2003: Formal Methods*, volume 2805 of *LNCS*. Springer, 2003.
6. F. Bouquet, F. Celletti, G. Debois, A. De Lavernette, E. Jaffuel, J. Julliand, B. Legeard, J. Lidoine, J.-C. Plessis, and P.-A. Masson. Model-based security testing, application to a smart card identity applet. In *eSmart 2006, 7th Int. Conf. on Smart Cards*, Sophia-Antipolis, France, September 2006.
7. Common Criteria for Information Technology Security Evaluation, Part 2: Security functional components. Technical Report CCMB-2006-09-002, version 3.1, sept 2006.
8. Common Criteria for Information Technology Security Evaluation, Part 3: Security assurance components. Technical Report CCMB-2006-09-003, version 3.1, sept 2006.
9. Common Criteria for Information Technology Security Evaluation, version 3.1. Technical Report CCMB-2006-09-001, sept 2006.
10. E.W. Dijkstra. *A discipline of Programming*. Prentice-Hall, 1976.
11. The Gixel web site. `http://gixel.fr`.
12. A. Haddad. Meca: a Tool for Access Control Models. In Julliand and Kouchnarenko [15].
13. Smart Card Standard: Part 4: Interindustry Commands for Interchange. Technical report, ISO/IEC, 1995.
14. E. Jaffuel and B. Legeard. LEIRIOS Test Generator: Automated Test Generation from B Models. In Julliand and Kouchnarenko [15].
15. J. Julliand and O. Kouchnarenko, editors. *B 2007: Formal Specification ans Development in B*, volume 4355 of *LNCS*. Springer, 2007.
16. Lamport. A temporal logic of actions. *ACM Transactions on Programming Languages and Systems*, 16(3):872–923, may 1994.
17. J-L. Lanet and A. Requet. Formal Proof of Smart Card Applets Correctness. In *CARDIS'98*, number 1820 in LNCS. Springer, 1998.
18. K. Li, L. Mounier, and R. Groz. Test Generation from Security Policies Specified in Or-BAC. In *COMPSAC – IEEE International Workshop on Secuirty in Software Engineering (IWSSE'07)*, Beijing, July 2007.
19. Fred B. Schneider. Enforceable security policies. *ACM Trans. Inf. Syst. Secur.*, 3(1):30–50, 2000.
20. N. Stouls and M-L. Potet. Security Policy Enforcement through Refinement Process. In Julliand and Kouchnarenko [15].
21. J. Tretmans. Conformance testing with labelled transition systems: Implementation relations and test generation. *Computer Networks and ISDN Systems*, 29(1):49–79, 1996.
22. M. Utting and B. Legeard. *Practical Model-Based Testing - A tools approach*. Elsevier Science, 2006. 550 pages.

An Implementation of a Privacy Enforcement Scheme based on the Java Security Framework using XACML Policies

Thomas Scheffler, Stefan Geiß, Bettina Schnor

Abstract In this paper we discuss implementation issues of a distributed privacy enforcement scheme to support Owner-Retained Access Control for digital data repositories. Our approach is based on the Java Security Framework. In order to achieve policy enforcement dependent on the accessed data object, we had to implement our own class loader that supports instance-level policy assignment. Access policies are described using XACML and stored together with the data as *sticky policies*. Enforcement of generic policies over sticky policy objects required the extension of XACML with XPath specific functions. Our use-case scenario is the user-controlled distribution of Electronic Health Records.

1 Introduction

The continuing advances in storage technologies allows the collection and storage of substantial data collections on mobile media such as smart cards. With the introduction and use of these mobile electronic data repositories for the storage and access of personal private data comes the requirement to securely enforce access policies for these repositories. Such an attempt requires the coordination between many parties, especially when the data on such media is used by many different principals and organisation. In this paper we propose a mechanism for the creation, distribution and enforcement of data-use-policies in distributed systems based on the Java Security Framework[11].

Many existing privacy protection techniques, such as P3P [7] and EPAL [3], are implemented by the custodian of the data. This protection model assumes that there are relatively few data release cases and the data itself is relatively immobile. With the use of mobile data repositories the data owner might want to implement

Thomas Scheffler, Stefan Geiß, Bettina Schnor
Department of Computer Science, University of Potsdam, 14482 Potsdam, Germany
e-mail: {scheffler,schnor}@cs.uni-potsdam.de

Please use the following format when citing this chapter:

Scheffler, T., Geiß, S. and Schnor, B., 2008, in IFIP International Federation for Information Processing, Volume 278; *Proceedings of the IFIP TC 11 23rd International Information Security Conference*; Sushil Jajodia, Pierangela Samarati, Stelvio Cimato; (Boston: Springer), pp. 157–171.

a need-to-know policy where data is only visible to the authorised data user and it is possible to maintain selective views on the repository. It would be beneficial to create the ability for Owner-Retained Access Control (ORAC), as described by McCollum [17], for the protection of mobile private data:

> "ORAC provides a stringent, label-based alternative to DAC[1] for user communities where the original owners of data need to retain tight control of the data as they propagate through copying, merging, or being read by a subject that may later write the data into other objects. ... The user who creates a data object is considered its owner and has the right to create an ACL *(Access Control List)* on the object. "

Enforcing data-use policies in a distributed environment requires a distributed architecture, where each distributed component supports the access control scheme. A *Reference Monitor*, as defined by Anderson [1], is a trusted component that validates each and every request to system resources against those authorised for the subject.

A distributed policy enforcement is necessary to control data access. It must be secured that access to data is only possible via a trusted intermediary that reliably enforces the defined policy. Otherwise policies and/or data could be accessed, altered and deleted without trace and protection would be lost. Maintaining a trusted, distributed reference monitor infrastructure is one of the main challenges in the proposed architecture. Every participating site needs to trust and to install the necessary components. We base our solution on the existing Java Security Framework which might already be installed and trusted by most sites.

The Java programming language already provides Reference Monitor functionality for the safe execution of untrusted code. It was our aim to re-use these proven mechanisms for the enforcement of data-use policies. Data-use policies are specified in the eXtensible Access Control Markup Language (XACML) [22]. The private data of the data owner is translated into a suitable XML record format and stored together with the corresponding policy as a single XML data object. The Reference Monitor needs to intercept data access and enforces the XACML policy through a mapping onto Java permissions for the accessing application instance.

This paper focuses on the task of expressing, managing and enforcing authorisations for distributed data access. We assume that a suitable encryption and authentication scheme, such as XML Encryption [13], is used to protect data and policies from modifications and make data securely available to the authorised data user.

The rest of the paper is organised as follows: Section 2 explains a motivating use case for the application of ORAC policies, Section 3 introduces the Privacy Enforcement Architecture and explains the use of XACML policies. In Section 4 we describe implementational details for the policy enforcement using the Java Security Framework. Section 5 presents related work and the paper concludes with Section 6.

---

[1] Discretionary Access Control (DAC) - is characterised by the capability of subjects with access permission to pass that permission (perhaps indirectly) on to other subjects

2 Use Case

Electronic Health Records (EHR) are a good example for mobile electronic data repositories. The work described in this paper has been motivated by the ability to store and process personal health record data on mobile media, such as a patient smart-card. The German government has mandated the use of patient smart-cards for general health care [5]. The health cards have the ability to store personal health record data of the patient, so that it can be accessed and exchanged by different practitioners participating in the treatment process and act as a repository for future diagnosis. While it is in the interest of the patient to have this data available, the data sharing needs to be controlled, since it involves sensitive private data.

Historically, health records have been created, stored and accessed locally by the practitioner or hospital. Data access was restricted through the fact that patient records were only locally available. When data will be stored in a mobile electronic repository, a similar level of separation between the different data sources needs to be maintained.

In our use case, practitioners can add medical data from examinations and treatment processes to the electronic repository. For this purpose the repository is substructured into separate compartments that will be guarded by an appropriate access policy. The implementation of a suitable policy-set guarantees the same level of privacy between the different visits to practitioners that the patient can currently expect.

2.1 Data Model

Repository data is stored in a structured way and data access policies can be applied to these structures. Several standards exist for the structured data representation in EHR (cf. [6],[14]). Since the focus of this work is not the exact representation of medical data, but rather the creation, management and enforcement of access decisions, the EHR is represented as a simple XML document which is flexible enough to incorporate standards-based data representation as necessary.

We propose to group all treatment records generated by the same practitioner into a virtual *Examination Room* (cf. Figure 1). A $1 : m$ relationship between practitioner and *Examination Room* is assumed. All treatment records generated by the practitioner are stored under this particular node and form a single zone of trust similar to the existing patient – practitioner relationship.

2.2 Use Case Policy Example

Hierarchical grouping is a widely used concept in the field of access control. It allows to minimise access rule management - rules can be defined and enforced at

```
<?xml version="1.0" encoding="UTF-8"?>
<healthRecord>
    <demographicData>
        <patient_id>CN=Homer J. Simpson, ... </patient_id>
        <dayOfBirth>19670904</dayOfBirth>
    </demographicData>
    <practitioners>
        <practitioner id="CN=Julius Hibbert, ...">
            <examinationRoom>
                <visit date="2007-11-28 15:06:37">
                    <description>X-Ray taken...</description>
                    <attachments>
                        <attachment filename="homer_brain.jpg"
                          mimetype="image/jpg" >...</attachment>
                    </attachments>
                </visit>
            </examinationRoom>
        </practitioner>
    </practitioners>
</healthRecord>
```

Fig. 1 Electronic Health Record Example

the group level, thus minimising the number of rules in the policy. The practitioner, as data author, has specific rights for his or her sub-tree in the patient health record. These can be specified as a generic rule affecting all groups of a certain type and be applied consistently for every instantiation of this type:

- Practitioner can create new examination entries in his/her personal examination room
- Practitioner can read examination entries from his/her personal examination room

A distinctive feature of the use case is the fact that data ownership and authorship are separated. The data owner determines the access policy for data access by other practitioners, but is constrained in the policy editing in order to avoid errors (e.g. revoke its own access rights) and inconsistencies (e.g. can not create a policy that allows him or her to act as a data author):

- Patients can grant access rights for practitioners to read examination entries of other practitioners
- Patients can grant the right to export entries from the health card into medical information system
- Patients have no right to create/modify entries in the examination rooms

3 Privacy Enforcement Architecture

The creation, distribution and enforcement of ORAC policies in a distributed environment requires the presence of an enforcement architecture that supports distributed policy creation and evaluation. Figure 2 shows a simplified version of the generic architecture described by the XACML standard [19]. The *Policy Administration Point* (PAP) is the entity that creates an access policy and makes this policy available to the *Policy Decision Point* (PDP). The data user tries to access a resource via a *Policy Enforcement Point* (PEP) and thus triggers a *Decision Request* to the PDP which will issue an appropriate *Decision Response* based on the available policy. The PEP then grants or denies access in accordance with this policy decision.

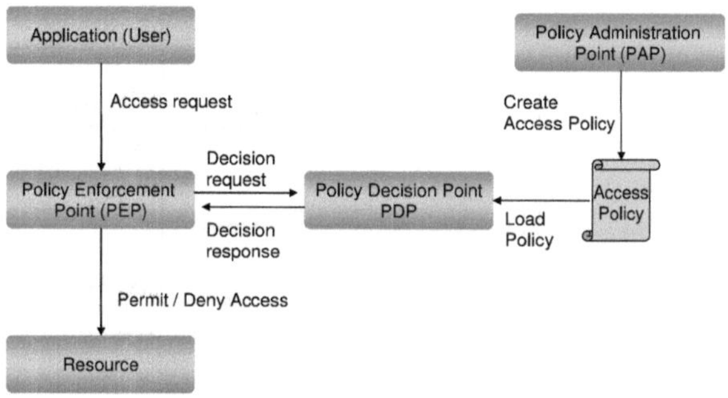

Fig. 2 Simplified XACML Access Control Architecture

Policy description languages, such as XACML are well suited to express usage policies for Electronic Health Records [2]. Policy languages have the ability to express policies for logically grouped objects and subjects and can express dependencies from environmental conditions (e.g. time of access). These properties allow the creation of concise policies that can be specified at high level of abstraction close to the intention of the policy creator.

XACML policies must be evaluated at the time of access in order to determine the access decision. This access decision is generated by the *Policy Decision Point* which implements a deterministic policy evaluation algorithm. In our architecture we use and extend a Java-based XACML implementation provided by Sun [21].

3.1 Sticky Policy Paradigm

Data access policies need to be referenced reliably throughout the distributed architecture. Policy storage and distribution becomes an important design choice for the implementation of the architecture. One possibility would be to store policies in a central repository. This requires the accessibility and availability of the policy store for every potential data user at any given time and would be suitable if the data is also centrally stored.

Our use case assumes that data is stored on a mobile media and thus needs to reference the policy independently. A policy distribution method, well suited for handling access to distributed data, is the *Sticky Policy* paradigm (cf. [15]). The data access policy is stored and distributed together with the data that it is protecting.

Together they form a sticky data object that allows the direct referencing of the policy as data needs to be accessed.

Figure 3 shows the enforcement architecture for the *Sticky Policy* model. Access to data and policy is mediated through the *Policy Administration Point*. The protected resource and its access policy are created and stored together.

Fig. 3 Access Control Architecture using 'Sticky Policies'

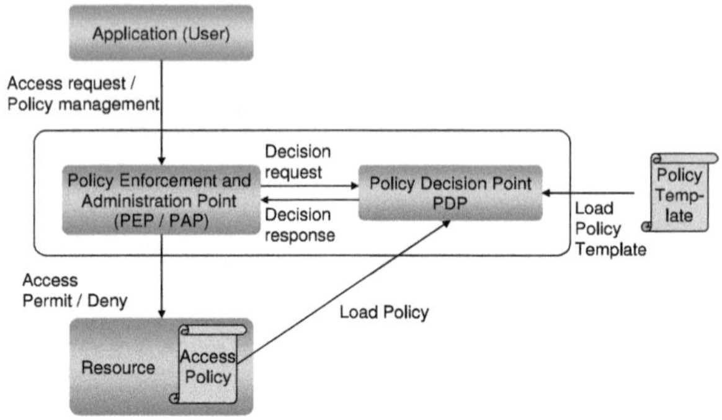

The XACML standard separates the description of authorisation policies from the actual resources. However, since policy and data are XML-based resources, policies can be included directly in the EHR document and referenced via XPath [9]. It then becomes the responsibility of the PEP to select the requested resource node from the XML document and query the PDP for a policy decision regarding the authenticated subject and the requested action for this resource.

3.2 Use case policy examples

Policy management will be controlled by a Policy Template (as shown in Figure 3), that also guides the policy creation process. The policy template has the function to apply a default policy for newly created EHR entries that already enforces a basic privacy protection level. Secondly, the default rules are needed to limit the data owner and data author in their administrative power over data and policies (e.g. the data owner should not be able to refuse data access to the data author).

The XACML policy-base contains two types of rules:

1. **Generic access rules** which define default behaviour for policies over the set of resources. These rules are static and immutable and based on the Policy Template.
2. **Specific access rules** define resource specific policies and are managed by the data owner to create specific access decisions (e.g. granting extended access to treatment records for an external practitioner)

Example 1. **Generic Rule:** A data owner has read access to his or her own resources

```
<Rule RuleId="dataOwnerRule0" Effect="Permit">
    <Target>
      <Subjects><AnySubject /></Subjects>
      <Resources><AnyResource /></Resources>
      <Actions>
        <ActionMatch MatchId="string-equal">
           <AttributeValue DataType="string">read</AttributeValue>
           <ActionAttributeDesignator AttributeId="action-id"
               DataType="http://www.w3.org/2001/XMLSchema#string" />
        </ActionMatch>
      </Actions>
    </Target>
    <Condition FunctionId="function:xpath-node-element-x500-compare">
       <Apply FunctionId="x500Name-one-and-only">
         <SubjectAttributeDesignator DataType="x500Name"
         AttributeId="subject-id" />
       </Apply>
       <Apply FunctionId="string-concatenate">
           <Apply FunctionId="string-one-and-only">
             <ResourceAttributeDesignator AttributeId="resource-id"
              DataType="http://www.w3.org/2001/XMLSchema#string" />
           </Apply>
           <AttributeValue DataType="string">
              /parent::attachments/parent::visit/parent::examinationRoom/
                            parent::practitioner/@id</AttributeValue>
       </Apply>
    </Condition>
</Rule>
```

Based on the requirements of our use case, new resource-trees can be added to the document anytime. In order to support dynamic comparison between the data user and the data owner of the currently selected resource sub-tree, we need to compare the current data user with the data owner of the sub-tree of the requested resource.

The XACML standard provides an XPath expression-based function for the selection of XML attributes. XACML uses the `<AttributeSelector>` element to identify a particular attribute value based on its location in the request context. The `RequestContextPath` attribute of the `<AttributeSelector>` element takes a static XPath expression and evaluates to a bag of values, given by the `DataType` attribute. The drawback of this function lies in the fact, that the attribute value for the `RequestContextPath` attribute handles only fixed XPath expressions that must be fully known at policy creation time.

We define a new XPath-based function that enables referencing and comparing of XML nodes relative to the currently selected resource:

> The function `<function:xpath-node-element-x500-compare>` takes two arguments. The first argument is of data type:
> `urn:oasis:names:tc:xacml:1.0:data-type:x500Name`
> and the second argument is of data type:
> `http://www.w3.org/2001/XMLSchema#string`
> which is interpreted as an XPath expression and evaluates to a
> `urn:oasis:names:tc:xacml:1.0:data-type:x500Name`

This function returns an `http://www.w3.org/2001/XMLSchema#boolean` and allows the dynamic creation of an XPath expression for the second argument, using the standard XACML string manipulation functions, such as concatenation. Both arguments are treated as `X500Name` values. The function compares the arguments and if they match, the function evaluates to **true**.

Example 2. **Specific Rule:** A practitioner is granted access to a treatment record for a limited time period

```
<Rule Effect="Permit">
   <Target>
    <Subject>
        <SubjectMatch MatchId="x500Name-match">
            <AttributeValue DataType="x500Name">CN=Julius Hibbert,
              ... </AttributeValue>
            <SubjectAttributeDesignator AttributeId="subject-id"
              DataType="x500Name"/>
        </SubjectMatch>
    </Subject>
    <Resources>
      <ResourceMatch MatchId="xpath-node-equal">/healthRecord/
                practitioners/practitioner/examinationRoom/visit/
        attachments/attachment/@filename='homer_brain.jpg'
      </ResourceMatch>
    </Resources>
    <Action>view</Action>
   </Target>
   <Condition FunctionId="date-less-than-or-equal">
      <Apply FunctionId="date-one-and-only">
         <EnvironmentAttributeDesignator DataType="date"
              AttributeId="current-date" />
      </Apply>
      <AttributeValue DataType="date">2009-03-22</AttributeValue>
    </Condition>
</Rule>
```

Generic rules capture the default behaviour of the system and can not be changed by the data owner or the data user. Specific rules can be added and deleted by the data owners depending on the different trust relationships and data exchange needs. These two rule-sets can be maintained separately using the existing XACML policy combining mechanism.

4 Reference Monitor Implementation

Implementation of the *Privacy Enforcement Architecture* requires the presence of a trusted system component at every data access location. An ideal *Policy Enforcement Point* would be based on a trusted virtual machine implementation that has the ability to enforce data use policies. We choose to base our implementation on the Java Security Framework and use the permission concept of the Java security manager for the enforcement of data use policies. Client applications will be started under the control of the Java security manager that controls resource access based on an appropriate data access policy for an application instance.

4.1 Java Security Architecture

The Java programming language provides a *Security Framework* that is aimed to protect the local system user from threats arising from untrusted Java code that is executed on the local system (such as Java Applets). Local programs typically have the full set of rights to access any resource on the system. Untrusted programs run under the supervision of the Java *SecurityManager* within a sandbox environment and are restricted in their access to system resources. For each Java Virtual Machine there exists exactly one instance of the *SecurityManager*. With the introduction of the Java 2 Security Architecture [11] the rigid sandbox model became much more refined and allows now the definition of application-specific security policies through the definition of permissions also for local programs.

Policies for resource access by Java applications started under the control of the SecurityManager are established through the Java `Policy` class. The default policy implementation uses text based configuration files to determine the actual set of permissions. The policy file(s) specify what permissions are granted for code from a specified *CodeSource* and support fine grained permissions.

All permissions granted to a class are encapsulated within a `ProtectionDomain` which is determined and irrevocably bound to the class at class loading time by the Java class loader. Permissions are granted depending on the origin of the code `CodeSource` and the user of the application `Principal` and bundled as a `PermissionCollection`. A `ProtectionDomain` for a class is constructed from the `CodeSource`, the `PermissionCollection`, a `ClassLoader` reference and the `Principal` who executes the code.

4.2 Assigning a XACML-Policy

In order to be enforceable through the Java Security Framework, XACML policies need to be translated into Java permissions. Only such policies that can be mapped to a corresponding Java permission can be directly enforced through the Reference Monitor without cooperation of the application. The set of permissions for the `ProtectionDomain` will be derived from the XACML policy description of the data object that is currently accessed.

The Reference Monitor is responsible for the translation of the XACML policy into a `PermissionCollection` and the launching of a restricted application component under the protection of the Java SecurityManager. Two alternatives exist to base permissions granted to code on XACML rather than the standard Java policy:

1. Write a new implementation of the `Policy` class, that derives permissions from XACML policies, rather than Java policy files
2. Implement a class loader that is able to derive and assign a `ProtectionDomain` from XACML policies

Writing a new `Policy` class would allow us to derive permissions from XACML. However, as permissions apply to the code source, we could not distinguish between different policies for application instances derived from the same code source. We therefore implement a custom class loader, because this gives us the possibility to assign different policies for application instances as we will see later. We started our implementation with the extension of the `SecureClassLoader` class. Our class loader overrides the `getPermissions()` method in order to allow the creation of the `ProtectionDomain` from the XACML Policy rather than the standard Java policy files. A XACML policy is typically much broader in scope than a Java permission that applies for a specific data object and the currently authenticated user. However, all granted actions need to be known at class loading time to be included in the `ProtectionDomain`. To determine the full set of permissions for a specific data object we execute several XACML requests, each against the corresponding data object and data user, but with different actions. We use the mapping in Table 1 to translate XACML policy responses into Java permissions.

The Reference Monitor generates a dedicated view on the data object for the called application, that is destroyed once the application quits. The actions *append* and *delete* therefore apply only to this view and require the cooperation of the Reference Monitor to persistently change the XACML data object. The Java `SecurityManager` enforces the permissions of the `ProtectionDomain` and intercepts actions that are not authorised.

Table 1 Mapping of XACML policy actions against Java Permissions

Java Permission	**XACML policy actions**					
	read	***copy***	***save***	***print***	***append***	***delete***
AWT:accessClipboard		x				
Runtime:queuePrintJob				x		
FilePermission:read	x					
FilePermission:write			x		x	
FilePermission:delete						x

4.3 Assigning Instance-Level Permissions

The current Java Security Architecture is targeted towards class based policing. Trust settings are applied by the code source and not by the running instance based on this code. For the realisation of Owner-Retained Access Control the reference monitor needs to enforce different policies depending on the current execution environment and data source.

An instance-based policing is necessary to distinguish between different instances of an application that simultaneously load data-sets with different access policies. Data users will be restricted in their actions based on the data that they are accessing. For each data object that is been accessed it becomes necessary to reference the corresponding policy before access is granted. When the data user is accessing different data objects during one session it becomes necessary to enforce more than one access policy.

Our class loader assigns a dedicated `ProtectionDomain` and loads the application class when data access is granted. The assignment of a new `ProtectionDomain` to a class is only possible at class loading time and can not be revoked or changed. Dynamic policy enforcement therefore requires the loading of a new class, including the construction of a new `ProtectionDomain`, for every data object that is accessed.

The default implementation of the `loadClass()` method in the `ClassLoader`, as described in [10], loads a class in the following order:

1. Call `findLoadedClass()` to check if the class is already loaded. If this is the case, return that object. Otherwise,
2. call the `loadClass()` method of the parent class loader, in order to delegate the task of class loading to the parent (this is done to ensure that system classes are only loaded by system class loaders).
3. If none of the parent class loaders in the delegation hierarchy is able to load the class, the `findClass()` method of this class loader is called in order to find and load the class.

With the behaviour of the default *loadClass* method the existing class would be found and re-used. In order to load a class with a new `ProtectionDomain` we load the class with a new instance of our class loader. The class loader uses a modified `loadClass()` method and no longer calls `findLoadedClass()` to check if the parent class loader already knows this class. Instead `findClass()` is called directly to load the class with a new `ProtectionDomain`.

Namespace separation in Java is enforced through the use of different class loaders. Two classes are considered distinct if they are loaded by different class loaders.

4.4 Use Case Implementation

To validate the protection concept outlined above we developed a prototypical implementation of a medical information system. Figure 4 visualises the interworking of the framework components. A resource browser component let the data user authenticate, select interesting events in the Electronic Health Record and start the Health Record Viewer (HRV) upon the selected entries. The HRV visualises the medical data of the health record such as images and diagnostic text and will be started under the control of the Java security manager. An appropriate permission setting will be derived from the XACML-policy part of the EHR. Since the HRV is under the complete control of the security manager the implementation of this component does not need to be fully trusted. The HRV can implement a superset of functions (such as print, save, etc.) whose execution will be restricted at runtime according to the specified data-use policy.

Multiple instances of HRV can be started simultaneously for different data objects and allow the comparison of different diagnoses or illnesses. Each instance of the HRV will carry its individual set of permissions based on the data that is being accessed.

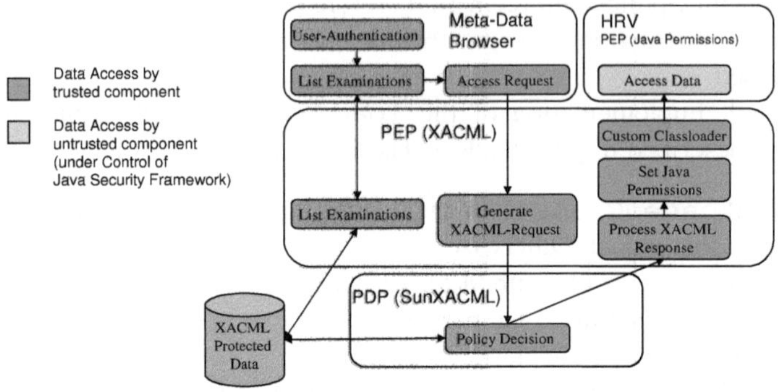

Fig. 4 Implemented Privacy Enforcement Framework

The XACML policy will be evaluated at the moment the application is loaded via the Reference Monitor. The Reference Monitor iterates through the set of actions contained in the policy-base for a given subject/resource pair to gather all the related permissions. An appropriate set of Java permissions is generated from the underlying XACML policy. The actual policy enforcement is offloaded to the Java Security Framework. No XACML requests have to be evaluated at the time of resource access of the HRV.

Policy enforcement is limited by the support of native permissions in Java – which are primarily focused on the Java threat model. Policies that can not be directly enforced through the native Java permission mechanism include the ability to control the file-append function and time based policies that enforce access time restrictions.

Time restricted policies can be handled at application start-up time by the Reference Monitor, but require reliable access to a trusted time-base.

The Java permission model can be extended through application specific extension of the policy class, however in this case the application needs to be trusted to correctly implement the necessary access checks. Implementation of new permissions would require the extension of our trust model, that currently only includes the Reference Monitor.

5 Related Work

Different policy schemes have been proposed to aid the data owner in the task of protecting his or her data.

Author-X [4] is a Java based data protection solution that allows the definition and enforcement of access restrictions on (parts of) XML-documents. It is a server-based solution where the document access is mediated by the access component, based on the collocated authorisation store. Access can be granted to parts of the complete document. No further protection mechanism exists once data access has been granted. While we realise a similar view on the document protections mechanism, our proposed protection scheme can enforce policies even after the data is released to the data user.

Damiani et al. [8] developed an access control system for XML documents that is able to describe fine grained access restrictions for the structure and content of XML documents. Their system generates a dedicated user view according to the permissions granted in a server-side authorisation file: the XML Access Sheet (XAS). The system does not implement any control over data that has been released by the server to the client. Consequently any information that is granted to be read by a user could be locally stored, copied and processed by the client. The generated view restricts data processing for single action classes only, e.g. the 'read' action. No support is given for orthogonal action sets, e.g. restricting a document to be read, but not to be printed.

Mont et al. [18] propose a privacy architecture that uses sticky policies and obfuscated data that can only be accessed if the requester can attest compliance with the requested privacy policy for this data. Data access is mediated via a Trusted Third Party that can reliably enforce time-restricted access. Our work aims to provide similar protection but does not depend on functions provided by another party. It uses the functions of a trusted reference monitor instead.

Sevinc and Basin [20] describe a formal access control model for documents based on the sticky policy paradigm. In their work they focus on document related actions such as read, print, change and delegate. Their model supports multiple owners and sub-policies for document parts and takes document editing into account, where merging and splitting of document content also influences the attached policies. We believe that our work fits within their problem definition but we focus mainly on implementational issues.

Lehmann and Thiemann [16] have developed a field access analyser that is able to analyse existing Java programs in order to determine the points in the program code where object methods are accessed. Static policy checking code is inserted to enforce access controls in accordance with the access-control policy for the program. In our work we choose to clearly separate the policy enforcement from program execution. No access to the application source code is necessary for the policy enforcement and policies can be expressed, evaluated and enforced independently from the application.

Gupta and Bhide [12] describe an XACML based authorisation scheme for Java that extends the Java Authentication and Authorisation Service. The work describes a generic implementation that extends the Java policy class with the ability to interpret XACML policies. While this work allows the Java Security Framework to enforce permissions for different users of an application, it might not be possible to enforce ORAC policies where different permissions need to be enforced depending on the data object that is currently accessed.

6 Conclusion

We investigated whether standard techniques like the Java Security Framework and XACML are sufficient for the implementation of privacy enforcement.

Our implementation allows the start of arbitrary, untrusted Java programs under the control of the Java Security Framework. The relevant access permissions of the application are derived at runtime from the policy of the data object that is being accessed. The developed architecture provides fine grained policy support for the enforcement of document policies at application level, independent from specific OS security mechanisms. We implemented a new class loader that supports instance level policy assignment. No new access control mechanism had to be added, as we use the existing implementation of the Java Security Manager.

The XACML policy language was used for the definition of data-use policies by the original data owner. The private data of the data owner is translated into a suitable XML record format and stored together with the corresponding XACML policy as a single XML data object. Data access policies are defined and bound to the data at creation time and revised later as access decisions need to be granted or revoked. Policy management is aided through the separation of generic default-policies from user-editable specific policies. The private data is referenced from the XACML policy via XPath.

References

1. Anderson, J.P.: Computer security technology planning study. Technical Report ESD-TR-73-51 (October 1972)
2. Apitzsch, F., Liske, S., Scheffler, T., Schnor, B.: Specifying Security Policies for Electronic Health Records. In: Proceedings of the International Conference on Health Informatics (HEALTHINF 2008), vol. 2, pp. 82 – 90. Funchal/Madeira, Portugal (January 2008)
3. Ashley, P., Hada, S., Karjoth, G., Powers, C., Schunter, M.: Enterprise Privacy Authorization Language (EPAL 1.2) (November 2003). URL http://www.w3.org/Submission/2003/SUBM-EPAL-20031110/
4. Bertino, E., Braun, M., Castano, S., Ferrari, E., Mesiti, M.: Author-X: A Java-Based System for XML Data Protection. In: Proceedings of the IFIP TC11/ WG11.3 Fourteenth Annual Working Conference on Database Security: Data and Application Security, Development and Directions, pp. 15–26. Kluwer, B.V. (2001)
5. Bundesgesundheitsministerium: Gesetz zur Modernisierung der gesetzlichen Krankenversicherung, SGB V, §291a. In: Bundesgesetzblatt, vol. 55 (2003)

6. CEN/TS-15211: Health informatics - Mapping of hierarchical message descriptions to XML. European Committee for Standardisation (2006). URL http://www.cen.eu
7. Cranor, L., Langheinrich, M., Marchiori, M., Presler-Marshall, M., Reagle, J.: The Platform for Privacy Preferences 1.0 (P3P1.0) Specification (April 2002). URL http://www.w3.org/TR/2002/REC-P3P-20020416/
8. Damiani, E., De Capitani di Vimercati, S., Paraboschi, S., Samarati, P.: A fine-grained access control system for XML documents. ACM Transactions on Information and System Security **5**(2), 169–202 (2002)
9. DeRose, J.C.S.: XML Path Language (XPath). W3C Recommendation (1999). URL http://www.w3.org/TR/1999/REC-xpath-19991116
10. Gong, L., Ellison, G., Dageforde, M.: Inside Java 2 Platform Security - Second Edition. Addison-Wesley, Boston (2003)
11. Gong, L., Mueller, M., Prafullchandra, H., Schemers, R.: Going Beyond the Sandbox: An Overview of the New Security Architecture in the Java Development Kit. In: USENIX Symposium on Internet Technologies and Systems. Monterey, California (1997)
12. Gupta, R., Bhide, M.: A Generic XACML Based Declarative Authorization Scheme for Java, *Lecture Notes in Computer Science: Computer Security - ESORICS 2005*, vol. Volume 3679/2005. Springer Berlin / Heidelberg (2005)
13. Imamura, T., Dillaway, B., Simon, E.: XML Encryption Syntax and Processing. W3C Recommendation (2002). URL http://www.w3.org/TR/2002/REC-xmlenc-core-20021210/
14. ISO/HL7-21731: Health informatics - HL7 version Reference information model Release 1) (2006)
15. Karjoth, G., Schunter, M., Waidner, M.: Platform For Enterprise Privacy Practices: Privacy-enabled Management Of Customer Data. In: 2nd Workshop on Privacy Enhancing Technologies (PET2002), vol. Lecture Notes in Computer Science 2482, pp. 69–84. Springer Verlag (2003)
16. Lehmann, K., Thiemann, P.: Field access analysis for enforcing access control policies. In: Proceedings of the International Conference on Emerging Trends in Information and Communication Security (ETRICS 2006), *Lecture Notes in Computer Science*, vol. 3995, pp. 337–351. Springer-Verlag, Berlin, Heidelberg (2006)
17. McCollum, C.J., Messing, J.R., Notargiacomo, L.: Beyond the pale of MAC and DAC-defining new forms of access control. In: IEEE Computer Society Symposium on Research in Security and Privacy, pp. 190–200 (1990)
18. Mont, M.C., Pearson, S., Bramhall, P.: Towards accountable management of identity and privacy: Sticky policies and enforceable tracing services. In: Proceedings of the 14th International Workshop on Database and Expert Systems Applications, p. 377. IEEE Computer Society (2003)
19. Moses, T.: eXtensible Access Control Markup Language (XACML) Version 2.0. XACML Core Standard (2005). URL http://www.oasis-open.org/committees/xacml
20. Sevinç, P.E., Basin, D.: Controlling Access to Documents: A Formal Access Control Model. Technical Report No. 517, Department of Computer Science, ETH Zurich, 8092 Zurich, Switzerland, (May 2006)
21. SUN: Sun's XACML implementation (2005). URL http://sunxacml.sourceforge.net/
22. XACML-2.0: eXtensible Access Control Markup Language (XACML). OASIS-Standard (2005). URL http://www.oasis-open.org/committees/xacml

Negotiation of Prohibition: An Approach Based on Policy Rewriting

Nora Cuppens-Boulahia, Frédéric Cuppens, Diala Abi Haidar, Hervé Debar

1 Introduction

Traditionally, access control is enforced by centralized stand-alone architectures. In this case, the access controller "knows" all information necessary to evaluate the access control policy. As a consequence, when a subject sends a query to the access controller, this access controller does not need to interact with this subject to decide if this query must be accepted or rejected.

However, in more recent architectures, such a centralized evaluation of the access control policy is no longer appropriate. When a subject sends a query to the access controller, this controller needs to interact with the subject through a negotiation protocol. The objective of this protocol is to exchange additional information necessary to evaluate the policy. This information generally correspond to credentials the subject has to provide to prove that he or she satisfies the requirements to execute the query.

Notice that the negotiation protocol can actually behave in a symmetric way in the sense that the access controller may also exchange credentials to provide the subject with guarantees that this subject can interact securely with the controller.

The objective of the negotiation is to exchange credentials in order to decide if the query must be accepted or not. When the access control policy corresponds to a set of *permission* rules, this consists in determining if the query matches one of these permission rules. However, the access control policy may also include *prohibitions* that act as exception to the permissions. In that case, the negotiation protocol must decide if (1) there is a permission to accept the query and (2) there is no prohibition that would apply to deny the query.

Nora Cuppens-Boulahia, Frédéric Cuppens and Diala Abi Haidar
TELECOM Bretagne, 2 rue de la châtaigneraie, 35512 Cesson Sévigné Cedex, France

Diala Abi Haidar and Hervé Debar
France Telecom R&D Caen, 42 rue des coutures BP 6243, 14066 CAEN, France

Please use the following format when citing this chapter:

Cuppens-Boulahia, N., et al., 2008, in IFIP International Federation for Information Processing, Volume 278; *Proceedings of the IFIP TC 11 23rd International Information Security Conference*; Sushil Jajodia, Pierangela Samarati, Stelvio Cimato; (Boston: Springer), pp. 173–187.

However, we claim that it would not be fair if the negotiation protocol ask for credentials in order to activate prohibitions. To illustrate this claim, let us consider the two following access control rules: (R1) a member of the medical staff is permitted to consult the patient's medical summary, (R2) a medical secretary is prohibited to consult the patient's medical summary. Let us also assume that rule R2 has higher priority than rule R1. Assigning priority to access control rules will be further discussed in the remainder of this paper.

Let us now consider a subject who asks to consult a given medical summary. We argue that the negotiation protocol should not ask this subject to provide a credential proving that he or she is a medical secretary in order to activate prohibition R2. Instead, the negotiation protocol should ask this subject to prove that he or she is a medical staff member (so that permission R1 applies) and not a medical secretary (so that prohibition R2 does not apply). For this purpose, the subject may provide a credential proving that he or she is a physician if this is sufficient to derive that (1) a physician is a medical staff member (due to an inclusion hierarchy) and (2) a physician cannot be a medical secretary (due to a separation constraint).

Since it is not possible to directly negotiate prohibitions, we suggest an approach to solve this problem. The central idea consists in rewriting an access control policy that contains both permissions and prohibitions into an equivalent policy that contains only permissions. We show that this approach applies to both open and close policies. The resulting policy only contains permissions but requires to negotiate negative attributes. For instance, in our above example, the negotiation protocol must get evidence that the subject is *not* a medical secretary. Thus, another contribution of this paper consists in adapting a negotiation protocol so that negotiation of negative attributes is possible.

The remainder of this paper is organized as follows. In section 2, we further develop a scenario to motivate the problem addressed in this paper. Section 3 presents the model we use to specify access control policies and explains how to manage conflicts between permissions and prohibitions by assigning priority levels to security rules. In section 4, we define a rewriting procedure that transforms an access control policy into an equivalent set of permissions and show how this procedure applies to both open and close policies. Since our rewriting procedure can generally generate negative conditions, section 5 explains how to adapt a negotiation protocol in order to negotiate such negative conditions. Section 6 presents a discussion of our approach and compares it with related work. Finally, section 7 concludes the paper.

2 Motivating example

In this section, we present an example to illustrate our approach. We consider a database used in an organization to manage medical records. There is special type of medical record called medical summary.

The database can be accessed by medical staff members. There are several sub roles of medical staff member: medical secretary, nurse and physician. There are also two sub roles of physicians: senior physician and junior physician.

Subjects can ask to execute the activity of managing a medical records. There are two sub activities of managing called consult and update.

The access control policy associated with this database management system corresponds to the following rules:

- R1: A member of the medical staff is permitted to manage the patient's medical summary,
- R2: A medical secretary is prohibited to manage the medical records,
- R3: In a context of urgency, a medical secretary is permitted to consult the patient's medical summary,
- R4: A nurse is prohibited to update the patient's medical summary,
- R5: A physician is permitted to manage medical records,
- R6: A junior physician is prohibited to update medical records.
- R7: In a context of urgency, a junior physician is permitted to update the patient's medical summary.

When a subject queries the database to get an access to a medical record, this subject has to provide credentials to prove that the requested access is actually permitted. For this purpose, a subject can give credentials proving his or her role (medical secretary, nurse, physician, junior physician or senior physician), credential proving that someone is his or her patient (if this subject is a physician) and credentials proving that the context of urgency is active.

When a subject queries the database, several rules of the security policy may potentially apply. For instance, when a subject asks to update some medical summary, all the rules of the above policy may potentially apply (since update is a sub activity of manage and medical summary is a special type of medical record).

Since these rules are conflicting, it is first necessary to solve these conflicts by assigning priority levels to these rules. This is further explained in section 3. Based on these priority levels, we define a process to rewrite the initial policy into an equivalent set of access control rules but that only contains permissions. For example, if we assume that rule R6 has higher priority than rule R5, then our rewriting process will rewrite rule R5 into the two following rules:

- R5.1. A physician who is not a junior physician is permitted to manage his or her patient's medical records,
- R5.2. A physician is permitted to manage without updating his or her patient's medical records.

Then, the database access controller has to determine which rule actually applies to take the decision to accept or deny the access. For this purpose, the access control must determine which credentials are sufficient to grant an access. For example, let us assume that the subject that queries the database provides his credential proving that he or she is physician. In this case, if the query consists in updating some medical record, then rule R5.1 potentially applies. Thus, the negotiation process may ask this subject to prove that he or she is not a junior physician.

As mentioned in the introduction, the net advantage of our approach is that the negotiation process will not ask the subject to prove that he or she is a junior physician to check if the prohibition associated with rule R6 actually applies. We claim that it is clearly better to ask this user to prove that he or she is *not* a junior physician in order to derive that rule R5.1 actually applies.

3 Policy specification and conflict management

3.1 Access control specification

Access control models provide means to specify which permissions and prohibitions apply to subjects when they execute actions on objects [3, 9]. These permissions and prohibitions are generally modelled by rules having the form[1] $condition \rightarrow permission(S,A,O)$ or $condition \rightarrow prohibition(S,A,O)$ where *condition* is a condition that must be satisfied on the state of the information system to derive the corresponding permission or prohibition. A conflict occurs if it is possible to derive that a given subject is both permitted and prohibited to execute a given action on a given object.

Managing conflicts in such models is a complex problem and [4] shows that detecting potential conflicts is actually undecidable. In [4], we also show the advantage of a more structured model as suggested in the OrBAC model [10, 11] and we shall use this model in the following to express the access control policy. One of the OrBAC contribution is the abstraction of the traditional triples $\langle subject, action, object\rangle$ into $\langle role, activity, view\rangle$. The entities *subject*, *action* and *object* are called *concrete entities* whereas the entities *role*, *activity* and *view* are called *organizational entities*.

A *view* is a set of objects that possess the same security-related properties within an organization thus these objects are accessed in the same way. Abstracting them into a view avoids the need to write one rule for each of them. Another useful abstraction is that of action into *activity*. An *activity* is viewed as an operation which is implemented by some actions defined in the organization. For example, the actions read (for a file) and select (for a database) may be considered as one *consult data* operation. This is why they can be grouped within the same activity for which we may define a single security rule. One of the main contributions of the OrBAC model is that it can model *context* that restricts the applicability of the rules to some specific circumstances [5]. Thus, *context* is another organizational entity of the OrBAC model.

---

[1] In the following, we shall assume that terms starting with a capital letter represent variables and that all free variables in formula are implicitly universally quantified.

The OrBAC model defines four predicates[2]:

- *empower*: *empower(s, r)* means that subject s is empowered in role r.
- *consider*: *consider(*α*, a)* means that action α implements the activity a.
- *use*: *use(o, v)* means that object o is used in view v.
- *hold*: *hold(s,* α*, o, c)* means that context c is true between subject s, action α and object o

Access control rules are specified in OrBAC by quintuples that have the following form:

- $SR(decision, role, activity, view, context)$

which specifies that the decision (*i.e.* permission or prohibition) is applied to a given role when requesting to perform a given activity on a given view in a given context. We call these *organizational security rules*. An example of such a security rule is:

- $SR(prohibition, nurse, update, medical\_summary, any_C)$

that corresponds to the rule R4 in our motivating example associated with the any_C context which is always true.

Concrete permissions or prohibitions that apply to triples $\langle subject, action, object\rangle$ are modelled using the predicate $sr(decision, subject, action, object)$ and logically derived from organizational security rules. The general derivation rule is defined as follows:

- $SR(Decision, R, A, V, C) \wedge empower(Subject, R) \wedge consider(Action, A) \wedge$ $use(Object, V) \wedge hold(Subject, Action, Object, C)$ $\rightarrow sr(Decision, Subject, Action, Object)$

3.2 Structuring organizational entities

The OrBAC model is based on four different types of organizational entities, namely *role*, *activity*, *view* and *context*. When defining our algorithm to rewrite a security policy in section 4, we shall need to aggregate elementary entities into composite entities. For instance, if r_1 and r_2 are two roles, then we shall consider that the intersection $r_1 \cap r_2$ and the disjunction $r_1 \cup r_2$ of these two roles is also a (composite) role. Similarly, the complement $\overline{r}$ or a role r is also a role.

For this purpose, we define an algebra for the four types of organizational entities. To simplify the presentation, we only formally define this algebra for the role entities. The algebras for the three other entities activity, view and context are similarly defined.

To define this algebra, we first consider a finite set $\mathscr{S}$ or subjects and a finite set $\mathscr{R}$ of elementary roles. The algebra associated with the role entity is then defined as follows:

---

[2] In OrBAC, the organization is made explicit in every predicate but here, to simplify, the organization is left implicit since we consider always only one organization.

Definition of the role algebra:

We define an algebra for the role entity as follows:

- no_R and any_R are two roles.
- If $r \in \mathscr{R}$ then r is an (elementary) role.
- If r is a role, then $\overline{r}$ is a role.
- If r_1 and r_2 are roles, then $r_1 \cap r_2$ and $r_1 \cup r_2$ are roles.
- Nothing else is a role.

In the following, we shall also use $r_1 \backslash r_2$ as a notation equivalent to $r_1 \cap \overline{r_2}$.

Interpretation of the role algebra:

To provide an interpretation of the algebra, we use the following notation for each elementary role r:

$| r | = \{s \in \mathscr{S}$ such that $empower(s,r)$ is true$\}$

Then the algebra is interpreted as follows:

- $| no_R | = \emptyset$
- $| any_R | = \mathscr{S}$
- $| \overline{r} | = C_{\mathscr{S}}^{|r|}$
- $| r_1 \cap r_2 | = | r_1 | \cap | r_2 |$
- $| r_1 \cup r_2 | = | r_1 | \cup | r_2 |$

Axiomatic:

The axiomatic of the role algebra is defined by axioms that specify that $\cap$ is commutative, associative, it distributes over $\cup$ plus the following axioms:

- $\overline{no_R} = any_R$
- $R \cap R = R$
- $R \cap no_R = no_R$
- $R \cap any_R = R$
- $\overline{\overline{R}} = R$
- $R_1 \cup R_2 = \overline{\overline{R_1} \cap \overline{R_2}}$

We also associates the four organizational entities with a hierarchy of inclusion and constraints of separation. We only present the model for the role entity. The models for the activity, view and context entities are similarly defined.

The inclusion hierarchy on the roles is defined using the *sub_role* predicate: If r_1 and r_2 are roles, then $sub\_role(r_1, r_2)$ means that r_1 is a sub role of r_2.

Separation constraints between roles are defined using the $separated\_role(r_1, r_2)$ predicate which states that role r_1 is separated from role r_2, *i.e.* a subject cannot be empowered in both r_1 and r_2.

We have the following axioms:

- $separated\_role(R_1, R_2) \leftrightarrow R_1 \cap R_2 = no_R$
- $sub\_role(R_1, R_2) \leftrightarrow R_1 \cap \overline{R_2} = no_R$
- sub_role is transitive
- $sub\_role(R_1, R_2) \wedge separated\_role(R_2, R_3) \rightarrow separated\_role(R_1, R_3)$

To illustrate this algebra, let *physician* be a role. According to our algebra $\overline{physician}$ is also a role which is defined through the complement of the role *physician*. That is, a subject is assigned to the role $\overline{physician}$ if he is not assigned to the role *physician*. If we have two roles *physician* and *employee* then $physician \cap employee$ and $physician \cup employee$ are also roles based respectively on intersection and disjunction of roles. A subject is empowered in the role $physician \cap employee$ if he or she is empowered in both roles *physician* and *employee*.

3.3 Prioritized access control rules

When the access control policy contains permissions and prohibitions, a conflict occurs when one can derive both $sr(permission, s, a, o)$ and $sr(prohibition, s, a, o)$ for some subject, action and object. The solution is based on assigning priorities to security rules so that when a conflict occurs between two rules, the rule with the higher priority takes precedence.

This is basically the approach suggested in the OrBAC model [4]. It actually provides means to detect and manage *potential* conflicts between organizational rules. A potential conflict exists between an organizational permission rule and an organizational prohibition rule if these two rules may possibly apply to the same subject, action and object. There is no such potential conflict between two organizational security rules if these rules are *separated*. Thus, in OrBAC, a potential conflict between two organizational security rules is defined as follows:

Definition 1. A potential conflict occurs between two security rules $SR(d_1, r_1, a_1, v_1, c_1)$ and $SR(d_2, r_2, a_2, v_2, c_2)$ if $d_1 \neq d_2$ and role r_1, activity a_1, view v_1 and context c_1 are respectively not separated from role r_2, activity a_2, view v_2 and context c_2.

Priorities should be associated with such potentially conflicting security rules in order to avoid situations of real conflict. Prioritization of security rules must proceed as follows [4]:

- Step 1: Detection of potentially conflicting rules.
- Step 2: Assignment of priority to potentially conflicting rules.

We then obtain a set of partially ordered security rules *SR(decision, role, activity, view, context, priority)*. Concrete security rules can be derived from the abstract security rules and are assigned with the same priority. It has been proved in previous works [4] the following theorem.

Theorem 1. *If every potential conflict is solved, then no conflict can occur at the concrete level.*

3.4 Application to our motivating example

The access control policy of our motivating example is formally specified by the following set of OrBAC security rules:

- R1: $SR(permission, medical\_staff, manage, medical\_summary, any_C)$
- R2: $SR(prohibition, secretary, manage, medical\_record, any_C)$
- R3: $SR(permission, secretary, consult, medical\_summary, urgency)$
- R4: $SR(prohibition, nurse, update, medical\_summary, any_C)$
- R5: $SR(permission, physician, manage, medical\_record, any_C)$
- R6: $SR(prohibition, junior\_physician, update, medical\_record, any_C)$
- R7: $SR(permission, junior\_physician, update, medical\_record, urgency)$

We also assume we have the following separation constraints:

- C1: $separated\_role(nurse, secretary)$
- C2: $separated\_role(nurse, physician)$
- C3: $separated\_role(secretary, physician)$

Notice that since we have $sub\_role(junior\_physician, physician)$ we can also derive:

- C4: $separated\_role(nurse, junior\_physician)$
- C5: $separated\_role(secretary, junior\_physician)$

Let us now detect and solve the potential conflicts of this access control policy:

- Step 1: Detection of potential conflicts.
  We have the following set of pairs of potentially conflicting rules:
  $Conflict = \{(R1,R2),(R1,R4),(R1,R6),(R2,R3),(R5,R6),(R6,R7)\}$
- Step 2: Resolution of potential conflicts.
  To solve the set of potential conflicts, we need to assign priority to every pair of potentially conflicting rules. For instance:
  $R1 < R2 < R3$
  $R1 < R4$, $R6 < R1$
  $R5 < R6 < R7$

4 Policy rewriting

We present an algorithm to rewrite a security policy that contains both permissions and prohibitions into an equivalent security policy that only contains permissions. In the initial policy we want to rewrite, we assume that every potential conflict is solved by priority assignment.

We first address the case of a close policy and then the case of an open policy. We recall that in the case of close policy, when no security rule applies to a given query, then the default decision is to reject the query. Whereas in an open policy, when no security rule applies to a given query, then the default decision is to accept the query.

4.1 Close policy case

Principle of the rewriting process: For every pair of potentially conflicting rule R_i and R_j such that R_i has higher priority than R_j and $decision(R_i) = prohibition$ and $decision(R_j) = permission$, rewrite R_i with R_j.
The rewriting process core: It keeps the rule with the higher priority R_i unchanged and it replaces the rule with the lower priority R_j by another rule after excluding from its application conditions the conditions of the higher priority rule R_i.
Let us write $SR(decision, r, ac, v, ctx, priority) = SR(decision, tuple_{SR}, priority)$, where $tuple_{SR} = \{(s,a,o,c)$ such that $s \in r, a \in ac, o \in v, c \in ctx\}$ and let us illustrate our algorithm using the following example of three conflicting rules:

$SR_1(permission, tuple_{SR_1}, priority_1)$
$SR_2(prohibition, tuple_{SR_2}, priority_2)$
$SR_3(permission, tuple_{SR_3}, priority_3)$

where each $tuple_{SR_i} = \{(s,a,o,c)$ such that $s \in r_i, a \in ac_i, o \in v_i, c \in ctx_i\}$ and $priority_1 < priority_2 < priority_3$.

The steps of our rewriting process are then the following:

1. The rule SR_3 is kept unchanged with its associated application condition $tuple_{SR_3}$.
2. Rewriting SR_2 with SR_3 is a process that replaces SR_2 by SR'_2 with:
   $tuple_{SR'_2} = \{(s,a,o,c)$ such that $(s,a,o,c) \in tuple_{SR_2} \backslash tuple_{SR_3}\}$
3. According to the principle of the rewriting process core, SR'_2 is kept unchanged and SR_1 is rewritten and replaced by SR'_1 with:
   $tuple_{SR'_1} = tuple_{SR_1} \backslash (tuple_{SR_2} \backslash tuple_{SR_3})$

$tuple_{SR'_1}$ can be simplified using some common properties of set theory. In a finite space E, we have the following properties over two sets S_1 and S_2:

$$S_1 \backslash S_2 = S_1 \cap C_E^{S_2} \quad (1)$$
$$C_E^{S_1 \cap S_2} = C_E^{S_1} \cup C_E^{S_2} \quad (2)$$
$$C_E^{C_E^{S_1}} = S_1 \quad (3)$$

Thus, using the property (1),(2) and (3), we get:

$$S_1 \backslash (S_2 \backslash S_3) = S_1 \cap (S_3 \cup C_E^{S_2}) \quad (4)$$

Coming back to our security rules and their associated conditions $tuple_{SR_i}$, $i \in \{1,2,3\}$, if we apply the above simplifications to $tuple_{SR'_1}$, we get:

$$tuple_{SR'_1} = tuple_{SR_1} \backslash (tuple_{SR_2} \backslash tuple_{SR_3}) = tuple_{SR_1} \cap (tuple_{SR_3} \cup C_E^{tuple_{SR_2}})$$

As the set $tuple_{SR_3}$ is already taken into account since we keep the rule of higher priority unchanged (*i.e* the rule SR_3), we can perform further simplification and we get:

$$tuple_{SR'_1} = tuple_{SR_1} \cap C_E^{tuple_{SR_2}} = tuple_{SR_1} \cap \overline{tuple_{SR_2}} \tag{5}$$

The simplification (5) is true in the case of 3 conflicting rules or even any number n of totally ordered conflicting rules. The correctness of this rewriting is proved in [6]. Thus, if we consider that we have n rules such as $priority_1 < priority_2 < priority_3 < ... < priority_n$ where $priority_n$ is the priority of SR_n, our rewriting algorithm for n ordered conflicting rules can be stated as the following:

- SR_n with its condition $tuple_{SR_n}$ are keep unchanged and
- for each j such that $1 \leq j, SR_{n-j}$ is replaced by SR'_{n-j} with the condition: $tuple_{SR'_{n-j}} = tuple_{SR_{n-j}} \backslash tuple_{SR_{n-(j-1)}}$

We get *in fine*:

$$\begin{aligned} tuple_{SR'_{n-j}} = & \mid r_{n-j} \backslash r_{n-(j-1)} \mid \times \mid ac_{n-j} \mid \times \mid v_{n-j} \mid \times \mid ctx_{n-j} \mid \\ & \cup \mid r_{n-j} \mid \times \mid ac_{n-j} \backslash ac_{n-(j-1)} \mid \times \mid v_{n-j} \mid \times \mid ctx_{n-j} \mid \\ & \cup \mid r_{n-j} \mid \times \mid ac_{n-j} \mid \times \mid v_{n-j} \backslash v_{n-(j-1)} \mid \times \mid ctx_{n-j} \mid \\ & \cup \mid r_{n-j} \mid \times \mid ac_{n-j} \mid \times \mid v_{n-j} \mid \times \mid ctx_{n-j} \backslash ctx_{n-(j-1)} \mid \end{aligned}$$

Actually, after applying the algorithm each rewritten rule is subdivided into four distinct sets of rules:

$$\begin{aligned} SR'_{n-j} \Leftrightarrow\ & SR'_{1.n-j}(decision, r_{n-j} \backslash r_{n-(j-1)}, ac_{n-j}, v_{n-j}, ctx_{n-j}, priority_{n-j}\} \\ & SR'_{2.n-j}(decision, r_{n-j}, ac_{n-j} \backslash ac_{n-(j-1)}, v_{n-j}, ctx_{n-j}, priority_{n-j}\} \\ & SR'_{3.n-j}(decision, r_{n-j}, ac_{n-j}, v_{n-j} \backslash v_{n-(j-1)}, ctx_{n-j}, priority_{n-j}\} \\ & SR'_{4.n-j}(decision, r_{n-j}, ac_{n-j}, v_{n-j}, ctx_{n-j} \backslash ctx_{n-(j-1)}, priority_{n-j}\} \end{aligned}$$

The rewriting process we have stated transforms a security policy into an equivalent policy that contains only permissions. All the conditions of prohibitions that are of higher priority are excluded from the permissions of less priority. Due to such an exclusion, if a prohibition rule of the policy before the application of our algorithm should have been applied to a given request, none of the resulting permissions of the rewritten policy should be matched. In this case, the default policy will be applied.

To illustrate our rewriting process, let us apply it to our motivating example. We shall obtain the following set of permissions:

- R1.1: $SR(permission, medical\_staff \backslash secretary \backslash nurse, manage, medical\_summary, any_C)$
- R1.2: $SR(permission, medical\_staff \backslash secretary, manage \backslash update, medical\_summary, any_C)$
- R3: $SR(permission, secretary, consult, medical\_summary, urgency)$

- R5.1: $SR(permission, physician \backslash junior\_physician,$
  $manage, medical\_record, any_C)$
- R5.2: $SR(permission, physician,$
  $manage \backslash update, medical\_record, any_C)$
- R7: $SR(permission, junior\_physician, update, medical\_record, urgency)$

Notice that the objective of the rewriting process is not to obtain a set of mutually independent permissions as suggested for instance in [1]. In our example, rules R5.1 and R5.2 are not mutually independent: if a subject assigned to role $physician \backslash junior\_physician$ asks for executing an action in $manage \backslash update$ on the view $medical\_record$, then both rules apply.

To obtain mutually independent rules, we could replace *physician* by *junior_physician* in rule R5.2. However, here, the objective of rewriting is actually not to obtain a "minimal" set of permissions. Instead, it is better for the negotiation process to obtain a set of "less" restrictive permissions. In our example, it would be inappropriate for the negotiation protocol to ask the subject to prove that he or she is a *junior_physician* if proving that he or she is a *physician* is sufficient to activate the rule.

4.2 Open policy case

The rewriting algorithm also applies when the security policy is open, i.e. when the default policy is to accept the request when no access control rule applies.

When the policy is open, we have simply to add a security rule specifying "everything is permitted":

- R0: $SR(permission, any_R, any_A, any_V, any_C)$

This security rule is associated with the lowest priority, i.e. for every other access control rule R_i of the policy, we have $R0 < R_i$.

We can then apply the rewriting algorithm without modification. Let us apply the approach to the following access control policy:

- R1: $SR(prohibition, secretary, manage, medical\_record, any_C)$
- R2: $SR(prohibition, nurse, update, any_V, any_C)$
- R3: $SR(permission, nurse, update, medical\_summary, urgency)$

Let us assume that R3 has higher priority than R2. After rewriting this policy, we shall get the following set of permissions:

- R0.1: $SR(permission, any_R \backslash secretary \backslash nurse, any_A, any_V, any_C)$
- R0.2: $SR(permission, any_R \backslash secretary, any_A \backslash update, any_V, any_C)$
- R0.3: $SR(permission, any_R, any_A \backslash manage, any_V, any_C)$
- R0.4: $SR(permission, any_R \backslash nurse, any_A, any_V \backslash medical\_record, any_C)$
- R0.5: $SR(permission, any_R, any_A \backslash update, any_V \backslash medical\_record, any_C)$

- R3: $SR(permission, nurse, update, medical\_summary, urgency)$

Rules R0.1 to R0.5 corresponds to rewriting rule R0 with prohibitions R1 and R2. Rule R3 is not rewritten since it has higher priority than rule R2 and is separated from rule R1.

5 Negotiation of negative attributes

The set theory we use in this paper is especially adapted to rewrite policies. We shall now explain how to define a negotiation protocol for the rewritten policies. For the purpose of negotiation, we need to specify conditions over attributes (*i.e.* credentials) to be requested from the requester. This is why we need to express our rewritten policy using conditions over the entities role, view, activity and context. Thus, we assume that every organizational entity involved in the negotiation is associated with a condition expressed in terms of attributes. This condition is a sufficient requirement to derive that a concrete entity (for instance a subject) is assigned to some organizational entity (for instance a role).

For example, the condition associated with the role *senior_physician* may be that the subject's occupation is *physician* and this subject starts this occupation for more than two years. Then, we have:

$occupation(S, physician) \wedge start\_occupation(S, physician, Start\_year) \wedge$
$year(current\_date, Current\_year) \wedge Current\_year - Start\_year \geq 2$
$\quad \rightarrow empower(s, senior\_physician)$

Now, if a subject involved in the negotiation has to prove that he or she is empowered in role *senior_physician*, then it will be requested to provide credentials to prove that his or her occupation is physician and that he or she is practicing this occupation for more than two years.

We have also to translate our set theory algebra into logical based conditions used in the negotiation process. This is straightforward because, if $Cond(E_1)$ and $Cond(E_2)$ respectively represent the sufficient conditions to be assigned into organizational entities E_1 and E_2, then we have the following equivalence:

$$Cond(E_1 \backslash E_2) \leftrightarrow Cond(E_1) \wedge not(Cond(E_2))$$
$$Cond(E_1 \cap E_2) \leftrightarrow Cond(E_1) \wedge Cond(E_2)$$
$$Cond(E_1 \cup E_2) \leftrightarrow Cond(E_1) \vee Cond(E_2)$$

As one can notice from the obtained rewritten security rules, we need to negotiate negative attributes such as $not(Cond(E_2))$. In the traditional centralized approach, the access controller will generally use "negation by failure" to evaluate negation. If the access controller cannot derive that some information is true, it will infer that this information is false. This corresponds to the close world assumption: The access controller knows every information necessary to evaluate the policy.

Of course, the close world assumption is not applicable to evaluate negative attributes in a negotiation process. Thus, the subject must provide credentials to prove that some condition is false.

If we assume that there is no credential that may be directly used to prove a negative attribute, then requester must provide credentials on positive conditions that are used to derive negative attributes proving that some condition is false. This derivation may be done using the inclusion hierarchy and separation constraint. For instance, having $separated\_entity(e_1, e_2)$, if the requester prove that he or she is assigned to the entity e_1, we can derive that he or she is not assigned to entity e_2. In addition to that if we have $sub\_entity(e_3, e_2)$, then we can derive that $separated\_entity(e_1, e_3)$. Thus, the given requester is not assigned to entity e_3.

For instance, in our motivation example, a subject can provide his or her credential proving that he or she is a senior physician to prove that he or she is not a medical secretary if (1) a senior physician is a sub role of physician (inclusion hierarchy) and (2) role physician is separated from role medical secretary (separation constraint).

6 Discussion and related work

Among other works done on negotiation of security policies we mainly discuss the Trustbuilder [15, 13, 14], Trust-χ [2] and XeNA [7] approaches.

TrustBuilder is a system for negotiation of trust in dynamic coalitions. It allows negotiating trust across organizational boundaries, between entities from different security domains. Using TrustBuilder, parties conduct bilateral and iterative exchanges of policies and credentials to negotiate access to system resources including services, credentials and sensitive system policies.

The TrustBuilder approach consists in gradually disclosing credentials in order to establish trust. The approach also incorporates policy disclosure; Only policies that are relevant to the current negotiation may be disclosed by the concerned parties. They specify what combinations of credentials one can present in order to gain access to a protected resource of the accessed service. In this way it is possible to focus the negotiation and base disclosures on need to know. Since these policies may contain sensitive information, their disclosure can also be managed by some strategies [12].

Trust-χ is another framework for trust negotiation specifically conceived for a peer-to-peer environment. Trust-χ proposes a language for the specification of policies and credentials needed in the negotiation process. Furthermore, it provides a variety of strategies for the negotiation. This latter consists of a set of phases to be sequentially executed. Trust-χ introduces *trust tickets* that are issued after a negotiation process succeeds. By certifying that previous negotiation process relative to a resource has succeeded, *i.e.* negotiating entities possess the required credentials, the trust tickets reduce as much as possible the number of credentials and policies needed in subsequent negotiation processes relative to the same resource thus speeding up these processes. Similarly to TrustBuilder, the Trust-χ disclosure policies state the conditions under which a resource can be revealed. Furthermore, *prerequisites*,(*i.e.* set of alternative policies to be disclosed before the policy they refer to) associated with sensitive policies manage their disclosure.

However, none of the previously described models deals with prohibitions.

XeNA is another negotiation approach based on the eXtensible Access Control Markup Language (XACML) [8, 7]. The proposed approach allows the expression of negative policies since XACML is a language that makes use of prohibitions. However, the authors do not explain how to deal with prohibitions in the negotiation policies. Their approach is based on a resource classification methodology [8]. It is the classification of a resource that determines if the access to this resource is negotiated (or not) and what are the negotiation requirements, *i.e.* needed credentials expressed in negotiation policies. They further propose a negotiation framework that uses this classification methodology and is based on the XACML architecture [7]. Two modules are introduced to manage the negotiation process: (1) the *negotiation module* is in charge of collecting the required information to establish a level of trust and to insure a successful evaluation of access and (2) the *exception treatment module* is called by the *negotiation module* in order to propose alternatives whenever an exception (*i.e.* non access or loop exception) is raised.

Thus, to our best knowledge, it is the first time that the problem of negotiating security policies that includes prohibition is addressed. We are currently implementing our approach as an extension of the above models.

7 Conclusion

We propose in this paper a new approach to negotiate security policies that include both permissions and prohibitions. Since it would be not fair to ask the subject to provide credentials in order to derive prohibitions, we suggest rewriting the policy so that it only contains permissions.

For this purpose and as suggested in the OrBAC model, the access control policy is defined in a structured way using the organizational entities of *role*, *activity*, *view* and *context* instead of the traditional concrete entities of *subject*, *action* and *object*. We also define a set theory algebra to aggregate elementary organizational entities into composite organizational entities. The rewriting algorithm uses, as preliminary steps, the approach suggested in [4] to detect and solve conflicts by assigning priorities to access control rules.

We then show that our rewriting algorithm provides means to transform an access control policy that contains both permissions and prohibitions into an equivalent one that only contains permissions. This rewritten access control policy is used in the negotiation process to determine which credentials are required to grant access to some requester. Since the rewritten policy generally specifies negative conditions, it is necessary to define strategies to negotiate these negative conditions. For this purpose, we actually assume that a credential cannot be directly used to prove a negative condition. Thus, we present an approach to derive negative attributes proving that some condition is false from credentials on positive attributes.

In future works we aim to implement this approach as an extension of existing prototypes, in particular TrustBuilder. We also plan to investigate how to negotiate policies that include obligations.

Acknowledgements This work is partially supported by the ANR Politess project.

References

1. J. G. Alfaro, F. Cuppens, and N. Cuppens-Boulahia. Towards Filtering and Alerting Rule Rewriting on Single-Component Policies. In *SAFECOMP*, Gdansk, Poland, September 2006.
2. E. Bertino, E. Ferrari, and A. C. Squicciarini. Trust-X: A Peer-to-Peer Framework for Trust Establishment. *IEEE Transactions on Knowledge and Data Engineering*, 16(7):827–842, 2004.
3. E. Bertino, S. Jajodia, and P. Samarati. Supporting Multiple Access Control Policies in Database Systems. In *IEEE Symposium on Security and Privacy*, Oakland, USA, 1996.
4. F. Cuppens, N. Cuppens-Boulahia, and M. Ben Ghorbel. High level conflict management strategies in advanced access control models. *Electron. Notes Theor. Comput. Sci.*, 186:3–26, 2007.
5. F. Cuppens and A. Miège. Modelling Contexts in the Or-BAC Model. *ACSAC*, page 416, 2003.
6. N. Cuppens-Boulahia, F. Cuppens, D. Abi Haidar, and H. Debar. Negotiation of prohibition: An approach based on policy rewriting. Technical report, TELECOM Bretagne, 2008.
7. D. Abi Haidar, N. Cuppens, F. Cuppens, and H. Debar. Access Negotiation within XACML Architecture. *Second Joint Conference on Security in Networks Architectures and Security of Information Systems (SARSSI)*, June 2007.
8. D. Abi Haidar, N. Cuppens, F. Cuppens, and H. Debar. Resource Classification Based Negotiation in Web Services. *Third International Symposium on Information Assurance and Security (IAS)*, pages 313–318, August 2007.
9. S. Jajodia, S. Samarati, and V. S. Subrahmanian. A logical Language for Expressing Authorizations. In *IEEE Symposium on Security and Privacy*, Oakland, CA, May 1997.
10. A. Abou El Kalam, R. El Baida, P. Balbiani, S. Benferhat, F. Cuppens, Y. Deswarte, A. Miège, C. Saurel, and G. Trouessin. Organization Based Access Control. In *8th IEEE International Workshop on Policies for Distributed Systems and Networks (POLICY 2003)*, Lake Como, Italy, June 2003.
11. A. Miège. *Definition of a formal framework for specifying security policies. The Or-BAC model and extensions.* PhD thesis, ENST, June 2005.
12. K. Seamons, M. Winslett, and T. Yu. Limiting the Disclosure of Access Control Policies During Automated Trust Negotiation. In Network and Distributed System Security Symposium, San Diego, CA, April 2001.
13. K.E. Seamons, T. Chan, E. Child, M. Halcrow, A. Hess, J. Holt, J. Jacobson, R. Jarvis, A. Patty, B. Smith, T. Sundelin, and L. Yu. TrustBuilder: negotiating trust in dynamic coalitions. *Proceedings DARPA Information Survivability Conference and Exposition*, 2:49–51, April 2003.
14. B. Smith, K.E. Seamons, and M.D Jones. Responding to policies at runtime in TrustBuilder. *Proceedings of the Fifth IEEE International Workshop on Policies for Distributed Systems and Networks (POLICY'04)*, pages 149–158, June 2004.
15. T. Yu, M. Winslett, and K. E. Seamons. Supporting structured credentials and sensitive policies through interoperable strategies for automated trust negotiation. *ACM Transactions on Information and System Security (TISSEC)*, 6(1):1–42, February 2003.

condition. Thus, we present an approach to derive negative attributes, proving that some condition is false from credentials on positive attributes.

In future works we aim to implement this approach as an extension of existing [illegible]

[illegible]

References

[illegible]

An Integrity Lock Architecture for Supporting Distributed Authorizations in Database Federations

Wei Li, Lingyu Wang, Bo Zhu, and Lei Zhang

Abstract In many data integration applications, a loosely coupled database federation is the underlying data model. This paper studies two related security issues unique to such a model, namely, how to support fine-grained access control of remote data and how to ensure the integrity of such data while allowing legitimate updates. For the first issue, we adapt the integrity lock architecture in multi-level database systems to a database federation. For the second issue, we propose three-stage procedure based on grids of Merkel Hash Trees. Finally, the performance of the proposed architecture and scheme is evaluated through experiments.

1 Introduction

Data integration and information sharing have attracted significant interests lately. Although web services play a key role in data integration as the main interface between autonomous systems, a loosely coupled database federation is usually the underlying data model for the integrated system. Among various issues in establishing such a database federation, the authorization of users requesting for resources that are located in remote databases remains to be a challenging issue in spite of many previous efforts. The autonomous nature of a loosely coupled federation makes it difficult to directly apply most centralized authorization models, including those

Wei Li, Lingyu Wang, and Bo Zhu
Concordia Institute for Information Systems Engineering
Concordia University
Montreal, QC H3G 1M8, Canada
e-mail: {w_li7, wang, zhubo}@ciise.concordia.ca

Lei Zhang
Center for Secure Information Systems
George Mason University
Fairfax, VA 22030-4444, USA
e-mail: lzhang8@gmu.edu

Please use the following format when citing this chapter:

Li, W., et al., 2008, in IFIP International Federation for Information Processing, Volume 278; *Proceedings of the IFIP TC 11 23rd International Information Security Conference*; Sushil Jajodia, Pierangela Samarati, Stelvio Cimato; (Boston: Springer), pp. 189–203.

proposed for tightly coupled database federations. The subject and object in an access request may belong to different participating databases that are unaware of each other's user accounts, roles, or authorization policies. Duplicating such information among the members is generally not feasible due to the confidential nature of such information. In addition, participating members in a database federation usually lack full trust in each other, especially in terms of authorizations and data integrity.

In this paper, we propose to support the distributed authorization in database federations by adapting the *integrity lock architecture*, which is originally designed for building multi-level database systems from un-trusted DBMS. Although intended for a different purpose, the architecture has some properties that are particularly suitable for database federations. First, the architecture does not require the DBMS to be trusted for authorizations or data integrity. Instead, it supports *end-to-end* security between the creation of a record to the inquiry of the same record. This capability is essential to a database federation where members do not fully trust each other for authorizations or data integrity. Second, the architecture binds authorization polices to the data itself, which can avoid duplicating data or policy across the federation, and also allows for fine-grained and data-dependent authorizations. A database federation under the adapted integrity lock architecture has some similarity with outsourced databases (ODB), such as the lack of trust in the remote database. However, a fundamental difference is that data in a federation of operational databases is subject to constant updates. This difference brings a novel challenge for ensuring integrity while allowing legitimate updates.

Motivating Example Consider the toy example depicted in Figure 1 (we shall only consider two databases unless explicitly specified otherwise since extending our solutions to a federation with more members is straightforward). Suppose a fictitious university and its designated hospital employ an integrated application to provide the university's employees direct accesses to their medical records hosted at the hospital. Bob and Eve are two users of the university-side application, and Alice is a user of the hospital-side application (we do not show details of those applications but instead focus on the interaction between the underlying databases).

In Figure 1, consider the two tables in the university and hospital's database, respectively. The two tables are both about employees of the university, and they have two attributes *ID* and *NAME* in common. As a normal employee of the university, Bob is not supposed to have free accesses to other employees' *DISEASE* attribute values hosted at the hospital. On the other hand, another user at the university side, Eve, may be authorized to access records of a selected group of employees due to her special job function (for example, as a staff working at the university clinic or as a secretary in a department). At the hospital side, Alice is prohibited from accessing the *INCOME* attribute of any university employee. However, as a doctor designated by the university, Alice is authorized to modify (and access) the *DISEASE* attribute.

The above scenario demonstrates the need for a federation of databases. We can certainly store the *DISEASE* attribute in the university-side database and thus completely eliminate the hospital-side table. However, such attribute (and other related medical data) will most likely be accessed and updated more frequently from the hospital side, so storing it at the hospital is a more natural choice. The above sce-

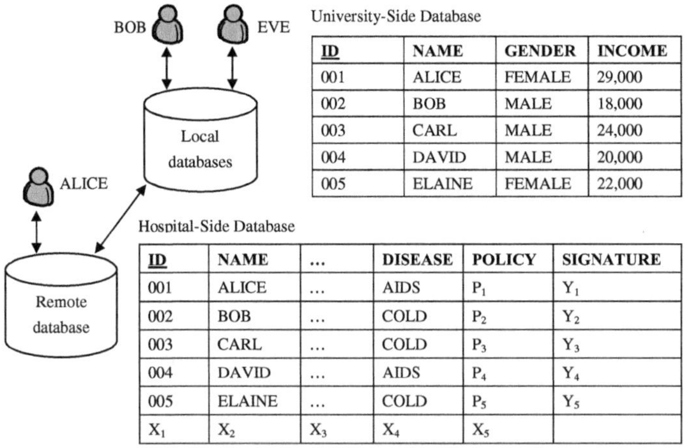

University-Side Database

ID	NAME	GENDER	INCOME
001	ALICE	FEMALE	29,000
002	BOB	MALE	18,000
003	CARL	MALE	24,000
004	DAVID	MALE	20,000
005	ELAINE	FEMALE	22,000

Hospital-Side Database

ID	NAME	...	DISEASE	POLICY	SIGNATURE
001	ALICE	...	AIDS	P_1	Y_1
002	BOB	...	COLD	P_2	Y_2
003	CARL	...	COLD	P_3	Y_3
004	DAVID	...	AIDS	P_4	Y_4
005	ELAINE	...	COLD	P_5	Y_5
X_1	X_2	X_3	X_4	X_5	

Fig. 1 An Example Database Federation

nario also shows the need for fine-grained and data-dependent access control of remote data. Row-level (or attribute-level) access control is clearly needed since Bob should normally only access his own records. Eve's job function may entitle her to only access records that satisfy certain conditions, such as *DISEASE* not equal to *AIDS*. That is, the access control policy may depend on actual data. Finally, the scenario shows the need for verifying the legitimacy of updates of remote data, such as that only a doctor designated by the university can modify the *DISEASE* attribute.

In the special setting of a database federation, we assume the university still *owns*, and is responsible for, its employees' medical records, even though the records are stored in the hospital. This is different from the case of two separate organizations where the university has no responsibility for its employees' interaction with a hospital. From this point of view, we can regard the university as *outsourcing* their employees' medical records to the hospital. However, different from the outsourced database (ODB) architecture where outsourced data are relatively static, the database federation we consider comprises of operational databases in which data are constantly being updated. As we shall show, existing solutions for ensuring the integrity of outsourced data in ODB are not sufficient for database federations.

The rest of the paper is organized as follows. Section 2 adapts the integrity lock architecture to database federations for fine-grained access control of remote data. Section 3 proposes a three-stage procedure for supporting legitimate updates of remote data while ensuring their integrity. Section 4 shows experimental results to evaluate different caching schemes. Section 5 reviews previous work. Section 6 concludes the paper.

2 Adapting The Integrity Lock Architecture to Database Federations

The *Integrity Lock architecture* is one of the *Woods Hole architectures* originally proposed for multi-level databases [19]. The integrity lock architecture depends on a trusted front end (also called a filter) to mediate accesses between users and the un-trusted DBMS (the original model also has an un-trusted front end, which is omitted here for simplicity) [5, 6, 8, 15]. Each tuple in tables has two additional attributes, namely, a security level and a cryptographic stamp. The stamp is basically a message authentication code (MAC) computed over the whole tuple excluding the stamp itself using a cryptographic key known to the trusted front end only.

The trusted front end determines the security level of the new tuple and computes the stamp to append it to the query when a tuple is to be inserted or updated. The query is then forwarded to the DBMS for execution. When users submit a legitimate selection query, the trusted front end will simply forward the query to the DBMS. Upon receiving the query result from the latter, the trusted front end will verify all tuples in the result and their security levels by recomputing and matching the cryptographic stamps. If all the data check out, the trusted front end will then filter out prohibited tuples based on their security levels, the user's security level, and the security policy. The remaining tuples are then returned to the user as the query result. The main objective of the integrity lock architecture is to reduce costs by building secure databases from un-trusted off-the-shelf DBMS components.

As described above, the cryptographic stamps provide *end-to-end integrity* from the time a record is created (or modified) to the time it is returned in a query result. The un-trusted DBMS cannot alter the record or its associated security level without being detected. Such a capability naturally fits in the requirements of a database federation illustrated before. More specifically, in Figure 1, we can regard the university-side database as the trusted front end, and the hospital-side database as an un-trusted DBMS in the integrity lock architecture. Suppose a user Eve of the university-side database wants to insert or update some records in the table stored at the hospital The university-side database will compute and append a cryptographic stamp to the tuple to be inserted or updated. When a user of the university-side database wants to select tuples in the hospital-side database, the university database will enforce any policy that is locally stored through either rejecting or modifying the original query posed by the user. Upon receiving query results from the latter, the university database will then verify the integrity of each returned tuple in the results through the cryptographic stamp in the tuple. It then filters out any tuple that Bob is not allowed to access according to the access control policy.

The adapted architecture also faces other issues. First, the original architecture requires a whole tuple to be returned by the un-trusted DBMS [8, 5], because the cryptographic stamp is computed over the whole tuple (excluding the stamp itself). This limitation may cause unnecessary communication overhead between databases in the federation. A natural solution to remove this limitation is to use a Merkle Hash Tree (MHT) [16]. Second, the integrity lock architecture can only detect modified tuples but cannot detect the omission of tuples in a query result. That is, the completeness of query results is not guaranteed. A similar issue has recently been addressed in outsourced databases (ODB) [7, 20, 14]. Two approaches can address this issue. A signature can be created on every pair of adjacent tuples (assuming the tuples are sorted in the desired order), and this chain of signatures is sufficient to prove that all tuples in the query result are contiguous and no tuple has been omitted. To reduce communication overhead and verification efforts, the signatures can be aggregated using techniques like the Condensed RSA [18]. Another approach is to build a MHT on the stamps of all tuples based on a desired order, so omitting tuples from query results will be detected when comparing the signature of the root to the stamp. However, applying the above solutions in ODB to the integrity lock architecture in database federations is not practical. A fundamental difference between ODB and database federations is that the former usually assumes a relatively static database with no or infrequent updates [1]. Data updates usually imply significant computational and communication costs. Such an overhead is not acceptable to database federations, because the members of such a federation are operational databases and data are constantly updated. We shall address such issues in the rest of this paper.

3 Supporting Frequent Updates While Ensuring Data Integrity

3.1 Overview

The previous section left open the issue of ensuring the integrity of data in remote databases while allowing for updates made by authorized users. First of all, we describe what we mean by *authorized users*. For simplicity, we shall refer to the database hosting data as *remote database* and the other database *local database*. We assume the federation provides each member the capability of authenticating users of a remote database. Such a capability should be independent of the remote database since we assume it to be un-trusted for authorizations. Our solutions will not depend on specific ways of authenticating remote users, although we shall consider a concrete case where a remote user possesses a public/private key pair and (queries issued by) the user is authenticated through digital signatures created using his/her private key.

Two seemingly viable approaches are either to verify the update queries, or to verify the state of remote data immediately after each update. First, in Figure 1, whenever Alice attempts to update a record, the hospital-side database can send the query and records to be updated, which are both digitally signed by Alice, to the university-side database for verification. The latter will verify the legitimacy of the update by comparing Alice's credential to the access control policies stored in the

---

[1] One exception is the recent work on accommodating updates while ensuring data confidentiality [4], which is parallel to our work since we focus more on data integrity.

records. However, this approach is not valid because the hospital-side database must be trusted in forwarding all update queries for verification and in incorporating all and only those legitimate updates after they are verified. Second, the university-side database can choose to verify the state of remote data after every update made to the data. However, this approach faces two difficulties. First of all, it is difficult to know about every update, if the remote database is not trusted (it may delay or omit reporting an update). Moreover, the approach may incur unnecessary performance overhead. For example, during a diagnosis, a doctor may need to continuously make temporary updates to a medical record before a final diagnosis conclusion can be reached. The university-side database should not be required to verify all those temporary updates.

We take a three-stage approach, as outlined below and elaborated in following sections.

- First, referring to the example in Figure 1, the university-side database will adopt a *lazy* approach in detecting modifications. More precisely, when Bob or Eve issues a selection query and the hospital-side database returns the query result, the university-side database will attempt to detect and localize any modifications related to tuples in the query result based on a two-dimensional grid of MHTs.
- Second, if a modification is detected and localized, then the local database will request the remote database for proofs of the legitimacy of such updates. The remote database then submits necessary log entries containing digitally signed update queries corresponding to those updates. The local database will check whether the queries are made by those users who are authorized for such updates and whether those queries indeed correspond to the modified data.
- Third, the local database will then disregard any tuples in the query result for which no valid proof can be provided by the remote database. To accommodate legitimate updates, the local database will incrementally compute the new MHTs and send them back to the remote database who will incorporate those new MHTs into the table.

3.2 Detecting and Localizing Modifications

We compute a two-dimensional grid of MHTs on a table to detect and localize any update to tuple or attribute level (a grid of watermarks is proposed for similar purposes in [10]). In Figure 2, $A_i(1 \le i \le n+1)$ are the attributes, among which we assume A_1 is the primary key and A_n the access control policy for each tuple. The MHT is built with a collision-free hash function $h()$ and $sig()$ stands for a public key signature algorithm. Each $y_i(1 \le i \le m)$ is the signature of the root w_i of a MHT built on the tuple $(v_{i,1}, v_{i,2}, \ldots, v_{i,n})$. Similarly, each x_i is a signature of the root u_i of the MHT built on the column $(v_{1,i}, v_{2,i}, \ldots, v_{m,i})$. Referring to Figure 1, for the hospital-side table, the signatures will be created by the university-side database using its private key. If a table includes tuples that are *owned* by multiple databases, then multiple signatures can be created and then aggregated (for example, using the

Condensed RSA scheme [18]) as one attribute value, so any involved database can verify the signature.

A_1	A_2	A_3	A_4	A_5	...	A_n	A_{n+1}
$v_{1,1}$	$v_{1,2}$	...				$v_{1,n}$	y_1
$v_{2,1}$	$v_{2,2}$	...				$v_{2,n}$	y_2
...	...	...				...	...
$v_{m,1}$	$v_{m,2}$	...				$v_{m,n}$	y_m
x_1	x_2	x_3	x_4	x_5	...	x_n	

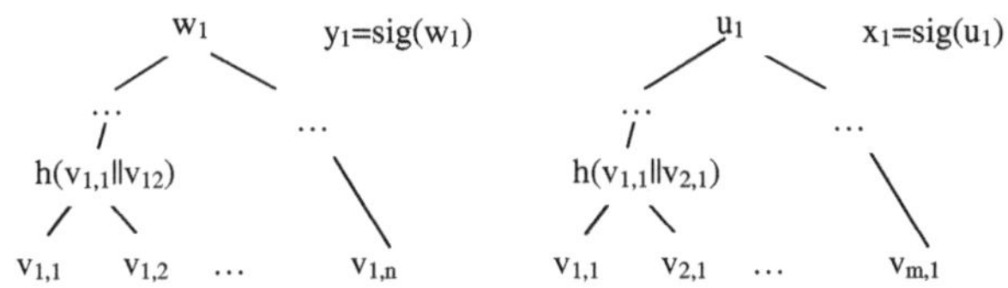

Fig. 2 A Grid of Merkel Hash Trees on Tables

Suppose Bob poses a selection-projection query whose result includes a set of values $V \subseteq \{v_{i,j} \mid 1 \leq i \leq m, 1 \leq j \leq n-1\}$. Then the hospital-side database needs to return the set V, the policy $v_{i,n}$ and the signatures x_i and y_j for each $v_{i,j} \in V$. Moreover, the siblings needed for computing the root of the MHTs from which the signatures have been computed should also be returned. Upon receiving the query result, the university-side database will first verify the signatures and the values in V by re-computing the root of the corresponding MHTs. If all the signatures are valid, then university database is ensured about the integrity of the query result. It will then examine the access control policies and filter out those tuples that are not allowed to be accessed by the user, and check the completeness of the query result based on the MHTs using techniques in [7, 20, 14]. If everything checks out, the query will be answered.

If some of the recomputed signatures do not match the ones included in the query result, then modified data must first be localized based on following observations [10]. If a value $v_{i,j}$ is updated, then the signatures y_i and x_j will both mismatch. The insertion of a new tuple $(v_{i,1}, v_{i,2}, \ldots, v_{i,n})$ will cause the signature $x_1, x_2, \ldots, x_n$ and y_i to mismatch, while all the $y_j (j \neq i)$ will still match. The deletion of a tuple $(v_{i,1}, v_{i,2}, \ldots, v_{i,n})$ will cause the signature $x_1, x_2, \ldots, x_n$ to mismatch, while all the $y_i (1 \leq i \leq n-1)$ will still match. The localization of modifications helps to reduce the amount of proofs that need to be provided (and thus the communication and computational costs) in the later verification phase. However, this mechanism does not guarantee the precise identification of every update made to the data. Fortunately, as we shall show, the verification phase does not rely on this localization mechanism.

3.3 Verifying the Legitimacy of Updates

Before we discuss the protocol for verifying updates, we need to describe how a remote database is supposed to handle updates. A remote database will need to record all the following into a log file: The update query, the signature of the query created with the user's private key, the current time, the current value before the update for deletion, and the current signatures involved by the update. Such information in the log file will allow the remote database to be rolled back to the last valid state. The information will thus act as proofs for the legitimacy of updates. When updates are detected and localized, the local and remote databases will both follow the protocol shown in Figure 3 to automatically verify the legitimacy of those updates and to accommodate legitimate updates by updating signatures stored in the table.

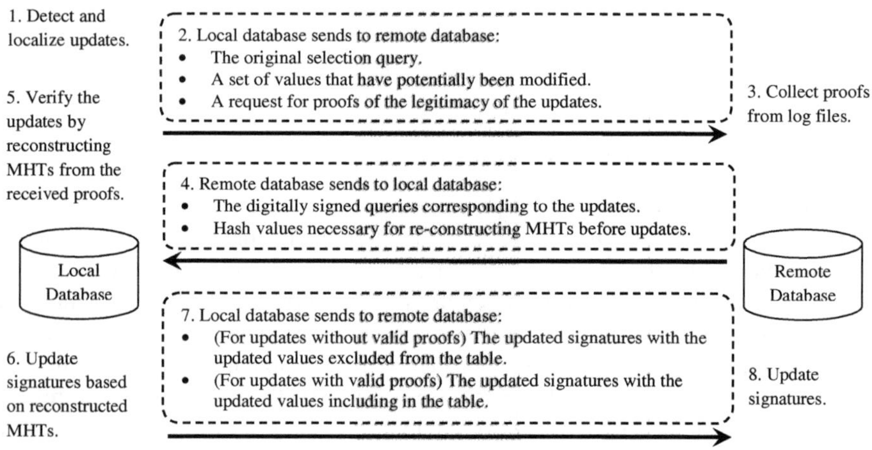

Fig. 3 The Protocol for the Verification of Updates

In step 1, the local database detects mismatches in signatures and localizes the updates to a set of values that may have been updated (recall that the localization does not guarantee the precise set of modified values). The local database will then send to the remote database the potentially updated values and related information, such as the original selection query in step 2. In step 3, the remote database examines its log files to find each update query that involves the received values. For each such query, the remote database will attempt to reconstruct the mismatched signatures using values and signatures found in the log file, which are supposed to be before the update. If a state is found in which all the mismatched signatures match again, then the involved queries will be collected as proofs and sent to the local database in step 4. Otherwise, the remote database will send to the local database a response indicating no proof for the updates is found.

In step 5, the local database will verify the signatures of the received update queries and ensure those queries are made by users who are authorized for such updates. The local database then attempts to reconstruct from the received queries a previous valid state in which all mismatched signatures match again. If such a state is found and all the update queries until that state are made by authorized users, then the detected updates are legitimate so the local database will create signatures by including the updated values (the details will be given in the next section) in step 6. Otherwise, the updates are unauthorized, so signatures are created by excluding the updated values in step 6. Upon receiving the updated signatures in step 7, the remote database will then update the received signatures in the table in step 8. The local database will only answer the original selection query if all the involved values are successfully verified.

3.4 Accommodating Legitimate Updates

To accommodate updates that are successfully verified to be made by authorized users, the local database needs to compute new signatures by including the updated values so the remote database can update the signatures in the table. Similarly, updates of signatures are also required for newly inserted tuples. Recomputing signatures for each record does not incur a significant performance overhead because the number of attributes in a table is limited. However, the signature of a column may be computed over a large number of records, and its computation is thus costly. Moreover, any insertion or update of a record will cause at least one of the signatures of columns to be updated. To reduce the computational cost of such updates, an obvious solution is to divide the table into smaller sub-tables with fewer records, and then apply the aforementioned grid of MHTs to each sub-table independently (instead of actually dividing the table, it is more convenient to simply change the way the grid of MHTs is computed).

However, upon a closer look, dividing the table does not solve all the problems. First, the table may need to be divided differently based on the ordering of tuples by different attributes. For example, in Figure 1, suppose we divide the table based on *ID*, then a query asking for tuples with a certain age may involve all the sub-tables, which essentially diminishes the value of dividing the table (diving the table will also cause more storage cost due to more signatures). Second, a more severe issue lies in the fact that even for a smaller sub-table, the local database cannot recompute signatures from all the values stored in the table simply because it does not have such values. Sending those values from the remote database will incur too much communication cost. Even to let the remote database compute the root will still incur high computational cost, considering that each insertion of a new tuple will cause the whole sub-table to be sent over.

Fortunately, a MHT can be incrementally updated. As illustrated in Fig 4, to update the hash value 3, the local database only needs the hash values 1, 2 in the MHT of each column, instead of all the leaves. To balance the MHT over time, for insertion of new tuples, we should choose to insert each value at an existing hash value that has the shortest path to the root (this may not be feasible for ordered attributes where the order of MHT leaves is used for ensuring the completeness of query results). The next question, however, is where to obtain the required hash values 1 and 2, given that recomputing them from the leaves is not an option. One possibility is to keep a cache of all or part of the non-leaf hash values in the MHT. If we keep all the non-leaf values in a cache, then a direct lookup in the cache will be sufficient for computing the root, which has a logarithm complexity in the cardinality of the table (or sub-table).

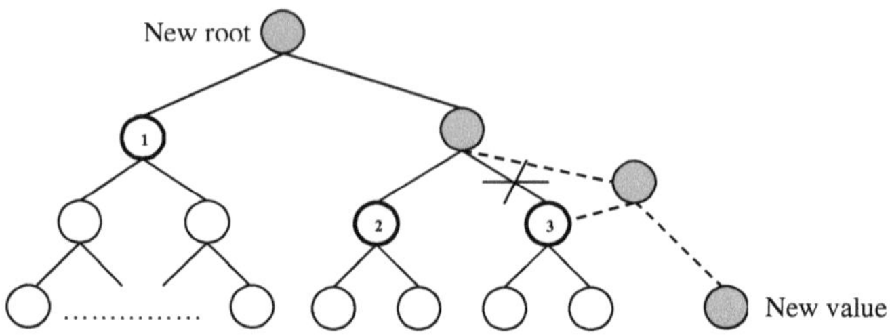

Fig. 4 Update the Root of a MHT

Considering the fact that the number of all non-leaf values is comparable to the number of leaves, the storage overhead is prohibitive. Instead, we can choose to cache only part of the MHT based on available storage. Two approaches are possible. First, we can use a static cache for a fixed portion of the MHT. If we assume a query will uniformly select any tuple, then clearly the higher a hash value is in the MHT, the more chance it will have to be useful in recomputing the new root of the MHT. For example, in Fig 4, the value 1 will be needed in the update of twice as much values as the value 2 will. Given a limited storage, we thus fill the cache in a top-down manner (excluding the root).

The assumption that queries uniformly select tuples may not hold in many cases. Instead, subsequent queries may actually select adjacent tuples in the table. In this case, it will lead to better performance to let the queries to drive the caching of hash values. We consider the following dynamic caching scheme. We start with the cache of a top portion of the MHT. Each time we update one tuple, we recompute the new root with the updated value using as much values as possible from the cache. However, for each non-leaf value we need to recompute due to its absence in the cache, we insert this value into the cache by replacing a value that is least recently used (other standard caching schemes can certainly be used). Among those that have the same timestamp for last use, we replace the value that has the longest path from the root.

3.5 Security Analysis

We briefly describe how the proposed scheme prevent various attacks using the previous example. Suppose in the hospital-side database, a malicious user inserts/deletes medical records or modifies some values. Such modifications will cause mismatches between recomputed MHT roots and those stored in the table, by which the university-side database will detect modifications. The hospital-side database, controlled by the malicious user, cannot avoid such a detection due to the security of MHT. The malicious user may attempt to modify the log entries to hide his activities by masquerading as users authorized for the updates. However, we assume the university-side database can authenticate remote users' queries through their signatures, so such signatures cannot be created by the malicious user without the private key of an authorized user. The malicious user can prevent the hospital-side database from sending proofs or reporting the absence of proofs, but this does not help him/her to avoid detection (a timeout scheme can be used for the case of not receiving proofs in a timely fashion). The malicious user can also reorder or mix up updates made by authorized users with his/her unauthorized updates. However, this will also be detected when the university-side database attempts to rebuild a previous valid state of data but fails. The only damage that can be caused by malicious users is a denial of service when too many tuples are excluded due to unauthorized modifications. However, as mentioned before, a database member may request the remote database to initiate an investigation when the number of such tuples exceeds a threshold. Ultimately, the use of signatures computed over the grid of MHTs provides the end-to-end integrity guarantee between the time of creating or updating (by both authorized users from the university or at the hospital) to the time of inquiry.

4 Experimental Results

We have implemented the proposed techniques in Java running on systems equipped with the Intel Pentium M 1.80GHz processor, 1024G RAM, Windows, and Oracle 10g DBMS. The main objective of the experiments is to compare the performance of different caching schemes, namely, a static cache of all the non-leaf values of each MHT, a static caches of partial MHTs of different sizes, and a dynamic cache of fixed size based on queries.

The left-hand side chart in Figure 5 shows the computation cost of updating a tuple in different size of databases when all non-leaf values are cached. We can see that at the cost of storage, there is only a relatively small difference between updating tuples without recomputing signatures (that is, ignoring the security requirement) and re-computing signatures from static cache. On the other hand, recomputing MHTs from scratch is very costly. The right-hand side chart in Figure 5 shows both the storage requirement and the performance of static caches of different sizes, which all hold a top portion of the MHT. We update one tuple in a database with 15,000 records. We reduce the cache size by removing each level of the MHT in a bottom-up fashion. The curve with square dots shows the number of values in the cache, that is, the storage requirement for caching. The other curve shows the computational cost. We can see that the overall performance is good in the range of (the hash tree height) -3 and -10 where both the storage requirement and the computational cost are acceptably low.

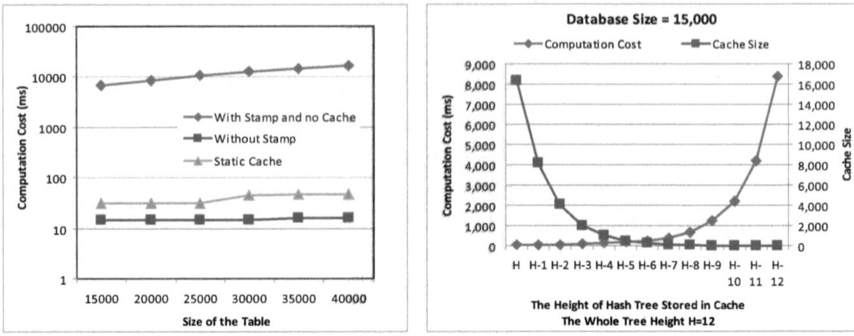

Fig. 5 The Performance of Static Cache

Figure 6 compares the computational cost of dynamic caching with that of the static caching under the same storage limitation. The database size is 15,000 records, and the cache is limited to store only 500 hash values in the MHT. To simulate queries that select adjacent tuples, we uniformly pick tuples within a window of different sizes. In Figure 6, *n* is the size of the window, *m* is the number of records involved by a query, the horizontal axis is the percentage of updated values within the window. We can see that as more and more values are updated, the performance of dynamic caching will improve since the cache hit rate will increase. The window size has a small effect on this result, which indicates that the dynamic cache is generally helpful as long as subsequent queries focus on adjacent tuples.

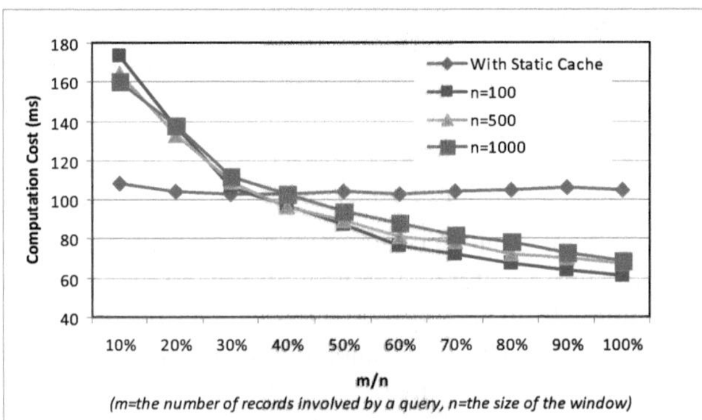

Fig. 6 The Performance of Static Cache and Dynamic Cache

5 Related Work

A Federated Database System (FDBS) is a collection of cooperating yet autonomous member database systems[21]. Member databases are usually heterogeneous in many aspects such as data models, query languages, authorization policies, and semantics (which refers to the fact that the same or similar data items may have different meanings or distinct intended usages among member databases). According to the degree of integration, FDBSs are mainly classified as *loosely coupled FDBS* and *tightly coupled FDBS*. A loosely coupled FDBS is rather like a collection of interoperable database systems. Most research efforts have focused on a tightly coupled FDBS, where the federation is created at design time and actively controls accesses through the federation. Although designing a tightly coupled FDBS from scratches has obvious advantages, in many cases it may not be feasible due to the implied costs. Our study assumes the loosely coupled FDBS model, and we do not require major modifications to existing DBMSs. This makes our approach more attractive to data integration applications. *Metadirectories* and *virtual directories* technology have similarity with our studied problem. They both can access data from different repositories by using directory mechanisms such as *Lightweight Directory Access Protocol (LDAP)*. When data in source directories changes frequently, it is a big headache to keep data updated. Which will have much more storage and computation cost when updating. However, our approach is based on the assumption that the remote database is untrusted to the local database, there is no authentication between the two databases.

Access control in FDBS is more complicated than in centralized databases due to the autonomy in authorization [2, 3, 9, 13, 23], which allows member databases to have certain control over shared data. Depending on the degree of such control, access control can be divided into three classes. For *full authorization autonomy*, member databases authenticate and authorize federation users as if they are accessing member databases directly. In the other extreme, *low authorization autonomy* fully trusts and relies on the federation to authenticate and authorize federation users. The compromise between the two, namely *medium authorization autonomy*, provides member databases with partial control on shared resources. Existing techniques, such as *subject switching*, usually requires members to agree on a loose mapping between user accounts and privileges in both databases such that one can help the other on making authorization decisions. Our approach does not require such a predefined mapping between databases but instead filters the result before giving it to the user. Several database recovery mechanisms based on trusted repair algorithms are adopted in commercial database systems. Each repair algorithm has static and dynamic version. There are various possibilities when maintaining read-from dependency information [1]. The survivability model extended from the class availability model is developed by using a state transition graph to model a ITDB (Intrusion Tolerant Database system), and it can provide essential services in the presence of attacks [22]. These works are similar to our approach in that they both need to isolate and recover from modified tuples. However, we focus more on the interaction between local and remote databases.

Multilevel databases have received enormous interests in the past, as surveyed in [19, 11, 12]. Various architectures have been proposed for building multilevel databases from un-trusted components [19]. The *polyinstantiation* issue arises when a relation contains records with identical primary key but different security levels [11]. A solution was given to the polyinstantiation problem based on the distinction between users and subjects [12]. The next section will review one of the architectures for multilevel databases in more details. More recently, outsourced database security has attracted significant interests [7, 18, 20, 17, 14]. One of the major issues in outsourced databases is to allow clients to verify the integrity of query results, because the database service provider in this model is usually not trusted. Various techniques based on cryptographic signatures and Merkle hash trees [16] have been proposed to address the integrity and completeness of query results. We have discussed the limitations in directly applying existing techniques in outsourced databases to the federation of operational databases in the paper. Parallel to our work, a recent effort is on accommodating updates while ensuring data confidentiality in ODB, The over-encryption model presents a solution for outsourced database to enforce access control and evolving polices using keys and tokens without the need for decrypting the resource to retrieve the original data and re-encryption [4].

6 Conclusion

We have addressed the issue of distributed authorization in a loosely coupled database federation. We revisited the integrity lock architecture for multi-level databases and showed that the architecture provides a solution to the authorization of accesses to remote data in database federations. We then proposed a novel three-stage scheme for the integrity lock architecture to ensure data integrity while allowing for legitimate updates to the data. We also devised a procedure for members of a database federation to update integrity stamps for legitimate updates. Our future work include the study of more efficient ways for handling concurrent updates made by multiple databases and the implementation and evaluation of a prototype based on the proposed techniques.

Acknowledgements The authors thank the anonymous reviewers for their valuable comments. This material is based upon work supported by Natural Sciences and Engineering Research Council of Canada under Discovery Grant N01035.

References

1. Paul Ammann, Sushil Jajodia, and Peng Liu. Recovery from malicious transactions. *IEEE Transactions on Knowledge and Data Engineering*, 14(5):1167–1185, 2002.
2. Jonscher D. and K.R. Dittrich. Argos - a configurable access control system for interoperable environments. In *IFIP Workshop on Database Security*, pages 43–60, 1995.

3. S. Dawson, P. Samarati, S. De Capitani di Vimercati, P. Lincoln, G. Wiederhold, M. Bilello, J. Akella, and Y. Tan. Secure access wrapper: Mediating security between heterogeneous databases. In *DARPA Information Survivability Conference and Exposition (DISCEX)*, 2000.
4. S. De Capitani di Vimercati, S. Foresti, S. Jajodia, S. Paraboschi, and P. Samarati. Over-encryption: Management of access control evolution on outsourced data. In *VLDB*, 2007.
5. D.E. Denning. Cryptographic checksums for multilevel database security. In *Proc. of the 1984 IEEE Symposium on Security and Privacy*, pages 52–61, 1984.
6. D.E. Denning. Commutative filters for reducing inference threats in multilevel database systems. In *Proc. of the 1985 IEEE Symposium on Security and Privacy*, pages 134–146, 1985.
7. Premkumar T. Devanbu, Michael Gertz, Chip Martel, and Stuart G. Stubblebine. Authentic third-party data publication. In *IFIP 11.3 Working Conference on Database Security*, pages 101–112, 2000.
8. R. Graubart. The integrity-lock approach to secure database management. In *Proc. of the 1984 IEEE Symposium on Security and Privacy*, page 62, 1984.
9. E. Gudes and M.S. Olivier. Security policies in replicated and autonomous databases. In *Proc. of the IFIP TC11 WG 11.3 Twelfth International Conference on Database Security*, pages 93–107, 1998.
10. H. Guo, Y. Li, A. Liu, and S. Jajodia. A fragile watermarking scheme for detecting malicious modifications of database relations. *Information Sciences*, 176(10):1350–1378, 2006.
11. S. Jajodia and R.S. Sandhu. Toward a multilevel secure relational data model. In M.D. Abrams, S. Jajodia, and H.J. Podell, editors, *Information Security An Integrated Collection of Essays*, pages 460–492. IEEE Computer Society Press, 1995.
12. S. Jajodia, R.S. Sandhu, and B.T. Blaustein. Solutions to the polyinstantiation problem. In M.D. Abrams, S. Jajodia, and H.J. Podell, editors, *Information Security An Integrated Collection of Essays*, pages 493–530. IEEE Computer Society Press, 1995.
13. D. Jonscher and K.R. Dittrich. An approach for building secure database federations. In *Proc. of the 20th VLDB Very Large Data Base Conference*, pages 24–35, 1994.
14. Feifei Li, Marios Hadjieleftheriou, George Kollios, and Leonid Reyzin. Dynamic authenticated index structures for outsourced databases. In *Proceedings of the 2006 ACM SIGMOD international conference on Management of data*, pages 121–132, New York, NY, USA, 2006. ACM Press.
15. C. Meadows. The integrity lock architecture and its application to message systems: Reducing covert channels. In *Proc. of the 1987 IEEE Symposium on Security and Privacy*, page 212, 1987.
16. R.C. Merle. A certified digital signature. In *Proc. of the Advances in Cryptology (CRYPTO'89)*, pages 218–238, 1989.
17. E. Mykletun and G. Tsudik. Aggregation queries in the database-as-a-service model. In *Proc. of the 2006 IFIP 11.3 Working Conference on Database Security*, 2006.
18. Einar Mykletun, Maithili Narasimha, and Gene Tsudik. Authentication and integrity in outsourced databases. *ACM Transactions on Storage (TOS)*, 2(2):107–138, 2006.
19. L. Notargiacomo. Architectures for mls database management systems. In M.D. Abrams, S. Jajodia, and H.J. Podell, editors, *Information Security An Integrated Collection of Essays*, pages 439–459. IEEE Computer Society Press, 1995.
20. HweeHwa Pang, Arpit Jain, Krithi Ramamritham, and Kian-Lee Tan. Verifying completeness of relational query results in data publishing. In *Proceedings of the 2005 ACM SIGMOD international conference on Management of data*, pages 407–418, New York, NY, USA, 2005. ACM Press.
21. A.P. Sheth and J.A. Larson. Federated database system for managing distributed, hetergeneous, and autonomous databases. *ACM Computing Surveys*, 22(3):183–236, 1990.
22. Hai Wang and Peng Liu. Modeling and evaluating the survivability of an intrusion tolerant database system. In *ESORICS*, 2006.
23. J. Yang, D. Wijesekera, and S. Jajodia. Subject switching algorithms for access control in federated databases. In *Proc. of 15th IFIP WG11.3 Working Conference on Database and Application Security*, pages 199–204, 2001.

3. S. Dawson, P. Samarati, S. De Capitani di Vimercati, P. Lincoln, G. Wiederhold, M. Bilello, J. Akella, and Y. Tan. Secure access wrapper: Mediating security between heterogeneous databases. In DARPA Information Survivability Conference and Exposition (DISCEX), 2000.
4. S. De Capitani di Vimercati, [illegible]

[illegible]

Role Signatures for Access Control in Open Distributed Systems

Jason Crampton and Hoon Wei Lim

Abstract Implementing access control efficiently and effectively in an open and distributed system is a challenging problem. One reason for this is that users requesting access to remote resources may be unknown to the authorization service that controls access to the requested resources. Hence, it seems inevitable that predefined mappings of principals in one domain to those in the domain containing the resources are needed. In addition, verifying the authenticity of user credentials or attributes can be difficult. In this paper, we propose the concept of *role signatures* to solve these problems by exploiting the hierarchical namespaces that exist in many distributed systems. Our approach makes use of a hierarchical identity-based signature scheme: verification keys are based on generic role identifiers defined within a hierarchical namespace. The verification of a role signature serves to prove that the signer is an authorized user and is assigned to one or more roles. Individual member organizations of a virtual organization are not required to agree on principal mappings beforehand to enforce access control to resources. Moreover, user authentication and credential verification is unified in our approach and can be achieved through a single role signature.

1 Introduction

The most problematic issue for an authorization service in any open distributed computing environment is that access requests may be received from a user that is not known to the authorization service. It is certainly possible to use signed assertions and a public key infrastructure (PKI) to determine that the user has been previously

Jason Crampton
Information Security Group, Royal Holloway, University of London, e-mail: jason.crampton@rhul.ac.uk

Hoon Wei Lim
SAP Research, France, e-mail: hoon.wei.lim@sap.com

Please use the following format when citing this chapter:

Crampton, J. and Lim, H.W., 2008, in IFIP International Federation for Information Processing, Volume 278; *Proceedings of the IFIP TC 11 23rd International Information Security Conference*; Sushil Jajodia, Pierangela Samarati, Stelvio Cimato; (Boston: Springer), pp. 205–219.

authenticated by some security domain D_1, even one not previously known to the security domain D_2 to which the request was directed. It may even be possible to use similar types of assertions to determine that a user has a particular attribute, role r, say, in D_1. However, there still remains the difficult problem of interpreting r in the context of D_2's authorization policy. It seems inevitable that there must be some prior agreement between D_1 and D_2 about what r should mean to D_2. This presupposes that D_2 is aware of the roles defined in D_1's security policy, which also means that D_1 is prepared to reveal role names and their authorization semantics (within D_1) to D_2.

In short, it seems inevitable that pre-defined mappings will need to be specified between principals in one security domain and those in another. It is fair to say, therefore, that authorization is considerably more difficult than authentication in open distributed systems. Indeed, it seems practically impossible to evaluate an access request from a user that is not previously known to the authorization service, unless there exists some *a priori* agreement between the domain containing the authorization service and the requester's domain.

In addition to the problem of principal mapping, we also note that all of the above approaches and existing authorization frameworks that we know of for open distributed computing environments, such as KeyNote [3], SPKI/SDSI [7] and RBTM [12], rely on some form of certificate-based PKI. Essentially these frameworks rely on signed statements or assertions, attesting to the user or the associated public key having a particular attribute. A set of such attributes is used to map the user to principals in the relevant authorization policy. The richer the policy language, the more complex the recovery of these assertions and subsequent computation of an authorization decision becomes. A considerable amount of research effort has been devoted to *credential chain discovery algorithms* in both SPKI/SDSI [5] and RBTM [13], for example. In essence, existing approaches require the processing, particularly verification, of a large number of digitally signed credentials.

In this paper, we consider the problems of *inter-domain principal mapping* and *verification of user credentials* that make authorization so difficult in open distributed environments. We believe the nature of a hierarchical structure within a virtual organization (VO) or a federation offers some opportunities to reduce the impact of the difficulties posed by principal mapping, credential verification and credential chain discovery.[1] Typically, a VO will have a hierarchical structure, enabling member organizations (MOs) and principals within those organizations to be identified uniquely within a hierarchical namespace. Access requests are signed using a hierarchical identity-based signature scheme (HIBS), in which signing keys correspond to role identifiers, hence the terminology *role signatures*. These identifiers are based on the hierarchical namespace in the VO and associated with some generic roles defined by the VO. If the identifiers are correctly formed and the associated signature on the request can be verified, then the user is known to be authorized for those roles in his home organization.

[1] Hereafter, a VO, a term commonly used in large-scale distributed computing systems [8], is assumed to be a collection of geographically dispersed organizations with heterogeneous systems, each of which has individual organizational autonomy.

We now summarize the main contributions of this paper.

- There does not need to be agreement between individual member organizations about how to map principal identifiers. This means that the composition of the VO can be dynamic without compromising the effectiveness of the authorization mechanisms in member organizations. New member organizations can join the VO and need only define some additional rules mapping their local roles to the VO roles.
- User authentication and credential verification is unified and credential verification is rendered trivial. The authorization service is required to verify a single role signature to both confirm that the user is an authenticated member of some other member organization and occupies a particular generic role within that organization.

In the next section, we provide a brief overview of identity-based cryptography, the Gentry-Silverberg HIBS scheme, and a recent extension to this scheme. In Section 3, we present the concept of role signatures and describe the use of a HIBS scheme for constructing and verifying such signatures. We also describe what policies need to be defined by member organizations. In Section 4, we describe a security architecture in which the concept of role signatures can be deployed. We discuss related work in Section 5.

2 Hierarchical Identity-Based Cryptography

The idea of generating public keys based on user names, or some other publicly available information that could uniquely identify a user (such as an email address), was conceived by Shamir more than two decades ago [20]. The corresponding private keys are computed and distributed by a trusted Private Key Generator (PKG). The usual role of a trusted third party (the CA) in a PKI is to attest to the authenticity of public keys. In identity-based cryptography, public keys are derived from public information and their authenticity can be assumed, obviating the requirement for certificates. Hence, the job of the trusted third party (the PKG) is to ensure the correct binding of private keys to identities.

Hierarchical identity-based signatures (HIBS) schemes were developed to reduce the burden of (private) key generation on the PKG. In such schemes, it is assumed that entities can be arranged in a rooted tree and that entities at one level are trusted to issue private keys to entities immediately below them in the tree. More specifically, the root PKG, located at level 0, produces private keys for entities at level 1, who in turn act as PKGs for entities in their respective domains at level 2, *etc.* In the context of this paper, the root PKG is the trusted authority (TA), who issues keys to VOs, who in turn issue keys to MOs, who in turn create role signing keys.

Each node in the tree has an identifer. The identifier of an entity is the concatenation of the node identifiers in the path from the root to the node associated with the entity. Hence, the string $id_1.id_2.\cdots.id_t$ represents an entity at level t whose ancestor at level 1 has identifier id_1 and whose ancestor at level j has identifier $id_1.\cdots.id_j$. In other words, the tree defines a hierarchical namespace.

We base our work around the Gentry-Silverberg HIBS scheme [10], which works in the following way. The root PKG computes a master secret s_0 and a set of system parameters, and every other entity chooses a secret value. Each non-leaf entity is a PKG and is responsible for computing private keys for each of its children using each child's identifier, the entity's secret information and the system parameters. Each entity may sign messages using the private key generated by its parent. Any other entity may verify the validity of a signature using the signed message, the signer's identifier and the system parameters as inputs.

The purpose of a role signature is to prove membership of a role. As we will see in Section 3.1.2, there may be situations in which it is useful to prove membership of multiple roles with a single signature.

There are other HIBS schemes in the literature, for example [4], that may be used for role signatures. Our proposal is based on Gentry-Silverberg's scheme because it can be extended to support "multi-key signatures" [14], in which several keys are used to generate a single signature, thereby enabling a user to sign a message to prove possession of two or more signing keys.

3 Role Signatures

We assume that there exists a hierarchical structure within an open distributed system, where a trusted authority (TA) is at the top of the hierarchy. Below the TA, we have the VOs who are formed by MOs. We assume that the VO specifies a small number of generic roles that can be used as principals in the authorization policy of each MO. We would argue that this is a much weaker assumption than assuming the existence of mappings between the principals referenced in each of the MOs' access control policies. It is also important to stress at this point that we are using *identifiers* (for VOs, MOs and generic roles), rather than (user) identities in our framework.

We treat the TA as a level 0 entity in a tree, the VOs as level 1 entities, the MOs as level 2 entities, and generic roles as level 3 entities. We then apply the Gentry-Silverberg HIBS scheme to this hierarchical structure. The TA is responsible for issuing signing keys to VOs. We view the issuance of a signing key as analogous to assigning a role to a principal. Hence, if the TA issues a signing key to principal VO_1, this means that VO_1 is a legitimate VO principal (recognized by the TA). This signing key will be derived from the identifier VO_1. Similarly, if the principal VO_1 issues a signing key to Org_1, this means that Org_1 is a legitimate MO principal in VO_1. This signing key will be derived from the identifier $VO_1.Org_1$. Finally, Org_1 may issue a signing key to user u, based on the generic role identifier $VO_1.Org_1.vr$. This is the simplest form of generic role identifier: additional information can be encoded in the identifier to specify the user to which the role is assigned or the lifetime of a key. We discuss these issues in more detail in Section 3.3.

3.1 RBAC Policies for Open Distributed Systems

In our proposal, we assume that a VO comprises a countable set of MOs, $Org_1, Org_2 \ldots$, and that membership of this set may change over time. We also assume that the VO defines a finite set of generic role identifiers $vr_1, \ldots, vr_m$.

Each MO Org_i defines and maintains role-based access control (RBAC) policies. As usual, a policy decision point (PDP_i) for a resource controlled by Org_i uses an access control policy (ACP_i) to decide requests for access to that resource from users authenticated directly by that organization. This is the *internal* ACP.

Each MO extends its ACP so that users in that MO are assigned to zero or more of the generic roles. These role identifiers will be used to map users in one MO to roles in another MO. In addition, the ACP must be extended to specify how members of generic roles in other MOs are mapped to local roles. This is the *external* policy.

3.1.1 Internal ACPs

We use RBAC96 syntax [19] for internal ACPs. We write VR for the set of generic roles identified within a VO. Given a set of internal role identifiers R, we write R^* for $R \cup VR$. Each MO Org_i defines an internal set of roles R_i and defines

- a user-role assignment relation $UA_i \subseteq U_i \times R_i^*$, where U_i is the set of authorized users in Org_i;
- a permission-role assignment relation $PA_i \subseteq P_i \times R_i^*$, where P_i is the set of permissions for resources maintained and protected by Org_i;
- a role hierarchy relation $RH_i \subseteq R_i^* \times R_i^*$, where the graph (R_i^*, RH_i) is directed and acyclic.

We write $(R_i^*, \leqslant)$ for the reflexive transitive closure of RH_i. Henceforth, we drop the subscript i whenever no ambiguity can arise.

Hence, a user $u \in U_i$ may be assigned directly to a generic role vr via the UA_i relation, or assigned implicitly via inheritance in the RH_i relation. This assignment may enable u to access resources in another organization Org_j, depending on the external policy defined by Org_j.

3.1.2 External ACPs

Informally, each member organization needs to decide which other member organizations it trusts, and which generic roles defined by those organizations can be mapped to internal roles. The RT family of languages [12] provides a natural way of stating these external policies. The RT_0 language defines four different types of rules:

- $A.r \leftarrow A'$ is an assertion made by principal A that principal A' is assigned to role r. Such an assertion is equivalent to saying that $(A, r) \in UA_A$, where UA_A

denotes the user-role assignment relation defined by A. In a distributed setting, the assertion may be presented by A' to another principal as a credential signed by A.

- $A.r \leftarrow A'.r'$ is a policy statement made by principal A that any member of role $A'.r'$ is also a member of the role r. In general, this assertion has no direct equivalent in RBAC96, which is concerned with RBAC policies in closed environments. (If, however, $A = A'$, then the statement is analogous to defining a child-parent relationship between r and r' in RBAC96.)
- $A.r \leftarrow A.r'.r''$ is a policy statement made by principal A that says any member of a role $B.r''$, where B is itself a member of role $A.r'$, is a member of role r. Statements of this form allow A to delegate responsibility (to members of $A.r'$) for assigning principals to role r''.
- $A.r \leftarrow A_1.r_1 \cap A_2.r_2$ is a statement made by principal A that says that any member of roles $A_1.r_1$ and $A_2.r_2$ is also a member of role r.

We now show how rules of this form can be used to encode our external policies. The RT rules

$$Org_i.memberOrg \leftarrow VO.memberOrg \tag{1}$$
$$Org_i.vr \leftarrow Org_i.memberOrg.vr \tag{2}$$

assume that (principal) VO defines a role called *memberOrg* and state that

- Org_i defines a role called *memberOrg* and any member of $VO.memberOrg$ is also a member of the local *memberOrg* role;
- any member of a generic role *vr* defined by a member of role *memberOrg* is also a member of the generic role defined by Org_i.

In other words, these rules state that if the VO says that Org_j is a member organization and Org_j says that u is a member of generic role *vr*, then Org_i is prepared to accept u as a member of *vr* as defined and used in ACP_i.

This means that any member of generic role *vr* defined by any MO is also a member of generic role *vr* in Org_i. In particular, in order to be assured that a user is authorized for generic role *vr*, Org_i needs to confirm that there exists a credential from the VO asserting that the MO is a legitimate member of the VO and a credential from the MO asserting that the user is a legitimate member of the role *vr*. In other words, if Org_j signs a credential of the form $Org_j.vr \leftarrow u$ (meaning u is a member of role *vr* defined by Org_j), then Org_i may deduce that u is a member of $Org_j.vr$, *provided* that Org_i can be convinced that Org_j is a genuine MO. The latter check requires the existence of a credential of the form $VO.memberOrg \leftarrow Org_j$ signed by the VO principal. In principle, then, the authenticity of two different credentials needs to be established by Org_i. Moreover, these credentials are issued by different entities. In Section 3.2 will show that these credentials can be encoded in a single role signature.

In fact, Org_i could map generic roles directly to local role r_i using the rules

$$Org_i.memberOrg \leftarrow VO.memberOrg, \tag{3}$$

$$Org_i.r_i \leftarrow Org_i.memberOrg.vr. \tag{4}$$

In general, the external ACP includes rules that map multiple generic roles to local roles and vice versa. For each generic role vr that Org_i chooses to recognize, Org_i defines one or more rules of the form

$$Org_i.r \leftarrow \bigcap_{j=1}^{m} Org_i.memberOrg.vr_j, \tag{5}$$

$$Org_i.memberOrg \leftarrow VO.memberOrg. \tag{6}$$

That is, any user who is a member of each of the generic roles $vr_1, \ldots, vr_m$ defined by any MO (that is recognized by the VO) is a member of role $r \in R_i^*$ in Org_i. It can be seen that this requires checking $m+1$ credentials. In Section 3.2, we show how key aggregation can be used to construct a single role signature, whose verification proves that all $m+1$ credentials are valid.

3.2 Access Request Signing And Verification

As we noted in the preceding section, in conventional RBTM (and other trust management frameworks) it may be necessary for the authorization service to obtain and verify the authenticity of a number of different credentials in order to evaluate an access request. We now demonstrate how hierarchical identity-based signature schemes can be exploited to simplify credential discovery and verification. Essentially, we associate each generic role with a unique identifer within the VO namespace and use this to generate a private key that is used to sign access requests — role signatures. Signature verification is performed using a key that can be derived from the identifier by any principal, thereby enabling that principal (or the PDP acting for that principal) to verify that the user is indeed a member of a particular generic role.

Note first that rules (3) and (4) can be reduced to the rule

$$Org_i.r_i \leftarrow VO.memberOrg.vr.$$

In other words, if a user can provide a credential proving that she is a member of a generic role vr in a member organization of the virtual organization, then she can be mapped directly to role vr in Org_i.

We adopt a push model in which the user supplies authorization credentials as part of an access request. In particular, a user u uses a signing key, such as the one associated with role identifier $VO_1.Org_1.vr$, to sign an access request. If the PDP in Org_2 can verify the signature on the request using the verification key associated with $VO_1.Org_1.vr$, then the PDP in Org_2 can be convinced that VO_1 is a legitimate VO (as far as the TA is concerned), Org_1 is a legitimate MO (as far as the VO is concerned), and u is a legitimate user assigned to role vr (as far as the MO is concerned). The PDP in Org_2 may then use its policy to map the generic role to local roles, and hence evaluate the access request. Note the definition of a comparatively small number of generic roles and a single signature verification are sufficient to both solve the principal mapping problem and eliminate credential chain discovery.

Moreover, the use of multi-key signatures enables a user to prove authorization for multiple roles in a single signature. Hence external policy rules (5) and (6), which can be reduced to the rule

$$Org_i.r \leftarrow \bigcap_{j=1}^{m} VO.memberOrg.vr_j,$$

can be matched using a single (multi-key) signature. In this case, the user should possess a set of signing keys associated with role identifiers $VO_1.Org_1.vr_1, \ldots, VO_1.Org_1.vr_m$.

3.3 Fine-Grained Identifiers

So far we have looked at how basic role-only identifiers are used to construct the associated signing keys. We now discuss more fine-grained ways of specifying identifiers.

Key Lifetimes It is well known that effective revocation of public-private key pairs is rather difficult to achieve. Within our framework, this is related to user-role revocation. Many practical applications prefer, instead, to use ephemeral keys that have a limited time period for which they are valid. In a grid environment, for example, short-lived keys are used for secure job submissions, to minimize the risk of exposing long-term keys. This is analogous to the relatively short lifetimes given to Kerberos tickets.

Therefore, we envisage that role identifiers will include a lifetime L. A typical identifier would have the form $VO_1.Org_1.vr\|L_1$, the interpretation being that the corresponding signing key would only be valid for time L_1 after its issuance. Note that L_1 can also be set to the validity period of the RBAC session[2] associated with role vr.

User-Role Bindings We remark that the use of signing keys based on role-only identifiers provides user privacy and pseudo-anonymity. However, in some applications, it may be desirable for a resource provider to keep track of the identities of users who accessed its resources for auditing and accountability purposes. This can be achieved by including a local user identifier u in a role identifier, $VO_1.Org_1.vr\|u\|L_1$, for example. The use of user identifiers and lifetimes may be essential for commercial grid applications when billing comes into play.

A role is likely to be shared by more than one user, and hence a signing key, which is based on a role-only identifier, may well be shared by a group of users. The

[2] In an RBAC session, a user activates a number of the roles to which he is assigned, thereby gaining the privileges associated with those roles for that interaction with the system.

inclusion of user identifiers within role identifiers obviates potential issues caused by key sharing. It is worth noting that although user identifiers may be used in role identifiers, principal mappings are still based on roles only.

Generic Role Sets There may also be situations where it is more appropriate for a user presenting all roles to which she is entitled within a single identifier. The user can obtain, from her organization, a signing key associated with all her roles $vr_1,\ldots,vr_m$. Her role identifier now becomes $VO_1.Org_1.(vr_1,\ldots,vr_m)\|u\|L_1$. One advantage of this approach is that the user is relieved of her responsibility in selecting the appropriate signing keys for a particular session. Clearly, on the other hand, the limitation of this method is that it would undermine the principle of least privilege, which may be desirable in some system environments.

3.4 Supporting Multiple Namespaces

It may well be useful to have a number of distinct hierarchical namespaces having different root TAs, with principals having distinct identities in different namespaces. We observe that Lim and Paterson's multi-key signature scheme [14] can be extended naturally to support multiple distinct hierarchical namespaces. The only requirement is that the root TAs of these distinct hierarchies must use the same group generator when computing their respective system parameters. Furthermore, the scheme can take as input private keys which correspond to entities at different levels in a hierarchy.

Consider, for example, an (imaginary) academic institution, the Missouri Institute of Science and Technology (MIST). We may have role identifier $VO_1.Org_1.vr_1$ in a 3-level hierarchical namespace rooted at TA_1 and role identifier $Uni_2.vr_2$ in a 2-level namespace rooted at TA_2, where $Org_1 = Uni_2 = mist$. Informally, the first identifier may be interpreted as: the Missouri Institute of Science and Technology is an accredited member of the virtual organization VO_1 working on data generated by the large hadron collider at CERN, where TA_1 is the EU Grid TA. On the other hand, the second identifier means: the Missouri Institute of Science and Technology is a higher education institution accredited by TA_2, the Accrediting Board for Universities, for example.

Supporting distinct hierarchical namespaces in role signatures is a very desirable feature in the sense that role signatures can now be used to articulate policy rules of the form $Org_i.r \leftarrow VO.memberOrg.vr_j \cap memberUni.vr_k$, where member organizations and universities belong to different hierarchical namespaces.

3.5 Supporting More Complex Namespaces

In the interests of simple exposition, we have assumed so far that the hierarchical namespaces are rather simple, being based on a model in which the level 1 entities are virtual organizations, level 2 entities are member organizations, and level 3 entities are generic roles. This type of structure is characteristic of certain large-scale distributed systems, for example computational grids, but not of open distributed systems in general.

We now discuss how we can build more complex namespaces. The basic ideas are to include the notion of a domain as a generic role and to generalize the binding of users to generic roles in identifiers.

More specifically, identifiers are formed from the concatenation of one or more identifier-role pairs. Hence, the root TA can create level 1 domains. Each level 1 domain is provided with a signing key and material with which to generate signing keys for generic roles, including level 2 domains. In this way, arbitrarily deep hierarchies can be constructed. Identifiers have the form $domain \| D_1 \| domain \| D_2 \| \ldots \| domain \| D_n \| vr \| u$, where vr is a generic role.

Then MIST might act as a level 0 TA and consider faculties to be level 1 entities. Each faculty is associated with a domain and a signing key. Each department within a faculty is treated as a level 2 domain. Each department is autonomous, in that each has a separate access control policy and is able to define child domains if desired. MIST identifies additional generic roles such as registered student and faculty.

Then a student *alice*, belonging to the computer science (CS) department, within the mathematical sciences (MS) faculty would have an identifier

$$domain \| MS \| domain \| CS \| student \| alice$$

and a signing key corresponding to this identifier. *alice* may send a signed request to the physics department and, for example, be assigned the guest role as a result of the department's external ACP, thereby enabling her to run a computer program using certain data collected and stored by the physics department.

There are other possibilities too. We could for example introduce different types of generic roles for level 1 entities. A computational grid, for example, might include partners from academia, industry and government agencies. In such a situation, it might be appropriate to define generic roles AMO, IMO and GMO, representing academic, industrial and governmental member organizations, respectively. We might then have identifiers $AMO \| MIST \| \ldots$, $IMO \| IBM \| \ldots$ and $GMO \| FBI \| \ldots$.

4 Security Architecture

The concept of role signatures can be easily integrated into a security architecture which makes use of hierarchical identity-based cryptography, for example a password-enabled and certificate-free grid security infrastructure (PECF-GSI) proposed by Crampton *et al.* [6]. PECF-GSI allows users to perform single sign-on based only on passwords and does not require a PKI. Nevertheless, it supports essential grid security services, such as mutual authentication and delegation, using public key cryptographic techniques. The fact that users are authenticated using only passwords significantly increases the user-friendliness of the infrastructure and allows users to join or leave a VO in a flexible way. This is mainly because users do not have to go through the hassle of obtaining a public key certificate when joining a VO. Moreover, this approach alleviates the typical private key distribution issue found in standard identity-based cryptosystems.[3]

We note that although identity-based techniques are certificate-free, an authentic set of the TA system parameters (or all sets of parameters for multiple hierarchies) must be made available to system users. One way to achieve this is by bootstrapping these parameters into the system, as with bootstrapping root CA certificates in existing certificate-based approaches. Alternatively, distribution of the parameters is also possible through the use of a certificate obtained from a conventional CA that certifies the parameters.

Using PECF-GSI, a user authenticates to a domain authentication server through a password-based TLS protocol [1]; hence authentication between the user and the server can take place without relying on a PKI. When performing single sign-on, the user establishes a secure TLS channel with the authentication server based on a shared password. The authentication server, which essentially acts as a MO (within a VO), then creates a proxy (short-lived) credential, comprising a role identifier and its corresponding signing key, and transmits it to the user. As explained in Section 3.3, there are several ways in which a role identifier can be specified. An authenticated copy of the TA system parameters are sent to the user, enabling her to execute the relevant cryptographic algorithms. In addition, the user is sent an up-to-date Identity Revocation List (IRL) so that she can be sure that a resource provider to which she submits her job request is still legitimate, respectively. The user is only required to sign-on once and use the fresh proxy credential generated by the authentication server until the credential expires.

Since our approach is applicable to the multiple hierarchical setting, we envisage that no centralized root TA is required in our architecture. Hence our approach is scalable in the sense that each VO or MO can be associated with a "decentralized" TA that it is willing to trust. Moreover, the multiple TAs setting seems to reflect well trust relationships and management in real world systems.

The use of role signatures seems to suit a decentralized access control model, provided that there exist a hierarchical structure which relates principals involved in access control, in such a way that higher-level authorities can delegate access control decisions to lower-level authorities/principals. This is often the case in many real world systems. For example in the finance sector, the head office of each global financial company can act as the root TA issuing credentials to regional main offices, which in turn, issue credentials to local branch offices. Each customer then is allowed multiple credentials, corresponding to different banks.

---

[3] Typically, a user of an identity-based cryptosystem is required to obtain her private keys from a TA through an independent secure channel or any out-of-bound mechanisms.

5 Related Work

The idea of generic roles is not entirely new. Li *et al.*, in describing role-based trust management [12], said:

> When an entity A defines $A.R$ to contain $B.R_1$, it needs to understand what B means by the role name R_1. This is the problem of establishing a common vocabulary.

Their solution to the problem was to introduce the concept of *application domain specification documents* (ADSDs), which serve to establish a common vocabulary. In particular, they can be used to define roles that are common to a number of different organizations. In a sense, role signatures provide a way of implementing ADSDs and role-based trust management in which credential verification is performed in a lightweight fashion.

A number of authors have considered the idea of *policy-based cryptography* [2, 21] in recent years. This can be used to implement access control by encrypting resources. A user is only able to read a resource if she has the appropriate encryption key. This approach is rather limited in the type of interactions that can be controlled between the user and the resource.

Bagga and Molva [2] recently introduced a policy-based signature scheme, derived from an identity-based ring signature scheme of [23], which provides the inspiration for our work. However, the policies are expressed as monotonic logical expressions involving complex conjunctions and disjunctions of conditions. Bagga and Molva cite a motivating example in which Bob has an ACP such that Alice is authorized to access some sensitive resource if she is an IEEE member *and* she is an employee of either university X *or* university Y.

The policy is expressed as $\langle \text{IEEE}, \text{Alice:member}\rangle \wedge [\langle X, \text{Alice:employee}\rangle \vee \langle Y, \text{Alice:employee}\rangle]$. This way of expressing policies does not seem to be practical, since Bob has to specify each policy for each requester who wants to access the resources. Moreover, it assumes that Bob knows something about every user that will make an access request. In short, while the cryptographic techniques they use to enforce such policies are interesting, it seems unlikely that such policies will be useful in practice.

We note in passing that (presumably the intent of) Bob's ACP could be expressed in the following way:

$$Bob.r \longleftarrow IEEE.member \cap Bob.uni.employee$$

where r is a role name mapped to some appropriate permissions. This style of ACP is far more appropriate in an open distributed environment. In this paper, we have shown how role signatures can be used to demonstrate that a user is authorized for a particular generic role within a single contiguous namespace. More importantly, our work examines the fundamental principal mapping problem which underlies the use of policy-based cryptography, rather than designing new cryptographic schemes that support access control and policy enforcement.

Apart from policy-based cryptography, there are also proposals for *attribute-based systems*, for example [11, 17], which are based on Sahai and Waters's attribute-based encryption (ABE) scheme [18]. ABE is closely related to the work of Bagga and Molva [2] and of Smart [21]. In ABE, the recipient's identifier comprises a set of attributes Ψ. A policy enforcer (sender) can specify another set of attributes Ψ', such that the recipient can only decrypt the ciphertext if his identifier Ψ has at least k attributes in common with the set Ψ'. Here k is a parameter set by the system.

As with [2, 21], the proposals of [11, 17] attempt to present constructions of more expressive cryptographic schemes in terms of policy specification and enforcement, without dealing with the underlying principal mapping issue. The central idea of their work is about using a threshold primitive to control access to some data (through encryption), whereby only users who fulfill k-of-n attributes can access the data (through decryption). On the other hand, we study how a hierarchical identity-based signature scheme can be used to provide role signatures that potentially greatly simplify inter-domain principal mappings and credential verification.

Perhaps the work that is most similar in spirit to ours, is that of Tamassia *et al.* on *role-based cascaded delegation* (RBCD) [22]. RBCD combines the advantages of RBTM with those of cascaded delegation [15]. Their proposal uses a hierarchical certificate-based encryption scheme [9] to simplify credential accumulation and verification. The basic idea is to encode the chain of credentials into a single signed delegation credential.

RBCD is only described using an extended example, making it difficult to analyze the approach formally. Each component of a delegation credential has the form (iss, r, p), where iss is the issuer of the credential, p is the subject of the credential who is authorized for role r. The delegation credential in the example has the form

$$\begin{array}{l}(H, H.guest, M.professor)\\(M, M.professor, Bob)\\(Bob, H.guest, L.assistant)\\(L, L.assistant, Alice)\end{array}$$

meaning that

- hospital H says that any member of the professor role at the medical school M is also a member of the role $H.guest$;
- M says that Bob is a member of the professor role;
- Bob says that any member of the lab assistant role at lab L is a member of role $H.guest$;
- L says that $Alice$ is a member of the lab assistant role.

It is suggested by the authors that this implies that H, on receipt of this delegation credential from $Alice$, can verify that she is indeed a member of the $H.guest$ role.

However, H needs to know about the professor role at M, and M is required to know that the professor role is important to H. RBCD also assumes that credentials of the form $(Bob, H.guest, L.assistant)$ are regarded as trustworthy by the hospital.

It also assumes that *Bob* is aware that he can issue credentials of this form, and knows to include the $(M, M.professor, Bob)$ credential in the delegation credential. In short, the problem of principal mapping is not addressed by RBCD.

6 Conclusions

We have proposed the use of role signatures for access control in open distributed systems. Our work is built on three assumptions:

- it is reasonable to define a comparatively small number of generic roles that will be recognized throughout a virtual organization;
- the structure of a virtual organization defines a hierarchical namespace;
- members of the virtual organization are trusted to assign their respective users to generic roles.

We have shown how an hierarchical identity-based signature scheme can be adapted to provide role signatures, where the corresponding verification keys are associated with generic roles.

Key management in our proposal is simple as role signatures can be used to both authenticate users and make access control decisions. Hence, we avoid the use of complex credential or certificate chain discovery mechanisms. Moreover, our approach allows signing with multiple keys. These keys, which are associated with multiple roles, can correspond to nodes at arbitrary positions within the same hierarchy or multiple hierarchies.

To conclude, our work provides nice balance between expressiveness of policy and ease of credential verification as compared to existing role-based access control and trust management frameworks.

Acknowledgements The second author was at Royal Holloway, University of London when he performed this work. He was supported by the UK Engineering and Physical Sciences Research Council (EPSRC) through Grant EP/D051878/1.

We would like to thank the anonymous referees for their helpful remarks, which have led to substantial improvements in the presentation and exposition of our work.

References

1. M. Abdalla, E. Bresson, O. Chevassut, B. Möller, and D. Pointcheval. Provably secure password-based authentication in TLS. In *Proceedings of the 1st ACM Symposium on Information, Computer and Communications Security (ASIACCS 2006)*, pages 35–45. ACM Press, March 2006.
2. W. Bagga and R. Molva. Policy-based cryptography and applications. In *Proceedings of the 9th International Conference on Financial Cryptography and Data Security (FC 2005)*, pages 72–87. Springer-Verlag LNCS 3570, February 2005.
3. M. Blaze, J. Feigenbaum, J. Ioannidis, and A.D. Keromytis. The KeyNote trust-management system version 2. *The Internet Engineering Task Force (IETF)*, RFC 2704, September 1999.

4. D. Boneh, X. Boyen, and E. Goh. Hierarchical identity based encryption with constant size ciphertext. In *Advances in Cryptology – Proceedings of EUROCRYPT 2005*, pages 440–456. Springer-Verlag LNCS 3494, May 2005.
5. D. Clarke, J. Elien, C. Ellison, M. Fredette, A. Morcos, and R. Rivest. Certificate chain discovery in SPKI/SDSI. *Journal of Computer Security*, 9(4):285–322, January 2001.
6. J. Crampton, H.W. Lim, K.G. Paterson, and G. Price. A certificate-free grid security infrastructure supporting password-based user authentication. In *Proceedings of the 6th Annual PKI R&D Workshop 2007*. NIST Interagency Report 7427, September 2007.
7. C. Ellison, B. Frantz, B. Lampson, R. Rivest, B. Thomas, and T. Ylonen. SPKI certificate theory. *The Internet Engineering Task Force (IETF)*, RFC 2693, September 1999.
8. I. Foster, C. Kesselman, and S. Tuecke. The anatomy of the Grid: Enabling scalable virtual organizations. *International Journal of High Performance Computing Applications*, 15(3):200–222, 2001.
9. C. Gentry. Certificate-based encryption and the certificate revocation problem. In *Advances in Cryptology – Proceedings of EUROCRYPT 2003*, pages 272–293. Springer-Verlag LNCS 2656, May 2003.
10. C. Gentry and A. Silverberg. Hierarchical ID-based cryptography. In *Advances in Cryptology – Proceedings of ASIACRYPT 2002*, pages 548–566. Springer-Verlag LNCS 2501, December 2002.
11. V. Goyal, O. Pandey, A. Sahai, and B. Waters. Attribute-based encryption for fine-grained access control of encrypted data. In *Proceedings of the 13th ACM Computer and Communications Security Conference (CCS 2006)*, pages 89–98. ACM Press, October 2006.
12. N. Li, J.C. Mitchell, and W.H. Winsborough. Design of a role-based trust management framework. In *Proceedings of the 2002 IEEE Symposium on Security and Privacy*, pages 114–130. IEEE Computer Society Press, May 2002.
13. N. Li, W.H. Winsborough, and J.C. Mitchell. Distributed credential chain discovery in trust management. *Journal of Computer Security*, 11(1):35–86, February 2003.
14. H.W. Lim and K.G. Paterson. Multi-key hierarchical identity-based signatures. In *Proceedings of the 11th IMA International Conference on Cryptography and Coding (IMA 2007)*, pages 384–402. Springer-Verlag LNCS 4887, December 2007.
15. N. Nagaratnam and D. Lea. Secure delegation for distributed object environments. In *Proceedings of the 4th USENIX Conference on Object-Oriented Technologies and Systems*, pages 101–116, April 1998.
16. K.G. Paterson. Cryptography from pairings. In I.F. Blake, G. Seroussi, and N.P. Smart, editors, *Advances in Elliptic Curve Cryptography*, pages 215–251, Cambridge, 2005. Cambridge University Press, LMS 317.
17. M. Pirretti, P. Traynor, P. McDaniel, and B. Waters. Secure attribute-based systems. In *Proceedings of the 13th ACM Computer and Communications Security Conference (CCS 2006)*, pages 99–112. ACM Press, October 2006.
18. A. Sahai and B. Waters. Fuzzy identity-based encryption. In *Advances in Cryptology – Proceedings of EUROCRYPT 2005*, pages 457–473. Springer-Verlag LNCS 3494, May 2005.
19. R.S. Sandhu, E.J. Coyne, H.L. Feinstein, and C.E. Youman. Role-based access control models. *IEEE Computer*, 29(2):38–47, February 1996.
20. A. Shamir. Identity-based cryptosystems and signature schemes. In *Advances in Cryptology – Proceedings of CRYPTO '84*, pages 47–53. Springer-Verlag LNCS 196, August 1985.
21. N.P. Smart. Access control using pairing based cryptography. In *Proceedings of the RSA Conference: Topics in Cryptology – the Cryptographers' Track (CT-RSA 2003)*, pages 111–121. Springer-Verlag LNCS 2612, April 2003.
22. R. Tamassia, D. Yao, and W.H. Winsborough. Role-based cascaded delegation. In *Proceedings of the 9th ACM Symposium on Access Control Models and Technologies (SACMAT 2004)*, pages 146–155. ACM Press, June 2004.
23. F. Zhang and K. Kim. ID-based blind signature and ring signature from pairings. In *Advances in Cryptology – Proceedings of ASIACRYPT 2002*, pages 533–547. Springer-Verlag LNCS 2501, December 2002.

Policies and Security Aspects For Distributed Scientific Laboratories

Nicoletta Dessí, Maria Grazia Fugini, R. A. Balachandar

Abstract Web Services and the Grid allow distributed research teams to form dynamic, multi-institutional virtual organizations sharing high performance computing resources, large scale data sets and instruments for solving computationally intensive scientific applications, thereby forming Virtual Laboratories. This paper aims at exploring security issues of such distributed scientific laboratories and tries to extend security mechanisms by defining a general approach in which a security policy is used both to provide and regulate access to scientific services. In particular, we consider how security policies specified in XACML and WS-Policy can support the requirements of secure data and resource sharing in a scientific experiment. A framework is given where security policies are stated by the different participants in the experiment, providing a Policy Management system. A prototype implementation of the proposed framework is presented.

1 Introduction

Web Services (WS) and the Grid have revolutionized the capacity to share information and services across organizations that execute scientific experiments in a wide range of disciplines in science and engineering (including biology, astronomy, high-energy physics, and so on) by allowing geographically distributed teams to form dynamic, multi-institutional virtual organizations whose members use shared community tools and private resources to collaborate on solutions to common problems. Since WS have been recognized as the logical architecture for the organization of

Nicoletta Dessí and R. A. Balachandar
Dipartimento di Matematica e Informatica, Universitá degli Studi di Cagliari, Via Ospedale 72, 09124 Cagliari, Italy, e-mail: dessi@unica.it, balsonra@yahoo.co.in

Maria Grazia Fugini
Dipartimento di Elettronica e Informazione, Politecnico di Milano, piazza L. da Vinci 32, 20133 Milano, Italy, e-mail: fugini@elet.polimi.it

Please use the following format when citing this chapter:

Dessí, N., Fugini, M.G. and Balachandar, R.A., 2008, in IFIP International Federation for Information Processing, Volume 278; *Proceedings of the IFIP TC 11 23rd International Information Security Conference*; Sushil Jajodia, Pierangela Samarati, Stelvio Cimato; (Boston: Springer), pp. 221–235.

Grid services, they can enable the formation of *Virtual Laboratories*, which are not simply concerned with file exchange, but also with direct access to computers, software, and other resources, as required by a dynamic collaboration paradigm among organizations [6].

As the community of researchers begins to use Virtual Laboratories, exploiting Grid capabilities [16], the definition of secure collaborative environments for the next generation of the science process will need further potentialities. In order to extend common security mechanisms such as certification, authorization or cryptography. These new functions include, for example, the definition and the enforcement of policies in place for single Virtual Laboratories in accordance with dynamically formed Virtual Organizations (VOs), and the integration of different local policies, in order to make the resources available to the VO members, who deploy their own services in the VO environment. These considerations motivate the approach that we propose in this paper, whose aim is to explore the security of environments supporting the execution of scientific experiments in a Virtual Laboratory. Specifically, the paper elaborates on extending usual control access mechanism by defining a general approach in which security policies are expressed and enforced to regulate *resource sharing* and *service provisioning*. In detail, the paper proposes a reference framework for secure collaboration where security policies can be formulated in order to regulate access to scientific services and to their provisioning. Since each Virtual Laboratory has a set of local security policies, we examine how these polices can be expressed and enforced such that the allocation process of resources to a distributed experiment is made aware of security implications. As a sample application of the proposed approach, some implementation hints are presented for distributed experiments that incorporate security policies. This paper is structured as follows. Section 2 reviews related work. Section 3 addresses requirements to be considered when security policies for experiments are defined. Section 4 presents our reference framework for Virtual Laboratories, with emphasis on security issues. Section 5 details our approach to Policy Management, giving a component architecture and providing implementation aspects. Finally, Section 6 contains the conclusions.

2 Related Work

A Virtual Laboratory for e-Science can be viewed as a cooperative System where WS are dynamically composed in complex processes (experiments) and executed at different organizations. WS security [19] is assuming more and more relevance since WS handle users' private information. WS-Trust [9] describes a framework for managing, assessing and establishing trust relationships for WS secure interoperation. In WS-based systems, security is often enforced through security services [20], for which new specifications have been developed to embed such security services in the typical distributed and WS-based elements, considering also security policies [18]. Examples are the SOAP header [19], the Security Assertion Markup Language (SAML) [12], XML Signature [4] and XML Encryption [14]. WS-Security [3] applies XML security technologies to SOAP messages with XML elements. Based on SOAP e-Services, [8] proposes an access control system, while XACML (XML Access Control Markup Language) [2] allows fine-grained access control policies to be expressed in XML. However, all these mechanisms prove useful in specifying specific aspects of security, but need to be selected first, and integrated later, into a uniform framework addressing all issues regarding e-collaboration.

Policies, as an increasingly popular approach to dynamic adjustability of applications, require an appropriate policy representation and the design and development of a policy management framework. Considering that security policies should be part of WS representations, [19] and [10] specify the Web Services Policy Framework (WS-Policy). Policy-based management is supported by standards organizations, such as the Internet Engineering Task Force (IETF). The IETF framework [13] defines a policy-based management architecture, as the basis for other efforts at designing policy architectures.

Existing technology for the Grid (e.g., see [11]) allows scientists to develop project results and to deploy them for ongoing operational use, but only within a restricted community. However, security is still implemented as a separate subsystem of the Grid, making the allocation decisions oblivious of the security implications. Lack of security [20] may adversely impact future investment in e-Science capabilities. The e-Science Core Programme initiated a Security Taskforce (STF) [http://www.nesc.ac.uk/teams/stf/], developing a Security Policy for e-Science (http://www.nesc.ac.uk/teams/stf/links/), while an authorization model for multi-policies is presented in [17]. An approach combining Grid and WS for e-Science is presented in [5, 1].

Authorizations in distributed workflows executed with their own distinctive access control policies and models has been tackled in [7]; security is handled through alarms and exceptions. In [15] access control for workflows is described explicitly addressing cooperation. However, decentralization of workflow execution is not explicitly addressed nor security policies handling is specifically tackled.

3 Basic Security Aspects for Virtual Laboratories

At least for certain domains, scientific experiments are cooperative processes that operate on, and manipulate, data sources and physical devices, whose tasks can be decomposed and made executable as (granular) services individually. Workflows express appropriate modeling of the experiment as a set of components that need to be mapped to distinct services and support open, scalable, and cooperative environments for scientific experiments [5]. We denote such scientific environments as Virtual Laboratories (VLs) or eLabs.

Each VL node (or *eNode*) is responsible for offering services and for setting the rules under which the service can be accessed by other *eNodes* through service invocation. Usually, the execution of an experiment involves multiple *eNodes* interacting to offer or to ask for services. Services correspond to different functionalities

that encapsulate problem solving and data processing capabilities. Services can be designed to use of VOs resources while the network infrastructure promotes the exploitation of distributed resources in a transparent manner. This offers good opportunities for achieving an open, scalable and cooperative environment.
We classify services in:

- *Vertical services*, that include components for a range of scientific domains, including various software applications.
- *Horizontal services*, that provide adaptive user interfaces, plug-and-play collaborative work components, interoperability functions, transaction co-ordination, and security.

Vertical services expose interfaces that convey information about specific application functions. Their interfaces are implemented from within the component embedding them and are assembled in a workflow that globally expresses the *experiment model*. Horizontal services allow for easier, more dynamic and automated *eNode* integration and for more precise run-time integration of remote services. They are designed to facilitate collaboration.
A VO member plans a complex scientific experiment by repeatedly choosing a sequence of services and including these services in a workflow. He can wait for the fulfilment of a specific workflow and/or choose the next service to invoke on the basis of the returned information. The workflow execution may require the collaboration of various services spread over different VLs whose owners must be confident that users accessing their software or data respect fine-grained access restrictions controlling the varying levels of access to the resource that a user may be granted for. For example, a service may require commodity processors or may have a limited choice of input data (possibly requiring a specific file-format or database access). Similarly, a scientist executing a service on a remote *eNode* must trust the administrator of the *eNode* to deliver a timely and accurate result (and possibly proprietary data sent to the site).
This requires the extension of security aspects related to resource sharing to those related to *service sharing*.
However, security is still currently unsupported in an integrated way by any of the available WS technologies, nor a standard method to enforce Grid security is defined. Moreover, security policy requirements have to be considered. The approach of this paper regards the definition of the basic aspects to be tackled when extending WS and Grid security infrastructures to VLs environments.

4 A Reference Framework for Virtual Laboratories

Based on what illustrated so far, we now introduce some basic modeling elements for the context of VLs security, by defining as an actor each relevant *subject* capable of executing experiments supported by *networked resources*, which we consider as *objects*. In detail:

- *Subjects* execute activities and request access to information, services, and tools. Among subjects we mention the remote user of a WS/Grid enabled application, which would generally be composed of a large, distributed and dynamic population of resources. Subjects may also include organizations, servers and applications acting on behalf of users. In this paper, we consider only *trusted* groups which are not requested to exchange security tokens or credentials during a scientific experiment, since they know and trust each other, and received authentication and authorization to access resources when first joining the VL.
- *Objects* are the targets of laboratory activities. Services are considered as objects. Methods are also regarded as objects, which can be grouped together to form experiments. Fine-grained access control would thus be required over input and output parameters, methods, WS and groupings among WS (to form a process) and among WS and other applications (e.g., legacy software or device control software). Other objects are the server hosting the WS, an IP address, or the URI of a WS. Internal data, kept in a database and other objects accessed by the WS, should also be considered as part of the list of objects to be managed.
- *Actions* that can be performed are various, depending on the type of subject issuing a request. Remote users or applications would generally be allowed to execute a WS method, or access a server hosting a number of WS objects or an application. Rights corresponding to actions such as place_experiment, or view_results, update_data could be granted.

The identification of subjects and objects in a scientific environment defines a framework for secure collaboration based on the idea of integrating components that control the workflow execution through a set of specific security components. Such framework, depicted in Fig. 1 comprises components (diamonds), their specific activities (ovals) and specific security aspects (double-border boxes).

The framework elements are as follows:

Process Manager - Each process manager supervises the execution of the workflow modeling the scientific experiment. It is responsible for the transformation of the abstract workflow into a concrete plan whose components are the executions of specific tasks/tools and/or actual accesses to data repositories. This planning process can be performed in cooperation with a service broker, acting as a mediator, in that it supplies, at run time, the description and location of useful resources and services.

Task Manager - This is in charge of executing a particular set of activities which are instances of the workflow plan. It is also responsible for collaborating with others components for managing the service execution. In fact, execution involves contacting data sources and components and requesting the appropriate execution steps.

Service Manager - This supervises the successful completion of each task request. In case of failure, the service manager takes appropriate repair actions. Repair may involve either restarting the task execution or re-entering the configuration component in order to explore alternative ways of instantiating the task execution to avoid service failures, e.g., due to a security attack or service misuse. In that case, the service flow can be rerouted to other services able to provide substitute functionalities, thus allowing redo or retry operations on tasks that were abnormally ended before

rerouting. Moreover, this component waits until completion of the task request, and notifies to the task manager the end of the activity.
Policy Manager - This component supports and updates the resource provision policy that regulates the flow of information through the applications and the network, and across organizational boundaries, to meet the security requirements established by members who are in charge of deploying their own services under their own policies that assert privileges and /or constraints on resource and services utilization.

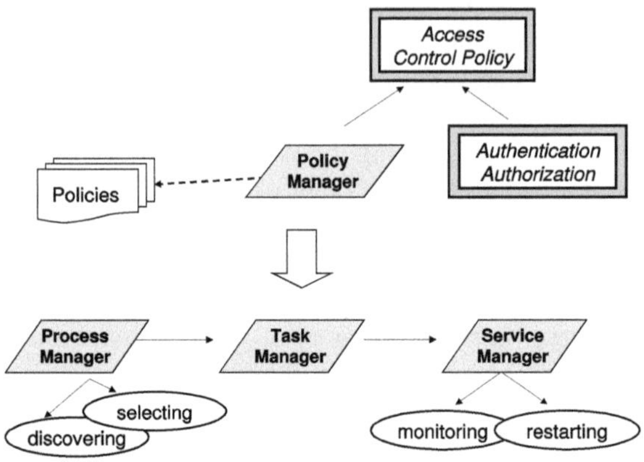

Fig. 1 Security Aspects and Related Components of a Virtual Laboratory

Two major concerns in this framework are: *structural and dynamic* concerns, and *security* concerns. i) *Structural and dynamic concerns* deal with the execution of a scientific experiment in a VL and incorporate controls on vertical services. ii) *Security concerns* refer to horizontal services supporting privileges and constraints on the of VL resources, and may differ from user to user for each individual service. The sequel of the paper presents how these policies can be implemented and how fine-grained constraints can be defined in the VL to gain restricted different access levels to services according to a policy that is fully decided by software owners themselves.

5 Policy Management

Policy management in VLs, as the ability to support an access control policy in accordance with the resource access control goals, should support dynamically changing decentralized policies, policy administration and integrated policy enforcement. A typical policy management system would include two components, namely the *Policy Enforcement Point* (PEP), and the *Policy Decision Point* (PDP), as shown in

Fig. 2. The *PEP* is the logical entity, or location within a server, responsible for enforcing policies with respect to authentication of subscribers, authorization to access and services, accounting and mobility, and other requirements. The *PEP* is used to ensure that the policy is respected before the user is granted access the WS resource. The *PDP* is a location where an access decision is formed, as a result of evaluating the user's policy attributes, the requested operation, and the requested resource, in the light of applicable policies. The policy attributes may relate to authorization and authentication. They may also refer to the attributes related to Quality of Service (QoS), or to service implementation details, such as transport protocol used, and security algorithms implemented. The *PEP* and the *PDP* components may be either distributed or resident on the same server. In our VL, access control works as follows. A user who wants to perform an experiment submits a request to the appropriate resource(s) involved in the experiments through a set of invocations to WS providers. The Policy Manager (see Fig. 2) located in each of the requested resources, implements the *PEP* and the *PDP* to take the access decision about the user access request. The *PEP* wraps up an access request based on the user's security attributes or credentials, on the requested resource, and on the action the user wants to perform on the resource. It then forwards this request to the *PDP*, which checks the request against the resource policy and determines whether the access can be granted.

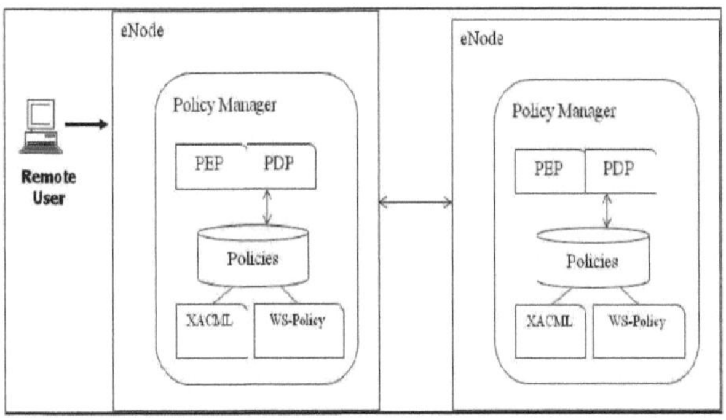

Fig. 2 Policy Management System

There is no standard way of implementing the *PDP* and *PEP* components; they shall either be located in a single machine or be distributed in the different machines depending on the convenience of the Grid Administrator and of the resource provider.

The *Policy Manager* (see Fig. 2) has the ability to recognize rules from the WS requestor and provider of relevant sources, and is able to correctly combine applicable access rules to return a proper, enforceable access decision.

Generally, policies are defined for access to a single resource; hence, the *PEP* and the *PDP* can be contained in a single eNode or be distributed. VL resources may be part of more than one application and therefore there should be a defined *access control service*. Further, these resources can be used contemporaneously by different applications with different associated policies; hence they will be processed by the applicable Policy Managers. In that case, the applications have their own *PEP* and *PDP*, which control user access to the applications. Further, the *Policy Manager* must be able to recognize the policy attributes related to access control, as well as, the information related to QoS. In the following subsection, we describe the implementation methodology employed for the *Policy Manager* and the standard specification used to express the access policy requirements for a resource.

The described access control mechanisms of the Policy Manager can be implemented using XACML, which includes both a policy language and an access control decision request/response language (both encoded in XML). The policy language is used to describe general access control requirements, and has standard extension points for defining new functions, data types, combining logic, etc. The request/response language allows queries on whether a given action should be allowed, and the interpretation of the result. The response always includes an answer about whether the request should be allowed using one of four values: Permit, Deny, Indeterminate (in case of error or required values missing, that so a decision cannot be made) or Not Applicable (the request can't be answered by this service). A Policy represents a single access control policy, expressed through a set of Rules. Each XACML policy document contains exactly one Policy or a PolicySet, that contains other policies or a reference to policy locations. For example, consider a scenario where a user wants to access and read a web page available in a resource. The XACML representation of this request in the PEP is as follows:

```
< Request >
  < Subject >
    < Attribute AttributeId = "urn : oasis : names : tc : xacml : 1.0 : subject : subject – id"
        DataType = "urn : oasis : names : tc : xacml : 1.0 : data – type : rfc822Name" >
    < AttributeValue > www.unica.it < /AttributeValue >
    < /Attribute >
    < /Subject >
  < Resource >
    < AttributeAttributeId = "urn : oasis : names : tc : xacml : 1.0 : resource : resource – id"
        DataType = "http : //www.w3.org/2001/XMLSchema#anyURI" >
    < AttributeValue > http : //webmail.dsf.unica.it/userGuide_gLite.html < /AttributeValue >
    < /Attribute >
    < /Resource >
  < Action >
    < AttributeAttributeId = "urn : oasis : names : tc : xacml : 1.0 : action : action – id"
        DataType = "http : //www.w3.org/2001/XMLSchema#string" >
    < AttributeValue > read < /AttributeValue >
    < /Attribute >
```

```
  < /Action >
< /Request >
```

The *PEP* submits this request form to the *PDP* component which checks this request against the policy of the resource hosting the intended web page. For example, the following policy states that the "developers" group is allowed to read the resource (i.e., the Web Page):

```
< RuleRuleId = "ReadRule"Effect = "Permit" >
  < Target >
    < Subjects >
    < AnySubject/ >
  < /Subjects >
  < Resources >
    < AnyResource/ >
  < /Resources >
< Actions >
< Action >
< ActionMatchMatchId = "urn : oasis : names : tc : xacml : 1.0 : function : string − equal" >
< AttributeValue
DataType = "http : //www.w3.org/2001/XMLSchema#string" > read < /AttributeValue >
< ActionAttributeDesignatorDataType = "http : //www.w3.org/2001/XMLSchema#string"
AttributeId = "urn : oasis : names : tc : xacml : 1.0 : action : action − id"/ >
< /ActionMatch >
< /Action >
< /Actions >
< /Target >
< ConditionFunctionId = "urn : oasis : names : tc : xacml : 1.0 : function : string − equal" >
< ApplyFunctionId = "urn : oasis : names : tc : xacml : 1.0 : function : string − one − and − only" >
< SubjectAttributeDesignatorDataType = "http : //www.w3.org/2001/XMLSchema#string"
AttributeId = "group"/ >
< /Apply >
< AttributeValue
DataType = "http : //www.w3.org/2001/XMLSchema#string" > developers < /AttributeValue >
< /Condition >
< /Rule >
```

The *PDP* checks this policy against the request and determines whether the read request can be allowed for the web page. It then forms a XACML response and forwards it to the *PEP* which eventually allows the user to read the page. The implementation of XACML provides a programming interface to read, evaluate and validate XACML policies. It can also be used to develop the Policy Manager containing the *PEP* and the *PDP*, and performs most of the functionalities of the Policy Manager. We can create a *PEP* which interacts with a *PDP* by creating requests and interpreting the related responses. A PEP typically interacts in an application-specific manner and there is currently no standard way to send XACML requests to an online PDP. Hence, we need to include code for both *PEP* and *PDP* in the same application. For instance, the following code snippet will create an XACML request and pass the same to the *PDP*.

```
RequestCtxrequest = newRequestCtx(subjects, resourceAttrs, actionAttrs,
environmentAttrs);
ResponseCtxresponse = pdp.evaluate(request);
```

The XACML based Policy Manager can recognize policy attributes related to authentication and authorization. Hence, they can be used only for implementing access control mechanisms. However, such authorization policies do not express the capabilities, requirements, and general characteristics of entities (i.e., users and resources) in an XML WS-based system and there are some more attributes, different from the access control attributes, that need to be examined before accessing a WS.
For instance, one may need to negotiate QoS characteristics of the service, or privacy policies and also the kind of security mechanism used in the WS. Unfortunately, XACML does not provide the grammar and syntax required to express these policies. For this aspects, we use WS-policy specifications which provide a flexible and extensible grammar for expressing various aspects of policy attributes, such as the used authentication scheme, the selected transport protocol, the algorithm suite, and so on. For example, the following specification represents the policy for the algorithm suite required for cryptographic operations with symmetric or asymmetric key based security tokens (it is also possible to include timestamps to the policy specifications to prevent any misuse of the policies).

```
< wsp : Policy
xmlns : sp = "http : //schemas.xmlsoap.org/ws/2005/07/securitypolicy"
xmlns : wsp = "http : //schemas.xmlsoap.org/ws/2004/09/policy" >
< wsp : ExactlyOne >
    < sp : Basic256Rsa15/ >
    < sp : TripleDesRsa15/ >
< /wsp : ExactlyOne >< wsp : All >
    < sp : IncludeTimestamp/ >
< /wsp : All >
< /wsp : Policy >
```

The Apache implementation of WS-Policy provides versatile APIs for programmatic access to WS-Policies. Under this approach, we can implement a policy matching mechanism to negotiate security attributes, and other QoS attributes, before actual access to the WS. Moreover, WS-policy APIs are a flexible tool to read, compare and verify the attributes present in WS-Policies. For instance, the following code snippet shall be used for creating a Policy Reader object to access a WS-Policy (here Policy_A) and to compare this object with another policy (Policy_B):

$$PolicyReaderreader =$$
$$PolicyFactory.getPolicyReader(PolicyFactory.DOM\_POLICY\_READER);$$
$$PolicyReaderreader =$$
$$PolicyFactory.getPolicyReader(PolicyFactory.DOM\_POLICY\_READER);$$
$$FileInputStreamPolicy\_A = newFileInputStream("ResA.xml");$$
$$PolicypolicyA = reader.readPolicy(Policy\_A);$$
$$FileInputStreamPolicy\_B = newFileInputStream("ResB.xml");$$
$$PolicypolicyB = reader.readPolicy(Policy\_B);$$
$$Booleanresult = PolicyComparator2.compare(Policy\_A, Policy\_B)$$

Through the combination of XACML and WS-Policy specifications, we can implement a full fledged Policy Management system for WS to manage authorization policies on resources as well as policies related to security and other QoS aspects. However, this Policy Management system cannot be used as such in Grid environments, considering the very nature of jobs and resources in the Grid. In fact, in the Grid, there are computationally intensive resources, such as clusters, that can either host an experiment as a service, or allow jobs to be executed in it. Hence, the policy requirements in this environment will be different from those of WS environments. For example, suppose that a resource wants to contribute up to (but not more than) 200MB of its memory for job execution in the Grid. To express such policy, currently existing policy languages do not offer enough grammar and syntax. Hence, we suggest to extend the existing policy language schema to include policies regarding elements typical of Grid Services, such as bandwidth information, memory, CPU cycle, etc. For our prototype implementation, we consider three attributes namely the memory, CPU cycle and the available nodes in the cluster resource and a schema is developed with these attributes. The APIs of the WS-Policy implementation are modified accordingly, to deal with this schema and be able to perform operations such as compare, read, normalize, and so on.

The schema that includes the attributes related to a Grid resource, and its usage in WS-Policy is as follows:

$$< xs : schema$$
$$targetNamespace = "http : //unica.it/gridpolicy.xsd"$$
$$xmlns : tns = "http : //unica.it/gridpolicy.xsd"$$
$$xmlns : xs = "http : //www.w3.org/2001/XMLSchema"$$
$$elementFormDefault = "qualified"$$
$$blockDefault = "\#all" >$$

$$< xs : elementname = "Mem"type = "tns : OperatorContentType"/ >$$
$$< xs : elementname = "ProcessorSpeed"type = "tns : OperatorContentType"/ >$$
$$< xs : elementname = "DiskSpace"type = "tns : OperatorContentType"/ >$$

The following WS-Policy uses this schema to represent the capabilities and policy information of a Grid resource:

$$wsp : Policyxmlns : sp = "http : //schemas.xmlsoap.org/ws/2005/07/securitypolicy"$$
$$xmlns : wsp = "http : //schemas.xmlsoap.org/ws/2004/09/policy"$$
$$xmlns : cs = "http : //schemas.mit.edu/cs" >< wsp : ExactlyOne >< wsp : All >$$
$$< cs : Mem > 1024 < /cs : Mem >$$
$$< cs : ProcessorSpeed > 2GHz < /cs : ProcessorSpeed >$$
$$< /wsp : All >$$
$$< wsp : All >< sp : Basic256Rsa15/ >< sp : TripleDesRsa15/ >< /wsp : ExactlyOne < wsp : All >$$
$$< /wsp : ExactlyOne >$$
$$< /wsp : Policy >$$

Through this policy, the Grid resource wants to advertise that it can allocate no more than 1GB of its free memory to Grid job execution, and that it is able to provide 2GHz of its processor speed. This policy information can be read and compared with other policies using the WS-Policy implementation libraries.

This prototype implementation modifies the WS-Policy specification to deal with a larger number of attributes. To implement these issues in a real time dynamic environment, an extensive survey of Grid resource usage policies and their representation in a WS-policy schema are needed. Our future research will investigate the development of a Policy Management system working for both WS and Grid environments.

6 Implementation Hints

The illustrated framework has been the basis for developing a prototype VL which, in an initial validation stage, has been used to test secure cooperation from the perspective of one scientific server only, for which a Security Server has been implemented, containing security functions deployed as Security WS. The prototype (see Fig. 3) is built on top of Taverna[1], a workflow composer that allows designers to map the initial abstract workflow into a detailed plan. Each Taverna workflow consists of a set of components, called Processors, each with a name, a set of inputs and a set of outputs. The aim of a Processor is to define an inputs-to-outputs transformation. Vertical services can be installed by adding to Taverna new plug-in processors that can operate alone or can be connected with data and workflows through control links. When a workflow is executed and the execution reaches a security Proces-

[1] Taverna is available in the myGrid open source E-science environment http://www.mygrid.org.uk/

sor, an associated invocation task is called that invokes a specific horizontal service implementing security mechanisms. The Scufl workbench included in MyGrid provides a view for composition and execution of processors. The internal structure of a VL includes four components: a Security Server, a Front-End, a Back-End, a Workflow Editor.

The Security Server exposes various functionalities aimed at data privacy and security both in the pole and during the interaction among poles. It manages User Authentication, Validity check of Security Contracts, Trust Levels, Cryptographic Functions, and Security Levels. The Security Server service communicates with the front-end scientific services by sending them the local Security Levels and the list of remote poles offering a specific resource. User authentications occurs through insertion of a secret code by the user requesting the execution of a protected workflow. The Front-end of the scientific pole is a set of WS that can be invoked by a workflow editor, after negotiation. These WS interact with the Security Server, from which they require information related to the local pole access policy. The Front-end includes services that do not hold their own resource trust level, but rather inherit the clearance level of the user executing the WS. However, the Front-end service receives, at creation time, a threshold security level, reflecting the quality and sensitiveness of the service.

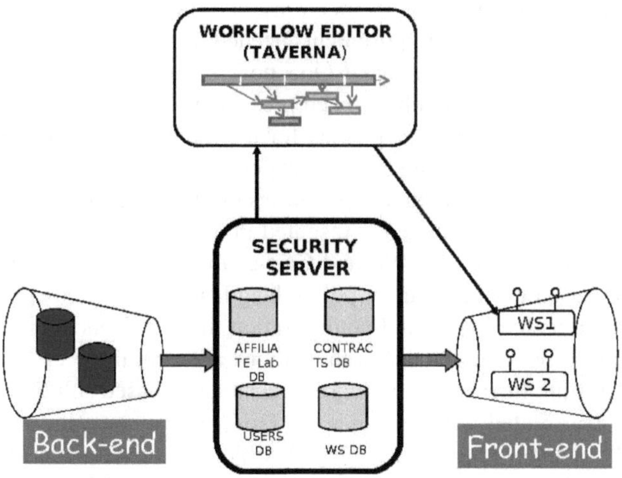

Fig. 3 Security Components Implementation Architecture

The Back-end of a scientific pole is constituted by the local resources of the scientific pole, e.g., calculus procedures or data stored in databases. All the resources in the Back-end are exposed as WS, and can be invoked by a remote Virtual Laboratory. Each resource has its own Resource Service Level assigned by an administrator. The applied policy is "no read up, no write down". The invocations of the Back-end services are protected via SSL. Finally, the scientific workflow is defined using the Taverna workflow editor of MyGrid [2]. Upon proper negotiation of security contracts, a download of the workflow modifier tool and the encryption/decryption module from the provider pole is required. The modifier tool modifies the scientific workflow, by adding crypt and decrypt activities and the input data related to access codes of services. The crypt/decrypt module implements cryptographic functions on exchanged data (we use AES). These editors are designed to be used by scientists teams, generally co-ordinated by a Chief Scientist. However, a workflow is not associated to a whole, given global Security Level, but rather each service of the workflow has an associated Security Level depending on the qualification of the user requiring the service.

7 Concluding Remarks

This paper has highlighted the requirements that should be considered when access control policies of Virtual Laboratories are written. To allow an access control policy to be flexible and dynamic, it can no longer be a high-level specification, but must become a dynamic specification that allows real-time access control administration of WS and the Grid resources. To this aim, we have presented the security requirements of a cooperative environment for executing scientific experiments. Namely, we have illustrated XACML policy specifications, and the use of the WS-Policy to define scientific resource sharing requirements needed to securely activate a collaboration in experiments with negotiating of QoS policy attributes. A security framework and a prototype environment have been presented, with the purpose of providing a uniform view of Grid service policies for a dynamic environment where a set of nodes cooperate to perform a scientific experiment. Currently there exists no standardized access control for virtual applications implemented with WS on the Grid. We plan to extend the requirements presented in this paper and define a formal security model and architecture for WS and Grid enabled scientific applications. The model will be based on the security policy languages used in this paper, independently of specific technologies and configuration models. This should ensure industry-wide adoption by vendors and organizations alike to allow cross-organization business integration. Interoperation requires a standard-based solution. In fact, a Virtual Laboratory, created with WS and the Grid, where scientific relationships may frequently change, requires a highly flexible, but robust security framework, based on approval and universal acceptance of standards. This would allow business partners to avoid interoperability problems among their disparate applications and maintain a security context to allow interoperation.

Acknowledgements This paper has been partially supported by the Italian TEKNE Project.

---

[2] Taverna, and other e-Science management tools, are freely available on the Internet, but to ensure encryption, decryption and server authentication capabilities they require additional features.

References

1. Amigoni F., Fugini M.G., Liberati D., "Design and Execution of Distributed Experiments", Proc. 9th International Conference on Enterprise Information Systems, (ICEIS'07), Madeira, June 2007
2. Anderson A. et. al., XACML 1.0 Specification, http://www.oasis-open.org/committees/tc_home.php?wg_abbrev=xacml, 2003
3. Atkinson B. et al., Web Services Security (WS-Security), 2002, Version 1.0 April 5, 2002, http://www.verisign.com/wss/wss.pdf
4. Bartel M., Boyer J., Fox B., LaMacchia B. and Simon, XML Signatures, http://www.w3.org/TR/2002/REC-xmldsig-core-20020212/E
5. Bosin A., Dess N., Fugini M.G., Liberati D., Pes B., "Supporting Distributed Experiments in Cooperative Environments", in Business Process Management, Springer-Verlag Bussler C., Haller A. (Eds.), vol. 25, 2006, pp. 281 - 292
6. Camarinha-Matos L.M., Silveri I., Afsarmanesh H., and Oliveira A.I., "Towards a Framework for Creation of Dynamic Virtual Organizations", in Collaborative Networks and Their Breeding Environments, Springer, Boston Volume 186/2005, 2005, pp. 69-80
7. Casati F., Castano S., Fugini M.G., "Managing Workflow Authorization Constraints Through Active Database Technology", Journal of Information Systems Frontiers, Special Issue on Workflow Automation and Business Process Integration, 2002
8. Damiani E., De Capitani di Vimercati S., Paraboschi S., Samarati P., "Fine Grained Access Control for SOAP E-Services", in Proc. of the Tenth International World Wide Web Conference, Hong Kong, China, May 1-5, 2001.
9. Della-Libera G. et al., Web Services Trust Language (WS-Trust), available at http://www.ibm.com/developerworks/library/ws-trust/index.html
10. Della-Libera G., et al, "Web Services Security Policy Language (WS-SecurityPolicy," July 2005. (See http://www.oasis-en.org/committees/download.php/16569/)
11. Foster, I. 2006. "Service-Oriented Science: Scaling e-Science Impact", Proceedings of the 2006 IEEE/WIC/ACM International Conference on Web intelligence, 2006
12. Hallam-Baker P., Hodges J., Maler E., McLaren C., Irving R., SAML 1.0 Specification, http://www.oasis-open.org/committees/tc_home.php?wg_abbrev=security, 2003
13. IETF Policy Framework Working Group, A framework for policy-based admission control, available at http://www.ietf.org/rfc/rfc2753.txt, 2003
14. ImamuraT., Dillaway B., Simon E., XML Encryption, http://www.w3.org/TR/xmlenc-core/
15. Jiang H., Lu S., "Access Control for Workflow Environment: The RTFW Model", in Computer Supported Cooperative Work in Design III, LNCS Springer Berlin / Heidelberg, Volume 4402/2007, 2007, pp. 619-626
16. Kim K.H., Buyya R., "Policy-based Resource Allocation in Hierarchical Virtual Organizations for Global Grids", 18th International Symposium on Computer Architecture and High Performance Computing (SBAC-PAD'06), 2006, pp. 36-46
17. Lang B., Foster I., Siebenlist F., Ananthakrishnan R., Freeman T., "A Multipolicy Authorization Framework for Grid Security," Fifth IEEE International Symposium on Network Computing and Applications (NCA'06), 2006, pp. 269-272
18. Mohammad A.,Chen A.,Wang G. W., Changzhou C., Santiago R., "A Multi-Layer Security Enabled Quality of Service (QoS) Management Architecture", in Enterprise Distributed Object Computing Conference, 2007 (EDOC 2007) Oct. 2007, pp.423-423
19. Nadalin A., C. Kaler, P. Hallam-Baker, R. Monzillo (Eds.) Web Services Security, available at http://docs.oasis-open.org/wss/2004/01/oasis-200401-wss-soap-message-security-1.0.pdf
20. Welch V., Siebenlist F., Foster I., Bresnahan J., Czajkowski K., Gawor J., Kesselman C., Meder S., Pearlman L., Tuecke S., "Security for Grid Services", Proc. 12th IEEE International Symposium on High Performance Distributed Computing, 22-24 June 2003, pp. 48- 57

A Fuzzy Model for the Composition of Intrusion Detectors

Inez Raguenet and Carlos Maziero

Abstract The performance of an intrusion detector depends on several factors, like its internal architecture and the algorithms it uses. Thus, distinct detectors can behave distinctly when submitted to the same inputs. The project diversity theory has been successfully used in the fault tolerance domain, and can also bring benefits to the intrusion detection area. The objective of this paper is to propose and evaluate a mathematical model, based on the fuzzy set theory, for the composition of heterogeneous intrusion detectors analyzing the same event flow. This model intends to combine the individual detectors' results into a more accurate global result. Experimental results show the usefulness of this approach.

1 Introduction

In most facilities where it is necessary to detect unauthorized access to sensitive resources and data, usually only one intrusion detection system (IDS) is deployed, for practical reasons. In some cases, there is more than one IDS program working collaboratively; when it happens, IDSs are generally located in distinct strategic places in the system, to detect and to analyze distinct events.

It can be difficult to deploy several IDS programs in the same installation, due to difficulties in tuning the software and consolidating data from different sources. On the other hand, replicating several copies of the same IDS program can lead to biased results, because the chosen IDS may replicate the same errors, warning about events that are not attacks (false positives) or ignoring attacks (false negatives).

The concept of project diversity [1] has proven to be very helpful in the fault tolerance and security areas [13]; it can also be applied to intrusion detection. In

Inez Raguenet
PPGIa PUCPR, Curitiba – Brazil, e-mail: raguenet@ppgia.pucpr.br

Carlos Maziero
PPGIa PUCPR, Curitiba – Brazil, e-mail: maziero@ppgia.pucpr.br

Please use the following format when citing this chapter:

Raguenet, I. and Maziero, C., 2008, in IFIP International Federation for Information Processing, Volume 278; *Proceedings of the IFIP TC 11 23rd International Information Security Conference*; Sushil Jajodia, Pierangela Samarati, Stelvio Cimato; (Boston: Springer), pp. 237–251.

[14] it was shown that the detection capacity of a specific IDS software is related to several factors, which include its internal architecture and algorithms. So, distinct detectors can perform distinctly when submitted to the same event flow. By applying project diversity to intrusion detection, we can obtain a composite IDS, based on individual detectors that can have distinct behaviors, not replicating the same errors, and with complementary results. This can potentially lead to better detection results.

This work introduces a mathematical model based on the Set Theory that leverages the results of individual heterogeneous intrusion detection programs, allowing us to build a composite intrusion detection system (CIDS) based on project diversity. This model is capable of mapping and evaluating the results of each individual IDS, and consolidating them in a final result which is more accurate and reliable than the individual results.

This article is divided in 6 sections: Section 2 introduces the CIDS concept; Section 3 presents some basic definitions and develops simple models, based on the traditional Set Theory; in Sect. 4 the model is extended through the use of the Fuzzy Set Theory and the *alarm relevance* concept is introduced; Section 5 shows some experiments that validate the proposition; Section 6 presents some possible extensions to the model; Section 7 discusses some related work; finally, Sect. 8 concludes the paper and discusses possibilities for future research.

2 Composition of Intrusion Detection Systems

Traditionally, the use of an IDS composition aims to cover a large distributed system whose size surpasses the capacity of any individual detectors. This approach, called *Distributed IDS*, consists of deploying detectors in distinct regions of the system, whose responsibility is to capture and analyze events in that part of the system. As the number of alarms each detector can generate may be huge, several techniques for managing and using such data were introduced, like standard alarm representations [3], centralized configuration [10], and alarm data correlation [4, 5, 6].

Another possibility of IDS composition is demonstrated by [2], who introduces the *Collaborative Intrusion Detection System* concept. It aggregates three different levels of detectors (network, kernel and application) and a level of components that help consolidating individual results. The aggregation of complementary detectors is also discussed in [7] and [9].

Recent studies have shown that distinct detectors can have distinct detection capabilities, which are sometimes complementary. For instance, [14] shows that anomaly-based detection algorithms are bound to "blind spots", and proposes to combine IDS programs based on algorithm diversity. The precision of IDS results is also discussed in [15], involving, among other things, the detection capacity, the probability of raising false alarms versus the probability of detecting a real attack, the strength against attacks to the IDS host itself, the scalability, and the capacity of detecting new attacks.

In the following sections, a mathematical model that combines the results of N distinct IDS programs treating the same event flow is proposed. It is important to stress that each detector is considered as a black box, so its internal architecture and internal algorithms are considered irrelevant for the composition. In this generic model, the input data can be packets from a network, system calls in an operating system, log files, and so on. A knowledge base stores rules that define known attacks (for a signature-based IDS) or the parameters that define a normal behavior (for abnormal behavior-based detectors). The detector applies the rules from the knowledge base in the input data and raises alarms when necessary.

3 A simple composition model

The mathematical approach used in this work will be based on the traditional set theory at first. Our intention is to point out each subset of entities occurring when an IDS is at work. A similar model was proposed by [11], but this one was restricted to a single IDS; our model considers N detectors.

3.1 Some definitions

Before introducing the model, some concepts should be defined, like events and attacks:

- *Event* (e_k): an action that occurs inside a host, between two hosts, or between a host and an user, which can be captured by an intrusion detector (such as packets in a network, system calls, and log files entries).
- *Attack* (a_k) : any event aiming at exploiting a vulnerability in a given system.
- *Normal event* (n_k): any event that is not an attack.
- *Intrusion detector* (d_i): a black-box capable of classifying input events as normal events or attacks[1].
- *Composite IDS* (*CIDS*): a group of N intrusion detectors $d_1, d_2, \ldots, d_N$ analyzing the same input event flow.

As our model is based on the set theory, some sets will also be defined, and shown in Fig. 1:

- *Universe set* ($\mathbb{U}$): comprises all possible events in any system, i.e. any access or operation in a computer-based system.
- *Normal events* ($\mathbb{N}$): comprises all events expected by a system, to which it is prepared to respond (i.e. they are in the system specification).

[1] We only consider stateless intrusion detection, in which individual input events are classified either as attacks or normal events. Stateful intrusion detection, in which specific sequences of input events can constitute an attack, is not considered here.

- *Events targeted to the system* ($\mathbb{T}$): comprises all events targeted to a system, including normal events and attacks. We assume that $\mathbb{N} \cap \mathbb{T} \neq \emptyset$, as this does not change the results and leads to a richer analysis.
- *Attacks* ($\mathbb{A}_i$): comprises all events classified by an intrusion detector d_i as attacks.

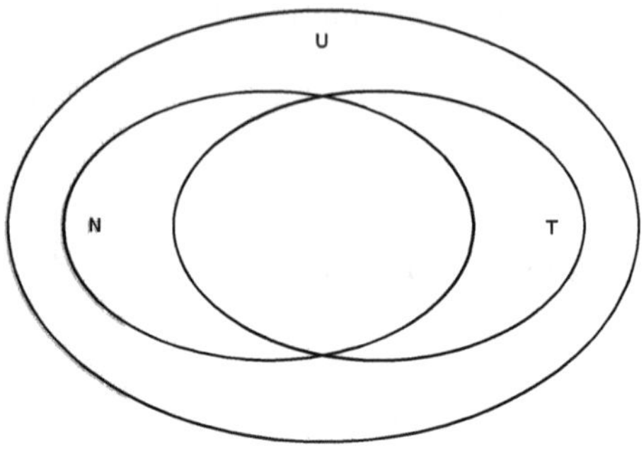

Fig. 1 The $\mathbb{U}$, $\mathbb{N}$, and $\mathbb{T}$ sets.

3.2 Modeling a single IDS

The first model considers a system with only a single detector d_1, which can detect the attacks defined in the $\mathbb{A}_1 \subset \mathbb{T}$ event set. As d_1 is not perfect, some events it classifies as attacks may be normal events (i.e. false positive detections) and some attacks may be misclassified as normal events (i.e. false negative detections). This behavior is represented in the Venn diagram of Fig. 2.

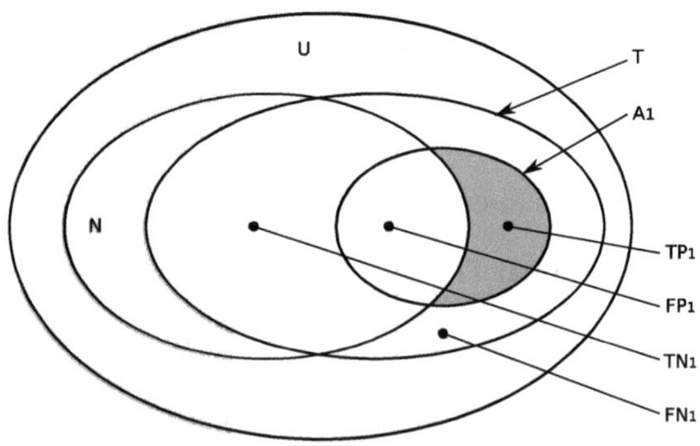

Fig. 2 Venn diagram for a single detector.

On the diagram shown in Fig. 2 it is possible to identify four subsets of interest:

- True positive alerts: $TP_1 = \mathbb{A}_1 - \mathbb{N}$ contains all attacks correctly detected by d_1 ; this area, in gray in Fig. 2, corresponds to the correct behavior expected from d_1 ;

- False positives alerts: $FP_1 = \mathbb{A}_1 \cap \mathbb{N}$ contains all normal events erroneously classified as attacks by d_1 ;
- True negatives: $TN_1 = (\mathbb{N} \cap \mathbb{T}) - \mathbb{A}_1$ contains all normal events targeted to the system that were correctly identified by d_1 .
- False negatives: $FN_1 = \mathbb{T} - (\mathbb{A}_1 \cup \mathbb{N})$ contains all attacks targeted to the system that were not recognized by d_1 ;

An ideal intrusion detector d_i should present $FP_i = FN_i = \emptyset$ (in other words, no classification errors). However, real detectors can fail, giving false positive or negative results.

3.3 Modeling a composite IDS

A model considering two detectors is presented in Fig. 3, in which the set of events perceived by each detector d_i is represented as $\mathbb{A}_i$.

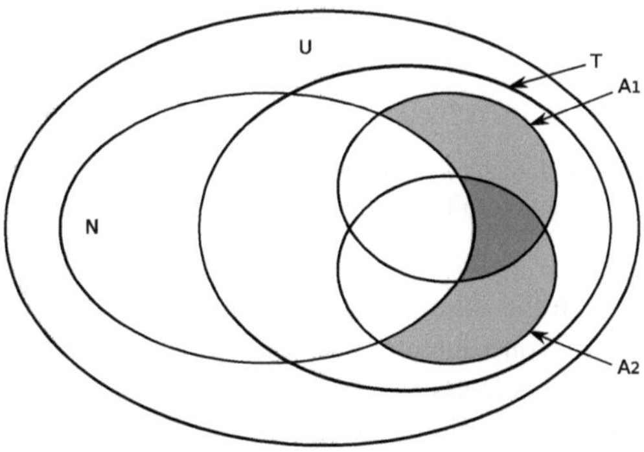

Fig. 3 Venn diagram for two detectors.

All $\mathbb{A}_i$ sets, generated by each d_i detector, can be combined together to generate a compound result $\mathbb{A}_c$, in two basic approaches:

a) by considering the attacks detected by both detectors: $\mathbb{A}_c = \mathbb{A}_1 \cap \mathbb{A}_2$
b) by considering the attacks detected by any detector: $\mathbb{A}_c = \mathbb{A}_1 \cup \mathbb{A}_2$

Their generalization for N detectors are, respectively:

$$\mathbb{A}_c = \bigcap_{i=1}^{N} \mathbb{A}_i \quad \text{or} \quad \mathbb{A}_c = \bigcup_{i=1}^{N} \mathbb{A}_i \tag{1}$$

The subsets of interest for the compound IDS are defined as:

$$TP_c = \mathbb{A}_c - \mathbb{N} \tag{2}$$

$$FP_c = \mathbb{A}_c \cap \mathbb{N} \tag{3}$$

$$TN_c = (\mathbb{N} \cap \mathbb{T}) - \mathbb{A}_c \tag{4}$$
$$FN_c = \mathbb{T} - (\mathbb{A}_c \cup \mathbb{N}) \tag{5}$$

The approach a is restrictive, because only attacks detected by all detectors will be considered as attacks (i.e. an event e is considered as an attack *iff* $\forall d_i\ e \in \mathbb{A}_i$). This leads to a smaller $\mathbb{A}_c$ set, and consequently to a smaller FP_c set. However, attacks not recognized by all detectors may be ignored in the final result, leading to false negative errors (i.e. a bigger FN_c set). So, it lowers false positive rates, but rises false negative rates (i.e. discards attacks that could have been detected only by some IDS). Therefore, if only one detector of the CIDS detects a given attack, this attack will not be in $\mathbb{A}_c$, but it does not necessarily mean that this event is unimportant. This approach is depicted in Fig. 4.

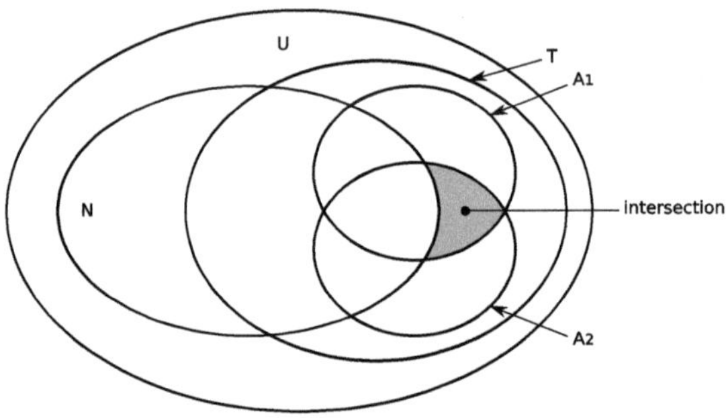

Fig. 4 Intersection of the individual results.

On the other hand, approach b is more comprehensive, as even attacks detected by just one detector are considered as attacks (i.e. an event *e* is an attack *iff* $\exists d_i \mid e \in \mathbb{A}_i$). This leads to a bigger $\mathbb{A}_c$ set, and consequently to a smaller FN_c set. However, there is a higher risk of false positive alerts (i.e. a bigger FP_c set). This approach is depicted in Fig. 5.

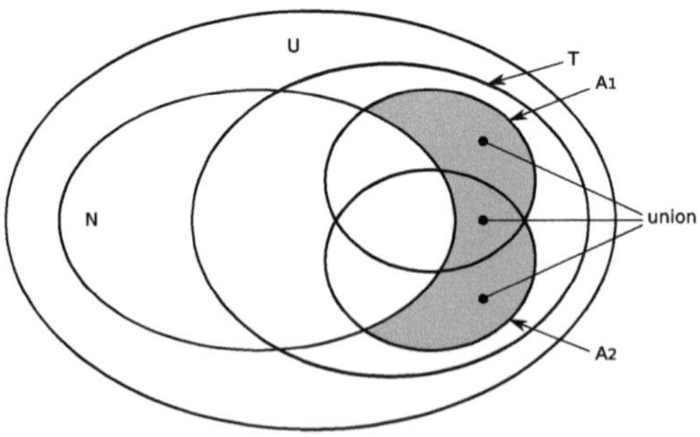

Fig. 5 Union of the individual results.

Both approaches represent extreme situations. In the next section, fuzzy sets are used to propose an intermediate model, mixing characteristics of both solutions.

4 A fuzzy composition model

The first CIDS model presented in Sect. 3 can discard important attacks not observed by all detectors. The second model considers a larger attack set, but increases the uncertainty on the results. Therefore, they should be improved to grasp the best of both worlds: the first model's accuracy and the second model's comprehensiveness. For that, some Fuzzy Set concepts are used to build a more general model. In this new model, the binary result of each detector (whether an event is an attack or not) will have some meaning in the collective result.

To consider all individual detector results, we need to define the *relevance* of a given event e as $r(e)$, meaning how much e is considered as an attack, according to the number of IDSs that detected it and the total number of detectors in the composition. Attacks detected by a larger number of detectors will have a bigger relevance than attacks detected by a smaller number of detectors. The relevance $r(e)$ of an event e can be seen as the *membership function* of a fuzzy set[2]. Thus, the relevance function $r(e)$ should satisfy the following properties:

a) it informs how much the event e can be considered as an attack: if $r(e) = 0$, e is a normal event (not an attack), and if $r(e) = 1$, e is surely an attack;
b) its input parameters are the number of detectors in the CIDS and the number of those that detected the event as an attack;
c) the number of elements in the CIDS should influence the result: it is better to have 100% of detection in a CIDS with 5 detectors than to have a 100% detection in a CIDS with just one detector;
d) it should have a negative exponential behavior, growing faster for the first values and tending to 1 as the number of detections increase; this provides a better sensibility in larger CIDS compositions.

Each intrusion detector d_i provides as output a binary result on each input event: for d_i, e is an attack ($e \in \mathbb{A}_i$) or e is not an attack ($e \notin \mathbb{A}_i$). From this, it is possible to define an *alarm count* $c(e)$, which indicates how many detectors in a CIDS consider the event e as an attack:

$$c(e) = \sum_{i=1}^{N} \left\{ \begin{array}{l} 0, e \notin \mathbb{A}_i \\ 1, e \in \mathbb{A}_i \end{array} \right\} \tag{6}$$

A first candidate for the relevance function would be $r(e) = c(e)/N$. However, although it satisfies the properties a and b, properties c and d are not satisfied. The exponential function $f(x) = 1 - 1/(x+1)$ satisfies properties c and d. The combination of both equations results in:

$$r(e) = \frac{c(e)}{N} \times \left(1 - \left(\frac{1}{c(e)+1}\right)\right) = \frac{c(e)^2}{N(c(e)+1)} \tag{7}$$

[2] A fuzzy set is defined as a pair (S, μ) where S is a set and $\mu : S \rightarrow [0,1] \in \mathbb{R}$ is a real function. For each $x \in S$, $\mu(x)$ represents how much x belongs to S. If $\mu(x) = 1$, x belongs totally to S, whereas if $\mu(x) = 0$, x does not belong to S at all [8].

The expected behavior of this $r(e)$ function can be seen in Table 1, which shows the relevance values for various CIDS configurations and detection levels. It shows that $r(e)$ values consider both the number of detectors in the CIDS and how many detectors classified e as an attack.

Table 1 Event relevance $r(e)$ in a CIDS with up to 6 detectors

Detections	Detectors in the CIDS (N)					
$c(e)$	1	2	3	4	5	6
0	0.000	0.000	0.000	0.000	0.000	0.000
1	0.500	0.250	0.167	0.125	0.100	0.083
2	-	0.667	0.444	0.333	0.267	0.222
3	-	-	0.750	0.563	0.450	0.375
4	-	-	-	0.800	0.640	0.533
5	-	-	-	-	0.833	0.694
6	-	-	-	-	-	0.857

To interpret $r(e)$ values, we propose defining a *relevance threshold* (r_t). This threshold defines the minimum relevance level for an event to be considered as an attack by the CIDS. For a given CIDS, its threshold should be tuned for the best results (as presented in the next section). Obviously, the CIDS behavior depends on the r_t threshold. For instance, considering $r_t = 0.5$, a CIDS with 4 detectors will consider an event as relevant only if all detectors detect it, but a CIDS with 6 detectors will do so if at least 4 detectors detect it. The next section presents the application of this model in a real scenario, and its evaluation.

5 Model evaluation

The proposed model was analyzed using data extracted from some controlled experiments. The CIDS performance was compared with individual detectors' performances using ROC curves [16], a technique frequently used to evaluate data classification algorithms.

The setup used for evaluating the proposed model consisted in a hub-based local area network with four distinct IDSs and an "attack generator". The DARPA Data Sets [12], commonly used for evaluating intrusion detectors, were not used here because they contain the MAC addresses of the target machines; some detectors we used only recognize attacks targeted specifically to the MAC addresses of the hosts they are installed in.

The IDSs used in our experiments are *KFSensor 4.2.0* (from *KeyFocus Ltd.*), *X-Ray* (from *GroundZero Security Research*), *HoneyBOT* (from *Atomic Software Solutions*), and *Snort 2.4.3 build 26* (from *Sourcefire, Inc.*), all updated and patched up to the date of the experiment. In order not to make direct comparisons, they will be referred here randomly as d_1, d_2, d_3, and d_4. The attack generator consisted in a computer running the *Nessus* vulnerability scanner, version 3.0.4 (from *Tenable*

Network Security, Inc). As the number of vulnerabilities scanned by *Nessus* is huge, we selected 25 distinct attacks that we found to be representative of frequent situations. Such attacks are presented in Table 2.

Table 2 Attacks used in the evaluation

Attack	Attack name	Nessus category
a_1	BackOrifice	Backdoors
a_2	BugBear	
a_3	DeepThroat	
a_4	FingerBackdoor	
a_5	IISPossibleCompromise	
a_6	PortalOfDoom	
a_7	Sygate BackDoor	
a_8	MyDoom	
a_9	IISFPDoS	DoS
a_{10}	PFPImageFile	
a_{11}	Winlogo.exe DoS	
a_{12}	Personal Web Sharing	
a_{13}	NetStat	Useless Services
a_{14}	Windows Terminal Service	
a_{15}	Telnet	
a_{16}	WriteSrv	
a_{17}	FrontPage Passwordless	WebServers
a_{18}	IISRemoteCommExecution	
a_{19}	CyDoor detection	Windows
a_{20}	GatorDetection+Gain	
a_{21}	I-Nav ActiveX BufferOverflow	
a_{22}	IE VersionCheck	
a_{23}	FTP Shell DoS Vuln	FTP
a_{24}	RPC Port Mapper	RPC
a_{25}	AliBaBa Port Climbing	Remote File Access

Two independent experiments were performed. The first one aimed at identifying the detection capabilities of each detector against such attacks, i.e. true positives (attacks correctly identified) and false negatives (attacks not detected). The second experiment analyzed the behavior of the detectors in the presence of a valid, normal background network traffic, in order to identify false positive detections. Both experiments are described next.

5.1 Experiment 1

In this experiment, each IDS was submitted to the 25 attacks of Table 2, one at a time. Each attack was tested against each IDS three times. Between two tests, the computer running the IDS was restarted, in order to prevent any cross-effects. During the tests, the network was isolated and there was no background traffic. The detection results are presented in Table 3 (each "•" corresponds to a raised alert).

This experiment allowed us to identify attacks correctly detected by the detectors (true positives) and attacks not detected by them (false negatives).

Table 3 Individual IDS alerts

Attack	d_1	d_2	d_3	d_4	$r(a_i)$	Attack	d_1	d_2	d_3	d_4	$r(a_i)$	Attack	d_1	d_2	d_3	d_4	$r(a_i)$
a_1	•	•	•	-	0.563	a_{11}	•	•	•	-	0.563	a_{21}	•	•	-	-	0.333
a_2	•	•	•	-	0.563	a_{12}	•	•	•	•	0.800	a_{22}	•	•	-	-	0.333
a_3	-	-	-	-	0.000	a_{13}	-	•	•	-	0.333	a_{23}	-	•	-	-	0.125
a_4	-	-	-	-	0.000	a_{14}	•	•	-	-	0.333	a_{24}	•	•	•	-	0.563
a_5	•	•	•	-	0.563	a_{15}	-	•	•	-	0.333	a_{25}	•	•	•	-	0.563
a_6	•	-	-	-	0.125	a_{16}	-	-	•	-	0.125						
a_7	•	•	-	-	0.333	a_{17}	•	-	•	-	0.333						
a_8	•	•	•	-	0.563	a_{18}	•	•	•	-	0.563						
a_9	•	-	•	-	0.333	a_{19}	•	•	-	-	0.333						
a_{10}	•	-	•	-	0.333	a_{20}	•	•	-	•	0.563						

5.2 *Experiment 2*

This experiment was conducted to identify false positive alerts generated by the detectors. For that, the detectors were deployed in a local area network with real traffic (DNS, HTTP, SMTP, POP, IMAP, Windows Terminal Service, NetBios, SNMP, and FTP traffic). The four detectors were deployed and their detections observed during some hours. Each generated alert was manually analyzed to verify its validity. False alerts were classified as false positives (only one instance of each type of event was counted for each detector). Results obtained from this experiment are summarized in Table 4 (each "•" corresponds to a raised alert).

Table 4 Individual false positive alerts

Event	Activity	d_1	d_2	d_3	d_4	$r(n_i)$	Event	Activity	d_1	d_2	d_3	d_4	$r(n_i)$
n_1	TCP 139	•	•	-	-	0.333	n_6	UDP 138	-	•	-	-	0.125
n_2	TCP 3088	•	-	-	-	0.125	n_7	UDP 1027	-	•	-	-	0.125
n_3	TCP 3089	•	-	-	-	0.125	n_8	UDP 2967	-	•	-	-	0.125
n_4	TCP 3090	•	-	-	-	0.125	n_9	UDP 38293	-	-	•	-	0.125
n_5	UDP 137	-	•	-	-	0.125	n_{10}	ICMP	•	•	-	-	0.333

5.3 *ROC analysis*

ROC (*Receiver Operation Characteristic*) analysis appeared in the 1950's, to help understanding radio signals contaminated by noise. It is frequently used in the medical area, to evaluate the efficiency of medical tests [16]. In computer science, it is used to evaluate data classification algorithms. A ROC analysis basically consists in comparing the *sensitivity* of a classifier (a value related to its True Positives count) with its *specificity* (a value related to its False Positives count). According to [16]:

$$Sensitivity = \frac{TP}{TP + FN} \quad (8)$$

$$Specificity = \frac{TN}{TN + FP} \quad (9)$$

$$TP\ Rate = Sensitivity \quad (10)$$

$$FP\ Rate = 1 - Specificity \quad (11)$$

When drawing the curve of specificity × sensitivity for a classifier (its ROC curve), it can be shown that its best operating point, in which it presents the best compromise between *FP* and *TP* rates, is the point nearest to $[0,1]$ in the curve (where $FP = 0$ and $TP = 1$).

An IDS can be considered as a classifier, as it classifies input events as attacks or normal events. So, it is possible to plot ROC curves from the values gathered in experiments 1 and 2, in order to evaluate our model and to identify the event relevance threshold r_t, as defined in Sect. 4. Table 5 presents the event relevance levels calculated for the attacks listed in Table 2 and the false positives listed in Table 4. Values were calculated according to the $r(e)$ definition in Sect. 4, and results are presented in increasing $r(e)$ order.

Table 5 Ordered event relevance

Event	$r(e)$	Event	$r(e)$
$a_3\ a_4$	0.000	$n_9\ n_2\ n_3\ n_4\ n_5\ n_6\ n_7\ n_8$	0.125
$a_6\ a_{16}\ a_{23}$	0.125	$n_1\ n_{10}$	0.333
$a_7\ a_9\ a_{10}\ a_{13}\ a_{14}\ a_{15}\ a_{17}\ a_{19}\ a_{21}\ a_{22}$	0.333		
$a_1\ a_2\ a_5\ a_8\ a_{11}\ a_{18}\ a_{20}\ a_{24}\ a_{25}$	0.563		
a_{12}	0.800		

Table 6 shows the *FP*, *TN*, *FN*, and *TP* counts, and the corresponding calculated *FP*/*TP* rates. Here, false/true positives and negatives are counted according to the CIDS point of view:

- TN_C: normal events n_i for which $r(n_i) < r_t$
- FP_C: normal events n_i for which $r(n_i) \geq r_t$
- TP_C: attacks a_i for which $r(a_i) \geq r_t$
- FN_C: attacks a_i for which $r(a_i) < r_t$

FP and *TP* rates can then be plotted in a ROC curve representing the CIDS behavior (Fig. 6). The points in the ROC curve correspond to rows in Table 6.

The best operating point for our CIDS is D, because it is the point nearest to the [0,1] coordinates. So, we can adopt $r_t = 0.333$ as the detection threshold for

Table 6 FP and TP rates for the CIDS

	$r(e)$	TN_C	FP_C	TP_C	FN_C	FP rate	TP rate
A	1.000	10	0	0	25	0.00	0.00
B	0.800	10	0	1	24	0.00	0.04
C	0.563	10	0	10	15	0.00	0.40
D	0.333	8	2	20	5	0.20	0.80
E	0.125	0	10	23	2	1.00	0.92
F	0.000	0	10	25	0	1.00	1.00

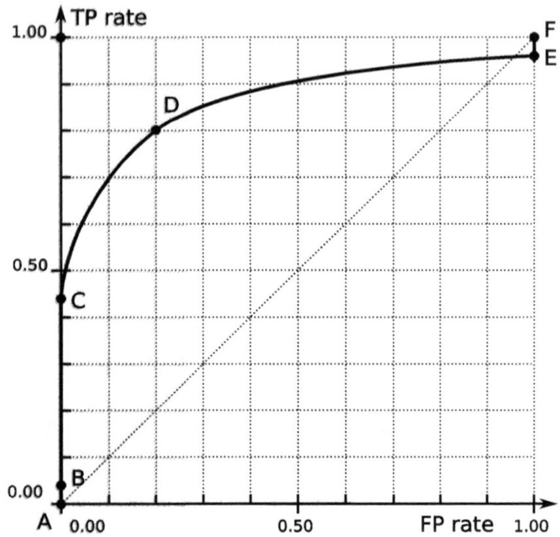

Fig. 6 ROC curve for the composite IDS.

the best detection results, in this case. Table 7 shows a comparison of CIDS results (operating at point D) with the individual detectors' results. Is shows clearly that (a) CIDS presents a smaller amount of false results (considering both false negatives and false positives), and (b) its true positive results are also better than any of the individual detectors.

Table 7 Comparing CIDS with individual detectors

Detector	CIDS	d_1	d_2	d_3	d_4
FN	5	4	5	8	21
FP	2	5	6	1	0
FN+FP	7	9	11	9	21
TP	20	19	18	15	2

To complement this comparison, we plotted the operating points for the individual detectors in the ROC space, using the experiments' data (Fig. 7). It can be seen that the CIDS operating point is closer to the [0,1] ideal point than the individual detectors. It also shows that the best individual detector would be d_3, in this case.

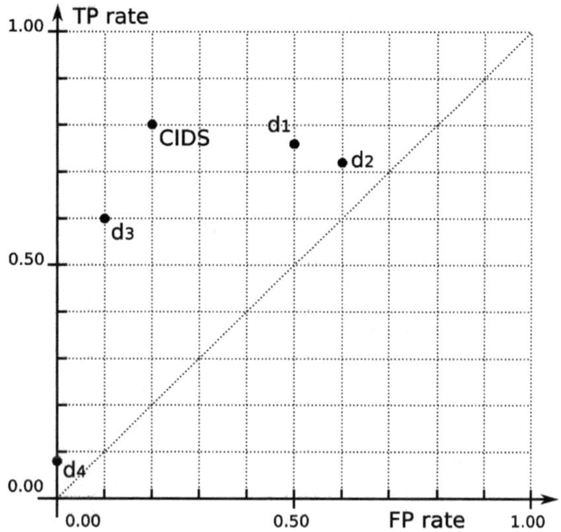

Fig. 7 ROC operating points for all the detectors

6 Model extensions

The experiments presented in Sect. 5 showed that detectors may have distinct detection performances. Consequently, the relevance function $r(e)$ could be adjusted to consider this. It is possible to define an "efficiency" factor $0 \leq \alpha_i \leq 1$ for each detector d_i based on its performance, leading to a new $c(e)$ definition:

$$c(e) = \sum_{i=1}^{N} \left\{ \begin{array}{l} 0, e \notin \mathbb{A}_i \\ \alpha_i, e \in \mathbb{A}_i \end{array} \right\} \tag{12}$$

The efficiency α_i of a given detector can be estimated from its *FP* and *TP* rates on the ROC curve. Usually, the euclidean distance from a detector's operating point $[FP_i, TP_i]$ to the $y = x$ diagonal is a good indicator of its efficiency [16]. In the ROC space, the $y = x$ line represents operating points in which FP and TP rates are equal. In such points, the detector's results are not better than random guesses. Thus, the $y = x$ line is also called the "random guess line".

Another possible extension to our model would be to define a "confidence" $0 \leq \gamma_i^k \leq 1$ of each detector d_i on each event e_k it classifies as an attack. This would be taken into account into $c(e_k)$ as:

$$c(e_k) = \sum_{i=1}^{N} \left\{ \begin{array}{l} 0, e_k \notin \mathbb{A}_i \\ \alpha_i \times \gamma_i^k, e_k \in \mathbb{A}_i \end{array} \right\} \tag{13}$$

However, this extension considers that each detector can inform its confidence on the alarms it produces, which it is not always the case. The manual definition of individual alarm confidences for each detector would not be feasible, either.

7 Related work

We identified some works that used mathematical models to represent and/or analyze intrusion detectors, some of them using fuzzy logic. Paper [11] defines a methodology to build anomaly-based IDSs called BSEADS (*Behavioral Secure Enclave Attack Detection System*). That methodology combines several data sources, like network traffic and user behavior, to identify anomalous behaviors. BSEADS analysis was done using a model similar to that presented in Sect. 3.2 (Fig. 2).

Article [18] presents *Vismath*, a geometric model that visually represents the variations in a computer environment. The model uses graphical structures called *spicules* to create vectorial representations of monitored variables, like processor usage, number of processes, and number of open files. Once the normal behavior of the system is defined, spicules monitoring allows identifying abrupt changes and anomalous behaviors.

Paper [17] is the closest one to our approach. It presents a method to evaluate the performance of an IDS using ROC curves and a cost-based decision-tree analysis. They also propose to build a composite IDS by the combinations of two individual detectors, but there are several differences between that work and ours. First, the behavior of their composite IDS is determined only by superposing the ROC curves obtained from individual detectors, instead of defining a generic composition model that would have its own ROC curve. Also, in the decision-tree approach they propose, the results obtained by a CIDS can be equivalent to those obtained by an individual IDS (if only the corresponding IDS in the CIDS detects the attack). This behavior is close to those for the simpler models presented here, in Sect. 3.3.

8 Conclusion

This article proposes building a Composite IDS (CIDS) from individual heterogeneous detectors, according to the project diversity principles. A first model allows us to treat the results of a CIDS in two possible ways: in the first, more restrictive, only attacks detected by all IDSs are considered; the second, more comprehensive, considers all attacks detected by any of the detectors. In order to use the best of both worlds, we propose another model, based on the fuzzy sets theory.

The proposed model was evaluated using two experiments, in which four individual detectors were tested against an "attack generator" (a vulnerability scanner). The results showed that the CIDS results are better than individual detector results, giving less false results and more true results for the attacks under consideration.

During our experiments, two instances of the same IDS, running in exactly the same operating system, but in distinct hardware, behaved distinctly and produced distinct results. This issue was also observed between instances of the same IDS running in the same hardware, but on top of distinct operating systems. This leads us to conclude that project diversity is not only a matter of IDS implementation, but also of running environment diversity (hardware and operating systems).

Possible future research includes a deeper analysis of the composition model, using the DARPA Intrusion Detection Evaluation Data Sets [12]. We intend also to evaluate the effectiveness of the extensions proposed in Sect. 6.

References

1. A. Avizienis and J. P. Kelly. Fault tolerance by design diversity: Concepts and experiments. *IEEE Computer*, pages 67–80, August 1984.
2. S. Bachi, Y. Mei, B. Boo B, and Y Wu. Collaborative intrusion detection system (CIDS): A framework for accurate and efficient IDS. In *Annual Computer Security Applications Conference*, 2003.
3. N. Carey, A. Clark, and G. Mohay. IDS interoperability and correlation using IDMEF and commodity systems. In *Intl Conference on Information and Communications Security*, 2002.
4. O. Dain and R. Cunningham. Fusing heterogeneous alert streams into scenarios. In *ACM Conference on Computer and Communications Security*, 2001.
5. F. Cuppens F. and Miège. Alert correlation in a cooperative intrusion detection framework. In *IEEE Symposium on Security and Privacy*, 2002.
6. K. Julisch. Clustering intrusion detection alarms to support root cause analysis. *ACM Transactions on Information and System Security*, November 2003.
7. C. Kahn, P. Porras, S. Staniford-Chen, and B. Tung. A common intrusion detection framework, 1998.
8. G. Klir and B. Yuan. *Fuzzy Sets and Fuzzy Logic: Theory and Applications*. Prentice Hall PTR, 1995.
9. K. Ko, T. Fraser, L. Badger, and D. Kilpatrick. Detecting and countering system intrusions using software wrappers. In *USENIX Security Symposium*, 2000.
10. C. Kreibich and R. Sommer. Policy-controlled event management for distributed intrusion detection. In *Intl Workshop on Distributed Event-Based Systems*, June 2005.
11. T. Leckie and A. Yasinsac. Metadata for anomaly-based security protocol attack deduction. *IEEE Transactions on Knowledge and Data Engineering*, 16(9):1157–1168, September 2004.
12. R. Lippmann, J. Haines, D. Fried, J. Korba, and K. Das. The 1999 DARPA off-line intrusion detection evaluation. *Computer Networks*, 34(4):579–595, 2000.
13. B. Littlewood and Stringini. Redundancy and diversity in security. In *European Symposium on Research in Computer Security*, France, 2004.
14. R. Maxion and K. Tan. The effects of algorithmic diversity on anomaly detector performance. In *IEEE/IFIP Intl Conference on Dependable Systems and Networks*, July 2005.
15. P. Mell, V. Hu, R. Lippmann, J. Haines, and M. Zissman. An overview of issues in testing intrusion detection systems. Technical Report Interagency Report 7007, National Institute of Standards and Technologies, June 2003.
16. C. E. Metz. Basic principles of ROC analysis. *Seminars in Nuclear Medicine*, 8(4):283–298, 1978.
17. J. Ulvila and J. Gaffney Jr. Evaluation of intrusion detection systems. *NIST Journal of Research*, 108(6), November 2003.
18. G. Vert, D. Frincke, and J. McConnell. A visual mathematical model for intrusion detection. In *21st NIST-NCSC National Information Systems Security Conference*, 1998.

Possible future research includes a deeper analysis of the composition model using the DARPA Intrusion Detection Evaluation Data Sets [12]. We intend also to evaluate the other items of the extensions proposed in Sect. 6.

References

[illegible]

Investigating the problem of IDS false alarms: An experimental study using Snort

G.C. Tjhai, M. Papadaki, S.M. Furnell, N.L. Clarke

Key words: Intrusion Detection System, False Alarm, Snort

1 Introduction

IDS can play a vital role in the overall security infrastructure, as one last defence against attacks after secure network architecture design, secure program design and firewalls [1]. Although IDS technology has become an essential part of corporate network architecture, the art of detecting intrusions is still far from perfect. A significant problem is that of false alarms, which correspond to legitimate activity that has been mistakenly classed as malicious by the IDS. Recognising the real alarms from the huge volume of alarms is a complicated and time-consuming task. Therefore, reducing false alarms is a serious problem in ensuring IDS efficiency and usability [2].

A common technique for reducing the false alarm rate is by performing a tuning procedure. This can be done by adapting the set of signatures to the specific environment and disabling the signatures that are not related to it [8], based on the fact that some vulnerabilities exist in a particular OS platform only. However, although this can offer a means of reducing the number of false alarms, the procedure can also increase the risk of missing noteworthy incidents. Therefore, the tuning process is actually a trade-off between reducing false alarms and maintaining the security level. This often leaves administrators with the difficulty of determining a proper balance between an ideal detection rate and the possibility of having false alarms. Furthermore, tuning requires a thorough examination of the environment by qualified IT personnel, and requires frequently updating to keep up with the flow of new vulnerabilities or threats discovered [26].

The authors are with the University of Plymouth, UK
e-mail: {gina.tjhai,maria.papadaki,s.furnell,n.clarke}@plymouth.ac.uk

Please use the following format when citing this chapter:

Tjhai, G.C., et al., 2008, in IFIP International Federation for Information Processing, Volume 278; *Proceedings of the IFIP TC 11 23rd International Information Security Conference*; Sushil Jajodia, Pierangela Samarati, Stelvio Cimato; (Boston: Springer), pp. 253–267.

This paper investigates the problem of false alarms based upon experiments involving the popular open source network IDS, Snort [7]. A number of potential issues are presented along with the analysis undertaken to evaluate the IDS performance on real network traffic. Section 2 critically reviews background information on the false alarm problem, and provides a critical analysis of existing research in the area. The methodology of the experiment is presented in section 3. Section 4 provides the findings from the private dataset, followed by conclusions in section 5.

2 Related work

The problem of false alarms has become a major concern in the use of IDS. The vast imbalance between actual and false alarms generated has undoubtedly undermined the performance of IDS [9]. For that reason, the main challenge of IDS development is now no longer focusing only upon its capability in correctly identifying real attacks but also on its ability to suppress the false alarms. This issue had been extensively explored and analysed by Axelsson [2] based on the base-rate fallacy phenomenon. At present, a solution to restrain the alarms is not close at hand, as numerous aspects (e.g. attack features) need to be considered as the prerequisites to develop a better alarm reduction technique [12]. Developing an alarms suppressing technique is a continuing process rather than an isolated, one-off action. The number of reported attacks (and the associated IDS signatures), increases each month, with the consequence that tuning becomes a requirement throughout the lifecycle of an IDS.

Similar to our research, an evaluation had been carried out by Brugger and Chow [4] to assess the performance of traditional IDS, Snort. This evaluation had been conducted using the baseline Defense Advanced Research Projects Agency (DARPA) dataset 1998 against a contemporary version of Snort. Although the use of DARPA dataset had been strongly criticised in IDS evaluation, it still serves as a benchmark by allowing the comparison of IDS tools with a common dataset [16]. This assessment was performed to appraise the usefulness of DARPA as an IDS evaluation dataset and the effectiveness of the Snort ruleset against the dataset. In order to analyse Snort's alarms, a perl matcher script was used to report the false negative and positive rates; thus generating the Receiver Operating Characteristic (ROC) curve for a given set of attacks. Given the six year time span between the ruleset and the creation of the dataset, it was expected that Snort could have effectively identified all attacks contained in the dataset. Conversely, what they found instead was the detection performance was very low and the system produced an unacceptably high rate of false positives, which rose above the 50% ROC's guess line rate. This might be due to the fact that Snort has a problem detecting attacks modelled by the DARPA dataset, which focused upon denial of service and probing activities [13]. In particular, Snort is alleged to commonly generate a high level of false alarms [17] and the alarm rate reported in this evaluation was not creditable enough to prove Snort's false positive performance in a real network, which might be much worse or much better. Moreover, the other experiments took place a few years ago, which means that Snort's performance may have changed since then. In view of that, our research decided to assess the performance of Snort on a more realistic data, as an attempt to critically evaluate the false positive issue of the system.

3 Experiment Description

In order to further explore the problem of false alarms faced by current IDS technology, an experiment was conducted to analyse and evaluate IDS alerts generated by real network traffic. In common with the earlier research referenced in the previous section, Snort, was chosen as the main detector. The reason for utilising Snort was due to its openness and public availability. Moreover, an investigation involving such a commonly used IDS can give an insight into the extent of the false alarm problem in other IDS systems as well.

A number of criticisms had been raised over DARPA dataset, questioning the use of synthetic data to picture a real world network as well as the taxonomy used to categorise the exploits involved in the evaluation [15]. Owing to these issues, our experiments involved the evaluation of Snort on both DARPA [23] and private dataset. However, this paper only presents an experiment using a private dataset, which was collected at University of Plymouth. The data was collected on a public network (100-150 MB/s network) over a period of 40 days (starting from May 17th to June 25th), logging all traffic to and from the University's web server. This includes TCP (99.9%) and ICMP (0.1%) traffic. The traffic collection was conducted with a conventional network analysis tool, tcpdump, and it involved the collection of the full network packet, including the packet payload. Although storing the full packet information significantly increased the storage requirements for the experiment, it was important to maintain this information for the validation and analysis of IDS alarms. The collected payload data was then further processed by Snort IDS in Network Intrusion Detection (NIDS) mode. It should also be noted that traffic containing web pages with the potential of having sensitive / confidential information was excluded from the packet capture, in order to preserve the privacy of web users. This was accomplished by applying filters on the traffic, prior to it being captured by tcpdump. Ngrep was used for this purpose [18].

The first stage of the experiment was to run Snort in NIDS mode, in its default configuration. This means that no tuning whatsoever was conducted. The aim of this phase is to investigate the extent of the false alarm problem with Snort's default ruleset. The next phase of the experiment involved the analysis of the same traffic, after tuning had been performed on Snort. A number of techniques were applied for the tuning, including setting up the event thresholds and adjusting Snort's rules [19]. A necessary requirement for this was the manual validation and analysis of alerts produced by Snort in the first phase, and identification of signatures that are prone to false alarms. The analysis of IDS alerts was supervised by a certified intrusion analyst, and the front-end tool Basic Analysis and Security Engine (BASE) was utilised to assist the intrusion analysis process [3].

The analysis of alerts was supervised by a GIAC Certified Intrusion Analyst [10]. Once the alerts were manually verified, the result was presented in a ROC diagram; a graphical plot of Snort alarm generation. In order to reveal a clear picture of the false alarm problem, a ROC plot is preferable. This type of graph can demonstrate the trade-off between the ability to identify correctly between true positives and the risk of raising too many false positives. Unfortunately, there were no true negative (number of benevolent activities passed) and false negative (number of real attacks missed) value known in this analysis since real network traffic was used as the input dataset. As an alternative, the plot diagram is drawn to represent the actual number of false and true alarms instead of their alarms rate. This diagram provides a simple graphical representation of the false alarm problem, thus enabling the analyzer to easily comprehend the trend of false alerts. By demonstrating the graphical plot of false positive versus true positive, this approach visibly explains the criticality of the false alarm issue. The alarm rate is calculated as follows:

$$\text{False Alarm Rate} = \frac{\text{False Alarm}}{\text{Total Alarm}} \times 100$$

$$\text{True Alarm Rate} = \frac{\text{True Alarm}}{\text{Total Alarm}} \times 100$$

4 Results

The lack of knowledge or awareness about the complexity of network by IDS technology has led to the generation of excessive amount of false alarms. Generally, there are three possible alert types raised by the system, namely true positives (alerts from real attacks), false positives (legitimate activities thought to be malicious) and irrelevant positive (alerts from unsuccessful attacks or attempts [12]. The last two alerts are the main concerns in this study.

This section presents the results of the experiment. Figure 1 depicts the ROC plot for the overall result, which represents the general detection performance of Snort IDS. In order to create a simpler illustrative graph, which facilitates the comprehension of Snort's detection ability, the false and true positives values are presented in a proportion of thousands. The number of false positives generated is presented per unit time (per day) for the X-scale, while true positives are portrayed for the Y-scale. This diagram also represents the random guess (known as non-discriminatory line), which gives a point along a diagonal line from the left bottom (0,0) to the top right corner (10,10). This diagonal line divides the space into two domains; namely good and bad classification. Ideally, a good detection system should yield a point above the line, meaning the number of real alerts (true positives) triggered should not be exceeded by the number of false positives generated.

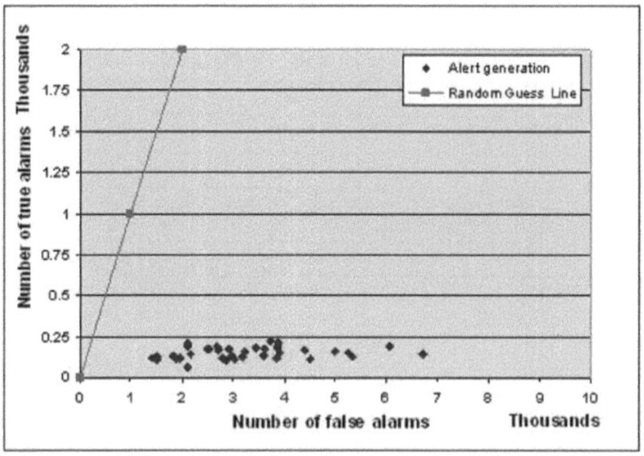

Fig. 1 Generation of alerts

Significantly, our research has also produced a similar result to that yielded in Brugger and Chow's evaluation. The number of false positives generated is massive. This indicates that the Snort's false positive performance on real network could be much worse than described in their evaluation.

This experiment focused on the analysis of false positive alarms, as opposed to other studies [14, 4], which were directed to explore the issue of false negatives. The main objective of this analysis is to merely provide a general view of the scale of false positives that may be generated by current IDS. The following subsections discuss this case in greater detail.

4.1 False Positives

A large volume of alerts, largely comprised of false alarms and irrelevant positives, drives the need to verify the validity of the alerts generated. Interestingly, apart from the false positives, our study reveals that some alerts were raised due to informational events, which merely occurred as a result of a network problem, not owing to the detection of real attacks. These types of alerts are known as irrelevant positives. Indeed, the unsuccessful attacks, or attempts that aim at an invincible target, might cause the system to generate such alarms.

Figure 2 provides a clear picture of the number of true and false alarms generated per day. In this context, it is obvious that the false alarms highly outnumbered the true alarms. Approximately 96% of alerts generated are asserted as false positives, while less than 1% of the total alerts are affirmed to be irrelevant positives. In order to make it simpler, irrelevant alarms are regarded as false positives alerts in this case since no immediate and crucial responses required from these events. By looking at the Snort alerts generated from the University's web server, most of the false positive alarms came from the category of web application activity. Table 1 shows

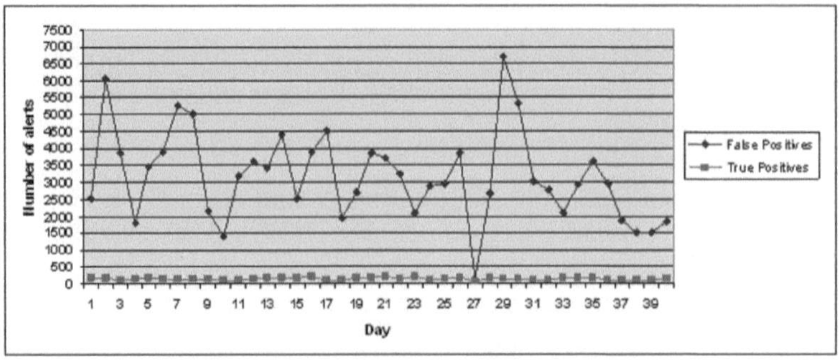

Fig. 2 Comparison between False Positive and True Positive alarms

a complete list of the Snort alerts triggered by the data. The first 3 alerts are the false positives alerts, which will be further investigated later in the subsubsections. The reason for focusing upon these alerts is due to the quantity generated, which is made up of more than 80% of total alerts raised by the system.

4.1.1 WEB-IIS view source via translate header

This event is categorized as web application activity, which targets the Microsoft IIS 5.0 source disclosure vulnerability [20]. Since Microsoft IIS has the capability of handling various advanced scriptable files such as ASP, ASA and HTR, the use of specialized header "Translate f" on HTTP GET request might force the web server to present the complete source code of the requested file to the client without being executed first by the scripting engine. In addition, this attack only works well if the trailing slash "/" is appended to the end of requested URL [5, 6].

Surprisingly, this single alert accounted for 59% of the total alerts. Therefore, approximately 1970 alerts were generated per day by this event. Although this event is deemed to be an attack that targets the Microsoft IIS source disclosure vulnerability, this could possibly be a false positive. Some applications, for example Web-based Distributed Authoring and Versioning (WebDAV) that make use of "Translate f" as a legitimate header, might cause this rule to generate an excessive amount of false alarms [25]. Moreover, WebDAV PROPFIND and OPTION methods also make use of this "Translate f" as a legitimate header to retrieve the information or properties of the resources identified by the Uniform Resource Identifier (URI) (nearly 96% of alerts generated by this event were not HTTP GET requests). Significantly, in this experiment, there is no alert generated by this signature, which required immediate action or indicated the occurrence of the real attack.

Table 1 Complete list of Snort alerts

No	Signatures	Total alerts
1	WEB-IIS view source via translate header	78865
2	WEB-MISC robots.txt access	30011
3	ICMP L3retriever Ping	10254
4	BARE BYTE UNICODE ENCODING	6392
5	POLICY Google Desktop activity	3258
6	SPYWARE-PUT Trackware funwebproducts mywebsearchtoolbar-funtools runtime detection	1873
7	ATTACK-RESPONSE 403 Forbidden	720
8	ICMP PING Cyberkit 2.2 Windows	651
9	DOUBLE DECODING ATTACK	504
10	ICMP Destination Unreachable Communication Administratively Prohibited	151
11	TCP Portsweep	124
12	SPYWARE-PUT Hijacker searchmiracle-elitebar runtime detection	80
13	WEB-MISC .DS_Store access	60
14	IIS UNICODE CODEPOINT ENCODING	49
15	WEBROOT DIRECTORY TRAVERSAL	35
16	SPYWARE-PUT Adware hotbar runtime detection - hotbar user-agent	27
17	WEB-IIS asp-dot attempt	26
18	TCP Portscan	19
19	SPYWARE-PUT Trackware alexa runtime detection	19
20	WEB-PHP IGeneric Free Shopping Cart page.php access	17
21	ICMP PING NMAP	17
22	ICMP Destination Unreachable Communication with Destination Host is Administratively Prohibited	13
23	WEB-CGI calendar access	11
24	MULTIMEDIA Quicktime User Agent Access	10
25	WEB-MISC intranet access	8
26	ICMP redirect host	8
27	ICMP PING speedera	7
28	SPYWARE-PUT Hijacker marketscore runtime detection	7
29	WARNING: ICMP Original IP Fragmented and Offset Not 0!	6
30	WEB-MISC WebDAV search access	5
31	WEB-FRONTPAGE /_vti_bin/access	5
32	Open Port	5
33	WEB-PHP remote include path	4
34	WEB-CGI formmail access	3
35	WEB-FRONTPAGE_vti_inf.html access	3
36	SPYWARE-PUT Trickler teomasearchbar runtime detection	2
37	WEB-PHP xmlrpc.php post attempt	2
38	WEB-CLIENT Microsoft wmf metafile access	2
39	WEB-MISC Domino webadmin.nsf access	2
40	OVERSIZE CHUNK ENCODING	2
41	ICMP Source Quench	2
42	WEB-PHP test.php access	2
43	WEB-PHP calendar.php access	1
44	WEB-PHP admin.php access	1

4.1.2 WEB-MISC robots.txt access

This event is raised when an attempt has been made to access robots.txt file directly [21]. Basically, robots.txt file is a file that is created to keep the web pages from being indexed by search engines. More to the point, this file provides a specific instruction and determines which part of a website a spider robot may visit. Interestingly, the problem is that the webmaster may detail sensitive and hidden directories or even the location of the secret files within the robots.txt file. This is considered extremely unsafe since this file is located in web server's document root directory, which can be freely retrieved by anyone.

Although this event is raised as the indicator of vulnerable information attack, there exists high possibility that all these alerts were raised due to legitimate activities from web robots or spiders. A spider is software that gathers information for search engines by crawling around the web indexing web pages and links in those pages. Robots.txt file is basically created to restrict the web spider from indexing pages that should not be indexed (e.g. submission pages or enquiry pages). As web indexing is regular and structurally repetitive, this activity tends to cause the IDS to trigger a superfluous amount of alerts. In this study, approximately 23% of total alerts (approximately 750 alarms per day) were accounted for by this web-misc activity. Given that all alerts generated from this event are owing to the activities of web spider, they are considered to be false positives. Significantly, this issue has apparently disclosed the drawback of Snort IDS in distinguishing legitimate activity from the malicious one; especially when it deals with the authorization or file permission.

4.1.3 ICMP L3retriever Ping

ICMP L3retriever Ping is an event that occurs when ICMP echo request is made from a host running L3Retriever scanner [22]. This type of ICMP echo request has a unique payload in the message, which significantly designates its distinctive characteristic. This traffic is considered to be an attempted reconnaissance since the attackers may use the ping command to obtain ICMP echo reply from a listening host. Surprisingly, in this analysis, quite a few alerts were generated from this event; contributing to 8% of the total alerts generated. This figure indicates that approximately 250 alerts were generated by this signature rule every day.

Considering the source IP address associated with these alerts, it is obviously clear that all ICMP requests were sent from the external hosts. Further investigation was conducted to critically analyse and discover if possible malicious events happened subsequent to the ICMP echo request. Surprisingly, there were no malevolent activities detected following the ICMP traffic. In addition, normal ICMP requests generated by Windows 2000 and Windows XP are also known to have similar payloads to the one generated by L3Retriever scanner [24]. Generally, this traffic is routine activities run by computer systems (especially Windows 2000 and XP systems) to communicate with their domain controllers or to perform network discovery. In view of this issue and given that no suspicious output detected following these ICMP requests; these alerts were likely false positives.

4.2 Fine Tuning

False alarm for one system might not be an erroneous alert for other systems. For example, port scanning might be a malicious activity for normal users, but it is a legitimate activity if it is performed by a system administrator. Figure 3 shows an example of an event which triggered both false alarms and true alarms from the experiment. From the IDS's perspective, as long the activity's pattern match to the signature defined in the rule database, it is considered to be a malicious event. In view of this, fine tuning is exceptionally required to maintain the IDS's performance and enable the administrator to adapt the signature rule to the protected environment.

In order to optimize Snort's performance, fine tuning is necessary to reduce the number of alerts raised. Since only 3 signatures were tuned in this experiment, the false alarm rate accounted for 86.8% of total alarms after tuning was performed. Figure 4 depicts the ROC plots for the overall result after tuning was performed. Obviously, only less than two thousands alerts per alert type have been generated by Snort. In order to understand the effectiveness of fine tuning, the alarm rate between default and tuned Snort is presented in Figure 5. This figure does not seem particularly impressive but fine tuning did fare well on those signatures; reducing up to 90% of false alarms per signature, excluding WEB-MISC robots.txt access. The following subsections discuss tuning processes in more details.

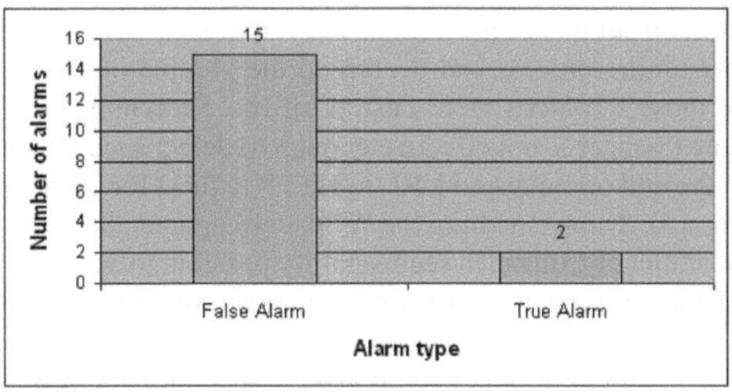

Fig. 3 "ICMP PING NMAP" event

4.2.1 WEB-IIS view source via translate header

Regarding the information disclosure vulnerability attack, Snort does not seem proficient enough to detect this type of event. The signature rule appears to be very loosely written, by searching for a particular string in the packet payload (in this case, "Translate: f"). Since the "Translate: f" is a valid header used in WebDAV application, as discussed previously, this rule tends to trigger a vast volume of alerts from the legitimate activities. Hence, tuning is needed to search for a more specific pattern of the attack signature.

As this attack is basically launched through HTTP GET request, searching for "GET" command in the content of analyzed packet can be a good start. Principally, this attack is performed by requesting a specific resource using HTTP GET command, followed by "Translate: f" as the header of HTTP request. In this case, a tuning can be performed by modifying the signature rule to:

```
alert tcp $EXTERNAL_NET any -> $HTTP_SERVERS $HTTP_PORTS
(msg:"WEB-IIS view source via translate header";
flow:to_server,established; content:"GET|20|";content:
"Translate|3A| F"; distance:0; nocase; reference:arachnids,
305; reference:bugtraq,14764; reference:bugtraq,1578;
reference:cve,2000-0778; reference:nessus,10491;
classtype:web-application-activity; sid:1042; rev:13;)
```

The tuning process significantly reduced the number of alerts, with only 3463 generated by this rule as against 78865 alerts in the first case (i.e. without tuning). Significantly, this tuned rule had been proved to effectively reduce up to 95% of the initial false alarms from this event.

Although the tuning process had decreased the volume of alerts, there is still a possibility that those 5% alerts were false positives. Searching for GET command and the Translate f header is not effective enough to detect such attack. Putting trailing slash "/" at the end of requested URL to HTTP request for example could lead in the security bug [5]. Thus, matching the "/" pattern against the packet payload will be helpful. Unfortunately, this idea seems hardly possible to achieve. Snort does not have a specific rule option that can be used to match a specific pattern at a particular location.

As to Snort's signature, looking for an overly specific pattern of a particular attack may effectively reduce the false alarms; however, this method can highly increase the risk of missing its range. A skilful attacker can easily alter and abuse the vulnerability in various ways as an attempt to evade the IDS. This might lead to false negatives as a consequence.

4.2.2 WEB-MISC robots.txt access

Since accessing the robots.txt file is a legitimate request for Internet bots (web spiders), a subjective rule, which mainly focuses on the source IP addresses, is necessary to verify user authorization in accessing a certain file. This approach, however, seems to be hardly feasible to deploy. Of course, identifying all authorized hosts from their source IP addresses is impractical. There is an infinite number of IP addresses need to be discovered before the rule can be written. Indeed, lawfully allowing specific hosts to access certain file might increase the risk of having false negatives.

In this case, the only solution to suppress the number of false alarms generated is by using event thresholding [19]. As robots.txt access requests generate regular and repetitive traffic, a "limi" type of threshold command is the most suitable tuning in this case. Such a threshold configuration would be as follows:

```
threshold gen\_id 1, sig\_id 1852, type limit,
track by\_src, count 1, seconds 60
```

This rule logs the first event every 60 seconds, and ignores events for the rest of the time interval. The result showed that approximately 10% of false alarms had been effectively reduced. This indicates that only an insignificant number of false alarms can be reduced in this scenario. The frequency of fetching robots.txt files greatly depends on the web spider's policy. Hence, deploying event suppression and thresholding cannot effectively trim down the number of false alarms logged by the system. Additionally, suppressing the number of alerts generated can also create

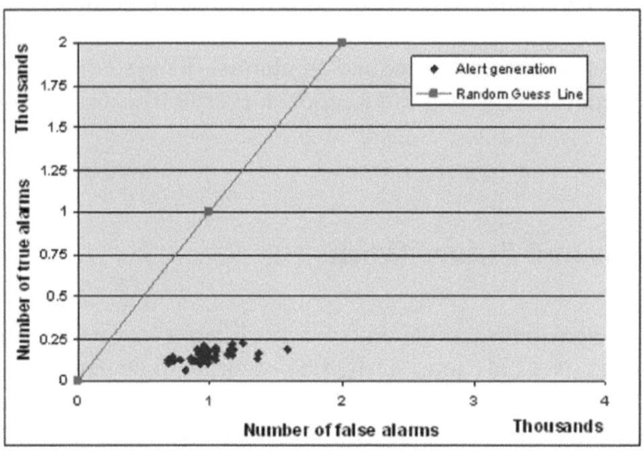

Fig. 4 Alerts generation after fine tuning

a possibility of ignoring or missing significant alerts. A malicious user can hide his/her action within the excessive number of alerts generated by using a spoofed address from web spider agent.

4.2.3 ICMP L3Retriever Ping

The only method that can be deployed to suppress the number of false positive triggered from this event is by applying event suppressing or thresholding command. Similar to the one applied to "WEB-MISC robots.txt access" signature, a threshold command is written to limit the number of alarms logged. Instead of using "limit" type of threshold command as previous signature, this rule utilized "both" type of command to log alerts once per time interval and ignore additional alerts generated during that period:

```
alert icmp $EXTERNAL_NET any -> $HOME_NET any (msg:"ICMP
L3retriever Ping"; icode:0; itype:8; content:
"ABCDEFGHIJKLMNOPQRSTUVWABCDEFGHI"; depth:32; reference:
arachnids,311; classtype:attempted-recon; threshold: type
both, track by_src, count 3, seconds 60; sid:466; rev:5;)
```

Similar to the previous signature (robots.txt access), the threshold applied will not prevent the generation of false positives, but it will highly reduce the number of redundant false positives triggered. Importantly, the threshold is written to detect brisk ICMP echo requests by logging alerts once per 60 seconds after seeing 3 occurrences of this event.

The result showed that only 1143 alerts had been generated from this event in 40 days experiment data. This experiment has also proved that the event thresholding can successfully reduce up to 89% of the false alarms generated by this activity. Despite its ability in suppressing redundant alarms, the system is prone to missing stealthy ICMP requests (e.g. requests sent once every 60 seconds can be missed by the system).

5 Conclusions and Future Work

The issue of false positives has become a critical factor in determining the success of IDS technology. Not only must an IDS be accurate in detecting real attacks, but it must also have the ability to suppress the number of unnecessary alerts generated. The experiment presented in this paper has revealed a similar result to the work of Brugger and Chow [4]. Over a span of two years since their research was published, the issue of false positives remains a critical challenge for the current Snort IDS.

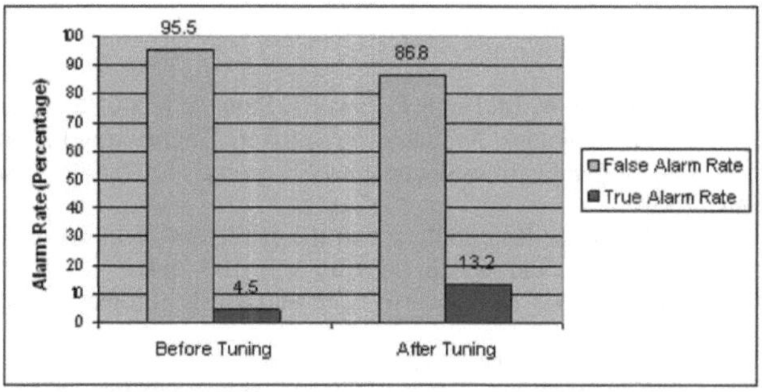

Fig. 5 Alarm rate before and after tuning

Obviously, Snort's performance does not look particularly remarkable as illustrated in Figure 1. The bottom right scattered plots demonstrate that the number of false positives largely overwhelms the number of true positives generated. Approximately 3,000 alerts had been generated per day, requiring manual verification to validate their legitimacy. Although the administrator can effectively distinguish the false and true positives from the alerts generated, the massive amount of false alarms triggered by one signature rule might cause the administrator to miss a malicious attack.

Principally, the overall effectiveness of Snort greatly hinges on the effectiveness of keyword spotting (i.e. matching the packet content to the signature rule). This has rendered the system prone to generating a superfluous number of false alerts. Interestingly, most of the rules looking for web traffic related attacks are loosely written and merely check for the presence of a particular string in the packet payload. This could trigger a large number of false alerts if a particular string is included in the content distributed by the web server. Hence, from this perspective, Snort is deemed not to be ideal enough to detect more complex attacks, which are not detectable by a pre-defined signature.

In view of these issues, an improvement is required to advance the performance of IDS technology. This involves developing an automatic alert verification, which no longer relies on human participation. Through this enhancement, it is expected that the number of false alarms can be substantially suppressed without increasing the possibility of false negatives. Also, a more intelligent system is required to help discover the logical relationship between alerts generated and to reveal the potential attack scenario; thus providing a better picture of the security issue to the system administrator. Given the complexity of systems and the ingenuity of attacks, an IDS will never be perfect, and there is still significant scope to enhance its performance.

Acknowledgements We want to thank Dr. Bogdan Ghita of University of Plymouth for his help in capturing the network traffic and for his support until the completion of this paper.

References

1. Allen J, Christie A, Fithen W, McHugh J, Pickel J, Stone E (2000) State of the Practice of Intrusion Detection Technologies. Available via Software Engineering Institute. http://www.sei.cmu.edu/publications/documents/99.reports/99tr028/99tr028abstract.html. Cited 9 January 2007
2. Axelsson S (2000) The Base-Rate Fallacy and the Difficulty of Intrusion Detection. ACM Transactions on Information and System Security 3(3), 186-205
3. BASE (2007) Basic Analysis and Security Engine (BASE) Project. Available via BASE Project. http://base.secureideas.net/. Cited 25 April 2007
4. Brugger ST, and Chow J (2005) An Assessment of the DARPA IDS Evaluation Dataset Using Snort. Available via UCDAVIS department of Computer Science. http://www.cs.ucdavis.edu/research/tech-reports/2007/CSE-2007-1.pdf. Cited 2 May 2007
5. Bugtraq (2007a) Microsoft IIS 5.0 "Translate: f" Source Disclosure Vulnerability. Available via Security Focus. http://www.securityfocus.com/bid/1578. Cited 9 June 2007
6. Bugtraq (2007b) Microsoft IIS WebDAV HTTP Request Source Code Disclosure Vulnerability. Available via Security Focus. http://www.securityfocus.com/bid/14764. Cited 9 June 2007
7. Caswell B and Roesch M (2004) Snort: The open source network intrusion detection system. Available via Snort. http://www.snort.org/. Cited 3 October 2007
8. Chapple M (2003) Evaluating and Tuning an Intrusion Detection System. Available online: SearchSecurity.com. http://searchsecurity.techtarget.com. Cited 1 November 2006
9. Chyssler T, Burschka S, Semling M, Lingvall T and Burbeck K (2004) Alarm Reduction and Correlation in Intrusion Detection Systems. Available via The Department of Computer and Information Science Linkopings Universitet. http://www.ida.liu.se/ rtslab/publications/2004/Chyssler04_DIMVA.pdf. Cited 15 June 2007
10. GCIA (2008) GIAC Certified Intrusion Analyst (GCIA). Available via Global Information Assurance Certification. http://www.giac.org/certifications/security/gcia.php. Cited 8 May 2007
11. Koziol J (2003) *Intrusion Detection with Snort*, 2Rev edition. Sams Publishing, United States of America
12. Kruegel C and Robertson W (2004) Alert Verification: Determining the Success of Intrusion Attempts, Proc. First Workshop the Detection of Intrusions and Malware and Vulnerability Assessment (DIMVA 2004). Available via Department of Computer Science, University of California, Santa Barbara. http://www.cs.ucsb.edu/ wkr/publications/dimva04verification.pdf. Cited 19 May 2007
13. Lippmann RP, Haines JW, Fried DJ, Korba J and Das KJ (2000) The 1999 DARPA off-line intrusion detection evaluation. Computer Networks 34:579–595
14. Mahoney MV and Chan PK (2003) An Analysis of the 1999 DARPA/Lincoln Laboratory Evaluation Data for Network Anomaly Detection. In Recent Advances in Intrusion Detection (RAID2003), Lecture Notes in Computer Science, Springer-Verlag 2820:220–237
15. McHugh J (2000) Intrusion Detection Systems: A Critique of the 1998 and 1999 DARPA Intrusion Detection System Evaluations as Performed by Lincoln Laboratory. ACM Transactions on Information and System Security 3(4), 262-294
16. Mell P, Hu V, Lippmann R, Haines J and Zissman M (2003) An Overview of Issues in Testing Intrusion Detection Systems. NISTIR 7007. Available via National Institute of Standards and Technology. http://csrc.nist.gov/publications/nistir/nistir-7007.pdf. Cited 7 July 2007
17. Patton S, Yurcik W and Doss D (2001) An Archilles' Heel in Signature-Based IDS: Squealing False Positives in SNORT. Recent Advanced in Intrusion Detection (RAID), Univ. of California-Davis.

18. Ritter J (2006) Ngrep - network grep. Available via SourceForge.net. http://ngrep.sourceforge.net. Cited 30 June 2007
19. Snort (2007a) Event Thresholding. Available via Snort. http://www.snort.org/docs/snort_htmanuals/htmanual_2.4/node22.html. Cited 1 July 2007
20. Snort (2007b) WEB-IIS view source via translate header. Available via Snort. http://snort.org/pub-bin/sigs.cgi?sid=1042. Cited 9 June 2007
21. Snort (2007c) WEB-MISC robots.txt access. Available via Snort. http://www.snort.org/pub-bin/sigs.cgi?sid=1:1852. Cited 9 June 2007
22. Snort (2007d) ICMP L3retriever Ping. Available via Snort. http://www.snort.org/pub-bin/sigs.cgi?sid=1:466. Cited 13 June 2007
23. Tjhai GC, Papadaki M, Furnell SM and Clarke NL (2008) The problem of false alarms: Evaluation with Snort and DARPA 1999 Dataset. Submitted to TrustBus 2008, Turin, Italy, 1-5 September 2008
24. Web Server Talk (2005) L3Retriever false positives. Available via Web Server Talk. http://www.webservertalk.com/message893082.html. Cited 12 July 2007
25. WebDAV (2001) WebDAV Overview. Available via Sambar Server Documentation. http://www.sambar.com/syshelp/webdav.htm. Cited 20 June 2007
26. Zhou A, Blustein J, and Zincir-Heywood N (2004) Improving Intrusion Detection Systems Through Heuristic Evaluation. 17th Annual Canadian Conference on Electrical and Computer Engineering. http://users.cs.dal.ca/ jamie/pubs/PDF/Zhou+CCECE04.pdf. Cited 25 June 2007

User Session Modeling for Effective Application Intrusion Detection

Kapil Kumar Gupta, Baikunth Nath (Sr. MIEEE) and Kotagiri Ramamohanarao

Abstract With the number of data breaches on a rise, effective and efficient detection of anomalous activities in applications which manages data is critical. In this paper, we introduce a novel approach to improve attack detection at application layer by modeling user sessions as a sequence of events instead of analyzing every single event in isolation. We also argue that combining application access logs and the corresponding data access logs to generate unified logs eliminates the need to analyze them separately thereby resulting in an efficient and accurate system. We evaluate various methods such as conditional random fields, support vector machines, decision trees and naive Bayes, and experimental results show that our approach based on conditional random fields is feasible and can detect attacks at an early stage even when they are disguised within normal events.

1 Introduction

Detecting intrusions is a challenge because it is important to detect malicious events at an early stage in order to minimize their impact. This becomes more important when attackers come up with previously unseen attacks even when the present systems are unable to detect all existing attacks with acceptable reliability [13]. Further, with more and more data becoming available in digital format and more applications being developed to access this data, the data and applications are a victim of malicious attackers who exploit the applications to gain access to sensitive data. Thus, there is need to develop robust and efficient intrusion detection systems which can detect such malicious activities at application layer.

Kapil Kumar Gupta, Baikunth Nath, Kotagiri Ramamohanarao
Department of Computer Science & Software Engineering, NICTA Victoria Research Laboratory, The University of Melbourne, Australia, 3010. e-mail: kgupta@csse.unimelb.edu.au, bnath@csse.unimelb.edu.au, rao@csse.unimelb.edu.au

Please use the following format when citing this chapter:

Gupta, K.K., Nath, B. and Ramamohanarao, K., 2008, in IFIP International Federation for Information Processing, Volume 278; *Proceedings of the IFIP TC 11 23rd International Information Security Conference*; Sushil Jajodia, Pierangela Samarati, Stelvio Cimato; (Boston: Springer), pp. 269–283.

Intrusion detection systems are classified as signature based, anomaly based or hybrid systems [5]. Hybrid systems generally employ machine learning methods while signature and anomaly based systems are often based on pattern matching and statistical methods. The advantage of hybrid systems is that they are trained using normal and anomalous data patterns together and hence can be used to label new unseen events reliably when compared with signature and anomaly based systems which are generally based on a threshold [21]. Intrusion detection systems can also be classified as network based, host based or application based [5].

In this paper, we propose an application intrusion detection system which models individual user sessions using a moving window of events. One of the main drawbacks of present application intrusion detection systems is that they are specific to a particular application and cannot be generalized [19], [20]. However, our proposed model is general and does not require application specific details to be encoded. It only needs to be trained with the logs associated with a particular application. As any application intrusion detection system, our system is meant to provide an additional line of defense and not to replace existing network based systems.

The rest of the paper is organized as follows; we explain our framework in Sect. 2 and discuss the data set in Sect. 3. We give our experimental results in Sect. 4. We then discuss related work in Sect. 5 and draw conclusions in Sect. 6.

2 Proposed Model

In general, there are two motives to launch an attack; either to force a network to stop some service that it is providing or to steal some information stored in a network. In this paper, we focus on the second motive, i.e., to detect malicious data access. However, what is normal and what is anomalous is not defined, i.e., an event may be normal when measured with respect to some criteria but the same may be called as anomalous when this criteria is changed. Thus, the objective is to find anomalous test patterns which are similar to the anomalous patterns which occurred during the training with the assumption that the underlying measuring criteria is unchanged and the system is trained such that it can reliably separate normal and anomalous events. The straight forward approach is to audit every data access request before it is processed and data is retrieved by the system. However, this is not the ideal solution due to the following reasons:

1. The number of data requests per unit time is very large and monitoring every request in real time applications severely affects system performance.
2. Assuming that we can somehow monitor every data request, the system must be regularly updated with new signatures to detect previously known attacks (it still cannot detect zero day attacks).
3. The system is application specific because the signatures are defined by encoding application specific knowledge.

Thus, monitoring every data request is often not feasible in real life environment. We also observe that real world applications generally follow the three tier architecture [1] which ensures application and data independence, i.e., data is managed separately and is not encoded into the application. Hence, to access data, an attacker has no option but to exploit this application. To detect such attacks, an intrusion detection system can either monitor the application requests or (and) monitor the data requests. As we discussed above, analyzing every data access is difficult and limits the detection capability of the intrusion detection system. Similarly, analyzing only the application requests does not provide useful information about the data accessed. Previous systems such as [6], [9] and [15] consider the application requests and the corresponding data requests separately and, hence, unable to correlate the events together resulting in a large number of false alarms. Before we explain our framework, we define some key terms which will be helpful in better understanding of the paper.

1. **Application:** An *application* is a software by which a user can accesses data. There exists no other way in which the data can be made available to a user.
2. **User:** A *user* is either an individual or any another application which access data.
3. **Event:** Data transfer between a user and an application is a result of multiple sequential events. Data transfer can be considered as a request-response system where a request for data access is followed by a response. An *event* is a single request-response pair. We represent a single event as an N feature vector. In this paper, we use the term *event* interchangeably with the term *request*.
4. **User Session:** A *user session* is an ordered set of events or actions performed, i.e., a session is a sequence of one or more request-response pairs. Every session can be uniquely identified by a session-id.

2.1 Framework

We represent a general framework for building application intrusion detection systems in Fig. 1. Our framework does not encode application specific knowledge making it useable for a variety of applications. To access data, a user accesses the application as in a simple three tier architecture. However, every request first passes through the session control. Session control is responsible for establishing new sessions and for checking the session-id for previously established sessions. For this, it maintains a list of all the valid sessions that are allowed to access the application and hence the data. Every request to access the application is checked for a valid session-id at the session control which can be blocked if it is found anomalous depending upon the installed security policy. The session control can be implemented as part of the application itself or as a separate entity.

Following checks from the session control, the request is sent to the application where it is processed. The web server logs every request. Similarly every data access is logged. The two logs are then combined to generate unified logs which are analyzed by the intrusion detection system as represented in the framework.

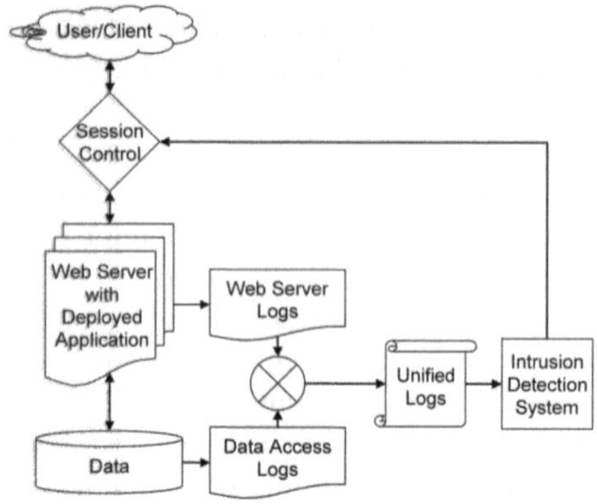

Fig. 1 Framework for building Application Intrusion Detection System

We represent the structure of a typical user session in Fig. 2. A user requests a resource which generates a web request. As we shall discuss later, we used a PHP application to generate data. We consider a web request to be a single request to render a PHP page by the web server and not a single HTTP GET request as it may contain multiple images, frames and dynamic content. The PHP page can be easily identified from the web server logs. This request further generates one or more data requests which depend on the logic encoded in the application. To capture user-application and application-data interactions, we utilize features of both the web server logs and the associated data access logs to generate unified logs. However, the number of data requests is extremely large as compared to the number of web requests. Hence, we first process the data access logs to generate simple statistics such as the number of queries invoked by a single web request and the time taken to process them rather than analyzing every data access individually. We then use the session-id which is present in both the web server logs and the associated data access logs to uniquely map the extracted statistics (obtained from the data access logs) to the corresponding web requests to generate unified logs.

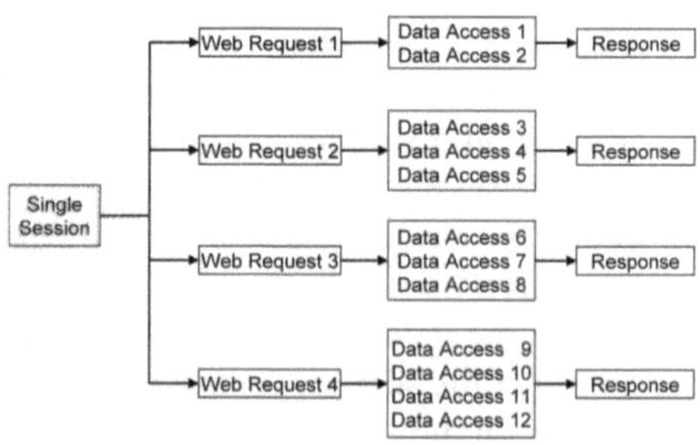

Fig. 2 Representation of a Single user Session

Thus, we generate a unified log format where every session is represented as a sequence of vectors and is represented by the following 6 features:

1. Number of data queries generated in a single web request.

2. Time taken to process the request.
3. Response generated for the request.
4. Amount of data transferred (in bytes).
5. Request made (or the function invoked) by the client.
6. Reference to the previous request in the same session.

Web access logs contain useful information such as the details of every request made by a client (user), response of the web server, amount of data transferred etc. Similarly, data access logs contain important details such as the exact data table and columns accessed, in case the data is stored in a database. Performing intrusion detection at the data access level, in isolation, requires substantially more resources when compared to our approach. Monitoring the two logs together eliminates the need to monitor every data query since we can use simple statistics. In order to gain data access an attacker follows a number of steps and hence, to reduce the number of false alarms and increase the attack detection accuracy, intrusion detection systems must be capable of analyzing entire sequence of events rather than considering every event in isolation [24]. To model such a sequence of event vectors, we need a method that does not assume independence among sequential events. Thus, we use conditional random field which we describe next.

2.2 Conditional Random Fields

Conditional random fields [18] offer us the required framework to build robust intrusion detection systems [11], [12]. The prime advantage of conditional random fields is that they are discriminative models which directly model the conditional distribution $p(y|x)$. Further, conditional random fields are undirected models and free from label bias and observation bias which are present in other conditional models [16]. Generative models such as the Markov chains, hidden Markov models, naive Bayes and joint distribution have two disadvantages. First, the joint distribution is not required since the observations are completely visible and the interest is in finding the correct class which is the conditional distribution $p(y|x)$. Second, inferring conditional probability $p(y|x)$ from the joint distribution, using the Bayes rule, requires marginal distribution $p(x)$ which is difficult to estimate as the amount of training data is limited and the observation x contains highly dependent features. As a result strong independence assumptions are made to reduce complexity. This results in reduced accuracy [22] and hence these methods are not considered in this paper. Instead, conditional random fields predict the label sequence y given the observation sequence x, allowing them to model arbitrary relationships among different features in the observations without making independence assumptions. The graphical structure of a conditional random field is represented in Fig. 3.

The following mathematical description of a conditional random field is motivated from [18]. Given X and Y, the random variables over data sequence to be labeled and the corresponding label sequences, let $G = (V, E)$ be a graph with vertices

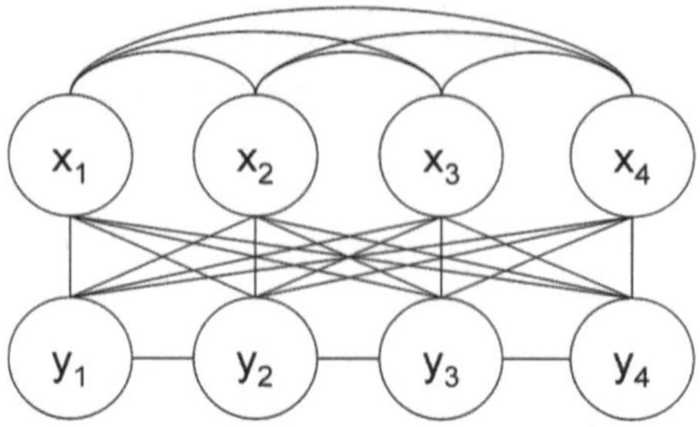

Fig. 3 Graphical Representation of a Conditional Random Field. x_1, x_2, x_3, x_4 represents an observed sequence of length four and every event in the sequence is correspondingly labeled as y_1, y_2, y_3, y_4. Further, every x_i is a feature vector of length '6'.

V and edges E such that $Y = (Y_v)$ where $v \in V$ and Y is represented by the vertices of the graph G, then, (X,Y) is a conditional random field, when conditioned on X, the random variables Y_v obey the Markov property with respect to the graph: $p(Y_v|X,Y_w,w \neq v) = p(Y_v|X,Y_w,w \sim v)$, where $w \sim v$ means that w and v are neighbors in G, i.e., a conditional random field is a random field globally conditioned on X. For a simple sequence (or chain) modeling, as in our case, the joint distribution over the label sequence Y given X has the form:

$$p_\theta(y|x) \propto \exp\left(\sum_{e\in E,k} \lambda_k f_k(e,y|_e,x) + \sum_{v\in V,k} \mu_k g_k(v,y|_v,x)\right) \quad (1)$$

where x is the data sequence, y is a label sequence, and $y|_s$ is the set of components of y associated with the vertices or edges in subgraph S. Also, the features f_k and g_k are assumed to be given and fixed. The parameter estimation problem is to find the parameters $\theta = (\lambda_1, \lambda_2, ...; \mu_1, \mu_2, ...)$ from the training data $D = (x^i, y^i)_{i=1}^N$ with the empirical distribution $\tilde{p}(x,y)$. Recently the conditional random fields have been shown to work very well for intrusion detection [11]. The reason for this is that they make no unwarranted assumptions about the data, and once trained they are very efficient and robust. During testing, the Viterbi algorithm is employed which has a complexity of $O(TL^2)$, where T is the length of the sequence and L is the number of labels. The quadratic complexity is problematic when the number of labels is large, such as in the language tasks, but for intrusion detection we have a limited number of labels (normal and anomalous) and thus the system is efficient.

3 Data Description

To perform our experiments we collected data locally by setting up an environment that mimics a real world application environment. We used an open source, online shopping application [2] and deployed it on a web server running Apache version 2.0.55 and connected to a database server running MySQL version 4.1.22. Every access to the web server and the data server was logged. We collected both the normal and the attack data. The data set is made freely available and can be downloaded from [10].

To collect the normal data we asked the students in the department to access the application. The system for data collection was online for five consecutive days. From the data we observed that about 35 different users accessed the application which resulted in 117 unique sessions composed of 2,615 web requests and 232,655 database requests. We then combined the web server logs with the data server logs to generate the unified logs in the format discussed in Sect. 2.1. Hence we have 117 sessions with only 2,615 events vectors which include features of both the web requests and the associated data requests. We also observed that a large number of user sessions were terminated without actual purchase resulting in abandoning the shopping cart. This is a realistic scenario and in reality a large number of the shopping carts are abandoned without purchase. A typical normal session in the data set is represented in Fig. 4.

```
0,0,301,369,GET /catalog HTTP/1.1,-,normal
0,0,200,28885,GET /catalog/ HTTP/1.1,-,normal
131,1,200,28480,GET /catalog/index.php,http://dummydata.xyz/catalog/,normal
108,1,200,27121,GET /catalog/product_info.php,http://dummydata.xyz/catalog/index.php,normal
```

Fig. 4 Representation of a Normal Session

To collect attack data we disabled access to the system by any other user and generated attack traffic manually based upon two criteria; first, the attacks which do not require any control over the web server or the database such as SQL injection and, second, the attacks which require some control over the web server such as website defacement and others. The events were logged and the same process to combine the two logs was repeated. We generated 45 different attack sessions with 272 web requests that resulted in 44,390 data requests. Combining them together we got 45 unique attack sessions with 272 event vectors. A typical anomalous session in the data set is represented in Fig. 5 which depicts a scenario where the deployed application has been modified by taking control of the web server.

```
98,1,301,369,GET /catalog HTTP/1.1,-,attack
113,0,200,28623,GET /catalog/index.php HTTP/1.1,-,attack
208,1,200,35467,GET /catalog/checkout_shipping.php HTTP/1.1,http://dummydata.xyz/catalog/index.php,attack
158,0,200,47801,GET /catalog/checkout_shipping_address.php HTTP/1.1,http://dummydata.xyz/catalog/checkout_shipping.php,attack
218,0,200,40401,GET /catalog/checkout_payment.php HTTP/1.1,http://dummydata.xyz/catalog/checkout_shipping_address.php,attack
```

Fig. 5 Representation of an Anomalous Session

4 Experiments and Results

We used the CRF++ toolkit [17] and the weka tool [23] for the experiments. Further, we developed python and shell scripts for data formatting and implementation. We perform all experiments ten times by randomly selecting training and testing data and report the average. We use exactly the same samples for all the four methods. It must be noted that methods such as *decision trees, naive Bayes and support vector machines* are not designed for sequence labeling. However, for our purpose these methods can be applied by treating the data as *relational rather than considering them as sequences.* To experiment with these methods, we convert every session to a single record by appending sequential events at the end of the previous event and then labeling the entire session as either normal or as attack. For the support vector machines we experimented with three kernels; *poly-kernel, rbf-kernel and normalized-poly-kernel*, and varied the value of c between 1 and 100 for all of the kernels [23]. In the experiments we *vary the window size 'S' from 1 to 20* and analyze its effect on the attack detection accuracy. Window of size $S = 1$ indicates that we consider only the current request and do not consider the history while a window of size $S = 20$ shows that a sequence of 20 events is analyzed to perform the labeling. We report the results for measuring the effectiveness of attack detection using *precision, recall* and *F-measure.* However, due to space limitations, we do not present the results for efficiency. Nonetheless, the efficiency for our system was comparable to that of other methods.

Very often, attackers hide the attacks within normal events, making attack detection very difficult. We define the *disguised attack parameter*, 'p' as follows:

$$p = \frac{number\ of\ Attack\ events}{number\ of\ Normal\ events + number\ of\ Attack\ events}$$

$where\ \ number\ of\ Attack\ events > 0\ \ and\ \ number\ of\ Normal\ events >= 0$

The value of 'p' lies in the range (0,1]. The attacks are not disguised when $p = 1$, since in this case the number of normal events is 0. As the value of 'p' decreases when the number of normal events is large, the attacks are disguised in a large number of normal events. In order to create disguised attack data, we add a random number of attack events at random locations in individual normal sessions and label the events as attack. This results in hiding the attacks within normal events such that the attack detection becomes difficult. We perform experiments to reflect these scenarios by varying the number of normal events in an attack session such that 'p' between 0 to 1.

4.1 Experiments with Clean Data (p = 1)

Figure 6 shows how the *F-measure* vary as we increase the window size 'S' from 1 to 20 for $p = 1$. We observe that conditional random fields and support vector machines perform similarly and their attack detection capability (*F-measure*) increases, slowly but steadily, as the number of sequential events analyzed together in a session increases. This shows that modeling a user session results in better attack detection accuracy compared to analyzing the events individually. However, decision trees and naive Bayes perform poorly and have low *F-measure* regardless of the window size 'S'.

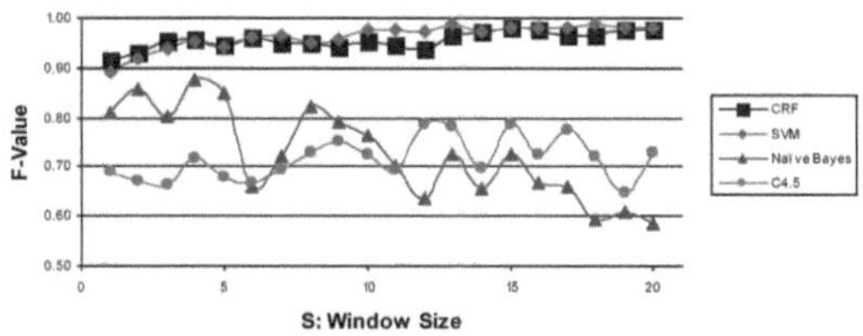

Fig. 6 Comparison of F-measure ($p = 1$)

4.2 Experiments with Disguised Attack Data (p = 0.60)

In order to test the robustness of the methods, we performed experiments with disguised attack data. We compare the results for all the four methods (conditional random fields, decision trees, naive Bayes and support vector machines) in Fig. 7 where we set $p = 0.60$. We observe that the conditional random fields performs best, outperforming all other methods and are robust in detecting disguised attacks. Their attack detection capability increases as the number of sequential events analyzed together in a session increases with the window size ‘S’. Support vector machines, decision trees and the naive Bayes did not perform well when the attack data is disguised in normal events.

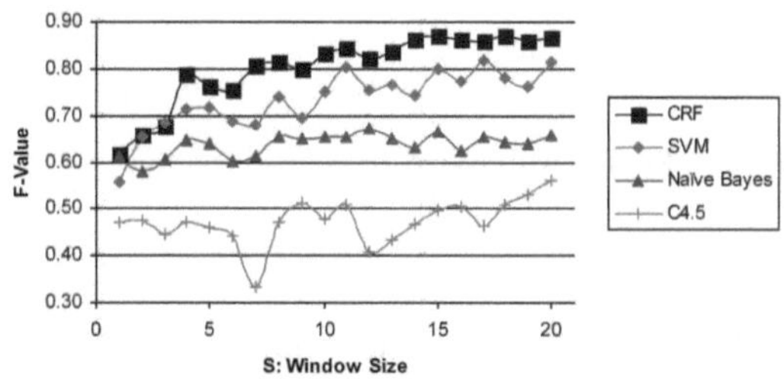

Fig. 7 Comparison of F-measure ($p = 0.60$)

Figures 8, 9, 10 and 11 represents the *precision, recall* and *F-measure* for conditional random fields, decision trees, naive Bayes and support vector machines.

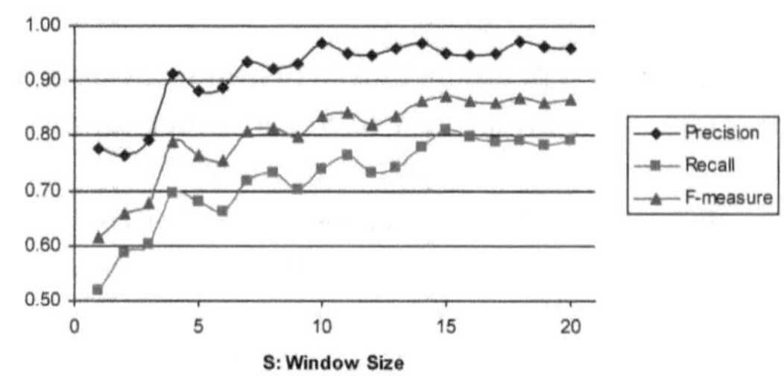

Fig. 8 Results with Conditional Random Fields

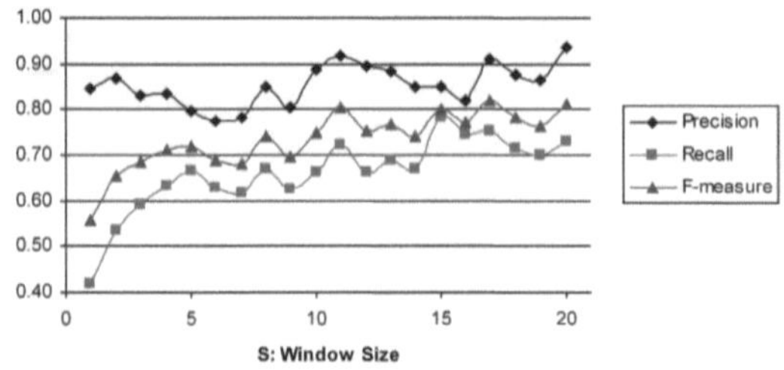

Fig. 9 Results with Support Vector Machines

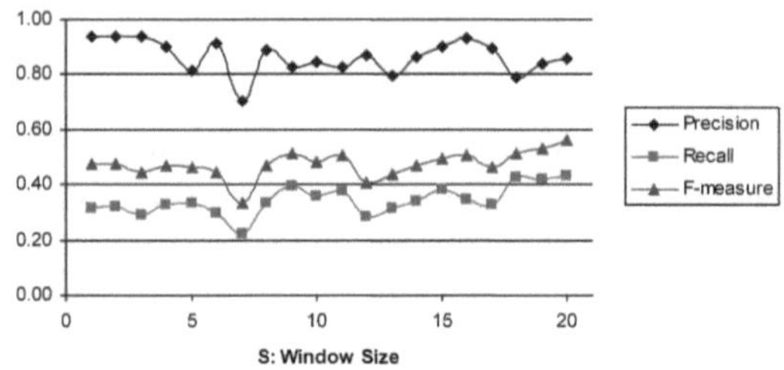

Fig. 10 Results with Decision Trees

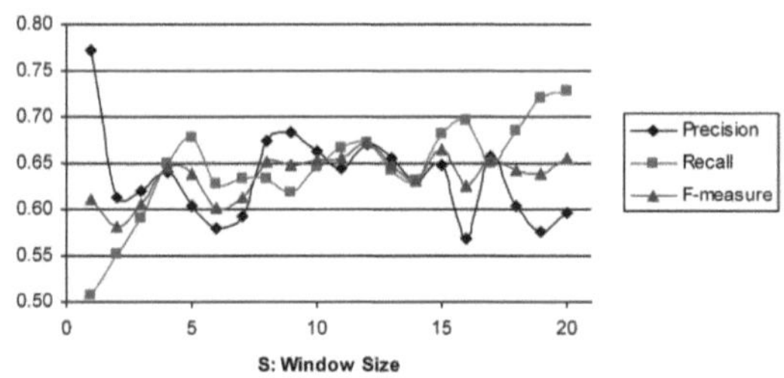

Fig. 11 Results with Naive Bayes

Figure 8 suggests that conditional random fields have high *F-measure* which increases steadily as the window size 'S' increases. The maximum value for *F-measure* is 0.87 at $S = 15$. This suggests that conditional random field generates less false alarms and the system performs reliably even when attacks are disguised.

For support vector machines, best results were obtained with *poly-kernel* and $c = 1$ and are reported in Fig. 9. We observe that support vector machines have moderate precision but low recall and hence low *F-measure*. The highest value for *F-measure* is 0.82 when $S = 17$.

Figure 10 represents that decision trees have very low *F-measure* suggesting that they cannot be effectively used for detecting anomalous data access when the attacks are disguised. The detection accuracy for decision trees remains fairly constant as 'S' increases. This is because the size of the decision tree remains constant even when the number of features increases since the goal of building a decision tree is to build a smallest tree with a large number of leaf nodes resulting in better classification. Hence, even when we increase the number of features, the size of the tree does not vary and their attack detection capability does not improve.

Results from Fig. 11 suggest that naive Bayes have low *F-measure* which fluctuates as the window size ‘S’ increases. There is little improvement in *F-measure* which remains low. The maximum value for *F-measure* is 0.67 at $S = 12$ suggesting that a system based on naive Bayes classifier is not able to detect attacks reliably.

4.3 Effect of ‘S’ on Attack Detection

In most situations, we want ‘S’ to be small since the complexity and the amount of history that needs to be maintained increases with ‘S’ and the system cannot respond in real time. Window size of 20 and beyond is often large resulting in delayed attack detection and high computation costs. Hence, we restrict ‘S’ to 20.

Table 1 Effect of ‘S’ on Attack Detection when $p = 0.60$

Size of Window ‘S’	Decision Trees	Naive Bayes	Support Vector Machines	Conditional Random Fields
1	0.47	0.61	0.56	0.62
2	0.47	0.58	0.66	0.66
3	0.44	0.61	0.69	0.68
4	0.47	0.65	0.71	0.79
5	0.46	0.64	0.72	0.76
6	0.44	0.60	0.69	0.76
7	0.33	0.61	0.68	0.81
8	0.47	0.65	0.74	0.81
9	0.51	0.65	0.70	0.80
10	0.48	0.65	0.75	0.83
11	0.51	0.66	0.80	0.84
12	0.41	**0.67**	0.75	0.82
13	0.44	0.65	0.77	0.84
14	0.47	0.63	0.74	0.86
15	0.50	0.66	0.80	**0.87**
16	0.50	0.63	0.77	0.86
17	0.47	0.65	**0.82**	0.86
18	0.51	0.64	0.78	0.87
19	0.53	0.64	0.76	0.86
20	**0.56**	0.66	0.81	0.86

We observe that conditional random fields perform best and their attack detection capability increases as the window size increases. Additionally, when we increase ‘S’ beyond 20 (not shown in the graphs), the attack detection accuracy for conditional random fields increases steadily and the system achieves very high *F-measure* when we analyze the entire session together. From Table 1, we observe that decision trees analyzes 20 events together to reach their best performance while conditional random fields achieve same performance by analyzing only a single event (i.e., $S = 1$). Similarly, naive Bayes peaked their performance at $S = 12$ while conditional random fields achieved the same performance at $S = 3$. Finally, support vector machines reach their best performance at window size $S = 17$ while the conditional random fields achieve the same performance at $S = 10$. *Hence, using conditional random fields attacks can be detected with higher accuracy at lower values of 'S' resulting in early attack detection and an efficient system.*

4.4 *Effect of 'p' on Attack Detection* $(0 < p < 1)$

We varied 'p', between 0 and 1 to analyze the robustness of conditional random fields with disguised attack data. In Fig. 12, we represent the effect of 'p' on conditional random fields for different values of 'S'. We make two observations; first, as 'p' decreases, it becomes difficult to detect attacks and second, irrespective of the value of 'p', the attack detection accuracy increases as 'S' increases.

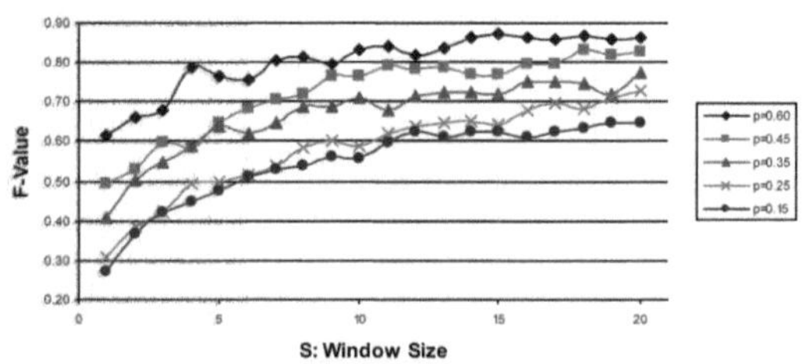

Fig. 12 Results for Conditional Random Fields when $0 < p < 1$

4.5 *Discussion of Results*

From the experiments, we observe that both conditional random fields and support vector machines performed very well when attacks were not disguised. However, support vector machines did not perform well while the conditional random fields were robust and detected disguised attacks reliably. This is because support vector machines perform classification in spatial domain thereby separating the classes by defining hyper-planes and distance measures. This results in higher attack detection accuracy when classes are distinct, but when the attacks are disguised, the system performs poorly. Decision trees and naive Bayes performed poorly in both cases. This is because they consider features of an event independently to label a particular event and then combine the results of all the features but do not consider the correlation between them. When the number of features is less, the error due to loss of correlation is less which increases with the number of features. Also, when 'S' increases, decision trees select subsets of features and does not use all of the input features and hence, their attack detection accuracy does not improve. However, conditional random fields can model long range dependencies among a sequence of events since they do not assume independence among the event vectors and perform effectively even when the attacks are disguised. This is critical as intrusion is not a one step process and an attacker performs sequence of steps to gain control of the data. Conditional random fields can capture long range dependencies in the sequence of events, and hence, perform better.

Also note that an experienced attacker may try to disguise attacks within more than 20 normal events. Even then, our system can detect attacks as the system does not consider events independently. Nonetheless, there is a tradeoff between disguise attack parameter 'p' and window size 'S'. In general, for better attack detection, 'S' must be increased when 'p' decreases. *The advantage of conditional random fields is that higher attack detection occurs at lower values of 'S' which is desirable.*

5 Related Work

The field of Intrusion Detection started in around 1980's and many techniques have been proposed for building intrusion detection systems. A number of surveys [4], [21] compare various well known intrusion detection methods such as data mining approaches which include association rules and frequent episodes, clustering, naive Bayes classifier, hidden Markov models, decision trees, support vector machines, Bayesian network approaches, neural networks, conditional random fields and others. Detecting data breaches has mainly focused on finding anomalous data queries based on these methods [6], [15]. These methods, however, consider data access patterns in isolation of the events which generates the data request. Similarly, systems which model application access such as web-application firewall [8] do not consider underlying data access and simply perform protocol analysis [9].

Methods for detecting malicious database modifications include mining data dependencies among data items to create dependency rules [15], clustering of data queries [26], modeling time difference between multiple transactions [14], building role profiles using naive Bayes classifiers to model normal behaviour [6], user profiling based on user query frequent item-sets [25], defining distance measures to determine the closeness of a set of attributes that are referenced together [7] and fingerprinting of data queries [19], [20]. These approaches are rule based, expensive to build and their signatures must be updated regularly. Additionally, they cannot detect previously unseen attacks and are specific to a particular application.

This is different from our work as we first combine the application access logs and the associated data requests to generate unified logs and then use session modeling to analyze a sequence of events together rather than analyzing them individually to detect malicious data access. Our system is application independent and therefore can be widely used. Finally, we model application-data interaction which does not depend upon a user and therefore does not change overtime when compared with user profiling based approaches. We also compare our work with [3] and [9]. In [3], the authors describe a tool for performing intrusion detection at application level. Their system uses Apache web server to implement an audit data source and the collected information is used to monitor the behaviour of the web server. This is different from our work as we are interested in analyzing the behaviour of a web application in conjunction to the underlying data. The system in [9] analyzes application layer protocols at the network level. This is also different from our work as we are interested in preventing malicious data access and our system operates at the application layer rather than at the network layer.

6 Conclusions

In this paper we proposed and evaluated a novel approach to analyze user sessions using sliding window for effective intrusion detection at application level. We also argued that combining application access logs and the corresponding data access logs to generate unified logs eliminates the need to analyze them separately thereby resulting in an efficient and accurate system. From our experiments we conclude that as the window size 'S' increases, the attack detection accuracy increases which justifies our motive of modeling user sessions rather than analyzing the events individually. Our results show that conditional random fields performed better than other methods and were robust to disguised attack data. Further, our framework is scalable for future applications and is not specific to any particular application except for data gathering. Finally, following good software engineering practices and taking care of logging mechanism during application development would not only help in application testing and related areas but would also provide necessary framework for building better and efficient application intrusion detection systems.

Acknowledgements We thank the students at the Department of Computer Science and Software Engineering, The University of Melbourne for helping us to collect data for our experiments.

References

1. ANSI/X3/SPARC Study Group on Data Base Management Systems: Interim Report, FDT (bulletin of ACM SIGMOD) 7, No.2, 1975.
2. osCommerce, Open Source Online Shop E-Commerce Solutions. Last accessed: January 08, 2008. `http://www.oscommerce.com/`.
3. M. Almgren and U. Lindqvist. Application-Integrated Data Collection for Security Monitoring. In *4th International Symposium on Recent Advances in Intrusion Detection*, pages 22–36. LNCS, Springer-Verlag, Vol (2212), 2001.
4. S. Axelsson. Research in Intrusion-Detection Systems: A Survey. Technical Report 98-17, Department of Computer Engineering, Chalmers University of Technology, 1998.
5. R. Bace and P. Mell. *Intrusion Detection Systems*. Gaithersburg, MD : Computer Security Division, Information Technology Laboratory, NIST, 2001.

6. E. Bertino, A. Kamra, E. Terzi, and A. Vakali. Intrusion Detection in RBAC-Administered Databases. In *21st Annual Computer Security Applications Conference*. IEEE, 2005.
7. C. Y. Chung, M. Gertz, and K. Levitt. DEMIDS: A Misuse Detection System for Database Systems. In *3rd International IFIP TC-11 WG11.5 Working Conference on Integrity and Internal Control in Information Systems*, pages 159–178. Kluwer Academic Pub., 1999.
8. L. Desmet, F. Piessens, W. Joosen, and P. Verbaeten. Bridging the Gap Between Web Application Firewalls and Web Applications. In *4th ACM workshop on Formal methods in security, FMSE*, pages 67–77. ACM, 2006.
9. H. Dreger, A. Feldmann, M. Mai, V. Paxson, and R. Sommer. Dynamic Application-Layer Protocol Analysis for Network Intrusion Detection. In *15th Usenix Security Symposium*, pages 257–272, 2006.
10. K. K. Gupta, B. Nath, and K. Ramamohanarao. Application Intrusion Detection Dataset. `http://www.csse.unimelb.edu.au/~kgupta`.
11. K. K. Gupta, B. Nath, and K. Ramamohanarao. Layered Approach using Conditional Random Fields for Intrusion Detection. *IEEE Transactions on Dependable and Secure Computing*. In Press.
12. K. K. Gupta, B. Nath, and K. Ramamohanarao. Conditional Random Fields for Intrusion Detection. In *21st International Conference on Advanced Information Networking and Applications Workshops*, pages 203–208. IEEE, 2007.
13. K. K. Gupta, B. Nath, K. Ramamohanarao, and A. Kazi. Attacking Confidentiality: An Agent Based Approach. In *IEEE International Conference on Intelligence and Security Informatics*, pages 285–296. LNCS, Springer Verlag, Vol (3975), 2006.
14. Y. Hu and B. Panda. Identification of Malicious Transactions in Database Systems. In *7th International Database Engineering and Applications Symposium*, pages 329–335. IEEE, 2003.
15. Y. Hu and B. Panda. A Data Mining Approach for Database Intrusion Detection. In *ACM symposium on Applied Computing*, pages 711–716. ACM, 2004.
16. D. Klein and C. D. Manning. Conditional Structure versus Conditional Estimation in NLP Models. In *ACL-02 Conference on Empirical methods in Natural Language Processing Vol (10)*, pages 9–16. Association for Computational Linguistics, Morristown, NJ, USA, 2002.
17. T. Kudu. CRF++: Yet another CRF toolkit. Last accessed: February 9, 2008. `http://crfpp.sourceforge.net/`.
18. J. Lafferty, A. McCallum, and F. Pereira. Conditional Random Fields: Probabilistic Models for Segmenting and Labeling Sequence Data. In *18th International Conference on Machine Learning*, pages 282–289, 2001.
19. S. Y. Lee, W. L. Low, and P. Y. Wong. Learning Fingerprints for a Database Intrusion Detection System. In *7th European Symposium on Research in Computer Security, Vol (2502)*, pages 264–279. LNCS, Springer-Verlag, 2002.
20. W. L. Low, J. Lee, and P. Teoh. DIDAFIT: Detecting Intrusions in Databases Through Fingerprinting Transactions. In *4th International Conference on Enterprise Information Systems*, pages 264–269, 2002.
21. A. Patcha and J.-M. Park. An Overview of Anomaly Detection Techniques: Existing Solutions and Latest Technological Trends. *Computer Networks*, 51(12):3448–3470, 2007.
22. C. Sutton and A. McCallum. An Introduction to Conditional Random Fields for Relational Learning. In *Introduction to Statistical Relational Learning*. MIT, 2006.
23. I. H. Witten and E. Frank. *Data Mining: Practical machine learning tools and techniques*. Morgan Kaufmann, 2005.
24. N. Ye, X. Li, Q. Chen, S. M. Emran, and M. Xu. Probabilistic Techniques for Intrusion Detection Based on Computer Audit Data. *IEEE Transactions on Systems, Man and Cybernetics, Part A: Systems and Humans*, 31(4):266–274, 2001.
25. Y. Zhong and Xiao-Lin-Qin. Research on Algorithm of User Query Frequent Itemsets Mining. In *3rd International Conference on Machine Learning and Cybernetics, Vol (3)*, pages 1671–1676. IEEE, 2004.
26. Y. Zhong, Z. Zhu, and X. Qin. A Clustering Method Based on Data Queries and Its Application in Database Intrusion Detection. In *4th International Conference on Machine Learning and Cybernetics, Vol (4)*, pages 2096–2101. IEEE, 2005.

6. E. Bertino, A. Kamra, E. Terzi, and A. Vakali. Intrusion Detection in RBAC-administered Databases. In 21st Annual Computer Security Applications Conference. IEEE, 2005.
7. C. Y. Chung, M. Gertz, and K. Levitt. DEMIDS: A Misuse Detection System for Database Systems. [illegible]

[illegible]

A Product Machine Model for Anomaly Detection of Interposition Attacks on Cyber-Physical Systems

Carlo Bellettini and Julian L. Rrushi

Abstract In this paper we propose an anomaly intrusion detection model based on shuffle operation and product machines targeting persistent interposition attacks on control systems. These attacks actually are undetectable by the most advanced system call monitors as they issue no system calls and are stealthy enough to transfer control to hijacked library functions without letting their saved instruction pointers get stored on stack. We exploit the fact that implementations of control protocols running in control systems, which in turn are attached to physical systems such as power plants and electrical substations, exhibit strong regularities in terms of sequences of function calls and system calls issued during protocol transactions. The main idea behind the proposed approach is to introduce NULL function calls within a Modbus binary and to apply the shuffle operation between them and existing function calls. We then devise and implement a product machine capable of recognizing the shuffle representation of function call and system call regularities. A sensor uses a unidirectional interprocess communication channel based on shared memory to receive profile data from a Modbus process, and subsequently submits them to the product machine. We describe an experimental evaluation of our model on an ARM-based Modbus device and demonstrate that the proposed model overcomes the limitations of state of the art approaches with regard to detection of persistent interposition attacks on control systems.

1 Introduction

With the advent of low cost computing the control systems industry is replacing its proprietary legacy hardware with state of the art devices. The interconnectivity of control systems has transitioned drastically from minimal communications over

Carlo Bellettini and Julian L. Rrushi
Università degli Studi di Milano, Dipartimento di Informatica e Comunicazione, Via Comelico 39/41, 20135 Milano, Italy, e-mail: {carlo.bellettini, julian.rrushi1}@unimi.it

Please use the following format when citing this chapter:

Bellettini, C. and Rrushi, J.L., 2008, in IFIP International Federation for Information Processing, Volume 278; *Proceedings of the IFIP TC 11 23rd International Information Security Conference*; Sushil Jajodia, Pierangela Samarati, Stelvio Cimato; (Boston: Springer), pp. 285–299.

dedicated serial-line channels to Ethernet TCP/IP networks connecting control systems to each-other and often to the enterprise network and/or Internet. Proprietary communication protocols and operating systems have been in part replaced with open standards such as IEC 61850, DNP3, Modbus, IEC 60870-5, etc., and modern operating systems such as Windows CE or real-time variants of Linux, respectively. The actually high connectivity of control systems along with their use of standard technology expose control networks to a variety of network attack vectors. In fact several studies have shown that control systems are subject to various kinds of vulnerability relying in their data, security administration, architecture, networks, and platforms[18]. In particular, low-level coding vulnerabilities exploitable by memory corruption attacks have been found to be widespread in control system code. Unclassified case studies include a heap overflow in Inter Control Center Protocol (ICCP)[19], a heap overflow in LiveData Protocol Server [8], faulty mappings between protocol elements, i.e. handles and protocol data unit addresses, and main memory addresses in OLE for Process Control (OPC)[13][20], and faulty mappings between data items in a protocol data unit (PDU) as addressed by Modbus and the memory locations where those data items are stored[3].
In this paper we provide an anomaly intrusion detection technique based on concepts which we borrowed and adapted from automata theoretic models of parallel computation, namely shuffle operations and product machines[5, 9]. The proposed technique has been devised to detect persistent interposition attacks[15] and is carried out through sensor agents placed in control systems. These sensor agents gather execution data from a process to be protected and apply an automata–based recognition algorithm for the purpose of determining whether an intrusion is taking place. In our opinion the very first line of defense from network attacks on control systems should be some host-based intrusion prevention approach such as the one provided in [4]. Nevertheless, counting for the highly sensitive role played by control systems in monitoring and controlling critical infrastructures, additional security levels are necessary for countering network attacks. Moving along this line the proposed intrusion detection technique is intended as an additional layer of defense.
The remaining of this paper is organized as follows. Section 2 provides the motivations behind our contribution and describes representative related work. Section 3 provides the main ideas behind the proposed intrusion detection model. Section 4 describes an experimental evaluation of this model on a Modbus device[12] running an embedded Linux operation system. Section 5 summarizes our contribution and concludes the paper.

2 Motivations and Related Work

Anomaly intrusion detection systems (IDS) based on system call information rely on monitoring interactions between a process in user land and an underlying operating system kernel. A process to be protected is sent regular data in input several times and in isolation, i.e. off line. All system calls which are issued to the kernel

by this process are analyzed for the purpose of building a normal execution profile. In literature such an operation is often referred to as the learning phase. In monitoring mode an anomaly IDS starts monitoring system calls issued by a process to be protected and compares. Such an IDS compares the information extracted from monitored system calls with the information extracted from system calls issued during the learning phase. If deviations are identified, then the IDS concludes that an intrusion has taken place, hence the detection type – anomaly detection.
Thus, a process–to–kernel interaction through system calls is used as a mechanism for profiling a process to be protected. Along their way system call based IDS have had various limitations in extracting information from system calls in a proper and thorough way. Nevertheless, modern system call based IDS are quite powerful in exploiting system call information. If we assume an ideal system call based IDS, i.e. an IDS which has the capabilities of capturing the whole context of process–to–kernel interactions through system calls, could we state that we have in hand an IDS which is capable of detecting all known attacks on a protected process ? The answer to our question comes directly from the research work discussed in [15] that describes an attack technique which has been demonstrated to be capable of evading powerful system call based IDS. Authors refer to such a technique as persistent interposition attack, and we verified its offensive capabilities on control systems.
A persistent interposition attack relies upon an initial shellcode injection attack. After gaining execution flow control, injected shellcode corrupts pointer tables such as the global offset table (GOT) in ELF, virtual table pointers in C++ code, or any specific support for plug-ins and modules. The aforementioned corruption is carried out in such a way that attack code interposes itself between a target process and *write()* & *read()* functions of a C library. A persistent interposition attack intercepts in a man in the middle (MITM) style and subsequently modifies either all or selected parts of data read and/or written by a target process. Taking into account that a persistent interposition attack only modifies the I/O data stream of a target process, and does so by limiting itself not to issue any system calls or corrupt any data stored on stack, in traditional computer systems it may not be sufficient for attackers to achieve their objectives. That said, from our evaluation of persistent interposition attacks as applied on control systems results that such attacks are extremely powerful and fully sufficient to achieve attacker goals. In fact relevant objectives of attacks on control systems center around gaining control over control protocol frames holding commands to underlying critical infrastructure utilities or status information to be processed by a master station.
Obviously all those IDS which rely only on sequences of system calls issued by a given process have no means of detecting a persistent interposition attack since the latter absolutely does not cause any changes to sequences of system calls. Thus, a persistent interposition attack issues no system calls on a target platform. The VtPath model[6] goes beyond sequences of system calls and points towards call stack information in conjunction with system call information. As a system call is issued by a given process, VtPath extracts the system call name and the value of instruction pointer (IP) register. Further, VtPath extracts from the stack all routine return addresses preliminarily saved on stack and puts them into what authors refer to as

a virtual stack list. The value of IP register is then added to the end of the virtual stack list. For the purpose of characterizing a transition from a system call A to another system call B VtPath employs virtual stack lists. It uses them to build a logical virtual path from A to B that abstracts execution from the moment the process issued system call A to the moment the process issued system call B. If during the monitoring phase VtPath cannot construct the virtual stack list, then it assumes that a successful attack has corrupted return addresses that were stored on it. This fact is referred to as a stack anomaly. If an address is missing in the virtual stack list, then we have a return address anomaly. If the extracted value of IP register does not correspond to the system call name, then we have a system call anomaly. If there are any deviations in the virtual paths between two system calls, then we have a virtual path anomaly.

The work in [7] also combines system call information with call stack information defining an observation as a vector of a system call number along with the return addresses present on the stack in the moment this system call is issued. Executions then are thought as arbitrary-length sequences of observations and are used to create the so-called execution graph characterizing the behavior of a process to be protected. In both the VtPath model and the execution graph model we can observe that the factors which create some kind of virtual fence to prevent injected shellcode from achieving attack goals without being detected from the IDS, i.e. call stack configuration and systems calls, are situated in the offensive space of injected shellcode itself. In fact nothing prevents injected shellcode from writing to a corrupted stack in order to restore return addresses before a system call is issued, hence evade detection. Further, although injected shellcode cannot issue a system call itself since that way it would cause what VtPath refers to as a system call anomaly, the work in [10] has demonstrated that the injected shellcode could jump to existing legitimate code in order to have that code execute the system call for it, i.e. for injected shellcode. Memory locations and registers are corrupted in such a way that the execution control is returned to injected shellcode after the issuance of a system call.

We deem approaches such as VtPath model and execution graph model to be still capable of detecting system call issuing attacks on control systems if an additional observable factor is employed, namely transaction response time. We exploiting the fact that industrial control communications are supposed to be real-time. In a typical Modbus transaction, for instance, a master station sends a Modbus request protocol data unit (PDU) to a slave device. The slave device examines the request and is supposed to reply with either a Modbus Response PDU or Modbus Exception Response PDU within a time limit which in most cases is in the range of just a few milliseconds. The response time of a slave device in normal transactions may slide between upper and lower time boundaries within the allowable response time. Let's take as an example a scenario where we have a sensor running on each slave device on a field. Let's assume that attackers acquire access to a process control network through a wireless node and start sending unauthenticated Modbus request PDU's to a target slave device on the field in order to exploit a memory corruption vulnerability in, say, a cryptographic routine.

If injected shellcode will try to reconstruct a corrupted stack each time it has existing legitimate code issue a system call for it, then the sensor on the compromised field device will notice a considerable variation in the response time of the compromised device. This is due to the fact that reconstructing a call stack several times and regaining execution control from existing code requires a considerable amount of time. Powerful IDS models such VtPath and execution graph though don't have the instruments necessary for detecting persistent interposition attacks. As stated above persistent interposition attacks issue no system call. Further, after having intercepted and possibly modified function call arguments stored on stack, a persistent interposition attack uses a jump instruction to transfer execution control to the real *read()* or *write()* functions of the C library. In a system running on an ARM microprocessor[2] we had injected shellcode which transferred execution control to the real *read()* or *write()* functions by writing directly to R15 register or executing an unconditional branch instruction. This way the return address of the injected shellcode will not be saved on stack and no virtual path anomaly will take place. For more information on persistent interposition attacks please refer to [15].

3 A Product Machine Model for Anomaly Detection

The information extracted from user land by powerful system call monitors such as VtPath model and execution graph model for the purpose of creating a process profile consists of the value of program counter (PC) and return addresses saved on stack. We deem PC is quite a suitable mechanism for forcing attack code not to issue any system calls, at least not by itself. With regard to return addresses saved on stack we see several weaknesses which could allow an attacker to evade intrusion detection, namely:

- Information used for detection is stored on buffers which attack code can easily corrupt. In fact nothing prevents attack code from writing to selected locations on stack before a system call is issued and intrusion verifications are made.
- If attackers perform a deep analysis on target code and are patient enough to go through it, detection information itself, i.e. return addresses, may be calculated by attack code and used to restore a corrupted stack in order to cover attack traces in the moment of intrusion verification.

In fact a good part of implementations of control protocols and/or related libraries are provided by third party software companies and are accessible to everybody with enough financial support. A dedicated attacker could get the code of a target control protocol and analyze how stack is laid out immediately after gaining the execution control of a target process by transferring it to injected shellcode. Function call paths could also be analyzed as they directly influence stack layout. Further, none of the information employed by other models for intrusion detection is actually usable in detecting persistent interposition attacks which limit themselves to intercepting and modifying the I/O data stream of a target process without issuing any system calls. The proposed detection model aims at avoiding these weaknesses.

On one hand the approach obfuscates legitimate function call paths, thus invalidates attacker's knowledge required for evasion. On the other hand it prevents attack code from corrupting profile data generated by a monitored process. We first explain the concepts of our anomaly detection model. Then in the other section we describe the application of the proposed model to ARM-based devices with the premise that it is straightforward to do the same on control devices equipped with other embedded CPU architectures.

In the proposed model the information used as a basic building block in the activity of creating the profile of a process to be protected consists of the memory address of an instruction which issues a call to a defined function and the memory address where execution control is transferred shortly thereafter. Thus, when execution flow moves from one function A to another function or code block B, we're concerned with extracting the address of the instruction in A which issued the function call and the address in B where execution control is transferred. As in different executions a parent process along with any child processes it forks could be loaded at different virtual memory locations, we use PC-relative addresses for identifying the memory locations in functions A and B where a function call is issued and where subsequently execution control is transferred, respectively. CPU architectures have a predefined register which acts as a PC. PC-relative addresses do not change in different runs, therefore they can be reliably used as profile data. In the proposed anomaly detection model we consider the PC-relative address of a memory location where execution flow is being transferred as a result of a function call.

That relative address in reality is an offset from PC in the moment a function call is issued. If we are working on a l-bit architecture and for the sake of simplicity assume that respective memory addresses will consist of l bits, by using PC-relative addresses we shrink the $2l$ bits needed as profile data, i.e. l bits of the address where a function call issuing instruction is stored + l bits of the address where execution flow is transferred, into only l bits of a PC-relative address. Thus, a PC-relative address serves as some sort of logical binding between the memory address of an instruction which calls a defined function and the memory address of an instruction to which execution control is transferred. If in formal language notation we define a letter as a PC-relative address, then the alphabet containing all letters which are of our interest, i.e. PC-relative addresses, may be defined as follows:

$$\Sigma = \{x \; / \; alph(x) = \{0,1\}, |x| = l\}$$

where $alph(x)$ denotes the symbols which appear in a given letter, and $|x|$ denotes a letter length in terms of number of symbols which appear in it along with their frequency.

If we start monitoring a process, extract a PC-relative address, where execution control is transferred, from each function call issuing instruction actually executed, and concatenate those PC-relative addresses, i.e. letters in formal language notation, in their order of appearance, then we get a word which characterizes important aspects of a process execution, namely what we refer to as inter-function transfer paths. At this point we could extend the concept of profile data to include the memory address of an instruction which issues a system call along with the system call number of a service requested to an operating system. The memory address of an instruction which issues a system call could still be relative to the value which PC register had at some predefined entry point in the beginning of process execution. Further, the system call number could be padded to l bits in order to give it an appearance which complies with how we define a letter. Thus, a given inter-function transfer path is an ordered sequence of l-bit values taken as a function call is issued or as an operating system service is requested through a system call.

Let Σ denote an alphabet, i.e. a finite set of symbols or letters. If we don't consider predefined address space ranges where a process may be loaded, then the set of all possible arbitrary behaviors of a given process running on a l-bit architecture is characterized by the set of words, i.e. letter concatenations, as shown in the following definition:

$$\Delta = (\cup_{j=1}^{2^l} x_j)^*$$

where U denotes the union operator, x_j is an arbitrary letter, i.e. $x_j \varepsilon \Sigma$, and $*$ denotes the Kleene closure, i.e. Kleene star operation.

At this point we decide to introduce diversity into legitimate inter-function transfer paths of a process to be protected. We do so by inserting some NULL functions into the code of that process. NULL functions are inserted in such a way that they preserve the correct computability of a given program. For instance, if before inserting the NULL functions, say *w()* and *v()* into a program which has three functions such as *a()*, *b()* and *c()*, and where *a()* calls both *b()* and *c()* in that order, then an instance of a valid sequence of functions where execution flow passes through as a process proceeds with its execution would be:

$$\{w, v, a, v, a, b, a, c, v\}$$

As a result of a correct insertion of NULL functions into a program to be protected, a new inter-function transfer path will be created upon the previous one. The insertion of NULL functions into a program generally may cause deviations from the logical bindings via PC-relative addresses which were already present in the program before it got instrumented. Let's refer to these deviations as jitter. The new inter-function transfer path then will be composed of those original logical bindings via PC-relative addresses as changed by jitter, interleaved with new logical bindings via PC-relative addresses. These new logical bindings are due to new function call issuing instructions inserted as a result of program instrumentation. NULL functions may be defined as having an arbitrary number of arguments and local variables with arbitrary lengths. Allocation of memory for these variables would contribute to further obfuscate the stack layout. Considering the motivation behind introducing function arguments and local variables in NULL functions, their values could be arbitrary as long as they respect the type of the variables to which they are assigned. In addition, it is also useful to insert NULL system calls into a program to be protected as well. Going back to our formal language parallelism, we may notice that the word which represents a given inter-function transfer path of an instrumented

program is the result of the shuffle operation between the word which represents the inter-function transfer path of the same program before getting instrumented as subjected to jitter, and the word created by concatenating the logical bindings of NULL functions inserted into the instrumented program.
At this point we've built the basis for discussing how to proceed with an application to anomaly detection of the concepts described above. According to our model we run an instrumented program on a control system to be protected by sending it regular PDUs, namely those frames which should be expected to be received by this control system when it will be operational in a PCN. While doing so we make sure that the control system in question is not under attack, such as for instance by testing it in isolated laboratory settings. As a process under observation replies to various normal PDUs, we extract information about the function calls along with system calls it issues. In order to facilitate construction of a product machine to be used to recognize legitimate process behaviors, we need to differentiate between PC-relative addresses in an inter-function transfer path which represent original function or system calls, and PC-relative addresses in that inter-function transfer path which represent NULL function or NULL system calls.
For such a purpose we first record only those PC-relative addresses which represent calls to functions found in the original version of a program to be protected. Thus, the inter-function transfer paths we obtain in this step are those inter-function transfer paths which could have been observed while learning the normal profile of an original program, but which have been altered by jitter. We then repeat the profile learning procedure, but this time we record all PC-relative addresses in each function or system call actually issued. As a result of such a learning phase we have in hand a set of inter-function transfer paths which characterize legitimate behaviors of a process to be protected. Furthermore, we know which PC-relative addresses in an inter-function transfer path are due to original function or system call issues, and which of them are due to NULL function or system call issues.

The language defined as:

$$\Gamma = \{y \; \varepsilon \; \Delta \; / \; y \; \textit{has been observed during learning phase}\}$$

defines all normal behaviors of an original program to be protected. Γ is a finite language since there is a defined finite number of different function call sequences which a process follows during different executions upon receipt of a finite set of input frames.

In general, if Θ is the language composed of words created by concatenating letters, i.e. PC-relative addresses, of NULL functions and NULL system calls, then the language Υ which defines all normal behaviors of a program instrumented in all possible ways is defined as:

$$\Upsilon = \Theta \,||\, \Gamma'$$

where Γ' is composed of words representing inter-function transfer paths in Γ as possibly altered by jitter.
Our anomaly detection model uses a product machine as a recognizer of normal behaviors, i.e. words representing inter-function transfer paths which have been ob-

served during the learning phases, of a process to be protected. While a shuffle automaton could instead have been used in our model since we use shuffle operation to affect the behavior of program, we deem a product machine to be more appropriate in our context since we do not use a shuffle closure operation. According to our model we build a first finite state machine for recognizing strings made of PC-relative addresses which represent original function or system calls as altered by jitter, and a second finite state machine for recognizing PC-relative addresses which represent NULL function calls or NULL system calls. The ultimate recognizer of legitimate behaviors of a protected process then is the product of these two finite state machines. During the monitoring phase complete words of PC-relative addresses are collected from a monitored process and fed to the product machine. If such a machine recognizes those words, then the monitored process is exhibiting normal behavior, otherwise our model deems that the execution control of a monitored process has been hijacked.

4 Experimental Evaluation and Technical Details

Fig. 1 depicts a cyber-physical system where an experimental evaluation of our anomaly detection model was carried out. Note that the physical system, i.e. a nuclear power plant in our case, is simulated. The experiments were carried out on a Modbus device based on a 32-bit ARM microprocessor and running an embedded Linux operation system. More precisely, we worked on FreeModbus[21], which is a free implementation of the popular Modbus protocol especially targeted for embedded systems. For the purpose of experimentation we integrated FreeModbus into uClinux[1], an embedded operating system most suited for use in microcontrollers. In ARM microprocessors it is the register R15 which acts as PC, consequently while applying our model to an ARM architecture we use R15 as a base register to allow relative addressing. In fact register R15 at any moment holds a value which is the sum of the memory address of an instruction currently executing and 8 (well, in most cases, depends on implementation), but this fact has no affect on our assumption of logical binding between the memory address of a function call issuing instruction and the memory address holding an instruction to which execution control is subsequently transferred as a result of that function call.

In an application of our model to ARM we extract from each actually executed *BL* (branch with link) instruction, i.e. an ARM function call issuing instruction, what in ARM is referred to as a target address. The target address is a R15-relative address where execution control is being transferred, and represents exactly what in our model we refer to as logical binding. Further, we extract the address of each actually executed *SWI* instruction, i.e. an ARM system call issuing instruction, along with the system call number of a service requested to an operating system. Each extracted *SWI* address will be relative to R15 in a predefined entry point. The Modbus processes we experimented with acted as slaves, in the sense that they received requests and responded with responses. In fact in general configurations control

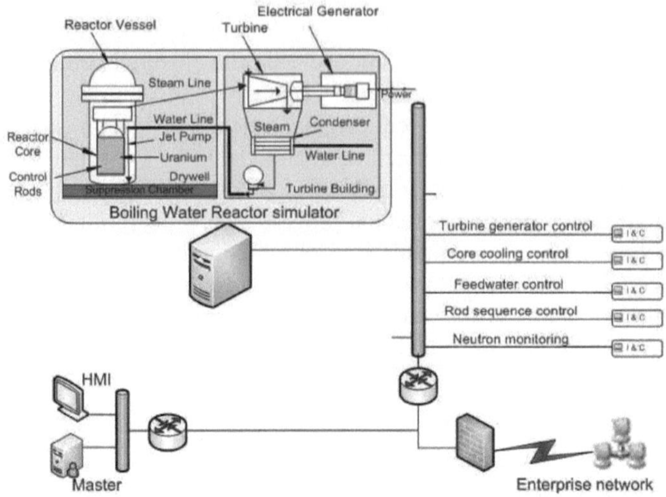

Fig. 1 An experimental testbed where the anomaly detection approach was practically evaluated

devices on a field act as slaves, except several cases in which they relay or even control protocol frames between other field devices. We coded a software agent which we used to extract data from a Modbus process as the latter proceeds with its execution. Further, we coded through the Concurrent Hierarchical State Machine language system[11] a small implementation of a product machine which we used as an intrusion detection mechanism following the proposed approach.

We started with a monitoring phase on FreeModbus tracing both its function calls and system calls in order to determine its actual inter-function transfer paths. We used testing utilities such as *modpoll* to send to the monitored process several Modbus request PDU's holding function codes of those which FreeModbus actually supports. We defined several NULL functions and a few NULL system calls which we inserted into the code of FreeModbus in such a way that the inter-function transfer paths newly formed were the result of a shuffle operation between R15-relative addresses of existing function calls and system calls as perturbed by jitter, and the inserted NULL function calls and NULL system calls. Rather than creating a profile of the whole FreeModbus code, we operated only on that part which actually executes during a Modbus transaction, which is from the moment a Modbus Request PDU is received from a socked till either a Modbus Response PDU or a Modbus Exception Response PDU is sent through a socket[12]. We used this defined interval as operational boundaries also during the monitoring phase.

Thus, the sensor agent starts to gather monitoring data from the Modbus process from the moment the latter receives a Modbus Request PDU. When a response is

generated by the Modbus process, the sensor agent feeds to the product machine implementation the string of monitoring data gathered that far. After doing so the sensor agent starts from the beginning. We set up an interprocess communication channel to allow the Modbus process send monitoring data to the sensor agent. The instrumentation of FreeModbus allowed us to also enable the Modbus process to send monitoring data to the sensor agent. We used shared memory as an interprocess communication mechanism. It is the sensor agent which creates a shared memory segment by issuing a *shmget()* system call. The shared memory permissions were such that the owner of the shared memory segment, i.e. the sensor agent, was allowed to attach to it in read mode, while others such as the Modbus process were allowed to attach to it in write mode. Thus, the Modbus process was supposed to write to the shared memory but not read from it, while the sensor agent was supposed to read from memory but not write to it. We used semaphores to synchronize the passage of monitoring data from the Modbus process to the sensor agent.
The intervention which enabled FreeModbus to send data to the sensor agent consisted in locating each *BL* instructions and subsequently inserting instrumentation instructions right before each one of them in order to extract their R15-relative *target_address* and write it to the shared memory so the sensor agent may grab it immediately. Further, we used the kernel to retrieve both the relative return address after a system call has been issued and the number identifying the service requested to the operating system. The defensive characteristics of our anomaly detection model which overcome the limitations of other powerful system call monitors described in previous sections are the following:

- As the sensor agent gathers monitoring data from the Modbus process throughout a transaction, an attacker cannot write valid data to the shared memory used for interprocess communication. This is due to the fact that an attacker does not know a valid inter-function transfer path as the original inter-function transfer paths have been shuffled with NULL function/system call R15-relative addresses.
- Attack code cannot overwrite monitoring data produced by legitimate FreeModbus instructions since due to process synchronization through semaphores those data are read by the sensor agent as soon as written on shared memory by FreeModbus.

Our anomaly detection model is devised to detect attacks which appear in an intra-process interposition form, therefore operating system security mechanisms should be properly employed to ensure that such attacks do not evolve into an inter-process interposition form. If a compromised Modbus process happens to run as a privileged account such as root in uClinux, then attack code could attach to a sensor process and take full control over its execution. In that case attackers could use DynInst API[14], which in earlier studies has turned out to be an easy to use and powerful attack tool[17]. An inter-process interposition form is also acquirable in the case both a Modbus process and a sensor process share user ID (uid) or group ID (gid). Therefore, a reasonable deployment of our anomaly detection model would consist in a Modbus process running as an unprivileged user, say *Modbus*, and in a sensor running as an unprivileged user, say *sensor*. Further, the uid and gid of user *sensor*

should be different than the uid and gid of user *Modbus*, respectively.
Let's see how our anomaly detection model behaves in front of a persistent interposition attack and an attack such as the one described in [10]. During the *initial exploit phase* phase of a persistent interposition attack a memory corruption vulnerability is used to transfer execution control to initial attack code. Such code is responsible for possibly downloading and storing bootstrap code, interposing that bootstrap code, and cleaning up any damage caused by the execution control hijacking. If the hijacking of execution control to the initial attack code is done through corruption of a return address or frame pointer stored on stack, our model is not likely to detect it since such a hijacking won't involve any of the *BL* instructions we keep under monitoring. If corruption of any function pointers within the address space of a target process is used to hijack execution control to the initial attack code, as it may be the case of a heap overflow or format string attack corrupting an entry in a function pointer table such as GOT, then our model will detect it. Considering that GOT in addition to ELF is also part of BFLT format[16], which in turn is used for formatting uClinux executables, let's take an example in which an attacker corrupts a GOT pointer to a library function *f()*. Let an original inter-function transfer path produced by a given application of a shuffle operation be $\{h, s, g, l, t, w, y, m, n\}$, where w is the address of function *f()* relative to R15, m is the address of a system call issuing *SWI* instruction relative to R15 in a predefined entry point, and n is a system call number padded to 32 bits.
Since the 32-bit data value in GOT which pointed to *f()* has been corrupted with a value which points to injected code, when function *f()* is called by the Modbus process execution control is transferred to injected code. During such a hijacking the *BL* instruction which was supposed to transfer execution control to the w R15-relative address, i.e. call function *f()*, in fact transfers execution control to, say, v R15-relative address, i.e. calls injected code. The inter-function transfer path extracted during the monitoring phase from such a hijacked process would be $\{h, s, g, l, t, v, y, m, n\}$. When this inter-function transfer path is fed by a sensor to the respective product machine, that product machine will not recognize such an observed inter-function transfer path, causing the IDS system to visualize intrusion alarms on HMI.
Regardless of detection of any hijackings of execution control to initial attack code, our model results to be capable of detecting a persistent interposition attack during what authors in [15] refer to as *bootstrapping phase*. In fact during the *interposing bootstrap code step* of *initial exploit phase* initial attack code modifies one or more function pointers in order to interpose bootstrap code. The effects of corruption of function pointers are observed in *bootstrapping phase* when bootstrapping code is invoked during all *read* and *write* operations. As each of these invocations takes place, a sensor registers from the *BL* instruction issuing the call the R15-relative address of the instruction of bootstrapping code where execution control is transferred. Such an address will cause a deviation in the legitimate inter-function transfer path making it unrecognizable by the product machine. The same consideration holds for *operational phase* during which execution control is continuously hijacked, consequently causing deviations in observed inter-function transfer paths which in turn

will not be recognized by the product machine.

Attack code itself cannot execute system calls without being detected. In fact, as a Modbus process requests an operating system service the kernel registers the return address and system call number. Such information is received by the sensor which incorporates it into the inter-function transfer path observed during the monitoring phase throughout a given Modbus transaction. The presence of NULL system calls in a shuffled behavior of a Modbus process would require attack code to scan most of existing instructions one by one in order to identify the system call numbers used in them. Walking through the executable segment though requires considerable time and processing logic. Further, if attack code issues a system call by itself, then its return address will be stored on stack and will lead to an easy calculation of the address of *SWI* instruction which issued the system call. The offset of the address of *SWI* instruction which issued the system call with respect to the value of R15 in a predefined entry point would cause a deviation in the observed inter-function transfer path.

Going back to our inter-function transfer path example and assuming a best case scenario for attackers, i.e. they make it to properly replay the NULL system call numbers, if such an offset is different than m, say q, then the following unrecognizable bahaviour representation will be observed on a compromised process: $\{h, s, g, l, t, w, y, q, n\}$. Thus, attackers would still need to issue system calls through *SWI* instructions in existing code and apply the IDS evasion techniques provided in [10] in order to regain execution control. Nevertheless, while reaching a returning point existing executing code may issue further function calls or even system calls, consequently additional R15-relative addresses or padded system call numbers may be inserted into the observed inter-function transfer path rendering it unrecognizable by the product machine applying the proposed intrusion detection model. The main techniques for regaining execution control according to [10] are modifying function pointers and return addresses stored on stack.

Modifying function pointers would immediately cause variations in inter-function transfer paths, thus their detection is straightforward. On the other hand, walking through the stack and searching for suitable return address values to corrupt requires time. Further, the knowledge required for locating a stack frame suitable for regaining control is not available since the sequence of original function calls has been shuffled with NULL function calls. Thus, an attacker does not know the stack layout and has to learn it. All these steps necessary for evasion cause a delay in both the total response time of a field device under attack and the time which passes between reception of consecutive R15-relative addresses in an observed inter-function transfer path. Our anomaly detection model takes into account these two different but inter-related delays for realizing that an evasion has potentially happened at a given field device.

The performance overhead induced by our anomaly detection model on a control system is dependent on the number of NULL function calls and NULL system calls inserted into a binary corresponding to an implementation of a control protocol. Inserting into FreeModbus from 2 to 4 NULL system calls and a number of NULL function calls which is a quarter of the overall number of function calls in the original FreeModbus code induces a performance penalty of 6% over the total response time of a Modbus process during a typical transaction. Such a performance cost is due to gathering inter-function transfer paths and processing them through a product machine.

5 Conclusion

In this paper we provide an anomaly detection model based on shuffle operations and product machines. The main idea behind the proposed model consists of inserting into a process what we refer to as NULL functions and NULL system calls. In this model we represent each issuance of a function call or a system call as an R15-relative address. We then apply a shuffle operation between R15-relative addresses of existing function calls and system calls, and NULL function calls and NULL system calls. With regard to the decision mechanism we employ a product machine which recognizes the result of the shuffle operation described above. If such an automaton does not recognize any single string of data gathered from a process running in a control system, then the proposed model deems that an attack is taking place in the control system in question. As a conclusion, we demonstrate the efficiency and feasibility of the proposed anomaly intrusion detection model. We show that it overcomes the limitations of state of the art system call monitors by providing an experimental evaluation on a Modbus ARM-based device running an embedded version of the Linux operating system.

Acknowledgment

We would like to thank Prof. Stefano Crespi Reghizzi of the Politecnico di Milano for useful discussions and suggestions that he provided throughout the implementation of this work. Julian Rrushi was supported in part on a doctoral scholarship from the Università degli Studi di Milano, and in part on a research scholarship from $(ISC)^2$. Opinions, findings, and conclusions expressed in this paper are those of the authors only.

References

1. Albanowski K, Dionne DJ Embedded Linux/Microcontroller Project. http://www.uclinux.org/pub/uClinux/ports/arm7tdmi/ Cited 14 Jan 2008
2. ARM Limited, ARM Technical Reference Manuals. http://www.arm.com/documentation/ARMProcessor_Cores/ Cited 14 Jan 2008
3. Bellettini C, Rrushi JL (2007) Vulnerability Analysis of SCADA Protocol Binaries through Detection of Memory Access Taintedness. In: Proceedings of the 8th IEEE SMC Information

Assurance Workshop, United States Military Academy, West Point, New York, USA, pp. 341–348
4. Chen Sh, Xu J, Nakka N, Kalbarczyk Z, Iyer RK (2005) Defeating Memory Corruption Attacks via Pointer Taintedness Detection. In: Proceedings of IEEE International Conference on Dependable Systems and Networks, Japan
5. Diekert V, Mètivier Y (1997) Partial commutation and traces, Handbook on Formal Languages, 3rd volume, Springer: 457–533
6. Feng H, Kolesnikov O.M., Fogla P., Lee W, Gong W (2003) Anomaly Detection Using Call Stack Information. In: Proceedings of IEEE Symposium on Security and Privacy, Oakland, California, USA
7. Gao D, Reiter MK, Song D (2004) Gray-box extraction of execution graphs for anomaly detection. In: ACM CCS
8. iDefense (2007) Livedata protocol server heap overflow vulnerability. http://labs.idefense.com/intelligence/vulnerabilities/display.php?id=523 Cited 14 Jan 2008
9. Jedrzejowicz J (1999) Structural properties of shuffle automata. In: Grammars 2, number 1, 1999.
10. Kruegel C, Kirda E, Mutz D, Robertson W, Vigna G (2005) Automating mimicry attacks using static binary analysis. In: Proceedings of 14th Usenix Security Symposium, Baltimore, USA
11. Lucas PJ, Riccardi F Concurrent Hierarchical State Machine. http://chsm.sourceforge.org Cited 14 Jan 2008
12. Modbus Organization (2004) MODBUS Application Protocol Specification V 1.1a. http://www.modbus.org/docs/Modbus_Application_Protocol_V1_1a.pdf Cited 14 Jan 2008
13. Mora L (2007) OPC server security considerations. In: Proceedings of SCADA Security Scientific Symposium, Miami, Florida, USA
14. Miller BP, Christodorescu M, Iverson R, Kosar T, Mirgordskii A, Popovici F (2001) Playing inside the black box: Using dynamic instrumentation to create security holes. In: Parallel Processing Letters
15. Parampalli C, Sekar R, Johnson R (2007) A Practical Mimicry Attack Against Powerful System-Call Monitors. Technical Report SECLAB07-01, Secure Systems Laboratory, Stony Brook University, USA
16. Peacock C uClinux - BFLT Binary Flat Format. http://www.beyondlogic.org/uClinux/bflt.htm Cited 14 Jan 2008
17. Rrushi JL, Rosti E (2005) Function Call Tracing Attacks to Kerberos 5. A presentation of Conference on Detection of Intrusions and Malware & Vulnerability Assessment, Vienna, Austria
18. Stamp J, Dillinger J, Young W, DePoy J (2003) Common Vulnerabilities in Critical Infrastructure Control Systems. A Technical Report of Sandia National Laboratories, Albuquerque, NM
19. US–CERT (2006) LiveData ICCP Server heap buffer overflow vulnerability. Vulnerability note VU#190617
20. US–CERT (2007) Takebishi Electric DeviceXPlorer OPC Server fails to properly validate OPC server handles. Vulnerability note VU#926551
21. Walter C FreeMODBUS library". http://www.freemodbus.org/ Cited 14 Jan 2008

Anomaly Detection with Diagnosis in Diversified Systems using Information Flow Graphs

Frédéric Majorczyk, Eric Totel, Ludovic Mé, Ayda Saïdane

Key words: anomaly detection, design diversity, COTS diversity, anomaly diagnosis, graph similarity

Abstract Design diversity is a well-known method to ensure fault tolerance. Such a method has also been applied successfully in various projects to provide intrusion detection and tolerance. Two types of approaches have been investigated: the comparison of the outputs of the diversified services without any knowledge of the internals of the server (black box approach) or an intrusive observation of the activities that occur on the diversified servers (gray box approach). Previous work on black-box approaches have shown that some types of attacks cannot be detected. In this paper, we introduce a gray-box approach, on the one hand to increase the detection coverage, and on the other hand to add some diagnosis capability to the IDS. Our gray-box approach is based on the comparison of information flow graphs generated by the activities on the servers.

1 Introduction

Intrusion detection includes misuse detection and anomaly detection. Misuse detection consists in detecting known attacks (and thus requires a base of signatures), as anomaly detection relies on the comparison of a system or application behavior with a previously defined "normal" behavior. Most of the time, anomaly detection requires to explicitly build the model of the normal behavior, either statically or dynamically (e.g., during a learning phase). Previous work [9, 6, 8] has introduced a

Frédéric Majorczyk, Eric Totel, Ludovic Mé
Supelec, Avenue de la Boulaie, 35575 Cesson-Sévigné Cedex, France, e-mail: frederic.majorczyk@supelec.fr, eric.totel@supelec.fr, ludovic.me@supelec.fr

Ayda Saïdane
University of Trento, via Belenzani, 12 I-38100 Trento, e-mail: ayda.saidane@unitn.it

Please use the following format when citing this chapter:

Majorczyk, F., et al., 2008, in IFIP International Federation for Information Processing, Volume 278; *Proceedings of the IFIP TC 11 23rd International Information Security Conference*; Sushil Jajodia, Pierangela Samarati, Stelvio Cimato; (Boston: Springer), pp. 301–315.

way to avoid building the behavior model explicitly, while allowing the built IDS to detect new or unknown attacks. This previous work is based on a dependability technique: N-version programming [1]. However, instead of developing specifically each variant like in classical N-version programming, latest work proposes the use of COTS (Components Off The Shelf) components. This reduces the cost of the architecture, and thus appears as the only viable approach, from an economic point of view. Nevertheless, the detection relies on the same hypothesises as in classical N-Version programming: the faults in the COTS (and thus the intrusions) are decorelated, to ensure that an intrusion on one of the server cannot occur on the others.

The basic approach of the intrusion detection consists in comparing the outputs of the diversified servers. Two types of comparisons can be performed at the IDS level as the servers can be considered as black-boxes or gray-boxes. In the first case, the outputs considered are the outputs of the servers. In the second case, the outputs are composed of both the internals of the servers (e.g., system calls) and the outputs of the servers.

In this paper, our objective is to present a new IDS based on COTS diversity, on one hand to correctly handle all types of attacks, on the other hand to add diagnosis capabilities to the intrusion detection system. We propose here an approach that exploits information about the activities occurring in the diversified servers: our gray box approach consists in dynamically building a view of the information flows that occur in the system, in order to be able to compare the behaviors of several diversified servers. The detection relies on the creation and comparison of information flow graphs generated by the activities on the servers.

The method we introduce provides the security administrator with an insight of what happens in the different servers. This brings some diagnosis capabilities to an anomaly detector. Indeed, a major drawback of anomaly detection is that no evidence is provided about the cause of the anomaly. No diagnosis is performed in order to help the administrator to identify whether an alert is a false positive or not; in the case of a true positive, no information is provided about the intrusion that has led to the anomaly.

In the following sections, we consider the various approaches that have been carried out in the domain of implicit model based anomaly detection (Section 2), and propose a technique to detect behavior variations of the diversified COTS in the architecture (Section 3). Then we show how we can propose a diagnosis of an intrusion using the graphs (Section 3.4). Finally a prototype is described to demonstrate the feasibility of the approach (Section 4).

2 Related Work

We present here the different work that have been carried out in the context of black-box and gray-box approaches.

Black-Box Intrusion Detection using Diversity

Three recent projects use diversity to detect intrusions with a black-box approach: DIT, HACQIT and DADDi.

DIT (Dependable Intrusion Tolerance) [9] is a project that proposes a general architecture for intrusion-tolerant systems and the implementation of an intrusion-tolerant web server as a specific instance. The architecture includes functionally redundant COTS servers running on diversified operating systems and platforms, hardened intrusion-tolerant proxies that mediate client requests and verify the behavior of servers and other proxies, and monitoring and alert management components based on the EMERALD intrusion-detection framework [7]. The architecture was then extended to consider the dynamic content issue and the problems related to on-line updating. The comparison of outputs is based on MD5 hashes of the web pages but the intrusion detection relies mainly on the host monitors and network intrusion detection systems.

HACQIT [6] (Hierarchical Adaptive Control for QoS Intrusion Tolerance) is a project that aims at providing intrusion tolerance for web servers. The architecture is made up of two COTS web servers: an IIS server running on Windows and an Apache server running on Linux. One of the servers is declared as the primary and the other one as the backup server. Only the primary server is connected to users. Another computer, the Out-Of-Band (OOB) computer, is in charge of forwarding the request of each client from the primary server to the backup one, and of receiving the responses from each server. Then, they compare the responses given by each server. The comparison is based on the status code of the HTTP response. In addition to this detection mechanism, host monitors, application monitors, a network intrusion detection system (Snort) and an integrity tool (Tripwire) are also used to detect intrusions.

DADDi [8] (Dependable Anomaly Detection with Diagnosis) implements an IDS for web servers with an architecture composed by three different COTS servers: an Apache on Mac-OS X, an IIS on Windows 2000 and a thttpd on Linux. The project extends the comparison to the complete network output of the COTS servers. Unlike the two projects presented above, the intrusion detection relies only on diversity. Neither mechanisms nor IDSes are used. The authors show that, depending on the algorithm used, the COTS diversity method can lead to many false positives due to design and specification differences. To solve this key issue, they propose the introduction of masking mechanisms to determine which output differences are the consequence of a design or a specification difference. This provides a model of the normal differences, which is much simpler to build than a complete web server model.

These three projects adopt a black-box approach. One major drawback is then that they are not able to detect all intrusions since they do not consider all outputs of the monitored services but only the network outputs. An intrusion against integrity can be missed: an attacker who has successfully compromised one server can forge a response identical to the ones from the other servers. It is necessary to add host and application monitors to be able to detect this kind of intrusions. Both the HACQIT and DIT projects add host monitors to detect this kind of intrusions but these host monitors do not use diversity. Gray-box approaches would also be able to detect this kind of intrusions since they monitor and compare the internal activity of the system.

Gray-Box Intrusion Detection using Diversity

Gao, Reiter and Song [4, 5] propose a way to compare system call sequences performed by different COTS on different operating systems. They introduce the notion of behavioral distance which is a measure of the deviation of the behaviors of two processes. They propose two ways to compute this distance: using evolutionary distance [4] and hidden Markov models [5]. The key idea is that an intrusion should thus modify the behavior of only one of the processes and should increase the behavioral distance. If the distance computed is above a given threshold then an alert is emitted. A drawback of this work is that it only takes the number of the system calls into account, while the operation performed by a system call often depends on its arguments. Moreover, no diagnosis of the alerts is provided to the administrator.

3 Intrusion Detection and Diagnosis by Comparison of Information Flow Graphs

Classical N-version programming requires to define which outputs must be compared, the system detects only errors that are propagating through these outputs. In the context of a black-box detection, only the intrusions affecting the server network outputs can be detected. In the context of a gray-box detection, other outputs, like system calls, can be compared. This approach is the one that has been used by [4, 5]. However, it is not straightforward to compare system calls on different operating systems as they are not equivalent namely and functionally.

The different server versions should behave the same with respect to the security policy. This security policy is generally implemented using access rights, and can be described as a set of permitted information flows in the system. This implies that a faulty service will not only invoke unauthorized system calls, but also produce illegal information flows generated by system calls. For example, an intrusion against confidentiality is seen as an illegal information flow between two objects. All the information flows generated by the processing of a request form an information flow graph. We argue here that comparing two information flow graphs, while not trivial, is easier than comparing two sequences of system calls produced on two different systems. An other advantage is that we do not have to monitor all the system calls, but only the subset of them that generates information flows.

In the following Sections we describe what is an information flow graph (Section 3.1), and the method we propose to use in order to compute the similarity between graphs (Section 3.2). Then we apply this method to detect intrusions in an architecture of diversified COTS servers (Section 3.3).

3.1 Information Flow Graphs

First of all, we must define the information flow notion. We consider an information flow has been produced from an object o_1 to an object o_2 if the state of the object o_2 causally depends [3] on the state of the object o_1.

An information flow graph is a set of information flows and objects that are involved during an invocation of the diversified service.

Formally, an information flow graph is a labeled graph, i.e., a directed graph $G = (V, r_V, r_E)$, of information flows between objects in the operating system, where: V is a set of vertices, $r_V \subseteq V \times L_V$ is the relation between the vertices and the vertex labels (L_V is the set of vertex labels), $r_E \subseteq V \times V \times L_E$ is the relation between the edges and the edge labels (L_E is the set of edge labels).

The vertices correspond to objects of the operating system. Currently, we consider processes, threads, files, sockets, pipes and memory mappings. The edges correspond to information flows between these objects. The labels are needed to calculate the similarity between two graphs, as explained in the next section.

In practice, each vertex or edge is associated with data items that define information required to characterize the edge or the vertex. For example, vertices are associated with a type (Process, Socket, File, Pipe, Mapping), edges with one of the types [1] (Process_to_file, File_to_process, Process_to_socket, ...). Moreover, depending on this type, additional information can be attached to each edge or vertex. For example, the vertices of type File are associated with a name, the file descriptor, the creation time and the destruction time of the file descriptor in the OS. Processes are associated with their name, their pid, the pid of their parent and a creation and destruction time. The edges are associated with the data transferred between the source and the destination of the flows as well as the time of the call.

The labels are in fact defined as a part of these data items chosen to compute the similarity, as explained in the following section: in our prototype, we use only the type as label. This implies that in our prototype, the data are not taken into account when we compute the similarity. In fact, we check the existence of information flows, instead of the contents of the information flows. This choice has been made for performance reasons.

[1] This information can seem redundant with the types associated with the vertices, but are in fact required to compute the graph similarity, see Section 3.2.

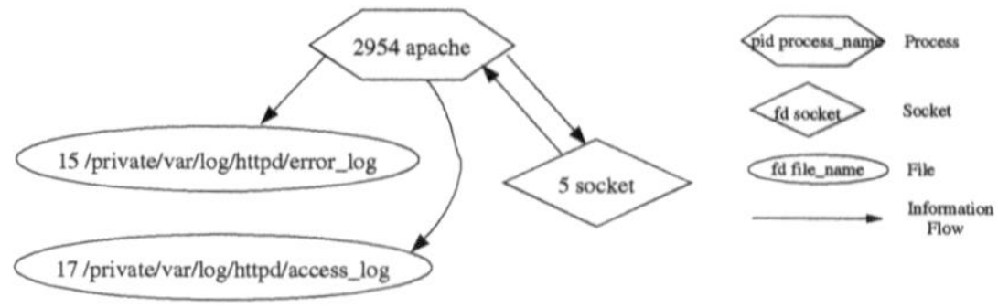

Fig. 1 Information flow graph for a HTTP request on the Apache web server

An example of information flow graph can be seen on Figure 1. This information flow graph is the one obtained for a single HTTP request. The type of a vertex is represented by its shape and information about vertices (name, pid, fd) is written inside. The graph Figure 1 shows that the Apache process reads from a socket, writes to two log files and writes to the socket (the time associated with the information flows allow to determine the chronology of the flows). The Section 4.2 explains how such a graph is built in practice, from system call monitoring.

3.2 Information Flow Graph Similarity

Since the COTS servers implement the same service, we expect that the information flow graphs on the different servers are quite similar. We need a way to assess if two graphs are similar or not. We use the model developed by Champin and Solnon [2] to measure the similarity between two labeled graphs. In their work, they propose an algorithm to calculate this similarity that we slightly change to optimize the computation to our particular case. We briefly present their approach and then detail the algorithm we use to compare information flow graphs.

To define the similarity between two graphs, we need to define the descriptor of a labeled graph: the descriptor of a labeled graph $G = (V, r_V, r_E)$ is defined by $desc(G) = r_V \cup r_E$.

We consider two labeled graphs $G_1 = (V_1, r_{V_1}, r_{E_1})$ and $G_2 = (V_2, r_{V_2}, r_{E_2})$ and we look for a measure of the similarity between those two graphs. In order to measure this similarity, the notion of mapping is defined: a mapping m is a relation $m \subseteq V_1 \times V_2$. m is a set of pairs of vertices. It must be noted that, in a mapping m, a vertex $v_1 \in V_1$ (resp. $v_2 \in V_2$) can be mapped with zero, one or more vertices in V_2 (resp. V_1). A functional notation may be used for m: $m(v)$ is the set of vertices which the vertex v is mapped with.

The similarity between G_1 and G_2 with respect to a mapping m is given by:

$$sim_m(G_1, G_2) = \frac{f(desc(G_1) \sqcap_m desc(G_2))}{f(desc(G_1) \cup desc(G_2))}$$

where f is a non-decreasing positive function with respect to inclusion (the cardinality is a function that respects these criteria, for example) and $\sqcap_m$, the intersection with respect to a mapping represents the set of labels corresponding to the vertices and to the edges in the mapping m:

$$\begin{aligned} desc(G_1) \sqcap_m desc(G_2) = & \{(v,l) \in r_{V_1} | \exists v' \in m(v), (v',l) \in r_{V_2}\} \\ & \cup \{(v,l) \in r_{V_2} | \exists v' \in m(v), (v',l) \in r_{V_1}\} \\ & \cup \{(v_i,v_j,l) \in r_{E_1} | \exists v'_i \in m(v_i), \exists v'_j \in m(v_j)(v'_i,v'_j,l) \in r_{E_2}\} \\ & \cup \{(v_i,v_j,l) \in r_{E_2} | \exists v'_i \in m(v_i), \exists v'_j \in m(v_j)(v'_i,v'_j,l) \in r_{E_1}\} \end{aligned}$$

A last concept is necessary to measure the similarity between two graphs. A vertex can indeed be mapped with more than one vertex. It can be interesting in our case, as we may need to map two processes in one operating system with one process in another operating system. The notion of *splits* can be added to take into account the mapping of a particular vertex to multiple vertexes. The *splits* of a mapping m represents the vertices that are mapped with more than one vertex in the mapping m:

$$splits(m) = \{(v,s_v) | v \in V_1 \cup V_2, s_v = m(v), |m(v)| \geq 2\}$$

The definition of the similarity with respect to a mapping m is changed to:

$$sim_m(G_1,G_2) = \frac{f(desc(G_1) \sqcap_m desc(G_2)) - g(splits(m))}{f(desc(G_1) \cup desc(G_2))}$$

where g is a positive, monotonic and non-decreasing function with respect to inclusion. We have defined the similarity between two graphs with respect to a mapping m. The similarity between two graphs can be defined by:

$$sim(G_1,G_2) = \max_{m \subseteq V_1 \times V_2} \frac{f(desc(G_1) \sqcap_m desc(G_2)) - g(splits(m))}{f(desc(G_1) \cup desc(G_2))}$$

So finding the similarity between two graphs G_1 and G_2 means finding the mapping m that maximizes this value.

Champin and Solnon [2] propose two algorithms to solve this problem: a complete search with some optimizations that allows to cut branches off the search tree and a greedy algorithm. In our prototype, we have used the complete search algorithm as we are more interested in the detection accuracy than in the temporal performance of the similarity computation, at least for a first implementation.

3.3 Intrusion Detection using Graph Similarity

In information flow graphs, an intrusion is characterized by the creation or modification of information flows, active objects (e.g., processes) and/or passive objects (e.g., files). An intrusion against confidentiality implies the creation of information flows and if necessary, the creation of new objects. An intrusion against integrity is characterized by the creation or modification of information flows and if necessary, the creation of new objects. Thus, an intrusion affects the value of the similarity between the information flow graph of a successfully attacked server and the one of a server which has not been compromised.

Similarity Threshold. The calculation of a similarity is a function taking two graphs as parameters. A high similarity means that the servers have behaved quite in the same way. A low similarity means that the servers have behaved quite differently, which can be the consequence of an intrusion, a design difference or specification difference. Our approach consists in learning what is an acceptable value of a similarity in the context of a normal behavior. This leads to determine a threshold to decide when an alert must be emitted, i.e., to determine the value of the similarity, under which it is symptomatic of an intrusion. If a similarity is lower than the threshold, we generate an alert.

This threshold must be determined experimentally for each pair of diversified services: the similarity depends on the cardinality of the descriptors of the graphs considered and then depends on the application considered. If the graphs are large, one or more vertices or edges that are not mapped have less influence on the similarity than in small graphs. So there cannot exist a unique threshold for all the applications. In order to calculate this threshold, we determine statistically which value corresponds to a normal behavior, i.e., a request that is not an attack.

Intrusion Detection Algorithm. In the context of an architecture with n COTS servers S_i, we must determine the similarity threshold $t_{i,j}$ for each pair of servers as explained in the previous paragraph. Detecting an intrusion requires calculating the similarities between all pairs of servers for a given service request. This leads to the computation of $C_n^2 = \frac{n!}{(n-2)! \times 2!}$ graph similarities, noted $s_{i,j}$. Since the similarity is symmetric, we can write $s_{i,j} = s_{j,i}$ for all (i,j) in $\{1,n\}^2$. We note $I_1^{i,j} = [0, t_{i,j}]$ and $I_2^{i,j} = [t_{i,j}, 1]$.

Currently, we use the following rules to determine the decision of our gray-box IDS for n servers:

$$\exists (i,j) \in \{1,n\}^2, i < j, s_{i,j} \in I_1^{i,j} \Rightarrow Alert$$
$$\forall (i,j) \in \{1,n\}^2, i < j, s_{i,j} \in I_2^{i,j} \Rightarrow No\ Alert$$

i.e., an alert is emitted as soon as one similarity is low, i.e., beneath $t_{i,j}$. If all the similarities are high, i.e., above $t_{i,j}$, no alert is emitted.

Intrusion Localization. Low similarities indicate that an incorrect activity has occurred in the architecture. Nevertheless, under the hypothesis that only one server can be compromised at a time, this server must be the only one leading to low similarities. In that case, the localization of the compromised server is possible. This localization is required to apply a reconfiguration to the architecture in order to mask the effects of the detected intrusion (e.g., the reconfiguration of a server). In

	$s_{2,3} \in I_1^{2,3}$		$s_{2,3} \in I_2^{2,3}$	
$s_{1,2} \in$ \ $s_{1,3} \in$	$I_1^{1,3}$	$I_2^{1,3}$	$I_1^{1,3}$	$I_2^{1,3}$
$I_1^{1,2}$	$A/?$	A/S_2	A/S_1	$A/?$
$I_2^{1,2}$	A/S_3	$A/?$	$A/?$	NA

Table 1 Alerts and localization of the server compromised in the case $N = 3$; A means Alert (gray cells), *NA* means No Alert (white cells), ? means no localization is possible, S_i means the server S_i is considered as being compromised

our prototype, the localization of the server compromised is based on the following rule:

$$\left.\begin{array}{l} \exists i \in \{1,n\}, \forall j \in \{1,n\}, j \neq i, s_{i,j} \in I_1^{i,j} \\ \wedge \\ \forall (k,l) \in \{1,n\}^2, k \neq i, l \neq i, s_{k,l} \in I_2^{k,l} \end{array}\right\} \Rightarrow S_i \text{ is compromised}$$

Three Server Instance. Table 1 sums up, in the case of three servers S_1, S_2 and S_3, in what conditions we decide to raise an alert and if we can localize the compromised server in function of the computed similarities.

Some cases should not happen: for example, for three servers, if $s_{1,2}$ and $s_{2,3}$ are high and $s_{1,3}$ is low. This means that the behaviors of S_1 and S_2 are close as well as the ones of S_2 and S_3, but the behaviors of S_1 and S_3 are really different. Since we have no evidence about the transitivity of the relation linked to the similarity, we consider that this case may be possible. An alert is emitted by the IDS but no localization is possible.

3.4 Diagnosis of Anomalies Detected

In classical anomaly detector, no diagnosis is associated with the alerts, which is one of the main drawbacks of this kind of detector. Here, as we capture information flows that can be viewed as an history of the system activity, we provide the security administrator with an evidence of what happens in the different servers: it is possible to explain an intrusion through the differences between the graphs: processes created, files read or written, sockets opened, etc.

By computing the similarity between the graphs, we identify also the active objects (processes), the passive objects (files, sockets, pipes, ...) and the information flows not mapped in the best mapping, i.e., the one for which the similarity is maximum. It must be noted that the best mapping depends on the computation of the similarity and thus on the functions f and g.

In case of an intrusion, the objects not mapped are visible effects at the OS level of an intrusion. By analyzing these objects, it is possible to gather some information about the intrusion: processes created, files written or read, sockets created, etc. If it is not possible to identify directly the vulnerability exploited, this information may lead to it. In the case of a zero-day, it even offers a good starting point to discover the currently unknown vulnerability.

We propose to show to the security operator the graphs of the different servers for the suspicious input and mark the objects and flows not mapped (This is illustrated in Section 4.3.4). We believe that this approach can be very helpful to a security operator and can be extended by automatically summing up the objects non mapped and their interactions. It is, as far as we know, the first anomaly-based approach in intrusion detection, which offers such a diagnosis capability.

4 Prototype and Experimental Results

We have implemented a proof-of-concept prototype of an IDS based on information flow graph similarity for web servers. After a brief presentation of the components of the architecture, we discuss the modeling of system calls. Finally some results show the performances of this prototype, in relation to its detection capabilities.

4.1 Intrusion Detection Architecture

We use three different web servers in our prototype: a thttpd (for tests with a static web server) or Lighttpd (for tests with a dynamic web server) web server running on Linux, an Abyss web server running on Windows 2000 Server and an Apache web server running on Mac-OS X. The architecture (Figure 2) is composed of several components: a HTTP proxy, a gray-box IDS based on information flow graph comparison and, on each server, a wrapper, a graph generator and a system call logger. The role of the wrapper is mainly to associate a request with its beginning and ending times. It receives an HTTP request from the proxy, stores the beginning time of the request and forwards the request to the web server. Then the wrapper forwards the response of the web server to the proxy and stores the time at the end of the response. Then it asks the graph generator for the information flow graph corresponding to the request by sending the beginning time and the ending time of the request considered and send the information flow graph to the proxy. Depending on the design of the web servers, it is not always easy to determine the correspondence between system calls and requests. To solve this problem, we choose in our prototype to serialize the requests to ensure that at one time only one request is processed. This proof-of-concept prototype has been developed to evaluate detection precision and reliability, its optimization in terms of real-time capability is left for future work.

The system call logger logs the system calls performed by the web server and sends them to the graph generator on demand. The graph generator builds information flow graphs from system calls and sends them to the wrapper.

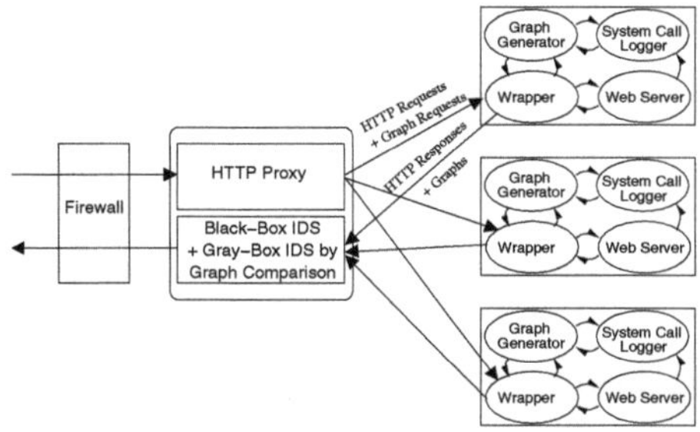

Fig. 2 Gray-box intrusion detection architecture

4.2 Monitoring System Calls Generating an Information Flow

About twenty system calls have been identified to generate information flows (For example, the *read* system call) and are thus monitored on each operating system. In the case of the *read* system call, the graph built is the following: the process which performs the system call *read* is an active object, the file, socket or pipe read is a passive object, and these two objects are linked.

However, some other information flows are difficult to build. The system calls that create another thread such as *clone* (on Linux) allow information flows between processes. In case of the system call *clone*, the child process is a copy of his parent process. The child process and the parent process share their memory and can thus communicate. It is possible to monitor whether one of the processes access to this data, but this has a significant impact on the performance. So we decided to model this system call by two information flows: one from the child to the parent process and the other one from the parent to the child. The information flow created this way has an empty label data.

A system call that creates another process such as *fork* corresponds to the execute operation of our model. For the same reason as the one mentioned above, the information flow which corresponds has an empty label data.

System calls such as *mmap* can also be the source of information flows which can not be modeled without observing memory accesses of processes. *mmap* allows a process to map a file in memory. Reading or writing in the file is simply performed by reading or writing to memory. Depending on the arguments of *mmap*, we decided to create information flows between the process which executes *mmap* and the file considered. If the mapping is read-only (resp. write-only), we create an information flow from the file (resp. process) object to the process (resp. file) object. If the mapping is read-write, we create two information flows: one from the file to the process object and the other one in the other way.

Our current prototype does not consider some IPC mechanisms (messages, shared memory) and signals. IPC mechanisms can be modeled as passive objects. Signals create information flows between the process that sends the signal and the process that receives it. They can be modeled by an information flow with a label data corresponding to the number of the signal sent.

4.3 Experimental Results

4.3.1 Detecting a Successful Attack Against Integrity

One of the motivations of defining a gray-box approach is to be able to detect successful attacks against integrity, where the network answers of the diversified servers does not reflect the intrusion. To demonstrate this detection capability, we have developped a small diversified php script, where, on the value of one parameter, a file write operation is performed on one server, but all the scripts return the same answer. This attack results in the creation of an information flow graph containing a write operation on the attacked server, and thus results in a low similarity between this server and the others. Consequently, this approach complementarize a black-box approach, where this type of attack were impossible to detect.

4.3.2 Evaluation of the False Positive Rate

In this Section, we evaluate the false positive rate of our prototype. For that purpose, we use a static web server, the one of our campus, and two sets of normal requests (real requests to this server).

Computation of the Thresholds $t_{i,j}$. As stated in Subsection 3.3, the thresholds $t_{i,j}$ must be chosen experimentally for each pair of servers used. We decide to set up the threshold so as to ensure that, for most of normal HTTP requests, our prototype does not raise an alert, i.e., the similarities computed for these requests are above the thresholds $t_{i,j}$.

For the normal requests, we use a set of HTTP requests logged on the website of our campus during a week. This set is composed of 71,596 HTTP requests. To check if this set contains only non-intrusive requests, we use WebSTAT [10] and the black-box IDS of [8]: all alerts generated have been confirmed to be false positives. Thus we have a high confidence in the fact that the traffic does not contain successful attacks. After this phase, we decide to set up all the thresholds to 0.7. More than 99.5% of the requests are thus considered as normal.

Results. In order to evaluate the false positive rate, we use another set of HTTP requests logged by the server of our campus during a week. This set is composed of 105,228 requests.

Table 2 sums up the 140 alerts raised by the gray-box IDS and the localization of the server considered as being compromised. All these alerts are false positives since they are not due to intrusions. It represents a false positive rate of 0.13% and 20 alerts a day, which is acceptable.

	$s_{2,3} \in I_1^{2,3}$		$s_{2,3} \in I_2^{2,3}$	
$s_{1,3} \in$ / $s_{1,2} \in$	$I_1^{1,3}$	$I_2^{1,3}$	$I_1^{1,3}$	$I_2^{1,3}$
$I_1^{1,2}$	0 (?)	0 (S_2)	120 (S_1)	1 (?)
$I_2^{1,2}$	2 (S_3)	1 (?)	16 (?)	105,088

Table 2 Number of alerts and localization of the server considered compromised for the test week; gray cells mean an alert is raised, white cells mean no alert is raised, ? means no localization is possible, S_i means the server S_i is considered compromised

Similarity between / Intrusions	SQL injection	write	execute 'whoami'	XSS (insertion)	XSS (read the corrupted entry)
Lighttpd and Apache	0.9655	0.725	0.5882	0.9677	0.9143
Apache and Abyss	0.7742	0.9715	0.6364	0.9677	0.9706
Lighttpd and Abyss	0.7838	0.7209	0.6667	1	0.9189
	detected	detected	detected	not detected	not detected

Table 3 Similarities between the graphs of the different servers for the intrusive requests

4.3.3 Detection Capabilities

In this Section, we test our prototype in the context of a dynamic web server and evaluate its detection capabilities.

We replace the thttpd server by the Lighttpd server on the Linux machine. For the web site, we choose an application named Bibtex Manager which is written in php and uses a database as a backend. This application manages a database of Bibtex citations. We log 86 HTTP requests that represent a normal use of the application. We introduce four vulnerabilities in one of the versions and develop corresponding exploits.

The similarities between the different graphs corresponding to the intrusions are lower than the ones for normal requests. While the similarity for normal requests is, in the mean, around 0.95, the similarity between the graph of a compromised server and a server not compromised is lower than 0.8. Table 3 sums up the similarities obtained for the intrusions.

By setting the threshold for each pair of servers to 0.8, our prototype IDS is able to detect all the intrusions except the XSS attack.The XSS attack is not detected as its impact on the similarities (see Table 3) is too low.

4.3.4 Diagnosis Capabilities

In order to show the diagnosis capabilities of our approach, we performed an intrusion against a tiny vulnerable web server developed for educational purpose (the result appears on Figure 3). The intrusion consists in a directory traversal so as to

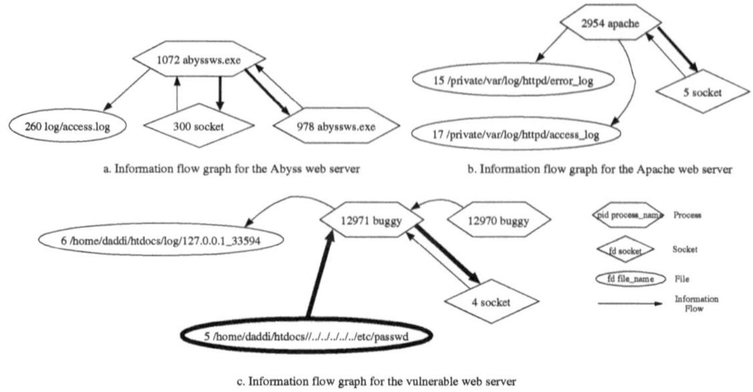

Fig. 3 Three information flow graphs linked to a HTTP request on different servers and identification of the objects not mapped

read the file */etc/passwd*. This server does not check the presence of '../' string in the url while the other servers refuse to serve such a request.

The file object representing the *passwd* file is not mapped with any objects in the other graphs as well as the information flows representing the read access to the *passwd* file and the write access to the socket. These objects are emphasized on Figure 3. For the Apache web server as well as for the Abyss web server, the information flows representing the write access to the socket are not mapped with their equivalent in the graph for the vulnerable server but are associated with each other.

5 Conclusion

Detecting intrusions by using COTS diversity proved to provide interesting results, both in terms of false positives and false negatives. However, the black-box approaches that have been investigated suffer from being incomplete, as they do not permit to detect intrusions that have no impact on the network outputs. To improve them, we have thus developed a gray-box approach that implements information flow graph comparisons.

As many IDSes, the method proposed can miss some attacks, if the objects involved in the system do not produce sufficient differences in the information flow graphs built on the different servers. This can lead to some false negatives. However, further work on the definition of the comparison algorithm (and the function f and g) should reduce the false negative rate.

Moreover, the current prototype is still far from being perfect, as it generates a too high false positive rate and exhibits low time performances. These flaws can be corrected by introducing design difference masking mechanisms on one hand (similarly to the black box approach in [8]), and a greedy algorithm on the other hand to decrease the similarity computation time significantly. This will motivate our future work.

Despite these current limitations, this approach and the experiments carried out with our proof-of-concept prototype show that our gray-box IDS is capable of detecting intrusions of all kinds as they imply a difference in the information flows observed in the servers.

Finally, the analysis of the differences between the information flow graphs has proved to be efficient to bring diagnosis capabilities to the IDS as it enlighten the effects of the intrusions at the OS level. The advantage of our approach is thus to propose to the administrator more than a simple intrusion detection mechanism: it brings him an evidence of the intrusion and its causes.

Acknowledgements This work has been funded by the region Bretagne and the French National Research Agency in the context of the DADDi project.

References

1. Bharathi, V.: N-version programming method of software fault tolerance: A critical review. In: National Conference on Nonlinear Systems and Dynamics (NCNSD). Kharagpur, India (2003)
2. Champin, P.A., Solnon, C.: Measuring the similarity of labeled graphs. In: in Proceedings of the 5th International Conference on Case-Based Reasoning (ICCBR 2003), pp. 80–95. Trondheim, Norway (2003)
3. d'Ausbourg, B.: Implementing secure dependencies over a network by designing a distributed security subsystem. In: Proceedings of the European Sysmposium on Research in Computer Security (ESORICS'94), pp. 249–266 (1994)
4. Gao, D., Reiter, M.K., Song, D.: Behavioral distance for intrusion detection. In: Proceedings of the 8th International Symposium on Recent Advances in Intrusion Detection (RAID 2005), pp. 63–81. Seattle, WA (2005)
5. Gao, D., Reiter, M.K., Song, D.: Behavioral distance measurement using hidden markov models. In: Proceedings of the 9th International Symposium on Recent Advances in Intrusion Detection (RAID 2006), pp. 19–40. Hamburg, Germany (2006)
6. Just, J.E., Reynolds, J.C., Clough, L.A., Danforth, M., Levitt, K.N., Maglich, R., Rowe, J.: Learning unknown attacks - a start. In: A. Wespi, G. Vigna, L. Deri (eds.) Proceedings of the 5th International Symposium on Recent Advances in Intrusion Detection (RAID 2002), *Lecture Notes in Computer Science*, vol. 2516, pp. 158–176. Zurich, Switzerland (2002)
7. Porras, P.A., Neumann, P.G.: EMERALD: Event monitoring enabling responses to anomalous live disturbances. In: Proc. of the 20th National Information Systems Security Conference, pp. 353–365. Baltimore, MD (1997). URL http://www2.csl.sri.com/emerald/emerald-niss97.html
8. Totel, E., Majorczyk, F., Mé, L.: COTS diversity based intrusion detection and application to web servers. In: Proceedings of the 8th International Symposium on Recent Advances in Intrusion Detection (RAID 2005), pp. 43–62. Seattle, WA (2005)
9. Veríssimo, P.E., Neves, N.F., Correia, M.P.: Intrusion-tolerant architectures: Concepts and design. In: Architecting Dependable Systems, *Lecture Notes in Computer Science*, vol. 2677. Sptringer-Verlag (2003)
10. Vigna, G., Robertson, W., Kher, V., Kemmerer, R.A.: A stateful intrusion detection system for world-wide web servers. In: Proceedings of the Annual Computer Security Applications Conference (ACSAC 2003), pp. 34–43. Las Vegas, Nevada (2003)

Behavioral Intrusion Detection Indicators

Jacques Saraydaryan, Luc Paffumi, Veronique Legrand and Stephane Ubeda

Abstract Monitoring and analysing Information system(IS)'s security events has become more and more difficult in the last few years. As IS complexity rises, the number of mandatory monitoring points has increased along with the number of deployed probes. Consequently, a huge amount of information is reported to the analyst which subsequently floods him and implies the implementation of very complex event analysis engines. In the behaviour analysis context in which sequences of events are studied, this information quantity issue makes it difficult to build automatable - not too complex - models. In order to cope with this increasing amount of information, we will describe a method to reduce the observation perimeter through the selection of most relevant indicators. Such indicators, which are defined thanks to users and attackers behaviour analysis, represent different actions that users or attackers perform in the IS. This method implies neither information loss nor significant detection rate decline. We experienced this indicators selection with a behaviour anomaly detection engines injecting few days of events. Results show that model complexity issues are significantly reduced while keeping detection rate almost the same.

Jacques Saraydaryan
ARES INRIA / CITI, INSA Lyon, F69621, France, Exaprotect, 149 bd Stalingrad 69100 Villeurbanne France e-mail: Jsaraydaryan@exaprotect.com

Luc Paffumi
Exaprotect, 149 bd Stalingrad 69100 Villeurbanne France e-mail: lpaffumi@exaprotect.com

Veronique Legrand
ARES INRIA / CITI, INSA Lyon, F69621, France, Exaprotect, 149 bd Stalingrad 69100 Villeurbanne France e-mail: vlegrand@exaprotect.com

Stephane Ubeda
ARES INRIA / CITI, INSA Lyon, F69621, France e-mail: stephane.ubeda@insa-lyon.fr

Please use the following format when citing this chapter:

Saraydaryan, J., et al., 2008, in IFIP International Federation for Information Processing, Volume 278; *Proceedings of the IFIP TC 11 23rd International Information Security Conference*; Sushil Jajodia, Pierangela Samarati, Stelvio Cimato; (Boston: Springer), pp. 317–331.

1 Introduction

The information security interest greatly increased in the last ten years. Securing large Information System (IS) communications, mobile users and sensitive data became one of the top priorities of private and governmental institutions. Helped by a multitude of security tools, security analysts and administrators organize and manage their IS defense. Classical security tools like firewalls, Host and Network Intrusion Detection Systems (HIDS-NIDS) are focused on local parts of the IS and are not sufficient anymore. These approaches are efficient for local detection but still need to be investigated to provide new methods to reduce data volume, increase alert semantics and detect global attack scenarios. Industrial and research communities show a great interest in the global Information System vision. Recent literatures aim at modeling and discovering global attack scenarios and Information System dependencies. Working on the global vision introduces two main limitations: the volume of computed data that can reach thousands of events per second and the complexity of attacks scenarios and IS dependencies that increase very quickly with the volume of data. Recent works provide three main functions to reduce the large volume of incoming events: normalization, aggregation and correlation. [4] describes an ontology of all actions (called moves) occurring on IS components. By normalizing all incoming events, redundant information are deleted and analysis and IS action modeling are possible. The aggregation approaches [12] gather events sharing the same semantics or same attributes. Correlation solutions follow the same objective by grouping incoming events through predefined models [15], precomputed data, or automatically generated models [7]. All these approaches aim at reducing the amount of data presented to the analysts and used for IS modeling. However, this data reduction is not always sufficient for an administrator's analysis as some hundreds of alerts can remain, the data volume remains an important issue for global analysis especially for global behavioral Intrusion Detection where all the events information are not relevant. In this paper, we introduce the notion of necessary transit actions for an attacker to achieve his objectives: these actions are called "checkpoints". We propose a selection of specific monitoring points (called indicators) in order to focus our analysis on specific local points in the IS. With the extraction of critical and relevant key points, we only provide necessary information for a global behavioral intrusion detection analysis. The section 2 introduces a survey of different observation points involved in anomalies detection. A user behavior analysis is realized on section 3. Section 4 and section 5 provide a classification and selection of behavioral indicators. Experimental results show our complexity reduction of anomaly models in section 6, followed by our conclusion in section 7.

2 Behavioral observation points

Since the beginning of the behavioral intrusion detection [8], several approaches aim at discovering anomalous behavior reflecting attacker's activities. In this section, we enumerate behavioral indicators described in Behavioral Intrusion Detection. This one tends to collect all types of behavioral observations in order to specify the relevance of each ones. Behavioral Intrusion Detection can be divided into two categories: Host intrusion detection System (HIDS) and Network intrusion detection system (NIDS).

2.1 Behavioral HIDS indicators

Traditional behavioral HIDS focus their analysis on particular points of observation inside the host. [14] realized an overview of intrusion detection methods and data sources. It describes information used by HIDS: system access information, system usage information, files usage information, application usage information and security violation information. System access information describes how someone or something accesses the system, how relevant information can be monitored like user or process/terminal ids, connection modes (local, remote) and time relation between connections. System usage information is focused on interactions between users and systems. [9] determinates the frequency of each user commands. User names, command types and times are the main properties of the used command. [6] models system command sequences. Each command is defined with pre and post conditions (file name, kind of agent, address and host name, source port, etc.). [1] determinates anomalies of proxylets by comparing CPU usage and memory use with actual CPU and memory load. File usage information determines how file can be accessed like access time, types (open, close, read, modify, etc.). As explained in [13], common intruder actions are visible thanks to the file manipulation monitoring. Intruders who successfully enter the IS often modify data. [13] stresses out four categories of *warning signs*: data/attribute modification, update pattern (deviation of "rotated" log file or modification of previous one), content integrity and suspicious content. Information hold by used applications gives detail about application properties installed on the host. [10] focus their work on system call modeling during application run to discover potential application misuse. [17] models temporal application relations of each user to discover unusual sequence application uses.

A last indicator, security violation information, defines anomaly behavior as a violation of specific rules. [5] defines specific policies for regulating access to system resources. Some strategic file access or bad privilege command execution are relevant about suspicious behaviors.

2.2 Behavioral NIDS indicators

While HDISs focus on the monitoring of specific components of the IS, NIDS became a complementary mechanism by monitoring network traffic. They are located in strategic network points of IS like network DMZ, firewall front or back head area. Although signature based NIDS are most popular inside commercial products, behavioral analysis becomes an alternative way to detect unknown attacks. Computing network flows modeling or determining threats threshold, behavioral NIDSs discover network flows anomalies. [11] classified network anomaly detection following three criteria: the Network feature Analyzed, the Behavior Model and the Analysis Scale. Network feature Analyzed expresses which data is monitored and modeling inside the IS. Behavior Model defines how behavioral NIDSs model usual IS activities (learnt models, specification-based models, etc.). Finally, Analysis Scale provides information about the level of analysis abstraction. For example, the monitoring of the number of packet can be viewed as a low level, the monitoring of connections or packet streams as a medium level and high level can be performed by the monitoring of several connections and event correlation within the whole network.In our context, we particularly focus on the Network feature Analyzed which defines different behavioral observation points. Network feature Analyzed criterion is divided into two main groups, the network traffic data source and the Network Elements/topology information. The Network Elements/topology information is not currently usable for classical wired networks and find its importance in emerging architecture like ad hoc networks. The Network Traffic data source constitute the major source of network behavioral analysis. Two Network Traffic properties (flows or protocols) can be analysed. On one side, flow analysis are characterized by the study of the evolution of traffic flows. Related data sources are various: number of bytes sent/received during a fixed time interval by a given final system, number protocol packets (TCP/UDP,etc.) packets sent/received, number of TCP/UDP connection, number of HTTP/DNS request,etc. On the other side, protocol analysis consists in discovering protocol misuse at different levels [2](Data Link, Network, Transport, Application). The analysis is realized on sequences of protocol steps and protocol transaction evolutions.This section tends to cover the monitored data frequently used for the behavioral analysis. All these data do not have any correspondence between each other. The next sections will explain logical links between behavioral observations and propose a selection of essential points of observations. These logical links will improve the interpretations of global behavioral anomalies study.

3 User-Oriented Behavioral Analysis

We focus our study on the selection of indicators for the global Behavioral Analysis of users actions. In order to define key points in the IS, we study the behavior of each users family in the IS. The IS behavior can be defined thanks to two main elements: the behavior of actions realized on the IS and the components states of the IS. Four different entities can be distinguished for the IS behavior definition: the behavior of classical user, the behavior of administrator of the IS, the behavior of the attacker and the behavior of the IS itself. Usually, the IS security is evaluated through a method which associates a number with attributes (called metrics) like:

Confidentiality, Integrity, Availability (CIA). Users' actions affect these metrics by increasing or decreasing their values (e.g. an Administrator increases confidentiality by configuring authentication, an Attack decreases the availability by flooding a server) (figure 1). In the following paragraph, we are going to describe each users family approach and involved actions affecting IS metrics.

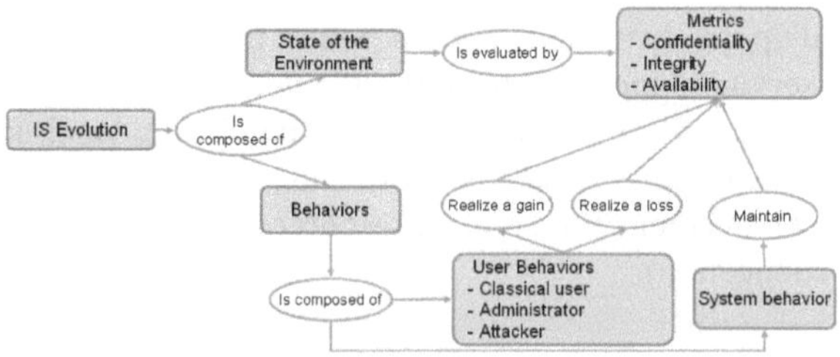

Fig. 1 Information System Composition

3.1 User actions modeling

Most of this work relies on the [4] ontology that provides a user actions description. It implies four parameters; the intention of the user, the realized actions, the target impacted by the action and the result of actions. An IS user has typically four types of goal: collecting information about a target (Recon), accessing the IS (Authentication), accessing IS resources (Authorization) and affecting IS resources (System). These four goals (called intention) describe the reasons why the user performs an action. In order to achieve his aim, the user (including classical users, administrators or attackers) performs actions directed on a target. These actions are differentiated according to their modes (activity, config, attack) and their natures (login , read, execute,etc.). Finally, each action has a result that reflects the gain of the user on the system i.e. whether the user succeeded its action attempt or not. For instance, a user that logs into an SSH server would be modeled in the ontology by a four-uplets : Authentication (referring to the intention), Activity Login (referring to the realized action), SSH (referring to the target) and Success (referring to the result). The resulted action model is noted Authentication.Activity.Login.SSH.Success.

3.2 Classical users approach

Classical users use the IS for professional or personal interest but always with respect to security policies. As described in section 3.1, we base our work on [4] and [3] which describe a wireless networks users analysis. We only extract the intention and the types of actions for our analysis, the other ones being too much specific and useless for the global behavior analysis. The *Recon* intention is not often achieved by classical users. For our study, we merge both authentication and authorization (often performed successively) in a unique authentication intention. The *System* intention is usually performed by classical users. As for the realized actions, we only use the *Activity* action for the classical user, the other ones representing attacker or administrator behaviors (described in section 3.3 and 3.4). Classical users activities could be summed up into two main action families; the local or remote connections/ authentications (services, applications of the IS ,etc.) and the use of local or remote resources. Two sequences of actions can be distinguished, local action sequences (authentication, resources use, disconnection) and remote action sequences (remote authentication, remote connection, remote resources use, remote service disconnection, system disconnection).

3.3 Administrator approach

An Administrator is a special IS user. Administrator inherits classical users behaviors and has special additional properties. One of the administrator characteristics is his ability to switch between classical user activities and administrative tasks. In addition to its classical user activities, an administrator has to manage and configure the IS. These functions need the use of special actions on specific targets, theoretically not accessible for classical users. In order to take into account these specific activities, the realized actions *Config* of [4] are used to describe a policy or configuration modification, add or deletion. Moreover, the intention *Recon* is also used to describe administrator activities as an administrator needs to get some information on its IS in order to monitor and manage it as well as possible. Configuration and maintenance actions form the administrator's main activities. He connects itself to the system with special logins (root) giving him full rights to the System. With such rights, an Administrator can effectively modify configurations and policies in the IS. Moreover, tests of accessibility and vulnerability (which take part of the *Recon* intention) can be launched in order to verify the performance of the system.

3.4 Attacker approach

The attacker's behaviour is the most complex and unpredictable one.[4] defines the first steps an attacker usually performs to enter an IS: information gathering and vulnerabilities exploitation. Sometimes, attackers can perform alternative initial actions; the attacker can also take advantage of backdoors or virus installed by users unaware of security risks during the metastasis phase.Despite various objectives, we can enhance the definition of necessary steps to achieve the attackers objectives. So as to mask his actions, an attacker would try to hide his malicious behaviour by

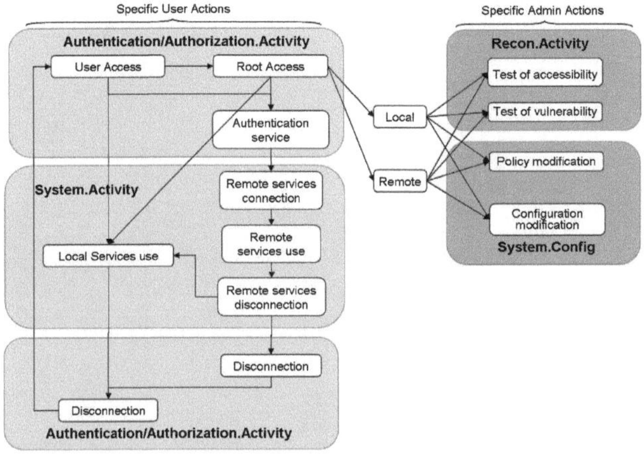

Fig. 2 Administrator approach

faking a classical user behavior. An attacker behavior inherits from classical user actions. An intermediate goal of an attacker is to gain administrative privileges in order to modify, alter or steal data in the IS. The figure 3 shows possible actions of an attacker on the IS. We can distinguish five objectives of an attacker; gain of privilege, gain of access, deny of service, bounce or data stealing (spying). In order to achieve these goals, following steps are essential. In the first step, an attacker has to locate the targeted system. In a second step, he needs to collect information about the system. Once the target located and analyzed (environment and vulnerabilities discovery), the attacker exploits a vulnerability to reach his final goal. An alternative sequence of action using automatic tools (malware like virus) exists. These malwares would automatically try to exploit some vulnerabilities. Once the system penetrated, the attacker would have a behavior close to classical users or administrators. All attacker actions are not always detectable (new attacks, miss of specific probes or non adequate probes in some locations of the IS), however it is possible to reveal important information about deviating users or administrator behaviors.

3.5 User-Attacker comparison

Normal IS users (classical users and administrator) share similar actions with attackers. These actions are bottlenecks in IS for all users. These actions reveal attackers checkpoints inside the user or administrator approach. As defined in section 1, these checkpoints define necessary actions for an attacker to reach his objectives. They constitute an essential behavioral monitoring for the detection of deviating behaviors subject to belong to an attacker. The figure 4 shows the interactions between the classical user/administrator approaches and attacker strategy. Arrows going through Vertical separators between both approaches represent merged points of both ap-

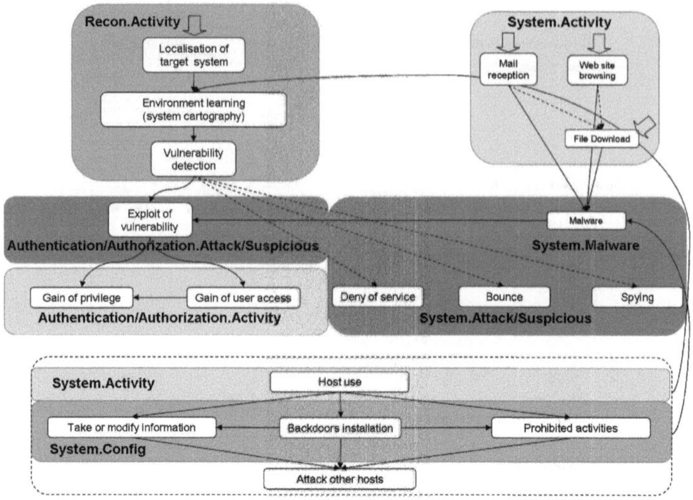

Fig. 3 Attacker approach

proaches. Two main checkpoints are enhanced. The connection action in the user approach side defines the first checkpoint. An attacker has no alternative way to reach his objective, he has to pass through classical authentication points to go into the IS. The second checkpoint is the transition from the user approach to the attacker strategy at the end of the attacker scenario. In order to achieve his malicious goals, the attacker would deviate from the original user or administrator behavior. This second checkpoint is less relevant because the deviance detection at this stage is not necessarily possible. For most of time, slight behavioral deviation on IS are not detectable and only effects of these actions differentiate attackers from normal IS users.

3.6 System Approach

The IS has to maintain its level of Confidentiality, Integrity and Availability (CIA). IS actions will represent internal actions by the system itself and not by a user interaction. Each component's behavior can be modeled as follow: after the physical start of the component, this one will launch services needed for its own operations or will try to load external services or information (load DHCP address, load list of services to start...). The started services could modify internal configuration of the system depending of the policies of the IS (network parameters modifications, restriction of some functionalities). After this starting step, the component will wait for external environment interactions. As soon as a user interaction occurred, the IS checks the security permission for the asked operation. The permissions are checked and the operation is launched. Information of the launched operation may be revealed through the state of the component (e.g. CPU overload representing by System.Information in [4]). The component can also execute operation by its own (component basic functions) as forwarding information, mail/packet reception and dispatch,etc. Then the component can be halted by an external intervention (System.Information.Stop) or by itself (System.Activity.Stop).

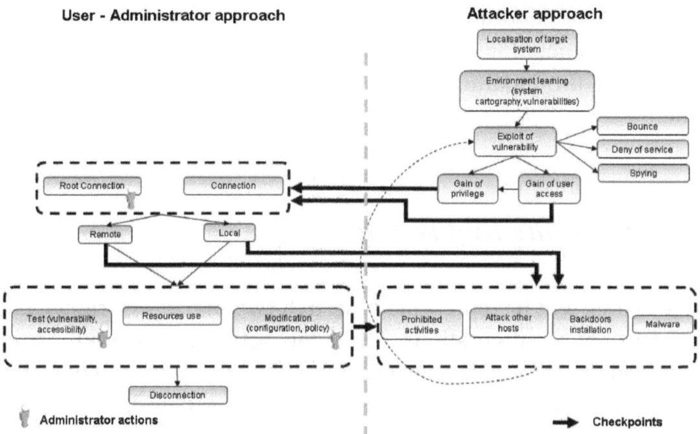

Fig. 4 Checkpoint

4 Indicators Selection

The description of IS user behaviour highlights different groups of actions. The main groups reflect actions about system access, usage/modification of authorization (called rigths) and usage/modification of the system. All users interact with the system through success or failure of these three groups. To determine which actions of success/failure are important for the user behaviour monitoring, we select all events reflecting system-user interactions. Trying to detect behavioral anomalies, our groups of observations (called meters) are focused on the evolution of classical user's and administrator's behaviors. Following users approach (described in section 3), each group is divided into different activities reflecting usage, modification or state information. The next paragraphs detail each group content in depth.

4.1 Indicators for the Access Meter

The access activities will be represented through three indicators: authentication activities, connection activities and modification of authentication configurations. The authentication activities correspond to the activities of login of an user or an administrator. The connection activities reflect the system activities during the process of authentication. These activities include the connection to an external service of authentication and other necessary transactions to identify the connected account. The monitoring of the modification of configuration is essential to detect potential intrusion activities since this one is the entry point for all IS users (section 3). All actions concerning the modification of authentication configuration will be taken into account.

4.2 Indicators for the Rights Meter

The rights activities will be represented through two indicators: rights activities and modification of rights configurations. The rights activities explain the use of special rights by a user in order to achieve an operation. The modification of rights activities describes the activities of modification by a user of its own rights or rights of other people or objects.

4.3 Indicators for the System Use Meter

Different activities can be operated on an IS. Files or objects can be of course read, written, deleted, but other special operations can be realized like executing a command, launching an application, starting/restarting/stopping a service. We can differentiate two IS activities; activities of user interactions and activities of IS itself (automated actions). Activities of user interaction include usage of services or applications and also services/applications configuration. Activities of IS describe related actions operate by IS itself like necessary packets transactions, files or configurations upload, etc. Moreover, the IS state reflects the actual load/status of service or IS components. This monitoring point can enhance the detection of abnormal action effects.The figure 5 sums up the selection of indicators for all meters.

5 Indicators Selection Refinement

Previous sections provide a set of relevant indicators to monitor user behaviors. Nevertheless, the set is still too large to be efficiently used as an anomaly detection. In order to reduce this set, this section presents two processes. One based on the selection of checkpoints (key points of observation), and the other one based on the delimitation of the observation perimeter.

5.1 Checkpoints Selection

As explained in section 3.5, attackers' actions pass through bottlenecks called attackers' checkpoints. In order to select the most relevant checkpoints, we analyzed each kind of attacks and determined their checkpoints. The attack-centric taxonomy defined by the DARPA advocates an attack classification through the attack effects. Five effect classes are distinguished: User to Root, Remote to local, Denial of service, Surveillance/probe, System Access/Alter data. We enrich these classes by adding for each class all possible attackers actions leading to a specific effect.

	Information	Gain	Loss
Access Meter	**Authentication Activities**		
	Authentication_Activity.login.XXX_Admin	Success	Failed/Denied
	Authentication_Activity.login.XXX_Account	Success	Failed/Denied
	Connection Activities		
	System_Activity.Connection.XXX	Success	Failed/Denied
		Success	Failed/Denied
	Authentication Modification		
	Authentication_Config.Add/Modify.XXX	Success	Failed/Denied
	Authentication_Config.Delete.XXX	Failed/Denied	Success
	Authentication_Config.Lock.XXX	Failed/Denied	Success
	Authentication_Config.UnLock.XXX	Success	Failed/Denied
	Authentication_Config.Repair.XXX	Success	Failed/Denied
Rights Meter	**Rights Activities**		
	Rights_Activity.Read/Write/Delete.XXX	Success	Failed/Denied
	Rights Modification		
	Rights_Config.Add.XXX.Admin/Account	Success	Failed/Denied
	Rights_Config.Modify.XXX.Admin/Account	Success	Failed/Denied
	Rights_Config.Delete.XXX.Admin/Account	Failed/Denied	Success
System Meter	**System Use**		
	System_Activity.Read/Write/Delete.XXX	Success	Failed/Denied
	System_Activity.Execute.XXX	Success	Failed/Denied
	System_Activity.Start/Restart/Stop.XXX	Failed/Denied	Success
	System Internal Activities		
	System_Activity.Forward.XXX	Success	Failed/Denied
	System_Activity.Send/Receive.XXX	Success	Failed/Denied
	Modification of System		
	System_Config.Add/Modify/Delete.XXX	Success	Failed/Denied
	System State		
	System_Information.Threshold.XXX	Success	Failed/Denied

Fig. 5 Indicators selection

We analyzed all checkpoints of all possible actions leading to one of these five effects. In order to illustrate our approach, we detail the attacker checkpoints for the User to Root effect. One of the main objectives of an attacker is to reach root rights on a host. The authentication and the connection to the IS are two requirements to achieve this objective. As soon as the attacker is connected, several actions are possible to realize this exploit. Checkpoints exist for each of these possible actions. Six actions can lead to a User to Root effect. The gain action consists in modifying the rights of a running session. The associated checkpoint is the modification of rights for this session. Another way of privilege escalation is the realization of an injection. An injection consists in launching an operation through a started session or service. The checkpoint needed to achieve this operation is the launch of the command. Furthermore, an overflow overloads a service in order to execute a command, can lead to gain upper rights.By flooding a buffer or a service, an attacker can overwrite another memory space and execute commands or scripts.To do this, a command or a request needs to be launched after the packet sending for the overload. The bypass attacker action which consists in bypassing authentication and rights by an exploit, is more difficult to be detected. Usually, a command execution is realized before an exploit. Finally, an attacker can elevate his rights using a virus or a Trojan. These Malwares are programs installed in the system with more rights and obviously need a program installation. The installation of a program or service defines a checkpoint for the Malwares usage. The checkpoint study leads to reduce the number of unavoidable checkpoint monitoring at a considerable degree. The final list of checkpoints are presented in figure 6.

5.2 Monitoring Perimeter Delimitation

The second reduction process consists in focusing on the monitoring of filtered indicators on special IS components. The relevancy of each indicator depends of the location where there are collected. The perimeter of observation of these indicators depends of the nature of the IS component from which there are collected. We separate IS components into three classes: components involved in work-oriented activities, components used for IS communications and one focused on security components. We differentiate components involved in work-oriented activities with their location in the IS and their criticality regarding their business importance (User Host LAN, Mobile User Host, Classical/sensitive LAN Server, Classical/sensitive private DMZ Server,Classical/sensitive public DMZ Server). The components of IS communications include the network components that manage and maintain the network activity (Network equipments). Moreover, we specify different network traffics, witnesses of network exchanges in the IS. (Internal LAN Traffic , LAN-DMZ traffic, LAN-Internet Traffic, DMZ Internet traffic). Then, components involved in the security management, detection and configuration compose the security components group (Firewall, Antivirus, IDS/IPS, Security Information Management). This classification of IS components allows defining appropriate information monitoring regarding their nature, location and sensitivity. The figure 6 sums up a proposition of indicators regarding the perimeter delimitation and checkpoints selection.

6 Experimentation

Anomaly detection used to test our approach is trained with normal event sequences [16]. Then, these sequences are transformed in a Bayesian Network where nodes represent events and linked nodes represent sequences of events. This approach highlights three anomaly classes: node anomalies (identification of unknown events), state anomalies (identification of unknown sources of events) and probability anomalies (identification of unfrequent sequences of events). We compared the detection rates of [16] with and without our indicators selection. The experimentation was realized on two datasets (training and test). The training data set is composed of 1500 events collected on heterogeneous probes. The test dataset is composed of 60 usual events and 30 events composed of attack scenarios (DoS, Bruteforce, Trojan contamination) and unusual system use. The resulting Bayesian Network model has been reduced by 36.60% for nodes and 54.83% for links.

		Work-oriented Activites								IS communications					
Checkpoint indicators	Ontology references	LAN HOST	Mobile User	Sensitive LAN Server	Common LAN Server	Sensitive Pr DMZ Server	Common Pr DMZ Server	Sensitive Pu DMZ Server	Common Pu DMZ Server	Network components	Traffic Internal-LAN	Traffic DMZ-LAN	Traffic Internet-LAN	Traffic Internet-DMZ	Security Components
resources cons	System_Information.Threshold.XXX			X	X	X	X	X	X	X					
Login Failed	Authentication_Activity.Login.XXX_Admin	X	X	X	X	X	X	X	X	X					X
packets sent	System_Activity.Send.XXX.										X	X	X	X	
Connection	System_Activity.Connection.XXX			X	X	X	X	X	X						X
command execution	System_Activity.Execute.Command			X		X		X							
Request execution	System_Activity.Execute.Request			X		X		X							
program Installation	System.activity.processe.start			X	X	X	X	X	X						
	System.activity.processe.stop			X	X	X	X	X	X						
	System.activity.execute.process			X	X	X	X	X	X						
Login system	Authentication_Activity.Login.XXX_Admin	X	X	X	X	X	X	X	X	X					X
Conf File modification	Authentication_Config.modify.XXX	/	/	X	X	X	X	X	X	X					X
rights modification	Authorization_Config.modify.XXX			X	/	X	/	X	/	X					X
Audit Files Modification	System_Config.Modify.XXX.LogFile			X	X	X	X	X	X	X					X
File System modification	System_Config.Modify.XXX.SysFile			X		X		X							X
packets reception	System_Activity.Receive.XXX										/	X	X	X	

XXX = Variable Field

Fig. 6 Perimeter Sum UP

Figure 7 shows the difference between detection rates. White columns represent the number of detected events through the anomaly detection engine without indicators selection. Grey ones represent the number of detected events through the anomaly detection engine with indicators selection. Black columns are the number of scenarios' events inside the test data set. We can notice that, for the events detection of attack scenarios, the same detection rates is found. However, the unusual system use detection rate is slightly lower. Moreover the indicators selection reduces the false positive rate. False positives have been reduced from 10.0% to 6.6%.

To enhance the complexity reduction, we compared the model computation time with and without our indicators reduction. The model computation was based on the training data set previously described and enriched by three other training data sets of 3000, 4500 and 6000 events. These training data sets share same types of events proportions. Figure 8 shows a significant reduction of the model computation time when only relevant indicators are selected. We can notice that for a low number of events, time reduction is of about 20% whereas for a higher number of events, time reduction is of about 40%. These results can be explained by the fact that new relations between events appear when the number of events is high. By deleting irrelevant information, indicators selection also deletes irrelevant relation. The invariability of the time reduction for a high number of events is due to the fact that no new relation between events has been found. The lack of new relations can be explained by the composition of the events which maintains the same proportion of alert's types.

More complex experimentations are under construction. We modeled a set of 86000 events following the [16] approach and highlight a node reduction of 24.40% and a link reduction of 34.12%. We presently work on the comparison of detection rates on large attack scenarios datasets.

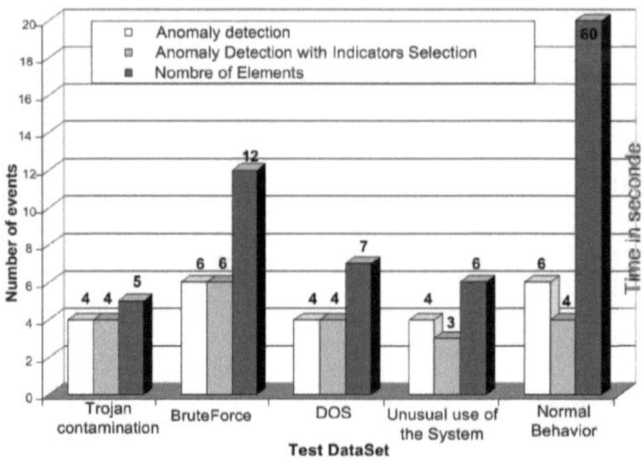

Fig. 7 Detection Rate Comparison

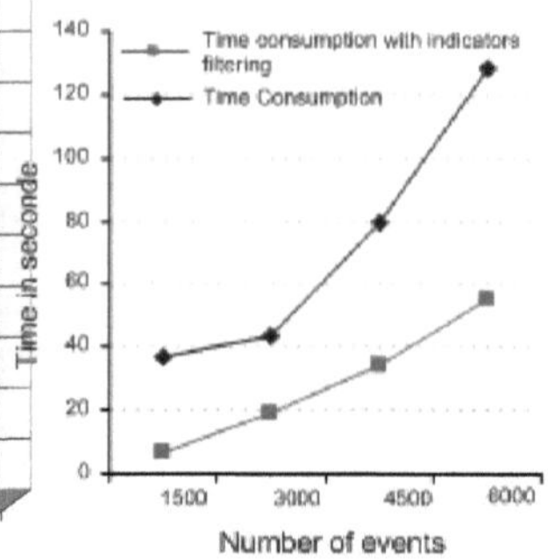

Fig. 8 Modeling Time Consumption

7 Conclusion and Discussions

In this paper, we presented both the benefit of the IS monitoring point selection (called indicators) that reduces the volume of data to handle and the selection method. After analyzing the significance and the relationships between each monitoring point (based on the state of the art) within IS user approaches, we emphasized necessary indicators for the monitoring of relevant behavioral deviances. Focused on the attackers' checkpoints, our set of indicators represents bottlenecks of attackers and legitimate users in the IS. Combined with business perimeter delimitations, we considerably lower the number of indicators, thus the number of sources observations. This complexity reduction allows a better scalability and the creation of more detailed models. We already tested our approach on anomaly detection engines and decreased significantly the complexity of the normal behavior model, slightly reducing the detection rate. We intended to realize deeper experimentations on large datasets with other anomaly detection engines.

The indicators reduction could also be applied to some global anomaly detections to compare and enhance our first results. In the same way, our further works tend to specify relevant sequence of events. This approach will enhance the complexity of the reduction of anomaly detection engines which exploit sequences of events.

References

1. Adballah Abbey Sebyala, Temitope Olukemi,Lionel Sacks. Active platform security through intrusion detection using naive bayesian network for anomaly detection. In *Proceedings of the London Communications Symposium 2002*, 2002.
2. A. Alharby and H. Imai. Security protocols protection based on anomaly detection. *IEICE Transactions on Information and Systems*, E89-D(1):189–200, 2006.
3. Anand Balachandran, Geoffrey M. Voelker, Paramvir Bahl, and P. Venkat Rangan. Characterizing user behavior and network performance in a public wireless lan. In *SIGMETRICS '02: Proceedings of the 2002 ACM SIGMETRICS international conference on Measurement and modeling of computer systems*, pages 195–205, New York, NY, USA, 2002. ACM Press.
4. Fatiha Benali, Veronique Legrand, Sephane Ubeda. An ontology for the management of heteregenous alerts of information system. In *SAM*, 2007.
5. S. Chari and P. Cheng. Bluebox: A policy-driven, host-based intrusion detection system, 2003.
6. Frédéric Cuppens, Fabien Autrel, Alexandre Miège, and Salem Benferhat. Recognizing malicious intention in an intrusion detection process. In *HIS*, pages 806–817, 2002.
7. Olivier M. Dain, Robert K. Cunningham. Building scenarios from a heterogeneous alert stream. In *IEEE SMC Information Assurance Workshop*, 2001.
8. D. Denning. An intrusion detection model. In *IEEE Transactions on Software Engeneering*, pages SE–13:222–232, 1987.
9. William DuMouchel. Computer intrusion detection based on bayes factors for comparing command transition probabilities. Technical report, National Institute of Statistical Sciences (NISS), 1999.
10. Eleazar Eskin, Wenke Lee, and Salvatore J. Stolfo. Modelling system calls for intrusion detection with dynamic window sizes. In *the DARPA Conference and Exposition on Information Survivability. DISCEX '01*, 2001.
11. Juan M. Estvez-Tapiador, Pedro Garcia-Teodoro, and Jess E. Daz-Verdejo. Anomaly detection methods in wired networks: a survey and taxonomy. *Computer Communications*, 27(16):1569–1584, 2004.
12. Annarita Giani, Ian Gregorio De Souza,Vincent Berk, George Cybenko. Attribution and aggregation of network flows for security analysis. In *FloCon 2006*, 2006.
13. Adam G. Pennington, John D. Strunk, John Linwood Griffin, Craig A.N. Soules, Garth R. Goodson, Gregory R. Ganger. Storage-based intrusion detection: Watching storage activity for suspicious behavior. In *the 12th USENIX Security Symposium*, 2003.
14. Ludovic Me and Cdric Michel. La dtection d'intrusions : bref aperu et derniers dveloppements. Actes du congrs EUROSEC'99, 1999.
15. B. Morin and H. Debar. Correlation of intrusion symptoms: an application of chronicles. In *6th International Conference on Recent Advances in Intrusion Detection (RAID'2003)*, 2003.
16. Jacques Saraydaryan, Veronique Legrand & Sephane Ubeda . Behavioral anomaly detection using bayesian modelization based on a global vision of the system. In *7eme Conference Internationale sur les NOuvelles TEchnologies de la REpartition (NOTERE 07)*, 2007.
17. Alexandr Seleznyov and Seppo Puuronen. Anomaly intrusion detection systems: Handling temporal relations between events. In *Recent Advances in Intrusion Detection*, 1999.

Leveraging Lattices to Improve Role Mining

Alessandro Colantonio, Roberto Di Pietro, Alberto Ocello

Abstract In this paper we provide a new formal framework applicable to role mining algorithms. This framework is based on a rigorous analysis of identifiable patterns in access permission data. In particular, it is possible to derive a *lattice* of candidate roles from the permission powerset. We formally prove some interesting properties about such lattices. These properties, a contribution on their own, can be applied practically to optimize role mining algorithms. Data redundancies associated with co-occurrences of permissions among users can be easily identified and eliminated, allowing for increased output quality and reduced processing time. To prove the effectiveness of our proposal, we have applied our results to two existing role mining algorithms: Apriori and RBAM. Application of these modified algorithms to a realistic data set consistently reduced running time and, in some cases, also greatly improved output quality; all of which confirmed our analytical findings.

1 Introduction

In recent years *role-based access control* (RBAC, [3]) has been spreading within organizations, greatly due to simplicity of the model: a role is just a set of access permissions, while users are assigned to roles based on duties to fulfill. However, companies still have considerable difficulty migrating to this model due to the com-

Alessandro Colantonio
Engiweb Security, Roma, Italy, e-mail: alessandro.colantonio@eng.it
Università di Roma Tre, Roma, Italy, e-mail: colanton@mat.uniroma3.it

Roberto Di Pietro
Università di Roma Tre, Roma, Italy, e-mail: dipietro@mat.uniroma3.it
Universitat Rovira i Virgili, UNESCO Chair in Data Privacy, Dept. of Computer Engineering and Maths, Av. Països Catalans 26, E-43007 Tarragona, Catalonia, e-mail: roberto.dipietro@urv.cat

Alberto Ocello
Engiweb Security, Roma, Italy, e-mail: alberto.ocello@eng.it

Please use the following format when citing this chapter:

Colantonio, A., Di Pietro, R. and Ocello, A., 2008, in IFIP International Federation for Information Processing, Volume 278; *Proceedings of the IFIP TC 11 23rd International Information Security Conference*; Sushil Jajodia, Pierangela Samarati, Stelvio Cimato; (Boston: Springer), pp. 333–347.

plexity involved in identifying a set of roles fitting the real needs of the company. Thus was born *role engineering*, the discipline of role definition based on actual company needs [5]. Various role engineering approaches proposed in literature are typically classified as: *top-down* or *bottom-up* [7,8,13]. The former carefully deconstructs business processes into elementary components, identifying system features necessary to carry out specific tasks. This activity is mainly manual, requiring a high level analysis of the business [10–12]. The latter class searches legacy access control systems to find *de facto* roles embedded in existing permissions. Automating this process with data mining techniques [4, 9, 13–16] is called *role mining*. All role mining techniques proposed to date in literature seek to derive candidate roles through the identification of data patterns in currently existing access rights. Despite important differences among the various techniques, almost all take advantage of some common principles summarized by the following:

- *If two access permissions always occur together among users, these should simultaneously belong to the same candidate roles.* Without further access data semantics, a bottom-up approach cannot differentiate between a role made up of two permissions and two roles containing individual permissions [15]. Moreover, defining roles made up of as many permissions as possible minimizes the administration cost by reducing the number of role-user assignments [4].
- *If no user possesses a given combination of access permissions, it makes no sense to define a role containing such combination.* Similar to the previous point, if no user actually performs a task for which a certain permission set is necessary, it is usually better not to define a role containing such an unassignable set.
- *It is quite common within an organization to have many users possessing the same set of access permissions.* This is one of the main justifications that brought about the RBAC model. The creation of a role in connection with a set of co-occurring permissions is typically more advantageous since the number of relationships to be managed is reduced [4].

The following example clarifies the assertions just made, particularly that of the first point presented. If of the given four permissions p_1, p_2, p_3, p_4, the pair p_1, p_2 is always found together with p_3, p_4, it is advisable not to define two distinct roles $\{p_1, p_2\}$ and $\{p_3, p_4\}$ but, rather, a single role $\{p_1, p_2, p_3, p_4\}$. This is different from saying that no user possesses only p_1, p_2 without also having some other permission. Suppose some users possess only p_3, others only p_4, others p_1, p_2, p_3 and still others p_1, p_2, p_4. In this case, even if p_1, p_2 never occur "by themselves", it could be convenient to define the role $\{p_1, p_2\}$ since roles $\{p_3\}$ and $\{p_4\}$ will certainly already exist individually. Thus, avoiding roles $\{p_1, p_2, p_3\}$ and $\{p_1, p_2, p_4\}$.

The cited role mining techniques do not always exploit the above-mentioned observations, even though analyzing such data "recurrences" could improve the quality of proposed candidate roles or increase computational efficiency of the algorithms.

Contributions. The mathematical analysis introduced in this paper provides a new model capable of increasing output quality and reducing process time of role mining algorithms. The model revolves around identifiable patterns in access permissions data. Through analysis of user permissions, a *lattice* [6] of candidate roles can be constructed from the permission powerset. Notable properties of this lattice will be discussed to substantiate their effectiveness in optimizing role mining algorithms. Leveraging our results, data redundancies associated with co-occurrence of permissions among users can be easily identified and eliminated, thus improving the role mining output.

To prove the merit of our proposal, we have applied our results to two algorithms: Apriori [1] and RBAM [4]. Applying them to a realistic data set yielded drastic reductions in running time and often provided significant redundancy elimination.

Roadmap. This paper is organized as follows: Section 2 cites the main related works. Section 3 reviews mathematical tools and RBAC concepts required for the analysis. Section 4 provides a description of how to define roles based on the permission-powerset lattice, and then Section 5 further analyzes this lattice by introducing the concept of equivalent sublattice and a few of its properties. Section 6 shows how to apply permission-powerset lattice properties to existing role mining techniques. We implement and test, over a real data set, our proposed framework with reference to two role mining algorithms, obtaining support for our theoretical findings. Finally, Section 7 reports concluding remarks and indicates further research directions.

2 Related Work

The proposed mathematical formalism is based on some well-known concepts such as the lattice, powerset, partial order, Hasse diagrams and directed acyclic graphs. The following section introduce these subjects; further details can be found in [6].

Various role mining techniques can benefit from this analysis. Due to space constraints, only a few of them will be summarized. The first improved algorithm is Apriori [1]. It is used in *Market Basket Analysis* (MBA, also known as *association-rule mining*), a method for discovering customer purchasing patterns by extracting associations or recurrences from store transaction databases. Role mining can be seen as a particular application of MBA, simply considering permissions, roles and users instead of products, transactions and customers, respectively. The RBAM algorithm [4] also benefits from the present analysis. It is a specialized implementation of Apriori in which any permission combinations increasing the RBAC model administration cost are rejected. This paper shows how data pruning operations can be conducted to improve RBAM efficiency without detracting from output quality.

There also exist some role mining techniques that take into account some properties described in the previous section. The most important is probably *subset enumeration* [15]. This algorithm starts from permission sets possessed by users and identifies potential candidate roles from all possible intersections among these sets. The resulting candidate role set presents analogies to a lattice of roles where all redundancies related to permission co-occurrence among users are eliminated.

3 Background and Preliminaries

3.1 Posets, Lattices, Hasse Diagrams and Graphs

In computer science and mathematics, a *directed acyclic graph* (DAG) is a directed graph with no directed cycles. For any vertex v, there is no non-empty directed path starting and ending on v, thus DAG "flows" in a single direction. Each DAG provides a *partial order* to its vertices. We write $u \succeq v$ when there exists a directed path from v to u. The *transitive closure* is the reachability order "$\succeq$". A *partially ordered set* (or *poset*) formalizes the concept of element ordering [6]. A poset $\langle S, \succeq \rangle$ consists of a set S and a binary relation "$\succeq$" that indicates, for certain element pairs in the set, which element precedes the other. A partial order differs from a total order in that some pairs of elements may not be comparable. The symbol "$\succeq$" often indicates a *non-strict* (or *reflexive*) partial order. A *strict* (or *irreflexive*) partial order "$\succ$" is a binary relation that is irreflexive and transitive, and therefore asymmetric. If "$\succeq$" is a non-strict partial order, then the corresponding strict partial order "$\succ$" is the reflexive reduction given by: $a \succ b \Leftrightarrow a \succeq b \wedge a \neq b$. Conversely, if "$\succ$" is a strict partial order, then the corresponding non-strict partial order "$\succeq$" is the reflexive closure given by: $a \succeq b \Leftrightarrow a \succ b \vee a = b$. An *antichain* of $\langle S, \succeq \rangle$ is a subset $A \subseteq S$ such that $\forall x, y \in A : x \succeq y \Rightarrow x = y$. We write $x \parallel y$ if $x \not\succeq y \wedge y \not\succeq x$. A *chain* is a subset $C \subseteq S$ such that $\forall x, y \in C : x \succeq y \vee y \succeq x$. Given a poset $\langle S, \succeq \rangle$, the *down-set* of $x \in S$ is $\downarrow x \triangleq \{y \in S \mid x \succeq y\}$, while the *up-set* of $x \in S$ is $\uparrow x \triangleq \{y \in S \mid y \succeq x\}$. Given $a \succeq b$, the interval $[a, b]$ is the set of points x satisfying $a \succeq x \wedge x \succeq b$. Similarly, the interval (a, b) is set of points x satisfying $a \succ x \wedge x \succ b$.

The *transitive reduction* of a binary relation R on a set S is the smallest relation R' on S such that the transitive closure of R' is the same as the transitive closure of R. If the transitive closure of R is antisymmetric and finite, then R' is unique. Given a graph where R is the set of arcs and S the set of vertices, its transitive reduction is referred to as its *minimal representation*. The transitive reduction of a finite acyclic graph is unique and algorithms for finding it have the same time complexity as algorithms for transitive closure [2]. A *Hasse diagram* is a picture of a poset, representing the transitive reduction of the partial order. Each element of S is a vertex. A line from x to y is drawn if $y \succ x$, and there is no z such that $y \succ z \succ x$. In this case, we say y *covers* x, or y is an *immediate successor* of x, also written $y \gtrdot x$. A *lattice* is a poset in which every pair of elements has a unique *join* (the least upper bound, or *lub*) and a *meet* (the greatest lower bound, or *glb*). The name "lattice" is suggested by the Hasse diagram depicting it. Given a poset $\langle L, \succeq \rangle$, L is a lattice if $\forall x, y \in L$ the element pair has both a join, denoted by $x \curlyvee y$, and a meet, denoted by $x \curlywedge y$ within L. Let $\langle L, \succeq, \curlyvee, \curlywedge \rangle$ be a lattice. We say that $\langle \Lambda, \succeq, \curlyvee, \curlywedge \rangle : \Lambda \subseteq L$ is a *sublattice* if and only if $\forall x, y \in \Lambda : x \curlyvee y \in \Lambda \wedge x \curlywedge y \in \Lambda$. In general, we define:

- $\bigcurlyvee \Lambda \triangleq \{x \in L \mid \forall \ell \in L, \forall \lambda \in \Lambda : \ell \succeq \lambda \Rightarrow \ell \succeq x\}$, the join of Λ (lub);
- $\bigcurlywedge \Lambda \triangleq \{x \in L \mid \forall \ell \in L, \forall \lambda \in \Lambda : \lambda \succeq \ell \Rightarrow x \succeq \ell\}$, the meet of Λ (glb).

In particular, $x \curlyvee y \triangleq \bigcurlyvee \{x, y\}$ and $x \curlywedge y \triangleq \bigcurlywedge \{x, y\}$. Both $\bigcurlyvee \Lambda$ and $\bigcurlywedge \Lambda$ are unique.

3.2 RBAC Model

We shall now review some of the concepts in the RBAC model according to the ANSI/INCITS standard [3]. The entities of interest for the present analysis are:

- $PERMS$, the set of all possible access permissions; $USERS$, the set of all system users; $ROLES \subseteq 2^{PERMS}$, the set of all roles.
- $UA \subseteq USERS \times ROLES$, the set of user-role assignments. Given a role, the function $ass\_users\colon ROLES \to 2^{USERS}$ identifies all the assigned users.
- $PA \subseteq PERMS \times ROLES$, the set of permission-role assignments. Given a role, the function $ass\_perms\colon ROLES \to 2^{PERMS}$ identifies all the assigned perms.
- $RH \subseteq ROLES \times ROLES$, the set of hierarchical relationships between pairs of roles. $\langle r_1, r_2 \rangle \in RH$ indicates that all the permissions assigned to r_1 are also assigned to r_2, and some more permissions are assigned to r_2.

The symbol "$\succeq$" indicates a partial order based on the role hierarchy. If $r_1 \succeq r_2$, then r_1 is referred to as the *senior* of r_2, while r_2 as the *junior* of r_1. If $r_1 \gtrdot r_2$ then r_1 is an *immediate senior* of r_2, while r_2 is an *immediate junior* of r_1. For the sake of simplicity, we define the functions $ass\_users()$ and $ass\_perms()$ indicating respectively the users and permissions *authorized* by a role—what a role inherits along the hierarchical path. This is slightly different from the definition given by the NIST standard: $ass\_users(r)$ thus indicates users possessing permissions assigned to role r instead of users assigned to role r but not to its seniors. In particular:

$$r_1 \succeq r_2 \Rightarrow ass\_users(r_1) \subseteq ass\_users(r_2) \land ass\_perms(r_1) \supseteq ass\_perms(r_2). \quad (1)$$

In addition to RBAC standard entities, the set $UP \subseteq USERS \times PERMS$ identifies permission to user assignments. In an access control system it is represented by entities describing access rights (e.g., access control lists). Given a permission, the function $perm\_users\colon PERMS \to 2^{USERS}$ identifies the set of users possessing it.

3.3 Support, Confidence and Equivalence

We now review some definitions given in [4]. Since RH defines a partial order on the role set, $\langle ROLES, \succeq \rangle$ is thus a poset on which the following definitions are based.

Definition 1. Given a role $r \in ROLES$, the *support* of that role is defined as $support(r) \triangleq |ass\_users(r)|/|USERS|$ and indicates the percentage of users possessing all permissions assigned to r.

Definition 2. Given $r \in ROLES$, the *degree* of that candidate role is defined as $degree(r) \triangleq |ass\_perms(r)|$ and indicates the number of permissions assigned to r.

Definition 3. Given a pair $r_1, r_2 \in ROLES : r_2 \succeq r_1$, the *confidence* between them is $confidence(r_2 \succeq r_1) \triangleq |ass\_users(r_2)|/|ass\_users(r_1)|$, namely the percentage of users possessing permissions of the junior also possessing permissions of the senior.

Lemma 1. *Given a role pair* $r_1, r_2 \in ROLES : r_2 \succeq r_1$*, the confidence between such a role pair is* $confidence(r_2 \succeq r_1) = support(r_2)/\, support(r_1)$.

Definition 4. Given a role pair $r_1, r_2 \in ROLES$, we call them *equivalent*, and indicate this with $r_1 \equiv r_2$, if and only if $ass\_users(r_1) = ass\_users(r_2)$.

The following properties are additionally demonstrated:

Lemma 2. *The equivalence relation is transitive, meaning that* $\forall r_1, r_2, r_3 \in ROLES$: $r_1 \equiv r_2 \wedge r_2 \equiv r_3 \;\Rightarrow\; r_1 \equiv r_3$.

Proof. According to Definition 4, $ass\_users(r_1) = ass\_users(r_2)$ and $ass\_users(r_2) = ass\_users(r_3)$, thus $ass\_users(r_1) = ass\_users(r_3)$. □

Lemma 3. *Given* $r_1, r_2 \in ROLES : r_1 \succeq r_2$*, if* $confidence(r_1 \succeq r_2) = 1$ *then* $r_1 \equiv r_2$.

Proof. From Def. 3, $confidence(r_1 \succeq r_2) = 1 \;\Rightarrow\; |ass\_users(r_1)| = |ass\_users(r_2)|$. From Eq. 1, $ass\_users(r_1) \subseteq ass\_users(r_2) \;\Rightarrow\; ass\_users(r_1) = ass\_users(r_2)$. □

4 Roles Based on the Permission-Powerset Lattice

We now introduce the model on which the following analysis is based. Consider the powerset of a set S (the set of all subsets of S) written as 2^S. The set 2^S can easily be ordered via subset inclusion "$\supseteq$". It can be demonstrated that $\langle 2^S, \supseteq, \cup, \cap \rangle$ is a lattice [6]. Setting $S = PERMS$ makes it possible to build an RBAC model based on all derivable roles from a given permission set. As the operator "$\succeq$" (see Section 3.2) is based on the inclusion operator "$\supseteq$" applied to permissions assigned to roles, it is thus natural to map the operators "$\curlyvee$" to "$\cup$" (the join of two roles represented by the union of all assigned permissions) and "$\curlywedge$" to "$\cap$" (the meet of two roles represented by shared permissions). Every permission combination of the lattice $\langle 2^{PERMS}, \succeq, \curlyvee, \curlywedge \rangle$ identifies the following: (1) an element of *ROLES*, (2) its corresponding relationships in *PA* to such permissions, (3) all permission inclusions in *RH* which involve the role and (4) all relationships in *UA* to users possessing such combination. *RH* is defined to represent the transitive reduction of the graph associated to the lattice. Moreover, if a user is assigned to a role r, then *UA* will contain relationships between r, its juniors and users assigned to them, namely $\forall r \in ROLES, \forall j \in \downarrow r : ass\_users(r) \subseteq ass\_users(j)$.

For simplicity sake, from now on the lattice $\langle 2^{PERMS}, \succeq, \curlyvee, \curlywedge \rangle$ is identified only with the set *ROLES*. The following are some basic properties of this lattice:

Lemma 4. *Removing a role* r *from ROLES, and its corresponding relationships in PA, UA, RH, such that* $ass\_perms(r) \neq \bigcap_{r' \in ROLES} ass\_perms(r')$ *and* $ass\_perms(r) \neq \bigcup_{r' \in ROLES} ass\_perms(r')$*, the resulting set ROLES is still a lattice.*

Proof. The role r such that $ass\_perms(r) = \bigcap_{r' \in ROLES} ass\_perms(r')$ represents a lower bound for any role pairs, similarly $ass\_perms(r) = \bigcup_{r' \in ROLES} ass\_perms(r')$ represents an upper bound, thus lattice properties are preserved. □

Table 1 An example of set *UP*

User	*Perms*	*User*	*Perms*	*User*	*Perms*	*User*	*Perms*	*User*	*Perms*
u_1	{1}	u_8	{1,3}	u_{15}	{3,6}	u_{22}	{1,3,5}	u_{29}	{2,4,6}
u_2	{2}	u_9	{1,4}	u_{16}	{4,5}	u_{23}	{1,3,6}	u_{30}	{1,2,3,5}
u_3	{3}	u_{10}	{1,5}	u_{17}	{4,6}	u_{24}	{1,4,5}	u_{31}	{1,2,3,6}
u_4	{4}	u_{11}	{1,6}	u_{18}	{1,2,3}	u_{25}	{1,4,6}	u_{32}	{1,2,4,5}
u_5	{5}	u_{12}	{2,5}	u_{19}	{1,2,4}	u_{26}	{2,3,5}	u_{33}	{1,2,4,6}
u_6	{6}	u_{13}	{2,6}	u_{20}	{1,2,5}	u_{27}	{2,3,6}	u_{34}	{2,3,4,5,6}
u_7	{1,2}	u_{14}	{3,5}	u_{21}	{1,2,6}	u_{28}	{2,4,5}	u_{35}	{1,2,3,4,5,6}

Note 1. Given $r \in ROLES$ then $\forall s \in \uparrow r : support(r) \geq support(s)$. In fact, users possessing permission combination $ass\_perms(r)$ do not necessarily possess other permissions. Analogously, $\forall j \in \downarrow r : support(r) \leq support(j)$. Apriori [1] and RBAM [4] algorithms use this property as a pruning condition to limit the solution space.

Based on the initial hypothesis of Section 1, *roles to which unused permission combinations are assigned do not represent significant candidate roles*. Such roles have support equal to 0 and can be eliminated from *ROLES*, except for the meet and join which are required to preserve lattice properties (see Lemma 4). Removing such roles results in a lattice that satisfies the following property:

Lemma 5. *The immediate seniors of a role $r \in ROLES$ differ from r by a single permission, that is* $\forall r, s \in ROLES : s \gtrdot r \Rightarrow degree(s) = degree(r) + 1$.

Proof. For Equation 1, any role represented by a subset of $ass\_perms(s)$ has support > 0 and is at least assigned to users $ass\_users(s)$. Thus, *ROLES* contains all roles obtained by removing a single permission from $ass\_perms(s)$, including *r*. □

5 Equivalent Sublattices

Let *ROLES* be the lattice based on 2^{PERMS} in which roles with support equal to 0 have been eliminated, except for the meet and join. Such set has a very simple property: *every candidate role set is contained within*, since it provides all user-assignable permission combinations. Beyond eliminating roles having support equal to 0, this section shows that *it is also possible to remove roles presenting equivalence with other roles*, as they do not belong to any "reasonable" candidate role set.

Table 1 shows an example of *UP* presenting equivalence relationships. By observing the data, it can be noted that all users simultaneously possessing permissions 3 and 4 also always have permissions 2, 5 and 6. Figure 1 shows the role lattice built on the given set *UP* with junior roles above and senior roles below. Despite this being a directed graph, direction indicators are absent (from top to bottom) to avoid complicating the figure. Thicker lines represent hierarchical relationships with confidence equal to 1, namely equivalence relationships (see Lemma 3).

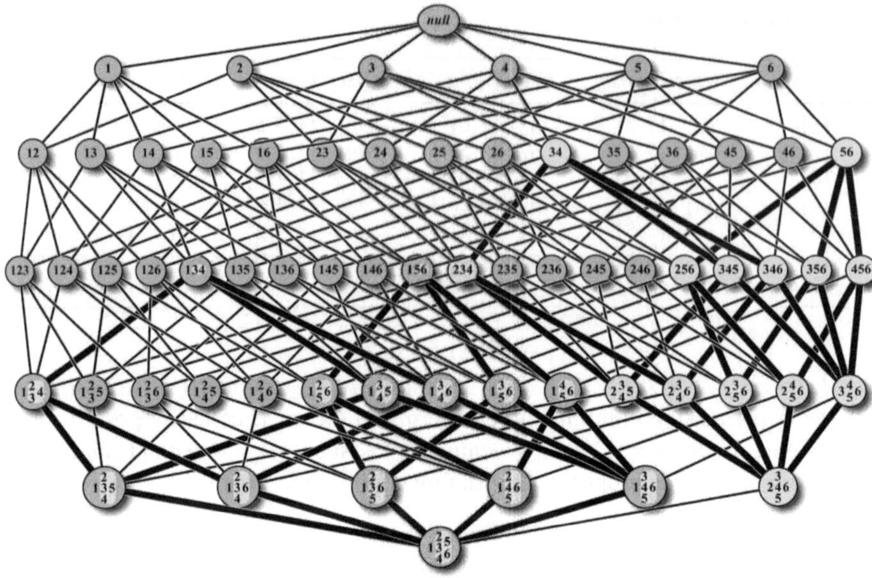

Fig. 1 Hasse diagram of the lattice based on permission powerset derived from Table 1

Next, we want to demonstrate that *when a role has more equivalent seniors, the combination of its assigned permissions still represents an equivalent role*. For example, $\{3,4\} \equiv \{2,3,4\}$, $\{3,4\} \equiv \{3,4,5\}$ and $\{3,4\} \equiv \{3,4,6\}$ implies $\{3,4\} \equiv \{2,3,4,5,6\}$. Moreover, the set of equivalent seniors forms a sublattice. We will now formalize this with a series of theorems demonstrating that: (1) given an interval of roles, if the bounds are equivalent then all roles on the interval are equivalent with each other; (2) by analyzing immediate equivalent seniors, the equivalent role with the maximum degree can be determined; (3) an interval of equivalent roles having the equivalent role with the maximum degree as upper bound is a sublattice of *ROLES*; (4) such sublattice is replicated in *ROLES* with the same "structure".

Theorem 1. *Given a role pair $r_1, r_2 \in ROLES$ such that $r_2 \succeq r_1$ and $r_1 \equiv r_2$, then all roles on the interval $[r_1, r_2]$ are equivalent to each other:*

$$\forall r, r_1, r_2 \in ROLES : r_2 \succeq r \succeq r_1 \land r_1 \equiv r_2 \quad \Rightarrow \quad r \equiv r_1 \equiv r_2.$$

Proof. According to Equation 1, $\text{ass\_users}(r_2) \subseteq \text{ass\_users}(r) \subseteq \text{ass\_users}(r_1)$. But $\text{ass\_users}(r_1) = \text{ass\_users}(r_2)$, so $\text{ass\_users}(r_2) = \text{ass\_users}(r) = \text{ass\_users}(r_1)$. □

Theorem 2. *A role $r \in ROLES$ is equivalent to the role represented by the union of permissions assigned to any set of its equivalent seniors:*

$$\forall r \in ROLES, \forall R \subseteq \uparrow r, \forall r' \in R : r' \equiv r \quad \Rightarrow$$
$$\Rightarrow \quad \exists s \in ROLES : r \equiv s \land \text{ass\_perms}(s) = \bigcup_{r' \in R} \text{ass\_perms}(r').$$

Proof. Users possessing a role are those possessing all the permissions assigned to that role, namely $\forall r' \in ROLES : ass\_users(r') = \bigcap_{p \in ass\_perms(r')} perm\_users(p)$. According to the hypothesis, $\forall r_i \in R : r_i \equiv r$, so all roles in R are assigned with the same users. Then $\bigcap_{r' \in R} \left(\bigcap_{p \in ass\_perms(r')} perm\_users(p) \right) = ass\_users(r)$. Such an equality can also be written as $\bigcap_{p \in \bigcup_{r' \in R} ass\_perms(r')} perm\_users(p) = ass\_users(r)$ but $\bigcup_{r' \in R} ass\_perms(r')$ represent the set of permissions assigned to the role s. □

Definition 5. Given $r \in ROLES$, the *maximum equivalent role* of r, written $\bar{r}$, is the role represented by the union of permissions of its immediate equivalent seniors:

$$ass\_perms(\bar{r}) = \bigcup_{r' \in ROLES \mid r' \gtrdot r \wedge r' \equiv r} ass\_perms(r').$$

The name attributed to the role $\bar{r}$ is justified by the following theorem:

Theorem 3. *Given $r \in ROLES$, $\bar{r}$ is the equivalent role with the highest degree:*

$$\forall r' \in ROLES : r' \equiv r \wedge r' \neq \bar{r} \quad \Rightarrow \quad degree(r') < degree(\bar{r}).$$

Proof. Seeking a contradiction, suppose that $r_{\max} \in ROLES : r_{\max} \neq \bar{r}$ is the highest degree role among all those equivalent to r. Since the same users possess both $\bar{r}$ and $r_{\max}$, then $ass\_perms(\bar{r}) \subseteq ass\_perms(r_{\max})$. If this was not the case, then there would exist another role within *ROLES* made up of the union of permissions assigned to $\bar{r}$ and $r_{\max}$ having a larger degree than both of these. This other role would also be equivalent to $\bar{r}$ and $r_{\max}$, since it is possessed by the same users. However, this contradicts the fact that $r_{\max}$ is of the highest degree.

Let $\Delta = ass\_perms(r_{\max}) \setminus ass\_perms(\bar{r})$. If $\Delta \neq \emptyset$, then it is possible to identify "intermediate" roles $\rho \in [r, r_{\max}]$ such that $\exists p \in \Delta : ass\_perms(\rho) = ass\_perms(r) \cup \{p\}$. For Lemma 5, $\rho \gtrdot r$, while for Theorem 1, $\rho \equiv r$. Since $\bar{r}$ is obtained by the union of all permissions assigned to all equivalent immediate seniors, it contains all the permissions of Δ. Consequently, it must be that $\Delta = \emptyset$ and so $\bar{r} = r_{\max}$. □

Theorem 4. *Given $r, s \in ROLES : s \succeq r$, the interval $[r, s]$ is a sublattice of ROLES.*

Proof. As long as $[r, s]$ is a lattice, it must be true that $\forall r_1, r_2 \in [r, s] : r_1 \curlyvee r_2 \in [r, s] \wedge r_1 \curlywedge r_2 \in [r, s]$. Given $r_1, r_2 \in [r, s]$, let r_{ub} be an upper-bound role such that $ass\_perms(r_{\text{ub}}) = ass\_perms(r_2) \cup ass\_perms(r_2)$. Since $s \succeq r_1, r_2$ then the permissions of s include the union of the permissions of r_1, r_2, so $s \succeq r_{\text{ub}}$. Thus, $r_{\text{ub}} \in [r, s]$. Similarly, it can be demonstrated that $[r, s]$ contains a lower-bound role r_{lb} such that $ass\_perms(r_{\text{lb}}) = ass\_perms(r_2) \cap ass\_perms(r_2)$.

Definition 6. Given a role $r \in ROLES$, we define the *equivalent sublattice* of r, indicated by $\varepsilon(r)$, the interval $[r, \bar{r}]$, that is $\varepsilon(r) \triangleq [r, \bar{r}]$.

Note 2. The set $\varepsilon(r)$ *does not* represent all the equivalent roles of r, rather, only a subset. In fact, we could have $r' \in ROLES$ such that $r \equiv r'$ even though $r \parallel r'$. However, for Theorem 3, from the union of permissions assigned to immediate equivalent seniors of r or r', the same maximum equivalent role is obtained, that is $\bar{r} \equiv \bar{r}'$. In fact, in Figure 1, roles $\{3,4\}$ and $\{5,6\}$ are antichain but, being equivalent to each other, they share the same maximum equivalent role $\{2,3,4,5,6\}$.

Note 3. If a role has equivalent seniors, then no user possesses only its permissions, namely if $\exists r' \in (\uparrow r) \setminus r : r \equiv r'$ then $ass\_users(r) \setminus \bigcup_{\rho \in (\uparrow r) \setminus r} ass\_users(\rho) = \emptyset$. The converse is not true. Particularly, if there is no user possessing a given permission combination, it is unknown whether the role made up of such permissions has immediate equivalent seniors. This is verified in Table 1. Permissions 3 and 4 are always found together with 2, 5 and 6. Thus, no user is assigned to role $\{3,4\}$ unless also assigned to one of its seniors. Yet, the contrary is not true: even though $\{2,3\}$ has no immediate equivalent seniors, it is not assigned with any user.

Theorem 5. *Given a role $r \in ROLES$, let $E = \{r' \in ROLES \mid r' \gtrdot r \wedge r' \equiv r\}$ be the set of immediate equivalent seniors of r. Then $|\varepsilon(r)| = 2^{|E|}$.*

Proof. For Lemma 5, $\forall r' \in E : degree(r') = degree(r) + 1$. Thus, permissions assigned to the maximum equivalent role of r include those of r plus a number of other permissions equal to $|E|$, that is $degree(\bar{r}) = degree(r) + |E|$. Further, $\varepsilon(r)$ contains all roles whose permission combinations are between $ass\_perms(r)$ and $ass\_perms(\bar{r})$, all of which have support greater than 0. Hence, the possible permission combinations between $ass\_perms(r)$ and $ass\_perms(\bar{r})$ are $2^{|E|}$.

Theorem 6. *Let there be $r,s \in ROLES$ such that s is an immediate equivalent senior of r. If there is $s' \in ROLES$, an immediate non-equivalent senior or r, then certainly there is a role $s'' \in ROLES$, an immediate equivalent senior of s' and immediate senior of s, represented by the union of permissions of s, s':*

$$\forall r,s,s' \in ROLES \; : \; s \gtrdot r \wedge s' \gtrdot r \wedge s \equiv r \wedge s' \not\equiv r \quad \Rightarrow \quad \exists s'' \in ROLES \; : \\ s'' \gtrdot s \wedge s'' \gtrdot s' \wedge s' \equiv s'' \wedge ass\_perms(s'') = ass\_perms(s) \cup ass\_perms(s').$$

Proof. The role s'' is a senior of both s, s' since $ass\_perms(s'') \supseteq ass\_perms(s)$ and $ass\_perms(s'') \supseteq ass\_perms(s')$. But $r \equiv s$, so $ass\_users(s'') = ass\_users(s) \cap ass\_users(s') = ass\_users(r) \cap ass\_users(s')$. But $ass\_users(s') \subseteq ass\_users(r)$ because of $s' \gtrdot r$, then $ass\_users(s'') = ass\_users(s')$. Finally, for Lemma 5 roles s and s' have an additional permission to that of r. If $s \neq s'$ then $degree(s'') = degree(r) + 2$. Hence, s'' is an immediate senior to both s, s'. □

Note 4. The previous theorem can be observed in Figure 1. The role $\{3,4\}$ has three immediate equivalent senior roles, while $\{1,3,4\}$ represents an immediate non-equivalent senior. For Theorem 6, this means that $\{1,3,4\}$ has *at least* three immediate equivalent seniors, identifiable by adding the permission 1 to equivalent seniors of $\{3,4\}$; according to Theorem 6, further immediate equivalent seniors of $\{1,3,4\}$ are allowed.

Theorem 7. *Let there be $r,s \in ROLES$ such that $s \gtrdot r$ and $s \not\equiv r$. Let also $p = ass\_perms(s) \setminus ass\_perms(r)$. Then there is a replica of the sublattice $\varepsilon(r)$ obtained by adding permission p to those of $\varepsilon(r)$.*

Proof. For Theorem 6, role s has among its immediate equivalent seniors at least those obtainable by adding permission p to immediate equivalent seniors of r. Let then $s' \in \mathit{ROLES}$ be the senior of s represented by the union of such immediate equivalent seniors, meaning $\mathit{ass\_perms}(s') = \mathit{ass\_perms}(\bar{r}) \cup \{p\}$. According to Theorem 2, $s \equiv s'$, while for Theorem 4 the interval $[s, s']$ is a sublattice. Let σ be a role defined from role $\rho \in \varepsilon(r)$ such that $\mathit{ass\_perms}(\sigma) = \mathit{ass\_perms}(\rho) \cup \{p\}$. Then, $s' \succeq \sigma$ since $\mathit{ass\_perms}(\bar{r}) \cup \{p\} \supseteq \mathit{ass\_perms}(\rho) \cup \{p\}$ and $\sigma \succeq s$ because $\mathit{ass\_perms}(\rho) \cup \{p\} \supseteq \mathit{ass\_perms}(r) \cup \{p\}$. Hence, $\sigma \in [s, s']$. □

A direct consequence of the preceding theorem can be seen in Figure 1. The equivalent sublattice $\varepsilon(\{1,3,4\})$ can be obtained from $\varepsilon(\{3,4\})$ by adding the permission 1 to all roles. In the Hasse diagram of *ROLES* it is therefore possible to identify a certain number of equivalent sublattice replicas determined by:

Theorem 8. *Given a role $r \in \mathit{ROLES}$ let S be the set of immediate non-equivalent seniors, $S = \{\rho \in \mathit{ROLES} \mid \rho \gtrdot r \wedge \rho \not\equiv r\}$. Then ROLES has a number of $\varepsilon(r)$ replicas between $|S|$ and $2^{|S|} - 1$.*

Proof. For Theorem 7, for all roles $s \in S$ the sublattice $\varepsilon(r)$ is replicated by adding permission $\mathit{ass\_perms}(s) \setminus \mathit{ass\_perms}(r)$ to every role in $\varepsilon(r)$. So, there are at least $|S|$ sublattice replicas. Starting from S, the set $P = \bigcup_{s \in S} \mathit{ass\_perms}(s) \setminus \mathit{ass\_perms}(r)$ of permissions added to r from non-equivalent seniors of r can be identified. For Lemma 5, the difference of degree between r and $s \in S$ is equal to 1, thus $|P| = |S|$. Every role $s \in S$ has at most $|S| - 1$ immediate non-equivalent seniors, meaning those represented by $\mathit{ass\_perms}(s)$ to which are added one of the permissions of $P \setminus (\mathit{ass\_perms}(s) \setminus \mathit{ass\_perms}(r))$. If, by contradiction, there was a role s', an immediate non-equivalent senior of s, for which $p = \mathit{ass\_perms}(s') \setminus \mathit{ass\_perms}(s) \wedge p \notin P$, then a role r' such that $\mathit{ass\_perms}(r') = \mathit{ass\_perms}(r) \cup \{p\}$ would have a support greater than 0 and would belong to S. This means that, still for Theorem 7, the role s can produce, at most, another $|S| - 1$ replicas. Reiterating the same reasoning for all seniors of r, it can be deduced that at most $2^{|S|} - 1$ replicas can be constructed by roles of $\varepsilon(r)$ to which are added permission combinations of $2^P \setminus \{\emptyset\}$. □

6 Discussion and Applications

The previous section analyzed some properties of a role lattice based on the powerset of permissions excluding combinations of support equal to 0. It was shown that a certain number of equivalent sublattice replicas could exist within such lattice. Based on the premises of Section 1, *all these replicas can be eliminated from the set of candidate roles except for maximum equivalent roles*. In fact, a maximum equivalent role can be considered a "representative" of all sublattices to which it belongs. Removing equivalent sublattices prunes the candidate role set solution space. Given a role $r \in \mathit{ROLES}$, let $E = \{r' \in \mathit{ROLES} \mid r' \gtrdot r \wedge r' \equiv r\}$ be the set of immediate equivalent seniors and $S = \{r' \in \mathit{ROLES} \mid r' \gtrdot r \wedge r' \not\equiv r\}$ be the set of immediate *non*-equivalent seniors. For Theorem 5, the equivalent sublattice generated by r contains $|\varepsilon(r)| = 2^{|E|}$ roles, all of which can be eliminated from *ROLES* except for $\bar{r}$.

Algorithm 1 Procedure Remove-Equivalent-Sublattices

Require: R_k, H_k, PA, UA, k
Ensure: R_k, H_k, PA, UA, M_i
$W \leftarrow \emptyset$ ▷ Set of equivalent roles to be deleted
$M_i \leftarrow \emptyset$ ▷ Set of maximum equivalent roles
for all $\rho \in \{h.junior \mid h \in H_k : h.confidence = 1\}$ **do**
  ▷ Identify equivalences in R_k to be deleted and maximum equivalent role permissions
  $E \leftarrow \{h.senior \mid h \in H_k : h.junior = \rho \wedge h.confidence = 1\}$ ▷ Equivalent seniors
  $S \leftarrow \{h.senior \mid h \in H_k : h.junior = \rho \wedge h.confidence < 1\}$ ▷ Non-equivalent seniors
  $P \leftarrow (\bigcup_{r \in E} \text{ass\_perms}(r)) \setminus \text{ass\_perms}(\rho)$ ▷ Perms diff between maximum equiv role
  $W \leftarrow W \cup E$ ▷ Mark equivalent immediate seniors for deletion
  ▷ Transform ρ into its maximum equivalent role. Enrich roles in S with permissions P.
  for all $\sigma \in S \cup \{\rho\}$ **do**
    $\sigma.degree \leftarrow \sigma.degree + |P|,\quad PA \leftarrow PA \cup (P \times \{\sigma\}),\quad M_i \leftarrow M_i \cup \{\sigma\}$
  end for
end for
▷ Delete equivalent roles in R_k
$R_k \leftarrow R_k \setminus W,\quad PA \leftarrow \{\langle p,r\rangle \in PA \mid r \notin W\},\quad UA \leftarrow \{\langle u,r\rangle \in UA \mid r \notin W\}$
$H_k \leftarrow \{h \in H_k \mid h.senior \notin W\}$

Based on the theorems of the preceding section, $\varepsilon(r)$ and $\bar{r}$ can be derived from r and E. Prospective algorithms calculating roles based on the permission-powerset lattice could benefit from eliminating equivalent sublattices if $2^{|E|} > |E| + 1$, namely when the cost of calculating $\varepsilon(r)$ is greater than the cost of calculating only the roles necessary for identifying $\bar{r}$. For simplicity, operating costs necessary for constructing role $\bar{r}$ from r and E are deemed negligible. The inequality $2^{|E|} > |E| + 1$ is always true when $|E| > 1$, namely when role r has more than one equivalent junior. For Theorem 8, every equivalent sublattice has at least $|S|$ number of replicas derivable from r, E, S. It is thus advantageous to remove these when $(|S|+1)2^{|E|} > |E| + |S| + 1$, that is true when $|E| > 1$, where $(|S|+1)2^{|E|}$ represent the amount pruned.

6.1 Equivalent Sublattice Deletion in Apriori

This section introduces the RB-Apriori (*Role-Based Apriori*) algorithm to identify roles based on permission-powerset lattices with no equivalent sublattices. Using the Apriori [1] algorithm makes it possible to generate a partial lattice by pruning permission combinations whose support is lower than a pre-established threshold $s_{\min}$ [4]. RB-Apriori extends Apriori removing equivalent sublattices except for the maximum equivalent roles. The following are the main steps of Apriori summarized. The set $R_k \subseteq ROLES$ denotes all roles calculated at step k of the algorithm, while $H_k \subseteq RH$ gathers the immediate hierarchical relations among roles in R_i and R_{i-1}.

Step 1 An initial analysis of UP provides the set R_1 containing candidate roles of degree 1 with a support greater than the minimum.

Step k When $k \geq 2$, the set R_k is generated merging all possible role pairs in R_{k-1} (*join step*). In order not to generate roles with the same permission set, only role pairs differing in the greater permission are considered. Combinations not meeting minimum support constraints are rejected (*prune step*). Hierarchical associations (H_k) are also identified, relating roles in R_k whose assigned permissions are a superset of permissions of roles in R_{k-1}.

Stop The algorithm completes when $R_k = \emptyset$, returning *ROLES* as the union of all calculated R_i and *RH* as the union of all calculated H_i.

RB-Apriori is obtained from Apriori by calling the Remove-Equivalent-Sublattices procedure at the end of every step k. The procedure is described in Algorithm 1. Given $r \in ROLES$, *r.degree* indicates the number of permissions assigned to it; given $h \in RH$, *h.junior* and *h.senior* indicate the pair of roles hierarchically related, while *h.confidence* is the confidence value between them. Step 3 of Algorithm 1 identifies all roles calculated in step $k-1$ presenting immediate equivalent seniors in R_k. For each of these roles, the steps immediately following determine sets E, S and the permission set P to be added to the role in order to obtain the maximum equivalent role. Steps 10–12 make up the maximum equivalent role by adding permissions P to the current role. The immediate non-equivalent seniors are also enriched with the same permissions; if not, eliminating roles E (Steps 8, 15–16) could prevent identification of the combination of permissions assigned to those roles during step $k+1$. Based on the Note 4, enriching permissions assigned to immediate non-equivalent seniors with P it is not definite that the respective maximum equivalent roles will be generated. This means that RB-Apriori *prunes only one sublattice at a time*, without also simultaneously eliminating any replicas.

As described in Note 2, there could exist $r_1, r_2 \in ROLES : r_1 \equiv r_2 \wedge r_1 \parallel r_2$. In Figure 1, roles $\{3,4\}$ and $\{5,6\}$ are equivalent and share the same maximum equivalent role $\{2,3,4,5,6\}$. According to Algorithm 1, the role $\{2,3,4,5,6\}$ is built twice. This means that after the last step ("Stop") of RB-Apriori it is necessary to check for duplicate roles. Particularly, given the set $M = \bigcup M_i$ of identified maximum equivalent roles, for every $m \in M$ each $r \in ROLES \setminus \{m\} : ass\_perms(r) \subseteq ass\_perms(m) \wedge support(r) = support(m)$ needs to be discarded.

6.2 Testing on Real Data

To assess the efficiency of the RB-Apriori algorithm described in the previous section, many tests have been conducted using real data. In order to highlight the properties of the algorithm, consider the results obtained from analyzing data of an application with a heterogeneous distribution of user permissions. In the analyzed data set, 954 users were possessing 1,108 different permissions. By applying the Apriori algorithm with $s_{\min} = 10\%$, a total of 299 roles were generated in about 119 seconds through the adopted Apriori implementation. These 299 roles were assigned with only 16 of the available 1,108 permissions resulting in 890 users possessing these permissions. Using the same minimum support, with RB-Apriori we obtained only

109 roles in 87 seconds, thus reducing the number of roles by 64% and the computation time by 27%. The difference in improvement between role number and computation time was due to time "wasted" in identifying equivalent sublattices. Actually, the algorithm identified 167 roles; although 58 of the 167 were subsequently eliminated as equivalents, time was saved avoiding computation of entire equivalent sublattices. Changing the minimum support to $s_{\min} = 5\%$, 8,979 roles were produced with Apriori in about 3,324 seconds, involving 31 permissions and 897 users. With RB-Apriori we obtained only 235 roles in 349 seconds, thus reducing the number of roles by 97% and computation time by 90%.

6.3 Comparison to the RBAM Algorithm

The RBAM [4] algorithm leverages the RBAC administration cost estimate to find the lowest cost candidate role-sets, implementing an extended version of Apriori to identify the optimal role set. Pruning operations are based on the variable minimum support concept. According to [4], a role $r \in ROLES$ can be removed when the percentage of users assigned to r but none of its seniors is below a threshold related to the administration cost of r. When r has equivalent seniors, this percentage is equal to 0 because of Note 3. Thus, RBAM always removes its equivalent sublattice. Since RBAM is an extended version of Apriori, it is easy to improve performances of the RBAM algorithm, basing it on RB-Apriori instead of Apriori. While producing the same candidate role sets, computation of the entire equivalent sublattices is avoided, thus improving the efficiency and obtaining performance comparable to RB-Apriori.

7 Conclusions and Future Work

This paper introduces a new formal framework based on a rigorous pattern analysis in access permissions data. In particular, it is possible to derive a *lattice* of candidate roles from the permission powerset. We have proved some interesting properties about the above-defined lattice useful for optimizing role mining algorithms. By leveraging our results, data redundancies associated with co-occurrence of permissions among users can be easily identified and eliminated, hence increasing output quality and reducing process time of data mining algorithms.

To prove the effectiveness of our proposal, we have applied our results to two role mining algorithms: Apriori and RBAM. Applying these modified algorithms to a realistic data set, we drastically reduced the running time, while the output quality was either unaffected or even improved. Thus, we confirmed our analytical findings.

As for future work, we are currently pursuing two activities: the first is to apply our findings to other role mining algorithms; the second is investigating equivalence relationships between a single role and a set of roles.

Acknowledgement

Roberto Di Pietro was partly supported by the Spanish Ministry of Science and Education through projects TSI2007-65406-C03-01 E-AEGIS and CONSOLIDER CSD2007-00004 ARES, and by the Government of Catalonia under grant 2005 SGR 00446. The authors would also like to thank Richard A. Parisi Jr. for his helpful comments and valuable review.

References

1. Agrawal, R., Srikant, R.: Fast algorithms for mining association rules. In: J.B. Bocca, M. Jarke, C. Zaniolo (eds.) Proceedings of the 20th International Conference on Very Large Data Bases, VLDB, pp. 487–499. Morgan Kaufmann (1994)
2. Aho, A.V., Garey, M.R., Ullman, J.D.: The transitive reduction of a directed graph. SIAM Journal on Computing **1**(2), 131–137 (1972)
3. ANSI/INCITS 359-2004, Information Technology – Role Based Access Control (2004)
4. Colantonio, A., Di Pietro, R., Ocello, A.: A cost-driven approach to role engineering. In: Proceedings of the 23rd ACM Symposium on Applied Computing, SAC '08, pp. 2129–2136. Fortaleza, Ceará, Brazil (2008)
5. Coyne, E.J.: Role-engineering. In: Proceedings of the 1st ACM Workshop on Role-Based Access Control, RBAC '95 (1995)
6. Davey, B.A., Priestley, H.A.: Introduction to Lattices and Order, 2 edn. Cambridge University Press (2002)
7. Epstein, P., Sandhu, R.: Engineering of role/permission assignments. In: Proceedings of the 17th Annual Computer Security Applications Conference, ACSAC, pp. 127–136. IEEE Computer Society (2001)
8. Kern, A., Kuhlmann, M., Schaad, A., Moffett, J.: Observations on the role life-cycle in the context of enterprise security management. In: Proceedings of the 7th ACM Symposium on Access Control Models and Technologies, SACMAT '02 (2002)
9. Kuhlmann, M., Shohat, D., Schimpf, G.: Role mining - revealing business roles for security administration using data mining technology. In: Proceedings of the 8th ACM Symposium on Access Control Models and Technologies, SACMAT '03, pp. 179–186 (2003)
10. Neumann, G., Strembeck, M.: A scenario-driven role engineering process for functional RBAC roles. In: Proceedings of the 7th ACM Symposium on Access Control Models and Technologies, SACMAT '02 (2002)
11. Röckle, H.: Role-finding/role-engineering. In: Proceedings of the 5th ACM Workshop on Role-Based Access Control, RBAC 2000, p. 68 (2000)
12. Röckle, H., Schimpf, G., Weidinger, R.: Process-oriented approach for role-finding to implement role-based security administration in a large industrial organization. In: Proceedings of the 5th ACM Workshop on Role-Based Access Control, RBAC 2000, vol. 3 (2000)
13. Schlegelmilch, J., Steffens, U.: Role mining with ORCA. In: Proceedings of the 10th ACM Symposium on Access Control Models and Technologies, SACMAT '05, pp. 168–176 (2005)
14. Vaidya, J., Atluri, V., Guo, Q.: The role mining problem: finding a minimal descriptive set of roles. In: Proceedings of the 12th ACM Symposium on Access Control Models and Technologies, SACMAT '07, pp. 175–184 (2007)
15. Vaidya, J., Atluri, V., Warner, J.: RoleMiner: mining roles using subset enumeration. In: Proceedings of the 13th ACM Conference on Computer and Communications Security (2006)
16. Zhang, D., Ramamohanarao, K., Ebringer, T.: Role engineering using graph optimisation. In: Proceedings of the 12th ACM Symposium on Access Control Models and Technologies, SACMAT '07, pp. 139–144 (2007)

Acknowledgement

Roberto Di Pietro was partly supported by the Spanish [illegible]

References

[illegible]

A Parallelization Framework for Exact Knowledge Hiding in Transactional Databases

Aris Gkoulalas-Divanis and Vassilios S. Verykios

Abstract The hiding of sensitive knowledge, mined from transactional databases, is one of the primary goals of privacy preserving data mining. The increased storage capabilities of modern databases and the necessity for hiding solutions of superior quality, paved the way for parallelization of the hiding process. In this paper, we introduce a novel framework for decomposition and parallel solving of a category of hiding algorithms, known as *exact*. Exact algorithms hide the sensitive knowledge without any critical compromises, such as the blocking of non-sensitive patterns or the appearance of infrequent itemsets, among the frequent ones, in the sanitized outcome. The proposed framework substantially improves the size of the problems that the exact algorithms can efficiently handle, by significantly reducing their runtime. Furthermore, the generality of the framework makes it appropriate for any hiding algorithm that leads to a constraint satisfaction problem involving linear constraints of binary variables. Through experiments, we demonstrate the effectiveness of our solution on handling a large variety of hiding problem instances.

Key words: Exact knowledge hiding, Parallelization, Constraints satisfaction problems, Binary integer programming.

1 Introduction

The hiding of sensitive knowledge has attracted increasing interest over the last decade, particularly due to two main reasons: (i) the protection of the privacy of the

---

Aris Gkoulalas-Divanis
Department of Computer and Communication Engineering, University of Thessaly, Volos, Greece.
e-mail: arisgd@inf.uth.gr

Vassilios S. Verykios
Department of Computer and Communication Engineering, University of Thessaly, Volos, Greece.
e-mail: verykios@inf.uth.gr

Please use the following format when citing this chapter:

Gkoulalas-Divanis, A. and Verykios, V.S., 2008, in IFIP International Federation for Information Processing, Volume 278; *Proceedings of the IFIP TC 11 23rd International Information Security Conference*; Sushil Jajodia, Pierangela Samarati, Stelvio Cimato; (Boston: Springer), pp. 349–363.

individuals to whom this knowledge may refer, and (ii) the protection of business' secrets that would allow business' competitors to gain advantage over their peers. A motivating example for the latter case involves the sharing of knowledge among competing parties. Consider, for instance, a set of organizations that want to gain knowledge by collectively mining their datasets, involving a set of similar activities that they typically conduct. First, each organization mines its own data and identifies a set of knowledge patterns, some of which are classified by the data owners as sensitive, since they reveal business' secrets. Thus, prior to sharing their data, the data owners want to prohibit the leakage of the sensitive knowledge to the other parties. To accomplish that, a knowledge hiding algorithm has to be employed.

There are several categories of hiding algorithms, depending on (i) the type of data they operate on, (ii) the type of knowledge they hide, and (iii) the hiding process they enforce. Frequent itemset hiding algorithms operate on transactional data, where the sensitive knowledge is depicted in the form of frequent patterns that lead to the production of sensitive association rules. The goal of these methodologies is to create a new - hereon called *sanitized* - dataset which achieves, when mined for frequent patterns using the same (or a higher) threshold of support, to identify all the frequent patterns except from the sensitive ones. When this goal is accomplished, the attained solution is *exact*. Two exact hiding algorithms have been proposed so far [7,8]. In both algorithms, the hiding process constructs a *Constraints Satisfaction Problem* (*CSP*) and solves it by using *Binary Integer Programming* (*BIP*). However, due to the large number of constraints that are typically involved in the *CSP*, even for medium size problems, these algorithms suffer from scalability issues.

In this work, we introduce a novel framework that is suitable for decomposition and parallelization of the approaches in [7, 8], and can be applied to substantially improve the scalability of both algorithms. The proposed framework aims at the decomposition of the *CSP* that is produced by the hiding algorithm, into a set of smaller *CSP*s that can be solved in parallel. First, the original *CSP* is structurally decomposed into a set of independent *CSP*s, each of which is assigned to a processor. Second, each independent *CSP* can be further decomposed into a set of dependent *CSP*s. In each step of the framework, a function is applied to question the gain of any further decomposition and allow the algorithm to take the appropriate action. Furthermore, the solutions of the various *CSP*s, produced as part of the decomposition process, can be appropriately combined to provide the solution of the initial *CSP* (prior to the decomposition). The generality of the proposed framework allows it to efficiently handle any *CSP* that consists of linear constraints involving binary variables and whose objective is to maximize (or minimize) the summation of these variables .

The rest of this paper is organized as follows. Section 2 provides the related work. In Section 3 we set out the problem of exact knowledge hiding and provide the necessary background for the understanding of the methodologies that are implemented as part of the proposed framework. The decomposition and parallelization framework is presented in Section 4. Finally, Section 5 contains the experimental evaluation, while Section 6 concludes this paper.

2 Related work

Clifton et al. [5, 6] are among the first to discuss the security and privacy implications of data mining and propose data obscuring strategies to prohibit inference and discovery of sensitive knowledge. Since then, several heuristics have been proposed for the hiding of frequent patterns and the related association rules [3, 10, 14, 15].

Menon et al. [13] present an integer programming approach for hiding sensitive itemsets. Their algorithm treats the hiding process as a *Constraints Satisfaction Problem CSP* and identifies the minimum number of transactions to be sanitized. The problem size is reduced to constraints involving only the sensitive itemsets. After solving the *CSP*, a heuristic is used to identify the transactions to be sanitized and perform the sanitization.

Sun and Yu [16] introduce a border based approach for frequent itemset hiding. The approach focuses on preserving the quality of the border constructed by the non-sensitive frequent itemsets in the lattice of itemsets. The authors use the positive border, after the removal of the sensitive itemsets, to keep track of the impact of altering transactions in the database.

Gkoulalas - Divanis and Verykios [7, 8] introduce two non-heuristic algorithms for frequent itemset hiding. Both approaches use border revision to identify the candidate itemsets for sanitization. The hiding process is performed by formulating a *CSP* based on the itemsets of the borders and by solving it through *Binary Integer Programming* (*BIP*). The attained solution leads to an exact hiding of the sensitive patterns, while a heuristic approach is used when the constructed *CSP* is infeasible.

In this paper, we propose a framework that is suitable for parallelization of the exact approaches in [7, 8], as well as on any hiding algorithm that is based on the construction of a *CSP* involving linear constraints of binary variables. Unlike distributed approaches [17], where the search for the CSP solution is conducted in parallel by multiple agents, our approach takes into consideration the binary nature of the CSPs to achieve a direct decomposition. Together with existing approaches for parallel mining of association rules, as in [2,9,18], our framework can be applied to parallelize the most time consuming steps of the exact hiding algorithms.

3 Notation and problem formulation

This section provides the necessary background regarding sensitive itemset hiding and allows us to proceed to our problem's formulation.

Let $\mathbf{I} = \{i_1, i_2, \dots, i_M\}$ be a finite set of literals, called *items*, where M denotes the cardinality of the set. Any subset $I \subseteq \mathbf{I}$ is called an *itemset* over $\mathbf{I}$. A transaction T over $\mathbf{I}$ is a pair $T = (tid, I)$, where I is the itemset and tid is a unique identifier, used to distinguish among transactions that correspond to the same itemset. Furthermore, a transaction database $\mathscr{D}$ over $\mathbf{I}$ is a $N \times M$ table consisting of N transactions over $\mathbf{I}$ carrying different identifiers, where entry $T_{nm} = 1$ if and only if the m-th item appears in the n-th transaction. Otherwise, $T_{nm} = 0$. A transaction $T = (tid, J)$ supports an itemset I over $\mathbf{I}$, if $I \subseteq J$. Given a set of items S, let $\wp(S)$ denote the powerset of S, which is the set of all subsets of S.

Given an itemset I over $\mathbf{I}$ in $\mathscr{D}$, we denote by $\sup(I,\mathscr{D})$ the number of transactions $T \in \mathscr{D}$ that support I. Moreover, we define the *frequency* of an itemset I in a database $\mathscr{D}$, denoted as $\text{freq}(I,\mathscr{D})$, to be the fraction of transactions in $\mathscr{D}$ that support I. An itemset I is *large* or *frequent* in database $\mathscr{D}$, if and only if, its frequency in $\mathscr{D}$ is at least equal to a minimum threshold minf. Equivalently, I is large in $\mathscr{D}$, if and only if $\sup(I,\mathscr{D}) \geq \text{msup}$, where $\text{msup} = \text{minf} \times N$. All itemsets with frequency less than minf are *infrequent*.

Let $\mathscr{F}_{\mathscr{D}} = \{I \subseteq \mathbf{I} : \text{freq}(I,\mathscr{D}) \geq \text{minf}\}$ be the frequent itemsets in $\mathscr{D}$ and $\mathbf{P} = \wp(\mathbf{I})$ be the set of all patterns in the lattice of $\mathscr{D}$. The *positive* and the *negative* borders of $\mathscr{F}_{\mathscr{D}}$ are defined as $\mathscr{B}^+(\mathscr{F}_{\mathscr{D}}) = \{I \in \mathscr{F}_{\mathscr{D}} |$ for all $J \in \mathbf{P}$ with $I \subset J$ we have that $J \notin \mathscr{F}_{\mathscr{D}}\}$ and $\mathscr{B}^-(\mathscr{F}_{\mathscr{D}}) = \{I \in \mathbf{P} - \mathscr{F}_{\mathscr{D}} |$ for all $J \subset I$ we have that $J \in \mathscr{F}_{\mathscr{D}}\}$.

Based on the notation presented above, we proceed to the problem statement for the exact hiding algorithms. In what follows, we assume that we are provided with a database $\mathscr{D}_{\mathscr{O}}$, consisting of N transactions, and a threshold minf set by the owner of the data. After performing frequent itemset mining in $\mathscr{D}_{\mathscr{O}}$ with minf, we yield a set of frequent patterns, denoted as $\mathscr{F}_{\mathscr{D}_{\mathscr{O}}}$, among which a subset $\mathbf{S}$ contains patterns which are considered to be *sensitive* from the owner's perspective.

$$\textbf{maximize}\left(\sum_{u_{nm} \in U} u_{nm}\right)$$

$$\textit{subject to} \begin{cases} \sum_{T_n \in D_{\{X\}}} \prod_{I_m \in X} u_{nm} < sup(I,\mathscr{D}), \forall X \in \mathbf{S} \\ \sum_{T_n \in D_{\{R\}}} \prod_{I_m \in R} u_{nm} \geq sup(I,\mathscr{D}), \forall R \in \mathbf{V} \end{cases}$$

Fig. 1 The Constraints Satisfaction Problem for the inline approach of [7].

Given the set of sensitive itemsets $\mathbf{S}$, we define the set $\mathbf{S}_{min} = \{I \in \mathbf{S}|$ for all $J \subset I, \;\; J \notin \mathbf{S}\}$ that contains all the *minimal* sensitive itemsets from $\mathbf{S}$, and the set $\mathbf{S}_{max} = \{I \in \mathscr{F}_{\mathscr{D}_{\mathscr{O}}} | \exists J \in \mathbf{S}_{min}, J \subseteq I\}$ that contains all the itemsets of $\mathbf{S}_{min}$ along with their frequent supersets. The goal of an exact hiding algorithm is to construct a new, sanitized database $\mathscr{D}$, which achieves to protect the sensitive itemsets from disclosure, while leaving intact the non-sensitive itemsets existing in $\mathscr{F}_{\mathscr{D}_{\mathscr{O}}}$. Thus, when the sanitized dataset $\mathscr{D}$ is mined, the frequent patterns that are discovered are *exactly* those in $\mathscr{F}'_{\mathscr{D}} = \mathscr{F}_{\mathscr{D}_{\mathscr{O}}} - \mathbf{S}_{max}$. This set is called *ideal*, as it pertains to an optimal hiding solution. When constructed, database $\mathscr{D}$ can be safely released since it protects sensitive knowledge. In the case of the inline approach, an exact solution is attained when the status (frequent vs infrequent) of the itemsets in $\mathbf{C} = \{I \in \mathscr{B}^+(\mathscr{F}'_{\mathscr{D}}) : I \cap \mathbf{I^S} \neq \varnothing\} \cup \mathbf{S}$ is properly controlled. This, is achieved by solving the *CSP* of Fig. 1, where $\mathbf{V} = \{I \in \mathscr{B}^+(\mathscr{F}'_{\mathscr{D}}) : I \cap \mathbf{I^S} \neq \varnothing\}$, $D_{\{I\}}$ denotes the set of supporting transactions for an itemset I and u_{nm} corresponds to the m-th item of the n-th transaction, while in the sanitization process.

4 A parallelization framework for exact knowledge hiding

Performing knowledge hiding by using the inline or the hybrid approach allows for the identification of exact solutions, whenever such solutions exist. However, the cost of identifying an exact solution is high due to the solving of the involved *CSP*s.

In this section, we propose a framework for decomposition and parallel solving that can be applied as part of the sanitization process of exact hiding algorithms. Our proposed framework operates in three phases, namely (i) the *structural decomposition* phase, (ii) the *decomposition of large individual components* phase, and (iii) the *parallel solving* of the produced *CSP*s. In what follows, we present the details that involve each phase of the framework.

4.1 Structural decomposition of the original CSP

The number of constraints in a *CSP* can be very large depending on the database properties, the minimum support threshold used, and the number of sensitive itemsets. Moreover, the fact that various initial constraints may incorporate products of u_{nm} variables, thus have a need to be replaced by numerous linear inequalities (using the *CDR* approach of [7]), makes the whole *BIP* problem tougher to solve. There is, however, a nice property in the *CSP*s that we can use to our benefit. That is, decomposition.

Based on the divide and conquer paradigm, a decomposition approach allows us to divide a large problem into numerous smaller ones, solve these new subproblems independently, and combine the partial solutions to attain the exact same overall solution. The property of the *CSP*s which allows us to consider such a strategy lies behind the optimization criterion that is used. Indeed, one can easily notice that the criterion of maximizing (equiv. minimizing) the summation of the binary u_{nm} variables is satisfied when as many u_{nm} variables as possible are set to one (equiv. zero). This, can be established independently, provided that the constraints that participate in the *CSP* allow for an appropriate decomposition. The approach we follow for the initial decomposition of the *CSP* is similar to the decomposition structure identification algorithm presented in [13], although applied in a "constraints" rather than a "transactions" level. As demonstrated on Fig. 2, the output of structural decomposition, when applied on the original *CSP*, is a set of smaller *CSP*s that can be solved independently. An example will allow us to better demonstrate how this process works.

Consider database $\mathscr{D}_{\mathscr{O}}$ of Fig. 3(a). Performing frequent itemset mining in $\mathscr{D}_{\mathscr{O}}$ using frequency threshold minf = 0.3, we compute the following set of large itemsets: $\mathscr{F}_{\mathscr{D}_{\mathscr{O}}} = \{A,B,C,D,AB,CD\}$. Suppose that we want to hide the sensitive item-

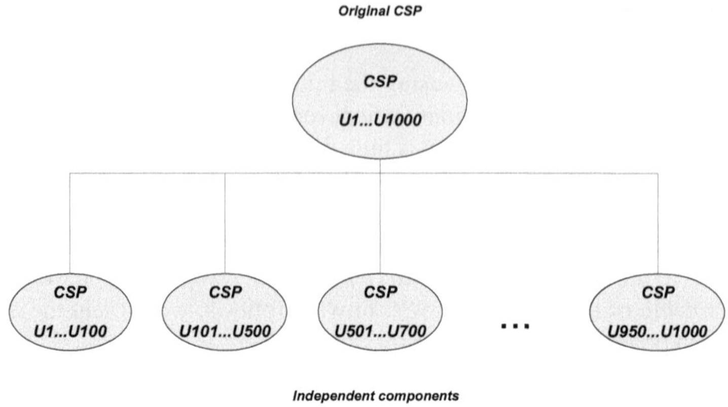

Fig. 2 Decomposing large *CSP*s to numerous independent components.

A	B	C	D
1	1	0	0
1	1	0	0
1	0	0	0
1	1	0	0
0	1	0	1
1	0	1	1
0	0	1	1
0	0	1	1
1	0	0	0
0	0	0	1

(a) Original database $\mathscr{D}_{\mathscr{O}}$.

A	B	C	D
1	u_{12}	0	0
1	u_{22}	0	0
1	0	0	0
1	u_{42}	0	0
0	u_{52}	0	1
1	0	u_{63}	u_{64}
0	0	u_{73}	u_{74}
0	0	u_{83}	u_{84}
1	0	0	0
0	0	0	1

(b) Intermediate form of $\mathscr{D}_{\mathscr{O}}$.

Fig. 3 The original and the intermediate form of database $\mathscr{D}_{\mathscr{O}}$ used in the example.

sets in $\mathbf{S} = \{B, CD\}$ using, for instance, the inline approach [1]. Then, we have that: $\mathbf{S}_{max} = \{B, AB, CD\}, \mathscr{B}^{+}(\mathscr{F}'_{\mathscr{D}}) = \{A, C, D\}$, and $\mathbf{V} = \{C, D\} \subset \mathscr{B}^{+}(\mathscr{F}'_{\mathscr{D}})$.

The intermediate form of this *CSP* is shown in Fig. 3(b) and its *CSP* formulation in Fig. 4 (left). Table 1 presents the various constraints c_r along with the variables that they control. As we can observe, we can cluster the various constraints into disjoint sets based on the variables that they involve. In our example, we can identify two such clusters of constraints, namely $\mathbf{M_1} = \{c_1\}$, and $\mathbf{M_2} = \{c_2, c_3, c_4\}$. Notice that none of the variables in each cluster of constraints is contained in any other cluster. Thus, instead of solving the entire problem, we can solve the two sub-problems shown in Fig. 4 (right), yielding, when combined, the same solution as the one of the initial *CSP*: $u_{12} = u_{22} = u_{42} = u_{63} = u_{64} = u_{73} = u_{74} = u_{83} = 1$ and $u_{52} = u_{84} = 0$.

[1] We need to mention that it is of no importance which methodology will be used to produce the *CSP*, apart from the obvious fact that some methodologies may produce *CSP*s that are better decomposable than those constructed by other approaches. However, the structure of the *CSP* also depends on the problem instance and thus it is difficult to know in advance which algorithm is bound to produce a better decomposable *CSP*.

$$\textbf{maximize}\ (u_{12}+u_{22}+u_{42}+u_{52}+u_{63}+u_{64}+u_{73}+u_{74}+u_{83}+u_{84})$$

$$\textit{subject to}\begin{cases} u_{12}+u_{22}+u_{42}+u_{52}<3\\ u_{63}u_{64}+u_{73}u_{74}+u_{83}u_{84}<3\\ u_{63}+u_{73}+u_{83}\geq 3\\ u_{64}+u_{74}+u_{84}\geq 1\end{cases}$$

$$\textbf{maximize}(u_{12}+u_{22}+u_{42}+u_{52})$$

$$\textit{subject to}\ u_{12}+u_{22}+u_{42}+u_{52}<3$$

and

$$\textbf{maximize}(u_{63}+u_{64}+u_{73}+u_{74}+u_{83}+u_{84})$$

$$\textit{subject to}\begin{cases} u_{63}u_{64}+u_{73}u_{74}+u_{83}u_{84}<3\\ u_{63}+u_{73}+u_{83}\geq 3\\ u_{64}+u_{74}+u_{84}\geq 1\end{cases}$$

Fig. 4 The original *CSP* (left) and its structural decomposition (right).

Table 1 The constraints matrix for the produced *CSP*.

	c_1	c_2	c_3	c_4
u_{12}	X			
u_{22}	X			
u_{42}	X			
u_{52}	X			
u_{63}		X	X	
u_{64}		X		X
u_{73}		X	X	
u_{74}		X		X
u_{83}		X	X	
u_{84}		X		X

4.2 Decomposition of large independent components

The structural decomposition of the original *CSP* allows one to divide the original large problem into a number of smaller subproblems which can be solved independently, thus highly reduce the runtime needed to attain the overall solution. However, as it can be noticed, both (i) the number of subproblems, and (ii) the size of each subproblem, are totally dependent on the underlying *CSP* and the structure of the constraints matrix. This fact means that there exist problem instances which are not decomposable and other instances which experience a notable imbalance in the size of the produced components. Thus, in what follows, we present two methodologies which allow us to decompose large individual components that are non-separable through the structural decomposition approach. In both schemes, our goal is to minimize the number of variables that are shared among the newly produced components, which are now *dependent*. What allows us to proceed in such a decomposition is the binary nature of the variables involved in the *CSP*s, a fact that we can use to our benefit to minimize the different problem instances that need to be solved to produce the overall solution of the initial problem.

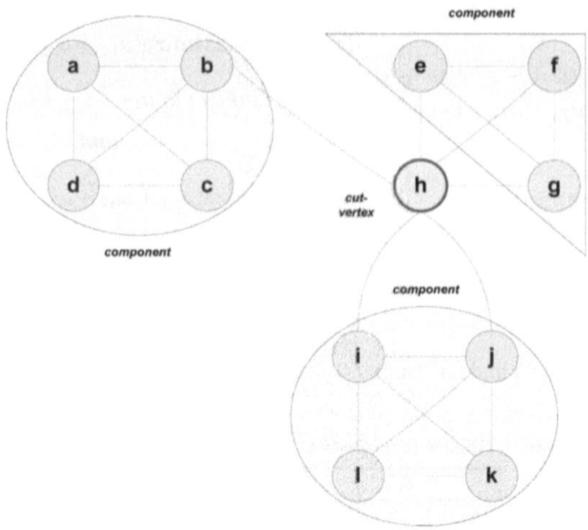

Fig. 5 An example of decomposition using articulation points.

4.2.1 Decomposition using articulation points

To further decompose an independent component we need to identify the least amount of u_{nm} variables which, when discarded from the various inequalities of this *CSP*, produce a *CSP* that is structurally decomposable. To find these u_{nm}s we proceed as follows. First, we create an undirected graph $\mathcal{G}(V,E)$ in which each vertex $v \in V$ corresponds to a u_{nm} variable, and each edge $e \in E$ connects vertexes that participate in the same constraint. Graph $\mathcal{G}$ can be built in linear time and provides us with an easy way to model the network of constraints and involved variables in our input *CSP*. Since we assume that our input *CSP* is not structurally decomposable, graph $\mathcal{G}$ will be connected.

After creating the constraints graph $\mathcal{G}$, we identify all its articulation points (a.k.a. cut-vertexes). The rationale here is that removal of a cut-vertex will disconnect graph $\mathcal{G}$ and the best cut-vertex u_{nm} will be the one that leads to the largest number of connected components in $\mathcal{G}$. Each of these components will then itself constitute a new subproblem to be solved independently from the others. To identify the best articulation point we proceed as follows. As is already known, a fast way to compute the articulation points of a graph is to traverse it by using DFS. By adding a counter to a table of vertexes each time we visit a node, we can easily keep track of the number of components that were identified so far. In the end of the algorithm, along with the identified articulation points we can have knowledge of the number of components that each of these articulation points decomposes the initial graph. This operation can proceed in linear time $O(V+E)$.

After identifying the best articulation point, our next step is to remove the corresponding u_{nm} variable from graph $\mathcal{G}$. Then, each component of the resulting graph corresponds to a new subproblem (i.e. a new *CSP*) that can be derived in linear time and be solved independently. To provide the same solution as the original *CSP*, the solutions of the various created subproblems need to be cross-examined, a procedure that is further explained in Section 4.3.

A final step to be addressed involves the situation in which no single cut-vertex can be identified in the graph. If such a case appears, we choose to proceed heuristically in order to experience low runtime of the algorithm. Our empirical approach is based on the premises that nodes having high degrees in graph $\mathcal{G}$ are more likely than others to correspond to cut-vertexes. For this reason, we choose to compute the degree of each vertex $u \in V$ in graph $\mathcal{G}(V,E)$ and identify the one having the maximum degree. Let $v = max_{u \in V}(degree(u))$ be the vertex whose degree is the maximum among all other vertexes in the graph. Then, among all neighbors of v we identify the one having the maximum degree and proceed to remove both vertexes from the graph. As a final step we use DFS to traverse the resultant graph to examine if it is disconnected. The runtime of this approach is linear in the number of vertexes and edges of graph $\mathcal{G}$. If the resultant graph remains connected, we choose to leave the original *CSP* as-is and make no further attempt to decompose it. Figure 5 demonstrates an example of decomposition using articulation points. In this graph, we denote as "cut-vertex", the vertex which, when removed, leads to a disconnected graph having the maximum number of connected components (here 3).

4.2.2 Decomposition using weighted graph partitioning

One of the primary disadvantages of decomposition using articulation points is the fact that we have limited control over (i) the number of components in which our initial *CSP* will eventually split, and (ii) the size of each of these components. This fact may lead to low CPUs utilization in a parallel solving environment. For this reason, we present an alternative decomposition strategy which can break the original problem into as many subproblems as we can concurrently solve, based on our underlying system architecture. The problem formulation is once more tightly related to the graph modeling paradigm but instead of using articulation points, we rely on *graph partitioning* algorithms to provide us with the optimal split.

By assigning each u_{nm} variable of the initial *CSP* to a vertex in our undirected graph, and each constraint c to a number of edges e_c formulating a clique in the graph (while denoting the dependence of the u_{nm} variables involved), we proceed to construct a *weighted* version of the graph $\mathcal{G}$ presented in the previous section. This weighted graph, hereon denoted as $\mathcal{G}^W$, has two types of weights: one associated with each vertex $u \in V^W$, and one associated with each edge $e \in E^W$. The weight of each vertex corresponds to the number of constraints in which it participates in the *CSP* formulation. On the other hand, the weight of each edge in the graph denotes the number of constraints in which the two vertexes (it connects) appear together. Using a *weighted graph partitioning algorithm*, such as the one provided by METIS [11], one can decompose the graph into as many parts as the number of available processors that can be used to concurrently solve them. The rationale behind the applied weighted scheme is to ensure that the connectivity between ver-

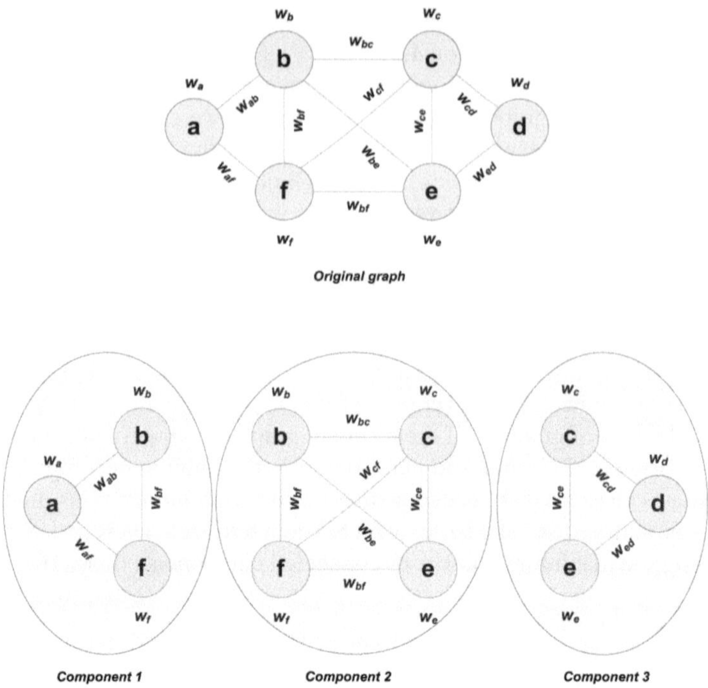

Fig. 6 An example of a three-way decomposition using weighted graph partitioning.

texes belonging in different parts is minimal. Figure 6 demonstrates a three-way decomposition of the original *CSP*, using weighted graph partitioning.

4.3 Parallel solving of the produced CSPs

Breaking a dependent *CSP* into a number of components (using one of the strategies mentioned earlier) is a procedure that should incur only if the *CSP* is large enough to worth the cost of decomposition. For this reason, it is necessary to define a function $\mathbf{F_S}$ to calculate the size of a *CSP* and a threshold, above which the *CSP* should be decomposed. We choose function $\mathbf{F_S}$ to be a weighted sum of the number of binary variables involved in the *CSP* and the associated constraints $\mathbf{C}$. The weights are problem-dependent. Thus, $\mathbf{F_S} = w_1 \times |u_{nm}| + w_2 \times |\mathbf{C}|$.

Our problem solving strategy proceeds as follows. First, we apply structural decomposition on the original *CSP* and we distribute each component to an available processor. These components can be solved independently of each other. The final solution (i.e. the value of the objective for the original *CSP*) will equal the sum of the values of the individual objectives; thus, the master node that holds the original *CSP* should wait to accumulate the solutions returned by the servicing nodes.

Each servicing node applies the function $\mathbf{F_S}$ to its assigned *CSP* and decides whether to further decompose it. To decompose the *CSP*, it uses one of schemes presented earlier and then assigns each of the newly created *CSP*s to an available processor. A mechanism that keeps track of the jobs distribution to processors and their status (i.e. idle vs occupied) is essential to allow for the best possible CPUs utilization. The same process continues until all *CSP*s are below the size threshold and therefore do not need further decomposition.

The handling of dependent *CSP*s by the servicing nodes, is complex. Let *border* u_{nm} be a variable that appears in two or more dependent *CSP*s. This means that this variable was either the best articulation point selected by the first strategy, or a vertex that was at the boundary of two different components, identified by using the graph partitioning algorithm. Border variables need to be checked for all possible values they can attain in order to provide us with the exact same solution as the one of solving the independent *CSP*. Suppose that p such variables exist. Then, we have 2^p possible value assignments. For each possible assignment, we solve the corresponding *CSP*s. In the objective functions of these *CSP*s, apart from the u_{nm} variables for the non-border cases, we include the values of the currently tested assignment for the p variables. After solving the *CSP*s for each assignment, we sum up the resulting objective values. The final solution will correspond to the maximum value among the different summations produced by the possible assignments[2].

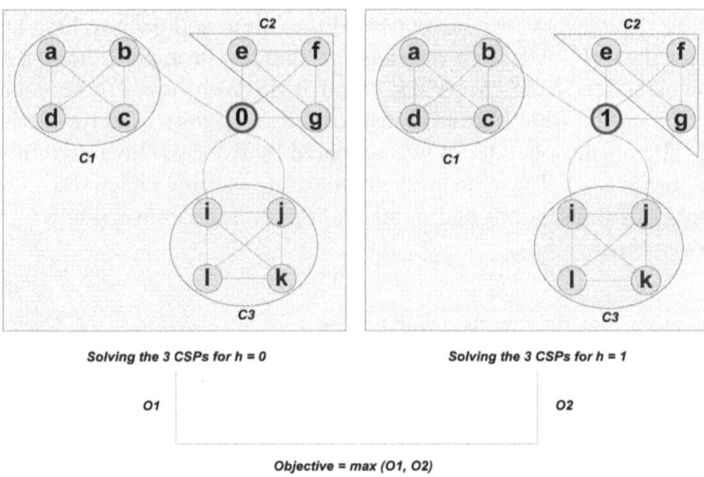

Fig. 7 An example of parallel solving after the application of a decomposition technique.

To make matters clearer, assume that an independent *CSP* is decomposed into two dependent *CSP*s, C_A and C_B, based on two border variables: u_1 and u_2. Since all possible assignments of u_1, u_2 should be tested, we have four different instances, namely: $C_{00}, C_{01}, C_{10}, C_{11}$. C_{xy} indicates the problem instance where $u_1 = x$ and $u_2 = y$; the rest variables' assignments remain unknown. Given two processors, the

[2] The proof of this statement was skipped due to the size limitations of the paper.

first solves the four instances for C_A, whereas the second one solves them for C_B. Suppose that the objective values for $C_{A,00}$ and $C_{B,00}$ are found. The objective value for C_{00} will then be the summation of these two objectives. To calculate the overall objective value and identify the solution of the initial *CSP*, we need to identify the maximum among the objective values of all problem instances. An example of parallel solving, after the application of decomposition, is depicted in Fig. 7. As one can notice, the solution of the initial *CSP* is provided by examining, for all involved *CSP*s, the two potential values of the selected cut-vertex h (i.e. solving each *CSP* for $h = 0$ and $h = 1$). The overall objective is the maximum of the two objectives, an argument that is justified by the binary nature of variable h.

5 Computational experiments and results

In this section, we provide the results of a set of experiments that we conducted to test our proposed framework. In what follows, we present the datasets we used and the different parameters involved in the testing process (such as the minimum support threshold and the number/size of the sensitive itemsets to hide), and we provide experimental results involving the structural decomposition process, where we demonstrate the major gain in the runtime of the hiding algorithm.

To test our framework, we encompassed the inline approach to hide knowledge in three real datasets. All these datasets are publicly available through the FIMI repository[3]. Datasets BMS-WebView-1 and BMS-WebView-2 both contain click stream data from the Blue Martini Software, Inc. and were used for the KDD Cup 2000 [12]. The mushroom dataset was prepared by Roberto Bayardo (University of California, Irvine) [4]. These datasets demonstrate varying characteristics in terms of the number of transactions and items and the average transaction lengths. Table 2 summarizes them.

Table 2 The characteristics of the three real datasets.

Dataset	*N*	*M*	Avg tlen	msup
BMS-1	59,602	497	2.50	30-70
BMS-2	77,512	3,340	5.60	2-10
Mushroom	8,124	119	23.00	10-50

In all tested settings, the thresholds of minimum support were properly selected to ensure an adequate amount of frequent itemsets and the sensitive itemsets to be hidden were selected randomly among the frequent ones. We conducted several experiments trying to hide sensitive 2-itemsets, 3-itemsets, and 4-itemsets. Our source code was implemented in Perl and C and we conducted all our experiments on a PC running Linux on an Intel Pentium D, 3.2 Ghz processor equipped with 4 GB of main memory. All integer programs were solved using ILOG CPLEX 9.0 [1].

[3] Available at: `http://fimi.cs.helsinki.fi/`.

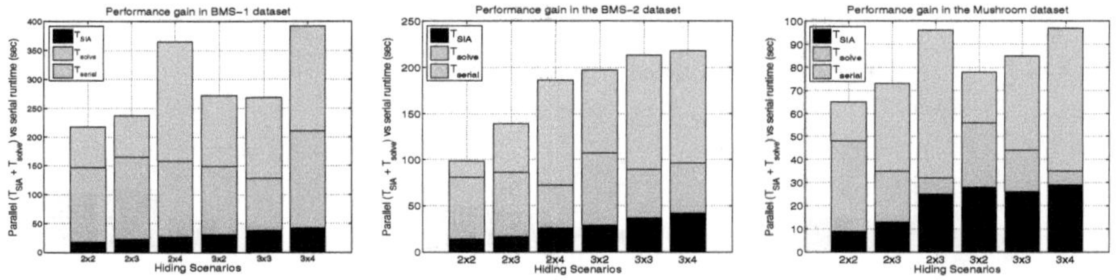

Fig. 8 Performance gain through parallel solving, when omitting the **V** part of the *CSP*.

CPLEX provides us the option of pre-solving the binary integer program, a very useful feature that allows the reduction of the *BIP*'s size, the improvement of its numeric properties (for example, by removing some inactive constraints or by fixing some non-basic variables), and also enables us to early detect infeasibility in the *BIP*'s solution. We used these beneficial properties of pre-solving to allow for early actions when solving the *CSP*s.

To conduct the experiments, we assume that we have all the necessary resources to proceed to a full-scale parallelization of the initial *CSP*. This means that if our original *CSP* can potentially break into *P* independent parts, then we assume the existence of *P* available processors that can run independently, each one solving one resultant *CSP*. Thus, the overall runtime of the hiding algorithm will equal the summation of (i) the runtime of the serial algorithm that produced the original *CSP*, (ii) the runtime of the *Structure Identification Algorithm* (SIA) that decomposed the original *CSP* into numerous independent parts, (iii) the time that is needed to communicate each of the resulting *CSPs* to an available processor, (iv) the time needed to solve the largest of these *CSP*s, (v) the communication time needed to return the attained solutions to the original processor (hereon called "master") that held the whole problem, and finally (vi) the time needed by the master processor to calculate the summation of the objective values returned in order to compute the overall solution of the problem. That is:

$$T_{\text{overall}} = T_{\text{HA}} + T_{\text{SIA}} + T_{\text{spread}} + T_{\text{solve}} + T_{\text{gather}} + T_{\text{aggregate}}$$

In the following experiments, we capture the runtime of (ii) and (iv), namely T_{SIA} and T_{solve}, since we consider both the communication overhead ($T_{\text{spread}} + T_{\text{gather}}$) and the overall solution calculation overhead ($T_{\text{aggregate}}$) to be negligible when compared to these run times. Moreover, the runtime of (i) does not change in the case of parallelization and therefore its measurement in these experiments is of no importance. To allow us compute the benefit of parallelization, we include in the results the runtime T_{serial} of solving the entire *CSP* without prior decomposition.

In our first set of experiments (presented in Fig. 8), we ensure the breaking of the original *CSP* into a controllable number of components by excluding all the constraints involving itemsets from set **V** (see Fig. 1). Thus, to break the original *CSP* into *P* parts, one needs to identify *P* mutually exclusive (in the universe of items) itemsets to hide. However, based on the number of supporting transactions for each

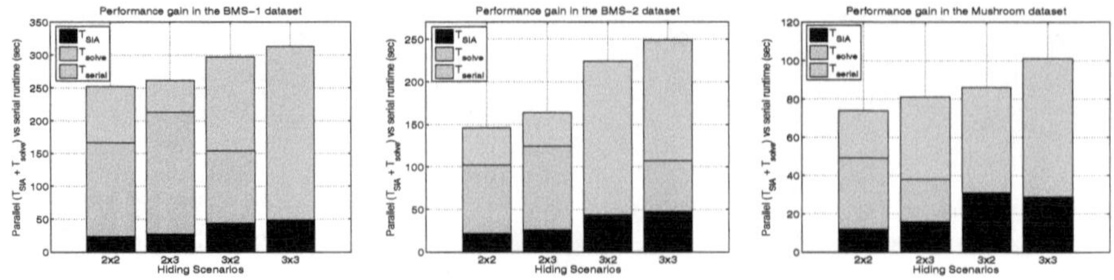

Fig. 9 Performance gain through parallel solving of the entire *CSP*.

of these itemsets in $\mathscr{D}_{\mathscr{O}}$, the size of each produced component may vary significantly. As one can observe in Fig. 8, the time that was needed for the execution of the *SIA* algorithm and the identification of the independent components is low when compared to the time needed for solving the largest of the resulting *CPS*s. Moreover, by comparing the time needed for the serial and the one needed for the parallel solving of the *CSP*, one can notice how beneficial is the decomposition strategy in reducing the runtime that is required by the hiding algorithm. For example, in the 2×2 hiding scenario for BMS-1, serial solving of the *CSP* requires 218 seconds, while parallel solving requires 165 seconds. This means that by solving the *CSP* in parallel using two processors, we reduce the solution time by 53 seconds.

In our second set of experiments, shown in Fig. 9, we included the **V** part of the *CSP*, produced by the inline algorithm. As one can observe, there are certain situations in which the original *CSP* cannot be decomposed ($T_{\text{solve}} = 0$). In such cases, one has to apply either the decomposition approach using articulation points or the weighed graph partitioning algorithm, in order to parallelize the hiding process.

6 Conclusions

In this paper, we introduced a framework for decomposition and parallel solving that is suitable for exact knowledge hiding. The proposed framework uses structural decomposition to partition the original *CSP* into independent components. Then, it offers two novel approaches for further breaking of these components into a set of dependent *CSP*s. By exploiting the features of the objective function, we provided a way of joining the partial solutions of the *CSP*s and deriving the overall hiding solution. Finally, through experimental evaluation on three real datasets, we demonstrated the benefit of decomposition towards speeding up the hiding process.

7 Acknowledgments

This work was partially funded by the European Union under the FP6-IST-FET programme, Project n. FP6-14915, GeoPKDD: Geographic Privacy-Aware Knowledge

Discovery and Delivery, www.geopkdd.eu. The authors would like to thank Dimitrios Syrivelis for his valuable comments and overall support in this work.

References

1. ILOG CPLEX 9.0 User's Manual. ILOG Inc., Gentilly, France (2003)
2. Agrawal, R., Shafer, J.C.: Parallel mining of association rules. IEEE Transactions on Knowledge and Data Engineering (TKDE) **8**(1), 962–969
3. Atallah, M., Bertino, E., Elmagarmid, A., Ibrahim, M., Verykios, V.S.: Disclosure limitation of sensitive rules. In: Proceedings of the IEEE Knowledge and Data Engineering Exchange Workshop (KDEX), pp. 45–52 (1999)
4. Bayardo, R.: Efficiently mining long patterns from databases. Proceedings of the ACM SIGMOD International Conference on Management of Data (1998)
5. Clifton, C., Kantarcioğlu, M., Vaidya, J.: Defining privacy for data mining. National Science Foundation Workshop on Next Generation Data Mining (WNGDM) pp. 126–133 (2002)
6. Clifton, C., Marks, D.: Security and privacy implications of data mining. In: Proceedings of the ACM SIGMOD International Conference on Management of Data, pp. 15–19 (1996)
7. Gkoulalas-Divanis, A., Verykios, V.S.: An integer programming approach for frequent itemset hiding. In: Proceedings of the ACM Conference on Information and Knowledge Management (CIKM) (2006)
8. Gkoulalas-Divanis, A., Verykios, V.S.: A hybrid approach to frequent itemset hiding. In: Proceedings of the IEEE International Conference on Tools with Artificial Intelligence (ICTAI) (2007)
9. Han, E.H., Karypis, G., Kumar, V.: Scalable parallel data mining for association rules. In: Proceedings of the ACM SIGMOD International Conference on Management of Data, pp. 277–288 (2007)
10. Kantarcioğlu, M., Clifton, C.: Privacy-preserving distributed mining of association rules on horizontally partitioned data. IEEE Transactions on Knowledge and Data Engineering (TKDE) **16**(9), 1026–1037 (2004)
11. Karypis, G., Kumar, V.: A fast and high quality multilevel scheme for partitioning irregular graphs. SIAM Journal of Scientific Computing **20**(1), 359–392 (1998)
12. Kohavi, R., Brodley, C., Frasca, B., Mason, L., Zheng, Z.: KDD-Cup 2000 organizers' report: Peeling the onion. SIGKDD Explorations **2**(2), 86–98 (2000)
13. Menon, S., Sarkar, S., Mukherjee, S.: Maximizing accuracy of shared databases when concealing sensitive patterns. Information Systems Research **16**(3), 256–270 (2005)
14. Oliveira, S.R.M., Zaïane, O.R.: Privacy preserving frequent itemset mining. In: Proceedings of the IEEE International Conference on Privacy, Security and Data Mining (CRPITS), pp. 43–54 (2002)
15. Saygin, Y., Verykios, V.S., Clifton, C.: Using unknowns to prevent discovery of association rules. ACM SIGMOD Record **30**(4), 45–54 (2001)
16. Sun, X., Yu, P.S.: A border-based approach for hiding sensitive frequent itemsets. In: Proceedings of the IEEE International Conference on Data Mining (ICDM), pp. 426–433 (2005)
17. Yokoo, M., Durfee, E.H., Ishida, T., Kuwabara, K.: The distributed constraint satisfaction problem: Formalization and algorithms. IEEE Transactions on Knowledge and Data Engineering **10**(5), 673–685 (1998)
18. Zaïane, O.R., M.El-Hajj, Lu, P.: Fast parallel association rule mining without candidacy generation. In: Proceedings of the IEEE International Conference on Data Mining (ICDM), pp. 665–668 (2001)

Efficient Coalition Detection in Traitor Tracing

Hongxia Jin, Jeffery Lotspiech and Nimrod Megiddo

abstract In this paper we study the traitor tracing problem for re-broadcasting attack. In this attack, instead of building a pirate clone device (or program) based on their secret keys and sell the clone, the attackers want to stay anonymous by redistributing the decrypted content or the actual encrypting keys for the content. To defend against this type of re-broadcasting attack, the content and its actual encrypting key must come with different versions. In our setting, content is divided into multiple segments, each segment comes with multiple variations and each variation is differently encrypted. Each user/device can only play back one variation per segment through the content. A typical traitor tracing scheme for re-broadcasting attack involves two basic steps, assigning the key/variation to devices (assignment step) and detecting at least a traitor in the coalition when a series of pirated key/content are recovered (coalition detection step). We take into considerations of some realities that have been overlooked in existing schemes. As a result, we have designed a probabilistic coalition detection algorithm that is not only closer to real world scenarios but also more efficient than existing approaches. The traceability is defined in terms of the number of recovered pirate copies of the content needed to detect traitor(s) as a function of the number of traitors involved in a coalition. While existing schemes try to identify traitors one by one, our probabilistic algorithm can identify multiple traitors simultaneously and deduce the coalition size during tracing. Therefore, for the same number of total traitors in a coalition, our scheme allows the detection of all the traitors using less number of recovered copies. The superior efficiency of the our coalition detection algorithm made its adoption by AACS (Advanced Access

Hongxia Jin & Nimrod Megiddo
IBM Almaden Research Center
San Jose, CA, 95120
e-mail: {jin,megiddo}@us.ibm.com

Jeffery Lotspiech
Lotspiech.com, Henderson, Nevada
e-mail: jeff@lotspiech.com

Please use the following format when citing this chapter:

Jin, H., Lotspiech, J. and Megiddo, N., 2008, in IFIP International Federation for Information Processing, Volume 278; *Proceedings of the IFIP TC 11 23rd International Information Security Conference*; Sushil Jajodia, Pierangela Samarati, Stelvio Cimato; (Boston: Springer), pp. 365–379.

Content System) content protection standards for next generation high-definition video optical disc.

1 Introduction

This paper is concerned with the protection of copyrighted materials. A number of business models has emerged whose success hinges on the ability to securely distribute digital content only to paying customers. Examples of these business models include pay-TV systems (Cable companies) or movie rental companies like Netflix, and massively distributing prerecorded and recordable media. These typical content protection applications imply a one-way broadcast nature. A broadcast encryption system [3] enables a broadcaster to encrypt the content so that only a privileged subset of users (devices, set up boxes) can decrypt the content and exclude another subset of users. When a broadcast encryption system is used for content protection, the enabling building block is a structure called Media Key Block (MKB) which is based on hybrid encryption. Each device is assigned a set of unique secret keys called device keys. The media key, which is indirectly used to encrypt the content, is encrypted by device keys again and again and put into MKB which is distributed together with the content. Each compliant device using its device key processes the MKB differently but gets the same correct media key to decrypt the content, while the excluded (revoked) devices cannot decrypt the MKB and get the correct media key.

Note that there can be different pirate attacks in the above content protection system. In one attack, a set of users (device owners) attack their devices, extract device keys out of the devices and use those keys collaboratively build a clone pirate device that can decrypt the content. When a pirate device is found, a traitor tracing scheme enables the broadcaster to find at least one of the users (called traitors) who have donated their device keys into the pirate device. Most existing broadcast encryption and traitor tracing schemes [2, 3, 4, 5, 6, 7, 8, 9, 10, 11, 12] targeted on this type of "pirate device attack".

This paper's focus is on a different attack, namely, the re-broadcasting attack as defined in [15, 16]. When an attacker re-broadcasts the content in the clear, the only forensic evidence is the unprotected copy of the content and the attackers can stay anonymous. The attacker can also simply re-broadcast the media key to stay anonymous and avoid being identified. To defend against the re-broadcasting attack, for different devices, not only the content needs to be in different versions, it also needs to be differently encrypted. Of course sending different versions to different users is oftentimes too costly in bandwidth or disc space needs. To reduce the cost, each content is divided into n segments and each segment is augmented by q different variations which are differently marked and encrypted. The underlying scene remains identical. To save cost, this same augmented content is distributed to every user. However, each user can only decrypt one of the variations at each segment. In other words, each recipient would follow a different path through the variations during playback time. In this way, even though each user does not receive a differently distributed content, it effectively creates different versions of the content for different users.

A traitor tracing scheme in this category usually consists of two basic steps:

1. *assignment step*: Assign a version of the content to the device by assigning the playback path, i.e., which variation to play for each augmented segment in the content.
2. *traitor/coalition detection step*: Based on the recovered pirated content/keys, trace back to the traitors.

The focus of this paper is on the traitor/coalition detection step. In literatures a traitor tracing scheme has been defined as a way to detect at least a traitor in the system when forensic evidence is recovered. Therefore the goal of the traitor detection step, as well as the design of a traitor tracing scheme, like [15, 16, 17, 18, 19], is to identify a traitor. It is assumed that the identified traitor can be disconnected from the system and the tracing continues after that. Indeed, for the *coalition/traitor detection* step existing schemes always use a highest-score approach, where each player is scored based on the number of matching between the recovered pirate movies and the versions assigned to the player, hoping the highest scored player is the guilty traitor. We believe using the one-by-one detection scheme for re-broadcasting attack is inefficient. We are motivated by the fact that in reality the ultimate goal is to detect all traitors in the coalition. If possible, one should try to detect multiple traitors simultaneously rather than detecting one by one. The efficiency of a tracing scheme is measured by the total number of recovered movies it needs in order to detect all traitors in a coalition of size T.

The second motivation of this work has to do with the fact that in reality the coalition size is usually unknown. As a result, the answers a traitor tracing scheme gets are always qualified in real applications. One cannot perform deterministic tracing as those shown in existing work. In reality, tracing will have to be probabilistic. Indeed, the real world question is how to accurately detect traitors without knowing the coalition size and with what probabilities.

We have designed the first traitor/coalition detection algorithm that tried to detect multiple traitors in the coalition together and also deduce the coalition size during tracing. In our algorithm, firstly, with the recovered movies, using set-cover, we try to detect which coalition of players may have involved in the attack, instead of which one particular player may have been involved. Second, when we find a suspect coalition, we cannot trivially incriminate all the players in the suspect coalition. We have designed ways to identify and incriminate the guilty individuals in the suspect coalition. As a result, we could incriminate more than one player at each iteration of the algorithm. Our goal is to correctly identify the actual traitors with high probability. In fact, our algorithm can identify traitors with any confidence the license agency wishes.

The above idea may look simple. But one might have been concerned with the theoretically exponential blow-up in computation time. Fortunately, in reality we find not only computational time is very manageable, we also find the computational time is less an issue than the demand for large number of pirate movies need to be recovered in order to detect traitors. After all, the tracing agency does not have control on how often attackers pirate and re-distribute movies, maybe every week or every month. Therefore, it is much more important to reduce the number of recovered movies that a traitor detection algorithm needs in order to detect traitors. Indeed as pointed out earlier, in this paper we define the efficiency of a traitor detection algorithm to be the number of pirate movies needed in order to detect traitors for a coalition of size T.

Furthermore, the efficiency of our algorithm derives from a very important but maybe counter-intuitive observation, it is much faster to eliminate the completely innocent coalitions than eliminating innocent individuals even though there exist a lot more (i.e., exponential number of)coalitions than individuals. This is because that it is much less likely that coalitions appear by random chance, than that individual players randomly have high scores. This truism is the essence of the efficient tracing underneath our new tracing algorithm.

The authors have been involved in what we believe is the first large-scale commercialization of a tracing traitors system for re-broadcasting attack within the AACS (Advanced Access Content System) content protection standards for next generation of high-definition optical DVDs. AACS adopts the use of the scheme in [20] as the assignment step to satisfy some practical restrictions for the assignment step. But the detection step shown in [20] is not efficient and practical enough. The algorithm we will show in this paper takes into considerations of those realities shown above that have largely been overlooked in existing work. As a probabilistic algorithm, it is not only more practical than deterministic tracing; it is also much more efficient due to the fact that it detects multiple traitors together. Furthermore, the entire tracing can be done in very reasonable time. As a result, AACS adopts the use of the scheme in [20] as the assignment step and adopts the work presented in this paper as the coalition detection step.

In rest of the paper, in Section 2, we will first provide more contextual background for designing a traitor tracing scheme for AACS for re-broadcasting attack, including some practical restrictions on the assignment step. Many schemes shown in literatures do not have those restrictions in mind and thus do not satisfy those restrictions. We will summarize the result in [20] to show how it can satisfy some of AACS' restrictions on assignment step. Then we will show our traitor/coalition detection algorithm in Section 3. We will analyze its false positive rate in Section 4 and its performance/efficiency in Section 5. We show simulation results in Section 6 and conclude in Section 7. For concreteness, we use movie as a sample content in this paper.

2 Background for traitor tracing in AACS

AACS founders find it acceptable to makes the following marking assumption on the pirate model. Given two variants v_1 and v_2 of a segment, the pirate can only use v_1

or v_2, not any other valid variant v_i. In a key-rebroadcasting attack, this assumption says if attackers have two valid random cryptographic keys, it is probable they will simply redistribute them instead of calculating a valid random key from the known two random keys since it is difficult if not impossible to do so. For content rebroadcasting attack, while watermarking is a common way to build variations, there are other better ways to exploit and satisfy the marking assumption. It is outside the scope of this paper to discuss why AACS adopts this attack model.

When a movie is divided into multiple segments and each segment is augmented with multiple (q) variations, as one can imagine, those variations take extra space on the disc. For content owners, a practical traitor tracing scheme on a prerecorded optical movie disc should take no more than 10% of the space on the disc to store the variations. This puts practical restriction on the number of variations one can put into a movie. The market for such discs is huge, involving literally a billion playing devices or more. This means a tracing scheme needs to be able to accommodate large number of devices. While these restrictions are inherently conflicting, a practical traitor tracing scheme must meet these requirements first. After meeting these requirements, it is also important to detect the coalition of traitors using as few recovered movies as possible.

In summary, a traitor tracing scheme for AACS needs to meet all the following requirements:

1. the number of variations for each movie cannot be big
2. the number of devices/users *must* be big
3. after the above two requirements are met, the number of movies necessary to detect a coalition of should be as small as possible

It is very important to notice that much of the literature on traceability codes has taken the approach of fixing the number of colluders and the number of recovered movies and trying to find codes to support an optimal number of devices/users for a given number of variations of each movie. For example, the code shown in [17] either has too few codewords (accommodates a small number of devices) or the number of variations is too large (requires too much space on the disc). In the AACS context, a traitor tracing scheme must first meet the two requirements on the number of variations and the number of devices, then its goal is to minimize the number of recovered movies to detect unknown number of colluders.

In existing literatures, the scheme shown in [20] can meet the first two requirements. In this scheme, basically for each movie, there is an "inner code" used to assign the different variations at the chosen points of the movie; it effectively creates different movie versions. Over a sequence of movies, there is an "outer code" used to assign movie versions to different players. Both assignments can be random or systematic. For example, one can use a Reed-Solomon code for both the inner and outer code. Suppose there are 16 variations created at each of the 15 points in the movie. Their scheme will create 256 versions in which any two versions will be guaranteed to differ at least 14 points. Once the "inner code" creates the multiple movie versions (e.g., 256), each player is assigned one of the 256 versions for each movie in a sequence of 255 movies. A Reed-Solomon code can create 256^4 codewords (thus billions players) with any two players differ at least 252 movies. By concatenating the two levels of codes, the assignments managed to avoid having a big number of variations at any chosen point but can still accommodate the billions of devices. These parameters can be good choices for AACS.

As mentioned above, the "outer code" is used to assign the movie versions to each player. For real use, the "outer code" can be used to assign the movie version keys to each player. Those keys will be burned into the player at manufacturer time and will not get updated afterwards. These keys are called "sequence keys" in the AACS specification. For example, each device is assigned a set of 255 keys, corresponding to the 255 movies in the sequence. Each key comes with 256 versions corresponding to the 256 movie versions created from the "inner code". During playback time, the device can use the sequence key for a movie to obtain the actual variation encrypting keys for each segment. More details are referred to [20].

The first two requirements have to do with the assignment step in a traitor tracing scheme. While AACS adopts [20] for its assignment step, the third requirement on the traceability cannot be met with the scheme [20], measured by the number of recovered movies needed in order to detect traitors involved in a coalition. In fact, the solution to the traceability problem has more to do with the actual traitor/coalition detection step.

As we mentioned earlier, there is one thing common with all the existing schemes including [16][17] and [20] on the tracing step. For each device, they calculate the number of matching that the observed pirate copies have in common with the versions assigned to that device. When the traitors in a coalition collude together in the pirate attack, these schemes are defined to detect and incriminate the one traitor who has the most matching. In fact if we use the highest score tracing approach on the above assignment, as shown in [20], for a coalition of 10 traitors one of them can be detected after 255 movies. This is not enough for practical use. In fact, the authors for [20] called for a more efficient probabilistic tracing approach.

3 Our traitor/coalition detection algorithm

Our algorithm works with both random and systematic assignment of the keys to devices. In this paper, for the sake of simplicity, we will just assume that the licensing agency assign the keys uniformly at random instead of using a Reed-Solomon code.

First of all, we want to make clearer of what we mean by "coalition". To our coalition detection algorithm, a coalition exists if illicit movies are coming from many players and we cannot otherwise determine which movies are coming from which players. For example, we recover re-broadcasted movies in a file sharing network. It does not mean that the people in the coalition are organized. It does not even mean that they know about each other's existence.

As mentioned earlier, traitor tracing schemes in literatures have been mostly focused on the assignment step. The actual detection algorithm is simple and straightforward: you take your sequence of recovered movies, and simply score all the devices based on how many movies match with what each device has been assigned. You incriminate the highest scoring device. Traitors are therefore detected one by one. But why not detect every member in the coalition all together? The classic one-by-one method has some obvious advantages:

1. It seems easier.
2. The number of coalitions of a certain size is exponential in the number of users in the system. For example, if there are 1,000,000,000 devices/users in the world, there are roughly 500,000,000,000,000,000 pairs of devices (i.e., coalitions of size 2).
3. It seems essential against the "scapegoat" strategy. In this strategy, the coalition sacrifices a few devices and uses them heavily while using the others lightly, to keep some in reserve. Note that even without the scapegoat strategy, simulation results usually show some unlucky innocent devices intermixed with guilty players when the devices are scored in the classic way.

It may seem counter-intuitive, but we believe it is easier to find the entire coalition than to sequentially find one individual traitor, disable him and find another one. It turns out that it is much less likely that coalitions appear by random chance, than that individual player randomly has high score. An example can informally illustrate the underlying idea. Suppose there are 4 people involved in a colluding attack, and we have a random sequence of 20 recovered movies. Each movie originally has 256 variations of which a given player only plays 1. The attackers wish to see that high scoring device can happen by chance. If the four attackers are using round robin, each guilty player will evenly score 5. Can we incriminate any player that share 5 movies with the recovered sequence? No, there will be about 15 completely innocent players scoring 5 or greater due to chance alone. What can you do then? You have to recover more movies before you can incriminate any player. In general, with N players and q variations for each movie, the expected number of individuals who can score x among m movies are:

$$N * (1/q)^x * \binom{m}{x} \tag{1}$$

However, the above 4 guilty players together can explain all the movies in the sequence. What is the chance that a coalition of size 4 might have all the variations in the sequence? The answer is roughly 0.04. In other words, while there are plenty of players that can explain 5 movies, it is unlikely that any four of them can "cover" all twenty movies. If we find four players that do cover the sequence, it is unlikely that this could have happened by chance. It is more likely that that some devices in the coalition are indeed guilty.

On the other hand, the attackers may use scapegoat strategy. Some player is used heavily, for example, score 9 or 10. The traditional approach can correctly identify him, but it is hard to find the lightly used player and the true coalition size. Our new tracing algorithm can nonetheless find the other members in the coalitions and find out the coalition size.

In section 3.1, we will show how we find a coalition to explain the recovered movies. After we find the suspect coalition, in section 3.2 we will show how we identify the actual guilty players in the suspect coalition and filter out the innocent ones.

3.1 Finding a coalition

Let us formalize the above intuition a bit more. If there are N players, and a sequence of m movies are selected, each movie having one random variation out of q, the expected number of coalitions of size T are:

$$\binom{N}{T} * (1-(1-1/q)^T)^m \qquad (2)$$

If the expected number of coalitions is less than 1, this formula also gives an upper bound on the probability that a random sequence of m movie variations is covered by a coalition of size T.

In AACS context, as a sample parameter, $q = 1024$ and a reasonable $T = 40$. If T is in fact noticeably less than q, a simplification of this is a close upper bound:

$$\binom{N}{T} * (T/q)^m \qquad (3)$$

The problem of finding a coalition of players that covers a sequence of movies is equivalent to a well-known problem in computer science called Set Cover. It is NP hard. Any set cover algorithm can be used here. But we find there is even no need to use a much elaborated set cover algorithm. Not only that computational time is not much an issue for AACS, but also in reality the calculation time is very reasonable for the parameters that AACS is concerned with. For example, using the simple set cover shown below, to detect coalitions that cover 20 movies, it takes about 5 seconds on a Thinkpad T30.

Assume the licensing agency has observed a sequence of movies and determined the particular variation (the "symbol") in use for each. We also introduce the parameter k, the number of symbols that would probabilistically identify a single player. For example, k could be set to $log_q N$, where N is the total number of players.

The following recursive procedure *COVER*, if given a suspected number of traitors T and a list of the m encoded symbols discovered, returns true if and only if there is at least one coalition of size T that can explain the observed symbols:

1. If $T * k$ is greater than the number of symbols, print "many" and return true.
2. Calculate the minimum number of symbols that the largest-scoring traitor must have:
$$min = \lceil \frac{m}{T} \rceil$$

3. For each possible combination of k symbols, calculate whether the single player assigned to that combination covers '*min*' number of symbols. If it does, perform the following:
   a. If $T = 1$, print the player ID and return true.
   b. If $T > 1$, recursively call *COVER* passing the symbol list after removing all the symbols from the suspect player and with $T = T - 1$.
      i. If the recursive call returns false, continue to loop through the other combinations.
      ii. If the recursive call returns true, print the player ID and return true.
   c. If all combinations have been checked, return false.

The tracing algorithm assumes that the size of the coalition is unknown, and proceeds to calculate both the size of the coalition as well as the actual players involved. Below is the method that uses the above procedure *COVER* (or any other Set Cover procedure):

1. Set T = 1.
2. Run *COVER*.
3. If *COVER* returns true, exit.
4. Otherwise set $T = T + 1$ and loop to step 2.

Eventually the procedure must exit at step 3. Why? Once the number of movies is less than $T * k$, *COVER* is guaranteed to return true (see step 1 in *COVER*). But the interesting thing happens if you exit "early". In this case, you have found a coalition, and you can calculate the probability that a larger completely different coalition could have incriminated this coalition of size T, as explained in Lemma 1.

3.2 Identify guilty individuals in the found suspect coalition

Once we have found a coalition, who in the coalition should we incriminate? What is the chance that some of the players in the purported coalition of size T might be actually innocent, being victimized by a scapegoat strategy that is hiding a few lightly used guilty players? We calculate this as follows:

For each combination of T players, perform the following steps:

1. Temporarily assume that the players in the particular combination are guilty.
2. If the number of players in this combination is c, subtract c from T
3. Temporarily subtract from the list of movies all the movies that can be explained by this combination of players.
4. Use the formula 2 above using the new number of movies m and T, to evaluate the probability that the remaining players are completely innocent. If the formula yields a number greater than 1, assume the probability is 1.

When this procedure has ended, there will be a list of all possible combinations of players together with the chance that the remaining players are innocent. If some of these combinations indicate that there is a good chance that a player is innocent under those circumstances, the licensing agency would be well advised not to take action against the player (yet). On the other hand, some players will seem guilty under all combinations. In other words, the license agency can use the minimum guilty probability of the each player under all combinations as the probability of guilt of the player. In general, players that score higher in terms of the number of movies they could have encoded are also more likely to show up as guilty after the procedure. It is also reassuring that after this procedure any player that is identified only as "many" in the *COVER* procedure will show up as likely innocent.

Note it is possible that two of the players in the coalition may have a high overlap in movies. In this case, the procedure above might reveal that if player A is guilty, there is a good chance that player B is innocent, and vice versa. In this case, the licensing agency would be well advised to avoid making a decision about either of them until more movies have pointed to one or the other. Note that using the "*min*" probability rule, both players show up as likely innocent for the time being. However, the policy used by the licensing agency is outside of the scope of this paper. This algorithm provides the necessary tool to the licensing agency: a short list of potentially guilty players and probability of their actual innocence or guilt.

We now discuss a few optimizations. Before calling *COVER* the first time, it is usually faster to pre-calculate the $\binom{m}{k}$ potential players. Then, in step 3 of cover, you simply iterate through the pre-calculated list, seeing if each player is still a candidate under the current circumstances. Determining which player corresponds to particular list of k symbols can often be optimized. It is always possible to exhaustively search through all the players to see which one is indicated, but this can be obviously sped up by well-known techniques like table look-up and hashing. Furthermore, if the encoding method used is a linear code, as it was shown in our previous paper [20], it is possible to identify the player by algebraic means. For example, each list of k symbols defines k equations in k unknowns, which can be solved by Gaussian elimination.

4 False positive

Our tracing algorithm assumes that the size of the coalition is unknown, and proceeds to calculate both the size of the coalition as well as the actual players involved. If the size of the coalition is known from other sources, the answers may be exact; otherwise, the answer is always probabilistic. The problem is, from the attackers side, they do not know what sequence would incriminate an innocent player, so they are just guessing. We can make the probability they guess correctly arbitrarily small by just collecting more movies. The following lemma shows the false positive rate in our detection.

Lemma 1. *Assume that a coalition of guilty players cannot deduce the movie assignment of any other player in the world, for a coalition C, $|C| = T$, found by algorithm* COVER, *the probability that every member in coalition C is innocent is* *bounded by formula 2. In other words, the formula gives the false positive probability in the detection.*

Proof: Imagine that the process of assignment is the opposite of the way it works in real life: instead of starting with the assignment of variations to the population, the coalition randomly picks their assignment and then picks the particular variations of m movies in any way they choose. Only then does the licensing agency, not knowing what the coalition has picked, assign the variations for the remaining innocent players randomly. The chance that this assignment would result in a coalition of size T amongst the innocent players is clearly bounded by equation 2. And since there is no way to distinguish the "real life" case from the "thought experiment" case based on the player assignment (they are both equally random), the equation does represent the best that the attackers can do. □

The licensing agency can choose any acceptable value for the false positive rate. The smaller the false positive rate, the more pirate movies it needs to recover. We can get any kind of confidence level desired, but it will just take us more recovered movies to achieve. If the attack is ongoing, we always have the option of increasing our confidence by recovering more movies. In general, for each movie recovered, our confidence that the guilty players are, in fact, guilty is increased by roughly q/T. Since our entire tracing is probabilistic, we can factor in some false positives from the underlying watermarking technology (that is determining which variations were recovered) as well.

5 Tracing efficiency

From formula 3, we can calculate the number of movies m it takes for a coalition of size T to achieve any level of confidence (or false positive rate), for example, λ. We obtained a superlinear relationship between m and T.

$$\binom{N}{T} * (T/q)^m = \lambda \tag{4}$$

Because N is much larger than T, $\binom{N}{T}$ can be approximated to be N^T. Solving the above equation gives us:

$$m = \frac{T * lnN - ln\lambda}{lnq - lnT} \tag{5}$$

For the parameters of our choice for AACS, it is easy enough to use a spreadsheet on the formula 3 to show the relationship among these numbers. The two graphs below show this relationship when the number of device is 1 billion.

Interestingly, it takes almost the same number of movies (roughly $6T$) to achieve a super high confidence (below 0.0001%) as it does to achieve a moderately high confidence (below 0.1%)

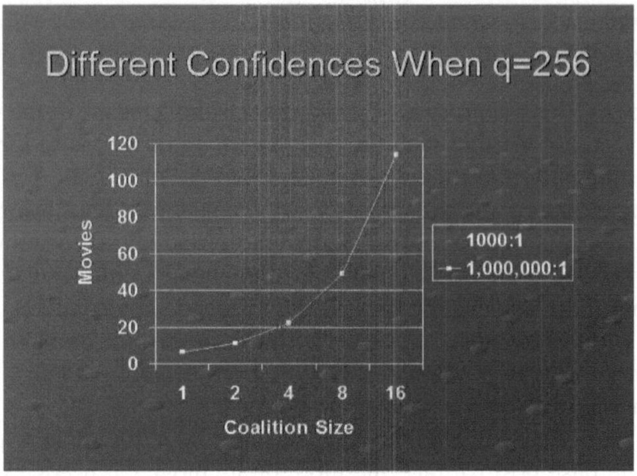

Now let us do some comparison with existing approaches. Of course in AACS context it is difficult to deploy a dynamic traitor tracing scheme like [15] because AACS has to assign the sequence keys to burn into devices during manufacture time and cannot easily update them afterwards. Among static schemes, a traceability codes is one of the traditional approaches that incriminates the highest score device, i.e. the device whose codeword is at the smallest Hamming distance from the pirated copy. Indeed a traceability code enables one to decode to the nearest neighbor of a pirate code and the nearest neighbor is deterministically a traitor.

Lemma 2. [5] Assume that a code $\mathscr{C}$ with length n and distance d is used to assign the symbols for each segment to each user and that there are t traitors. If code $\mathscr{C}$ satisfies

$$d > (1 - 1/t^2)n, \tag{6}$$

then $\mathscr{C}$ is an t-traceability-code.

In [20], it showed the tracing results based on the above formula when using the parameters of choice for AACS. It can deterministically identify traitors in a coalition of nine after recovering 256 movies. In contrast, for the same coalition size, our algorithm takes 56 movies and the false positive rate can be low at 0.0001%. Indeed [20] called for probabilistic tracing to improve efficiency as well as fit more with the reality that coalition size is unknown in advance.

As another one-by-one detection scheme, the static sequential traitor tracing scheme shown in [16] can detect T traitors with $T^2 + T$ movies. For the reasonable coalition size that AACS is concerned with, for example, a dozen to several dozens traitors, our superlinear results shown in Formula 5 is much more efficient.

Please also note that the probabilistic tracing we have is also different from the probabilistic tracing in [4, 5]. Their goal is to make the probability of exposing an innocent user as small as possible, while we try to make the probability of catching the actual traitor to be reasonably high.

6 Simulation results

We have also performed simple simulations to confirm the above analysis. Because of the nature of the probabilistic detection, it means some false positive. For a coalition of size 4, we know it takes about 22 movies to detect the traitors with very high confidence. Of course, to confirm a very low probability like that would take an unreasonably large number of simulations. Instead, we used a test with a larger false positive rate, namely a 20 movie sequence. We randomly picked a coalition of size 4, and create 20 pirate movies out of the chosen 4 traitors. We tried both random and round robin methods for the traitors' strategy. We confirmed (at the 95% confidence level) that equation 2 holds. Similarly, for a coalition size of 6, from the formula we know it takes about 34 movies to reach a confidence 0.005% false positive. We simulated using only 32 movies. After 100 simulations we tested, we found 6 cases that involve a completely innocent coalition, which is consistent with the bound from equation 2, which is 9.5%.

We also notice a slight difference of the behavior when we use round robin to create the pirate movies than when we use random selection. In the case of random selection, one player often contributes a lot. This partially explains why traditional score ranking could work to some extent against the random selection attacker strategy. But with our new tracing scheme, the other coalition members are nonetheless found, unless they made a negligible contribution to the attack.

On the other hand, in the case of round robin, the movies are contributed evenly from the attackers. It is hard to incriminate the highest scoring player in this case. For example, in the case of a coalition of size 4 and with 20 movies, all 4 players explain 5 movies. In our simulation, in most cases, the new tracing algorithm found the exact one coalition that together can explain all 20 movies. Once again, this explains why our new tracing algorithm is more efficient than the traditional approach.

7 Conclusions

In this paper, we study the problem of traitor tracing for re-broadcasting attack where the legitimate users (traitors) who instrument their devices and illegally resell the pirated copies by redistributing the content or the decryption keys on the Internet. We have designed an efficient traitor detection algorithm for AACS (Advanced Access Content System) copy protection standard for the next generation of high-definition DVDs. The efficiency is measured by the number of recovered movies it takes to identify all the traitors in the coalition.

We take into considerations of some realities that have been overlooked in existing work. We designed a probabilistic tracing scheme that is closer to the real world situation more than deterministic tracing. It also achieves super linear traceability, much more efficient than existing approaches. Different from existing approaches which try to detect traitors one by one, we detect multiple traitors in the coalition together. This idea enables faster tracing with less recovered content, at the cost of higher computational overhead. We take advantage of the fact in reality this tradeoff is gladly made.

The superior traceability achieved by the algorithm described in this paper made its commercial adoption by AACS to protect the next generation DVDs. In the future, we will continue to improve its traceability, not only theoretically, but also by taking into consideration of real implementations. Technically we are interested in improving the filtering algorithm. We would also like to consider the case when the coalition size is large to anticipate new types of attacks enabled by future new technologies.

References

1. http://www.aacsla.com
2. D. Naor, M. Naor and J. Lotspiech, "Revocation and Tracing Schemes for Stateless Receivers", *Crypto 2001, Lecture Notes in computer science*, Vol. 2139, pp 41-62, 2001.
3. A. Fiat and M. Naor, "Broadcast Encryption," *Crypto'93, Lecture Notes in computer science*, Vol. 773, pp480-491. Springer-Verlag, Berlin, Heidelberg, New York, 1993.
4. B. Chor, A, Fiat and M. Naor, "Tracing traitors," *Crypto'94, Lecture Notes in computer science*, Vol. 839, pp480-491. Springer-Verlag, Berlin, Heidelberg, New York, 1994.
5. B. Chor, A, Fiat, M. Naor and B. Pinkas, "Tracing traitors," *IEEE Transactions on Information Theory*, Vol 46(2000), 893-910.
6. M. Naor and B. Pinkas, "Efficient Trace and Revoke Schemes", Financial Cryptography'2000, Lecture Notes in Computer Science, Vol. 1962, pp. 1-20.
7. D. boneh, C. Gentry and B. Waters, "Collusion Resistant Broadcast Encryption With Short Ciphertexts and Private Keys", Crypto'05. pp.258-275.
8. D. Boneh, A. Sahai and B.Waters, "Fully Collusion Resistant Traitor Tracing With Short Ciphertexts and Private Keys", EuroCrypt'06, pp.573-592.
9. D. Boneh and M. Franklin, "An efficient public key traitor tracing scheme", Crypto'99. LNCS 1666, pp.338-353.
10. D. Boneh and B. Waters, "A collusion resistant broadcast, trace and revoke system", ACM Communication and Computer Security, 2006.
11. K. Kurosawa and Y. Desmedt, "Optimum traitor tracing and asymmetric schemes", EuroCrypt'98, pp.145-157.
12. H. Chabanne, DH. Phan and D. Pointcheval, "Public traceability in traitor tracing schemes", Eurocrypt, 2005, pp.542-558.
13. D.R.Stinson and R. Wei, "Key preassigned traceability schemes for broadcast encryption", ACM SAC'98, 1998.
14. E. Gafni, J. Staddon and Y.L.Yin, "Efficient methods for integrating traceability and broadcast encryption", CRYPTO'99, Lecture Notes in computer Science, Vol. 1666, 1999, pp. 537-554
15. A. Fiat and T. Tassa, "Dynamic traitor tracing," *Crypto'99, Lecture Notes in computer science*, Vol. 1666, pp354-371. Springer-Verlag, Berlin, Heidelberg, New York, 1999.
16. R. Safani-Naini and Y. Wang, "Sequential Traitor tracing," *IEEE Transactions on Information Theory*, 49, 2003.

17. Tran van Trung and Sosina Martirosyan, "On a class of Traceability Codes", *Design, code and cryptography*, 31(2004), pp 125-132.
18. J. N. Staddon, D.R. Stinson and R. Wei, "Combinatorial properties of frameproof and traceability codes," *IEEE Transactions on Information Theory*, 47 (2001), 1042-1049.
19. D.R.Stinson and R. Wei, "Combinatorial properties and constructions of traceability schemes and frameproof codes," *SIAM Journal on Discrete Mathematics*, 11:41-53, 1998.
20. H. Jin, J.Lotspiech and S.Nusser, "Traitor tracing for prerecorded and recordable media", ACM DRM workshop, Oct. 2004.
21. G. Tardos, "Optimal Probabilistic fingerprint codes", in proceedings of the *Theory of Computing*, pp. 116-125, June 9-11, 2003, San Diego, CA.

SPIT Identification Criteria Implementation: Effectiveness and Lessons Learned

S. Dritsas, Y. Soupionis, M. Theoharidou, Y. Mallios, D. Gritzalis

Abstract While VoIP enables new means for communication, it may also provide a new way of transmitting bulk unsolicited messages and calls, namely SPam over Internet Telephony (SPIT). In this paper, we present the phases of a SPIT management process and we form a set of SPIT identification criteria, which are needed in order to characterize a call as SPIT, or a caller as spitter. Then, we present briefly the currently existing anti-SPIT frameworks, so as to examine which of the SPIT identification criteria is fulfilled by each framework, thus providing an insight on which criteria a technique should cope with, as well as how one can evaluate and combine existing approaches, in order to effectively mitigate SPIT. Finally, we implement a list of the criteria in our lab environment in order to examine the applicability of these controls in a Session Initiation Protocol (SIP) environment.

Stelios Dritsas
Dept. of Informatics, Athens University of Economics and Business, 76 Patission Ave., Athens, GR-10434, Greece, e-mail: sdritsas@aueb.gr

Yannis Soupionis
Dept. of Informatics, Athens University of Economics and Business, 76 Patission Ave., Athens, GR-10434, Greece, e-mail: jsoup@aueb.gr

Marianthi Theoharidou
Dept. of Informatics, Athens University of Economics and Business, 76 Patission Ave., Athens, GR-10434, Greece, e-mail: mtheohar@aueb.gr

Yannis Mallios
Information Networking Institute, Carnegie Mellon University, 4616 Henry St., Pittsburgh, PA 15213, USA, e-mail: imallios@andrew.cmu.edu

Dimitris Gritzalis
Dept. of Informatics, Athens University of Economics and Business, 76 Patission Ave., Athens, GR-10434, Greece, e-mail: dgrit@aueb.gr

---

Please use the following format when citing this chapter:

Dritsas, S., et al., 2008, in IFIP International Federation for Information Processing, Volume 278; *Proceedings of the IFIP TC 11 23rd International Information Security Conference*; Sushil Jajodia, Pierangela Samarati, Stelvio Cimato; (Boston: Springer), pp. 381–395.

1 Introduction

Voice-over-IP (VoIP) increasingly gains ground compared to traditional telephony. Its penetration and attractiveness is mainly due to its seamless integration with the existing IP networks, to its low-cost, and to the provision of sophisticated end-user services based on computer-based soft-phones. Currently, VoIP services drift towards the Session Initiation Protocol (SIP), due to its simplicity and its strong market acceptance. SIP is a protocol used for establishing communications between users, providing services such as voice telephony and instant messaging (IM) [14].

An identified threat to VoIP is the voice spam, referred to as Spam over Internet Telephony (SPIT). SPIT initiators, called spitters, use the IP network to generate bulk, unsolicited calls (or instant messages), mainly for commercial reasons. If SPIT prevalence becomes proportional to the one of spam, then the acceptance of VoIP will be encumbered. However, SPIT only recently received attention and only few solutions to it have been proposed (see section 4). Recent analyses show that SIP is more vulnerable to SPIT than it was initially estimated [5].

In this paper we argue that the effectiveness of any anti-SPIT technique is equally important to the actual technique itself. In this context we propose a set of SPIT identification criteria that will facilitate through their application a more concrete SPIT recognition and management process. Furthermore, we examine how the state-of-art antiSPIT mechanisms and frameworks handle the proposed criteria and finally, we present two different approaches that a VoIP system administrator could follow to implement these criteria in the domain that she is responsible for.

The paper is organized as follows: First, we illustrate some of the SIP features and present a macroscopic view of the SPIT management process. Then, we define a set of SPIT identification criteria needed to identify a SPIT call/message or a spitter. In Section 5, we briefly present existing anti-SPIT mechanisms. In section 6 we evaluate these mechanisms in terms of which SPIT identification criteria they cope with. Finally, we present two different ways of implement the predefined SPIT identification criteria and we conclude by providing the reader with some noteworthy remarks.

2 SPIT Phenomenon

SIP is an application layer protocol used to create, maintain, and terminate multimedia sessions. It supports five main services to multimedia communication: (a) user location, (b) user availability, (c) user capabilities, (d) session setup, and (e) session management. The basic SIP entities that support these services are User Agents (UA), which act as communication end-points, and SIP servers (proxies and registrars servers), which help and support the SIP sessions.

In this context, SPIT constitutes a new type of threat in VoIP environments. However, despite illustrating several similarities with email spam, there are certain differences between SPIT and spam, among them being the synchronous and real-time nature of VoIP services, which hinder the adoption of email spam filtering techniques (i.e. Bayesian filters). Hence, new mechanisms should be adopted in order to handle effectively SPIT.

SPIT is defined as a set of bulk unsolicited phone calls or instant messages. Currently, three different types of VoIP spam forms have been recognized, namely: (a) *Call SPIT*, which is defined as bulk, unsolicited session initiation attempts to establish a multimedia session, (b) *Instant Message SPIT*, which is defined as bulk, unsolicited instant messages, known as SPIM, and (c) *Presence SPIT*, which is defined as bulk, unsolicited presence requests so as the malicious user to become a member of the address book of a user or potentially of multiples users.

The identified threats regarding SPIT are classified into four categories: (a) threats due to SIP protocol vulnerabilities, (b) threats due to the SIP protocol optional recommendations, (c) threats due to interoperability with other protocols, and (d) threats due to other (generic) security risks. These threats exploit specific SIP protocol vulnerabilities and can be used by a potential spitter in order to transmit SPIT calls and/or messages [5].

2.1 SPIT Management

The real-time nature of VoIP services led us to consider that it is more efficient to handle SPIT in the SIP signaling phase, than real-time filtering of a session (i.e. voice analysis). In general, a SPIT management process requires three distinct steps (see Fig. 1):

- ***Prevention***. This step prevents SPIT a priori, i.e., it impedes a potential SPIT message to be sent or a SPIT call to be established. In the context of SIP, prevention is responsible for blocking the spitter (caller) at her outgoing proxy. This requires a priori identification of SPIT, based on specific criteria. In order to be

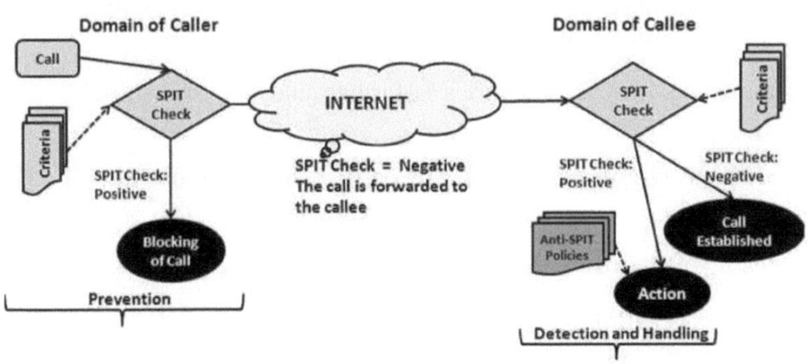

Fig. 1 A macroscopic view of SPIT Management

more efficient it should consider the overall SPIT policies that her domain has adopted.

- ***Detection***. This step detects a SPIT call or message when it reaches the callee's domain. It depends on pre-identified criteria and it is influenced by the preferences-interests of the callee, in terms of the attributes of the call or message, or the anti-SPIT policies of the domain of the callee.
- ***Reaction***. This step applies specific actions in case a call or a message has been identified as SPIT. These reactions, i.e. the application of specific anti-SPIT measures, are defined by the anti-SPIT policies adopted by the callee's domain.

3 SPIT Identification Criteria

SPIT management requires, first, appropriate criteria in order to identify SPIT calls and/or messages. In this section we present such a list of criteria, categorized according to their role in SPIT calls/messages. The same criteria can be used as detection rules, on both sides of a SIP session (i.e. outgoing or incoming proxies), according to their role in terms of handling SPIT. More specifically, when these criteria are used on an outgoing proxy (i.e. sender-caller's domain), we characterize them as preventive criteria, as they aim to prevent a call/message to leave the domain. When these criteria are applied by incoming proxies, they are characterized as detective criteria, as they aim to identify a SPIT call/message at the receiver point of a SIP session. The effectiveness of these criteria increases when they are applied in conjunction with strict identification and authentication mechanisms adopted by every SIP-participating domain. In this context, we propose two generic categories of SPIT identification criteria:

- ***SIP Message criteria***: This category includes the criteria that are related to attributes of SIP messages.
- ***SIP User Agent criteria***: This category includes the criteria that are related to attributes of a SIP User Agent.

Each one of the above generic categories is further analyzed into sub-categories, namely:

- Call and Message Origin as well as SIP participants' relationship (SIP User Agent oriented).
- Call and Message Patterns (SIP Message oriented);
- Headers' Semantics (SIP Message oriented).

A description of these criteria is presented in the sequel.

3.1 Call and Message Origin and SIP participants' relationship Criteria (SIP User Agent Oriented)

This category includes criteria that examine the characteristics of a SIP session, regarding the SIP addresses of the sender/caller (i.e. SIP URI or IP address), as well as the domain the session was initiated in[1]. Furthermore, through this analysis the relationship of the participants of a SIP session is examined, i.e. whether the caller/sender is trusted by the callee/receiver. Typical examples include whether a caller is known to the callee (included in his address book), whether she is included in a white list or contrary she is blacklisted.

- *Caller SIP URI*: It detects and analyzes the SIP URI of the sender of a call/message, so as to determine if she is a potential spitter or not.
- *Caller IP Address*: It analyzes the IP address of the sender/caller so as to characterize her as spitter.
- *Caller Domain*: It analyzes the identity of the domain of the caller (sender), which is determined either by SIP URI of the caller, or through DNS lookup from her IP address. If the identity of the domain is a well-known SPIT source, then the call or the message is characterized as potentially SPIT.

3.2 Call-Messages Patterns (SIP Message Oriented)

This category includes criteria that analyze specific call or message characteristics or patterns, in order to determine whether a call (message) is a possible SPIT.

- *Path traversal*: A call or a message might pass through many intermediates before reaching its final destination. This path is denoted in the Via header. Thus, if in the Via header a SPIT domain is recognized, the call or the message may be a potential SPIT.
- *Number of calls-messages sent in a specific time frame*: It analyzes the number of calls (messages) made in a specific time period by a user. If this number is above a specific pre-defined threshold then the call (message) is characterized as a possible SPIT call.
- *Static calls' duration*: If the calls initiated by a single user have a static duration, then the user is a potential spitter and it is possible to use an automated script (e.g. bot software) in order to make the calls.
- *Receivers' address patterns*: If the receivers' addresses follow a specific pattern (e.g. alphabetical SIP URI addresses), then the call (message) is flagged as SPIT.

---

[1] The specific controls require a database that stores the source of well-known spitters' domain or specific spitters identities (SIP URIs).

- *Small percentage of answered/dialed calls*: It indicates the number of successful call completions from this caller per a pre-defined time period, which is relative to the number of failed ones.
- *Large number of errors*: When a user send a large number of INVITEs and the SIP protocol returns a large number of error messages (e.g. 404 Not Found) then it is probable this user be a potential spitter, therefore the calls made by her/him are blocked.
- *Size of SIP Messages*: In this case a set of SIP messages sent by a user to other users is analyzed. If those messages have a specific size then it is very possible to be sent by a "bot" software, therefore the call is characterized as SPIT.

3.3 SIP Headers' Semantics (SIP Message Oriented)

This category includes criteria that identify a SPIT call or message through a semantic analysis of the contents of the SIP messages. Through the analysis one can apply well-known anti-spam techniques (e.g. Bayesian filters), in order to determine if a call/message is SPIT.

These particular criteria are further categorized, according to the different parts of SIP messages that could be used. These are: (a) a message's headers, (b) a message's body, and (c) the reason phrases of a message.

In addition, we have identified three possible types of SPIT that could be injected in a SIP message, namely: (a) text SPIT injected in a header field, (b) media SPIT carried in the message's body, and (c) hyperlink to a SPIT message injected in a header field).

Tables 1 to 3 depict the specific SIP header fields that can be used for a detailed semantic analysis, so as to detect a SPIT call or message alongside with the type of the SPIT that could be sent. Hence, Table 1 presents the header fields of the SIP request or response messages that should be examined in order to check if they include SPIT content. For instance, the header *Subject* might contain a suspicious text, i.e. the word pornography, which in most cases might be considered as SPIT. Moreover, the *Alert-Info* header might include a hyperlink that directs a user to a specific site used for promotional-commercial reasons.

Table 2 presents the types of SIP messages that could contain a body field. This field should be examined as it may include suspicious content, characterized as SPIT. The message types are grouped in Request and Response Messages. The SPIT conained in the message body can be text, media or hyperlink.

Table 3 presents the Reason Phrases of Response Messages that could be used by a malicious user so as to generate SPIT message. More specifically, the Reason Phrases may consist of plain text or hyperlink, which forms the SPIT message sent to the receivers.

Table 1 SIP Headers that could include SPIT content

Header Fields	SPIT Type	Request Messages	Response Messages
Subject	Text	✓	✓
From	Text	✓	✓
Call-Info	Hyperlink	✓	✓
Contact	Text	✓	✓
To	Text	✓	✓
Retry After	Text	✓	✓
Alert-Info	Hyperlink	✓	✓
Reply To	Text	✓	–
Error-Info	Hyperlink	–	✓
Warning	Text	–	✓
Header Fields related to SIP messages' bodies *notcarryingSPIT"directly*"			
Content-Disposition	Displayed Message Body	✓	✓
Content-Type	Displayed Message Body	✓	✓

Table 2 Request-Response Messages that could include SPIT content

Message Type	**Message**
Request Messages	INVITE
	ACK
Response Messages	180 Ringing
	183 Session Progress
	200 OK
	300 Multiple Choices
	380 Alternative Service
	488 Not Acceptable Here
	606 Not Acceptable

Table 3 Request-Response Messages that could include SPIT content

Response Messages Possibly Carrying Reason Phrases
182 Queued
183 Session Progress
200 OK
400 Bad Request
480 Temporarily Unavailable
484 Address Incomplete

4 Anti-SPIT Mechanisms Overview

As mentioned, SPIT may influence the future use and adoption of the VoIP technology. So far, some general frameworks from the email spam paradigm have been discussed as candidates for SPIT handling [13]. Furthermore, some of them appear to be basic building blocks of the anti-SPIT architectures that have been proposed in the literature. In the sequel, we discuss the anti-SPIT architectures that have been proposed so far.

AVA (Anonymous Verifying Authorities). The Anonymous Verifying Authorities approach, presented in [2], is based on the introduction of a "call-me-back" scheme and the use of two new entities, namely: (a) the Mediator and (b) the Anonymous Verifying Authority (AVA). The authors try to mitigate SPIT by anonymously blocking unwanted calls through AVA and the Mediator. Thus, in the case of not call establishment, the caller is not aware for the existence of the callee.

Anti-SPIT Entity. A network-level entity, placed in the edge of the network, is proposed in [8]. The role of this entity is to filter and analyze the transmitted SIP packets, and to detect SPIT according to certain criteria. By using these criteria, a weighed sum is introduced, namely spitLevel, which serves as a threshold. If the spitLevel is exceeded specific actions are performed depending on the policies adopted by the callee's domain. Experimental data are provided.

Reputation/Charging Mechanism. The work in [13] proposes two techniques for handling SPIT. The first is based on reputation builds trust within different SIP communities and uses the resulting trust networks for detecting SIP spam. The second is a variant of the payment at risk proposal. Implementation details are not provided by the authors.

DAPES (Domain-based Authentication and Policy-Enforced for SIP). In this framework, any SIP-based communication passes through two stages of verification; namely, verification of the caller's identity, and mutual authentication of the participated proxies alongside with verification of the outbound proxy [17].

PGM (Progressive Multi Gray-Levelling). The approach proposed in [4], stems from the antiSPAM framework graylisting. Accordingly, it calculates and assigns a non permanent gray level for each caller, in order to check if a message is SPIT or not. This level is calculated based on previous call patterns of a particular caller. Depending on the level's value, appropriate actions are taken.

Biometrics Approach. In [1], the authors propose the use of global servers that bind users' identities to personal data; they select biometric data, such as a person's voice. The proposal is based on the concept of binding identities to persons that cannot change globally. User interference and threats taken into account are also mentioned.

RFC 4474. An end-user authentication scheme is discussed in RFC 4474 [11], based on Public Key Infrastructures (PKI) and Certificate Authorities (CA). Although this approach is not oriented specifically towards SPIT handling, the identity control mechanism is useful for controlling SPIT. Two new SIP header fields are used and their manipulation is done only by proxy servers within the domain of the calling UA, through appropriate authentication and certificates.

SIP-SAML. The approach presented in [18] uses the Security Assertion Markup Language (SAML) for SIP authentication and authorization through asserted traits. The authors aim at a strict identity control accomplishment, in order to prevent spitters from changing their identity frequently.

DSIP (Differentiated SIP). In [6], an extension to SIP is proposed. It tries to handle SPIT through the classification of callers into three categories of lists, namely: white, who are legitimate callers, black, who are spitters, and grey list, who are not yet classified. Through this classification of users, the handling of calls is conducted accordingly. When the caller is unknown, a human verification test is imposed, in order to prove that she is not a SPIT automated machine.

VoIP Seal. The work in [9] presents a system that operates in two stages. During the first stage, modules that are not transparent to the caller, examine the call. Each module of the first stage contributes a score in [-1,1], where high score corresponds to a high probability that the call is SPIT. Each module is associated with a weight, and the final score is compared with two thresholds. If the score is within acceptable threshold range, then the call passes to the second stage of checking the call. This stage includes modules that require interaction with the user. For instance, they could be a Turing test that checks whether the caller is spitter or not. If this test fails, the call is rejected.

VSD (Voice Spam Detector). The [3] framework combines many of the anti-SPIT approaches presented in [15]. The system is a multi-stage SPIT filter based on trust and reputation, and uses feedback between the different stages. Presence filtering, the first step, depends on the current status of the callee. The next step, that is the traffic pattern filter, analyzes the rate of incoming calls. This step is followed by the white/black lists' filtering. Bayesian filtering is the fourth step, where a call is checked regarding the behavior of the participated entities. Finally, reputation techniques are used to check the acceptance of a call based on social relationships that an end- user maintains with other entities in the VoIP environment.

5 Compliance of SPIT mechanisms to Identification Criteria

In this section we identify the SPIT identification criteria which have been used by the aforementioned mechanisms. Our analysis, in conjunction with the analysis presented in [7] provides the reader with a point of reference, in terms of which mechanisms should be selected in a specific context. In this context, Figure 2 presents which of the mechanisms takes into account the SPIT identification criteria we defined. For this purpose we took under consideration only an abstract description of each mechanism as implementation details are not fully discussed and described, in their relative publications. Furthermore, we do not consider whether the mechanisms meet the criteria well or not, but we rather provide the mere existence of each criterion in the mechanisms' description. For example, in the description of Reputation/Charging mechanism, the use of Black and White lists requires the existence of a way to identify and handle users, either by SIP URI, IP address or even domain of origin. However, as something like that is not explicitly mentioned, we put the appropriate negative value in the table.

Furthermore, the table can be used as a reference to choose the appropriate mechanism for SPIT handling in a given context. For example the call and message patterns might be costly to implement, in terms of data gathering and analysis, thus mechanisms that focus on and fulfill the other criteria might be of preference.

Finally, the table can be read as a concentrated area of further research directions regarding anti-SPIT countermeasures. Some of the questions that one can answer using the table include how can a particular mechanism contribute in terms of prevention, detection or handling of SPIT, which combinations of techniques should someone use in order to fight SPIT more effectively, etc.

6 Implementation

A key question regarding the proposed criteria is whether they can be applied on a SIP environment. In order to examine their applicability, we first implemented the following test computing environment, which is depicted in Fig. 3. It consists of a SIP Proxy Server, which is established in our laboratory environment. The SIP server application is a scalable and reliable, open source software called SIP Express Router (SER 2.0) [16]. It can act as a SIP registrar, proxy, or redirect server. We have extended its functionality to support our implementation of the above mentioned criteria. All the laptops and the PCs are equipped with soft-IP-phones (X-lite), which can use the SIP server in order to establish a call.

Having the above testbed in a full functional status, we implemented the proposed identification criteria so as to examine their applicability in real VoIP settings. From

SPIT Identification Criteria / Anti-SPIT Mechanisms	Call-Message Origin Caller/Callee Relationship				Calls-Messages patterns							SIP Headers Semantics
	Caller SIP URI	Caller IP address	Caller domain	White/Black list	Path of message	Number of Calls	Calls duration	Sequential Call Numbers	Dialed/answered calls	Large number of errors	Size of SIP message	Message Headers, Bodies, and Reason Phrases
AVA	☑	–	–	–	–	–	–	–	–	–	–	–
Anti-Spit Entity	☑	☑	–	☑	–	☑	☑	☑	–	☑	–	–
Reputation/Charging	–	–	–	☑	–	–	–	–	–	–	–	–
DAPES	☑	☑	☑	–	☑	–	–	–	–	–	–	–
PMG	☑	–	–	☑	–	☑	–	–	–	–	–	–
Biometrics	–	–	–	–	–	–	–	–	–	–	–	–
RFC 4474	☑	–	☑	–	–	–	–	–	–	–	–	–
SIP SAML	☑	–	☑	–	–	–	–	–	–	–	–	–
DSIP	☑	–	☑	☑	–	–	–	–	–	–	–	–
VoIP Seal	–	–	–	☑	–	–	–	–	–	–	–	–
VSD	☑	☑	☑	☑	☑	☑	–	–	–	–	–	–

Fig. 2 A macroscopic view of SPIT Management

the list of the criteria, presented in section 3, we selected the (a) Call and Message Origin and (b) SIP participants' relationship criteria, as well as the (c) SIP Headers' Semantics criteria. Regarding the Call-Messages Patterns category, we implemented only the path traversal (path of message), because the remaining ones require historical and statistical data in order to generate metrics and define thresholds. For instance, the numbers of calls criterion requires the historical logs per caller which might introduce modifications in the setup of our environment.

We have used two different approaches to put in practice the criteria. In the first technique, we alter the main configuration file of the SIP Server. In the second one, the main parameters of the criteria are stored into an external MySQL database (ver. 5.0) and for each SIP message we query the database in order to find out if it is SPIT message or not. MySQL database is also used by SER for storing users, as a part of the typical setup of the SER server. In the following, we present two implementation examples and then we compare the two techniques.

6.1 Implementation with configuration file

The SER configuration file consists of the main SIP Server attributes and the routing rules of the SIP messages. The SPIT criteria are applied by adding a small portion of additional code in the configuration file for each criterion, which is identified by the SIP server administrator.

An example of an implemented criterion, which is mentioned in paragraph 3.3, is stated below. *Example code 1* shows a SIP message, in which the Error-Info (highlighted) contains a Hyperlink. Therefore Bob's SIP proxy server will reject the incoming call.

The proposed addition in the configuration file so as to discover this vulnerability is described in *example code 2*. The first line is used to discover the proposed criteria, the second line is used to write in a log file the reason for which the message was

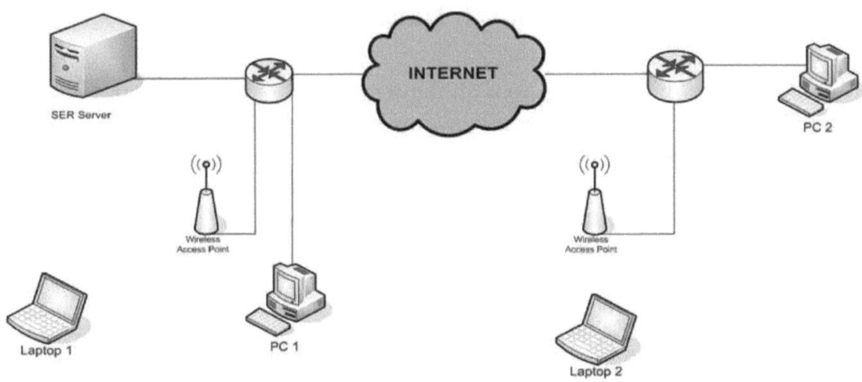

Fig. 3 A macroscopic view of SPIT Management

rejected, the third line is used to send a response SIP message to the caller explaining the cause of the rejection and the forth line is used to terminate the connection.

Example Code 1: *SIP Message (Error-Info header field contains a hyperlink)*

```
1: SIP/2.0 200 OK
2: Via: SIP/2.0/UDP pc1.example.com
3: To: "Bob" <sip:bob@example.com>;tag=987
4: From: "Alice" <sip:alice@aueb.gr >;tag=123
5: Call-ID: 6543219999@172.1.2.2
6: CSeq: 1 INVITE
7: Contact: <sip:bob@example.com>
8: Content-Type: application/sdp
9: Content-Length: 200
::
21: Error-Info: <http://www.sell.com/yourshoe.jpg>
```

Example Code 2: Error-Info criterion script (part of SER conf.file)

```
1: if (search("^Error-Info:\s<http://.*"))
2: {
3: log("LOG: alert: someone trying to send an
      http link through Error-Info\n");
4: sl_send_reply("476", "No Hyperlink Text is
      permitted through Error-Info" );
5: break;
6: \};
```

6.2 Implementation with MySQL Database

The MySQL database is used to store all the parameters which assist to identify a possible SPIT. For example it stores all the domains and URIs of callers for which it is decided whether they are spitters or not. Therefore, each newly received SIP message is partially passed to an external script which performs a query to the database and checks if the message violates any of the given SPIT rules.

A script, which finds out if the user's URI (mentioned in paragraph 3.1.) is acceptable, appears in the sequel (*example code 3*).

Example Code 3: External script accessing database

```
#!/bin/sh
m=`echo $1 | sed -e 's/^sip://'`
num=("echo 'SELECT count(*) FROM users
     WHERE user_uri=\"$m\";'
| mysql -u ser -h localhost --password=heslo -D ser")
if [ $num != 0]; then
    exit 0
else
    exit 1
fi
```

6.3 Implementation Results and Comparison

The main advantage of the first technique is the speed of (a) handling the SIP messages and (b) deciding whether the message is SPIT or not. This occurs because, for routing every SIP message, the configuration file is accessed. On the other hand, it is really complex to insert a new SPIT criterion. For example, if the administrator decides to reject all incoming calls from a certain domain, he has to find out the exact position in the configuration file to place the script and afterwards he has to restart the SER server in order this modification to take effect.

The second method helps the administrator to add and modify values of SPIT criteria without the reloading of the SER instance being mandatory. The main drawback of this method is the time overhead as it has to access the database for every message and actually execute a query for each criterion in each message.

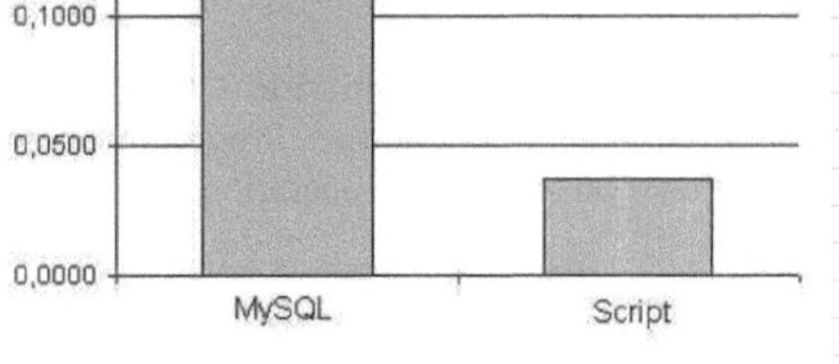

Fig. 4 Performance Comparison of two suggested methods

The performance comparison of the two techniques is presented in the figure 4, where we examined the time required for extracting and checking the SIP URI address of a SIP packet. The related time was 0,21748 sec for database script and 0.0371 for SER configuration script respectively.

7 Discussion and comments

VoIP technology and SIP raised significant concerns, as to whether SPIT phenolmenon will be equivalent to the current spam prevalence. In order to address and evaluate these concerns, we provided a macroscopic view of SPIT management, alongside with an extensive list of SPIT identification criteria that can be used by anti-SPIT mechanisms in the prevention and detection stages of SPIT management.

VoIP infrastructures have recently gained a (still) small, but recognizable market share. Thus, only recently, and prior to the SPIT phenomenon prevailing, some anti-SPIT mechanisms have been suggested. The majority of them focus on the prevention, detection, and handling stages of SPIT management. Most of them seem not to take into account the results of an appropriate threat and vulnerability analysis regarding SPIT, thus SIP protocol vulnerabilities are usually not considered.

On the other hand, the proposed anti-SPIT mechanisms aim at fulfilling qualitative and quantitative criteria. In this paper we used a two-fold evaluation framework. First, we defined a set of parameters that each mechanism should address in order to counter SPIT efficiently, and we identified how each class should be evaluated, in terms of effectiveness. Second, we analyzed which of the SPIT identification criteria each SPIT mechanism takes into account. Finally, we implement two methods of discovering the possible SPIT messages. It is clearly demonstrated that not only it is achievable to put in practice the proposed criteria, but also that the methods are considerably effective since, as they check every SIP message for possible SPIT attributes. A possible extension of the proposed implementation would aim at taking into account the criteria presented in section 3.2.

Finally, the proposed evaluation framework provides insight on how the effectiveness of a mechanism can be evaluated, as well as how combinations of relevant mechanisms should be selected, in order to effectively mitigate SPIT in a given context. In this context, we are planning to implement an automatic solution that allows us to evaluate each anti-SPIT mechanism based on the criteria and choose the best one.

Acknowledgements This work has been partially performed within the SPIDER (COOP-32720) project, which is partly funded by the European Commission under Framework Programme 6. We would like to thank our partners in the consortium for their constructive co-operation.

References

1. Baumann R., Cavin S., Schmid S.: Voice Over IP - Security and Spit. Swiss Army, FU Br 41, KryptDet Report, Univ. of Berne (2006)
2. Croft, N., Olivier, M.: A Model for Spam Prevention in Voice over IP Networks using Anonymous Verifying Authorities. In: Venter, H.S. et al. (eds.) Proc. of the 5th Annual Information Security South Africa Conf., South Africa (2005)
3. Dantu R., Kolan P.: Detecting Spam in VoIP Networks. In: Proc. of Steps to Reducing Unwanted Traffic on the Internet Workshop, USA (2005)
4. Dongwook S., Jinyoung A., Choon S.: Progressive Multi Gray-Leveling: A Voice Spam Protection Algorithm. IEEE Network, 20(5), 18-24 (2006)
5. Dritsas S., Mallios J., Theoharidou M., Marias G., Gritzalis D.: Threat Analysis of the Session Initiation Protocol Regarding Spam. In Proc. of the 3rd IEEE Int. Workshop on Information Assurance (26th IEEE International Performance Computing and Communications Conference), IEEE Press, pp. 426-433, New Orleans (2007)
6. Madhosingh B.: The Design of a Differentiated SIP to Control VoIP Spam. Technical Report, Computer Science Department, Florida State University (2006)
7. Marias G., Dritsas S., Theoharidou M., Mallios J., Gritzalis D.: SIP vulnerabilities and anti-SPIT mechanisms assessment. In Proc. of the 16th IEEE Int. Conf. on Computer Communications and Networks (ICCCN '07), IEEE Press, Hawaii, pp. 597-604 (2007)
8. Mathieu, B. et al.: Spit Mitigation by a Network-Level Anti-Spit Entity. In: Proc. of the 3rd Annual VoIP Security Workshop, Germany (2006)
9. Niccolini S.: Spit prevention: State of the art and research challenges. Network Laboratories, NEC Europe, Germany (2006)
10. Park S., Kim J., Kang S.: Analysis of applicability of traditional spam regulations to VoIP spam. In: Proc. 8th Int. Conf. of the Advanced Communication Technology, Phoenix Park, Korea (2006)
11. Peterson J., Jennings C.: Enhancements for Authenticated Identity Management in the Session Initiation Protocol. RFC 4474 (2006)
12. Rebahi Y., Sisalem D.: SIP service providers and the spam problem. In: Proc. of the Voice over IP Security Workshop, Washington, USA (2005)
13. Rebahi, Y., Sisalem, D., Magedanz T.: SIP Spam Detection. In: Proc. of the Int. Conf. on Digital Telecommunications, pp. 29-31, France (2006)
14. Rosenberg, J. et al.: Session Initiation Protocol. RFC 3261 (2002)
15. Rosenberg J., Jennings C.: The Session Initiation Protocol (SIP) and Spam. draft-ietf-sipping-spam-03 (2006)
16. SER server version 2.0, Available via www.iptel.org/ser. Cited 10 Jan 2008
17. Srivastava K., Schulzrinne H.: Preventing Spam For SIP-based Instant Messages and Sessions. Technical Report, University of Columbia (2004)
18. Tschofenig H. et al.: Using SAML to Protect the Session Initiation Protocol. IEEE Network, 20(5), 14-17 (2006)

References

Detecting More SIP Attacks on VoIP Services by Combining Rule Matching and State Transition Models *

Dongwon Seo, Heejo Lee, and Ejovi Nuwere

Abstract The Session Initiation Protocol (SIP) has been used widely for Voice over IP (VoIP) service because of its potential advantages, economical efficiency and call setup simplicity. However, SIP-based VoIP service basically has two main security issues, malformed SIP message attack and SIP flooding attack. In this paper, we propose a novel mechanism for SIP-based VoIP system utilizing rule matching algorithm and state transition models. It detects not only two main attacks, but also covers more SIP attacks. Instead of simply combining rule comparison and counting number of SIP messages, we develop secure RFC 3261 rules based on existing RFC 3261 rules, so that proposed mechanism shows 26% higher detection rate for malformed attack. Moreover, we utilize session information and define the features of each state in order to detect abnormal situations including SIP flooding. As the result, it is shown that the proposed mechanism provides not only higher accuracy, but also covering more SIP attacks including two main attacks.

1 Introduction

Telephone is definitely an important communication tool. As the Internet is being popular, Voice over IP (VoIP), also called Internet telephony, has become a promising communication medium owing to its economical rates and additional features such as video conversation, SMS and messenger services. It also means that VoIP services are facing on known and unknown security threats. As shown in several studies on VoIP security [7, 15, 5], there are lots of security problems in VoIP services. Actually, there are some existing tools to verify vulnerabilities of VoIP soft-

D. Seo and H. Lee are with Korea University, Seoul 136-713, Korea, and E. Nuwere is with SecurityLab Technologies, e-mail: {aerosmiz, heejo}@korea.ac.kr, ejovi@ejovi.net.

* This work was supported in part by the ITRC program of the Korea Ministry of Knowledge Economy.

Please use the following format when citing this chapter:

Seo, D., Lee, H. and Nuwere, E., 2008, in IFIP International Federation for Information Processing, Volume 278; *Proceedings of the IFIP TC 11 23rd International Information Security Conference*; Sushil Jajodia, Pierangela Samarati, Stelvio Cimato; (Boston: Springer), pp. 397–411.

wares. However, most of them simply scan known vulnerabilities and produce a report. For more robust VoIP services, it is necessary to design a mechanism which is capable of detecting specific suspicious packets and attack conditions without interrupting existing VoIP services.

There are two VoIP session protocols, SIP and H.323. However, SIP is recently being chosen because its simpler connection process and easier implementation for the Internet [9]. Therefore, we focus on the security issues of SIP-based VoIP services. Nonetheless, the principles of our study can be applicable to H.323 VoIP services.

Technically, SIP-based VoIP services consist of two different protocols, SIP and RTP (Real-time Transport Protocol). SIP is a signaling protocol to establish and terminate sessions. On the other hand, RTP is a media protocol to transfer multimedia data. Thus, there are two categories of attack along with the two protocols. One is SIP related attacks, which cause unexpected results such as service malfunction, session connection between wrong users, and incorrect billing to wrong users. Another is RTP related attacks, which include voice eavesdropping and media spamming. In exploring the questions of both SIP and RTP attacks, we first consider SIP attacks due to their growing impacts on VoIP services.

SIP protection is very important in the sense that SIP is in charge of session initiation, connection and termination. Especially, SIP is susceptible to two types of attacks, malformed message attacks and SIP flooding attacks. It is easy to forge the header fields of a SIP message since the message is based on plain text. And there are many tools to generate SIP packets for launching SIP flooding attacks. However, previous works do not consider both attacks simultaneously, but detect only one type of attacks at a time, either malformed messages [3] or flooding attacks [1].

Main contributions of this study are twofold.

1. Unlike existing researches which detect two main SIP attacks (malformed and flooding attacks) separately, we develop a new approach by combining rule matching and state transition models, and it detects not only two main attacks, but also covers three more SIP attacks as utilizing SIP features with affordable overhead.
2. Because of plain text-based SIP message, it is difficult to cover all variant malformed messages which can exploit vulnerabilities of SIP-based VoIP services such as buffer overflow and string format exception. Especially, there is no research that provides statistical experiment for detecting malformed SIP messages so far. Therefore, we develop secure RFC 3261 rules using regular expression based on RFC 3261 ABNF rules. As a result, from the experiment based on 2426 malformed cases of PROTOS test suite, our proposed approach shows 26% higher detection rate than using original RFC 3261 rules.

The rest of this paper is organized as follows. In Sect. 2, we introduce related works. Threat models for SIP and RTP are discussed in Sect. 3. And, we propose a novel mechanism for detecting more SIP attacks in Sect. 4. The evaluation of the proposed mechanism is shown in Sect. 5. Finally, we summarize our result and conclude the paper in Sect. 6.

2 Related Work

There exist some researches using state machines for intrusion detection. One of them is State Transition Analysis Technique(STAT) [6], which is a rule-based intrusion detection approach. STAT is a general method that recognizes computer penetrations easily using rule-based state diagram. There are different versions of STAT. NetSTAT [12] is to determine which network event should be monitored, and WebSTAT [13] is to detect malicious behaviors for web servers according to analyzing web requests.

In addition, Snort is the most broadly deployed IDS around the world and it has many attack patterns, over 6000. To protect VoIP system, it may be possible to apply to an existing IDS. However, there are some problems when we use a current IDS directly to protect VoIP system [16]. First, VoIP service is based on session while IDS detects attacks based on packets. It means that IDS monitors every single packet and compares it with pre-defined rules, but it is necessary for a VoIP service to distinguish which session the packet belongs to. Second, although Snort provides stateful detection for TCP-based protocols like HTTP and FTP, it does not help in processing stateful VoIP sessions. Finally, VoIP service is formed combining of multi-protocol, such as the signaling protocol SIP and the media protocol RTP. If an attack is performed across protocols, conventional IDSs fail to detect it. Therefore, we need to develop intrusion detection technologies dedicated to VoIP services.

Several studies have been done for protecting VoIP services. SCIDIVE by Yu-Sung Wu [16] is an architecture which provides stateful and cross protocol detection. SCIDIVE is able to detect attacks in both protocol, SIP and RTP. To examine SIP format, SCIDIVE uses rule sets including standard SIP rules. However, there are many malformed SIP messages which is formed as standard but dangerous. For example, %s%d%caaa.com follows a standard form, even though it may be dangerous because of format string like %s%d.

Hemant Sengar also proposed a VoIP defense mechanism by the use of state machines [10]. The mechanism uses cross protocol state machines which define attack detection patterns. The mechanism also has an advantage of detecting across two protocols. However, it is not a flexible mechanism because it needs lots of state machines to protect against various attacks.

There is a similar approach to detect malformed SIP messages [3]. It proposes a framework based on the rules for valid SIP messages. The key idea is that normal SIP messages should have mandatory fields and fit to pre-defined byte size. Nonetheless, this mechanism allows to pass malformed SIP messages, which include the messages whose mandatory fields and byte sizes are even less than pre-defined ones. Considering that SIP header fields use plain text, we have to examine the content of each header that may contain abnormal string formats such as non-ASCII, malformed UTF-8 and escape characters, and so forth.

Eric Y. Chen proposed DoS detecting method on SIP systems [1]. It also utilizes RFC 3261 state transition models, and defines additional state and upper bounds for error conditions. One drawback of this approach is that malformed SIP messages are not considered properly. Although this mechanism is very effective to detect DoS or flooding attacks, malformed SIP messages are definitely hazardous because they cause the malfunction of a VoIP service. In contrast to this approach, we propose a mechanism that is able to detect both malformed SIP messages and flooding attacks at the same time.

3 Threat Model

From the previous researches, [7]and [1], we could categorized VoIP attacks into six groups (three SIP related and three RTP related attacks) by their protocols and behaviors.

VoIP attacks can be divided into two categories: SIP attacks and RTP attacks. Since SIP takes significant roles of session initiation, connection and termination, we need to consider SIP attacks first. RTP attacks are briefly discussed in this Sect., and they are out of our scope. We do not consider all kinds of SIP attacks like the attacks derived from IP features such as spoofing attack. Our attention is directed to SIP attacks derived from SIP features such as malformed message and SIP flooding attacks [11]. These two attacks are strongly connected to SIP systems and exploit their vulnerabilities. In the light of this consideration, we propose a novel approach that is able to handle with those two attacks simultaneously.

Malformed Message Attack: This is one of the most representative case using the vulnerabilities of text-based protocol. Attackers are able to cause malfunctions of proxy server or UA by manipulating SIP headers. For instance, overflow-space, overflow-null, specific header deletion and using non-ASCII code are involved in malformed message attacks.

SIP Flooding Attack: IP phones generate requests or responses to send to a specific UA, called by `victim`. As a result, a single UA is overwhelmed by receiving excessive SIP messages within a short duration of time, so that the UA cannot provide normal services. INVITE flooding is one of the most typical attacks. Basically, flooding attack is also the issue of IP layer. In case of INVITE flooding, however, it could be more annoying attack for the VoIP user because the one should see many call requests and hear ringing.

Spoofing Attack: Two kinds of spoofing attacks are possible, IP spoofing attack and URI spoofing attack. IP spoofing attack is to forge IP source addresses in order to pretend a trusted user. And, IP spoofing is the intrinsic security problem in TCP/IP protocol suites and it is not in the scope of our study on VoIP security. URI spoofing attack is a particular case in malformed message attacks. The attacker who hijacked SIP messages between two UAs forges their URI field, so the attacker can hide himself from tracebacks. If spoofed BYE requests (BYE DoS attack) are sent to a victim, the call will be terminated by the attacker.

In addition to the SIP attacks, there are several kinds of RTP attacks. RTP attacks can be classified into three categories: RTP flooding attacks, media spamming attacks, and man-in-the-middle (MITM) attacks. RTP flooding attacks are similar to SIP flooding attack, but they use RTP packets. Media spamming attacks, also known as SPIT (Spam over Internet Telephony), have been an annoying problem that disturbs a user who does not want to receive a call for advertisement. Finally, MITM attacks are similar to eavesdropping. It is one of the most critical issues in RTP attacks.

4 The Proposed Mechanism

In this Sect., we propose a new approach to detect SIP attacks including two main types of SIP attacks, malformed messages and flooding attacks.

4.1 Background

This part gives an overview of basic knowledge about the constitution of SIP message and how to call-setup and tear-down on SIP.

4.1.1 SIP Messages

A SIP message basically consists of two parts, message header and body. A message header contains essential user information such as URI (Uniform Resource Identifiers), method and Call-ID. A message body is described as SDP (Session Description Protocol) which are informed for media encoding scheme [4].

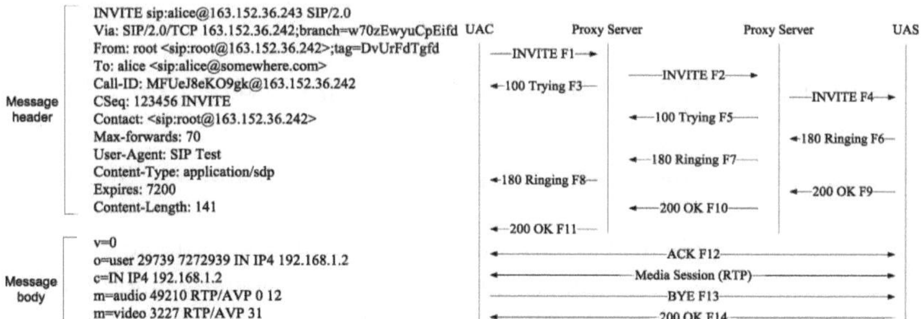

Fig. 1 Normal INVITE request (left) and SIP call-setup and tear-down process (right).

There are six general requests; INVITE, ACK, BYE, OPTIONS, REGISTER, and CANCEL. INVITE is for making a call to the other, ACK is corresponding request to response, BYE is to terminate a call, OPTIONS is for getting information such as user capability, REGISTER is for signing in or out from VoIP provider, and

CANCEL is to abort last request. Responses, which are three digit numbers, comprise six classified groups; Provisional, Success, Redirection, Client Error, Server Error, and Global Failure. Figure 1 (left) is an example of a normal INVITE request.

4.1.2 The Call-setup and Tear-down Process on SIP

In order to set up a call, UAC (User Agent Client, caller) sends an INVITE request to UAS (User Agent Server, callee). Proxy server forwards it to UAS and sends 100 Trying response to UAC. After the UAS receives INVITE request, it transfers 180 Ringing and 200 OK responses subsequently. Finally the UAC gets OK response, sends ACK request and the connection is established. Figure 1 (right) indicates such a process.

4.2 The Concept of the Proposed Mechanism

The VoIP service uses SIP when it makes call-setup and tear-down and takes RTP while transmitting media stream data. Since SIP is on the upper layer of IP layer, SIP also has weak points such as flooding Besides, text-based message header is always exposed to various text-modified attacks such as string overflow. To corresponding SIP attacks, we design a detection mechanism which consists of three parts: malformed SIP detection, session management, and state verification. The most significant modules are malformed SIP detection module that performs rule matching and header field categorization, and state verification module that is related to four state transition models [2]. Figure 2 is an overall flow chart of our mechanism.

4.3 Malformed SIP and Invalid Header Field Detection

Malformed SIP detection module covers two SIP attacks, malformed SIP and invalid header field attacks.

First of all, to apply RFC 3261 rule sets for real VoIP services, we convert RFC 3261 ABNF rules into regular expressions. Rule matching algorithm decides whether the header of a packet follows its standard forms. Malformed SIP packets including unmatched or undefined headers can be blocked or considered to pass.

There are over 280 rules in RFC 3261, and we can define the standard forms of the SIP messages in the rules. However, we found that the original RFC 3261 rules have some vulnerabilities to cover many kinds of malformed SIP messages. For instance, the regular expression corresponding to the `userinfo` rule in RFC

[2] INVITE server, INVITE client, Non-INVITE server, and Non-INVITE client transition models

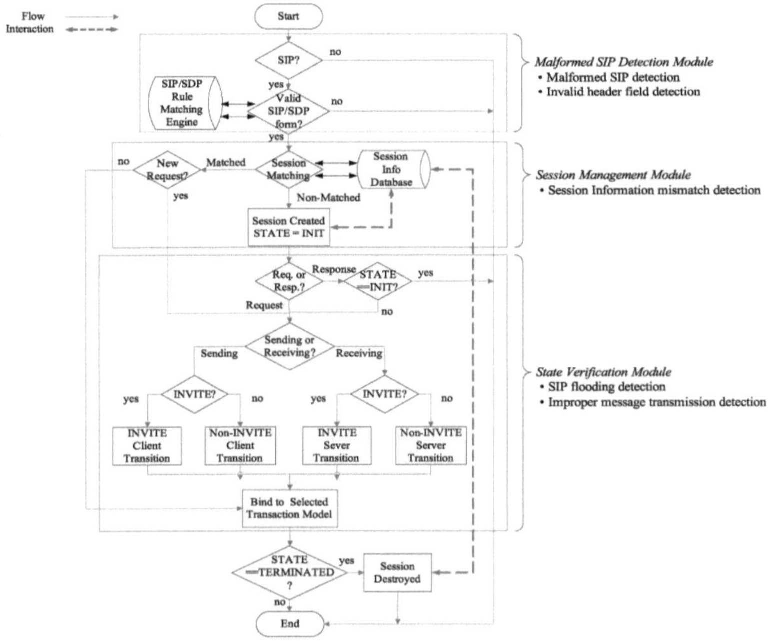

Fig. 2 Overall flowchart of proposed mechanism

3261 is like this, **userinfo:((#user#)(:#password#)?)**. What if an input is for extremely long user ID or password? It may cause unexpected result such as overflow exception. For one more simple example, there is an ABNF rule for port number:

port=1*DIGIT

The corresponding regular expression for the ABNF rule is

port=\d+

which means that a port should be a number more than one digit. Nonetheless, the rule does not check length of the port number causing overflow-integer. Thus, we change from the original rule to a secure one,

port=(\d{0,4}|[1-5]\d{4}|6[0-4]\d{3}|65[0-4]\d{2}|655[0-2]\d|6553[0-5])

because port number is from 0 to 65535. For instance, port number **65540** is mismatched by the port rule, **655[0-2]\d**. An adversary can make a lot of exceptional cases like the example, and they may cause malfunctions of SIP-based VoIP services. For that reason, we apply secure SIP rules that restrains size and format of string and number. Table 1 shows that some example of comparison between regular expressions based on RFC 3261 ABNF rules and secure regular expressions. For instance, `user` field allows only alphabet, number, '_', '-' and must not be over twelve characters. Formalizing of SIP standard form is capable of recognizing not

Table 1 Rule comparison between original and secure regular expressions

<table>
<tr><th>RFC3261 regular expressions</th><th>Secure RFC3261 regular expressions</th></tr>
<tr><td>user:((#unreserved#|#escaped#|#user_unreserved#)+)</td><td>user:((#alphanum#|_|\-){1,12})</td></tr>
<tr><td>password:((#unreserved#|#escaped#|\&|\=|\+|\$|\,)*)</td><td>password:(((#unreserved#|#escaped#|\&|\=|\+|\$|\,)*){0,12})</td></tr>
<tr><td>SIP_Version:(SIP\/\d\.\d)</td><td>SIP_Version:((SIP\/\d\.\d){7,9})</td></tr>
<tr><td>extension_method:(#token#)</td><td>extension_method:(#ASCII_NAME#{1,20})</td></tr>
<tr><td>protocol_version:(#token#)</td><td>protocol_version:(\d{1,2}\.\d{1,2})</td></tr>
<tr><td>display_name:((#token##LWS#)*|#quoted_string#)</td><td>display_name:((\w){1,32}|#quoted_string#)</td></tr>
<tr><td>callid:(#word#(\@#word#)?)</td><td>callid:(#ASCII#{1,50}(\@(\w\.*){1,32})?)</td></tr>
<tr><td>Max-Forwards:(Max-Forwards#HCOLON#\d+#CRLF#)</td><td>Max-Forwards:(Max-Forwards#HCOLON#\d{1,4}#CRLF#)</td></tr>
</table>

only known malformed SIP packets, but also unknown ones. In addition, it is very flexible to being adapted reformed standard by adding or editing existing rules.

Moreover, categorizing mandatory and optional header fields for each SIP message in our secure RFC 3261 rule sets, it is possible to filter out suspicious SIP messages which is well-formed SIP but includes non-allowed header fields. For instance, SIP requests must contain `Call-ID`, `CSeq`, `From`, `Max-Forwards`, `To`, and `Via` header fields. Also, ACK should not contain `Subject` header field. Through these kinds of rule grouping, malformed SIP detection module performs stronger rule matching. Table 2 is a categorized table to detect invalid header field for ACK message.

Table 2 Categorized header fields table for ACK to detect invalid header field

Types	Header fields
Mandatory (6)	Call-ID, CSeq, From, Max-Forwards, To, Via
Optional (13)	Authorization, Contact, Content-Disposition, Content-Encoding, Content-Language, Content-Length, Content-Type, Date, MIME-Version, Record-Route, Route, Timestamp, User-Agent
Non-allowed (25)	Accept, Accept-Encoding, Accept-Language, Alert-Info, Allow, Authentication-Info, Call-Info, Error-Info, Expires, In-Reply-To, Min-Expires, Organization, Priority, Proxy-Authenticate, Proxy-Authorization, Proxy-Require, Reply-To, Require, Retry-After, Server, Subject, Supported, Unsupported, Warning, WWW-Authenticate

4.4 Flooding and Improper Message Transmission Detection

State verification module decides whether or not each SIP message is normal based on current state. We adopt four modified state transition models from RFC 3261, and focus on `INVITE server transition model` to describe how it works in this paper. The dashed lines indicate an abnormal (either attack or suspicious) condition for each state.

Figure 3 describes `INVITE server transition model`. The model is selected when a host receives INVITE message. Each state compares number of messages with threshold in order to check flooding condition. Especially, in `Confirmed` state, receiving INVITE and all kinds of responses are identified as abnormal conditions. Like these, through state verification module, it is possible to detect flooding attack and improper message transmission. Figure 4 shows an example of improper message transmission. Bob is now on `Confirmed` state, which allows only ACK message. If Trudy sends INVITE message, however, we can detect it.

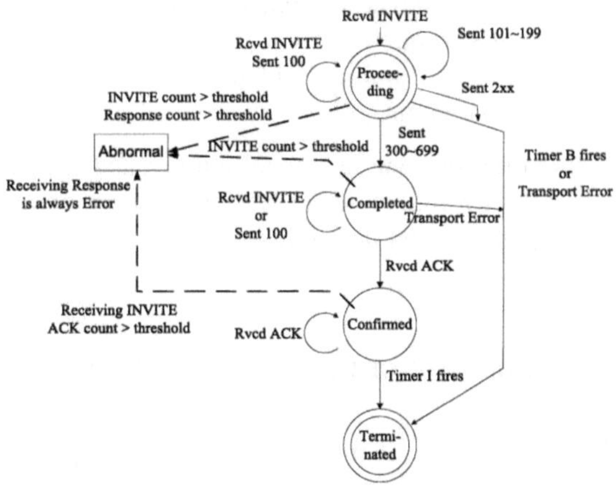

Fig. 3 INVITE server transition model: `Abnormal` state handles flooding condition and improper message transmission.

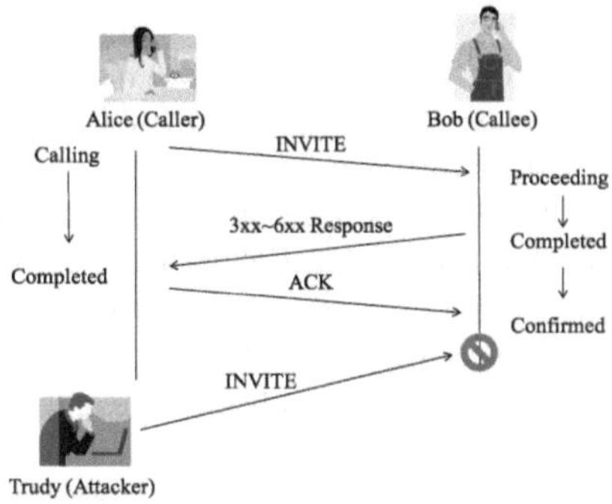

Fig. 4 Improper message transmission: Trudy sends INVITE message to Bob, which is unacceptable to Bob's current state, `Confirmed`.

4.5 Session Information Mismatch Detection

Session management module creates a new session after receiving or sending INVITE request, and destroys the session after receiving or sending BYE request. The followings are the information which should be stored in session management module.

- URI: to distinguish UAC and UAS.
- Selected state transition algorithms: the form of queue containing history of selected state transition algorithms.
- Current state: current state of most recent selected state transition algorithm.
- Error code: there are three levels, e.g. pass, warning and abnormal.
- `Sequence number`: 32-bit unsigned integer. A response copies the sequence number from received request, and it adds certain increment like 256 when sending a new request.
- `Call-ID`: it uniquely identifies a particular invitation or all registrations of a particular client.

Comparing current sequence number and Call-ID of each session with previous ones, we are able to detect session information mismatch. this module has a similar concept to stateful inspection.

5 Evaluation of the Proposed Mechanism

In order to measure the effectiveness of the proposed mechanism, we used publicly available attacking tools such as PROTOS [2] and SiVuS [14]. PROTOS is a popular VoIP vulnerability assessment tool and `PROTOS test-suite:c07-sip` provides a lot of malformed SIP messages. SiVuS is used for launching SIP flooding attacks by generating overwhelming SIP messages. The PROTOS suite has been widely used and publicly available to evaluate the implementation level security and robustness of Session Initiation Protocol (SIP) implementations. There are 4527 malformed SIP test cases. SiVuS is a free VoIP vulnerability scanner which has the ability to generate packets and SIP header fields can be edited by a user.

Moreover, we developed two application programs, namely `VoIPDefender` and `VoIPAttaker`. VoIPDefender is a prototype implementation of the proposed mechanism, and VoIPAttacker is a SIP attacking tool whose input is a file name for the PROTOS suite and generates attack patterns according to each test case.

At last, to verify whether our proposed mechanism disturbs existing VoIP services, five SIP softphones are chosen from "myvoipprovider.com" web site [8], which offers top 100 raking of 155 international VoIP providers. The last comparison is updated on December 2007. We picked five softphones providing free PC to PC VoIP services based on SIP. The five softphones are Globe7, Vbuzzer, VoIPGo, Gizmo Project and SJPhone.

5.1 The Result for Malformed SIP Attacks

A subset of SIP from PROTOS suite, namely INVITE messages, was chosen as the subject protocol for vulnerability assessment through syntax testing and test-suite creation. An exceptional element is a piece of data designed to provoke undesired behavior of the test subject. An exceptional element can violate the protocol specification, but often it is legal or in the hazy region between legal and illegal constructs [2]. We could get 4527 test cases of malformed SIP packets, and 2426 cases

Table 3 SIP exceptional cases in PROTOS test suite

# Case	Exceptional Elements	Description
1	Overflow-general, space and null; Format string; UTF-8; ANSI-escape	Repetition of general character, space or null; Using format string. Ex) %s%d%f; UTF-8 code. Ex) Chinese characters; Start with characters ESC (ASCII 27d / 1Bh / 033o) and [(left bracket).
2	SIP-URI	Invalid SIP-URI form. Ex) sip: aaa:bbb@ccc.ddd, port number should be a number not character like "bbb."
3	SIP-Version	"SIP/" must have existed. Ex) SIP:2.0
4	IPv4-ASCII	The number range should be from 0 to 255.
5	Integer-ASCII	Number ranges are needed. Ex) port number
6	Overflow-colon	Only one colon is allowed. Ex) sip::::::::invalid.com
7	SIP-tag	Only one semi-colon is allowed for any option tag. Ex) <sip:<From>>;;;;;=token
8	Overflow-bracket	Only one bracket (< or >) is allowed.
9	Overflow-at	Only one at (@) is allowed.
10	CRLF(Carriage Return/Line Feed)	Every single line should have only one CRLF at the end.

of them are associated with SIP message header. SIP exceptional cases are categorized in Table 3.

To simulate 2426 test cases of PROTOS, we implemented an application, VoIPAttacker, which is capable of sending specific range of PROTOS test cases. Input values are in the range of PROTOS file names, e.g. 000001-000100. Figure 5 (left) shows VoIPDefender detects PROTOS malformed cases from 1 to 193 which are a part of case group number 1; overflow-general, overflow-space, overflow-null, format string, UTF-8 and ansi-escape. `SIP message view` dialog box in Fig. 5 (left) shows detail header field information of 193th test case, which does not have a method name in the first line.

While testing the PROTOS exceptional cases, we found that there are a number of ambiguous cases in the middle of valid forms and invalid forms. For example, `aaaaa@sip.invalid.com` can be a valid URI form, but it is included as an exceptional case in the PROTOS suite. Thus, we identify those 217 cases as legitimate SIP messages, so the total exceptional cases are 2209. When applying original RFC 3261 rules, 1837 of 2209 (74%) exceptional cases are detected as malformed messages while our secure rules detects 100% of them. Figure 5 (right) indicates how many exceptional cases are detected by each rule. The group ID in Fig. 5 (right) is the same as the one in Table 3.

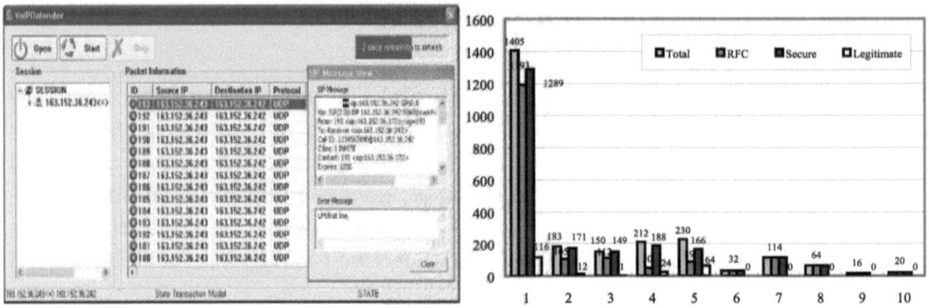

Fig. 5 VoIPDefender (left) and the comparison between original rules and secure ones (right).

5.2 *The Result for SIP Flooding Attacks*

Before explaining the result, we would like to mention the interesting things that we found while we were testing existing VoIP services. Each VoIP service has been adding specific message header fields such as `PortaBilling` for billing information in Globe7. Vbuzzer is also using `Warning` header fields to transmit noisy feedback. Gizmo Project also defines extra header fields, `JabberID`, `CQBM` and `RemoteIP`. On the other hand, VoIPGo uses a format string when there is a space in a user name. For example, if user name is `voip go`, it is going to change to `voip%20go` because 0x20 is the ASCII code for the space character. Format string is also included PROTOS exceptional cases, so that it may cause erroneous operation.

The most significant fact for SIP flooding detection is how to decide the threshold. The threshold is not supposed to disturb existing VoIP services. Figure 6 (left) depicts the number of transmitted SIP messages for each existing VoIP service.

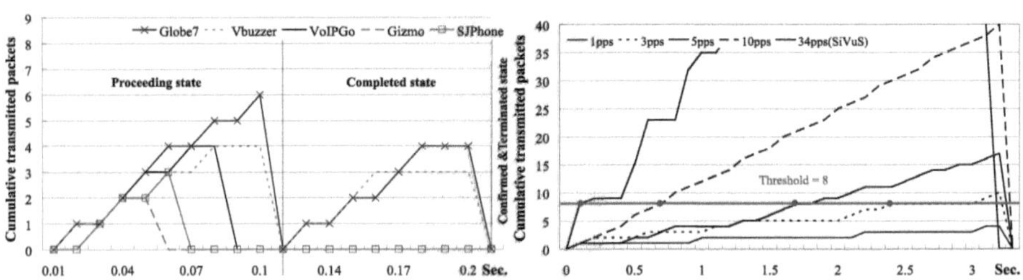

Fig. 6 Number of SIP messages for each state (left) and the result of SIP flooding test (right).

To find an appropriate threshold, we employed the proposed mechanism in the UAC part of SIP system and monitored SIP messages during call-setup process and distinguish the messages according to state. It shows that all five VoIP services send SIP messages under 6 pps (packet per second) per state. From the result, we could infer how many SIP messages were transmitted under the normal VoIP service condition.

To simulate flooding attack conditions, we applied five different pps (packet per second) cases in SiVuS; 1pps, 3pps, 5pps, 10pps and 34pps. Generating one packet per second is not a big burden in current computer system, but over 3pps starts consuming computer resources.

Figure 6 (right) shows SIP flooding simulation. 1pps is under the threshold, so that it is regarded as a normal condition. Actually it stands to the reason that 1pps is not flooding attack condition because it consumes just little resources. However, 34pps, 10pps, 5pps, and 3pps flooding tests reach to the threshold respectively at 0.2, 0.8, 1.9, and 2.3 second. Using the threshold, we detect flooding attack in 2.3 second that allows only ringing once.

We assume that there is no packet missing and retransmission. Under our experimental environment, small VoIP network between UAC and UAS, proper threshold is 8pps. It means that the average number of transmitted SIP messages from an initial state to its terminate state are normally lower than 6pps. We give 2pps gap as a tolerable range between threshold (8pps) and estimated max value (6pps) because the range is wide enough to reduce false alarm in our assumption. However, there is a possibility to transmit SIP messages more than the threshold under the larger VoIP networks. To adopt different environment, dynamic threshold is necessary but the principle of proposed approach is still useful.

5.3 The Overhead of Proposed Mechanism

We implemented an application, VoIPDefender, based on our detection mechanism. The developing environments are as follows: 3.0 GHz CPU, 2GB DDR2 memory, Windows XP service pack 2, Visual studio 2005 and MFC.

We estimate how many memory it requires and how long it takes to load the rules. VoIPDefender requires about 11 MB to and it is light enough to load for most systems. In fact, 11MB is not necessary because most of 11 MB is used for GUI (Graphic User Interface) such as dialog and window controls. It implies that there is the possibility of reducing the resource consumption. Moreover, it takes only 0.015 second and 352 KB to load the rules and creating session needs 40 KB. As a result, it turns out that VoIPDefender does not consume too much resources, so that it is suitable for applying to modern computer systems.

5.4 The Comparison with The Other Approaches

We presented that proposed mechanism is capable of detection two main SIP attacks in the previous Subsects. 5.1 and 5.2. Furthermore, Table 4 shows our proposed approach is able to detect additional SIP attacks compared with existing similar approaches. Three additional SIP attacks that proposed approach covers are follows.

- Invalid header field: a message missing the mandatory header or containing the non-allowed header.
- Improper message transmission: a message that is unacceptable to current state.
- Session information mismatch: a message containing wrong `CSeq` or `Call-ID`.

Neither rule matching nor state machine approach detects any of three SIP attacks. Also, simple combination approach of rule matching and state machine only covers two main SIP attacks, malformed and flooding attacks. However, proposed approach covers all SIP attacks by using SIP features, and shows higher detection rate for malformed SIP attack as applying secure rule sets that we developed.

Table 4 The comparison with the other approaches

Attack/Approach	Rule matching	State transition	Simple combination (Rule+State)	Proposed approach
Malformed	74%	X	74%	100%
Flooding	X	O	O	O
Invalid header field	X	X	X	O
Improper message transmission	X	X	X	O
Session information mismatch	X	X	X	O

6 Conclusion

We propose a complementary mechanism for detecting both malformed SIP messages and SIP flooding attacks. Moreover, proposed mechanism covers three additional SIP threats and shows 26% higher detection rate for malformed SIP attacks. To sum up, there are three strengths of proposed mechanism. First, the secure rules that we propose show the improvement apparently for detecting malformed SIP messages than original RFC 3261 ones. Also, the result shows that all PROTOS malformed SIP messages can be detectable by our rule matching algorithm, and it is confirmed that the algorithm is effective to protect VoIP services from variant malformed message attacks. Second, we modify the original state transitions and utilize a threshold based on practical VoIP services. Proposed state transition models with the threshold have not interrupted existing VoIP services, and it is possible to recognize flooding conditions. Lastly, through using SIP features from the rule sets and state machines, proposed mechanism catches three more SIP attacks; invalid header field, improper message transmission, and session information mismatch.

As a consequence, we insist that it is possible to build more robust the VoIP systems by applying our proposed mechanism. Furthermore, our mechanism can be adopted as a lower layer detection module to protect higher layer VoIP applications.

For future works, we have a plan to extend the rule matching algorithm to apply for SDP (Session Description Protocol) because the header fields of SDP are also plain texts. In addition, we will study how to apply the proposed approach to a complicated network system, such as a system with SIP proxy servers and gateways.

References

1. Chen, E.: Detecting DoS attacks on SIP systems. In: Proc. of VoIP Management and Security (2006)
2. Computer Engineering Laboratory, University of Oulu: PROTOS Test-Suite:c07-sip (2005). URL http://www.ee.oulu.fi/research/ouspg/protos/testing/c07/sip/index.html
3. Geneiatakis, D., Kambourakis, G., Dagiuklas, T., Lambrinoudakis, C., Gritzalis, S.: A framework for detecting malformed messages in SIP networks. In: Proc. of Local and Metropolitan Area Networks (LANMAN) (2005)
4. Handley, M., Jacobson, V.: RFC2327: Session description protocol (SDP) (1998)
5. Hung, P., Vargas Martin, M.: Security issues in VoIP applications. In: Proc. of Electrical and Computer Engineering, Canadian Conference (2006)
6. Ilgun, K., Kemmerer, R., Porras, P.: State transition analysis: A rule-based intrusion detection approach. IEEE Trans. on Software Engineering (1995)
7. McGann, S., Sicker, D.: An analysis of security threats and tools in SIP-based VoIP systems. In: Proc. of the 2nd Workshop on Securing Voice over IP, Cyber Security Alliance (2005)
8. MyVoIPProvider.com: Rank and Compare the Worlds Top 100 VoIP Providers (2007). URL http://www.myvoipprovider.com/
9. Packetizer, Inc.: H.323 versus SIP: A comparison (2007). URL http://www.packetizer.com/voip/h323_vs_sip
10. Sengar, H., Wijesekera, D., Wang, H., Jajodia, S.: VoIP intrusion detection through interacting protocol state machines. In: Proc. of Int'l Conf. on Dependable Systems and Networks (DSN) (2006)
11. Sisalem, D., Kuthan, J., Ehlert, S.: Denial of service attacks targeting a SIP VoIP infrastructure: attack scenarios and prevention mechanisms. IEEE Network (2006)
12. Vigna, G., Kemmerer, R.: NetSTAT: A network-based intrusion detection approach. In: Proc. of the 14th Annual Computer Security Application Conference (ACSAC) (1998)
13. Vigna, G., Robertson, W., Kher, V., Kemmerer, R.: A stateful intrusion detection system for world-wide web servers. In: Proc. of the Annual Computer Security Applications Conference (ACSAC) (2003)
14. Voice over Packet Security Forum: SiVuS: the VoIP Vulnerability Scanner (2006). URL http://www.vopsecurity.org/html/downloads.html
15. Walsh, T., Kuhn, D.: Challenges in securing voice over IP. IEEE Security & Privacy (2005)
16. Wu, Y.S., Bagchi, S., Garg, S., Singh, N.: SCIDIVE: a stateful and cross protocol intrusion detection architecture for voice-over-IP environments. In: Proc. of Int'l Conf. on Dependable Systems and Networks (DSN) (2004)

As a consequence, we insist that it is possible to build more robust the VoIP systems by applying our proposed mechanisms. Further more, our mechanism can be [illegible]

References

[illegible]

A Decentralized Bayesian Attack Detection Algorithm for Network Security

Kien C. Nguyen, Tansu Alpcan, and Tamer Başar

Abstract Decentralized detection has been an active area of research since the late 1970s. Its earlier application area has been distributed radar systems, and more recently it has found applications in sensor networks and intrusion detection. The most popular decentralized detection network structure is the parallel configuration, where a number of sensors are directly connected to a fusion center. The sensors receive measurements related to an event and then send summaries of their observations to the fusion center. Previous work has focused on separate optimization of the quantization rules at the sensors and the fusion rule at the fusion center or on asymptotic results when the number of sensors is very large and the observations are conditionally independent and identically distributed given each hypothesis.

In this work, we examine the application of decentralized detection to intrusion detection with again the parallel configuration, but with joint optimization. Particularly, using the Bayesian approach, we seek a joint optimization of the quantization rules at the sensors and the fusion rule at the fusion center. The observations of the sensors are not assumed to be conditionally independent nor identically distributed. We consider the discrete case where the distributions of the observations are given as probability mass functions. We propose a search algorithm for the optimal solution. Simulations carried out using the KDD'99 intrusion detection dataset show that the algorithm performs well.

Kien C. Nguyen
Department of Electrical and Computer Engineering and the Coordinated Science Laboratory, University of Illinois at Urbana-Champaign, 1308 W Main St., Urbana, IL 61801, USA,
e-mail: knguyen4@uiuc.edu

Tansu Alpcan
Deutsche Telekom Laboratories, Ernst-Reuter-Platz 7, D-10587 Berlin, Germany,
e-mail: tansu.alpcan@telekom.de

Tamer Başar
Department of Electrical and Computer Engineering and the Coordinated Science Laboratory, University of Illinois at Urbana-Champaign, 1308 W Main St., Urbana, IL 61801, USA,
e-mail: tbasar@control.csl.uiuc.edu

Please use the following format when citing this chapter:

Nguyen, K.C., Alpcan, T. and Başar, T., 2008, in IFIP International Federation for Information Processing, Volume 278; *Proceedings of the IFIP TC 11 23rd International Information Security Conference*; Sushil Jajodia, Pierangela Samarati, Stelvio Cimato; (Boston: Springer), pp. 413–427.

1 Introduction

There is pressing need for extensive research and development of novel approaches to address security problems in networked systems. The current cost of security-related issues is on the order of billions of dollars in terms of lost productivity, prevention, and clean-up. This affects individuals, businesses, and organizations on a global scale. For an example, the Code Red worm, which infected some 360,000 servers, cost about $1.2 billion in damage to computer networks [1]. As a result of the general-purpose nature of current computing systems and due to their social underpinnings, network security poses significant challenges that require innovative security architectures.

The problem of decentralized detection has been addressed in many works ([2], [3], [4], [5], [6], and [7]). The concepts and taxonomy of intrusion detection systems can be found in [8] and [9]. Reference [10] provides a survey on intrusion detection for mobile *ad hoc* networks. Furthermore, the authors in [11] have proposed an algorithm for decentralized intrusion detection in the context of wireless sensor networks. The use of Principal Component Analysis (PCA) to detect network anomalies has been examined in [12], [13] and [14], while reference [15] uses a Markov chain model to learn the normal behavior and then detect the anomalies. Also, application of game theory to intrusion detection has been examined in [16] and [17].

A variety of network security issues such as attack and anomaly detection can be addressed within the framework of Bayesian hypothesis testing. In such a framework, one considers networked security systems with multiple virtual sensors (detection units) implemented as software agents that report various measurements or observations. In many cases, sending all this information to a centralized location for processing (attack detection) has several disadvantages such as traffic overhead and need for extensive computing resources at the center. To remedy these issues, we resort in this paper to decentralized hypothesis testing for attack detection.

KDD[1] Cup 1999 [18] is a dataset extracted from the TCP dump data of a Local Area Network (LAN). The LAN was set up to simulate a United States Air Force LAN and speckled with different kinds of attacks. From this dataset, it can be shown that the observations from different sensors (parameters) are not necessarily identically distributed and may also be strongly correlated. Thus the analyses and results developed under the assumption of conditionally independent and identically distributed (*i.i.d.*) observations with a large number of sensors will not be applicable here. We therefore attempt to analyze a sensor network with a finite number of sensors. We do not assume that the observations are conditionally *i.i.d.* We use the Bayesian criterion, i.e., the cost function is the average probability of error at the fusion center.

The main contributions of this paper are: (i) applying decentralized hypothesis testing to intrusion detection, where each sensor observes a parameter of the system or current connection; (ii) proposing a search algorithm for the optimal (Bayesian)

[1] KDD stands for Knowledge Discovery and Data Mining [18].

thresholds for the general case of non-*i.i.d.* observations, provided that the sensors are restricted to use likelihood ratio tests; and (iii) deriving some relationships between the majority vote and the likelihood ratio test for a parallel configuration.

The rest of the paper is organized as follows. The background theory is presented in Section 2. In Section 3, we derive some relationships between the majority vote and the likelihood ratio test at the fusion center. We then propose a search algorithm to find the optimal thresholds for the sensors in Section 4. Section 5 gives a brief overview of the KDD 1999 dataset, discusses the application of hypothesis testing in attack and anomaly detection, and presents the simulation results using the dataset. Finally, some concluding remarks end the paper.

2 Decentralized hypothesis testing with non-*i.i.d.* observations

In this section, we formulate the problem of decentralized hypothesis testing with non-*i.i.d* observations. We first discuss centralized detection before proceeding with the decentralized problem. Extensive discussion on both models can be found in [4]. In Subsection 2.2, we provide details on the fusion rule and the average probability of error at the fusion center.

2.1 From centralized to decentralized detection

Centralized detection. First we consider the configuration given in Figure 1. This is a parallel configuration with a finite number of sensors and a data fusion center. The sensors observe two hypotheses, H_0 and H_1, corresponding, for example, to the normal state and an attack, respectively. Let $Y_1, Y_2, \ldots, Y_N$, the observations of the sensors, be N discrete random variables that take values in finite sets $\mathscr{Y}_1, \mathscr{Y}_2, \ldots, \mathscr{Y}_N$, respectively. The observations are not assumed to be conditionally independent nor identically distributed. In this model, we suppose that the fusion center has full access to the observations of the sensors. It then fuses all the data to finally decide whether H_0 or H_1 is true. From the result of centralized Bayesian hypothesis testing [19], the rules can be stated as follows:

$$\gamma_0(y_1, y_2, \ldots y_N) = \begin{cases} 1 & \text{if } \frac{P_1(y_1, y_2, \ldots y_N)}{P_0(y_1, y_2, \ldots y_N)} \geq \frac{\pi_0}{\pi_1} \\ 0 & \text{otherwise,} \end{cases} \tag{1}$$

where $P_1(y_1, y_2, \ldots y_N)$ denotes the joint probability of the Y_i's under hypothesis H_1, i.e., $P(Y_1 = y_1, Y_2 = y_2, \ldots Y_N = y_N | H_1)$; $P_0(y_1, y_2, \ldots y_N)$ denotes the joint probability of the Y_i's under hypothesis H_0, i.e., $P(Y_1 = y_1, Y_2 = y_2, \ldots Y_N = y_N | H_0)$; π_0 and π_1 are the prior probabilities of H_0 and H_1, respectively; and γ_0 is the fusion rule at the fusion center. Throughout this paper, we use the indices of the hypotheses (0, 1) to indicate the hypotheses (H_0, H_1) in the equations. Note that the fusion rule

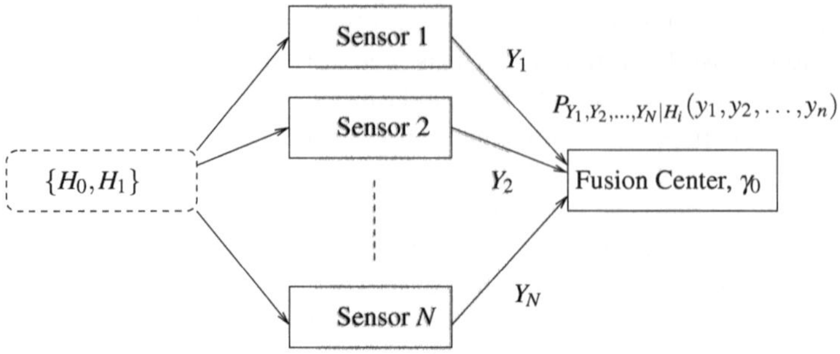

Fig. 1 Centralized detection, where the fusion center has full access to the observations of the sensors.

involves a threshold which is the ratio of π_0 to π_1, and the likelihood ratio (ratio of probabilities under the two hypotheses) is tested against that threshold.

Decentralized detection. In the decentralized detection model, instead of providing the full observation, each sensor only transmits 1 bit of information (which is a local decision whether H_0 or H_1 is true) to the fusion center, which will fuse all the bits to finally decide between H_0 or H_1. The communication channels between the sensors and the fusion center are assumed to be perfect. We seek a joint optimization of the quantization rules of all the sensors $(\gamma_1(.), \ldots, \gamma_N(.))$ and the fusion rule of the fusion center $(\gamma_0(.))$ to minimize the average probability of error of the system. The configuration of N sensors and the fusion center are shown in Figure 2.

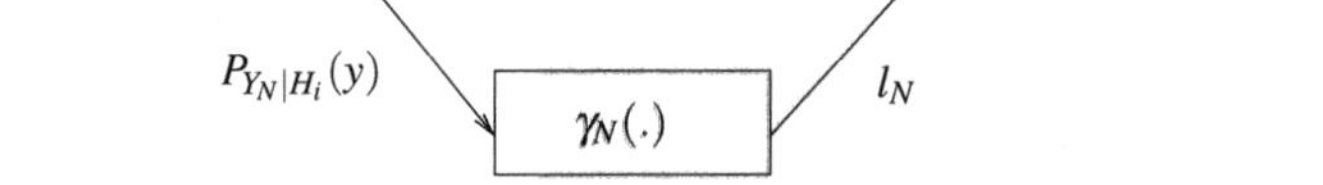

Fig. 2 Decentralized detection model, where each sensor transmits 1 bit of information to the fusion center, which will fuse all the bits to finally decide whether H_0 or H_1 is true.

Naturally, given the same *a priori* probabilities of the hypotheses and conditional joint distributions of the observations, the decentralized configuration will yield an average probability of error that is higher than or equal to that of the centralized configuration. The reason is that we lose some information after the quantization at the sensors [4]. Putting it another way, given the observations of the sensors and assuming the use of a likelihood ratio test at the fusion center in the centralized configuration, the test in (1) will yield the minimum probability of error. The decentralized configuration, however, can always be considered as a special setup of the fusion center in the centralized case, where the observations from the sensors are quantized before being fused together.

Under the assumption that the observations are conditionally independent, it has been shown in [4] that there exists an optimal solution for the local sensors, which is a deterministic (likelihood ratio) threshold strategy. When the observations are conditionally dependent, however, the threshold rule is no longer necessarily optimal [4]. In this case, obtaining the overall optimal non-threshold rule is a very challenging problem. In view of this, we restrict ourselves to threshold-type rules (which are suboptimal) at the local sensors and seek optimality within that restricted class. The optimal fusion rule, as shown next, will also be a likelihood ratio test.

2.2 *The fusion rule and the average probability of error*

For each combination of the thresholds at the sensors $\{\tau_1, \tau_2, \ldots, \tau_N\}$, the fusion rule ($\gamma_0$) is determined based on the likelihood ratio test at the fusion center:

$$\gamma_0(l_1, l_2, \ldots, l_N) = \begin{cases} 1 & \text{if } \frac{P_1(l_1,l_2,\ldots,l_N)}{P_0(l_1,l_2,\ldots,l_N)} \geq \frac{\pi_0}{\pi_1} \\ 0 & \text{otherwise.} \end{cases} \tag{2}$$

Here $P_i(l_1, l_2, \ldots, l_N)$ is the conditional joint probability mass function (*pmf*) given H_i, $i = 0, 1$.

This result can be derived from the solution of the one-sensor Bayesian detection problem [19], where the fusion center is considered as a sensor with the local decisions (from the connected sensors) as its observations [4].

The average probability of error at the fusion center is then given by:

$$\begin{aligned} P_e &= \pi_0 P_0\left(\frac{P_1(l_1,l_2,\ldots,l_N)}{P_0(l_1,l_2,\ldots,l_N)} \geq \frac{\pi_0}{\pi_1}\right) + \pi_1 P_1\left(\frac{P_1(l_1,l_2,\ldots,l_N)}{P_0(l_1,l_2,\ldots,l_N)} < \frac{\pi_0}{\pi_1}\right) \\ &= \pi_0 \sum_{l_1,l_2,\ldots,l_N : L_a \geq \frac{\pi_0}{\pi_1}} P_0(l_1,l_2,\ldots,l_N) + \pi_1 \sum_{l_1,l_2,\ldots,l_N : L_a < \frac{\pi_0}{\pi_1}} P_1(l_1,l_2,\ldots,l_N) \\ \text{where } L_a &= \frac{P_1(l_1,l_2,\ldots,l_N)}{P_0(l_1,l_2,\ldots,l_N)}. \end{aligned} \tag{3}$$

As we are considering the discrete case, where the conditional joint distributions are given as *pmf*s, the conditional joint distributions of the local decisions can be written as:

$$P_i(l_1, l_2, \ldots, l_N) = \sum_{Y_N \in R_{Ni_N}} \cdots \sum_{Y_1 \in R_{1i_1}} P_i(Y_1, Y_2, \ldots, Y_N) \tag{4}$$

where $i_n = 0, 1$, and R_{ni_n} is the region where Sensor n decides to send bit i_n, $n = 1, \ldots, N$:

$$R_{n1} = \left\{ Y_n \in \mathscr{Y}_n : L_{Y_n} = \frac{P_1(Y_n)}{P_0(Y_n)} \geq \tau_n \right\} \tag{5}$$

$$R_{n0} = \left\{ Y_n \in \mathscr{Y}_n : L_{Y_n} = \frac{P_1(Y_n)}{P_0(Y_n)} < \tau_n \right\}. \tag{6}$$

where $L_{Y_n} = P_1(Y_n)/P_0(Y_n)$ is the likelihood ratio at Sensor n.

Our goal is to find the combination $\{\tau_1, \tau_2, \ldots, \tau_N\}$ that yields the minimum probability of error at the fusion center. If the number of threshold candidates for every sensor is finite, the number of combinations of thresholds will also be finite. Then there is an optimal solution, i.e., a combination of thresholds $\{\tau_1, \tau_2, \ldots, \tau_N\}$ that yields the minimum probability of error. In Section 4, we show how to pick the threshold candidates for each sensor.

3 The majority vote versus the likelihood ratio test

In this section, we first show that if the observations of the sensors are conditionally independent, given the set of thresholds at the local sensors, any sensor switching from decision 0 to decision 1 will increase the likelihood ratio at the fusion center. Furthermore, if the observations are conditionally *i.i.d.* and the sensors all use the same threshold for the likelihood ratio test, the likelihood ratio test at the fusion center becomes equivalent to a majority vote. In the general case, where the observations are not *i.i.d.*, this property no longer holds; we provide towards the end of the section an example where the likelihood ratio test and the majority vote yield different results.

Recall that the fusion rule at the fusion center is given by (2). If the observations of the sensors are conditionally independent, the likelihood ratio at the fusion center becomes:

$$\frac{P_1(l_1, l_2, \ldots, l_N)}{P_0(l_1, l_2, \ldots, l_N)} = \frac{\prod_{n=1}^N P_1(l_n)}{\prod_{n=1}^N P_0(l_n)} = \prod_{n=1}^{N} \frac{P_1(l_n)}{P_0(l_n)}.$$

Let us denote by $\mathscr{N}$ the set of all local sensors (represented by their indices). We divide $\mathscr{N}$ into two partitions: $\mathscr{N}_0$, the set of local sensors that send 0 to the fusion center, and $\mathscr{N}_1$, the set of local sensors that send 1 to the fusion center. Then we have $\mathscr{N}_0 \bigcup \mathscr{N}_1 = \mathscr{N}$ and $\mathscr{N}_0 \bigcap \mathscr{N}_1 = \emptyset$. Note that, given the conditional joint probabilities of the observations, $\mathscr{N}_0$ and $\mathscr{N}_1$ are set-valued functions of the thresholds $\{\tau_1, \tau_2, \ldots, \tau_N\}$. Let N_0 and N_1 denote the cardinalities of $\mathscr{N}_0$ and $\mathscr{N}_1$, respectively. Obviously, $N_0, N_1 \in \mathscr{Z}$ (where $\mathscr{Z}$ is the set of all integers), $0 \leq N_0, N_1 \leq N$, and $N_0 + N_1 = N$. Now the likelihood ratio can be written as:

$$\frac{P_1(l_1, l_2, \ldots, l_N)}{P_0(l_1, l_2, \ldots, l_N)} = \prod_{n \in \mathscr{N}_0} \frac{P_1(l_n = 0)}{P_0(l_n = 0)} \prod_{m \in \mathscr{N}_1} \frac{P_1(l_m = 1)}{P_0(l_m = 1)}. \tag{7}$$

From the definitions of the decision regions in (5), (6) we have that

$$P_1(l_n = 1) = \sum_{Y_n : L_{Y_n} \geq \tau_n} P_1(Y_n) \text{ and } P_0(l_n = 1) = \sum_{Y_n : L_{Y_n} \geq \tau_n} P_0(Y_n).$$

Consider the region where Sensor n decides 1 (defined in (5)), $\{R_{n1} : Y_n \in \mathscr{Y}_n : L_{Y_n} = P_1(Y_n)/P_0(Y_n) \geq \tau_n\}$. We have that

$$P_1(l_n = 1) = \sum_{Y_n : L_{Y_n} \geq \tau_n} P_1(Y_n) \geq \tau_n \sum_{Y_n : L_{Y_n} \geq \tau_n} P_0(Y_n) \geq \tau_n P_0(l_n = 1),$$

or

$$\frac{P_1(l_n = 1)}{P_0(l_n = 1)} \geq \tau_n. \tag{8}$$

Similarly, summing over the region where Sensor n decides 0 (defined in (6)), $\{R_{n0} : Y_n \in \mathscr{Y}_n : L_{Y_n} = P_1(Y_n)/P_0(Y_n) < \tau_n\}$, we have that

$$\frac{P_1(l_n = 0)}{P_0(l_n = 0)} < \tau_n. \tag{9}$$

From (7), (8) and (9), we can see that any sensor switching from decision 0 to decision 1 will increase the likelihood ratio at the fusion center.

Now, if the observations are conditionally *i.i.d.* and all the sensors use the same threshold then

$$P_i(l_n = 1) = \sum_{Y_n : L_{Y_n} \geq \tau} P_i(Y_n) = P_i(l_m = 1)$$

where $i = 0, 1;\ 0 \leq m, n \leq N$. Thus we can write (7) as follows:

$$\frac{P_1(l_1, l_2, \ldots, l_N)}{P_0(l_1, l_2, \ldots, l_N)} = \left(\frac{P_1(l = 0)}{P_0(l = 0)}\right)^{N - N_1} \left(\frac{P_1(l = 1)}{P_0(l = 1)}\right)^{N_1}. \tag{10}$$

The fusion rule compares the likelihood ratio in (10) with the ratio π_0/π_1. Again, using (8) and (9), it can be seen that the likelihood ratio is a non-decreasing function of N_1. Therefore the likelihood ratio test becomes equivalent to a majority vote rule in this case.

In what follows, we give an example where $L(001) > L(110)$ for the case of three sensors. The observations are supposed to be conditionally independent but not conditionally identically distributed. If we use the majority vote, the fusion center will output H_1 if it receives $(1,1,0)$ and H_0 if it receives $(0,0,1)$. On the contrary, we will show that, if the likelihood ratio test is used, the fusion center will pick $(0,0,1)$ against $(1,1,0)$ for H_1. Using the independence assumption, we have that:

$$L(110) = \frac{P_1(110)}{P_0(110)} = \frac{P_1(l_1 = 1)}{P_0(l_1 = 1)} \frac{P_1(l_2 = 1)}{P_0(l_2 = 1)} \frac{P_1(l_3 = 0)}{P_0(l_3 = 0)},$$

$$L(001) = \frac{P_1(001)}{P_0(001)} = \frac{P_1(l_1=0)}{P_0(l_1=0)}\frac{P_1(l_2=0)}{P_0(l_2=0)}\frac{P_1(l_3=1)}{P_0(l_3=1)}.$$

Consider the ratio

$$\begin{aligned}\frac{L(001)}{L(110)} &= \frac{P_1(l_1=0)P_0(l_1=1)}{P_1(l_1=1)P_0(l_1=0)}\frac{P_1(l_2=0)P_0(l_2=1)}{P_1(l_2=1)P_0(l_2=0)}\frac{P_1(l_3=1)P_0(l_3=0)}{P_1(l_3=0)P_0(l_3=1)}\\ &= \frac{[1-P_1(l_1=1)][1-P_0(l_1=0)]}{P_1(l_1=1)P_0(l_1=0)}\frac{[1-P_1(l_2=1)][1-P_0(l_2=0)]}{P_1(l_2=1)P_0(l_2=0)}\\ &\quad \frac{P_1(l_3=1)P_0(l_3=0)}{[1-P_1(l_3=1)][1-P_0(l_3=0)]}. \end{aligned} \tag{11}$$

As l_1, l_2, and l_3 are conditionally independent given each hypothesis, we can choose their conditional probabilities such that the ratio in (11) is larger than 1. For example, we can choose the conditional probabilities as follows:

$$\begin{aligned}&P_1(l_1=1) = P_0(l_1=0) = P_1(l_2=1) = P_0(l_2=0) = 0.6,\\ &P_1(l_3=1) = P_0(l_3=0) = 0.9.\end{aligned}$$

Such conditional probabilities can be obtained if we choose P_0 and P_1 as in Figure 3 with $k = 2.5$ for Sensor 1 and Sensor 2, and $k = 10$ for Sensor 3; and the thresholds for all three quantizers satisfy $1/(k-1) < \tau < k-1$.

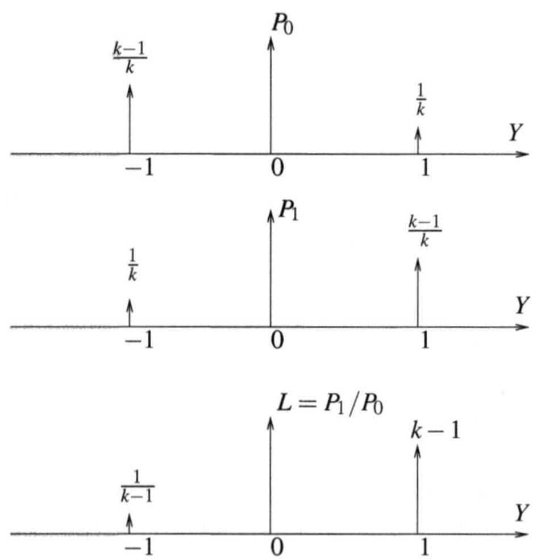

Fig. 3 The majority vote versus the likelihood ratio test: If P_0 and P_1 of each sensor is as shown, the thresholds for all three quantizers satisfy $1/(k-1) < \tau < k-1$ with $k = 2.5$ for Sensor 1 and Sensor 2 and $k = 10$ for Sensor 3, then $L(001) > L(110)$. A majority vote will output H_1 if it receives $(1,1,0)$ and H_0 if it receives $(0,0,1)$, while the likelihood ratio test favors $(0,0,1)$ for H_1.

4 An algorithm to compute the optimal thresholds

As mentioned in the introduction, the binary decentralized detection problem with two sensors, binary messages, and the fusion rule fixed *a priori* is NP-complete [20]. We thus propose in this section a brute-force search algorithm to solve the optimization problem. (For a discussion on the complexity of this kind of algorithms, see [4], [20].) This algorithm is suitable for small sensor networks. Suppose that we are given a training dataset each record of which has been labeled with either "Normal" or "Attack". Suppose further that each record consists of N parameters, each of which takes values in a finite set. We do not assume that the observations of the sensors (the parameters) are conditionally independent nor identically distributed. The *a priori* probabilities and the conditional joint *pmf*s given each hypothesis then can be learnt from the training dataset. The search algorithm for the optimal thresholds is as follows.

The algorithm to compute the optimal thresholds at the sensors:

1. Group all possible values of each parameter into equally spaced bins with the number of bins for the n-th parameter denoted by b_n. In general, b_n's do not have to be equal. This operation is done for both "Normal" and "Attack" modes.
2. Compute the *a priori* probabilities of "Normal" and "Attack", π_0 and π_1.
3. Compute the conditional joint *pmf*s and the conditional marginal *pmf*s for each hypothesis.
4. Compute the likelihood ratio for each parameter. There are b_n possible values of likelihood ratio for the n-th parameter, $0 \le \tau_n^1 \le \tau_n^2 \ldots \le \tau_n^{b_n} \le \infty$.
5. The threshold candidates for the local likelihood ratio test of each parameter are

$$\tau_n^0 = 0 < \tau_n^1 < \tau_n^2 \ldots < \tau_n^{b'_n} < \tau_n^{b'_n+1} = \infty, \tag{12}$$

   where $\tau_n^1, \tau_n^2, \ldots, \tau_n^{b'_n}$ are the b'_n values of likelihood ratio of the n-th parameter from Step 4, where duplications have been removed ($b'_n \le b_n$).
6. For each combination $\{\tau_1, \tau_2, \ldots, \tau_N\}$ where τ_n takes a value in $\{\tau_n^0, \tau_n^1, \ldots, \tau_n^{b'_n+1}\}$, determine the fusion rule (γ_0) based on the likelihood ratio test at the fusion center given in (2).
7. For each combination $\{\tau_1, \tau_2, \ldots, \tau_N\}$, evaluate the average probability of error P_e using (3) and (4).
8. Choose the combination that minimizes P_e.

Once the optimal thresholds for the sensors have been computed (off-line), we can carry out the following steps to detect attacks in the system.

Using the optimal thresholds for attack detection:

1. For each record, each local sensor quantizes the parameter into a single bit (indicating whether an attack exists or not).

2. The fusion center collects all the bits from the local sensors and computes the likelihood ratio using (4) (the joint conditional *pmf*s are drawn from the training data).
3. The fusion center makes the final decision using (2).

If we have a labeled dataset where each record has been marked as "Normal" or "Attack", we can compute the error probabilities as follows:

Computing the probabilities of error:

1. Compute the actual *a priori* probabilities ($\overline{\pi_0}$ and $\overline{\pi_1}$), the false alarm probability ($P_f = P_0(\gamma_0(.) = 1)$ and the misdetection probability ($P_m = P_1(\gamma_0(.) = 0)$.
2. Compute the average probability of error using the equation:

$$P_e = \overline{\pi_0} \times P_f + \overline{\pi_1} \times P_m. \tag{13}$$

5 KDD Cup 1999 data and simulation results

In this section, we first introduce the KDD Cup 1999 data and discuss the application of decentralized detection to these data. We then present the results of the simulation of the algorithm proposed in the previous section using the KDD data.

5.1 KDD Cup 1999 data

As mentioned in the introduction, KDD Cup 1999 [18] is a dataset extracted from the TCP dump data of a LAN. The network was set up to simulate a U.S. Air Force LAN and was speckled with different types of attacks. Each connection (record) consists of 41 parameters and is labeled with either "Normal" or some type of attack. Table 1 describes some parameters of a TCP connection. To apply hypothesis

Feature name	Description	Type
duration	length (number of seconds) of the connection	continuous
protocol_type	type of the protocol, e.g. tcp, udp, etc.	discrete
service	network service on the destination, e.g., http, telnet, etc.	discrete
src_bytes	number of data bytes from source to destination	continuous
dst_bytes	number of data bytes from destination to source	continuous
flag	normal or error status of the connection	discrete
land	1 if connection is from/to the same host/port; 0 otherwise	discrete
wrong_fragment	number of "wrong" fragments	continuous
urgent	number of urgent packets	continuous

Table 1 Basic features of individual TCP connections [18].

testing for network intrusion systems, we can consider the state "Normal" as hypothesis H_0 and a particular type of attack as hypothesis H_1. (For a more general setting, we can group all types of attack into one hypothesis "Attacks" or deal with "Normal" and all types of attacks separately as a multiple hypothesis testing problem with the number of hypotheses, $M > 2$.) We can use the labeled data to learn the conditional distributions of the parameters given each hypothesis. These conditional distributions will then be used to decide the rules for the "sensors" (each of which represents a parameter) and the fusion center. Here, instead of observing the same event, each sensor looks at an aspect of the same event.

For example, we extracted all the records labeled with "Normal" and "Smurf" (which means the connection is a Smurf attack) in the 10% portion of the data given in [18]. We examined the following parameters of all the normal and Smurf connections:

- **duration**: Length (in seconds) of the connection (Table 1).
- **src_bytes**: Number of data bytes from source to destination (Table 1).
- **dst_bytes**: Number of data bytes from destination to source (Table 1).
- **count**: Number of connections to the same host as the current connection in the past two seconds.
- **srv_count**: Number of connections to the same service as the current connection in the past two seconds.

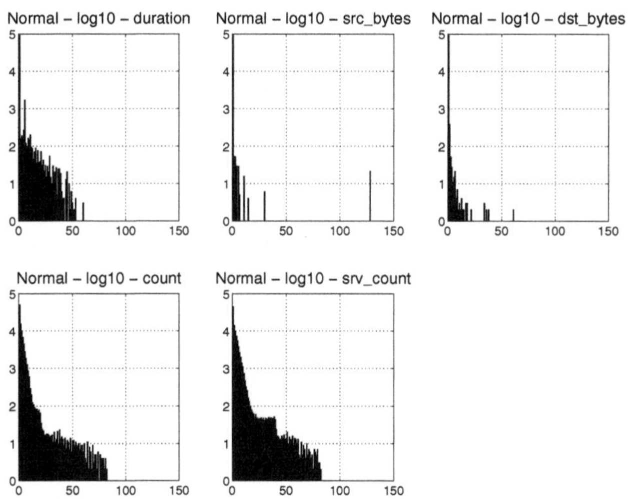

Fig. 4 Probability distributions of some parameters when the LAN is normal. A base-10 logarithmic scale is used for the Y-axis.

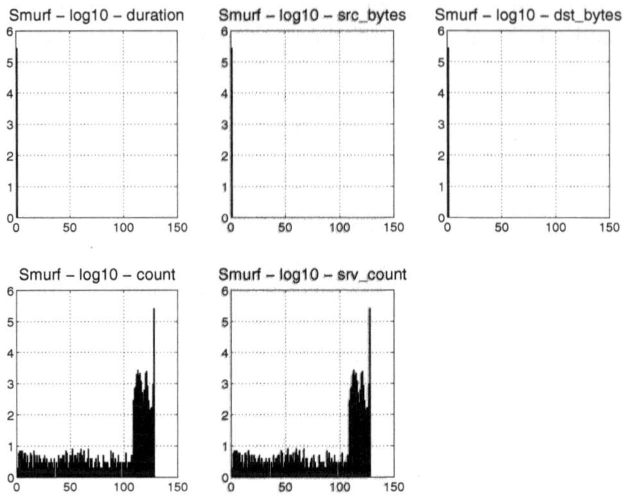

Fig. 5 Probability distributions of some parameters when there are Smurf attacks. A base-10 logarithmic scale is used for the Y-axis.

Figures 4 and 5 show that the conditional distributions of the parameters given either hypothesis can be very different. Also, some parameters are strongly correlated (for example, *count* and *srv_count* given a Smurf attack). Thus, as mentioned earlier, the asymptotic results for large values of N will not be applicable.

5.2 Simulation results

In these simulations, we employ the algorithm and procedures given in Section 4 to detect Smurf attacks against Normal connections in the KDD data ([18])[2].

We use the 10% portion of the dataset (given in [18]) as the training data. The proportion of Normal connections is $\pi_0 = 0.2573$, and the proportion of Smurf connections is $\pi_1 = 0.7427$. Four parameters (*duration*, *src_bytes*, *dst_bytes*, and *count*) are used. The number of bins for each of the parameters is 8.

The threshold candidates for the four parameters *duration*, *src_bytes*, *dst_bytes*, and *count* are given in Table 2. The minimum probability of error computed using the algorithm is $9.3369E-4$. The results show that this probability of error is obtained at different combinations of thresholds, one of which, for example, is $\{1.0082, 1.0003, 1.0004, 1.67\}$.

[2] A Smurf attack can be detected using rule-based detection [21], however, here we just use the dataset as a demonstrative example to illustrate our approach.

duration	0								1.0082	∞
src_bytes	0								1.0003	∞
dst_bytes	0								1.0004	∞
count	0	2.81E-4	3.88E-2	9.60E-2	2.04E-1	2.65E-1	1.67	2.21E2	1.37E4	∞

Table 2 The threshold candidates computed for each parameter. The threshold duplications in the first three parameters have been removed.

The detection procedures are then applied to the whole KDD dataset, which is divided into 10 files for ease of handling. Table 3 provides the simulation results. The probabilities of misdetection, probabilities of false alarm, and the average probabilities of error are plotted in Figures 6 and 7.

File	N̲o Normal	N̲o Smurf	$\overline{\pi_0}$	$\overline{\pi_1}$	P_m	P_f	P_e
1	379669	105556	0.7825	0.2175	0.0061	1.1326E-4	0.0014
2	182718	86493	0.6787	0.3213	0.0028	5.4729E-6	9.1007E-4
3	149880	117038	0.5615	0.4385	0.0035	8.0064E-5	0.0016
4	0	489843	0	1	0.0013	n/a	0.0013
5	0	489843	0	1	0	n/a	0
6	0	489843	0	1	0	n/a	0
7	31046	456829	0.0636	0.9364	0	0	0
8	36798	8189	0.8180	0.1820	0.1260	0	0.0229
9	4061	478090	0.0084	0.9916	6.6724E-4	0	6.6162E-4
10	188609	86162	0.6864	0.3136	0.0037	9.7026E-4	0.0018

Table 3 Probabilities of error for 10 portions (files) of the KDD dataset. We only consider Normal and Smurf connections. *N̲o Normal*: Number of Normal connections in the file; *N̲o Smurf:* Number of Smurf connections in the file. We use *n/a* (not available) for the entries of P_f corresponding to the files with no Normal connections.

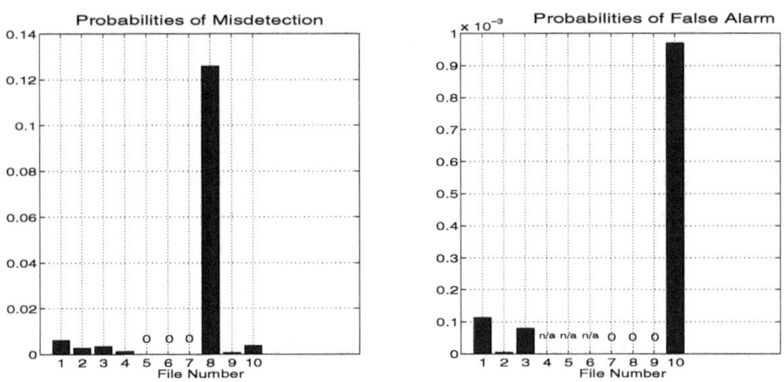

Fig. 6 Misdetection probabilities (left) and false alarm probabilities (right) against file indices (data from Table 3).

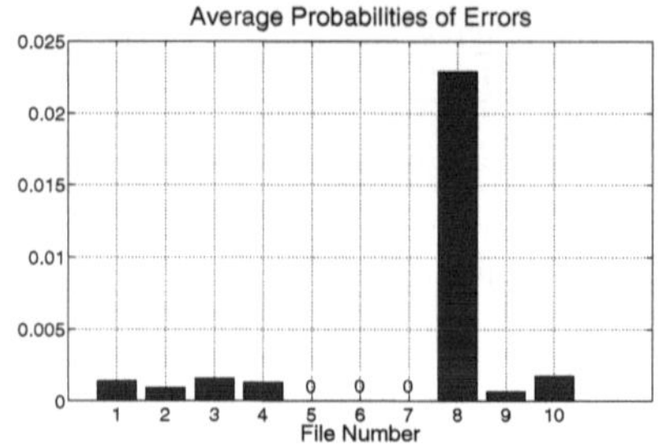

Fig. 7 Average probabilities of error against file indices (data from Table 3).

From the simulation results, we can see that, as expected, the probabilities of error change from file to file, depending on how close the *a priori* probabilities and the conditional joint probabilities of each file are to those of the training data (the simulation of detection using the training data provides exactly the error probability computed from the algorithm, which is $9.3369E-4$). Also, it can be noted that the minimum probability of error should also depend on the number of bins and the way of binning for each parameter. The overall results of the simulation are good, which shows that the algorithm performs well with this dataset.

6 Concluding remarks

In this paper, we have considered the problem of decentralized hypothesis testing with non-*i.i.d.* observations. We have presented the theoretical background for the joint optimization of the likelihood ratio thresholds at the sensors and the fusion rule at the fusion center. We have also derived some relationships between the majority vote and the likelihood ratio test at the fusion center. Building on the theoretical background, we have proposed a search algorithm to compute the optimal thresholds for the sensors. Simulations carried out using the KDD'99 dataset have shown that the algorithm performs well as expected.

Some possible extensions are as follows. First, we can consider the case where the sensors send multiple-bit summaries to the fusion center. Second, multiple-hypotheses testing ($M > 2$) can be used to detect more types of attack. Next, when more parameters are used in detection, PCA can be used to reduce the number of dimensions of the problem. Finally, the tree structure with non-*i.i.d.* observations is an intriguing research direction.

Acknowledgements This work was supported by Deutsche Telekom Laboratories and in part by the Vietnam Education Foundation (VEF). The opinions, findings, and conclusions stated herein are those of the authors and do not necessarily reflect those of VEF. We are grateful to the anonymous reviewers for their valuable comments. The first author would also like to thank Dr. Akshay Kashyap and Jayakrishnan Unnikrishnan for helpful discussions on this subject matter.

References

1. Reuters, The cost of 'code red': $1.2 billion, *USA Today*, Aug. 1, 2001. Available at http://usatoday.com/tech/news/2001-08-01-code-red-costs.htm.
2. J. N. Tsitsiklis, Decentralized detection by a large number of sensors, *Math. Control Signals Syst.*, Vol. 1, No. 2, 1988, pp. 167-182.
3. J. N. Tsitsiklis, Extremal properties of likelihood-ratio quantizers, *IEEE Transactions on Communications*, Vol. 41, No. 4, 1993, pp. 550–558.
4. J. N. Tsitsiklis, Decentralized detection, *Advances in Signal Processing*, JAI Press, 1993.
5. J. Chamberland, V. V. Veeravalli, Asymptotic results for decentralized detection in power constrained wireless sensor networks, *IEEE Journal on Selected Areas in Communication*, Vol. 22, No. 6, 2004, pp. 1007-1015.
6. A. Kashyap, T. Başar, R. Srikant, Asymptotically optimal quantization for detection in power constrained decentralized networks, *Proceedings of the American Control Conference*, Minnesota, USA, 2006.
7. I. Y. Hoballah, P. K. Varshney, Distributed Bayesian signal detection, *IEEE Trans. Inform. Theory*, Vol. 35, 1989, pp. 995–1000.
8. A. K. Jones, R. S. Sielken, Computer system intrusion detection: A survey, Technical Report, Computer Science Department, University of Virginia, 2000.
9. S. Axelsson, Intrusion detection systems: A survey and taxonomy, Technical Report 99–15, Department of Computer Engineering, Chalmers University, 2000.
10. T. Anantvalee, J. Wu, A survey on intrusion detection in mobile ad-hoc networks, *Wireless/Mobile Network Security*, Y. Xiao, X. Shen, D. -Z. Du (eds.), Springer, 2007.
11. A. P. da Silva, M. Martins, B. Rocha, A. Loureiro, L. Ruiz, H. C. Wong, Decentralized intrusion detection in wireless sensor networks, *Proceedings of the 1st ACM International Workshop on Quality of Service & Security in Wireless and Mobile Networks*, ACM Press, 2005, pp. 16-23.
12. A. Lakhina, M. Crovella, C. Diot, Diagnosing network-wide traffic anomalies, *Proceedings of the ACM SIGCOMM Conference on Applications, Technologies, Architectures, and Protocols for Computer Communication*, Portland, Oregon, USA, 2004.
13. L. Huang, X. L. Nguyen, M. Garofalakis, M. Jordan, A. D. Joseph, N. Taft, In-network PCA and anomaly detection, *Advances in Neural Information Processing Systems 19*, MIT Press, Cambridge, MA.
14. L. Huang, X. L. Nguyen, M. Garofalakisy, J. M. Hellerstein, M. I. Jordan, A. D. Joseph, N. Tafty, Communication-efficient online detection of network-wide anomalies, *Proceedings of the 26th Annual IEEE Conference on Computer Communications*, Anchorage, Alaska, 2007.
15. N. Ye, X. Li, A Markov chain model of temporal behavior for anomaly detection, *Proceedings IEEE Systems, Man, and Cybernetics Information Assurance and Security Workshop*, 2000.
16. T. Alpcan, T. Başar, A game theoretic analysis of intrusion detection in access control systems, *Proceedings of the 43rd IEEE Conference on Decision and Control*, Paradise Island, Bahamas, 2004, pp. 1568–1573.
17. T. Alpcan, T. Başar, An intrusion detection game with limited observations, *Proceedings of the 12th Int. Symp. on Dynamic Games and Applications*, Sophia Antipolis, France, 2006.
18. KDD Cup 1999 Data. Available at http://kdd.ics.uci.edu/databases/kddcup99/kddcup99.html
19. V. H. Poor, *An Introduction to Signal Detection and Estimation*, 2nd Ed., Springer, 1994.
20. J. Tsitsiklis, M. Athans, On the complexity of decentralized decision making and detection problems, *IEEE Transaction on Automatic Control*, Vol. AC–30, No. 5, 1985, pp. 440–446.
21. W. Lee, S. J. Stolfo, A framework for constructing features and models for intrusion detection systems, *ACM Transactions on Information and System Security*, Vol. 3, No. 4, 2000, pp. 227-261.

References

An Operation-Based Metric for CPA Resistance*

J. Pan, J.I. den Hartog, and E.P. de Vink

Abstract Differential power analysis (DPA) is a strong attack upon cryptographic devices such as smartcards. Correlation power analysis (CPA) is a specific form of DPA where the Hamming-weight and the correlation coefficient are employed. In this paper we investigate the intrinsic vulnerability of the individual operations that are targeted in DPA attacks. We find that under the typical circumstances, there is a difference in resistance to the attack between the operations. We then provide a precise definition of CPA resistance and capture it in a simple yet effective metric to rank operations. The metric is validated with both simulations and experiments on actual hardware.

1 Introduction

Since the well-known work of Kocher *et al.* [7] and the research following [1, 2, 3, 8, 11, 12, 15], side-channel attacks and particularly Differential Power Analysis (DPA) have become a major security concern for the implementation of cryptographic algorithms on small devices such as smartcards. The side-channel exploited in DPA attacks is the power consumption of a cryptographic device that usually reveals some information about the data being processed. Unlike traditional cryptanalysis, a DPA attack targets a small part of the key at a time. This is possible because the power consumption of a cryptographic device at a point in time usually depends on only a few bits of the processed data.

Correlation power analysis (CPA) [3], as a specific form of DPA attack, employs the Hamming-weight model and the correlation coefficient. In this attack, the power consumption of the device is assumed to be linked to the Hamming-weight of the

Eindhoven University of Technology, Den Dolech 2, 5612 AZ, Eindhoven, the Netherlands.
Corresponding author e-mail: j.pan@tue.nl.

* This work is funded by Sentinels-project PinpasJC TIF.6687.

Please use the following format when citing this chapter:

Pan, J., den Hartog, J.I. and de Vink, E.P., 2008, in IFIP International Federation for Information Processing, Volume 278; *Proceedings of the IFIP TC 11 23rd International Information Security Conference*; Sushil Jajodia, Pierangela Samarati, Stelvio Cimato; (Boston: Springer), pp. 429–443.

data. By looking at the correlation between the Hamming-weight of the predicted values and the actual power consumption, the hypothetical key values and the actual key of the device are compared.

In this paper, we study the resistance to CPA by examining the individual operations executed on the cryptographic device. The resistance of fundamental operations in the algorithm determines the basic resistance of the algorithm as a whole. Knowing which operation is the weakest, and how likely a CPA attack on this location is to succeed given a certain level of noise in the measurements, is an important starting point in defending the implementation of a cryptographic algorithm.

Our analysis of commonly used operations in smartcards indeed shows that there are differences in the success rate of CPA attacks (assuming there is some noise involved in the measurement of the power consumption, which is in practice always the case). We demonstrate this by simulated attacks and discuss the underlying statistics. The main goal of this paper is to provide an easy to use yet effective method for ranking operations based on their resistance to CPA attacks.

After formally defining the CPA resistance of operations, we introduce a metric which captures this resistance. The metric is simple to calculate as it is purely based on the correlation values for the different key candidates, using the operation and an estimated noise level of the target device. We show why it is reasonable to build our metric on these values and subsequently validate the metric. The validation is done for four operations with simulated attacks as well as experiments based on physical measurements in practice and then comparing the results with the ranking obtained from the metric. The validation shows that the metric can capture the CPA resistance of the operations on the device.

Prouff [13] investigated the problem of DPA vulnerability of S-boxes from a cryptographic point of view and defined the notion of a 'transparency order' of an S-box, meant to capture its resistance to a particular DPA attack [2]. The conclusion of [13], that some of the very properties which cryptographically enhance operations, weaken them on the other hand to power analysis, corresponds to our general observation (a point also made in [6]). Compared to the approach in [13], we define a metric that is simpler and more general in the type of operations that can be addressed. The notion of 'transparency order' is complex and requires rapidly increased computations regarding to the bit size. This is not really an issue for typical S-boxes, as cryptographic devices generally do not have the storage space to deal with large S-boxes, but it can become a practical problem for other types of operations. Individual operations were analyzed in [10] for DPA resistance as well, with both simulated and physical means, but not compared with respect to a metric. In the framework presented in [15], our approach fits in the class of strong implementation with an adequate leakage model and sufficient many queries.

The paper is organized as follows. Section 2 starts with a description of the simulated CPA attacks. Sections 3 and 4 demonstrate the simulation on some examples where noise is ignored and regarded, respectively. The essentials are then analyzed in Section 5, where a metric for ranking operations regarding to their resistance to CPA attacks is proposed and exampled. In Section 6, experimental results are shown validating the ranking given by our metric. The last section provides conclusion.

2 CPA Simulation

A comprehensive description of CPA simulation can be found in [11]. We here summarize the general technique with emphasis to the characteristics of our experiment.

2.1 Modeling of Power Consumption

For the modeling of the power consumption signals, we employ the decomposition pattern from [11] as shown below,

$$P_{total} = P_{data} + P_{op} + P_{noise} + P_{const} \,,$$

where the total power consumption P_{total} at a single point in time can be decomposed into four disjoint components: the data-dependent consumption P_{data}, the operation-dependent consumption P_{op}, the electronic noise P_{noise} and the constant component P_{const}. The P_{data}, P_{op} and P_{noise} are the most important. The attacker can learn about confidential information by analyzing P_{data} and P_{op}. Electronic noise reflects the fluctuation that occurs when a fixed measurement is repeated. The bigger P_{noise} is, the more difficult the analysis is. The electronic noise in most cryptographic devices can be assumed to have a Gaussian distribution (see e.g. [9, 12]). In the presence of P_{const}, the expected value of P_{noise} equals zero. The standard deviation is, of course, specific to a device. We thus denote that $P_{noise} \sim \mathcal{N}(0, \sigma)$. The constant component P_{const} occurs independently of the operation performed and the data processed, and is therefore not relevant to CPA attacks.

2.2 The Attack Strategy

Let f denote the operation under attack and let $f(d,k)$ be the output of performing f on input d and key k. Input d can in general be calculated by the attacker based on the input to the device. The key material k is often a small portion of the secret key of the device.

In an CPA attack one can distinguish three phases – measurement, prediction, and analysis. In the first phase, the power consumption of a device is physically measured while the device performs cryptographic operations. In second phase, we predict the power consumption P_{data} for hypothetical key values, by constructing the output $f(d,k)$ for chosen d. In the analysis phase, the predicted power consumption values are compared with the measurements. The result determines which key guess used for power prediction can be a candidate for the key of the device. In our work, the measurements in the first phase is simulated based on the power model in Section 2.1. This implies we are supposed to know the key of the device in this phase, so that given an operation and its input message, the output can be computed based on the key. We will next present the attack strategy in more details.

Phase 1: measurement. We compute the output $f(d,k)$ for different input d using the key k from the device. For this purpose, we generate an input vector $\mathbf{d} = (d_1, d_2, \ldots, d_m)'$ such that $\mathbf{d}$ includes all possible values for d. This allows us to obtain maximal information about the operation and, subsequently, about the key. The computation results in a vector of output values $\mathbf{v} = (v_1, v_2, \ldots, v_m)'$. They are then mapped to power consumption values $\mathbf{h} = (h_1, h_2, \ldots, h_m)'$ using the Hamming-weight power model, which projects a value X to the number of bit set in it, here referred to as $HW(X)$. To model the P_{noise} while each value in $\mathbf{v}$ is computed on the device, we use a vector of noise values $\mathbf{p} = (p_1, p_2, \ldots, p_m)'$ sampled from normal distribution $\mathcal{N}(0, \sigma)$. Since we perform the analysis for specific operation individually, P_{op} is constant for each measurement and is thus captured by P_{const}. As stated before, component P_{const} is not relevant in determining the correct key value. Hence, by omitting P_{op} and P_{const} from our simulation, the power consumption of the device at the point in time when an output value v_i is handled, is modeled as $t_i = HW(f(d_i,k)) + p_i$, yielding a vector of simulated power consumption values $\mathbf{t} = (t_1, t_2, \ldots, t_m)'$.

Phase 2: prediction. In this phase, we compute $f(d_i, k_j)$ with the input vector $\mathbf{d}$ from Phase 1 and a key hypotheses vector $\mathbf{k} = (k_1, k_2, \ldots, k_n)$ containing all possible choices for k. The simulation of P_{data} when $f(d_i, k_j)$ is processed is similar to that in Phase 1, however, it now needs to be done for each $k_j \in \mathbf{k}$. This leads to a matrix $\mathbf{H}$ of power consumption values, where $h_{i,j} = HW(f(d_i, k_j))$. Because P_{data} is the only relevant power component for determining the key in a CPA attack, the matrix $\mathbf{H}$ is then the result of this phase. Since $\mathbf{k}$ contains all possible choices for k, the key of the device is then among $\mathbf{k}$. We refer to the index of this element as ck and the key of the device as k_{ck}. Column $\mathbf{h}_{ck}$ of $\mathbf{H}$ is correspondingly derived based on k_{ck}.

Phase 3: analysis. After having obtained the simulated power consumption data and the predicted power consumption data, we next compare them and determine the correct key value. The comparison is based on the correlation coefficient, which is commonly used to express the linear relationship of two random variables, defined as:

$$CC(X,Y) = \frac{Cov(X,Y)}{\sqrt{Var(X) \cdot Var(Y)}}.$$

Based on N samples for X and Y each, the value of $Cov(X,Y)$, $Var(X)$ and $CC(X,Y)$ can typically be assessed by the following estimators, respectively:

$$W(\mathbf{x},\mathbf{y}) = \frac{1}{N-1} \cdot \sum_{i=1}^{N} (x_i - \bar{x}) \cdot (y_i - \bar{y})$$

$$S^2(\mathbf{x}) = \frac{1}{N-1} \cdot \sum_{i=1}^{N} (x_i - \bar{x})^2$$

$$R(\mathbf{x},\mathbf{y}) = \frac{\sum_{i=1}^{N} (x_i - \bar{x}) \cdot (y_i - \bar{y})}{\sqrt{\sum_{i=1}^{N} (x_i - \bar{x})^2 \cdot \sum_{i=1}^{N} (y_i - \bar{y})^2}}$$

The correlation between **t** and each column of **H** is estimated by R, resulting in a vector $\mathbf{r} = (r_1, r_2, \ldots, r_n)$, where r_j compares the j-th column of **H** to **t**. Recall that column $\mathbf{h}_{ck}$ has been processed with the key hypothesis k_{ck}, which has also been used to simulate **t**. Therefore, column $\mathbf{h}_{ck}$ and **t** are assumed to be strongly related and the corresponding correlate coefficient r_{ck} is the highest in **r**. Other values of **r** are expected to be lower because the other columns of **H** and **t** are less correlated. Following this line of reasoning, the index of the correct key hypothesis ck is revealed.

A minor point suppressed in the sequel is the following. If the power consumption increases with the Hamming-weight, k_{ck} has a positive correlation coefficient; otherwise it has a negative correlation coefficient. The linear dependency is determined by specific cryptographic device, which, if is unknown beforehand to the attacker, a brute-force analysis needs to be applied. Therefore, we consider both positive and negative correlation peaks as possible candidates. Consequently, the absolute values of the correlation coefficients $(|r_1|, |r_2|, \ldots, |r_n|)$ are taken as references for the analysis, instead of the actual values. Some wrong key hypotheses cause what are often referred to as 'ghost peaks' in context of CPA attacks. The presence of ghost peaks typically requires additional brute-force methods to identify the correct key; and the cost increases exponentially on the number of ghost peaks. Therefore, we say that the more ghost peaks there are, the more resistant an operation is to CPA attacks.

2.3 Demonstration

In order to demonstrate the attack simulation, we take as examples four operations that are typically targeted in DPA attacks for software implementations of AES [4], TEA [16] and Edon [5]. The operations are: exclusive-or, modular addition, modular multiplication, and AES AddRoundKey plus SubBytes. In this paper, we refer to them as operations `XOR`, `ADD`, `MUL`, and `AES`, respectively. To achieve a fair comparison between the operations, they are all carried out with 8-bit data.

A note for `MUL` (see [5]) is that to avoid multiplications by zero, the inputs are mapped from $\mathbb{Z}_{255}$ to $\mathbb{Z}^*_{256}$ by a function g and the output is projected from $\mathbb{Z}^*_{256}$ back to $\mathbb{Z}_{255}$ by the inverted function g' after modular multiplication. The f-function is then: $f(d,k) = g'(g(d) \times g(k) \bmod 257)$.

3 Idealized Simulation

This section provides examples of CPA attacks for the idealized case, where the electronic noise component P_{noise} is omitted in the simulation and only the data-dependent component P_{data} is taken into account in the measurements. Clearly, this situation never occurs in practice. However, it is useful for better understanding the dependency between the processed data and the power consumption of the device. Technically, column $\mathbf{h}_{ck}$ of $\mathbf{H}$ and vector $\mathbf{t}$ now contain the same values, which results in the maximum correlation coefficient value 1 for r_{ck} for all operations.

We have performed this simulated attacks on every operation. The resulting correlation coefficients are plotted in Fig. 1. Note that for operations that are bijective, which is the case for our examples, the frequency distribution of the correlation coefficients is subject to the operation only, independently from the choice of the correct key. Based on the results in Fig. 1, we will next analyze the characteristics of the operations individually.

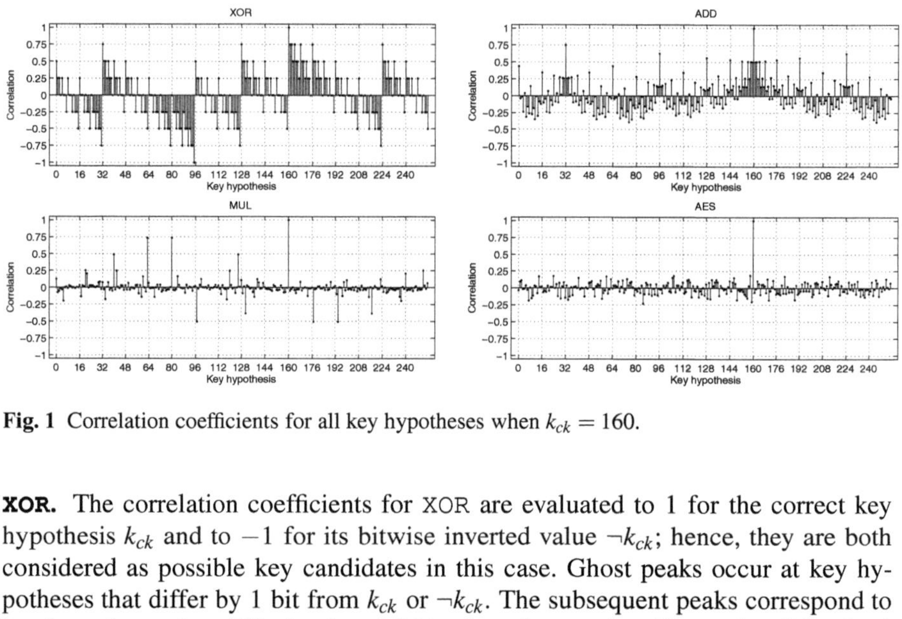

Fig. 1 Correlation coefficients for all key hypotheses when $k_{ck} = 160$.

XOR. The correlation coefficients for XOR are evaluated to 1 for the correct key hypothesis k_{ck} and to -1 for its bitwise inverted value $\neg k_{ck}$; hence, they are both considered as possible key candidates in this case. Ghost peaks occur at key hypotheses that differ by 1 bit from k_{ck} or $\neg k_{ck}$. The subsequent peaks correspond to key hypotheses that differ by 2 and 3 bits from k_{ck} or $\neg k_{ck}$. Those that differ by 4 bits from $\neg k_{ck}$ are not correlated and hence lead to zero correlation.

ADD. Operation ADD is similar to XOR except for the bit carry propagation. The wrong key hypotheses that cause ghost peaks can be ranked as: $k_{ck} \pm 2^7$, $k_{ck} \pm 2^6, \ldots,$ $k_{ck} \pm 2^0$, $k_{ck} \pm 2^7 \pm 2^6$, $k_{ck} \pm 2^7 \pm 2^5$, ..., $k_{ck} \pm 2^7 \pm 2^0$, ... For instance, the output of $f(d, k_{ck} \pm 2^7)$ differs by one bit from $f(d, k_{ck})$ for any input d; and $f(d, k_{ck} \pm 2^6)$ differs from $f(d, k_{ck})$ for $2^8/2$ values by one bit, for $2^8/4$ values by zero bit and for $2^8/4$ values by two bits.

MUL. A few wrong key hypotheses show ghost peaks here. Employing the method in [10], we summarize the correlated key hypotheses in four sequences $K_{1,i}$, $K_{2,i}$, $K_{3,i}$ and $K_{4,i}$ as follows:

$$K_{1,i} = g'(2^i \cdot g(k_{ck}) \bmod 257)\ ;\ K_{2,i} = g'(257 - g(K_{1,i}))\ ;$$
$$K_{3,0} = k_{ck}\ ,\ K_{3,i+1} = g'(\tfrac{g(K_{3,i})}{2}) \text{ for } g(K_{3,i}) \text{ even },$$
$$K_{3,i+1} = g'(\tfrac{257-g(K_{3,i})}{2}) \text{ for } g(K_{3,i}) \text{ odd };\ K_{4,i} = g'(257 - g(K_{3,i}))\ ,$$

where $i = 0, 1, \ldots, 8$. To give an example, the key hypotheses that cause the peaks in Fig. 1 are: $k_{ck} = 160$; $K_{1,i} = \{160, 63, 126, 252, \ldots\}$; $K_{2,i} = \{97, 194, 131, 5, \ldots\}$; $K_{3,i} = \{160, 80, 40, 20, \ldots\}$; and $K_{4,i} = \{97, 177, 217, 237, \ldots\}$.

AES. In contrary to the other operations, no ghost peak occurs for AES. This is due to the fact that the AES S-box has been well chosen regarding to the non-linearity criterion. Although it is an advantage to resist linear cryptanalysis, this optimization allows CPA attacks to succeed easily.

4 Simulation with Noise

We now discuss more realistic DPA attacks where electronic noise is involved. A notion for the failure of CPA attacks is introduced, and experiments using the simulated CPA attacks based on this notion are presented.

Again, CPA selects possible key candidates according to the absolute values of the obtained correlation coefficients. A straightforward CPA chooses only the most significant correlation peak as the candidate. Due to the noise, the highest peak may not exactly occur at the correct key hypothesis and thus a wrong candidate could be returned. In this case, the attack is deemed to be failed. Intuitively, an attack can easily fail this way when the noise is high. As stated in Section 2.1, the influence of the electronic noise on the measurement is typically characterized by its standard deviation σ. The greater σ is, the higher P_{noise} is. Given the standard deviation σ for the noise P_{noise}, we refer to the resulting correlation coefficients based on P_{noise} as $(r_1^\sigma, r_2^\sigma, \ldots, r_n^\sigma)$. Accordingly, the correlation values obtained in the idealized case (see Section 3) are denoted as $(r_1^0, r_2^0, \ldots, r_n^0)$. Using these notations, we define the difference between the absolute correlation values for k_{ck} and k_j, for some σ, as follows:

$$\delta_j^\sigma = |r_{ck}^\sigma| - |r_j^\sigma|\ . \tag{1}$$

We introduce notion $\mathscr{F}(\sigma)$ for the event that CPA fails when the standard deviation of noise equals σ. Notion $\mathscr{F}(\sigma)$ can then be formulated as a set of boolean outcomes that if there is any ghost peaks higher than the peak at k_{ck}:

$$\mathscr{F}(\sigma) = \{\, \delta_j^\sigma < 0 \mid 1 \le j \le n \,\}\ .$$

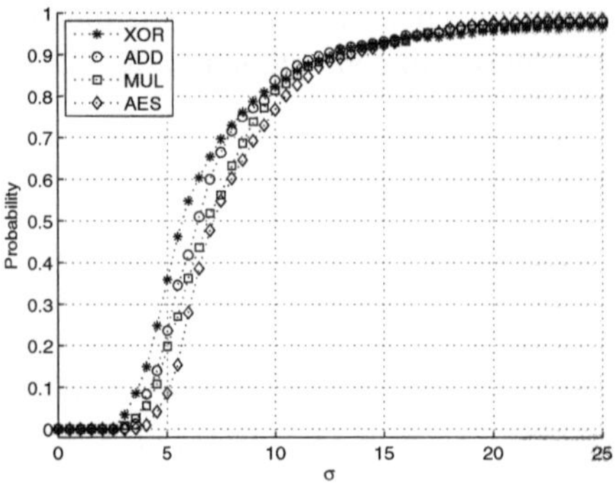

Fig. 2 *Prob*($\mathscr{F}(\sigma)$) for all operations.

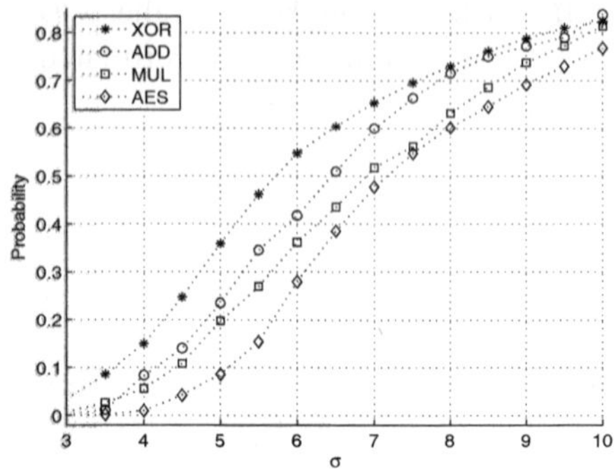

Fig. 3 A zoom of Fig. 2.

Next, we perform simulated CPA attacks according to the strategy presented in Section 2. In contrast to the idealized case, the noise values in vector $\mathbf{p}$ are now added to the power consumption values in $\mathbf{t}$. To model different levels of electronic noise, we generate a set of possible values $\{0.5, 1, 1.5, \ldots, 13\}$ for σ. In order to deliver a promising assessment for the probability that an attack fails, which is referred to as *Prob*($\mathscr{F}(\sigma)$), we have repeated each experiment for 500 times[2] with the same input d and k and different values for p. The number of times that the attacks fail is recorded for each choice of σ. Dividing these numbers individually by 500 yields the probabilities *Prob*($\mathscr{F}(\sigma)$) for each value of σ.

The above experiment has been performed to all the operations and the results are plotted in Fig. 2. The overall rising of the probabilities agrees that the attacks fails more often for all the cases as the noise is turned up. As the figure presents, after an initial leveling down at 0%, the failure rates start growing for all the cases. The increase is the most rapid for XOR. When $\sigma = 4$, for instance, the probability for XOR is close to twice as much as that for ADD and almost three times as much as that for MUL; and, it exceeds the one for AES by a ratio of 1.5 to 0. The ranking of the operations by their failure probabilities stays this way until σ hits 10. After that, they all converge to 1. As can be seen, in majority of the cases, the failure rates remain in the order: XOR > ADD > MUL > AES, which is, hence, taken as the ranking of the operations for the resistance to CPA attacks in our experiment.

5 A Metric for Resistance to CPA attacks

Above, we have shown the results of CPA simulation for both the noise-free case and the noise-involved case. In this section, we analyze the probability of CPA failure in Section 4 and show it primarily depends on the correlation values obtained in the idealized case in Section 3. We then integrate the results from both sections

[2] The number 500 is chosen as a trade-off of precision and cost of experiment.

and propose a metric for evaluating the resistance of an operation to CPA attacks, based on correlation values in the idealized simulation. Additionally, we show by examples how this metric can be used to rank operations.

5.1 Reasoning about Prob($\delta_j^\sigma < 0$)

As previously assumed, a CPA attack fails when at least one ghost peak is higher than the resulting correlation by the correct key hypothesis. The difference δ_j^σ defined in (1) is modeled as in (2). Random variables H_j and P_{noise}^σ are used to denote respectively the hypothetical power consumption values in column j of $\mathbf{H}$ and the simulated noise values in $\mathbf{p}$ with a standard deviation of σ.

$$\begin{aligned}\delta_j^\sigma &= |CC(H_{ck}, H_{ck} + P_{noise}^\sigma)| - |CC(H_j, H_{ck} + P_{noise}^\sigma)| \\ &= \frac{1}{\sqrt{Var(H_{ck} + P_{noise}^\sigma)}} \cdot \Big(\sqrt{Var(H_{ck})} \cdot \big(|CC(H_{ck}, H_{ck})| - |CC(H_j, H_{ck})| \big) \\ &\qquad + \big(\frac{\pm|Cov(H_{ck}, P_{noise}^\sigma)|}{\sqrt{Var(H_{ck})}} - \frac{\pm|Cov(H_j, P_{noise}^\sigma)|}{\sqrt{Var(H_j)}} \big) \Big) \\ &\approx \frac{1}{\sqrt{S^2(\mathbf{h}_{ck}) + \sigma^2}} \cdot \Big(\sqrt{S^2(\mathbf{h}_{ck})} \cdot (1 - |r_j^0|) + \big(\frac{\pm|W(\mathbf{h}_{ck}, \mathbf{p})| \mp |W(\mathbf{h}_j, \mathbf{p})|}{\sqrt{S^2(\mathbf{h}_{ck})}} \big) \Big).\end{aligned} \tag{2}$$

One assumption underlying the deduction in (2) is that the attacked operation is assumed to be balanced [13], which is the case for most of the operations used in cryptographic algorithms. So that, given uniformly distributed random input and key, the output of the operation is also uniformly distributed. This assumption yields that the variances of the Hamming-weight of the outputs for different key hypotheses are constant when all input values are used, i.e., $Var(H_i) = Var(H_j)$ for any $1 \le i, j \le n$.

In Eq. (2), the variables are in the end substituted by their estimators. The exact value for $Prob(\delta_j^\sigma < 0)$ is difficult to derive analytically based on this model, requiring statistical methods out of the scope of this paper. However, we have discovered some interesting properties for the probability $Prob(\delta_j^\sigma < 0)$ based on (2). Since $Var(H_{ck})$ is constant, $S^2(\mathbf{h}_{ck})$ tends to constant when all possible input values are used. Because P_{noise}^σ and H_j are independent, by the Central Limit Theorem [14], when all possible values for input are used, the distribution of $W(\mathbf{h}_j, \mathbf{p})$ is approximately normal with expectation zero and some variance $Var[W(\mathbf{h}_j, \mathbf{p})]$, which increases on σ. Therefore, considering two arbitrary key hypotheses k_i and k_j, we can assume that $W(\mathbf{h}_i, \mathbf{p})$ and $W(\mathbf{h}_j, \mathbf{p})$ have nearly the same distribution for a fixed σ. Consequently, we can assume that when all inputs are used, δ_j^σ can be seen as a function of $|r_j^0|$. Hence, the probability $Prob(\delta_j^\sigma < 0)$ depends only on $|r_j^0|$ for some fixed σ and the relation of $Prob(\delta_j^\sigma < 0)$ between different key hypothesis can be approximated by their relation for $|r_j^0|$. As shown in (3), for two key hypotheses k_i and k_j where $i \neq j$, their probabilities of resulting a higher correlation peak than that by k_{ck}, are approximately equal if $|r_i^0| = |r_j^0|$ and have the same relation as $|r_i^0|$ and $|r_j^0|$ if otherwise. Note that when $|r_i^0|$ is smaller than but very close to $|r_j^0|$, the probability $Prob(\delta_i^\sigma < 0)$ can be approximately equal to and not necessarily smaller than $Prob(\delta_j^\sigma < 0)$.

$$\begin{aligned} |r_i^0| = |r_j^0| &\Longrightarrow Prob(\delta_i^\sigma < 0) \approx Prob(\delta_j^\sigma < 0) \\ |r_i^0| < |r_j^0| &\Longrightarrow Prob(\delta_i^\sigma < 0) < Prob(\delta_j^\sigma < 0)\,. \end{aligned} \tag{3}$$

When two balanced operations op_1 and op_2, both processing with b-bit data, are considered, we have that $Var(H_i^{op_1}) = Var(H_j^{op_2}) = b/4$ for any i and j, when all input values are used. As P_{noise}^σ is also independent of the operation, similar arguments as previously regarding $W(\mathbf{h}_j, \mathbf{p})$ can also be applied here. Hence, we can conclude that the properties in (3) hold independently of operations as long as they are carried out with data of the same sized.

5.2 Assessing Prob($\delta_j^\sigma < 0$) and Prob($\mathscr{F}(\sigma)$)

Based on the relation between $|r_j^0|$ and $Prob(\delta_j^\sigma < 0)$ as in (3), we define a function $h(r,\sigma)$ which takes non-negative inputs r and σ, and returns the probability that a key hypothesis with correlation coefficient $\pm r$ in the noise-free simulation, becomes the key candidate in an attack when the standard deviation of noise equals σ. Thus, the probability $Prob(\delta_j^\sigma < 0)$ can be expressed as $h(|r_j^0|, \sigma)$.

We estimate the function $h(r,\sigma)$ by applying the CPA simulation performed in Section 4 on the four demonstrated operations with 500 repetitions each. Unlike the previous experiment, we have now recorded the number of times that each hypothesis k_j results in a negative δ_j^σ, i.e. when the absolute value of the correlation by k_j is higher than that by k_{ck}, for $\sigma = 0.5, 1, 1.5, \ldots, 13$. The ratios of these numbers to 500 are then the estimation of $h(r,\sigma)$. Note that this assessment for $h(r,\sigma)$ covers only a part of the possible values for r, which however, as we will show later, is sufficient to capture the characteristics of $h(r,\sigma)$.

The results of this experiment agrees with our analyzed properties about relations between r and $h(r,\sigma)$ as in (3). Due to the lack of space, we do not show the result for each individual experiment. In order to give a clear illustration of $h(r,\sigma)$, we plot the averaged results in Fig. 4 for a few representative values of r. Figure 5 gives an example when $\sigma = 7$, which is the column of Fig. 4 where $\sigma = 7$. The plottings indicate that $h(r,\sigma)$ monotonically increases on σ for every r, and grows rapidly on r in most of the cases for σ.

We now discuss how to reason about $Prob(\mathscr{F}^\sigma)$ using $h(r,\sigma)$. An assessment of $Prob(\mathscr{F}^\sigma)$ can be derived as in (4), where every step of approximation is la-

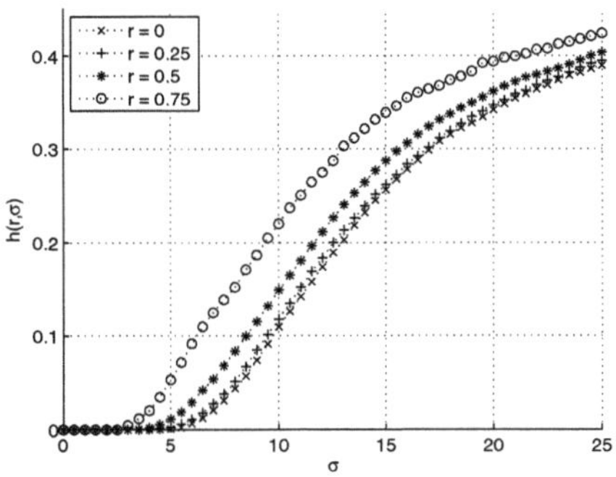

Fig. 4 Function $h(r,\sigma)$.

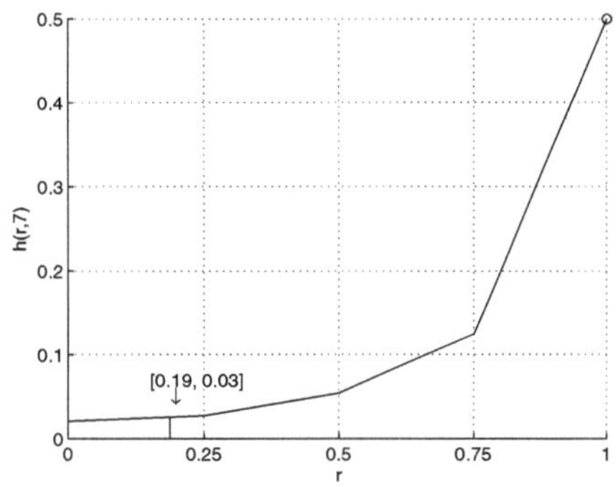

Fig. 5 Function $h(7,\sigma)$.

beled with the amount of errors that this approximation causes. That is, for $X \overset{\varepsilon}{\approx} Y$, $\varepsilon = Y - X$. Therefore, a positive ε represents overestimating and a negative one represents underestimating. We will later investigate into the precision of each individual and the overall approximations.

$$\begin{aligned} Prob(\mathscr{F}^{\sigma}) &= Prob(\{\,\delta_j^{\sigma} < 0 \mid 1 \le j \le n\}) \\ &\overset{\varepsilon_1}{\approx} \sum_{j=1}^{n} Prob(\delta_j^{\sigma} < 0) \;=\; \sum_{j=1}^{n} h(|r_j^0|,\sigma) \\ &\overset{\varepsilon_2}{\approx} \sum_{j=1}^{n} h(|r_j^0|,\sigma) \qquad \text{for } 1 > |r_j^0| \ge \rho \\ &\overset{\varepsilon_3}{\approx} \frac{h(1,\sigma)+h(\rho,\sigma)}{2} \cdot \#\{\,j \mid 1 > |r_j^0| > \rho\,\}\,. \end{aligned} \tag{4}$$

For ε_1, outcomes $\{\delta_j^{\sigma} < 0\}$ for all j are not mutually exclusive. Hence, this error is related to the dependency between the outcomes, which is unknown. However, we can give a translation of ε_1 in the context of CPA attacks. Let us consider a stronger attacker who always takes the highest N correlation peaks from an attack, and later determines the correct key by brute-force methods in the order of the height of the peaks. In this case, the expected maximum number of trials that the attacker performs for each operation under attack before he finds the correct key hypothesis (or gives up) can be computed by $E[min(\#\{\,j \mid \delta_j^{\sigma} < 0\},N)]$. Intuitively, the attacker can tolerate N wrong key candidates at maximum and a CPA attack can succeed if $|r_{ck}^{\sigma}|$ is ranked in the top N correlation peaks. Using this notation, the probability $Prob(\{\delta_j^{\sigma} < 0\})$, on the left hand side of ε_1, is equal to $E[min(\#\{\,j \mid \delta_j^{\sigma} < 0\},1)]$ and can be interpreted as the expectation of the number of trials that an attacker performs on brute-force, when he takes only one key candidate in an attack. On the other hand, the sum of $Prob(\delta_j^{\sigma} < 0)$ equals, by definition, the expectation of the total number of wrong candidates a CPA attack returns, i.e. $E[\#\{\,j \mid \delta_j^{\sigma} < 0\}]$, which is no less than $E[min(\#\{\,j \mid \delta_j^{\sigma} < 0\},1)]$. Therefore, ε_1 is non-negative and increases

Table 1 The value of ρ for selected σ.

σ	–2.5	3	3.5	4	4.5	5	5.5	6	6.5	7	8	9	10	11	12	13–
ρ	$\frac{13}{16}$	$\frac{12}{16}$	$\frac{11}{16}$	$\frac{8}{16}$	$\frac{7}{16}$	$\frac{6}{16}$	$\frac{11}{32}$	$\frac{5}{16}$	$\frac{4}{16}$	$\frac{3}{16}$	$\frac{5}{32}$	$\frac{2}{16}$	$\frac{1}{32}$	$\frac{1}{64}$	$\frac{1}{128}$	0

on σ. For example, when σ is small, noise influences less and the correlation peak for the correct key hypothesis is likely to be the highest so that ε_1 is small; and when σ is big, noise influences more and $|r^{\sigma}_{ck}|$ is unlikely to be the highest resulting a big ε_1.

The second estimation ignores the case when r is smaller than some threshold ρ. Hence, $\varepsilon_2 = -\sum_{j=1}^{n} h(|r^0_j|, \sigma) \leq 0$, for $r < \rho$. Figure 5 shows an example when $\rho = 0.19$. Although $h(r, \sigma)$ can be small when r is small, the correlation values resulted from an attack can very likely be close to zero, referring to the demonstrations in Fig. 1. Therefore, the sum of $h(r, \sigma)$ for $r < \rho$ is not necessarily small. Generally speaking, ε_2 decreases on σ and ρ for all operations. When σ grows, $h(r, \sigma)$ rises for every r and the sum of $h(r, \sigma)$ increases for $r < \rho$; when ρ increases more cases for r will be ignored by this approximation.

By making the third approximation in (4), we are actually assuming that r is equally distributed for $r \geq \rho$. This may in practice not be the case for an operation. The value of ε_3 depends on the distribution of r for $r \geq \rho$, which is subject to the operation. Taking Fig. 5 as an example, at interval $r = [\rho, 1)$, ε_3 is positive if the distribution of r is denser in the area close to ρ and is negative if the distribution of r is denser in the area close to 1. The amount ε_3 approaches zero when σ increases, whereas its relation to ρ requires more details on the distribution of r.

In summary of the previous analysis, ε_1 is non-negative and increases on σ, whereas ε_2 is non-positive and decreases on σ and ρ, somehow compensating ε_1. Amount of ε_3 is uncertain, depending on specific operations. Therefore, we can claim that our approximation for $Prob(\mathscr{F}^{\sigma})$ in (4) is not too rough and can be very close to the true value if the threshold ρ is well chosen. Deriving a function for ρ based on σ, however, requires information that is unknown to us, such as the distribution of correlation coefficient for a random operation and the exact value for $h(r, \sigma)$. Nonetheless, the values for ρ can be assessed based on our experimental results for $h(r, \sigma)$ and $Prob(\mathscr{F}^{\sigma})$ (see Section 4). The approximated ρ for selected values of σ is shown in Table 1.

5.3 A Metric for CPA Resistance

Previous section shows that given an estimated standard deviation σ for noise P_{noise}, one can find a value for ρ in Table 1 such that $Prob(\mathscr{F}(\sigma))$ can be assessed using (4). The resulting formula indicates that when σ and ρ are fixed, the probability that a CPA fails is proportional to the number of correlation peaks that are smaller

Table 2 Metrics for the operations for selected values of σ.

σ	–2.5	3	3.5	4	4.5	5	5.5	6	6.5	7	8	9	10	11	12	13–
XOR	0	16	16	72	72	72	72	72	184	184	184	184	184	184	184	254
ADD	0	1	1	15	17	19	27	31	71	99	125	157	237	247	255	255
MUL	0	0	2	5	7	9	9	9	11	17	21	29	115	177	209	255
AES	0	0	0	0	0	0	0	0	0	4	17	35	188	223	241	255

than 1 and higher than or equal to ρ in the results of the idealized attack simulation. Intuitively, the more high correlation peaks an operation results in from a noise-free CPA attack, the more wrong key hypotheses are correlated to the correct one and the more likely the real CPA attack on this operation, where the noise fluctuates the power consumption measurements, is going to fail.

Therefore, we can deliver a metric for the resistance of an operation to CPA attack:

Definition 1. Given correlation coefficient values $\mathbf{r}^0 = (r_1^0, r_2^0, \ldots, r_n^0)$ obtained from the idealized CPA simulation on an operation, a metric for its resistance to CPA attacks where the electronic noise has a standard deviation approximately equal to σ, is the number of elements in $\mathbf{r}^0$ whose absolute values fall into interval $[\rho, 1)$, i.e.,

$$\#\{j \mid 1 > |r_j^0| \geq \rho, 1 \leq j \leq n\},$$

where, knowing σ, the threshold ρ can be obtained from Table 1.

Using Definition 1, we have calculated the metrics in Table 2 for the operations used in demonstration. It shows that the ranking of the failure rates for the operations previously obtained by attack simulations (see Section 4) is now well captured by the metrics of those operations in Table 2.

6 Validating the Metric

In this section, we discuss executing the exemplary operations on a Atmel AVR microcontroller with all switchable countermeasures off. Nowadays, most cryptographic devices available on the market come with countermeasures against side-channel analysis. Information leakage in the Atmel AVR microcontroller reports similarity to that in cryptographic devices such as smartcards, but with a customizable setting for the countermeasures. Hence, it is typically seen as a good representative for predicting the leakage of cryptographic devices in the worst scenario at an earlier stage.

Usually for a practical CPA, one needs to record the power consumption values for a large number of time samples during execution. Therefore, each input results in a power trace consisting of numerous power consumption values each of which corresponds to a single time sample. However, only the time sample at which the output of the attacked operation is processed is relevant to an CPA attack. We denote this point of time using τ. Hence, we firstly apply the CPA attack using the complete power traces for all input and then identify this concerned time sample τ based on the resulting correlation values. The power consumption values at τ then corresponds to the power consumption vector $\mathbf{t}$ in our simulation (see Section 2). Accordingly, the correlation values at τ are then captured in $\mathbf{r}$.

We have performed the attack for a number of traces (input). In general, the more resistant an operation is to CPA attacks, the more traces is needed to obtain a clear correlation peak. The resulting correlation values at τ are shown in Fig. 6. The correct key hypothesis is plotted in black. The plotting for XOR is vertically symmetric every key hypothesis and its bitwise inverted value report exactly negated correlation values. Although the correct key hypothesis always results in the highest correlation coefficient after about 250 traces, ghost peaks are still very significant. For ADD, only one ghost peak, which is caused by the key hypothesis $k_{ck} \pm 2^7$, remains very high after 400 traces. The results for MUL shows that the peak for k_{ck} becomes clear after about 250 traces, followed by a few of ghost peaks. In case of AES, the peak at k_{ck} stands out very obviously after only about 50 traces. The results show that the physical measurements from these experiments are in conformance with our previous simulation results, thereby validating the ranking and the metric of the operations in Section 5.

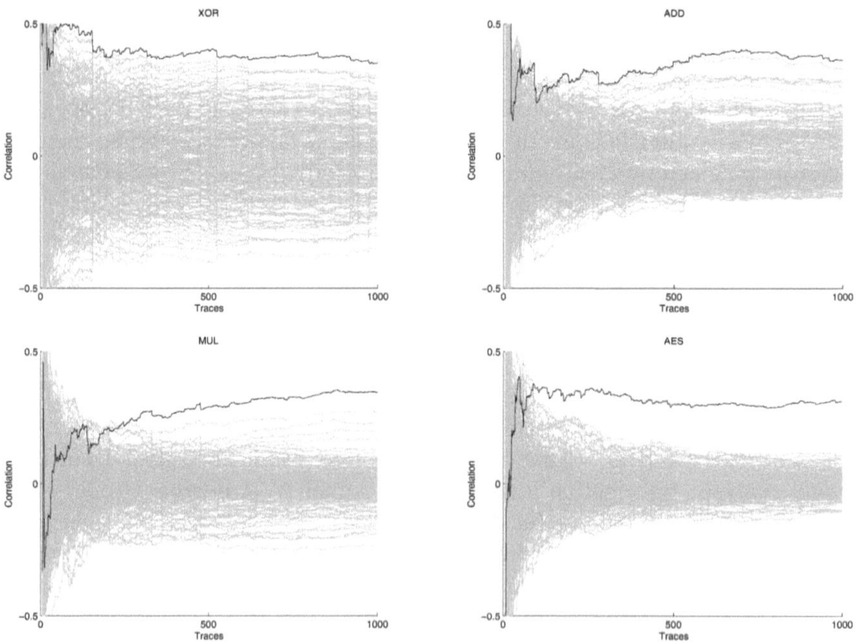

Fig. 6 The correlation values for different number of traces at τ.

7 Conclusion

In this paper, we analyze the resistance to CPA attacks for fix-sized primitive operations. By studying the results from simulated CPA attacks on a few operations that carry out 8-bit data, we provide a model for the resistance to CPA attacks. Based on this reasoning, we propose a convenient metric for measuring the resistance of an operation to the attacks and argue its validity. By demonstration, we show how this metric can be employed to rank operations with respect to their CPA resistance. Additionally, physical attacks are applied on the operations in practice on a Atmel AVR micro-controller and the results of agree well with the ranking metric proposed.

Acknowledgements We thank Jaap de Vos and Lex Schoonen for experimental support and stimulating interaction.

References

1. M.-L. Akkar, R. Bevan, P. Dischamp, and D. Moyart. Power analysis, what is now possible... In *ASIACRYPT*, pages 489–502. Springer, 2000.
2. R. Bevan and E. Knudsen. Ways to enhance differential power analysis. In *ICISC*, pages 327–342. Springer, 2002.
3. E. Brier, C. Clavier, and F. Olivier. Correlation power analysis with a leakage model. In *CHES*, pages 16–29. Springer, 2004.
4. J. Daemen and V. Rijmen. *The Design of Rijndael*. Springer-Verlag New York, Inc., Secaucus, NJ, USA, 2002.
5. D. Gligoroski. Stream cipher based on quasigroup string transformations in $\mathbb{Z}_p^*$. *Computing Research Repository (CoRR)*, cs.CR/0403043, 2004.
6. S. Guilley, P. Hoogvorst, and R. Pacalet. Differential power analysis model and some results. In *CARDIS*, pages 127–142. Kluwer, 2004.
7. P. Kocher, J. Jaffe, and B. Jun. Differential power analysis. In *CRYPTO*, pages 388–397. Springer, 1999.
8. T.-H. Le, J. Clediere, C. Serviere, and J.-L. Lacoume. A proposition for correlation power analysis enhancement. In *CHES*, pages 174–186. Springer, 2006.
9. T.-H. Le, J. Clediere, C. Serviere, and J.-L. Lacoume. How can signal processing benefit side channel attacks? *IEEE Workshop on Signal Processing Applications for Public Security and Forensics*, pages 1–7, April 2007.
10. K. Lemke, K. Schramm, and C. Paar. DPA on n-bit sized boolean and arithmetic operations and its application to IDEA, RC6, and the HMAC-construction. In M. Joye and J-J. Quisquater, editors, *CHES*, pages 205–219. Springer, 2004.
11. S. Mangard, E. Oswald, and T. Popp. *Power Analysis Attacks: Revealing the Secrets of Smart Cards*. Advances in Information Security. Springer, 2007.
12. T. Messerges, E. Dabbish, and R. Sloan. Examining smart-card security under the threat of power analysis attacks. *IEEE Trans. Computers*, 51(5):541–552, 2002.
13. E. Prouff. DPA attacks and S-boxes. In *FSE*, pages 424–441. Springer, 2005.
14. A. Siegel. *Statistics and data analysis: an introduction*. John Wiley & Sons,, 1988.
15. F.-X. Standaert, E. Peeters, C. Archambeau, and J.-J. Quisquater. Towards security limits in side-channel attacks. In *CHES*, pages 30–45. Springer, 2006.
16. D. Wheeler and R. Needham. TEA, a tiny encryption algorithm. In *FSE*, pages 363–366. Springer, 1994.

7 Conclusion

In this paper, [illegible]

YASIR: A Low-Latency, High-Integrity Security Retrofit for Legacy SCADA Systems

Patrick P. Tsang and Sean W. Smith

Abstract We construct a bump-in-the-wire (BITW) solution that retrofits security into time-critical communications over bandwidth-limited serial links between devices in legacy Supervisory Control And Data Acquisition (SCADA) systems, on which the proper operations of critical infrastructures such as the electric power grid rely. Previous BITW solutions do not provide the necessary security within timing constraints; the previous solution that does is not BITW. At a hardware cost comparable to existing solutions, our BITW solution provides sufficient security, and yet incurs minimal end-to-end communication latency.

1 Introduction

1.1 SCADA Systems

Supervisory Control And Data Acquisition (SCADA) systems are real-time process control systems that monitor and control local or geographically remote devices. They are widely used in industrial facilities and critical infrastructures such as electric power generation and distribution systems, oil and gas refineries and transportation systems, allowing operators to ensure their proper functioning.

Electric power utilities, for instance, were among the first to widely adopt remote monitoring and control systems. Their earliest SCADA systems provided simple monitoring through periodic sampling of analog data, but have evolved into more complex communication networks. In this paper, we focus on SCADA systems for electric power generation and distribution. However, our proposed solution and discussion are applicable to many other SCADA systems.

Patrick P. Tsang and Sean W. Smith
Department of Computer Science, Dartmouth College, Hanover, NH 03755, USA,
e-mail: {patrick, sws}@cs.dartmouth.edu

Please use the following format when citing this chapter:

Tsang, P.P. and Smith, S.W., 2008, in IFIP International Federation for Information Processing, Volume 278; *Proceedings of the IFIP TC 11 23rd International Information Security Conference*; Sushil Jajodia, Pierangela Samarati, Stelvio Cimato; (Boston: Springer), pp. 445–459.

Devices and Communications A SCADA system consists of *physical devices*, as well as *communication links* (we simply call them *links* from now on) that connect them together. Typical communications in a SCADA system include exchanging control and status information between master and slave devices. Master devices, most of which are PCs or *programmable logic controllers (PLCs)*, control the operation of slave devices; a slave device, e.g., a *remote terminal unit (RTU)*, can be a sensor, an actuator, or both. Sensors read status or measurement data of field equipments such as voltage and current, whereas actuators send out commands or analog set-points such as opening or closing a switch or a valve.

Most SCADA systems have traditionally used low-bandwidth links, e.g., radio, direct serial and leased lines, with typical baud rates from 9600 to 115200. They are known as *serial-based SCADA systems*. Communication protocols used in these systems are very compact—messages are short, and slave devices send information only when polled. Popular protocols include Modbus (`http://www.modbus.org/`) and DNP3 (`http://www.dnp.org`).

Security Trouble Many serial-based SCADA systems in operation today were deployed decades ago with availability and personnel safety as the primary concerns, rather than security. As with any complex systems not designed to withstand adversarial action, these systems are vulnerable to a variety of malicious attacks such as sniffing and tampering. The risks due to such a lack of security in these systems are ever increasing, as an initial protection of "security through obscurity" breaks down.

First, after initial dependence on proprietary elements, it is now common to build SCADA systems using commercial off-the-shelf (COTS) hardware and software that speak open communication protocols, the technical internals of which are often easily accessible. Second, many utilities have replaced, to various extent, their private networks by public ones such as the Internet. Their SCADA networks and corporate networks have also become highly inter-connected to achieve efficient information exchange—leading to increased risks of intentional or inadvertent exposure to the Internet. Finally, teams of sophisticated hackers are now employed by criminal organizations or terrorists to break into these systems.

Retrofitting Security Failures of critical infrastructures could lead to devastating consequences. As an example of cyber-attacks on critical infrastructures, in 2001, an Australian man hacked into a computerized sewage management system and dumped millions of liters of untreated waste into local parks and rivers [9]. It is therefore paramount to secure SCADA systems against malicious attacks. In the long run, existing insecure SCADA systems may eventually be replaced by newer ones built with better technologies and with security as a primary goal—we will gradually see devices that are computationally more powerful, links with higher bandwidths, as well as devices and protocols with built-in security, e.g., DNPSec [7] and IEC 61850 (`http://www.61850.com/`).

Nonetheless, for the next several decades (the expected lifetime of many SCADA equipments spans from 20 to 50 years), achieving security requires *non-intrusively retrofitting it* to existing insecure and legacy SCADA systems, as it is economically infeasible, if not technically impossible, to simply throw away the existing infras-

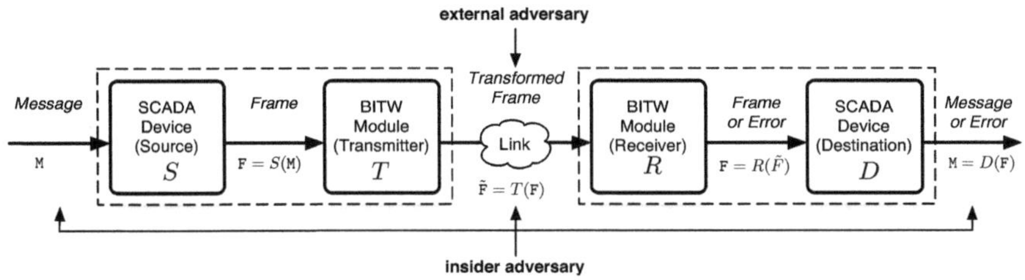

Fig. 1 System and attack model for "bump-in-the-wire" approach.

tructures overnight. In such an effort, several *"bump-in-the-wire" (BITW)* solutions have been developed. In a BITW solution, two hardware modules are inserted into the link connecting two communicating SCADA devices, one next to each of the device, as depicted in Figure 1. These modules transparently augment the necessary security through mechanisms such as encryption and authentication.

1.2 The Challenge

BITW solutions secure SCADA communications at the expense of incurring end-to-end communication delay, due to the processing and buffering in the BITW modules. Buffering can be prohibitively expensive in low-bandwidth links. For instance, a serial link at 9600 baud per second has a *byte time* (i.e., the time to send one byte of data) of roughly 1ms. If each of the two BITW modules buffers up a message of 20 bytes before processing it, then a timing overhead of 40ms is incurred, due to buffering alone. If the message has 250 bytes, the overhead becomes 0.5s.[1]

Such an overhead could be intolerable for serial-based SCADA systems that have timing constraints on communication latencies. For example, the exchange of event notification information for bus and transformer protection function between *Intelligent Electronic Devices (IEDs)* within a power substation must be accomplished within 10ms, and the maximum delivery time for information such as response to data poll and phasor measurements is up to 0.2s [5].

As we will see in Section 2 when we review some of the existing solutions, retrofitting *data privacy* to the communications in serial-based SCADA systems, even the time-critical ones, is a relatively trivial task; the real challenge lies in retrofitting *data authenticity and freshness* in a timely manner, as the straightforward application of conventional data authentication techniques does not provide the required timing guarantee: the BITW module at the receiving end of the communication must *"hold back"* the message, i.e., it must wait until the receipt of the entire message and its authentication information, before relaying the message to

[1] A typical SCADA message has a length of roughly 20 bytes. However, some SCADA protocols allow a maximum message-length of more than 250 bytes.

the destination SCADA device, if the message is indeed authentic and fresh. This incurs a latency dependent linearly on the length of the message being secured.

1.3 Our Contributions

We present *Yet Another SecurIty Retrofit*, or *YASIR*, which is a novel BITW solution for retrofitting security to time-critical communications in serial-based SCADA systems. To the authors' best knowledge, our solution is the first that achieves all of the following goals simultaneously:

- **High Security.** *YASIR* provides data authenticity and freshness, and optionally data privacy, against not only eavesdroppers but stronger adversaries such as insiders, at a security level of 80 bits.[2]
- **Low Latency.** *YASIR* incurs an overhead of at most 18 byte times, irrespective of the length of the message being authenticated, and can hence secure time-critical SCADA communications.
- **Comparable Cost.** *YASIR*'s BITW modules have hardware costs comparable to many existing solutions. Deploying *YASIR* is thus economically practical.
- **Standard and Patent-free Tools.** All cryptographic tools and techniques used in *YASIR*, such as AES-CTR and HMAC, are NIST-standardized and patent-free.

The rest of this paper is organized as follows. In Section 2, we review several existing BITW solutions. Section 3 covers SCADA preliminaries. Section 4 studies the threat model and security goals of BITW solutions. We give an overview to our solution in Section 5 and provide the details of its actual construction in Section 6. Section 7 concludes the paper. In the extended version of this paper [10], we evaluate *YASIR*'s security, performance and costs in depth. We also report on a micro-controller prototype of *YASIR*.

2 Existing Solutions

We do not consider encryption-only solutions as retrofitting only data privacy does not provide sufficient security. Also, since we are interested in non-intrusively retrofitting security into legacy SCADA communications, we do not consider non-BITW solutions, i.e. solutions that require replacing the link with one of a higher bandwidth, e.g., from RS-232 to Ethernet, and/or upgrading the (software or hardware of) the SCADA devices to allow for newer technologies such as IPSec [6].

Below, we review several existing BITW solutions, all of which fall short in some critical property: they don't provide data authenticity against realistic attacks, or they delay messages too long. Table 1 summarizes this picture.

---

[2] A security solution attains a security level of ℓ bits if brute-forcing a space of 2^ℓ possibilities is the most effective strategy for an adversary to break the solution's security.

Approach	Bump-In-The-Wire?	Confidentiality?	Integrity?	Strong Threat Model?	High Security Level?	Low Latency? (byte times)
SEL 3021-1	Yes	Yes	No	No	Yes	Yes (5)
SEL 3021-2	Yes	Yes (option)	Yes	Yes	Yes	No
AGA12/Cisco, PE mode	Yes	Yes (option)	Yes	No	No	Yes (~32)
AGA12/Cisco, other modes	Yes	Yes (option)	Yes	Yes	Yes	No
PNNL SSCP BITW	Yes	Yes (option)	Yes	Yes	Yes	No
PNNL SSCP embedded	No	Yes (option)	Yes	Yes	Yes	Yes (<10)
YASIR (our approach)	**Yes**	**Yes** (option)	**Yes**	**Yes**	**Yes**	**Yes (≤18)**

Table 1 Previous BITW solutions for securing legacy SCADA communications all fall short in some critical property; the one previous approach that provides the critical property is not BITW. Our approach meets all the criteria.

2.1 SEL's Serial Encrypting Transceiver

The SEL-3021 Serial Encrypting Transceiver from Schweitzer Engineering Laboratories, Inc (SEL, `http://www.selinc.com`) is a BITW module for securing RS-232 serial links between SCADA devices against malicious attacks. Both available models, SEL-3021-1 and SEL-3032-2, support all standard SCADA protocols, including DNP3-Serial and Modbus/RTU, at data rates up to 115200 bps.

The *SEL-3021-2* provides data authenticity through HMAC-SHA-1/-256. It also optionally provides data privacy through AES-CTR-128. Unfortunately, SEL-3021-2 does not provide an upper-bound on the delay it may incur [8]. In fact, SEL suggests that SEL-3021-2 *"may not be suitable to secure links that require time-critical communications with low latency (i.e., links for electrical tele-protection)"* [8]. Another model in the family, the *SEL-3021-1*, is an encryption-only solution.

2.2 AGA's SCADA Cryptographic Module

The American Gas Association (AGA) (`http://www.aga.org/`) Task Group 12 designed the *SCADA Cryptographic Module (SCM)* [1] as a BITW solution that retrofits data authenticity to SCADA communications while maintaining the performance requirements. AGA's SCM provides several cipher-suites to choose from. The most secure ones use AES-CTR for data privacy and HMAC-SHA-1/-256 for data authenticity. Unfortunately, messages must be held back by the receiving SCM using these cipher-suites.

PE Mode of Operation In one of the cipher-suites provided by AGA's SCM, data authentication is achieved by operating AES in the *Position-Embedded (PE) mode* [11]. Using this cipher-suite, SCMs provide data authenticity with an overhead of only 32 byte times, regardless of the message-length. To the best knowledge of the authors, AGA's SCM and our *YASIR* are the only BITW solution for legacy SCADA systems that provide data authenticity without message hold-back.

Unfortunately, AES operating in the PE mode attains a security level of only 16 bits at maximum, which is far below the generally accepted minimum of 80-bit level of security: with a probability of at least 2^{-16}, SCADA devices protected by SCMs will accept maliciously crafted messages as authentic. As a remedy, SCMs rely in addition on traditional HMAC for more secure data authentication. However, as pointed out by Majdalawieh et al [7], although unauthentic messages can eventually be detected by the SCM, the late detection can't stop the SCM from forwarding them to the SCADA devices. Moreover, AES in PE mode is proven secure only under known-plaintext attacks [11]. Hence, this solution is not guaranteed to be secure against stronger and yet realistic attacks, such as chosen plaintext and/or ciphertext attacks launched by, e.g., a compromised employee working in the control center.

2.3 PNNL's Secure SCADA Communications Protocol

A SCADA communications authenticator technology is under development by a group led by Mark Hadley at the Pacific Northwest National Laboratory (PNNL, `http://www.pnl.gov/`). In PNNL's solution, SCADA messages are "wrapped" by an authenticator and potentially some other information such as a unique identifier. Their solution is effectively a protocol wrapper that converts an insecure SCADA protocol into their Secure SCADA Communications Protocol (SSCP).

PNNL's technology is being implemented both as a BITW solution and an embedded solution [3]. The BITW solution requires message hold-back. The embedded solution is fast but is not a BITW solution: it requires upgrading the hardware and/or software of the SCADA devices.

3 Preliminaries

SCADA Protocols The data link layer of a SCADA protocol specifies how control and data messages are encoded into bit-sequences known as *frames* for transmission over the communication link. Let $||$ denote the concatenation of (bit- or octet-) strings. A frame $\mathtt{F}$ has the form $\mathtt{s}||\mathtt{H}||\mathtt{P}||\mathtt{e}$.

The header $\mathtt{H}$, if present,[3] may contain control information about the frame such as its length. The payload $\mathtt{P}$ contains a message in its encoded form and usually has variable length. The starting symbol $\mathtt{s}$ and the ending symbol $\mathtt{e}$ are bit-sequences distinct from any code symbols used in the rest of the frame so that a SCADA device can detect frame boundaries unambiguously. In many asynchronous protocols including Modbus/ASCII and DNP3-Serial, frame boundaries can be recognized

[3] In some SCADA protocols such as Modbus, frames do not have a header.

within two byte times. In Modbus/RTU, which is a synchronous protocol, a silence of 3.5 byte times indicates the end of a frame.

A Classification of Legacy SCADA Protocols There are more than a hundred SCADA protocols in use today, many of which are closed and proprietary. A practical BITW solution should make few assumptions about the SCADA protocol it is protecting, so that it can be used to, upon simple configuration, protect a majority of protocols.

Our solution to be presented in Section 6 does require certain assumptions to be made about the underlying protocols, but is otherwise designed so that those assumptions hold for the majority of SCADA protocols. Specifically, we introduce a classification of SCADA protocols into Type-I and Type-II in the following; our solution assumes that a SCADA protocol is of Type-I or Type-II, or both.

- *Type-I Protocols.* The last few octets in the frame is a checksum of (a part of) the rest of the frame produced according to certain known CRC algorithm. A receiving SCADA device flags an error and drops the frame if the checksum is incorrect. For example, in Modbus/ASCII (resp. DNP3), the last two octets is a CRC-16 on the rest of the payload (resp. the previous 16 bytes).
- *Type-II Protocols.* A frame contains in its fixed-sized header information from which the length of the frame (and thus that of the payload) can be calculated. If the actual length of the frame is *smaller than*[4] the length as calculated using the header information, a receiving SCADA device flags an error and drops the frame.[5] For example, DNP3 frames contain in the header the size (in terms of the number of 16 octets) of the payload excluding the CRCs.

Most existing SCADA protocols are of Type-I or Type-II: it has long been a commonly adopted practice to append CRC checksums to frames at the data-link layer of a communication protocol for detecting transmission errors. Similarly, length verification is employed in many communication protocols as a mechanism for detecting errors. Moreover, it is fairly easy to check if a protocol is of one of the types and determine the CRC algorithm used. Even if the protocol is closed and proprietary, one can do so by examining several actual frames coming out of a real SCADA device speaking that protocol.

Formalizing BITW Solutions As Figure 1 illustrates, a *source* SCADA device S converts messages such as data or control information into frames for transmission. We overload S to denote the function that models the device, which takes a message $\mathtt{M}$ as input and outputs the corresponding frame $\mathtt{F}$. Similarly, the *destination* SCADA device D is modeled as a function D, which takes a frame $\mathtt{F}'$ as input and output an *error*, if $\mathtt{F}'$ fails to pass certain conformance checks such as the random-error detection, or else the corresponding original message $\mathtt{M}'$.

---

[4] Replacing "smaller than" with "different from" results in a more restrictive assumption as there may exist protocols that reacts to frames longer than what is specified in the header by, rather than dropping them as error, truncating them to the specified length and operating on the truncation.

[5] This implicitly implies that the device will do the same if the frame is shorter than a header.

If no error was introduced (randomly or maliciously) into $\mathtt{F}$ during its transmission (i.e., if $\mathtt{F}' = \mathtt{F}$), then a correct pair of S and D must always give $D(\mathtt{F}') = D(\mathtt{F}) = D(S(\mathtt{M})) = \mathtt{M}$. If $\mathtt{F}' \neq \mathtt{F}$, then D may or may not return an error, depending on whether F' passes the conformance checks in D. Virtually all SCADA devices have random-error detection mechanisms such as CRCs, and are thus capable of catching most random errors.

Now, any BITW solution injects two hardware modules into the link in the model, one next to S and the other next to D, which we call the *Transmitter* T and the *Receiver* R respectively. Refer to Figure 1 again for a diagrammatic illustration. Again T is overloaded to denote the function that models the Transmitter, which takes each frame $\mathtt{F}$ output by S as input and returns the corresponding transformed frame $\tilde{\mathtt{F}}$ to be transmitted over the insecure channel. Similarly, the Receiver R is modeled as a function R that takes in a transformed frame $\tilde{\mathtt{F}'}$ and outputs either an *error*, or the corresponding original frame $\mathtt{F}'$ to be given to D. If no error was introduced (randomly or maliciously) into $\tilde{\mathtt{F}}$, i.e., $\tilde{\mathtt{F}'} = \tilde{\mathtt{F}}$, a correct pair of T and R must always give $R(\tilde{\mathtt{F}'}) = R(\tilde{\mathtt{F}}) = R(T(\mathtt{F})) = \mathtt{F}$. In most existing BITW solutions that provides data authenticity and freshness, if for whatever reason $\tilde{\mathtt{F}'} \neq \tilde{\mathtt{F}}$, then R should output an error with overwhelming probability. Effectively, R acts as a guard in these solutions and discards all malformed frames so that D won't even see them.

We note that while S and D do not output the corresponding output until they receive the input in its entirety, this is not necessarily the case for T and R: they could start outputting part of the output after having received only part of the input. For example, T and R output data of size equal to an AES-block for every receipt of data of the same size in AGA's SCMs; in the solution we are going to propose, T and R output a byte upon receiving a byte.

Finally, a SCADA device can be the source at one time and the destination at another (but never at the same time). A BITW module in operation will thus switch between the role of a Transmitter and that of a Receiver accordingly.

4 Security Requirements

A BITW solution retrofits security to legacy SCADA communications to thwart adversarial attacks. Here we study the adversary's goals and capabilities when attempting to launch those attacks and the security properties a BITW solution must possess to defend against them. A more formal treatment of the discussion in this section can be found in the extended version of this paper [10].

4.1 Threat Model

When attempting to break the security provided by a BITW solution, the adversary may interact with the various components in the SCADA system through all interfaces exposed to him in any malicious and arbitrarily intelligent way, in order to increase his advantage in launching a successful attack. Formalizing a threat model by correctly identifying the adversary's capabilities is thus critical in the evaluation of the security of any BITW solution.

Communication Links It is impossible to keep the adversary away from the entirety of links as they travel through a long distance to connect end SCADA devices together. This is the case for private leased lines, and even more so for public networks such as the Internet. As Figure 1 shows, in our threat model, *links are insecure:* an adversary may arbitrarily sniff, tamper, inject and replay communications.

SCADA Devices and *YASIR* Modules We assume that the adversary knows how S, D, T and R operate, i.e., the complete specification of how they convert an input into the corresponding output. For SCADA systems that speak open protocols, such information is readily available to the public. Even for systems that use closed and proprietary standards, one should that the same information can be obtained by the adversary through reverse-engineering or insider leaks.

However, we assume that the adversary can't physically tamper with any of them, e.g., manipulate their internal operations, or extract or overwrite their internal states, including the secret keys in the case of T and R. Assumptions on physical tamper-resistance as such are inevitable for most cryptographically secure hardware. One usually achieves physical tamper-resistance by carefully controlling who can have physical accesses to the hardware, and/or by introducing tamper-resistant/-responsive mechanisms to the hardware itself.

Insider Attacks If there existed security boundaries around the substations and the control centers, then attacking the communication links would be all the adversary could possibly do. Unfortunately, such security boundaries do not exist. For example, an adversary may physically break into an under-guarded substation, compromise an employee working in the control center, or remotely hack into the computers auditing the SCADA devices.

In our threat model, *SCADA devices and the attached YASIR modules are insecurely located:* as depicted in Figure 1, an adversary may feed D with maliciously crafted inputs and learn the corresponding outputs at T; he may also feed R with maliciously crafted inputs and learn the corresponding outputs at D.

As we have discussed, the security of AGA's SCMs using AES operating in PE mode assumes the absence of any insider. We think that this is a rather unrealistic assumption. The actual security of their solution is unclear in practice when the assumption ceases to hold.

4.2 Security Goals

A BITW solution must provide data authenticity and freshness to SCADA communications. If desired, it must also provide data privacy.

Data Authenticity and Freshness A destination SCADA device D equipped with a *YASIR* Receiver R only accepts a transformed frame $\tilde{\mathtt{F}}$ as valid, i.e., it outputs the corresponding original message $\mathtt{M}$ instead of flagging an *error*, if:

- *(Authenticity.)* $\mathtt{M}$ was an input to a source SCADA device S equipped with the *YASIR* Transmitter T that shares its secret keys with R.
- *(Freshness.)* $\tilde{\mathtt{F}}$ is fresh, i.e., not a replayed/re-ordered frame. More precisely, if T output any other transformed frame $\tilde{\mathtt{F}'}$ after outputting $\tilde{\mathtt{F}}$, R has not been given $\tilde{\mathtt{F}'}$ as an input.

Data Privacy No information about the corresponding original frame can be inferred from a transformed frame in transit, except perhaps its size. More precisely, an adversary is allowed to choose two messages $\mathtt{M}_0$ and $\mathtt{M}_1$ such that their corresponding frames, $\mathtt{F}_0$ and $\mathtt{F}_1$ respectively, as output by S, are distinct but of the same length. The goal of data privacy is so that when given the transformation $\tilde{\mathtt{F}}$ by T of either $\mathtt{F}_0$ or $\mathtt{F}_1$, the adversary does not know which is the case.

We remark that there are scenarios when data privacy is *not* a concern. For example, it is fine for an IED to report the current temperature reading to another IED within the same substation over an unencrypted channel because an adversary who has broken into the substation might as well go to read off the temperature directly from the sensing IED instead of tapping into the serial link. There are even scenarios when data privacy is *undesirable*, such as when a message has multiple recipients. One example is when the control center wants to broadcast the same control message to all RTUs. Also, one might want to install a logging device that audits all the messages leaving or entering a SCADA device.

As will become clear, our proposed solution provides both data privacy and data authenticity and freshness by default, and yet can easily be modified to provide only data authenticity and freshness and send transformed frames in cleartext.

5 Solution Overview

An Observation Recall that the BITW receiver module R acts as a guard for the destination SCADA device D in most existing solutions. R can't decide if a frame is authentic and fresh and hence can't start relaying it until the receipt of the entire frame and its authentication tag. The latency thus grows linearly with the frame length. AES in PE mode used in AGA's SCM as previously discussed is, however, a novel exception. R starts relaying the frame to D before the authenticity of the frame is known. However, R operates on the frame in such a way that, with probability close to 1, D will flag a CRC error and drop the frame if it has been tampered.

In a sense, AGA's solution converts random-error detection, already built in to the legacy SCADA devices, into a mechanism for verifying data authenticity against malicious attacks. In their solution, the conversion relies on the "real-or-random indistinguishability" property [2] of AES when used as a block cipher. However, this solution has three drawbacks: (1) one 16-byte block of data must be buffered at each of both BITW modules. (2) There is a non-negligible probability (as high as 2^{-8} or 2^{-16}, depending on the underlying protocol) that a maliciously tampered frame can get through *R* and be operated on by *D*. (3) This approach is proven secure only against known-plaintext attacks, but not against stronger and yet still very realistic attacks such as chosen-plaintext and/or chosen-ciphertext attacks.

Our Approach Our solution shares the same idea of converting random-error detection to data authenticity and freshness checking, but is different in how that conversion is done, which enables our solution to offer three advantages: (1) our BITW modules operate on a frame as a stream of bytes instead of 16-byte blocks so that latency to due buffering is minimal. (2) Our solution uses HMAC (but in a way so that no message hold-back is required) so that *R* knows, at a 80-bit security level, when a frame has been tampered with, in which case *R* is always capable of forcing *D* to drop the frame. (3) The use of HMAC also allows our solution to be secure against stronger and yet realistic attacks, namely chosen-plaintext-and-ciphertext attacks.

To provide data privacy and freshness, our solution makes appropriate use of encryption and sequence numbers respectively, as we will describe in details in the next section. However, if we ignore data privacy and freshness for now, the following explains at a high level how our solution provides data authenticity.

For each frame F the BITW Transmitter *T* receives from the source SCADA device *S*, *T* appends an HMAC-SHA-1-96 on F to the back of F and sends it off to the insecure channel. This can done without holding back the frame. At the other end, the BITW Receiver *R* relays every byte it gets from the insecure channel to the destination SCADA device *D*, but with a delay of 14 byte times. Since a HMAC-SHA-1-96 MAC has 12 bytes, by the time *R* is about to relay last byte, it will have already received the whole HMAC and will thus be able to verify the authenticity of the received frame. Now if the HMAC verifies, all *R* has to do is to finish up relaying the frame by sending the last byte. However, if the HMAC does not verify, *R* manipulates the last byte to cause the conformance checks at *D* to fail.

6 Solution Details

We now present the construction for our *YASIR* Transmitter and *YASIR* Receiver. Our single *YASIR* Transmitter construction works for both Type-I and Type-II SCADA protocols; we have two *YASIR* Receiver constructions, one for each type of SCADA protocols. If a SCADA protocol to be secured is of both Type-I and Type-II, then either *YASIR* Receiver construction may be used.

Due to space limitation, we omit the presentation of our *YASIR* Receiver construction for Type-II SCADA protocols, and an in-depth analysis of *YASIR*'s security. They can be found in the extended version of this paper [10].

Let HASH denote the cryptographic hash function SHA-1, the output of which has an octet-length of $\ell_H = 20$. Let HMAC denote the HMAC function HMAC-SHA-

1-96, the output of which has an octet-length of $\ell_M = 12$. Further let ENCRYPT denote the encrypting (resp. decrypting) function AES-CTR-128, which takes a nonce of octet-length $\ell_N = 4$, and a plaintext (resp. ciphertext) of any length, and outputs the corresponding ciphertext (resp. plaintext) of the same length. Finally, let CRC denote the CRC algorithm used by the Type-I SCADA protocol, which takes a frame and outputs boolean answer of the validity of a frame, as described in Section 3.

The BITW Transmitter T and Receiver R share a 128-bit AES key ek and a 160-bit HMAC-SHA-1 key hk. These keys are re-negotiated on a regular basis, such as once every day.[6] T and R keep counters ctr_T and ctr_R of octet-length $\ell_S = 4$ respectively, both of which are reset to zero every time keys are re-negotiated.[7]

6.1 YASIR Transmitter

On input an incoming frame $\mathtt{F} = \mathtt{s}||\mathtt{H}||\mathtt{P}||\mathtt{e}$, the *YASIR* Transmitter T does the following:

1. Output the corresponding transformed frame $\tilde{\mathtt{F}} = \mathtt{s}||\mathtt{CTXT}||\mathtt{x}||\mathtt{MAC}||\mathtt{SEQ}||\mathtt{e}$, where

$$\mathtt{CTXT} = \text{ENCRYPT}_{\mathsf{ek}}(\mathsf{ctr}_T, \mathtt{H}||\mathtt{P}),\ \mathtt{MAC} = \text{HMAC}_{\mathsf{hk}}(\mathsf{ctr}_T||\mathtt{CTXT}),\ \mathtt{SEQ} = \mathsf{ctr}_T,$$

   and $\mathtt{x}$ is, like $\mathtt{s}$ and $\mathtt{e}$, a special symbol distinct from any code symbol used in the rest of the frame. It indicates the end of CTXT and hence the start of MAC.[8]
2. Increments ctr_T by 1.

In a nutshell, T transforms F to $\tilde{\mathtt{F}}$ by first encrypting F's content (i.e., header and payload) for data privacy, then appending a "time-stamp" on the ciphertext with a unique sequence number for data authenticity and freshness, and finally appending the sequence number itself.

The above describes how T operates on an input to produce the corresponding output, without detailing the timeliness of the operation, i.e. which part of the output is available when. We specify this in the following.

Operation Timeliness T leverages the "stream"-nature of AES-CTR, which, upon receiving one byte in the plaintext, can compute the corresponding byte in the ciphertext. Consequently, T processes each of the bytes in the incoming frame F as they come in, and immediately outputs a byte in the corresponding transformed frame $\tilde{\mathtt{F}}$. The processing of each byte involves only a byte-wise XOR operation in the critical path, which incurs negligible latency.

When T has received F in its entirely, it immediately computes the HMAC on the internal counter and the ciphertext and starts outputting the result as well. We adopt

---

[6] Key management is outside the scope of this paper. One can borrow key distribution and re-negotiation techniques from other existing BITW solutions.

[7] There is no practical chance of exhausting a 4-byte counter in any SCADA deployment.

[8] Alternatively, one can use a character escaping mechanism to allow for proper frame parsing.

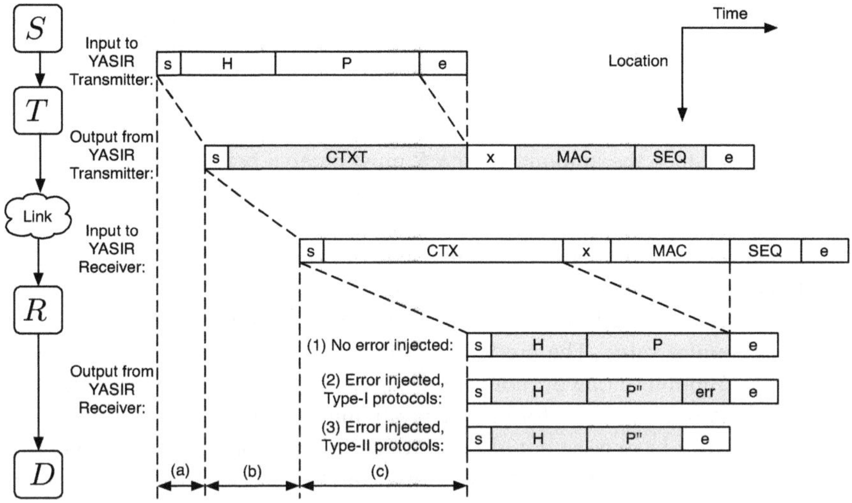

Fig. 2 Latency incurred by (a) *YASIR* Transmitter, (b) the communication link itself, and (c) *YASIR* Receiver. Shaded boxes indicates values computed by the *YASIR* components.

an iterative computation of HMAC so that both the latency and storage requirement of this HMAC computation is a small constant independent of the length of the ciphertext, and thus that of F.

Consequently, the transformation done by T incurs no delay, except the time needed to decode a code symbol or detect frame boundaries in the input frame, which takes at most 4 byte times in almost all protocols, as discussed in Section 3.

Figure 2 gives a pictorial illustration of this.

6.2 YASIR Receiver for Type-I Protocols

On input a transformed frame $\tilde{\mathtt{F}}' = \mathtt{s}||\mathtt{CTXT}'||\mathtt{x}||\mathtt{MAC}'||\mathtt{SEQ}'||\mathtt{e}$, denote

$$\mathtt{H}'||\mathtt{P}' = \textsc{Encrypt}_{\mathsf{ek}}(\mathsf{ctr}_R, \mathtt{CTXT}'),\ \mathtt{MAC}'' = \textsc{Hmac}_{\mathsf{hk}}(\mathsf{ctr}_R||\mathtt{CTXT}'),$$

and $l = |\mathtt{P}'|$. The *YASIR* Receiver R does the following:

- If $\mathtt{MAC}' = \mathtt{MAC}''$ then output the frame $\mathtt{F}' = \mathtt{s}||\mathtt{H}'||\mathtt{P}'||\mathtt{e}$. and increment ctr_R by 1.
- Otherwise, output the frame $\mathtt{F}'' = \mathtt{s}||\mathtt{H}'||\mathtt{P}''||\mathtt{e}$, where $\mathtt{P}'' = \mathtt{P}'[1\ldots(l-1)]\,||\mathtt{err}$ and $\mathtt{err}$ is any single octet such that $\textsc{Crc}(\mathtt{F}'')$ is invalid. Furthermore, if $\mathtt{SEQ}' > \mathsf{ctr}_R$ and $\mathtt{MAC}' = \textsc{Hmac}_{\mathsf{hk}}(\mathtt{SEQ}'||\mathtt{CTXT}')$, set $\mathsf{ctr}_R = \mathtt{SEQ}' + 1$.

In other words, R reconstructs $\mathtt{F}'$ from $\tilde{\mathtt{F}}'$ simply by decrypting $\mathtt{CTXT}'$ if $\mathtt{F}'$ contains a valid HMAC. Otherwise, R replaces the last byte of $\mathtt{F}'$ with a byte $\mathtt{err}$ during its reconstruction in such as way that the error-injected frame $\mathtt{F}''$ will fail the conformance check in D. R calculates `err` by first computing the correct CRC for F'' and then choosing `err` to be any byte different from the last byte of the correct CRC.

Sequence Numbers Contrary to many other protocols in which sequence numbers are contained in frame headers, T in *YASIR* puts the sequence number at the end of a frame to reduce the amount of data R must receive before it can reconstruct a frame and decides on the authenticity and freshness of the frame. Since *YASIR* uses a 4-octet sequence number, the latency at R is reduced by 4 byte times.

Note that R does not know the actual sequence number of a frame by the time it has finished relayed the frame to D. To properly decrypt and verify the integrity the incoming transformed frame, R predicts the sequence number of the frame using its internal counter value. The prediction will be correct if there was no random or malicious corruption in one or more frames recently sent. The sequence number at the back of the frame is used for re-synchronizing the internal counters between T and R in case they have gone out of synchronization, but only when the integrity of the frame can be verified using that sequence number, to prevent malicious manipulation of the value of R's counter.

Operation Timeliness Similar to T, R is designed to minimize the latency it incurs by attempting to start outputting bytes of the detransformed frame once they become available. The use of AES-CTR once again allows R to reconstruct the original frame at a per-byte basis by decrypting the input bytes as they arrive.

The output of R depends on the validity of the HMAC inside the transformed frame it receives. R behaves indifferently until when it has finished outputting the second to last byte in the payload and has to decide whether it should inject an error or not, depending on the validity of the HMAC. This implies that R must have received the entire 12-byte-long HMAC in the input at that moment. To ensure this, R must delay its operation by at least 12 byte times.

As argued in Section 6.1, decrypting a byte and verifying a HMAC both take negligible time. Also, the CRC checksum for F'' and thus the value of `err` can be computed in negligible time and even pre-computed. Therefore, if we assume that the symbol `x` can be decoded in 2 byte times, the total latency incurred by R is thus $12+2=14$ byte times. Finally, while R may operate on the sequence number in the input, the operation does not incur additional latency as the detransformation does not depend on it.

Figure 2 illustrates this.

7 Conclusions

In this paper, we have proposed *YASIR*, which is a BITW solution for retrofitting security to serial-based SCADA systems where communications are time-critical, such as those for electric power generation and distribution. As Table 1 has shown, our solution is the first to provide data integrity in a timely manner, at a high security level even against strong and yet realistic adversaries. Hence, *YASIR* is a pragmatic solution to a high-threat security problem we are facing right now.

We have implemented our solution as a proof-of-concept prototype. As our next step towards a real industrial deployment of *YASIR*, we are going to implement it on FPGA for better cost-effectiveness. Furthermore, we have been in contact with Working Group C6 in the Substation Committees of IEEE. The group is drafting a standard for a cryptographic protocol for cyber security of substation serial links [4]. We are working on the potential incorporation of *YASIR* into that standard.

Acknowledgements This work was supported in part by the National Science Foundation, under grant CNS-0524695, the U.S. Department of Homeland Security under Grant Award Number 2006-CS-001-000001, and the Institute for Security Technology Studies, under Grant number 2005-DD-BX-1091 awarded by the Bureau of Justice Assistance. The views and conclusions do not necessarily represent those of the sponsors.

References

1. American Gas Association. Cryptographic Protection of SCADA Communications Part 1: Background, Policies and Test Plan. Technical Report AGA Report No. 12, American Gas Association, March 2006. `http://www.gtiservices.org/security/AGA%2012%20Part%201%20Final%20Version.pdf`.
2. M. Bellare, A. Desai, E. Jokipii, and P. Rogaway. A concrete security treatment of symmetric encryption. In *FOCS*, pages 394–403, 1997.
3. M. Hadley. Personal communication, Aug 2007.
4. IEEE Substation Committees, Working Group C6. IEEE Trial Use Standard for a Cryptographic Protocol for Cyber Security of Substation Serial Links. IEEE P1711 Draft, Feb 2007.
5. IEEE standard communication delivery time performance requirements for electric power substation automation. IEEE Std 1646-2004, 2005.
6. S. Kent and R. Atkinson. Security Architecture for the Internet Protocol. Internet Engineering Task Force: RFC 2401, November 1998. `http://www.ietf.org/rfc/rfc2401.txt`.
7. M. Majdalawieh, F. Parisi-Presicce, and D. Wijesekera. DNPSec: Distributed Network Protocol Version 3 (DNP3) Security Framework. In *Advances in Computer, Information, and Systems Sciences, and Engineering: Proceedings of IETA 2005, TeNe 2005, EIAE 2005*, pages 227–234. Springer, 2006.
8. Schweitzer Engineering Laboratories, Inc. SEL-3021-2 datasheet. `http://www.selinc.com/datasheets/3021-2_DS_20070109.pdf`.
9. T. Smith. Hacker jailed for revenge sewage attacks. *The Register*, Oct 31 2001. `http://www.theregister.co.uk/2001/10/31/hacker_jailed_for_revenge_sewage/`.
10. P. P. Tsang and S. W. Smith. YASIR: A Low-Latency, High-Integrity Security Retrofit for Legacy SCADA Systems (Extended Version). Technical Report TR2008-617, Dartmouth College, Computer Science, Hanover, NH, April 2008.
11. A. K. Wright, J. A. Kinast, and J. McCarty. Low-latency cryptographic protection for scada communications. In *ACNS*, volume 3089 of *LNCS*, pages 263–277. Springer, 2004.

Adversary Modeling and Simulation in Cyber Warfare

Samuel N. Hamilton and Wendy L. Hamilton

Abstract Modeling and simulation provide many excellent benefits in preparation for successful cyber operations. Whether used for creating realistic training environments, testing new cyber warfare techniques, or predicting possible adversary actions, it is critical for such simulations to take into account the possibility of an active cyber adversary, able to adapt its plans to network conditions. Without real-time high fidelity modeling and simulation, training fails to address how to cope with intelligent and adaptive opponents, and operations become trial and error exercises rife with high-risk improvisation in situations where the adversary does not follow a well defined script. Unfortunately, current simulation techniques are insufficient to model adversaries capable of dynamic adjustment to changes in the simulation environment. Either adversary actions are completely pre-scripted, or live red teams are required to be on hand to tailor adversary actions to circumstances. In this paper, we present a technique for avoiding the prohibitive cost associated with requiring live red team participation during each use of a simulation environment while still providing the advantages dynamic adversary modeling provides. Our approach utilizes game theoretic techniques, using a new probability based search technique to curtail the search-space explosion issues that previous attempts in this area have encountered. This technique, entitled **Partially-Serialized Probability Cutoff Search**, also includes a new approach to modeling time, allowing modeling of anticipatory strategies and time-dependent attack techniques.

1 Introduction

The success of game theory in creating world-class competitors in domains such as chess, checkers, backgammon, and othello is well known. The strongest effect this

---

Distributed Infinity Inc., La Mesa CA 91941
e-mail: shamilton@distributedinfinity.com; whamilton@distributedinfinity.com

Please use the following format when citing this chapter:

Hamilton, S.N. and Hamilton, W.L., 2008, in IFIP International Federation for Information Processing, Volume 278; *Proceedings of the IFIP TC 11 23rd International Information Security Conference*; Sushil Jajodia, Pierangela Samarati, Stelvio Cimato; (Boston: Springer), pp. 461–475.

has had in the gaming community is not the entry of these programs in competition, but in helping human players with preparation and analysis. By considering huge numbers of possibilities, computers have been shown capable of finding exceptions to general rules and exploiting them mercilessly. In some cases, whole new theories on how to play are developed because of this [1]. We believe game theory will not ultimately replace the human analyst in the domain of cyber warfare, but can supply him with a powerful tool for suggesting approaches, techniques, or potential threats that might not occur to him, and provide the ability for better and more detailed analysis by simulating possible futures. In some sense, this can already be done, in that network simulation techniques have been dramatically improving in the last few years, allowing people to provide training in simulated cyber environments such as in [4], or to determine the efficacy of their tools and techniques in simulated environments before deploying them for network defense. What has been missing from these simulated environments, however, is the ability to actively model adversaries with the potential to sense, interact and plan based on the effects produced by the tools or techniques being tested. Even in [4], adversaries are simulated more in lines with Sim-City AI techniques than those applied to model sophisticated plan development such as used by chess players. This is understandable, since researchers have had much less success applying standard game theoretic techniques in this area, due to the number of complexities involved in modeling the cyber warfare game space compared to well defined games such as chess.

To overcome these challenges, we have developed a new search that addresses many of the fundamental problems with applying standard search approaches to the domain of cyber warfare. The search has the following characteristics:

- each player may simultaneously initiate multiple moves.
- moves have explicit time durations and affect state upon initiation, during, and upon completion.
- moves may have multiple possible outcomes from the same starting conditions.
- each player has a separate explicitly modeled view of the game space that may be inaccurate.
- each player has a separately modeled set of goals that may or may not come into conflict.

Each of these features are a distinct departure from previous approaches to game theoretic modeling, and would act to further exacerbate the search space explosion if not accompanied by the partially-serialized probability cutoff search presented here. Figure 1 presents a summary of the partially-serialized probability cutoff search technique utilized to curtail this search explosion. Results for this new technique, described in detail in section 4, have been gathered and published in a final report by the Disruptive Technology Office [16]. Success rate was measured by predicting incident response team actions during a red on blue cyber warfare exercise hosted by the Space and Naval Warfare Center. In over 70% of the scenarios, our search was able to pick the identical action chosen by the incident response team. A more detailed result analysis can be found in section 4.

2 Related Work

In this section we describe the current state of research in game theory, concentrating on areas relevant to tactical analysis in cyber warfare. There are two fundamental pieces to a tactical analysis engine: the search technique, and the evaluation function. The evaluation function reports how good a position looks to the player whose move it is.

The search technique determines which moves to consider, and returns the move or series of moves it considers best at the end of the search. The search forms a tree of moves and counter moves, and the leaves are judged using an evaluation function. While our search populates the tree with moves from both sides, in a majority of cyber warfare research to date the tree is populated by only moves by a single side. In this case, such as when using the planning techniques applied by Adventium Labs in [2], these techniques lack the ability to anticipate opponent actions. The same holds true for most attack graph generation techniques, such as those used in [3]. Such techniques can be quite useful for identifying security holes, since the depth of search enabled by simulating only actions by a single side is greater, but they do not provide the dynamic interactive plan generation necessary for simulating live network attackers or defenders.

When generating a tree populated by moves from two parties, the most popular technique is to use a derivative of the mini-max search [6], which propagates leaves back to the root by having parents alternatively assigned the minimum/maximum value of its children, ending with the root maximizing. This works under the assumption that ε_{p_1}, the evaluation function of player 1, is the opposite of ε_{p_2}, the evaluation function of player 2. Thus, $\varepsilon_{p_1} = -\varepsilon_{p_2}$. In other words, this assumes that what is bad for you is good for your opponent, and vice-versa. This assumption is clearly valid in normal game arenas such as chess and othello, where the resources, goals, and moves allowed by both parties are the same. These conditions do not hold in the domain of command and control planning. There are a variety of reasons

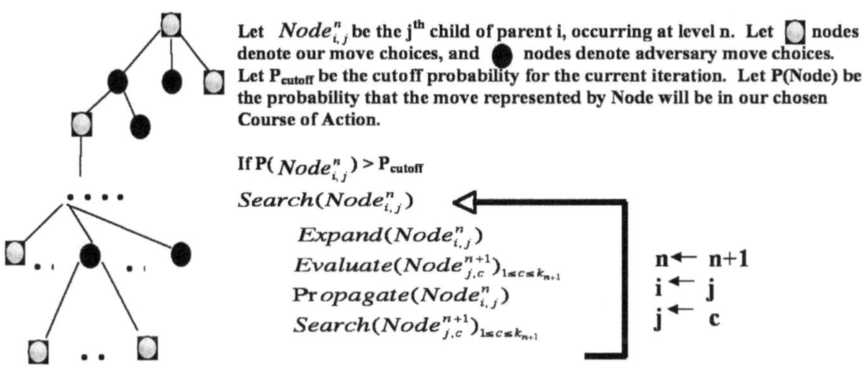

Fig. 1 Partially-Serialized Probability Cutoff Search

for $\varepsilon_{p_1} \neq -\varepsilon_{p_2}$. First, your opponent likely has different goals and priorities than you. Second, both sides are unlikely to have the same view of state. Even so, in the domain of command and control planning, there has been some limited success based on the assumption that , $\varepsilon_{p_1} = -\varepsilon_{p_2}$ [5]. We believe, however, that in the domain of cyber warfare improved results can be obtained by considering alternative evaluation functions.

To address this issue, our previous work section concentrates on three areas of game theory because of their particular relevance to cyber warfare. The first is pruning, as the difference between our evaluation function and an opponent evaluation function invalidates many of the traditional techniques. The second is opponent modeling, since it is necessary to define the opponent evaluation function. The third is tuning our own evaluation function.

2.1 Pruning

While we cannot use a mini-max derived search due to its reliance on the assumption that $\varepsilon_{p_1} = -\varepsilon_{p_2}$, we can use what we will refer to as a max-max' search, where nodes in the tree alternate between passing the maximum child according to the evaluation function of the player whose turn it is. Unfortunately, pruning techniques available in a max-max' search are much more limited than in mini-max searches, where alpha-beta pruning [6] can mathematically eliminate many possibilities. In alpha-beta pruning, moves are eliminated by showing that searching a move cannot change the outcome of the search. Unfortunately, in max-max' searches, it has been shown that no such pruning method is possible [7].

Since in any sufficiently complex game some type of pruning is necessary to limit the explosion of the search space with each increase in search depth, alternative techniques have been explored. One group of techniques is derived from best-first searches. In a best-first search, a tree of explored possibilities is kept open, and each leaf is judged as to how promising it is. The most promising node is then expanded, and its children added to the queue. In this scenario, the most promising move is defined as the most likely to be in the final predicted move group. The problem with best-first searches is that the memory requirements are explosive, so in a game where a large number of positions must be considered this solution is not feasible.

β-pruning [8] has been explored specifically with respect to max-max' searches. In β-pruning, the opponent evaluation function and search depth are assumed to be known, and the opponent is assumed to search using a mini-max based strategy. These assumptions allow the use of weaker versions of alpha-beta pruning. It is unclear how realistic these assumptions are unless playing against a known computer opponent running on inferior hardware.

Another search technique proposed for max-max' searches is $\alpha\beta*$ [7]. This technique assumes that the opponent uses an evaluation function similar to your own (i.e. it uses the same heuristics to judge a position) but weights them differently. The technique takes into account the fact that the opponent evaluation function is not completely accurate, but assumes it is correct within a certain error range. Pruning is then done for values outside of that range, using techniques derived from the motivating principals of the alpha-beta search. We found the limitations on the evaluation function in this case to be too restrictive in the chosen domain, thus is $\alpha\beta*$ is not applicable to our search.

2.2 *Modeling the opponent evaluation function* ε_o

Most literature in this area assumes that the opponent uses some type of mini-max search that goes to a fixed depth [7, 8]. The problem then reduces to determining what that depth is, and what evaluation function is in use.

One approach to identifying depth and evaluation characteristics is to iteratively increase model depth, and use reinforcement techniques to learn which depth best predicts opponent behavior. If the evaluation function is given, this technique works quickly and effectively [8].

For the evaluation function, the usual assumption is that an opponent evaluation function uses a subset of the heuristics in our own evaluation function, with different weights. A hill climbing algorithm can then be used based on a function of the number of correct opponent move predictions taken from a list of previous opponent moves or games. A linear programming technique using pattern recognition methods was proposed in [11], and used with some success to find optimal weights in a follow up pass after hill climbing in the domain of checkers [10].

2.3 *Determining self evaluation function* ε_s

Over the years some very effective techniques have been developed for tuning evaluation functions. In [10], a method was proposed for tuning the weights in a list of heuristics in the domain of checkers. This turned out to be good enough to build a World Champion checker program. A world-class backgammon program used neural networks to learn using similar techniques [11]. In computer chess, Deep-Blue and its predecessor Deep-Thought rose to the top riding an evaluation function that was also automatically tuned [12].

While there are some differences between the techniques used in each case, there are some significant similarities. First, a human comes up with a list of heuristics expected to be correlated with success or failure. Then, a large number of master level games are analyzed at a low depth, and the best move is selected. This move is checked against the actual move played. If the move matches, the heuristic weighting is reinforced.

There has also been some work on automated methods for heuristic generation in the domain of othello [13]. This work was successful in finding valid heuristics, though they did not actually improve the program results since the slow evaluation function was more of an impediment than the improved accuracy could compensate for. A method of linearly combining Boolean feature lists into heuristics and then weighting them has also been explored [14].

In the domain of command and control planning, there are no large databases of games at any level, and the heuristics are constantly changing. Thus, within this domain this approach is currently untenable as a viable solution.

3 Partially-Serialized Probability Cutoff Search

We have developed a new search that addresses many of the fundamental problems with applying standard search approaches to the domain of cyber warfare. Fundamentally, the primary challenge in this domain is that the search space is significantly more complex than traditional games, and a number of characteristics of this domain not modeled in traditional game theory approaches (time, simultaneous moves, stochastic move outcomes, non-symmetric player goals) either threaten the validity of the approach if not modeled, or exacerbate the search-space explosion if modeled. A more complete enumeration of these challenges can be found in [15].

The approach presented here addresses these issues by introducing a pruning method that enables significant improvements in tree analysis, sufficient to model human blue and red team[1] reasoning. It does this while simultaneously blending the state and move representation issues listed above that normal game theoretic approaches ignore.

Figure 2 shows the basic architecture of the search engine. The output of the engine is a course of action recommendation, which consists of a series of actions and expected adversary actions, with timing sequence information included. The output will be in tree format, and response suggestions to non-primary adversary actions are included in this tree.

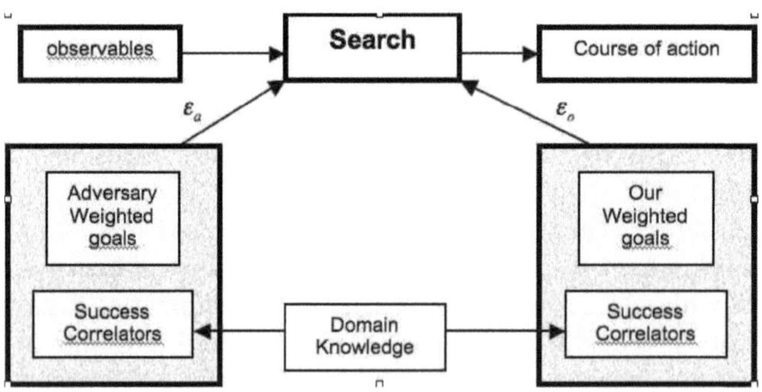

Fig. 2 Search Architecture

[1] For those not familiar with this terminology, a blue team is assigned a defensive role, and a red team is assigned a mission in conflict with the blue team goals.

The input to the search comes from three sources. The first is a list of observables, which is information about the perceived state of the network. This information may include inaccuracies, and is in fact expected to contain some in certain cases as moves by both parties may be designed to mislead adversaries by producing inaccurate observables.

The second and third input sources are in the form of evaluation functions, one representing our mission and associated goals, and one representing a hypothesized adversary's mission and associated goals. Note that there is no linkage between our evaluation function and that of the adversary. This means that while the search uses both functions, neither evaluation function has direct knowledge of the goals of the opponent. Each evaluation function is generated by weighting each goal, and applying these weights to state characteristics correlated with achieving these goals (taken from a database derived from domain knowledge expertise).

In the work presented herein, the concentration our research has been on the development of the search itself, not on the design of the evaluation function, which was done only as a pre-requisite for gathering meaningful results when comparing our search effectiveness to human analyst teams. Evaluation function design is a very interesting area in itself, and it is our intent to pursue this area further in subsequent work. For example, multiple hypothesized adversaries could be generated and modeled simultaneously using a modified version of this algorithm, with a worst-case linear increase in the search time with respect with the number of adversaries modeled. In cases where adversary goals overlapped, the increase would be much less. How to best generate adversary hypotheses could also be a fruitful area of future research.

In the next two sections, we will describe how a game tree is formed and the search algorithm applied.

3.1 Move Definition and Game Tree Construction

A cyber warfare move is defined to have the following characteristics:

- A list of preconditions.
- Effect on state upon initiation.
- Effect on state upon completion.
- A list of conditional effects during execution.
- Timing information for the entire move and each effect.
- A list of possible outcomes and probabilities for each effect.

Note that one of the possible effects is to generate an observable for one or both players, which is what changes their perception of state.

In addition to explicitly modeling timing effects and stochastic move outcomes, our move set differs from traditional game move sets in another fundamental way. In a traditional game, two opposing players alternate moves. In most real-world domains such as cyber-warfare, this is simply not the case. Each player has the option of choosing multiple moves that are executed simultaneously. In fact, both players will frequently be executing multiple actions at the same time.

To accommodate this, our search utilizes an untraditional approach to tree construction. All simultaneously chosen moves are serialized, such that they are listed in order in the tree despite the fact that they will be executed at the same time.

This is accomplished by introducing a new move type: Pass. A pass indicates that the player will not be choosing to begin any additional actions until the next time slice. All moves chosen before a pass are interpreted as beginning at the same time. Figure 3 shows a simple example of this.

When there are no players left to choose a move at a particular time slice, each action chosen is entered into a queue of actions that have been initiated but not completed, and time is advanced. Time is advanced to the next "interesting time" which is defined as the first of the following events.

- a move in the action queue completes
- a move in the action queue produces an observable
- a predefined objective/goal relevant time is reached
- a maximum Pass time is reached

While each move has a duration and set of possible outcomes associated with it, both players may or may not be aware of these outcomes. Awareness of the state of the network is based on available resources, and may be contingent on making moves to gain information. Even when a move produces an observable, such as a message logged by a deployed Intrusion Detection System, the players may not be in a position to see the observable without further action. In the event that a player can see the observable the system will give that player a chance to see and respond to the observed event.

Note that both players are not necessarily given the option of moving during a particular slice of time. Players only move if one of the defined events occurs such that they are aware of it. Thus, if the defender completes a move, the defender will have the option to choose more moves but the attacker will only have that option if the event has produced an observable.

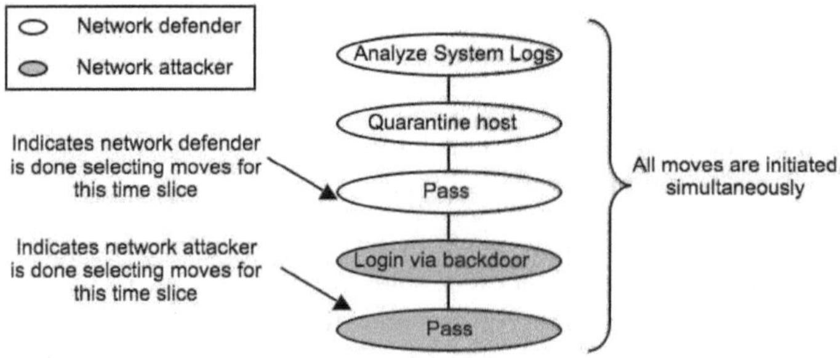

Fig. 3 Snippet of a Partially-Serialized Game Tree

3.2 Search

The Partially-Serialized Probability Cutoff Search is designed to deal with a much more complicated search environment than in most traditional games. Instead of having a single game space represented, we have five. Attacker Opinion, Defender Opinion, Attacker Opinion of Defender, Defender Opinion of Attacker, and Ground Truth. Each move updates these states independently depending on the observables produced over the duration of the move. In addition, each player may have asymmetric goals and objectives. To further complicate things, moves can be defined to have multiple stochastic outcomes. The benefit of these five opinions of state over traditional methods is increased realism, since in the real world the attacker and defender rarely know for sure the true state of things.

The interaction between the two players and the Ground Truth value is worth expounding upon, because of the significant impact it has on the search results. While it is true that neither evaluation function has explicit knowledge of the adversary's evaluation function, there is an interaction between these two functions through observables generated in the Ground Truth state representation and propagated to both parties within the search. That means that the course of action generated for player 1 does take into account actions that player 2 (given its evaluation function) might want to take for those actions that produce observables. The result of this is that while the search does effectively generate moves that can foil multiple courses of action an opponent might take to reach its objectives, it does not currently consider methods for foiling multiple possible adversaries. While we consider this an extremely interesting direction to explore in the future, we view the current approach sufficient for current training and simulation needs, for which even modeling a single group of sophisticated adversaries united in a single set of goals would be a major leap forward. Until the issue of efficient multiple adversary support is addressed, we have found it possible to roughly simulate this scenario by designing adversary evaluation functions that weight numerous separate goals and objectives such that the goal set of a single adversary becomes a super-set of the goals of a hypothesized group of adversaries.

To address the multitude of challenges presented by maintaining an ongoing interaction between a complex move representation and five separate states , we designed a search capable of taking both players separate perspectives into account. The search does not rely on depth cutoffs, which would interact harshly with the partially serialized game tree. Instead it utilizes a probability cutoff. The search will continue to expand all nodes that have a probability equal to or higher than the probability cutoff. The probability cut-off is then iteratively decreased, improving the quality of the search continuously and updating the user with an improved set of analyses after each iteration.

Probabilities are not expert defined (except in the case of stochastic move outcomes) but are instead generated automatically within the context of the algorithm. The algorithmic search is executed as follows:

1. generate children of node n for player whose move it is in the partially serialized tree.
2. generate position value for each child from each player's perspective
3. propagate values up the tree
4. propagate probabilities down the tree
5. select a child whose probability is above the cutoff and repeat

The memory requirements of the search are linear with respect to the depth of the tree, as is the amount of time to analyze a single node. Thus, for roughly balanced trees, these characteristics are approximately logarithmic with respect to the number of nodes. Values are calculated for leaf nodes n (such as when a child is first generated) as follows:

$$V_{n,1} = \varepsilon_{p_1}(S_{n,p_1,p_2})$$

and

$$V_{n,2} = \varepsilon_{p_1}(S_{n,p_1,p_2})$$

Where $V_{n,1}$ is the value for player 1 from player 1's perspective, $V_{n,2}$ is the value for player 1 from player 2's perspective, ε_{p_1} is the evaluation function of player 1, and S_{n,p_1,p_2} is a state estimate at node n for player 2 from player 1's perspective. Note that the evaluation function results are a product of state estimates, which may include values related to anticipated adversary goals. In this fashion, it is not necessary to model all characteristics of an anticipated adversary's goals within the evaluation function as it can be dynamically hypothesized and weighed within the state representation given previously encountered evidence.

The values are propagated up the tree using one of two methods. A node with a stochastic outcome has a child with each outcome, and the value is propagated for each player p as follows:

$$V_{n,p} = \sum_{i=1}^{c} V_{i+j,p} \cdot \rho_{i+j,p}$$

Where c is the number of children, j is the starting node number of the first child, and ρ_{i+j} is the probability of the outcome of child $i+j$. Note that the probability can be different for both players as their opinion of the stochastic nature of the result may differ. The linear weighting by estimated probability implicit here is likely non-optimal, but was chosen for the purposes of speed of calculation.

If the children of a node are choices of player p_1, then values are propagated by:

$$V_{n,1} = \max_{i=1}^{c}(V_{i+j,1})$$

and

$$V_{n,2} = \max_{i=1}^{c}(V_{i+j,2})$$

This is based on an assumption by both players that the player whose move it is will be optimizing their own result. Note that both players may have very different perspectives on what state is, so these results may be very different.

Propagation of the score goes up the tree, and upon reaching the root node triggers the calculation of probabilities. Probabilities of node n with parent σ and sibling children i through j are calculated as follows:

$$\rho_{n,1} = normalize(V_n, \{V_i \ldots V_j\}) \cdot \rho_{\sigma,1}$$

and

$$\rho_{n,2} = normalize(V_n, \{V_i \ldots V_j\}) \cdot \rho_{\sigma,2}$$

By normalizing based on the value, we ensure that moves with higher scores from the perspective of the player who is choosing the move have higher probabilities than lower valued moves. Multiplying by the parent probability ensures that the probability of children nodes always add up to the probability of the parent, from both players perspective. Of course, the probability of the root node for both players is 1.

Note that the normalization technique chosen can have a significant effect on the results of the search. If the result of normalization generally produces values with a small range, the result is a broad shallow search tree, where all possibilities are explored to relatively the same extent. If normalization generally results in a large spread between the highest values and the smallest values, then the search tree is longer and skinnier, such that high probability moves are deeply considered while other possibilities are explored more shallowly.

Figure 4 shows an example tree generated using this technique. Each node is annotated with two scores, one from the perspective of player 1, the second from the perspective of player 2.

The propagation of probabilities down the tree is what enables our aggressive pruning technique. By using these probabilities instead of arbitrary depth values to direct our search, the search trees generated become deeper and less broad, more

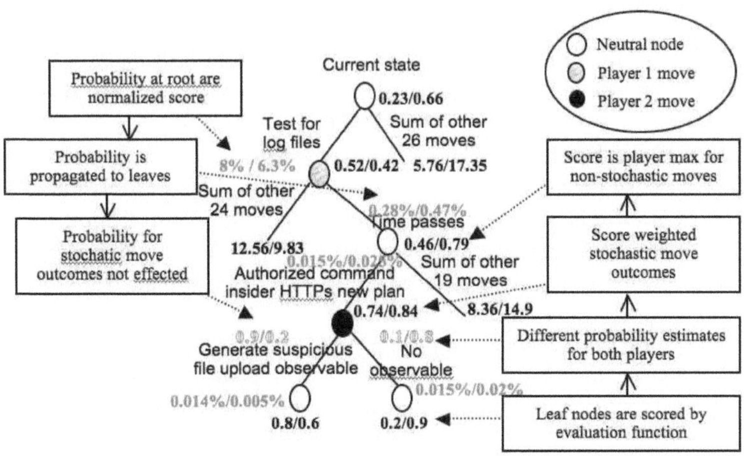

Fig. 4 Snippet of a Partially-Serialized Game Tree

similar to human generated attack trees than most computer generated trees. Of course, since the search is extremely fast, unlike human generated trees, they can contain hundreds of thousands or even million of nodes.

4 Results

The search described above was implemented using a move set developed by the Disruptive Technology Office (formerly ARDA) during the Cyber Strategy and Tactics Workshop. This workshop, held at the Space and Naval Warfare Center (SPAWAR) in San Diego, conducted attacker - defender cyber warfare exercises where the blue teams (defenders) were pitted against red teams (attackers) in a series of three cyber warfare scenarios. The missions and scenarios tested included timing based attacks, which exploited the need for certain cyber resources to be available during particular times. Any automated search approach that did not explicitly model time would be severely challenged to perform in these situations. The attacker and defender evaluation functions were hand-crafted before the experiment was begun, using input from members of both the blue and the red team regarding possible goals, and network state characteristics correlated with achieving success. Software was developed that allowed the blue team and red team to sit in separate rooms, enter their chosen courses of action, and simulate the effect of those actions which would then effect what both teams would see in terms of future observables. Noise events were also simulated, to help disguise which observables were the result of actions by the other team, and which were non-malicious events caused through normal network use (or misuse) by valid operators.

The original experimental design was that the blue team would compete head to head defending the network against our algorithm, with a pre-defined algorithm for success disclosed apriori to both parties. The blue-team experts objected to this experimental design, however, since they felt that defining success in terms of an explicit algorithm would give the computer program an unfair and unrealistic advantage, as it would be able to "game the system." Instead, blue team results were gathered against a live red team using several different attack scenarios, and the blue team decisions were labeled the "gold standard" against which our algorithm was tested. Thus, success for our algorithm was to duplicate the decisions made by the blue team at each critical juncture. There were three blue teams composed of two members each, a cyber security researcher and an experienced cyber defender. These teams were given an unlimited amount of time to discuss their decisions at each junction to maximize the quality of their decisions. Each situation they faced was fed to our algorithm as well, under a strict time limitation of ten seconds per decision. Figure 5 shows our results. In the figure, first indicates that the blue team move choice was ranked first by our algorithm. Second indicates that our algorithm ranked the blue team move as the second best option. On average, at any given point there were over fifty possible choices.

In general, the search proved highly successful, choosing the same move as the blue team over 70% of the time. The remaining cases were shown to blue team members for discussion. A large majority of these cases fell into one of two categories. The first category (roughly 14% of the cases) consisted of situations where the search listed the move chosen by the blue team as one of the top six moves, with a top move whose effect was largely similar to the move chosen by blue. For example, the blue team chose to "monitor logs in real-time" while the search selected the "monitor host real-time" move. The second category of moves was the set of moves where the machine selected a more aggressive course of action than the human blue-team. The general conclusion of the blue teams was that during the exercise, the machine-selected moves would have been more effective at catching the attacker, but would have been over-reaction in real-life.

While the conclusion of this experiment with regards to the effectiveness of the search was extremely positive, a number of suggestions were captured in post-experiment interviews with the blue team members. The general conclusions regarding the experimental conditions were:

1. **Larger move set needed.** The blue teams in particular felt that larger numbers of moves were needed. We have subsequently tested our approach with over 6 times as many move types defined and believe the probability search scales well in this area, but have not repeated a full-scale study with the larger move set.
2. **Effective training environment.** The time model, particularly the effect of the 'Pass' move was difficult for some participants to understand when initially explained, but was intuitive and worked well when they actually saw it in action after play began. The general consensus for both blue and red teams was that the experimental setup would be very effective for training.
3. **More realistic noise needed.** At first, the noise moves were effective, but after a while the human teams were able to reliably identify what was an adversary driven observable, and what was computer generated.

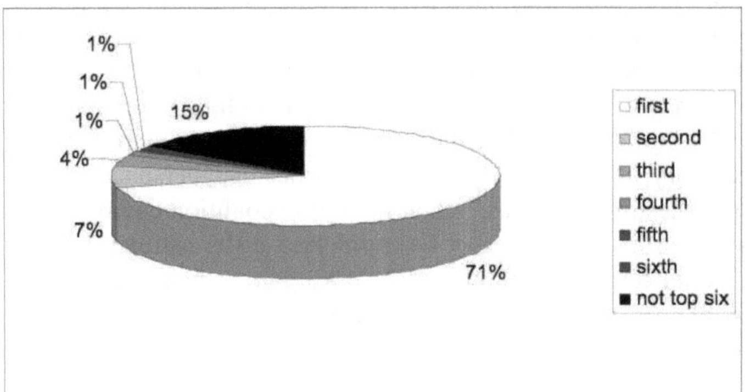

Fig. 5 Search Results Compared to Human Blue Teams

Overall, we considered the experimental results highly gratifying. While it was clear that at the time of the experiment we did not have a mature, ready-to-deploy piece of training software (nor was that the expectation of any of the parties) the capabilities of the search did receive a thorough comparison with highly trained experts in the cyber warfare domain, and proved extremely effective. This is the first example of an automated course-of-action generation algorithm being so tested within this domain that we are aware of.

5 Conclusion

In this paper, we have presented a new type of search designed for application to the cyber warfare domain. The Partially-Serialized Probability Cutoff Search we have developed has proven extremely effective on the benchmarks tested, successfully modeling the dynamic interaction of network attackers and defenders well enough to suggest the same course of action as domain experts over 70% of the time. It does so without the limitations of most search based approaches by allowing multiple simultaneous moves, asymmetric goals, inaccurate state perception by both attacker and defender, explicitly modeling time, and allowing for moves with multiple stochastic outcomes. This strongly differentiates our approach from all other published approaches to date.

The current version of the search is well adapted to dynamically simulate either network attacker or defender activities, and could be easily adapted to provide an automated red-team capability. Currently, the reasoning model has only been tested in two sided warfare situations, where one side is defending a set of resources, and another side has a mission that includes interfering with one or more of the protected assets. What have not been actively explored are situations where there are more than two active parties. Note, each active party could have thousands of resources, including large networks of computers and cyber warriors of varying degrees of skill, and still fit within the models presented here. As long as the ultimate goal of each member of the party remains roughly the same, simulation of an adversary can remain at the two party level without increasing complexity. When it becomes necessary to model more than two sets of goals, however, the modeling complexity can significantly increase the search space. For the purposes of most simulation needs, this is currently unnecessary, as the complexity of two parties in cyberspace is sufficient for most training or testing purposes. When modeling coalition environments with multiple interested parties, such as may be of interest at the national level, it may be necessary to model significant numbers of clashing goals and interests. We believe this to be possible, but anticipate future work in this area will be necessary to overcome these challenges.

References

1. Tesauro, G.: Temporal Difference Learning and TD-Gammon. Communications of the ACM. **38(3)**, 58–68 (1995)
2. Body, M., Gohde, J., Haigh, T., Harp, S.: Course of Action Generation for Cyber Security Using Classical Planning. ICAPS. (2005)
3. Wang, L., Noel S., Jajodia, S.: Minimmum-Cost Network Hardening using Attach Graphs. Computer Communications. **29(18)**, 3812–3824 (2006)
4. Cone, B., Irvine, C., Thompson, M., Nguyen, T.: A Video Game for Cyber Security Training and Awareness. Computers and Security. **26(1)**, 63–72 (2007)
5. Katz, A., Butler, B.: "Game Commander" - Applying an Architecture of Game Theory and Tree Lookahead to the Command and Control Process. Conference on AI, Simulation and Planning. (1994)
6. Winstron, P.: Artificial Intelligence. Addison-Wesley (1992)
7. Carmel, D., Markovitch, S.: Learning and using Opponent Models in Adversary Search. Technical Report CIS9606. (1996)
8. Donkers, H. et al.: Implementing β-pruning Opponent-Model Search, Technical Report CS 00-05 IKAT, Universiteit Maastricht, Maastricht, The Netherlands. (2000)
9. Duda, R., Hart, P.: Pattern Classification and Scene Analysis. Wiley and Sons (1973)
10. Samuel, A.: Some studies in Machine Learning using the Game of Checkers.: IGM Journal of Research and Development **3(3)**, 211–229 (1959)
11. Tesauro, G.: TD-Gammon, a Self-Teaching Backgammon Program, reaches master-level play.: Neural Computation **6(2)**, 215–219 (1994)
12. Hsu, F. et. al.: Deep Thought. In T. A. Marsland and J. Schaeffer (eds.) Computer Chess and Cognition pp.55-78. Spinger Verlag (1990)
13. Buro, M.: Statistical Feature Combination for Evaluation of Game Positions.: JAIR **3**, 373–382 (1995)
14. Utgoff, P.: Constructive Function Approximation.: Technical Report 97-4, University of Mass. (1997)
15. Hamilton, S., Miller, W., Ott, A., Saydjari, O.: The Role of Game Theory in Information Warfare.: The Information Survivability Workshop (2001)
16. Meyers, K., Saydjari, O.: ARDA Cyber Strategy and Tactics Workshop Final Report. (2002).

Interactive Selection of ISO 27001 Controls under Multiple Objectives

Thomas Neubauer, Andreas Ekelhart, and Stefan Fenz

Abstract IT security incidents pose a major threat to the efficient execution of corporate strategies. Although, information security standards provide a holistic approach to mitigate these threats and legal acts demand their implementation, companies often refrain from the implementation of information security standards, especially due to high costs and the lack of evidence for a positive cost/benefit ratio. This paper presents a new approach that supports decision makers in interactively defining the optimal set of security controls according to ISO 27001. Therefore, it uses input data from a security ontology that allows the standardized integration of rules which are necessary to model potential countermeasure combinations based on the ISO 27001 standard controls. The approach was implemented into a tool and tested by means of a case study. It not only supports decision makers in defining the controls needed for certification but also provides them with information regarding the efficiency of the chosen controls with regard to multiple definable objectives.

1 Introduction

IT security incidents such as computer virus contaminations and unauthorized access to information, caused total losses of about 52 million US dollars among 313 U.S. respondents in 2005, coming from the commercial and governmental sector [12]. The Information Security Breaches Survey 2006 [21] estimates the overall costs of U.K. security breaches, mainly caused by virus infection and disruptive

Thomas Neubauer
Secure Business Austria, Vienna, Austria, e-mail: tneubauer@securityresearch.ac.at

Andreas Ekelhart
Secure Business Austria, Vienna, Austria, e-mail: aekelhart@securityresearch.ac.at

Stefan Fenz
Secure Business Austria, Vienna, Austria, e-mail: sfenz@securityresearch.ac.at

Please use the following format when citing this chapter:

Neubauer, T., Ekelhart, A. and Fenz, S., 2008, in IFIP International Federation for Information Processing, Volume 278; *Proceedings of the IFIP TC 11 23rd International Information Security Conference*; Sushil Jajodia, Pierangela Samarati, Stelvio Cimato; (Boston: Springer), pp. 477–491.

software, in the order of ten billion pounds per year. To protect their organization against such threats, 41 percent of U.K. businesses utilize an IT service provider or consultancy, 46 percent an internal audit function, and 42 percent personal contacts within the business or security community [21]. Only 7 percent of U.K. businesses carried out certification initiatives [21], in terms of BS7799 [4], ISO 17799 [14] or ISO 27001 [15] to strengthen the security of their processes and systems. Nine-tenths of businesses that have implemented an information security standard benefit in the following ways: (1) raising staff awareness, (2) pushing security up to the management agenda, (3) better business continuity, (4) formal accreditation, and (5) marketing reasons [21].

Most organizations carry out certification initiatives to become more commercially acceptable in sensitive business sectors (e.g., financial or health sector) or to comply to legal regulations such as Basel II [3] or the Sarbanes Oxley Act [22]. Especially in highly integrated businesses it is crucial that business partners can trust each other regarding the correct implementation of IT security measures in order to ensure that the integration of external IT services does not pose a risk to the own organization. However, in spite of these benefits, most companies refrain from the implementation of information security standards, especially due to high costs, the bureaucratic certification process and the lack of methods for measuring the cost/benefit ratio [21]. The major problem with information security standards is their abstract control definition, which leaves space for interpretation. Not the standard, but the certification auditor decides if certain security measures are compliant to the standard or not. Organizations which are required to obtain a formal certification often focus on satisfying the auditor and forget to evaluate and subsequently implement the optimal security measures in line with their specific corporate requirements. But investments into security should precisely target a company's specific business needs (and not only the requirements of the certification), as competitive advantages can only be accrued by aligning security investments to the corporate business processes as well as strategic and legal objectives. Thus, companies often fail in introducing standards because their primary focus lies on fulfilling the requirements given by the auditors, while they are frequently unaware of the level of their capital expenditure and/or – even more importantly – whether these investments are effective (cf. [16]).

In order to address these reservations and demands outlined above, we developed a new (two-phase) approach that supports decision makers in interactively defining the optimal set of security safeguards according to ISO 27001. In the first step, the security ontology (cf. [8], [9]), which comprises knowledge about the IT security domain including relationships among threats, vulnerabilities, countermeasures, and assets, serves as a knowledge base for potential countermeasure implementations. By now we have incorporated relevant parts of the German IT Grundschutz Manual [5] into the security ontology, to provide the organization with fundamental information security knowledge. While the initial ontology creation step has to be conducted by information security experts, the final information security knowledge base can be reused without expert support. Using an ontological knowledge base allows to model the IT security domain in a standardized way, enables ontological reasoning support to maintain consistency, and enables the standardized integration of rules which are necessary to model potential countermeasure combinations. In the second step, Atana (a decision support approach which is derived from "AlTernative ANAlysis"; cf. [17], [18], [19]) determines solution alternatives that are both feasible with respect to given constraints and Pareto-efficient with respect to a number of objectives that have been identified as the most relevant ones for the given decision setting. Furthermore, Atana supports decision makers such as the Chief Security Officer in interactively exploring the determined solution space until they find their individually "best" solution. This paper describes the new approach and provides a case study.

2 Ontology-based Determination of Security Controls

Checklist-based tools are one approach to support the certification process. The assigned employee completes a questionnaire which reveals potential weaknesses and provides corresponding security recommendations. The questions, as well as the pre-defined sets of recommendations, are often based on best-practices. One weakness of checklists is that they usually offer general, high-level recommendations and cannot support organization specific threat scenarios. Furthermore, no underlying data model exists, which defines connections between the involved entities explicit to allow modification and reuse. Information security standard support tools (e.g., GSTool or EBIOS) are a further certification assistance possibility. Such tools facilitate a structured approach to comply to a defined certification standard, but cannot assist in the actual decision for appropriate security measures, as only the high-level control definitions are presented. To support the certification process in a standardized way, a conceptual and machine-readable model of IT security is required. Such a model has to incorporate best-practice knowledge about threats, threatened infrastructure classes, vulnerabilities, and countermeasures. One possibility to model the IT security domain and make it accessible for machines are ontologies. According to Gruber [13] an ontology is the explicit formal specification of the terms in the domain and the relations among them.

2.1 Security Ontology

We utilized the security ontology classification proposed in [8], [9], [10] which is based on the security relationship model presented in the National Institute of Standards and Technology Special Publication 800-12 [20]. Figure 1 shows the high-level concept of the ontology in which threats, vulnerabilities, controls and their implementation (safeguards) are the pivotal elements: a threat represents, through an existing vulnerability, any potential danger to the organizations' assets and affects specific security attributes (confidentiality, integrity, and/or availability). To pose a

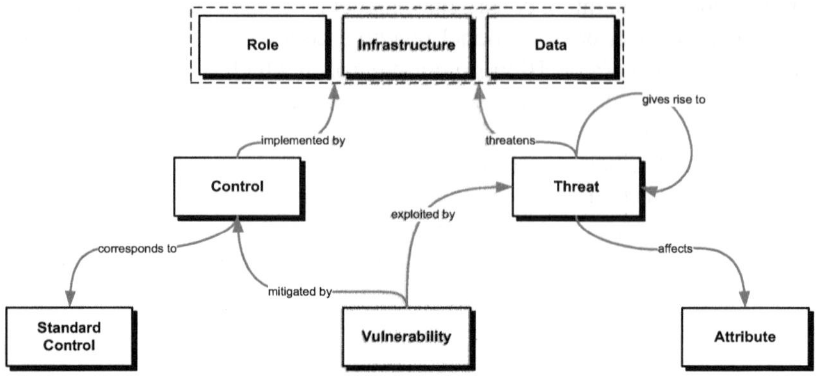

Fig. 1: Conceptual model of IT security

risk to an organization, a threat has to exploit a vulnerability, via a physical, technical or administrative weakness, and cause damage to defined assets. Controls have to be put into place to mitigate an identified vulnerability and to protect the corresponding assets by either preventive, corrective or detective measures. Each control is implemented by role, infrastructure, or data concepts or combinations thereof. Controls are derived from best-practice and information security standard controls (e.g., German Baseline Protection Manual, ISO 27001, or EBIOS) to ensure that the knowledge is widely accepted. The controls are modeled on a highly granular level and thereby reusable for different standards. The ontology follows the OWL-DL standard [24] and ensures that the knowledge is represented in a standardized and machine-readable form. As already mentioned, controls are implemented by role, infrastructure, or data concepts or combinations thereof. The connection between the control and its implementation (role, infrastructure, and/or data) is realized by a 1:n relation. Controls can be implemented in different ways. Therefore, we utilized the concept of OWL property restrictions in order to express these relationships in an ontological form. The universal OWL property restriction (∀) is used to constrain the 'implementation' side to specific concepts. For example, to implement the *Access Regulation Control* a security guard, an entry checkpoint, or an access system is required, which is expressed as follows:

∀ *sec:implementedBy only*
  (ent:SecurityGuard ∨ *ent:AccessSystem* ∨ *ent:EntryCheckpoint)*

Up to that point, the ontology is aware of which concepts (Role, Infrastructure and/or Data) are required to implement a certain control, but a description of the possible combinations is still missing. Therefore, we utilized the existential OWL property restriction (∃), which states that at least one value for that property is of a certain type [24].

For example, the *Access Regulation Control* requires in all implementation variations an access system and either a security guard or an entry checkpoint:

$\exists$ *sec:implementedBy some ent:AccessSystem*
$\exists$ *sec:implementedBy some (ent:SecurityGuard* $\vee$ *ent:EntryCheckpoint)*

On this account, two possible implementation combinations are possible, namely access system and security guard, or access system and entry checkpoint.

The security ontology provides a set of evaluation criteria (benefit and resource categories) and a list of potential investment candidates including potential countermeasure implementations that are needed for the definition and selection of Pareto-efficient solutions (described in the following subsections). Each of these potential investment candidates is rated in every of the defined benefit and resource categories. The data needed for the rating is taken from the security ontology which contains specifications from the providers of the potential investment candidates, empirical evaluations and experience from the project team.

2.2 Determining Efficient Solutions

The first task in the Atana approach lies in determining efficient solution alternatives. Solving this problem that technically constitutes a multiobjective combinatorial optimization (MOCO; for a survey cf. [7]) problem involves the identification of Pareto-efficient combinations of controls in which the binary variables $x_i \in \{0,1\}$ indicate whether or not a control i is selected ($x_i = 1$ if so, and $x_i = 0$ otherwise).

A solution can be represented as vector $x = (x_1, \ldots, x_N)$, where N denotes the number of proposed controls or necessary choices between controls, respectively. The MOCO problem comprises the maximization of K objectives (such as costs, availability or usability)

$$\text{maximize} \quad u_k(x) \qquad \text{for } k = 1, \ldots, K. \tag{1}$$

Objective functions referring to criteria that should naturally be minimized (e.g., costs) can easily be transformed by simply multiplying the underlying objective values with (-1). The functions $u_k(x)$ may take any form (linear, non-linear, etc.) as long as they are defined for all (feasible) alternatives x. Note, that finding proper functions for criteria such as the expected availability of a given combination of controls may prove challenging, but this difficulty also holds true to the same degree for all other decision support approaches.

All solutions taken into consideration must be feasible with respect to two sets of constraints. The first set comprises limited resources (e.g., initial costs or running costs). For binary variables x_i constraints may be formulated simply as

$$\sum_i r_{iq} x_i \leq R_q \qquad \text{for } q = 1, \ldots, Q, \tag{2}$$

where r_{iq} represents the amount of resources of type q required by countermeasure i and R_q stands for the maximum available amount of resources. Corresponding terms must be added in the event of synergy or cannibalism effects that influence the total resource consumption. The second set ensures that at most a maximum – or at least a minimum – number of countermeasures from given subsets is included in the set of feasible solutions. For instance, a constraint may require that at least two defined countermeasures (referring to the corresponding countermeasures having assigned indices 1 to 6) but not more than four countermeasures must be selected and, thus, takes the form

$$2 \leq \sum_{i=1}^{6} x_i \leq 4. \tag{3}$$

Accordingly, decision makers can define that certain countermeasures should only be selected in combination with each other (e.g., the standard demands the combined use of a Security Guard and an Access System) and/or they can take into consideration that their combination yields synergy effects (e.g., the use of two countermeasures from the same vendor might result in reduced costs). Other countermeasures are mutually exclusive (e.g., countermeasures that provide exactly the same functionality) or cause cannibalism effects. For example, the use of a countermeasure fulfilling only part of the needed functionality might demand the use of a second countermeasure and thus would result in higher costs or reduced performance (cf. [23]).

2.3 Interactive Exploration of Solution Space

In Atana's second phase, the decision maker is supported in making a final determination of the solution that best fits his/her notions out of the possibly hundreds (or even thousands) of Pareto-efficient alternatives identified in the first phase. As we are using search-based procedures, we start from an efficient portfolio and allow the decision maker to iteratively "move" around in solution space towards more attractive alternatives until no better portfolio can be found (cf. an application by Focke and Stummer [11]). The Atana approach is based on interactive modifications of lower and upper bounds for one or more objectives. The decision support system (DSS) starts with displaying K "flying" bars (cf. Fig. 2).

For each objective (cf. Fig. 4) the system provides information on what can be achieved by (i) the efficient solutions (the corresponding marks may visually grow together to vertical blocks), and (ii) the alternatives that have remained after the decision makers have made decisions in their interactive exploration of the solution space.

Two moveable horizontal lines with small arrows at one side represent lower and upper bounds and are intended to restrict the set of remaining solutions in a step-by-step manner (e.g., by raising the minimum bound in one of the objectives) or for

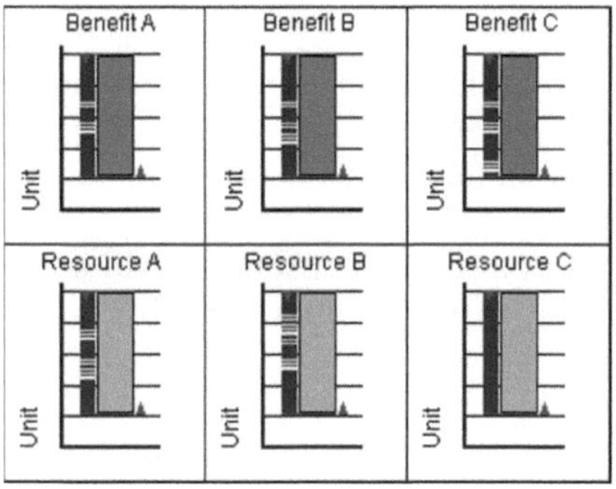

Fig. 2: Status of the DSS at the beginning

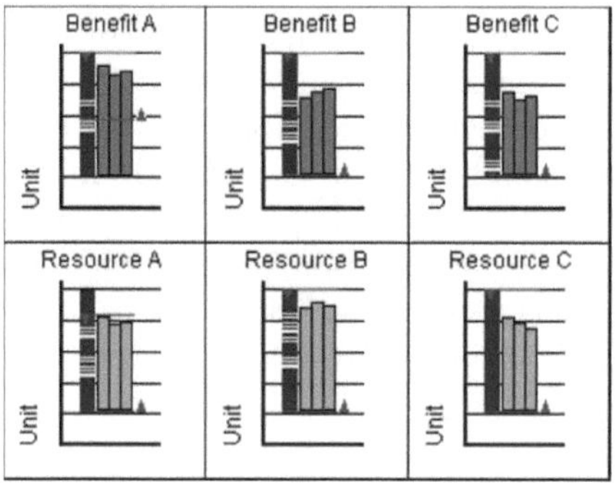

Fig. 3: Status of the DSS after two settings

expanding it (e.g., by once again relaxing some bounds) according to the decision makers' preferences. In all of these cases, the system provides immediate feedback about the consequences of such choices in terms of the remaining alternatives.

First the maximum allowance for resource A is reduced. Because this setting has primarily filtered those solutions that come with a relatively high value in "Resource Category A" (and, on average, a somewhat higher need for resource C) but still values in "Benefit Category A", the options in the other objectives have been reduced as well and the position and size of the flying bars have changed accordingly. Raising the minimum value for Benefit A (e.g., functionality) narrows the set of remaining alternatives even further, since many alternatives with low resource values (e.g., price) drop out (cf. Fig. 3).

In further iterations, the decision maker continues playing with minimum and maximum bounds and by doing so can learn about the consequences of his/her decisions and, thus, gain a much better "feeling" for the problem in terms of what can be achieved in some objectives at what "price" in terms of opportunity costs in other objectives. After several cycles of restricting and once again expanding the opportu-

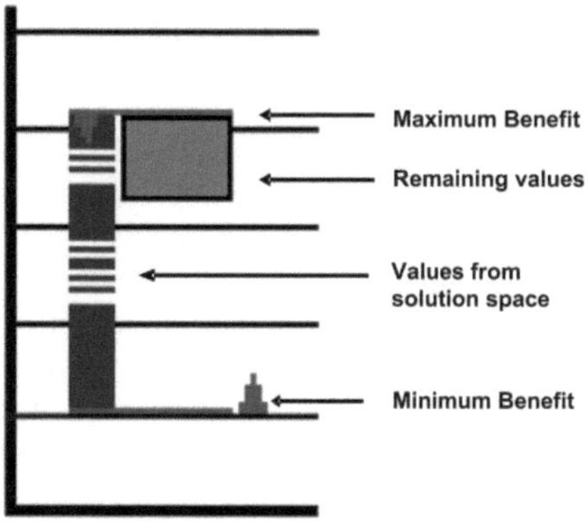

Fig. 4 Subwindow details

nity set, the decision maker will finally end up with a solution alternative that offers an individually satisfying compromise between the relevant objectives. The decision makers do not need to explicitly specify (i) weights for objectives, (ii) the form of their preference function or (iii) how much one solution is better than another during any stage of the whole procedure. Instead, the system provides ample information on the specific selection problem while it ensures that the final solution will be an optimal (i.e., Pareto-efficient) one, with no other feasible solution available that is better from an objective point of view.

3 Case Study

The case study was carried out in the social security sector in Austria. The goal of the organization was to obtain an ISO 27001 certification to comply to legal regulations and to further improve their commercial acceptance within the very sensitive social security sector. Therefore, we aimed at supporting the certification process by supporting decision makers in selecting Pareto-efficient implementation portfolios, which fulfill those ISO 27001 controls which require physical countermeasure implementations (e.g., ISO 27001 A.9.1.4 Control: Protecting against external and environmental threats). As described in Section 2, the security ontology splits all ISO 27001 controls into more granular controls, which are equipped with concrete implementation requirements that are necessary to fulfill the corresponding control. Figure 5 shows an example for ISO 27001 control A.9.1.1 and A.9.1.4 and the corresponding security ontology controls.

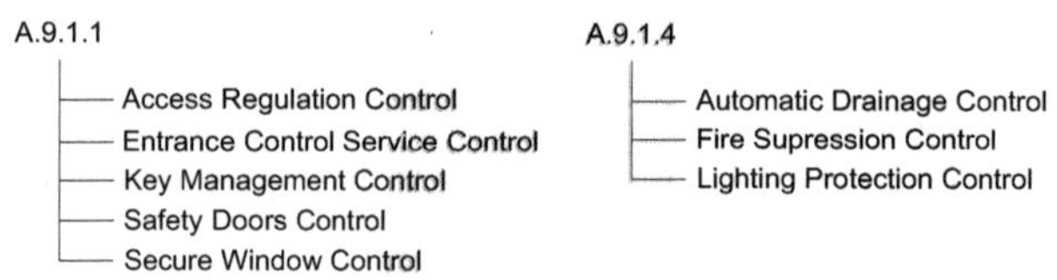

Fig. 5: ISO 27001 control A.9.1.1 and A.9.1.4

Splitting up the abstract ISO 27001 controls into more granular controls enables the definition of concrete implementation requirements. Figure 6 exemplarily shows the implementation requirements for the *Access Regulation Control*.

To fulfill the control the organization has to implement one access system (X1, X2, X3, or X4) and either one security guard (Sec Guard 1, Sec Guard 2, or Sec Guard 3) or one entry checkpoint (Ent Check 1, Ent Check 2, or Ent Check 3) at all entrances which connect sensitive to non-sensitive areas (e.g., main entrance of the building). Naturally only implementations should be contained in the final portfolio that support a successful certification and, thus, provide a strategic value for the company.

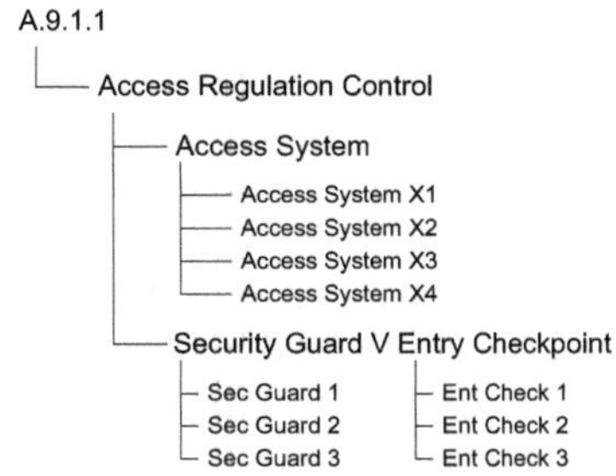

Fig. 6 Access Regulation Control implementation

3.1 Elicitation of Criteria

The criteria set defined in this section serves as main measurement objective for the evaluation of the investment candidates. Due to the multicriterial nature of our approach, a set of criteria is needed that is in line with the strategic objectives of the company. The primary goal of the company under consideration is to pass the certification process (achieved by considering the dependencies defined in section 3.2). At the same time, the company aims to implement measures that optimally cover the need for protection and are cost-efficient. Therefore, the criteria set includes financial criteria and security related objectives taken from literature (cf. [2]):

- Effectiveness (cf. [6]) is defined as the ability to achieve stated goals or objectives, judged in terms of both output and impact. Although our potential countermeasure implementations are not directly related to a specific threat (i.e., defined goals or objectives are missing), their effectiveness can be rated based on their primary purpose. For example, the main purpose of a fire detector is to detect fire and so we rate its effectiveness based on its ability to detect fire. At the current stage of research we are not considering side-effects of countermeasures (e.g., a security guard's primary purpose is to prevent unauthorized access but he would be also able to detect fire).
- Maintainability is a characteristic of design and installation, expressed as the probability that an item will be retained in or restored to a specified condition within a given period of time, when the maintenance is performed in accordance with prescribed procedures and resources [1].
- Reliability is defined by IEEE as the ability of a system or component to perform its required functions under stated conditions for a specified period of time (from 0 up to t). $R(t) = 1 - F(t)$ is the distribution function of the time to the first malfunction. $F(t) = exp(-t/T)$ in the case of an exponentially distributed time to malfunction, where parameter T defines the mean time to malfunction.
- The term running costs $q_{rc}(i)$ should be self-explanatory. They either depend on the maintenance costs or the number of requests.
- Finally, the initial costs $q_{ic}(i)$ represent the amount of money an enterprise has to invest in order to integrate a countermeasure i into its corporate environment.

An in-depth analysis then led to the criteria set summarized in Table 1. Note that depending on whether criteria can be measured in "real units" (e.g., monetary units, time units or measurable resource consumption), different scales are applied. If a category can be measured using a discrete number that relates to a real unit, investment candidates are assigned their absolute value. Otherwise (i.e., in case of intangible assets such as *Maintainability*), an abstract scale of *points* that ranges from 0 to 10 is used. Further note that each criteria is either of type *benefit* or if type *resource*, depending on whether the portfolios' category values should be maximized or minimized.

Code	Description	Unit	Limit
EF	Effectiveness	Pts.	Benefit
MA	Maintainability	Pts.	Benefit
RE	Reliability	Pts.	Benefit
IC	Initial Costs	€ 1,000	Resource
RC	Running Costs	€ 1,000	Resource

Table 1: Final set of objectives (selection criteria)

3.2 Definition of Investment Candidates

Prior to evaluating investment candidates, a set of feasible candidates is pre-selected from the ontological database. This selection is conducted by considering existing components and by performing a rough selection of potential investment candidates and comparing their main characteristics to the decision situation's base line parameters (knock-out criteria), such as available monetary or performance parameters. The number of investment candidates to include in individual evaluation strongly depends on several factors, including application domain and dependencies among the investment candidates – in this specific case, 26 candidates are selected. According to these preconditions and the requirements of the given certification controls, the components chosen for further evaluation are denoted with the letters A to Z and divided into ten groups: Access System (A, B, C, D), Security Guard (E, F, G), Entry Checkpoint (H, I, J), Safety Door (K, L, M), Acrylic Window (N, O), Security Film Window (P, Q), Tempered Window (R, S), Automatic Drainage System (T, U), Fire Extinguisher (V, W, X), and Lighting Arrester (Y, Z). Investment Candidates are rated based on data taken from the security ontology which incorporates specifications, empirical evaluations or estimations (cf. Table 2 for the rating of all investment candidates). Note that the ranges of the ratings differ depending on whether values naturally can be measured quantitatively (e.g., monetary units, time units or resource consumption). If so, investment candidates are directly assigned their absolute values for this criterion. Otherwise, an abstract scale of points is applied.

Candidate	EF	MA	RE	IC	RC
Access System					
Candidate A	2	9	2	9	5
Candidate B	7	9	9	1	7
Candidate C	0	1	6	6	7
Candidate D	0	1	3	17	34
Security Guard					
Candidate E	3	0	8	15	145
Candidate F	2	6	2	0	93
Candidate G	9	6	5	28	56
Entry Checkpoint					
Candidate H	5	3	3	7	12
Candidate I	0	0	9	4	6
Candidate J	5	1	10	27	55
Safety Door					
Candidate K	8	5	6	4	24
Candidate L	6	9	2	9	2
Candidate M	3	2	3	26	82
Acrylic Window					
Candidate N	0	3	6	23	45
Candidate O	2	6	8	1	120
Security Film Window					
Candidate P	9	1	1	9	71
Candidate Q	1	1	7	19	68
Wired Window					
Candidate R	10	4	8	29	26
Candidate S	9	7	7	11	49
Automatic Drainage System					
Candidate T	3	0	3	9	43
Candidate U	2	2	2	32	84
Fire Extinguisher					
Candidate V	8	6	6	20	40
Candidate W	10	2	7	2	22
Candidate X	2	5	8	2	9
Lighting Arrester					
Candidate Y	5	8	2	8	49
Candidate Z	2	6	3	40	70

Table 2: Ratings of investment candidates

3.3 Definition of Dependencies

Some (combinations of) decision alternatives entail dependencies. The ontological database provided the following interdependencies that we used as input for our interactive selection approach:

- **Access Regulation Control**
  $\forall$ *sec:implementedBy only*
  (ent:SecurityGuard $\vee$ *ent:AccessSystem* $\vee$ *ent:EntryCheckpoint)*;
  $\exists$ *sec:implementedBy some ent:AccessSystem*;
  $\exists$ *sec:implementedBy some (ent:SecurityGuard* $\vee$ *ent:EntryCheckpoint)*;
  in other words: the control is fulfilled if an access system or either an entry checkpoint or a security guard is in place.
- **Entrance Control Service Control**
  $\forall$ *sec:implementedBy only (ent:SecurityGuard* $\vee$ *ent:EntryCheckpoint)*;
  $\exists$ *sec:implementedBy some (ent:SecurityGuard* $\vee$ *ent:EntryCheckpoint)*;
  in other words: the control is fulfilled if either an entry checkpoint or a security guard is in place.
- **Safety Doors Control**
  $\forall$ *sec:implementedBy only ent:SafetyDoor*;
  $\exists$ *sec:implementedBy some ent:SafetyDoor*;
  in other words: the control is fulfilled if a safety door is in place.
- **Secure Window Control**
  $\forall$ *sec:implementedBy only*
  (ent:WiredWindow $\vee$ *ent:AcrylicWindow* $\vee$ *ent:SecurityFilmWindow)*;
  $\exists$ *sec:implementedBy some*
  (ent:WiredWindow $\vee$ *ent:AcrylicWindow* $\vee$ *ent:SecurityFilmWindow)*;

in other words: the control is fulfilled if either a wired window, a acrylic window, or a security film window is in place.

- **Automatic Drainage Control**
  ∀ *sec:implementedBy only ent:AutomaticDrainageSystem*;
  ∃ *sec:implementedBy some ent:AutomaticDrainageSystem*;
  in other words: the control is fulfilled if an automatic drainage system is in place.
- **Fire Supression Control**
  ∀ *sec:implementedBy only ent:FireExtinguisher*;
  ∃ *sec:implementedBy some ent:FireExtinguisher*;
  in other words: the control is fulfilled if a fire extinguishing system is in place.
- **Lighting Protection Control**
  ∀ *sec:implementedBy only ent:LightningArrester*;
  ∃ *sec:implementedBy some ent:LightningArrester*;
  in other words: the control is fulfilled if a lighting arrester is in place.

3.4 Interactive Selection of ISO 27001 Controls

Following the multiobjective decision support procedure described in section 2.2, the process starts by importing the categories together with potential controls and dependencies from the ontology. Depending on the number of objectives, constraints and business processes, Atana is capable of evaluating about 40 investment candidates per decision situation. In our case study (which includes five objectives plus 26 investment candidates) the underlying MOCO problem can be solved on an average workstation in less than one minute. Thus, 249 non-dominated (i.e., Pareto-efficient) feasible portfolios are identified. These solution alternatives are further evaluated using Atana's interactive decision support module.

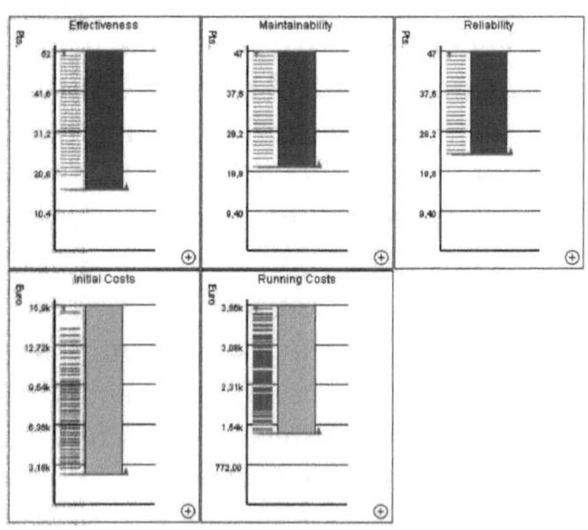

Fig. 7 Initial mask of the Atana analysis tool

Figure 7 shows the initial screen of the analysis tool. By moving the red upper and lower rulers, aspiration levels are set (for minimum or maximum values in a given objective category) and, thus, the number of remaining solutions can be reduced in a straightforward manner. In our example, this is performed as follows: at first, the maximum initial costs are reduced to a value of 6k and the running costs to a level of 2k, which reduces the number of portfolios from 249 to 23 (cf. Fig. 8).

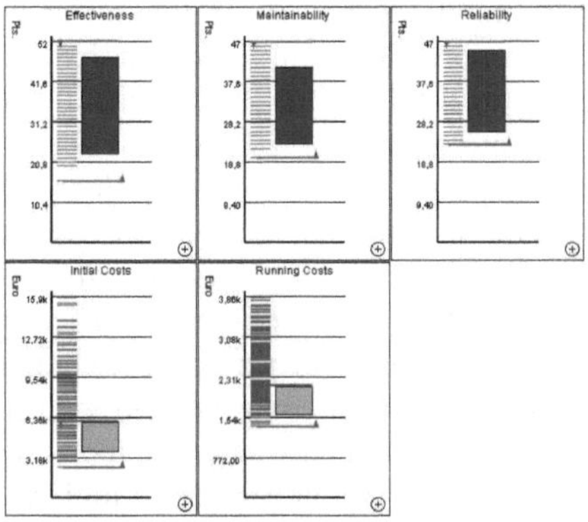

Fig. 8: Mask after the user's first setting

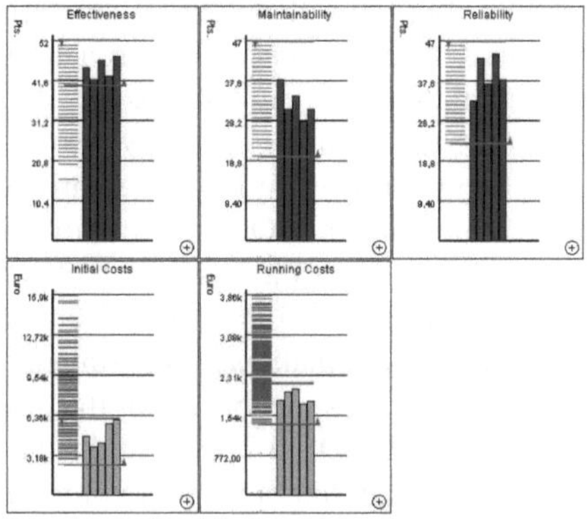

Fig. 9: Mask after the user's final setting

After this, the minimum requirement for effectiveness is set to a value of 40 points, while the corresponding values for maintainability and for reliability remain unchanged. Afterwards, the remaining five portfolios are visualized side by side (cf. Fig. 9). The remaining portfolios (cf. Table 3) provide benefits on an average level

Portfolio	Controls	EF	MA	RE	IC	RC
1	B, H, L, S, T, W, Y	45	38	33	4700	1800
2	B, I, K, S, T, W, Y	42	31	43	3900	2000
3	B, H, K, S, T, W, Y	47	34	37	4200	2060
4	B, I, K, R, T, W, Y	43	28	44	5700	1770
5	B, H, K, R, T, W, Y	48	31	38	6000	1830

Table 3: List of the remaining portfolios

and are associated with average resource consumptions. Note that the second and fourth portfolio provide the highest values for reliability, but also the lowest values for effectiveness and maintainability. Portfolios two and three come with the lowest initial costs but have the highest running costs of all solutions, whereas their benefits are on an average level. Depending on the decision makers preferences, one of these can either be selected or the evaluation process can be continued by picking other portfolios and/or (re-)setting the aspiration levels.

4 Conclusions and Further Work

Although an organization benefits from an information security certification in several ways, most companies refrain from the implementation of information security standards, amongst other reasons due to the lack of methods for measuring the cost/benefits ratio of potential countermeasure implementations. In this paper we proposed a new two-phase approach, which supports decision makers in defining the optimal set of countermeasures complying to the ISO 27001 standard. In the first step, the security ontology serves as an ontological knowledge base for potential countermeasure implementations (and combinations thereof), which are required to obtain an ISO 27001 certification. In the second step, the decision support system Atana determines solution alternatives that are both feasible with respect to given constraints and Pareto-efficient with respect to multiple objectives. Thereby we give decision makers an instrument that allows them to interactively select tangible countermeasures based on the abstract descriptions of controls from security standards such as ISO 27001. In the case study we showed how Atana supports decision makers in interactively exploring the determined solution space to find their individually "best" solution. While this paper addresses mainly physical countermeasure implementations (e.g., fire extinguisher, secure windows, or safety doors), further research activities will address the inclusion of organizational aspects (e.g., policy components, legal regulations) to support the ISO 27001 certification in the most holistic way. We will also consider the dependencies among countermeasures and vulnerabilities to ensure that potential countermeasure side-effects are regarded within the Atana methodology.

Acknowledgements This work was performed at Secure Business Austria, a competence center that is funded by the Austrian Federal Ministry of Economics and Labor (BMWA) as well as by the provincial government of Vienna.

References

1. Federal standard 1037c. URL http://www.its.bldrdoc.gov/fs-1037/fs-1037c.htm, last access: 7 April 2008
2. Avizienis, A., Laprie, J.C., Randell, B., Landwehr, C.: Basic Concepts and Taxonomy of Dependable and Secure Computing. IEEE Transactions on Dependable and Secure Computing **1**(1), 11–33 (2004)
3. BASEL2: Basel Committee on Banking Supervision (BCBS), Basel 2 - International Convergence of Capital Measurement and Capital Standards - A Revised Framework (2001)
4. British Department of Trade and Industry (DTI): BS7799-2:2002 Information security management systems - Specification with guidance for use (2002)
5. BSI: IT Grundschutz Manual. Online: http://www.bsi.bund.de/gshb/ (2004).
6. Bureau of Justice Assistance: Center for Program Evaluation - Glossary. Online: http://www.ojp.usdoj.gov/BJA/evaluation/glossary/glossary_e.htm, last access: 7 April 2008 (2007)

7. Ehrgott, M., Gandibleux, X.: A survey and annotated bibliography of multiobjective combinatorial optimization. OR Spectrum **22**(4), 425–460 (2000)
8. Ekelhart, A., Fenz, S., Klemen, M., Weippl, E.: Security Ontology: Simulating Threats to Corporate Assets. In: A. Bagchi, V. Atluri (eds.) Second International Conference, ICISS 2006, December 19-21, *Lecture Notes in Computer Science*, vol. 4332/2006, pp. 249–259. Springer Berlin / Heidelberg, Kolkata, India (2006). DOI 10.1007/11961635_17
9. Ekelhart, A., Fenz, S., Klemen, M., Weippl, E.: Security ontologies: Improving quantitative risk analysis. In: 40th Hawaii International Conference on System Sciences (HICSS'07), pp. 156–162. IEEE Computer Society, Los Alamitos, CA, USA (2007).
10. Fenz, S., Goluch, G., Ekelhart, A., Riedl, B., Weippl, E.: Information security fortification by ontological mapping of the ISO/IEC 27001 Standard pp. 381–388 (2007).
11. Focke, A., Stummer, C.: Strategic technology planning in hospital management. OR Spectrum **25**(2), 161–182 (2003)
12. Gordon, L., Loeb, M., Lucyshyn, W., Richardson, R.: 2006 CSI/FBI Computer Crime and Security Survey (2006)
13. Gruber, T.: A translation approach to portable ontology specifications. Knowledge Acquisition **5**(2), 199–220 (1993).
14. International Organization for Standardization and International Electrotechnical Commission: ISO/IEC 17799:2005, information technology – code of practice for information security management (2005)
15. International Organization for Standardization and International Electrotechnical Commission: ISO/IEC 27001:2005, information technology - security techniques - information security management systems- requirements (2005)
16. Ittner, C.D., Larcker, D.F.: Coming Up Short On Financial Measurement. Harvard Business Review **81**(11), 88–95 (2003)
17. Neubauer, T., Stummer, C.: Extending business process management to determine efficient IT investments. In: Proceedings of the 2007 ACM Symposium on Applied Computing, pp. 1250–1256 (2007)
18. Neubauer, T., Stummer, C.: Interactive decision support for multiobjective cots selection. In: Proceedings of the 40th Annual Hawaii International Conference on System Sciences, 01 (2007)
19. Neubauer, T., Stummer, C., Weippl, E.: Workshop-based Multiobjective Security Safeguard Selection. In: Proceedings of the First International Conference on Availability, Reliability and Security ARES, pp. 366–373. IEEE Computer Society (2006)
20. NIST: An introduction to computer security - the nist handbook. Tech. rep., NIST(National Institute of Standards and Technology) (1995). URL http://csrc.nist.gov/publications/nistpubs/800-12/handbook.pdf. Special Publication 800-12
21. PriceWaterhouseCoopers: Information Security Breaches Survey. www.dti.gov.uk/industries/information_security, last access: 7 April 2008 (2006)
22. SOX: One hundred seventh congress of the United States of America, Sarbanes Oxley Act - to protect investors by improving the accuracy and reliability of corporate disclosures made pursuant to the securities laws, and for other purposes. (2002)
23. Stummer, C., Heidenberger, K.: Interactive R&D portfolio analysis with project interdependencies and time profiles of multiple objectives. IEEE Transactions on Engineering Management **50**(2), 175–183 (2003)
24. World Wide Web Consortium: OWL - Web Ontology Language. http://www.w3.org/TR/owl-features/, last access: 7 April 2008 (2004)

Feasibility of Automated Information Security Compliance Auditing

Longley D., Branagan M., Caelli W.J. and Kwok LF

1 Introduction

According to AS/NZS ISO/IEC 27001:2006 [11], management of an organization should provide evidence of its commitment to the establishment, implementation, operation, monitoring, review, maintenance and improvement of the organization's information security management system. The objective of this research project was to explore the feasibility of designing an intelligent documentation system to assist information security managers in meeting this commitment. In particular, this documentation system would assist in the associated tasks of risk assessment and information security compliance auditing.

The proposed documentation system, comprising both supporting software and a database model of the organizational information security environment, together with formalized compliance requirements, may be used both for automated and on-going compliance testing as well as risk assessment. The risk assessment aspect of the documentation system has been described in previous papers [3, 14]. This paper will deal with a feasibility study of automated compliance auditing. Such automated compliance auditing would enable security managers to readily benchmark their current systems against the appropriate information security standards.

This study was undertaken to specifically explore the feasibility of automated compliance auditing against an international information security standard. The standard originally selected for the study was AS/NZS ISO/IEC 17799:2001) [9]

Dennis Longley and William J Caelli
International Information Security Consultants Pty Ltd, 21 Castle Hill Drive South, Gaven, Queensland 4211 Australia e-mail: d.longley@iisec.com.au,w.caelli@iisec.com.au

Mark A. Branagan
Information Security Institute Queensland University of Technology, GPO Box 2434, Brisbane, Qld, Aust 4001 e-mail: m.branagan@isi.qut.edu.au

Lam-for Kwok
Department of Computer Science, City University of Hong Kong, 83 Tat Chee Avenue, Kowloon, HKSAR, PRC e-mail: cslfkwok@cityu.edu.hk

Please use the following format when citing this chapter:

Longley D., et al., 2008, in IFIP International Federation for Information Processing, Volume 278; *Proceedings of the IFIP TC 11 23rd International Information Security Conference*; Sushil Jajodia, Pierangela Samarati, Stelvio Cimato; (Boston: Springer), pp. 493–507.

but during the course of the project this standard was replaced by AS/NZS ISO/IEC 17799:2006 [10]. However, since the objective of the study was to explore the feasibility of automated information security compliance auditing in general, the decision was taken to complete the detailed work on the previous standard.

Bellamy et al [4] warn against the concept of automatic compliance systems *"because ultimately one or more persons must take personal and legal responsibility for compliance."* Nevertheless the use of automation to significantly reduce the manual effort, currently required by information security personnel, and thus the cost of compliance auditing is a worthwhile venture. It is postulated that automated compliance auditing would significantly reduce the auditing effort currently faced by security personnel. This would enable audits to be routinely performed: as part of a continuing security improvement process, when reporting on the security implications of proposed developments, etc. The provision of audit reports for governance purposes would be a natural byproduct of this process.

The implementation of automated compliance testing is not a cost free process. However, by minimizing duplication of effort and removing the need to have experienced security staff undertake many of the required auditing tasks the overall cost is reduced. With the proposed system, the significant effort of converting a text based standard to a series of logical statements is undertaken by some central body, e.g. an appropriate standards authority or the head office of a large organization. The auditing data collection / collation effort is then simplified to the point where it can be handled by junior technical or administrative staff.

A major component of this research project lay in the experimental conversion of a text based standard into a series of logical statements to be used for automated compliance testing. An idealized view of the proposed system is illustrated in Fig. 1. The compliance auditing software processes the standards requirements and organizational system documentation to produce audit data, subsequently evaluated by an experienced auditor to produce a final report for senior management. The audit data output itself would also provide useful information to security managers.

The study did not assume that standardized system documentation would be readily available to security managers or that current organizational documentation could be readily reformulated. It is however postulated that an interface to the system documentation and data can be developed to facilitate the task of querying

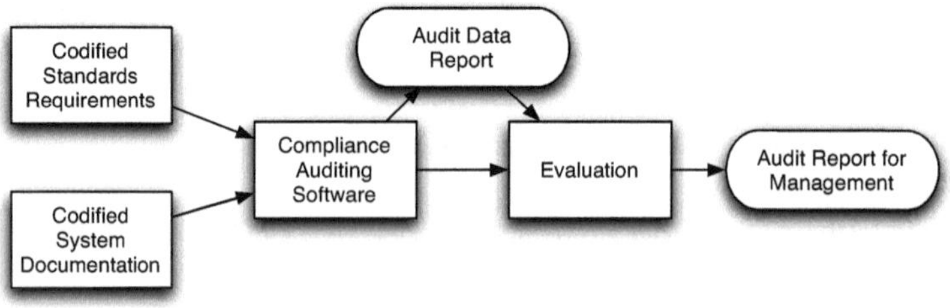

Fig. 1 Automated Compliance Auditing Standards Requirements

organizational security relevant information. This study encompassed: conversion of the ISO/IEC 17799:2001 document into a series of codified compliance requirements (CCR), development of an interface to facilitate querying of organizational security relevant data, and development of prototype compliance auditing software.

The results of this research study demonstrated an automated compliance audit for a small system against the requirements of AS/NZS ISO/IEC 17799:2001 providing useful experience in establishing an automated compliance auditing regime.

2 Governance and Compliance Auditing Background

The U.S. government has been active in information security governance for several decades. Creation and dissemination of standards and guidelines commenced in the early 1970s under the auspices of the National Bureau of Standards (NBS), the predecessor of the National Institute of Standards and Technology (NIST). In 1992, the OECD Guidelines for the Security of Information Systems [15] defined nine principles to address concerns for the dangers of weak information security. The UK Governments Department of Trade and Industry (DTI) published a Code of Practice for Information Security Management [18], amended and re-published by the British Standards Institute as BS 7799 in 1995[5]. This standard was revised in 1999 evolving into ISO/IEC 17799 in 2000 [8]. BS 7799-2, an Information Security Management Specification, was published in 2002 [6]. Currently ISO/IEC 17799:2006 and ISO 27001:2006 [11, 10] represent the latest versions of these standards.

The massive expansion of government and corporate ICT systems in the last decade, coupled with growing concerns about corporate governance practice, have increased the demands made upon management to demonstrate the effectiveness of their information security systems and procedures. Hence legislation has been enacted related to corporate financial governance (the USA's Sarbanes-Oxley Act [17]), maintenance of healthcare information systems (HIPAA [16]), and confidentiality of personal information held by companies (California's SB1386 [2]). These and other similar pieces of legislation require an enterprises management to demonstrate the scope and effectiveness of their information security systems and procedures.

These governance demands have placed a heavy load on corporate management and an estimated cost of $27.9 billion for compliance testing in the U.S alone in 2007 has been quoted [1]. This level of governance implies that management should move beyond a mere demonstration of the "health" of the current ICT system to the adoption of enterprise architectures incorporating information security.

3 An overview of Automated Compliance Auditing

Financial auditing has a centuries old tradition and a financial auditor undertakes two tasks:

- Examination of the organizations financial records against audit requirements to produce a set of audit data indicating any areas of apparent incompatibilities etc.
- Production of a report on the financial situation of the audited organization based upon a detailed evaluation of that audit data.

The first process is normally delegated to junior accounting staff and their task is simplified by the standardization of normal financial documents. This standardization allows them to cope readily with financial records from a variety of sources. The information security manager is usually in a less enviable position since the limited history of information security auditing has not produced detailed guidance on security documentation. Hence, currently, compliance auditing frequently involves significant cross correlation of conventional organizational documentation never designed for that purpose. Consider for example, AS/NZS ISO/IEC 17799:2001 Para 7.1 which includes the statement:

> Critical or sensitive business information processing facilities should be housed in secure areas, protected by a defined security perimeter, with appropriate security barriers and entry controls. They should be physically protected from unauthorized access, damage and interference.

In the late 1980s a mainframe computer centre manager would probably know from memory the details of any computing systems processing sensitive data, their locations and the physical security of those locations. Current, complex distributed information processing presents an entirely different scenario. The information security auditor must now cross-correlate sensitive information assets with processing systems, identify each component of the distributed system, determine its location and cross correlate its location with any security barriers and entry controls. For present systems, even if this information is documented, there may be no guarantee that system changes are accurately reflected in this documentation.

In these circumstances the compliance auditor is faced with, at best, the difficult task of gleaning the requisite system data from a variety of document sources, and at worst with a major data collection task involving interviews and physical inspections. This data collection task may need to be repeated for each audit. The prime benefit of automated compliance auditing is that it encourages the standardization of the requisite documentation, reducing the effort involved in multiple data collection activities and of cross correlating this data with standards requirements.

3.1 Security Documentation for Auditing

Previous work on security documentation has been reported [3, 14, 13, 12, 7]. Given the problems of reformulating the total set of existing relevant organizational documentation to a form suitable for information security auditing, a proposed alternative approach is illustrated in Fig. 2. Here a database providing a template for an information security model (ISM) of the organization, is developed, e.g. by the standards authority, to facilitate querying for standards compliance checking.

The information security model firstly represents each item relevant to information security in an organization, i.e. IT systems and components, locations, services, documentation etc., as an entity with attributes and inter-relationships. These entities are organized hierarchically in a tree structure. Each database entry thus represents a node of the tree structure and stores the attributes of that entity, e.g. the date of a document, the security sensitivity of an information asset, etc. The inter-relationships between entities are themselves considered as system entities, and their components are similarly stored in database entries.

This template database thus contains entries for entities such as *information processing system* and *buildings*, and relationships between those entities (e.g. *located_in*). This template database reduces duplication of security documentation design effort amongst security managers by providing an operational framework.

When populated the Standardized ISM Database contains: cross-references to the organization's documentation set, information on requisite entities from the documentation, and additional data on entities required for compliance auditing and not available from the current organizational documentation.

The task of implementing and updating the standardized model database is discussed in more detail below (See 5.3). The manual effort required to establish and update the model database depends, to some extent, on the form and content of existing organizational documentation. If the existing documentation can be queried electronically, incorporating the data into the database will involve minimal effort. If the documentation is not in electronic form then populating the database initially will be more labour intensive, as in a manual audit. This initial effort will nevertheless be repaid by the reduction in effort required for subsequent compliance auditing and risk analysis data collection. Further, the end result will be a comprehensive information security database for the security manager. In any event, the use of the template database implies that much of the work can be delegated to junior staff.

The Standardized ISM Database serves as a standards requirements interface to the organizations IT documentation, systems and environment and significantly reduces the task of formulating codified standards requirements to be used in automated compliance auditing. In particular, when a standards requirement makes a reference to a model entity, e.g. a security policy document, that database entry is available to the designer of the codified compliance requirement (See Fig. 3).

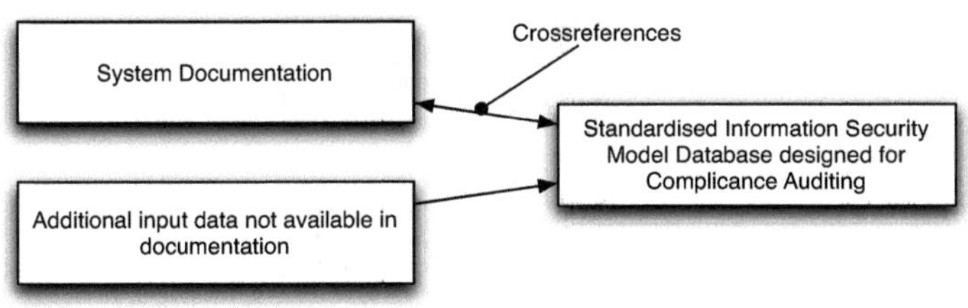

Fig. 2 A Documentation Database for Compliance Auditing

The security manager populates the database by adding organizationally specific information to entries in the template. For example, ISO 17799:2001 specifies the requirement for a management approved security policy document with various subsections. Entities for that document and its subsections would be included as named entities in the database template. The manager would then enter certain attributes of these entities, such as cross-references to the corresponding organizational security policy and its subsections, date and confirmation of management approval, etc. as specified by the compliance requirements.

The security manager is also required to add *children* entities to nodes of the template tree such as, rooms, information processing systems, networks etc. and to add relationship entities indicating, for example, the *location of information processing systems*, *interconnections of networks*, etc. Relationships inherently required by the content of various standards paragraphs are defined in the template database.

When the database has been populated it can be queried via the codified compliance requirements to produce an audit data report (Fig.5). The database is moreover a valuable documentation resource and the model data can also be used for risk assessment studies as described in a previous paper [14].

3.2 Codified Compliance Requirements

A number of the sections of AS/NZS ISO/IEC 17799:2001 [9] are purely informative from the viewpoint of the standard itself, e.g. Sections 1 and 2. In addition, the subsequent sections sometimes contain informative subsections that may be included in the local internal security manual.

The remaining standards paragraphs specify requirements and need to be transformed from simple text format to a series of logical statements for automated compliance auditing. These codified compliance requirements (CCRs) are formulated at a central authority, e.g. by the standards body, and supplied to the security manager with the template ISM database.

Using the ISM database as an interface to organizational information security documentation implies that standards compliance requirements may be specified in

Fig. 3 Standardised ISM Database

terms of ISM database entities, their attributes and interrelationships. Each of these entities may be specified in turn as the address of the corresponding database entry.

The degree of complexity associated with the various sections of information security standards varies widely. Some merely refer to the contents of certain documents, whilst others involve attributes and inter-relationships of users, systems, assets, documentation etc. Experience in developing the CCRs for the various chapters of 17799:2001 indicated the value of a relatively simple basic form of codified requirement, as a building block for the various compliance requirements (Fig. 4).

The codified compliance requirement format developed in this study comprises the following components, compliance reference and brief description, starting entities, relationship between target entities and starting entity, criteria to be met by the target entities, output entities, and audit data.

The starting entity refers to an entry in the ISM Database (See Sect 3.2), and is included as an address in the CCR. This illustrates the advantage of the standardized model in that the designer of the CCR can directly access the entity of concern, once accessed the data included for that entry is queried for compliance checking.

3.3 Information Security Model Database

The ISM database was developed originally for risk assessment [3] and risk assessments may utilize the data entered for compliance auditing and vice versa. The ISM data are stored in a tree structure. There are no constraints on this structure and the ISM software does not assume any particular model or contain any security information; it merely manipulates the entities as required. The parent nodes of the tree hierarchy used in the compliance auditing study were:

- System: Platforms (information processing systems), hardware, networks, software, assets, users and security components
- Environment: Location (sites, buildings, rooms...) and services (power supplies...)
- Security: (not used for compliance testing but retained for risk assessment studies)

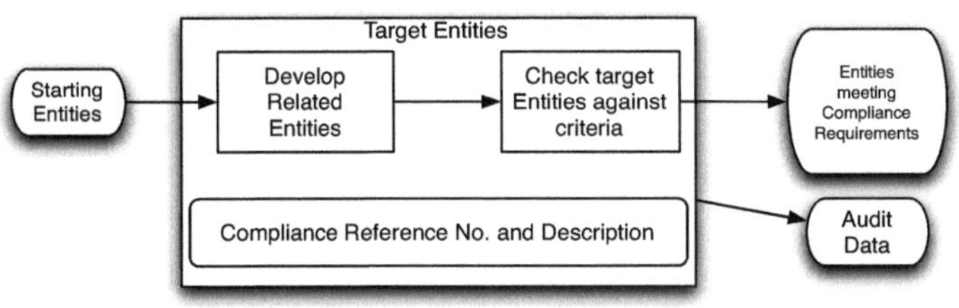

Fig. 4 Codified Compliance Requirement (CCR) Requirements

- Procedures: (documentation, organization, CCRs)
- Relationships

The software displays the tree as a conventional directory tree and entities can be accessed with the conventional GUI for accessing files in a directory structure. The details of each entity: name, description, attributes and relationships, are displayed as the entity is selected Entities can be added or modified manually, but for this study entities were input in the form of an XML file.

Entities may be assigned attributes defined in tag-value format. The value may be a text string, any defined object or another entity. Relationships between entities are themselves treated as entities and are used to define linkages between entities.

3.4 Compliance Software

Development of the compliance software was facilitated by the availability of routines used in the risk assessment studies. Nevertheless there was a considerable degree of experimentation and trouble shooting initially, due to the lack of experience in the interpretation of the standards, design of CCRs and the model template, etc.

A number of valuable lessons were learnt in this development process:

- complex CCRs should be developed as combinations of basic standard forms;
- the correctness of CCRs should be assured before compliance testing;
- the audit data output should be designed to provide maximum information to the auditor rather than as a final report to management.

3.5 Auditing

The immediate output from the automated compliance auditing process is a set of audit data (Fig. 5) representing the detailed results arising from the application of the CCRs to the populated ISM database. The audit data contain details of the standards section, conformance/non conformance to the compliance requirements, names of the starting and target entities and, if required, attributes of those entities.

AUDIT RESULT Seq No. 1.1 Section 17799. Sect 3.1.1

RESULT ConditionResult: initialEntity = Security Policy Document

resultEntity = Security Policy Document targetEntity = Security Policy Document

Decision = true

Candidate attr list

URL doc/policy

Fig. 5 Audit Report

The compliance software creates audit data reports on the information contained in the ISM database but the auditor needs to evaluate this data. For example:

- Do the organizational document subsections cross-referenced in the database actually contain the information specified in the textual standards?
- Is the ISM database content complete and accurate, e.g. is there a sensitive information processing system located in an insecure environment that is not entered in the ISM database?

The automated compliance auditing will have supplied the auditor with a cross-reference to the requisite document subsection, and ideally this will take the form of a URL to that subsection, allowing the auditor to randomly sample the specified document subsections.

The auditor should also seek assurance that the ISM database truly reflects the state of organizational information security by requesting that it be certified by organizational management. For example, the ISM database contents may be recorded as an XML document and signed off by organizational management.

Management in turn will need to seek assurances on the validity of the database contents prior to providing such certification. Such assurances may result from internal audits, facilitated by the format of the ISM database. For example, security managers may run partial audits related to sections of the standards, e.g. physical and environmental security, after known system changes or on a regular basis with a frequency related to the volatility in a particular sector and compare audit results with their local knowledge. Such proposed procedures for updating and checking the ISM database are described in more detail below (See 5.4).

The audit data produced by the compliance software contains a great deal of detail which is useful to the auditor and security manager, as described above, but is superfluous from a governance viewpoint. It is therefore suggested that the audit data be evaluated, and processed into a final audit report, for submission to management (see Fig.1).

4 Designing Codified Compliance Requirements

This study was designed to explore, inter alia, the problem of converting a text based standard to a series of logical statements for automated compliance auditing. In this process it became clear that considerable care was required to ensure that this translation conformed to the intentions of the standards authors. Whilst conventional security auditors have the task of interpreting the individual sections of the standards in the context of their local system, the CCR designer must undertake this interpretation in a much wider context. It is therefore important that some higher authority examines the subsequent set of codified requirements to ensure that they truly reflect the intentions of the standards authority. Codification of legal documents in this regard provides a useful precedent.

The CCRs were developed in this study to indicate the feasibility of such an approach. They were based upon best endeavor interpretation and were not intended as an authorized version for general usage. One of the major concerns in this interpretation process was that of deciding the level of compliance checking. Consider for example: 17799:2001 Section 8.1.4 *Segregation of duties* referring to the danger of fraud if personnel have excessive access privileges.

Bracketing the potential compliance levels one might consider the upper and lower levels of compliance to be:

- **Least Stringent:** insert a paragraph in the local security manual to the effect that managers were to apply segregation of duties principles when allocating access privileges
- **Highly Stringent:** checking the access privileges of every individual member of staff to ensure adequate segregation of duties.

In some cases it may prove impossible to agree upon a single codified compliance for all organizations. In this case categories of organizations could be defined, and CCRs developed for each category. In summary, the CCR designer requires guidance on the interpretation of the text based standard, and the subsequent codified compliance requirements should be subjected to approval from a higher authority.

4.1 Basic Compliance Requirements

A codified compliance requirement (CCR) is essentially an IF-THEN statement. Nevertheless, considerable experimentation with the format of CCRs occurred in the course of this project. The lesson learnt from this experimentation was that a simple basic format, capable of parameterization and combination, presented the best solution. The basic format selected is illustrated in Fig. 4. The parameterization comprised the routines used to relate target entities to individual starting entities and apply criteria for the target entities.

A target entity will satisfy one or more of the following conditions in relation to the starting entity:

- any immediate child of the starting entity, from the viewpoint of sub trees in the model database;
- any descendent of the starting entity;
- any entity linked to the starting entity in a specified model database relationship;
- any entity linked recursively to the starting entity in a specified model database relationship;
- any entity contained in the starting entity when the latter is a specified relationship.

In some cases a simple Boolean AND was used to combine conditions. It was found that all the compliance requirements of 17799:2001 could be formulated using this approach. The criteria used for 17799:2001 requirements were that the target entity must be an entity:

- with the same model database address as a CCR specified entity;
- with the same name as a CCR specified entity;
- which is a child of a CCR specified entity;
- with a CCR specified attribute, or set of attributes;
- with a CCR specified attribute value.

This basic CCR was adequate for one of the most common compliance requirements, i.e. for those sections of the standard recommending that specified subsections be included in a given document.

4.2 Serial Compliance Requirements

A serial combination of CCRs was commonly used to report upon situations related to operational documentation concerning a given set of entities, e.g. documentation for processing systems, information assets etc. For example, 17799:2001 section 8.1.1 Documented Operating Procedures states, *The operating procedures identified by the security policy should be documented and maintained.* Audit of this requirement essentially involves a multi stage operation: select all the information processing systems; retrieve the operating procedure documentation for each information processing system; and check that each operating procedure document contains the subsections specified in Section 8.1.1.

Whilst the number of stages could be reduced by the use of AND conditions the multistage CCR was used to ensure comprehensive reporting in the audit data, e.g. it was important to report if there were no operating procedures for a particular information processing system.

5 Implementation

There are three parties in the proposed scheme:

- the body responsible for the design of the ISM database template and codified compliance requirements (CCR). It is expected that the software comprising the ISM template, CCRs and compliance checking software would be supplied to security managers;
- security managers responsible for populating the ISM database and maintaining and certifying the database contents for audit purposes;
- compliance auditors responsible for checking and evaluating the audit data.

The first task in the process leading to the automated compliance system lies in the definition of the ISM template database providing an indication of the assumed IT environment for the audit. The CCRs utilizing the template database must then be produced and tested.

Organizations will then be supplied with software comprising the ISM template database, compliance checking software and CCRs. The security managers will then populate the ISM database with details of the organizational IT environment, and accept responsibility for checking and maintaining this database for use in audits.

The information security auditors will run the compliance checking software with the CCRs to produce the audit data and make checks on the validity of this data, before evaluating it and producing an audit report for management. Each of these processes is described in more detail in the following sections.

5.1 Defining the Information Security Model Template

In this study the information security model template was defined and the database was populated with model data to test the codified compliance requirement (CCR) design. There were two major aspects of the template model developed for compliance auditing: documentation entities and system entities. A high proportion of the 17799:2001 sections refer to implied organizational documentation and experience of codifying those requirements suggested that the requisite documentation entities fell into four categories: security policy; internal security manual; operational security documentation; and reports, contracts, logs, reviews etc.

The requirements for the security policy document are described in 17799:2001 Section 3.1.1 and enhanced in subsequent sections e.g. Section 8.3.1: *"a formal policy requiring compliance with software licences and prohibiting the use of unauthorized software."*

The internal security manual informs all organizational parties of the security requirements and is, in effect, an edited version of the standards document translated for the local environment. The corresponding operational security documentation entities represent the documents recommended within the security manual for the various system entities, e.g. the documented operating procedures for each information processing system as described in 17799:2001 Section 8.1.1

The first three categories of documentation have a one-to-one relationship with the standards and hence represent entities defined by the CCR designer, having addresses in the database known to the designer. The fourth category of documentation entities *reports, contracts, logs, reviews etc.* represent multiple documents produced by the organization and are listed under headings specified by the CCR designer.

The model system entities were added as they were mentioned within the various sections of the standards. These system entities included: platforms (i.e. information processing systems), hardware, software, networks, users, information assets, security, locations and services, and the various subheadings were added as they arose in the standard.

The relationships were also defined as the need was indicated by the standards, e.g. systems were *located_in* in sites/buildings, and were *supplied* by power supplies, cabling was *installed_in* locations, gateways were *connected_ to* networks and so on.

5.2 Designing the Codified Compliance Requirements

The conversion of textual standards statements into CCRs is not a mechanical process. Standards authors assume that the requirements will be interpreted by auditors in the context of a local IT environment. The ISM database template serves to give some context for the design of the CCRs and this template must therefore be defined as the first task in the translation process. The translation of some standards requirements, e.g. those dealing with documentation, was reasonably straightforward. For others the design of the CCRs was not so clear. Many standards requirements related to system entities necessitated careful analysis of the standards text and significant assumptions related to the organizational context when designing CCRs. It is likely that for some standards statements a number of organizational contexts may need to be postulated and CCRs specified for each.

Following the requirements translation the design of the CCRs may be undertaken in a four stage process:

- commence with a classification of the various sections of the translated standard into CCR categories,
- design CCRs for each of these categories;
- translate the standards textual statements into these CCRs categories;
- produce the CCRs.

The experience of CCR design described above (See 3.2) may well assist in the procedure. In this study the CCR design proceeded quite rapidly once the foundations on CCR formats and template design had been established. It is recommended that software be developed to aid CCR designers in the production of CCR XML documents. Checking the CCR format before it is processed by the compliance checking software significantly reduced the complexity of that software, and facilitated trouble shooting in the CCR design.

5.3 Implementing and Maintaining the ISM Database

There are perhaps three potential classes of organizational information security documentation:

- Case 1: comprehensive, in electronic form and containing all the information required by the standard;
- Case 2 : reasonably comprehensive, in electronic form but not sufficiently complete in terms of the standards requirements;
- Case 3: not comprehensive and only partially or not in electronic form.

In the first case the codified compliance requirements could be formulated to allow for direct access to the organizational information, and the ISM database would not be required. Tools used to explore and report upon networks would probably produce this form of documentation, but other aspects of the documentation, e.g.

personnel, physical and environmental security would also need to be in this format.

In the second case effort required to bring the documentation to the level of Case 1 would probably be greater than that of implementing the ISM database. It should, in any case, be possible to arrange for much of the electronic documentation to be queried so to produce the data for direct entry into the ISM database.

In the third case there would be a significant amount of effort expended in extracting the requisite input data for the ISM database. However, this would be a once-off task, the alternative approach of conventional manual auditing would involve this amount of effort for every audit. In any event much of this work related to the population of ISM database is a of routine nature and may be delegated to junior staff.

5.4 Conducting Audits

The objective of automated compliance auditing is to transform the audit process from a major manual task, which may be viewed as a bureaucratic burden by information security managers, to a routine activity, conducted periodically to provide feedback on the organizational information security stance.

Audits for governance purposes will follow the process illustrated in Fig. 1. The auditor will evaluate the audit data from the viewpoint of ensuring its correctness, completeness and significance. The audit data is a reflection of the contents in the ISM database and the auditor will seek some re-assurance that it reflects the true organizational situation hence the auditor may conduct additional investigations to:

- ensure that cross-references lead to documents that do indeed have the requisite contents;
- check that the documentation has a valid certification and that there is evidence of periodic internal audits verifying the ISM database contents;
- check that some random samples of the database contents are consistent with the results of interviews and physical inspections.

Once the audit data has been subject to verification as described above the auditor will then consider the significance of the audit data in relation to the management intentions on information security and produce a final report for senior management.

6 Conclusion

The objective of information security standards is to raise the level of information security in an organization to an optimum state. If the auditing process is a periodic and highly onerous task undertaken merely to satisfy governance requirements, there is a danger that it can simply serve to increase the burden on the information security manager without materially improving the actual level of information security in the enterprise. Automated compliance auditing as described here provides the information security officer with a valuable resource in terms of the ISM database which can be used both for compliance auditing and associated risk assessment [14]. The compliance audits can moreover be undertaken more routinely, allowing the security manager take a more proactive role in terms of continuous improvement and quick reaction to system changes.

References

1. C. Abrams, J. vonKänel, S. Müller, B. Pfitzmann, and S. Ruschka-Taylor. Optimized enterprise risk management. *IBM Systems Journal*, 46 (2):219–234, 2007.
2. California Security Breach Information Act. SB 1386, 2003.
3. Alison Anderson, Dennis Longley, and Lam For Kwok. Security modelling for organisations. In *CCS '94: Proceedings of the 2nd ACM Conference on Computer and communications security*, pages 241–250, New York, NY, USA, 1994. ACM.
4. R.K.E Bellamy, T. Erickson, B. Fuller, W.A. Kellogg, R. Rosenbaum, J.C. Thomas, and T. Vetting Wolf. Seeing is believing: Designing visualizations for managing risk and compliance. *IBM Systems Journal*, 46 (2):205 –218, 2007.
5. British Standards Institute. BS 7799, Code of Practice for Information Security Management, 1995.
6. British Standards Institute. BS 7799-2, Information Security Management Specification, 2002.
7. W.J. Caelli, G. Gaskell, LF Kwok, and D. Longley. A model to support information security governance. *Journal of Information Risk Management and Audit*, 16(1):7–24, 2006.
8. International Standards Organisation. ISO/IEC 17799:2000, Information technology—Code of practice for information security management, 2000.
9. Joint Australian and New Zealand Standard. AS/NZS ISO/IEC 17799:2001 Information technology—Code of practice for information security management, 2001.
10. Joint Australian and New Zealand Standard. AS/NZS ISO/IEC 17799:2006 Information technology — Security techniques— Code of practice for information security management, 2006.
11. Joint Australian and New Zealand Standard. AS/NZS ISO/IEC 27001:2006 Information technology — Security techniques — Information security management systems- Requirements, 2006.
12. L-F Kwok and D. Longley. Information security management and modelling. *Information Management and Computer Security*, 7(2):3–4, 1999.
13. Lam For Kwok and Dennis Longley. A security officer's workbench. *Computers & Security*, 15(8):695–705, 1996.
14. Lam-for Kwok and Dennis Longley. Security modelling for risk analysis. *Security and Protection in Information Processing Systems*, pages 29–45, 2004.
15. Organisation for Economic Co-operation and Development, Directorate for Science Technology and Industry. Guidelines for the security of information systems, 1992.
16. Health Insurance Portability and Accountability Act of 1996. Public law 104-191, united states senate and house of representatives in congress, 1996.
17. Sarbanes-Oxley Act of 2002. Public law 107-204 (116 statute 745), united states senate and house of representatives in congress, 2002.
18. U.K. Department of Trade and Industry. Code of practice for information security management, 1992.

security manager without manually improving the actual level of information security in the enterprise. Automated compliance auditing as described here provides the information security officer with a valuable resource in scope of the ISMS. Insofar [illegible]

[illegible]

[illegible]

Software Licence Protection and Management for Organisations

Muntaha Alawneh and Imad M. Abbadi

Abstract Most organisations have recently converted their physical assets into digital forms. This underlines the needs to have different types of software products to manage such information, and raises security concerns for protecting software products from being illegally used in organisations. This paper proposes a licence management solution that protects software products from being illegally used. The proposed scheme is based on dividing an organisation devices into dynamic domains, each of which is bound to a single software product. Each dynamic domain has a predefined number of devices that can use the dynamic domain-specific software product. This number is specified by the software provider and is stored in the software licence file. In this case a software product can be installed on multiple devices, and a device can possess multiple software products by joining multiple dynamic domains. The proposed mechanism ensures that the number of used copies of software product does not exceed the limit that is agreed with the software provider.

1 Introduction

Consumers and organisations are moving into digitising content, which becomes more convenient than physical forms. Organisations in its wider definition including private and public sectors, universities, governments and many others, have replaced their system and workflow so that everything is digitised. Digitised information requires software products to process it, stores it and enables it to be easily accessed so that it achieves organisations' main functionality.

Software providers understand the importance of providing appropriate software products that meet the current and expected future needs for managing and accessing digitised information. However, one of the main problems facing software providers

Muntaha Alawneh and Imad M. Abbadi
Information Security Group, Royal Holloway, University of London, Egham, Surrey, TW20 0EX, UK, e-mail: {M.Alawneh,I.Abbadi}@rhul.ac.uk

Please use the following format when citing this chapter:

Alawneh, M. and Abbadi, I.M., 2008, in IFIP International Federation for Information Processing, Volume 278; *Proceedings of the IFIP TC 11 23rd International Information Security Conference*; Sushil Jajodia, Pierangela Samarati, Stelvio Cimato; (Boston: Springer), pp. 509–523.

is that their copyright is not sufficiently protected within organisations. Many organisations abuse the weak protection for software products by using the software product on many devices they have without paying usage fees. Currently, more than one out of three software applications are pirated. It is expected that US$300 billion will be spent on PC software over the next five years. During the same period it is expected that almost US$200 billion worth will be pirated [5].

Most researches in this area focus on personal networks. Personal networks have different requirements than organisations [3, 4]; for example, an organisation has larger size, more users, different mechanisms for licence enforcement and different copyright law regulations [6]. This in turn demonstrates the importance of finding a proper solution focusing on both organisations and software providers requirements. There are few schemes attempting to address software protection for organisations; however, these schemes have many problems and security flows in addressing organisation requirements. These are discussed in section 2.

Software protection is not only for the benefits of software provider (i.e. licence enforcement), but it is also important for organisations. For example, some organisations need to securely protect their own specific-software products from getting leaked outside it and used by others, e.g. to protect their own secrets, specific design, etc. Moreover, protecting a software product from getting leaked helps, in someway or another, in protecting content. This is because leaking an organisation-specific software product enables a third party to create, using the leaked software, a forged content in the same format that could be created in the organisation.

This paper proposes a mechanism for addressing software licence management for organisations. In this scheme we analyse the main security concerns facing software providers, specifically for organisations. Next, we propose a solution for managing software licencing for organisations.

Our novel idea is based on organising an organisation devices into dynamic domains. Each dynamic domain is bound to a single software product, which is itself bound to a licence file. The licence file specifies the rules for using the software product, and it includes the maximum number of devices that can use the software product at any time. These are stored in the licence file and are agreed between software providers and organisation administrators. The licence file also specifies the dynamic domain unique identifier to which this licence file is bound.

Using dynamic domains not only provides software protection, but it also helps organisations to manage their own licences. The latter is ensured, as each software product only requires a single licence file for all devices that require using the software product. This reduces the total number of licences required per software product in an organsation, hence helps in managing software licencing, storing it, and using it. In addition, the proposed solution considers organisations needs by adding to dynamic domains other features that are required by organisations, such as: expandability and shrinking; i.e. domains can be expanded or shrink based on organisations dynamic structure and needs, devices can move between different dynamic domains and use each dynamic domain-specific software product without requiring to go through the process of ordering new licences or even to pay for new licence fees (i.e. a device can join the domain, which it needs to use its software product, or leave the domain that it does not need to use its software product. This is conditional by having the number of devices in a domain does not exceed the limit permitted by software provider, as stored in the domain associated licence file). Moreover, the proposed solution is designed in such a way it is easy to use, and provides ease of recovery. Hence, the proposed solution satisfies both software providers and organisations needs.

2 Problem Definition

Software products licensing are, typically, charged based on number of devices, or, sometimes, on number of users, which use a software product. Although there are different techniques trying to enforce the rules included inside software licences; however, most of these techniques have many security flows, also, some of them have usability limitations (as described below). Moreover, these techniques have been abused many times, e.g. an organisation could buy one licence for a software product, and then illegally installs it (using the same licence) on unlimited number of devices; see, for example, [1, 2]. This is a clear breach of copyright law, and certainly software providers are not happy with such mechanisms.

Each software product, typically, has a licence-agent that regularly checks the availability and validity of a proper licence for the associated software product. Licences are protected using software-only techniques, a combination of both software and hardware protection techniques, and/or deterrent measures. In the remaining part of this section we discuss these techniques, which are used by software providers for protecting their own software products. In addition, we discuss other issues related to managing software licences for organisations.

2.1 Software-only Techniques

A software-only technique is based on having a software agent that is installed on a consumer device, and which requests a serial key or a password to enable the accessing of an associated software product. This serial key/password is provided by the software provider to the consumer after paying a proper licencing fees, and which needs to be inserted by the consumer whilst installing the software product. The licence-agent protects the serial key and stores it somewhere inside the consumer device. It then regularly checks the availability and the validity of this key to authorise the associated software to run.

The serial key/password is either bound to a single device, or it can work on any device. In the latter case, the software product is easier to be hacked; for example all devices in an organisation can use the same serial key to run a software product, which is originally bought to work on a single device. In the earlier case a serial key is bound to a permanent factor inside a device. Such a technique is implemented by some vendors such as Sun Microsystems [12] and weblogic [15]. This typically would be based on either a device hardware-id or IP address. However, such a mechanism has been attacked, as the hardware-id (after the system starts up) is stored in unprotected area inside the device memory, which can be bypassed or changed [1]. Binding the serial number with an IP address could also be easily hacked; a machine could have multiple network cards with different IP addresses, so a network card (which should not be connected to the main network to prevent address conflict) could be configured to have the right IP address that the software checks before starts up; for example, a company can buy a software product to work on a single machine that has a predefined IP address, and later on, the company can configure all its PCs to have two network interfaces each has two IP addresses. The first interface to have the same IP address used for licencing, and which needs to be disconnected from the main network (to prevent address conflict). The second network interface to have a public IP address and is connected to the main network.

2.2 Software and Hardware Techniques

Other solutions are mainly based on combinations of both software and hardware mechanism. Although these mechanisms are much secure than software-only techniques; however, they still have security flows and usability limitations. Such techniques are mainly based on using a tamper-resistant component storing, for example, a serial key that the licence-agent checks every time it runs. A common example of this type what is know by a 'dongle', which is "a small hardware device that connects to a computer and acts as an authentication key for a particular piece of software" [16]. Using a dongle does not solve the defined problem, as it is not robustly and securely integrated with computer devices [11]. Moreover, and most importantly, dongles are not practical and more expensive to have. This is because a dongle is a software-product specific, and a device, typically, has multiple software products from different vendors each requiring a specific-dongle to be connected to a device port all the time a software is running. This raises serious usability limitations for small devices. Also a device normally has a limited number of ports that are usually used for other purposes; e.g. connecting a printer or scanner, so it is not practical to have multiple software products using this technique on a device.

2.3 Deterrent Measures

Other software vendors, such as Oracle [9], do not enforce licences using cryptographic techniques; i.e. this licensing mechanism relies upon deterrent measures, which is based on copyright law enforcement.

2.4 Other Issues

In addition to the problems associated with each technique described in the previous sections, these techniques mainly focus on enforcing licences rules on a single device (except for the case of site licence, where a licence can be used on any device). This raises serious licence manageability problems for organisations, as an organisation, usually, has hundreds or even thousands of devices each run multiple software products from different vendors. Hence an organisation ends up with thousands, and even tens of thousands, of different licences each of which is bound to a single device and a single software product.

From the above we can see the importance of finding an acceptable solution for the problem of software licence management for organisations. In order to find a practical ground, such solutions should satisfy organisations, software providers, and copyright law requirements.

3 Dynamic Domains

Software providers need a solution which solves the problems defined in section 2. Using dynamic domains, which can be reallocated dynamically between organisation devices, helps to solve these problems. A dynamic domain is a domain consisting of one or more devices chosen from the organisation devices, each dynamic domain is bound to a single software product. The number of devices in a dynamic domain must not exceed the number of devices that can use the software product bound to that domain, as specified in the licence file which is provided by the software provider. This ensure that the maximum number of devices using the assigned software product do not exceed the maximum permitted number of devices agreed with the software provider. Each dynamic domain has a unique identifier, and a unique symmetric key. The dynamic domain symmetric key is used to protect the software product inside the dynamic domain devices. This key is only available inside devices member of the domain, so that only these devices can access the software product bound to the domain.

The dynamic domain creation process is performed by an organisation authorised security administrators, who choose devices that need to be bound to one or more dynamic domains. This binding is performed using a master control device, which needs to be trusted by software providers. The master control device intermediates the communication process between software providers and devices in an organisation that is going to use a software product. In addition, the master control device enforces the limits inside the licence file by ensuring the number of devices assigned to a dynamic domain does not exceed the authorised number of devices in the licence file, which are provided by the software provider whose software product is binded to the dynamic domain. These are explained in detail in section 5.

4 Proposed Model

In this section we describe the main entities constituting the proposed model.

4.1 Hardware Requirement

4.1.1 Devices.

Devices are commercial off-the-shelf PC hardware enhanced with trusted computing technology as defined by the Trusted Computing Group (TCG[1]) specifications [13, 14]. TCG compliant trusted platforms (TP) are not expensive, and are currently available from a range of PC manufacturers, including Dell, HP and Intel [10].

4.1.2 TCG Overview.

TPM: The TCG specifications require each TP to include an additional inexpensive hardware chip to establish trust in that platform. This chip is referred to as the Trusted Platform Module (TPM), which has protected storage and protected capabilities. The TPM is typically implemented as a processing engine that is separate from the TP's main processing environment.

Protected Storage: The TP protects all secret keys required by devices. Stored secrets are only released after the platform's software state has been measured and checked. Storage, and retrieval are carried out by the TPM. Therefore, if a software process relies on the use of secrets, it cannot operate unless it and its software environment are correct. The latter ensures that the software process operates as expected. Once a TPM has been assigned an owner, it generates a new Storage Root Key pair (SRK), which is used to protect all TPM keys. The private part of the SRK is stored permanently inside the TPM. Other TPM objects (key objects or data objects) are protected using keys that are ultimately protected by the SRK in a tree hierarchy structure. The entries of a TPM platform configuration registers (PCRs), where integrity measurements are stored, are used in the protected storage mechanism. This is achieved by comparing the current PCR values with the intended PCR values stored with the data object. If the two values are consistent, access is then granted and data is unsealed.

Attestation: Establishing trust in a TP is based on the mechanism that is used for measuring, reporting and verifying platform integrity metrics. TP measurements are performed using the RTM (Root of Trust for Measurement), which measures software components running on a TP. The RTS (Root of Trust for Storage) stores these measurements inside TPM shielded locations, which is referred to as the Platform Configuration Registers (PCR). Next, the RTR (Root of Trust for Reporting) mech-

[1] http://www.trustedcomputinggroup.org

anism allows TP measurements to be reliably communicated to an external entity in the form of an integrity report. The integrity report is signed using an AIK (Attestation Identity Key) private key, and is sent with the appropriate identity credential. This enables a Verifier to be sure that an integrity report is bound to a genuine TPM[2].

4.2 Master Control Device

The master control device is a trusted device that has all TP features, as defined in section 4.1. The master controller is a single logical entity, although its implementation may be a distributed one[4]. Each organisation has a specific master control device in charge of managing the organisation dynamic domains and all devices membership in each dynamic domain. The master control device has the following main functionalities.

- ► The master control device communicates with third parties, i.e. software providers, for downloading software products associated with proper licence files. The licence file, associated with the software product, contains a limit specifying the total number of devices that can use the software product. The master control device enforces this limit
- ► Creating and managing dynamic domains. This includes the following:
  - Securely generating and storing each dynamic domain-specific unique identifier, protection key, and a public key list which includes the public keys for all devices member in the dynamic domain.
  - Attesting to the execution environment status of devices added to a dynamic domain, ensuring they are trusted to securely store dynamic domain keys and execute as expected.
  - Adding devices to a dynamic domain by releasing the dynamic domain-specific key (i.e. the software protection key) to devices member of the dynamic domain.
- ► Managing software licencing, by ensuring each software product is bound to a single dynamic domain that has a maximum number of devices does not exceed the number of devices in the licence file associated with the software product.

5 Process Workflow

The workflow of the proposed system is divided into the following phases.

---

[2] One might argue that the device states might change after getting attested. This is solved by using the new generation of Intel/AMD hardware technology that stops DMA or by using Virtualisation technology as has been described in [10].

5.1 Master Control Device Initialisation

This section describes the process of initialising a master control device, which establishes the dynamic domains. The first time a master control device is initialised, the master control device instructs the organisation security administrators to provide their authentication credentials. The master control device then stores in its protected storage[3] the authentication credentials of the organisation security administrators associated with its trusted execution environment state (which is stored in the TPM's PCR based on TCG specification; see, for example, section 4.1). The authentication credential is used to authenticate security administrators before using the master control device. The master control device is used each time the security administrators want to create, expand, shrink or change a dynamic domain.

5.2 Buying Software Licences

This section describes the process of buying and downloading software products, which involves the following steps (figure 1 summarises the protocol for this stage).

1. The organisation administrators need to specify the number of licences the organisation need for a software product, say X (the number of devices in a dynamic domain that will use this software product should not exceed the value of X).
2. An organisation then negotiates the price with the software provider, for X licences. If the organisation agrees on a price, a formal contract is established between the software provider and the organisation that specifies the software product terms and conditions of usage and the maximum number of devices permitted to use the software product.
3. Next, the organisation administrators instructs the master control device to send a request to the software provider to download the software product. The software provider and the master control device exchange each other certificate, extracts the signature verification key from the certificates, and checks that it has not been revoked, e.g. by querying an Online Certificate Status Protocol (OCSP) service, [8]. If so, the software provider attests to the execution status of the master control device based on TCG specifications; see, for example, section 4.1. If the attestation shows that the master control device is trusted, the software provider encrypts the software product with a symmetric key k_S, and creates a licence file containing a one-way hash value of the encrypted software product. This is to bind the software product with the licence file. The licence file also contains the following: the software product encryption key k_S encrypted using the master control device public key, the value of X, the soft-

[3] We mean by storing data in a protected storage is protecting data using the SRK, which its private key part is stored inside the TPM. The protected data is then stored in an unprotected storage (see section 4.1).

ware product identifier *id*, and other usage rules. The software provider signs the licence file and sends the encrypted software product associated with the licence file to the organisation master control device.

4. The master control device verifies the software provider signature, and verifies the content is bound to the licence file by recomputing a one-way hash value of the received encrypted software product and comparing it with the one stored in the licence file. If the verifications succeed, the master control device signs the licence file, and then stores the encrypted software product associated with the signed licence file. Before installing the software product into devices, the master control device should first bind the software product to a specific dynamic domain. This binding could be performed by storing the dynamic domain specific identifier *i* in a specific field inside the software product licence file. This filed is exclusive for only one dynamic domain identifier, which ensures that each software licence is bound to a single dynamic domain.

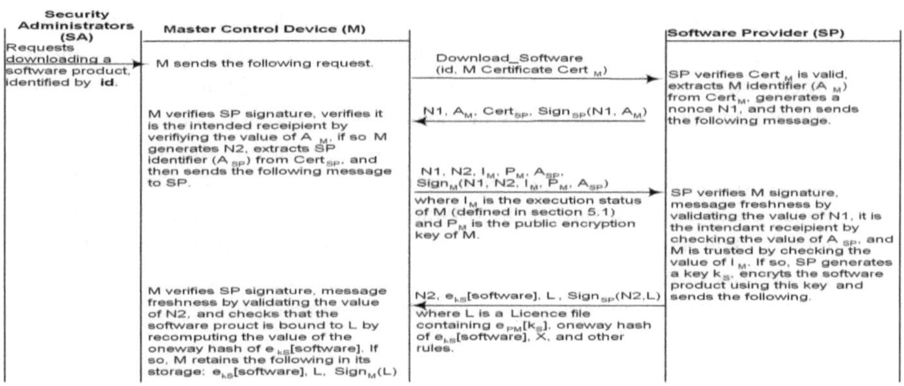

Fig. 1 Buying Software Licence Protocol

5.3 Dynamic Domain Establishment

Whenever an organisation wishes to install a software product into a set of devices, it must do the following (figure 2 1 summarises the protocol for this stage).

1. The organisation system administrators decide how many devices need to use a specific software product at this stage, say N. N would be the initial size of a dynamic domain, and it should not exceed the value of X stored in the licence file (it can be less than that).
2. The organisation system administrators decide which devices that will use the software product; the selection process is based on organisation needs, for example, a dynamic domain could consist of devices owned only by managers

layer, seniors layer, or mixed between different layers. These devices constitute the dynamic domain.

3. The security administrators instruct the master control device to create a new dynamic domain. The master control device then authenticates the organisation security administrators, e.g. using a password.
4. If authentication succeeds, the master control device instructs the security administrators to provide the number N, the public keys of devices that will be in the dynamic domain, and the identifier of the software product *id* that will be used on this dynamic domain.
5. The master control device verifies that the software licence is not bound to an existing domain, by verifying a field in the licence file showing whether it is used by another domain or not, as described in section 5.2, point (4).
6. If the above succeeds, the master control device then securely generates a dynamic domain specific symmetric key k_D, and a dynamic domain specific identifier i. The master control device creates a public key list for this domain consisting of the provided public keys. It then ensures that the size of the public key list equals to N, and verifies that the value of N does not exceed the value of X. k_D and i are associated with the public key list and the value of N, and then stored in the master control device protected storage and bound to a trusted execution environment based on TCG specifications; see, for example, section 4.1. The dynamic domain specific identifier i is also stored in the software product licence file. This is to bind the software product licence with a specific dynamic domain, and to make sure each software licence is bound to a single dynamic domain. The master control device then decrypts the software product encryption key (as stored in the licence file; see section 5.2 point 3), and re-encrypts it using the dynamic domain key k_D and stores the result in the licence file.

5.4 Adding Devices into a Domain and Software Installation

This section describes the process for adding a device into a dynamic domain and the process of software installation, which are performed as follows (in this section we describe the process using bull technique; i.e. a device sends a join request to the master control device. The same process applies using push technique; i.e. when a master control device sends a join domain requst to all devices in the domain. Which way to go for depends on the organisation policy).

1. From each device in the public key list, the organisation security administrators sends a join domain request to the master control device to install the dynamic domain specific key. This request includes the dynamic domain specific identifier i identifying which domain to join.
2. The master control device and the joining device mutually authenticates each other conforming to the three-pass mutual authentication protocol described in

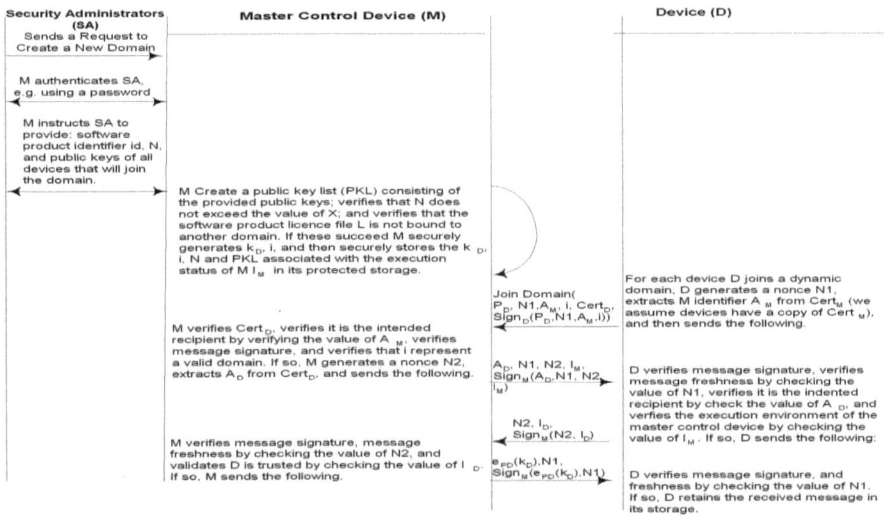

Fig. 2 Domain Establishment and Adding Devices Protocols

[7]. The master control device then attests to the execution environment of the joining device and validates its trustworthiness; as described in section 4.1.
3. If the joining device execution environment is trusted, the master control device checks if the device's public key is included in the public key list for the dynamic domain (as specified in step (1) above). If so, it securely releases the dynamic domain specific key to the device.
4. The device stores the domain key in its protected storage, and binds it to a specific execution environment. This device is now part of the domain, as it possesses a copy of the domain key and its public key matches the one stored in the master control device.
5. Now, all devices member of the domain can download from the master control device the encrypted software product associated with the licence file, which is bound to the domain. All these devices have a copy of the dynamic domain-specific key k_D. Therefore, these devices can decrypt the software encryption key, which is stored inside the licence file encrypted with the key k_D. These devices can then decrypt the software product and access it.

6 Domain Management

In order for a solution to be accepted and be widely used, it should adapt with organisations dynamic structure; for example, an organisation might need to change its strategy, layout, business work flow, and/or replace its devices. In this section we discuss how the proposed scheme covers these requirements, i.e. removing a device from a dynamic domain, adding a device into a dynamic domain, and key revocation.

6.1 Domain Shrinking

An organisation might need to use a software product on fewer number of devices than it is currently use, or it might need to replace its devices for several reasons, e.g. a hardware failure and the device cannot be recovered, or replace the device with newer technology. In these cases the organisation should still have the right to use the software product on other devices by adding them to the domain, as long as the number of devices in a domain N does not exceed the value of the maximum number of devices X that can use a software product, as stored in the licence file.

The way to remove a device from a dynamic domain is as follows. The master control device needs to attest to the execution status of the device ensuring it is trusted to remove the dynamic domain key from its storage (based on TCG specifications; see, for example, section 4.1). If the device is trusted, the master control device (for each dynamic domain) instructs the device to delete the dynamic domain key. The master control device then removes this device public key from the public key list of the dynamic domain, and decrements the value of N. On the other hand, if the execution status of the device is not trusted, the master control device will not remove this device; i.e. it will not decrement the value N and will not remove the device public key from the dynamic domain-specific public key list.

6.2 Domain Expansion

An organisation can expand a dynamic domain as long as the value of N does not exceed the value of X. In this case, the master control device instructs the security administrators to enter the public keys of the new devices. The master control device then add the number of the new devices to N. The master control device check the new value of N is still less than or equal the value of X. If so, the master control device securely stores the new value of N and updates the public key list with the added values, and finally it allows the new devices to join the domain as described in section 5.4.

6.3 Key Revocation

Hacking a dynamic domain specific key only affects the dynamic domain-specific software product protection. As a precautionary measure, security administrators need to revoke the domain key, and generate a new domain key, which can be done as follows. The security administrators instruct the master control device to change the key for a specific dynamic domain. The master control device then authenticates the organisation security administrators. If authentication succeeds, the master control device generates a new domain-specific key, and then decrypt the domain-specific software protection key stored in associated licence file with the old domain key, and re-encrypts it with the new domain key. The master control device then re-install this key and the licence file on domain devices; the master control device identifies devices using their public keys, which are securely stored inside the master control device, as described in section 5.3. For each device, the master control device releases the licence file, and the new value of the domain key encrypted using the device public key. The device replaces the old licence file, and stores the domain key in its protected storage and binds it to the same execution environment used for the old key, as it has already been verified as trusted; see section 5.4 point (3).

7 System Analysis

In this section we discuss the pros of using dynamic domains, which are summarised as follows.

- Software Protection and Licence Enforcement. A software is protected from being abused in organisations, as each software product is bound to a single domain with a maximum number of devices must not exceed the number of devices allowed to use the software product. This latter number is specified in the licence file associated with the software product. Having a trusted master control device enforces this limit. Each domain has a unique key, which is used to encrypt the software protection key. This encrypted key is stored in the software-specific licence file. The domain key is securely stored in domain devices, so only domain devices can decrypt the software protection key and access the software product. Moreover, the domain key is bound to a trusted execution environment that should work as expected. Hence, these devices are trusted to enforce the rules stored inside the associated licence file.
- Licence management. By using dynamic domains a software product is protected with a single licence file shared between a set of devices, rather than having a device-specific licence for each software product. Hence, this reduces the total number of required licences, and so it eases licence management.
- Flexibility. This is realised as follows.
    - As it is known, organisations have different layers, e.g. managers, seniors. In addition, organisations are organized in different business processes, e.g. a newspaper type of organisation has an editorial work flow, a publishing work flow, and page layout. A dynamic domain can contain devices from a single layer, or from different layers, based on organisation requirements. This provides an organisation the flexibility to layout its software products on devices based on the organisation functionality.

- An organisation can dynamically move devices between dynamic domains based on changes in its needs. For example, if an organisation requires to change its layout, say after one year, this might require software re-allocation. Assuming dynamic domains are not implemented, some software licences require renewing based on redistributing software products on different organisation devices. This is because a software licence would typically be bound to a device hardware id or an IP address (as discussed in section 2). On the other hand, by using dynamic domains, an organisation does not require renewing software licences. In this case, when a device is reallocated to be used by a new layer (i.e. different business process) that require different software products than it already has, it can join all dynamic domains where the new software products are bound, as long as the number of devices in each domain does not exceed the domain-specific number X stored in each domain licece file. The device also needs to remove all softwares it no longer needs to give chance for another device to use it.
- As we said earlier, the security administrators can make a dynamic domain with a number of devices less than the number of devices allowed to use the software licence, which is bound to the domain. We propose this feature, to add more flexibility and to cover organisations requirements. Having the number of devices less than the number of licences allows the organisation administrators to add devices in future time i.e. if the organisation changes its layout by moving devises between different layers, or if the organisation expanded. For example, system administrators could buy a 50 user licence for a software product and install it on 30 devices (still has the right to use the remaining 20 user devices at a later time), If the corporation expanded after 6 months and decided to add 10 more devices to use that software, the organisation can use the 10 licences as it has the right to use them, also, it is still has the rights to use the remaining 10 licences. One reason for doing this is cost, as the more number of devices that can use a software lincece the cheaper the licence would be per device. In addition, going into the process of buying another licence would, typically, require repeating the process of buying licences and many other procurement procedures, which we manage to eliminate in our solution.
- Removing a device from a domain does not mean loosing the licence associated with the device, as dynamic domains provide the flexibility to shrink domains and re-allocate licences to new devices that can replace the leaving one (now or in the future).

► Using a software-specific dynamic domain provides better protection for software products. For example, hacking the key of a dynamic domain affects only the protection of a single software product, i.e. it does not cause a global impact on other software products protection.

► Ease of Recover. Using a software-specific dynamic domain provides ease of recovery for a hacked software product. For example, hacking the key of a dynamic domain requires the recovery of only one dynamic domain.

8 Conclusion

In this paper we propose a solution to protect software products and manage licence files used by organisations. The proposed solution uses dynamic domains, consisting of devices owned by an organisation, which can be dynamically reallocated between dynamic domains, following the organisation needs. The proposed solution ensures that software products are protected from being illegally used.

References

1. spoofing hostids, 2005. http://blogs.sun.com/relling/entry/spoofing_hostids.
2. Spoofing time and space with DTrace, 2005. http://blogs.sun.com/relling/entry/spoofing_time_and_space_with.
3. Imad Abbadi. Digital asset protection in personal private networks. In *8th International Symposium on Systems and Information Security (SSI 2006), Sao Jose dos Campos, Sao Paulo, Brazil*, November 2006.
4. Imad Abbadi. Digital rights management using a master control device. In I. Cervesato, editor, *ASIAN '07: Proceedings of the 12th Annual Asian Computing Science Conference Focusing on Computer and Network Security*, volume 4846 of *Lecture Notes in Computer Science*, pages 126–141. Springer-Verlag, Berlin, December 2007.
5. BSA and IDC Global Software. 2005 piracy study, 2005. http://www.bsa.org.
6. Natali Helberger, Nicole Dufft, Stef van Gompel, Kristof Kerenyi, Bettina Krings, Rik Lambers, Carsten Orwat, and Ulrich Riehm. Digital rights management and consumer acceptability. Technical report, DG Information Society, December 2004. http://www.indicare.org/soareport.
7. International Organization for Standardization. *ISO/IEC 9798-3, Information technology — Security techniques — Entity authentication — Part 3: Mechanisms using digital signature techniques*, 2nd edition, 1998.
8. M. Myers, R. Ankney, A. Malpani, S. Galperin, and C. Adams. X.509 Internet Public Key Infrastructure Online Certificate Status Protocol — OCSP. RFC 2560, Internet Engineering Task Force, June 1999.
9. Oracle, 2007. http://www.oracle.com.
10. A. Sadeghi. Trusted computing — special aspects and challenges. In V. Geffert et al., editor, *SOFSEM*, volume 4910 of *Lecture Notes in Computer Science*, pages 98–117. Springer-Verlag, Berlin, 2008.
11. A. Sadeghi, M. Wolfl, C. Stble, N. Asokan, and J. Ekberg. Enabling fairer digital rights management with trusted computing. In J. Garay et al., editor, *Information Security, 10th International Conference*, volume 4779 of *Lecture Notes in Computer Science*, pages 53–70. Springer-Verlag, Berlin, 2007.
12. Sun Microsystems Inc. Licensing center, 2007. http://www.sun.com/software/licensingcenter/.
13. Trusted Computing Group. *TPM Main, Part 1, Design Principles. Specification version 1.2 Revision 94*, 2006.
14. Trusted Computing Group. *TPM Main, Part 2, TPM Structures. Specification version 1.2 Revision 94*, 2006.
15. Weblogic, 2007. http://www.bea.com.
16. Wikipedia. Dongle, 2007. http://en.wikipedia.org/wiki/Dongle.

8 Conclusion

References

A Vulnerability Prioritization System Using A Fuzzy Risk Analysis Approach

Maxwell G. Dondo

Abstract In this work, we present a fuzzy systems approach for assessing the relative potential risk associated with computer network assets exposed to attack by vulnerabilities. We use this approach to rank vulnerabilities so that analysts can prioritize their work based on the potential risk exposure of assets and networks. We associate vulnerabilities with individual assets, and therefore networks, and develop fuzzy models of the vulnerability attributes. Fuzzy rules are then used to make an inference on the risk exposure and the likelihood of attack, which allows us to rank the vulnerabilities and show which ones need more immediate attention. We argue that our approach has more meaningful vulnerability prioritization values than the severity level calculated by the popular Common Vulnerability Scoring System (CVSS) approach.

1 Introduction

Vulnerability assessment analysts have the task to deal with all vulnerabilities affecting their assets. In many cases, they must handle hundreds of vulnerabilities at a time. This can be a tedious process that can be made worse when the client is big and has many assets connected to many different networks. To prioritize their work, ranking the vulnerabilities is important to the analysts.

In this work, we will use a risk analysis method to rank vulnerabilities in order to assist the analyst in prioritizing events and improve network situational awareness. In information technology, risk is defined as the possibility for loss of confidentiality, integrity or availability (CIA) due to a specific threat [1]. We determine the risk associated with each vulnerability on a given asset (and therefore network) by

Maxwell G. Dondo
Defence Research & Development Canada (Ottawa) , Ottawa ON, Canada, e-mail: maxwell.dondo@drdc-rddc.gc.ca

Please use the following format when citing this chapter:

Dondo, M.G., 2008, in IFIP International Federation for Information Processing, Volume 278; *Proceedings of the IFIP TC 11 23rd International Information Security Conference*; Sushil Jajodia, Pierangela Samarati, Stelvio Cimato; (Boston: Springer), pp. 525–539.

determining the potential loss in value of a given asset when a threat exploits a vulnerability on that asset. We then rank the calculated risk values in order of priority.

1.1 Network Risk Analysis

In computer risk analysis, there are typically three overlapping tasks [7]. The first task is to identify everything possible that could go wrong in the network. The second task is to estimate how often the event can occur. The final task is to know the implications of an event.

An important category of things that can go wrong on computer networks is that a threat may exploit a vulnerability resulting in resources being compromised. Historical data have shown that there are many types of computer threats with varying complexity/lethality. Computer vulnerabilities are also well documented and collective efforts have resulted in the compilation of lists like the National Vulnerability Database (NVD) and Common Vulnerabilities and Exposures (CVE) [9]. In some cases, there are also unpublished vulnerabilities which may only be locally known.

We are unlikely to know exactly when or how often an attack will happen, but we know that the consequences can be a loss in confidentiality, integrity and/or availability of computer resources. This results in a loss in asset value [4]. To determine this loss in value, the value for the likelihood of attack is required. Due to the lack of extensive historical data covering a wide range of vulnerabilities, and that the relevant factors change with time, determining a likelihood of attack with current methods is not possible. This is a subject of substantial current research.

In our earlier work [3], we showed that the classical steps of calculating risk R_i for vulnerability v_i in a computer network with N nodes leads to the following equation:

$$R_i = \sum_{j=1}^{N} c_j \sum_{k=1}^{K_j} t_{kj}(v_i)(1-\mu_{ijk})p(t_{kj},v_i) \tag{1}$$

where $p(t_{kj},v_i)$ is the likelihood of threat t_{kj} exploiting a vulnerability v_i on asset j and μ_{ikj} is the safeguard factor for threat t_{kj} on vulnerability v. In this work, the numerical value of $t_{kj}(v)$ is termed the *impact value* because it represents the fractional potential loss in value on a given asset. This equation can also be further split into its CIA components of computer security [3].

In this work, we assume that physical and logical connections, and asset dependencies are modeled in the value of c.

1.2 The Challenges

Determining the likelihood of an attack $p(t_i,v)$ is not necessarily intuitive; this is even made difficult by the fact that there often is not enough data available to make a statistical inference on the likelihood of an attack. Fortunately, there are experienced analysts who can make educated guesses on the likelihood of an attack based on what they can "read" from vulnerability attributes. We intend to explore this path in our work.

The impact of an event on an asset, represented by $t_i(v)$, needs to be quantified as well. This is not intuitive either, and approaches that use questionnaires have shown that this is very subjective [10]. In the absence of a proper asset value model, it is difficult to come up with a value of $t_i(v)$ that includes all dependencies. Using vulnerability events and asset attributes we could give an estimate of the impact value for a given attack.

The classical approach described by Equation 1 has one additional weakness: overlap. Most computer related attacks consist of one or more attack steps. For example the `HP-UX dtmail/rpc.ttdbserverd` vulnerability can allow unauthorized access through a buffer overflow. What the attacker does after gaining unauthorized access can be considered another stage of an attack. There are many possibilities of what an attacker can do once an asset has been compromised. Quantifying each of the possibilities could be a tedious task. In fact, analysts often identify complete attack paths and usually base their analysis on the worst case scenario.

1.3 Previous Work

One approach being used is the Common Vulnerability Scoring System (CVSS)[1] [11]. It has the advantage that it takes into consideration vulnerability attributes and uses them to calculate a severity score which can be used for relative comparison. However, as we will show in this work, this approach's coarse-grained handling of relative asset values and assets exposed as well as its omission of the time variable, shows some weaknesses that can lead to misleading comparisons.

The *Delphi* approach [10] is a basic approach in which several raters estimate priority based on predetermined metrics like the likelihood of exploitation. However, the resultant ratings are based on a limited number of metrics which can be applicable to individual assets, and it would be difficult, if not impossible, to use this method on a network or a group of networks.

Probabilistic approaches like the one by Mosleh *et al.* [7] (Bayesian) offer a sound theoretical approach to this problem. They model the potential loss due to the occurrence of an event as a family of normal distributions. In the absence of enough statistical data, which is usually the case in these types of problems, it is difficult to make an inference on the statistical distributions of asset losses, and therefore the likelihood of attack. Other approaches, such as Fault Trees Analysis (FTA), Event Trees Analysis (ETA), and Markov Analysis [6], determine the likelihood of attack through sequences of steps. Although these methods could give relatively accurate

[1] In this work, references to CVSS imply the original version, and not CVSS 2.

rankings for individual assets, it is not trivial to handle a network or a group of networks.

Fuzzy systems have also been widely used in risk analysis [2, 12]. In these approaches, researchers used fuzzy logic to determine the probability of failure or likelihood of an attack. Chen *et al.* [2] go further by improving on previous fuzzy systems' approaches while introducing dependencies to component failures. Their fuzzy models are based on the severity and likelihood fuzzy numbers (FNs). Shah [12] used several key risk indicators (KRIs) (operational variables that provide the basis for estimating losses corresponding to risk), to determine risk based on their linguistic descriptors.

The biggest shortcoming in traditional approaches is incomplete representation of KRIs. They make estimates of the likelihood of an attack, but they do not model the relative importance of each to the final risk value. As we will show in our work, all attributes of KRIs should be included in the model that contributes to the final solution.

2 Proposed Solution

We propose an approach that exploits human reasoning, linguistic in particular, to model what the expert analyst knows and use it to model a fuzzy system risk model. Our approach is similar to the approaches taken by Shah [12] and Ng *et al.* [8], but on a broader scale. We identify and use different types of KRIs. We go deeper, by performing analysis on individual attributes of the KRIs.

We start by assuming that the asset value is a known fixed quantity. We associate each vulnerability with an asset on our network. Vulnerabilities which do not affect our assets are not considered for calculations, but are listed in a database. We then identify the KRIs for a given vulnerability and asset. These are the attributes of the vulnerability, asset and safeguards.

We model each attribute as a fuzzy variable [5]. Fuzzy variables have the advantage of being able to model KRIs using linguistic declarations such as *low*, *medium*, *high*, *etc*. Variable qualifiers such as *very* and *somewhat* can also be used with each FN. Each FN is assigned a range of values representing the expert linguistic descriptors of the attributes. We then make an inference on these fuzzy variables, using fuzzy *IF–THEN* rules, to determine the fuzzy risk value represented by its CIA components. Finally, we defuzzify the result back into a crisp value and compare the results for each vulnerability in order to rank them.

2.1 Vulnerability FIS

Our vulnerability fuzzy inference system (VFIS) approach is illustrated in Figure 1 and its stages are described in detail in the next sections. Figure 1 shows the list

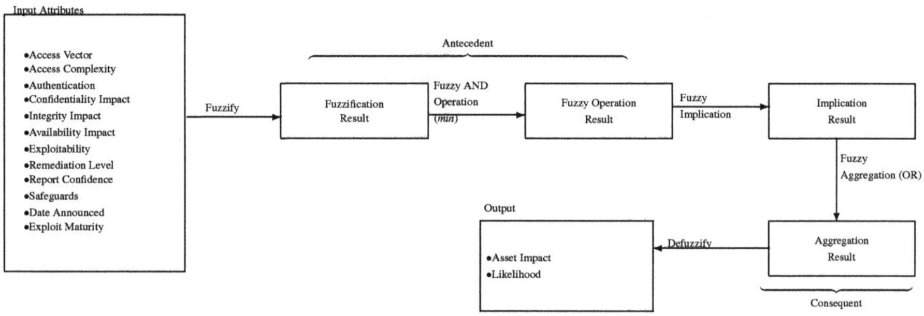

Fig. 1 Layout of the vulnerability FIS (VFIS).

of vulnerability attributes identified for this work. We fuzzify them and apply the fuzzy AND operator on the set (*antecedent* or *premise*). The *implication* completes the rules that govern the functional relationships between the fuzzy attributes. The results from individual rules are combined through *aggregation* to give the *consequent*. We defuzzify the fuzzy impact and likelihood values to obtain the final crisp metrics for the calculation of risk.

Fuzzification of Attributes: We model a vulnerability as a set of fuzzy attributes. If V is the set of vulnerability attributes (universe of discourse), and its elements are denoted by x, then the fuzzy set $\tilde{v}$ in V is denoted by:

$$\tilde{v} = \{x, \mu_v(x) \mid x \in V\} \tag{2}$$

where $\mu_v(x)$ is the membership function (MF) of x in $\tilde{v}$. It is bounded in $[0,1]$. To simplify the fuzzy definitions of input attributes, we use *straight line* MFs, namely *trapezoidal* and *triangular*.

The number of FNs defining an attribute is not fixed, but depends on the linguistic declarations about that attribute. Some attributes are defined using two FNs, while others are defined by as many as 5 FNs. The rule of thumb is that when the number of FNs used does not provide adequate distinction for some sets of input attributes, then increase the number of FNs.

Fuzzification Approach: Figure 2 shows triangular and trapezoidal MFs. The degree of truth ranges from 0 (uncertainty) at b to 1 (certainty) at a. Similarly, on the opposite edge of the MF, the degree of truth varies from 1 (certainty) at a to 0 (uncertainty) at c and beyond. The slopes of these lines are determined by the designer of the MF based on the linguistic declarations about the variable (i.e. values of b and c). In this case, a linguistic declaration that would result in this FN is as follows:

The value is "LOW" when it is a. The value is never known to be lower than b and is no longer classified as "LOW" if it exceeds c.

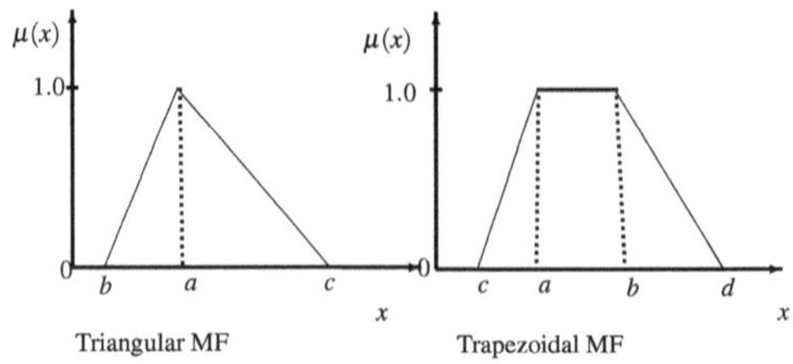

Fig. 2 The triangular MF represents a fuzzy variable"LOW", for example. The triangular edge between a and b represents the degree of truth that the respective values of x are the values of "LOW". The trapezoidal MF is a special case of a triangular MF.

The lower and upper bounds (b and c), outside which the degree of truth is 0, help the designer to determine the slopes of the FNs.

A similar approach is used to convert linguistic declarations to trapezoidal MFs, which have more than one value at $\mu(x) = 1$. An example of a linguistic declaration that could result in this FN is as follows:

The value is "LOW" when it is between a and b. It is never known to be lower than c and it is no longer classified as "LOW" when it exceeds d.

We use this general approach in the next sections to fuzzify each of the KRIs used in this work.

Input Attributes: The first attributes we will look at are the access vector (AV), access complexity (AC), authentication (Au), and the CIA impact bias values. Some of the value ranges used to fuzzify them in this work correspond to the value definitions used in CVSS [11]. This choice of values is not necessary, but we used the CVSS ranges to simplify the task of choosing appropriate values of attribute ranges, and also to capitalize on the expertise put into establishing these values.

The fuzzy AV attribute is shown in Figure 3(a). The "Local" FN represents a

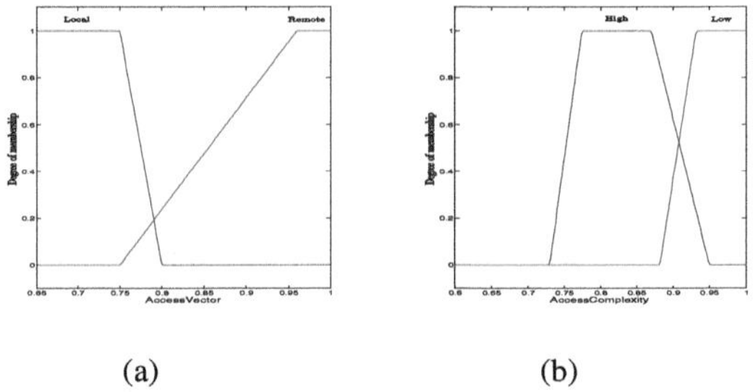

Fig. 3 Trapezoidal fuzzy numbers; they represent "Local" and "Remote" access for AV in (a) and, "High" and "Low" access complexity for AC in (b).

linguistic value that lies between 0.65 and 0.75, but *never exceeds* 0.8. Similarly, the "Remote" access FN represents a linguistic value that is *never below* 0.75, but is *most certainly* between 0.95 and 1.0. Figure 3(b) shows the fuzzy AC attribute. The "High" FN represents a linguistic value that lies between 0.77 and 0.87, but *never exceeds* 0.95, and is *never below* 0.74. The "Low" access FN represents a linguistic value that is *never below* 0.88, but is *most certainly* between 0.93 and 1.0.

The fuzzy authentication attribute is shown on Figure 4(a). The "Required" FN represents a linguistic value that *certainly* lies between 0.6 and 0.7, but *never exceeds* 0.79. Similarly, the authentication "NotRequired" FN represents a linguistic value that is *never below* 0.82, but lies between 0.82 and 1.0.

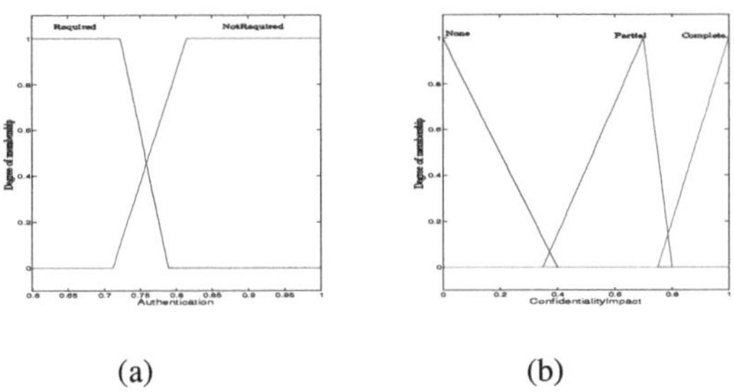

Fig. 4 Trapezoidal FNs representing authentication "Required" and "NotRequired" in (a). Triangular CI FNs representing "None", "Partial" and "complete" in (b).

There are three impact bias attributes, each corresponding to the security confidentiality, integrity or availability (CIA) elements. Since they are similar, they each have the same shapes and definitions. We therefore picked one for presentation. Figure 4(b) shows the FN for confidentiality impact which is defined by three triangular FNs representing "None", "Partial", and "Complete". The "None" FN represents a linguistic score of *around* 0 but *never exceeds* 0.4. Similarly, the "Partial" bias FN represents a linguistic score of *around* 0.7 and is *always between* 0.35 and 0.8. The "Complete" FN represents a linguistic score of *around* 1 but is *never less than* 0.75.

A similar approach was used to fuzzify *exploitability*, *remediation level*, *report confidence*, *safeguards*, and *time*. The *time* attribute is calculated from the vulnerability or exploit announcement date, whichever comes first. It is also used as indication of exploit maturity.

Vulnerabilities and threats evolve along a life cycle. As a result, we define the time fuzzy attribute with five FNs in order to have the flexibility of making inferences that best reflect a threat's life cycle. The probability of a threat exploiting a vulnerability on an asset tends to start low, then grows over time until it stabilizes at a constant value. The Symantec Internet Security report [13] states that the average number of days for exploit development was 6.0 for the period of Jan-June 2005. We used this data to define part of the time fuzzy set. The attribute is defined by "Very Low", "Low", "Medium", "High", and "Very High". The FN ranges are: [0 8] for "Very Low", [7 21] for "Low", [15 28] for "Medium", [25 35] for "High", and [32 ∞] [2] for "Very High".

Fuzzy Output Attributes and Rules: For every fuzzy inference system (FIS), a fuzzy output variable has to be defined before any inference is performed. The

[2] In this work we use 50 days as the upper limit.

above input fuzzy attributes are combined using fuzzy rules to give a fuzzy output value; an example of such a rule is as follows:

$$\text{if } A \text{ is "Low" and } B \text{ is "High" then } C \text{ is "Medium"} \tag{3}$$

Equation 3 cannot be solved without first defining "Medium" in the fuzzy number C. In this section, we therefore define the outputs for our inference system. The FN values are our interpretation of the consequent as expressed in the linguistic declarations.

The two output MFs, the impact and likelihood, are shown in Figures 5(a) and 5(b) respectively. As the final fuzzy outputs, we define them using smooth Gaussian MFs in order to be able to distinguish between small inference differences.

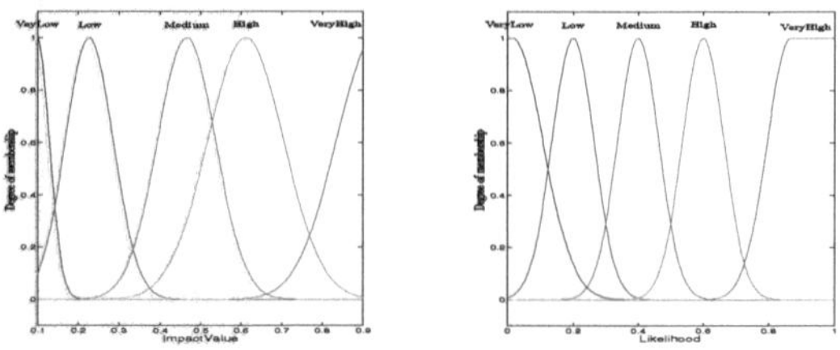

(a) Impact. (b) Attack Likelihood.

Fig. 5 The output attributes are each defined by 5 FNs, namely "Very Low", "Low", "Medium", "High", and "Very High".

Due to the size and number of attributes used, we break down the problem into four small FISs as illustrated in in Figure 6. The ImpactValue and Attacklikelihood fuzzy output values are used to compute the crisp risk values. We use *if- then-* rules to combine the attributes based on the linguistic declarations about the attributes. Rules can be given weights depending on the importance of a rule over others. As an example, 5 of the 24 fuzzy rules defining FIS1 are listed in Table 1. Rule weighting

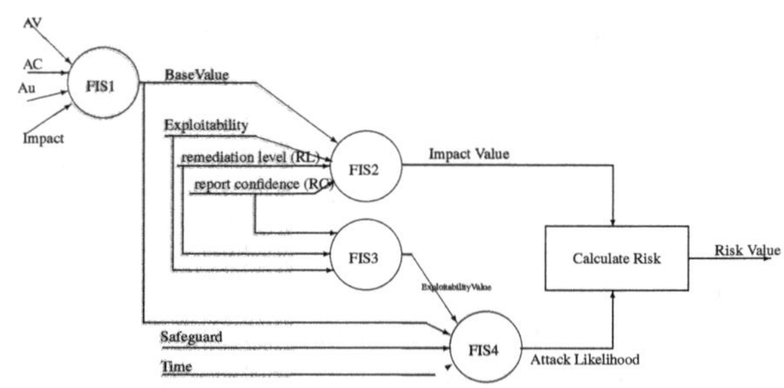

Fig. 6 In this VFIS implementation, the outputs of FIS1, FIS2, FIS3, and FIS4 are combined with other input attributes to give the final two outputs, Impact value and Attack Likelihood. The risk value is calculated from the Impact Value and Attack Likelihood.

Table 1 Fuzzy rules for BaseValue (FIS1).

```
1. If (AV is Local) and (AC is High) and (Auth is Required) and (Impact is None) then (BaseValue is VeryLow) (1)
2. If (AV is Local) and (AC is High) and (Auth is Required) and (Impact is Partial) then (BaseValue is Low) (1)
3. If (AV is Local) and (AC is High) and (Auth is Required) and (Impact is Complete) then (BaseValue is Medium) (1)
4. If (AV is Local) and (AC is High) and (Auth is NotRequired) and (Impact is None) then (BaseValue is VeryLow) (1)
5. If (AV is Local) and (AC is High) and (Auth is NotRequired) and (Impact is Partial) then (BaseValue is Medium) (1)
```

factors vary in $[0,1]$; in our case, all rules were given equal weights of 1. This is the value indicated in brackets at the end of each rule in Table 1.

Defuzzification: For decision making purposes, the fuzzy outputs from FIS2 and FIS4, which respectively represent the fuzzy impact value $\tilde{t}$ and attack likelihood $\tilde{p}$, are defuzzified and the crisp values are used to calculate the risk values for each vulnerability. In this work, we used the centroid method for defuzzification. We then sum the risk values over the number of vulnerabilities to represent the overall risk for a given asset. We also use the defuzzified impact value to compare vulnerability rankings of our approach with those produced by CVSS.

3 Experimentation and Results

In this section, we present the experimental results of our work. In Section 3.1, we present the outputs from the VFIS implementation. Finally, we present a sample set of results from our model in Section 3.2.

3.1 FIS Output

The impact value is one of the two important outputs in our work. In the implementation, it is represented by the output of FIS2. The output curve is shown in Figure 7.

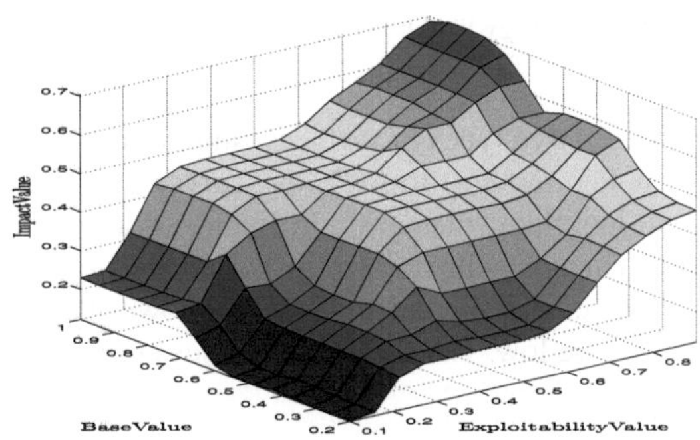

Fig. 7 The output value for FIS2, Impact Value; it is a result of two attributes going into FIS2, the `BaseValue` and `ExploitabilityValue`.

The output curve in Figure 7 is representative of the final value obtained from the inference. Thus, we expected the output value to range in $(0\ 0.7]$ as represented by the vertical axis (`ImpactValue`). This value represents the fraction of the asset value exposed to risk due to the expected exploitation of a given vulnerability. A value of 0 means no exposure, while a value of 0.7 means maximum exposure in this case.

It should also be noted that the value of 0.7 as the maximum risk exposure was not predetermined; it was determined through the inference rules that governed the FIS outputs. The specific numerical value of this maximum is not important on its own; it is a relative quantity that can be used to compare and rank vulnerabilities of different attributes. To compare with CVSS, we ranked vulnerabilities based on their impact values produced by this defuzzified output[3]. The results will be presented below. The other important FIS output for our work is the attack likelihood $\tilde{p}$ as implemented by FIS4. The output curves for $\tilde{p}$ are shown in Figure 8. The results

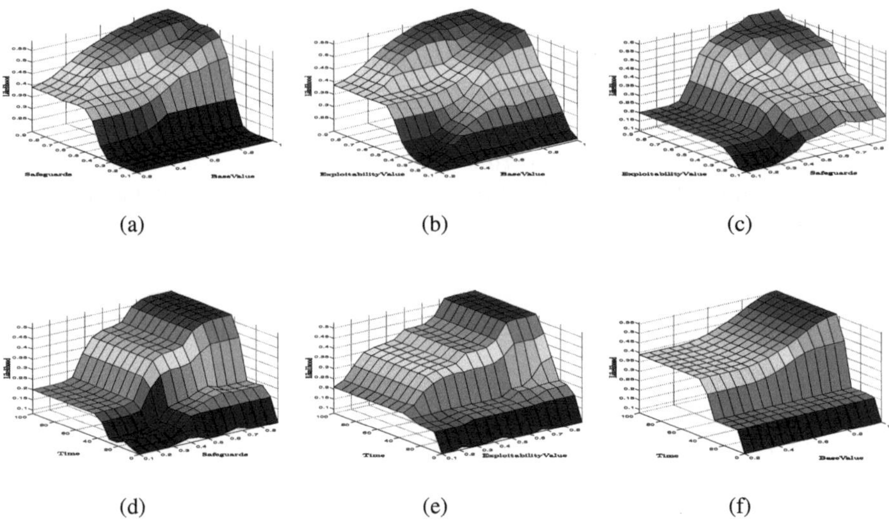

Fig. 8 Final fuzzy likelihood value.

produced two types of surfaces: smooth-continuous and flat-topped.

In Figures 8(a) to 8(c), the curves are relatively smooth with a few cases of what look like "plateaus". In Figures 8(a) to 8(c), the likelihood values show very little change with respect to variations in `Safeguards` at low values. As expected, the likelihood of attack at low values of `Safeguards` (fuzzy attribute `High`) are low. The likelihood values are high for high values of `BaseValue` and `ExploitabilityValue`.

[3] We fix the likelihood of attack during these comparisons.

The other set of plots are slightly different. All of them have a "plateau" at large values of the `Time` attribute. We defined the fuzzy `Time` attribute to be maximum for any time difference of over 50 days. Any time duration exceeding that would result in the maximum likelihood value. This explains the "flat" top part of the plots shown in these curves.

We use the defuzzified values of $\tilde{t}$ and $\tilde{p}$ to calculate risk as represented by Equation 1. In summary, the risk value r, for a given vulnerability on a given asset, would be,

$$r = c \times t \times p \tag{4}$$

where c is the asset value. This is also split up into the CIA components [3]. We then use the calculated risk value to rank[4] vulnerabilities as explained in the next section.

3.2 Sample Vulnerability Ranking Results

In this section, we present the results of our approach in three stages. We first present ranking results for individual assets. Then we present the results for individual networks, and finally the overall vulnerability ranking for the organisation owning the networks. Vulnerability data was downloaded from known vulnerability databases like CVE or NVD [9]. Data from NVD now comes with CVSS score values. These can be used to compare the CVSS ranking with the risk rankings of our model.

We also use a colour coding system to visually assist the analyst. The colour code ranges from green to red. Green represents a lowest risk level while red indicates high risk. Intermediate colours like yellow and orange represent intermediate risk levels. The absolute values of the calculated risk values provide relative levels of risk exposure for the assets in the organisation; this can be used for decision-making purposes using our approach.

3.2.1 Asset Vulnerability Ranking

We defined hypothetical assets and associated real vulnerabilities with each of them. For illustrative purposes, we mixed up vulnerabilities with those from different asset types, e.g. in some cases, we mixed vulnerabilities for Unix and Windows OS type assets. We applied our ranking approach and ranked the vulnerabilities for that asset.

In Figure 9, we show the results of ranking vulnerabilities on asset 123 of network 234. The table in Figure 9 shows columns for vulnerability ID, Name, Status, Risk Level, and CVSS Score. The Name column gives a brief description of the vulnerability. The Status shows the vulnerability handling stage within an organi-

[4] In this work, *ranking* refers to the ordering of vulnerabilities based on a relative numerical value; in our approach, this is the calculated risk value.

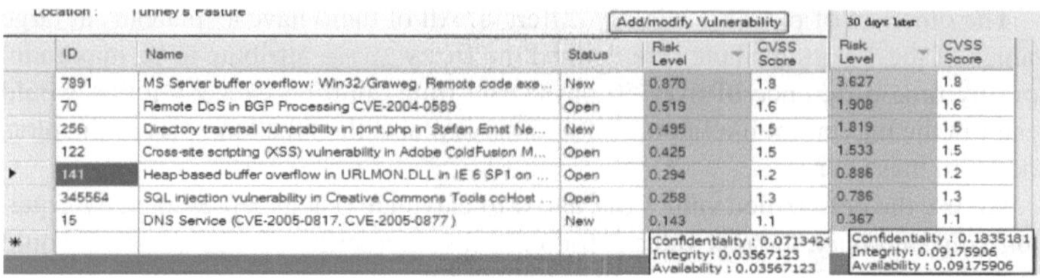

Location : Tunney's Pasture

Add/modify Vulnerability | 30 days later

ID	Name	Status	Risk Level	CVSS Score	Risk Level (30 days later)	CVSS Score (30 days later)
7891	MS Server buffer overflow: Win32/Graweg. Remote code exe...	New	0.870	1.8	3.627	1.8
70	Remote DoS in BGP Processing CVE-2004-0589	Open	0.519	1.6	1.908	1.6
256	Directory traversal vulnerability in print.php in Stefan Ernst Ne...	New	0.495	1.5	1.819	1.5
122	Cross-site scripting (XSS) vulnerability in Adobe ColdFusion M...	Open	0.425	1.5	1.533	1.5
141	Heap-based buffer overflow in URLMON.DLL in IE 6 SP1 on ...	Open	0.294	1.2	0.886	1.2
345564	SQL injection vulnerability in Creative Commons Tools ccHost ...	Open	0.258	1.3	0.786	1.3
15	DNS Service (CVE-2005-0817, CVE-2005-0877)	New	0.143	1.1	0.367	1.1

Confidentiality : 0.0713424
Integrity: 0.03567123
Availability : 0.03567123

Confidentiality : 0.1835181
Integrity: 0.09175906
Availability : 0.09175906

Fig. 9 Vulnerability ranking for asset 123.

Table 2 Attribute values for asset 123 vulnerabilities.

ID	Vulnerability attribute values										
	LA	AC	Auth	CI	II	AI	IW	RL	EC	CVSS	Risk
7891	False	False	False	Partial	Partial	Partial	Normal	Unavailable	High	1.8	3.627
70	False	False	False	Partial	Partial	Partial	Integrity	Unavailable	Unproven	1.6	1.908
256	False	False	False	Partial	Partial	Partial	Confidentiality	Unavailable	Proof of Concept	1.5	1.819
122	False	False	False	Partial	Partial	Partial	Integrity	Workaround	Unproven	1.5	1.533
141	False	True	False	Partial	Partial	Partial	Integrity	Official Fix	Functional Code	1.2	0.886
345564	False	False	False	Partial	Partial	Partial	Normal	Official Fix	Unproven	1.3	0.786
15	False	True	False	Partial	Partial	Partial	Confidentiality	Official Fix	Unproven	1.1	0.367

sation. The Risk Value column represents the crisp (non-fuzzy) value calculated by our approach.

The yellow box, near the bottom right hand corner of Figure 9, shows the different CIA components of the risk value listed in column 4. In this example, the risk value for vulnerability 15 is 0.133 and can be split into 0.071 for confidentiality, 0.035 for integrity and 0.035 for availability.

Figure 9 shows the ranking of vulnerabilities in descending order of the risk values associated with them. Table 2 shows the list of vulnerability attributes that produced these rankings. For this asset, the vulnerability dates were intentionally fixed for all vulnerabilities in order to compare the ranking with CVSS rankings. As shown above, all our ranking matched the CVSS rankings. For accuracy, our CVSS scores were the same as calculated by NVD [9].

To show the difference between our approach and CVSS, we changed the time attribute for all the vulnerabilities of asset 123 to 30 days later. All the other attributes were left as they were. The vulnerability rankings produced after this change are shown in Figure 9 (column 6). As expected, the ranking matched the ranking produced by the CVSS scores. The risk values in our calculations are higher than they were 30 days ago. This is also expected since our approach is time dependent. In contrast, CVSS scores remained the same[5].

[5] This assumes, plausibly, that nothing is known to affect the CVSS temporal scores during this time.

3.2.2 Network Vulnerability Ranking

In this section, we present results for two individual networks. These results show the ranking of all the vulnerabilities in a given network. Figure 10 shows an example

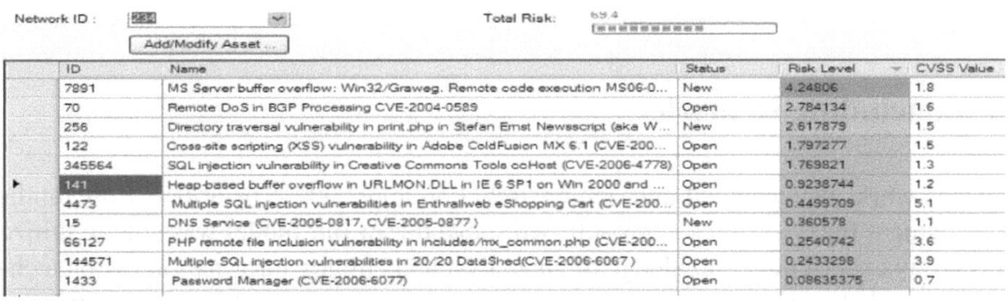

Network ID : 234
Add/Modify Asset ...
Total Risk: 69.4

ID	Name	Status	Risk Level	CVSS Value
7891	MS Server buffer overflow: Win32/Graweg. Remote code execution MS06-0...	New	4.24806	1.8
70	Remote DoS in BGP Processing CVE-2004-0589	Open	2.784134	1.6
256	Directory traversal vulnerability in print.php in Stefan Ernst Newsscript (aka W...	New	2.617879	1.5
122	Cross-site scripting (XSS) vulnerability in Adobe ColdFusion MX 6.1 (CVE-200...	Open	1.797277	1.5
345564	SQL injection vulnerability in Creative Commons Tools ccHost (CVE-2006-4778)	Open	1.769821	1.3
141	Heap-based buffer overflow in URLMON.DLL in IE 6 SP1 on Win 2000 and ...	Open	0.9238744	1.2
4473	Multiple SQL injection vulnerabilities in Enthrallweb eShopping Cart (CVE-200...	Open	0.4499709	5.1
15	DNS Service (CVE-2005-0817, CVE-2005-0877)	New	0.360578	1.1
66127	PHP remote file inclusion vulnerability in includes/mx_common.php (CVE-200...	Open	0.2540742	3.6
144571	Multiple SQL injection vulnerabilities in 20/20 DataShed(CVE-2006-6067)	Open	0.2433298	3.9
1433	Password Manager (CVE-2006-6077)	Open	0.08635375	0.7

Fig. 10 Vulnerability rankings for network 234.

of the vulnerability rankings for network 234, which consists of two assets, 120 and 123. Vulnerabilities for asset 123 were shown in the previous section. The rest of the vulnerabilities in Figure 10 represent those for asset 120.

At this point, the CVSS value ranking did not match our approach. Vulnerabilities from asset 123, still matched the ranking approach of our method and the CVSS approach. This is because none of the vulnerabilities in asset 123 appear anywhere else in the same network, and the vulnerability attributes were still fixed for the comparison we showed in the previous section. However, vulnerabilities in asset 120 were not fixed this way, and therefore did not get ranked according to the CVSS scores.

3.2.3 Overall Vulnerability Ranking

The final set of results shows the overall ranking of vulnerabilities in the network. The vulnerabilities in the network are listed in order in Figure 11. These vulnerabil-

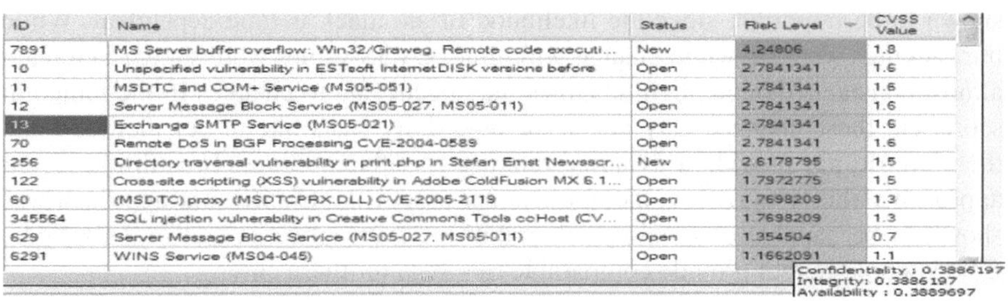

ID	Name	Status	Risk Level	CVSS Value
7891	MS Server buffer overflow: Win32/Graweg. Remote code executi...	New	4.24806	1.8
10	Unspecified vulnerability in ESTsoft InternetDISK versions before	Open	2.7841341	1.6
11	MSDTC and COM+ Service (MS05-051)	Open	2.7841341	1.6
12	Server Message Block Service (MS05-027, MS05-011)	Open	2.7841341	1.6
13	Exchange SMTP Service (MS05-021)	Open	2.7841341	1.6
70	Remote DoS in BGP Processing CVE-2004-0589	Open	2.7841341	1.6
256	Directory traversal vulnerability in print.php in Stefan Ernst Newsscr...	New	2.6178795	1.5
122	Cross-site scripting (XSS) vulnerability in Adobe ColdFusion MX 6.1...	Open	1.7972775	1.5
60	(MSDTC) proxy (MSDTCPRX.DLL) CVE-2005-2119	Open	1.7698209	1.3
345564	SQL injection vulnerability in Creative Commons Tools ccHost (CV...	Open	1.7698209	1.3
629	Server Message Block Service (MS05-027, MS05-011)	Open	1.354504	0.7
6291	WINS Service (MS04-045)	Open	1.1662091	1.1

Confidentiality : 0.3886197
Integrity: 0.3886197
Availability : 0.3889697

Fig. 11 Vulnerability rankings for all networks.

ities are a combination of all the vulnerabilities on an organization's networks.

From the preceding sections, the columns and rankings are self-explanatory. The most important thing to note is that we were able to rank vulnerabilities based on the risk they pose to organizational assets. It is also evident from the risk values and CVSS scores that the latter is not capable of prioritizing vulnerabilities where many assets or networks are involved, or where time is involved.

4 Concluding Remarks

In this work, we designed and demonstrated an approach to prioritize vulnerabilities using a fuzzy systems approach. We showed how our model was able to utilize everyday experiential knowledge of an analyst and employ information fusion techniques with fuzzy logic to model the risk associated with each vulnerability on a given asset. With this model, the analysts could be able to priorities and schedule their work in order to handle the most critical events at a given time.

Our approach capitalizes on the ability of fuzzy systems to model known key risk indicators (KRIs) based on a combination of experience, expertise, or historical input. Using a fuzzy information fusion technique, the fuzzy inference system (FIS), we were able to combine all the identified KRIs to come up with a final risk value. This final result is a relative risk quantity for each vulnerability which can be used to prioritize work or investments (such as buying safeguards, reconfiguring or upgrading the network) in protecting the network.

We tested our approach using vulnerability data from well known vulnerability databases such as the National Vulnerability Database (NVD), and Common Vulnerabilities and Exposures (CVE). We were also able to compare the results of our approach with a new, currently used vulnerability scoring system, the Common Vulnerability Scoring System (CVSS). When we fixed our KRIs to match the CVSS attributes, all our vulnerability ranking order matched those produced by CVSS. With this successful comparison with CVSS, our approach was used to rank other vulnerabilities over the full set of KRIs; the results are a very promising for testing in an operational environment.

We went on to show the advantages of our approach over CVSS rankings. Unlike CVSS, our approach models time and existing safeguards. The time attribute was shown to be important since the likelihood of an attack is time-dependent. While our rankings were shown to change with time, CVSS values were shown to remain almost constant (though slight changes may occur due to changes in the temporal score, but these changes may not occur on a daily basis like in our method), and therefore do not provide a dynamic ranking of vulnerabilities. In addition to our approach's ability to rank vulnerabilities per asset (like CVSS), our approach was shown to be capable of ranking vulnerabilities over networks and organizations; CVSS scores cannot provide comparable rankings for these cases.

References

1. Anderson, K.E.: Intelligence-based threat assessments for information networks and infrastructures: A white paper. Global Technology Research, Inc. (1998)
2. Chen, S., Chen, s.: Fuzzy risk analysis based on similarity measures of generalized fuzzy numbers. IEEE Transactions on Fuzzy Systems **11**(1), 45–56 (2003)
3. Dondo, M.: A fuzzy risk calculations approach for a network vulnerability ranking system (2007)
4. FEMA: Asset value, threatharzard, vulnerability and risk. URL `http://www.fema.gov/pdf/fima/426/fema426_ch1.pdf`
5. H-J. Zimmerman: Fuzzy Sets, Decision Making and Expert Systems. Kluwer Academic Publishers (1987)
6. Isograph: FaultTree+ - Event Tree Analysis (2005). URL `http://www.isograph-software.com/ftpovereta.htm`
7. Mosleh, A., Hilton, E.R., Browne, P.S.: Bayesian probabilistic risk analysis. ACM SIGMETRICS–Performance Evaluation Review **13**(1), 5–12 (1985)
8. Ng, G.W., Ng, K.H., Yang, R., Foo, P.H.: Intent inference for attack aircraft through fusion. In: B.V. Dasarathy (ed.) Proceedings of SPIE, vol. 6242–06. Orlando, Fl (2006)
9. NVD: National vulnerability database. URL `http://nvd.nist.gov`
10. Pfleeger, C.P.: Security in Computing, 2 edn. Prentice Hall PTR, Upper Saddle River, NJ (1997)
11. Schiffman, M.: The common vulnerability scoring system (CVSS). URL `http://www.first.org/cvss/cvss-guide.html`
12. Shah, S.: Measuring operational risk using fuzzy logic modeling. URL `http://www.irmi.com/Expert/Articles/2003/Shah09.aspx`
13. Symantec Enterprise Security: Symantec internet security threat report: Trends for july 05-december 05. Symantec Enterprise Security **IX**, 1–106 (2006)

Acronyms and Abbreviations

AI	availability impact
AC	access complexity
Au	authentication
AV	access vector
CI	confidentiality impact
CIA	confidentiality, integrity or availability
CVE	Common Vulnerabilities and Exposures
CVSS	Common Vulnerability Scoring System
EC	exploit code
ETA	Event Trees Analysis
FIS	fuzzy inference system
FN	fuzzy number
FTA	Fault Trees Analysis
II	integrity impact
IW	impact weight
KRI	key risk indicator
LA	local access
MF	membership function
NVD	National Vulnerability Database
RC	report confidence
RL	remediation level
VFIS	vulnerability fuzzy inference system

References

ASTRA : A Security Analysis Method Based on Asset Tracking

Daniel Le Métayer and Claire Loiseaux

Abstract ASTRA is a security analysis method based on the systematic collection and analysis of security relevant information to detect inconsistencies and assess residual risks. ASTRA can accommodate organizational as well as technical aspects of security and it can be applied to innovative products for which no security data (e.g. vulnerability or attack database) is available. In addition, ASTRA explicitly deals with the notion of responsibility and naturally leads to an iterative refinement approach. This paper provides an introduction to the method and comparison with related work.

1 Context and motivations

A broad variety of methods and techniques have been proposed for IT security analysis, both by the academic world and by industry, with a number of differences in terms of scope, objectives and approaches. Actually, even the perimeter of what is called "security analysis" and the meaning of the basic terms used in this area are subject to subtle variations [8]. In this paper, we refer to security analysis as a part of a more general "security management" (or "risk management") process, the goal of the security analysis being to prepare the technical arguments for a subsequent "decision making" phase, which typically involves business related considerations[1].

The context in which the ASTRA method has been devised is the delivery of security services for the design or certification of innovative IT products. Our ex-

Daniel Le Métayer
Inria Rhône-Alpes, 655 venue de l'Europe, Montbonnot e-mail: Daniel.Le-Metayer@inrialpes.fr ·
Claire Loiseaux
Trusted Labs, 5 rue du Bailliage, Versailles, e-mail: Claire.Loiseaux@trusted-labs.com

[1] Possible outcomes of the decision phase being to accept the risks, to mitigate them (e.g. through the implementation of additional countermeasures), to transfer them (e.g. to an insurance company) or to avoid them (e.g. by deciding not to distribute a new product or functionality).

Please use the following format when citing this chapter:

Le Métayer, D. and Loiseaux, C., 2008, in IFIP International Federation for Information Processing, Volume 278; *Proceedings of the IFIP TC 11 23rd International Information Security Conference*; Sushil Jajodia, Pierangela Samarati, Stelvio Cimato; (Boston: Springer), pp. 541–555.

perience is mostly with companies offering new solutions in the field of telecommunications, banking or e-administration. As far as technology is concerned, such products and services are usually based on smart cards, mobile phones and/or security modules. The needs of these companies in terms of security analysis typically occur at two stages of the life cycle of the new products: before the design phase, for example as part of a feasibility study, and during (or even after) development, to prepare a subsequent certification procedure.

The first qualities of a security analysis method in this context are rigour, generality and incrementality:

- *Rigour* is obviously a virtue of any method, but it is a prerequisite for any method to be used in a certification process (especially if the highest levels of assurance are to be targeted). Rigour can be achieved through the application of systematic rules. Systematization itself brings additional benefits: it improves the efficiency of the process (and therefore reduces delays and costs, which are crucial factors in the case of innovative products for which time-to-market is often decisive) and enhances repeatability and maintenance.
- *Generality* is the ability to cope with all security aspects, including organizational, technical as well as management issues. The lack of generality, or the inability to provide a complete view of all security aspects, may lead to overlook significant issues or to spend too much energy and time on minor items when other, more significant, aspects, are underestimated.
- *Incrementality* is also crucial because, in practice, security analyses can rarely be one shot undertakings. Most companies prefer to start with a preliminary analysis, which should produce first conclusions as soon as possible at a moderate cost, before deciding to embark on more extensive studies.

From our experience, one of the main challenges for the security analyst is to be able to provide a representation of security which is both sufficiently complete and sufficiently rigorous. Actually, rigour is necessary at two levels:

- At the descriptive level: in most cases (and not only in large organizations), security information is spread over different groups of actors (architects, developers, suppliers, managers, security experts, etc.). One of the main tasks of any security analysis is therefore to gather all relevant information and build an overall picture of the security of the system. Needless to say, one usually observes different views among different actors. In any complex system, inconsistencies may also arise within individual representations of the system[2]. Such inconsistencies are typical symptoms (if not the sources) of misconceptions and vulnerabilities: detecting them is thus the first major outcome of a security analysis, which is possible only through a rigorous approach.
- At the analysis level: one of the main goals of a security analysis is to provide technical arguments for further decisions concerning the system (e.g. enhancement, deployment, security certification level, etc.). The key issue to this respect

[2] Typically, different assumptions can be made about the security features or available functionalities of a component at different design stages.

is to be able to justify such decisions: to this aim, the results of the security analysis should come with sound rationales and tracing facilities. Traceability and precise rationale, which are required by certification procedures such as the Common Criteria [4], also facilitate the maintenance of the security of the system.

Last but not least, a sufficient level of rigour is also necessary in order to establish the precise responsibilities of all actors and stakeholders. Responsibility can be understood here both in the technical sense and the legal sense (liability). Indeed, a large number of actors are usually involved in the design and operation of modern IT products and systems[3] and security issues may increasingly become a matter of liability, especially when substantial valuables are at stake.

Evaluating existing security analysis methods by the above yardsticks leads us to their classification into two main categories:

- In the first category, which includes most industrial methods and standards [1, 11, 15, 16], some level of systematization is attained through the use of catalogues or checklists. Checklists are a very effective way to capitalize on past experience and reduce the dependency of an organization with respect to a small group of experts. However, apart from systematization, they do not introduce by themselves a high level of rigour. In addition, they are appropriate only for the analysis of established (and relatively stable) categories of products such as operating systems or firewalls: they cannot be applied to the analysis of new products in emerging markets for which, typically, no data base of vulnerabilities is yet available.
- Methods in the second category provide a systematic approach based on semi-formal or formal models of the system under study [2, 3, 7, 12, 13]. Different levels of rigour can be attained depending on the formalism used to represent the models and the tools available to analyse them. However theses methods, which originate mostly from the academic world, usually focus on technical issues and leave organizational aspects out of their scope.

The ASTRA method has been devised precisely to fill this gap and provide a framework for the systematic security analysis of innovative products, addressing in an incremental and uniform way both organizational and technical aspects. The method is iterative and relies on the systematic collection and analysis of all security relevant information to detect inconsistencies and assess residual risks. In this paper, we present an introduction to the method and relate it with previous work. The framework is introduced in Section 2, followed by a presentation of the method itself in Section 3. Section 4 discusses related work and Section 5 summarizes the benefits and limitations of the method.

[3] For a device as small as a mobile phone, one can think of the device provider, operating systems and software suppliers, content providers, the operator, not to mention the user himself who plays an increasing role in the management of his device.

2 The Framework

The core of the ASTRA method is the construction and analysis of functions representing different views of the system (*Security Views*). Before entering into the presentation of the method itself in Section 3, we first provide the basic notions in Subsection 2.1 and introduce the three main components of the *Security Views* in the following subsections: right functions in Subsection 2.2, responsibility functions in Subsection 2.3 and dependency relations in Subsection 2.4.

2.1 Basic Notions

As its name suggests, ASTRA is based on the idea of *asset tracking*. In addition to assets, the basic ingredients of the method are locations, subjects, access rights, contexts, trust levels and sensitivity levels:

- An *asset* can be anything (part of the IT product or under its control) which has a value and needs to be protected. Assets can be digital (e.g. health record, cryptographic key, PIN, etc.) or physical (e.g. USB key, computer, network, official authorization letter, etc.). In the following, A denotes the set of assets.
- In order to track assets, we use the notion of *location*: a location can be seen as a container for assets; in other words, access to assets is possible only through locations. Locations can take different forms: computer memory, compact disk, network (cable or wireless), office cabinet, computer room, etc. The set of locations is denoted by L.
- As usual, *subjects* are the active entities in the system: subjects can have access to assets and locations. Again subjects can be digital (software code) or physical (developer, security officer, night-watchman, etc.). Note that the notion of subject used here is different from the notion of *legal entity* which can be considered in an extension of the method as set forth in Section 5. U denotes the set of subjects.
- Subjects may have *access rights* to assets and to locations. At first glance it could seem that considering both types of access rights just introduces useless redundancies. We believe that there are good reasons to include both of them though: first, they do not convey exactly the same kind of information and, from our experience, some actors feel it more natural to reason in terms of assets and others in terms of locations; also, one of the goals of security analysis is precisely to detect inconsistencies: in this context, offering the possibility to introduce redundancies is thus an advantage rather than a weakness.
- Access rights may depend of the current *context*. The context is a property of the state of the system, it being understood that states can encompass technical as well as procedural information (e.g. execution mode, security status, presence of a security officer, official authorization letter, etc.). For the sake of uniformity, we consider that the state Δ is a set of designated assets.

- Each subject s is associated with a *trust level T(s)* and each asset a is associated with a *sensitivity level S(a)*. Trust and sensitivity levels play an instrumental role in the evaluation of risk levels. They should thus be chosen with great care by the security analyst. To remedy any potential misjudgement in their assessment, the ASTRA method makes it easy to play *what-if games*, typically by making different assumptions about trust levels and analysing their consequences in terms of risks. In addition, as further detailed below, trust levels can be used to place different levels of constraints (whether technical, organizational or legal) on subjects.

2.2 Right functions

The three main functions which form the core of the ASTRA method are the Subject-Location function, the Subject-Asset function and the Asset-Location function:

- The Subject-Location function $SL_r(s,l)$ defines, for each subject s and each location l, the context c in which subject s has access right r to location l. More precisely, s may not have access right r to l, except when $SL_r(s,l)$ holds. The access right r can be *read* or *write*.
- The Subject-Asset function $SA_r(s,a)$ defines, for each subject s and each asset a, the context c in which subject s has access right r to asset a. More precisely, s may not have any access to a, except when $SA_r(s,a)$ holds. The semantics of *read* for assets is the possibility to obtain information about a while *write* includes the modification, creation, deletion and copy of the asset (all operations modifying the set of values of the asset in the system).
- The Asset-Location function $AL(a,l)$ defines, for each asset a and each location l, the context c in which location l may contain information about asset a. More precisely, l may not contain any information about a, except when $AL(a,l)$ holds.

2.3 Responsibility Functions

As set forth in the introduction, we believe that responsibilities should be dealt with explicitly in a security analysis method. Responsibilities can be specified through the following E (for *Ensures*) functions in ASTRA:

- $E(SL_r)(s,l) = \{s'\}$ specifies that subject s' is responsible for ensuring that subject s has access to location l only in context $SL_r(s,l)$. Obviously, we may have $s = s'$, which means that the subject is responsible for its own access to l, but it is not necessarily the case (and it should not be for subjects with low trust levels).
- $E(SA_r)(s,a) = \{s'\}$ specifies that subject s' is responsible for ensuring that subject s has access to asset a only in context $SA_r(s,a)$. In contrast with $E(SL_r)$,

which must return a non empty set of subjects, we may have $E(SA_r)(s,a) = \emptyset$, which means that no subject is explicitly designated as responsible for this rule. Instead, the rule has to be ensured indirectly, through conditions imposed by the SL_r and AL functions. Such under-specifications are often used for Subject-Asset relations because their implementation can be indirect: typically, a subject may have no access to a given asset because it has no access to a location which may contain this asset. Note that this does not mean that such rule will be left without any responsible subject: as shown in Section 3, responsibilities will instead be derived by the method. In addition, we impose that $\forall a \in \Delta, E(SA_{write})(s,a) \neq \emptyset$: in other words, the subjects responsible for context changes must be explicitly identified. This constraint is both reasonable, because of the instrumental role played by contexts, and useful from a technical point of view (see Subsection 3.2).

- $E(AL)(a,l) = \{s\}$ specifies that subject s is responsible for ensuring that information about asset a can be found in location l only in context $AL(a,l)$. For the same reason as $E(SA_r), E(AL)$ can return $\emptyset$, which means that the responsibilities for the corresponding rule will be derived by the method.

To conclude this subsection, let us note that, for the sake of generality, responsibility functions return sets of subjects. In most cases however, it is advised that this set should be reduced to a singleton.

2.4 Dependency Relations

For better clarity and conciseness it is useful in practice to define dependencies between assets and between locations: for example a message asset may be made of several fields, each of them containing another asset; an asset (e.g. ciphered text) can be derived from other assets (e.g. clear text and cryptographic key); a location can be a memory zone containing several buffers, each of them considered as another location. To address this need, we consider simple dependency relations between locations and assets respectively:

- $l \subseteq l'$ specifies that location l is included into location l'.
- $a_1, \ldots, a_n \rightarrow a$ means that the knowledge of information about assets $a_1, \ldots$ and a_n may provide information about asset a.

The dependency relations are implicitly closed by transitivity. Note that $a_1, \ldots, a_n \rightarrow a$ does not necessarily entails $a \rightarrow a_i$ for any a_i because a may be obtained from $a_1, \ldots, a_n$ through a one-way function. More sophisticated dependencies can be considered but we found the above relations sufficient in practice.

3 The Method

In the following, we introduce successively the two main phases of the method: the collection of information and detection of inconsistencies in Subsection 3.1 and the risk assessment in Subsection 3.2. Both phases are iterative. The first one constitutes the initial phase of the analysis, whose goal is to build a consistent and comprehensive view of the security of the system. The second one is repeated, possibly with intermediate decision making steps (e.g. to decide the implementation of additional countermeasures) until a stable state is reached. The two phases identify different kinds of pathological situations: sheer contradictions for the first phase and high risk levels for the second one.

3.1 Collection of Information and Detection of Inconsistencies

Before starting the collection of information, the very first task of any security analysis should be to precisely fix the perimeter of the analysis and assumptions about the actors involved. In ASTRA, the perimeter is defined by the sets of assets, locations and subjects, with the associated assumptions about levels of trust and levels of sensitivity and the dependency relations. This task is crucial because it defines the objectives and limitations of the analysis. The assessment of trust and sensitivity levels is especially delicate and should take account of technical as well as business considerations. This issue is further analysed in Subsection 3.2 where trust and sensitivity levels are used to derive risk levels.

As set forth in the introduction, various pieces of information about the security of a system are usually spread over several groups of actors. In addition, different actors may have different views about the functionalities and the security of the system. Such differences sometimes reveal serious misconceptions about the system which may lead to major security holes. To tackle this issue, the first task in ASTRA is to consolidate all relevant information in the form of *Security Views*: each *Security View* consists of SL_r, SA_r, AL and E functions representing the view of one actor or group of actors (e.g. requirements team, security expert, architect, developer team, integrator, etc.). Two types of inconsistencies may occur in *Security Views*, inconsistencies between different views and inconsistencies within a single view, which are defined in the following subsections.

3.1.1 Inter-view inconsistencies

Inter-views inconsistencies occur when $F_1(x,y) \neq F_2(x,y)$ where F_1 and F_2 stand for the versions of one of the SL_r, SA_r, AL and E functions in *Security Views* 1 and 2 respectively. From our experience, the two most common cases of inter-view inconsistencies are the following:

- For SL_r, SA_r and AL functions, one of the two conditions (or state properties) may be strictly weaker than the other one, that is $F_1(x,y) \Rightarrow F_2(x,y)$ or $F_2(x,y) \Rightarrow F_1(x,y)$, which means that one category of actors has placed stronger security requirements on a component than the other one.
- For E functions, $F_1(x,y) \neq F_2(x,y)$ reveals different assumptions about the subjects responsible for ensuring a security rule.

If not simple oversights, both kinds of inconsistencies may be the symptoms of serious discrepancies about security issues among different teams and have to be solved through discussions between these teams. As a result, one *Security View* at least has to be modified. The impact is sometimes confined to the presentation of the requirements or share of responsibilities but it may also happen that the implementation itself is affected.

3.1.2 Intra-view inconsistencies

We distinguish two kinds of intra-views inconsistencies: right inconsistencies and responsibility inconsistencies, which are defined in Definitions 1 and 2 respectively.

Definition 1. A *right inconsistency* occurs within a view if one of the following conditions holds:
(1) $l \subseteq l'$ *and* $\neg(SL_r(s,l) \Rightarrow SL_r(s,l'))$
(2) $a_1,\dots,a_n \rightarrow a$ *and* $\neg(SA_r(s,a_1) \wedge \dots \wedge SA_r(s,a_n) \Rightarrow SA_r(s,a))$
(3) $l \subseteq l'$ *and* $\neg(AL(a,l) \Rightarrow AL(a,l'))$
(4) $a_1,\dots,a_n \rightarrow a$ *and* $\neg(AL(a_1,l) \wedge \dots \wedge AL(a_n,l) \Rightarrow AL(a,l))$

Definition 2. A *responsibility inconsistency* occurs within a view if the following two conditions holds:
(5) $E(SA_r)(s,a) = \emptyset$
(6) $\exists l \in L, \neg(AL(a,l) \wedge SL_r(s,l) \Rightarrow SA_r(s,a))$

Right inconsistencies occur when the rights defined through the SL_r, SA_r and AL functions are in contradiction with the dependencies between locations or assets. A contradiction derives from (1) in Definition 1 in a situation where, for example, a memory zone l' contains a block l (thus $l \subseteq l'$), subject s has unconditional access rights to l (thus $SL_r(s,l) = True$), but no access right on l' (thus $SL_r(s,l') = False$). Note that the opposite condition is not imposed, which means that access rights to a location can be restricted to certain subsets of this location[4].

The second condition in Definition 1 identifies situations where access is allowed to intermediate assets $a_1,\dots,a_n$ which, together, can be used to get information about an asset a which should not be accessible.

Condition (3) mirrors Condition (1) for Asset-Location rights: if a memory zone l' contains a block l (thus $l \subseteq l'$), which can contain information about an asset a

[4] This is consistent with the semantics of $SL_r(s,l)$ presented above : subject s may not have any access right r to l, except when $SL_r(s,l)$ holds

(thus $AL(a,l) = True$), then l' should also be allowed to contain information about a (thus $AL(a,l') = True$).

Finally, Condition (4) mirrors Condition (2): if location l is allowed to contain intermediate assets $a_1,\ldots,a_n$ which, together, can be used to get information about an asset a, then l should be allowed to contain information about asset a.

Right inconsistencies thus stem from overlooked dependencies: sometimes they can be corrected without deep impact on the design of the product (e.g. through the extension of unduly restricted access rights in the *Security View*) but there are also cases where they call for more drastic modifications to some components or even to the architecture of the product (e.g. when the current design does not allow for sufficient protection of intermediate assets).

A responsibility inconsistency occurs when the *Security View* does not specify any responsible subject for a Subject-Asset access rule and does no provide any way to ensure this access rule indirectly. As set forth in Subsection 2.3, $E(SA_r)(s,a) = \emptyset$ means that the condition $SA_r(s,a) = c$ is to be ensured indirectly, through conditions imposed by SL_r and AL. The property to be checked is thus $\forall l \in L, SL_r(s,l) \wedge AL(a,l) \Rightarrow SA_r(s,a)$, which expresses the fact that if subject s can get access to a location l which may contain asset a, then such access is permitted only in the context specified by $SA_r(s,a)$. If this property is not satisfied, a contradiction occurs in the *Security View* because the responsibility to ensure $SA_r(s,a)$ cannot be assigned to any subject.

Information collection and detection of inconsistencies is an iterative and interactive process: when inconsistencies are discovered, either intra-view or inter-view, discussions are organized with the concerned teams to further study the conflicting rules and strengthen the overall understanding of security issues. In the most serious cases, it may even be necessary to set up global project meetings to converge towards a common view. From our experience, this first phase goes much further than a simple collection of information: the elucidation of the expectations and assumptions of the different actors already makes it possible to uncover major gaps or misconceptions about security issues.

3.2 Risk Assessment

The result of the first phase is a single consolidated *Security View* consisting of SL_r, SA_r, AL and E functions. Trust and sensitivity levels are also attached to subjects and assets during this first phase. The second phase consists in identifying and classifying risks based on the consistent set of information resulting from the first phase. In contrast with the inconsistencies identified in the first phase, risks are not sheer contradictions: they represent potentialities of attacks which can be classified on a severity scale.

In ASTRA, risks are identified and assessed based on a ternary relationship between the rights, the subject responsible for those rights and the assets at stake. More precisely, for each right specified by a function F in SL_r, SA_r or AL, we derive:

- The set $C(F)$ of assets concerned by the right and
- The set $R(F)$ of subjects responsible for enforcing the right.

The risk level associated with the right is then derived from the sensitivity level of the most sensitive asset in $C(F)$ and the trust level of the less trustable subject in $R(F)$. Different scales can be used to express sensitivity and trust levels, depending on the complexity of the system under study and the types of actors involved (authorized as well as malicious). Similarly, different algorithms can be used to derive risk levels. For the sake of illustration, we use very simple scales and algorithm here, that we found sufficient in most situations:

- Trust levels take integer values in a range from 1 to 4 (4 corresponding to the less trustable subjects).
- Sensitivity levels take integer values in a range from 1 to 4 (4 corresponding to the most sensitive values).
- The risk level associated with a right specified by F is the sum of the sensitivity level of the most sensitive asset in $C(F)$ and trust level of the less trustable subject in $R(F)$.

A risk level of 8 corresponds to the worst situation (the less trustable subjects being responsible for the security of the most sensitive assets), 7 corresponds to an unacceptable risk and 6 to a significant risk. Risks from level 5 to 2 are considered as "tolerable" (5 being the minimum level of risk for assets of sensitivity 4). Obviously, this interpretation depends very much on the interpretation of the trust and sensitivity levels themselves, and can be adapted to fit the needs of each project.

We proceed now with the definition of the risk levels, which are computed from the sets of responsible subjects and concerned assets.

Definition 3. The sets of responsible subjects R, the set of assets concerned C, and the derived risk level $Risk$ are defined as follows for, espectively, SL_r, SA_r and AL:

(1) $R(SL_r)(s,l) = E(SL_r)(s,l)$

(2) $C(SL_r)(s,l) = D(\{a \mid AL(a,l) \neq False\})$

(3) $Risk(SL_r)(s,l) =$
$$Max(\{T(s') \mid s' \in R(SL_r)(s,l)\}) +$$
$$Max(\{S(a) \mid a \in C(SL_r)(s,l)\})$$

(4) $R(SA_r)(s,a) =$
$$if\ E(SA_r)(s,a) \neq \emptyset$$
$$then\ E(SA_r)(s,a)$$
$$else \bigcup \{R(SL_r)(s,l) \mid l \in L\} \bigcup \{R(AL)(a,l) \mid l \in L, SL_r(s,l) \neq False\}$$

(5) $C(SA_r)(s,a) = D(\{a\})$

(6) $Risk(SA_r)(s,a) =$
$$Max(\{T(s') \mid s' \in R(SA_r)(s,a)\}) +$$
$$Max(\{S(a) \mid a \in C(SA_r)(s,a)\})$$

(7) $R(AL)(a,l) =$
$$if\ E(AL)(a,l) \neq \emptyset$$
$$then\ E(AL)(a,l)$$

$$else \bigcup \{R(SL_r)(s,l) \mid s \in U\} \bigcup \{E(SA_{write})(s,a') \mid s \in U, a' \in \Delta\}$$

(8) $C(AL)(a,l) = D(\{a\})$

(9) $Risk(AL)(a,l) =$
$$Max(\{T(s') \mid s' \in R(AL)(a,l)\}) +$$
$$Max(\{S(a) \mid a \in C(AL)(a,l)\})$$

Definition 4. $D(A)$ is defined as the minimal superset of A such that
$$\forall a_1 \in D(A), \ldots, \forall a_n \in D(A),\ a_1, \ldots, a_n \rightarrow a \Rightarrow a \in D(A)$$

Generally speaking, when specified in the *Security View* through the E function, the responsible subject is as defined by E ((1) and (4) in Definition 3).

When no responsible subject is specified for a Subject-Asset right $SA_r(s,a)$, then a subject is considered responsible for this right either if ((4) in Definition 3) it is responsible for the access right to a location by s (and thus it belongs to $R(SL_r)(s,l)$) or if it is responsible for the right for a location to contain a (and thus it belongs to $R(AL)(a,l)$). The motivation is that, as set forth in Subsection 3.1.2, the Subject-Asset right is ensured indirectly in such case, through Subject-Location and Location-Asset rights.

As far as Asset-Location rights are concerned, $AL(a,l)$ is an invariant property which can be breached by two kinds of actions: accesses to location l resulting in information about asset a being available in location l in an unauthorized context or changes of context. Responsible subjects are thus members of $R(SL_r)(s,l)$ and $E(SA_{write})(s,a')$, as set forth in (7) above[5].

The set of concerned assets is straightforward in the cases of $SA_r(s,a)$ and $AL(a,l)$ which apply directly to asset a ((5) and (8) in Definition 3). Note however that asset dependencies are taken into account through function D: if assets $a_1, \ldots, a_n$ are concerned by a rule and information about asset a can be derived from $a_1, \ldots, a_n$ then a is also concerned (Definition 4). The assets concerned by $SL_r(s,l)$ are all the assets which can reside in location l ((2) in Definition 3). Finally risk levels are defined for each function as set forth above, based on the trust levels of responsible subjects and the sensitivity levels of the concerned assets (lines (3), (6) and (9) in Definition 3).

To conclude this subsection on risk assessment, let us stress the fact that the above definitions allow us to separate the issues of defining the set of responsible subjects and evaluating of the risk level. Whereas the risk level depends on the initial assumptions about trust and sensitivity of subjects and assets, the definition of responsible subjects does not rely on such assessments. An interesting property of the definition of R above is that it leads to a confinement of responsibilities which can stated as follows:

Confinement Property:

1. If all the subjects in $R(SL_r)(s,l)$ comply with their responsibilities, as defined by R, then $SL_r(s,l)$ will be guaranteed by the system.

[5] Note that, as set forth in Subsection 2.3, $\forall a' \in \Delta, E(SA_{write})(s,a') \neq \emptyset$.

2. If all the subjects in $R(SA_r)(s,a)$ comply with their responsibilities, as defined by R, then $SA_r(s,a)$ will be guaranteed by the system.
3. If all the subjects in $R(AL)(a,l)$ comply with their responsibilities, as defined by R, then $AL(a,l)$ will be guaranteed by the system.

The proof of this property, which is omitted here for space considerations, is based on a case analysis of Definitions 3 and 4. The significance of this confinement property is that it holds disregarding the behaviour of the other subjects, that is to say even if they do not comply with their own responsibilities. This confinement property shows that Definitions 3 and 4 form a sound basis for risk assessment, independently of the validity of the assumptions about trust and sensitivity levels. Actually different assumptions about these levels can be made during the analysis to study their impact on the resulting risk based on the above definition of R.

4 Related Work

The security analysis methods used in industry fall essentially into two categories [10]: commercial methods and standards. As far as standards are concerned, [5] is essentially a code of good practices: it offers guidelines and very general principles, with strong emphasis on management and organizational issues while [4] as an international standard for the evaluation of IT products. [1] puts forward a general three phases approach based on (1) the establishment of an asset-based threat profile, (2) the identification infrastructure vulnerabilities and (3) the development of security strategy and plans. [15] is also very generic but more technical than [1]; it puts emphasis on the integration of risk management into the software development life cycle and proposes a decomposition of the analysis into a series of predetermined phases split into a number of steps with specified inputs, outputs and guidance (checklists, definitions, questionnaires, interview outline, etc.).

Turning to commercial methods, [11] is consistent with the recommendations in [15]; its main emphasis is cost-effectiveness and it provides organizational rules for conducting the analysis process based on brain storming meetings (people involved, roles, responsibilities, required material, meeting preparation, duration, objectives, checklists, etc.). The methods put forward by Microsoft [16, 6] are based on a range of information representation patterns (tables), classification lists (e.g. the STRIDE checklist for threats: Spoofing, Tampering, Repudiation, Information disclosure, Denial of service, Elevation of privilege) and semi-formal representations (data flow diagrams, attack trees).

Attack trees [14] are a natural way to represent security attacks which is used by several methods. The root of an attack tree represents the goal of the attack and the nodes correspond to subgoals linked by *AND* and *OR* relations. Most interestingly, different kinds of attributes can be assigned to the leaves (cost, risk for the attacker, required equipment or expertise, etc.) and propagated to the root. Attack trees are rather popular in industry because they can be used in a pragmatic, incremental process in which leaves requiring deeper investigation can be progressively decomposed into subtrees. Attack trees have limitations though; in particular, they provide a convenient framework for presenting, categorizing and analyzing attacks but they offer little help for the discovery of these attacks, which still relies on the expertise of the analyst.

Attack trees were originally presented in an informal way. Two main approaches have been followed to provide a formal framework for attack trees:

- The first approach consists in enhancing the attack tree notation with statements expressed in an attack specification language: the attack tree notation is then used as a structuring framework or glue syntax for the formal statements [17].
- The second approach is to endow the attack tree notation itself with a mathematical semantics, which makes it possible to study attack trees as mathematical objects of their own [9]. This approach can be used to define a class of "reasonable attributes" which can correctly be propagated bottom-up.

The attack tree approach has also been extended to *attack graphs* and techniques have been proposed for the automatic generation of attack graphs (based on attack templates) and their analysis (based on graph algorithms) [2, 7, 12], which is especially useful for the network security analysis.

A more detailed introduction to existing security analysis methods can be found in [8]. This quick review reveals several gaps in the security analysis landscape: first, most methods fall into one of the following two categories: they are either (1) general purpose with, usually, much emphasis on organizational issues or (2) based on a formalism with, usually, strong emphasis on systematization (or even automation) and rigour. As set forth in the introduction, attaining high levels of both generality and rigour (or systematization) remains a challenge. Attack trees and attack graphs go in the right direction but, as mentioned above, they offer little help to discover attacks in the first place. It remains necessary to rely on the expertise of the analyst or on the existence of catalogues or checklists which are usually not available for new, innovative products.

5 Conclusion

The method presented in this paper was devised precisely to fill the gaps identified in the previous section. The framework provided by ASTRA is:

- Rigorous : it can serve as a basis for inconsistency detection.
- General: it can accommodate organizational as well as technical aspects of security.
- Suited to innovative products for which no security data (e.g. vulnerability or attack database) is available.

In addition, the method naturally leads to an iterative refinement approach: inconsistencies or high risk levels can be solved through different kinds of refinements: decomposition of a subject (or code) into several subjects (for a more appropriate allocation of responsibilities), decomposition of a context into more precise state conditions (to refine access rights), decomposition of a location into different sublocations (which should be associated with different access rights).

An important aspect of ASTRA is that organizational rules can be handled in exactly the same way as technical rules: individual actors such as security officers or a night-watchers can be represented as subjects, physical goods or authorization documents can be represented as assets, rooms or premises are represented as locations, etc. Actually malicious actors can also be included in the *Security Views* (with an extended trust level range to take into account the very low, or negative, level of trust associated with such subjects) and possibilities such as monitoring the electrical activity of a device to perform a DPA (Differential Power Analysis) attack can be represented as a form of location access (access to the room and access to the device, possibly in specific contexts such as the absence of security officer and night-watcher, etc.). Another possibility of the framework which has not been presented here is the use of sensitivity levels depending on rights: for example, for some assets *read* is a more sensitive type of access than *write*, for others the opposite holds.

Among the benefits of the method let us also stress the significance of the notion of responsibility: in practice, it turns out to be very useful to be able to separate the specification of the behaviour of a subject from the definition of the responsibilities for this behaviour. Indeed, many security holes in a system come from misunderstandings or conflicting views about responsibilities. The next step in this direction will be the introduction of legal entities associated with subjects, which will allow us to encompass legal liability.

As far as limitations are concerned, the method, in its current state, is targeted towards the study of invariant security properties such as confidentiality and integrity. More work is needed to extend it to denial of service or liveness properties (such as agreement properties). Last but not least, the application of a method like ASTRA should obviously be supported by a tool because the amount of available information is usually so large that its analysis by human beings would be cumbersome and error prone. The two main features of such a tool are its interface and its rule based engine. The role of the engine is to implement the rules set forth in Section 3 and to sort access rules according to associated the risk levels. The most challenging part of the tool is actually the user interface, which should be easy to use both by analysts (to enter security information, e.g. through dedicated text processing and spreadsheet functionalities and to trace the risk level calculation in order to understand how to improve the situation) and by decision makers (with simplified presentations of the results and alternative options). Dedicated graphical features are necessary, especially to support "what-if games" (changing assumptions about trust and studying the consequences in terms of risk levels) and to provide user-friendly representations of access rights.

Acknowledgements This work has been partially funded by the ANR (Agence Nationale de la Recherche) under the grant ANR-07-SESU-007 (project LISE: Liability Issues in Software Engineering).

References

1. Alberts, C., Dorofee, A., Stevens, J., Woody, C.: Introduction to the OCTAVE approach. Carnegie Mellon, SEI (2003).
2. Ammann, P., Wijesekera, D., Kaushik, S.: Scalable, graph-based network vulnerability analysis. Proceedings of the 9th ACM conference on Computer and Communications Security CCS'02(2002).
3. Besson, F., Jensen, T., Le Métayer, D., Thorn, T.: Model checking security properties of control flow graphs. Journal of Computer Security, Vol. 9 (2001).
4. Common Criteria for Information Technology Security evaluation. http://www.commoncriteriaportal.org/, CC V3.1 (2006).
5. ISO/IEC 17799:2005, Information technology - security techniques - code of practice for information security management (2005).
6. Howard, M., LeBlanc, D.: Writing secure code. Microsoft Press (2003).
7. Jha, S., Sheyner, O., Wing, J.: Two formal analyses of attack graphs. Proceedings of the 15th Computer Security Foundations Workshop, IEEE Computer Society (2002).
8. Le Métayer, D.: IT Security analysis: best practices and formal approaches. Proceedings of FOSAD Summer School (Formal Security Analysis and Design), Springer Verlag LNCS 4677 (2007).
9. Maw, S., Oostdijk, M.: Foundations of attack trees. International Conference on Information Security and Cryptology, Springer Verlag LNCS 3935 (2005).
10. McGraw, G.: Software security: building security in. Addison Wesley Professional (2006).
11. Peltier, T. R.: Information Security Risk Analysis. Auerbach Publications (2005).
12. Phillips, C., Swiler, L. P.: A graph-based system for network-vulnerability analysis. Proceedings of the 1998 Workshop on New Security Paradigms, ACM Press (1998).
13. Ramakrishan, C. R., Sekar, R.: Model-based vulnerability analysis of computer systems, Second International Workshop on Verification, Model Checking and Abstract Interpretation, (VMCAI'98) (1998).
14. Schneier, B.: Attack trees, modeling security threats. Dr Dobbs Journal (1999).
15. Stoneburner, G., Goguen, A., Feringa, A.: Risk management guide for information technology systems. NIST Special Publication 800-30 (2002).
16. Swiderski, F., Snyder, W.: Threat modeling. Microsoft Press (2004).
17. Tidwell, T., Larson, R., Fitch, K., Hale, J.: Modeling internet attacks. Proceedings of the 2001 IEEE Workshop on Information Assurance and Security (2001).

A Knowledge-Based Bayesian Model for Analyzing a System after an Insider Attack

Qutaibah Althebyan, Brajendra Panda

Abstract Many consider insider attacks to be more severe than outsider attacks due to the nature of such attacks that involve people who have knowledge of their own organization. In this work, we presented a new model to evaluate and analyze a system after the occurrence of an insider attack. By evaluating and analyzing the system after detecting such attack, we classified systems' objects into a list of non affected objects and a list of affected objects. We also introduced a new graph called knowledge Bayesian attack graph (KBAG). KBAG represents possible candidate paths that malicious insiders may follow to achieve their goal of compromising critical objects. KBAG also enables us to calculate risk values for different objects using Bayesian inference techniques. These risk values will be considered as measurements for the likelihood of possible occurrence of other insider attacks that have not yet been detected by the underlying system.

1 Introduction

Nowadays, computer security issues have become a great concern for both individuals and organizations. Users have been increasingly concerned about sensitive information that can be revealed if they face an attack. Consequences of attacks can be as small as stealing small portion of an individual's critical information and as severe as destruction of an organization's entire information base. Several kinds of attacks may affect an organization. Among such attacks are insiders' attacks which are considered, according to many experts, among the most devastating ones.

Insider attacks involve individuals who work for an organization and who have justifiable privileges to access sensitive data in the organization. During this kind of attacks privileged individuals accumulate enough knowledge about their organiza-

Qutaibah Althebyan and Brajendra Panda
Department of Computer Science and Computer Engineering, University of Arkansas, Fayetteville, Arkansas 72701, USA, e-mail: {qaltheb, bpanda}@uark.edu

Please use the following format when citing this chapter:

Althebyan, Q. and Panda, B., 2008, in IFIP International Federation for Information Processing, Volume 278; *Proceedings of the IFIP TC 11 23rd International Information Security Conference*; Sushil Jajodia, Pierangela Samarati, Stelvio Cimato; (Boston: Springer), pp. 557–571.

tion. Both privileges and knowledge help individuals in planning successful attacks while making it difficult for the organization to discover and/or prevent them. In this paper, we assume that such an attack has been detected by the underlying system and it affected a specific object or set of objects. In our effort to resolve the problem and recover the system, we use Bayesian networks [1] as well as knowledge graphs (KGs) and dependency graphs (DGs), which were proposed in [2], to analyze the system that suffered from a successful attack. Analysis of the system includes identification of the source of the attack and after identifying the source, an evaluation of all objects in the system must be performed.

In general, an attack can be of many forms. However, in our work we focus on attacks that involve modification of a given document or a set of documents. It is important to mention that this work is suitable only for insider attacks. So, the reader should realize that attempts to use this work to evaluate a system suffering from an outsider attack may not be successful. Our model helps in narrowing down the investigation process by classifying objects into a list of unaffected objects and a list of affected objects. The set of aunaffected objects can then be made available to users while all affected objects go through further invistigation.

2 Our Model

Many definitions have been proposed for the insider. For example, Mark Maybury et al. [3] introduced malicious insider as "one motivated to adversely impact an organization's mission through a range of actions that compromise information confidentiality, integrity, and/or availability". Boanerges Aleman-Meza1, Phillip Burns et al. [4] mentioned that "insider threat refers to the potential malevolent actions by employees within an organization, a specific type of which relates to legitimate access of documents." However, in our model, we define an insider as [2]: *An insider is an individual who has access to and has some knowledge of the organization's information system.*

The above definition involves individuals with assigned privileges with a concentration on knowledge of insiders. Throughout this paper, we consider any piece of information as an object. Hence, usernames, passwords, dates, paper documents, digital documents, e-mails, etc. are all valid examples of objects. An insider upon accessing an object increases his/her knowledge. We assume that any knowledge an insider gains is saved in his/her knowledgebase, and it is saved as units. Usually insiders have knowledge about their own organization. They know other insiders in the organization and may know others' responsibilities. This includes the knowledge of the overall network topology of the organization which makes it easy to know where to get information and where to find sensitive data. He/she also gains knowledge by accessing documents through his/her valid account. This accumulated knowledge gives him/her the advantage to extract sensitive data, which he/she is not authorized to get. However, he/she increases these chances by adding to his/her knowledgebase the knowledge of existing dependencies among various objects in the system.

Our model "Knowledge-Based Bayesian Graph Model" uses knowledge graphs (KGs), dependency graphs (DGs), and knowledge Bayesian attack graphs (KBAGs) to analyze the system after a detected attack that is initiated by an insider of the underlying system. Before going into details in describing our model, it is important to give brief descriptions of KGs and DGs in order to familiarize the reader with these concepts. Both KGs and DGs are used in constructing KBAGs and implementing algorithms in our model. We start with a brief description of KGs.

2.1 Knowledge Graphs (KGs)

A Knowledge Graph [2], denoted by KG, is a graph that represents different knowledge units of an insider. Knowledge units are any piece of information an insider gets access to and are saved in his/her knowledgebase. Knowledge units are denoted by K_i. A given insider has a specific KG that is initiated the first time he/she accessed the organizations' resources. It is updated after each access to any object of the system. *Definition: A Knowledge Graph* is a directional graph represented by G(V, E) where V is:

- A set of non-leaf nodes representing the user's knowledge that is gained from objects in the underlying system
- A set of leaf nodes representing the objects that the user has had access to

E is the set of edges among vertices of the graph. An edge E = (V_i, V_j) exists in G iff the knowledge unit in V_j can be obtained from V_i. V_i, V_j, respectively belong to any of the following set of vertices:

- An object O_i and its corresponding knowledge unit K_i
- Two knowledge units K_i and K_j
- A knowledge unit K_i and the vertex of the composed knowledge CK, where the composed knowledge CK is a node in the KG that represents the total knowledge accumulated for the corresponding insider, and equals to the union of knowledge units that exist in the knowledgebase of the insider

Fig. 1 illustrates an example of Knowledge Graph of an insider S_i:

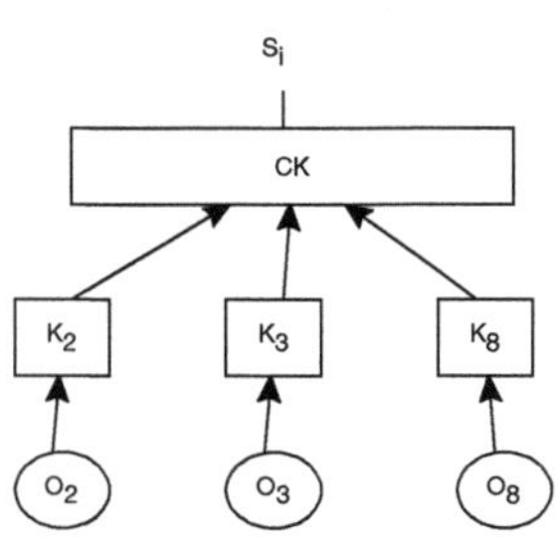

Fig. 1 An Example of a Knowledge-Graph

So, a KG contains knowledge units K_i's that are saved in S_i knowledgebase. We used ontological methods to extract knowledge facts (saved as units) from documents' contents using the concept of relatedness of documents to the current active domain of the corresponding insider. All knowledge units that are extracted from documents related to the user's current domain constitute the insider's knowledge. However, this does not constitute his/her total knowledge. In fact, an insider can obtain a new higher knowledge by combining existing knowledge units. To illustrate, consider the following example of a document d_1 represented by table 1(a):

Table 1 Original and related attributes of d_1 to the domain of access for S_i

	Name	ID	Age	Salary
1	A	1	30	$1000
⋮	...			
100	K	100	27	$1600

(a) D_1's Attributes.

	Name	ID
1	A	1
⋮	...	
100	K	100

(b) Related Attributes.

Table 1(b) contains the attributes that are related to the current insider's domain. S_i is interested only in names and id's of employees. Since there are 100 names then the set of related attributes (knowledge units) are: $U_1 \rightarrow A$, $U_2 \rightarrow B, \ldots, U_{100} \rightarrow k$. Therefore, 100 knowledge units $U_1, \ldots, U_{100}$ are saved in his/her knowledgebase. Another 100 knowledge units (100 ID's) are also saved in his/her knowledge units. That is: $U_{101} \rightarrow 1$, $U_{102} \rightarrow 2, \ldots, U_{200} \rightarrow 100$ are another 100 knowledge units. Moreover, S_i can extract a higher level of knowledge from the 200 knowledge units he/she already gained. This can be obtained by combining existing knowledge units which will be represented as new knowledge units. Fig. 2 (a) illustrates the combining of two knowledge units to form a new higher-level knowledge unit:

(a)Combining two knowledge units.

Name-Id
A, 1
...
K, 100

(b) Knowledge unit Name-Id.

Fig. 2 Relation of combining two knowledge units and the corresponding new knowledge unit.

The table in Fig. 2 (b) illustrates the process of combining the two knowledge units: Name and ID which results in knowledge unit "Name-ID". This associates names of employees with their id's. This adds 100 new knowledge units to his/her knowledgebase, giving a total of 300 knowledge units.

2.2 Dependency Graphs (DGs)

A *Dependency graph* (DG) [2] is a global hierarchal graph that shows all dependencies among various objects in the system. Usually, objects, especially documents, are created depending on other objects of the same system. This dependency relationship is an important one through which insiders may predict contents of important objects that they do not have privileges to access. By following dependencies among different objects, insiders may locate critical objects, and hence get a chance to obtain critical information for which they are not authorized to access. A DG contains nodes for all objects in the system. Our concept of a DG is similar to the System Dependency Graph, SDC, presented by Larsen and Harrold [6] for modeling an object-oriented program.

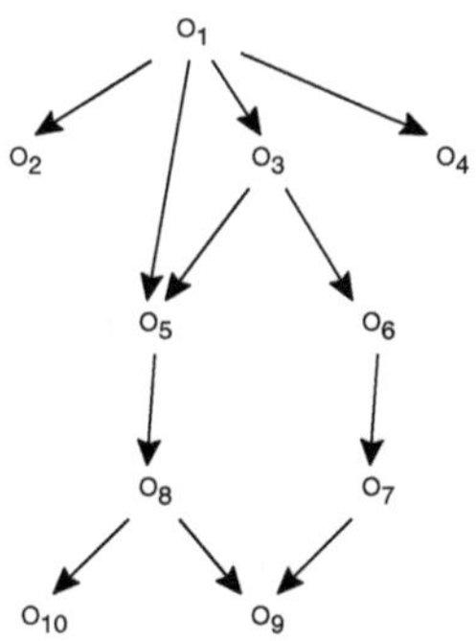

Fig. 3 An Example of a Dependency Graph

Fig. 3 represents an example of a DG of objects. It is important to mention that the DG is a dynamic graph that is updated for every newly created object in the system. A new edge is added between the new object and the object (or objects) which the new object relies on. Also, the DG is updated periodically to reflect operations affecting the objects. A DG is a directional graph in which the direction of the edge indicates the dependency direction which can be verified from Fig. 3. Throughout this paper, we follow the top down approach for representing dependencies among different objects. So, if we consider the dependency relation between any two objects as a function F, then we can verify the following relations from Fig. 3 to be true: $O_3 = F(O_1)$, $O_4 = F(O_1)$, $O_5 = F(O_1, O_3)$,... etc.

It is important to clarify the meaning of dependency relations that exist among nodes in a DG. For example, in Fig. 3 the following relation $O_5 = F(O_1, O_3)$ exists. This relation indicates that O_5 is a function of O_1 and O_3. In reality this relation has a meaning that is consistent with the context for which this relation has been created. Generally speaking, this relation means that some information in O_1 and O_3 has been used to derive some information in O_5. This contributes to some or all knowledge units that O_5 contains. An example of the above argument is:

- Object O_1 contains salary rates of all sets of employees in the organization. Employees are distinguished into several sets that involve categorizing employees with the same rank into the same set
- Object O_3 contains the total number of employees in each set or group
- Object O_5, as a result, uses the information in both objects O_1 and O_3 to calculate the total amount of money consumed for salaries out of the total budget of the organization

Having the knowledge of both O_1 and O_3 gives an insider the ability to "get the knowledge" of object (O_5) probably without having the right privilege to access O_5.

Before we go into describing KBAGs, it is necessary for the reader to have some familiarity with the concept of Bayesian networks. We start by giving a brief description of Bayesian networks. We then describe KBAGs.

2.3 Bayesian Networks

Bayesian network (or Bayes net) is modeled as a directed acyclic graph over a set of variables which associates these variables with a set of conditional probability distributions, one for each variable [5]. It is a graphical representation which shows probabilistic relationships among a set of variables and is used in modeling situation with uncertainty. Fig. 4 shows a simple Bayesian network with three variables A, B and C. Bayesian network uses the available prior probabilities or knowledge for cal-

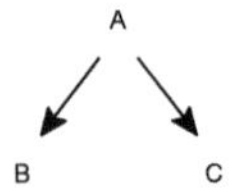

Fig. 4 A simple Bayesian netowrk with three variables

culating new probability values using Bayesian inference techniques. For example, if we consider Fig. 4, then the joint probability distribution function for the above three variables is P(A, B, C), and this joint probability distribution function equals to:

$$P(A, B, C) = P(A/B)*P(C/B)*P(B)$$

The above formula can be extended to any number of variables. It also draws some dependency relations among variables in which a change in the state (value in our case) in one variable results in a change in the state of one or more other variables. The change takes effect when one or more variables of the Bayesian network have a dependent relation with the variable that has been changed. For example, any change in the value of variable B results in an effect in variable A, affecting the joint probability distribution function. Moreover, any change in variable B (for instance) will not have any direct effect in variable C because both B and C are independent.

However, the joint function is still affected by this change because of the dependency relation between C and A which (i.e., A) has a dependency relation with B. In the following section we introduce KBAG which is a basic component in our model of evaluating and analyzing an attack initiated by an insider of the underlying system.

2.4 Knowledge Bayesian Attack Graphs (KBAGs)

Knowledge Bayesian Attack Graph (KBAG) is a top-down directed graph that shows probabilistic relationships among different objects (representing nodes) of the graph. It involves similar characteristics of both Bayesian networks and attack graphs [7, 8, 9]. Each node of a KBAG (represents an object) is assigned a probability value that represents the probability of a successful attack at that node. That is, this probability represents a measurement which quantifies the fact that a given node of KBAG had been attacked (maliciously modified). Different levels of conditional probabilities are assigned to different nodes. More details for how to create KBAGs and how to assign probability values for their nodes are presented in section 3.2.

A KBAG is created using information from the knowledge graph (KG) of an insider and the dependency graph (DG) of different objects in the system. It consists of a set of variables (representing nodes) that represents a set of objects that can be accessed by an insider. These nodes will be associated with probability values as mentioned earlier. It also consists of a set of directed edges that indicates a directed dependency from the parent node to its descendent nodes. Hence, a path from one node to another node represents a dependency relation that exists between the two nodes. Conditional dependency has only the top-down direction which is the direction from the parent node to children nodes.

A candidate path in a KBAG represents a series of accesses for objects. This series of accesses may lead to a successful attack to any node in the underlying system. So, a path from a root node to a descendent intermediate or leaf node represents a candidate for a successful attack. By creating this graph and identifying all possible paths from a root node to either a leaf node or a critical node (a critical node is a node that has critical information and will be called "hot node") we can learn how insiders initiate a set of accesses or actions for launching an attack. Further, we can narrow down the list of affected objects by calculating risk values for all nodes in the KBAG. More details on how to create and implement KBAGs is provided in section 3.1.

3 Evaluating and Analyzing the System after an Insider Attack

In this section, we introduce a new algorithm for evaluating and analyzing a system after undergoing an insider attack. We assume that the system has been affected by an attack launched by an insider of the system. Although our model can be extended to cover all kinds of attacks, we limit ourselves to cover only attacks that involve modefying an object. In what follows we introduce a new algorithm which uses KBAGs to calculate risk values for different objects in the system. Through risk values we can find a list of possible affected objects by the same insider in case other attacks have been performed to other objects.

3.1 Creating Knowledge Bayesian Attack Graph (KBAG)

A KBAG is a directed graph that consists of:

1. A set of nodes each of which representing an object of the system
2. Top-down directed edges among different nodes of KBAG; and
3. Probability values assigned to all nodes.

To build KBAG, both KG and DG are compared in parallel. Nodes that belong to the knowledgebase of the insider create the new set of nodes. That is, part of the nodes of the considered KG represent the set of nodes of the KBAG. Directed edges are obtained by traversing the DG of different objects in the system. That is, we are computing kind of transitivity closure of the DG. After building the KBAG, probability values are assigned to different nodes of the KBAG. More details on assigning these probability values follows in section 3.2.

The algorithm below illustrates creating KBAG. In this algorithm, we assume that an attack has been detected which affected a specific object identified as O_{hacked}. A list of hot nodes is determined. A hot node is a node that has high importance value and its corresponding access list is limited to some high privileged users. This indicates that hot nodes contain very sensitive information that should not be accessed except by very high privileged users of the organization. After determining hot nodes, all paths from different nodes in the KBAG to these hot nodes are specified. The paths are possible candidates for attack paths. We assume that attackers try one of these paths to get access to one or more of these hot nodes in their effort to compromise one of them. It is important to mention that hot nodes are not the only nodes that will be investigated. In fact, our model considers identifying attacks that might have been carried out on any node in the underlying system and yet have not been detected. However, identifying hot nodes guides us in building KBAG. It is also right (according to our assumption) that insiders try to compromise several nodes (to accumulate enough knowledge) before attacking a node that has sensitive information. So, although our model use hot nodes to build KBAGs, the reader should realize that all nodes of KBAGs are considered. This means that all nodes of the KBAG will be evaluated and investigated for any expected attack that might have been carried out without being detected by the underlying system. Consider the following segments of a DG which is illustrated in Fig. 5(a) and the segment of a KG of an insider which is illustrated in Fig. 5(b).

Fig. 6 shows the corresponding partially constructed KBAG (yet without implementing the last step, i.e., assigning probability values for the nodes). It shows

```
Algorithm : Creating KBAG {
/* Given that O_hacked is the object that has been maliciously modified */
/* KG(S_i) is the knowledge graph of insider S_i */
/* DG is the dependency graph of objects in the system */
 Create a new graph G* = (V*, E*) where
 V* =        /* V* is empty */
 E* =        /* E* is empty */
 V* = V*  O_hacked
 V* = V*  O_hot
 for every insider S_i do
          for each vertex v_j  KG(S_i)
            V* = V* U  v_j
 for each vertex vk  belongs to V* {
          Starting with the vertex v_k
          Traverse DG and add edges between vertices v_k and v_j (v_k, v_j)  G* such that
          there is a direct edge connecting v_k and v_j in DG}
 for each vertex v_i belongs to V* do{
          if v_i does not have any incoming or leaving edge from it then{
            v_i is an isolated vertex
            V* = V* - vi } }
 for each vertex v_i   belongs to V* do {
          if there is no direct edge between v_i and O_hot in G* then do {
          Traverse DG
          if there is a path from v_i to {v_j}and a path from {v_j} to O_hot such that
          /* {v_j} represents one or more vertices */
          both vertices v_i and v_j (v_i, v_j)  G* then add a series of edges
          between v_i and O_hot adding edges among all intermediate nodes
          {v_j} between v_i and O_hot  } }
G* is the new KBAG
}
```

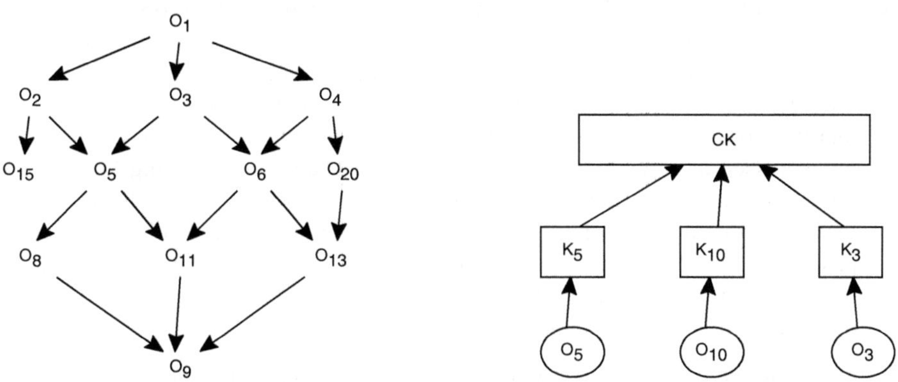

(a) An example of a DG. (b) A snapshot of a KG.

Fig. 5 A DG and a KG of a specific insider.

the partial KBAG with nodes (objects) and edges (dependency relationships among nodes). Once the KBAG is constructed, probability values will be assigned to each node. From Fig. 6 we can observe the following facts:

- A KBAG may, in some cases, consist of only one node. This case happens when an attacked object does not have any dependency relationship with any other

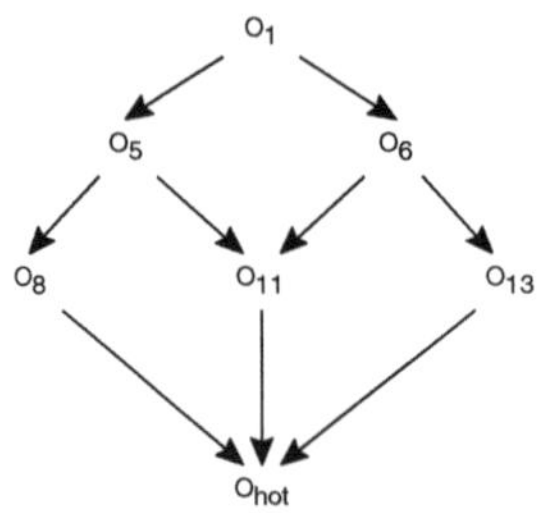

Fig. 6 A partially constructed KBAG.

object in the system. In such a case, the insider can not launch an attack on any other node if he/she relies on dependency relationships exist among objects

- The risk of compromising a set of descendent nodes does not depend on the number of the ongoing edges from the parent node of these descendent nodes. For example, consider O_5, O_8, and O_{11} in Fig. 6. O_5 is the parent node of both O_8 and O_{11}. Consider that the probability of compromising O_5 is high (say 0.75), then, the risk value of compromising O_5 is also high. This high value results in a high risk of compromising all descendent nodes of O_5 (O_8, and O_{11}). The same example can be applied to cases where the probability value of O_5 is low which results in low chances of compromising any of the descendent nodes. So, if the probability of a node is high, then probability of compromising all its descendent nodes is high
- The risk of compromising a descendent node depends on the probability values of compromising all its parent nodes. That is, the risk of compromising a specific node depends on the number of incoming edges to this node. To illustrate, consider O_5, O_6, O_{11}. These objects have the relation $O_{11} = F(O_5, O_6)$. Consider that their probability values are (0.2, 0.3, 0.7), respectively. The risk values can be expressed as (low, low, high), respectively. Then compromising O_{11} is very low. Since compromising O_{11} is low, then compromising O_5 is also low. The fact that compromising O_6 is high does not contribute much in the likelihood of compromising O_{11}. However, it can be deduced that compromising O_{13} is likely to be very high because the probability of compromising O_6 is high and O_{13} is a descendent of O_6 (as explained in the previous case)

From the above cases, one can conclude that what contributes more to the likelihood of compromising a node is the number of incoming edges to the node, not the number of outgoing edges from that node (taking into consideration the probability values of nodes). The following section illustrates the process of assigning these probability values to the corresponding KBAG.

3.1.1 Assigning Probabilities to KBAGs' Nodes

To use Bayesian networks in modeling KBAG, probability values need to be assigned to each node in the KBAG. Our proposed approach uses the fact that an attack which affected node O_{hacked} has been detected. It also aims to make sure that no other nodes in the system have been maliciously modified without being detected. In the proposed approach we follow a similar procedure used by [10] to assign different probability values for all nodes of the corresponding KBAG, where two cases can be classified:

- Base Case: Indicates the probability of only one node and takes the form P(A = yes/no). This shows the probability of an attack of node A. Here, "yes" means that the node has been compromised and "no" indicates that node A is not compromised. An example is: $P(O_1{=}yes) = 0.3$. This probability means that the probability of a successful attack on O_1 equals to 0.3.
- Inductive Case: Indicates the probability of one or more nodes given the knowledge of a fact of one or more other nodes. This probability takes the form: P(A= yes/no / B= yes/no). This indicates a dependency relation among nodes in the KBAGs and is a conditional dependency from the parent node to the child node as indicated in the definition of KBAGs. So, the above probability shows the probability of an attack at node A by a specific insider given that this node has dependency with another node B that may or may not be compromised by the insider. An example is: $P(O_i = no\ /\ O_j = yes) = 0.41$. It means that the probability of node O_i is not compromised considering the dependency of its parent node O_j which has been compromised equals to 0.41.
  Note: the two objects O_i and O_j have the parent/child relationship as indicated earlier in the definition of KBAGs.

Therefore, probability by the inductive case (which draws the probability of a node X_i in the KBAG) is given by: $P(X_i) = P(X_i\ /\ parent(X_i))$

Expert knowledge and past observations are used to assign the initial probability values to nodes in a KBAG. To clarfiy how initial values are assigned for different nodes, let us consider the following example:

(a) A KBAG of four nodes. (b) A segment of KBAG given in Fig. 6.

Fig. 7 Two KBAGs of four nodes

The following probability values are associated with nodes of the KBAG of Fig. 7(a):

P(A) = 0.6, P(B) = 0.4, P(C) = 0.2, P(D) = 0.7, P(B = yes / A = yes) = 0.3, P(C = yes / A = yes, D = no) = 0.4

Below we explain what the above probabilities mean:

- P(A)= 0.6 means that 60% of insiders trying to access node A were able to access it. If 100 insiders try to access this node, then on average 60 of them will be able to access it.
- P(B), P(C), and P(D) have the same meaning.
- P(B = yes / A = yes) = 0.3 means that if given that node A had been compromised, then there is a probability of 0.3 for node B to be also compromised. In other words, according to system previous knowledge and experience if node A had been compromised, there is a probability of 0.3 for node B to be also compromised. That is, system experience indicates that 30% of attackers try to compromise node B after compromising node A.
- P(C = yes / A = yes, D = no) = 0.4 means that if given the fact that node A had been compromised and node D had not been compromised, then there is a probability of 0.4 for node C to be compromised. In other words if an attacker wants to compromise node C then he has a choice of following a path from A going to C or following a path from D going to C. However, according to system experience and knowledge 40% of attackers follow the path from A to C.

Based on the above discussion, the system realizes that the attacker most likely follows the path with the higher probability value. In fact, the above fact will be captured in our method of calculating risk values. That is, in the method of calculating risk values, higher probability values contributes more in the new risk values and hence may give more insight for a node to be compromised by an insider. The above discussion gives a clear idea about the way of calculating new risk values and hence a new evidence for a node to be compromised. This method of calculating risk values has been adapted from [10].

3.2 *Calculating Risk Values for Nodes of KBAGs with an Example Scenario*

Risk value for a specific node A in a KBAG can be achieved by calculating a new probability value of that node given the occurrence of an attack at a descendant node that has dependency with it. To illustrate the process of dynamically updating new probability values for nodes based on the occurrence of an attack that affected other nodes in the KBAG, we consider a segment of the KBAG we gave earlier, illustrated in Fig. 7(b):

The example shows how to compute the inferred probability at node O_5 for observed evidence at node O_{11}. "Observed evidence" means that the object O_{11} had been successfully attacked. In light of previous experience and system knowledge and according to our previous discussion we assume that initial probability values for the nodes of the KBAG are:

$P(O_5 = yes) = 0.4$, $P(O_6 = yes) = 0.1$, $P(O_{11} = yes) = 0.3$, $P(O_8 = yes / O_5 = yes) = 0.3$, $P(O_8 = yes / O_5 = no) = 0.2$, $P(O_{11} = yes / O_6 = yes, O_5 = no) = 0.3$, $P(O_{11} = yes / O_6 = yes, O_5 = yes) = 0.15$

If an evidence of an attack has been detected at O_{11} by insider S_i, then the probability that an attack at O_5 was carried out can be calculated by computing the probability $P(O_5/O_6, O_8, O_{11})$; this is computed as:

$$P(O_5/O_6,O_8,O_{11}) = \frac{P(O_5,O_6,O_8,O_{11}}{\sum P(O_5,O_6,O_8,O_{11})} \tag{1}$$

$$= \frac{P(O_{11} = yes/O_6 = yes, O_5 = yes) * P(O_8 = yes/O_5 = yes) * P(O_5 = yes)}{\sum P(O_{11}/O_6,O_5) * P(O_8/O_5) * P(O_5)} \tag{2}$$

$= 0.4929$

This new probability value of O_5 (represents risk value) is compared with a threshold value. If it is less than the threshold value, it does not indicate a high risk of compromising that node. However, if it is equal to or more than the threshold value, then it indicates a very high risk of an attack at that node which causes an alarm to be raised. Legal actions should be initiated to resolve this situation.

This process of calculating risk values for different nodes in the KBAGs which involves updating probability values is repeated for all nodes. It shows which nodes may be compromised (maliciously modified), and which other nodes do not have any indication of a compromise. The above process of dynamically updating probability values takes care of any risk that may arise from an insider that accesses several documents and tries to access some critical documents. If the risk reaches a sensitive point that is high enough for the insider to compromise a critical object, the above procedure will detect that and raise an alarm. Raising an alarm informs legal parties about the situation. Hence, legal actions should be initiated to resolve the problem. The following table 2 describes different risk values for nodes of the KBAG described in Fig. 7(b), given that O_{11} has been attacked (maliciously modified). Risk values have been calculated using the above procedure. As can be seen from table 2, risk values might increase having the fact that other nodes might have been compromised. From table 2, we conclude that increased knowledge of a malicious insider increases his/her chances of compromising more objects in the underlying system. Hence, a direct relation exists between the knowledge of a malicious insider and the risk of compromising more objects. This can also be captured by Fig. 8(b) which illustrates results of the table in Fig. 8(a). In Fig. 8, risk1 represents risk values of O_6 considering the fact that one, two or three ascendant or sibling nodes of O_6 have been compromised. For example, risk value of O_6 considering that one of the ascendant nodes (O_6 and its parent O_1 results in 2 nodes) equals

Table 2 Calculated risk values of nodes of KBAG given in Fig. 7(b)

Risk	$P(O_5)$	$P(O_5/O_{15})$	$P(O_6/O_{15})$	$P(O_8/O_1)$	$P(O_6/O_1)$	$P(O_5/O_{15},O_6,O_1)$	$P(O_6/O_{15},O_5,O_1)$
Value	0.4	0.55	0.49	0.53	0.48	0.61	0.54

Knowledge	Risk1(for O_6)	Risk2 (for O_5)
1	0.22	0.40
2	0.48	0.53
3	0.54	0.61

(a)Knowledge vs Risk relation

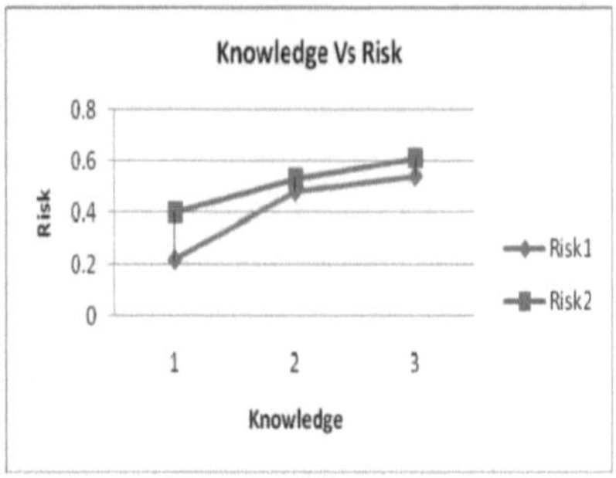

(b) Knowledge vs Risk

Fig. 8 Knowledge VS Risk

0.48. The same can be applied to risk2 to get the same meaning of risk1. Knowledge indicates that the insider gets the knowledge of the corresponding node(s). For example two in the knowledge column of Fig. 8(a) indicates that the insider gets the knowledge of two objects (O_6 and O_1 as an example)

4 Conclusion

In this paper, we introduced a new model of evaluating and analyzing a system after an insider attack. In this work, we introduced a new graph called Knowledge Bayesian Attack Graph (KBAG) that uses Bayesian network concepts as well as knowledge graphs (KGs) and dependency graph (DG) of different objects in the underlying system. KBAG helps in reasoning about attacks on the underlying system because its paths are considered as candidate paths that (according to our assumptions) malicious insiders may follow to achieve their goals of compromising critical objects. It also helps in calculating risk values for each node in the KBAG. The model should calculate and update risk values regularly using Bayesian inference techniques. Regularly updating risk values reflects the likelihood of the possible occurrence of an attack on other nodes by the same insider. Risk values also help in classifying objects into a list of non affected objects and a list of possible affected objects. Consequently, an increased risk of a node in the KBAG indicates a possible compromise of that node by the insider. It is important to mention that this work is suitable only for insider attacks. So, the reader should realize that attempts to use this model to outsider attacks may not be successful. The compromises that are suspected by our model, that may impose a great risk on the system, represent compromises that are not detected by the underlying system. So, our model helps in uncovering these compromises and also helps in understanding the ways that malicious insiders may use to launch their attacks.

Acknowledgements This work has been supported in part by US AFOSR under grant FA 9550-04-1-0429. We are thankful to Dr. Robert. L. Herklotz for his support, which made this work possible. We are also thankful to the anonymous reviewers for their valuable remarks.

References

1. D. Burroughs, L. Wilson and G. Cybenko. Analysis of Distributed Intrusion Detection System Using Bayesian Methods. In Proceedings of the twenty first IEEE International Performance, Computing and Communications Conference, 2002.
2. Q. Althebyan, B. Panda. A Knowledge-Base Model for Insider Threat Prediction. In Proceedings of the 2007 IEEE Workshop on Information Assurance United States Military Academy, West Point, NY 20-22 June 2007.
3. M. Maybury, P. Chase, B. Cheikes, D. Brackne, S. Matzner, T. Hetherington, B. Wood, C. Sibley, J. Marin, T. Longstaff, L. Spitzner, J. Haile, J. Copeland, S. Lewandowski. Analysis and Detection of Malicious Insiders. In Proceedings of the 2005 International Conference on Intelligence Analysis. Sheraton Premiere, McLean, VA. May 2-4.
4. B. Aleman-Meza, P. Burns, M. Eavenson, D. Palaniswami, A. Sheth. An Ontological Approach to the Document Access Problem of Insider Threat. In Proceedings of the IEEE International Conference on Intelligence and Security Informatics, ISI 2005, Atlanta, Georgia, USA, May 19-20, 2005, 486-491.
5. J. Pearl. Probabilistic Reasoning in Intelligent Systems: Networks of Plausible Inference. Morgan Kaufman, San Mateo, CA, 1988.
6. L Larsen, M. Harrold. Slicing Object-Oriented Software. In Proceedings of the 18th International Conference in Software Engineering, March 1996.
7. L.P. Swiler, C. Philips, D. Ellis, S. Chakerian. Computer-Attack Graph Generation Tool. In Proceedings of the IEEE Symposium on Security and Privacy 2001.
8. A.P. Moore, R.J. Ellison, R.C. Linger. Attack Modeling for Information Security and Survivability. Technical Note, CMU/SE1-2001-TN-001, March 2001.
9. O. Sheyner, J. Joshua Haines, S. Jha, R. Lippmann, J.M. Wing. Automated Generation and Analysis of Attack Graphs. In Proceedings of the IEEE Symposium on Security and Privacy, 2002.
10. R. Dantu, P. Kolan. Risk Management Using Based Behavior Bayesian Networks. In Proceedings of IEEE International Conference on Intelligence and Security Informatics, ISI'2005, Lecture Notes in Computer Science (LNCS), pages 115-126, Springer-Verlag, May, 2005.

Acknowledgements This work has been supported in part by US AFOSR under grant FA 9550-04-1-0129. We are thankful to Dr. Robert Herklotz for his support, which made this work possible. We are also thankful to the anonymous reviewers for their valuable comments.

References

[illegible]

Portable User-Centric Identity Management

Gail-Joon Ahn, Moo Nam Ko and Mohamed Shehab

Abstract User-centric identity management has recently received significant attention for handling private and critical identity attributes. The notable idea of user-centric identity management allows users to control their own digital identities. Current user-centric identity management approaches are mainly focused on interoperable architectures between existing identity management systems. Normally, users can access the Internet from various places such as home, office, school or public Internet café. We observe that the importance of portability of the a user's digital identity should be addressed in the user-centric identity management practices. In other words, users should be able to export their digital identities and transfer them to various computers in a secure manner. In this paper, we focus on the portability issue of the Identity Metasystem and describe three possible types of portability-enhanced Identity Metasystem model including our implementation experience.

1 Introduction

The Internet has dramatically changed the way people communicate and do business. Businesses heavily depend on the Internet to draw in commerce and make information available on demand. Managing bank accounts, paying bills and purchasing goods via Internet are commonly exercised. The diverse Internet services

Gail-Joon Ahn
Arizona State University, Ira A. Fulton School of Engineering, Department of Computer Science and Engineering, 699 S. Mill Avenue, Tempe, AZ 85281, e-mail: gahn@asu.edu

Moo Nam Ko
The University of North Carolina at Charlotte, 9201 University City Blvd., Charlotte, NC 28223, e-mail: mnko@uncc.edu

Mohamed Shehab
The University of North Carolina at Charlotte, 9201 University City Blvd., Charlotte, NC 28223, e-mail: mshehab@uncc.edu

Please use the following format when citing this chapter:

Ahn, G.-J., Ko, M.N. and Shehab, M., 2008, in IFIP International Federation for Information Processing, Volume 278; *Proceedings of the IFIP TC 11 23rd International Information Security Conference*; Sushil Jajodia, Pierangela Samarati, Stelvio Cimato; (Boston: Springer), pp. 573–587.

and the tremendous amounts of personal data collected over the Internet have raised various problems such as identity theft, fraud, and privacy breaches [22]. Numerous identity management systems have been introduced to solve the identity management problems of business domains [1]. Different identity management systems have their strengths and weaknesses and have been deployed in different contexts. Most identity management systems were designed mainly from the business's perspective. Users were not considered carefully in the design stage which led to serious identity related problems. In addition, most identity management systems have focused on identity management issues in an isolated domain and federation issues between identity management systems in the circle of trust.

The digital identity industry recognizes that identity management systems are designed without the consideration of user experience and the non-interoperability between current identity management systems which restricts the growth of e-commerce activities. As a result, user-centric identity management has recently received significant attention for handling private and critical identity attributes. The main objective of user-centric identity management is to put the users in control of their identity information. Users are allowed to select their credentials that are used to respond to an authentication or attribute requester. Through the user-centric identity management, the users have more rights and responsibilities for their identity information than before. In this paper, we articulate the portability issues of the user-centric identity management system, attempting to enhance an existing Identity Metasystem. The paper is organized as follows. Section 2 overviews the digital identity management and discusses the related technologies. Section 3 describes our portability enhanced Identity Metasystem approaches. Section 4 describes implementation details followed by the related works in Section 5. Section 6 includes the concluding remarks.

2 Digital Identity Management

In this section, we first start with the discussion of digital identity and digital identity management. We then discuss the user-centric identity management approach, portability issues and the related technologies.

2.1 Digital Identity

There are various definitions of digital identity. Depending on organizations, systems and contexts, the diverse definitions of digital identity have been created and used. From our perspective, we define a user's digital identity as the global set of attributes that make up an online representation of who and what an entity is. It can

[1] Such identity management systems include IBM Tivoli [11], Liberty Alliance [18], LID [19], OpenID [24], Sxip [31], Microsoft CardSpace [40] and Live ID [41]

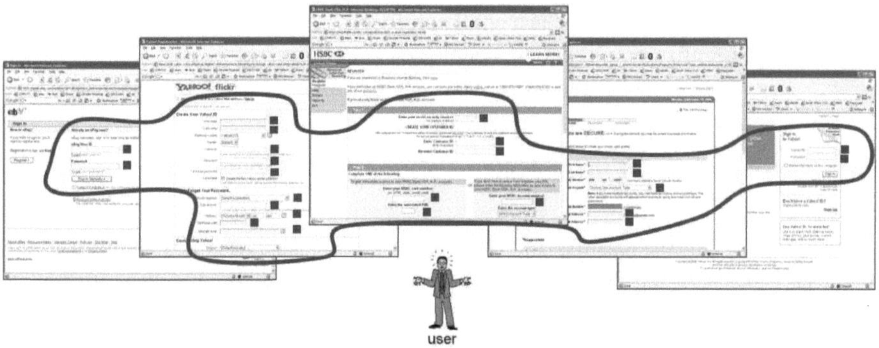

Fig. 1 Digital Identity: Global Set of Attributes of a User

include access credentials, personal attributes and personal references. Over the Internet, a user has numerous access credentials that are issued from different sites and different or duplicated personal attributes and references on each site. We believe all of these attributes should be considered as the user's digital identity as shown in Figure 1. In each site, a user can be represented by subsets of these attributes. Depending on the situation and the context, different subsets of attributes are used to represent the same user in the Internet. For example, in an auction site, a subset of a user's attributes such as username, password, shopping history, and reputation record represent the user's identity in this site, while a subset of the user's attributes such as a student ID number, class record, and GPA may represent the user's identity in an university site.

2.2 Digital Identity Management

Digital identity management consists of several tasks such as maintaining user attributes and using subsets of attributes to enable secure online interactions between users or between users and systems. Digital identity management enables the addition, utilization, and deletion of identity attributes. In [2], the identity management systems are categorized into three models: isolated, centralized, and distributed identity management. In the isolated identity management model, each site has its own identity management domain and its own way of maintaining the identities of users including employees, customers, and partners. The centralized identity management model has a single identity provider that brokers trust to other participating members or service providers in a circle of trust. The distributed identity management model provides a frictionless identity management solution by forming a federation and making authentication a distributed task. Every member agrees to trust user identities vouched for by other members of the federation. These identity management models were mostly focused on the domain centric approach. Our analysis and observation indicate that most identity management systems neglect user-friendliness and usability issues. Therefore, it leads users to be the weakest link in digital identity management systems.

2.3 User-Centric Identity Management and Portability

Under domain centric identity management systems, a user's information is collected and managed by service providers so it is difficult for the user to manage their identity information located at service providers and to monitor the usage of the user's private information. Putting the owner of the identity information into the transaction gives the user-centric identity management approach the ability to solve identity related problems. To achieve the goal, several requirements from the user's perspective need to be accommodated in the design of user-centric identity management systems. As the users have more rights on their own identity information, they can decide what information they want to share, how much information to be disclosed with other trusted service providers, and under what circumstances. Thereby better protection of the user's private information is enabled by user.

Domain centric identity management systems focus on the user authentication to protect their properties from malicious users. However, the authentication of service providers is equally important for a user to figure out the trustworthiness of the service providers. Current browsers provide the padlock icon to give notice to the users for the SSL communication between the users and service providers but it is not enough for the users to figure out the trustworthiness of the service providers [44]. By providing the identity information of service providers clearly to the users in web-based interactions enables the users to distinguish trusted service providers from malicious service providers. The users can then decide to disclose their information to only trusted service providers. Hence, the users can protect their information from phishing attacks and possible frauds.

In the current Internet environments, a user has to create a separate account for each web site the user wishes to access. The user also has to maintain multiple separate accounts, which would be a tedious job. In addition, the users often choose insecure passwords, rarely change their passwords, and use the same password across different accounts [1]. These trends make the password-based authentication systems insecure. New strong authentication methods are required to overcome the security problems of the password-based authentication method. The new methods should be easy for the users to manage their digital identities. Existing identity management systems provide different user experiences and interfaces that could lead the users to improperly interact with different entities in Internet environments. Under the user-centric identity management systems, the users manage their identity information directly through a proper interface which provides a consistent experience to control their identity information legitimately.

People carry identity cards such as a driver license card, a student ID card, and an employee ID card in their wallet and they use each identity card in its appropriate context. Similar to the identity cards in the real world, the digital identity should be carried by the users and it should be used without the limitation of locations and devices. Actually, people access the Internet from different sites such as home, office, school, public Internet café, and so on. Therefore, the digital identity should be both interoperable and portable.

2.4 Related Technologies

The Identity Metasystem is an interoperable architecture for digital identity management [6]. It is defined based on the "Laws of Identity" which are intended to codify a set of fundamental principles to which any universally adopted, sustainable identity architecture must conform [5]. The Identity Metasystem provides interoperability between existing and future identity systems using Web Services (WS-*) protocols which is a set of specifications built on the web service platform. Specifically, WS-Trust [38], an encapsulation protocol, is used for the claim transformation. WS-MetadataExchange [35] and WS-SecurityPolicy [37] are used to conduct the format and claim negotiations between participants. Finally, WS-Security [36] is used to secure transmitted messages. The Identity Metasystem can transform the claims of one type into the claims of another type and WS-* protocols negotiate the acceptable claim type between two parties to provide interoperability between them. The Identity Metasystem also provides a consistent and straightforward user interface to all the users. There are three roles within the identity metasystem: *Identity Providers* who issue digital identities, *Relying Parties* who require identities, and *Subjects* who are individuals and other entities about whom claims are made. To build an identity metasystem, the system is required to follow five key components [22]:

1. A way to represent identities using claims.
2. A means for identity providers, relying parties, and subjects to negotiate.
3. An encapsulating protocols to obtain claims and requirements.
4. A means to bridge technology and organizational boundaries using claims transformation.
5. A consistent user experience across multiple contexts, technologies, and operators.

CardSpace [40], is an implementation of the Identity Metasystem, provides the consistent user experience required by the Identity Metasystem. When a user needs to authenticate to a relying party, CardSpace interprets the security policy of the relying party and displays an Identity Selector containing a set of information cards which satisfy the requested claims in the relying party's security policy. Once the user selects a card, CardSpace contacts the relevant identity provider and requests a security token. The identity provider generates a signed and encrypted security token which includes the required information and returns it to the Identity Selector. The user then decides whether to release this information to the relying party. If the user approves then the token is sent to the relying party where the token is processed and the user is authenticated.

Java Card is a Smart Card running a small Java based operating system. It is useful in the areas of personal security and can be used to add authentication and secure access to information systems that require a high level of security. The user can carry around valuable and sensitive personal information such as medical history, credit card numbers and private key in the Java card. The Java Card technology enables Smart Cards and other devices with very limited memory to run small applications (applets) and provides Smart Card manufactures with a secure and interoperable execution platform that can store and update multiple applications on a single device [14]. Java-powered iButton is based on Java Card technology and provides the processing features which include a high-speed 1024 bit RSA encryption, Non-Volatile RAM(NVRAM) capacity, and unalterable realtime clock [8]. It utilizes NVRAM for program and data storage. Unlike electrically erasable programmable read-only memory, the NVRAM iButton memory can be erased and rewritten as often as necessary without wearing out. Therefore multiple applets can co-exist in NVRAM and control the sensitive data in a secure way. It can be attached to accessories such as a key fob, watch, and finger ring so the users can easiliy carry the iButton. We adopt this technology to demonstrate the feasibility of our approach.

3 PORTABILITY IN IDENTITY METASYSTEM

In this section we discuss the principles behind the Identity Metasystem and seek methods to extend the Identity Metasystem for addressing portability aspects. We focus on the information card and security token service modules in the Identity Metasystem.

3.1 Information Card

The users of Identity Metasystem can manage their digital identities using visual information cards in the Identity Selector. The information card draws a line between the self-issued card and the managed card. Both types of information cards do not contain personally identifiable information (PII). The information card generally contains the card name, card image, a list of claims, and issuer information. However, there are differences between the two types of information cards. In case of the self-issued card, after the user provides the general user's information such as last name, first name, and e-mail address, the Identity Selector grants the user a self-issued card. The self-issued card is stored in the local machine. Although the self-issued card includes general PII, it is not supposed to include the sensitive user information such as social security number, bank account and credit card number. On the other hand, the managed cards are obtained from identity providers such as employers, financial institutions, or the government. Like the self-issued information card, the managed card can be stored in local machines but the PII associated

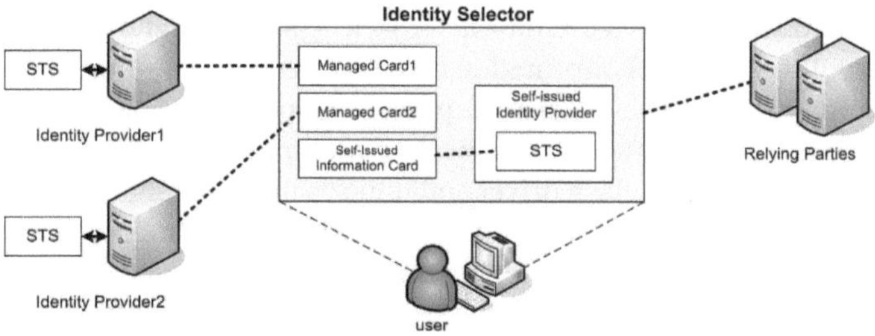

Fig. 2 STSs and Information Cards in Identity Metasystem

with the card is not stored in the local machine. The PII is stored and managed by each identity provider. The managed card enables the identity providers to issue their own set of claims. For example, credit card companies can design a set of claims such as card name, card number and expiration date in their managed card and the DMV can design a set of claims such as driver license number, license class and expiration date in their managed card.

3.2 Security Token Service

When the digital identities are transmitted on the network, every digital identity is presented by some sort of security tokens such as X.509 certificate [42], Kerberos ticket [16], and SAML assertion [28]. The Identity Metasystem generates a security token by contacting the Security Token Service (STS) in the identity provider. When the Identity Selector sends a "RequestSecurityToken" message to the identity provider, the STS in identity provider responds back with a "RequestSecurityToken-Response" message that contains a new security token. The current implementation of Identity Metasystem has two STSs as illustrated in Figure 2. The STS located at the third party identity provider generates security tokens for the managed cards, whereas the STS in Identity Selector at the user's local machine generates the security tokens for the self-issued cards.

3.3 Portability of Information Cards and STS

The CardSpace stores the information cards in a local machine and provides basic import and export functions for information cards. Using these functions, the users can export their information cards to portable storage devices such as portable USB flash drive, mobile phone, and PDAs and import the information cards into other machines. When the information cards are exported, the information cards are encrypted using a key derived from a user-selected pass-phrase [7]. Hence, if a user loses a portable storage device with the exported information cards, other people cannot decrypt the exported information cards unless they know the pass-phrase of the information cards. However, these export and import functions are not sufficient to support the various practical scenarios. For example, a user carries the exported information cards in a USB flash driver and imports the information cards in a kiosk machine from the USB flash driver. After using the information cards in the kiosk machine, if the user forgets to delete the imported information cards, then the next user of the kiosk machine can access the previous users' information cards without any restrictions. The bottom line is to enable the users to carry the information cards in a secure manner, considering the portability of STS as well. To achieve such an intrinsic goal, we categorize the portability enhanced Identity Metasystem into three models based on the location of the information cards and STS as follows:

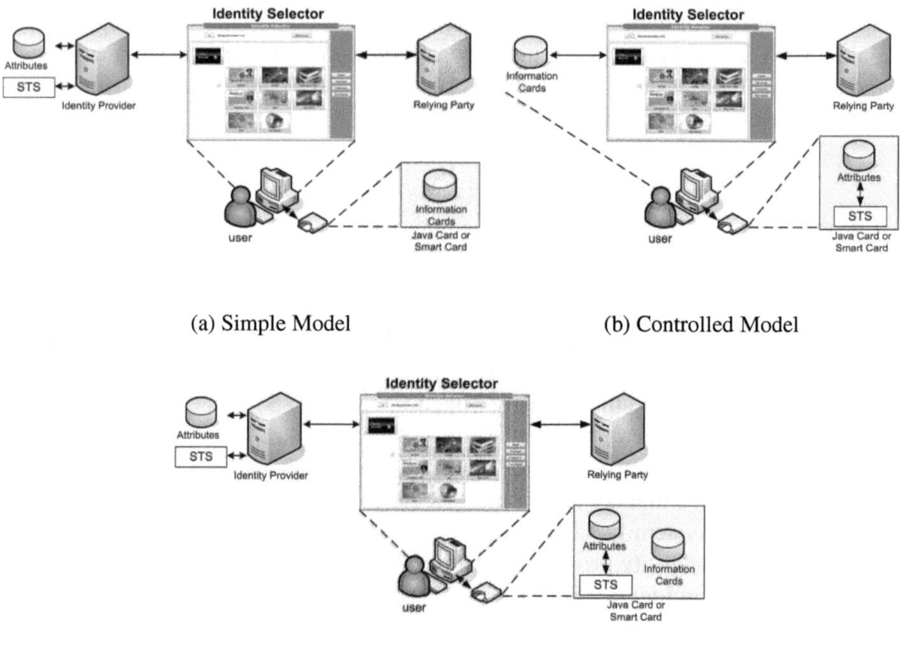

(a) Simple Model (b) Controlled Model

(c) Integrated Model

Fig. 3 Portability-enhanced User-centric Identity Management

- ***Simple Model:*** This model is similar to the general architecture of the Identity Metasystem. Figure 3(a) shows the simple portability enhanced Identity Metasystem model. The STS is located in the identity provider and the users carry their information cards using portable secure devices such as Java Card or Smart Card. By storing the information cards in portable secure devices, only a user who knows the PIN number of the secure device can access the information cards and is able to export their information cards to multiple machines. When the user removes the secure device from a machine, the imported information cards should be removed from the machine automatically. This model can be applied between different machines to synchronize the information cards.

- ***Controlled Model:*** This model shifts the role of identity provider to the portable secure device. The user's attributes and STS are located in a portable secure device and the information cards are located in a local machine. The user carries the STS and attributes in portable secure devices so the Identity Selector does not have to contact the identity provider to get a secure token. The Identity Selector directly contacts the STS in the portable secure device and gets the security token. The Figure 3(b) shows the controlled portability enhanced Identity Metasystem model. This model can be applied to the one-time credit number system [4, 39], where A credit card company issues a portable secure device with STS to the customers. The customers can treat the portable secure device with STS as a portable identity provider. When a customer does an online purchase, the Identity Selector gets a secure token from the STS in the portable secure device directly. The issued secure token includes the one-time credit card number so the user can protect the real credit card number. The drawback of this model is that information cards are still in a local machine and a high expense is expected to distribute the portable STS devices
- ***Integrated Model:*** This model is a combination of the Simple and Controlled models. The users carry the information cards, STS and attributes in a portable secure device, this enables them to directly manage their identity. When a user plugs a portable secure device into a machine and provides the PIN number, the identity selector imports and shows the information cards in a portable secure device to the user. After the user selects a managed information card which requests a token from the STS in the portable secure device, the Identity Selector directly gets the request token from the STS in the portable secure device. This model combines the advantages of previous models so the user can carry their information cards, portable STS and attributes in a secure device according to the user's purpose. This model gives the user more flexibility and extensibility to manage his/her digital identities. Figure 3(c) shows the integrated portability enhanced Identity Metasystem model.

4 Implementation Details

Based on our analysis of the Identity Metasystem and articulation of potability-enhanced models, we developed a prototype of the Identity Selector, which is a Java-based implementation of Identity Metasystem. Furthermore, we enhanced the Identity Selector to support our portability enhanced Identity Metasystem models. In this section we give an overview of our implementation experience and outcomes.

4.1 Identity Selector

Identity Selector is an important component in Identity Metasystem. Using the visual information card, the users can select their identity cards with the same experience as the one in their real life. Figure 4 illustrates our Java-based prototype of CardSpace-compatible Identity Selector. Each information card contains a subset of the available user attributes that are used to represent the user's identities in different contexts. Each card mainly includes meta information required to acquire the real attributes from the identity provider. The meta information includes the necessary user attribute fields, identity provider contact information, and token related information.

Our Identity Selector consists of seven components: Information Card Manager, Graphical User Interface, Card Store, iButton/Smartcard Agent, Web Service Client, Local STS/Token Issuer, and libraries as shown in Figure 4 (b). The Information Card Manager handles all events generated by users and systems, and performs the appropriate action. It also provides the card creation, editing, and deleting functions for the self-issued information card. The Graphical User Interface component manages the user interface of Identity Selector. It consists of a set of screens such as the creation of new card, the examination of cards and the selection of a card. The Card Store contains information cards, which are usually stored in XML format. The Web-Service Client supports the communication between identity provider and Identity Selector. The iButton/Smartcard agent manages the communication between the Identity Selector and the Java-powered iButton. It sends the PIN number and token request message to iButton and receives the issued token from iButton. The iButton/Smartcard agent and the Java-powered iButton exchange messages using the APDU (Application Protocol Data Unit). The Java-powered iButton includes the Java Applet which provides STS module, user attribute storage, and information card storage. The Java Applet is designed based on our integrated model. The Local STS/Token Issuer generates CardSpace compatible security token for self-issued information card and also transforms the token issued from iButton to the CardSapce compatible security token. Using openSAML 1.1 [25], Bouncy Castle API [32] and our libraries, the local STS/Token Issuer encrypts and signs the XML token. The libraries include the required standard and customized modules that are necessary for supporting the functionalities of Identity Selector.

4.2 Portable Security Token Service

To generate a CardSpace-compatible security token in portable secure devices, the Portable Security Token Service (PSTS) needs to support strong cryptographic algorithms. Moreover, portable secure devices should be able to generate SAML asser-

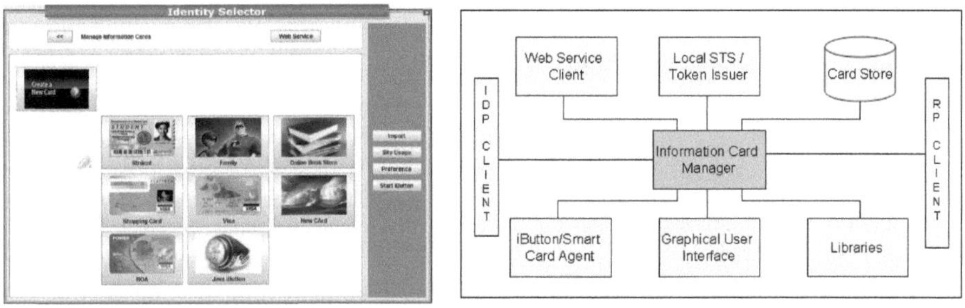

(a) Interface (b) Components

Fig. 4 Java version of Identity Selector

tions. We identify three approaches to address how CardSpace-compatible security tokens can be generated by Java Card technology [2].

- *Basic Mode*: The PSTS in Java Card generates its own token and the local STS in Identity Selector transforms the issued token into a CardSpace compatible security token. The local STS signs and encrypts the token for the relying party. This PSTS approach is only available for self-issued cards.
- *Non-auditing Mode*: The PSTS in Java Card generates a SAML assertion and then the local STS in Identity Selector encrypts it for the relying party. This is a "non-auditing" mode of Identity Metasystem [4], as the identity provider has no knowledge of the relying party to protect the user's privacy for Internet activities. In other words, when Identity Selector receives a singed token from Identity provider, PSTS can generates the SAML assertion by using a predefined XML SAML assertion document and dynamically generated assertion data such as digested value, signature values, and RSA public key value. Identity Selector then encrypts the SAML assertion for the relying party. This approach can be applied to both self-issued information cards and managed information cards.
- *Auditing Mode*: The PSTS in Java Card directly generates CardSpace compatible security token for the relying party under the assumption that Java Card supports the WS-Trust standard with strong cryptographic algorithms. When the PSTS generates the security token, the PSTS knows the identity of relying party and generates the security token for relying party directly. This is in "auditing" mode of Identity Metasystem [4]. When PSTS receives "RequestSecurityToken" message from Identity Selector, the PSTS generates a security token for the relying party and sends it to Identity Selector using "RequestSecurityTokenResponse" message. This approach is similar to current .NET Smart Card approach and it is

[2] .Net Smart Cards such as Gemalto Cryptoflex NET [9] and MXI security Stealth MXP [30] can also provide cryptographic functions necessary to implement the PSTS.

can be easily implemented when Java Card supports the WS-Trust standard with strong cryptographic algorithms.

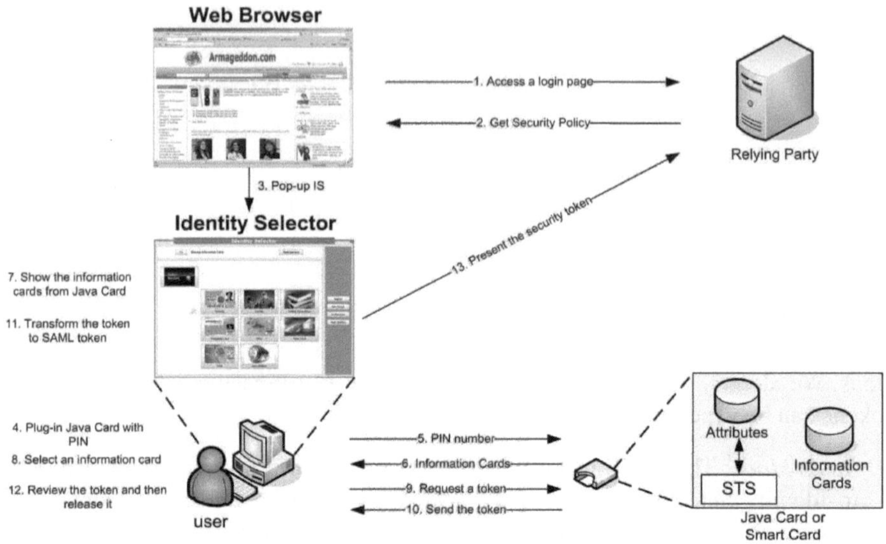

Fig. 5 System Flows and Corresponding Messages

Our prototype of the PSTS applet and iButton/ SmartCard agent is based on the *Basic Mode*. Using a predefined protocol, iButton/ SmartCard agent requests a token for self-issued card to PSTS applet. The PSTS applet is a PIN protected applet and provides card storage, user attribute storage, and token generation service.

Figure 5 depicts the system flow diagram and corresponding messages in our portability-enhanced user-centric identity management model. The process begins when a user accesses a login page at a relying party's web site. The site sends a login form to the browser. The login form contains a specific OBJECT tag which includes the site's security policy and invokes the Identity Selector, which displays the information cards that satisfy the relying party's security policy. On the other hand, when the user accesses a kiosk machine, the Identity Selector does not contain any cards because the kiosk machine should not store the user's information cards. In that case, the user needs to select the iButton mode and insert a Java-Powered iButton into the kiosk machine. The iButton agent in Identity Selector immediately recognizes the iButton and asks for the PIN to reads the information cards from iButton. Next, the user selects an information card and the Identity Selector sends the token requests to iButton. The Identity Selector transforms the token issued by iButton into a CardSpace compatible security token using the local STS module and displays the attribute information. If the user consents to release the security token, the Identity Selector presents the security token to the relying party. Finally, the relying party verifies the security token as part of the authentication process. With this scenario, we believe our prototype enable users to carry their digital identities using portable secure devices.

5 Related Works and Discussion

There are several open source projects for user-centric identity management systems or related technologies. To address the interoperability issue among those identity management systems, the Open-Source Identity Systems (OSIS) working group was formed [33]. The OSIS fosters several identity-related open-source projects such as Bandit [3], Heraldry [12], Higgins [10], OpenSSO [26], OpenXRI [27], Shibboleth [29], and xmldap [43] and harmonizes the construction of an interoperable identity layer for the Internet.

In [23], the authors pointed out the portability problem of client side storage of user profile information. Once the user stores their information in a local machine, it assures that the user has as much control over their information as possible. However, the personal information stored on a local machine is not portable. The authors briefly suggested smart card or other portable devices to solve the portable problem in client side storage of user information. Another approach is to use IDRepository [17], IDRepository approach is to separate user profile information from the services, and store the identity in a central place where it can be maintained and accessed by appropriate entities. In [15], the authors allowed users to store identifiers and credentials from different service providers in a personal authentication device (PAD). The functionality of a PAD could be integrated into other approach.

In our work, the secure channel between smart card and smart card application and the trust of client machine might be issues in using portable secure device on various machines. Our approach assumes both secure channel and trustworthiness are intact. If the communication channel between smart card and smart card application is not secure, the communication can be monitored by malicious software on client machine. Markantonakis et al. [20] proposed a secure channel protocol between smart card and smart card application using the Diffie-Hellman protocol [34]. Using their approach we can further establish a secure channel between Identity Selector and Java Card as needed. In case of CardSpace, it runs on Secure Desktop in .NET Framework 3.0 [21] for preventing any distrusted activities in a client machine. To support this security feature, we would require trust computing technologies that can be either software or hardware-based solutions. These issues are currently being explored as ongoing research tasks.

6 Conclusion and future work

In this paper, we have articulated three types of portable Identity Metasystem models and explored the applicable environments of each model. To demonstrate our models, we have developed our own prototype of a CardSpace-compatible Identity Selector using the Java language and extended the portability using Java Card technologies. We also proposed three possible approaches to generate CardSpace compatible security tokens using the Java Card. We believe our implementation demonstrated the feasibility of proposed portable user-centric identity management models that effectively enable the users to carry information cards and user attributes in a secure manner.

Our future work would include possible enhancements of our Identity Metasystem to support Web 2.0. Mashups and Social network service environments.In these environments users can share their information attributes with other users more frequently and easily through creative and innovative Web 2.0 based applications. Also, our work would include the development of metrics to characterize and measure user-centricity in the digital identity management that eventually leads us to have the common understanding of principles and practices. In addition, we strongly believe that private and critical identity attributes exchanged in our portable user-centric identity management models should be also protected based on the users' preferences. Such privacy-preservation techniques will be studied as part of our future works.

References

1. Adams, A. and Sasse, M. A. 1999. Users are not the enemy. Commun. ACM 42, 12 (Dec. 1999), 40-46. DOI= http://doi.acm.org/10.1145/322796.322806
2. Ahn, G. and Lam, J. 2005. Managing privacy preferences for federated identity management. In Proceedings of the 2005 Workshop on Digital Identity Management (Fairfax, VA, USA, November 11 - 11, 2005). DIM '05. ACM, New York, NY, 28-36. DOI= http://doi.acm.org/10.1145/1102486.1102492
3. Bandit-project.org Home. Available at http://www.bandit-project.org/
4. Cameron, K.: Kim Cameron's Identity Weblog. Available at http://www.identityblog.com/
5. Cameron, K.: The Laws of Identity. Microsoft Corporation, White Paper, May 2005
6. Cameron, K. and Jones, M.: Design Rationale behind the Identity Metasystem Architecture. Microsoft Corporation, White Paper, May 2005
7. Chappell, D.: Introducing InfoCard. Microsoft Corporation, Draft version for MIX, March 2006
8. Curry, S.:An introduction to the Java Ring, Java Wrold, April 1998
9. Gemalto Cryotoflex.NET. Available at http://www.cardsolutions.se/Cryptoflex.NET.pdf
10. Higgins Trust Framework Project Home. Available at http://www.eclipse.org/higgins/
11. Identity Management solutions from IBM Tivoli software. Available at http://www-306.ibm.com/software/tivoli/solutions/identity-mgmt/
12. Incubation Status for Heraldry. Available at http://incubator.apache.org/projects/heraldry.html
13. Java Card Technology. Available at http://java.sun.com/products/javacard/index.jsp
14. Java Card Technology Overview. Available at http://java.sun.com/products/javacard/overview.html
15. Jsang, A. and Pope, S.: User Centric Identity Management. Proceedings of AusCERT, Gold Coast, May 2005
16. Kerberos Token Profile 1.1. Available at http://www.oasis-open.org/committees/download.php/16788/wss-v1.1-spec-os-KerberosTokenProfile.pdf
17. Koch, M.:Global Identity Management to Boost Personalization, 9th reserch sysmp. on Emerging Electronic Markets, 137-148, 2002

18. Liberty Alliance Project. Available at http://www.projectliberty.org/
19. LID Wiki. Available at http://lid.netmesh.org
20. Markantonakis, K. and Mayes, K.: A Secure Channel Protocol for Multi-Application Smart Card Based on Public Key Cryptography, IFIP CMS, 2004
21. Microsoft .NET Framework 3.0 Community (NetFx3). Available at http://www.netfx3.com/
22. Microsofts Vision for an Identity Metasystem. Microsoft Corporation, White Paper, May 2005
23. Mulligan, D. and Schwartz, A. 2000. Your place or mine?: privacy concerns and solutions for server and client-side storage of personal information. In Proceedings of the Tenth Conference on Computers, Freedom and Privacy: Challenging the Assumptions (Toronto, Ontario, Canada, April 04 - 07, 2000). CFP '00. ACM, New York, NY, 81-84. DOI= http://doi.acm.org/10.1145/332186.332255
24. OpenID: an actually distributed identity. Available at http://openid.net/
25. OpenSAML - an Open Source Security Assertion Language toolkit. Available at http://www.opensaml.org/
26. OpenSSO Home, Available at https://opensso.dev.java.net/
27. OpenXRI.org Home. Available at http://openxri.org/
28. SAML Token Profile 1.1. Available at http://www.oasis-open.org/committees/download.php/16768/wss-v1.1-spec-os-SAMLTokenProfile.pdf
29. Shibboleth Project- Internet2 Middleware. Available at http://shibboleth.internet2.edu/
30. Stealth MXP. Available at http://www.mxisecurity.com/docs/mxi_stealth_mxp.pdf
31. Sxip identity. Available at http://www.sxip.com/
32. The Legion of the Bouncy Castle. Available at http://www.bouncycastle.org/
33. OSIS: Open Source Identity Systems. Available at http://osis.idcommons.net/
34. Ueli M. Maurer, Stefan Wolf: The Diffie-Hellman Protocol. Des. Codes Cryptography 19(2/3): 147-171 (2000)
35. Web Services Metadata Exchange(WS-MetadataExchange). Available at http://specs.xmlsoap.org/ws/2004/09/mex/W S-MetadataExchange.pdf
36. Web Services Security: SOAP Message Security 1.0 (WS-Security 2004). Available at http://docs.oasis-open.org/wss/2004/01/oasis-200401-wss-soap-message-security-1.0.pdf
37. Web Services Security Policy Language(WS-SecurityPolicy). Available at http://specs.xmlsoap.org/ws/2005/07/securitypolicy/ws-securitypolicy.pdf
38. Web Services Trust Language (WS-Trust). Available at http://specs.xmlsoap.org/ws/2005/02/trust/WS-Trust.pdf
39. What is ShopSafe. Available at http://www.bankofamerica.com/creditcards/index.cfm?template=faq
40. Windows CardSpace. Available at http://cardspace.netfx3.com/
41. Windows Live ID. Available at https://accountservices.passport.net/ppnetworkhome.srf?lc=1033
42. X.509 Token Profile 1.1. Available at http://www.oasis-open.org/committees/download.php/16785/wss-v1.1-spec-os-x509TokenProfile.pdf
43. xmldap.org - cardspace/infocard resources. Available at http://xmldap.org/
44. Ye, Z. and Smith, S. 2002. Trusted Paths for Browsers. In Proceedings of the 11th USENIX Security Symposium (August 05 - 09, 2002). D. Boneh, Ed. USENIX Security Symposium. USENIX Association, Berkeley, CA, 263-279

Ubiquitous Privacy-Preserving Identity Managment

Kristof Verslype and Bart De Decker

Abstract The increasing use of digital credentials undermines the owner's privacy. Anonymous credentials offer a powerful means to improve this. However, more is needed w.r.t. usability. A user will indeed have to manage dozens of credentials in the future: sporting club credentials, a digital driving license, e-tickets, etc. The owner will want to use these anytime at any place. The credentials must remain manageable as well and, in case of theft or loss, they must become unusable by others and recoverable by the legitimate owner. A possible solution based on smart card or SIM tokens is presented, in which user privacy is maximized. An evaluation reveals both strengths and future challenges.

1 Introduction

A credential is a piece of information attesting to the integrity of certain stated facts: properties about or rights of its owner. Examples are a driving license, money, an identity card and a ticket.

Traditional digital credentials (e.g. X.509 certificates) pose a threat to the privacy of the owner since they generally contain a unique identifier together with other personal data. This data is registered in databases, potentially with other data (shopping behaviour, medical records, etc.). These data are not only interesting to the entity to which the user shows the credential, but also to insurance companies, to marketeers, etc. Databases containing personal data are thus very valuable and a point of attraction for (internal or external) attackers. They can also get lost, and possibly fall in the wrong hands, as we saw recently in the UK.

Moreover, a user will have to manage dozens of credentials in the future: a sporting club credential, a digital driving license, digital prescriptions, cinema e-tickets, etc. The problem of loss of privacy and identity theft will thus aggravate if we do

---

Department of Computer Science, K.U.Leuven, Celestijnenlaan 200A, B-3001 Leuven, Belgium
e-mail: firstname.lastname@cs.kuleuven.be

Please use the following format when citing this chapter:

Verslype, K. and De Decker, B., 2008, in IFIP International Federation for Information Processing, Volume 278; *Proceedings of the IFIP TC 11 23rd International Information Security Conference*; Sushil Jajodia, Pierangela Samarati, Stelvio Cimato; (Boston: Springer), pp. 589–603.

not offer the proper techniques to the users in a practical way. At the same time, the user needs access to these credentials anywhere at any place. E.g., it is not acceptable that the user has a smart card for each credential or that the credentials can only be used on a single computer. The credentials must thus remain easily manageable. In case of theft or loss, credentials must be useless for others and recoverable by the legitimate owner.

Privacy enhancing credentials are being developed and implemented. These allow the user to select what data will be released. However, more is needed. This paper examines how a user can manage and use credentials such that the above requirements hold. Therefore, a portable user-unique token (e.g. a smart card) is introduced, as well as an online server where credentials can be stored in a privacy-preserving way, while preventing loss and exposure of credentials and related credential data. This paper is the result of an exercise in which we tried to maximize the privacy of the user, while still taking into account the other requirements. The exercise revealed future problems and challenges that must be tackled in order to have a deployable system.

Section 2 touches cryptographic and technology related aspects. Section 3 discusses the storage and management of credentials. Section 4 presents the roles and high level interactions. Section 5 presents the requirements. The protocols are described in section 6, and evaluated in section 7. Section 8 refers to related work. Section 9 concludes and discusses future work.

2 Technologies

This section briefly touches aspects about modular exponentiations, zero-knowledge proofs and key lengths and discusses anonymous credentials.

2.1 Some Cryptographic Aspects

A **modular exponentiation** (modex) has the form $h \leftarrow g^a \bmod n$. Finding a out of h, g and n is infeasible for sufficiently large numbers (DL assumption).

A **zero-knowledge proof** proves some knowledge of the prover to a verifier, without revealing any other information. The notation in [9] will be used in this paper: $PK\{\alpha : y = g^\alpha \bmod n\}$ denotes a *"zero-knowledge proof of knowledge of an integer* α *such that* $y = g^\alpha \bmod n$ *with* y, g *and* n *publicly known"*. A message can be added to the proof: $PK\{\alpha : y = g^\alpha \bmod n\}(message)$. The proof can only be correctly verified if the message is not modified.

As technology is evolving, 1024 bits **modulus length** will soon be insufficient; 2048 bits, both for DL and RSA, will suffice till 2022 and symmetric keys need to have a length of at least 109 bits to be secure till 2050 [12].

2.2 Anonymous Credentials

Anonymous credentials were introduced by Chaum [10]. Idemix [8] and U-Prove [7] are two credential systems that are being developed. They allow for anonymous yet accountable transactions between users and organizations and allow to show properties of some credential attributes while hiding the others. E.g. using an anonymous credential containing one's name, date of birth and address, one can prove that he is older than 18, without revealing anything else. Credentials can have features such as an expiry date, the number of times it can be shown and the possibility to be revoked. A mix network ([15], [11]) is required for network layer anonymity. The two most important (simplified) anonymous credential protocols are $getCred()$ and $showCred()$.

- In $cred \leftarrow getCred(attributes, features)$ an *issuer* issues a new credential *cred* to the *receiver*. The credential attributes and features are given as input.
- In $trans \leftarrow showCred(cred, props, [msg])$, the *prover* shows properties *props* of credential *cred* to the *verifier* resulting for the verifier in a transcript that can serve as proof in case of disputes. By giving message *msg* as (optional) input, the prover additionally signs *msg* anonymously: the verifier knows that the signer fulfills the revealed properties.

A U-Prove modification was proposed [7] to enforce the collaboration of a smart card or SIM token, containing a credential secret, during a credential show by a device. A similar Idemix modification exists. The notation becomes:

- $(secret; cred) \leftarrow getCred(attributes, features)$. The credential issue results in a credential on the device and a secret on the token.
- $trans \leftarrow showCred(secret; cred, props, [msg])$. The credential is shown by the user's computer, with the help of the token, which needs to know the corresponding secret. The secret never leaves the token in cleartext.

Anonymous credential systems heavily rely on complex zero-knowledge proofs an thus on modular exponentiations. Both $getCred()$ and $showCred()$ require only a single modex on the token if the token is involved.

3 Credential Manager and Credential Repository

We distinguish between the Credential Repository and the Credential Manager. The former stores the user's credential data such as credentials, but also transcripts, while the latter enables usage and management of this data.

The **Credential Repository** can be situated locally at the user's side, on a remote server or even a hybrid combination is possible. A purely local credential store, on a device such as a USB-stick, smart card, PDA or mobile phone, can have dramatic consequences in case of loss, theft or damage of the device. If a server-based solution is applied, tampering, deletion, reading or use of credential data and linkage of credential data to the owner by the server must be prevented. Also, an Internet connection is required, which will not always be available, and which potentially slows down the system. Therefore, a hybrid solution is presented; permanent remote storage is combined with local caching.

The **Credential Manager** runs the credential protocols and therefore, it must be trusted by the user; e.g. it should never show a credential to another party without the user's consent. The Credential Manager is the only place where credential data may exist in cleartext. If the Credential Manager runs on a server, it cannot be trusted by the user, as it is completely outside the user's control. Also, network access is required. If the Credential Manager runs locally on a device which is a user's PDA, mobile phone or PC, it is relatively trustworthy, but a Trojan horse or malware cannot be excluded in case of a software implementation. A Credential Manager that runs on a computer outside the user's control is much more dangerous (e.g. a computer in a public library or shop). If the Credential Manager runs entirely on a secure token such as a smart card, the Credential Manager is trustworthy. This paper focuses on a more realistic approach, where most of the computation is outsourced by the token to the client device to which the token is connected.

4 Roles and Interactions

An overview of the roles and their most important interactions is given in figure 1. Token T is a SIM or smart card owned by the user who inserts it in a client device D in order to manage or use his credentials. Token T locally caches a part of the credential data. The client device D will do most of the computations (outsourced by T). D is also responsible for the network connection and for the token-user interactions. The dashed part of D is trusted by the user. This part can for instance be a sealed smart card reader with limited user interaction capabilities (e.g. small screen) on a public computer. The Online Repository OR stores almost all the user's credential data. The credential issuer I issues new credentials to the user. These credentials can be shown to a service provider SP and stored on the OR. During token issuance and initialisation, as well as during token recovery, a token issuer TI and and a notary[1] are needed.

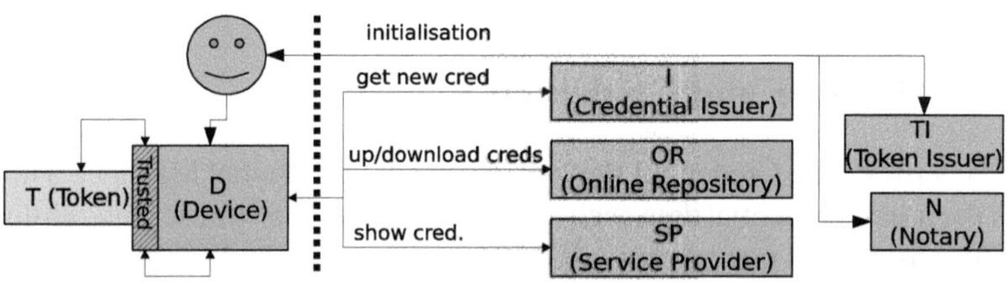

Fig. 1 Overview of the different roles and their interactions.

5 Requirements

The requirements on which we focus are now summed up.

[1] A trusted intermediary in contract signing, testaments, etc. Exists in many countries.

- **User privacy.** The *OR* must be unable to link actions or data stored on the *OR* to an identifiable user (P1). The anonymity set w.r.t. the *OR* must thus also be kept as large as possible, i.e. profiling must be minimized. The amount of personal data the (potentially untrustworthy) device *D* can extract must be minimized (P2). Eavesdroppers and attackers must not be able to derive any personal information (P3).
- **Integrity.** The *OR* must be unable to tamper with uploaded credential data (I1). This also means that the *OR* is unable to add or delete credential data. Abuse must be provable (dispute handling). It must be impossible to tamper with messages by external attackers (I3) or by the intermediary *D* (I2).
- **Confidentiality.** It must be impossible for anyone to get hold of the sensitive data such as protocol keys and credential secrets (C1).
- **Access Control.** In order to use/manage credential data, the user needs to authenticate to the token, using a sufficiently strong user authentication mechanism (A1). If there is a possibility that a thief obtains access to the owner's token (e.g. using the proper PIN), the legitimate owner should be able to revoke further usage of the token and access to the *OR* (A2). The *OR* must be ensured that the user indeed has the right to use its services and that the user is indeed the owner of the *OR* record he wants to access (A3). The user must be ensured that he is communicating with the right *I*, *OR* and *SP* and vice versa (A4).
- **Efficiency.** Computational, interaction and storage efficiency are especially important w.r.t. the token, which has limited capabilities (E1).
- **Functionality.** Even without Internet connection, the user must be able to use a limited set of credentials (e.g. a one show digital cinema ticket) (F1). The *OR* must be able to limit the amount of storage space that can be used by a single user (F2). Loss, theft or damage of the token should not result in loss of any credentials or other credential data (F3).

6 Protocols

We start by presenting the most important data structures; next we describe the protocols for issuing credentials, uploading credentials to the *OR*, downloading credentials from the *OR* and showing a credential to a service provider *SP*. We also discuss some other protocols and aspects in lesser detail.

6.1 Data structures

This section shows the data structures on the online repository and token.

Each user has exactly one **token** T, which contains:
- An unextractable user-specific *user master secret* S. This secret is required to access the user's credential data (both locally and on the *OR*).
- A credential $cred_T$ and a corresponding secret $secret_T$. These allow to authenticate anonymously to the *OR*. To do so, $cred_T$ is off-loaded to the device D. $secret_T$ never leaves the token. This way, the credential is linked to the token.

- X.509 certificates $cert_{OR}^{sig}$ and $cert_{OR}^{auth}$ of the *OR* which allows to verify signatures from and authentications of the *OR*.
- Locally cached credentials.
- The credential *index file* $file_{index}$, containing for each credential a tuple $(i, desc, receipt)$:

- i is an index for the credential, used only inside the token.
- $desc$ contains a user-friendly credential name, a short description, and the credential attribute names. This allows T to locally search for the proper credential. E.g. with what credential is it possible to prove that $age > 18$.
- $receipt$ is a proof attesting that a credential is stored by the *OR*.

The **Online Repository (OR)** contains:
- Secret keys SK_{OR}^{sig} and SK_{OR}^{auth} and the corresponding certificates $cert_{OR}^{sig}$ and $cert_{OR}^{auth}$ for signing and authentication purposes.
- For each upload credential, an $(id, cred^E, receipt_{OR})$-tuple is stored:

- id is the unique index of the *OR*-record where the credential is stored. Each credential of each user has its unique index.
- $cred^E$ is the credential and credential (token) secret encrypted by T.
- $receipt_{OR}$ is the receipt, anonymously signed with $cred_T$. The *OR* can use it as a proof in case of dispute. The signature (i.e. a transcript) can be deanonymizable by a trusted third party.

6.2 Assumptions and Notation

We assume that (1) the user is already authenticated to the token, (2) all secret data loaded in T's volatile memory will be removed from that memory by the T as soon as it is no longer required in the protocol session and (3) the user is informed by T about the protocol status at the end.

All the network connections involving D are integrity and confidentiality preserving in which *OR*, *I* and *SP* identify and authenticate to D, while the client stays anonymous. $user \leftrightarrow D$ and $D \leftrightarrow T$ connections are direct connections. We assume that during one protocol execution, the same (secure) connection is used between two parties, introducing linkabilities of actions during the protocol.

All the ciphers are integrity preserving. This can easily be done by adding a MAC before encryption. The numbers g and p are generated by *OR*, publicly available and stored by T. p is prime and g is a generator of a multiplicative group with order q with $q|p-1$ and p and q sufficiently large.

The method $genKey(seed)$ generates a symmetric key. The method $sendEncrypted(PK, data)$ sends data to a receiver, via the potentially untrusted device D. Therefore, the data is encrypted using the public key of the receiver.

Superscripts ^{E} and ^{S} denote a cipher and a signed message: $M^E \leftarrow encrypt(K,M)$, $M \leftarrow decrypt(K,M^E)$), and $M^S \leftarrow (M)sig_K$. The initiating entity is put in bold: $\mathbf{X} \rightarrow Y$. Optional steps are between square brackets $[\ldots]$.

6.3 Token Issuance and Deployment

We focus on the realistic business model where the token issuer *TI* and the online repository *OR* are two roles which may collaborate in order to obtain user information; e.g., the *TI* and *OR* can be owned by the same company.

In order to obtain a token for getting access to the OR, the user first needs to register to the *OR*. Therefore, payment and/or identification might be necessary. What exactly is required, depends upon the applied business model. E.g. the government can offer for free access to the *OR* for all its citizens and thus, it issues exactly one token to each citizen. Therefore, the citizens need to prove their identity, e.g. with their eID card.

To guarantee the user's privacy and security, the user secret *S* on the token must not be known by the *OR* or the *TI* and must thus be generated at the user side. On the other hand, it is unacceptable that loss of *S* (e.g. damaged token) obliges the user to renew all his - potentially expensive - credentials. Therefore, a secret sharing scheme can be applied. E.g. *TI* could generate half of *S*, store it together with the user id and put it on the token *T*. During token initialisation by the user, the other half is generated on the token and sent to a user-chosen notary. Using both secret halves, *S* is generated (e.g. by xoring) and the TI generated secret part is removed from *T*.

Different parties can deploy our system. The government can issue eID cards, combined with the credential management functionality. The government can manage the *OR* itself, or can outsource it to a commercial company. Other potential token issuers are banks (bank card issuers), and GSM operators (issuers of SIM tokens for mobile phones).

Although we focus on anonymous credentials, it is possible to extend the protocols to support other credential types as well, although this will have a negative impact on the privacy. Computationally, it will be less intensive.

6.4 Receiving a Credential

In table 1, a credential is issued to the user (1). This results in a credential on the device *D* and a corresponding secret on *T*. The credential is transfered by *D* to *T* (2). Then, *T* generates a local index *i* for the new credential (3). This *i* is used together with the user's master secret *S* to generate a credential specific symmetric key *K* (4). This *K* is used to encrypt both the credential and the corresponding secret (5). The resulting cipher is stored (6). Potentially with the help of the user, a description of the credential is made (7) and together with *i* added to the index file (8). The *null*-value indicates that there is no receipt; the credential has not yet been uploaded to the *OR*.

6.5 Upload Credential

Now, the credential is only stored on the token, making it vulnerable to loss. Therefore, it is uploaded (see table 2). Afterwards, the credential can be deleted from the token.

1	$T \leftrightarrow \mathbf{D} \leftrightarrow I$	$(secret;cred,\ldots) \leftarrow getCred(\ldots)$
2	$T \leftarrow \mathbf{D}$	$send(cred)$
3	$\mathbf{T}$	$i \leftarrow getFreeLocalIndex()$
4	$\mathbf{T}$	$K \leftarrow genKey(i\|\|S)$
5	$\mathbf{T}$	$cred^E \leftarrow encrypt(K,(secret,cred))$
6	$\mathbf{T}$	$store(cred^E)$
7	$\mathbf{T}[\leftrightarrow U]$	$desc \leftarrow composeDescription(cred)$
8	$\mathbf{T}$	$addToIndexFile(i,desc,null)$

Table 1 The 'Receive Credential' protocol

To upload the credential to the *OR*, the credential cipher stored by T is retrieved from T's local storage (1). The corresponding symmetric key K is calculated (2). Based on this K, the *OR* specific, global *id* for that credential is calculated (3). The user proves with the help of both T and D that he is allowed to use the *OR* by showing $cred_T$ (4, 5). T now sends *id* and $cred^E$ to *OR* (6, 7) and proves that he is the owner of the *OR*-record with index *id* (8). By linking the zero knowledge proof with $cred^E$, the *OR* is sure that D did not tamper with the credential cipher.

The *OR* generates for the user a receipt (9), stating that at a given moment, an encrypted credential with a certain hash value was uploaded to record *id*. Newer receipts invalidate older ones. The signed receipt is sent to and verified by T with $cert_{OR}^{sig}$ (10, 11).

T now signs anonymously that receipt with $cred_T$ (12). The resulting transcript (signature) is stored by the *OR*, together with the credential cipher, *id* and *receipt* (13). T adds the receipt to the index file (14). Both user and *OR* now have a proof that can be used in case of dispute (e.g. user claims that a credential has been removed by *OR*.

1	$\mathbf{T}$	$cred^E \leftarrow retrieveLocalCred(i)$
2	$\mathbf{T}$	$K \leftarrow genKey(i\|\|S)$
3	$\mathbf{T}$	$id \leftarrow g^K \bmod n$
4	$\mathbf{T} \rightarrow D$	$send(cred_T)$
5	$T \leftrightarrow \mathbf{D} \rightarrow OR$	$showCred(secret_T;cred_T,possession)$
6	$\mathbf{T} \rightarrow D \rightarrow OR$	$sendEncrypted(PK_{OR},id)$
7	$\mathbf{T} \rightarrow D \rightarrow OR$	$send(cred^E)$
8	$\mathbf{T} \rightarrow D \rightarrow OR$	$PK\{K : id == g^K \bmod n\}(cred^E)$
9	$\mathbf{OR}$	$receipt \leftarrow (id,H(cred^E),timestamp_{OR})sig_{OR}$
10	$T \leftarrow D \leftarrow \mathbf{OR}$	$send(receipt)$
11	$\mathbf{T}$	$verify(cert_{OR}^{sig},receipt)$
12	$T \leftrightarrow \mathbf{D} \rightarrow OR$	$trans_{OR} \leftarrow showCred(secret_T;cred_T,possession,receipt)$
13	$\mathbf{OR}$	$store(id,cred^E,receipt,trans_{OR})$
14	$\mathbf{T}$	$updateIndexFile(i,receipt)$

Table 2 The 'Upload Credential' protocol

6.6 Show Credential

Table 3 shows how a credential is shown after it has been retrieved from the *OR*. First, T searches for a credential able to prove the requested properties $properties_{show}$ (1,2). If more credentials can be shown, the user selects the most appropriate one. The credential decryption key K is calculated and the credential's OR-index *id* is retrieved from the receipt (3,4). D and T show together $cred_T$ to the *OR* (5,6) to prove that the user is allowed to use the *OR*. Now the *OR*-index *id* of the required credential is sent to the *OR* (7). The *OR* replies with the credential cipher and the corresponding receipt (8). We will later argue why this receipt is required although it is not used in this protocol. T decrypts the credential cipher. This results in a credential and its corresponding secret. No proof of possession of the *OR*-index *id* is required as no changes on that record are performed and only the owner of the record can decrypt the content. Finally, the credential is shown (11, 12) after the user has given his consent (10).

1	$T \leftarrow D \leftarrow \mathbf{SP}$	$send(properties_{show})$
2	$\mathbf{T}[\leftrightarrow U]$	$(i, desc, receipt) \leftarrow find(properties_{show})$
3	$\mathbf{T}$	$K \leftarrow genKey(i\|\|S)$
4	$\mathbf{T}$	$id \leftarrow receipt_T.id$
5	$\mathbf{T} \rightarrow D$	$send(cred_T)$
6	$T \leftrightarrow \mathbf{D} \rightarrow OR$	$trans_{OR} \leftarrow showCred(secret_T; cred_T, possession)$
7	$\mathbf{T} \rightarrow D \rightarrow OR$	$sendEncrypted(PK_{OR}, id)$
8	$\mathbf{T} \leftarrow D \leftarrow OR$	$send(cred^E, receipt')$
9	$\mathbf{T}$	$(secret; cred) \leftarrow decrypt(K, cred^E)$
10	$U \leftrightarrow \mathbf{T}$	*user gives permission*
11	$\mathbf{T} \rightarrow D$	$send(cred)$
12	$T \leftrightarrow \mathbf{D} \rightarrow SP$	$showCred(secret; cred, properties_{show})$

Table 3 The 'Show Credential' protocol

6.7 Other Relevant Aspects and Protocols

We touch *token recovery* and *limiting the usage of the OR*. Other protocols such as $file_{index}$ *upload* are not discussed in this paper.

Token recovery. The user requests a new token from the token issuer TI, which then revokes the previous $cred_T$ and puts a new one on a new token, as well as one half of the user master secret S. After having contacted the notary, S is regenerated. If the last version of the index file is not uploaded as a cipher to the *OR*, it can be recovered by requesting for each *id* owned by that user the credential data from the *OR*, as it is done in our show credential protocol, where the *OR* not only returns the credential cipher, but the receipt as well. The index file can thus be regenerated/updated. For each credential recovery, a new connection with the *OR* needs to be made to avoid linkabilities. The credential data that were not yet uploaded to the *OR* are lost. Thus, some credentials potentially need to be revoked and reissued.

Limiting usage of the OR. As a result of the unlinkability of *OR* records, the user has a potentially unlimited online storage space. Limiting the size of a record is one part of the solution. Secondly, the number of records per user can be limited. The token issuer TI can issue two credentials $cred_T^{\infty}$ and $cred_T^{k}$ instead of a single $cred_T$. The former is an unlimited show credential, the latter a k-show. $cred_T^{k}$ is only used for step 5 in the upload protocol, in all the other situations, $cred_T^{\infty}$ is used. If the user removes an *OR* record, he obtains a proof thereof, blindly signed by *OR*. Later, the user can use these proofs to update (reload) the k-show credential.

Keeping track of your anonymity. Different shows of the same U-Prove credential are linkable, as well as shows of Idemix credentials over the same nym. The user's willingness to reveal personal data to a service provider might depend upon the amount of data that has been revealed previously. Therefore, the user can decide to store a profile tuple $(id_{SP}, spec, i_{cred}, timestamp)$ on the token. $spec$ describes (a simplified $properties_{prove}$) what properties of the credential referred to by i_{cred} were shown. As the tokens usually do not have a clock, timestamp must be provided by the client device D. For each service provider whereof the user stores such tuples, a different OR-record is needed. Each such profile record thus contains a set of profile tuples. This can be uploaded in a similar way as the credentials. However, each time a tuple is added, the record changes and thus a new receipt must be generated. This receipt has the form $(id, nb, acc, timestamp)$. nb is the number of tuples, acc has the form $H(...H(H(tuple_1), tuple_2, ..., tuple_{nb})$ and avoids tampering by the OR. Later, the user can merge tuples, but this must be done in a trusted environment.

7 Evaluation

In this section, the requirements listed in section 5 are evaluated.

7.1 Privacy

The level of privacy is evaluated by analysing what personal information the different entities can or cannot obtain. An overview is given in table 4.

OR	1.1 Size and time of action on *OR*-record with id *id*
	1.2 Number of tuples per profile record
	1.3 No inter-credential or credential-owner linkability
Eavesdropper	2.1 No linkability of packets
	2.2 No information leakage on network layer.
Device	3.1 When, for how long are what entities contacted.
	3.2 Credential and show specification, but no secrets or keys.
	3.3 [I/O via client] Interception of commands, PINs, etc.
	3.4 More properties can be revealed during a single show.
Illegal token access	4.1 [$cred_T$ valid] Access to all credential data, not to secrets, keys.
	4.2 [$cred_T$ revoked] Access to local credential data, not to secrets, keys.

Table 4 Overview of the data the different entities can obtain.

P1 - During authentication, the OR first receives a $cred_T$ credential show. If $cred_T$ is an Idemix credential, the OR cannot link different shows thereof. The proof of possession of the record with index id does not reveal anything else. The OR can thus not link records to each other or to the same user. A mix-network is required and delay might be necessary to avoid time-based linking. The OR cannot distinguish between credential retrieval for recovery or show purposes. We thus can theoretically have total unlinkability of credential records stored by the OR (1.3).

OR knows the index id, receipts and ciphers of credentials and privacy tuples. The only evidence it can collect is the time actions on records are performed and the cipher sizes (1.1). This can be reduced by increasing the amount of credential data

cached by T and by padding uploaded data. *OR* also knows the number of uploaded tuples per profile record (1.2). The *OR* thus only obtains a very limited usage profile per credential record and per profile record.
P2 - The device D can get hold of credentials and show specifications during the protocol executions (3.2). D also knows when actions are performed, and to whom (3.1). D can thus get hold of many personal data. Users should be aware of this when they use potentially untrusted computers.

In the absence of a sealed token reader with user I/O capabilities, D can eavesdrop on the interactions between user and T, however this does not reveal new personal attributes (except the user's PIN!) (3.3). D can never get hold of *id*s, preventing it from collaborating with *OR*, nor does it ever see credential secrets or the master secret. However, by synchronizing and collaborating with *OR*, linkabilities can be revealed.

D can show more (or other) properties to the *SP* than what is required in $properties_{show}$. Showing insufficient properties to D will be detected because the user will not obtain the expected privileges. The required user consent to T before a credential is shown and the corresponding secret on T prevents D from surreptitiously showing a credential (3.4).
P3 - Eavesdroppers or external entities cannot link different sessions if a mix network is used (2.1). Secure network connections prevent eavesdropping (or tampering) on the sent data (2.2).

If an attacker obtains access to T (e.g. by obtaining the PIN), the privacy is evidently further reduced because he can access many locally stored data (4.2). If $cred_T$ is not yet revoked, the attacker can get hold of the other, *OR*-stored, data as well (4.1). As long as the tamper resistance is maintained, the attacker cannot get hold of keys or secrets.

7.2 Integrity

I1 - Tampering with individual ciphers stored by the *OR* will be detected as the ciphers are integrity preserving. Deletion of an individual cipher in a profile record can be detected by verifying the receipt. The *OR* also stores an (anonymous) signature on the receipt from T, to prevent charges based on out-dated receipts of T. By slightly modifying the protocol, the proof generated in step 8 in the upload credential protocol can serve as a pre-proof that can be used by *OR* in case the protocol is interrupted after step 11.

An unsolved problem is that token (and thus $cred_T$) renewal results in an invalidation of the user's anonymous signatures on the receipts, invalidating the *OR*'s evidence. Renewal of other certificates such as $cert_{OR}^{sig}$ must also be possible in a transparent way.
I2 - T cannot be sure whether there is indeed a secure connection between D on the one side and *OR*, *I* or *SP* on the other side. Therefore, *OR*, *I* and *SP* need to have and enforce policies that require D to set up such a connection.
I3 - If there is no sealed card reader with I/O capabilities, the communications between T and user need to pass D, which can do modifications. This is a typical

smart card/SIM token problem. Everything else sent or forwarded by D to T or an external party is integrity protected. However, T is unable to check the integrity of anonymous credentials due to T's computational limitations. *OR* signatures (e.g. on receipts) can be verified by T as it has the right *OR* certificate, but still, D is needed to check the validity of that certificate. Even if $properties_{show}$ is signed and T has the corresponding certificate, T cannot verify whether the certificate corresponds to the right *SP*.

7.3 Access control

A1 - A PIN or biometric data can be used for user authentication to the token. No credential (including $cred_T$) secret ever leaves T in an unencrypted form. The token is thus required to access the *OR* or credentials. However, if no sealed token reader with user I/O capabilities is used, D can intercept the PIN, giving it complete control over the usage of T.
A2 - By revoking $cred_T$, further access to the *OR* by an illegitimate user is prevented. However, this user can still access and use the locally cached credential data. These credentials need to be revoked as well. Quickly revoking $cred_T$ and all the locally cached credentials is thus of utmost importance. Caching too many credentials locally should be discouraged. Access by an illegitimate user to the locally cached profile tuples or the index file cannot be prevented if he knows the PIN.
A3 - Only users having a valid token (i.e. containing a valid $cred_T$) can use the *OR*. If a user wants to change something in *OR*-record with index *id*, he needs to prove that his token knows the corresponding key K. Thus, only the owner of that record can do changes. Because the user's token is the only entity that knows K, only the owner can decrypt the data in the *OR*-record. A proof of ownership is not necessary in this case.
A4 - D is trusted to connect to the proper *I*, *SP*. If it connects to the wrong (fake) *OR*, that *OR* will not be able to issue valid receipts or show the right data.

7.4 Confidentiality.

C1 - We assume that the notary does not collaborate with the *OR* and that the token is tamper proof such that secret data cannot be extracted. Each record on the *OR* is encrypted using another key. If such a credential-specific key is leaked, only a single credential record is compromised.

7.5 Storage

Our reference credential has 7 attributes. Tests showed that Idemix needs about 4.5Kb and about 7KB when using respectively 1024 and 2048 bit keys. This included the credential itself, an XML description and the public key data.

Based on the assumptions in Figure 2 on the observation that T stores $file_{desc}$, $cred_{OR}$, $secret_{OR}$, S, and a two *OR* certificates, about 50KB is needed to manage 50 credentials stored on the *OR*.

Additionally managing 25 profile records (25 different *SPs*) requires about 7KB as the receipts are about the same size as the credential receipts. The size of a single privacy tuple will be dominated by the size of *spec*, which will seldom be larger than 0.5KB if expressed in a compact way.

Thus, a realistic token with 100KB storage space satisfies in our setting.

Cred. Description	
Cred. desc.	64 byte
att. names	7 * 32 byte
TOTAL:	288 byte

Receipt	
id	128 byte
hash	20 byte
$time_{OR}$	8 byte
sig_{OR}	128 byte
TOTAL:	284 byte

$file_{index}$ **entry**	
counter	2 byte
desc	288 byte
receipt	284 byte
TOTAL:	572 byte

Other	
single character	1 byte
master secret S	256 byte
small cert.	< 5 KB

Fig. 2 Estimated size of a credential description, a receipt, an index file entry and other data.

7.6 Performance

Token T will be the bottleneck in the protocols. Especially modex operations are cumbersome. RSA signature verification as well as RSA encryption can be done efficiently if the exponent is well chosen. Modex operations with a small, numerical, values (e.g. numerical attributes) are no problem either. The Chinese Remainder Theorem can never be applied in our protocols. Based on these observations, only the underlined step in the protocols require a 'hard' modex by T: credential receive, upload and show, need respectively one, four and two modex. This can be done in 174, 696, and 348 ms for 2048 bit moduli by a state-of-the-art smart cards (Infineon SLE 88CFX4002P). Less expensive, but still considered as fast, smart cards require much more time. E.g. the ST22N144 requires 1.7, 6.8 and 3.4 seconds to do the same operations. The remaining operations on T are lightweight: sending, receiving, storing, reading, en- and decryption of small amounts of data, user interactions and generation of symmetric keys.

The *showCred*() and *getCred*() methods will dominate the steps performed by the other entities. The time required by client and *I*, *OR* or *SP* to issue a credential or to prove properties highly depends upon the involved attributes and properties. Issuing our reference credentials required 25 modex for Idemix at 2048 bit. Show tests required between 12 and 106 hard modex. Even the latter was only proving that one's age is in a given interval. We did not consider the use of Idemix pseudonyms. Usually, the big half of the modex are on the user side. An Intel 1.83GHz CPU needed on average about 80 ms for a 2048 bit modex.

The proposed protocols are thus computationally feasible and acceptable on ths fastest smart cards. Theoretically, the prover part of very simple credential shows can be done solely on these smart cards. However, even for these cards, still help of the client device is indispensable to do more complex operations on credentials. Future improvements (more powerful tokens, more efficient implementations, etc.) will improve this, enhancing the security and privacy. Then, a secure connection could be established between T and *OR*, *I* or *SP*. Still, a trusted sealed token reader is required for user I/O.

Only small packets are transfered. The use of mix networks will likely introduce most delay on the network level. By caching, network interactions are reduced. An implementation is required to test the real-life performance and feasibility of our proposed protocols.

8 Related Work

Online Credential Repositories can be categorized in mechanism-aware or mechanism-neutral systems [6]. Mechanism-aware repositories (e.g. MyProxy [13], CredEx [16]) can support mechanism-specific protocols for credential retrieval. The disadvantage of such systems is that only few types of credentials are supported. Furthermore, the repository can access the credentials. Our repository can store every type of credential and does not know the credential data. Several credential repositories (Entrust Roaming PKI [1], Verisign roaming [5], etc.) are described in [14], which lists some problems that most current repositories suffer from. First, compromising the credential repository allows the attacker to perform an offline attack on each credential [6, 14]. This can be a serious threat if the credentials are encrypted using a password. Our approach uses strong encryption for credentials. Furthermore, because the users's credentials are unlinkable, it is infeasible to gain access to all the credentials of one particular user. Second, most repositories use a potentially untrusted client that can directly access the credentials. On public workstations, this of course poses a big security risk. Our approach minimizes trust put in the client.

Multiple **Identity Management Systems** exist. *Microsoft CardSpace* [3] enables the user to request from identity providers security tokens asserting claims (e.g. age > 21). Although computationally less demanding, each show of a security token requires a new interaction with the identity provider if unlinkability of shows has to be achieved. More trust is put in the identity provider (the issuer). This entity must also be trusted not to collaborate with service providers. *Liberty alliance* [4] is based on federated identity management; service providers exchange personal data about the user to facilitate user's authentication. The default setup is thus not privacy-friendly. However, the user can setup his own identity provider or strong privacy preference can be set to the identity provider. *The Higgins framework* [2], of which Idemix is part of, is a young project aimed at creating a common interface layer that will allow various existing identity management systems to interoperate.

9 Conclusion and Future Work

This paper tried to maximize the user's privacy, as well as the usability of his credentials. Although feasible on the fastest smart cards, a number of problems appeared, that are likely to appear in other similar solutions as well. E.g. the trust put in the client device. The paper revealed those challenges that will need to be tackled in order to have a deployable system that satisfies the user's needs.

A prototype implementation is necessary and aspects such as the use of Idemix nyms and mix network latency need to be looked at. A study of the evolution of token crypto co-processors w.r.t. the available computer power would reveal whether it will once become possible to run the protocols always entirely on the token. Other challenges are updating the security parameters, using ECC and examining to what extent Trusted Computing Base (TCB) can offer a solution for the untrustworthy client problem. Development of similar protocols for e.g. Microsoft CardSpace are likely to be possible.

Acknowledgements. This research is a contribution to the European PRIME project and is partially funded by the Interuniversity Attraction Poles Programme Belgian State, Belgian Science Policy, the Research Fund K.U.Leuven and the IWT-SBO project (ADAPID) "Advanced Applications for Electronic Identity Cards in Flanders".

References

1. Entrust authority roaming server. http://www.entrust.com/pki/roaming/index.htm.
2. Higgins trust framework project home. http://www.eclipse.org/higgins/.
3. Introducing windows cardspace. http://msdn2.microsoft.com/en-us/library/aa480189.aspx.
4. Liberty allicance project. http://www.projectliberty.org/.
5. Verisign roaming. http://www.verisign.com/products-services/security-services/pki/pki-security/wireless-roaming/index.html.
6. J. Basney, W. Yurcik, R. Bonilla, and A. Slagell. The credential wallet: A classification of credential repositories highlighting myproxy. In *Proceedings of the 31st Research Conference on Communication, Information and Internet Policy*, 2003.
7. Stefan A. Brands. *Rethinking Public Key Infrastructures and Digital Certificates: Building in Privacy*. MIT Press, Cambridge, MA, USA, 2000.
8. Jan Camenisch and Anna Lysyanskaya. An efficient system for non-transferable anonymous credentials with optional anonymity revocation. In *EUROCRYPT '01: Proceedings of the International Conference on the Theory and Application of Cryptographic Techniques*, pages 93–118, London, UK, 2001. Springer-Verlag.
9. Jan Camenisch and Markus Stadler. Efficient group signature schemes for large groups (extended abstract). In *CRYPTO '97: Proceedings of the 17th Annual International Cryptology Conference on Advances in Cryptology*, pages 410–424, London, UK, 1997. Springer-Verlag.
10. David Chaum. Security without identification: transaction systems to make big brother obsolete. *Commun. ACM*, 28(10):1030–1044, 1985.
11. Matt Hooks and Jadrian Miles. Onion routing and online anonymity. *CS182S*, 2006.
12. Arjen K. Lenstra and Eric R. Verheul. Selecting cryptographic key sizes. *Journal of Cryptology: the journal of the International Association for Cryptologic Research*, 14(4):255–293, 2001.
13. J. Novotny, S. Tuecke, and V. Welch. An online credential repository for the grid: Myproxy. In *Proceedings of the Tenth International Symposium on High Performance Distributed Computing (HPDC-10)*. IEEE Press, 2001.
14. G. Sarbari. Security characteristics of cryptographic mobility solutions. In *Proceedings of the 1 Annual PKI Research Workshop, Gaithersburg, Maryland*, 2002.
15. Paul F. Syverson, David M. Goldschlag, and Michael G. Reed. Anonymous connections and onion routing. In *SP '97: Proceedings of the 1997 IEEE Symposium on Security and Privacy*, page 44, Washington, DC, USA, 1997. IEEE Computer Society.
16. David Del Vecchio, Marty Humphrey, Jim Basney, and Nataraj Nagaratnam. Credex: User-centric credential management for grid and web services. In *ICWS '05: Proceedings of the IEEE International Conference on Web Services (ICWS'05)*, pages 149–156, Washington, DC, USA, 2005. IEEE Computer Society.

Facilitating Privacy Related Decisions in Different Privacy Contexts on the Internet by Evaluating Trust in Recipients of Private Data

Indrajit Ray and Sudip Chakraborty

Abstract Every time a user uses the Internet, a wealth of personal information is revealed, either voluntarily or involuntarily. This often causes privacy breaches, specially if the information is misused. Ideally, a user would like to make a reasoned decision about who to release her information to and what to release. For this purpose, we propose using the level of trust that a user has on the recipient regarding not to misuse her private data. To measure this trust level, we adapt the vector model of trust proposed earlier. We formalize a notion of privacy context and show how a privacy context ontology can be used to determine trust values for previously unencountered situations.

1 Introduction

Researchers are getting increasingly concerned about protecting the user's privacy in an electronic world. Unfortunately, most of us would find it difficult to provide a concrete definition of privacy with enough information to be able to apply it to our real lives. As individuals, each of us have unique needs and views of what constitute personal and private data [1]. The task is considerably more difficult when we have to define what privacy means to us as we use the Internet. Efforts to define and develop technologies that support the specification of consumer privacy requirements as well as help protect them, are evolving at a considerably slower pace. Efforts like the Platform for Privacy Preferences (P3P) Project of the World Wide Web consortium [4] and the related Privacy Bird project [3], and works based on the *k-anonymity* and *ℓ-diversity* models, provide solutions to some facets of electronic consumer privacy. For example, the P3P project attempts to provide a framework for service providers to express their privacy policies to the user with the goal that a user can form a reasoned opinion about the state of her privacy at the service provider. The related work on Privacy Bird [3] provides a user-friendly mechanism by which a user can determine if a service provider's P3P policies match the user's privacy preferences. The understanding is that such compliance will enhance the user's trust

Indrajit Ray and Sudip Chakraborty
Computer Science Department, Colorado State University, Fort Collins, CO 80523 e-mail: indrajit, sudip@cs.colostate.edu

Please use the following format when citing this chapter:

Ray, I. and Chakraborty, S., 2008, in IFIP International Federation for Information Processing, Volume 278; *Proceedings of the IFIP TC 11 23rd International Information Security Conference*; Sushil Jajodia, Pierangela Samarati, Stelvio Cimato; (Boston: Springer), pp. 605–619.

in the service provider. However, P3P is only able to provide a technical mechanism by which service providers can describe their use of personal information. P3P does not provide mechanisms by which policies are enforced. Nor can policies be used to verify or prove that the services accurately reflect the original policies. The *k-anonymity* model [12, 14], *ℓ-diversity* model [8] and similar works like [11], on statistical databases [5], and deductive databases [2] address the problem of releasing personal information so that the subjects of the data cannot be identified uniquely. Proponents argue that these efforts enable the users to act on what they see and thereby help protect their private information. However, often privacy is breached by factors that the users cannot see or control – for example, misjudged trust and misuse of information. Thus, these models and technologies solve only parts of the problem of protecting user privacy.

The last observation indicates that trust plays an important role in the problem of preserving privacy. Ultimately, the user needs to trust the recipient with her private information. A number of researchers have previously explored the idea of modeling privacy using a trust centric approach [6, 13, 9]. Goecks and Mynatt treat reputation and trust as separate independent entities and propose an approach to combine trust networks with reputation to provide privacy [6]. Shand et al. [13] rely on recommendation to direct the sharing of private information. Nguyen and Mynatt [9] address the problem of trust in pervasive computing environment. Their goal is to make the user more aware of privacy issues. The goal of enhancing consumer confidence in privacy practices of service providers has been explored by privacy seal programs such as TrustE (http://www.truste.org). However, it relies heavily on policy statements similar to P3P statement.

We believe that trust based approach to preserving privacy is promising. The problem with this group of work is that the trust models used are not very expressive. Moreover, none of these works discuss how to evaluate trust for the purpose of privacy preservation. In this work, we adapt and extend the vector model of trust we had proposed earlier [10] to help the user decide how much to trust the recipient of private data to preserve her privacy. We specify the user's different Internet activities like browsing a website, downloading content, purchasing, etc., as privacy contexts. The user is likely to have different privacy preferences for different contexts and may switch context anytime during an online session. Sometimes the user may not have enough information to calculate trust about a trustee in a new context. Or, the user may have no predefined preference rules in that context. We show how, in the above scenarios, the user can extrapolate a trust or a privacy preference rule-set using trust and preference rules for existing contexts. For this purpose, we define an ontology of privacy contexts containing a similarity relationship between different contexts. This similarity relationship is represented by a context similarity graph. Using the degree of similarity between contexts, the user can extrapolate trust or can set up privacy preferences in the context for which she does not have any a priori information.

The rest of the paper is organized as follows: Section 2 describes the vector trust model summarizing the main features and discussing our adaptation. Section 3 describes how this model can be used to evaluate the trust in the recipient for privacy related issues. In section 4 we formalize the notion of privacy context. We show in section 5 how we can reason about privacy preferences and trust in different privacy contexts based on information about related contexts. Finally, we conclude in section 6 with some discussion on our future plans to extend this work.

2 The Trust Model

We adapt our previously proposed trust model [10]. Trust is specified as a trust relationship between a truster, A, a trustee, B, in a particular context, c and denoted as $(A \xrightarrow{c} B)$. The trust relationship is expressed as a vector where components are the parameters influencing trust. We identify three such parameters and express each of them in terms of a numeric value in the range $[-1,1] \cup \{\perp\}$. The three parameters may not have equal importance in determining a trust level. The *trust policy vector* specifies a normalization factor that gives the relative weight of each parameter. Applying the normalization factor to the trust relationship gives a *normalized trust relationship*, which we denote by $(A \xrightarrow{c} B)^N$. We also associate a numeric value in the range $[-1,1] \cup \{\perp\}$ to this normalized trust relationship. If the trust value is $1(-1)$ then we call the trustee completely trustworthy (untrustworthy). The trustee is semi-trustworthy (semi-untrustworthy) if the trust value is between $(0,1)$ $((-1,0))$. The truster professes a neutral trust level about the trustee if the trust value is 0. We use the symbol $\perp$ to denote an unknown trust value. We define the following properties of $\perp$. If $\mathbf{R}$ is the set of real numbers and $a \in \mathbf{R}$ then (i) $a \times \perp = \perp \times a = \perp$, (ii) $a + \perp = \perp + a = a$, (iii) $\perp + \perp = \perp$ and (iv) $\perp \times \perp = \perp$.

Trust Parameters

The three parameters for evaluating trust relationship – *properties*, *experience* and *recommendation* – are formalized as follows.

Properties:

Definition 1. The *properties* of the truster regarding a trustee for a particular context is defined as a measure of the characteristic attributes or information of the trustee for which the truster can have some assertion to be truly related to the trustee.

Each truster must initially define its own criteria for the gradation of properties regarding a particular entity. We can have *positive properties*, *negative properties*, and *neutral properties* where positive properties contribute towards increase in trust, negative properties contribute towards increase in distrust and neutral properties contribute neither way. To assign a value to the *properties* component, the truster must assign a value between -1 and $+1$ for each attribute of the trustee. This is done using a function, called *property evaluation function*. It is formally defined as,

Definition 2. Let p be a property. The property evaluation function of truster A, denoted by P_A is defined as a function that associates a value in the range $[-1,1] \cup \{\perp\}$ with the property p. Formally, $P_A(p) = v$, where $v \in [-1,1] \cup \{\perp\}$.

Different trustees may have properties that are not exactly same, but similar. For example, a trustee may use SSL as a communication protocol, whereas other uses TLS. Though the trustees use different protocols, they have similar properties as both of them use 'secure communication protocol'. However some trustee may not use any secure protocol at all during communication. To differentiate between these, we categorize properties of trustee into classes and subclasses where each class (or, subclass) has a finite set of possible items. For example, *communication protocol* used by the trustee is considered to be a property and thus can be represented as a class with possible items like SSL and TLS. The truster may choose to have subclasses within a property class. For example, within communication protocol, the truster may look for subclasses like *encryption algorithm* and *key-size*. The subclass key size may be, for example, represented by $\{[1-56],[57-128],[129-512],[513-1024]\}$. The truster needs to build these classes and subclasses according to her own criteria. To evaluate the property, the truster assigns value to each class (and subclass) as well as each of the attributes contained in them.

The truster A gathers the property information and evaluates it using P_A. If the truster is unable to obtain any information about the existence of any of the elements of a particular class (or subclass) CL, the class (or subclass) is considered to be empty and the truster assigns a value $\perp$ for the whole class (or subclass). Therefore, we extend the definition of property evaluation function for a class or subclass $CL = \{p_1, p_2, \ldots, p_n\}$ as

Definition 3. The property evaluation function extended for a class or subclass is denoted by $P_A : CL \rightarrow [-1,1] \cup \{\perp\}$ and is defined as

$$P_A(CL) = \begin{cases} \{v_1, v_2, \ldots, v_n\} & \text{where } \forall i, v_i = P_A(p_i) \\ \perp & \text{if } \forall i, P_A(p_i) = \perp \end{cases}$$

We do not dictate how a truster designs the function P_A. It will depend on the truster's domain knowledge, the scheme and trust evaluation criteria. Average of the property values gives the value for the component *properties*. If the truster is aware of k attributes of the trustee, then properties of trustee B according to truster A in context c is evaluated as ${}_AP_B^c = \frac{1}{k}\sum_{i=1}^{k} v_i$ where $v_i \in [-1,1] \cup \{\perp\}$, $\forall i = 1,2,\ldots,k$. v_i is the value assigned to i^{th} attribute of B. Note, ${}_AP_B^c = \perp$ is different from ${}_AP_B^c = 0$. Value 0 implies that after evaluating the information, the truster's decision is neutral. The value '$\perp$' implies "lack of information", i.e., there is not enough data to determine 'properties' of the trustee.

Experience:

Definition 4. The *experience* of a truster about a trustee is defined as the measure of the cumulative effect of a number of events that were encountered by the truster with respect to the trustee in a particular context and over a specified period of time.

The trust of a truster on a trustee can change because of the the truster's experiences with the trustee in the particular context. Each event that can influence the degree of trust is interpreted by the truster as either a *positive event*, a *negative event* or a *neutral event*. We believe, events far back in time does not count as strongly as very recent events for computing trust values. Hence we introduce the concept of *experience policy* which specifies a length of time interval subdivided into non-overlapping intervals.

Definition 5. An *experience policy* specifies a totally ordered set of non-overlapping time intervals together with a set of non-negative weights corresponding to each element in the set of time intervals.

The whole time period $[t_0, t_n]$ is divided in such intervals and the truster A keeps a log of events occurring in these intervals. If e_k^i denote the kth event in the ith interval, then $v_k^i = +1$, if $e_k^i \in \mathbf{P}$, $v_k^i = -1$, if $e_k^i \in \mathbf{Q}$, and $v_k^i = 0$, if $e_k^i \in \mathbf{N}$, where $\mathbf{P}$ = set of all positive events, $\mathbf{Q}$ = set of all negative events and $\mathbf{N}$ = set of all neutral events.

The *incidents* I_j, corresponding to the jth time interval is the sum of the values of all the events, positive, negative, or neutral for the time interval. If n_j is the number of events that occurred in the jth time interval, then $I_j = \sum_{k=1}^{n_j} v_k^j$. If there is no event in $[t_{j-1}, t_j]$, then $I_j = \perp$.

Events far back in time does not count as strongly as very recent events for computing trust. We give more weight to events in recent time intervals than those in distant intervals. To accommodate this, we assign a *non-negative* weight w_i to the ith interval such that $w_i > w_j$ whenever $i > j$. To ensure that we compute the weight w_i for the ith interval as $w_i = \frac{i}{S}$, $\forall i = 1, 2, \ldots, n$, where $S = n(n+1)/2$. Then the *experience* of A with regards to B in context c is given by ${}_AE_B^c = (\sum_{k=1}^{n} w_k I_k)/(\sum_{k=1}^{n} n_k)$.

Recommendation:

Definition 6. A *recommendation* about a trustee is defined as a measure of the subjective or objective judgment of a recommender about the trustee to the truster.

We assume that the user is a member of a 'community' where each member can act as client (truster), service provider (trustee) or simply a third party (peer). The trust value of a truster on a trustee can change because of a *recommendation* for the trustee, provided by other members of the community. However, some members are more attributable to provide a 'good' feedback. Therefore truster partition the whole community in two different groups – attributable sources, having a trust relationship of certain level with the truster; and non-attributable sources, having no or very low valued trust relationship. For computing recommendation, the truster considers only those feedback that are provided by attributable sources. In section 3 we show how a truster choose the attributable sources.

A recommender sends her opinion or feedback about the trustee in the specified context, in terms of a numeric value in the range $[-1, 1] \cup \{\perp\}$. If Ψ is a group of n recommenders, $v(A \xrightarrow{c} r_j)^N$ (> 0) is trust value of jth member (r_j) in Ψ, and $F_j = j^{th}$ recommender's feedback about trustee B in context c, then the truster A computes the recommendation component ${}_AR_B^c$ as, ${}_AR_B^c = (\sum_{j=1}^{n} [v(A \xrightarrow{c} r_j)^N \times F_j]) / \sum_{j=1}^{n} v(A \xrightarrow{c} r_j)^N$.

Note, the truster A has a trust relationship with the recommender r_j. We consider the context of this trust relationship as *negotiating*. Requesting for a recommendation and receiving it can be viewed as a negotiation where the truster is concerned about certain amount of her privacy. For example, the truster may be interested to share the following information with the recommender but does not want to make this public: (i) her identity (may be the IP address or other identifying information), (ii) identity of the trustee, (iii) the details of recommendation request, (iv) the context in which the trustee is being evaluated.

Scaling the recommendation score based on the trust relationship between the truster and the recommender has one important benefit. Suppose that the recommender tells a lie about the trustee in the recommendation in order to gain an advantage with the truster. If the truster does not have trust on the recommender to a great degree then the trust on the recommendation will be low with the truster.

Normalization

Having determined the values for each component of trust we specify the simple trust relationship between the truster A and the trustee B in a context c as $(A \xrightarrow{c} B)$. During evaluation of a trust value, a truster may assign different weights to the different factors that influence trust. The weights indicate relative importance of the parameters. We capture this factor using the concept of a *normalization policy* and is represented by a vector called *trust policy vector*.

Definition 7. The *trust policy vector*, ${}_AW_B$, is a vector that has the same number of components as there are parameters for influencing trust. The elements are real numbers in the range $[0,1]$ and the sum of all elements is equal to 1.

The normalized trust relationship $(A \xrightarrow{c} B)^N$ is obtained from the simple trust relationship, after combining the former by component-wise multiplication with the trust policy vector. Suppose ${}_AW_B = [w_P,\ w_E,\ w_R]$ is the trust policy vector, where $w_P, w_E, w_R \in [0,1]$ and $w_P + w_E + w_R = 1$. Then $(A \xrightarrow{c} B)^N = {}_AW_B \cdot (A \xrightarrow{c} B) = [w_P \times_A P_B^c,\ w_E \times_A E_B^c,\ w_R \times_A R_B^c]$.

Value of Trust Relationship

The values of the components of normalized trust relationship $(A \xrightarrow{c} B)^N$ are added to obtain the value corresponding to the trust relationship. This value is denoted by $v(A \xrightarrow{c} B)^N$. Formally, $v(A \xrightarrow{c} B)^N = {}_A\hat{P}_B^c + {}_A\hat{E}_B^c + {}_A\hat{R}_B^c$ where ${}_A\hat{P}_B^c = w_P \times_A P_B^c$, ${}_A\hat{E}_B^c = w_E \times_A E_B^c$, and ${}_A\hat{R}_B^c = w_R \times_A R_B^c$.

3 Preserving Privacy Using The Trust Model

We look into the privacy preservation scheme from a client's perspective. That is, we investigate how a user can have a reasonable control over her privacy while interacting with a server. Before each transaction, a user evaluates the trustworthiness of the server using the trust model described in section 2. To evaluate this trust the client uses information about characteristics of the server, her personal experience with the server, and information that she gathers from other members in the community. In the following sections, we describe how properties, experience, and recommendation can be evaluated.

Evaluating *Properties*

To quantify the 'properties' component of the trust relationship, the client A (truster) needs to gather information about the attributes of the server B (trustee) and classify them. We give some examples of classes and subclasses of attributes of a trustee that a truster may define to evaluate properties component. (a) *Communication protocol* – Presence of a secure communication protocol like SSL helps preventing confidentiality breach, integrity breach, identity theft and thereby can prevent other indirect violations of privacy. In this class the truster may have the following subclasses: (i) Encryption algorithm – which encryption algorithm (e.g., AES or DES or RSA) is being used, (ii) Key-type – what type of key (e.g., symmetric key or asymmetric key) is used, (iii) key-size – what is the key size (e.g., 56-bit or 128-bit or 512-bit), (iv) Message digest algorithm – what type of message digest algorithm is used (e.g., MD5 or SHA), (v) Authentication – what authentication mode is used (e.g., authentication of both ends, or only B's authentication or, it is totally anonymous), (vi) Key exchange – which key exchange algorithm is used (e.g., RSA or Diffie-Hellman), (b) *Credential* – Presence of a certificate from a well-known certifying authority (e.g., Verisign) about policies, methods and tools applied and used by B in a particular transaction. The truster A can have following subclasses: (i) Certifying authority – who the certifying authority is (i.e., how well-known the certifying authority is), (ii) Validation period – how long the certificate is valid. For example if it is an old certificate and is still valid for sufficiently long, then that would create a positive impression about B.

Once some or all of these information are available, A evaluates 'properties', according to her own policies, as described in section 2.

Evaluating *Experience*

Most of the information that goes toward forming the properties of the trustee B in a particular privacy context by itself does not necessarily enhance/diminish the truster's trust on B. This is because majority of the above criteria are examples of self-assertions. There is no guarantee that B conforms to these self-assertions. B's behavior as an entity (it includes behavior as a service provider, recommender or just as a community member) in a transaction manifests in the form of *events*. If there are events that conforms to the properties that A has gathered then these events will be termed positive. If the events are contrary to the properties then they are negative. A false or misleading recommendation is also a negative event. Otherwise the events are neutral.

Categorizing an event to positive or negative depends on the truster A's policy, specific activities and violations. Experience is computed by counting how many times (i.e., in how many events) B has deviated from or conformed to self-assertions or provided wrong information. During a specific period of time, number of deviations from the stated self-assertions give number of negative events in that period. The events where B adhered to the self-assertions or provided correct feedback generate positive events.

Evaluating *Recommendation*

As mentioned earlier, evaluation of recommendation involves measuring the feedback provided by other members in the community. Note, however, a group of malicious members can send false good/bad reviews about the server (trustee) to influence the trust decision of the client (truster). The server may or may not be a member of that malicious group. To diminish the effect of such collusion while computing the recommendation, that is to select 'attributable sources' from the whole community, we propose the concept of 'trusted neighbors'. Note, we do not use the term 'neighbor' to mean the physical distance (in terms of length or hop) of a member from the client. We intend to measure how 'close' the member is with the client in terms of trust relationship. We now discuss how a truster builds this set.

Trusted Neighbors

Let there be m members in the community M. To choose the trusted neighbor set, a truster A sets up a neighbor_trust threshold τ_A^{nbr}. Then A broadcasts a ('neighbor_invitation') message to each of the members with whom A has a trust relationship and the value of the trust relationship is $\geq \tau_A^{nbr}$. A considers all members as her trusted neighbor from whom she gets back acceptance message. Therefore 'trusted neighbors' can be defined as

Definition 8. The trusted neighbors of a truster A is the set $TNBR_A$ of all members j where the trust value of j as evaluated by A is greater than or equal to the neighbor_trust threshold set by A and A receives an acceptance of neighbor_invitation from j. Formally, we can write, $TNBR_A = \{j \in M | \ v(A \xrightarrow{c} j)^N \geq \tau_A^{nbr} \wedge A \text{ receives acceptance of neighbor\_invitation}\}$.

The next algorithm formally describes the process of creating trusted neighbor set.

Algorithm 1 *Get the trusted neighbors*
Input: *(i) M – the community of members, (ii) A – the truster whose neighbor set is to be determined, (iii)* $\tau_A^{nbr} (> 0)$ *– neighbor_trust threshold set by A*
Output: $TNBR_A$ *– set of trusted neighbors of A*

Procedure $FindTrustedNeighbor(M, A, \tau_A^{nbr})$
begin
  $TNBR_A = \{\};$
  for *each* $j \in M$
    if $v(A \xrightarrow{c} j)^N \geq \tau_A^{nbr}$
      Send 'neighbor_invitation' message to j;
      if *A receives an acceptance of neighbor_invitation from j*
        $TNBR_A = TNBR_A \cup \{j\};$
  return $TNBR_A;$
end

After computing the trust, the truster checks the privacy policy of the trustee. If it conforms with her privacy preferences in that context, then she controls the disclosure of her information based on the evaluated degree of trust.

4 Privacy Context

As mentioned in section 2, a trust relationship between A and B is never absolute. In privacy platform, a user's trust on another user (service provider or recommender) will depend on how the other user is capable of keeping A's privacy in a specific context. For example, A (truster) can trust the entity B (trustee) to protect her private information collected during a registration procedure. However, that does not necessarily mean that A also trusts B to protect the private information collected while A is making a purchase from B. This leads us to associate a notion of *privacy context* with a trust relationship.

A user typically performs different activities during an online session. These activities can be categorized by their type. We denote each type as a 'context' of user activity. For example, a user may *search* for some document, and when found, she may *download* the corresponding file. The above involves two different contexts of activities, 'searching' and 'downloading'. Some examples of context are *Browse, Download, Purchase, Register, Log-in* etc. We assume the universe of contexts is finite. We observe that context should be defined such that the model is interoperable. Different entities often use different words to describe the same context. Alternately, the same word can be used for describing different contexts. These are example of semantic conflicts in the use of terminology. To solve these problems we borrow some ideas from the work on ontologies [7, 15]. Next, we present our privacy context ontology.

Privacy Context Ontology

Our ontology consists of a set of contexts together with relationships defined among them. First, we formally define the privacy context and later define the relationships between them.

Definition 9. A privacy context C is represented by a set of semantically equivalent keywords, denoted by $keywords(C)$.

Each keyword in $keywords(C)$ is used to describe the privacy context C. The keywords in $keywords(C)$ are semantically equivalent because they express the same context. For each context C we assume that the set $keywords(C)$ is non-empty and finite. Also, for any two semantically distinct privacy contexts C_1 and C_2, we require $keywords(C_1) \cap keywords(C_2) = \emptyset$. That is, any keyword belongs to exactly one context.

We give an example to illustrate the notion of privacy context. Consider the usual registration process in an Web-service. Some sites call it *registration*, some call it *register*, and some sites specify it as *sign-up*. All these different terminologies describe the same process. Therefore we specify any of these privacy contexts by the keyword set {register, registration, sign-up}. Using this notion, we define equality of two contexts as

Definition 10. Two privacy contexts C and C' are said to be equal, denoted by $C = C'$, if and only if $keywords(C) = keywords(C')$.

In the above example, the privacy contexts *register* and *sign-up* are equal.

Relationship Between Privacy Contexts

We define a relation called 'similarity' between distinct privacy contexts. This relation is defined for every pair of contexts in the privacy context set. The similarity relation is reflexive, symmetric, but not transitive. Each similarity relationship is associated with a *degree of similarity*. For two contexts C and C', we denote the degree of similarity by the symbol $sim(C,\ C')$. This indicates the semantic closeness of the two contexts. Since two distinct privacy contexts related by similarity are not exactly identical, the degree of similarity is denoted as a fraction. The exact value of the fraction is determined by the truster using her domain knowledge. Therefore, for two privacy contexts C and C' we have,

$$sim(C,\ C') = \begin{cases} 1 & \text{if } C = C' \\ 0 & \text{if } C \text{ and } C' \text{ are unrelated} \\ d \in (0,1) & \text{otherwise} \end{cases}$$

The similarity relationship will be used in setting up privacy preference rule-set when there is no such preference available in the privacy preference repository for a new context. It will also be used to calculate the initial trust about the trustee on that new context. The degree of similarity together with the trust on the entity in known privacy context will be used to extrapolate the trust on the entity in the new privacy context.

Privacy Context Similarity Graph

The privacy contexts and the similarity relationships between them is represented using a single graph which we refer to as the *privacy context similarity graph*. Each node n_i in the graph corresponds to a context C and is labeled by the set $keywords(C)$. We draw a weighted, undirected edge between two nodes n_i and n_j if degree of similarity between the corresponding contexts is between $(0,1)$. The weight on the edge indicates the degree of similarity between the nodes n_i and n_j. We formally define privacy context similarity graph as

Definition 11. A privacy context similarity graph $PCSG = \langle \mathscr{N}, \mathscr{E} \rangle$ is a weighted undirected graph satisfying the following conditions

1. $\mathscr{N}$ is a set of nodes where each node n_i is associated with a privacy context C_i and is labeled with $keywords(C_i)$, which is the set of keywords associated with the privacy context C_i.
2. For each edge $(n_i, n_j) \in \mathscr{E}$, the weight on the edge (n_i, n_j), denoted by $w(n_i, n_j)$, is in $(0,1)$ and equals to $sim(C_i,\ C_j)$, where C_i and C_j are represented by n_i and n_j respectively.

Figure 1 gives an example of privacy context similarity graph that involves four privacy contexts – *Browse*, *Search*, *Register* and *Log-in*. The weights are assigned by the truster according to her domain knowledge about these four contexts.

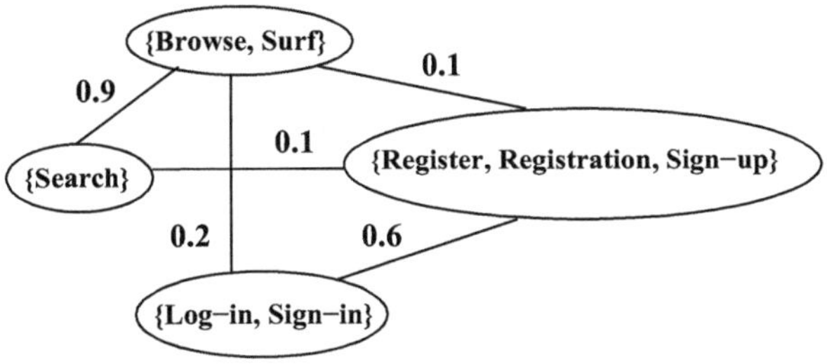

Fig. 1 An example privacy context similarity graph

5 Reasoning about Privacy Preferences and Trust in Different Privacy Contexts

A user (truster) is likely to have different privacy preferences for different privacy contexts, that is user's privacy preferences depend on underlying contexts. In other words, the user will perform certain actions, during a communication with a trustee, in one context and other actions in a different context. For example, a user may disclose her address information while making a 'purchase', but not when she is just 'searching' or 'downloading' something on or from the Web. Such actions, that are to be performed during a communication in a particular privacy context, are specified by the user, according to her own policies, as a set of rules. We call this rule-set for a particular privacy context as *privacy preference rule-set* and formally define it as

Definition 12. A user's privacy preference rule-set for a privacy context C, denoted by $\mathscr{R}_C$, is a set of rules regarding the actions or steps to be performed by the user (truster) when interacting with another entity (trustee) in the privacy context C.

A user (truster) can add/delete/modify these rule-sets according to her own policies. The privacy context keeps switching as the user continues her online activities, thereby continuously changing her privacy preferences. A user maintains a *privacy preference repository* where she keeps her privacy preference rule-sets for entities (trustees) in specific privacy contexts. However, the user may have a privacy preference rule-set for an entity in some context C, but may not have any preference rule-set in context C' in the repository. In this scenario the user, while interacting with that entity, needs to make decision about using some existing privacy preference rule-set.

A user also maintains a trust repository where she keeps the trust about entities in different privacy contexts. For a particular trustee, the user will not have a trust in a new privacy context, irrespective of whether she has or does not have a privacy preference rule-set for that context. After setting up a rule-set the user needs to initiate a trust relationship with the trustee in the new privacy context. This initial trust is calculated using the trust on the trustee in some existing privacy context.

Using an existing privacy preference rule-set from the repository when encountering a new privacy context, or an existing privacy context for which no rule-set is available is reasonable only when the new context is 'similar' to the context for which a privacy preference rule-set is available in the repository. This is also true when extrapolating the initial trust in the new privacy context. The initial trust should be calculated from the trust on the trustee in some 'similar' privacy context available in trust repository. A privacy context may be related to several other privacy contexts through 'similarity' relationship. Nonetheless, we need to find out which context or set of contexts is conceptually closest to the given context. In other words, we need to find the privacy context or set of privacy contexts that has the highest similarity degree with the given privacy context. For this, we first define the concept of *closest privacy context*.

Definition 13. Let C be a privacy context. The set of privacy contexts $\mathscr{C}(C) = \{C_1, \ldots, C_n\}$ is defined to be *closest* to C if the following conditions hold:

1. for all $i \neq j, 1 \leq i, j \leq n$, $sim(C, C_i) = sim(C, C_j)$
2. for all $i = 1, \ldots, n$, $sim(C, C_i) = max(sim(C, C'))$, where C' is any privacy context that is related to the privacy context C.

Note, the set $\mathscr{C}(C)$ can be a singleton set. The following algorithm describes the method for finding the closest privacy context(s) of a given privacy context.

Algorithm 2 *Get the closest privacy context*
Input: *(i) C – the privacy context whose closest one needs to be determined. (ii) PCSG – the privacy context similarity graph in which C is a privacy context*
Output: $\mathscr{C}(C)$ *– set of privacy contexts closest to C*

Procedure $FindClosestContext(C, PCSG)$
begin
  $\mathscr{C}(C) = \{\}$, $relatedContext(C) = \{\}$;
  for *each* $C_i \in PCSG$
    if *there is an edge between nodes corresponding to C and* C_i *in PCSG*
      $relatedContext(C) = relatedContext(C) \cup \{C_i\}$;
  for *each* $C_j \in relatedContext(C)$
    if $sim(C, C_j) = max(sim(C, C_k))$ *where* $C_k \in relatedContext(C)$
      $\mathscr{C}(C) = \mathscr{C}(C) \cup \{C_j\}$;
  return $\mathscr{C}(C)$;
end

Example 1. Consider the privacy context similarity graph shown in figure 1. Suppose a user *Alice* wants to find the closest contexts of the privacy context {Log-in, Sign-in}. The *relatedContext* set for this privacy context is {{Browse, Surf}, {Register, Registration, Sign-up}}. The graph shows that *sim*({Log-in, Sign-in}, {Browse, Surf}) = 0.2 and *sim*({Log-in, Sign-in}, {Register, Registration, Sign-up}) = 0.6. Therefore, $\mathscr{C}$({Log-in, Sign-in}) is found to be the context {Register, Registration, Sign-up} as it has highest similarity degree with the privacy context {Log-in, Sign-in}.

If the privacy context similarity graph *PCSG* has n nodes, then the node corresponding to the privacy context C can be related to at most $n-1$ nodes in the graph. Therefore, at most $n-1$ edges can be in the set $relatedContext(C)$, from which the closest privacy contexts are determined. Thus the algorithm has complexity $O(n)$, where n is the number of nodes in the privacy context similarity graph $PCSG$. However, note, if C was not present in $PCSG$, then the truster needs to update the existing $PCSG$ by including a node corresponding to C and determining the weighted edges between the new node and the existing nodes. This updated $PCSG$ is then used in the above algorithm 2 to find $\mathscr{C}(C)$.

Extrapolating Privacy Preferences from Similar Privacy Contexts

When a user A does not have privacy preferences in a particular privacy context C, we show how she can select one such preference rule-set using one or more similar privacy contexts. Suppose the user A encounters a privacy context C with an entity B and A does not have a privacy preference rule-set for C in the repository. A finds the set of closest privacy context $\mathscr{C}(C)$ using the algorithm 2. If $\mathscr{C}(C)$ is a singleton set, say $\{C'\}$, then the preference rule-set corresponding to C' is retrieved from the repository and set for context C. Now, suppose $\mathscr{C}(C) = \{C_1, C_2, \ldots, C_k\}$ i.e., $\mathscr{C}(C)$ is not a singleton set. Suppose for all $i = 1, \ldots, k$, $\mathscr{R}_{C_i}$ is the privacy preference rule-set corresponding to privacy context C_i. The user A has two choices in this case to set the rule-set for C. She can choose an $\mathscr{R}_{C_i}$ arbitrarily from the available $\mathscr{R}_{C_i}$s. Alternatively, she constructs the rule-set by taking union of all available $\mathscr{R}_{C_i}$s. Algorithm 3 describes the method.

Algorithm 3 *Extrapolate privacy preference rule-set for a new privacy context*
Input: *(i) C – the privacy context for which preference rule-set needs to be set (ii) PCSG – the privacy context similarity graph in which C is a context (iii) The privacy preference rule-set repository* $\mathscr{R}$
Output: $\mathscr{R}_C$ *– privacy preference rule-set for privacy context C*

Procedure $ConstructPreferenceRules(C, PCSG, \mathscr{R})$
begin
  $\mathscr{R}_C = \{\}$; $\mathscr{C}(C) = FindClosestContext(C, PCSG)$;
  if $\mathscr{C}(C) = \{C'\}$
    if $\mathscr{R}_{C'} \in \mathscr{R}$
      $\mathscr{R}_C = \mathscr{R}_{C'}$;
    else *exit;*
  if $\mathscr{C}(C) = \{C_1, C_2, \ldots, C_k\}$
    Case 1: $\mathscr{R}_C = \mathscr{R}_{C_j}$ *for an arbitrary* j *such that* $1 \leq j \leq k$ *and* $\mathscr{R}_{C_j} \in \mathscr{R}$;
    Case 2: $\mathscr{R}_C = \bigcup \mathscr{R}_{C_j}$ *for all* $1 \leq j \leq k$ *such that* $\mathscr{R}_{C_j} \in \mathscr{R}$;
  return $\mathscr{R}_C$;
end

Extrapolating Trust from Similar Privacy Contexts

As mentioned earlier, if a truster A does not have a trust about a trustee B in a privacy context C in her trust repository, then she calculates the initial trust about B in C using the similar privacy contexts of C. For this evaluation, we discuss two scenarios:

Scenario 1: $\mathscr{C}(C) = \{C'\}$ i.e., the closest privacy context set is a singleton set.

In this case A retrieves the normalized trust vector $(A \xrightarrow{C'} B)^N$ with B in privacy context C' and assigns the value $sim(C, C') \times v(A \xrightarrow{C'} B)^N$ as the initial value for the trust relationship $(A \xrightarrow{C} B)^N$. If $v(A \xrightarrow{C'} B)^N = \perp$, i.e., A has no information about trust on B in privacy context C', then she needs to extrapolate $(A \xrightarrow{C'} B)^N$.

Therefore, this extrapolation can be a recursive process.

Scenario 2: $\mathscr{C}(C) = \{C_1, C_2, \ldots, C_k\}$.

A retrieves all the normalized trust vectors $(A \xrightarrow{C_i} B)^N$, $i = 1, 2, \ldots, k$. The initial value for the trust relationship $(A \xrightarrow{C} B)^N$ is calculated as $v(A \xrightarrow{C} B)^N = \frac{1}{k}\sum_{i=1}^{k}[sim(C, C_i) \times v(A \xrightarrow{C_i} B)^N]$. To illustrate the above, we continue with our earlier example.

Example 2. Let *Alice* now want to extrapolate her trust on www.Books.com in the privacy context {Log-in, Sign-in}. In our earlier example, *Alice* finds the closest privacy context of the privacy context {Log-in, Sign-in} as {Register, Registration, Sign-up}. For the sake of brevity, let us denote the privacy context {Log-in, Sign-in} by *Log-in* and the privacy context {Register, Registration, Sign-up} by *Register*. Suppose *Alice* has a trust relationship $(Alice \xrightarrow{Register} www.Books.com)^N$ with the server www.Books.com (trustee) in her trust repository. Suppose $v(Alice \xrightarrow{Register} www.Books.com)^N = 0.8$. Then the initial value of the trust relationship $(Alice \xrightarrow{Log-in} www.Books.com)^N$ is evaluated as $0.6 \times 0.8 = 0.48$.

6 Conclusion and Future Work

In this paper, we introduce a framework that helps the Internet user make reasoned decision regarding release of her private information. Using the framework, a user can make sound choice regarding to whom she should release, why to release, and to what extent, during a transaction in specific privacy context. The framework uses a trust model which is build upon our earlier proposed trust model. In this model trust is expressed as a numeric value within the range $[-1, 1] \cup \{\perp\}$. We identify parameters that influence this trust and propose methods to evaluate them. A mechanism to define relative importance of parameters is also proposed. We posit that a user switch privacy contexts during online sessions and is likely to have different privacy preferences for a trustee in different contexts. We also argue that it is possible that the user does not have a privacy preference as well as a trust in some privacy context. To solve this issue we define an ontology on privacy context. The ontology defines relationship between privacy contexts. This helps a user to extrapolate trust and privacy preferences for a new privacy context from existing privacy contexts.

We plan to extend this work in future. We are currently investigating how to define an operator to combine two privacy context similarity graphs. It will be useful for group of users, working collaboratively, to make privacy related decisions. We need to investigate the possibility of other relationships between contexts, for example generalization/specialization or composition, in the privacy context ontology. We also have plan to evaluate the model by implementing it and then analyzing its performance for privacy protection.

Acknowledgements This work was partially supported by the U.S. Air Force Office of Scientific Research under contract FA 9550-07-10042. The views and conclusions contained in this document are those of the authors and should not be interpreted as representing official policies, either expressed or implied, of the U.S. Air Force or other federal government agencies.

References

1. Ackerman, M., Cranor, L., Reagle, J.: Privacy in E-Commerce: Examining User Scenarios and Privacy Preferences. Communications of the ACM (1999)
2. Bonatti, P., Kraus, S.: Foundations on Secure Deductive Databases. IEEE Transactions on Knowledge and Data Engineering **7**(3), 406–422 (1995)
3. Corp., A.: Privacy Bird Project. http://www.privacybird.org
4. Cranor, L., et al.: The Platform for Privacy Preferences 1.1 (P3P 1.1). Tech. rep., World Wide Web Consortium (2004)
5. Domingo-Ferrer, J.: Inference Control in Statistical Databases from Theory to Practice. Volume 2316. Springer (2002)
6. Goecks, J., Mynatt, E.: Enabling Privacy Management in Ubiquitous Computing Environments Through Trust and Reputation. In: Proceedings of CSCW 2002 Workshop on Privacy in Digital Environments. New Orleans, LA (2002)
7. Gruber, T.R.: A Translation Approach to Portable Ontology Specifications. Knowledge Acquisition **5**(2), 199–220 (1993)
8. Machanavajjhala, A., Kifer, D., Gehrke, J., Venkitasubramaniam, M.: ℓ-diversity: Privacy beyond k-anonymity. ACM Transactions on Knowledge Discovery from Data **1**(1), Article 3 (2007)
9. Nguyen, D., Mynatt, E.: Privacy Mirrors: Understanding and Shaping Socio-technical Ubiquitous Computing Systems. Technical Report GIT-GVU-02-16, Georgia Institute of Technology (2002)
10. Ray, I., Chakraborty, S.: A Vector Model of Trust for Developing Trustworthy Systems. In: Proceedings of the 9th European Symposium on Research in Computer Security, pp. 260–275. Sophia Antipolis, France (2004)
11. Samarati, P.: Protecting Respondents' Identities in Microdata Release. IEEE Transactions on Knowledge and Data Engineering (TKDE) **13**(6), 1010–1027 (2001)
12. Samarati, P., Sweeney, L.: Generalizing Data to Provide Anonymity When Disclosing Information. In: Proceedings of the 17th ACM SIGACT-SIGMOD-SIGART Symposium on Principles of Database Systems. Seattle, WA (1998)
13. Shand, B., Dimmock, N., Bacon, J.: Trust for Ubiquitous, Transparent Collaboration. In: Proceedings of the 1st IEEE International Conference on Pervasive Computing and Communications. Dallas, TX (2003)
14. Sweeney, L.: K-Anonymity: A Model for Protecting Privacy. International Journal on Uncertainty, Fuziness and Knowledge-based Systems **10**(5), 557–570 (2002)
15. Uschold, M., Grüninger, M.: Ontologies: Principles, Methods, and Applications. Knowledge Engineering Review **11**(2), 93–155 (1996)

Acknowledgements This work was partially supported by the U.S. Air Force Office of Scientific Research under contract FA 9550-07-1-0042. The views and conclusions contained in this document are those of the authors and should not be interpreted as representing official policies, either expressed or implied, of the U.S. Air Force Office of Scientific Research or the U.S. Government.

References

[illegible]

Using Virtualization to Create and Deploy Computer Security Lab Exercises

Brian Hay, Ronald Dodge, and Kara Nance

Abstract Providing computer security laboratory exercises enables students to experience and understand the underlying concepts associated with computer security, but there are many impediments to the creation of realistic exercises of this type. Virtualization provides a mechanism for creating and deploying authentic computer security laboratory experiences for students while minimizing the associated configuration time and reducing the associated hardware requirements. This paper provides a justification for using virtualization to create and deploy computer security lab exercises by presenting and discussing examples of applied lab exercises that have been successfully used at two leading computer security programs. The application of virtualization mitigates many of the challenges encountered in using traditional computer laboratory environments for information assurance educational scenarios.

1 Introduction

Creating authentic physical computer security scenarios is a challenging undertaking, requiring a significant commitment of time and effort on the part of the instructor and lab support personnel, but the benefits of hands-on lab experiences is an important part of computer security education. Traditional computer lab environments are typically unsuitable for computer security, information assurance, and networking research and classwork, for a variety of reasons, including a lack of network isolation, the challenges associated with the creation and deployment of scenarios,

Brian Hay, Kara Nance
Department of Computer Science, University of Alaska, Fairbanks, AK 99775,
e-mail: brian.hay@uaf.edu

Ronald Dodge
Department of Electrical Engineering and Computer Science, United States Military Academy, West Point, NY 10996, e-mail: ronald.dodge@usma.edu

Please use the following format when citing this chapter:

Hay, B., Dodge, R. and Nance, K., 2008, in IFIP International Federation for Information Processing, Volume 278; *Proceedings of the IFIP TC 11 23rd International Information Security Conference*; Sushil Jajodia, Pierangela Samarati, Stelvio Cimato; (Boston: Springer), pp. 621–635.

and the legal and ethical issues associated with computer security lab experiences [4]. Virtualization provides a mechanism to mitigate the challenges associated with traditional lab environments, allowing an instructor to easily create and deploy authentic and applicable computer security lab scenarios that allow students to gain practical experience of the concepts presented during classroom lectures.

2 Virtualization

Virtualization provides the ability to create and host multiple machines within one physical machine, thereby allowing the development of complex scenarios with a minimal hardware commitment [2, 17]. To be able to evaluate a student's mastery and understanding of the underlying principles associated computer security scenarios; typically a student demonstrate proficiency. This presents several challenges as identified above. Because the construction of the virtual environment is carefully controlled by the developer, it is possible to create isolated virtual environments within one physical host where the deployment of a virus, which could be difficult to control in a traditional lab environment, can be easily controlled. Another identified challenge, recreation of scenarios, is markedly simple in a virtual environment. Virtualization includes "the ability to create standard configurations for virtual machines, which can then be essentially cloned and used by others[4]." In addition to the great flexibility offered by the virtual machines, the target computers are generally very small, offering the ability to distribute authentic scenarios in virtual environments on a DVD. This simplifies the distribution process as well as the setup time required to recreate a scenario. The use of virtual machines presents students with a full spectrum of hands-on opportunities to learn about, experiment with, analyze, build, and demonstrate competency in a wide range of scenarios.

3 Lab Exercises

The following sections describe the components of various lab exercises supported by multiple virtual machines. While a wide range of commercial and open source virtualization products exist, including Virtual PC/Server [8], VMware [20], QEMU [16], KVM [5], Xen [23], and Parallels [12], the examples presented in this paper were constructed on VMware Workstation. The four examples provide a sampling of computer security scenarios, but are by no means a comprehensive coverage of the rich arena of computer security problems that students are likely to encounter when working as professionals. They are intended to provide instructors with starting points from which additional scenarios can be derived and shared. For standardization, the following scenarios were created using VMware Workstation and use the terminology associated with VMware technologies. The tools used in the labs, at the extent possible, are all open source, freeware tools, or demo versions.

The intent was to design labs with the least possible support overhead. The subject matter and hands-on nature of the labs is such that students will employ procedures and build, configure, and use malware with the intent of exploiting systems (in our case, virtual systems). This methodology is founded on the principle that learning how defensive technologies and practices work is facilitated by understanding the attacks first. As an example, in learning how firewalls work and are configured, it is important to understand how various scanning techniques work to map open firewall ports. A very important precursor to this type of exploration is the explanation of the legal and ethical obligations the student must agree to. Typically this is accomplished through a written agreement between the student and the instructor that explicitly outlines the environment in which the student must operate within.

3.1 Lab Exercise 1 - Demonstration of Basic Security Concepts

The objective of Lab Exercise 1 is to increase students understanding of some of the basic computer security concepts that they are likely to encounter in day-to-day computer use. The target audience for most of the examples given is entry-level computer science students, although components of this lab have been used as a basis for K-12 outreach as well as an example for non-majors. Upon completion of this lab experience, students should be able to define some basic security concepts and also to make informed choices when faced with computer security decisions regarding the associated concepts.

3.1.1 Introduction

Although the majority of computer science students will not focus exclusively on security in their post graduation careers, it is vital that all computer science students have an understanding of the basic concepts of computer security if many of the security failures of the past (and present) are to be avoided in the future. Programmers, IT architects, and managers all need to be aware of the ways in which security vulnerabilities can be introduced into the products they will be responsible for if the state of computer security is to improve. At the University of Alaska Fairbanks (UAF) modules are incorporated into all core classes in the computer science curriculum to address some important practical computer security concepts, such as:

- Carefully validating input rather than blindly trusting it.
- Including security requirements in the initial stages of a project rather than attempting to add them in once the product is functional.
- Understanding the concept of least privilege.
- Building more secure software.

While in-class discussion of these concepts is useful, some lab exercises using virtual machines have been developed at UAF to allow students to observe some classic examples of failures in computer security.

3.1.2 Configuration

The laboratory environment consists of two virtual machines (VMs), named *client* and *server*, connected by a virtual network as shown in figure 1. CentOS[24], a Linux distribution that is a Red Hat Enterprise Linux clone, was chosen as the operating system for both VMs, primarily because it is not only freely available, but also licensed in such a manner that the virtual machines can be easily distributed to students at UAF, and even to other institutions, without violating licensing agreements. However, similar environments demonstrating the same concepts could be constructed using any other mainstream operating systems. The client system includes a web browser (Firefox), a secure shell client, a telnet client, an FTP client, the *passwordDemo* program, the *wget* utility, the *strings* utility, and a network traffic sniffer (*Wireshark*). The server system includes a web server (Apache, listening on ports 80 and 443), a database (MySQL), and the *simpleFileServer* program.

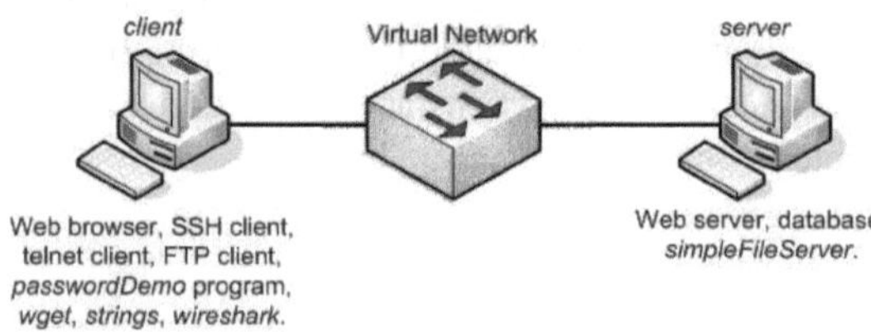

Fig. 1 Network diagram and installed programs/services for the basic security concepts exercise.

3.1.3 Lab Activity

The lab consists of the following activities which can be conducted as one lab or a sequence of lab experiences:

1. **Encrypted versus unencrypted network traffic.** The student starts the network packet sniffer on *client*, then initiates a telnet session to *server*, performs a few basic operations, such as a directory listing and the display of file contents using cat, then logs out. The student can then review the data captured by the packet sniffer, which clearly shows the contents of the session, including the login name, password, and the results of all operations performed in plaintext. The exercise is then repeated using secure shell rather than telnet, at which point the packet sniffer does show that encrypted traffic flowed between *client* and *server*, but there is little additional information revealed, such as the plaintext user name, pass-

word, and operations performed. FTP and SFTP, or HTTP and HTTPS can also be used, and provide similar examples of the use of plaintext versus encrypted network communications. The placement of the packet sniffer on *client* in this exercise rather than on a third system, which would have been more realistic, was the subject of some debate and careful consideration. Ultimately its placement on *client* was chosen in part to simplify the environment, but also to reduce the risk associated with demonstrating packet sniffing to students, particularly if the scenario is distributed beyond the classroom environment. In this configuration the concept of monitoring plaintext and encrypted network traffic can be demonstrated while not providing a system that would gather additional packets in a commonly deployed switched environment, thereby placing the student in a potentially problematic legal situation. On some occasions students have raised the question of whether these techniques only work when the monitor is placed on one of the endpoints, at which point further explanation, and even instructor led demonstrations, can be provided at a level that is appropriate for the maturity of the students in question.

2. **Storing secrets.** A small program named *passwordDemo* is installed on *client*, which ask the user to enter a password, and then responds with either "Access granted" if the correct password is entered, or "Access Denied" otherwise. The goal is for the student to determine the correct password, which is not provided to them, when presented with the executable but not the source code. However, through the use of the *strings* command the students can quickly find all ASCII character sequences in the password, and then use that information to determine what the correct password is. An alternative, although more complex, approach to solving this problem is to patch the *passwordDemo* binary to either modify the password with the program, or even alter the execution sequence.
3. **Buffer overflows.** A small program named *simpleFileServer* is installed on *server*. The program allows a remote user to make a request for a file, which is then returned if it exists within a preconfigured directory, which is essentially the functionality of a very basic web server. The program was written specifically for this exercise, and contains multiple vulnerabilities, including a buffer overflow resulting from a read of up to 255 bytes into a 25 byte array in the *handleConnection()* function. This vulnerability can be trivially used to cause the *simpleFileServer* program to crash, and can, with some additional effort, be used to execute remote user supplied code on server. The program also contains many other relevant problems, including a violation of the least privilege concept (it must be run with elevated privileges in order to bind to port 81, but does not drop to a lower privilege level once that has been accomplished), a time of check versus time of use (TOC/TOU) issue in the *handleGet()* function, and the ability for a remote user to successfully retrieve files outside the designated directory using a directory traversal attack.
4. **Failure to Validate Input.** The web server on server includes a page which performs user authentication based on a username/password combination entered by the user, and which then displays some confidential data if the user is authenticated. The connection between the client and server is secured using SSL,

and as such an attacker monitoring the connection would be unable to view the data, such as the password or confidential data, passed between *client* and *server*. However, the web page uses the username and password supplied by the user directly in an SQL statement, which allows an attacker to perform a classic SQL injection attack which bypasses the username/password check altogether, and allows unauthorized viewing of the confidential material.

5. **Bypassing client verification.** The web server on *server* includes a second page which is very similar to the one used in the previous example, with the exception that it includes JavaScript code to ensure that prior to submission to the web server the username consists of between 1 and 10 alphanumeric characters, and that the password consists of between 1 and 8 digits. These checks appear to provide a defense against the SQL injection attack previously demonstrated, but the attacker can easily bypass this by either creating a modified version of the page that omits the check, by typing the page request directly into the browser's address box, or by using an alternate client, such as *wget*, to send the page request.

3.1.4 Discussion

While these examples are all certainly contrived for use in the lab, there are many real world examples of all of these vulnerabilities which resulted in successful exploits. While these example do not cover all of the ways in which vulnerabilities can be introduced into computer systems, the intent is that students will gain some understanding of how simple (and unfortunately all too common) programming and architectural mistakes can result in devastating exploits. While this lab can be used as an introduction to computer security issues, any of the components can be used as a starting point for a more in depth discussion of computer security topics. For example, programs often need to be able to store and use secrets, such as encryption keys, and while the demonstration showed that hard coding these secrets in executables is likely to be problematic, it is interesting to work through other approaches to solving that problem with students, either as a class lecture, group discussion or individual assignment.

3.2 Lab Exercise 2 - Digital Forensics Investigation

The objective of Lab Exercise 2 is to increase students understanding of the process associated with incident response and addresses a key research area identified in the virtualization in digital forensics research agenda [14]. The target audiences for the examples are extremely varied. Note that the following lab activity description has been necessarily summarized for this paper and can be adjusted to meet the education needs of most digital forensics audiences. The labs are all part of one single larger investigation. Through the completion of the labs, the students will find conflicting indicators and will have to separate out these factors. As an example, content found on the machine under a given user's profile has a created date when a different user was logged in. Upon completion of this lab experience, students should be able to respond to incidents and to help develop policy for incident response at a level consistent with the depth of the laboratory experience.

3.2.1 Introduction

The second lab explores what to do after an incident whether it is malware initiated or the result of illegal activity. Forensics exercises involve many stages of evidence recovery and analysis. To completely evaluate a students understanding of the techniques and requirements for all stages, typically a student needs multiple physical machines. We focus on four primary objectives for our curriculum where multiple computers are needed; chain of custody, network activity monitoring, volatile evidence collection, and hard drive imaging. It is hard to learn these objectives without investigator and target machines. (Typically, if the instructor provides the students with a hard drive image, only chain of custody and image analysis be done without the need for a multiple system environment.) The use of virtual machines presents students with a full spectrum of hands-on opportunities to learn and demonstrate all aspects of digital forensics. The following section describes the components of various digital forensics lab exercises supported by multiple virtual machines. The virtual forensics environment can exist between a physical host and a virtual machine or two virtual machines. Depending on the objectives, the most flexible configuration consists of multiple virtual machines. This setup allows for the investigator's machine to take many forms - from a platform to use standard *nix utilities to full Windows based forensic suites or bootable platforms (for example, Helix, FIRE, or Knoppix). The use of virtual machines is also valuable for the target computer as well. Various operating systems present unique requirements for investigators from analysis of network traffic to log file analysis. As mentioned previously, the examples will use terminology based on VMware workstation. This example lab configuration combines the four objectives identified above and includes only basic tasks for the student to perform. In practice, each objective can be implemented separately and expanded to evaluate tasks in detail as appropriate for varying curricula. More detailed documentation is available through contact with the authors.

3.2.2 Configuration

The laboratory environment consists of two virtual machines, a target machine that is the subject of an investigation, and an investigator's machine. The target computer is configured to dual boot into Windows XP system and Ubuntu 7.2 (minimal install) and the investigator's machine is a Windows XP system configured with a forensic tool suite and other free tools (for example windows dd.exe, Windows Forensic Toolkit, or tools from sysinternals). The virtual machines are configured to connect to a virtual network (VMnet 2). This configuration allows for many options.

First, the target system can be booted to either operating system and placed into a suspend state. The student could then un-suspend the system, presenting each student with identical target computer. Based on the scenario, evidence can be present on both operating systems, requiring the student to understand the differences in how the systems store and interact with files and memory and perform authentication. Second, the investigators system could use either the installed tool suite and freeware tools or be booted into a forensics platform.

3.2.3 Lab Activity

Lab example: The target computer booted in Win XP. Based on the collection exercise, the investigator's system will vary.

1. **Chain of Custody.** Evidence chain of custody is arguably the most important step in a digital forensics investigation. This lab requires the student to identify the objectives of an investigation, determine the support requirements, develop a case outline, and implement chain of custody documentation.
2. **Network Traffic Analysis.** The network activity of a computer may be very useful in determining where to start an investigation, if the incident has spread to other computers in the network, and possible attribution to the source of the compromise. In this exercise, the student may use a variety of tools including wireshark [22], tcpdump [19], SNORT [18], and Nmap [10] to capture and analyze the network traffic of a compromised computer. As part of the preparation for the lab, the target machine was compromised and from the network activity the student should identify that the computer is sending out data to an IP address using UDP. Additionally from a port scan, the student should identify several open ports with established connections indicating malicious services including IRC [11].
3. **Image Capture.** Proper image capture is essential for a complete and valid investigation. Use dd to remotely (over the virtual network) image the target system or read-only mount the virtual disk file an image locally (done using a Linux based investigation platform). Students are taught how a virtual disk can be mounted in a different virtual machine. Since the mounting will not take place using a physical write block device, part of the student instruction is how to mount a device in read only mode. As a demonstration of a capability, the students also use Liveview [6] to create VMware virtual machine from the newly acquired dd image.
4. **Volatile Memory Collection.** An area that is often overlooked is the capture of volatile memory. Students use a collection of tools, such as dd, pmdump [13] to collect and WinHex [21] to analyze the contents of volatile memory.
5. **System Log Collection.** Like virtual memory collection, system logs present on a system can provide a valuable source of information, ranging from service failures to failed/successful login-ins. In some instances, an investigator will want to extract these logs prior to shutting down a target system. The student can

use psloglist [15] or dumpel.exe [3], a tool in the Microsoft Product Support Reporting Tool Suite, to collect system logs from the Windows target system.
6. **Analyze the imaged disk.** The area where significant information is gained is through direct interaction with the target data. While this could be done without the aide of virtual machines, it is an important step in the progression of labs. The student uses forensics suites, freeware tools, or booted investigation platform to complete the investigation of various file system and partition artifacts.

3.2.4 Discussion

Each of these steps could be completed using the tools indicated or others available either from a commercial or open source suites running on Windows, Linux, or a booted platform (Helix). The depth of the labs provided here is presented as an overview and provide only an example of the breadth of capability. In practice each topic within the labs is richly expanded to include additional methods to obtain the needed information or a detailed series of questions about the state of the target system, and the amount of information. The amount of detailed guidance provided to the students can be adjusted to meet the needs of the target population. Examples of extensions to the lab include activities such as mining files for information. This topic can be developed further to discuss file type obfuscation to alternative data streams to data carving. This ability to incorporate a depth component in a versatile environment provides a scalable experimentation environment for education and training.

3.3 Lab Exercise 3 - Botnets

The objective of Lab Exercise 3 is to increase student understanding of the concept of a botnet and the security measures associated with managing this threat. The target audiences for the examples are entry-level computer science students, but more advanced students also find this lab intriguing. Upon completion of this lab experience, students should understand how botnets can be created and deployed.

3.3.1 Introduction

Much like the previous example, investigation of malware from an attacker's perspective benefits as well from virtualization. This example details an environment to build and deploy a botnet. The exploit will start like many others; a user visits a compromised website and gets compromised. The bot will then not only allow control over the compromised computer, but it will also seek out other vulnerable systems and extend the size of the botnet. The lab exercise is configured to allow for exploration of malware signatures of a compromise on the target system as well from the network.

3.3.2 Configuration

As in the previous lab environments, we can elect to use a variety of operating systems for the lab based on the tools selected. The specific lab described here uses a Windows XP virtual machine for the attack computer, a Linux based firewall/router, and Windows XP and 2003 virtual machines for the target computers. The configuration of the laboratory environment is shown in Figure 2.

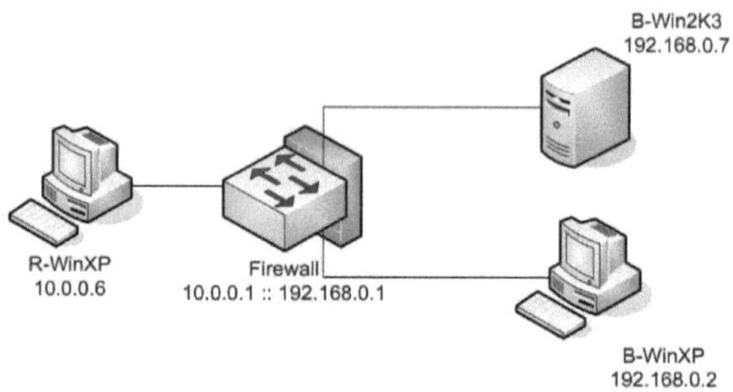

Fig. 2 Botnet lab virtual machine network

3.3.3 Lab Activity

The lab is broken down into four major phases as described below. As with the previous lab, the phases have been necessarily summarized and more information can be provided upon request.

1. **Setting up the attack computer.** The attack computer is set up in three stages. First, the development environment needs to be setup to compile the bot. For simplicity, we use lcc-win32 [7]. The student installs the executable (accepting all defaults). The next step is to configure the control channel using Office IRC. The student would install Office IRC and then launch the Remote Control application to configure a new IRC channel (call it "#botc0ontrol"). in the next step the student will mIRC (an IRC client) [9] to issue commands to your army of bots. The student will configure mIRC to connect to OfficeIRC on localhost and connect to the new control channel, "#botcontrol".
2. **Compiling sdBot.** On the attack computer, start the lcc-win32 and open the sdBot C code file (this can be found through Google, however it is provided to the students). The students will analyze the code to understand how it works and ensure the parameters are set to connect to the IRC server previously setup. After

the code is compiled, a new file called "sdbot06b.err.exe" is created; this is the payload.
3. **Infecting the victim(s).** On the attack computer, the student verifies the file "bot.htm" is in the c:\ Inetpub\ wwwroot directory and copys in the "sdbot06b.err.exe" file. On the target Windows XP virtual machine, the student opens an IE browser and navigates to the web site on the attack computer (http://10.0.0.6/bot.htm). On the victim Windows XP virtual machine, the student should run the *netstat* command and should then see an outbound connection to the IRC server and several connection requests on port 445 (this is the bot trying to spread!).
4. **Wreaking havoc.** On the firewall, the student will start monitoring traffic flowing over the firewall using *Wireshark*. From the attack Windows XP virtual machine, the student will use mIRC to tell the bot to ping the firewall 100 times. This should see the pings on the *Wireshark* monitor on the firewall.

3.3.4 Discussion

This lab provides a brief example of how you can, in an isolated and secure environment, create, configure, and experiment with malware. As described earlier, the full labs (available from the authors) have much more detail and additional steps designed to explore techniques to prevent, discover, mitigate, and recover from exploitation. The focus of the lab is for the student to understand how malware gets on a target system, installed, and what it is capable of doing. In the context of the whole course, the intent behind using and understanding the malware is to understand how to detect, mitigate, and defeat it. Once the malware (whether it be a bot or another example) is understood, the student can follow additional labs that demonstrate the effectiveness of various defensive technologies.

3.4 Lab Exercise 4 - War Games

The objective of Lab Exercise 4 is to provide students with experience with offensive and defensive techniques related to computer security. The target audiences for is exercise is advanced computer science students with experience in computer security. Upon completion of this lab experience, students should understand some of the steps that can be taken to defend a system against threats they may encounter.

3.4.1 Introduction

This exercise has been used on several occasions towards the end of an upper division computer security course, and it involves the use of both defensive and offensive techniques. The class is divided into groups of 4-5 students, and the exercise is typically held over the course of 10-14 days near the end of the semester.

3.4.2 Configuration

Each group of students is given access to 1 or more physical hosts, on which virtualization software, such as VMware Workstation, is installed. The systems are connected by a wired network which is physically isolated from any other network to ensure that any malicious traffic during the exercise cannot impact production systems. Figure 3 shows the network configuration for this exercise.

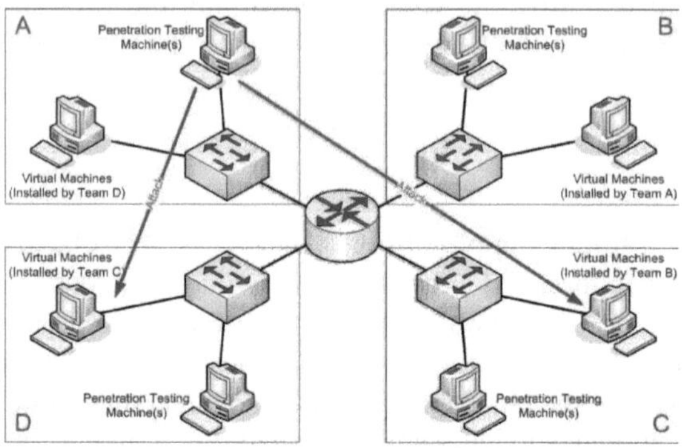

Fig. 3 War Games network configuration for example class consisting four teams.

3.4.3 Lab Activity

The exercise consists of four components, three of which are undertaken in the lab environment. The initial task is for each group of students to install and configure a small number (3-4) of virtual machines on one of their physical hosts. Students are free to select the operating system and installed applications for each VM, but they are required to include at least 5 network accessible services, which must remain accessible to all participants throughout the exercise. Groups are free to configure the operating systems, services, and applications, and can also optionally install additional services and applications, extra accounts, rootkits, scheduled tasks, etc. Routing between the subnets assigned to each of the teams is disabled at the central router during this period to ensure that teams do not begin the second and third components of the exercise prior to the scheduled start date. The second and third components of the exercise occur concurrently, and involve the teams attempting to defend their systems, while also attempting to compromise the systems assigned to other teams. This section of the exercise begins with an exchange of systems, so that each team is charged with defending a set of systems installed by another team.

Team leaders are required to meet to exchange the virtual machines, which really just involves moving to a new physical workstation rather than moving the virtual machines themselves. Administrator/root passwords for the physical workstations and virtual machines, and the list of 5 required services are also passed on at this point. For example, in an exercise with six teams Team A would pass their configured virtual machines, Administrator/root passwords, and required services to Team B, while receiving a set of virtual machines, Administrator/root passwords, and required services from Team F. Once the exchange has occurred, the central router is reconfigured to allow network communication between the teams, and the teams are immediately responsible for defending their systems from attack, while ensuring that their required services remain operational. As part of this defensive effort, teams are free to modify the configurations of the services, disable unnecessary services, install additional tools or systems, and change operating system, application, or service vendors, versions or patch levels. During this process the team that installed the systems can also monitor the system to ensure that the required services remain functional, as can the instructor (who can attempt to connect to the services from any of the subnets, ensuring that filtering based on source IP address is not an effective defense). Each team is also charged with penetration testing the other teams' systems, with the exception that they are not permitted to attempt to compromise the systems they designed, nor are they permitted to share information about the configuration with other teams. For example, Team A will perform a penetration test on the systems being defended by Team C, Team D, Team E, and Team F. (They are not permitted to perform penetration tests on the systems defended by Team B as they designed and built that system.) They will have no information about these systems other than their subnet, and as such will begin by attempting to map the systems, followed by a vulnerability analysis, and ultimately culminating in a successful exploit if time and conditions permit. The penetration testing is conducted from one or more additional physical workstations assigned to each team, on which they were allowed to preload virtual machines for use in the penetration testing effort. These active components of the exercise are typically conducted over 2 days, which allows each of the team members an opportunity to participate regardless of their class/work schedule. In addition, scheduling the exchange of systems for the start of a class period, and then immediately starting this phase of the exercise gives students a guaranteed session in which they can participate when they are most needed (i.e., when the systems they are defending and attacking are likely to be most vulnerable). The final component of the exercise is the preparation of a report and a presentation to the class by each group. The reports include:

- A description of the environment that the team installed, including the required services, known vulnerabilities, and other relevant information.
- A description of the systems they were given to defend, including the vulnerabilities they discovered and the steps they took to address them.
- A description of attacks that were detected. In some cases these are attacks that were prevented, and in other cases the attacks were successfully executed and only discovered at some later point.

- The results of their penetration testing efforts, including the tools used, information gathered, exploits attempted, and successful compromises (if any).

3.4.4 Discussion

While there are other approaches to running this type of exercise, such as those modeled around the Collegiate Cyber Defense Competition [1], this approach provides many of the same opportunities with significantly fewer people involved in running the exercise, and can essentially be organized by a single instructor. It is important that the students involved in this effort are sufficiently mature to be charged with the use of offensive tools, despite the environment being carefully controlled and physically isolated from any other network. In the past students have been encouraged to be creative during this exercise, but also encouraged to check for instructor permission prior to attempting anything they have any doubt about, and certainly prior to doing anything that involves the use of systems other than those assigned directly to their team. Examples of activities that students have requested clarification for which were subsequently disallowed include physical access to other team's workstations, access to the core router configuration, and spoofing email messages outside the lab environment. However, on two occasions a team requested and was given permission to create a new webmail account in an attempt to acquire password information from the other teams. As a result, a hotmail account was created which contained the name of the instructor, which was then used, successfully in two independent cases, to request password information from the members of other teams. Other teams recognized the attempted attack, and in some cases changed their communication processes to include encryption or digital signatures to thwart further attempts. The in-class presentations often spark interesting discussion amongst the students, and in some cases the vulnerabilities found and exploited were not known to the team charged with initially configuring the environment.

4 Summary

The primary purpose of this paper was to provide examples of real labs being used in university settings to teach information assurance concepts. There has been much discussion on how to best design the physical architecture of information assurance labs, but little on the learning modules themselves. In this paper we discussed, in a summary fashion, four exercises that demonstrate the technique for applying virtualization in the classroom or lab. The exercises described, provide students with hands-on opportunities to learn concepts ranging from introductory to complex. It is important to note that while virtualization makes it trivial to create multiple copies of systems and distribute them with ease, that doesn't mean it is legal. When doing this, one must ensure that the quantity of software licenses (for applications and operating systems) is appropriate. A further consideration is that students are working with malware and learning techniques that may be applied maliciously and the associated legal and ethical considerations should be directly addressed. The authors have implemented the exercises described in this paper with great success. Additional material covering the physical infrastructure for virtual laboratories, extensions to the exercises described in this paper, and additional exercises are available through direct contact with the authors.

References

1. Official Collegiate Cyber Defense Competition Web site (n.d.) Retrieved December 18, 2007 from http://www.nationalccdc.org/
2. Crosby, S. and Brown, D. The Virtualization Reality. ACM Queue, December/January 2006-2007, pp.34-4
3. Dumpel.exe. Retrieved from the Microsoft Product Support's Reporting Tools web site on December 18, 2007 from http://www.microsoft.com/downloads/details.aspx?FamilyID=cebf3c7c-7ca5-408f-88b7-f9c79b7306c0displaylang=en)
4. Hay, B., K. Nance, and C. Hecker. Evolution of the ASSERT Computer Security Lab. Proceedings of the 10th Colloquium for Information Systems Security Education. Adelphi, MD. June 2006.
5. Kernel based Virtual Machine. Retrieved November 18, 2007 from http://kvm.qumranet.com/kvmwiki.
6. Liveview sourceforge website retrieved December 18, 2007 from.http://liveview.sourceforge.net/
7. lcc-win32 retrieved on December 18, 2007 from http://www.cs.virginia.edu/ lcc-win32/
8. Microsoft Virtual PC Server. Retrieved July 15 from http://www.microsoft.com/windowsserversystem/virtualserver/
9. mIRC retrieved on December 18, 2007 from http://www.mirc.com/
10. Nmap website retrieved December 18, 2007 from http://nmap.org/
11. Office IRC retrieved on December 18, 2007 from http://www.officeirc.com/
12. Parallels. Retrieved July 25, 2007 from http://www.parallels.com/
13. Pmdump website retrieved December 18, 2007 from http://www.ntsecurity.nu/toolbox/pmdump/
14. Pollitt, M., Nance, K., Hay, B., Dodge, R., Craiger, P., Burke, P., Marberry, C., and Brubaker, B. Virtualization and Digital Forensics: A Research and Education Agenda in Journal of Digital Forensic Practice. Taylor and Francis, Philadelphia, PA.
15. psloglist retrieved from the Microsoft sysinternals web site on December 18, 2007 from http://technet.microsoft.com/en-us/sysinternals/default.aspx
16. QEMU (nd) Open Source Process Emulator. Retrieved on November 18, 2007 from http://fabrice.bellard.free.fr/qemu/.
17. Rosenblum, M. (2004) The Reincarnation of Virtual Machines. ACM Queue. July/August 2004 ACM.
18. Snort website retrieved December 18, 2007 from http://www.snort.org/
19. TCPdump website retrieved December 18, 2007 from http://www.tcpdump.org/
20. VMware. Retrieved November 18, 2007 from http://www.vmware.com.
21. Winhex website retrieved December 18, 2007 from http://www.winhex.com/winhex/
22. Wireshark website retrieved December 18, 2007 from http://www.wireshark.org/
23. Xensource. Retrieved July 27, 2007 from http://www.xensource.com/xen/xen/nfamily/virtualpc/default.mspx
24. CentOS. Retrieved December 17, 2007 from http://www.centos.org/modules/tinycontent/index.php?id=15

DigForNet: Digital Forensic in Networking

Slim Rekhis, Jihene Krichene, and Noureddine Boudriga

Abstract Security incidents targeting information systems become more complex and sophisticated, and intruders might evade responsibility due to the lack of supporting evidences to convict them. In this paper, we develop a system for Digital Forensic in Networking (DigForNet) which is useful to analyze security incidents and explain the steps taken by the attackers. DigForNet uses intrusion response team knowledge and formal tools to reconstruct potential attack scenarios and show how the system behaved for every step in the scenario. The attack scenarios identification is automated and the hypothetical concept is introduced within DigForNet to alleviate lack of data related to missing evidences or investigator knowledge.

1 Introduction

Faced to the increase and sophistication of security incidents, security experts have started giving a great interest to the digital forensic investigation of security incidents. Defined in the literature as *preservation, identification, extraction, documentation and interpretation of computer data* [1], digital investigation aims to perform a post-incident examination of the compromised systems to identify conducted attack scenarios and attackers source, understand what occurred to prevent future similar incidents, and argument the results with non refutable proofs.

Performing a digital investigation is a challenging task. First, attacks may use multiple sources and become difficult to trace using available traceback techniques. Second, systems may not be initially prepared for investigation, leading to the absence of effective logs and alerts to be used for understanding the incident. In addition, the attackers may use a number of techniques to hide traces left on the compro-

---

Slim Rekhis[1], Jihene Krichene[2], and Noureddine Boudriga[3]
Communication Networks and Security Research Lab. University of the 7th of November at Carthage, Tunisia, e-mail: [1]slim.rekhis@isetcom.rnu.tn, [2]jkrichene@gmail.com, [3]nab@supcom.rnu.tn

---

Please use the following format when citing this chapter:

Rekhis, S., Krichene, J. and Boudriga, N., 2008, in IFIP International Federation for Information Processing, Volume 278; *Proceedings of the IFIP TC 11 23rd International Information Security Conference*; Sushil Jajodia, Pierangela Samarati, Stelvio Cimato; (Boston: Springer), pp. 637–651.

mised system. Third, attack scenarios may use several automated tools that create intensive damaging activities. A large amount of data should thus be analyzed.

To face the above complexity, the digital investigation should, first, be well structured by reconciling both the expertise of the incident response team (IRT) and the use of formal reasoning techniques about security incidents. This reconciliation allows to: a) better filter the data to be analyzed and source of evidences to be explored, based on the skills developed by the IRT, and b) validate the results of the formal techniques by the IRT before presenting them and exploit them to accumulate knowledge about security incident. Second, digital investigation should integrate the use of formal techniques that are useful to develop non-refutable results and proofs, and avoid errors that could be introduced by manual interpretations. Moreover, it should consider the development of tools to automate the proof providable by these formal methods. Third, since the collected evidences may be incomplete and describing all potential malicious events in advance is impractical, hypotheses need to be put forward in order to fill in this gap.

Despite the usefulness of formal approaches, digital investigation of security incidents remains scarcely explored by these methods. Stephenson took interest in [8] to the root cause analysis of digital incidents and used Colored Petri Nets to model occurred events. The methodology may become insufficient if there is a lack of information on the compromised system that requires some hypotheses formulation. Stallard and Levitt proposed in [7] an expert system with a decision tree that exploits invariants relationship between existing data redundancies within the investigated system. To be usable with highly complex systems, it is imperative to have a prior list of *good state* information, otherwise the investigator has to complete its analysis in Ad-hoc manner. Gladychev provided in [2] a Finite State Machine (FSM) approach to the construction of potential attack scenarios discarding scenarios that disagree with the available evidences. However, if some system transitions (e.g., malicious event) are unknown, the event construction may freeze.

We develop in this paper, a system for Digital Forensic in Networking (DigForNet). It integrates the analysis performed by the IRT on a compromised system, through the use of the Incident Response Probabilistic Cognitive Maps (IRPCMs). DigForNet provides a formal approach to identify potential attack scenarios using I-TLA logic. The latter allows to specify different forms of evidences, and identify an attack scenario as a series of elementary actions retrieved from a used library, that, if executed sequentially on the investigated system, would produce the set of available evidences. To develop the concept of executable attack scenarios showing with details how an attack is performed progressively on the system, DigForNet uses I-TLC, an automated verification tool for I-TLA specifications. To handle unknown attacks, DigForNet integrates a technique for generating hypothetical actions to be appended to the scenario under construction.

DigForNet contribution is three-fold. First, to the best of our knowledge, it is the first investigation system that reconciles in the same framework conclusions derived by the incident response team and theoretical and empirical knowledge of digital investigators. Second, using the concept of hypothetical actions, DigForNet stands out from the other existing approaches and allows to generate sophisticated and unknown attack scenarios. Third, most of the techniques brought by DigForNet can be automated which makes it a promising computer-assisted investigation tool.

This paper is organized as follows. Section 2 describes the DigForNet's methodology for reasoning about security incidents. The use of the IRPCM technique is described in Section 3. Section 4 describes I-TLA as a logic for specifying evidences and identifying potential attack scenarios that satisfy them. It also shows how to pass from IRPCM to I-TLA specification. Section 5 introduces I-TLC showing how it can be used to generate executable attack scenarios. Section 6 illustrates with an example the use of DigForNet in investigating a real security incident. Finally, Section 7 concludes the paper.

2 Methodology of structured investigation

DigForNet methodology is composed of five steps in a waterfall model as shown in Figure 1. The first step collects evidences available within three different sources, namely the operating systems, networks, and storage systems. DigForNet integrates the incident response team contributions under the form of Incident Response Probabilistic Cognitive Maps (IRPCMs). An IRPCM is nothing but a directed graph representing security events, actions and their results. It is built during the second step with a collaborative fashion by the IRT members based on the information collected on the system. IRPCMs provide a foundation to mainly investigate and explain occurred security attacks.

The third step generates a formal specification. Sets of evidences and actions are extracted from the cognitive map for the formal specification of the potential attack scenarios. A formal approach is necessary for this purpose. DigForNet uses a logic, referred to as I-TLA, to generate a specification containing a formal description of the set of extracted evidences and actions, the set of elementary attack scenario fragments retrieved from the library of elementary attacks, and the initial system state. In this step, DigForNet uses I-TLA to prove the existence of potential attack scenarios that satisfy the available evidences. To be able to generate a variety of attack scenarios, DigForNet considers the use of a library of elementary actions supporting two types of actions: legitimate and malicious. Malicious actions are specified by security experts after having assessed the system or appended by investigators upon the discovery of new types of attacks.

The fourth step generates of executable potential attack scenarios using a model checker tool associated with the formal specification. DigForNet uses Investigation-based Temporal Logic Model Checker called I-TLC. The latter rebuild the attack scenarios in forward and backward chaining processing, showing details of all intermediate system states through which the system progresses during the attack. I-TLC provides a tolerance to the incompleteness of details regarding the investigated incident and the investigator knowledge. It interacts with a library of hypothetical atomic actions to generate hypothetical actions, append them to the scenarios under construction, and efficiently manage them during the whole process of generation.

The library of hypothetical atomic actions is composed of a set of entries showing interaction between a set of virtual system components and a set of rules used to efficiently create hypothetical actions as a series of hypothetical atomic actions.

The fifth step uses the generated executable potential attack scenarios to identify the risk scenario(s) that may have compromised the system, the entities that have originated these attacks, the different steps they took to conduct the attacks, and the investigation proof that confirms the conclusion. These results are discussed with the IRT members to check the hypotheses added by I-TLC and update the initial IR-PCM where concepts can be omitted because they do not present an interest for the attack scenario construction, while other concepts corresponding to the hypothetical actions can be added to the IRPCM and linked to the other concepts. Links in the IRPCM are deleted in the case where the concepts at their origin or end are omitted. Hypothetical actions are also added to the attack library. In addition, tools collecting the evidences are enhanced to detect the newly discovered vulnerabilities.

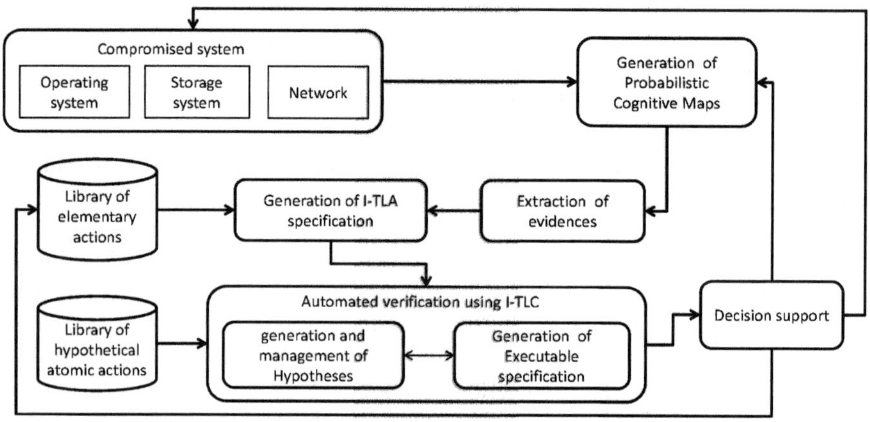

Fig. 1 DigForNet Methodology

3 Intrusion Response Probabilistic Causal Maps

We have studied in [3] a new category of cognitive maps to support intrusion response. In this paper, we provide an extension to these cognitive maps referred to as Incident Response Probabilistic Cognitive Maps (IRPCMs) by introducing the notions of probability and activation degree of concepts. IRPCMs provide a foundation to investigate and explain security attacks which have occurred in the past and predict future security attacks. These aspects are important for negotiation or mediation between IRT members solving thus disparities which are generated by the difference in their view points and which can lead to conflict between them.

3.1 IRPCM definition

An Incident Response Probabilistic Cognitive Map (IRPCM) is a directed graph that represents intrusion response team members' experience-based view about security events. In this graph, the nodes represent concepts belonging to the network security field, while the edges represent relationships between the concepts.

IRPCM concepts can be symptoms, actions, and unauthorized results related to network security field. Symptoms are signs that may indicate the occurrence of an action (e.g., system crashes, existence of new user accounts or files). An action is a step taken by a user or a process in order to achieve a result (e.g., probes, scans, floods). An unauthorized result is an unauthorized consequence of an event (defined by an action directed to a target, e.g., increased access, disclosure of information). IRPCM concepts are labeled by values in the interval $[0,1]$ informing about the activation of the correspondent concepts.

IRPCM edges link concepts to each others. Each edge e_{ij} linking concept c_i to concept c_j is labeled as (π_{ij}, q_{ij}) where π_{ij} is the predicate expressing the relationship between the two nodes (examples include $<_t$, I/O, CE) and q_{ij} (taking values in $]0,1]$) is the probability expressing the certitude degree that the relationship π_{ij} really exists between concepts c_i and c_j. Quantitative values are given by security experts. Notice that the predicate π_{ij} depends on the nature of the concepts c_i and c_j. For the reason of simplicity, we consider four cases in this paper:

1. c_i is a symptom and c_j is a symptom or an action: π_{ij} expresses an input/output relationship ($\pi_{ij} = I/O$). Part of output of c_i is the input of c_j.
2. c_i and c_j are two actions: π_{ij} expresses a temporal relationship between the two concepts ($\pi_{ij} =<_t$). c_i is an action that precedes c_j.
3. c_i is an action and c_j is an unauthorized result: π_{ij} expresses the causality existing between the action and the unauthorized result ($\pi_{ij} = CE$).
4. c_i and c_j are the same concept: π_{ij} is the identity.

3.2 Building IRPCMs

The IRT members are responsible for building the IRPCM (second step in the DigForNet methodology). The basic elements needed in this activity are the events collected on the Information System. These events may be IDS alerts, compromises of network services, or any sign indicating the occurrence of a malicious action against the network. IRT members analyze these signs and define the appropriate symptoms, actions and unauthorized results and assign the appropriate probabilities and relationships to the edges linking the defined concepts. The process of building an IRPCM has two properties: completeness (if an attack has occurred and a sufficient number of events are collected to identify this attack, then we can find an IRT able to build an IRPCM allowing to identify the attack) and convergence (if an IRPCM is built and is large enough to collect all the events related to a given attack, then the IRT must build in a finite time an IRPCM allowing to provide the right solution to protect against this attack).

The building of an IRPCM follows seven steps:

1. Collect security events observed in the compromised system or detected by security tools.
2. Build an IRPCM based on the collected events.
3. Continue to collect security events.
4. Update the IRPCM based on the collected events. Events which do not belong to the previous IRPCM are added. Links related to the newly considered concepts are also added to the IRPCM.
5. Refine the IRPCM by omitting the nodes that the IRT members find not interesting for the investigation activity.
6. Update the probabilities of the links and the activation degree of the concepts.
7. If the stopping criterion is satisfied, stop the IRPCM building process; else, return to step 4.

Two criteria can be considered to decide about the end of the IRPCM building process. The first is when all the candidate actions in the library (those which have a relationship with the collected events) are present in the IRPCM. The second is based on the decision of the IRT members. If the latter agree that the IRPCM is large enough, then the building process is stopped. The IRT decision can be shared by all the members or it can be taken by a mediator.

3.3 Activation degree of a concept

IRPCM concepts values give indications about their activation. These values, referred to as activation degrees, belong to the interval $[0,1]$. We define the function dac to assign activation degrees to the concepts as follows:

$$\begin{aligned} dac\colon\ C &\rightarrow [0,1] \\ c &\mapsto dac(c) \end{aligned}$$

A concept is said to be dac-activated if its activation degree is equal to 1. In the following, we show how to build a dac function based on a given set of selected concepts in the IRPCM. Let I be the set of concepts related to collected events of involvement in attack with respect to detected intrusions. $I = \{c_1 \cdots c_n\} \subseteq C$.

1. Let $dac(c_i) = 1$, $i = 1 \cdots n$.

2. Compute iteratively the remaining activation degrees as follows: Let F be the set of the concepts for which we have already computed the activation degree. F is initially equal to the set I.
3. Let G be the set of concepts that have a relation with one or more concepts belonging to F. $G = \{c \in C/\exists d \in F, (d,c) is\, a\, relation\}$. Then, $dac(c) = sup_{d \in G}\{q_{dc}dac(d)\}$.
4. $F := F \cup G$ and return to step 3 if $F \neq \varnothing$.

In the case where the IRT members have detected malicious actions against the secured system, they construct the IRPCM corresponding to this situation. The concepts that represent the collected events are activated and will form the set I. The activation degree of the remaining concepts is determined according to the previous algorithm. The *dac* function is used in the third step of the DigForNet methodology to extract nodes having a degree greater than a predefined threshold. These nodes will be used as evidences for the formal specification.

4 Generation of a formal specification of attack scenarios

The Investigation-based Temporal Logic of Actions, I-TLA [6], is a logic for the investigation of security incidents. It is an extension to S-TLA logic [5], which is itself an extension to the TLA logic [4]. I-TLA is provided with I-TLA$^+$, a highly expressive formal language that defines a precise syntax and module system for writing I-TLA specifications. I-TLA will be used in this paper to model and specify available set of evidences, and generate a specification describing potential attack scenarios (as a series of elementary actions extracted from a library describing legitimate and malicious events) that satisfy these evidences. In the sequel, we focus on describing the different forms of evidences supported by I-TLA, showing how they can be specified and how they should be satisfied by the expected attack scenario. The reader is referred to [6] for a complete understanding of I-TLA and I-TLA$^+$ and a complete semantic and syntactic description.

4.1 Modeling scenarios and evidences in I-TLA

I-TLA is typeless and state-based logic that allows the description of states and state transitions. A state, while it does not explicitly appear in a I-TLA specification formula, is a mapping from the set of all variables names to the collection of all possible values. An I-TLA specification ϕ generates a potential attack scenario in the form of: $\omega = \langle s_0, s_1, ..., s_n \rangle$, as a series of system states s_i ($i = 0$ to n). This form of representation allows a security expert to observe how its system progresses during the attack and how it interacts with the actions executed in the scenario. I-TLA supports four different forms of evidences, namely history-based, non-timed events-based, timed events-based, and predicate-based evidences.

- **History-based evidences:** I-TLA encodes a history-based evidence, say E, as an observation over a potential attack scenario ω, generated by $Obs(\omega)$. $Obs()$ is the observation function that characterizes the ability of a security solution to provide evidences as histories of the value of the monitored system components, during the spread of an attack scenario. $Obs(\omega)$ is obtained as follows:

    1. Transform very state s_i to $\hat{s}_i$ using a labeling function that makes the value of every variable v in s_i be: invisible (in that case it will be represented by ε), equal to a fictive value, or unmodified.
    2. Delete any $\hat{s}_i$ which is equal to null value (i.e., all values are invisible) and then collapse together each maximal sub-sequence $\langle \hat{s}_i, ..., \hat{s}_j \rangle$ such that $\hat{s}_0 = ... = \hat{s}_i$, into a single $\hat{s}_i$.

    Taking into consideration the availability of a history-based evidence E, consists in generating, an attack scenario ω such that $Obs(\omega) = E$.
- **Ordering of observations:** As the scope of observations differs, they may not allow to notice that the system has progressed during the attack at the same time. I-TLA allows to specify for two given history-based evidences, which one is expected to vary first/last when the attack scenario starts/finishes. Consider the following example involving an attack scenario ω, and two history-based evidences $OBS = [e_1, ..., e_n]$ and $OBS' = [e_1^{'}, ..., e_m^{'}]$, generated by observation functions $Obs()$ and $Obs'()$, respectively. OBS allows to notice the occurrence of an incident before OBS', if and only if: $\exists \omega_x$ such that: $\omega = \omega_x \omega_y \wedge Obs(\omega_x) = [e_1, ..., e_j] \wedge Obs'(\omega_x) = e_1^{'}$ for some j $(1 < j \leq m$.
- **Non-timed events based evidences:** Constructed attack scenarios may differ by the manner in which observations are stretched and stuck together to generate intermediate states of the execution. I-TLA defines non-timed events based evidences in the form of predicates over I-TLA executions, that specify the modification pattern of variables values through an execution. The following evidence E, for instance, states that predicate p_1 switches to value true in the same state the predicate p_2 switches to value false ($E \triangleq \forall \langle s_i, s_{i+1} \rangle \in \omega : (s_i \nvDash p_1 \wedge s_{i+1} \vDash p_1) \Rightarrow s_i \vDash p_2 \wedge s_{i+1} \nvDash p_2)$). Taking into consideration the availability of a non-timed event-based evidence E, consists in generating, an attack scenario ω such that $\omega \vDash E$.
- **Timed events-based evidences:** Starting from a set of available alerts, an investigator can extract some indications related to occurred events. I-TLA defines a timed event-based evidence $E = [A_0, ..., A_m]$ as a set of ordered actions (A_0 to A_m) that should be part of an expected execution without requiring that these events be contiguous. Given a timed event-based evidence $E = [A_0, ..., A_m]$, an execution $\omega = \langle s_0, ...s_n \rangle$ satisfies evidence E if and only if: $\forall (A_x, A_{x+1}) \in E$: $\exists (s_i, s_{i+1}) \in \omega$ such that: $(A_x(s_i, s_{i+1}) = \mathit{true} \wedge A_{x+1}(s_j, s_{j+1}) = \mathit{true}$ for some $j \geq i+1)$.
- **Predicate-based evidences:** An unexpected system property, is a preliminary argument supporting the incident occurrence (e.g., the integrity of a file was violated). I-TLA defines a predicate-based evidence as a predicate, say E, over system states, that characterizes the system compromise. An execution ω satis-

fies evidence E, if E divides ω into two successive execution fragments ω_1 and ω_2. ω_1 is composed of secure states ($\forall s \in \omega_1$: $s \nvDash E$), while ω_2 is composed of insecure system states ($\forall s \in \omega_2$: $s \nvDash E$).

4.2 Illustrative example

We consider a system under investigation which is specified by three variables x, y, and z. The initial system system state, described in advance, states that x, y, and z are all equal to 0. The library of elementary actions, contains two actions A_1 and A_2 that can be executed by the system: $A_1 \triangleq (x' = x) \wedge (y' = y+1) \wedge (z' = z+2)$ and $A_2 \triangleq (x' = x+1) \wedge (y' = y) \wedge (z' = z/2)$.

Action A_1, for instance, keeps the value of variable x in the new state unchanged with respect to the previous state, and sets the values of y and z in the new state 1 and 2 higher than its values in the old state, respectively.

Three different evidences are provided. The first two represent history-based evidences, defined as $E_1 = \langle 0\varepsilon\varepsilon, 1\varepsilon\varepsilon, 2\varepsilon\varepsilon \rangle$ and $E_2 = \langle \varepsilon 0 \varepsilon, \varepsilon 1 \varepsilon, \varepsilon 2 \varepsilon, \varepsilon 3 \varepsilon \rangle$. They are generated by observation functions $Obs_1()$ and $Obs_2()$, respectively. The first observation function $Obs_1()$, allows a security solution to only monitor variable x, meaning that, when applied to a state s, it makes the value of y and z both equal to ε, and keeps the values of variable x unchanged. The second observation function $Obs_2()$ allows a security solution to only monitor variable y. The ordering of observations indicates that observation provided by $Obs_2()$ allows to notice the occurrence of an incident before the observation provided by $Obs_1()$. The third evidence E_3, is provided as a predicate-based evidence defined as $E_3 \triangleq z \geq 1$. The fourth evidence E_4, defined as $E_4 \triangleq \forall \langle s_i, s_{i+1} \rangle \in \omega : (s_i \nvDash p_1 \wedge s_{i+1} \vDash p_1) \Rightarrow s_i \vDash p_2)$, is an non-timed evidence, stating that predicate $p_1 \triangleq x = 1$, which is false in a state s_i, could not switch to true in the next state s_{i+1}, unless predicate $p_2 \triangleq z \neq 4$ is true in that state. Finally, evidence E_5, indicates that sequence of events (A_1, A_2) is part of the attack scenario.

Figure 2 shows how I-TLA guarantees the satisfaction of evidences during construction of the potential attacks. Two potential attack scenario satisfying the available evidences are provided by I-LA, namely ω_1 and ω_2. The first scenario ω_1 is described as $\omega_1 = \langle s_1, s_3, s_4, s_7, s_{12}, s_{15} \rangle$, and consists in consecutively executing the five following actions $A_1 \rightarrow A_1 \rightarrow A_1 \rightarrow A_2 \rightarrow A_2$. The second scenario ω_2 is described as $\omega_1 = \langle s_1, s_3, s_5, s_9, s_{11}, s_{18} \rangle$.

Starting from state s_1, I-TLA cannot execute action A_2 as it moves the system to a state that does not satisfy the ordering of observations. In fact, the sub-scenario $\langle s_0, s_1 \rangle$ is observed by $Obs_1()$ as $\langle 0\varepsilon\varepsilon, 1\varepsilon\varepsilon \rangle$ and by $Obs_2()$ as $\langle \varepsilon 0 \varepsilon \rangle$. The event A_2 is thus detected by E_1 but not by E_2. Starting from state s_4, I-TLA does not execute action A_2 as it moves the system to a state that violates evidence E_4. State s_8 could not be considered in the construction process as it violates predicate E_3. In fact, the predicate $p1$ has became already true in state s_3 and should not change again to false in state s_8. I-TLA discards states s_{13}, s_{14}, and s_{19} as each one of them would create an execution that violates evidence E_2 if appended to the scenario under construction. In the same context, state s_{16} is also not added to the scenario under construction as it creates an execution that violates E_1.

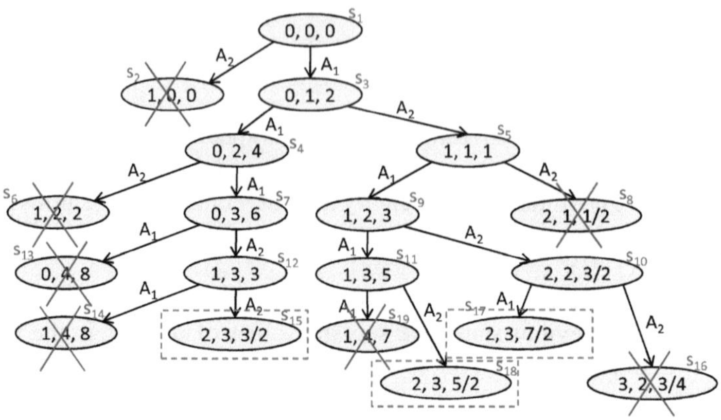

Fig. 2 I-TLA attack scenario generation: an illustrative example

4.3 From IRPCM to I-TLA specification

Starting from the IRPCM built by the IRT, useful information, in the form of symptoms, unauthorized results, or actions, will be extracted and used to formally describe different type of evidences with I-TLA. We denote by useful information, any concept in the IRPCM having a degree of activation value that exceeds some predefined threshold, denoted by extraction threshold.

Symptoms are typically extracted from log files, traffic capture, or even keystrokes. They can be traduced to history-based evidences by transforming the whole content of the log file (including the record indicating the symptom itself) into an I-TLA history-based evidence. Symptoms extracted from alert files indicate the occurrence of events whose position in the constructed attack scenario cannot be determined. They will typically be transformed to a non-timed I-TLA based evidence.

Actions selected from an IRPCM represent steps taken by a user or a process in order to achieve some result. A well intentioned reader has noticed that actions in the I-TLA library and actions in the IRPCM may not have the same form, and are not of the same granularity. In fact, an IRPCM action can be traduced to one or several consecutive I-TLA actions. In this context, for every selected IRPCM action an investigator has to extract sequence of elementary actions from the I-TLA library. The different obtained sequences will represent Timed events-based evidences.

Unauthorized results represent unauthorized consequence of events. They are traduced to I-TLA predicate-based evidences. An investigator identifies the system variable affected by the unauthorized consequence and then uses it to describe the evidence.

5 Executable scenarios generation using I-TLC

To automate the proof in the context of digital investigation and generate executable attack scenarios showing with details how the attack was conducted and how the system progressed for each action part of the scenario, I-TLC [6], a model checker for I-TLA$^+$ specifications can be used. I-TLC is somehow an extension to TLC, the model checker of TLA$^+$ specification.

I-TLC represents a node in the graph as a tuple of two information: *node core* and *node label*. The node core represents a valuation of the entire system variables, and the node label represents the potential sets of hypothetical actions under which the node core is reached. A reading of the node label indicates a) the state of the system in the current node, and b) the alternatives (hypothetical action sets) under which the system state is reachable.

As the generation of potential attack scenarios may fail if the library of actions is incomplete, I-TLC tries to generate a hypothetical action and append it to the graph under construction, whenever available evidences are not completely satisfied. The idea behind the generation of hypothetical actions is based on the fact that unknown actions can be generated if additional details about internal system components (i.e., those abstracted by the specification) is available. This detail involves a description of how these internal system components are expected to behave (if an atomic actions is executed on them) and how they depend on each other. These internal system components are modeled by a specific set of variables denoted by internal variables. The other variables specified by I-TLA are denoted by external variables.

Semantically, a hypothetical action is true or false for a pair of states $\langle s, t \rangle$. Syntactically, a hypothetical action is modeled as a series of hypothetical atomic actions, executed one after the other from state s to move the system to state t. It is defined in the following form $H = m_{ie} h_0 \rightarrow ... \rightarrow h_n m_{ei}$. m_{ie} defines a mapping from the external variables values to the internal variables values in state s and m_{ei} defines a mapping from the internal variables to the external variables in state t. The set of h_i (i from 0 to n) represents executed hypothetical atomic actions. A hypothetical atomic action h_i only modifies a single internal variable, and represents a relation between two consecutive internal system states. During hypothetical actions generation, I-TLC needs access to the library of hypothetical atomic actions. This library describes all the potential hypothetical atomic actions that can be executed on the investigated system.

During scenarios generation, several hypothetical actions may be appended whenever needed. I-TLC manages hypotheses following the two key ideas. First as hypotheses are not completely independent from each others and some hypotheses are contradictory, I-TLC avoids reaching a state under a contradictory situation. In this context, the library of hypotheses indicates potential contradictory sequences of hypothetical atomic actions. Second, in order to ensure that generated hypothetical actions are at the maximum close to real actions performed on the system, I-TLC defines techniques to refine the selection of hypothetical atomic actions.

To generate potential scenarios of attacks, DigForNet uses I-TLC Model Checker, which follows three phases. The reader is referred to [6] for a detailed description of I-TLC algorithms.

1. Initialization phase: During this step, the generated scenarios graph is initialized to empty, and each state satisfying the initial system predicate is computed, appended to the graph with a pointer to the *null* state, and a label equal to $\emptyset$ (as no hypothetical action is generated).

2. Forward chaining phase: The algorithm starts from the set of initial system states, and computes in forward chaining manner all the successor states that form scenarios satisfying evidences described in I-TLA. Successor states are computed by executing an I-TLA action or by generating a hypothetical action and executing it. When a new state is generated, I-TLC verifies if another existing node in the graph has a node core equal to that state. If the case is false, a new node, related to the generated state, is appended to the graph under construction, and linked to its predecessor state. If the case is true, the label of the existing node is updated so that it embodies a sound, consistent, complete, and minimal the set of hypothetical actions under which the new system state is reachable.

3. Backward chaining phase: All the optimal scenarios that could produce terminal states generated in forward chaining phase and satisfy the available evidences, are constructed. This helps obtaining potential and additional scenarios that could be the root causes for the set of available evidences. The new generated predecessor states are managed and appended to the graph under construction with the same manner followed in forward chaining phase.

All potential scenarios are supposed to be generated by I-TLC. The only exception may occur due to the lack of actions in the library of elementary actions. Nonetheless, the use of hypothetical actions allows to alleviate this problem.

6 Case study

We concentrate on the following case study, related to the investigation of a DoS attack against a web server. Upon the occurrence of the incident, DigForNet collects traces from the network IDS, the web server log files, and the storage-based IDS located in the web server.

IRPCM generation

The IRT members analyze the compromised system and the output of the security tools to build the IRPCM. The generated graph is represented in Figure 3 and is composed of six symptoms, seven actions, and two unauthorized results. They appear in by dashed, continuous, and dotted ellipses, respectively. The first steps of the construction process are described as follows. Snort IDS provided two alerts related to the occurrence of a buffer overflow attack and a reconnaissance attack. The web server log file indicates that a malformed URL was used by some users. These alerts form the symptoms linked to the action "probe the web server version". This action precedes the action "Launch a remote buffer overflow on HTTP service". The occurrence of the latter is vindicated by the alert provided by the network monitoring tool. The remote buffer overflow action is used to execute some privileged commands aiming at sending network traffic to an unused port.

Having appended the set of concepts, IRT members define the edges linking the nodes and set their labels. We highlight here the existence of some high probabilities related to edges linking the concepts $S4$ to $A2$, $S5$ to $A6$, and $A6$ to $U2$. The degree of activation of the concepts $S4$, $S5$, $A1$, $A6$ and $U2$ are set to 1 as their existence is well vindicated by the content of the log and alert files provided by the web server, the network monitoring tools, and the NIDSs.

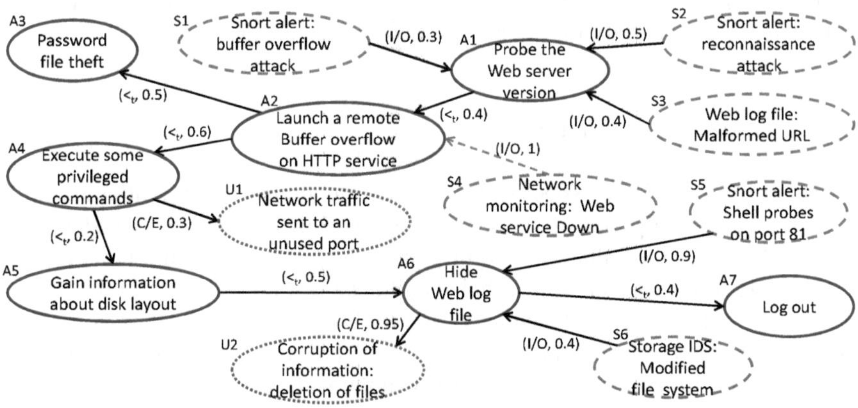

Fig. 3 Case study: Generation of the IRPCM

Extracting evidences from IRPCMs

To extract useful information from the IRPCM, the IRT members defined an extraction threshold equal to 0.9. Concepts in the IRPCM having a degree of activation value that exceeds 0.9 are retained to be translated into I-TLA evidences. The investigated system is modeled using four variables, namely Pr, $Srv80$, $Weblog$, $Srv81$. They represent the privilege granted to the remote user, the service granted on port 80, the tail of the content related to the web service log, and the service granted on port 81. Symptoms $S4$ and $S5$ are traduced to a history-based evidence described in I-TLA in the form of $\langle \varepsilon\text{"}http\text{"}\varepsilon\varepsilon,\ \varepsilon\text{"}noservice\text{"}\varepsilon\varepsilon \rangle$, and $\langle \varepsilon\varepsilon\varepsilon\text{"}noservice\text{"},\ \varepsilon\varepsilon\varepsilon\text{"}/bin/sh\text{"} \rangle$, respectively. The first evidence is generated by the network monitoring tool that allows to monitor variable $srv80$. The second evidence is generated by the NIDS that verifies that none traffic is directed to unused server ports. In other words, it monitors variable $srv81$. The unauthorized result $U2$ is traduced to a predicate-based evidence in the form of $weblog = "\_"$. Each one of actions $A1$ and $A6$ is mapped to a single action in the I-TLA library. These actions are described as follows:

$$Act1 \triangleq \wedge Pr = 0 \wedge Srv80 = "http" \wedge Pr' = 1 \wedge Weblog' = "get/?" \wedge \text{UNCHANGED } \langle Srv81, Srv80 \rangle$$

$$Act3 \triangleq \wedge Pr \geq 2 \wedge Weblog' = "\_" \wedge \text{UNCHANGED } \langle Pr, Srv81, Srv80 \rangle$$

Action $A1$, for instance, cannot be executed unless Pr and $Srv80$ values are set to 0 and "$http$", respectively. Once executed, it sets the value of Pr equal to 1 (a non privileged access is granted), and the value of $Weblog$ equal to "$get/?$" (the tail of the web log file indicates that a specific URL was requested to probe the web server version). Actions $Act1$ and $Act3$ form a timed event-based evidence indicating that sequence $(Act1, Act3)$ is part of the attack scenario. The evidences extracted from the IRPCM in conjunction with the library of elementary actions are then used by the I-TLA logic to specify the set of potential attack scenarios.

Executable scenarios generation by I-TLC

Starting from the I-TLA$^+$ specification, I-TLC generates one potential executable attack scenario, composed of six states, described in Figure 4. Every state in the scenario describes the value of the four system variables used in the I-TLA$^+$ specification. Edges linking states, are labeled by the name of the executed I-TLA action. An attacker gets an unprivileged access to the web server and requests a specific URL that probes the web server version. After that, it conducts a buffer overflow attack, by exploiting a remote vulnerability in the web service. The web service becomes down and the intruder escalates its privilege on the compromised system. In the third step, the intruder executes an anti-investigation attack on the file system, hiding the content of the blocks related to the web log file.

I-TLC has generated some hypothetical actions. For the lack of space, we only kept one hypothesis among those generated. Starting from state s_4, I-TLC could not find in I-TLA specification an action which can be executed. It looks within the library of hypotheses if it is possible to generate a hypothetical action, which if executed, will let the system progress to a state that satisfies all available evidences. I-TLC generates a hypothetical action H and executes it to move the system to state s_6. The hypothetical action consists in attaching a shell to port 81 to be used by a backdoor allowing the intruder to maintain his access to the system. Later the intruder logs out. I-TLC specifies that states s_6 and s_7 are reachable under the hypothetical action H by setting their label equal to the singleton $\{H\}$.

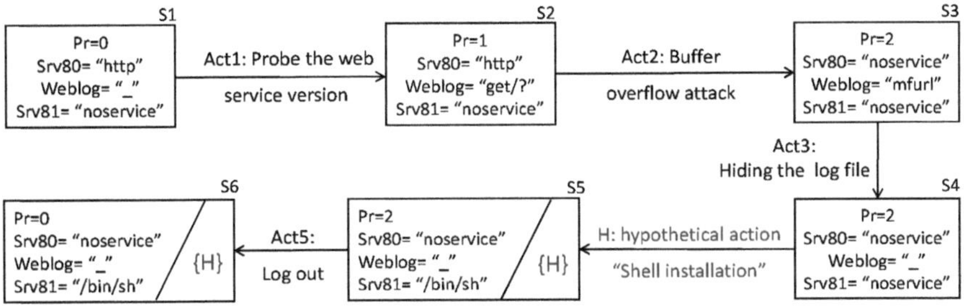

Fig. 4 Executable scenarios generation by I-TLC

7 Conclusion

In this paper we have developed a system for digital investigation of networks security incidents. This system uses formal techniques as well as the IRT members knowledge to analyze the attacks performed against the networks. We have introduced the intrusion response probabilistic cognitive maps that are constructed by the IRT upon the occurrence of the attack. A formal language has been introduced to help specifying the attack scenarios based on the cognitive map. A model checker was built to automatically extract the attack scenarios and a hypothetical concept is introduced here to help in the construction process. To illustrate the proposed system, we used it in a real case of security attack.

References

1. P.D. Dixon. An overview of computer forensics. *IEEE Potentials*, 24(5):7–10, dec 2005.
2. Pavel Gladyshev. Finite State Machine Analysis of a Blackmail Investigation. *International Journal of Digital Evidence*, 4(1), May 2005.
3. Mohamed Hamdi, Jihene Krichene, and Noureddine BOUDRIGA. Collective computer incident response using cognitive maps. In *Proceedings of IEEE conference on Systems, Man, and Cybernetics (IEEE SMC 2004)*, The Hargue, Netherland, October 10-13 2004.
4. Leslie Lamport. The Temporal Logic of Actions. *ACM Transactions on Programming Languages and Systems*, 16(3):872–923, May 1994.
5. Slim REKHIS and Noureddine BOUDRIGA. A temporal logic-based model for forensic investigation in networked system security. In LNCS 3685 Springer Verlag, editor, *Third International Workshop Mathematical Methods, Models and Architectures for Computer Networks Security*, pages 325–338, St. Petersburg, Russia, September 2005.
6. Slim REKHIS and Noureddine BOUDRIGA. A formal approach for the reconstruction of potential attack scenarios. In *Proceedings of the International Conference on Information & Communication Technologies: from Theory to Applications (ICTTA)*, Damascus, Syria, April 2008.
7. Tye Stallard and Karl Levitt. Automated analysis for digital forensic science: Semantic integrity checking. In *Proceedings of the 19th Annual Computer Security Applications Conference*, Las Vegas, Nevada, USA, December 2003.
8. Peter Stephenson. Modeling of post-incident root cause analysis. *International Journal of Digital Evidence*, 2(2):1–16, 2003.

A Live Digital Forensic system for Windows networks

Roberto Battistoni†, Alessandro Di Biagio†, Roberto Di Pietro‡⋆, Matteo Formica†, and Luigi V. Mancini†

Abstract This paper presents *FOXP* (computer FOrensic eXPerience), an open source project to support network *Live Digital Forensics* (LDF), where the network nodes run a Windows NT family Operating System (OS). In particular, the FOXP architecture is composed of a set of software sensors, once for every network node, that log node activities and then send these logs to a FOXP collector node; this collector node analyzes collected data and manages the sensors activities. Software sensors, implementing the technique called *System Call Interposition* for Win32, intercepts all the kernel API (native API) invoked by the OS of the node. Thanks to the fine granularity of the logs, FOXP can intercept malicious activities. Centralized logs collected in the collector node, allow to detect coordinated-attacks on network nodes: attacks that would not be detectable with a single node analysis only. Note that the implemented System Call Interposition technique has allowed to intercept and redirect all of the 284 Windows XP system calls. The technique is exposed in detail and could be considered a contribution on its own. Finally, an overview of next steps to complete the FOXP project is provided.

Acknowledgements This work was partly supported by the Spanish Ministry of Science and Education through projects TSI2007-65406-C03-01 E-AEGIS and CONSOLIDER CSD2007- 00004 ARES, and by the Government of Catalonia under grant 2005 SGR 00446.

---

† "Sapienza" Università di Roma, Dipartimento di Informatica, Via Salaria n. 113, 00197 - Roma, Italy; e-mail: {battistoni, dibiagio, formica, mancini}@di.uniroma1.it

‡ Università di Roma Tre, Dipartimento di Matematica, L.go S. Leonardo Murialdo n.1, 00146 - Roma, Italy; e-mail: dipietro@mat.uniroma3.it
⋆ Universitat Rovira i Virgili, UNESCO Chair in Data Privacy, Dept. of Computer Engineering and Maths, Av. Països Catalans 26, E-43007 Tarragona, Catalonia; e-mail: roberto.dipietro@urv.cat

---

Please use the following format when citing this chapter:

Battistoni, R., et al., 2008, in IFIP International Federation for Information Processing, Volume 278; *Proceedings of the IFIP TC 11 23rd International Information Security Conference*; Sushil Jajodia, Pierangela Samarati, Stelvio Cimato; (Boston: Springer), pp. 653–667.

1 Introduction

Vulnerabilities are constantly growing (see Figure 1), and new vulnerabilities are the pre-requisite for new attacks. One difficulty for network administrator and police forces to deal with attacks, is that smart attackers attempt to erase or to hide proofs of their intrusion: log deleting, changing files timestamp or rootkit installation. These considerations show the need for new generations of Live Digital Forensic (LDF) tools [26] that could enforce responsibility attribution [12].

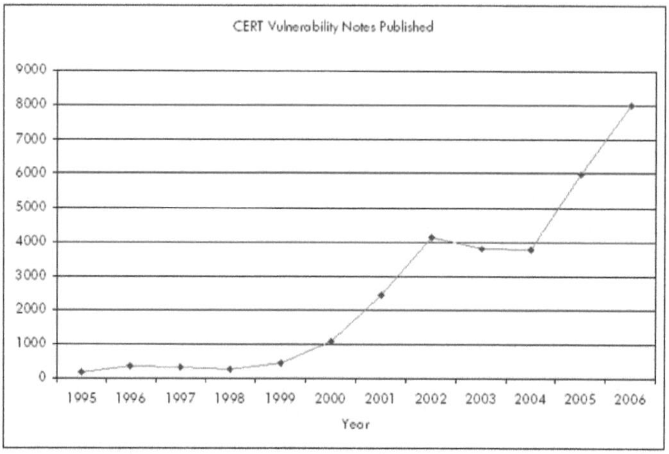

Fig. 1 CERT reported vulnerability in 1996-2006

In this context, network administrators need tools to support analysis and audit tasks and to detect intrusions and malicious activities. Suppose, for example, that in a time interval an attacker is able to exploit a node new vulnerability to attack other nodes of the network. If the administrator has not the right tool, she cannot detect neither the node generating the attack, nor when the attack started. In this type of context, tools that allow to reconstruct the entire activities of a system in a determined time interval, collecting evidences of the activities carried out in that interval, are needed. To date, there are two possibilities to accomplish this goal: traditional Computer Forensics (CF) and Live Digital Forensics (LDF). While the former approach is a static analysis of electronic supports only after a damaging event, the latter is able to represent the state of a live system for a determined time interval [2] [11].

The main contribution of this paper is to detail the architecture of *FOXP*, *computer FOrensic eXPerience*, an open source project [5] to support network LDF. FOXP traces activities at a kernel level in the node OS (Windows NT family based), with the primary goal of detecting malicious activities that are trying to subvert (or subverted) the node. In compliance with the LDF approach, FOXP is able to monitor activities in the system at every moment, and it allows both a live and a *post-mortem* analysis of the system. We also detail the corner stone of this architecture: the Logger; a software module that implements the system call interposition technique at kernel level within Windows NT family OS based nodes.

Architecture components can be grouped in two distinct sets: *client side* and *server side* components (figure 2):

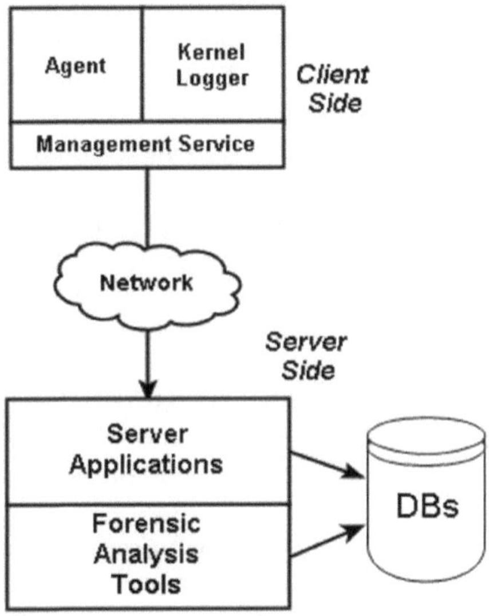

Fig. 2 FOXP architecture

1. Client side components are located on every node of the network. One component is the Logger, that allows to collect all the information needed to reconstruct the activity of the single node.
2. Server side components could be located on a single server node or on multiple server nodes, and their task is to collect nodes logs and organize them in an RDBMS for the successive forensic analysis.

The sequel of the paper is organized as follows. Section 2 reports some related works.

In Section 3 the FOXP architecture is introduced. Section 4 is focused on the Logger: the main technical component of the system. The Logger allows, extending technique called *System Call Interposition*, to intercept and monitor the entire set of Windows NT family system calls. Thanks to the ability to monitor system calls and their parameters, it will be possible to create a first dangerousness classification of Windows system call. Section 5 reports some concluding remarks and the activities currently under development to fully implement the FOXP architecture.

2 Related Work

IDSs are key to the protection of computing systems and computer networks: they allow to control systems and to react to attacks. In [3] it is shown the role of IDS in complex organization and some guidelines are provided for the development, operational conduct and management of IDS. IDS can be used as COTS or can be customized [27] to support CF or LDF.

Intrusion Detection named *anomaly based* is based on network traffic analysis. Its funding principle is that attacker behavior is different from normal user behavior and that the differences can be detected. Provided a definition of what a *normal* behavior is, anomaly based IDS could detect if the behavior is not *normal*, hence are able to detect unknown attacks or attacks for which patterns are not known yet [4] [23]. The main issue with this type of IDS is that there can be just a slight difference between *normal* and *anomalous* system behaviour. These two concepts can overlap producing a *false positive*, hence denying the access to system to a legitimate user. To reduce this problem, one could try to relax the definition of what is *normal*. However, this could produce *false negatives*: attacks could successfully run without being detected.

A subset of the IDS family are Host-based IDSs (HIDS) [4] [23]: these particular IDSs are the last line of defense in a system, because they try to detect and prevent an intrusion occurring within the system. HIDSs monitor both malicious and suspicious activities.

A subset of HIDS is constituted by the *Host Intrusion Prevention System* (HIPS) that also prevents attacks stopping invocation of malicious system calls. An example of HIPS are WHIPS [6] and REMUS [9] that use *System Call Reference Monitor* paradigm [9]. REMUS (REference Monitor for Unix System) is a prototype to monitor system calls that could be used to subvert privileged applications. REMUS uses a simple mechanism to implement the interception of the system calls at OS kernel level. Fundamentally, the execution of system calls is allowed only when the parameters of a certain set of system calls match a rule in an *Access Control Database* (ACD) in the kernel. That is, REMUS follows an *Anomaly Detection* approach.

WHIPS (Windows NT family Host based Intrusion and Prevention System) [6] is a system similar to REMUS that implements detection and prevention in Windows OSs and uses the *Reference Monitor* paradigm too.

In figure 3 we report the scheme of WHIPS, while details on the techniques implemented in WHIPS can be found in [14]. WHIPS and REMUS are on *SourceForge* as Open Source projects and it is possible to download them[7] [8].

An example of CF architecture is *Forensix* [21] for UNIX system. Similarly to FOXP, Forensix allows to control all the activities in the OS kernel space sending logs to a central server to structure logs in an RDBMS to implement CF high level analysis.

BluePipe [18] is another LDF system for *NIX platforms that is an alternative to a classic *post-mortem* analysis. It first performs a so called *on-the-spot* analysis, then results go to a central server for detailed analysis (as FOXP and Forensix, Bluepipe implement a client/server paradigm too).

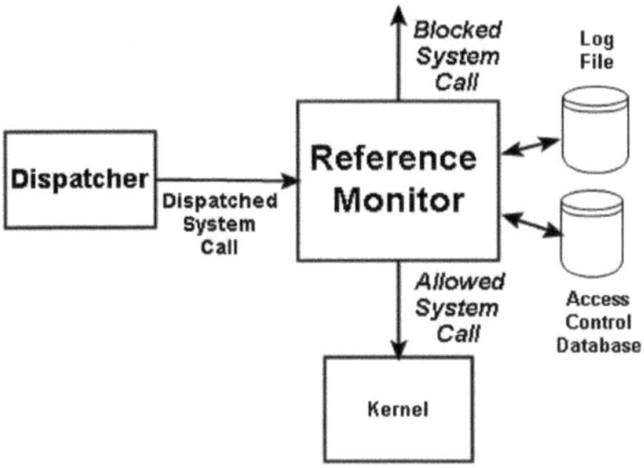

Fig. 3 WHIPS module

FOXP is similar to previous mentioned systems, but it has also some important differences:

- As Forensix and BluePipe, FOXP is based on a distributed agent (Logger) architecture, whereas WHIPS and REMUS are made of a single kernel module implementing system call interposition technique.
- Development of Forensix, Bluepipe and REMUS are just suitable for open source (well documented) OS. FOXP (as WHIPS) is developed for Windows NT family based OS. This introduces a critical level of complexity: Windows is a closed source OS, with little documentation available, especially for the native API realm.
- As Forensix and Bluepipe, FOXP uses an RDBMS too. This allows to store lot of logs in a structured way, useful to perform efficient analysis thanks to the expressivity of SQL.

3 FOXP Architecture

The aim of the FOXP architecture is to monitor the activities of the nodes in a network; when the client running on a node detects a malicious or suspicious activity, it will record the activities running on that node for a suitable time interval. Recorded data will be then sent to a centralized analysis system for CF purpose. In the following we provide a detailed discussion of the FOXP architecture.

Note that it is out of the scope of this paper to address the issue of communication security. Indeed, in this paper we focus on the forensics components of our proposed architecture only. However, note that the cited issue, together with the issues needed to provide a complete and deployable architecture, such as authenticity and non-repudiability of collected logs, are currently under investigation and will be presented in a different paper.

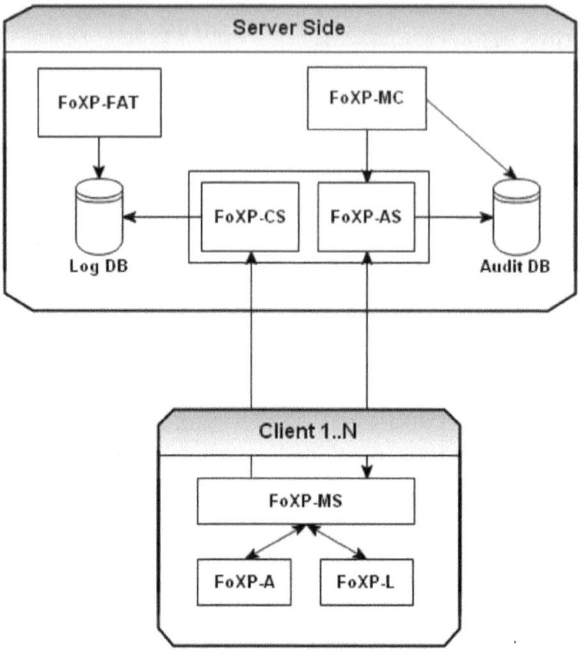

Fig. 4 Detail of FOXP Architecture

As shown in Figure 4, we assume a network of N nodes, where on each node it is installed a software module called *FOXP Agent* (FOXP-A): when this module detects an anomaly in the behavior of the system, it activates the *FOXP Logger* (FOXP-L) that starts collecting and sending data to a dedicated server machine. FOXP Architecture is composed by client-server subsystems (Figure 2): the client subsystem is located on every node of the network, and it controls the activities of the single node in order to detect anomalous behaviors.

Client subsystem is composed by:

- *FOXP Agent* (FOXP-A): it performs the analysis of the node activities. If an anomaly is detected, than the logging is activated (Section 3.1).
- *FOXP Logger* (FOXP-L): it intercepts the system calls invoked on the node and keeps track of them in a logging file (Section 3.1).
- *FOXP Management Service* (FOXP-MS): it manages the Agent and the Logger on every node as well as their communications with the centralized server of the architecture (Section 3.1).

Server-side subsystems are represented by one or more dedicated servers: these systems store the logs sent from every network node and collect these logs into a database for a successive forensic analysis. The server-side subsystems are:

- *FOXP Collector Server* (FOXP-CS): it receives and stores logs from every network node (Section 3.2).
- *FOXP Audit Server* (FOXP-AS): it receives and stores the state of the nodes (Section 3.2).
- *FOXP Management Console* (FOXP-MC): it remotely manages network nodes communicating with the FOXP-MS on every node (Section 3.2).
- *FOXP Forensic Analysis Tool* (FOXP-FAT): it executes the analysis of the collected logs and states (the Section 3.2).

3.1 Client-side Components

Client-side components reside on every node of the network and have the task to intercept and to log system calls invoked on the analyzed node. Recorded logs are sent to a dedicated server node (*Collector Server*) that stores their data in an RDBMS. As shown in Figure 5, the main components are:

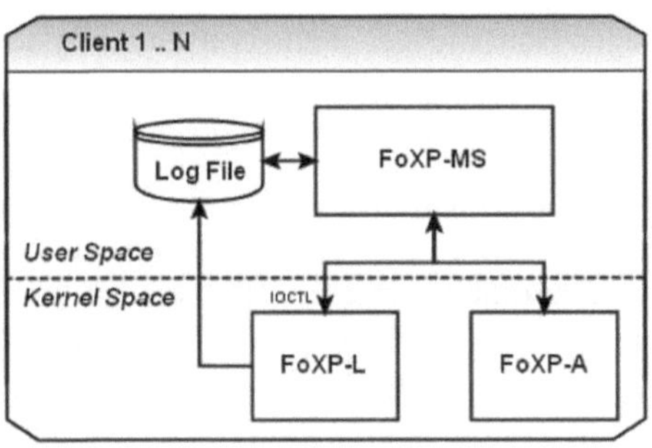

Fig. 5 Client-Side Components

- FOXP Agent
  it is an IDS (based on the Anomaly Detection [4] [23] paradigm) installed on every network node, that executes basic analysis of the node activities. All the FOXP Agents realize a Distributed IDS (DIDS) [1]: in this type of IDS, the role of the traditional IDS is delegated to a group of agents equipped with some intelligence (at the moment still not formalized and implemented in the system [14]). FOXP Agent will be able to detect malicious activities; the consequent action is then to send an alarm to the *Management Service* that will activate the *Logger*.

- FOXP Logger
  it is the main module of the FOXP architecture; it can be manually activated from the system administrator through the (server-side) *Management Console* or automatically by the (client-side) *Agent*. Through the system call interception in the Windows kernel, FOXP Logger captures and records every system generated event. Such module is implemented as a kernel driver: it is loaded and run in a reserved (and not paged) zone of kernel memory. FOXP Logger is loaded in the kernel by the *Management Service* and then it is launched together with the OS. Because the kernel module resides in the kernel space, it is not directly accessible from the user space programs, and it only accepts commands from the *Management Service*: module loading or unloading from the kernel memory, starting or stopping the interception of the system calls, and log writing on a file. Further details of this module will be given in Section 4.
- FOXP Management Service
  it performs the following tasks:
  - it receives commands from the *Management Console* for the *Agent* rules update;
  - it forwards commands directly to the *Logger* (through IOCTL channels [28]) without using the *Agent*.
  - it sends to the *Audit Server* periodic messages on the node live state (*heartbeat*), as well as the notifications of all the actions completed on the node from the *Agent* and the *Logger*.
  - it receives messages from the *Agent* and consequently sends commands to the *Logger*;
  - it sends to the *Collector Server* the data collected from the *Logger*.

  This module has been implemented as an OS service: it runs in background and supplies functionality not tied to the single user (services of Windows are similar to UNIX daemons). The requirement to use a service in order to communicate with driver when in user mode, derives from the fact that only an application with specific privileges can interact with a kernel module. The Management Service is initially installed by the system administrator and configured in automatic mode at start-up, so it will be started automatically at OS startup.

3.2 Server-side Components

On the Server-side, as synthesized in Figure 6, the tasks are the following: to receive, to store and to analyze logs received by the nodes of the network. It is fundamental that the reception is not compromised in some way (for example with DoS attacks), that the sent data are neither accessed nor alterable from unauthorized entities, and that the log storage support is adequately protected. These requirements, that could be achieved with standard network security techniques, are out of the scope of this paper and we assume them fulfilled. In detail, Server-side components are:

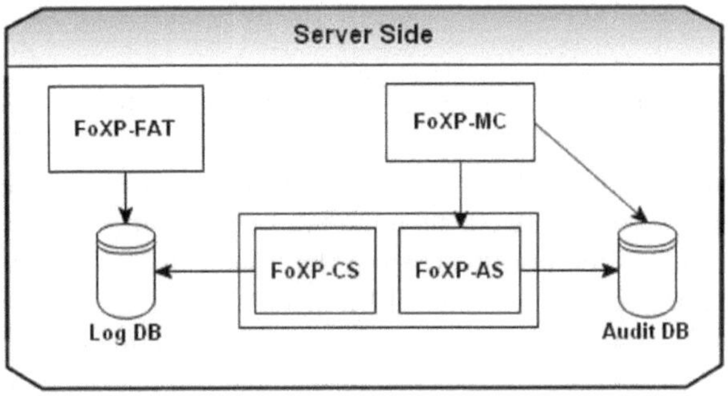

Fig. 6 Server-side Components

- FOXP Collector Server
  it is a server application that receives, over a TCP channel, the logs from the *Management Service* installed on every node and stores these logs into an RDBMS (*Log DB*). The server is a multithreaded application and the number of the thread is correlated to the number of the network nodes that are sending their log; it implements load balancing techniques with other server processes or with other *Collector Server* in cluster configuration.
- FOXP Audit Server
  it is a server application that receives, over a TCP channel, commands from the *Management Console* and forwards them to the *Management Service* of the destination nodes. Moreover, the *Audit Server* receives the notifications about the state and the completed operations from the *Agent* and the *Logger*; each of these pieces of information is to be inserted in a relational database (*Audit DB*).
- FOXP Management Console
  it is an administration console that is used to manage the entire FOXP architecture. It is used by the network administrator to monitor the state of the nodes (query on *Audit DB*), to configure (or to update) the FOXP *Agent* rules, and to manage the *Logger*.
- FOXP Forensic Analysis Tool
  it is a tool for the forensic analysis of the data stored in the Log DB. The main task of this component is the detection and the acquisition of the evidences to be used in a legal procedure to prosecute computer crimes perpetrators. This analysis methodology has not been defined yet at the moment, but will be addressed in future work. Some guidelines on Forensic Analysis methodology can be found in [16] and [15]. In particular, in [24] it is defined a formal model for the definition of forensic analysis procedures.

4 Logger

The *Logger* is implemented as a kernel driver. We chose this technique because in Windows NT family based OS (as well as in *NIX) any code can be injected into the kernel through a driver. However, note that this is critical for the stability and the security of the system. Indeed, such modules operate in Ring 0 [1] and constitute an extension of the kernel. For this reason, third party drivers — usually employed to control hardware devices — should be installed only if certified from *trusted* entities. In the following we detail the techniques used to implement this feature.

4.1 Interception of system call

The purpose of the FOXP Logger is the interception of all the Windows system calls, in order to monitor the entire activity of the system. The interception technique, that constitutes a contribute on its own, is described in detail in the following.

The paradigm of *system call interposition (SCI)* has already been used, for instance for the development of: sandboxing systems [20], process confinement, intrusion detection, auditing and privilege elevation [25] [17]. Although the SCI paradigm is a powerful method to monitor application behavior, it is a very error prone technique. In particular, Garfinkel [19] shows some of the difficulties and provides some guidelines to cope with them.

The interception technique was introduced by M.Russinovich in [13] (based on the SCI paradigm). Basically, this technique replaces the pointers to the original system calls in the SSDT table [2] with pointers to new functions. This substitution is not a trivial task: in fact, in the most recent Windows versions, it is not possible to write in certain regions of the kernel space, in particular the region where the SSDT resides. This makes the traditional technique of SCI useless: if someone tries to modify the SSDT, writing in a protected region, this would cause a Blue Screen of Death [3] [28].

To avoid experiencing a BSOD due to the violation of the memory protection mechanism, the solution is based on applying a patch to the SSDT [10] [22] [29]. In particular, this technique leverages the use of a *Memory Descriptor List* (MDL), to allocate a zone of non paged memory with the same interval of addresses of the virtual memory of the original SSDT. The fundamental difference is that this new zone of memory can be accessed in write mode.

A function in the MDL replacing an original system call (in agreement with the SCI technique) is called *wrapper*. Each wrapper is coded to perform logging and control operations. These activities carried out, the wrapper completes its last

[1] Windows has two modes (or rings) [28]: user mode (Ring 3) and kernel mode (Ring 0)

[2] System Service Dispatch Table, a kernel data structure where every system call has associated an index and a pointer to the memory zone that hosts the system call code

[3] BSOD, an error not recoverable that requires to reboot the system

function: it invokes the original system call. This way, the intended functionalities associated to the invocation of the system call are performed. A limited disadvantage of this technique is that, for every system call that must be intercepted, it is necessary to write a new wrapper.

To save (in *OldAPIPtr*) the pointer to the original system call (the *APIName*) and to exchange this one with the pointer to the wrapper (*NewAPIPtr*), it will be used the *HOOK* macro:

```
HOOK(APIName,NewAPIPtr,OldAPIPtr)
OldAPIPtr=ExchangePointers(
              &SSDT[Index(APIName)],
              NewAPIPtr)
```

Listing 1 HOOK macro

For example, if we want to intercept the Windows NT *ZwOpenFile* system call, we would use the HOOK macro in the following way:

```
HOOK(ZwOpenFile,NewZwOpenFile,OldZwOpenFile);
```

Listing 2 ZwOpenFile API

After the completion of this operation the OS will execute, when invoked, the new function *NewZwOpenFile* and not the *ZwOpenFile*; in *OldZwOpenFile* will be stored the memory address of the original system call (necessary for its restoration when the wrapper returns).

4.2 The Wrapper functions

In this subsection we detail the structure of the wrapper, focusing on the *NewZwOpenFile* introduced above:

```
NewZwOpenFile(OUT PHANDLE phFile,
              ..,IN ULONG OpenMode) {
  doLog("ZwOpenFile", phFile, .., OpenMode);
  OldZwOpenFile(phFile, .., OpenMode);
}
```

Listing 3 NewZwOpenFile API

Remind that the goal of the FOXP system is to trace the invocation of every system call. The main operation executed by each wrapper will be to write into a file some information about the intercepted system call: the name, the parameters, the date and the time of the invocation, the information on the current user and, at last, the complete path of the process that invoked the system call. The last operation of every wrapper will be to recall the original system call not to interfere with the normal evolution of the computation.

4.3 Interruption of the interception

It can happen that the administrator requires to unload the Logger. In this case, the original system calls must be restored. This action, issued via the management module of the Logger (*Agent* or *Management Console*), invokes the UNHOOK macro:

```
UNHOOK(APIName, OldAPIPtr)
ExchangePointers(&SSDT[Index(APIName)],
                 OldAPIPtr)
```

Listing 4 UNHOOK macro

After this operation the driver will be unloaded from memory by the *Management Service* using the Logger *UnLoad* function.

In the following we report an issue we had to deal with to implement the unload function. In the first stage of the implementation, the restoration of the original pointers of the system call (*UNHOOK* macro) and the unload of the logger (the *Unload()* function) was executed in one phase only, often generating (but in a non-deterministic fashion) a BSOD with error:

```
DRIVER_UNLOADED_WITHOUT_CANCELLING_PENDING_OPERATIONS
```

Listing 5 BSOD error

We figured out the reason: some system calls delay their own execution till the moment they are called again. This behavior can be due to the fact that the release of the resources held by the driver overlaps with the instant when these resources are requested by the pending system call. This problem has been superseded by separating the restoration phase from the unload phase.

4.4 Extension of the System Call Interposition technique

The system calls that can be intercepted with the macro previously described are only 104 out of a total of 284: for each of them, it exists an exported symbol [4] in the *ntoskrnl.lib* library, that allows to invoke the system call using its name. Note that trying to invoke a system call from a driver, a system call that has an unexported symbol (as for example *ZwAddAtom*) would generate the linking error:

```
error LNK2019:
unresolved external symbol
__imp__ZwAddAtom@24
referenced in function
_Hook@0sys\i386\Logger.sys:
error LNK1120: 1 unresolved externals
```

Listing 6 Linking error

[4] The symbols are special strings that identify a function within a program and link it to the respective code in a library

For the *Logger* module to intercept also those system calls for which the symbol from *ntoskrnl.lib* is not exported, the original technique has been extended as follows.

First, observe that, in the SSDT, a system call is clearly identifiable not only through its name, but also via its numerical index within the same SSDT. Then, the basic idea is to recall a system call just using its corresponding index in the SSDT (and not its name). The HOOK macro has been therefore extended through new *HOOK_NE* macro:

```
HOOK_NE(IndexAPIName,NewAPIPtr,OldAPIPtr)
OldAPIPtr=ExchangePointers(
                      &SSDT[IndexAPIName],
                      NewAPIPtr)
```

Listing 7 HOOK_NE macro

Using this macro the Logger will be able to intercept, without generating any error, the not exported system call (for example the *ZwCreateProcess*):

```
HOOK_NE(0x002f,NewZwCreateProcess,
        OldZwCreateProcess);
```

Listing 8 ZwCreateProcess API

Consequently, we define the *UNHOOK_NE* macro:

```
UNHOOK_NE(IndexAPIName,OldAPIName)
ExchangePointers(&SSDT[IndexAPIName],
                     OldAPIName)
```

Listing 9 UNHOOK_NE macro

4.5 Getting the image path of a process invoking a system call

Remind that, among the items that are collected by the logger, the complete process path of the process invoking the system call is an important one. Indeed, this would greatly help in both LDF and post-mortem analysis, to attribute responsibilities.

However, it is necessary to emphasize as finding this path has not been an easy task. Indeed, in principle there exist several ways to obtain this piece of information, when programming within the user space. However, many of these methods fail when adapted to the kernel mode, or just cause instability of the system, carrying to non deterministic BSOD generation.

We were able to devise an effective method, reported in the following. It is based on the usage of the *ZwQueryInformationProcess* system call, that takes three formal parameters. We have to pass to it, as parameters, both (*ProcessInformationClass* type) and *ProcessImageFileName* value (defined in *PROCESSINFOCLASS*). The third parameter is used to collect the return value. Hence, invoking the *ZwQueryInformationProcess* system call with the described parameters, returns —within the third parameter— the string containing the complete path calling process.

5 Conclusions and Future Work

In this paper we have presented FOXP, an open source project to support network LDF where nodes run a Windows NT family based OS. In particular, we have detailed the architecture components of FOXP. Further, we have shown the first implementation achievement: the Logger module of the *FOXP agent*. This module is the one that presents the major technical difficulties within the project, and its implementation could be considered a contribution on its own. In particular, the Logger *extends* the system call interposition technique. As a result, all of the 284 system call in Windows XP OS have been mapped, and therefore FOXP is able to reconstruct all the system activities on such system. Note that the completeness of system call interception is a very important aspect for a system to support computer forensic activities.

As for future work, we are undergoing the following steps: to classify the system calls according to their level of dangerousness, to assess the overhead introduced by our Logger. We are also striving to extend our SCI technique on VISTA 32-bit OS. Preliminary results are quite encouraging.

Finally, note that two of the described architecture components have not been implemented yet: FOXP Agent and FOXP Management console. These development activities will be carried out as soon as the previously described steps complete; note that a preliminary feasibility study supported out intuition that their implementation should not present technical difficulties.

References

1. Abraham, A., Thomas, J.: Distributed intrusion detection systems: A computational intelligence approach. Applications of Information Systems to Homeland Security and Defense (Chapter 5), 105–135 (2005)
2. Adelstein, F.: Live forensics: Diagnosing your system without killing it first. Communications of the ACM **49**(2), 63–66 (2006)
3. Allen, J., McHugh, J., Christie, A.: Defending yourself: The role of intrusion detection systems. IEEE Software **17**(5), 42–51 (2002)
4. Axelsson, S.: Intrusion detection systems: A taxomomy and survey. Tech. rep. (2000)
5. Battistoni, R., Di Biagio, A., Di Pietro, R., Formica, M., Mancini, L.V.: The foxp project. SourceForge.net, http://foxp.sourceforge.net/
6. Battistoni, R., Gabrielli, E., Mancini, L.V.: A host intrusion prevention system for windows operating systems. In: Computer Security ESORICS 2004, vol. 3193, pp. 352–368. LNCS (2004)
7. Battistoni, R., Mancini, L.V.: The whips project. SourceForge.net, http://whips.sourceforge.net/
8. Bernaschi, M., Gabrielli, E., Mancini, L.V.: The remus project. SourceForge.net, http://remus.sourceforge.net/
9. Bernaschi, M., Gabrielli, E., Mancini, L.V.: Remus: A security-enhanced operating system. ACM Transactions on Information and System Security pp. 36–61 (February 2002)
10. Butler, J., Hoglund, G.: Rootkits: Subverting the Windows Kernel. Addison Wesley Professional (2005)

11. Carrier, B.D.: Risks of live digital forensic analysis. Communications of the ACM **49**(2), 56–61 (2006)
12. Casey, E.: Investigating sophisticated security breaches. Communications of the ACM **49**(2), 48–55 (2006)
13. Cogswell, R., Russinovich, M.: Windows nt system call hooking. Dr. Dobb's Journal (January 1997)
14. Di Pietro, R., Durante, A., Mancini, L.: Formal specification for fast automatic ids training. In: Ali Abdallah, Peter Ryan, and Steve Schneider, editors, article from the BCS-FACS International Conference on Formal Aspects of Security 2002, vol. 2629, pp. 191–204. LNCS (Spring 2003)
15. Di Pietro, R., Mancini, L.V.: A methodology for computer forensic analysis. article of the 3rd Annual IEEE Information Assurance Workshop pp. 41–48 (2002)
16. Di Pietro, R., Me, G., Mochi, M., Strangio, M.A.: An effective methodology to deal with slack space analysis. article of the International Conference on E-Crime and Computer Evidence (ECCE'05) (2005)
17. Forrest, S., Pearlmutter, B., Warrender, C.: Detecting intrusions using system calls: Alternative data models. In: article of 1999 IEEE Symposium on Security and Privacy, pp. 133–145. IEEE (1999)
18. Gao, Y., Richard III, G.G., Roussev, V.: Bluepipe: A scalable architecture for on-the-spot digital forensics. International Journal of Digital Evidence **3**(1) (2006)
19. Garfinkel, T.: Traps and pitfalls: Practical problems in system call interposition based based security tools. article of the ISOC Symposium on Network and Distributed System Security Symposium (2003)
20. Garfinkel, T., Pfaff, B., Rosenblum, M.: Ostia: A delegating architecture for secure system call interposition. Internet Society's 2003 Symposium on Network and Distributed System Security (2004)
21. Goel, A., chang Feng, W., chi Feng, W., Maier, D., Walpole, J.: Forensix: A robust, high-performance reconstruction system. International Conference on Distributed Computing Systems Security Workshop (SDCS-2005) (1999)
22. Hoglund, G., McGraw, G.: Exploiting Software: How to Break Code. Addison-Wesley (2004)
23. Jones, A.K., Sielken, R.S.: Computer system intrusion detection: A survey. Tech. rep. (1999)
24. Leigland, R., Krings, A.W.: A formalization of digital forensics. International Journal of Digital Evidence **3**(2) (2004)
25. Provos, N.: Improving host security with system call policies. Tech. rep. (2002)
26. Richard III, G.G., Roussev, V.: Next-generation digital forensics. Communications of the ACM **49**(2), 76–80 (2006)
27. Ruighaver, A.B., Tan, K.M.C., Thompson, D.: Intrusion detection systems and a view to its forensic applications. Tech. rep. (2000)
28. Russinovich, M., Solomon, D.: Microsoft Windows Internals. Microsoft Press, 4th edition (2004)
29. Schreiber, S.: Undocumented Windows 2000 secrets : A programmers cookbook. Addison-Wesley (2001)

7. Carrier, B.D.: Risks of live digital forensic analysis. Communications of the ACM 49(2), 56–61 (2006)
8. Casey, E.: Investigating sophisticated security breaches. Communications of the ACM 49(2), 48–55 (2006)
[illegible]

HoneyID : Unveiling Hidden Spywares by Generating Bogus Events

Jeheon Han, Jonghoon Kwon, Heejo Lee

Abstract A particular type of spyware which uses the user's events covertly, such as keyloggers and password stealers, has become a big threat to Internet users. Due to the prevalence of spywares, the user's private information can easily be exposed to an attacker. Conventional anti-spyware programs have used signatures to defend against spywares. Unfortunately, this mechanism cannot detect unknown spywares. In this paper, we propose a spyware detection mechanism, called HoneyID, which can detect unknown spywares using an enticement strategy. HoneyID generates bogus events to trigger the spyware's actions and then detects hidden spywares among running processes which operate abnormally. We implemented the HoneyID mechanism as a windows based, and evaluated it's effectiveness against 6 different known spywares(3 keyloggers and 3 ftp password sniffers). From this study, we show that the HoneyID can be effective to detect unknown spywares with high accuracy.

1 Introduction

Spyware has become one of the most serious Internet phenomena. A recent report stated that 9 out of 10 computers connected to the Internet are infected [6]. However, most users are unaware of the presence of spywares due to the evasive behavior. This makes it difficult for the user to prevent it from causing damage.

Today, many signature based anti-spyware solutions have been used to defence from spyware. However, these solutions cannot detect unknown spywares. Therefore, the users are exposed to the threat of spyware before the corresponding signature update. Behavior-based spyware detection has been studied in several ways such as Gatekeeper [5], Behavior-based Spyware Detection [3]. Although these behavior-based approaches provide good detection results for particular behavior,

J. Han, J. Kwon and H. Lee are with the Division of Computer and Communication Engineering, Korea University, Seoul 136-713, Korea. e-mail: {getroot, signalnine, heejo}@korea.ac.kr. This work was supported in part by the ITRC program of the Korea Ministry of Knowledge Economy.

Please use the following format when citing this chapter:

Han, J., Kwon, J. and Lee, H., 2008, in IFIP International Federation for Information Processing, Volume 278; *Proceedings of the IFIP TC 11 23rd International Information Security Conference*; Sushil Jajodia, Pierangela Samarati, Stelvio Cimato; (Boston: Springer), pp. 669–673.

they have less eppectiveness against spywares which are triggered by a user's activity. In addition, there are also flow based approaches to detect spywares which use a honeytoken. For example, Siren [1], SpyCon [2] were proposed, which induce a spyware to make additional network request. Unfortunately, these approaches cannot detect spywares which do not send the stolen user's information to a remote server and cannot obtain infected spywares information. For solving these problems, in this paper, we propose a novel spyware detection mechanism called HoneyID.

2 Detection Mechanism

HoneyID is a mechanism that detects dialog spyware processes actively in a local machine. The dialog spyware is one of the most significant spyware, since it works using specific user activity. To steal and handle the user's activities, it uses generated events. Thus, HoneyID causes dialog spywares to fall into a trap by generating specific bogus events.

HoneyID consists of the trap and bogus events, as shown in Fig. 1. The trap is a component which monitors the changes of each process and the bogus event is a mimic user event which can make the dialog spyware operate. To detect spyware processes, HoneyID sets up a trap in the operating system and generates bogus events. When these events induce a dialog spyware behavior, HoneyID can detect dialog spyware processes by checking the changes of the processes.

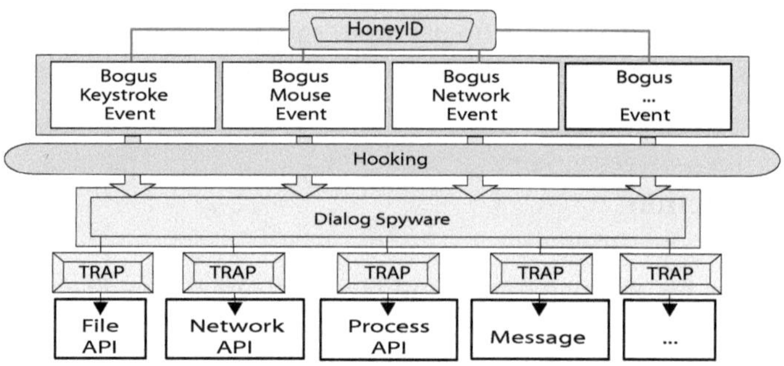

Fig. 1 The basic concept of HoneyID to detect dialog spywares.

If a process responds to bogus events whenever they are generated, HoneyID classifies it as a dialog spyware. Hence, dialog spyware can be classified by Eq. (1), where E is the number of bogus events generated per second, N is the period during which the bogus events occur continuously and T is the number of jobs of the process used for transacting bogus events. The job is a set of operations required for the target process.

$$T = E \cdot N \quad (1)$$

A dialog spyware steals and processes generated events immediately before the next event generation. Otherwise, it will fail to steal the next events. Therefore, the number of jobs of a dialog spyware process invoked by the bogus events and the number of generated bogus events is the same. So satisfying Eq. (1) means that the process can be regarded as a dialog spyware.

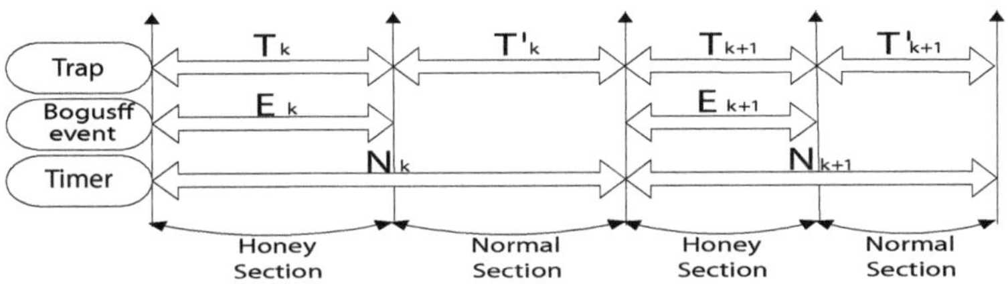

Fig. 2 Divided two sections with variables

In order to classify the jobs of normal processes and dialog spyware processes, HoneyID separates them into two sections. The first one is honey section with bogus event and other one is normal section. If HoneyID begins to generate bogus events and pauses repeatedly, and a process operates only in the honey section, HoneyID can check that the process operates as a result of the bogus events. If this method is repeated k times, the probability that a normal process runs in each honey section is $\frac{1}{2}^k$. Hence, the probability of a false alarm is very low.

Fig. 2 shows the two sections with three variables. The trap counter counts the number of jobs in both sections, the bogus event counter counts the number of bogus events per second, and the timer measures the time of each section. Eq. (1) can be represented by the divided section as the process reaction degree defined by Eq. (2).

$$R_k = \frac{T_k - T'_k}{E_k \cdot N_k/2} \quad (2)$$

Eq. (2) measures the number of jobs induced by the bogus event. T_k include the number of malicious jobs and normal jobs while T'_k includes only normal jobs. $T_k - T'_k$ becomes the number of malicious operations because the normal jobs are distributed both sections. In the case of a dialog spyware process, R_k will become one and normal process. From this distinctiveness, HoneyID can determine the threshold to distinguish between normal processes and spywares to be 0.5.

There is some possibility of errors in R_k because a dialog spyware could use delayed processing. This error can be reduced by obtaining the average value of R_k after z times iterations of C_k. Therefore, HoneyID can detect the dialog spyware process with less error by calculating the reaction degree(Φ) using Eq. (3).

$$ReactionDegree(\Phi) = \frac{\sum_{k=0}^{z} R_k}{z} \quad (3)$$

3 Evaluation

The HoneyID architecture is composed of three modules, the trap manager, the bogus event generator and the spyware detector. The trap manager sets up traps in the operating system and gathers the number of jobs of processes. The bogus event generator generates bogus events in response to commands from the spyware detector. The spyware detector controls the other two modules and measures the process condition used to distinguish between normal processes and spyware processes.

We developed two types of bogus events, the virtual keystroke event using the SendInput API function and the virtual ftp login event modifying the CInternetSession of MFC, respectively. The trap is implemented by means of the Win32 hook and Paladin Hook technique [4], for monitoring at the kernel level.

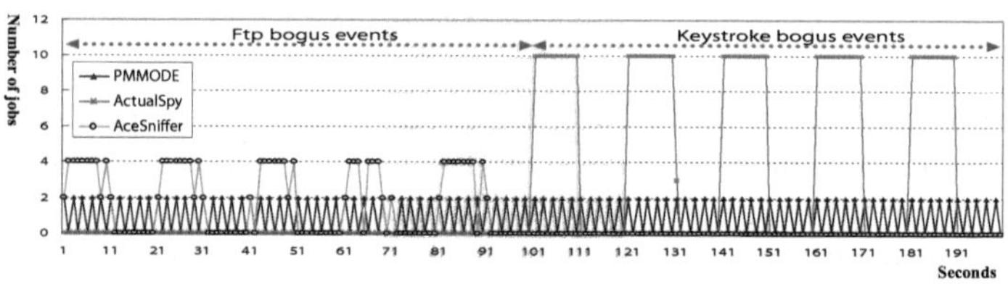

Fig. 3 The number of jobs of processes according to bogus events in a second

We collected three keyloggers and three ftp password stealers. Fig. 3 shows the fluctuations in the number of jobs of three processes : the normal process(PMMODE), the keylogger(ActualSpy) and the password stealer(AceSniffer). HoneyID generates ftp connection bogus events for the initial 100 seconds, and then generates keystroke events for the next 100 seconds. We can see that the PMMODE works irrespective of the bogus events, whereas the AceSniffer and the ActualSpy only works when relational bogus events are generated.

Table 1 show the results obtained from the experiment designed to detect keyloggers and password stealers, respectively. HoneyID operated for 100 seconds and was repeated five times. Bogus events for keyloggers are generated 10 times per second. The three keyloggers were identified. Bogus events for the password stealer are generated 3.6 times per second. Since an ftp connection event needs more resources, we generate ftp connection events as often as possible. The password stealers were also correctly identified.

When HoneyID was running, there were 36 processes. HoneyID found the three keyloggers that were installed and there were no false positives. One of the Internet messenger program is in close proximity to the threshold 0.5. This process may

Table 1 Password stealer detection (E=3.6 & N=100) and keylogger detection(E=10 & N=100).

Process	R_1	R_2	R_3	R_4	R_5	Φ	—	Process	R_1	R_2	R_3	R_4	R_5	Φ
Winsniffer	0.83	0.94	1	1	0.94	0.94	—	Family	1	1	1	1	1	1
Sniffpass	1	0.89	0.89	0.89	0.78	0.89	—	ActualSpy	1	0.97	1	1	1	0.99
AceSniffer	0.94	1	0.89	0.78	0.78	0.88	—	BPK	1	1	1	1	1	1

make use of keystroke events to notify friends of the user's status. When password stealers were found, the alg process is identified as the password stealer with no false negatives. However, the alg process is a core process for Windows. Since the alg process monitors ftp packets, HoneyID identifies the alg process as a password stealer. However these false positives can be solved by means of a white list filter.

4 Conclusion and Future Work

In this paper, we present a novel mechanism that detects spyware actively in a local machine. It causes spywares to exhibit malicious behavior by generating bogus events and it can detect dialog spyware processes by checking response to these bogus events. This approach is a powerful method of detecting dialog spywares that use the information of a user or PC. Future work will focus on extending our approach. We also plan to experiment on a large scale with a large number of spywares and normal applications installed.

References

1. Borders, K., Zhao, X., Prakash, A.: Siren: Catching evasive malware (short paper). In: Proceedings of IEEE Symposium on Security and Privacy (2006)
2. Chandrasekaran, M., Vidyaraman, S., Upadhyaya, S.: Spycon: Emulating user activities to detect evasive spyware. In: Proceedings of IEEE Int'l Conf. on Performance, Computing and Communications (IPCCC) (2007)
3. Kirda, E., Kruegel, C., Banks, G., Vigna, G., Kemmerer, R.A.: Behavior-based spyware detection. In: Proceedings of the 15th USENIX Security Symposium (2006)
4. pudn.com: HookAPI Source Code (2005). http://www.codeproject.com/system/Paladin.asp
5. Wang, Y.M., Roussev, R., Verbowski, C., Johnson, A., Wu, M.W., Huang, Y., Kuo, S.Y.: Gatekeeper: Monitoring auto-start extensibility points (aseps) for spyware management. In: Proceedings of Usenix Large Installation System Administration Conference(LISA) (2004)
6. Webroot Software, Inc.: Spyware info and facts that all internet users must know (2006). http://www.webroot.com/resources/spywareinfo

A Security Protocol for Self-Organizing Data Storage

Nouha Oualha, Melek Önen and Yves Roudier

Abstract This paper describes a cryptographic protocol for securing self-organized data storage through periodic verifications. The proposed verification protocol, which goes beyond simple integrity checks and proves data conservation, is deterministic, efficient, and scalable. The security of this scheme relies both on the ECDLP intractability assumption and on the difficulty of finding the order of some specific elliptic curve over $\mathbb{Z}_n$. The protocol also makes it possible to personalize replicas and to delegate verification without revealing any secret information.

1 Introduction

Online data storage has become an increasingly popular and important application, especially given the increasingly nomadic use of data and the ubiquity of data producing processes. As illustrated by P2P infrastructures like AllMyData, Wuala, or Ubistorage, self-organization today represents a promising approach to achieving scalable and fault-tolerant storage, even though it proves far more demanding in terms of security than plain distributed storage. This paper considers such a self-organizing storage application in which a peer, the data *owner*, replicates its data by storing them at *holder* peers.

Ensuring the availability of stored data in particular requires periodic verifications of the remote storage at peers for detecting voluntary data destruction by holders, which simple integrity checks cannot achieve. Such an interactive check may be formulated as a proof of knowledge in which the holder attempts to convince the verifier that it possesses some data, which is demonstrated by correctly responding to queries that require computing on the very data. Such a verification should neither require transferring back the entire data nor make it necessary to store large data at a verifier. Some authors have emphasized the difference between this type

EURECOM, France, e-mail: {Nouha.Oualha|Melek.Onen|Yves.Roudier}@eurecom.fr

Please use the following format when citing this chapter:

Oualha, N., Önen M. and Roudier, Y., 2008, in IFIP International Federation for Information Processing, Volume 278; *Proceedings of the IFIP TC 11 23rd International Information Security Conference*; Sushil Jajodia, Pierangela Samarati, Stelvio Cimato; (Boston: Springer), pp. 675–679.

of proof and classical proof of knowledge protocols through the use of a specific terminology: proofs of data possession for [3, 1], and proofs of retrievability for [5].

This paper introduces a secure self-organizing storage protocol for highly dynamic P2P environments, with scalability as an essential objective. It notably makes it possible to generate an unlimited number of verification challenges from the same small-sized security metadata and is the first, to our knowledge, to introduce the secure delegation of data storage verification. This enables verification, and not only storage, to be distributed, thereby balancing verification costs among several peers while suppressing a single point of failure. It aims at the following objectives: (1) Remote detection of data destruction. (2) Collusion-resistance, in particular to selfish holders trying to optimize their resources. (3) Denial-of-Service prevention, in particular to prevent storage disruption through *flooding* holders with bogus verification requests, or the malicious *replay* of a valid challenge or response message.

2 Secure Storage Scheme

This section describes our three-party secure storage protocol. The protocol relies on the hardness of two different problems in the context of elliptic curve cryptography. The first problem is the elliptic curve discrete logarithm problem (ECDLP) which is to find r given two elements P an element of a finite field G and $Q = rP$. The second problem is related to the order of an elliptic curve, which has been proved to be computationally equivalent to factoring the corresponding composite number for some set of elliptic curves [6].

The scheme consists in four phases of Setup, Storage, Delegation, and Verification executed between an owner, a holder, and a verifier. The owner communicates the data to the holder at the storage phase and the meta-information to the verifier at the delegation phase. At the verification phase, the verifier interactively checks the holder's possession of data, which can be executed an unlimited number of times. In the following, we assume that the data is uniquely mapped into a number $d \in \mathbb{N}$ (e.g., conversion from a binary to a decimal representation). The secure storage scheme is described in Figure 1, and relies on the following polynomial time algorithms:

- `Setup`: The algorithm is run by the owner at the *setup* phase. Given a chosen security factor k ($k > 512$ bits), the algorithm outputs the parameters for generating an elliptic curve whose order N_n is hard to compute as previously explained. N_n is thus kept secret by the owner.

- `Personalize`: This algorithm prevents collusion between holders. It is run by the owner at the *setup* phase. It takes in input data d and a secret random number s. It returns d' the encryption of d with a keyed pseudo-random function such as AES.

- `MetaGen`: The algorithm is run by the owner at the *delegation* phase. It takes in input d' and returns $T = (d' mod N_n)P$. T is stored by the verifier.

- `Challenge`: The algorithm is run by the verifier at the *verification* phase. It takes in input a random number r and returns point $Q = rP$. Q will be sent to the holder as a challenge.

- `Response`: The algorithm is run by the holder at the *verification* phase. It takes in input a point Q and an integer d' and outputs $R = d'Q$. R is sent to the verifier as a response to a challenge.

- `Check`: The algorithm takes in input the response R, the random number r of the challenge, and the metadata T. Checking if $R = rT$ decides on the holder's proof acceptance or rejection.

An improved version of this protocol whereby the computational complexity at the holder can be reduced by splitting data into m chunks is described in more detail in [8] together with solutions to DoS issues. Such an extension also makes it possible to consider our scheme in a probabilistic setting similar to [1].

Phases	Description		
Setup	**Owner** (public = (n, b, P), secret = N_n) ← `Setup`(k)		
Storage	**Owner** d' ← `Personalize`(d, s)	d' →	**Holder** store d'
Delegation	**Owner** T ← `MetaGen`(d', n, b, P)	T →	**Verifier** store T
Verification	**Verifier** Q ← `Challenge`(r, n, b, P) {"*accept*", "*reject*"} ← `Check`(R, r, T, n, b)	Q → ← R	**Holder** R ← `Response`(d', Q, c, b)

Fig. 1 Secure Storage Verification Protocol

Security analysis. This section essentially discusses completeness and soundness of the protocol, the two essential properties of a proof of knowledge protocol [4]. An extended version of the protocol [8] addresses other security attacks.

Theorem 1. *The proposed protocol is* ***complete****: if the verifier and the holder correctly follow the proposed protocol, the verifier always accepts the proof as valid; and* ***sound****: if the claimant does not store the data, the verifier will not accept the proof as valid.*

Proof. Thanks to the commutative property of point multiplication in an elliptic curve, we have $d'rP = rd'P$. Therefore, since $d'Q = rT$, the proposed protocol is *complete*. Furthermore, there are only three ways to generate a correct response without storing the data. The first one is to store $d'P$ (which is much smaller that the full data size) instead of d. In this case, the holder would have to find r which is equivalent to solving ECDLP. Another option for the holder is to compute N_n, the order of the elliptic curve, in order to store $\{d' mod N_n\}$ instead of d'. However, this is hard in our particular setting as explained above. The last option for the holder is to collude with other holders storing the data. This option cannot be considered either since data at each holder is personalized and the only peer that knows the secret s used for personalization is the owner. Therefore the proposed protocol is *sound*.

3 Related Work

Deterministic Verification. Deterministic solutions allow verifying the remote storage of the full data at a holder through a single operation. The use of precomputed but limited series of time-variant challenges stored at the verifier has been suggested early on: [2] describes a time-variant MAC. Approaches with an unlimited number of challenges instead rely on the use of homomorphisms. In the SEC scheme [4], tags are stored with data chunks and a subset of these are combined with chunks using a discrete logarithm based homomorphic scheme. Thanks to his knowledge of the secret used to make up these tags, only the verifier can directly check the proof. [2] describes a technique, later rediscovered [3], that makes use of an RSA-based hash function H: the prover hashes the combination of a nonce sent by the verifier with the data to prove it still holds them. The verifier stores $H(data)$ and the RSA public key as a secret key: he can compute his own proof using RSA homomorphic properties and compare it with the prover's. The whole data is however used as an exponent, which is computationally intensive for the prover. [12] addresses this concern at the expense of additional storage at the verifier, the data being split into m chunks.

Probabilistic Verification. Probabilistic verification methods rely on the verification of randomly sampled stored data. They have been favored in many proposals to lessen the performance impact of verification on holders. In a first type of schemes, the verifier compares the value of a stored chunk with the value of a reference data chunk. The probability of detecting selfish holders increases with the number of chunks verified at the expense of linearly increasing communication costs. [10] proposes such a scheme which improves on [7] and the Merkle-based solution by Wagner mentioned in [4], by transferring the role of protecting reference data from the verifier to the prover using signatures. The POR protocol [5] is based on verification of random values signed and hidden within the data. The verification is probabilistic with the number of verification operations allowed being limited to the number of sentinels. Another probabilistic approach proposed in [11] makes use of Rabinesque algebraic signatures of data blocks stored at different holders, and on the homomorphic properties of the signatures with respect to parity. This approach however makes it difficult to recognize a faulty holder if the parity blocks do not match. The PDP model [1], which combines a certain number of randomly selected homomorphic verifiable tags compressed into one result far smaller in size than that of the tags, seems one of the most promising of recent schemes proposed.

4 Conclusion

This paper introduces a protocol that satisfies the security needs of self-organizing storage applications, in particular through the introduction of delegated verifications, and which also meets their performance requirements. The scheme security relies on an elliptic curve cryptographic scheme in which each challenge-response message mainly consists of an en elliptic curve point on $\mathbb{Z}_n$. The size of messages between the verifier and the prover is independent from the size of data and only a function of the security parameter k of the `Setup` algorithm: a smaller number of resources may be used at the expense of a reduction in the security of our scheme however. The verifier needs to store only one elliptic curve point to produce challenges at will. Finally, the construction and verification of the proof rely on point multiplication operations only. We are actively investigating the use of this protocol as an observation primitive to both stimulate peer cooperation [9] and to evolve active replication strategies to rejuvenate the replicas of some data under attack.

Acknowledgements The work presented here has been partially funded by Institut Telecom Initiative program on autonomic and spontaneous networks, projects PACALAB and SPREADS (ANR), and the ReSIST IST-026764 NoE.

References

1. Ateniese, G., Burns, R., Curtmola, R., Herring, J., Kissner, L., Peterson, Z., Song, D.: Provable data possession at untrusted stores. In: CCS '07: Proceedings of the 14th ACM conference on Computer and communications security, pp. 598–609. ACM, New York, NY, USA (2007)
2. Deswarte, Y., Quisquater, J.J., Saidane, A.: Remote integrity checking. In: Conference on Integrity and Internal Control in Information Systems '03 (2003)
3. Filho, D.L.G., Barreto, P.S.L.M.: Demonstrating data possession and uncheatable data transfer. Cryptology ePrint Archive, Report 2006/150 (2006). http://eprint.iacr.org/
4. Golle, P., Jarecki, S., Mironov, I.: Cryptographic primitives enforcing communication and storage complexity. In: Financial Crypto (2002)
5. Juels, A., Burton S. Kaliski, J.: PORs: proofs of retrievability for large files. In: CCS '07: Proceedings of the 14th ACM conference on Computer and communications security, pp. 584–597. ACM, New York, NY, USA (2007)
6. Koyama, K., Maurer, U., Okamoto, T., Vanstone, S.: New public key schemes based on elliptic curves over the ring zn. In: LNCS (ed.) Advances in Cryptology - CRYPTO'91, vol. 576, pp. 252–266 (1991)
7. Lillibridge, M., Elnikety, S., Birrel, A., Burrows, M., Isard, M.: a cooperative Internet Backup Scheme. In: Usenix Annual Technical Conference (General Track), pp. 29-41 (2003)
8. Oualha, N., Önen, M., Roudier, Y.: A Security Protocol for Self-Organizing Data Storage. Tech. Rep. EURECOM+2399, Institut Eurecom, France (2008)
9. Oualha, N., Roudier, Y.: A game theoretic model of a protocol for data possession verification. In: IEEE International Workshop on Trust, Security, and Privacy for Ubiquitous Computing (TSPUC'07). Helsinki, Finland (2007)
10. Oualha, N., Roudier, Y.: Securing ad hoc storage through probabilistic cooperation assessment. In: 3rd Workshop on Cryptography for Ad hoc Networks (WCAN'07). Wroclaw, Poland (2007)
11. Schwarz, T.S.J., Miller, E.L.: Store, forget, and check: Using algebraic signatures to check remotely administered storage. In: ICDCS '06: Proceedings of the 26th IEEE International Conference on Distributed Computing Systems, p. 12. IEEE Computer Society, Washington, DC, USA (2006)
12. Sebe, F., Domingo-Ferrer, J., Martnez-Ballest, A., Deswarte, Y., Quisquater, J.J.: Efficient remote data possession checking in critical information infrastructures. In: IEEE Transactions on Knowledge and Data Engineering. IEEE Computer Society Digital Library (2007)

Protecting Financial Institutions from Brute-Force Attacks

Cormac Herley and Dinei Florêncio

Abstract *We examine the problem of protecting online banking accounts from password brute-forcing attacks. Our method is to create a large number of honeypot userID-password pairs. Presentation of any of these honeypot credentials causes the attacker to be logged into a honeypot account with fictitious attributes. For the attacker to tell the difference between a honeypot and a real account he must attempt to transfer money out. We show that is simple to ensure that a brute-force attacker will encounter hundreds or even thousands of honeypot accounts for every real break-in. His activity in the honeypots provides the data by which the bank learns the attackers attempts to tell real from honeypot accounts, and his cash out strategy.*

1 Introduction and Related Work

The majority of banking and financial institutions in the US authenticate users with a simple userID-password pair. The main encouragement for brute-force attackers is the notorious weakness of user-chosen passwords, first observed three decades ago by Morris and Thompson [7]. A more recent study of web password habits by Florêncio and Herley [1] showed that weak passwords are still very common. Much of the work on password attacks has focussed on off-line attacks. Instead of focussing exclusively on keeping the attacker out we propose to let him in and, as Provos and Holz put it [6], "look at the bright side of break-ins." Break-ins are a problem because it can be hard to tell the fraudulent activity in an account resulting from a break-in from the legitimate activity of the account owner. By allowing the attacker into many honeypots for every one real account we will learn detailed information on his strategy both for cash-out and to tell honeypots from real accounts. In addition we slow him down more effectively than a lockout rule, without the Denial of Service hole that lockouts create. Pinkas and Sander [5] examine a question close to our problem: their motivation is to prevent brute-force attacks without resorting to a lockout policy. The lockout policy opens a Denial of Service vulnerability, and, as [5] points out, this can be a very serious issue for some classes of accounts: *e.g.* the possibility of eliminating a rival

Microsoft Research
One Microsoft Way
Redmond, WA

Please use the following format when citing this chapter:

Herley, C. and Florêncio, D., 2008, in IFIP International Federation for Information Processing, Volume 278; *Proceedings of the IFIP TC 11 23rd International Information Security Conference*; Sushil Jajodia, Pierangela Samarati, Stelvio Cimato; (Boston: Springer), pp. 681–685.

from an online auction by locking their account would be unacceptable to eBay for example. Pinkas and Sander's raise the attacker's cost by requiring that a Human Interactive Proof (HIP) be solved after a threshold number of attempts has been exceeded. Van Oorschoot and Stubblebine [4] enhance the scheme by better use of the recent account login history; they are able to improve the protection and simultaneously reduce the number of HIP's that legitimate users will be asked to solve.

2 Attacks

Brute-force and guessing attacks In a brute-force attack repeated credential pairs are tried in an attempt to gain access to an account. The simplest is directed against a single account: the attacker tries all possible passwords for one userID until one succeeds. For non-numeric passwords he might increase his yield by trying passwords in order of likelihood. Simple brute-force attacks like this are generally stopped by a "three strikes" type lockout policy (but such policies open up a Denial of Service attack as below). Far more likely to succeed is a bulk guessing attack against a large number of accounts [5, 3]. Instead of trying different passwords for a single userID the attacker tries different userID-password pairs. Since only a small number of unsuccessful logins are attempted at any individual userID the attack is far harder to detect. Observe that a bulk guessing attacker knows very little about his victims. For example an attacker who forces entry will generally not know the name, address or any other information about the victim until he logs in.
Cash-out strategies: Once an attacker forces entry, the server has few means to distinguish him from the legitimate user. It might seem that all is now lost, but in fact the attacker's task is just beginning. The assets in the compromised account is all potential gain, but to turn the potential into reality he must move the assets to a "safe place," by which we mean cash or an account the attacker controls that is beyond the reach of the bank or law enforcement and cannot be frozen. It is important that any transfers he performs cannot be reversed when the break-in is detected; it is also important that none of the intermediate accounts can be used to identify the attacker. For example, wiring money from a compromised account at BigBank to an account at AnotherBigBank will naturally draw scrutiny to the holder of the second account. This task is far from trivial. Thomas and Martin [8] describe a complex ecosystem that has developed around harvesting stolen credentials. Cashiers and drop men are used to pick up money moved from the compromised accounts.
Do we care about brute-force anymore? The existing approach to brute-force attacks is a combination of:

- password strength policies,
- "three strike" type lockout rules and

- fraud and anomaly detection at the backend server.

Passwords strength policies are unpopular and users demonstrate considerable preference for short passwords. Three strikes type lockout rules suffice to slow down attacks on a single account, but do little against the bulk guessing attacker. Further, in some cases any lockout on an account can be very undesirable. Three well-timed failed logins can deny access a rival in an auction, for example [5]. Equally, an attacker who gains access to the list of userID's at a bank can halt all online access at a cost three times as many form submits as their are accounts. And this attack can be repeated. Details on the backend fraud detection employed by banks is understandably not made public.

The prevalence of brute-force attacks is itself hard to estimate. One might argue that in the age of better attacks such as phishing and keylogging brute-force is no longer an issue. However, banks are unable to lower the defences against it. And these defences result in burdensome password policies for users, and lockout policies, which generate the Denial of Service (DoS) vulnerability. It is argued by Florêncio *et al.* [2] that bulk guessing brute-force attacks are the main reason for strong password policies on online accounts. The approach we introduce in the next section makes brute forcing a great deal harder. Thus, we claim it carries two great advantages. First, it removes the need to encumber users with strong password policies. Second, it removes the need for a lockout rule and thereby eliminates a lockout based DoS threat.

3 Method

A Simple Honeypot account: A honeypot account at a financial institution is an account that appears exactly like a real account, except of course there is no real money there. In every other respect it is indistinguishable from a real account. It has all the attributes that a real account would have: name, address, email account of record, beneficiary information, account history, balance, holdings *etc.* When logging in to any account a user generally expects to be able to:

- Change account information (*e.g.* name, address, beneficiaries *etc*)
- Buy or sell instruments (*e.g.* move money from checking to savings, buy or sell stock *etc*).
- Send money to previously used accounts (*e.g.* utilities, mortgage)
- Send money to a new recipient

An attacker who enters a honeypot account will have access to the full range of services, with the exception of course that the bank will not actually remit any money to anyone. It will however pretend that it has done so. Only attackers will enter a honeypot, and the goal of the account is to create the illusion of reality. Thus the bank will do everything possible to perpetuate the illusion except part with money.

Generation of Honeypot accounts: To protect against brute-force attackers a bank may need thousands, or even millions of honeypot accounts. Hence it is important to be be able to generate such accounts at will. This is actually simple. Our solution is to copy attributes from a the pool of real accounts, but enter fictional attributes for name, address, beneficiaries *etc.* This guarantees that the honeypot contains valid account history and transaction details. For example an attacker would see real online bill pay details, together with the amounts and dates, but for a fictionally generated user. Accounts are generated on-demand at the time of first entry, but account information persists through successive logins.

Distribution of Honeypot accounts: Consider an institution BigBank which assigns users a b_u bit userID and enforces that passwords are at least b_p bits. Together the userID-password pair form the credential that grants access to a user account. In general entry of a wrong userID or wrong password or both results in a "login failed" message to the user.

In our solution the bank in addition to the credentials of real users allows access to a honeypot account when any of a number of honeypot credentials is presented. The size of the combined userID-password search space, at $2^{b_u+b_p}$, is far larger than the number of real user accounts the number of honeypot accounts can outnumber real accounts. For example, for a given userID if a single 8-digit PIN results in login there is one correct password, and almost one million incorrect possibilities. Instead of having each of these incorrect passwords results in a "login failed" page we have the bank assign 10000 of the incorrect passwords to honeypot accounts. Thus an attacker who mounts a brute-force attack on the password of that userID is 10000 times more likely to gain entry to a honeypot account than a real account. With an 8-digit PIN we can still ensure that a legitimate user who types two digits of his PIN incorrectly (there are $\binom{8}{2} \cdot 10^2 = 2800$ such possibilities) will still never enter a honeypot.

Honeypots associated with a userID assigned at setup: To ensure that a user who types the userID correctly, and gets no more two characters of the password incorrect, never enters a honeypot we must ensure that honeypot passwords, for that userID, are a sufficient distance from the true password. Since the salted hash is all that is required for authentication, passwords are generally not stored on the server. Thus the only time the server can determine which passwords are close to the true password for a particular userID is when the account is being set up. At this time, when it salts and hashes the password, it should also generate as many honeypot passwords as required and also salt and hash them. In this way there is no change in the existing arrangements for storing credentials. The details associated with a honeypot need not be generated only when an attacker enters the account.

Cashing-out must be done on real accounts only: If an attacker forces entry he must first determine if he is in a real or a honeypot account and then cash-out. He would be very foolish to attempt cash-out on all accounts: since stepping stone accounts and the services of cashiers are expensive [8], he cannot risk a cash-out attempt on a honeypot. Should he do so he identifies his cashier, and the bank will suspect any attempt to transfer to the cashier from a real account.

Telling them Apart Without Getting Caught: Suppose the attacker has compromised N accounts, of which $M \ll N$ are real and the remainder honeypot. The attacker and the bank each have partial and different information about the break-ins. The attacker knows all N of the accounts he has broken, but does not know which M are real. The bank knows only that the $N - M$ logins to the honeypot accounts must be the work of an attacker, but does not know which M real accounts are also compromised.

To distinguish the real from the honeypots, but with the constraint that his activity must vary from account to account. Suppose the attacker sends funds for a small purchase (from an innocent retailer) from each of the N accounts and arranges to have mail sent to a hotmail account when the item ships. This can be done, but is cumbersome. The attacker must choose a retailer who will accept a transfer or check and then arrange for funds to be sent from the compromised account. This would enable him to identify the M real accounts that are active. But it also notifies the bank that these M real accounts have something in common with the $N - M$ honeypot accounts. Clearly a one-size-fits all strategy will not work to distinguish accounts if he is to remain undiscovered. To avoid linking a real account, when he finds it, to the known-bad work of an attacker he must employ N different retailers to probe his collection of accounts. While he may be able to write a script that programmatically arranges a transfer from each of the N accounts, it is not possible to set up purchases at N different retailers this way. This is expensive: the attacker must expend individual effort for a retailer on each of the N accounts. Thus the attacker's effort increases with N, while the bank can generate honeypot accounts at will. For large enough N the attacker is faced with great effort for minimal return.

References

1. D. Florêncio and C. Herley. A Large-Scale Study of Web Password Habits. *WWW 2007, Banff.*
2. D. Florêncio, C. Herley, and B. Coskun. Do Strong Web Passwords Accomplish Anything? *Proc. Usenix Hot Topics in Security*, 2007.
3. K. J. Hole and V. Moen and T. Tjostheim. Case Study: Online banking Security. *IEEE Security & Privacy Magazine*, 2006.
4. P.C. van Oorschot, S. Stubblebine. On Countering Online Dictionary Attacks with Login Histories and Humans-in-the-Loop. *ACM TISSEC vol.9 issue 3*, 2006.
5. B. Pinkas and T. Sander. Securing Passwords Against Dictionary Attacks. *ACM CCS*, 2002.
6. N. Provos and T. Holz. *Virtual Honeypots.* Addison Wesley, 2007.
7. R. Morris and K. Thompson. Password Security: A Case History. *Comm. ACM*, 1979.
8. R. Thomas and J. Martin. The Underground Economy: Priceless. *Usenix ;login:*, 2006.

Agency Theory: Can it be Used to Strengthen IT Governance?

Shaun Posthumus and Rossouw von Solms

Abstract In recent years it has become questionable whether corporate boards are able to direct and control IT effectively. There seems to be a general lack of board-level information regarding IT which may lead to ineffective governance over it. The aim of this paper is to demonstrate how this scenario relates to the agency problem and how agency theory may be used to offer a theoretical framework for addressing IT-related issues more effectively at board level.

1 Introduction

The board of directors is generally responsible for defining an organization's overall mission and vision as well as setting its overall strategic direction so that the organization can achieve its goals (vision) and accomplish its purpose (mission). The strategic direction is usually implemented and maintained through a system of directing and controlling. [7] describe this as the direct-control cycle, claiming it to be central to corporate governance.

2 Directing and Controlling

A board issues directives on how an organization should function. These directives need to be translated into organizational policies, standards and procedures, which

---

Shaun Posthumus
Nelson Mandela Metropolitan University, PO Box 77000, PORT ELIZABETH, South Africa, 6031, e-mail: shaun.posthumus@nmmu.ac.za

Rossouw Von Solms
Nelson Mandela Metropolitan University, PO Box 77000, PORT ELIZABETH, South Africa, 6031, e-mail: rossouw.vonsolms@nmmu.ac.za

---

Please use the following format when citing this chapter:

Posthumus, S. and von Solms, R., 2008, in IFIP International Federation for Information Processing, Volume 278; *Proceedings of the IFIP TC 11 23rd International Information Security Conference*; Sushil Jajodia, Pierangela Samarati, Stelvio Cimato; (Boston: Springer), pp. 687–691.

will enable strategic, tactical and operational alignment with the company's corporate vision and mission. The board also needs to control an organization by ensuring that there is compliance with all directives, policies, standards, procedures and any relevant laws and regulations [7]. Therefore, to properly control (i.e., manage), thus ensuring compliance with directives and policies, there exists a need to measure. In order to measure, there exists a need to identify and collect the correct information to measure against [7]. Any directive issued by the board which cannot be measured in some particular way is of little value because compliance and adequate control cannot be achieved [7]. The board should extend this strategic directing and controlling responsibility into IT to ensure that it supports the corporate vision and mission. This can be accomplished through IT governance.

3 IT Governance

IT governance is concerned with aligning IT with an organization's vision, mission and corporate strategy, thus achieving a link between IT and the business. IT governance builds structure around how organizations typically align their IT strategy with the business strategy, ensuring that they remain on course to accomplish their strategies and goals, and put into practice effective means to measure IT's performance [6]. Achieving adequate control over IT is necessary, but it is not a simple task. There still exist many problems that need to be addressed before IT governance will become effective in fulfilling its intended purpose.

[5] claim that most boards remain fairly ignorant as far as IT spending and strategy is concerned. Very few grasp the degree to which their organizations depend operationally on IT systems or the degree to which IT participates in forming business strategy. Ultimately, a lack of board-level oversight for IT activities is unsafe because this creates similar risks to not properly auditing its books would [5]. [2] states that "busy executives and board members need more specific guidance on how to achieve that vaunted goal of effective control". A practical approach to acquiring such guidance would focus on examining how similar issues, not specifically related to IT, have been addressed. Thus, exploring the practices and theories implemented in other disciplines may be beneficial. One theory that may be of potential use is agency theory.

4 Agency Theory

Agency theory is concerned with the "ubiquitous agency relationship" in which one party (i.e., the principal) assigns tasks to another party (i.e., the agent) [1]. The agency problem arises due to a conflict of interest between the principal and the agent in terms of work that has been delegated to the agent by the principal. This occurs because the principal and agent may have differing levels of risk acceptance

[1]. Additionally, it may be difficult for the principal to verify that the agent has behaved in an appropriate manner due to moral hazard and adverse selection [1]. Moral hazard refers to the general lack of effort applied by the agent in carrying out his/her tasks. Adverse selection refers to the falsification of ability by the agent. It is important to address these issues between the principal and the agent to resolve the agency problem effectively.

Without appropriate governance mechanisms in place to acquire necessary information about agent behaviour, the agent is more likely to act in a self-interested way [1]. [1] explains that an agent's actions can be revealed to a principal through the use of information systems such as budgeting systems, reporting procedures, the board of directors, and additional layers of management. Additionally, the principal can contract on the results of the agent's behaviour. This is achieved by measuring the proficiency of their work which motivates the agent to align his/her interests with that of the principal [1]. Furthermore, task programmability can also affect the ease of measuring the agent's behaviour while they carry out a task. [1] claims that known means/end relationships (i.e., task programmability) enables agent behaviour control, as well as crystallized goals (i.e., measurable outcomes), which then enable the principal to control outcomes. An important point to consider would be how the resolutions to the agency problem could be applied to IT governance to offer a means of addressing its many challenges.

5 IT Governance and Agency Theory

Agency theory may be applied to IT where the board (i.e., the principal) delegates responsibilities for IT to management (i.e,. the agent). Their relationship, as [4] put it, can be explained through the metaphor of a contract, which, in this case, could be linked to a policy issued by the board that governs the use of IT within an organization. This policy wold then be implemented by middle management through the development of procedures that explain how to comply with policy. Furthermore, middle to low level management would then draw up HR contracts and employees would normally also attend a Security Education Training and Awareness (SETA) course and they would have to sign off that they will comply with the procedures that represent the implementation of policy.

However, since many boards are in the dark about IT-related issues, they may not be able to verify that the IT-related decisions and actions of management effectively portray the best interests of the organization. This may be due to moral hazard and adverse selection, explained through agency theory. Moral hazard may occur because the board may not necessarily be involved in ensuring that IT delivers its said value. Additionally, adverse selection may occur because the board may not know the full degree of the organization's reliance on IT. Thus, it may not be able to certify that management is ensuring that IT is aligned effectively with the organization's business goals. Management could be making IT strategy-related decisions that may not fully support the organizational strategy due to the lack of board-level knowledge and involvement. Thus, it is important to ask: "How can a board acquire the essential information needed to gain such control and ensure that management's actions are aligned with the best interests of the organization in terms of IT strategy?"

The solutions to the agency problem provide a possible means to answering this question. In this regard, the concepts of monitoring and measuring play significant roles in helping the board to attain the much needed information required to direct and control effectively and reduce a conflict of interest in the sense that IT may not be aligned with business strategy. Therefore, the board should monitor the actions and decisions of management and intervene, where necessary, to maintain alignment. Furthermore, it should also measure how IT is performing in order to gauge whether value is being produced. This would serve to mitigate the problems of moral hazard and adverse selection. Monitoring and measuring provide a board with information about what is currently taking place in terms of its IT strategic direction in the organization. This information also enables the board to become comprehensive in terms of its own and management's responsibilities to keep IT aligned with the business goals. Thus, the concept of task programmability, discussed in agency theory, also plays a role as it enables behaviour control as well as crystallized goals (i.e., outcomes that are measurable) and outcome control, which [1] has claimed.

6 Conclusion

The [3] states that the aligning of IT investments with business strategy is one of the largest issues organizations currently face. It is important that organizations implement appropriate governance over IT because many do not have formalized structures in place to ensure IT and business alignment [3]. Agency theory can be used to achieve this by offering a simple proven theoretical framework that merges the interests of management and the board to ensure that IT fully supports the organization's strategic direction.

References

1. Kathleen M. Eisenhardt. Agency Theory: An Assessment and Review. *Academy of Management Review*, 14(1):57 – 74, 1989.
2. Gary Hardy. Using IT Governance and COBIT to Deliver Value with IT and Respond to Legal, Regulatory and Compliance Challenges. *Information Security Technical Report: Legal, Regulatory and Compliance Aspects of Information Security*, 11(1):55 – 61, 2006.
3. IT Governance Institute. *IT Governance Domain Practices and Competencies: IT Alignment - Who Is in Charge?*, 2005.
4. M. Jensen and W. Meckling. Theory of the firm: Management behaviour, agency costs, and ownership structure. *Journal of Financial Economics*, 3:305 – 360, 1976.
5. Richard Nolan and F. Warren McFarlan. *Information Technology and the Board of Directors.* Harvard Business Review, 2005.

6. Karen D. Schwartz. Abc: An introduction to it governance. *[WWW document]. URL http://www.cio.com/article/111700*, 2007.
7. R. Von Solms and S.H. Von Solms. Information security governance: A model based on the direct-control cycle. *Computers and Security*, 25:408–412, 2006.

7 ACKNOWLEDGEMENTS

The financial assistance of National Research Foundation (NRF) toward this research is hereby acknowledged. Opinions expressed and conclusions arrived at are those of the authors and not necessarily those of the National Research Foundation.

A new Accounting Mechanism for Modern and Future AAA Services

Alexandros Tsakountakis, Georgios Kambourakis, and Stefanos Gritzalis

Abstract Accounting along with Authentication and Authorization comprise the concept of AAA provided by IETF (Internet Engineering Task Force). In heterogeneous environments, where different administrative domains and different wired and wireless technologies are utilized, those principles are often hard and complex to correctly implement and evaluate. Specifically, accounting which is our topic of interest, is in many cases a complicated procedure since many aspects need to be taken into consideration. In this respect, a distributed, flexible, robust, secure and generic accounting system needs to be implemented in order to provide the ability to determine which user has acquired which services and for how long at each operator domain. This work examines different scenarios applicable to such 3G/4G hybrid mobile environments and suggests a novel, generic mechanism to support accounting.

Key words: AAA, Accounting, 3G/4G Environments, RADIUS, DIAMETER

This paper is part of the 03ED375 research project, implemented within the framework of the "Reinforcement Programme of Human Research Manpower" (PENED) and co-financed by National and Community Funds (25% from the Greek Ministry of Development-General Secretariat of Research and Technology and 75% from E.U.-European Social Fund).

Alexandros Tsakountakis · Georgios Kambourakis · Stefanos Gritzalis
Laboratory of Information and Communication Systems Security, Department of Information and Communication Systems Engineering, University of the Aegean, Karlovassi, GR-83200 Samos, Greece, e-mail: {atsak, gkamb, sgritz}@aegean.gr

---

Please use the following format when citing this chapter:

Tsakountakis, A., Kambourakis, G. and Gritzalis, S., 2008, in IFIP International Federation for Information Processing, Volume 278; *Proceedings of the IFIP TC 11 23rd International Information Security Conference*; Sushil Jajodia, Pierangela Samarati, Stelvio Cimato; (Boston: Springer), pp. 693–697.

1 Introduction

Once a user successfully authenticates with the network and gains the appropriate authorization privileges she is granted access to network resources. From that time on, the user activities need to be constantly tracked and metered, in order for the network operator to calculate and accordingly charge the user. This procedure is called accounting. The main purpose of the accounting procedure is to bind user-related activities with accounting data. The latter may be the time spent connected to the network, the Kilobytes of data downloaded, or even some pre-defined tariffs correlated with a specific service.

The idea of AAA services has been under constant study and attention by researchers especially the last few years. However, as far as accounting is concerned, little work has been conducted as researchers mostly focus on the Authentication/Authorization functions and on security considerations of AAA architecture [1, 2, 3]. Accounting is considered straightforward and the IETF draft [4] directions are followed by all implementations. Most studies in the literature so far propose accounting systems that build on standard AAA protocols like RADIUS and are suited for specific environments and technologies [5]. At the same time these schemes usually rely on predefined number of users and relationships between those users and existing network providers [6, 7]. In our opinion though accounting should be performed in a more generic way thus avoiding the limitations stemming from the underlying network technology or the specific AAA protocol being utilized.

The rest of this paper is organized as follows. Section 2 covers some important background aspects of accounting in greater detail. In section 3 the requirements of the new accounting mechanism are presented and the analysis concentrates on the description of the proposed architecture. Last section offers concluding thoughts and future directions for this work.

2 Accounting

In a typical accounting scenario several entities are involved. First the customer who holds a subscription with a network operator who is responsible for offering and supporting network access to his customers. That operator is called the Home Operator (HO) and is the only party holding a user profile, consisting of detailed information regarding the user as well as the user SLA (Service Level Agreement). An external or foreign network operator may be utilized in case of roaming to allow the user to continue network access outside the Home Operator's covered area and is called Foreign Operator (FO). In most cases an FO holds a roaming agreement with the HO. The last party involved is called Foreign Service Provider (FSP) and is actually a third party capable of providing add-value services to users requiring them. These services are in most cases charged separately, but the cost is added to the cost of network access. Figure 1 shows all participants in an accounting scenario along with the connections between them.

Accounting can be a relatively straightforward process or become highly complicated as more and more network operators and service providers are participating in. The factors affecting the accounting procedure are bipartite. On the one hand lay the different administrative domains the user visits during vertical hand-offs. Whilst on the other emerge the technological variations, as more and more different technologies are available to the user.

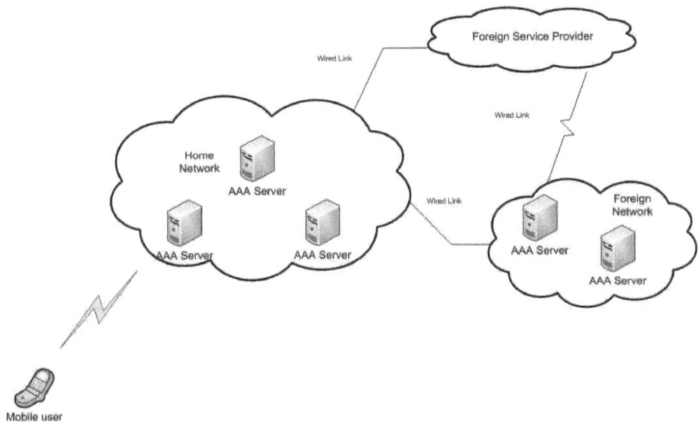

Fig. 1 Generic AAA Network architecture

In this respect, technological hand-offs and administrative domain hand-offs often become intertwined as the user enjoys the benefits of the new heterogeneous environments and their services, which in turn are derived from the use of innovative network technologies. Thus, modern accounting systems need to meet and satisfy several challenges and demands in order to provide robust and foolproof services to network operators.

3 Accounting architecture

3.1 Architecture requirements

Every new accounting system should take into consideration all the parameters related to: (a) the heterogeneous environment, (b) the multi-network operator relationship model, (c) the existence of many innovative technologies frequently incompatible and (d) the large number of mobile user population. In a nutshell the desirable requirements a new accounting system must meet are the following:

- **Generic.** The new accounting system should be applicable regardless of the underlying network access technology used.

- **Distributed.** The magnitude and complexity of current accounting demands can only be tackled with distributed architectures that mitigate future problems and technical failures.
- **Secure.** Data privacy, confidentiality and integrity should be ensured. Of utmost importance is the protection of user personal information. Private personal data should be safely stored and never be transmitted to any party other than the one the user has a contractual relationship with. At the same time accounting data regarding a user should securely and reliably travel between administrative parties.
- **Transparent to users.** Users must receive one single bill regardless of the number of operators or other charging parties involved in the process of accounting.

3.2 Proposed Architecture

According to our model during the accounting process an AAA Server can take either the role of the Root Server or the Administrative Server. The Root Server is an AAA Server inside the HO the user first attaches to. From now on, in terms of Accounting, the Root Server will be responsible for that specific user and will be used for collecting accounting events throughout the entire user session within the HO. The Root Server initializes and terminates the accounting process. Upon granting network access to the user the Root Server creates a unique identification number (ID) and stores a record mapping the newly created ID with the actual user. The actual user ID may be the user's International Mobile Station Identifier (IMSI) or Network Access Identifier (NAI). The first ID that the Root Server creates is called Master ID and is only altered, updated or deleted by the Root Server. Finally, the Root Server is responsible for the preparation of the final invoice to be sent to the subscriber.

The Administrative Server is initially the same as the Root Server. As the user moves, hand-offs occur and the user may need to attach to a different NAS Server or even require the services of a new AAA Server. Consequently, the Administrative Server is the local AAA, which is at the given moment responsible for the user. It is important to note that the Administrative Server can be an AAA Server that is located in the administrative domain of a foreign network operator. The administrative Server keeps track of where the user is physically located and thus minimizes data transfer requirements and bandwidth allocation for accounting purposes. This server is responsible for collecting accounting records while the user remains under his surveillance. Each Administrative server holds only limited information about the actual user, keeping only the required SLA information needed for charging as well as a reference to an ID (Master ID) sent to it by the previous Administrative Server.

Each time the user initializes an event that needs to be tracked the Administrative Server will create a new unique ID (called Event ID) mapped to that event. The Server will securely store in the corresponding database the correlation between the newly created Event ID and the received Master ID as well as the correlation between the Event IDs with accounting data. When a user leaves the current Administrative Server, or when required for other purposes, all accounting data gathered will be sent to the Root Server. The Root Server will eventually combine all events and store a single record for each user.

In case the user moves to the domain of a FO the same principles apply but the Master ID sent to the new Administrative Server inside the FO (by the Administrative Server inside the HO) is now an Event ID created by the Administrative Server in HO. The current Administrative Server takes the role of the Root Server inside the FO. When the user leaves the domain of the FO all the engaged Administrative Servers will send the relevant accounting data to the Root Server, which forwards them back to the corresponding Administrative Server inside the HO. That server will later send them along with its own collected accounting data to the Root Server in HO. If a FSP interferes, the current Administrative Server will allocate an ID to be mapped with the accounting data sent by the FSP.

4 Conclusions and Future work

The proposed accounting system is generic, provides secure means to transfer and store sensitive data, is distributed thus mitigating network failures and most importantly does not rely on, or affect by any means, existing technologies or protocols. On the contrary, it can be easily incorporated into the network operator existing mechanisms regardless of the underlying network technology. At the same time this generic behavior allows for interoperability between different network operators and service providers. The next steps of this work include the implementation and evaluation of a prototype system. DIAMETER will be used as the AAA protocol in charge and the test-bed will include both wireless and cellular networks.

References

1. Kim, H., Afifi, H.: Improving mobile authentication with new AAA protocols. Communications, 2003. ICC '03. IEEE International Conference.
2. Perkins, C.E.: Mobile IP joins forces with AAA, Personal Communications, IEEE,Volume 7, Issue 4, Aug. 2000 Page(s):59 - 61(2000).
3. Meng, Fang, An, Changqing, Yang, Jiahai: Implementing a Secure AAA System in IPv6 Network Communication Technology, 2006.
4. Authentication, Authorization and Accounting services, http://tools.ietf.org/wg/aaa/
5. Lopez, R.M., Perez, G.M., Gomez Skarmeta, A.F.: Implementing RADIUS and diameter AAA systems in IPv6-based scenarios, Advanced Information Networking and Applications, 2005.
6. Janevski, T., Janevska, M., Tudzarov, A., Stojanovski, P., Temkov, D., Stojanov, G., Kantardziev, D., Pavlovski, M.; Bogdanov, T., Interworking of cellular networks and hotspot wireless LANs via integrated accounting system, Wireless Internet, 2005.
7. Chaouch, H., A new policy-aware terminal for QoS, AAA and mobility management, International journal of network management.

A user survey on the sense of security, Anshin

Yasuhiro Fujihara, Yuko Murayama and Kentarou Yamaguchi

Abstract Traditional research on security has been based on the assumption that users would feel secure when provided with secure systems and services. In this research we address factors influencing users' sense of security. This paper reports our recent discoveries regarding the structure of the sense of security – Anshin. We conducted a questionnaire survey with one hundred and nine civil servants working for a local government regarding the sense of security. This paper reports our survey.

1 Introduction

The evaluation of security technology has been concerned with how secure a system is from the theoretical and performance viewpoints. On the other hand, the majority of computer users have not been sure about how secure the systems and services which they use really are. What has been missing is evaluation from users' viewpoints. Not so much work has been done on how well systems and services incorporate users' subjective feelings such as the sense of security. In this research, we try and identify the factors influencing the sense of security.

Throughout this paper, we use a Japanese word for the sense of security, Anshin. Anshin is a Japanese noun which is composed of two words: An and Shin. "An" is to ease, and "Shin" indicates mind. Anshin literally means to ease one's mind [1, 2].

According to Yamagishi [3], Anshin is the belief that we have no social uncertainty, whereas trust is needed when we have high social uncertainty. Traditional studies on trust were concerned primarily with cognitive trust, however, Lewis [4]

Yasuhiro Fujihara and Yuko Murayama
Faculty of software and Information science, Iwate Prefectural University, 152-52 Sugo, Takizawa-mura, Iwate 020-0193 JAPAN, e-mail: {fuji/murayama}@iwate-pu.ac.jp

Kentarou Yamaguchi
Graduate School of Information Security, Institute of Information Security, 2-14-1 Tsuruya-cho, Kanagawa-ku, Yokohama-shi 221-0085 JAPAN, e-mail: mgs064512@iisec.ac.jp

Please use the following format when citing this chapter:

Fujihara, Y., Murayama, Y. and Yamaguchi, K., 2008, in IFIP International Federation for Information Processing, Volume 278; *Proceedings of the IFIP TC 11 23rd International Information Security Conference*; Sushil Jajodia, Pierangela Samarati, Stelvio Cimato; (Boston: Springer), pp. 699–703.

defined another type of trust, viz. emotional trust. Xiao [5] suggests that the emotional aspect of trust is defined as an emotional security, or feeling secure, or comfortable. Pu [6] reports that how information was presented affected trust building in user interfaces. Yamazaki and Kikkawa [7] identifies that there is a structure in Anshin through their study on Anshin in epidemic disease.

2 User survey on Anshin

We conducted a questionnaire survey on Anshin with about four hundred university students, performing factor analysis on the responses [8]. We identified the six factors contributing to Anshin: security technology, usability, experience, preference, knowledge and assurance. Our previous user survey presented included two types of subjects: those with education in software technology and the others without such an education. The structure of Anshin differs according to whether the subjects know about software technology or not [9]. While the students whose major is Software and Information Science have Anshin based on their knowledge and understanding, those with other majors rely more on Preference and Assurance. This suggests that the two types of the students have different structures of Anshin. The number of subjects without the knowledge was not enough for further analysis. We conducted an additional survey on users without technical knowledge in December 2007. This section describes the previous survey and the new one.

In the future we plan to conduct a larger-scale survey with civil servants. As the survey subjects(civil servants) are somewhat different from the previous ones(students), we conducted an experimental survey. In the current survey, we used a revised questionnaire based on the results from the previous survey. Our new survey includes the following question: "Do you feel that the following thirty four items account for Anshin when you use a service or system through the Internet on a personal use?" Some of the items are listed in Table 1. We used the seven-point Likert scale system ranging from strongly disagree (1) to strongly agree (7), as many such survey have used this scale.

We asked two hundred civil servants working for a local government to answer our questionnaire though e-mail. One hundred and nine civil servants responded via the web. All answers were valid for statistical analysis. All the subjects have basic knowledge of how to operate a computer and they use the Internet on a daily basis. Of the one hundred and nine subjects, seventy one were male, and thirty eight were female, and the average age about 39.3.

3 Factor Analysis results

We analyzed the current survey data using explanatory factor analysis (EFA). In this study, we examined the factors of Anshin that existed behind between questionnaire items, by using EFA. The main results were as follows: EFA using maximum-likelihood method and promax rotation found that seven factors are present. We tried the analysis several times to derive the effective items out of thirty four and found that the twenty eight items would be feasible as contributing to Anshin. All items have factor loading above 0.581. The seven factors explained by 73.13% of the total variance.

We present a brief summary of each factor. Each factor is composed of multiple questionnaire entries. Following items contained in each factor, which is represented in descending order of factor loading.

Factor 1: *Security Technology* consists of six items (Q15, Q08, Q14, Q07, Q13, Q04, Q01) about security technology. Most items indicate measures for security such as protection of personal data.

Factor 2: *Usability* consists of five items (Q26, Q24, Q25, Q23, Q27) items about satisfaction with the user interface (UI). Especially, it has subjective assessment of the quality of UI; for example, usability, attractive design and user-friendliness.

Factor 3: *Preference for Interface* consists of three items (Q21, Q22, Q20) about preference for interface design. In other words, it shows the user's likes and tastes on interface.

Factor 4: *Knowledge* consists of four items (Q18, Q19, Q16, Q17) about knowledge of information technology. It shows the perception of risk, and understanding of risk or threat based on a user's prior knowledge.

Table 1 Item details

Factor	Items
Factor 1	Q15 Companies care about security.
	Q08 Personal information which I input is managed carefully and it will not be leaked to the outside.
	Q14 I feel secure when I use the system/service.
Factor 2	Q26 Compared to other systems, we need only a few cumbersome operations and it is easy to use the system/service.
	Q24 The usability of the system is excellent.
	Q25 Since the system/service provides deliberate explanation on how to use it, I get the impression that I am treated well.
Factor 3	Q21 The system design is attractive.
	Q22 The layout and color of the system design are attractive.
	Q20 I feel familiar about the system design.
Factor 4	Q18 I know quite a lot about information technology.
	Q19 I know the risks and security threats when I use the system/service.
	Q16 I know something about the mechanism of security tools.
Factor 5	Q32 I like the system/service without any specific reason.
	Q31 I feel secure without any specific reason when I use the system/service.
	Q29 Since I frequently use the system/service, I am not worried about its security.
Factor 6	Q02 The service provider and its owner company have the confidence of society.
	Q06 The systems and services provided by a large company are secure.
	Q03 I am confident in the competence of the provider and its owner.
Factor 7	Q10 Even if I had a trouble, I would be protected by a guarantee.
	Q12 Even if I had a problem, the system would assist me to solve it.
	Q11 Even if I had a problem, it would be fixed when the system restarts.

Factor 5: *Intuitive Impression* consist of three items (Q32, Q31, Q29) about impression based on intuition. It is a fully subjective factor such as user's experience, user's preference of the service, and recommendation of one's family and friends.

Factor 6: *Assurance* consists of three items (Q02, Q06, Q03) concerned with how much confidence the user feels in society and the user's expectation ability of the others, security, safety, and so forth.

Factor 7: *Action on a trouble* consists of three items (Q10, Q12, Q11) about expected action of the system on a trouble. In other words, it shows the system would assist the user to solve the problem or the problem would be fixed when the system restarts.

4 Discussion

Based on the current survey, the seven factors including the newly found two factors of *Intuitive Impression* and *Action on a trouble* have been found. The items belonging to *Intuitive Impression* were composed of user experience, preference, impression and so on. The factor of *Intuitive Impression* included the items that made up the Experience factor in the previous survey. While *Action on a trouble* was included in the factors of Information security in the previous survey, it was found as an independent factor this time.

We asked the subjects a question about knowledge of information security on current survey. We classified the subjects in three groups of "those who know in details" (seventeen people), "those who know like everyone else" (fifty people), "those who do not know" (forty two people), compared with ordinary people. In order to study the relationship between the knowledge of information security and each respective factor, we made an analysis of variance that made the knowledge of information security as a factor. As a result of analysis, there are significant differences only in the *usability* factor ($F(2,108)=3.710$, $p<.05$), and the *intuitive impression* factor ($F(2,108)=3.163$, $p<.05$). That is, those who do not have information security knowledge, tended to understand the degree of security based on *usability* and *intuitive impression*. Accordingly it indicates that the structure of Anshin is different according to the knowledge of information security.

5 Conclusions

We conducted a user survey with civil servants, concerning Anshin in information security. We had one hundred and nine cases of data used in this analysis, which is not quite a sufficient number to make a detailed analysis. As the current survey was a preliminary experiment to prepare for a larger-scale survey, we cannot lead to a conclusion from the results of this survey. Some items in the questionnaire were hard to answer, according to users who do not know much about information security. In the future, we plan to improve the questionnaire and conduct a user survey with a greater number of subjects for various groups, finding out the structure of Anshin in information security.

Acknowledgements Special thanks to Natsuko Hikage of Nippon Telegraph and Telephone, and Dr. Carl Hauser of Washington State University. Without their help this research was not possible. We thank Ginny Hauser for her assistance with our translation of our questionnaire into English.

References

1. Murayama, Y., Hikage, N., Hauser, C., Chakraborty, B. and Segawa, N. (2006) An Anshin Model for the Evaluation of the Sense of Security, Proc. of the 39th Hawaii International Conference on System Science (HICSS'06), Vol.8:205a
2. Hikage, N., Murayama, Y. and Hauser, C. (2007) Exploratory survey on an evaluation model for a sense of security, Proc. of the 22nd IFIP TC-11 International Information Security Conference (SEC2007):121–132
3. Yamagishi, T. (1998) The structure of trust: The evolutionary games of mind and society, Tokyo University Press. English version is available at : http://lynx.let.hokudai.ac.jp/members/yamagishi/english/ (Cited 14 Jan 2008)
4. Lewis, J. D. and Weigert, A. (1985) Trust as a Social Reality, Social Forces, Vol.63, No.4:967–985
5. Xiao, S. and Benbasat, I. (2003) The formation of trust and distrust in recommendation agents in repeated interactions: a process-tracing analysis, Proc. of the 5th international conference on Electronic commerce (ICEC'03):287–293
6. Pu, P. and Chen, L. (2006) Trust building with explanation interfaces, Proc. of the 11th international conference on Intelligent user interfaces (IUI'06):93–100.
7. Yamazaki, M. and Kikkawa, T. (2006) The Structure of Anxiety Associated with Avian Influenza and Pandemic Influenza, the 47th annual conference of the Japanese Society of Social Psychology:676–677(in Japanese)
8. Hikage, N., Hauser, C. and Murayama, Y. (2007) A statistical discussion of the sense of security, Anshin, Information Processing Society of Japan (IPSJ) Journal, Vol.48, No.9:3193–3203(in Japanese)
9. Murayama, Y., Hikage, N., Fujihara Y. and Hauser C. (2007) The structure of the sense of security, Anshin, 2nd International Workshop on Critical Information Infrastructures Security:85–96

Multi-Layer Encryption for Multi-Level Access Control in Wireless Sensor Networks

Po-Yuan Teng, Shih-I Huang, and Adrian Perrig

Abstract The purpose of Multi-Layer Encryption (MLE) is to have only one cipher text, but users with different keys (e.g., in different groups) will obtain different levels of data after they decrypt with their own key. This property is especially useful in surveillance applications, which requires an efficient mechanism for multi-level data access. In this paper, we first address specific requirements for Wireless Sensor Networks (WSNs), and then propose a MLE scheme which has good properties of forward/backward secrecy, without the necessity of time synchronization. In this scheme, users only need to store a constant number of keys regardless of defined secret layers, and higher-level users are able to decrypt more data than lower-level users.

Key words: Security, Multi-Layer Encryption, Forward Secrecy, Wireless Sensor Networks, Multi-Level Access Control

1 Introduction

Some applications with multiple priority groups need different layers of sensed data (e.g., in a metropolitan surveillance application, the police can see all data, but citizen can only see a subset of the data), this requirement is the main reason to develop MLE. In our architecture, we expect a data server to store encrypted data from sensor nodes, and this data server will authenticate users whenever they request reading specific data.

Po-Yuan Teng
Industrial Technology Research Institute (ITRI), Taiwan. e-mail: pppk@itri.org.tw

Shih-I Huang
Industrial Technology Research Institute (ITRI), Taiwan. e-mail: si.huang@gmail.com

Adrian Perrig
Carnegie Mellon University (CMU). e-mail: adrian@ece.cmu.edu

Please use the following format when citing this chapter:

Teng, P.-Y., Huang, S.-I. and Perrig, A., 2008, in IFIP International Federation for Information Processing, Volume 278; *Proceedings of the IFIP TC 11 23rd International Information Security Conference*; Sushil Jajodia, Pierangela Samarati, Stelvio Cimato; (Boston: Springer), pp. 705–709.

In the following section, we shortly describe our target environment, and supply a summary of notation used throughout this paper. We will precisely describe our multi-layer encryption schemes in Section 3 and discuss some possible attacks in Section 4, then make a conclusion in Section 5.

2 Background

In this section, we briefly describe the fundamental network architecture applied in our scheme, and the notations we used throughout this paper.

- Sensor Network Environments

In general, sensor nodes face some limitations, including constrained computational power, limited battery life, limited storage space, and deployments in networks [5].

Because of these sensor node limitations, one popular solution is to have a data server as a supplementary controller (also known as base station [4]). In this architecture, the data server stores sensed data from sensor nodes, broadcasts beacon signals periodically to maintain the routing topology, and schedules the duty cycle for each node. This periodically broadcasted beacon signals are utilized to develop our MLE scheme.

- Notation

For clarity, we list the symbols and notations used throughout this paper below:

Table 1 Notation

MK	Master Key
M_i	Plaintext of layered message i
C_i	Cipher text of corresponding M_i
ID_i	The identity of sensor node i
UID_i	The identity of user i
UK_i	User key for user i
K_{G_i}	Group Key (ex. K_{G_1} for Group G_1)
$Enc(K,M)$	Encrypt message M using key K
$\{M\}_K$	Encrypted message M by K
$H^n(M)$	Hash n times of message M
$H(M_1,M_2)$	Hash of M_1 concatenates M_2
KB_{ID_i,L_n}	Base key for layer n of node ID_i
KE_{ID_i,L_n,T_j}	Encryption key for layer n of node ID_i, during time period T_j
T_i	The ith Time period
TMK_{ID_i}	Time Master Key for node ID_i
TK_{ID_i,T_j}	Time Key for node ID_i, during time period T_j

3 Multi-Layer Encryption Scheme

Informally, forward secrecy ensures that the past messages are protected even if the current secret key is exposed [3], and backward secrecy means that the exposed secret key is no longer useful in the future.

As shown in Fig. 1, this scheme requires the data server to hold one master key MK. The data server randomly generates K_{G_1} and computes K_{G_2}, K_{G_3} by performing one-way hash function, and then gives these keys to G_1, G_2, and G_3 users respectively.

The data server periodically broadcasts $seedT_i$ to sensor nodes, the value of $seedT_i$ could be a computational result of time period T_i. For example, as Fig. 1 shows, the date "2007-10-15" could be the 18th time period of our system, so the value of $seedT_i$ that the server broadcasts in this time period is $seedT_{18}$, where $seedT_{18} = AES(MK, \text{"2007-10-15"})$.

Basically, $seedT_i$ are used to update encryption keys, since these $seedT_i$ values are broadcasted in plaintext, an attacker could record all the values and endanger the system. To avoid this problem, the server gives each sensor node an unique time master key (TMK_{ID_i}) through function $TMK_{ID_i} = Enc(MK, ID_i)$. TMK_{ID_i} are used to generate time keys (TK_{ID_i,T_j}), and time keys are aimed to update encryption keys for each secret layer through hash function $KE_{ID_i,L_n,T_j} = H(KB_{ID_i,L_n}, H^{L_n - 1}(TK_{ID_i,T_j}))$. The reason to perform one-way hash on time keys in each secret layer here is to prevent colluding attack.

The server gives each sensor node a different key set, here we denote it as base key (KB_{ID_i,L_n}), where the subscript ID_i denotes that this key belongs to node ID_i and L_n denotes the secret level of the key. Combining base keys and TK_{ID_i,T_j} values can generate encryption keys (KE_{ID_i,L_n,T_j}). This is known as key-insulated methods which are mainly used to provide forward/backward secrecy.

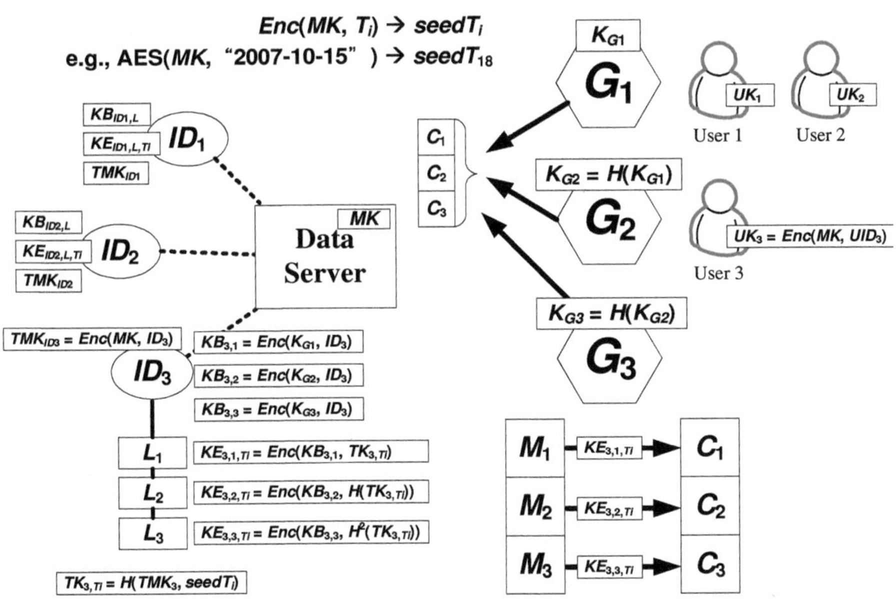

Fig. 1 Our MLE scheme

In this scheme we also give each user an user key (UK_i) by the generating function $UK_i = Enc(MK, UID_i)$. These user keys can be used to perform user authentication and encrypt time key (TK_{ID_i,T_i}) before sending to users.

We use the example that user 1 requests data "2007-10-15" from node ID_3, the flow is as follows:

1. User 1 requests data from ID_3 in time period "2007-10-15"
2. Server authenticates user 1 by UK_1
3. Server compute $Enc(MK, \text{"2007-10-15"}) = seedT_{18}$
4. Server computes $Enc(MK, ID_3) = TMK_3$
5. Server computes $H(TMK_3, seedT_{18}) = TK_{3,18}$
6. Server sends $Enc(UK_1, TK_{3,18}) = \{TK_{3,18}\}_{UK_1}$ for user 1
7. User 1 decrypts $\{TK_{3,18}\}_{UK_1}$ and obtains $TK_{3,18}$
8. User 1 owns K_{G_1} and now she has $TK_{3,18}$
   a. User 1 has K_{G_1} and knows ID_3 (public information), so she can derive node's base key $KB_{3,1}$ by computing $Enc(K_{G_1}, ID_3) = KB_{3,1}$
   b. User 1 knows $TK_{3,18}$, so she can derive node's encryption key $KE_{3,1,18}$ by computing $Enc(KB_{3,1}, TK_{3,18}) = KE_{3,1,18}$
   c. Then user 1 has encryption key $KE_{3,1,18}$ and can decrypt C_1 to obtain M_1
   d. Because user 1 has K_{G_1}, she can deduce K_{G_2} and K_{G_3} by performing one-way hash function, then she can derive base key $KB_{3,2}$ and $KB_{3,3}$ by computing $Enc(K_{G_2}, ID_3) = KB_{3,2}$ and $Enc(K_{G_3}, ID_3) = KB_{3,3}$
   e. User 1 can derive encryption key $KE_{3,2,18}$ and $KE_{3,3,18}$ to decrypt C_2 and C_3, where $KE_{3,2,18} = Enc(KB_{3,2}, H(TK_{3,18}))$ and $KE_{3,3,18} = Enc(KB_{3,3}, H^2(TK_{3,18}))$
9. User 3 in group G_2 only has K_{G_2} and can deduce K_{G_3}. If user 3 requests time key from the server, after authenticated herself using UK_3, the server will know she is in group G_2, and gives her the value of $H(TK_{3,18})$ instead of $TK_{3,18}$. This can prevent the colluding attack because even though user 3 can get K_{G_1} from a left G_1 user, she still cannot obtain $TK_{3,18}$ value, so user 3 can at most obtain M_2 and M_3

4 Discussion

There are many known attacks in sensor networks, including Denial-of-Service, blackhole, wormhole, Sybil, traffic analysis, node replication, and so on [1, 2]. As a complementary solution, we concentrate on the security of our MLE scheme. There are some possible attacks to our proposed scheme and we evaluate the security here.

- **Eavesdropping** In our proposed scheme, the only plaintext data adversaries can get is $seedT_i$ value, but without the time master key TMK_{ID_i}, the $seedT_i$ value is useless because it is only a seed value for generating the time key TK_{ID_i,T_j}.
- **Colluding Attack** If a user in lower privileged level collude with a left user in higher privileged level (e.g., user 3 colludes with user 1), although she can get the

group key of higher level, after authenticated, the data server will only give the time key of corresponding privileged level (i.e., $H^{L_{n-1}}(TK_{ID_i,T_j})$) to her. Without time keys of higher level, the user cannot derive specific encryption keys to obtain the data.

- **Compromised sensor nodes** In our scheme, each sensor node is given a set of distinct keys, and these keys are only the computational results. Even if specific sensor node is compromised, the adversary will only know these computational results and cannot take any advantage to compromise the other nodes, so the damage will be limited in the range of compromised nodes.

5 Conclusion

With the proliferation of sensor networks, the amount of privacy-sensitive data that is collected increases continuously. Based on the inherent properties of numerous applications, we observe a tension and tradeoff between privacy and the usefulness of information: very fine-grained data often contains privacy-sensitive information but is the most useful, whereas coarse-grained data protects privacy but is often less useful.

In this paper, we observe that we can break this tradeoff by simultaneously providing access to varying granularities of information, based on the access right of the data consumer. In fact, our efficient cryptographic construction enables sensor nodes to encrypt different granularities of data under different cryptographic keys. We find that our approach is viable even on highly resource-constrained sensor nodes, enabling us to simultaneously achieve several points in the tradeoff space between fine granularity/resolution of data and privacy.

Acknowledgements Special thanks to Lee-Chun Ko for inspecting the article and providing precious comments.

References

1. Akyildiz LF, Su W, Sankarasubramaniam Y and Cayirci E (2002) A survey on sensor networks. In IEEE Communications Magazine, 40(8):102–114
2. Callaway EH (2004) Wireless Sensor Networks: Architectures and Protocols. CRC Press.
3. Itkis G (2006) Forward Security: Adaptive Cryptography - Time Evolution. Invited chapter for the Handbook of Information Security, John Wiley and Sons, Inc.
4. Perrig A, Szewczyk R, Wen V et al (2002) SPINS: Security Protocols for Sensor Networks. In Wireless Networks Journal (WINE), September 2002.
5. Walters JP, Liang Z, Shi W, and Chaudhary V (2006) Wireless sensor network security: A survey. In Security in Distributed, Grid, and Pervasive Computing, Chapter 17, Auerbach Publications, CRC Press.

A Comparative Study of Anomaly Detection Techniques in Web Site Defacement Detection

Giorgio Davanzo, Eric Medvet and Alberto Bartoli

Abstract Web site defacement, the process of introducing unauthorized modifications to a web site, is a very common form of attack. Detecting such events automatically is very difficult because web pages are highly dynamic and their degree of dynamism, as well as their typical content and appearance, may vary widely across different pages. Anomaly based detection can be a feasible and effective solution for this task because it does not require any prior knowledge about the page to be monitored. This study enables gaining further insights into the problem of automatic detection of web defacements. We want to ascertain whether existing techniques for anomaly intrusion detection may be applied to this problem and we want to assess pros and cons of incorporating domain knowledge into the detection algorithm.

1 Introduction

The defacement of web sites has become one of the most widely diffused security incident categories in the Internet and "continues to plague organizations" [4]. Anecdotal evidence about this phenomenon is abundant and steadily expanding (e.g., http://www.zone-h.org, http://www.serapis.net/), with more than 480.000 defacements stored at Zone-H, a public web-based archive devoted to gathering evidences of defacements, during 2007 alone. A defaced web site typically contains only a few messages or images, perhaps including disturbing contents and/or political messages.

We proposed a technology for implementing a *defacement detection service*, in which a single organization could monitor the web sites of hundreds or thousands of web sites of other organizations [1]. The crucial feature of our proposal is that it does not require any participation from the monitored site, in particular, it does not require the installation of any infrastructure at the monitored site, nor does it require the knowledge of the officially approved content of the web page. Our approach is

DEEI - Università degli Studi di Trieste

Please use the following format when citing this chapter:

Davanzo, G., Medvet, E. and Bartoli. A., 2008, in IFIP International Federation for Information Processing, Volume 278; *Proceedings of the IFIP TC 11 23rd International Information Security Conference*; Sushil Jajodia, Pierangela Samarati, Stelvio Cimato; (Boston: Springer), pp. 711–715.

based on *anomaly detection*: we build automatically a profile of the monitored web page and then generate an alert to the relevant monitored organization whenever something "unusual" shows up.

In this work we broaden our analysis and compare our domain-knowledge based approach with anomaly detection techniques that have been proposed earlier for host/network-based intrusion detection systems. This study enables gaining further insights into the problem of automatic detection of web defacements. We want to ascertain whether techniques for anomaly-based intrusion detection may be applied also to anomaly detection of web defacements and we want to assess pros and cons of incorporating domain knowledge into the detection algorithm.

2 Experimental Evaluation

We provide only essential information about our monitoring framework. Full details can be found in the accompanying report [3]. We observe the monitored resource at regular intervals. Each reading of the resource is transformed into a numerical array of 1466 elements. This array is then classified by a detector as being *negative* (legitimate) or *positive* (anomalous).

We experimented with the following detectors, that implement techniquespreviously used for detecting intrusions in host or in network based IDSs. We used as baseline the detector based on domain-knowledge that we developed in our earlier work.

- **K-th Nearest** [9, 6] is distance-based, often computed using Euclidean metric; basically it measures the minimum distance required to include at least k points: an anomaly is detected when that distance is greater than a provided threshold.
- **Local Outlier Factor** [2, 6] is an extension to the k-th nearest distance, assigning to each evaluated point an outlying degree.
- **Mahalanobis Distance** [7, 6] is a measure based on the correlation between variables; an anomaly is detected when the distance of the inspected value from the mean is greater than that of the element composing the profile.
- **Hotelling's T-Square** [5, 10] is very similar to Mahalanobis distance; its main difference is that it considers the number of sampled elements.
- **Parzen Windows** [11] provide a method to estimate the probability density function of a random variable;we experimented with two basic distributions: Gaussian and Pulse.
- **Support Vector Machines** [8, 6] uses hyperplanes to maximally separate N classes of data. In anomaly detection, only $N = 2$ classes of objects are used, providing positive readings during the learning.

We use each technique to build a profile by passively observing the inspected resource—our experience shows that profiling for two weeks is enough. When the profile is complete, the system is then able to judge the content of the observed page by comparing it against the profile accordingly with the given technique.

We observed 15 web pages for two months, collecting a reading for each page every 6 hours, thus totaling a *negative sequence* of 240 readings for each web page. We visually inspected them in order to confirm the assumption that they are all genuine. The observed pages differ in size, content and dynamism and include pages of e-commerce web sites, newspapers web sites, and alike. We also collected an *attack archive* composed by 95 readings extracted from a publicly available defacements archive (http://www.zone-h.org).

We used False Positive Ratio (FPR) and False Negative Ratio (FNR) as performance indexes computing average, maximum and minimum values among web pages. For each page: (i) we built a *learning sequence* S^+ of positive readings composed by the first 20 elements of the attack archive; (ii) we built a sequence S^- of negative readings composed by the first 50 elements of the corresponding negative sequence; (iii) we trained the SVM detector with $S = S^- \cup S^+$ and all the other detectors with $S = S^-$. Then, for each page:(i) we built a *testing sequence* S_t by joining a sequence S_t^-, composed by the remaining 190 readings of the corresponding negative sequence, and a sequence S_t^+, composed by the remaining 75 readings of the attack archive; (ii) we fed each algorithm with each reading of S_t—as if it was the first reading to be evaluated after the learning phase—counting false positives and false negatives.

3 Results

A first crucial result is that only the detector based on domain-knowledge delivers acceptable results when fed with the entire array of 1466 features. A *feature selection* turned out to be necessary for all the other techniques. The results below have been obtained with detectors focussing only on 10-20 features selected as described in the companion report.

We provide FPR that we obtained experimenting first with the first 75 readings of S_t^- and then on all the 190 readings of S_t^-. In other words, we assessed the effectiveness of each technique separately on the *short term* and on the *long term*—about 19 and 48 days respectively. We also provide FNR computed on all readings of S_t^+.

Table 1 shows results obtained in the short term: FNR values suggest that all the algorithms proved to be effective when detecting defacements. On the other hand, they behaved differently when analyzing genuine readings.

Domain Knowledge performed well on many web pages, although on some of them it exhibited very high FPR; Mahalanobis, Hotelling and LOF did not score well, being unable to classify genuine pages for many pages. Both Parzen methods proved to be acceptably effective on many pages, although on some of them they worked as badly as Mahalanobis and Hotelling.

An excellent result comes from K-th Nearest and Support Vector Machines: both techniques managed to correctly classify all the negative readings, while still detecting a large amount of attacks.

Table 1 Short term results (75 readings).

Aggregator	FPR % AVG	FPR % MAX	FPR % MIN	FNR % AVG	FNR % MAX	FNR % MIN
Domain Knowledge	1.3	13.3	0.0	0.1	1.3	0.0
K-th Nearest	0.0	0.0	0.0	0.1	1.3	0.0
Local Outlier Factor	6.6	94.7	0.0	0.3	4.0	0.0
Hotelling	10.9	94.7	0.0	0.0	0.0	0.0
Mahalanobis	11.5	94.7	0.0	0.2	1.3	0.0
Parzen Pulse	1.2	16.0	0.0	0.0	0.0	0.0
Parzen Gaussian	4.1	40.0	0.0	0.0	0.0	0.0
Support Vector Machines	0.0	0.0	0.0	0.0	0.0	0.0

Table 2 shows results obtained in the long term. FNR is the same as Table 1, since both aggregator internal state and the positive testing sequence S_t^+ remain the same. Results in terms of FPR are slightly worse for all the evaluated techniques, as expected; the only aggregator that managed to perform almost as good as in short term is the one based on the Support Vetor Machines. As a matter of fact, both K-th Nearest and Pulse Parzen managed to maintain a low FPR, but raised many false alarms on some web pages.

Table 2 Long term results (190 readings)

Aggregator	FPR % AVG	FPR % MAX	FPR % MIN	FNR % AVG	FNR % MAX	FNR % MIN
Domain Knowledge	2.7	26.3	0.0	0.1	1.3	0.0
K-th Nearest	1.8	18.9	0.0	0.1	1.3	0.0
Local Outlier Factor	11.0	97.9	0.0	0.3	4.0	0.0
Hotelling	14.7	97.9	0.0	0.0	0.0	0.0
Mahalanobis	16.2	97.9	0.0	0.2	1.3	0.0
Parzen Pulse	1.3	15.3	0.0	0.0	0.0	0.0
Parzen Gaussian	4.5	40.0	0.0	0.0	0.0	0.0
Support Vector Machines	0.0	0.5	0.0	0.0	0.0	0.0

According to our experimental evaluation, almost all techniques (with the exception of LOF and Hotelling/Mahalanobis) show results, in terms of FNR and FPR, which are sufficiently low to deserve further consideration. In particular, most techniques achieve an average FPR lower than 4%, while being able to correctly detect almost all the simulated attacks (FNR $\simeq$ 1%). We remark that such a lower FPR is equivalent, in our scenario, to about 4 false positives raised every month. Such a finding suggests that, with most of the proposed techniques, the realization of a large-scale monitoring service is a feasible solution.

Support Vector Machines are the most promising alternative to our earlier Domain Knowledge proposal in terms of effectiveness. Since that technique requires an archive of attacks, however, it may be useful to investigate more deeply the relation between quality of that archive and resulting performance.

On the other hand, we believe that a domain knowledge-based detection algorithm benefits from two important advantages:

First, an intrinsic feature of Domain Knowledge is that the framework can provide the human operator with meaningful indications in case of a positive. For example, the operator could be notified with some indication about an anomalous number of links in the page or about a tag that was not present in the page despite being supposed to be. These indications can hardly be provided using the other techniques.

Second, the Domain Knowledge aggregator does not require a feature selection. While increasing performance for the techniques we tested, thus definitely making defacement detection effective with them, feature selection introduces more opportunities for attacks that remain hidden within the analyzed profile. Any attack affecting only elements that are not taken into account after the feature selection, cannot be detected by a detection algorithm that requires feature selection. The practical relevance of this issue (i.e., which attacks indeed fall in this category) certainly deserves further analysis.

References

1. Bartoli, A., Medvet, E.: Automatic integrity checks for remote web resources. IEEE Internet Computing **10**, 56–62 (2006)
2. Breunig, M.M., Kriegel, H.P., Ng, R.T., Sander, J.: Lof: identifying density-based local outliers. SIGMOD Rec **29**, 93–104 (2000)
3. Davanzo, G., Medvet, E., Bartoli, A.: A comparative study of anomaly detection techniques in web site defacement detection - long version (2008). URL http://www2.units.it/̃bartolia/download/ComparativeStudyLong.pdf
4. Gordon, L., Loeb, M., Lucyshyn, W., Richardson, R.: CSI/FBI Computer Crime and Security Survey. Computer Security Institute (2006)
5. Hotelling, H.: The generalization of student's ratio. The Annals of Mathematical Statistics **2**, 360–378 (1931)
6. Lazarevic, A., Ertoz, L., Kumar, V., Ozgur, A., Srivastava, J.: A comparative study of anomaly detection schemes in network intrusion detection. Proceedings of the Third SIAM International Conference on Data Mining (2003)
7. Mahalanobis, P.C.: On the generalized distance in statistics. In: Proceedings of the National Institute of Science of India, vol. 12, pp. 49–55 (1936)
8. Mukkamala, S., Janoski, G., Sung, A.: Intrusion detection using neural networks and support vector machines. In: Neural Networks, 2002. IJCNN '02. Proceedings of the 2002 International Joint Conference on, vol. 2, pp. 1702–1707 (2002)
9. Ramaswamy, S., Rastogi, R., Shim, K.: Efficient algorithms for mining outliers from large data sets. SIGMOD Rec **29**, 427–438 (2000)
10. Ye, N., Chen, Q., Emran, S.M., Vilbert, S.: Hotelling t2 multivariate profiling for anomaly detection. Proc. 1st IEEE SMC Inform. Assurance and Security Workshop (2000)
11. Yeung, D.Y., Chow, C.: Parzen-window network intrusion detectors. In: Pattern Recognition, 2002. Proceedings. 16th International Conference on, vol. 4, pp. 385–388 vol.4 (2002)

Managing the lifecycle of XACML delegation policies in federated environments

Manuel Sánchez, Óscar Cánovas, Gabriel López, Antonio F. Gómez-Skarmeta

Abstract This paper presents an infrastructure that enables the use of administrative delegation in an effective way, reducing the complexity in the policy management for some specific scenarios. This infrastructure is in charge of managing the policies of the system during its lifecycle, for example when they are created by the users or when they are collected to take an authorization decision. The proposal makes use of a robust and extensible language as XACML in order to express the authorization policies. However, as we will see, the management infrastructure has been designed in a way that facilitates the task of the different users involved, assuming that those users do not have to be security experts or XACML-aware.

1 Introduction and motivation

Nowadays we are experiencing the emergence of federated approaches to resource sharing, like eduroam [5]. In this approaches, trust links are established among different autonomous institutions in order to grant users in any of them access to shared resources with a single identity, stated by the institution the user belongs to. Moreover, this kind of agreements is facilitating mobility of users among institutions. In this scenarios, access control policies are used in order to manage the access of users to the services and resources offered by an institution. But due to the dynamic nature of this kind of scenarios, the management of that policies becomes more difficult. In this situations, *administrative delegation* [6] can help to reduce this complexity. It means that the system administrator can delegate in another person, the *delegate*, to make part of the work by managing a subset of the policies.

Manuel Sánchez, Gabriel López, Antonio F. Gómez-Skarmeta
Department of Information and Communications Engineering, University of Murcia, Spain
e-mail: {manuelsc, gabilm, skarmeta}@um.es

Óscar Cánovas
Department of Computer Engineering, University of Murcia, Spain e-mail: ocanovas@um.es

Please use the following format when citing this chapter:

Sánchez, M., et al., 2008, in IFIP International Federation for Information Processing, Volume 278; *Proceedings of the IFIP TC 11 23rd International Information Security Conference*; Sushil Jajodia, Pierangela Samarati, Stelvio Cimato; (Boston: Springer), pp. 717–721.

A scenario that shows this situation could be a meeting of an international project. In this meeting there are people from different institutions who belong to the same federation. During the meeting time, the host institution wants to provide to the members Internet access. Besides, some constraints such as the use of a specific Virtual LAN (VLAN) or a Quality of Service (QoS) profile must be enforced. In this case, administrative delegation can be used to assign the responsability of managing the access control properties to a user more closely related to the mentioned scenario. For example, the person who is organizing the meeting can be the delegate in this situation, because he knows all the necessary information such as the identity of the audience or the schedule of the meeting. In this way, the system administrator will create one policy to delegate the network access management to the meeting organizer. Then, the meeting organizer will create the specific policies to control the access to the network.

This scenario can help us to show the different issues involving the administrative delegation. For example, the delegate does not usually know anything about policy management, therefore it is necessary to help them to develop a correct access control policy. Moreover, we have additional policies in the system to specify the delegation. Thus, despite the work of the system administrator is reduced, the management of the policies is more complex from a global point of view. An infrastructure for managing the policies is necessary in order to help the system administrator and delegates to carry out their tasks. Thus, our main contribution in this paper is the definition of a complete infrastructure that provides the means of controlling how the policies are created, where they are stored or how the appropriate policies are collected and evaluated when it is necessary to take an authorization decision.

The rest of this paper is structured as follows. Section 2 shows the access control language used in this proposal and its extension to enable the use of administrative delegation. Finally, section 3 describes the proposed infrastructure.

2 Administrative delegation in XACML

XACML (eXtensible Access Control Markup Language) [3] is a standard XML-based access control language proposed by OASIS to represent access control policies in a standard way. This specification includes the definition of an access control policy language and a representation format to encode access control requests and responses. An XACML delegation profile [8] was produced to support administrative and dynamic delegation. The purpose of this profile is to specify how to express permissions about the right to issue policies and to verify issued policies against these permissions. Basically, it defines that an XACML policy may contain a *PolicyIssuer* element that describes the source of the policy. Then, the authority of the issuer needs to be verified in order to consider this policy as valid. The essence of the verification is that the issuer of the policy is checked against the trusted policies, directly or through other policies with issuers.

This profile is the key element upon we have based our work to define an infrasctructure for management of delegation policies, as described below.

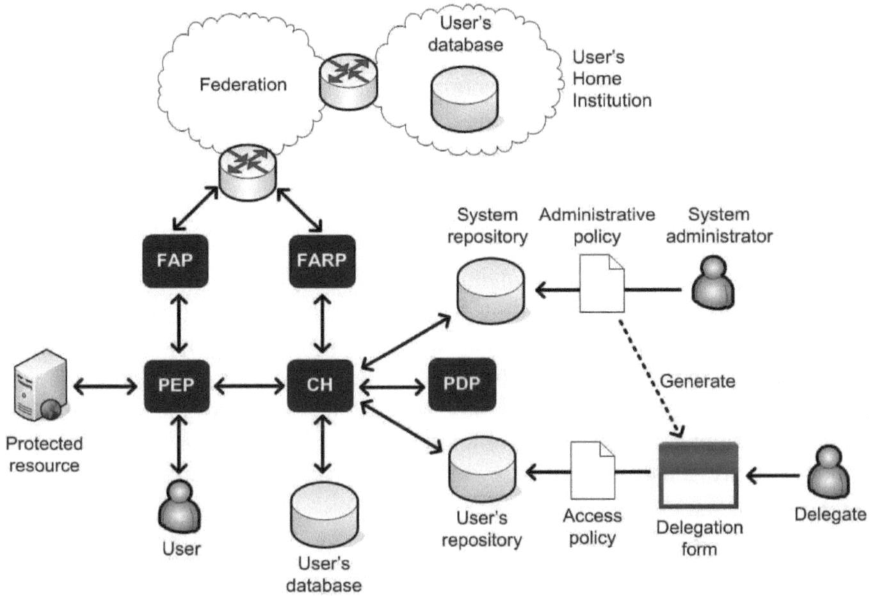

Fig. 1 Proposed architecture

3 Delegation infrastructure

3.1 Architecture

Usually, in the federated environments, the authentication of roaming users is carried out in their home institutions while the authorization to access a specific service is done at the remote institution based on some attributes associated with them. Thus, the federation offers common services to the member institutions to authenticate roaming users and to request their associated attributes through the federation. From this point of view, we can consider that, in a general way, the federation offers two different entities: a *Federation Authentication Point (FAP)* which authenticates a remote user and returns to the user a handle (identifier), and a *Federation Attribute Requester Point (FARP)* which returns the attributes associated with the user identified by the handle. Specifically, the work presented in this paper is based on the DAMe project [1], where authentication is based on eduroam [5] and the attribute requests are carried out through eduGAIN [4].As Figure 1 shows, the FAP in our architecture is provided by eduroam while the FARP is provided by eduGAIN. Both services forward the corresponding requests to the user's home institution, where they can be answered properly.

The figure also shows a *Policy Enforcement Point* or *PEP*, which is responsible for protecting the resources and enabling the access only to authorized users, and a

Policy Decision Point or *PDP*, which takes the authorization decisions based on the XACML policies and the user's attributes. Finally, we can see the *System and the User's repositories* that contains the policies generated by the system administrator and the delegates respectively. In the example described previously, the protected resource is the network, and the PEP is the access point (AP) that is providing wireless access.

3.2 Policy management

The first type of policy we have to define in our system is an administrative policy expressing the delegation of the administrative rights to the delegate. It is created by the system administrator in the usual way, although to simplify the task, some XACML editor can be used [7, 2]. This policy should specify the delegate by means of the identity, or in a more general way, specifying some attributes that must be held. An important advantage of defining the delegate by means of attributes is that the policy can previously exist in the system, and the only step to take is the issuance of the appropriate attributes for the delegate. Moreover, this policy can specify some network properties to be enforced during the network connection and some access conditions for the final users, by means of obligations and the condition elements. In our example, the administrator assigns the *meeting_delegate* attribute to the meeting organizer to allow him to create the proper policies, and specifies a *high* level of QoS. However, he does not specify time conditions because he does not know the meeting schedule.

Once this policy is defined, the delegate is able to create the access policies. He is a common user of the institution without specific knowledge about the policy language, so instead of building this policy from scratch, he can use some kind of form or template. Therefore, we need a *Policy Management Tool (PMT)* to build the access policy form. This tool can be an XSLT transformation that extracts the appropriate data from the delegation policy to generate the form. In this way, the delegate only has to fill in this form to create the access policy. Additionally, this form must include an option to refine the network properties specified by the administrator, but checking the properties specified by the delegate against the others specified by the administrator. We have to take into account that the access to this form must be restricted to the the proper delegates. Therefore, the PMT must also generate a XACML policy to control the access to the policy itself. Finally, the administrative policy and the access control policy are stored in the system repository, Figure 2 on the left. In the meeting example, after the delegate is successfully authenticated in the system, he can fill in the form to generate the access policies. In the form, he also can specify the time allowed to access to the network from 9h to 18h.

There is still an open issue with the management of the access policies, because somebody has to delete them from the repository when they become invalid, for example when the meeting is finished. Despite the system administrator might be responsible for that task, the sense of administrative delegation is to free the administrator of doing this kind of tasks. Another option is to assign that responsability to the delegate. However, he is a common user not worried about these policy management tasks, and therefore he can forget to do it. As a solution, the access policy form can force the delegate to specify the validity time for this policy. Then, as Figure 2 shows on the right, when the policies are stored in the repository, the max validity date is also specified. Thus, the list of expiration dates can be checked periodically to automatically delete the policies that have expired.

Once the policies have been successfully generated, meeting attendants can try to access to Internet. First, rhe AP authenticates them by means of the FAP. Later, their attributes are revocered via the FARP and an authorization request is sent to the PDP, but an administrative request is also needed to check whether the issuer is a right delegate. If all the authorization decisions are successful and the time condition is satisfied, the AP enables the Internet access to the user with the specified QoS. Once the meeting is finished, the access policies are deleted automatically from the user's repository because they become invalid. Finally, the system administrator de-assigns the *meeting_delegate* attribute.

References

1. *DAMe Project web site*. http://dame.inf.um.es.
2. *UMU XACML Editor Home Page*. http://xacml.dif.um.es.
3. A. Anderson et al. *EXtensible Access Control Markup Language (XACML) Version 1.0*, February 2003. OASIS Standard.
4. D.R. López et al. *Deliverable DJ5.2.2,2: GÉANT2 Authorisation and Authentication Infrastructure (AAI) Architecture - second edition*, April 2007. GN2 JRA5. GÉANT 2.
5. T. Kersting et al. *Deliverable DJ5.1.5,2: Inter-NREN Roaming Infrastructure and Service Support Cookboook - Second Edition*, August 2007. GN2 JRA5. GÉANT 2.
6. E. Rissanen and B.S. Firozabadi. *Administrative Delegation in XACML - Position Paper*, 2004.
7. M. Sánchez, G. López, O. Cánovas, and A.F. Gómez-Skarmeta. Using Microsoft Office InfoPath to Generate XACML Policies. In *Proceedings of the International Conference on Security and Cryptography (SECRYPT)*, 2006.
8. OASIS Access Control TC. *XACML v3.0 Administration and Delegation Profile Version 1.0*, October 2007. OASIS Working Draft.

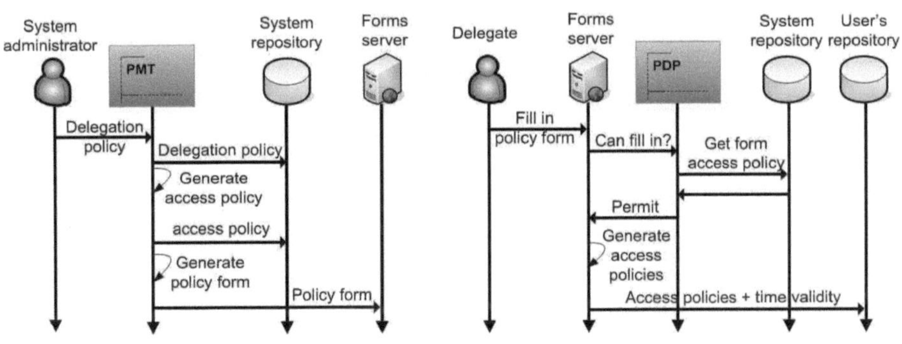

Fig. 2 Policy management

Assessing the Likelihood of Privacy Policy Compliance

George O.M. Yee, Larry Korba, and Ronggong Song

Abstract Individuals interact with organizations in many different capacities (e.g. as clients, as employees). Many of these interactions require the individual to submit her personal information to the organization, which may claim compliance with privacy policy. It is important to assess this compliance quantitatively. This paper describes an approach for quantitatively assessing the likelihood that an organization will comply with privacy policy.

1 Introduction

Individuals interact with organizations in various roles that require them to submit their private information to the organization (e.g. health care patient, buyer). Given that how well an organization protects privacy is usually a matter of how well it complies with either its own privacy policy or the privacy policies of personal information owners, it is important to be able to assess this compliance quantitatively. If such assessments are publicly available, a) organizations could be challenged if their assessments are below a pre-established threshold (assuming a higher assessment is better), b) individuals could select organizations that have high compliance with which to do business, and c) organizations may be encouraged to pay more attention to protecting privacy. However, assessing an organization's actual compli-

George O.M. Yee
National Research Council Canada, Institute for Information Technology, 1200 Montreal Road, Building M-50, Ottawa, ON, Canada K1A 0R6 e-mail: george.yee@nrc.ca

Larry Korba
National Research Council Canada, Institute for Information Technology, 1200 Montreal Road, Building M-50, Ottawa, ON, Canada K1A 0R6 e-mail: larry.korba@nrc.ca

Ronggong Song
National Research Council Canada, Institute for Information Technology, 1200 Montreal Road, Building M-50, Ottawa, ON, Canada K1A 0R6 e-mail: ronggong.song@nrc.ca

Please use the following format when citing this chapter:

Yee, G.O.M., Korba, L. and Song, R., 2008, in IFIP International Federation for Information Processing, Volume 278; *Proceedings of the IFIP TC 11 23rd International Information Security Conference*; Sushil Jajodia, Pierangela Samarati, Stelvio Cimato; (Boston: Springer), pp. 723–727.

ance performance may be difficult to do - the organization may be hesitant to report data needed to determine this performance, especially where the performance is bad, and even if the required data is reported, it would be difficult to ensure the reliability of the data. On the other hand, an organization's likelihood to comply with privacy policy may be more easily determined, since it could be based on what provisions it has implemented to protect privacy. In addition, an organization would welcome any opportunity to make known its investments in the protection of privacy in order to attract clients. This paper proposes a straight-forward approach for estimating the likelihood that an organization will comply with privacy policy.

Privacy refers to the ability of individuals to *control* the collection, use, retention, and distribution of information about themselves. This is the same definition as in [3] except that we also include *use*. An organization's *compliance with privacy policy* refers to the organization's use of provisions to give the protected person (PP) control over the organization's collection, use, retention, and distribution of information about the protected person, where this control is specified in the organization's privacy policy or the PP's privacy policy. An *internal violation (IV)* (or an inside attack) of privacy policy is one that is carried out by an insider of the organization (i.e. someone who has special data access privileges by virtue of the person's association with the organization, e.g. employee), whose access and use of the private information does not comply with the privacy policy. An *external violation (EV)* (or an outside attack) of privacy policy is one that is carried out by a non-insider of the organization, whose access and use of the private information does not comply with the privacy policy.

The literature appears empty of works dealing directly with estimates of an organization's likelihood to comply with privacy policy. Only works that are indirectly related were found, such as privacy impact assessment (PIA) (e.g. [6]), privacy risk analysis (e.g. [5]), and privacy audits (e.g. [2]).

2 Likelihood Estimates of Complying with Privacy Policy

A *likelihood estimate* of an organization's likelihood of complying with privacy policy is a set of numerical values that indicate the degree to which the organization will likely avoid IV and EV. The likelihood of avoiding IV and EV depends on protective provisions that the organization has in place to prevent violations. Let E denote a likelihood estimate. E will need to account for the provisions used against both IV and EV.

To account for the provisions against IV, we propose that a special PIA [6], extended to identify vulnerabilities that can lead to malicious IV, be carried out to identify IV vulnerabilities. Suppose that such an assessment identified m IV vulnerabilities and countermeasures (provisions against IV) are in place for p of these vulnerabilities. To account for provisions against EV, we propose that a special security threat analysis [5], oriented towards discovering EV vulnerabilities be carried out. Suppose that this analysis identified n security vulnerabilities and countermeasures (provisions against EV) are in place for q of these vulnerabilities. Then, one formulation of E is

$$E_1 = (p+q)/(m+n), \text{ if } m+n > 0,$$
$$= 1, \text{ if } m+n = 0.$$

Let e_i account for the provisions used against IV and e_e account for the provisions used against EV. Then, another formulation of E is

$$E_2 = (e_i, e_e) = (p/m, q/n), \text{ if } m > 0,\ n > 0,$$
$$= (1, q/n), \text{ if } m = 0,\ n > 0,$$
$$= (p/m, 1), \text{ if } m > 0,\ n = 0,$$
$$= (1,1), \text{ if } m = 0,\ n = 0.$$

Note that $0 \leq E_1, E_2 \leq 1$. In practice, the quantities E_1, e_i, e_e are expressed as percentages. E_1 has the advantage of providing a single number for ease of comparison between different organizations. A percentage threshold t for E_1 may be predetermined such that for E_1 above t, the provisions against IV and EV are deemed sufficiently likely to protect from violations. E_2 has the advantage of identifying where an organization stands in terms of its specific provisions for IV or EV. By predetermining percentage thresholds t_i and t_e for e_i and e_e respectively (thresholds above which the corresponding provisions for IV and EV are sufficiently likely to protect from privacy policy violations), E_2 defines a region in a 100 x 100 plane in which an organization's likelihood to comply with privacy policy (avoid privacy policy violations) is acceptable (shaded region in Figure 1).

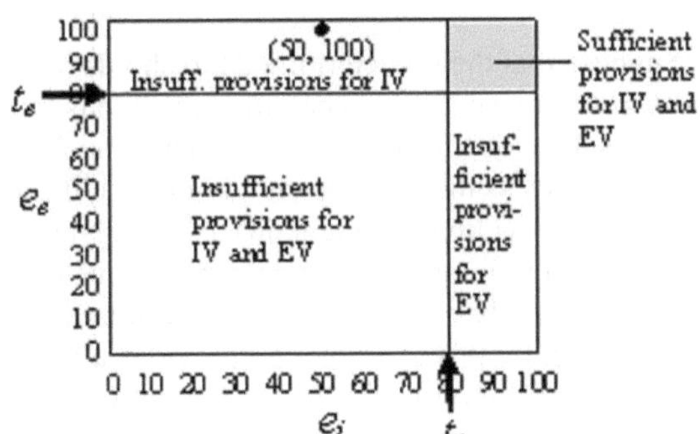

Fig. 1 Plot of E_2 = (50, 100) indicating that the corresponding organization has insufficient provisions to protect against IV.

We next give an application example. Suppose that a bank branch keeps the following personal information about its clients: name, social insurance number, home address, phone number, and financial assets. Suppose that the branch keeps this data stored within the branch itself. The branch decides to hire a privacy auditor, certified to apply the above estimation method, to estimate its likelihood of privacy policy compliance, with the intention of using the results in its advertising.

To determine values for m and p, the auditor puts together a team to do a PIA. The team analyzes where personal information originates, how it is stored, and how it is used. The PIA uncovers the following IV issues: a) there is no one accountable for private information, b) the database containing client personal data is not protected from illegal access, c) the branch's employees have been unhappy over the reduction in branch contributions to the employee pension plan, and d) the branch only does a minimal background check before hiring a new teller. The auditor is told by the branch manager that he has assigned himself to be accountable for private information in the branch's possession, and that a more thorough background check for job applicants has been initiated. However, the branch puts off any new measures to protect the database citing the fact that it already has a firewall in place. The branch also cannot do anything about the employee pension plan for the time being. Thus, $m = 4$ and $p = 2$.

To obtain values for n and q, the auditor assembles a team (with some members from the team for the PIA) to perform a threat analysis. Some examples of threats identified in this analysis are: a) the personal information flow is vulnerable to man-in-the-middle attacks (from the personal information path going into and out of the branch), b) the personal information database is vulnerable to attacks from inside and outside (via the Internet) the branch, and c) the bank tellers are vulnerable to social engineering attacks. The number of vulnerabilities n is found to be 6. Suppose that the branch has put in place countermeasures against each of these vulnerabilities, resulting in q also having the value 6. Thus,

$$E_1 = (p+q)/(m+n) = (2+6)/(4+6) = 8/10 = 4/5,$$
$$E_2 = (e_i, e_e) = (p/m, q/n) = (2/4, 6/6) = (1/2, 1).$$

Suppose that the predetermined thresholds for E_1, e_i, and e_e are t=85%, t_i=80%, and t_e=80% respectively. Then the branch has failed E_1 evaluation (since 80% for E_1 is less than the threshold of 85%). The branch has also failed E_2 evaluation (since 50% for e_i is less than the threshold of 80%). It is clear that this failure is due to the branch not providing sufficient provisions against IV (Figure 1). This branch would be motivated to improve its provisions against IV if other banks or branches of this bank are similarly evaluated and have results in the shaded area of Figure 1.

As shown by this example, E_1 provides a single number that shows whether or not the organization is likely to have sufficient provisions against IV and EV to avoid future violations. If E_1 is calculated for a number of similar organizations, the PP could easily see which organization is likely to comply with privacy policy. On the other hand, E_2 not only indicates the likelihood of an organization's future compliance, but also shows how strong the organization is in terms of its specific provisions against IV or EV. If the organization failed E_2 evaluation, it would know where it needs to make improvements in terms of provisions for IV, EV, or both.

3 Conclusions and Future Research

This work[1] has proposed estimates for evaluating the likelihood that an organization will comply with privacy policy. The estimates allow organizations to be challenged if their likelihood to comply is perceived to be inadequate. They also allow consumers to choose organization with high likelihoods of compliance.

The proposed estimates are straightforward and should be acceptable to the general public. We envision that organizations will want to publicize their estimates to show that they exceed the thresholds (which could be standardized by an international body) as for ISO 9000 [4]. This could encourage organizations to achieve higher levels of privacy policy compliance.

We suggest that the proposed approach be applied by a separate, impartial firm specialized in performing PIA and threat analysis. Application guidelines could be developed and standardized by a privacy authority, and only firms certified by the authority would be authorized to apply the approach (as done for ISO 9000 and CMMI (Capability Maturity Model Integration) [1]). This would ensure that the calculation of the estimates is done fairly and consistently across organizations.

Future research includes looking at ways to improve the accuracy of the estimates, such as incorporating the impact of past violations, as well as improving the methods for calculating the estimates, such as increasing the effectiveness of threat analysis through automation.

References

1. Carnegie Mellon Software Engineering Institute: Welcome to the CMMI Web Site. Visited April 14, 2008 at: http://www.sei.cmu.edu/cmmi/
2. Enright, K.P.: Privacy Audit Checklist. Visited May 6, 2006 at: http://cyber.law.harvard.edu/clinical/privacyaudit.html
3. Goldberg, I., Wagner, D., Brewer, E.: Privacy-Enhancing Technologies for the Internet. Proceedings, 42nd IEEE Computer Society International Conference (COMPCON'97), 103-109 (1997)
4. International Organization for Standardization: Management Standards. Visited April 16, 2008 at: http://www.iso.org/iso/management_standards.htm
5. Salter, C., Sami Saydjari, S., Schneier, B., Wallner, J.: Towards a Secure System Engineering Methodology. Proceedings of the New Security Paradigms Workshop (1998)
6. Treasury Board of Canada: The Privacy Impact Assessment Guidelines: A Framework to Manage Privacy Risk. Visited May 6, 2006, at: http://www.tbs-sct.gc.ca/pgol-pged/piatp-pfefvp/course1/mod2/mod2-5_e.asp

[1] NRC paper number: NRC 50328

Classification features for detecting Server-side and Client-side Web attacks

Benferhat Salem and Tabia Karim

Abstract During last years, the number and cleverness of attacks against Web related applications are steadily growing as Web services become more popular. In this paper, we propose relevant classification features for detecting Web attacks targeting either server-side or client-side applications. Four kinds of features are provided: Request general features, Request content features, Response features and Request history features. Experimental studies carried on real[1] and simulated *http* traffic including normal data and several attacks show the efficiency of our feature set in detecting Web related attacks.

1 Introduction

Web technologies are widely deployed in nowadays information systems. For the attackers, this fact offers two opportunities: Firstly, *http/https* traffic is often the only service allowed through fire-wall and filtering technologies. The second opportunity lies in increasing numbers of Web related application vulnerabilities. In spite of the importance of Web application security, there are few works proposing classification features in order to detect malicious Web activities using machine learning and data mining techniques. Moreover, most proposed feature sets in intrusion detection are network oriented [5][6] while most nowadays attacks are targeting Web related applications [4][7]. In addition, to our knowledge there is currently no preprocessing tool for extracting Web oriented features directly from network traffic.
This paper proposes a relevant feature set suitable for detecting Web related attacks. Our feature set includes basic features of *http* connections as well as derived fea-

Benferhat Salem and Tabia Karim
CRIL - CNRS UMR8188, Université d'Artois,
Rue Jean Souvraz SP 18 62307 Lens, Cedex, France, e-mail: {benferhat, tabia}@cril.univ-artois.fr

[1] Thanks to DADDi project for providing us such real network traffic (URL: http://www.rennes.supelec.fr/DADDi/)

Please use the following format when citing this chapter:

Salem, B. and Karim, T., 2008, in IFIP International Federation for Information Processing, Volume 278; *Proceedings of the IFIP TC 11 23rd International Information Security Conference*; Sushil Jajodia, Pierangela Samarati, Stelvio Cimato; (Boston: Springer), pp. 729–733.

tures summarizing past *http* connections and providing useful information for revealing suspicious behaviors involving several *http* connections. While most works focus on *http* requests, we designed features characterizing both *http* requests and their corresponding responses. Note that our feature set is directly extracted from network packets instead of using Web application logs. Processing whole *http* traffic is the only way for detecting suspicious activities and attacks in both inbound and outbound traffic.

2 Web attacks

Web attacks use Web protocols (namely *http* [1] and *https* [2]) to perform malicious actions exploiting Web application vulnerabilities. They target either Web servers, Web clients or any Web related application using Web connections. Most Web attack taxonomies [11] [4] rely on attack techniques and group them into the following categories:

1. **Input validation attacks:** Input validation attacks refer to those bypassing input validation procedures in order to exploit Web application vulnerabilities. The strategy of such attacks is to send especially crafted requests exploiting vulnerabilities in Web server/client applications. Buffer-overflow, SQL injection, Directory traversal, Cross Site Scripting, etc. are well-known examples of input validation attacks Note that input validation attacks can cause denial of service, unauthorized access or command execution and full control of victim systems.
2. **Web authentication/authorization attacks**: They are Web attacks bypassing authentication/authorization restriction mechanisms. For example, some authentication mechanisms which aim at authenticating users, can be bypassed by brute-force and dictionary attacks.
3. **Web site scan and flooding attacks**: As the number of Web sites and contents grow rapidly, attackers often use scripted and automated scanning tools such as W3af [10] to search for possible vulnerabilities in Web sites. As for flooding attacks, users may abuse in some functionalities in order to prevent other legitimate users for having access to services.

3 Classification features for detecting Web attacks

In order to design effective feature set for detecting Web attacks, we analyzed several Web-based attacks and extracted features according to common attacks techniques. Our classification features are grouped into four categories:

1. **Request general features**: They are features that provide general information on *http* requests. The following table gives detailed examples of request general features:

Table 1 Request general features

Name	Description	Type	Target attacks
Req-length	Request length	Positive Integer	Buffer overflow attacks
URI-length	URI length	Positive integer	Buffer overflow, Value misinterpretation, URI decoding errors
Req-method	Request method (GET, POST HEAD...)	Symbolic	–
Req-resource-type	Type of requested resource (html, asp, cgi, php, exe, ...)	Nominal	–
Num-param	Number of parameters	Positive Integer	Input validation
Num-arg	Number of arguments	Positive Integer	Input validation
Is-req-correct	Does the request comply with *http* protocol (ex. Is there a request method in the request?)	Boolean	URL anomalies, URL decoding errors

2. **Request content features**: These features search for particularly suspicious patterns in *http* requests. The number of meta-characters, number of directory traversal patterns, etc. are examples of features describing request content.

Table 2 Request content features

Name	Description	Type	Target attacks
Num-NonPrintChars	Number of special and meta-characters and shell codes in the *http* request (x86, carriage return , semicolon...)	Positive Integer	Buffer overflows, shell codes, URL decoding errors and anomalies
SQL-cmds-tricks	Does the request contain SQL commands ("- -, OR 1 == 1, ...)	Boolean	SQL injection
Shell-cmds	Does the request contain shell commands (All operating systems shell commands)	Boolean	Command injection
Sensitive-files	Does the request reference sensitive files? (etc/passwd,...)	Boolean	Information leak, unauthorized access, ...
Directory-traversal	Does the request contain directory traversal tricks (Presence of token like "../",...)	Boolean	Directory traversal
Oversized-values	Does the request contain potentially oversized numeric values	Boolean	Value misinterpretations
Default-login-passwd	Does the request include factory default logins and passwords (Guest, anonymous, root, admin,...)	Boolean	Dictionary attacks, brute-force...
Script-injection	Does the URI contain a script tag ("<script", "<meta",...)	Boolean	Cross Site Scripting

3. **Response features**: These features can for instance reveal suspicious *http* content in the response, in which case Web clients are targeted by a possible attack. Table 3 provides detailed response feature examples:

Table 3 Response features

Name	Description	Type	Target attacks
Resp-Code	Response code to *http* request (200, 404, 500...)	Nominal	–
Is-html-Response	Is the response an *html* file?	Boolean	–
Response-time	Time elapsed since the corresponding http request	Real	DoS
Script-type	The type of script included in the response (Java, Visual basic, ...)	Nominal	Cross Site Scripting
Writing-script	Does the response flow include script writing functions (document.write()...)	Boolean	Session ID fixation,...

4. **Request history features**: In section 2, we pointed out that there are Web related attacks that perform through several connections. We accordingly designed derived features summarizing past *http* connections. Note that these features can be computed using a time-window or a connection-window that is fixed accord-

ing to the needed tradeoff between processing overload and detection rate. The following table contains examples of request history features:

Table 4 Request history features

Name	Description	Type	Target attacks
Num-Req-Same-Host	Number of requests issued by same source	Positive integer	Flooding, vulnerability scans
Num-Req-Same-URL	Number of requests with same URL	Positive integer	Flooding from same source/multiple sources
Num-Req-Same-Host-Diff-URI	Number of requests issued by same source and requesting different URLs	Positive integer	Vulnerability scans
Inter-Req-Interval	Inter request time interval	Positive integer	Flooding and vulnerability scans...

4 Experimental studies

In order to evaluate the relevance of our classification feature set, we carried out experimental studies on real and simulated *http* traffic using a C4.5 decision tree [15] which is among the most efficient classifiers. We extracted *http* traffic and preprocessed it into connection records using only packet payloads. Each *http* connection is characterized by the four feature categories presented in Section 3. Note that in order to label the preprocessed *http* traffic, we analyzed this data using Snort IDS[12] as well as manual analysis. As for other attacks, we simulated most of the attacks involved in [13][14] which is to our knowledge the most extensive and uptodate Web-attack data set. In addition to these Web attacks, we played vulnerability scanning sessions using W3af [10]. The following table provides details about our experimentations:

Table 5 Training and testing data set distributions and C4.5 evaluation results

	Training data		Testing data		Evaluation on Training data	Evaluation on Testing data
	Number	%	Number	%		
Normal	55342	55.877%	61378	88.88 %	100%	99.8%
Vulnerability scan	31152	31.453%	4456	6.45 %	99.99%	0.00%
Buffer overflow	9	0.009%	15	0.02%	100%	20%
Input validation	44	0.044%	4	0.01 %	99.99 %	99.99 %
Value misinterpretation	2	0.002%	0	0%	0.00%	–
Poor management	3	0.003%	0	0%	66.76%	–
URL decoding error	3	0.003%	0	0%	0.00%	–
Flooding	12488	12.609%	3159	4.57	99.99%	99.99%
Cross Site Scripting	0	0%	**6**	**0.01 %**	–	0.00%
SQL injection	0	0%	**9**	**0.01 %**	–	0.00%
Command injection	0	0%	**12**	**0.02 %**	–	0.00%
Total	99043	100%	69059	100%	PCC=99.93%	PCC=93.31%

In order to evaluate the ability to detect new attacks, we build a testing data set including normal real *http* connections as well as known attacks and new ones. When trained and tested using the same training data, the decision tree's PCC (Percent of Correct Classification) is too close to 100%. Then this is the indication that training data set is free from incoherences. The results of building the C4.5 decision tree on training data and evaluating it on testing data set show that in spite of a good PCC, new attacks are not detected since they are completely different from those included in training data. This is a recurring problem affecting most classifiers in intrusion detection [16][17]. Note that most miss-classifications are false negatives as it is the case with most classifiers used in intrusion detection [16][17].

5 Conclusion

In this paper, we proposed a relevant feature set for detecting Web attacks. We proposed four classification feature categories relative to *http* request general features, content features, response features and finally history features. Experimental studies carried out on real and simulated *http* traffic showed that most tested attacks are correctly detected and identified using our feature set. Future work will address extending this feature set in order to take into account most Web attacks as well as building an extensive and open data set of Web related attacks.

References

1. www.ietf.org/rfc/rfc2616.txt
2. www.ietf.org/rfc/rfc2818.txt
3. www.securityfocus.com/
4. http://cwe.mitre.org/documents/vuln-trends.html
5. W. Lee, A Data Mining Framework for Constructing Features and Models for Intrusion Detection Systems, PhD thesis, Columbia University, 1999.
6. I. V. Onut, A. A. Ghorbani, A Feature Classification Scheme for Network Intrusion Detection, In International Journal of Network Security, Vol. 5, N. 1, pp. 1-15, July 2007.
7. Common Vulnerabilities and Exposures, http://cve.mitre.org/
8. C. Krugel, G. Vigna: Anomaly detection of web-based attacks, ACM Conference on Computer and Communications Security, pp:251-261, 2003.
9. C. Kruegel, G. Vigna, W. Robertson, A multi-model approach to the detection of web-based attacks, In Computer Networks 48(5), pp. 717-738, 2005.
10. A. Riancho, w3af - Web Application Attack and Audit Framework, 2007. http://w3af.sf.net/
11. J. Undercoffer and J. Pinkston, Modeling Computer Attacks: A Target-Centric Ontology for Intrusion Detection, The Sixth International Symposium on Recent Advances in Intrusion Detection, Pittsburgh, PA, 2003.
12. www.snort.org/
13. K. L. Ingham, Anomaly Detection for HTTP Intrusion Detection: Algorithm Comparisons and the Effect of Generalization on Accuracy, PhD thesis, B.S. cum laude, University of New Mexico & M.S., University of New Mexico, May 2007.
14. http://www.i-pi.com/HTTP-attacks-JoCN-2006.
15. J. R. Quinlan,C4.5 : Programs for Machine Learning, Morgan Kaufmann Pub., San Mateo, CA, 1993.
16. C. Elkan, Results of the KDD'99 Classifier Learning, In ACM SIGKDD International Conference on Knowledge Discovery and Data Mining, Boston, MA 1(2), pp.63-64, 2000.
17. S. Benferhat, K. Tabia, Y. Djouadi, Integrating Anomaly-Based Detection with Bayesian-Decision tree Classifiers, International Conference on Advances in Information and Communication Technologies ICICOT07, Manipal, India, 2007.

Index

A

Abbadi, Imad M. 509
Abi Haidar, Diala 173
Ahn, Gail-Joon 573
Alawneh, Muntaha 509
Alpcan, Tansu 413
Althebyan, Qutaibah 557

B

Başar, Tamer 413
Baek, Joonsang 95
Balachandar, R. A. 221
Bao, Feng 47
Barni, M 33
Bartoli, Alberto 711
Battistoni, Roberto 653
Bellettini, Carlo 285
Bianchi, T 33
Boudriga, Noureddine 637
Branagan, M. 493

C

Caelli, W.J. 493
Caini, M 33
Canovas, Oscar 717
Chakraborty, Sudip 605
Clarke, N.L. 253
Colajanni, Michele 79
Colantonio, Alessandro 333
Crampton, Jason 205
Cuppens, Frédéric 173
Cuppens-Boulahia, Nora 173

D

Dadeau, Frédéric 141
Das, Tanmoy Kanti 125
Davanzo, Giorgio 711
De Decker, Bart 589
de Vink, E. P. 429
Debar, Hervé 173
den Hartog, J. I. 429
Dessí,Nicoletta 221
Di Biagio, Alessandro 653
Di Pietro, Roberto 333, 653
Dodge, Ronald 621
Dondo, Maxwell G. 525
Dritsas, S. 381

E

Ekelhart, Andreas 477
Espelid, Yngve 63
Evans, David 1

F

Fenz, Stefan 477
Florêncio, Dinei 681
Formica, Matteo 653
Fugini, Maria Grazia 221
Fujihara, Yasuhiro 699
Furnell, S.M. 253

G

Gei, Stefan 157
Gkoulalas-Divanis, Aris 349
Gomez-Skarmeta, Antonio F. 717
Gozzi, Daniele 79

Gritzalis, D. 381
Gritzalis, Stefanos 693
Gupta, Kapil Kumar 269

H

Hamilton, Samuel N. 461
Hamilton, Wendy L. 461
Han, Jeheon 669
Hay, Briani 621
Herley, Cormac 681
Hole, Kjell J. 63
Huang, Shih-I 705

J

Jin, Hongxia 365

K

Kambourakis, Georgios 693
Karim, Tabia 729
Kerschbaum, Florian 17
Klingsheim, André N. 63
Ko, Moo Nam 573
Korba, Larry 723
Krichene, Jihene 637
Kwok, L.F. 493
Kwon, Jonghoon 669

L

Le Métayer, Daniel 541
Lee, Heejo 397
Lee, Heejo 669
Legrand, Veronique 317
Li, Wei 189
Lim, Hoon Wei 205
Loiseaux, Claire 541
Longley, D. 493
Lopez, Gabriel 717
Lopez, Javier 125
Lotspiech, Jeffery 365

M

Majorczyk, Frédéric 301
Mallios, Y. 381
Mancini, Luigi V. 653
Marchetti, Mirco 79
Maziero, Carlos 237
Me, Ludovic 301
Medvet, Eric 711
Megiddo, Nimrod 365
Murayama, Yuko 699

N

Nance, Kara 621
Nath, Baikunth 269
Netland, Lars–Helge 63
Neubauer, Thomas 477
Nguyen, Kien C. 413
Nohl, Karsten 1
Nuwere, Ejovi 397

O

Ocello, Alberto 333
Onen, Melek 675
Orlandi, C 33
Oualha, Nouha 675

P

Paffumi, Luc 317
Pan, J. 429
Panda, Brajendra 557
Papadaki, M. 253
Perrig, Adrian 705
Piva, A 33
Posthumus, Shaun 687
Potet, Marie-Laure 141

R

Raguenet, Inez 237
Ramamohanarao, Kotagiri 269
Ray, Indrajit 605
Rekhis, Slim 637
Roudier, Yves 675
Rrushi, Julian L. 285

S

Saïdane, Ayda 301
Salem, Benferhat 729
Sanchez, Manuel 717
Saraydaryan, Jacques 317
Scheffler, Thomas 157
Schnor, Bettina 157
Seo, Dongwon 397
Shehab, Mohamed 573
Smith, Sean W. 445
Song, Ronggong 723
Soupionis, Y. 381
Strangio, Maurizio Adriano 109

T

Tan, Han Chiang 95

Teng, Po-Yuan 705
Theoharidou, M. 381
Tissot, Régis 141
Tjhai, G. C. 253
Totel, Eric 301
Tsakountakis, Alexandros 693
Tsang, Patrick P. 445

U

Ubeda, Stephanei 317

V

Verslype, Kristof 589
Verykios, Vassilios S. 349
von Solms, Rossouw 687

W

Wang, Lingyu 189
Wong, Jun Wen 95
Wu, Yongdong 47

Y

Yamaguchi, Kentarou 699
Yao, Haixia 47
Yee, George O.M. 723

Z

Zhang, Lei 189
Zhou, Jianying 95, 125
Zhu, Bo 189

MIX
Papier aus verantwortungsvollen Quellen
Paper from responsible sources
FSC® C105338

If you have any concerns about our products,
you can contact us on
ProductSafety@springernature.com

In case Publisher is established outside the EU,
the EU authorized representative is:
Springer Nature Customer Service Center GmbH
Europaplatz 3, 69115 Heidelberg, Germany

Printed by Libri Plureos GmbH
in Hamburg, Germany